Y0-DHD-566

MASS MEDIA, FREEDOM OF SPEECH, AND ADVERTISING

A Study in Communication Law

Daniel Morgan Rohrer

Boston College
Chestnut Hill, Massachusetts

KENDALL/HUNT PUBLISHING COMPANY

2460 Kerper Boulevard,
Dubuque, Iowa 52001

Copyright © 1979 by Kendall/Hunt Publishing Company

ISBN 0-8403-1988-6

All rights reserved. No part of this publication may be reproduced, stored in a retrieval system, or transmitted, in any form or by any means, electronic, mechanical, photocopying, recording, or otherwise, without the prior written permission of the copyright owners.

Printed in the United States of America

B   401988   01

With gratitude and thanks to the contributors whose gracious efforts made this work possible.

Contents

Preface   ix
Introduction   *Arthur L. Berney*   xv
               Chapter I: Problems in Free Speech and Advertising
Section 1: A Rationality Standard for the First Amendment   *Daniel M. Rohrer*   1
Section 2: Media Images of Alcohol: The Effects of Advertising and Other Media on Alcohol Abuse, 1976   *Wilson Bryan Key*   35
Section 3: Television, Violence and Advertisers: A Select Review   *Martin P. LoMonaco*   46
Section 4: Advertising: New Arena of Rights Battle   *A. Kent MacDougall*   57
               Chapter II: Commercial Speech
Section 1: The Rise and Fall of Commercial Speech   *William J. Rooney, Jr.*   67
Section 2: Advertising of Prescription Drug Prices as Protected Commercial Speech   *Cameron F. Kerry*   73
Section 3: The Advertising Challenge: An Alternative to Individual Lawyer Advertising   *John Stewart Geer*   94
Section 4: American Bar Association Recommendations on Lawyer Advertising   99
    Part A: Report to the Board of Govenors of the Task Force on Lawyer Advertising   *S. Shepherd Tate*   99
    Part B: Advertising: Making the Best of a Good Thing   *William B. Spann, Jr.*   103
Section 5: Cases   107
    Valentine v. Chrestensen (1942)
    Railway Express Agency v. New York (1949)
    New York State Broadcasters Association v. United States (1969)
    Capital Broadcasting Co. v. John Mitchell (1971)
    HM Distributors of Milwaukee v. Department of Agriculture (1972)
    Holiday Magic, Inc. v. Warren (1973)
    Pittsburgh Press Co. v. Pittsburgh Commission on Human Relations (1973)
    Lehman v. Shaker Heights (1974)
    Eisenstadt v. Baird (1972)
    Bigelow v. Virginia (1975)
    Carey v. Population Services International (1977)
    Virginia State Board of Pharmacy v. Virginia Citizen Consumer Council, Inc. (1976)
    Bates and Van O'Steen v. State Bar of Arizona (1977)
    Ohralik v. Ohio State Bar Association (1978)
    In Re Edna Smith Primus (1978)
    Talsky v. Department of Registration and Education (1977)
    Linmark Associates, Inc. and William Mellman v. Township of Willingboro and Gerald Daly (1977)
    Zacchini v. Scripps-Howard Broadcasting Co. (1977)
    First National Bank of Boston v. Bellotti (1978)

FCC v. National Citizens Committee for Broadcasting; Channel Two Television Company v. National Citizens Committee for Broadcasting; National Association of Broadcasters v. FCC; American Newspaper Publishers Association v. National Citizens Committee for Broadcasting; Illinois Broadcasting Company v. National Citizens Committee for Broadcasting; Post Company v. National Citizens Committee for Broadcasting (1978).
Action for Children's Television v. FCC (1977)
FCC v. Pacifica Foundation (1978)
NBC v. Niemi (1978)

Chapter III: False and Deceptive Advertising

Section 1: Deceptive Business Practices: Federal Regulations *Daniel M. Rohrer* **249**
Section 2: Deceptive Business Practices: State Regulations *Daniel M. Rohrer* **259**
Section 3: The Law, Consumer Research, and the Question of Puffery *Herbert J. Rotfeld* **269**
Section 4: Adult-Oriented Businesses: A Case Study of Deceptive Advertising *Richard A. Kallan* **276**
Section 5: Improbable Claiming *Evan Blythin* **284**
Section 6: Cases **289**
  FCC v. ABC, NBC & CBS (1954)
  Testing Systems, Inc. v. Magnaflux Corp. (1966)
  FTC v. Colgate-Palmolive Co. (1966)
  J.B. Williams (Geritol) (1965)
  Libbey-Owens-Ford Glass Co. v. FTC (1965)
  J.B. Williams C., Inc. v. FTC (1967)
  J.B. Williams (Vivarian) (1972)
  Consumers Assoc. of DC v. CBS & WTOP-TV (1971)
  FTC v. Sperry & Hutchinson Co. (1972)
  American Home Products v. Johnson & Johnson (1977)
  Warner-Lambert Co. v. FTC (1977)
  U.S. v. STP (1978)

Chapter IV: Censorship and the Media

Section 1: The Promotion of Obscenity and Pornography *Daniel M. Rohrer* **341**
Section 2: Cases **359**
  Roth v. U.S. (1957)
  Memoirs v. Massachusetts (1966)
  Ginzburg v. United States (1966)
  Paris Adult Theatre I v. Slaton (1973)
  Miller v. California (1973)
  Jenkins v. Georgia (1974)
  Ward v. Illinois (1977)
  Splawn v. California (1977)
  Smith v. U.S. (1977)
  People v. Llewellyn (1977)
  Western Corp. v. Kentucky (1977)
  Pussycat Theatre v. State of Florida (1978)

St. Martin's Press v. Carey (1977)
Pinkus, dba "Rosslyn News Co." v. United States (1978)

Chapter V: Public Access to the Media

Section 1: The Fairness Doctrine and Equal Protection   *Daniel M. Rohrer*   **421**

Section 2: Cases and Hearings   **427**

   Poughkeepsie Buying Service, Inc. v. Poughkeepsie Newspapers, Inc. (1954)
   Miami Herald Publishing Co. v. Tornillo (1974)
   Banzhaf, III v. FCC (1968)
   Red Lion Broadcasting Co. v. FCC (1969)
   Retail Store Employees Union v. FCC (1970)
   Brandywine-Maine Line Radio v. FCC (1972)
   CBS v. DNC (1973)
   Council for Employment and Economic Energy v. FCC (1978)
   Congressional Statement on the Fairness Doctrine, *U.S. Rep. Robert Drinan,* former Dean, Boston College Law School (1975)
   Congressional Statement on the Fairness Doctrine, *U.S. Rep. Robert Drinan,* former Dean, Boston College Law School (1975)
   Georgia Power Project v. FCC (1977)
   National Citizens Committee for Broadcasting v. FCC (1977)
   Sec. 315, Federal Communications Act of 1934

Chapter VI: Warranty Limits on Free Speech and Advertising

Section 1: From Advertising to Warranties   *Daniel M. Rohrer*   **497**

Section 2: Cases   **509**

   Part A. *Offer*   **509**
      Craft v. Elder and Johnston Co. (1941)
      Steinberg v. Chicago Medical School (1976)
      Steinberg v. Chicago Medical School (1977)

   Part B. *Acceptance*   **518**
      Carlill v. Carbolic Smoke Ball Co. (1892)
      Georgian Co. v. Bloom (1921)

   Part C. *Consideration*   **522**
      Cole-McIntyre-Norfleet Co. v. Holloway (1919)
      Morris Lefkowitz v. Great Minneapolis Surplus Store (1957)
      Jenkins Towel Service, Inc. v. Fidelity-Philadelphia Trust Co. (1960)

   Part D. *Contract and Tort*   **530**
      Jacob E. Decker and Sons, Inc. v. Capps (1942)
      Henningsen v. Bloomfield Motors, Inc. (1960)
      Lasky v. Economy Grocery Stores (1946)
      Imperial Ice Co. v. Rossier (1941)

   Part E. *Warranties and the Pre-Existing Duty Rule*   **546**
      Wood v. Lucy, Lady Duff-Gordon (1917)

   Part F. *Warranties and Deceptive Advertising*   **547**
      Auto-Teria, Inc. v. Ahern (1976)
      Lantner v. Carson (1978)

Chapter VII: Defamation and Advertising

Section 1: The Role of Advertising in Defamation of Character   *Daniel M. Rohrer*, with *Martin P. LoMonaco*   **559**

Section 2: First Amendment Restrictions on the Public Disclosure Tort   *Joyce Rechtschaffen*   **581**

Section 3: Cases   **600**

    Kilian v. Doubleday & Co., Inc. (1951)
    New York Times Co. v. Sullivan (1964)
    Gertz v. Robert Welch, Inc. (1974)
    Greenbelt Cooperative Publishing Assoc. v. Bresler (1970)
    Time, Inc. v. Firestone (1976)
    Paul v. Davis (1976)
    Sharratt v. Housing Innovations, Inc. (1974)
    Flake v. Greensboro News Co. (1938)

Chapter VIII: Privacy and Advertising

Section 1: The Role of Advertising and the Right of Privacy   *Daniel M. Rohrer,* with *Martin P. LoMonaco*   **631**

Section 2: The First Amendment and the Abridgement of Individual Privacy   *Joyce Lindmark* and *Donald Fishman*   **668**

Section 3: Cases   **675**

    Haelan Laboratories, Inc. v. Topps Chewing Gum, Inc. (1953)
    Tollefson v. Price (1967)
    Time, Inc. v. Hill (1967)
    Cabaniss v. Hipsley (1966)
    Florida Publishing Company v. Fletcher (1977)
    Jeppson v. United Television (1978)
    Neff v. Time, Inc. (1976)

Preface

This text is designed as a stepping stone for the study of communication law. Its purpose is to serve as a beginning only, not as an end in itself.

As a result cases are reprinted in partial form, and internal citations have been deleted. As an aid to further research and investigation, however, the introductory sections to each chapter are intended to open new areas of interest which both explain the cases and advance the reader from the elementary application of case law to social, political, philosophical and historical perspectives that transcend the opinions of judges, clerks and lawyers' briefs.

The essence of each chapter is as follows:

Chapter I: Problems in Free Speech and Advertising

The purpose of this chapter is to introduce a variety of challenging concepts and practices in the context of limitations which are placed upon First Amendment rights. Subliminal advertising and violence on television comprise controversial topics that are of interest to scholars and critics alike. Recommendations for improvement, control and change are discussed from the viewpoint of academicians and journalists as well.

The first section summarizes and analyzes traditional theories of free speech, including the Bad Tendency Test, the Clear-and-Present Danger Test, the Incitement Test, the Balancing Test and the hypothetical Absolute Test. This section further develops a new theory of free speech, the Rationality Standard, which can permit a wide scope of expression and yet resist attrition by interpretation. The doctrine asserts that all advocacy warrants unqualified protection, unless it is presented in such a context that the listener does not have an opportunity to decide rationally whether or not to heed the speaker's appeal. Conditions to which this standard may be applied include mind control and subliminal advertising. With the exception of advertising and commercial speech, the roots and applications of these areas are expanded in a companion book entitled *Freedom of Speech and Human Rights: An International Perspective* (1979), by the same author and publisher.

Subsequent sections in Chapter 1 define areas in which arguments and cases can be made for both the increased and decreased regulation of advertising and commercial speech. They include subliminal advertising, crime and violence on television, and a whole new area of rights in which the media has an interest.

Chapter II: Commercial Speech

The rise and fall of commercial speech are traced from court rulings in recent decades. Here the current trend toward First Amendment protection of advertising is analyzed in the context of overbreadth and the need for greater regulation to meet the new and wider range of allowable advertising.

Areas addressed in this context include prescription drug prices, birth control devices, legal fees for services rendered, and the possibility of advertising the price of medical care. The question of whether corporations should be permitted to finance the advertising and promotion of political issues bridges the gap between commercial and political speech. Further consideration is given to the issue advanced by challenges to the integrity of sex and violence aired on television and the question as to whether there is any transfer effect to real life activity or actions on the part of some who view such acts on the broadcast media. Finally the questions concerning whether interests of Action for Children's Television should be pursued, and whether the media conglomerates should be dispersed, are discussed and illustrated.

Chapter III: False and Deceptive Advertising

An attempt is made here to scrutinize both the methods and effects of false and deceptive advertising. A variety of approaches to this kind of promotion is viewed from both a theoretical and case study approach. Lotteries are included, while similar techniques employed in TV quiz shows are reserved for Chapter 8, Privacy and Advertising. The role of the Federal Communication Commission and the Federal Trade Commission in regulating the electronic media is also considered, with an emphasis on the FTC and the control of advertising.

Section One contends that federal regulations intended to prevent deceptive advertising seek to balance the advertiser's freedom of speech with protection of the consumer. It discusses what the FTC has done to regulate advertising, evaluates the adequacy of its controls, and overviews its use of cease-and-desist orders, affirmative disclosure, corrective advertising, and advertisement substantiation requirements as its advertising controls. A review of court cases involving the FTC and advertisers attempts to determine whether the Commission has broad latitude in determining what advertising is deceptive, and whether the courts tend to uphold the decisions of the Commission.

Further review is made of the relationship between the FTC and the courts, and an attempt is also made to determine whether the FCC refers to the FTC most of the questionable broadcast advertising brought to its attention. Finally the National Association of Broadcasters is evaluated in terms of whether it has developed self-regulatory advertising codes that serve the radio and television milieu effectively and responsibly. The section also considers whether definitive steps have been taken against "psychological" advertising and whether, in light of regulation on the federal and state level, more can reasonably be expected for further control of false and deceptive advertising on the part of the government.

Section Two observes that although efforts have been made at the federal level to control deceptive advertising practices, many states have repealed such laws recently. This section examines attempts on the part of the states to balance the advertiser's freedom of speech with the consumer's need for information concerning products by comparing state legislation with five descriptive elements of the term "deception" and seven provisions concerning deceptive business practices outlined in the Model Penal Code of 1962.

Some of the unacceptable practices include mislabeling or adulterating products and making false or misleading statements. The section reflects the assumption that the line of demarcation between legitimate, desirable business conduct and illegitimate business conduct is continually in flux and is subject to great controversy (which can account for the variety of legal interpretations made by the states).

Section Three approaches the question of "psychological" advertising and puffery in advertising from an empirical effectiveness point of view. Sections Four and Five scrutinize the subject of false and deceptive advertising in the adult entertainment field on the basis of case studies in Las Vegas.

Chapter IV: Censorship and the Media

The question of whether, or the extent to which, obscenity and pornography should be censored is addressed as a problem that merits greater judicial attention, scrutiny, and consistency. Special consideration is given to the advertising methods employed in the promotion of these controversial interests. The possibility of a single federal standard is compared to the varying community standard application which predominates at the present time. Radio and television, billboards, and child pornography are addressed as areas that can be regulated without violating the First Amendment. The question whether these areas fall within the First Amendment is resolved in Chapter 5 in terms of limited air waves, and in this section in terms of distinguishing between speech and action. Prior restraint, on the other hand, is considered as it relates to the areas of interest in this chapter.

Chapter V: Public Access to the Media

In this chapter the advantages and disadvantages of the Fairness Doctrine are analyzed as a problem with which broadcasting stations and networks must contend. Comparisons are made to the print media, and the differences between the print and electronic media are contrasted as they relate to the need for varying degrees of information control and regulation.

It is noted that in general the advertising and print media are excepted as requiring equal time or space, and that a new bill in the House of Representatives, HR 13015, calls for the broadening of these exceptions to include all of radio and television. It would eliminate the FCC altogether, replacing it with a new and different form of regulation.

Chapter VI: Warranty Limits on Free Speech and Advertising

The bridge from advertising to warranties is surveyed as a means of understanding the point at which an advertisement may become so specific a commitment that it binds the advertiser and client to fulfill the terms of an unintended contract. When this occurs, innumerable consequences (both expected and unexpected, favorable and unfavorable) may affect the advertisers, clients, and customers. The results are studied as they affect contracts and tort liability, pre-existing duty, and the relationship between warranties and deceptive advertising.

Chapter VII: Defamation of Character and Advertising

Section One, an overview of the subject, considers the use of name or likeness as defamation of character. It provides an overview for the basis of liability, mitigating circumstances in action for libel and slander, the effect of retraction, defamation by radio and television, libel and slander in the electronic media, defamation and appropriation through cable television, and copyright law as it relates to defamation and cable television.

Here a study is made of the elements of defamation of character, of immunity for those who are protected from liability, and of use of libel for purposes of advertising or trade, for purposes of increasing the circulation of printed publications, and for purposes of increasing the listening and viewing audiences in the electronic media. The mitigating circumstances and degrees of immunity include absolute privilege, qualified privilege, journalists' privilege, fair comment, matter of public interest, government information, executive, legislative and judicial privileges and proceedings, truth of the statement, good faith in trustworthy information, malice or evil design, knowledge of falsity or reckless disregard for the truth, the entertaining of grave doubts standard, compensatory efforts, and consent.

Finally the area of requisite special damages is viewed as an inherent part of defamation in contrast to traditional liability and recovery. Libel *per se* and libel *per quod* are also distinguished in terms of their damages, proof requirements, and relative applications in majority and minority states respectively.

Chapter VIII: Advertising and Invasion of Privacy

Serving as the most extensive introduction to a chapter in the book, Section One analyzes the basis for invasion of privacy as well as privileges and immunities viewed in terms of the use of name, voice, picture, likeness or image for purposes of advertising or trade, for purposes of increasing the circulation of printed matter, and for purposes of increasing the listening and viewing audiences of the electronic media.

Here public figures are considered as newsworthy items; consent is discussed as a limitation upon liability. Employment, lapse of time, or revocation are discussed as mitigating circumstances against using the identity of a person for purposes of advertising or trade; malice is given equal attention as a prerequisite for liability in the privacy invasion of a public or newsworthy figure. The question as to whether a public figure, public interest or newsworthy interest standard should be employed is also discussed and analyzed.

These criteria are considered in the context of indorsement of products or services; the use of one's name on products; the use of one's name as part of a corporate name; the use of one's name for display purposes, in newspapers or other printed publications, on television or in motion pictures, and in newspapers or magazines.

The question of prior restraint is considered as it relates to the substance of the subject matter described above. This issue is addressed most directly in the context of censorship and the media in Chapter 4. The topic of prior restraint is pursued in greater breadth and depth in *Freedom of Speech and Human Rights: An International Perspective*.

The materials in these books seem to suggest that any form of speech or communication should be protected and permitted unless it violates the Espionage Act or involves mind control, racial discrimination, subliminal advertising, child pornography, obscene or offensive billboards; any form of advertising which intrudes substantially upon the privacy rights of others or upon their reputation or livelihood in a false or untrue way; and unless it is restricted by contract or warranty—in effect, other forms of consent. The privacy section written by Joyce Lindmark and Donald Fishman makes a special attempt to equate privacy rights with freedom of speech, placing a high premium upon the individual right of privacy and protection against public intrusion, disclosure or appropriation.

When community values come into play, they affect the First Amendment in terms of privacy rights. Justice Black underscored this principle for the majority of the Court in the case of *Village of Belle Terre* v. *Boraas,* 416 U.S. 1 (1974). Here he wrote the opinion and position of the Court to the effect that there becomes a point whereby the community should have the option of deciding for itself its internal restrictions, limitations, and privacy rights. Only Justice Marshall dissented on the merits of the case, and Justice Brennan dissented on procedural grounds. Surely such restraints should not include racial or religious discrimination, however.

On these terms, it is suggested that the community should decide issues involving questions of obscenity, pornography, and even subliminal advertising. While the use of community standards may invoke some uncertainty as to permissible limits of free speech and press, there seems to be no solution to this dilemma, short of the Absolute or Rationality Standards.

The only reasonable objection to the use of the Rationality Standard is that it is difficult to decipher borderline cases. Yet this difficulty is seldom compared to the uncertainty of not knowing whether the Incitement Standard, the Clear-and-Present-Danger Standard or the Balancing Standard will be invoked in a given case.

The problem of uncertainty over which free speech standard the Court may employ in a given instance has existed since it abandoned the newly adopted Clear-and-Present-Danger Standard, returning to the Bad Tendency Standard the very same year in the *Abrams* case. The criteria employed by the Supreme Court in determining which free speech standard it will apply under a given set of circumstances remains unclear. How to determine such criteria would provide the basis for a substantial doctoral dissertation or treatise of equal vigor.

The author wishes to extend his thanks to the many contributors and others whose patience and assistance made the completion of this work possible.

DMR

Introduction

Arthur Berney*

How pure and simple is the ideal that John Milton expressed in 1644:

And though all the winds of doctrine were let loose to play upon the earth, so truth be in the field, we do injuriously, by licensing and prohibiting, to misdoubt her strength. Let her and Falsehood grapple; who ever knew truth put to the worse, in a free and open encounter?

How beclouded and complex the matter has become in the three centuries in which we, Milton's heirs, have committed ourselves in significant measure to the pursuit of that ideal.

As the first chapter of this book about the unfolding of the ideal in modern America reveals, not even the underlying assumptions go unchallenged. We are, after all, the heirs of Freud as well, and as such we no longer are certain of Reason, not to speak of Truth. Perhaps an updated version of *Areopagitica* would rest on the less ambitious premise that free and open communication will at least serve to encumber the concentration of power. And in a world where truth is relative and reason is dubious, only the division of power may avert disaster.

The American system of government—of political, social, and economic order—is grounded in a more positive assertion of this same basic premise: *power must be and remain divided*. There are many provisions in our Constitution, even including its intrinsic framework, that serve this basic premise. But none serves it more dynamically or vitally than the First Amendment; for whatever else changes in human systems, the dynamic force of knowledge and beliefs remains a constant. Even revolutionaries know this and move swiftly to seize the public means of communication.

Freedom of expression, as the materials of this text richly demonstrate, is not a self executing principle of governance. It is a dynamic force and as such it must contend with other sources of power and the interests these serve in our society. In the nature of things this must be so. This very division of power that comes to be, will naturally resist alteration. It is thus not surprising that the communication of ideas that challenges the existing order, criticizes those in power, and questions popular beliefs, is that which will face the greatest resistance. Correlatively, the existing order will more often than not reflect very important, established social and political ideas. It is for these reasons that in the almost endless contexts in which the expression cases arise, another significant interest is in contention. The resolution process in such cases therefore, invariably appears to be that of balancing our commitment to freedom of expression against that other interest—be it security, health, quiet, privacy, economic well being, or whatever.

This balancing process takes place essentially in the courts of the land—ultimately in the Supreme Court. This is why, of course, materials on Communications Law are, as this book is, largely a compilation of leading cases. There is, however, an explanation for this that goes beyond the fact that

---

*Professor, Boston College Law School.

the right of expression is enshrined in our Constitution. The explanation lies in the relationship of the First Amendment right and the vindication of individual and minority interests in judicial forums. Political majorities and their causes need neither the First Amendment nor the courts. The will of the majority is expressed in the legislative forum. Individuals and dissidents require both the First Amendment, and the courts, where the "majority of one" is heard, to make their contribution to democratic rule. It is also because of this special relationship that courts are never comfortable merely balancing the First Amendment claim to free expression against whatever interest stands counterpoised. Thus, the Supreme Court in the speech cases has devised a series of standards that amount to a presumption in favor of the exercise of the First Amendment claim. Nevertheless each test the Court devises, short of absolute protection of First Amendment exercises, merely shifts to another level the balancing decision the Court must make.

The student should make a special effort to discover this process replayed in each series of cases offered in the various classes of disputes presented in the chapters of the book. In that fashion you will come to see that the different standards the courts devise in various contexts, over time, are analogs of one another. You will also recognize that the difficulty the courts face arises not only from resolving the important interests at stake, but also arises from the tension the judiciary must feel when it substitutes its judgment for that of the majority will.

In order to avoid the onus of substituting its judgment for that of the legislature or the executive, the Court has sometimes resorted to techniques of averting the clash of interests at stake. These techniques, such as the "overbreadth doctrine," may confuse the beginning student. What you should realize is that such techniques reflect the courts' effort to protect the free exercise of expression without directly declaring the official curtailment of the exercise specifically improper. Instead the court, under this doctrine, charges that the curtailment is invalid because it might have been more narrowly drawn. Whether or not it improperly curtails the exercise of rights of the claimant, the curtailment is invalidated because in its overbroad form it chills the exercise of First Amendment rights of others.

This "latest" ground of decision is mentioned, not only to suggest its connection with earlier tests, and certainly not to suggest that through it the courts can avert the basic dilemma of overriding democratic decisions (of majority rule) in the name of higher democratic principle (free speech), but also to recall the candor with which Justice Holmes answered this fundamental dilemma:

> But when men have realized that time has upset many fighting faiths, they may come to believe even more than they believe the very foundations of their own conduct that the ultimate good desired is better reached by free trade in ideas . . . . That at any rate is the theory of our Constitution. *It is an experiment, as all life is an experiment.* (emphasis added). *Abrams* v. *United States* , 250 U.S. 616, 630 (1919); Holmes, J., joined by Brandeis, J., dissenting.

Chapter I

Problems in Free Speech and Advertising

Section 1

A Rationality Standard for the First Amendment

*Daniel M. Rohrer**

INTRODUCTION

This section will attempt to formulate the general standards for determining the permissible limits of free expression. Because these guidelines seek to distinguish speech that forfeits constitutional protection, they cut across special cases and seek to define the extent to which any dissenting opinion may be controlled. The question of determining the permissible limits of free speech has been the subject of several articles in recent years, including "The Fighting Words Doctrine: From Chaplinsky to Brown" by Franklyn S. Haiman (*Iowa Journal of Speech*, Fall 1972); "Free Speech Decisions and the Legal Process: The Judicial Opinion in Context" by Don R. LeDuc (*The Quarterly Journal of Speech*, October 1976); and "The Art of Implying More Than You Say" by Sherida Bush (*Psychology Today*, May 1977). In particular, LeDuc, while discussing the role a scholar should play in the "development of a freedom of expression doctrine in law," suggests that:

> The typical lawyer is too immersed in day-to-day problems to gain a broader vision of the path free speech law should follow. Thus it seems up to the scholar not simply to follow legal techniques or a legal approach, but to use a synthesis of legal methodology and communication research techniques in perceptive fashion to develop a philosophy for the area of law of greatest concern to communication scholarship, that law defining rights in the vital process of communication.[1]

Thus, as the above reference suggests, there is an increasing need for communication scholars to consider seriously the direction or "path" that free speech will take in the future. This section will examine several contemporary speech standards including the Bad-Tendency Standard, Clear and Present Danger Standard, Balancing Standard, Incitement Standard, and Absolute Standard tests. Both their strengths and weaknesses will be highlighted and supported by Supreme Court precedents.

Furthermore, a new theory of speech, a Rationality Standard, will be presented. This doctrine suggests that all advocacy warrants unqualified protection unless it is presented in such a context that the listener does not have an opportunity to rationally decide whether to heed the speaker's appeal.[2]

---

*My thanks to Professor Arthur Berney of Boston College Law School, Professor Allan Lichtman of The American University, Mark Bly of Yale University and Martha, Martin LoMonaco, Laura Tramontozzi, Eric Woodbury, Stephen Kelly, and John P. Hart of Boston College for recommendations and assistance with this section.

Finally, this section in concluding will suggest alternative means of redress through the passage of laws and court litigation for those citizens who have grievances that fall outside the protection of the Rationality Standard, but are presently precluded by the exclusive jurisdiction of the Federal Trade Commission; specifically, those grievances produced by mind control and subliminal manipulation—the usage of subliminal perception devices and unconscious indoctrination techniques.

BAD–TENDENCY TEST

The Supreme Court initially formulated a First Amendment philosophy in the context of World War I indictments for disloyal and dangerous advocacy. These prosecutions, the first of their kind in over a century, were based on the Espionage Acts of 1917 and 1918. These statutes proscribed a variety of expression that was deemed inimical to the war effort. In their final form, the Espionage Acts prohibited (among other things):

> . . . false reports or false statements with intent to interfere with the operation or success of the military or naval forces of the United States or to promote the success of its enemies . . . attempts to cause insubordination, disloyalty, mutiny, or refusal of duty in the military or naval forces . . . attempts to obstruct the recruiting or enlistment services . . . saying or doing anything with intent to obstruct the sale of United States bonds . . . uttering scurrilous or abusive language, or language intended to cause contempt, scorn, contumely, or disrepute as regards the form of government of the United States; or the Constitution; or the flag; or the uniform of the Army or Navy . . . words or acts supporting or favoring the cause of any country at war with us, or opposing the cause of the United States.

Under the umbrella legislation, a motley collection of war protesters and radicals were prosecuted, few of whom posed the slightest danger to the war effort. Some of the prosecutions rivaled the theatre of the absurd. Mrs. Rose Pastor Stokes was indicted and convicted for declaring in a letter that "I am for the people and the government is for the profiteers." A farmer was imprisoned for using blasphemous and unpatriotic language at his dinner table in the presence of two guests. Others were convicted for expressing pacifist views, for questioning the constitutionality of the draft, for profanity uttered in the heat of argument, for criticizing the YMCA and the Red Cross, and (under state law) for discouraging women for knitting socks for the troops.[3]

Efforts to control the so-called Bad-Tendency speech may tend to inhibit freedom of expression, and furthermore require wasteful and unnecessary policing measures. The standard employed by the Supreme Court for distinguishing constitutional utterances from those subject to the Espionage Acts was the Bad-Tendency Test. Under this doctrine, any speech that has a tendency, however remote, to evoke substantial evil, forfeits the right to constitutional protection. As the previous examples show, the test is so broad that it virtually repeals the First Amendment. The standard was not rejected in the calm of normalcy, and was used to evaluate state laws against subversive expression in the 1920s and 1930s. It was not until 1937, with the decision in *Herndon* v. *Lowry*, 301 U.S. 242 (1937), that the Bad-Tendency Test was superseded by the Clear-and-Present-Danger Rule.[4]

CLEAR-AND-PRESENT-DANGER TEST

The Clear-and-Present-Danger Standard was first enunciated by Justice Oliver Wendell Holmes in *Schenk* v. *United States*, 249 U.S. 47 (1919), one of the World War I Espionage Act cases. "The question in every case is whether the words are used in such circumstances and are of such a nature as to create a clear and present danger that they will bring about the substantive evils that Congress has the right to prevent." This guideline was not long lived, however; for by the early 1950s it had been tacitly abandoned in favor of the Ad Hoc Balancing Test.[5]

The Clear-and-Present-Danger Rule represents an improvement over the Bad-Tendency Test in that it requires the state to justify the restriction of freedom of speech by establishing a more direct link between utterance and illegal or dangerous conduct. Yet, it is hardly a potent instrument for safeguarding free speech.[6]

First, it fails to recognize that expression, even when it poses a clear and present danger of substantive evil, may merit protection. Free expression is bound to conflict with societal interests and should not automatically be forced into a subordinate position in view of its vital importance. Witness, for example, Daniel Ellsberg and the Pentagon Papers; Woodward and Bernstein, and the Watergate affair; and finally Daniel Shorr and the CIA.

Second, the test is too vague. The phrase "clear and present danger" is subject to a variety of interpretations, and each word affords a wide latitude for subjective judgment. In difficult cases, this standard forces judges to rely on intuition.

Third, to effectively implement the test, there must be a factual determination of the sort normally beyond the scope of judicial inquiry. It requires the prediction of individual and mass behavior—a difficult and sometimes impossible task that involves the sophisticated manipulation of a vast quantity of unreliable data.

BALANCING TEST

At its fringes, the Clear-and-Present-Danger Rule touches upon another test which explicitly rejects any attempt at an *a priori* classification of speech. This is an Ad Hoc Balancing Test which, in each instance, involves a weighing of the value of the self-expression the government seeks to restrict against the social objective preserved through such regulation. Justice Felix Frankfurter was the foremost advocate of the Balancing Standard, employed most frequently in cases involving the indirect infringement of free speech.

The Balancing Test also has some serious defects. First, it entails even more difficult factual investigation than the Clear-and-Present-Danger Test, as both sides of the balance must be appraised.

Second, the standard may bias the judicial judgment in favor of the legislative decision, as Justice Frankfurter's opinions in First Amendment cases would indicate. First Amendment rights are generally asserted by the poor and minorities, while control is based on the broad interest in law and order. Yet the protection of such minorities from the tyranny of the majority is a major goal of the Constitution.

Third, the rule fails to specify the standards that should form the balancing procedure. Should the scales tip but a feather's weight in favor of the government to justify abridgement of speech, or must the state satisfy a more stringent requirement? Fourth, the standard makes the protection of free speech almost wholly dependent upon the attitudes of judges.

Fifth, the test confronts the judicial system with a different dilemma. Legitimate balancing would have to consider the possibility that the state could achieve its objectives through less restrictive means; yet it is extremely hard for the courts to discuss such potential legislation without encroaching upon the legislature's prerogatives or rendering advisory opinions.[7] Sixth, the Balancing Standard cannot afford police, prosecutors, other government officials, or private citizens adequate notice of which rights must be protected and which may be overruled.

THE INCITEMENT TEST

The most popular free speech standard today is the Incitement Test. As expressed in *Brandenburg* v. *Ohio*, 395 U.S. 444 (1969), "The constitutional guarantees of free speech and free press do not permit a state to forbid or proscribe advocacy of the use of force or of law violations except for where such advocacy is directed to inciting or producing imminent lawless action and is likely to incite or produce such action." The Incitement Standard is, in effect, a narrower and more precise restatement of the Clear-and-Present-Danger Rule. As such, it is probably the best guideline yet employed by the court. Brandenburg offers the most extensive protection to date of individual rights against state and local prosecution. Nonetheless, it suffers from all the defects of the original doctrine, at least to some degree.

ABSOLUTE TEST

An Absolute Test has never been an accepted standard as promulgated by a majority of the Supreme Court. Even for the primary advocates, Justice Black and Douglas, absolutist doctrine is still in an ill-defined state. It is based upon the premise that the founding fathers literally meant that the freedom of speech should not be abridged at all. Thus, it seeks to distinguish protected speech by "defining," rather than balancing. Certain types of expression, it argues, can be termed "speech" under the meaning of the First Amendment, and cannot be abridged. Other expression may be termed "action" and thereby subjected to some type of Balancing Test.

Thomas I. Emerson has extended and refined this formulation in an attempt to devise a First Amendment theory based upon the difference between speech and action, the definition of the words "law and abridge," and the delineation of "those sectors of social activity which fall outside the area in which, under the basic theory, freedom of expression must be maintained."[8] Emerson undertakes a lengthy and elaborate analysis of the way in which application of these principles would alter the practical application of First Amendment guarantees.

Admittedly, Emerson's ideas bring the interpretation of the First Amendment into a new context, that of classification. Nevertheless, they do not guide this process adequately. Nothing in this theory prevents the same considerations that underlie a balancing approach from determining the distinction between "speech and action;" the definition of "law and abridge ;" and delineation of the areas in which usual rights of expression do not operate. For example, suppression of the Communist Party could be justified on the grounds that the organization and operation of a political party constitutes action rather than speech. Although Emerson's concretization of his ideology advances civil liberties in specific instances, the same process, if undertaken by a scholar with different intuitions might yield opposite results.

RATIONALITY STANDARD

The following paragraphs suggest a new theory of free speech, one that is libertarian enough to permit a wide scope for expression and yet be sufficiently demanding to foreclose attrition by interpretation. The suggested doctrine is that all advocacy warrants unqualified protection, unless it is presented in such a context that the listener does not have an opportunity to rationally decide whether or not to heed the speaker's appeal. Although this test adequately applies to the straightforward assertion of unpopular or subversive opinions, it does not cover all types of advocacy, such as: 1) speech that is an integral part of a criminal act; 2) speech that conflicts with other provisions of the Bill of Rights; and 3) speech that includes a substantial part of conduct.

Condition 1 poses no serious problem. Crimes may involve the use of speech or other forms of communication: order may be given, plans laid, gunmen hired, etc., or expression may be used to bribe or defraud or swindle. Current doctrines recognize that such communications may be proscribed and few difficult cases arise.[9]

Condition 2 relates to the interface between privacy and free expression: two absolute rights cannot simultaneously exist. Some regulation of expression is necessary to maintain sanctity in our personal lives. The trade-off between privacy and free speech is so complex that general standards can hardly be given, except that there is now a far greater need to shield privacy from the government than from private individuals.

Condition 3 pertains to the indirect regulation of symbolic speech. Clearly, the government cannot give free reign to all forms of symbolic speech regardless of the conduct involved. This issue would need resolution by some type of Balancing Test.

All three conditions are simply an admission that not all free speech issues can be encompassed in a single comprehensive standard. Other special cases include freedom of religion, indirect controls on speech, and the regulation of public facilities. Two current practices which would be prohibited by the Rationality Standard, however, include mind control and subliminal advertising.

Mind Control

Perhaps the greatest threat to world stability and national security is unconscious manipulation of thought processes and emotional reactions. When powerful agents, such as the government, political candidates, business, or industry, find it necessary to resort to such measures, the most significant question should be not how effective such measures are, but what is the intent behind them. If the intent is to subvert the pursuit of rational decision making or belief, then the degree of success resulting from such efforts should be secondary, thought not unimportant, in an assessment of whether such practices should be permitted on any level or to any extent. These efforts have occurred in contemporary American society through organized attempts to control and manipulate the human mind for purposes of enhancing governmental objectives and enriching business or industry.

BUSINESS AND INDUSTRY

One example of a special case, which would be banned under the Rationality Standard, is concerned with the practice of unconscious indoctrination. This of course is a form of subliminal manipulation, and in the past this process has taken place in some mind control classes, sessions, and seminars.

An unacceptable form of mental conditioning was displayed by trained employees of Mind Dynamics Corporation, a subsidiary of U.S. Universal. The purpose of the course offered by Mind Dynamics was to train subscribers to take themselves into their "mental levels."

During the training session, subscribers were put into a state of relative unconsciousness. While in this state, subjects were conditioned, without their knowledge or consent, to invest in Holiday Magic, Inc., another subsidiary of U.S. Universal. This company was selling distributorships—the equivalent of franchises—the sale of which, for a variety of reasons, was subsequently banned by the Federal Trade Commission.[10] The franchises were promoted deceptively and fraudulently, yet the FTC ban on further sales fell short of requiring the corporation and its executives to return investments to those individuals who had been misled. Subsequently, the Securities and Exchange Commission sought to meet the latter need, but failed to accomplish its objective.

A second form of mind manipulation utilized by Holiday Magic, Inc., was that of misrepresenting to the public the success of the company's executives and salespersons for the purpose of promoting the sale of franchises or distributorships. Such personnel operate a chain distributor scheme which is:

> "a sales device whereby a person, upon a condition that he make an investment, is granted a license or right to recruit for profit one or more additional persons who also are granted such license or right upon condition of making an investment and may further perpetuate the chain of persons who are granted such license or right upon such condition." *Holiday Magic, Inc.* v. *Warren*, 357 F.Supp. 20 at 23 (1973).

Under this plan, persons licensed to sell licenses to other persons fabricated their own record of success in the business in corroboration with their district manager. Fabricated bills of sale were endorsed by the distributor in the presence of, and under the direction of, his district manager.

Sidestepping the issue, two courts in one state decided the question in terms of regulating the content of commercial speech without regard to falsehood. Nevertheless the decisions proscribed speech that furthered illegal activities. Here the court upheld a state prohibition upon "pyramid" sales schemes, including a prohibition on the "promotion" of such schemes. "Promotion was a form of commercial activity and the fact '(t)hat commercial activity takes the form of speech does not necessarily immunize it from regulation.'" *Id.* at 26. See also *H.M. Distributors* v. *Department of Agriculture*, 55 Wis. 2d 261, at 198, NW F.2d 205 (CA 4), cert. den., 409 U.S. 934 (1972).

These cases involving Holiday Magic, Inc. illustrate the failure of the Supreme Court "to provide any principled justification other than precedent for a commercial speech exception."[11] What may be needed is a more penetrating First Amendment standard that prohibits explicitly appeals to the human mind and emotions that are grounded upon irrational and untrue criteria that are not readily perceivable to the conscious mind.

Furthermore, to be legal under the Rationality Standard, the subject must know the purpose of the conditioning before it takes place. For example, a subject must first agree to unconsciousness conditioning for the purpose of giving up smoking, if such conditioning is to take place constitutionally under hypnosis. Any process of mental conditioning for a specific purpose must be known and agreed to by the patient or client before any such objective is pursued when the subject allows himself to be placed in a state of relative unawareness.

The relative success of hypnotic suggestion is not the point; for intent as well as effect raises the constitutional issue in question. Such is the case with all forms of mind control and subliminal advertising as well.

GOVERNMENT

The process of controlling, or attempting to control, the human mind may take a variety of forms. Another example of such a method may be found in activities of the CIA. For example, unwitting U.S. citizens have been subjected to drug testing by this government agency as part of its apparently unsuccessful research seeking various means of manipulating and controlling the human mind against the will of the subject.[12]

1. The Testing of Drugs

In his opening statement at Senate Subcommittee Hearings, where such efforts were verified, Senator Edward Kennedy explained that:

> The question is not whether a free society can accommodate the need for covert intelligence activities. The question is how those activities can be made accountable; how they can be carried out without jeopardizing the very freedoms they are supposed to protect.[13]

The Senator from Massachusetts pointed out that:

> . . . well motivated, patriotic Americans . . . , by their work, eroded the freedom of individuals and of institutions in the name of National security. . . . What we have seen over the issue of behavioral health research, which is the area of interest of this committee, during this period of time is that the agency worked effectively without accountability and, in so many instances, really basically without basic regard for the protection of the human subjects.[14]

In the following words Senator Kennedy, Chairman of the Subcommittee, summarized the Senate hearings on the CIA mind control operations:

> Individual Americans from all social levels, high and low, were made the unwitting subjects of drug tests; scores of universities were used to further CIA research objectives without their knowledge, thus threatening in a fundamental way their traditional independence and integrity; other Government agencies, such as the Bureau of Narcotics, the National Institutes of Health, and the Internal Revenue Service, were used to further the programs and mission of the Central Intelligence Agency.
> These projects were not the creation of low-level agency bureaucrats working against the wishes or without the knowledge of the Agency's leadership. The collection of activities now known as MK-ULTRA were approved, after personal review including briefings, by the Director of the Agency, Mr. Dulles.
> It is well known that another CIA Director, Mr. Helms, approved the destruction of the MK-ULTRA records in 1972. This has made the task of reconstructing those events very

difficult—both for the CIA and for interested Senate committees. What is clear now, from the witnesses we have heard and will hear, and from the few records that have been found, is the following:

1. When MK-ULTRA was phased out, it was replaced by MK-SEARCH. MK-SEARCH represented a continuation of a limited number of the ULTRA projects. It is now clear that the records of this project have also been destroyed. In fact, the records of all drug research projects available to the Director of the Technical Services Division of the CIA were destroyed at the same time.
2. Some operational activities utilizing the fruits of this research were carried out.
3. The bulk of the research effort led nowhere.
4. The Bureau of Narcotics was heavily involved in all the drug projects involving unwitting subjects.
5. The CIA had available certain documents pertaining to these activities in 1975, when this subcommittee's inquiry began, which they did not make available until 2 weeks ago; and that the Agency only discovered that some MK-SEARCH materials were available after the August 3 hearing.[15]

During the course of the hearings, the claims described above were substantiated by Dr. Charles F. Geschickter, Sr., Professor Emeritus of Research Pathology, Georgetown University Medical Center; David Rhodes and Phillip Goldman, former CIA employees; Adm. Stansfield Turner, Director, CIA; Harry E. Gordon, CIA Office of Research and Development; Ray Reardon, CIA Office of Security; Frank Laubinger, Office of Technical Services; Alan Brody, Office of Inspector General; Deanne C. Siemer, General Counsel, Department of Defense; and Sidney Gottlieb, M.D., former CIA agent.

Many of the activities described by these officials violate a Rationality Standard for the First Amendment, and would be proscribed by its provisions. However, it should be noted that the CIA appears to have curtailed such experimentation, at least in terms of conducting tests on unwitting U.S. citizens, and that individuals who implemented such experiments appeared to be reasonably open and candid about such work when they appeared before the Senate Subcommittee on Health and Scientific Research on September 20–21, 1977.

Nevertheless, more recently the CIA has apparently engaged in another infringement upon the Rationality Standard for the First Amendment. This activity, though apparently curtailed at the moment, involves manipulation of the news media.

2. Manipulation of the News Media

Evidence of such happenings was first revealed in newspapers, magazines, and the media in general. Consequently the House Intelligence Committee held hearings concerning the matter from December 27, 1977 to January 5, 1978. Here Stuart H. Loory of the *Chicago Sun-Times* explained that former CIA Director, William E. Colby, had revealed in November, 1973 that the CIA had retained American journalists as paid agents. "Colby at that time said there were 'some three dozen' American newspersons on the CIA payroll."[16]

In his opening statement for the hearings, Chairman Edward P. Boland explained: "We know that in the past the CIA has had contractual relationships—paid and unpaid—with individual journalists in both American and foreign news organizations."[17] Elaborating on this observation, Colby noted that: "While some 'black' propaganda was, indeed, produced by CIA and circulated abroad, for the largest part of its efforts fell in the so-called 'grey' area."[18]

The significance of this practice was noted by Gilbert Cranberg, editor of the editorial pages, *Des Moines Register and Tribune*, in the following words: "We print on our pages a substantial number of articles from foreign sources. Members of our editorial page staff rely on U.S. and foreign publications for information in forming the judgments we express. I am concerned, therefore, about the possibility of being an unwitting mouthpiece for CIA propaganda. I know many editorial page editors share the concern."[19]

The CIA viewpoint toward Cranberg's comment was answered in the hearings a day earlier by Morton H. Halperin, Director of the Center for National Security Studies. He explained that:

> As you will no doubt have been told in these hearings, members of the press, on their own initiative, talk frequently to officials of the CIA both at home and abroad as part of their regular newsgathering activities. No one would want to prevent this. The difficulty arises when the CIA exploits these relations or uses its network of foreign propaganda assets to influence American perceptions or to affect politics in the United States.
>
> The CIA's position is that it simply supplies information to American reporters at their request (presumably as its contribution to keeping the American public informed), and that when it supplies false and misleading information to its foreign assets, it views the feedback into the United States as an unintended and undesired consequence.[20]

Halperin continued by pointing out that there is "considerable evidence that the CIA has in the past and continues to use its various disinformation techniques to influence what appears in the American press, either to indirectly influence events abroad or to affect events in the United States."[21] He proceeded to review in detail several episodes which have come to light. They included: a) The CIA effort to discredit studies critical of the Warren Commission Report; b) The CIA effort to present Salvador Allende as a threat to a free press in Chile; c) The CIA exploitation of the murder of Robert Welch, its station chief in Greece; and d) The CIA effort to discredit Elias Demetracopoulos.[22]

a. The Warren Commission Episode

According to Halperin, "on April 1, 1967, the CIA sent a dispatch to some of its field offices directing them to take action where there was discussion of the John F. Kennedy assassination to discredit and counter the claims of American authors challenging the results of the Warren Commission Report."[23] Halperin continued his prepared statement with the explanation that:

> The cable provided a list of themes to be used and directed the stations "to employ propaganda assets to answer and refute the attacks of the critics. Book reviews and feature articles are particularly appropriate."
>
> . . . its spill back effects in the United States should have been clearly anticipated.[24]

b. *Allende and the Chilean Press*

As part of the effort to prevent Salvadore Allende from coming to power or remaining in office, the CIA spread the word through its media assets that he would abolish freedom of the press in Chile. The recent *New York Times* series on the CIA and the press reports that the CIA arranged for the Inter-American Press Association to issue a statement charging that freedom of the press was being jeopardized in Chile. This statement was reported in the U.S. as well as the Latin Press.

The CIA . . . went a step further in providing a briefing to *Time* magazine, at its request, and perhaps to other magazines as well. The Church Committee described this episode as follows:

"Third, special intelligence and inside briefings were given to U.S. journalists, at their request. One *Time* cover story was considered particularly noteworthy. According to the CIA documents, the *Time* correspondent in Chile apparently had accepted Allende's protestations of moderation and constitutionality at face value. Briefings requested by *Time* and provided by the CIA in Washington resulted in a change in the basic thrust of the *Time* story on Allende's September 4 victory and in the timing of that story."

. . . the CIA provided *Time* with the same information that was being put out to its assets in Latin America. In particular, the documents emphasized the threat to freedom of the press in Chile.

This was done despite the fact that the DDI intelligence estimates were apparently suggesting that no U.S. vital interests would be threatened by an Allende regime. *Time* requested a briefing on Chile. It was given a propaganda document by an official of the clandestine services.[25]

c. *The Welch Assassination*

The Welch Assassination case is the only episode that I am aware of where there is clear evidence of CIA manipulation of the American press for the purpose of influencing events in the United States. The CIA successfully exploited the murder of one of its station chiefs to set back efforts to bring the CIA under constitutional control.

The facts are no longer in serious dispute.

Sometime before Welch went to Greece, an American magazine, *Counter-Spy*, identified him as station chief in Peru. This did not lead to cancellation of his assignment. When Welch arrived in Athens he decided to live in the home that CIA station chiefs had occupied for many years. A cable from Langley urged him to live elsewhere, pointing out that it was widely known in Athens' political circles that the CIA chief lived in that house. Welch was warned that with anti-American feeling running high, he risked assassination if he remained in the house. He tragically rejected the advice.

When word of Welch's murder reached Washington, the CIA assistant to the Director for press relations, Angus Thuermer, called many Washington reporters and told them on deep background, that an American magazine had published Welch's name and that he was now dead. Lest the point be missed, Thuermer, or some other CIA official, said on background—for attribution to "a U.S. intelligence source"—that "we've had an American gunned down by other

Americans fingering him—right or wrong—as a CIA agent." Thuermer did not tell anyone that the Agency had warned Welch not to live in that house. Indeed, Daniel Schorr reported in the *Washington Post* on December 27 that, months later, when the Senate Intelligence Committee was investigating this episode, the CIA Director sought to persuade the committee not to make that fact public.

American newspapers the next day reported, on their own authority that Welch's name had been published in an American magazine and now he was dead. Consider how different the Welch episode would have been if the stories had begun: "Two months after he was warned not to live in a notorious house long known to be occupied by CIA station chiefs, Richard Welch was murdered as he returned to the house late last night." That the stories instead suggested that *Counter-Spy* was responsible for his death was the result of a deliberate CIA manipulation of the American press.[26]

d. *The Demetracopoulos Episode*

On December 6, 1977, the *New York Times* carried an article by David Binder, describing the activities of Elias P. Demetracopoulos. The story contained the following sentence: "*CIA records* show that in 1951 Mr. Dimitracopoulos (sic) offered his services to the agency and was turned down. They show that he offered to work for United States Army Intelligence in August 1951 and was again turned down. The CIA further alleged that in the 1950's he was associated with both Yugoslavia and Israeli intelligence services." I understand that Mr. Binder has since confirmed to journalists that he was shown portions of Mr. Demetracopoulos' CIA file.

Mr. Demetracopoulos has been seeking his files under the FOIA. He has seen, I understand, no files showing the alleged contacts with U.S. intelligence. He has been given a CIA memorandum saying that agency had no record of his having worked for any foreign intelligence service.

Why did a CIA official show portions of Mr. Demetracopoulos' file to a *New York Times* reporter? I urge this committee to explore whether this was not part of a deliberate CIA effort by the clandestine services to discredit a persistent critic. Whatever the motive the CIA cannot be permitted to deliberately provide information from its files about individuals without their permission. Such action may well violate the Privacy Act. It certainly violates the CIA charter.[27]

The four examples described above involve the planting of articles and editorials without attribution in publications to which the CIA has special access. As a recent series of articles in the *New York Times* brings out, "A lot of this sort of thing goes on, or used to."[28] William C. Trueheart pointed out in his opening statement of committee hearings, however, that he does not recall any such activities that were remarkably effective.[29] Trueheart contended further that: ". . . the exposure of such involvements has on occasion been an embarrassment in our foreign relations and the overall effect on our national reputation may be significant."[30] Finally, Trueheart argued that: ". . . perhaps the most serious problem about these activities is that they are not susceptible to the sort of high level review and supervision which should be accorded covert action operations."[31]

Trueheart recommends that: ". . . there should be a strict arms-length relationship between CIA (and other U.S. intelligence agencies) and the American press. I would favor a statutory ban on operational use of American media for clandestine intelligence or covert action purposes."[32] So long as the CIA refrains from providing slanted or fabricated stories in the interests of deception, there may very well exist a worthy relationship between the CIA and the media.

Legislation curbing such a relationship would probably be unnecessary or even undesirable in the opinions of some journalists. According to Joseph Fromm, Deputy Editor of *U.S. News and World Report*, "Existing legislation, if effectively enforced, would prevent the Agency from engaging in domestic activities—and that could be interpreted to apply to deliberate attempts to engage in disinformation in this country. A new law seeking to regulate CIA relations specifically with the news media would, in my judgment, raise more questions than it would answer—both with respect to freedom of the press and the future effectiveness of legitimate clandestine collection of intelligence."[33]

Herman Nickel of *Fortune Magazine* expressed it well in his opening statement as follows: "In the end the problem can't be solved by CIA policy directives, and certainly not by Congressional action which would probably violate the First Amendment. This principal burden, I firmly believe, rests on the press itself."[34]

In keeping with a substantial interest in such an alternative, an October 1976 resolution by the Board of Directors of the American Society of Newspaper Editors bars any CIA relationships with fulltime or parttime journalists.[35] Following this action, on November 30, 1977, the CIA implemented a resolution governing relations with the media. It almost eliminated the relationship between CIA overseas and American journalists.[36] However, even before that George Bush, Director, on February 11, 1976, advised the CIA not to enter any future contractural relationship with any fulltime correspondents of American news media. Subsequently Bush and CIA representatives gave assurance to the National News Council, on June 24, 1976, that this directive prohibits CIA employment of American news executives, stringers for American news organizations, foreign nationals working as newsmen for American news organizations, and freelance writers who would be interpreted in any manner as being journalists.[37]

It would seem that such sanctions may be sufficient, for the ". . . credibility of American news media is damaged when evidence is produced, and even when mere rumor is circulated, that reporters, editors, and publishers are used to support and promote governmental policy."[38] It should be noted, furthermore, that control over CIA manipulation of the media would not violate the First Amendment because CIA manipulation of information is government action. Moreover, such activity is deceptive, fraudulent, and violates the CIA charter. For these reasons such conduct may be regulated by the government without contravening the First Amendment. Under present circumstances, however, it does not appear necessary for such regulation to occur. Problems which have existed in the past have been insignificant, and have since become curtailed internally both by the media and by the CIA. In contrast a study of mind control in the Soviet Union is provided in *Freedom of Speech and Human Rights* by this writer.

An area that violates the Rationality Standard and is currently uncontrolled either internally or externally should be of greater concern at this time. It is the use of subliminal techniques for purposes of advertising or increasing the circulation of a publication. Measures that might be required to regulate such activity would not involve the "least reasonable man" principle,[39] which merely suggests that the ignorant are entitled to special legal protection solely because they are ignorant or uneducated. The Rationality Standard, on the other hand, presumes that if any individuals, including intelligent and well educated people, are not given the opportunity to rationally assess the information presented to them, should they desire to do so, then something is inherently wrong with the means or methods of presentation of the information in question. A contemporary area of study whereby such conditions exist involves the use of subliminal techniques in the news media, in the entertainment field, and in advertising, as well as in television commercials.

*Subliminal Advertising**

Another special case, the illegal usage of subliminal perception devices, would also be banned under the Rationality Standard. One example of such conduct would be the use of tachistoscopes. The tachistoscope was initially used in the 1960s to flash messages superimposed over motion pictures in theatres or upon film being transmitted through television. The highspeed messages were invisible to the conscious mind, but planted messages in the viewer's subconscious. They were designed to induce film viewers to buy products, and in some cases they were effective. During one six-week test of the tachistoscope in a movie theatre involving 45,699 patrons, messages were flashed on alternate days: "Hungry? Eat Popcorn," and "Thirsty? Drink Coca-Cola." As a result of this test, popcorn sales increased 57.7 percent and Coca-Cola sales increased 18.1 percent during that six-week period.[40]

Another example of the usage of subliminal perception devices occurred shortly before Christmas in 1973, when it was called to the attention of the Federal Communications Commission that some television stations had broadcast an advertisement that contained the subliminal message: "Get It!" "Commission inquiry revealed that the NAB-TV Code Authority had learned of the use of the subliminal messages in late November and had received a statement from the advertising agency to the effect that it was dispatching telegrams to all stations to which the advertisements had been sent, informing them of the subliminal statements, authorizing the stations to delete the statements from the spots and informing the stations that film prints that did not contain the 'Get It!' flashes would be sent to them . . . ." Despite the Code Authority's action, some stations apparently continued to broadcast spots containing the "Get It!" statement, and some state they have no record of having received the telegram from the agency.[41]

Then too, in March, 1976, Dr. Wilson Bryan Key in his statement before the Congressional Subcommittee on Alcoholism and Narcotics alluded to many illegal usages of subliminal manipulation in the media. In one case, Key pointed out that he had several photographs from *Time* Magazine which according to him had the word "sex" embedded in them numerous times (Figures 1 and 2). Key also stated that subliminal manipulation techniques had been employed in various political campaigns including one in the United States: "I looked at one Congressional campaign in the United States—right here in Arlington, Virginia. Subliminals were being used almost universally by the candidates. I think, in all fairness however, without the candidates' awareness. It is done by the advertising agencies as a standard production technique."[42] According to Key, an example of this occurred in the Rufus Philips' campaign posters where the word "sex" was again supposedly embedded (Figure 3).

In assessing the question whether legal measures should be taken for the purpose of controlling the use of subliminal advertising, it is important to consider the following issues: 1) Is the use of a given subliminal technique in advertising intentional? 2) Is the use of a given subliminal technique in advertising effective? 3) Is there any viable means of regulating the use of subliminal advertising?

---

*Note: The first three illustrations in this discussion of subliminal advertising are based on the research of Wilson Bryan Key as produced in his books, *Subliminal Seduction* (Signet) and *Media Sexploitation* (Prentice-Hall) and as given in his statement to the Subcommittee on Alcoholism and Narcotics of the Committee of Labor and Public Welfare. The use of illustrative material within this discussion is for the sole purpose of viewing the effects of advertising media rather than reflecting adversely on the advertiser.

14 Problems in Free Speech and Advertising

Courtesy of Wilson Bryan Key, PhD.

Figure 1

A Rationality Standard for the First Amendment

Courtesy of Wilson Bryan Key, PhD.

Figure 2

16 Problems in Free Speech and Advertising

Rufus Phillips for Congress

Courtesy of Wilson Bryan Key, PhD.

Figure 3

1. Is the use of a given subliminal technique in advertising intentional?

The examples of the six-week test of the tachistoscope in a movie theatre, of the Vietnam collage, and of the campaign poster were cited for the reason that they might illustrate possible cases of what appears to be the intentional usage of subliminal imbeds for the purpose of increasing the circulation of a publication or a political candidate's image.

If it can be established that an attempt has been made to defraud and deceive the human mind for commercial or political reasons, by appealing to the unconscious or subconscious senses, then the success or lack of success, effectiveness or ineffectiveness, of the effort should not be dispositive of the issue. On the contrary, in such an action the intent should be decisive regardless of the impact resulting from attempted action.

In his books entitled *Subliminal Seduction* and *Media Sexploitation*,[43] Wilson Bryan Key illustrates and describes a wide variety of subliminal advertising forms. They range from images that may or may not involve intentional attempts to employ subliminal techniques to images of a more subjective nature which require conjecture and explanation.

An example of the latter category may be found in the work of art. It is often difficult to determine the intent behind images which may or may not have been designed with subliminal content in mind. One instance of this uncertainty may be viewed on the cover of the North Suburban Boston telephone directory.

Courtesy of Arthur L. Griffin.

Figure 4

18   Problems in Free Speech and Advertising

Apparently unknown to Arthur Griffin, the artist and photographer responsible for what appeared, the phone company, and anyone else who saw it, "the seemingly innocent picture of Woburn's Horn Pond concealed what some see as visual dynamite. Only after thousands of phone books had been distributed to homes and businesses across the state did people begin to notice the interesting shape produced by the overhanging tree and its reflection: when the book was turned sideways, the symmetrical image can be interpreted as a picture of a nude female body."[44] When turned to the other side, the appearance is that of a nude male body. The neck of the female, when the picture is turned to one side, is the penis of the male, when the picture is turned to the other side.

The artist responsible for the drawing claimed that he "had no idea of the hidden picture in it until it came out on the telephone cover." He agrees that he now sees it too.[45] In Griffin's opinion: "It's actually an accident of nature. I've taken thousand's of shots all over the world and this is the first time I found a real double meaning in any of my transparencies."[46]

Now 75 years of age, Griffin began as a commercial artist. After studying at Boston's New School of Design, he joined the art staff of the *Boston Globe* in 1929. Gradually he moved on to photography. Later he left the *Globe* to freelance, and since 1946 has spent 22 years traversing the planet on assignment for the *Saturday Evening Post, Time, Fortune, Colliers, Holiday,* and the Eastman Kodak Corporation.

© 1976 Pro Arts, Inc., Medina, Ohio. Reprinted with permission.

Figure 5

A second instance of subliminal seduction, which may to some extent be unintentional, is that of the famous and best selling Farrah Fawcett-Majors poster. One *Playboy* magazine reader, Jeff Kimelman of Philadelphia, wrote in to inform the editors of the publication that the poster was subliminal. He suggested that the interested viewer observe the word "sex" spelled out in Farrah's tresses.[47] Whether of not this appearance was intended remains an open question.

It is quite possible that the illustrations above constitute mere illusions of subliminal imbeds rather than serving as examples of such imbeds. If that is true, to suppress them through any legal sanctions or with any legal measures whatsoever would be to intrude upon the rightful domain of the First Amendment and freedom of speech.

On an earlier occasion, Judge Learned Hand described a subliminal illusion in the following way:

Two photographs were inserted; the larger, a picture of the plaintiff in riding shirt and breeches, seated apparently outside a paddock with a cigarette in one hand and a cap and whip in the other. This contained the legend, "Get a lift with a Camel"; neither it, nor the photograph is charged as part of the libel, except as the legend may be read upon the other and offending photograph. That represented him coming from a race to be weighed in; he is carrying his saddle in front of him with his right hand under the pommel and his left under the cantle; the line of the seat is about twelve inches below his waist. Over the pommel hangs a stirrup; over the seat at his middle a white girth falls loosely in such a way that it seems to be attached to the plaintiff and not to the saddle. So regarded, the photograph becomes grotesque, monstrous, and obscene; and the legends, which without undue violence can be made to match, reinforce the ribald interpretation. (*Burton* v. *Crowell Pub. Co.*, 82 F.2d 154 (1936).)

A subliminal imbed, on the other hand, is another matter. It is real rather than a mere illusion. While such techniques may have been employed in art and sculpture throughout history, it is only in advertising, commercial, political and religious speech that a Rationality Standard for the First Amendment would prohibit its use.

In the pages that follow, methods for regulating subliminal advertising are suggested. A rationality interpretation of the First Amendment should protect such legal remedies. This is not to suggest that such measures are necessary, however. For the mere threat of exposure may serve as a deterrent to the future use of subliminals by the industry involved.

The inhibiting effects of exposure of mind control activities can be seen in the curtailment of CIA efforts to manipulate the press and to test drugs on unwitting individuals. (See CIA hearings discussed above and John Marks, "Sex, Drugs and the CIA," *Saturday Review* (February 3, 1979), 12–16.)

Furthermore, it should be kept in mind that laws and regulations intended to or purported to protect the consumer often do quite the opposite. As will be suggested under the Pre-Existing Duty Rule in Sections One and Two of Chapter Six, for example, the consumer might be in a better position without a warranty because it simply limits liability and serves as a substitute for a more rewarding common law warranty.

Although examples of subliminal imbeds are neither illustrated with certainty nor cited through explanation and fair use commentary in this text, it is apparent that the use of such subliminals in advertising has continued at least throughout the year 1978. Evidence and explication of their existence and implementation remains for another publication.

In the meantime one must resort to observing what is considered by Dr. Key to be subliminal illusions in the advertisements not only of the products discussed above but of L. and M. Cigarettes and

Benson and Hedges cigarettes as well. Furthermore, such appearances are apparent in advertisements for numerous alcoholic beverages, such as Gilbey's Gin, Dewars Whiskey, Tanguaray Gin and Johnnie Walker Scotch, according to Wilson Bryan Key.

The three examples above suggest how it may be possible to observe in a picture or drawing foreign images which do not seem to belong in the context of a given advertisement or promotional device. They may result from the natural shading and lining in the background, or they may have been designed willfully on the part of the artist, photographer or scene designer. This writer has been informed directly from the original source that such subliminal devices have been employed intentionally and deliberately in the preparation of cosmetic commercials for television viewing.

Unless it can be demonstrated that a prohibited form of subliminal advertising has been practiced intentionally, it is impossible to establish a *prima facie* case against the offender. Thus it is necessary not only to isolate an unambiguous form of subliminal advertising, but it must be shown to have resulted from knowledge or awareness on the part of its creator and there must be a law prohibiting such conduct. Presently there is none in the United States.

2. Is the use of a given subliminal technique in advertising effective?

Once intent has been proven, the question of whether the use of subliminal advertising has an impact upon the receiver's belief or behavior must be considered as a possible element of the offense. Studies have been conducted to measure the degree of such effects upon individuals who have been exposed to sublimination.

The question of whether subliminal advertising is effective has been tested on a number of occasions. The results have been mixed, and fall short of resolving the issue. According to the results of empirical studies conducted by Dr. Lloyd H. Silverman of New York Veterans Administration Hospital and New York University, in each of 18 studies, the presentation of drive related stimuli to subjects at a subliminal level has proven capable of evoking pathological manifestations.[48]

Dr. Silverman discovered further that the subliminal exposure of wish-related stimuli can be expected to influence psychopathology since they stimulate such wishes "silently," for example, without allowing them to emerge into consciousness.[49] Many studies have now shown the effectiveness of subliminal psychodynamic activation. It is now evident that a subliminal stimulus can bring about behavior change as a result of activating psychodynamic processes.[50]

It has been shown that the use of subliminal techniques can affect individual responses. However, such conclusions are not being identified here for the purpose of implying that the degree of impact resulting from such practices should be a decisive factor as to whether such practices should be permitted or restricted. Surely a significant effect upon the behavior or attitudes of individuals, resulting from the use of subliminal methods, would serve as an equally significant reason for regulating the use of such practices. Nevertheless, such a conclusion is not intended to suggest that subliminal advertising should not be controlled for less cause.

It should be noted that the term "significant" is relative to its context. The degree of significance required to justify a change in policy should outweigh the risk of uncertainty that unknown adverse consequences will occur should the change be implemented. Known adverse results of change would also be a consideration mitigating the basis for change.

For example, if there is only a small chance that the use of subliminal advertising may affect any of the subjects upon whom it is employed, and if only a small economic loss is suffered as a result of curtailing such activity, there would be greater reason for curtailing the activity than for permitting it to continue. In the case of subliminal advertising, a specific comparison can be made in terms of the advantages and disadvantages of curtailing its use.

Subliminal advertising is obviously a form of commercial speech. It is employed for the purpose of increasing the sales of the products advertised. If the use of subliminal advertising is effective, there would be ample reason for curtailing it by its very nature—by virtue of the fact that it is subliminal. If, on the other hand, the use of subliminal advertising is ineffective, there would be no loss to anyone if its employment were curtailed, since it achieves nothing and therefore gains no one anything.

In other words, if the use of subliminal advertising is effective, that is *prima facie* evidence justifying the regulation of all such activity. If the use of subliminal advertising is ineffective, on the other hand, there would be no loss suffered by anyone who might be denied its further use as an advertising technique. Thus the regulation of subliminal advertising could meet the balancing test of the First Amendment even if its effects upon individuals could be shown to be ineffective. Furthermore, the question as to whether subliminal advertising should be regulated may be decided solely on constitutional grounds, regardless of any balancing criteria or empirical data relating to its effects upon individuals who may see and/or hear any form of its manifestations. Examples of governmental regulation for constitutional reasons, regardless of empirical effects, may be found in the areas of school busing for racial integration and limits upon the use of capital punishment as a deterrent to crime and violence.

a. *School Busing*. It has been well established in court decisions that racial integration is an end in itself, and in the educational system should take first priority regardless of whether it can be demonstrated empirically that the quality of education *per se* is improved as a result of implementing such a program nationally. While educational improvement in the traditional sense is a desired goal of school busing for racial integration, the latter is an independent end for its own sake and thus takes priority over any of its effects. Thus racial integration is an end in itself regardless of whether it can be shown empirically that it results in an improved quality of education for anyone.

b. *Capital Punishment*. Likewise, there are overriding reasons for refusing to impose blanket capital punishment upon the law at either the federal or state level. These reasons transcend any established basis for more law and order, regardless of its basis. The question is not a matter of empirical data, although such information should be at least a consideration; it is first a question of constitutional principle.

c. *Civil and Criminal law*.

While it is quite possible that the use of subliminal advertising has little or no effect upon many and perhaps most individuals are not affected significantly by exposure to subliminal advertising, should not the few who Silverman found may be affected by it receive legal or regulatory protection when the sole intent behind such use could be none other than its effect? Indeed, intent to do the act is the key to a battery, not the intent to harm. (*McGuire* v. *Almy*, 8 N. E. 2d 760 (1937).)

As in the case of battery, the tort of assault need not require a showing of harm or effect, although the latter may serve as criteria in assessing damages. For example, "(I)f one strike another upon the hand, or arm, or breast in discourse, it is no assault, there being no intention to assault; but if one, intending to assault, strike at another and miss him, this is an assault." *Tuberville* v. *Savage*, 1 Mod. Rep. 3, 86 Eng. Rep. 684 (1669). Again, the critical issue is one of intent rather than harm or effect.

As long as the defendent intends to recklessly cause an apprehension in the mind of the plaintiff, he may be liable even if the apprehension is not created. *Allen* v. *Hannaford*, 138 Wash. 423, 244 P. 700

(1926). Thus it is unnecessary and irrelevant to consider the severity of the apprehension in order to determine whether there has been an assault. *Tuberville, supra.*

Along with battery and assault, false imprisonment has now become exclusively an intentional tort. The *Restatement* (Second) *of Torts* Section 35, Comment *h,* points out, however, that for negligence resulting in the confinement of another a negligence action will lie, but only if some actual damage results. *Cf. Mouse* v. *Central Savings and Trust Co.,* 120 Ohio St. 599, 167 N.E. 868 (1929). Thus it is suggested once again that when intent is demonstrated a showing of damages is unnecessary.

Likewise mental distress is a tort the harm or effect of which is not essential for recovery when inflicted intentionally. Here the Supreme Court extended the right of recovery to situations where no physical injury follows the suffering of mental distress, saying that: "(A) cause of action is established when it is shown that one, in the absence of any privilege, intentionally subjects another to the mental suffering incident to serious threats to his physical well-being, whether or not the threats are made under such circumstances as to constitute a technical assault." *State Rubbish Collectors Association,* 38 Cal.2d 330, 240 P.2d 282 (1952); also see *Taylor* v. *Vallelunga,* 171 Cal. App.2d 107, 339 P.2d 910 (1959).

In a later case the Supreme Judicial Court of Massachusetts overruled an 80-year-old precedent and abandoned the requirement that the plaintiff must suffer some "impact" in order to be permitted to recover damages for negligently caused emotional distress. The court upheld a claim for damages made by the estate of a mother who died from the emotional shock, distress and anguish which she experienced when she learned that her daughter had been struck by a motor vehicle while alighting from a school bus. The court denied recovery for the death of the child's father, however, who himself died when he learned about his wife and child. While the mother had come on the scene soon after the child was injured, the allegations in the complaint concerning the father did not reveal where, when, or how he had come to know of the injury to his daughter and death of his wife. *Dziokonski* v. *Babineau,* 380 N.E.2d 1295 (1978).

The reasoning of the seven-judge court ruling concerning a new "impact" standard was explained by Justice Wilkins in the following words:

> At the heart of the plaintiffs' claims is the argument that this court should abandon the so called "impact" rule of *Spade* v. *Lynn & Boston R.R.,* 168 Mass. 285, 290, 47 N.E. 88 (1897), which denies recovery for physical injuries arising solely from negligently caused mental distress. We agree that the rule of the *Spade* case should be abandoned. *Ibid,* 1296.

The Court explained the relevance of intent in the following way suggesting "We have never applied the *Spade* rule to bar recovery for (the tort of) intentionally caused emotional distress. The Spade opinion itself recognized that the result might be different if the defendant's conduct had been intentional and not negligent. We left that question open in *Smith* v. *Postal Tel. Cable Co.,* 174 Mass. 576, 578, 55 N.E. 380 (1899), and it so remained until 1971, when we decided *George* v. *Jordan Marsh Co.,* 359 Mass. 244, 268 N.E.2d 915 (1971)." The Court said:

> The question of liability for intentionally or recklessly caused severe emotional distress in the absence of bodily harm came before us in *Agis* v. *Howard Johnson Co.,* 355 N.E.2d 315 (1976). There, we held that a complaint alleging extreme, outrageous, and unprivileged conduct by the defendant stated a cause of action in favor of both the female plaintiff who sustained emotional

distress but no bodily harm and her husband for loss of consortium. We rejected arguments that we should deny recovery for emotional distress where there is no physical injury because of the insurmountable difficulties of proof and the danger of fraudulent or frivolous claims. Although we recognized these problems, we rejected them as an absolute bar in all such cases and concluded that these were proper matters for consideration by the trier of fact in the adversary, trial process. 355 N.E.2d 315.

Thus the Court seemed to suggest that proof of impact is unnecessary when intent can be established, leaving open need for impact in other cases.

Furthermore, the tort of trespass to land is concerned primarily with the question of intent. While there may be negligent trespass, it is governed by the ordinary rules applicable to negligence actions. "One of these is that when the entry upon the land is merely negligent, proof of some actual damage is essential to the cause of action." William L. Prosser, *et. al., Cases and Materials on Torts* (1976), 71. When the trespass is intentional, there may nevertheless be nominal damages despite the fact that the trespass does no harm to anyone or anything.

While it may be argued that some forms of subliminal advertising may be beneficial to both the individual and society, when a trespassory invasion is found, the fact that the defendant's conduct was useful in a social sense or even advantageous to the plaintiff was usually considered immaterial. See *Harmony Ditch Co.* v. *Sweeney,* 31 Wyo. 1, 222 P. 577 (1924); *Longenecker* v. *Zimmerman,* 175 Kan. 719, 267 P.2d 543 (1954).

The tort of nuisance, on the other hand, may take into account the social utility of the defendant's activity, but the protection of the plaintiff's use and enjoyment of his land can be measured on more tangible criteria than can the use of a form of advertising that it may be impossible for the plaintiff to be aware. Indeed, in the case of nuisance it is the plaintiff's very awareness of the intrusion that constitutes the harm and serves as the basis for relief or recovery. However, the fact that the subject may not know of its existence is the essence and nature of the problem and danger in the case of subliminal advertising. This was certainly true when the Germans were bombarded with subliminals imbedded in Hitler's Nazi propaganda, which resulted in the Second World War.

Surely such a result would be considered more than a nuisance. Notwithstanding such a conclusion, none of the other torts discussed above involve a weighing of positive and negative effects. Furthermore, if it is impossible to determine the effects of subliminal advertising, or if it is difficult to measure the effects of subliminal advertising with any degree of certainty, it would then seem unrealistic to attempt any process of weighing its positive against its negative effects, or to attempt making any such comparison based upon probable outcome. Moreover, if it were possible to measure the effects of subliminal advertising, any attempt to evaluate the social utility of such effects would depend upon the subjective goals and relative instincts and interpretations of the evaluator who might himself be a subject of subliminal manipulation without his knowledge and against his will. While it may be possible to balance the social utility of nuisance in terms of time, location, degree, etc., it is not so easy to measure the effects of subliminal advertising in light of the same criteria.

Just as assault may be only potentially threatening and not necessarily harmful at all, and battery not even potentially harmful in some cases, so too may the effects of subliminal advertising vary with the nature of the input, the extent of the exposure, and the temperament or psychological predisposition of the receiver, as Silverman discovered. The question thus becomes whether assaults upon the unconscious mind should continue receiving greater legal protection than do assaults upon the human body.

If the cause of subliminal imbeds appearing in advertising is a result of mere negligence, then perhaps the damages should be based upon harmful effect as well as upon intent, as is the case in trespass to land. Nevertheless, there is no basis or precedent in the law for requiring a showing of harmful effect in cases of intentional infliction of some undesirable action simply because such a showing is necessary in actions based upon negligence alone.

Also analogous closely to the question concerning whether it should be necessary legally to demonstrate harmful effects that may potentially result from subliminal advertising is the question of professional solicitation. Here the Court held such a burden of proof is unnecessary in the interest of better protecting the needs of the consumer from potentially undesirable exploitation resulting from a given form of commercial speech. The high Court ruled that: "Under our view of the State's interest in averting harm by prohibiting solicitation in circumstances where it is likely to occur, the absence of explicit proof or findings of harm or injury is immaterial." *Ohralik v. Ohio State Bar Association*, 436 U.S. 447, 468 (1978).

This is not to deny, however, that in most commercial speech cases the Court would hold the contrary view as was its decision concerning *In re Edna Smith Primus,* 436 U.S. 412 (1978), on the strength of the argument that it lacked the inherent dangers described above. "Accordingly, nothing in this opinion should be read to foreclose carefully tailored regulation that does not abridge unnecessarily the associational freedom of nonprofit organizations, or their members, having characteristics like those of the NAACP or the ACLU." (*Ibid*).

In the following terms the Court attempted to reconcile or equate the different outcome in *Primus* with that of *Ohralik:* "Although a showing of potential danger may suffice in the former context, appellant may not be disciplined unless her activity in fact involved the type of misconduct at which South Carolina's broad prohibition is said to be directed." (Ibid).

Thus, at least since the case of *Virginia Board of Pharmacy* v. *Virginia Citizen Consumer Council, Inc.,* 425 U.S. 748 (1976), the Court has based its judgment as to whether to allow the prohibition of a particular form of commercial speech on the following criteria: "Whatever may be the proper bounds of time, place, and manner, restrictions on commercial speech, they are plainly exceeded by this Virginia statute, which singles out speech of a particular content and seeks to prevent its dissemination completely."

The Court concluded further that "the First Amendment disabled the State from achieving its goal by restricting the free flow of truthful information "when such restriction is intended to disrupt the process of racial integration." *Linmark* v. *Township of Willingboro,* 431 U.S. 85 (1977).

The regulation of the intentional use of subliminal imbeds in advertising, on the other hand, obviously does not interfere with constitutional objectives such as racial integration, discouraging any form of class discrimination, or equal opportunity, but rather suggests that subliminal advertising should be controlled because its manner is intended to manipulate the unconscious mind of the consumer without providing the opportunity for the consumer to resist, discern, or ignore such forms of commercial speech.

Consequently, it is possible for the State to proscribe carefully and narrowly defined forms of subliminal advertising in the interest of protecting the consumer's privacy interest despite the fact this writer would agree that when commercial speech is presented in such a manner that the interested and willing consumer is able to evaluate its content and form objectively, it "may be restricted if its 'impact be found detrimental' by a municipality." (*Ibid.,* footnote 6). The latter classification, for example, might apply quite appropriately to limited cases of puffery in which the commercial messages are clear, explicit, and not erroneous or inaccurate factually. (See Chapter 3, Section I). However, those appeals attempting to dispel rational decision-making would be called into question, and it is in those cases that the *Ohralik* standard would apply within the context of this author's analysis concerning the regulation of subliminal advertising.

It should be noted, furthermore, that the *Ohralik* standard is consistent with a much larger framework of invasion of privacy cases and decisions. (See Chapter 8). It is only in cases of libel and defamation of character that damages must be based upon perceived and demonstrated harm to the plaintiff. (See Chapter 7). Subliminal advertising might be equated more with intrusion upon seclusion which requires a lesser standard of effect in the sense that no harm need be demonstrated for relief or recovery.

The case of *Bates and Van O'Steen* v. *State Bar of Arizona,* 433 US 350 (1977), underpins further the Court's view that reasonable limits, without a showing of harm or deleterious effect, may be placed upon the time, place and manner of commercial speech. Referring to place, the Court suggests that: "As with other varieties of speech, it follows as well that there may be reasonable restrictions on the time, place, and manner of advertising. Advertising concerning transactions that are themselves illegal obviously may be suppressed. And the special problems of advertising on the electronic broadcast media will warrant special consideration."

Finally, it will be suggested in Chapter 3 that false advertising may be punished without a showing of harm or detrimental effect. (See Sections I and II, and the case of *Testing Systems, Inc.* v. *Magnaflux Corp.,* in particular). The Supreme Court's decisions in the major commercial speech cases of the 1970s specify, moreover, that advertising of professional fees or services may be proscribed merely for being deceptive. Indeed, there is not a single instance in which the Court has required a showing of harm, evil consequences, or effect of any kind in cases of this nature. Neither in cases of false advertising in general nor of professional deceptive advertising in particular is a showing of effects or impact upon the consumer or harm to a competitor a necessary prerequisite for proscription, relief, or punishment. The relevant issues are intent, existence and form of regulation, but effect is only a secondary consideration that may determine the amount of damages in a given case.

> Addressing a relevant illustration, the court exclaimed: Moreover, since cigarette smoking is psychologically addicting, the confirmed smoker is likely to be relatively unreceptive to information about its dangers; his hearing is dulled by his appetite. And since it is so much harder to stop than not to start, it is crucial that an accurate picture be communicated to those who have not yet begun. *Banzhaf* v. *F.C.C.,* 405 F.2d 1082, 1099 (1968).

In light of this viewpoint, and in consideration of findings concerning the harmful effects of smoking (see for example Richard D. Lyons, "U.S. Cites 'Overwhelming Proof' That Tobacco Causes Lung Cancer, *New York Times* (January 12, 1979); "Those Killer Cigarettes," *New York Times* (January 12, 1979), A22; "Study Says Smoking Perils Baby Even If Halted Before Pregnancy," *New York Times* (January 17, 1979), A11), might it not seem at least at a minimum that the use of subliminal advertising to promote some products should be reconsidered in light of intent as well as impact.

Is it consistent, for example, to maintain that the construction of nuclear power plants should be discontinued or curtailed unless they can be proven safe, but that the use of subliminal advertising should be continued until it is proven unsafe? Should the standard not be the same in both cases?

Perhaps effects should be viewed in light of the fact that industries in certain areas flourish despite the well established fact that "under certain circumstances an advertiser may be required to make affirmative disclosure of unfavorable facts"? *Warner-Lambert Company* v. *FTC,* 562 F.2d 749, 759 (1977); also see *Banzhaf, III* v. *FCC,* 405 F.2d 1082 (1968). Is there possibly a need to update traditional notions of causality, as well as to improve upon the basis of its determination?

As has been and as will be suggested in the following section on regulation, the burden of proof may be shifted or reversed depending upon the circumstances. For example, the employee need only prove an involuntary termination of the employment contract and the burden immediately shifts to the employer to prove that he had reasonable grounds for the termination. If the jury concludes that the asserted justification is not reasonable grounds for terminating the employment contract, the employer is liable to the employee for breach of contract. Alan S. Polackwich, "Contracts—Employment At Will: Contractual Remedy For Discharge Motivated By Bad Faith, Malice, Or Retaliation," 16 *Boston College Law Review* 232 (1975); also see *Monge* v. *Beebe Rubber Co.,* 316 A.2d 549 (1974).

The burden of proof has been altered in areas in which the issue of causality is highly complex, sometimes unknown, and difficult to ascertain. If for example, one could not establish that a child was gnawing on paint as a result of some diet deficiency, one might be inclined to either change the paint or keep the child away from the paint.

A majority of the states assume that the question of insanity or suffering under some kind of delusion is no defense against the commission of a crime or accident, and do not relieve the defendant of any culpability whatsoever. See *Breunig American Family Inc. Co.,* 45 Wis.2d 536, 173 N.W.2d 619 (1970).

Consistent with that philosophy, the CIA did not discontinue its practice of testing drugs on human beings because one of its members committed suicide after drugs were tested on him (see hearings, *supra.*), but rather for constitutional reasons. While some courts hold that it is possible to determine the cause of suicide (see *Tate* v. *Canonica,* 180 CA2d 898, 5 Cal. Rptr. 28 (1960)), CIA agents have been known to commit suicide for other reasons. See Tad Szulc, "The Missing C.I.A. Man," *New York Times Magazine* (January 7, 1979). The field of psychiatry addresses the effects of such problems as much and as often as it addresses the cause(s) of such problems. See Jim Jerome, "Catching Them Before Suicide," *New York Times Magazine* (January 14, 1979). It is not assumed that the causes of any given problem can always be known with either certainty or high probability.

Nevertheless, well advised attempts will continue to be made in terms of establishing causes as well as effects in complex areas such as suicide and other subliminal effects. For example, Florida's Third District Court of Appeal has ruled, in a first-degree murder prosecution wherein the defense of insanity was based upon so-called "involuntary subliminal television intoxication" that the trial judge did not commit reversible error by failing to allow psychologists to testify at trial on the effect of television violence upon adolescent viewers. *Ronny A. Zamora* v. *State of Florida,* 316 So.2d 776 (1978).

Policy oriented decisions often necessitate effect oriented rather than cause oriented criteria simply due to complexity and unknown variables that are difficult to determine. Policy has been defined as a system of interrelated yet not necessarily logically consistent principles of forces of action. It therefore functions to shape the quality of life or level of well being of members in society to determine interrelationships among members of society. In a decisionmaking framework such as this one, it is often difficult or impossible to draw causal correlations with any degree of reliability.

Such a determination is based not only upon the examples given above, but upon conclusions derived from both court decisions and empirical evidence. For example, proof of causation in terms of the likelihood of success is difficult to establish in the fields of both legal and medical malpractice. Here litigants attempt to avoid trying all or nothing cases, but rather place a value on them and settle them out of court. The damages are based upon the chance of recovery, and the strengths and weaknesses of the evidence available on both sides. (See, for example, *Hodges* v. *Carter,* 239 N.C. 517, 80 S.E.2d 144 (1954); *Boyce* v. *Brown,* 51 Ariz. 416, 77 P.2d 455 (1938).)

This method is employed not only because of the difficulty involved in establishing causality, but because the process is too slow, too expensive, and often impossible. Indeed, it has been established that in several areas, each involving subliminal impact at least potentially, that it is impossible to determine either the causes or the effects with any degree of certainty. This reduces or elevates the decision making mechanism to one based upon either the results of empirical studies or those results in combination with broader philosophical and constitutional judgments made by the judge and jury in each given case.

These criteria combine to suggest that it is impossible, for example, to verify the qualities which will produce a charismatic leader and produce given results in his or her followers. (See Marilyn J. Matelsky, "Universal Appeals Used by Charismatic Leaders: A Content Analysis," PhD dissertation, Department of Communication, University of Colorado (1978); Nancy Lynch Street, "Dialectical and Mythical Dimensions for Rhetorical Theory and Criticism: An Evolutionary Perspective," PhD dissertation, Department of Communication, University of Colorado (1979); Nancy Lynch Street, "Rhetorical Criticism and Commitment: Implications for a Person-Centered Rhetoric of Protest and Assent," Paper Presented to the "Modern and Contemporary Rhetorical Theory, 1770–1970's" Panel at the Western Speech Communication Association, Phoenix, Arizona (November 1977); James MacGregor Burns interviewed by Doris Kearns Goodwin, "True Leadership," *Psychology Today* (October 1978); Barbara Lovenheim, "A Test to Uncover Managerial Skills," *New York Times* (January 21, 1979).)

These studies and others cited above create and leave an open question in regard to the effectiveness of subliminal advertising, the causes and effects of delusion and leadership qualities, and the causes of insanity and suicide. Other elements of the First Amendment involving constitutional applications of mind control will be considered in Chapter III on False and Deceptive Advertising.

Establishing a universal standard for the determination of causality and the measuring of effects may very possibly create as many problems as it solves, and raise more questions than it answers. Such an outcome would not necessarily minimize the need or desirability of pursuing a likely course. In the meantime, while progress is made in refining methods of testing subjective and intangible qualities, additional criteria must be applied in making policy decisions. They may involve tradition, vested interest, and philosophical predisposition. These influences currently permit the use of subliminal advertising in the United States. The merits of such permissiveness are difficult to assess, and the practice continues on the assumption of business that the use of such techniques produces the desired and predicted effects pursued. Whether this is good or bad has not been proven, and may be unprovable on the basis of any presently existing or universally acceptable standards or criteria.

Under such circumstances it would seem that, at minimum, the burden of proof should be reversed. That is, it should be the burden of business and industry to prove that subliminal advertising has no effect on its customers before such advertising shall be permitted. Clearly, if this could be established, there would be no need for regulation because the cost of the practice would render it an unproductive pursuit. Indeed, the curtailment of subliminal advertising would be advantageous economically in that case. Reversing the burden of proof is not new. It has been employed in pollution control.[51] The method of regulation, however, leads to the third question essential to whether the use of subliminal advertising should be regulated.

3. What form of regulation should the use of subliminal advertising take?

Perhaps the most critical issue is whether any regulation of subliminal advertising would violate the First Amendment. Surely it would not be unconstitutional for the Federal Communication Commission to regulate such conduct in the electronic media in light of the limited frequences and captive audiences involved.

Furthermore, the First Amendment question can be interpreted in at least two distinct ways as it relates to the use and regulation of subliminal advertising. One has to do with the transmission of the message, and the other has to do with the reception of the message. The importance of either should not be diminished.

For example, the right to receive the message one wishes to receive is as important as the right to transmit the message one wishes to transmit or to have another receive. However, when the two interests come into absolute conflict with each other, one must give way to the other. In this case, the rights of the receiver prevail over the rights of the sender.

The question in this instance is one of commercial speech. Consequently, it is the receiver or consumer rather than the sender or transmitter who should be granted the presumption. Unless it can be demonstrated that the consumer is not being exploited by virtue of being exposed to repetitious subliminal advertising, the consumer has the basic right to be freed from such exposure. In such a case the right of free speech for the transmitter must give way to the right of privacy for the consumer, and the right of privacy for the consumer becomes his constitutional right of free speech.

The receiver has the First Amendment right to be free from potentially undesirable, perhaps hazardous, unwanted communication when by himself the consumer may be in no position to knowingly, consciously, and objectively resist. For the unwitting, though presumably rational, consumer is not given the reasonable opportunity to decipher subliminal from nonsubliminal advertising, even if he wishes to do so.

Consequently, the assistance of some well motivated, well intended, and adequately funded regulatory agency is required. Also needed is a specific law which defines carefully and delimits narrowly the forms of subliminal advertising that will be proscribed as unconstitutional under the Rationality Standard for the First Amendment. It has been established here that such a law would fall well within the Balancing Standard for the First Amendment as well.

There are presently two federal agencies entrusted with regulating problems in the media: the FCC and the Federal Trade Commission. In its code the FCC has expressed only an aversion to, but not a regulation against, the usage of subliminal perception techniques or devices. However, it can neither police such activities realistically nor does its present position serve as an effective deterrent. Furthermore, the FCC invariably abdicates any involvement in the regulation of advertising to the FTC. *Consumers Association of District of Columbia* v. *CBS and WYOP-TV*, 32 FCC 2d 405 (1971).

Moreover, in his statement given before the Congressional Subcommittee on Alcoholism and Narcotics, Wilson Bryan Key suggested clearly how difficult it would be to police such activities:

> I do not know a reliable way to detect subliminals. I counseled the House of Commons in Ottawa that attempting to pass laws against this is almost absurd. There are ways I know to circumvent

any law that could be written. They would be unenforceable. The National Association of Radio and TV Broadcasting have a prohibition on subliminals in their code—which of course is not a law—which is unenforceable. Again, you would have to catch them and this is most difficult.[52]

At the present time no law exists in the U.S. prohibiting or restricting the use of subliminal advertising. As a result only the FTC remains as an agency actively commissioned to regulate the use of such devices.

In February 1977 the Director of the FTC Bureau of Consumer Protection was asked the following: "1) What laws or ruling have been established against the usage of subliminal perception devices in advertising both for the screen and printed matter? 2) What effect has the ruling or law had on the prevention or deterrence of the practice? 3) How many cases involving the usage of subliminal perception devices have been tried by the Federal Trade Commission, and what were the results?" These questions produced the circular response from the FTC that: "There have not been any cases because there is no regulation prohibiting the use of subliminal advertising . . . and there is no regulation prohibiting the use of subliminal advertising because there have not been any cases reported."

Nevertheless, Wilson Bryan Key has documented that in 1977 incidents of subliminal advertising had not subsided. Quite certainly there is a danger as Earl Kintner suggests in his book *A Primer on the Law of Deceptive Practices*: "Production is no longer measured by consumer satisfaction. Moreover, the use of such deceptive techniques is not uncommon in the advertising field."[53]

While there is a significant need to curtail such forms of advertising, the FTC is reluctant to use its power of class reparations. Despite the fact that the FTC has the power to obtain class reparations, it seldom does, preferring in the vast majority of cases to opt for injunctive relief in order to spread its limited enforcement powers over a larger number of cases.[54] As a result its deterrent effect is substantially undermined.

Administrative agencies, such as the Securities and Exchange Commission and the Federal Trade Commission "do not have the tools available to remedy the many claims of persons injured." Thus a significant responsibility for the protection of the consumer is left to the private sector.[55] Governmental agencies usually have limited budgets and staffs, and thus are incapable of adequately protecting small claimants. Both the Federal Trade Commission and the Security Exchange Commission have experienced these problems in the past.[56] The government rarely has either the resources or the inclination to prosecute many of the actions that could be brought in the name of consumer protection.[57]

There are many reasons why a government agency may not institute a meritorious law suit. These include subtle or direct political influence, budgetary limitations, the policies and priorities of a particular administration, honest but erroneous interpretations of statutes and precedents, and simple bureaucratic inertia, incompetence, or oversight.[58] Yet better business bureaus and other nongovernmental groups, although successful in resolving relatively minor complaints, lack statutory enforcement authority. In contrast, those governmental agencies having enforcement authority are characteristically allocated limited funds and staff.[59] Consequently, there is respected opinion that neither administrative nor public agencies can adequately protect the consumer by their own enforcement powers.[60]

It has been implied that the U.S. Supreme Court has not adopted a Rationality Standard for the First Amendment. While such a standard might permit a common law remedy against the use of subliminal advertising, without such a standard, any law abridging the right to employ subliminal advertising might very well be found to violate the First Amendment. In other words, a Canadian law that bars the use of subliminal advertising (a partial text of which is given in Section Two) might be found unconstitutional based upon the First Amendment if it, or one similar to it, were passed in the U.S.

Aside from the First Amendment problems a law against the usage of subliminal advertising might pose, and aside from the legal dilemmas a Rationality Standard for the First Amendment might create in terms of any or all emotional speech and communication, in theory it might be worthwhile to consider some ways in which a ban on the usage of subliminal advertising might be enforced, short of the possible First Amendment limitations upon such an imposition.

Essentially, there are four ways in which a law against subliminal advertising might be implemented and enforced: 1) through regulatory agency rulings or criminal laws to be enforced by regulatory agencies and/or law enforcement agencies; 2) through civil laws that might be employed by a single plaintiff as a basis for private litigation; 3) through civil laws that would liberalize class action procedures as well as provide relief for each member of the class in private actions against the usage of subliminal advertising; 4) through actions raised by individuals as friends of the FTC.

The four enforcement measures suggested above are by no means mutually exclusive. In fact the usage of more than one would undoubtedly augment the deterrent effect.

Conclusion

As noted before, the Rationality Standard is premised on libertarian arguments. Society, in order to promote its long term welfare and provide for individual fulfillment, should allow maximum scope for expression. It simultaneously recognizes that the community must protect itself from direct encroachment on its security. Given this dialect, the only restriction upon speech that can be tolerated is that which, because of its content and the circumstances of its delivery, provides the listener with no opportunity to rationally evaluate the speaker's words. Such expression may constitute a direct threat to law and order, and at the same time be virtually of no value to the development of the individual, the search for truth, or the preservation of democracy.

It relates to some extent to the promotion of change, but only insofar as it provokes violence; and when the forces of change operate at this level, society has the right and responsibility to protect itself. If one person advocates violence and another individual decides to heed such advice, the crime is clearly the responsibility of the listener. Only if the listener is unable to control himself, if he is moved to violence by forces beyond his control, such as a mob or riot, is the responsibility placed upon a speaker.

The suggested rule is sufficiently narrow to avoid the wide range of interpretations that reflect the prejudices of judges. Under its guidance, the rationale for limiting speech is not an assessment of public danger, which leaves great room for subjective opinion, but simply whether or not the nature or context of the speech preclude rational consideration.

This is strictly a question of fact—value judgments do not intrude. The judgment it requires is admittedly difficult, but it should be recalled that the only question is whether the listener has a reasonable amount of time to react rationally—not whether in fact he did react rationally. Moreover, through expert testimony and the evolution of precedent, specific guidelines could be developed. Broadly conceived, the doctrine would do no more than prohibit incitement in a situation so emotionally charged that it would be unreasonable to expect a rational response from listeners. Aside from such special cases as the use of false or untrue advertising, and the kind of subliminal advertising which employs hidden embeds that cannot be verified without the assistance of technical or mechanical devices, individuals would be free to express any opinion, however noxious. Thus society would allow the advocacy of revolution, but would draw the line at the actual inciting of violence.

The Rationality Standard is far more libertarian than those employed currently. It would mandate the repeal of virtually all statutes that punish expression. These include the Smith Act of 1940 (18 USC 2385, 54 Stat. 670) which makes it illegal for any individual to 1) knowingly or willfully advocate or teach the overthrow or destruction of any government in the United States by force or violence; 2) print, publish, or disseminate written matter advocating such overthrow; 3) participate in the organization of any group dedicated to such purposes; and 4) acquire and hold membership in such a group with knowledge of its purposes.

Also subject to repeal would be the McCarran Act of 1950 (50 USC 781, 64 Stat. 987) which 1) prohibits the advocacy of, conspiring to advocate, or knowing participation in any organization desiring or attempting to establish a totalitarian dictatorship; 2) denies passports to members of Communist organizations; 3) requires registration and annual reports of Communist organizations; 4) defines the term "person" as an individual or an organization; etc., and other statutes which proscribe dangerous advocacy or belief, such as the Communist Control Act of 1954 (50 USC 841, 68 Stat. 775) which declares that the Communist Party and its subdivisions should be outlawed for they are not entitled to any of the rights, privileges, and immunities attendant upon legal bodies and therefore should be terminated. Thus the range of First Amendment cases that could be brought before a jury would be substantially curtailed. Moreover, if narrowly written law should survive judicial review, and cases be presented before juries, the jury would have to base its verdict in part on whether the conduct fits the factual context of the Rationality Test.

These guidelines would also prohibit civil disabilities based upon expression. It would require the repeal of loyalty oaths and loyalty investigations into First Amendment activities, as formerly conducted under the Communist Control Act. Such suggestions are expanded further in *Freedom of Speech and Human Rights: An International Perspective* (1979) by the same author and publisher.

CONCLUSION

The need for such a broadened interpretation of the First Amendment is not based solely on theoretical considerations; it derives as well from an analysis of our society, from an atmosphere of repression. America's often hysterical fear of radical upheaval and her distrust of strange ideas and practices has become institutionalized in a vast, impersonal bureaucracy that is armed with the most modern, intrusive technology. Moreover, the intolerance latent in the general public is constantly being stirred up by politicians seeking an easy way of election. Given this uncertain climate, the unscrupulous, deceptive system of legal safeguards becomes especially significant.

Freedom of speech is a broad area with constantly changing definitions and emphases. Encompassing everything from press, association, expression, privacy, defamation, obscenity, nuisance, privilege, immunity, public access to the media, commercial speech, warranty limits on speech, and advertising, to equal protection, civil rights, and political dissent, the issue to be determined remains the same. It is the question whether all forms of communication shall be permissible or what forms of communication shall be deemed impermissible. The answer to this dilemma is a matter of conscience, perception, philosophy, and law.

Because of the varying interpretations of the First Amendment, ranging from Bad-Tendency, Clear-and-Present-Danger, Absolute, and Balancing, to Incitement and the Rationality Standard, the issue of constitutionality becomes a matter of will and perspective. This question can be answered only by a consideration of the specific elements of communication as they relate to society and government in light of the kind of society and government desired.

There is enough overlap of issues involved to make any determination of one specific example in isolation from the others moot and potentially invalid. For instance, the legitimacy or acceptability of subliminal advertising cannot be decided on the basis of its frequency or how serious a given occurrence might be. Requiring such criteria only explains why it took two world wars rather than one to succeed in dividing Germany and ending its military aggression; why it took publication of the Pentagon Papers to produce a law making the reproduction of classified documents illegal; and why it took a Watergate to curtail the power of the Presidency. In all of these cases, previous warnings fell on deaf ears and insufficient efforts were made to deter the harm before it was done. Crisis intervention has been America's weakness, limitation and enigma.

Neither the frequency of cases occurring nor the magnitude of any given case should be the basis for determination of legitimacy when the issue involves the use of subliminal advertising. The potential for harming society is weighed against the benefits to society if the Balancing, Bad-Tendency, or Clear-and-Present-Danger Standards are employed, and the degree of action is considered if the Incitement or Absolute Tests are applied. In none of these instances is any clear standard involved. They are all based on degree and ambiguity. Only in the case of the Rationality Standard does the evaluation of acceptability of speech transcend any kind of weighing process or empirical consideration. It is not based on these criteria because such standards are too subjective, as was suggested in the early pages of this chapter.

A far more valid speech standard is one in which the communication can be perceived by the listener or viewer. If it cannot be seen or heard consciously by the listener or viewer, it is unconstitutional *per se*. In this case, damages need not be proven for the Constitution has already been violated.

The advantage of such a free speech standard would not only be the curtailment of mind manipulation on the part of the sender and involuntary action on the part of the receiver, but it would preserve society against dangers from which the other free speech standards were intended to protect the individual as well. Both government and industry would be deterred from using a number of devices with which to subvert the people without their knowledge or against their will. Such safeguards may not be necessary today, but surely they are desirable, for their employment will result in no harmful side effects, and they may very possibly have profound effects upon the quality of life tomorrow.

NOTES

[1] Don R. Le Duc, "Free Speech Decisions and the Legal Process: The Judicial Opinion in Context," *The Quarterly Journal of Speech* (October 1976), p. 287.
[2] Daniel M. Rohrer, *Justice Before the Law* (1971), pp. 223–229.
[3] Zechariah Chafee, *Free Speech in the United States* (1941), pp. 36–80.
[4] Robert G. McCloskey, *The American Supreme Court* (1960), pp. 172, 178.
[5] Samuel Krislov, *The Supreme Court and Political Freedom* (1968), pp. 120–21.
[6] Thomas I. Emerson, *Toward A General Theory of the First Amendment* (1966), pp. 51–56.
[7] "Less Drastic Means and the First Amendment," *Yale Law Journal* (1969), pp. 462–72.
[8] Emerson, pp. 56–62.
[9] Ibid., p. 83.

[10] United States of America Before Federal Trade Commission; Docket No. 8834, "In the matter of Holiday Magic, Inc., a corporation and William Penn Patrick, individually as Chairman of the Board of Directors of Holiday Magic, Inc., and Fred Pape and Janet Gillespie, individually." Initial Decision, Edgar A. Buttle, Administrative Law Judge (May 31, 1973), 1–407.

[11] Norman Dorsen, Paul Bender and Burt Neuborne, *Political and Civil Rights in the United States*, Ed. IV, Vol. I (Boston: Little, Brown and Co., 1976), p. 562.

[12] "Human Drug Testing by the CIA, 1977," Hearings Before the Subcommittee on Health and Scientific Research of the Committee on Human Resources, U.S. Senate, 95th Congress, 1st Session on S. 1893 (Washington, D.C.: U.S. Government Printing Office, September 20–21, 1977).

[13] Id., p.1.

[14] Id., pp. 1 and 37.

[15] Id., p. 2.

[16] Stuart H. Loory, statement before the permanent Select Committee on Intelligence, unpublished manuscript, January 4, 1978, p. 1.

[17] Edward P. Boland, id., December 27, 1977, p. 3.

[18] William E. Colby, id., p. 4.

[19] Gilbert Cranberg, id., January 9, 1978, p. 1.

[20] Morton H. Halperin, id., January 4, 1978, p. 1.

[21] Id., p. 2.

[22] Id.

[23] Id.

[24] Id., p. 3.

[25] Id., p. 4.

[26] Id., p. 6.

[27] Id., p. 7.

[28] William C. Trueheart, id., December 29, 1977, p. 4.

[29] Id.

[30] Id., p. 5.

[31] Id.

[32] Id., p. 6.

[33] Joseph Fromm, id., December 28, 1977, p. 4.

[34] Herman Nickel, id., p. 5.

[35] Eugene Patterson, id., December 27, 1977, p. 1.

[36] Robert J. Myers, id., January 5, 1978, p. 1.

[37] American Society of Newspaper Editors Bulletin (January 1977), p. 5.

[38] Clayton Kirkpatrick, House Intelligence Committee, Oversight Subcommittee hearings, unpublished manuscript, January 5, 1978, p. 1.

[39] See Isabella C.M. Cunningham and William H. Cunningham, "Standards for Advertising Regulation," 41 *Journal of Marketing (October 1977), pp. 92–97.

[40] Wilson Bryan Key, *Subliminal Seduction* (1973), pp. 22–23.

[41] "Subliminal Advertising," *Federal Trade Regulation Reports*, 50, 198 (February 25, 1974).

[42] U.S. Congress, Senate, Committee On Labor and Public Welfare, Wilson Bryan Key, "Media Images of Alcohol: The Effects of Advertising and Other Media on Alcohol Abuse," 1976, (Hearings Before the Subcommittee on Alcoholism and Narcotics, Senate, 94th Congress, 2nd Session, March 11, 1976), pp. 179–82.

[43] Wilson Bryan Key, *Subliminal Seduction*, op. cit., pp. 1–205; *Media Sexploitation* (1976), pp. 1–204; see also, Stuart Ewen, *Captains of Consciousness* (1976); Mary P. Ryan, *Womanhood in America from Colonial Times to the Present* (1975); N.F. Dixon, *Subliminal Perception: The Nature of Controversy* (1971).

[44] Jon Jacobs, "Naked Came the Phone Book," The *Boston Phoenix* (February 28, 1978), p. 3.

[45] Id.

[46] Id.

[47] *Playboy* Magazine (January 1978), p. 201.

[48] Lloyd H. Silverman, "Drive Stimulation and Psychopathology: On the Conditions Under Which Drive-Related External Events Evoke Pathological Reactions," in R.R. Holt and E. Peterfreund, eds., *Psychoanalysis and Contemporary Science*, I (1972), pp. 306–325.

[49] Lloyd H. Silverman, "An Experimental Method for the Study of Unconscious Conflict: A Progress Report," *Journal of Medical Psychology*, 48 (1975), pp. 291–298.

[50] Lloyd H. Silverman, "Ethical Considerations and Guidelines In the Use of Subliminal Psychodynamic Activation," unpublished manuscript (1977), pp. 1–38; also see Silverman, *et al.*, "A Clinical Application of Subliminal Psychodynamic Activation," *Journal of Nervous and Mental Disease*, 161 (1975), pp. 379–392; Silverman *et al.*, "The Further Use of

the Subliminal Psychodynamic Activation Method for the Experimental Study of the Clinical Theory of Psychoanalysis: On the Specificity of the Relationship Between Symptoms and Unconscious Conflicts," *Psychotherapy: Theory, Research, and Practice*, 13 (Spring 1976), pp. 2–16.

[51] See Daniel M. Rohrer, *et al.*, *The Environment Crisis* (1970), p. 61; Rohrer, "Reversing the Burden of Proof in Legal Suits Involving Pollution," *Issues*, IV (November 1970), pp. 1–16.

[52] Key, "Media Images of Alcohol: The Effects of Advertising and Other Media on Alcohol Abuse," pp. 179, 182.

[53] Earl W. Kintner, *A Primer on the Law of Deceptive Practices* (1971), p. 2.

[54] Beverly Moore Jr., *Class Action Reports* (Second Quarter, 1974), p. 43.

[55] 18 *UCLA Law Review* 1021 (1971).

[56] *Creighton Law Review* (1974), p. 506.

[57] 18 *UCLA Law Review* 1021 (1971).

[58] Beverly Moore, Jr., *Class Action Reports* (Second Quarter, 1974) p. 45.

[59] 26 *University of Florida Law Review* 58 (1973).

[60] J. Kelley, California Rural Legal Assistance Corporation Legal Services Center, *Consumer Class Action Hearings* (April 27, 1971), p. 89.

Section 2

Media Images of Alcohol: The Effects of Advertising and Other Media on Alcohol Abuse, 1976

Hearings before the Subcommittee on Alcoholism and Narcotics of the Committee on Labor and Public Welfare, U.S. Senate, 94th Congress, 2nd Session, on:

Examination of the Effects of Advertising and Other Media on Alcohol Abuse

March 8 and 11, 1976

Statement of Wilson Bryan Key*

Dr. Key. I did not have an opportunity to prepare a statement. I was only notified about this hearing 3 days ago. I submit by book *Subliminal Seduction* as a statement.

I have conducted over 300 research studies over a period of some 15 years, mainly for business corporations. Among my clients were Seagram's, Amstel Breweries in Holland, and the Schlitz Brewing Company, in Milwaukee. For the past 2 years I have been a consultant on subliminal media influences in media to a member of the Canadian House of Commons, who is attempting to initiate legislation which would govern or control the situation and also the Canadian Radio and Television Commission. I have been a professor at the University of Western Ontario for the past 6 years.

My research on subliminal influences produced two books: *Subliminal Seduction* (Signet) and a new book that will be out next September titled *Media Sexploitation* (Prentice-Hall).

I get the very definite feeling from listening to the earlier industry and administration testimony, described in the old adage: If you are careful that no one asks the right question, you really do not have to worry about what answer they come up with.

So if I could have someone turn on my projector, the best introduction to the subject is simply to show you subliminal techniques in advertising.

(Film slide.)

Dr. Key. This particular ad appeared in Playboy, in the January 1976 issue. The ad had been kicking around for about 2 years. It appeared in most of the national magazines. We estimated that at least $250,000—perhaps as much as $500,000—was spent buying space to display this piece of art.

For just the one insertion in Playboy, the space rate would be something like $55,000. If you add to that another $5,000, at least, for the art work, you would have roughly a $60,000 investment for one appearance of this ad in Playboy magazine. It appeared in many other publications, of course.

According to the Department of Commerce last year, alcoholic beverage advertisers put 6 percent of their gross receipts back into advertising. Round this off at 5 percent. Multiply this $6,000 for one insertion by 20. This gives you about $1.2 million in product sales as a break-even point for this ad.

*President, Media Probe, Inc.; Author of *Subliminal Seduction* and *Media Sexploitation*.

If this ad is not capable of selling at least $1.2 million worth of Johnny Walker scotch, there is going to be a great deal of difficulty in the advertising agency. Actually, this ad would be capable of selling somewhere between $2 million and $5 million just on the one insertion. We are involved here in a very major economic transaction.

You have had a chance to look at this and indeed it appears to be a harmless picture. You would think with all the money involved, someone would look at this ad carefully. We have filmed individuals with video cameras through a one-way mirror reading the magazine. No one looks at the ad for more than 2 to 3 seconds. There's really nothing to see, is there?

(Film slide.)

Dr. Key. What I have done is simply move the camera in close and look at the small details in the ice cubes. The copy reads, "The road to success is paved with rocks—let us smooth them for you."

Now look at how Johnny Walker smooths these rocks. The ice cube close up is like something out of a William Blake or a Dali surrealistic painting—a screaming, agonizing face was carefully painted on the ice cube surface. On another ice cube appears a turbaned head, a face, someone in the seated position with a snake—probably a snake charmer—looks like there could be a cobra dancing in front of him. On another ice cube is a little teddy-bear monster. You see the eyes, nose, mouth, and an arm or flipper. On another ice cube appears more surrealistic screaming faces which seems to be melting away while they scream. You can clearly see the eyes, noses, and mouths. These are bizarre things to put into an expensive advertisement published in almost every leading magazine in North America.

In another cube is a figure with a devil's mask. You can see the body, the genital area, and the arms. And, here is another of those melting, distorted faces.

Many of these pictures seem to relate to nightmare experiences. They are certainly far removed from conscious experience.

(Film slide.)

Dr. Key. This is curious. On another ice cube a man is suspended in mid-air, his feet and shoes dangling in space. A rather common dream experience for many people. Another monster appears on another cube. You can see the eyes, mouth, and the encircling arms. Again, a bizarre portrait to include in a liquor advertisement.

(Film slide.)

Dr. Key. Another ice cube portrait of a most curious bird. You can see the eye, the bird's head, and the bird's pecker.

Can you move the projector to the right just a bit?

Now you can see this object underneath the bird's pecker.

(Film slide.)

Dr. Key. I will show you another perspective of the bird, turning upside down.

There you are.

You can see the bird's eye. The pecker is here just above, a castrated male penis. The drawing is anatomically correct—a castrated penis with the two chambers. Behind it is a skull, a symbol of death.

(Film slide.)

Dr. Key. Now, with a photograph of the whole ad, I will take you through very quickly the entire sequence—the screaming faces, the legs suspended upside down; the melting, screaming faces upside down; the monster—its eyes and the encircling arms. The little teddy-bear monster with the eyes and flipper, and the other melting faces. The distorted face is here in the top cube. Here is the bird's eyes, the bird's pecker and body, and the castrated penis with the skull behind it.

It would be quite interesting if we could get the originator of this ad in to testify under oath just what it was he had in mind. I can assure you of one thing, this technique sells alcohol—Johnny Walker Scotch—extremely well. If it did not sell, it would not be used as consistently with as much money invested. And this, of course, is only one example.

(Film slide.)

Dr. Key. I have over a thousand of these kinds of advertisements collected over the past 6 years. The subliminal content appears to be about two things—sex and death. Death images are used extensively. These are subliminal stimuli not perceived at any conscious level. The other is sex, the origin of life, procreation. Love and death in the American media, but at the subliminal, not the conscious level.

Indeed, these two areas reflect man's main preoccupation throughout the history of his cultures.

(Film slide.)

Dr. Key. This ad does not involve liquor, but the technique is often used in alcohol advertising. This example was so well done I could not really leave it out. This one appeared in the *Family Circle*, that bastion of middle class morality, and sold the Kraft Corporation's soft Parkay Margarine. The copy advises consumers to "Take Advantage of a Softie."

If you want to see the "softie," it is protruding from the right of the Parkay patty on the end of the knife blade. It is a male genital. Indeed, the whole chunk of Parkay was drawn in the shape of the glands—the head of the penis. A sort of a penis within a penis, a rather astounding ad illustration for *Good Housekeeping, Family Circle*, and half the women's magazines in North America.

(Film slide.)

This ad I think you might call a subliminal masterpiece. The principle has been known a long time. This is a synchrotristic illusion such as the Ruben's profiles, the young woman or old woman, the duck or rabbit, or the vases or faces—drawings with two interpretations.

This ad appeared in *Playboy* and other men's magazines selling Kanon Men's cologne. The ad is directed at men, of course.

Now, this is a curious hand. Women often spot the illusion but men do not, including myself. I looked at this for 10 minutes when it was first shown to me. I kept mumbling "What am I supposed to see?" And suddenly I consciously perceived it. What I saw was unsettling. This palm became two testicles and this thumb an erect penis.

All the artist did was simply take the old synchrotism concept and load one side of the illusion with a subject that is highly taboo in our society. If you want to express this in psychoanalytical terms, the appeal is to latent homosexuality. We do not really know what is going on in the human brain. We can only theorize about it, but if you were to use a psychoanalytic theory as an explanation for how this ad works you could probably discuss latent homosexuality as a basic unconscious appeal that all men share in one degree or another.

Now, if the unconsciously perceived erect penis does not grab you, this knife—at the top of the illustration—that has split the edge of the cork cologne bottle stopper and is about to slip downward where it would cut the thumb (or penis) threatens a fear most men share in one measure or another. In the ad, there is also a hidden dog—you can see the nose, the eye, and the floppy ear, but the dog has a chisel through its head. It has been killed. Why subliminal dogs work in ads, I do not know. We find these very often embedded in women's hygienic products, sanitary napkins, things of this sort.

(Film slide.)

Dr. Key. There were several ad executives I personally met connected with this ad in Canada. Jerry Maclear, Vice President of Toronto's Baker & Lovick agency, purchased this painting in New York, or so he told me. He went around in affidavits swearing that all they did was put a bottle and glass on the table and simply take a picture.

If you ever have been around commercial photography you would know that this is an absolute impossibility. You can't photograph ice, the stuff melts under hot lights. Ice cubes will not conveniently contain alphabetic letters. You can see the letter "E" in the third ice cube from the top.

In the second ice cube from the top, silhouetted between the ice cube and the lime slice, you can trace the letter "S," neatly imbedded in the design. So you can see—in the second and third cubes appears an "S" and an "E." In the fourth ice cube, you can see diagonal tracks. We looked at these ices cubes miscroscopically. They are masterpieces, painted under a magnifying lense a dot at a time. One slip of the brush and the whole thing becomes openly available to conscious perception. In the fourth ice cube appears the letter "X." So you now have "S," "E," and "X," cleverly hidden in the ice cubes.

Further, in the fourth cube behind the "X" you can see eyes, a nose, and a mouth down here and up there a forehead and long hair. It seems to be a woman. She appears to be looking down left at the bottle cap. Look at the shadow of the bottle cap. Consider the shadow of the bottle a man's legs and consider the bottle cap shadow a male genital.

Now, if you want to carry this story line a little further, you can see the slit between the bottle and glass shadows. Lips have been shaded in very, very lightly on each side of it, forming a recognizable female vagina.

(Film slide.)

Dr. Key. This was a very touching ad put out by the Seagram Corporation—one of their ads designed to encourage "reasonable" or "responsible" drinking. The copy says, "A trigger cannot think." A finger is on the trigger of a rifle. When you think about the trigger that cannot think, this finger is remarkably similar to an erect male penis with the testicles formed by the other fingers.

A rather curious way to encourage people to drink responsibly, I think.

(Film slide.)

Dr. Key. Very quickly, there is quite a bit of material in this Walker DeLuxe Bourbon ad. I want to bring your attention only to the ice cube at the top and what you will see looking at it upside down. A very macabre skull appears. It is very clear—another example of using skulls as a device for merchandising alcoholic beverages. This technique is used by all of the wineries, distilleries, and brewers. It is a common device also used in merchandising a great many other things.

(Film slide.)

Dr. Key. This Galiano ad appeared very widely in magazines such as *Gourmet*. In this ice cube here in the background in the darker area, appears this bizarre looking skull.

(Film slide.)

Dr. Key. Again Beefeater Christmas tradition—an ad which appeared in *Time* and many other publications. Notice the wrapping. This ad appears in my new book. You can see the shadow of an eye, a nose, and a gaping mouth with teeth—either a death mask or a skull. Again, we are involved here—and I hope you understand—in a multimillion dollar transaction in the merchandising of alcoholic beverages. This material was not intended to be consciously perceived, but will be perceived instantly—at the unconscious level—by anyone who views the ads for one second, possibly even faster than that.

(Film slide.)

This Black Velvet ad was banned by the State of Oregon's Liquor Commission because of its overt relationship to sex and alcohol. One thing the commission did not notice, however, was in this ice cube—very lightly shaded into the small glass at the bottom—it is a skull. This ad was on billboards all over the United States and Canada, and appeared in a number of newspapers as well as magazines in both countries.

(Film slide.)

Dr. Key. This one is remarkable. Another ad where over half a million dollars was spent by Philip Morris International. The ad was done by the Mary Wells Agency in New York.

Now, there is quite a bit going on here in this ad showing a fight on a hockey rink. But these men are not fighting. They are laughing, rough-housing, funning. You can see the laugh-wrinkles in the corners of their eyes. One pretends to strike the other. You do not strike anyone like that if you really wish to hurt them. The focal point is in this triangular central area of the picture. Now, the curious part of this ad is this hand down at the bottom. The hand does not belong to any of the three bodies in the pile up. It could be the referee's hand, but you would have to sever his forearm and drag the stump through the pile of bodies which does not seem reasonable, even for Madison Avenue.

Notice the referee. We do not know what he is thinking because we cannot see his eyes, but his whistle is way out here at arms length. He is not about to blow it yet and decide the issue whatever it may be. Anyhow, this hand brings viewer's subliminal attention to the hockey glove or gauntlet lying empty on the ice.

A glove or a gauntlet cast down, for at least a couple of thousand years in at least four cultures, has symbolized a challenge. A right hand glove challenges a superior, the left hand an inferior. This is a left hand glove. The wording on the back of the glove, which is too small to see in this slide reads—

(Film slide.)

Dr. Key (continuing). The word is "cancer." The word originally had been "Cooper," but was manipulated with an airbrush into the word "cancer."

Cancer, of course, is one of the most terrifying symbols of death in our society. Now, if the subliminal, or unconscious, fear of death—or as in Freud's theory of the death wish compulsion—if these aspects of behavior can be successfully utilized in product marketing, then such warnings as the Surgeon General's which appears on cigarette packages actually becomes an effective advertising stimuli. Indeed, it would appear, self-destruction—especially with young experiencing puberty—could be a motive for smoking and drinking within some individuals. It is entirely conceivable that many people who drink do so as a means of courting death.

(Film slide.)

Dr. Key. This Dewars Whiskey ad shows a young professional woman—a physicist—lecturing before a blackboard. A young woman in San Francisco who was very troubled over this ad sent it to me. The ad made her quite uncomfortable, but she could not figure out why. It turned out to be very simple. The young woman in the ad, Ann T. Long, is surrounded by "sin." You can see "sin" there, there, over there—the word is part of the mathematical formulas and equations on the blackboard. If you connect people to an electroencephalograph as they perceive material with such hidden words, and compare their reactions toward the same material with the words removed, different unconscious reactions will appear. This would also apply to subliminally perceived words such as "cancer," "sex," or other four letter words.

(Film slide.)

Dr. Key. The word "sex" appears hidden in the glass in this Puerto Rican Rum ad. You can see it quite distinctly, looking from the right side at the glass by the model's feet. This ad shows a male and female model dressed in white, the male seated in a rocking chair. The ad has appeared in virtually all U.S. national magazines.

(Film slide.)

Dr. Key. Again, another Johnny Walker ad—this one for Red Label, showing the bottle two-thirds empty with ice cubes inside the bottle. If you turn to the left side, you can see the face of a man, the eyes, the nose, the moustache, and kind of a turban, and, curiously, there is an axe imbedded in the back of its neck. This is a beheading in the Johnny Walker ice cubes. In art, cutting off a man's head is a symbolic castration—an interesting unconscious motive, for some of these devices become humorous, but it is often difficult to decide whether you should laugh or cry.

I purposely kept away from the theory because it is detailed in my two books. In any respect, this introduces a whole new dimension to the consumer manipulation game and to the current way in which human behavior is viewed in North American universities.

Senator Hathaway. Have you talked to the creators of these ads and asked them if they intentionally put these in?

Dr. Key. Yes.

Senator Hathaway. Have they admitted it?

Dr. Key. Yes.

Senator Hathaway. What was the basis for putting it in there?

Dr. Key. Simply to increase the ad's effectiveness, to sell. Last year in the beverage industry they spent $600 million, roughly half on beer, most of which utilized subliminals. This year, the ad industry estimated it will spend in the United States over $31 billion. This is a massive media environment created to modify human behavior in the interest of consumption. Now, with this enormous budget, year after year, they try a lot of techniques. Those things which appear to succeed are repeated. The development of subliminal techniques were probably as simple as that.

There is a billion-dollar research industry in the United States which, as you probably know, is dedicated to testing audience reactions to advertising. If an ad does not work, the client usually knows about it rather quickly.

Senator Hathaway. So what you are saying is we should screen for subliminal content before approving them?

Dr. Key. No, not really. What I have shown you here were easily perceived dramatic examples that my students and I collected over a six-year period. I do not know a reliable way to detect subliminals.

I counseled the House of Commons in Ottawa that attempting to pass laws against this is almost absurd. There are ways I know to circumvent any law that could be written. They would be unenforceable. And, I am sure there are people around who know more about this than I do.

You can do the same things, I've shown you here visually, with sound. It is often done in motion pictures, for example, such as "The Exorcist." Mr. Friedkin at Warner Brothers admitted using subliminal tachistoscopy in his film flashes. This is a very old technology. Several subliminal induction devices were patented by Dr. Hal Becker, a professor at the Tulane Medical School in 1962 and 1966. Dr. Becker told me he has been able to lower dystolic pressure—hypertension—with subliminal inductions.

This works similarly to post-hypnotic suggestion. Subliminals set up a delayed reaction response mechanism that was described about 1917 by Dr. Otto Poetzle and is still called the Poetzle alarm clock effect.

You perceive a subliminally imbedded ad, let us say for 2 seconds. Three days, 3 weeks, 3 months later you walk into a liquor store. The thought might come to mind, "Gee, Johnny Walker Red might really put a head on a party." You opt for the brand without any knowledge at the conscious level of what is motivating your brand preference.

As I said, the Poetzle effect has been known for a very long time in the advertising field—at least for 50 years.

Senator Hathaway. Let me ask this question. Is there actually any deception here: deceptive practices?

Dr. Key. It is not practiced just in liquor advertising. It is practiced in the media generally, the use of tachistoscopic displays in TV commercials, in such as *Time* magazine news pictures. I have Vietnam atrocity photographs from *Time* with "sexes" lightly imbedded all over the bodies. I have similar imbedded news photographs from the *New York Times*.

We are into something here that is almost beyond comprehension in terms of what we have traditionally known about the mass media and human perception. The words deceit and deception are inadequate to describe what has been going on here.

I spent the first two years after *Subliminal Seduction*'s publication defending my sanity. The whole thing is too outrageous for most people to accept. Now, I do not have to do that quite as intensely any more. As a society, we are into this form of manipulation very deeply—in all forms of mass media. There are ways of doing it in sound for example, that are, for all practical purposes, undetectable. It is done very often in rock music. In fact, you can say almost with certainty, any successful rock music album of the past ten years has had extensive subliminal imbedding done to it. The Beatles were masters at the art.

And as I said, there is virtually no place in the mass media you can find this practice not being done, especially when large amounts of money, heavy investments in advertising expenditures, are involved.

Senator Hathaway. I suppose it is deceptive just by the fact that people do not know it is there.

Dr. Key. It is more than deceptive. In the entire development of Western civilization's democratic concepts the political, economic, religious, and social institutions, were based upon the concept of free will—the idea that you and I have a right in our own interest to determine what we are going to become, what we will do, who we will vote for, etc. These subliminal techniques subvert the whole concept of free will. This is a technique of managing group behavior which most individuals cannot resist. There is no defense.

I recently spent an all-night session with several priests discussing the traditional concepts of pornography. The techniques I've shown you make hardcore porno almost an exercise in mental hygiene. At least with porno, you can look at it or not look at it, or perhaps consider whether or not to look. You are in control.

These subliminal stimuli are in your brain instantly. There is some evidence which suggests subliminals may stay in your brain throughout life.

As I said, all this is really not new. It is not difficult to understand why advertising people resort to these with the enormous pressure in our society to sell. And, they are not illegal. They might well be immoral, but as yet they are not illegal. Almost everything I found in advertising I also located in the work of Renaissance artists such as Heironymus Bosch, Rembrandt, and di Vinci, who were very clever at it. It is nothing new.

It is, however, astonishing we do not know about it.

Senator Hathaway. Why do you say that we cannot prohibit it?

Dr. Key. Because there are ways of doing it that are undetectable. You could not enforce the law. There are, for example, ways of doing this in sound where no one—unless you had extremely elaborate equipment, the design of which I cannot conceive of at this point—would be able to detect it.

Let me give you an example. The tachistoscopy was discussed by Vance Packard in his book *Hidden Persuaders*. Dr. Hal Becker later patented the machine. These high speed flashes, however, were consciously perceived by some people. They flashed at one three-thousandths of a second every five seconds. A few people consciously picked up the messages. On an oscilloscope, these flashes are detectable. You can see the lines jump.

Early in the development of our research, I asked an executive of a large American corporation whom I know had used one of these tachistoscopes if I could borrow one. He told me they had gotten rid of them years ago. They were obsolete.

He told me how to make a more effective device which would do the same job better. Simply take a projector, he said, and wire a wide-range rheostat into the power cord. When you run your movie, project your subliminal message over the movie with the light intensity lowered to where it is no longer consciously perceivable, where you cannot see it but the projector lamp is still on.

The subliminal message is in the signal all the time. It is completely undetectable. It works much better than a tachistoscope.

The political implications of all this are also unsettling. I studied a Canadian Federal election where every candidate's campaign material utilized one type or another of subliminal technique. There are about eight or nine more or less specific techniques which I have included under the label "subliminal."

I looked at one Congressional campaign in the United States—right here in Arlington, Virginia. Subliminals were being used almost universally by the candidates. I think, in all fairness, however, without the candidates' awareness. It is done by the advertising agencies as a standard production technique.

Senator Hathaway. Can you give us a list of those agencies?

Dr. Key. I would be delighted.

Senator Hathaway. Senator Williams.

Senator Williams. Thank you very much, Mr. Chairman. I was not here for the opening of your presentation so I am not exactly sure how you introduced this subject to the committee. Maybe my questions will seem a little bit uninformed. This is because I was not here.

Now, we have assumed and legislated with the assumption we can deal with fraud and falsehoods in advertising, particularly in the drug areas. We have legislated authority to test advertising in terms of its being accurate and whether it is misleading, and there are prohibitions set into the law to prohibit false, fraudulent, misleading advertisement.

I just wonder how you would describe subliminal advertising and its infamy. I am sure in your judgment a wrong is being perpetrated.

Dr. Key. I think indeed under the rules of the game as we have known them for the past century and a half in the United States, we would have to agree a wrong is being perpetrated. But it is more complicated than that.

Senator Williams. As I would describe the rules, we have been living with fraudulent and misleading falsehoods. Does this fit into any of the accepted rules that we have legislated?

Dr. Key. Perhaps. The National Association of Radio and TV Broadcasting has a prohibition on subliminals in their code—which of course is not law—which is unenforceable. Again, you would have to catch them and this is most difficult.

Senator Williams. How do they describe what they are doing which is prohibited?

Dr. Key. The Canadian Radio and Television Commission defined this very well in a ruling they made last spring prohibiting the use of subliminal techniques.

They define it, as I recall, as anything designed to manipulate or motivate behavior of which the recipient has no conscious awareness, something generally—and I can give you a copy. (Copy of CRTC Announcement, 27 June 1975 is attached.)

(The information referred to follows:)

Canadian Radio-Television Commission

Counseil de la Radio-Télévision Canadienne

PUBLIC ANNOUNCEMENT

AVIS PUBLIC

Ottawa, June 27, 1975

Amendments to the Television Broadcasting Regulations

(Subliminal Advertising)

Following an announcement on February 3, 1975 and a Public Hearing held in Ottawa on March 11, 1975, the Commission has issued today the following amendments to the Television Broadcasting Regulations:

1. The *Television Broadcasting Regulations* are amended by adding thereto, immediately after section 9 thereof, the following section:

"9.1 (1) No station or network operator shall knowingly broadcast any advertising material that makes use of any subliminal device.

(2) In subsection (1), "subliminal device" means a technical device that is used to convey or attempt to convey a message to a person by means of images or sounds of very brief duration or by any other means without that person being aware that such a device is being used or being aware of the substance of the message being conveyed or attempted to be conveyed."

Guy Lefebvre
Director-General of Licensing

Ottawa, le 27 juin 1975

Modification au Reglement Relatif a la Telediffusion

(Publicité subliminale)

Suite à l'avis public du 3 février 1975 et à l'audience publique tenue à Ottawa le 11 mars 1975, le Conseil publie aujourd'hui les modifications suivantes au Règlement relatif à la télédiffusion:

1. Le *Règlement relatif à la télédiffusion* est modifié par l'adjonction, immédiatement après l'article 9, de l'article suivant:

"9.1 (1) Il est interdit à une station ou à un exploitant de réseau de diffuser sciemment du matériel publicitaire qui fait usage d'un dispositif subliminal.

(2) Aux fins du paragraphe (1), "dispositif subliminal" désigne un dispositif technique utilisé pour transmettre ou tenter de transmettre un message à une personne au moyen d'images ou de sons de très courte durée ou par tou autre moyen sans que celle-ci ait conscience qu'un tel dispositif est utilisé ou sans qu'elle ait conscience de la teneur du message que l'on transmet ou que l'on tente de transmettre ainsi."

Guy Lefebvre
Le directeur général
Gestion des politiques de licences

Senator Williams. It would be good to have that. That is on the private side in Canada, the radio broadcasting—

Dr. Key. No. That is the Federal CRTC.

Senator Williams. This is ours?

Dr. Key. No. Last spring the Canadian Radio and Television Commission, our counterpart of the FCC, attempted to regulate this. A law was subsequently introduced into the House of Commons by Lloyd Francis (MP from Ottawa West). In my opinion, the CRTC regulation was weakened by inclusion of a clause which stated station operators must "knowingly" broadcast subliminals to determine what a person "knowingly" does. This makes it impossible to obtain a prosecution under the regulation.

Senator Williams. Quite frankly, in the ice cube I consciously found no assault upon my conscious perception.

Dr. Key. Did you see the first one? I would be delighted to run again for you the Johnny Walker Black Label ad that included the castrated penis and the skulls.

Senator Williams. Yes. I did see it, and I saw the other ads. I never, however, saw this content, but that again is something you are suggesting we do not consciously see. It is something less than a clear definition that you could state as to what you see.

Dr. Key. It is not quite that simple.

One of the things you have to eventually deal with when you spend any time working with subliminals is that the artist is not hiding anything. The instant I show one of these, everyone sees them. I have been on lecture tours now for over one year. At least 10,000 people, consciously perceived these once I showed them how to do it.

The problem seems to be we are repressing—I used the term "repressing" in a loose sense as I am not sure what it might include—perceptually defending ourselves against these visual stimuli. We apparently do not want to consciously deal with them.

We did some limited experiments showing subliminally imbedded art to the Invit, Eskimo peoples native to Canada. They perceived the hidden material easily, but often did not want to tell us because they realized it might upset us. They appeared to believe we also perceived embeds, but preferred not to discuss them.

Subliminals seem to be culture-bound. I think you could define culture, as has been done by anthropoligists like Ed Carpenter, as a tacit, unverbalized group of agreements we make within a culture about things which we will not perceive consciously, and a group of agreements we tacitly make about things we will consciously perceive. Both conscious and subliminal stimuli are perceived by everyone instantly, the unconscious portions are repressed. We appear to be defending ourselves against them.

Consider the hand in the Kanon cologne ad, the hand holding the bottle. That ad was directed at men. We found in experiments with women that many consciously perceive the male genital. They are not threatened with the social taboo of homosexuality as intensely as are men. The whole idea of homosexuality in our society is very difficult for men to cope with. Most men would predictably repress the male genital in the ad and consciously perceive only a hand. The ones who are less able to consciously deal with the taboo would be the ones most susceptible to the technique.

There was an experiment done in Britain by a psychologist named Fisher that suggests there are differences in how subliminals will affect people. Some are more susceptible than others. Perceptual rigidity appears to be involved with susceptibility.

Senator Williams. Let me ask you—you say perceived by those who are most—

Dr. Key. Let us say everyone perceives and represses perception, but some will repress more than others. They are not affecting everybody in a uniform way.

In marketing research, you deal with statistically significant numbers of people moving from one brand preference to another. It is impossible to predict individual behavior, but often relatively simple to predict group or social behavior. Probable change in response to advertising stimuli is rather easily calculated. If ads do not work, they are dropped instantly.

Senator Williams. Among other things, I would judge you are an art critic.

Dr. Key. I find myself at the moment getting into that. Yes. But not a critic in any traditional sense of the word.

Senator Williams. Some of that art work with the ice cubes—though I am not an art critic—would impress me as rather high quality abstract art.

Dr. Key. Yes, indeed. In fact, abstract art has a great deal to do with all this. Subliminals also relate to poetics. As I said, these are very old art forms.

Strangely, we seem very reluctant to call advertising an art form. We want to consider it as something else—something very special but not really art. This may be one of the reasons it is difficult for us to look seriously at advertising. Of course, that is exactly what the advertisers desire as this view increases our vulnerability. They'd much rather we look at these no more than a couple of seconds.

We went over the Gilbey's Gin ad with a microscope, a linen tester, a machine that lets you look at the engraving's dot structures. You can see extensive air brush retouching has been done. It is extremely skillful work. With that Gilbey's ad, one slip of the brush and the whole show might have become consciously available to readers. Then, both agency and client are in trouble. They would have to explain what they were doing, and they would find it quite embarrassing.

Senator Williams. Why wouldn't anyone look at it?

Dr. Key. It was designed not to be consciously perceived, specifically for subliminal perception.

Senator Williams. So the advertising team is much more than the simple photographer and the still life pictures it used to be.

Dr. Key. We have looked at photographic work by artists, people like Yousef Karsch of Montreal—a portrait artist who uses an air brush to retouch photographs. The "sex" imbeds are apparent in his portraits of Eleanor Roosevelt, Churchill, etc.

Senator Williams. One of your missions, I would assume, is to alert the public to the possibility of this subliminal assault?

Dr. Key. It is not just subliminal advertising. There is a vested interest in our society to not deal with this subject. I am sure you are finding it a very, very perplexing thing to have to confront. It gets you into all kinds of problems and moral issues. What do you do once you know? It seems my book has been quite successful. It is less difficult to deal with this now than it was. The subject of subliminal manipulation must be made part of education.

I think, probably, that in drug, alcohol, and tobacco advertising—all of which involve mutually reenforcing promises of a chemical solution to problems of emotional adjustment—there has to be some kind of legislative intervention. But, subliminal techniques generally cannot be prohibited. Our society must start asking questions of itself such as do we really need drug, alcohol, and tobacco advertising? Aside from that, the subliminal issue should be handled through education. If you could take the subliminal stimuli out of a Beethovan symphony, you would not want to do it. Nor, remove them from a T.S. Eliot poem. We should know much more about this aspect of human perception . . .

Section 3

Television, Violence, and Advertisers: A Select Review

*Martin P. LoMonaco**

INTRODUCTION

In 1975 Action for Children's Television, a Newton, Massachusetts based consumer group, sued the Federal Communications Commission for abdicating its responsibility as a guardian of the public's airwaves in allowing children's programs to contain questionable content and advertising. The decision in this case and the events leading up to it present a unique case study of the legal and extralegal processes in media regulation.

Probably the most widely discussed issue that concerns parents, program executives, and advertisers is the effects of television violence. There are three theories on television violence and how it influences viewers: the Facilitation Effect, the Arousal Effect, and the Catharsis Effect.

FACILITATION EFFECTS

Stated in very general terms the hypothesis for studies that deal with this effect is: Subjects (usually children) imitate aggressive behavior they see on television. The principel proponent of this research hypothesis, and its most productive author, is Alvert Bandura.

In Bandura's experiments (1961 and 1962), the typical methodology is an experiment that presents children with a novel behavioral response via television (like seeing other children attacking a Bobo doll). Then, after a frustration inducing experience, the child is put into a play situation that contains a Bobo doll. The researchers found that the subjects who were shown the TV aggression were more prone to attack the Bobo doll. Subsequent experiments introduced other variables such as fantasy creatures performing the violent televised act instead of a real child, or showing scenes in which the aggressor was reinforced.

A number of studies have dealt with facilitation effects through observational learning. The results can be summarized as follows: 1) Viewers learn aggressive behavior via TV regardless of reinforcement results; 2) When televised violent behavior is rewarded, imitation is more likely to occur overtly; 3) Violence on TV which goes unrewarded lowers succeeding violence when the play situation is perceived as being the same. Punishment also deters aggressive behavior when it is perceived as such and caused by violence. (Meyer and Anderson, 1973).

AROUSAL EFFECTS

Whereas the imitative behavior theorists have been concerned with the modeling of a specific, novel behavior, those who hypothesize that viewing television violence leads to violent behavior are concerned with a broad class of behaviors. This generalization of behavior can be manifested in an example such as a child, seeing a gun fight, might break a dish.

*Assistant Professor of Speech Communication at Boston College.

It seems that it is in this area of increased aggression that the greatest body of literature on violence effects exists. It is not within the scope of this section to review all of that literature; however, we will review select studies.

The major theorist of the increase aggressive point of view is Leonard Berkowitz. He theorized that "anger arousal increases aggressive tendencies, but that the likelihood of intensity of their expression is a function of the degree of anger, the strength of past learning to be aggressive, and the presence of situational cues inhibiting or facilitating aggression against the anger arouser." (Weiss, 1971, pp. 318–19.)

The studies of Berkowitz (1964) and Berkowitz and Geim (1966) dealt with subjects who were angered by a target. They viewed a fight scene from the movie "The Champion" and then were allowed to administer shocks to the target. The control group saw a neutral movie on canal boats. Those who saw the fight movie shocked more. Berkowitz and his associates introduced other variables in subsequent experiments. These included:

—Justified vs. unjustified aggressive behavior in the film (when behavior is justified more shocks).
—Similarity of target to film aggressor (the greater the identification the more shocks there are).
—Same name as target (again more shocks).

There were some inconsistencies in Berkowitz's experiments (Boksen, Berkowitz, 1965; and with Gein, 1966; and with Rawlings, 1963; and with Corwin and Hieronymous, 1963), but these have been explained in a "post facto" rationale: a slight but significant increase in shock aggression is formed when a particular conjunction of conditions occurs: an angered subject witnesses a justified beating given to someone who bears a similar name or role. But experimental arousal of anger alone produces a greater increase in shocks than did the fight film or the similarities alone (Weiss, 1969).

The conclusion based upon this research is that some people are affected by some violence sometimes. The conclusions of Himmelweit, Oppenheim, and Vince (1958), and Schramm, Lyle, and Parker (1961) are still valid—namely that aggressive tendencies do not relate *so much* to the medium as to the person. The media does play some role, however.

CATHARSIS EFFECTS

This theory is based upon the Aristotelian belief that viewing drama will drain off (cathart) one's emotional feelings—including aggression. The major proponent of this theory is Seymour Fishback.

In his major study, published in 1971, Fishback along with Robert D. Singer tried to control TV viewing in a natural setting—at a number of boys schools. The conclusions they reached were:

1. Exposure to aggressive content for six weeks did not produce an increase in aggressive behavior.
2. Boys exposed to aggressive TV content manifest significantly less behavioral aggression toward peers and authority than boys exposed to nonaggressive TV contents.

Fishback feels that aggressions are worked out internally through fantasies. These he feels purge the aggressive attitudes of the viewer as well as the aggressive behavior. He took attitude measures to demonstrate this. He also concluded that aggressive content controls aggressive behavior in those from low socio-economic backgrounds, especially.

CRITIQUES OF THE THREE THEORIES

Each of the three theories that has tried to explain the effects of televised violence on the viewer has certain flaws. These arise in most cases from the methodology that has been used to test them. In other instances, criticism has been leveled on theoretical grounds.

This latter posture has been used as a criticism of the facilitation effect. Weiss (1969 and 1971) alludes to the fact that those who follow the theory of imitative behavior are behavioralists. He criticized this research on that ground. Weiss, as well as others, feel that not only should the overt behavior be studied, but also the motivations for it. He refers to this as the subjective meaning of the behavior to the children.

Of further importance is the fact that the measures used (electric shocks to a target or hits to a Bobo doll) do not measure aggression. The "Why?" of the behavior of the subjects was never addressed.

Hartley (1964), by writing a CBS research memo has brought up the fact that children may accept, what adults feel is aggression, as play. He describes the "play culture" of the child. (This aspect of play will be mentioned below in reference to a more recent study).

Finally, there is a problem of generalizing from lab experiments to real situations, especially when the lab experiment is contrived, replete with the aggressor's target and often lacking in social controls.

Arousal effects come under much of the same type of criticism. Most of the research was experimental and took place in laboratories, not in natural settings. This can lead to subject bias. The subjects were also put in a peculiar situation: they were forced to view the program. Therefore their increased anxiety may have been a function of their lack of choice in viewing material. One cannot easily ascertain which types of material the subject of an experiment such as Berkowitz's would choose to view voluntarily. This is based upon the subject's predispositions. Experiments that have dealt with the arousal effects of television violence have done a poor job of pretesting "state" aggressiveness (which is temporary) and "trait" aggressiveness which can be considered a permanent state due to long term behavior patterns or neurochemical imbalance.

One problem mentioned above as a critique of the arousal effects theory can also be applied to the catharsis theory, namely that the limiting of viewer's choices can be a cause of their greater aggressive tendencies. But Fishback's research, which were field studies, did show a reduction in aggression. In their review, Meyer and Anderson (1973) present three arguments for this reduction in addition to catharsis:

—inhibition in motivational system to be aggressive;

—inhibition of an aggressive response due to projected consequences;

—perceived lowered probability of positive reinforcement.

Of greatest concern to those who analyze research dealing with the effects of television violence is that little has been done in analyzing individual differences in the viewer. Each user of the mass media has selective perception—s/he chooses what s/he wants to see. This can lead to complicating factors in a research model as well as in any conclusions one would draw from the research. Should the potentially violent predispositions of certain viewers, who may be in a small minority, exclude a certain type of programming from a vaster majority of the population? When does minority rule stop and minority concerns begin? When are we concerned with mass entertainment? These questions have yet to be adequately answered by the researchers and the formulators of public policy that rely on their findings.

J.M. Ziman has commented on what many fail to realize:

> A regular journal carries from one research worker to another the various . . . observations which are of common interest . . . . A typical scientific paper has never pretended to be more than another little piece in a larger jigsaw—not significant in itself but as an element in a grander scheme. This technique, of soliciting many modest contributions to the store of human knowledge, has been the secret of Western science since the seventeenth century, for it achieves a corporate, collective power that is far greater than one individual can exert.

THE SURGEON GENERAL'S REPORT

It was the need to put all of the existing knowledge in meaningful cohesive context that prompted the National Institute of Mental Health and the Office of the Surgeon General to sponsor the two-year inquiry started in 1969. The report of the Surgeon General's committee was published in 1972.

The report was important because it included field studies, studies that dealt with the long term effects of viewing television violence and studies dealing with the effect of television violence on adolescents, an age group that previously had been ignored.

FINDINGS

The general conclusion of the committee was: ". . . we can conclude that there is a modest relationship between exposure to television viewing and aggressive behavior or tendencies, as the latter are defined in the studies at hand."

There are two reasons for this cautious tone. One is that studies revealed correlations from null to plus .30. The other is that industry members of the committee had to be true to their social science professions as well as to their employers.

The committee observed two possible explanations for their relationships:

—TV violence viewing may lead to aggression;

—both aggression and violence viewing may be joint products of a third set of circumstances.

They generally favored the first explanation due to two studies showing a plus .30 correlation between earlier viewing and later aggression.

ADVERTISING TO CHILDREN: ECONOMIC EXPLOITATION

The question of violence and its effects aside, there is another side to the television controversy, especially when the programs are aimed at children. In a revealing 1973 book, *Children's Television: The Economics of Exploitation*, William Melody discusses the unique role of the child as an audience for television programming. Melody traces the historical development of children's programs. These programs began as a way of building a quality base for advertisers, but after this base had been built, the number of advertisers increased as well as the value of the advertising time.

Since children are a highly specialized market, the advertising strategy to reach them is a high response rate based upon a deep immediate impression followed by a quick sale. Because of this, manufacturers of children's products create a need for new products and new advertisements to sell them. This escalation has been looked upon as a dangerous and artificially contrived situation by consumer groups. The problem is compounded by the fact that the need for constant new advertising has created a "traffic jam" effect with many advertisers vying for positions on network schedules. The immediate impact necessary for the deep impression has usually lead to a talent tie-in. In this case the programs' stars deliver the pitch for the advertised product. Critics have charged that this confuses young viewers since the program content and its advertising flow together.

These two interrelated problems have lead Melody to make a number of recommendations for the reform of children's programming. His plan calls for a review of existing programs to specify those that are acceptable. He would then have it that an alternative form of financing children's programs be established. This would eliminate advertising. It is not specified in the Melody plan, but he estimates that the cost for a weekly, hour-long series for a season would run about one million dollars. Melody suggests that stations and networks can begin to pick up the tab for this cost. He then advocates that programming decisions be taken out of the hands of network and station officials. In this way the needs of the children will be served. The plan should not be implemented overnight according to Melody, but rather in a phased adoption lasting five to seven years. As Melody states:

> The issue has been narrowed down to the purposes for which children are classified as special. As a special television audience, they need protection from pinpoint advertiser exploitation. In addition, they may require special programming directed to their needs and interests. (p. 138.)

It should be noted that Melody's work was supported by Action for Children's Television.

THE FAMILY VIEWING HOUR DECISION

The FCC felt the pressure of ACT and other citizens' groups in the wake of the evidence on violence and the economic realities of children's programming. In response to the issue of violence the then FCC chairman, Richard E. Wiley, made numerous references in 1974 and 1975 to the broadcasting of adult content during the early evening. Wiley made reference to the stations' public service responsibilities and went so far as to threaten license renewal based upon the inclusion of adult-oriented programs at times when children might be watching.

The National Association of Broadcasters, self regulatory agency of the industry, decided that it was better to regulate internally rather than formalizing a federal policy. With that the NAB instituted its Family Viewing Hours policy. As part of the Television Code, the self-regulation stated that there should be no adult-oriented programming on the air between 7:00 and 9:00 p.m. Eastern Time. The Writers Guild of America, a union for those who write television programs, did not like the code's restriction. It contended that the Family Viewing plan infringed upon First Amendment rights to create programs without governmental restriction. A U.S. district court in Los Angeles agreed.

Judge Warren J. Ferguson ruled that the Family Viewing was unconstitutional. Relevant excerpts from the decision state:

> . . . 3. The adoption of the family viewing policy by each of the networks constituted a violation of the First Amendment. The networks are free to continue or discontinue the policy or any

variant of the policy provided that such programing decisions are made independent of concern for government action.

4. The adoption of the family viewing policy by the NAB involved a First Amendment violation by each of the defendants.

5. NAB attempts to enforce the family viewing policy in any way would violate the First Amendment.

6. The networks are required to independently program and may not without violating the First Amendment enter into agreements with the NAB which condition their membership on adherence to the family viewing policy or enter into any other agreements which delegate their programing authority over family viewing matters to the NAB. Their delegation of authority in this case violated the First Amendment.

7. Each of the government defendants violated the First Amendment by issuing threats of government action (through Chairman Wiley) should industry not adopt the family viewing policy or the equivalent thereof.

8. FCC enforcement of the family viewing policy (or of commitments associated with the policy) through the licensing process would violate the First Amendment.

9. Each of the government defendants has violated the Administrative Procedure Act . . . , *Writers Guild of America* v. *FCC*, 423 F. Supp. 1064 (1976).

Judge Ferguson's decision not only supported the constitutional rights of broadcasters, but it also temporarily shifted the countervailing power which they possess. The concept of countervailing power is important in broadcasting. Many decisions are not made through regulatory statute, but rather through political pressure. This pressure and the way it works is integral to an understanding of the broadcasting industry.

THEORY OF COUNTERVAILING POWER AND THE BUSINESS OF BROADCASTING

Classical economics dictates that restraint between competitors comes from the same side of the market, that is, from other competitors. John Kenneth Galbraith points out, however, that competition in its classical form, namely where the market is open to anyone, has been replaced by oligopoly or monopolistic competition. This has caused a new restraint to be placed on private power; a restraint that is devised from customers or suppliers. Galbraith calls this restraint "countervailing power." This countervailing power is a self-generating force in that when strong sellers arise, so do strong buyers. (Galbraith, 1956).

Countervailing power is at work in the broadcasting industry. Here there are three large, strong competitors. They are buyers in terms of labor and government approval; they are sellers in terms of the audience. The networks' relationship with advertisers is two-fold. They are buyers in that they need advertisers to exist and they therefore "shop" for the best; and they are sellers in that advertisers are interested in reaching the networks' audiences.

The labor unions in broadcasting, as in other industries, are known for their high pay scales, minimum work-hours, seniority clauses, and strict delineation of employee duties. This may appear to be countervailing power in action. It has progressed to a stage where networks fill certain positions by contacting the union, not an individual employee.

The networks, because they own stations, must also "buy" government approval. If there is any impropriety in programming, their stations (and affiliates) will suffer the consequences. As Head writes:

> Ownership of stations gives the network a licensee status, for networks as such are not licensed. They have no legal status under the Communications Act, and therefore appear in legal proceedings before the FCC primarily as licensees of stations rather than as networks *per se*. (Head, 1956, p. 229.)

The fact that affiliates are responsible for programs broadcast, no matter what the source, was established in the 1938 "Mae West" incident. In a letter sent to all NBC affiliates after an objectionable broadcast material incident, the FCC stated:

> Each licensee carries his own definite responsibility for the character of the programs he broadcasts, and he must be held to account regardless of the origin of the program. (Summers, 1966, C–26.)

The FCC is merely a governmental reaction to the strong power that broadcasters can wield. This reaction is countervailing power.

The networks as sellers must have a product that is appealing to viewers. Only recently however have viewers gained a countervailing power of their own. In the past viewers have covertly relied on the power that has been exercised by the Federal Communications Commission. This is changing. The most formidable example is Action for Children's Television (ACT), which as a citizen's group has applied pressure on the networks to improve the quality of and decrease the commerical quantity in children's programming. This was seen as only the beginning by former FCC Commissioner Nicholas Johnson, who actively advocates viewer involvement in station programming decisions. Johnson is now the chairperson of the National Citizens' Committee for Broadcasting (NCCB), a consumer activist group working for more responsive and responsible broadcasting.

Older and more developed is the countervailing power exhibited by advertisers. Although it is not openly acknowledged, advertisers do control the content of commerical programs. (Chester, et al., 1963, 104.) But an opposite, if not equal power, is exercised by the networks where more than one advertiser may be vying for an opening in an important prime time slot. Network television and advertising are both big businesses.

Although on a smaller scale, these same countervailing powers are present at the local level. If there is no union present at a station, employees may use threat of joining one as their countervailing power for higher wages. Advertisers and government also exercise some measure of control on stations.

It can be seen that countervailing power from various sources restrains networks and stations as much as competing networks and stations.

COUNTERVAILING POWER AND THE VIOLENCE ISSUE

The countervailing power exerted by advertisers has become most apparent in the violence issue. A number of large budget television advertisers have decided to boycott those television programs that are especially violent. Among the growing list are such sponsors as Sears, General Foods, Best Foods, General Motors, Gillette, Proctor and Gamble, Kodak, and McDonald's. In addition, pressure is being applied by certain church groups whose stock portfolios contain sponsors of violent programs. The unfortunate aspect of this withdrawal is that at this writing it has had little effect on the networks.

As the big advertisers move out of a program, there is still a smaller advertiser waiting to buy time. These smaller advertisers who have had smaller budgets and less clout, now have the opportunity to buy time that was taken by larger advertisers. The networks are still making their profits. The countervailing power will not have an effect until there is unified action in the advertising agency business. This may come about as the American Association of Advertising Agencies is presently reviewing matters related to the sponsorship of violent programs. Then the countervailing power will play its part. A few advertisers, no matter how prestigious will not affect the institution of television; it takes the institution of advertising, as a whole, to effectuate such a change.

THE ACTION FOR CHILDREN'S TELEVISION CASE

With the above mentioned concepts in mind, let us return to the case of *Action for Children's Television* v. *FCC and U.S.* In 1970, ACT proposed that the FCC rule that sponsorship of children's programs be prohibited, that there be no mention of products in blocks of time devoted to children's programs, and that there be a specified minimum number of hours of programs for children in specific age groups. This proposal was accepted by then FCC chairman Dean Burch as a petition for a rulemaking. As per FCC administrative guidelines, two rounds of arguments, three days of oral arguments and three days of panel discussions on the ACT proposal followed.

The National Association of Broadcasters, in its usual way in order to avoid a direct government rule, reinterpreted its television code in regard to deceptive advertising practices. Then the NAB and the Association of Independent Television Stations agreed to reduce the amount of time member stations would include in children's programs.

Finally after some four years of hearings, debates, and private meetings, the FCC issued a nonbinding policy statement. The commission cited the sensitive First Amendment issues involved and emphasized the need for stations to make a meaningful effort in providing a reasonable amount of educational programs for children. The policy statement also said that the abolition of sponsorship for children's programs would be self-defeating since the revenue from these commercials is the *raison d'etre* for children's programming. It stressed, however, that if self-regulation did not work, *per se* rules would have to be adopted. Finally, the commission noted that commercial tie-ins and host selling was undesirable; it reminded stations to keep a distinct separation between program content and commercial content.

The nonbinding nature of this policy statement outraged ACT. As a result it sued the FCC. The case was heard before a three judge panel of the U.S. Court of Appeals in Washington, D.C.

The judicial panel ruled that the commission acted properly in only issuing a policy statement. The court agreed that self-regulation is the most appropriate means for solving the issue of programs for children. ACT is not pleased with the most recent decision and will ask the full nine judge bench of the District of Columbia circuit court to hear the case. In addition, ACT will attempt to prove to the FCC that the self-regulation is not working and will not work.

There is even more to this case than seems apparent on the surface. One will note that in *ACT* v. *FCC and U.S.*, the court reaffirmed the FCC's right to rely on industry-wide self-regulation as well as the threat of appropriate action that might have to be taken against those stations that do not follow the vague guidelines. This is in contrast to the decision in *Writers' Guild of America* v. *FCC* discussed above. The commission is expected to use the discussion of the ACT case in its briefs to be filed in appeals of the *Writers' Guild* case as well as the pay cable case (*Home Box Office, Inc.* v. *FCC and U.S.*) which is discussed in Chapter 8, Section One. In the latter case, the FCC was reprimanded for carrying on informal off-the-record discussions with *ex parte* interests. This aspect and most other parts of the HBO case were appealed to the United States Court of Appeals for the District of Columbia Circuit (denied 98 S.Ct.Ill (1977)), and to the United States Supreme Court (denied 98 S.Ct. 621 (1978)).

THE CASE OF STATE OF FLORIDA V. RONNEY A. ZAMORA

As FCC lawyers began preparing briefs for their Supreme Court appeal, Ellis Rubin, a Miami attorney prepared papers for a criminal case in which, to his mind, television violence played an integral role. Ronney Zamora, a 15-year old, was charged by Miami police with killing his 83-year old neighbor and stealing $415 from her along with her car. According to police, Zamora then treated four of his friends to a weekend spree at Disney World.

As the boy's attorney, Rubin argued that the boy was a victim of "involuntary subliminal television intoxication." According to Rubin, Zamora had seen too much violence on television. The boy allegedly planned the crime based upon a "Kojak" episode he had seen. The youth viewed television with quite a bit of zeal. His parents, who had been upset with his constant diet of crime shows, sent him to a psychologist a week before the murder was committed.

Rubin's attempts at bringing the court to examine the effects of violent programs on the young were halted by Judge H. Paul Baker. Baker would not allow testimony concerning television violence because he saw no direct link between it and Zamora's crime. The boy was found guilty as charged and Rubin has appealed the conviction.

THE CASE OF NBC V. NIEMI

Another case and one that is more interesting in its implications dealt with the responsibilities that a broadcaster has as a result of the programs he broadcasts. Popularly known as the *Born Innocent* case, NBC and its San Francisco affiliate KRON-TV, were sued by the mother of a 9-year old girl who was raped by girls wielding a Coca-Cola bottle in a fashion, the suit alleges, presented in the network's broadcast of the movie *Born Innocent*. 98 S. Ct. 705 (1978).

The suit, for $11 million in damages, was initially dismissed by California Superior Court Judge John Ertola. Judge Ertola, after viewing the film, ruled without calling a jury that the First Amendment protects broadcasters against such suits. He said, "The state of California is not about to begin using negligence as a vehicle to freeze the creative arts."

The decision was appealed by the mother and the California Court of Appeals overturned the lower court decision and returned the case to the lower court where, it insisted, a jury trial be held. It was at this point that the defendents, NBC and KRON-TV, asked the U.S. Supreme Court to consider the case based upon their First Amendment protection. In their petition to review, NBC and KRON-TV said that the plaintiff's theory that "the tort of 'imitation' may, consistently with long-standing First Amendment principles, be permitted to survive" is "simplistic . . . novel . . . insidious . . . (and) unbounded." CBS and the National Association of Broadcasters filed friend-of-the-court briefs, with all parties arguing that trial of the suit would not only violate the First Amendment, but also inhibit broadcasters from presenting news and dramatic programs that portray harsh realities of life.

By refusing to grant a stay, the Supreme Court seemed to agree at least implicitly that the lower court in California should hear the case with a jury trial. First Amendment protections are not to be ruled out, however, as the California appellate court said that the First Amendment argument could be considered following the jury trial. In August 1978 the San Francisco trial judge dismissed the complaint rather than sending it to the jury as the California Court of Appeals had suggested, thus facilitating its possible return to the high Court.

Violence and economic exploitation are two areas that affect advertisers and broadcasters. The legal right to regulate such program and advertising content is weakened by the First Amendment rights of broadcasters. The manner in which these programs can be regulated is through the extralegal process of countervailing power.

REFERENCES

"Advertisers Take Aim on TV Violence," *Media Decisions* (February, 1977) 12:2, pp. 64–67, 109–112.

Atkins, Charles K., John P. Murray, and Oguz B. Nayman, "The Surgeon General's Research Program on Television and Social Behavior: A Review of Empirical Findings," *Journal of Broadcasting* (Winter, 1971–72), 16:1, pp. 21–36.

Baran, Stanley J., "Prosocial and Antisocial Television Content and Modeling by High and Low Self-Esteem Children," *Journal of Broadcasting* (Fall, 1974), 18:4 pp. 481–495.

Belson, William A., "Mass Communications," *Annual Review of Psychology* (1965), p. 16.

Bogart, Leo, "Warning: The Surgeon General has Determined that TV Violence is Moderately Dangerous to Your Child's Mental Health," *Public Opinion Quarterly* (Winter, 1972–73), 36:4, pp. 491–521.

Canadian Royal Commission, *Violence in the Communications Industry* (New York: Renouf, 1977).

Chester, Giraud, Garnet Garrison, and Edgar E. Willis, *Television and Radio*, 3rd ed. (Englewood Cliffs, N.J.: Prentice-Hall, 1963).

"FCC Upheld in ACT Decision; Ruling may bear on other cases," *Broadcasting* (July 11, 1977), pp. 19, 22.

Galbraith, John Kenneth, *American Capitalism* (Boston: Houghton-Mifflin Company, 1956).

Greenberg, Bradley S., "British Children and Televised Violence," *Public Opinion Quarterly* (Winter, 1974–75), 38:4, pp. 531–547.

Greenberg, Bradley S. and Thomas F. Gordon, "Critics' and Public Perceptions of Violence in Television Programs," *Journal of Broadcasting* (Winter, 1970–71), 15:1, pp. 29–44.

Greenberg, Bradley S. and C. Edward Wotring, "Television Violence and Its Potential for Aggressive Driving Behavior," *Journal of Broadcasting* (Fall, 1974), 18:4, pp. 473–480.

Head, Sydney W., *Broadcasting in America* (Boston: Houghton-Mifflin, 1956).

Hoyt, James L., "Effect of Media Violence 'Justification' on Aggression," *Journal of Broadcasting* (Fall, 1970), 14:4, pp. 455–464.

Howill, Dennis and Guy Cumberbatch, "Audience Perceptions of Violent Television Content," *Communication Research* (April, 1974), 1:2, pp. 204–223.

"Judge Says Networks, NAB, FCC all Acted Illegally on Family Viewing," *Broadcasting* (November 8, 1976), 91:19, pp. 20–21.

Krugman, H.E., "The Impact of Television Advertising: Learning without Involvement," *Public Opinion Quarterly* (Fall, 1965), 29, pp. 349–356.

Liebert, Robert M., John M. Neale, and Emily S. Davidson, *The Early Window: Effects of Television on Children and Youth* (New York: Pergamon Press, Inc., 1973).

Melody, William, *Children's Television: The Economics of Exploitation* (New Haven, Conn.: Yale University Press, 1973).

Meyer, Timothy P., "Some Effects of Real Newsfilm Violence on the Behavior of Viewers," *Journal of Broadcasting* (Summer, 1971), 15:3, pp. 275–286.

Meyer, Timothy P., "The Effects of Verbally Violent Film Context on Aggressive Behavior," *Audiovisual Communication Review* (Summer, 1972), 20:2, pp. 160–69.

Meyer, Timothy P., "Children's Perceptions of Justified/Unjustified and Fictional/Real Film Violence," *Journal of Broadcasting* (Summer, 1973), 17:3, pp. 321–332.

Meyer, Timothy P. and James A. Anderson, "Media Violence Research: Interpreting the Findings," *Journal of Broadcasting* (Fall, 1973), 17:4, pp. 447–458.

Milgram, Stanley and Lance Shotland, *Television and Antisocial Behavior: Field Experiments* (New York: Academic Press, 1973).

Roberts, Donald F., "Communication and Children: A Developmental Approach," *Handbook of Communication*, Wilber Schramm and Ithiel de Sola Pool (eds.) (Chicago: Rand-McNally, 1973).

Schramm, Wilber and D.F. Roberts, *The Process and Effects of Mass Communication*, rev. ed. (Urbana, Ill.: University of Illinois Press, 1971).

Sheikh, Anees, V. Kanti Prasad, and Tanniru R. Rao, "Children's Television Commercials: A Review of Research," *Journal of Communication* (Autumn, 1974), 24:4, pp. 126–136.

"Slaying by Teen-ager Blamed on Insanity from TV Violence," Allentown, Penn. *Morning Call* (August 19, 1977), p. 13.

Summers, Harrison B., *Communications Law Handbook* (Columbus, Ohio: Ohio State University Press, 1966).

Tannenbaum, Percy H., "Mass Communication," *Annual Review of Psychology* (1968), 19, pp. 351–385.

Thain, Gerald, "Suffer the Hucksters to Come Unto the Little Children? Possible Restriction of Television Advertising to Children Under Section 5 of the Federal Trade Commission Act," *Boston University Law Review* (1976), 56, pp. 651–684.

Watt, James H., Jr. and Robert Krull, "An Examination of Three Models of Television Viewing and Aggression," *Human Communication Research* (Winter, 1977), 3:2, pp. 99–112.

Weiss, W., "Effects of the Mass Media of Communication," *Handbook of Social Psychology*, G. Lindzey and E. Aronson (eds.) (Reading, Mass.: Addison-Wesley, 1968).

Weiss, W., "Mass Communications," *Annual Review of Psychology* (1971), 22, pp. 309–336.

Ziman, J.M., "Information, Communication, Knowledge," *Nature* (1969), 224, pp. 318–24.

Section 4

Advertising: New Arena of Rights Battle

*A. Kent MacDougall**

Boys' Life magazine accepts advertisements for rifles and shotguns, but turns down ads for boomerangs.

The *New York Times* takes ads for abortion referral services, but not for abortion clinics or contraceptives.

The CBS television station in New York recently aired a commercial that showed an Irish Catholic priest being converted to kosher hot dogs, but the CBS television network would not touch it.

Magazines, newspapers, and television broadcasters routinely find themselves in inconsistencies such as these in the course of deciding which ads to accept and which to reject. Sometimes they explain their decisions. *Boys' Life* says its boy scout readers can learn firearms safety in summer camp, but instruction in boomerang-throwing is unavailable. "A kid could kill himself with a boomerang," ad director Frank Rowe said. Often, however, an advertiser is turned away with no explanation other than that his ad "doesn't meet our standards" or is unacceptable because of considerations of "taste."

With or without explanation, refusals to sell space and time increasingly are being challenged as artitrary censorship, an abridgment of the right to advertise implicit in the First Amendment guarantee of freedom of speech. The critics include advertisers, public interest groups, lawyers, and academics.

Sex film producers and exhibitors are angry because of a spreading blackout of newspaper ads for pornographic movies. Mobil Oil Corporation is angry because it cannot buy television time to air its views on energy and other issues. Public interest groups are angry at the media's power to consign unpopular products and services, ideas and lifestyles to obscurity or underground status by refusing ads for them.

No one is disputing the media's right to reject ads that are misleading or fraudulent—ads for miracle cures, home improvement frauds, worthless desert real estate, and the like. But a growing number of advertisers and their legal and academic allies are contending that the media have a moral, even a legal obligation to accept ads for any product, service, or cause that is not expressly forbidden by law.

The right-to-advertise forces have been winning considerable support—though not specifically against privately owned publications. Courts, departing from a long tradition of depriving advertising (or commercial speech as it is known in legal circles) of First Amendment protection, in recent years have:

- —upheld the right of political candidates, antiwar activists, and others to advertise in such public places as buses, subway platforms, train terminals, and shopping centers;
- —struck down state bans on the advertising of prescription drug prices, abortion referral services, contraceptives, and lawyers' services;

*Published October 24, 1977. Copyright 1977, *Los Angeles Times*. Reprinted by permission.

—ruled that public high school and college newspapers and state bar association journals cannot reject advertising for causes they dislike;

—recognized that the public has a right to receive the often valuable information and views that ads contain.

"Advertising, however tasteless and excessive it sometimes may seem, is nonetheless dissemination of information as to who is producing and selling what product, for what reason, and at what price," the Supreme Court declared last year in voiding Virginia's ban on drug price advertising.

One thing no court has yet done is force a privately owned periodical to accept an ad—or anything else, for that matter. Newspaper and magazine publishers insist that their First Amendment right to decide what goes in and what stays out of their publications is absolute. The Supreme Court has agreed, most notably three years ago when it struck down a Florida law that had given candidates for public office the right to reply to criticism in newspapers.

Hence, the press continues to control the flow of information on many products and services. Take, for example, information about automobile buying. There is a company in Brooklyn named Car/Puter International Corporation that, for $10, will provide any person contemplating buying a new car with a computer printout of the list price and dealer's cost for that car and the accessories and options available with it. For another $10, Car/Puter will order the car from one of 900 participating dealers at $125 above dealer's cost, far below the usual markup.

Millions of Americans have had access to information about this unusual service through newspaper and magazine articles. But many of the same periodicals that have reported favorably on Car/Puter in their editorial columns have denied the firm access to advertising columns. At last count 42 newspapers and magazines had rejected Car/Puter ads, almost always without explanation. One, however, was remarkably candid.

In a letter to Car/Puter, a sales executive of *Reader's Digest* explained that the problem with Car/Puter advertising was "its direct competitiveness with automotive dealers. I know you will understand that manufacturers do not like to advertise in media which dealers do not heartily endorse . . . In our judgment it would be foolish to deliberately accept advertising which might tend to destroy (the dealer support) it has taken years to build."

Car/Puter, using the letter as evidence, filed a $6 million antitrust suit alleging a conspiracy among *Reader's Digest* and the Big Four domestic auto manufacturers. The suit was dropped, however, when Car/Puter President Arnold Wonsever learned it would cost $50,000 to $100,000 to carry it through.

"I am tired of paying legal fees to defend what I consider is 100 percent right," he said. "We have survived since 1964 largely on the favorable notices of reporters and columnists, but I have given up trying to buy space. We would have done a lot more business if we had been able to advertise regularly."

Another innovative enterprise that charges that rejection of its advertising is hurting its business is Teleprompter Corporation. Teleprompter is the nation's largest community antenna cable television operator. Its hookups allow television viewers to tune in distant stations they could not otherwise receive. For an additional monthly fee, Teleprompter supplies some original entertainment programs and motion pictures.

The best way to make TV viewers aware of Teleprompter's cable and pay TV services is to advertise them on TV. But TV stations are not eager to sell time to a competitor. Five of 21 stations, including two of three in El Paso, Texas, have rejected Teleprompter's ads. Teleprompter has filed a complaint with the Federal Trade Commission, asserting that denial of access to TV places the company "at a distinct competitive disadvantage," and asking the FTC to investigate for possible antitrust violations.

Although the power to keep a commercial off the air can be the power to destroy a little-known product or service, it seems to have little effect on overall demand for such well established, sought-after products as cigarettes. The evidence: Americans are smoking more cigarettes (205 packs for the average adult last year) than they did before cigarette commercials were banned from television and radio in 1971.

The loss of cigarette ads has not prevented broadcasters from increasing their total advertising revenues faster than other media. And other media have found the ban a boon. Magazines took in three times more revenue from cigarette advertising last year than they did in 1970. Newspapers carried 12 times more cigarette advertising, and outdoor billboards took in 15 times more. Total cigarette ad spending rose to $435 million from $288 million.

The Tobacco Institute attributes the increase to higher ad rates, a proliferation of aggressively promoted low-tar brands, and the decreased impact of less obtrusive print and outdoor ads.

Cigarette advertisers' free-spending ways have proved too much of a temptation for some newspapers and magazines that once rejected cigarette ads. *Better Homes and Gardens* cut out cigarette ads in 1971, but reinstated them four years later. Last year it carried $4.4 million worth of such advertising and expects at least $6 million in cigarette ad revenue this year.

Magazines that continue to hold the line include *Reader's Digest, National Geographic, Good Housekeeping* and *The New Yorker*. Somewhat self-righteously, *The New Yorker* devoted a recent "Talk of the Town" comment to cigarette advertising, drawing a connection between the print media's growing dependence on cigarette ads and the fact that "the press has been paying very little attention to the issue of cigarettes and public health." It singled out the *Columbia Journalism Review* for specific criticism, suggesting that its acceptance of cigarette ads was incompatible with its "purpose of subjecting the reporting standards of the American press to critical examination."

In a rejoinder in its own pages, the *Columbia Journalism Review* pointed to "the solid research indicating that cigarette advertising rarely influences decisions to smoke or not to smoke, but that its effect and purpose is to influence the choide of brands." It also cited "substantial medical opinion that use and misuse of alcoholic beverages damage Americans' health at least as much as do use and misuse of cigarettes," and chided *The New Yorker* for accepting liquor ads.

If some Americans had their way, there would be no advertising for either cigarettes or liquor, in any medium. Bills to disallow cigarette and liquor advertising as deductible business expenses are perennially introduced in Congress.

Forty-four years after the repeal of Prohibition, drinking is still such a sensitive issue in the U.S. that more than 200 of the nation's 1,700 daily newspapers refuse ads for beer, wine, or liquor—or all three. Of 21 daily newspapers in Mississippi, only two accept liquor ads.

Although beer and wine are commonly advertised on radio and television around the country, hard liquor is not. Distillers and broadcasters fear that radio and television commercials would offend many persons and strengthen the position of those who want to outlaw all alcoholic beverage advertising.

To avoid offending viewers and to head off government restrictions, the broadcast industry has adopted comprehensive guidelines on what is acceptable advertising and what, including liquor, is not. These do's and don't's are codified and administered by the National Association of Broadcasters. There is one code for radio and another for television. Compliance with the codes is voluntary and is easiest for the highly profitable national networks and the stations they own or are affiliated with. Small, nonaffiliated stations are financially less able to be selective and many do not subscribe to the codes. Of the nation's 7,300 radio stations, only 35 percent are code subscribers. Two-thirds of the 700 television stations subscribe.

In recent years, some code restrictions have been tightened and others loosened. Restrictions on commercials aimed at children have been tightened in response to complaints from parents and activist groups and prodding by the Federal Communications Commission. Hosts on children's programs no longer may make product pitches. Toys no longer may be shown performing feats they cannot actually perform. Viewers may no longer be exhorted to "ask your mom to buy this doll."

The restrictions go too far to suit some advertisers and their agencies. "Children are far sharper about what's going on than adults," and many of the NAB code restrictions are "simply ridiculous," said John Bergin, the father of five children and executive vice president of SSC&B, Inc., a large ad agency.

But the restrictions do not go far enough to suit Action for Children's Television. This citizen's group would like all commercials aimed at preschool children taken off the air, along with children's commercials for candies and highly sugared cereals and snack foods. It has filed formal complaints with the Federal Trade Commission against four candy manufacturers and the makers of two brands of presweetened cereals, contending that commercials for the products mislead children about their nutritional value.

The National Association of Broadcasters code bans on "personal products" have been relaxed in recent years. At one time, commercials for toilet paper were unacceptable. Since 1969, however, the TV code in several steps has approved advertising of genital deodorants, hemorrhoid remedies, enema products, douches, tampons, and sanitary napkins. "Jock itch" and bed-wetting remedies are still barred from TV, although they are allowed on radio.

Contraceptives are about the only significant personal products still banned. This is regarded by birth control advocates as hypocritical, inasmuch as advertisers are allowed to use sexy commercials to sell shaving cream, cologne, and other products. They also think the ban is against the national interest, considering the high rate of unwanted pregnancies, especially among unwed teenagers.

Harriet F. Pilpel, counsel to Planned Parenthood Federation of America, questions the legality of the code ban on contraceptives. "For a group of media people to get together and decide collectively that they will carry certain types of advertising but not other types seems to me to raise serious antitrust questions, and possibly First Amendment questions as well," she said.

NAB code officials stress that code compliance is strictly voluntary and that they have not forever closed the door to contraceptive advertising. Instead, they have agreed to discuss testing contraceptive commercials to gauge audience reaction. That precaution is understandable in light of the vituperative telephone calls and letters that halted soft-sell commercials for Trojans condoms on TV stations in Canton, Ohio and San Jose, California two years ago.

Youngs Drug Products Corporation, which makes Trojans condoms, said it had encountered no comparable hostility with radio commercials and magazine ads, and fortunately does not need TV commercials to keep its "plant running full tilt." Marketing director Milton Bryson said that the widely publicized complications that oral and intrauterine contraceptives can cause had brought the condom and the diaphragm back into favor. "Our business is out of sight," he said.

Each network has a staff of six or more editors who screen about 40,000 television commercials a year. A commercial usually is submitted in the form of a storyboard—drawings and words—so that any change required by the editors may be made before the commercial is filmed.

Commercials that name competing brands and claim superiority over those brands require documentation. Before clearing a commercial for one nonprescription drug, NBC sent it back to the ad agency that created it 26 times for revisions and documentation of claims.

Even documentation can cause problems. Makers of two competing household detergents recently showed CBS "independent" test results "proving" that each brand was superior to the other in precisely the same way. Rather than confuse viewers' CBS turned down commercials for both brands.

To avoid offending viewers, the networks watch out for ethnic stereotyping. ABC sent back an automobile commercial because the Charlie Chan character in it spoke pidgin English; after he changed it to full sentences the commercial was approved.

The CBS television network rejected the commercial with "Father O'Neill" pushing Hebrew National Kosher frankfurters as inappropriate use of religion as a selling tool. But its New York outlet, WCBS, and CBS stations in several other cities found it acceptable. "These are judgment calls," said Donn O'Brien, CBS network vice president in charge of commercial clearance. "We try to run a consolidated, centralized clearing house, but the CBS stations are autonomous, and the final call on commercials, unless there is a legal problem, is theirs."

Inconsistent TV clearance policies often force advertisers to prepare two and even three versions of the same commercial—one for each network.

CBS reported that it turned down 30 percent of the commercials submitted to it last year. NBC reported that it rejected only 1 percent of submissions last year but required 35 percent to be revised, documented, or both. ABC said it rejected 5 percent and required revisions in 80 percent.

As tough as all three networks may be, they nonetheless approve some commercials that are found later to be misleading by the national advertising division of the Council of Better Business Bureau and the Federal Trade Commission. And the network blue-pencil artists seem to have little success winning viewers' respect for TV commercials. A recent Louis Harris poll found that 46 percent of the public considered most or all of TV advertising "seriously misleading," compared with 28 percent for newspaper and magazine ads.

Television's severest critics, though, are less concerned with product commercials that are on the air than with public-issue commercials that are kept off the air. These critics include such unlikely allies as Mobil Oil, the Sierra Club, public-interest law firms such as Media Access Project, National Citizens Committee for Broadcasting, and others who believe that television's refusal to accept ads that take positions on public controversies is arbitrary and undemocratic.

Broadcasters give several reasons for their refusal to air public-issue commercials. One is that a complex issue such as energy policy cannot be dealt with adequately in a 60-second commercial, that the appropriate forum is in news programs. The critics reply that news coverage of issues is typically sporadic and superficial, often being condensed into one- or a two-minute summaries. Herbert Schmertz, Mobil Oil Vice President for Public Affairs, said, "Generally speaking, TV coverage of energy matters has tended to be simplistic and often inaccurate."

The critics also note that broadcasters find short spot announcements perfectly adequate for the presentation of controversial issues during election campaigns. But then, federal law requires the broadcasters to sell time to candidates for federal office, a right accorded no one else. They do not have to sell more than brief spots, however, and generally reject requests to purchase larger blocks, fearing politicians will draw smaller audiences than regularly scheduled situation comedies and cop shows. Ronald Reagan was able to buy one half-hour of prime time on NBC last year, after ABC and CBS had turned him down, because he preempted the low-rated "The Dumplings," which NBC was eliminating anyway.

Beyond fears that public-issue commercials will bore or antagonize some viewers, network officials do not want to change the complexion of an industry that depends on bland programming to draw huge audiences which are then sold to advertisers at high prices. Mass merchandising, not proselytizing, is what TV is all about.

Broadcasters are also afraid that public-issue ads would obligate them under the Fairness Doctrine to provide free time to those expressing opposing viewpoints. The Fairness Doctrine, laid down by the Federal Communications Commission in 1949 and later upheld by Congress and the courts, requires television and radio to deal with controversial issues of public importance and to present contrasting viewpoints on them.

The FCC first applied the Fairness Doctrine to commercials in 1967 when it ruled that cigarette commercials raised the controversial and important public issue of smoking. The FCC required countercommercials against smoking, which the American Cancer Society was delighted to supply.

In 1974 the FCC ruled that the Fairness Doctrine could not be applied to ordinary commercials promoting the sale of a product even when the commercials were misleading and use of the product was controversial. The only commercials that carry Fairness Doctrine obligations, the FCC said, are those that directly comment on important controversies.

These guidelines have given broadcasters added incentive to reject public-issue ads. The trouble is, it is not always easy to distinguish an ordinary commercial from an issue ad. When Texaco, Inc. made a commercial showing a jigsaw puzzle falling into place because Texaco was represented in all aspects of the oil industry, the TV networks and stations that accepted it judged that it simply provided information in how Texaco efficiently served its customers.

But the pro-consumer Energy Action Committee and two senators pushing legislation to break up the major oil companies deemed the Texaco commercial antidivestiture propaganda. They asked for air time for rebuttal and when they were denied it, appealed to the FCC. The FCC ruled that the commercial did indeed take a position on an important issue and that the station that had aired the spot most often had violated the Fairness Doctrine by disallowing rebuttal.

To make amends, WTOP in Washington, D.C. recently ran counter-commercials prepared by the Energy Action Committee. One spot showed a U.S. oil executive, disguised as an Arab, mugging an American consumer in a dark alley. Sticking a gasoline nozzle in the citizen's back, the mugger lifted his wallet. The message, "We'd better break up the oil monopoly before it breaks us."

To get more such commercials on the air, public-interest groups are moving on several fronts. Some have asked a federal appeals court to overturn the 1974 FCC ruling that television and radio stations airing ads for controversial products need not present opposing viewpoints. Others plan to appeal the FCC's refusal to increase the number and diversity of the public service announcements the commission requires stations to carry without charge.

Public Media Center, an alternative ad agency in San Francisco, contends that as things stand now, television stations typically carry few public service ads, bury them in non-prime time, and depend on the business-dominated Advertising Council to supply or approve most of those they do carry. This acts to keep off the air issue-oriented ads, especially from grassroots citizen organizations that raise substantive issues such as nuclear power, unemployment, and resource depiction and that assess corporate responsibility for those and other national problems.

The main obstacle to access for such populist views is a 1973 Supreme Court decision that TV and radio stations are not required by existing federal regulations to accept public-issue ads. This decision overturned a federal appeals court ruling that broadcasters' refusals to accept issue ads from the Democratic National Committee and Business Executives Move for Vietnam Peace violated the free speech provision of the First Amendment.

Chief Justice Warren E. Burger, who wrote the 7–2 majority opinion, argued that if stations were required to accept public-issue ads, "the views of the affluent could well prevail over those of others, since they would have it in their power to purchase time more frequently." Critics would add that affluent corporations already prevail with endless ads for nasal sprays, oven cleaners and pet foods while, as Justices William J. Brennan Jr. and Thurgood Marshall pointed out in a vigorous dissent, those "seeking to discuss war, peace, pollution, or the suffering of the poor" are denied comparable access.

Chief Justice Burger also complained that applying the Fairness Doctrine to public-issue advertising could deprive broadcasters of revenue by forcing them to give free response time for opposing views.

The fact that the networks fear more than loss of revenue seems apparent from their rejection of Mobil Oil's standing offer to buy time for its critics, providing the networks allow Mobil to buy an equal number of commercials to state its own views on energy policy. The networks fear that accepting the offer would set a dangerous precedent.

Mobil, which reports no problems getting its issue ads published weekly in hundreds of newspapers, remains convinced that broadcasters are badly shortchanging the public. Said Mobil Vice President Schmertz: "My complaint is that broadcasters claim the same First Amendment rights as newspapers, but they don't accord the same First Amendment opportunities in the form of access." Whereas newspapers publish letters from readers, and articles and columns by nonstaffers, broadcasting is a "closed operation."

Legally, he might have added, newspapers have even more right to be closed operations than broadcasting. Unlike television and radio licensees, who have public-service reply and other obligations because of their use of the public airwaves, privately owned newspapers have no obligation to provide space for reply, debate, or access. Nor must they accept any given ad.

Because the First Amendment prohibits only government abridgment of speech, a privately owned newspaper may be held to violate an advertiser's freedom of speech only if it can be shown to a court's satisfaction that the paper enjoys delegated governmental power or exercises a governmental function.

Far from finding newspapers tinged with governmental function, courts have repeatedly upheld a newspaper's right to reject advertising, as long as the paper acts independently of other advertisers. The most frequently cited case involves an attempt by the Amalgamated Clothing Workers to place an ad in four Chicago daily newspapers. The ad complained that imported clothing was taking jobs from American clothing workers. It explained that the union was picketing the Marshall Field department store in downtown Chicago because it sold imported clothing. All four papers rejected the ad. The courts upheld the blackout.

There are limits to newspapers' discretion on advertising, however. The First Amendment does not give a newspaper the right to publish an ad that libels someone or invades his privacy. Nor may it run an ad that violates laws banning racial and sexual discrimination.

Cases involving discriminatory advertising got newspaper publishers considerably worked up several years ago. At issue was the right of a Maryland weekly to publish an ad for a furnished apartment "in a private white home," and a Pittsburgh daily's right to segregate help wanted ads under separate "male" and "female" headings. Although both actions were found to violate antidiscrimination laws, the papers and the American Newspaper Publishers Association argued vehemently, if futilely, against any restraint on newspapers' discretion to accept and classify ads at will.

Even after the Supreme Court ruled against the *Pittsburgh Press,* it petitioned for a rehearing, contending that the court had "inadvertently provided states, counties, and municipalities with awesome and devastating power sufficient to choke off the economic lifeblood of newspapers and to destroy the press."

An increasing number of newspapers are voluntarily choking off ad revenue from another source, pornographic movie theaters. The *New York Times,* which had been taking in $750,000 a year in such ads, has run only one since July, when it began restricting them to small, unillustrated notices that porno theaters have disdained buying.

The *Los Angeles Times,* which had been running about $1 million a year in porno movie ads, cut them out entirely in August, prompting a group of producers, distributors, and exhibitors to file a $45 million damage suit alleging "arbitrary, irrational, and discriminatory" censorship. Eight other California dailies and several others elsewhere have recently announced similar restrictions, joining about 35 dailies known to have banned X-rated movie ads for years.

Many readers approve of the bans. At last count, the *Los Angeles Times* had received 2,403 letters supporting its stand and only 211 expressing disapproval. However, civil libertarians are disturbed. Fred Okrand, legal director of the American Civil Liberties Union of Southern California, said the ban arbitrarily denied advertisers the right to be heard and adult movie patrons the right to receive information. "Irrespective of what the law is, a publication in the business of accepting advertising has a moral obligation to everybody to accept all legal advertising," he said.

Porno movies aside, newspapers generally seem to be relaxing their advertising acceptance policies. The *New York Times,* which decreased its advertising acceptability staff from seven to two several years ago, no longer airbrushes out the navels of bikini beauties pictured in travel ads. It now permits ads that use the word "gay" (homosexual). Superlatives such as "the best buy in town" are now permitted, although "the best lawyer in town" is not permitted.

The *New York Times* recently accepted an ad for Christian Dior sunglasses showing a glamorous model with a smoking revolver. Some readers complained the ad lent acceptability to the use of handguns. Replied *Times* advertising acceptability manager Robert P. Smith: "We don't feel there was a serious enough problem with that ad to tell the advertiser he couldn't do it his way. It's an example of trying to keep the columns as open as possible."

Keeping columns as open as possible "is not only good business but good faith" with the public, according to a former newspaperman who now teaches journalism at the University of Arkansas at Little Rock. Professor Peter Donaghue recently proposed a right-of-access code under which newspapers would voluntarily agree, among other things, not to reject any legal ad. "Adoption of the voluntary code provisions would be a good faith indication that the press intends to use its favored position to produce diversity and fairness across the board, not just for 'press people'," Donaghue argued.

As for access to the airwaves, something stronger than a voluntary code is needed, right-to-advertise advocates agree. For starters, they would like to see Congress and the Federal Communications Commission obligate broadcasters to accept public-issue advertising. Gary W. Maeder, author of a definitive article in the *UCLA Law Review* on access to radio and television for issue advertising, proposed that broadcasters be required to set aside 10 percent of the time they sell for standard product commercials for public-issue commercials.

The Supreme Court left the door open to the possibility of some such statutory requirement in its 1973 decision that broadcasters need not accept issue ads. As Chief Justice Burger put it. "Conceivably at some future date, Congress or the commission—or the broadcasters—may devise some kind of limited right of access that is both practicable and desirable."

Chapter II

Commercial Speech

Section 1

The Rise and Fall of Commercial Speech

*William J. Rooney, Jr.**

The doctrine of commerical speech can be thought of as an exception to the area of communication protected by the First Amendment. As the Supreme Court stated in the case of *Valentine* v. *Chrestensen*,[1] "We are equally clear that the Constitution imposes no such restraint on government as respects purely commercial advertising." One rationale for this exception is that, unlike ordinary speech, commercial speech is profitable and therefore less subject to the chilling effect the Court has found so obnoxious to the First Amendment.[2] Another is that the subject matter of commercial speech is of little value to society.[3]

This section will deal with the doctrine of commercial speech in two parts. It will deal first with the development of the commercial speech doctrine, and then with the impact of recent cases limiting the doctrine.

I

Valentine v. *Chrestensen*[4] was the first case to state a doctrine of commercial speech. In *Valentine* a submarine operator was foreclosed from passing out handbills to advertise his submarine rides by a New York law barring the distribution in the streets of *commercial advertising*. The purpose of the law was apparently to prevent littering of the city streets. In an effort to circumvent the law, the submarine operator had a protest against the actions of the City Dock Department printed on the back of his advertisements. The police department advised that the distribution of the protest would not violate the law,[5] but the distribution of the double faced bill was prohibited.

The submarine operator brought suit to enjoin the police from interfering with the distribution of the leaflets. The district court granted the injunction,[6] and the Court of Appeals affirmed.[7]

The Supreme Court held that the streets are proper places for the exercise of the freedom of communicating information and disseminating opinions and that, though the states and municipalities may appropriately regulate the privilege in the public interest, they may not unduly burden its employment in these public thoroughfares. As to commercial speech, however, the constitution imposes no similar restraint on government, so states and municipalities may regulate it as they see fit.[8]

This distinction between commercial and noncommercial speech explains the case of *Breard* v. *City of Alexandria*.[9] In *Breard* a municipal ordinance that prohibited peddlers or canvassers from calling upon the occupants of private residences without having been requested or invited to do so was

---

*Mr. Rooney, Esq., represents McCabe and Sidel Attorneys at Law, Inc., in Boston.

held not to violate the due process clause by depriving peddlers and canvassers of their means of livelihood, or to violate the commerce clause, or, as applied to solicitors or magazine subscriptions, to unconstitutionally abridge freedom of speech and press.

In reaching this conclusion, the Court distinguished *Martin* v. *Struthers*,[10] which held that a municipal ordinance forbidding anyone from summoning the occupants of a residence to the door to receive advertisements was invalid as applied to the free distribution of leaflets advertising a religious meeting. The *Breard* court explained the distinction: "As no element of the commercial entered into this free solicitation, and the opinion was narrowly limited to the precise fact of the free distribution of an invitation to religious services, we feel it is not necessarily inconsistent with the conclusion reached in this case."[11]

Breard was followed by *New York Times* v. *Sullivan*,[12] which was an action for libel brought in the Circuit Court of Montgomery County, Alabama, by the city commissioner of public affairs against the *New York Times*.[13] The commissioner alleged he was libeled by a paid advertisement in the *New York Times* which purported to describe the maltreatment in the city of black students protesting segregation. The Circuit Court found for the commissioner and awarded him $50,000 in damages. The verdict was affirmed by the Supreme Court of Alabama and the defendants appealed to the Supreme Court of the United States.

The Supreme Court reversed the judgment below, holding that the rule of law in Alabama did not provide proper safeguards for the freedom of speech and press. The Court dismissed the contention that the First Amendment did not apply because this was part of a paid commerical advertisement stating:

> The publication here was not a "commercial" advertisement in the sense in which the word was used in *Chrestensen*. It communicated information, expressed opinion, recited grievances, protested claimed abuses, and sought financial support on behalf of a movement whose existence and objectives are matters of the highest public interest and concern . . . . That the *Times* was paid for publishing the advertisement is as immaterial in this connection as is the fact that newspapers and books are sold . . . . Any other conclusion would discourage newspapers from carrying "editorial advertisements" of this type, and so might shut off an important outlet for the promulgation of information and ideas by persons who do not themselves have access to publishing facilities—who wish to exercise their freedom of speech even though they are not members of the press . . . . The effect would be to shackle the First Amendment in its attempt to secure "the widest possible dissemination of information from diverse and antagonistic sources. ". . . To avoid placing such a handicap, upon the freedoms of expressions, we hold that if the allegedly libelous statements would otherwise be constitutionally protected from the present judgment, they do not forfeit that protection because they were published in the form of a paid advertisement.[14]

The issue of commercial speech arose again in *Pittsburgh Press Co.* v. *Pittsburgh Commission on Human Relations*,[15] in a somewhat different context. The Pittsburgh Commission on Human Relations found that the *Pittsburgh Press* violated the city's Human Relations Ordinance by placing help wanted advertisements in columns captioned "Jobs—Male Interest," "Jobs—Female Interest," and "Male-Female." The Commission ordered the newspaper to cease such violations and utilize a classification system with no reference to sex.

On certiori, the Supreme Court affirmed the order. The Court held that the help wanted advertisements were commercial speech, and any First Amendment interest that might be served by advertising an ordinary commercial proposal was absent because the commercial activity was illegal and the restrictions on advertising were incidental to a valid limitation on economic activity. The Court further held that the order was not unconstitutional as a prior restraint on free speech.

Distinguishing *New York Times* v. *Sullivan* the Court said:

> In crucial respects, the advertisement in the present record resembles the *Chrestensen* rather than the *Sullivan* advertisement. None expresses a position on whether, as a matter of social policy, certain positions ought to be filled by members of one or the other sex, nor does any of them criticize the Ordinance or the Commission's enforcement practices. Each is no more than a proposal of possible employment. The advertisements are thus classic examples of commercial speech.[16]

Two years later the issue was again before the Court in *Bigelow* v. *Virginia*.[17] In *Bigelow*, a newspaper editor who printed an advertisement for an out of town organization that aided in procurring abortion, was convicted of violating a Virginia statute which made it a misdemeanor to encourage or prompt in the procurring of an abortion by the sale or circulation of any publication. On appeal, the Virginia Supreme Court affirmed, holding that the advertisement was a commercial one which could be constitutionally prohibited by the state, particularly since the advertisement related to the medical, health field. On appeal, the Supreme Court reversed, holding that the editor's First Amendment rights of free speech and press were not lost merely because a commercial advertisement was involved, where the advertisement conveyed information of potential interest and value to a diverse audience.

Although it may appear that *Bigelow* would mean the end of the commercial speech exception, hope for the continuing validity of the commercial speech exception might have persisted due to the subject matter of *Bigelow*. As the Court would point out in *Virginia State Board of Pharmacy* v. *Virginia Citizens Consumer Council*:[18]

> We noted that in announcing the availability of legal abortions in New York, the commercial advertisement "did more than simply propose a commercial transaction. It contained factual material of clear public interest" . . . and of course the advertisement related to an activity with which the State could not interfere . . . . Indeed we observed: "We need not decide in this case the precise extent to which the First Amendment permits regulation of advertising that is related to the activities the state may legitimately regulate or even prohibit."[19]

After *Bigelow* the exception to the First Amendment of commerical speech was still valid law, although severly questioned. The Court had yet to hold that a bare statement of the form, I will sell X product at Y price, should be afforded First Amendment rights. This would be squarely dealt with in *Virginia State Board of Pharmacy* v. *Virginia Citizen Consumer Council*[20] and *Bates* v. *State Bar of Arizona*.[21]

II

In *Virginia State Board of Pharmacy* the plaintiffs, consumers of prescription drugs, brought suit against the State Board of Pharmacy and its individual members challenging the validity, under the First and Fourteenth Amendments, of a Virginia statute declaring it unprofessional conduct for a licensed pharmacist to advertise the prices of prescription drugs. A three judge District Court declared the statute void and enjoined its enforcement.[22]

The Supreme Court held that the advertiser's purely economic interest in a commercial advertisement does not disqualify him from protection under the First and Fourteenth Amendments since both the individual consumer and society in general may have strong interests in the free flow of commercial information. The ban on advertising prescription drug prices could not be justified on the basis of the State's interest in maintaining the professionalism of its licensed pharmacists. Although the state may require whatever professional standards it wants of its pharmacists, and may subsidize and protect them in other ways, it may not do so by keeping the public in ignorance of the lawful terms that competing pharmacists are offering. Finally, since no claim was made that the prohibited prescription drug advertisements are false, misleading, or propose illegal transaction, the State could not suppress the dissemination of concededly truthful information about entirely lawful activity, out of fear of that information's effect upon its disseminators and their recipients.

Although *Virginia State Board* held that First and Fourteenth Amendment rights applied to the advertisement of standardized products, it was not completely dispositive of the commercial speech exceptions. Advertisements of more personalized services were not within the scope of the *Virginia State Board* decision. As the court explained:

> We stress that we have not considered in this case the regulation of commercial advertising by pharmacists. Although we express no opinion as to other professions, the distinctions, historical and functional, between professions, may require consideration of quite different factors. Physicians and lawyers, for example, do not dispense standardized products; they render professional services of almost infinite variety and nature, with the consequent enhanced possibility for confusion and deception if they were to undertake certain kinds of advertising.[23]

The question of advertisement of professional services was dealt with the next year in *Bates v. State Bar of Arizona*.[24] In *Bates* two attorneys opened a "legal clinic" and advertised the prices they charged for certain routine services. The court found that the almost absolute prohibition on advertising in effect violated the First and Fourteenth Amendments since it was overbroad, but the Overbreadth Doctrine (which holds that government regulation, at least in the area of speech, cannot sweep unnecessarily broadly and thereby invade the area of protection freedoms) would not be available in the case because:

> The justification for the application of overbreadth analysis applies weakly, if at all, in ordinary commercial context. As was acknowledged in *Virginia Pharmacy Board* v. *Virginia Consumer Council* (sic) 425 U.S. at 771 n24, there are "common sense differences" between commercial speech and other varieties. Since advertising is linked to commercial well being, it seems unlikely that such speech is particularly susceptible to being crushed by overbroad regulation.
>
> Moreover concerns for uncertainty in determining the scope of protection are reduced, the advertiser seeks to disseminate information about a product or service that he provides, and presumably he can determine more readily than others whether his speech is truthful and protected. Since overbreadth is strong medicine, which has been employed sparingly and only as a last resort, it will not be applied to professional advertising, a context where it is not necessary to further its intended objective.[25]

Deciding whether the blanket prohibition on advertising was unconstitutional as applied to the defendants, the court held:

> The constitutional issue in this case is only whether the State may prevent the publication in a newspaper of appellants' truthful advertisement concerning the availability and terms of routine legal services. The flow of such information may not be restrained, and the present application of the disciplinary rule against appellants is violative of the First Amendment.[26]

Relying upon *Bates*, in at least one state the Court subsequently held in *Revieve* v. *Ohio State Dental Board*[27] that Ohio's regulations regarding advertising by dentists were unconstitutional insofar as they barred price advertising and certain methods of advertising—such as the use of "glittering light signs" and large displays. Statements of superior services and painless treatment could be constitutionally regulated, however.

The Court refused to extend *Bates* to in-person solicitation by an attorney for remunerative employment in *Ohralik* v. *Ohio Bar Association*.[28] Although granting that the solicitation was entitled to some First Amendment protection, the Court held that it was subject to regulations in furtherance of the state's important interest in preventing fraud, undue influence, intimidation, overreaching, and other forms of vexatious conduct. The Court distinguishes the companion case, *In Re Primus*,[29] in which an attorney wrote a letter advising a woman, who had been sterilized allegedly as a condition of continued receipt of medicaid benefits, that free legal assistance was available from the ACLU to sue the doctor who performed the operation. The Court held that the attorney's activity came within the "generous zone of protection" reserved for associational freedoms because she engaged in solicitation by mail on behalf of a bona fide, nonprofit organization that pursues litigations as a vehicle for effective political expression and association, as well as a means of communicating useful information to the public. In reaching this conclusion the Court noted that:

> Unlike the situation in *Ohralik*, . . . appellant's act of solicitation took the form of a letter to a woman . . . . This was not in-person solicitation for pecuniary gain.[30]

Revieve, *Ohralik* and *Primus* indicate that although advertisement of the price of standardized professional services, like standardized goals, would be protected by the First and Fourteenth Amendments; advertisements that go beyond this may be subject to severe regulation.

CONCLUSION

The commercial speech exception which originated with *Valentine* v. *Chrestensen* has been consistently limited by subsequent cases. Now, with the exception of the area of professional services, only a vestige of the exception remains which says that the Overbreadth Doctrine will not be employed in the context of commercial speech.

NOTES

[1] 315 U.S. 52, 54 (1941).
[2] See *New York Times* v. *Sullivan*, 376 U.S. 254, 278–283 (1964).
[3] *Cf, Valentine* v. *Chrestensen*, 316 U.S. 52, 55 (Court distinguished between communication for public interest and what is merely for private profit).

[4] 316 U.S. 52.
[5] The distribution of a political protest on city streets is constitutionally protected. See *Lovell* v. *Griffin*, 303 U.S. 444 (1938).
[6] 24, F. Supp. 596.
[7] 122 F.2d 511.
[8] 316 U.S. at 54.
[9] 341 U.S. 622 (1951).
[10] 319 U.S. 141 (1943).
[11] 319 U.S. at 643.
[12] 376 U.S. 254 (1964).
[13] Besides the *New York Times*, there were four other defendants in the case.
[14] 376 U.S. at 266 (Citations omitted).
[15] 413 U.S. 376 (1973).
[16] 413 U.S. at 385.
[17] 421 U.S. 809 (1975).
[18] 425 U.S. 748 (1976).
[19] Ibid.
[20] Ibid.
[21] 433 U.S. 350 (1977).
[22] 373 F. Supp. 683 (E. E. Va 1974).
[23] 425 U.S. 748, 771, n.24.
[24] 433 U.S. 350 (1977).
[25] Ibid.
[26] Ibid.
[27] 358 NE 2d 1384 (Ohio Common Pleas, 1978).
[28] 436 U.S. 447 (1978).
[29] 436 U.S. 412 (1978).
[30] Ibid.

Section 2

Advertising of Prescription Drug Prices as Protected Commercial Speech

*Cameron F. Kerry**

INTRODUCTION

Although the precise contours of the First Amendment remain undefined, the expression that it protects has been seen to serve three broad functions. First and most clearly, the First Amendment is seen to protect democratic self-government by promoting public discussion of matters broadly relevant to public decision making, and protecting against governmental suppression of ideas. A second function of the First Amendment is to promote individual self-fulfillment by permitting self-expression and the development of rational faculties through exposure to ideas. The third broad function of freedom of expression is to foster the attainment of truth through competition of ideas.

Historically, "commercial speech"[1] has been viewed as categorically outside the scope of First Amendment protection without examining whether it may serve the functions of the First Amendment.[2] In a series of recent decisions, however, culminating in the 1975 term in *Virginia State Board of Pharmacy* v. *Virginia Citizens Consumer Council, Inc.,* the Supreme Court has broadened the scope of First Amendment protection to include commercial expression. The decision in *Virginia Board of Pharmacy* abrogated what remained of the doctrine that commercial expression is wholly outside the protection of the First Amendment.

In *Virginia Board of Pharmacy,* the Supreme Court squarely addressed the question whether there is an exception from the First Amendment for commercial speech. The Court answered this question unequivocally in the negative. Yet, while bringing commercial speech within the boundaries of the First Amendment, the Court did not extend to such expression the same degree of protection accorded to other forms of speech. Rather, the Court appears to have adopted a two-tiered protective approach[3] in which commercial speech is considered to be in a ". . . second class (of) First Amendment rights." This article will examine the conceptual basis for the Court's two-tiered approach in terms of the relationship of commercial expression to the theoretical values of the First Amendment. It will then examine the method by which the Court determined that Virginia's prohibition of prescription drug price advertising was impermissible, with a view toward determining what is permissible governmental regulation of commercial advertising under the Court's two-tiered approach . . .

I. *The First Amendment Values of Commercial Speech*

The place of commercial expression in the framework of First Amendment values has been the underlying issue in determining whether such expression should be protected. The traditional doctrine that commercial speech is wholly outside the First Amendment necessarily rested on the premise that

---

*Law Clerk to Elbert P. Tuttle, U.S. Senior Circuit Judge, Fifth Circuit, Atlanta, Georgia. This article was written when the author was a law student and staff member of the *Boston College Industrial and Commercial Law Review,* prior to his executive editorship of that journal. Subsequently, the article has been revised and updated for publication in this book.

commercial speech is beneath the dignity of First Amendment "speech." In *Virginia Board of Pharmacy,* the Supreme Court identified affirmative advertising which bring it within the scope of the First Amendment. Yet in placing commercial advertising in a second tier of First Amendment protection, the *Virginia Board of Pharmacy* Court apparently concluded that the affirmative values of commercial advertising do not raise such expression to the dignity of other protected speech. Thus, by corollary, the Court incorporated aspects of the doctrine displaced in *Virginia Board of Pharmacy*. This section of the article will examine the Court's conflicting doctrines of commercial speech and will analyze the Court's two-tiered approach to commercial speech as a synthesis of these doctrines.

A. Lack of First Amendment Values in Commercial Speech—The *Chrestensen* Doctrine

Although it held sway for over thirty years, the doctrine that commercial speech is outside the scope of First Amendment protection was never coherently explicated by the Court. The doctrine was enunciated in a brief opinion without citation, in *Valentine v. Chrestensen*. Pursuant to a municipal ordinance forbidding distribution of commercial advertising matter in the streets, Chrestensen, the owner of a submarine exhibited for profit, was ordered by the New York City Police not to distribute handbills advertising his exhibit. Chrestensen obtained an injunction against enforcement of the statute from the federal district court, which ruled that the New York City ordinance constituted an unreasonable restraint on the time, place, or manner of handbill distribution. The Second Circuit affirmed, reasoning that there was no valid distinction between ideological speech and speech "in the market place." The Supreme Court reversed the circuit court, holding that the constitutional protection of freedom of expression did not apply to commercial advertising such as Chrestensen's.

Although no rationale for the Court's treatment of commercial speech was advanced in *Chrestensen,* one explanation does emerge from that case. The *Chrestensen* Court stated: "whether, and to what extent, one may promote or pursue a gainful occupation in the streets, to what extent such activity shall be adjudged a derogation of the public right of user, are matters for legislative judgment." Implicit in this conclusion is the premise that commercial advertising essentially involves the pursuit of "a gainful occupation," which "relates to a separate sector of social activity involving the system of property rights rather than free expression."[4] Under this view, commercial speech is not "speech" for First Amendment purposes; rather, it is economic conduct, the regulation of which is subject chiefly to the generally minimal limitations of the Fifth and Fourteenth Amendments. As the *Chrestensen* Court seemingly presumed, commercial advertising is largely economic activity. While it may have aspects which are expression touching public affairs or self-fulfillment, advertising is primarily marketing designed to garner private profits. Viewed solely as such, commercial advertising is within the state's well-established power to regulate. On the other hand, advertising by its nature engages in communication. As such, even though it may remain primarily conduct, it partakes of expression. Where conduct and expression are combined and First Amendment protection is asserted, the Court will as a rule attempt to determine whether the challenged regulation is directed at the conduct or the expression at issue. Thus, merely to dispose of advertising by labelling it conduct ignores its expressive aspect and consequently avoids the question whether the First Amendment has any bearing. It is perhaps for this reason that the advertising-as-pure-conduct rationale implied in *Chrestensen* has yielded to a second rationale which treats advertising as speech and focuses on its value as speech.

This second basis for excluding commercial speech from the protection of the First Amendment can be abstracted from the landmark political libel decision in *New York Times Co. v. Sullivan*. That case involved an advertisement which, in seeking financial and other support for a civil rights organization, made false statements about police officials in Montgomery, Alabama. Establishing that public officials may not recover for defamation without showing that the defamatory statement was made with knowing or reckless disregard of its truth or falsehood, the Supreme Court reversed an Alabama state court judgment for the police officials. The *Sullivan* Court premised its discussion on "a profound national commitment to the principle that debate on public issues should be uninhibited, robust, and wide-open . . . ." In this light, the Court distinguished the advertisement at issue from the advertisement in *Chrestensen*. It found that the former "communicated information, expressed opinion, recited grievances, protested claimed abuses, and sought financial support on behalf of a movement whose existence and objectives are matters of the highest public interest and concern." The implication of this distinction is that communications which are purely commercial as in *Chrestensen* are not sufficiently related to discussion of public issues to warrant First Amendment protection. Indeed, as expressed by Judge Bazelon, commercial advertising

> is not ordinarily associated with any of the interests that the First Amendment seeks to protect. As a rule, it does not affect the political process, does not contribute to the exchange of ideas, does not provide information on matters of public importance, and is not, except perhaps for the ad-men, a form of individual self-expression.[5]

In this analysis, then, commercial speech is viewed as separated from the dialogue of public affairs, and therefore without social importance. Unlike the *Chrestensen* approach, which appears to have viewed advertising as amounting only to conduct, this approach recognizes that advertising has aspects which are expression. Yet, under *Sullivan,* commercial speech is distinguished from protected debate and hence is unworthy of First Amendment protection.

B. The Affirmative Values of Commercial Speech: The *Chrestensen* Doctrine Reconsidered

The traditional exclusion of commercial speech from First Amendment protection placed advertising in the same category as "the lewd and obscene, the profane, the libelous, and insulting, or 'fighting' words. . . ." Advertising is an anomaly in the company of such words "which by their very utterance inflict injury or tend to incite an immediate breach of the peace."[6] While, like all speech, it is certainly capable of being harmful, commercial speech is not harmful, per se. In its last two terms, the Supreme Court has re-examined this anomalous treatment of commercial speech. In so doing, the Court has considered the ways in which commercial expression can serve the functions of the First Amendment.

The *Chrestensen* doctrine was largely abrogated in the Supreme Court's 1975 decision in *Bigelow* v. *Virginia*. There, Bigelow, the editor of a weekly newspaper in Virginia, published an advertisement for a commercial abortion referral agency located in New York. He was convicted in state court of violation of a Virginia statute which prohibited the prompting of an abortion by advertising or any other means. Subsequently, his conviction was affirmed on appeal by the Virginia Supreme Court. On appeal to the United States Supreme Court, his conviction was reversed. Justice Blackmun, writing for the majority, as he did in *Virginia Board of Pharmacy,* found "clear public interest" in the advertisement at issue. First, although the advertisement offered a commercial service, it also contained factual information about abortion laws in New York and the availability of abortions there. Second, the subject matter—abortion—touched on matters of Constitutional interest. On the basis of this public interest content, the Court found Bigelow's advertisement protected by the First Amendment. Accordingly, the Court concluded that his First Amendment interests must be balanced against the governmental interests involved. Examining the justifications for the restriction of Bigelow's First Amendment rights, the Court found only the barest state interest in protecting Virginia citizens from possible harm from abortion agencies, an interest characterized as one in "shielding . . . citizens from information about activities outside Virginia's borders." Hence, the Court ruled the prohibition against abortion advertising an unconstitutional infringement of the freedom to express the ideas contained in the advertisement published by Bigelow.

The decision in *Bigelow* represented a major abridgment of the *Chrestensen* doctrine. Most significantly, the *Bigelow* Court adopted by reference criticism of that case by Justices in previous cases, and recast the decision on its facts as one involving restrictions of the manner of speech in the public forum. The *Bigelow* Court concluded that "(*Chrestensen*) obviously does not support any sweeping proposition that advertising is unprotected per se." In place of the *Chrestensen* doctrine the decision in *Bigelow* established that courts may not categorically exclude commercial advertising from First Amendment protection. Rather, they must first examine the advertising at issue to determine whether and to what extent there are First Amendment interests involved, and then balance the latter against the relevant governmental interests.

Despite the *Bigelow* Court's departure from *Chrestensen,* however, the doctrine of the latter case retained at least an appearance of vitality. This faint life sign was the result of the Court's First Amendment analysis in *Bigelow*. The First Amendment protection of Bigelow's advertisement stemmed from extrinsic importance in the particular advertisement, not any generic value in commercial speech in general. Indeed, the Court differentiated between the advertisement in Bigelow's newspaper and Chrestensen's advertisement on the basis that Bigelow's advertisement "did more than simply propose a commercial transaction," whereas Chrestensen's was viewed as "purely commercial." Hence, it was possible to construe *Bigelow* as holding that purely commercial speech remains outside the scope of First Amendment protection.[7]

In *Bigelow* a specific advertisement was in controversy. By contrast, in *Virginia Board of Pharmacy,* no particular advertisement was at issue. As a result the Court could only consider the values inherent in commercial advertising rather than those which might be imported by particular content. The Court identified the broad interests in commercial advertising as those of the advertiser, the consumer, and society at large. In characterizing the interest of the advertiser as "purely economic," the Court didn't reason that this interest has affirmative weight requiring First Amendment protection, but rather discerned that its economic character is no basis for its disqualification from such protection. The interest of consumers is similarly economic. As characterized in *Virginia Board of Pharmacy,* the interest is one in purchasing drugs at the lowest possible cost. While in that case the Court was able to find this interest especially "convincing" due to the health needs of poor, aged, and infirmed consumers, this interest will rarely be as convincing where commodities less vital than prescription drugs are involved. In the case of many commodities, it will often be trivial. As such, like the advertiser's interest, the interest of consumers in commercial advertising does not require exclusion of commercial speech from the First Amendment sphere, but neither does this interest require its inclusion. Thus, the fundamental basis for extending First Amendment protection to commercial expression must lie in the social value which the Court discerns in advertising in general, rather than the value of a particular subject matter.

The Court identified three functions of commercial advertising which have broad social value. The first function the Court identified is the promotion of rational private economic decisions. This goal of enlightened private decision making reflects the views of the First Amendment both as a means of approaching an understanding of truth and as a means to individual self-fulfillment. The effect which advertising may have on individual consumers' economic decisions is well-established; it is the raison d'etre of advertising. The Court apparently adopts the view that through competing information about goods and services the best decisions by individuals will emerge. Moreover, the Court's decision may also reflect the view that the process of discernment which an individual undergoes in making such decisions serves the purpose of rational self-fulfillment.[8]

Yet, both these views of the First Amendment are circumscribed as rationalizations for the extension of protection to commercial speech. First, the concept of a "marketplace of ideas" has only limited applicability in the commercial arena. This concept posits that a false or valueless idea is corrected "by the competition of other ideas." In the commercial arena, however, where the competition is less between ideas than between products or services, such ideas as are expressed are rarely countered by other ideas. Instead, it is the value of the products or services themselves, and not the ideas expressed about them, which determines their ultimate acceptance. Moreover, even to the extent that commercial ideas survive independently of the products to which they relate, such ideas do not depend on acceptance for their survival, because commercial ideas buy their way into the ideological marketplace and therefore are largely exempt from its dynamics. On the other hand, commercial expression does present the consumer with a modicum of information and competing claims, by which rational decisions may be reached better than in a total absence of information. Second, the value of commercial speech to self-fulfillment is an unpersuasive rationale, since the value at best is marginal; the degree of self-fulfillment achieved by evaluating commercial information may not be comparable to the self-fulfillment derived by appreciating artistic creation. Still, the First Amendment does not demand exceptional value to self-fulfillment. Protection of artistic works has included such creations as magazines devoted to "crime, violence, and lust stories," which can hardly contribute more to individual discernment than can commercial advertising. Thus, while the Court's conclusion that commercial information is "indispensable" to rational decision making may be somewhat overstated, it is reasonable to conclude that commercial advertising has some affirmative value as speech in this respect.

The second societal function discerned by the Court in commercial advertising is its effect, through private economic decisions, on the allocation of resources in society. The effect which individual consumer decisions in the aggregate have on the allocation of resources in the market system is a matter of established economic theory. A significant aspect of market theory is that the proper functioning of the market system requires "perfect information;" that is, individual buyers and sellers must be able to act rationally with knowledge of existing market conditions. In rationalizing the social interest in commercial expression as "the proper allocation of resources in a free enterprise system," the Court appears to adopt as a basis for First Amendment protection the perfect information aspect of market theory.

Justice Rehnquist criticized this approach in his dissent as a form of substantive due process which elevates the free enterprise system to Constitutional status and thereby contradicts the history of judicial restraint in the economic area. The essential criticism of the substantive due process decisions has been that the Court, in judging the reasonableness of governmental economic regulation, could substitute its own views concerning the substance of economic regulaton for that of legislatures, often frustrating political decisions based on judicially imponderable values. Reflecting this criticism, the Court in recent times has adopted a posture of deference to legislative judgments concerning the functioning of the economic system. But when Justice Blackmun reasoned in *Virginia Board of Pharmacy* that the proper allocation of resources in a free enterprise system "is a matter of public interest" on which First Amendment protection of advertising is based, he appeared to be tinkering with the economic system. This apparent intrusion into an area traditionally reserved to the political branch seemingly weakens the Court's rationale for First Amendment protection of commercial advertising.

It is not clear from the language of the *Virginia Board of Pharmacy* opinion what Justice Blackmun intended when he wrote, "so long as we preserve a predominantly free enterprise economy," advertising is necessary to ensure proper flow of commercial information. On the one hand, this argument may be understood as proposing that commercial information is functionally, and therefore Constitutionally, necessary to the proper functioning of a free enterprise economy. If so, then the Court's reasoning does resemble substantive economic due process analysis. Alternatively, Justice Blackmun's argument may be interpreted as viewing the economic system, in whatever form the political branch chooses, as a public institution affecting the general welfare. Since private economic decisions in the aggregate affect the operations of this institution, commercial information affecting private decision making takes on public importance. Accordingly, it should be protected. Under this interpretation, the *Virginia Board of Pharmacy* decision does not give Constitutional status to any particular economic system. Rather, it leaves the choice of system to legislative discretion, and holds that within the framework of any chosen system, the legislature may not unduly restrict the flow of information relating to that system. Commercial speech is thus viewed as important not because it has an economic function to perform, but because it is information per se. Since it is unlikely that the Court would disregard the history of economic substantive due process, the second interpretation of Justice Blackmun's language would seem to be the better one. Hence, Justice Rehnquist's characterization of the majority opinion as substantive due process, while it raises a troublesome point, seems in the final analysis misplaced.

The third aspect of commerical speech which the Court identified as socially important is its relevance to self-government. In the Court's view, this relevance exists because commercial information is "indispensable to the formation of intelligent opinions as to how (the free enterprise) system ought to be regulated or altered." The Court thus reflects the view of the First Amendment as an instrument of self-government. Relevance to democratic decision making has been broadly defined to include "all issues about which information is needed or appropriate to enable members of society to cope with the exigencies of their period."[9] In this consumer age, it is possible within this definition to construe the types of private economic decisions to which commercial speech is relevant as "exigencies of (our) period." Moreover, to the extent that the economic system is viewed as an institution through which decisions are made affecting the public welfare, the private decisions affected by commercial advertising become analogous to decision making in an explicitly public context. In this respect, the significance of commercial speech to self-government and its significance within the economic system overlap. Justice Blackmun's reasoning indicates, though, that the Court defines the relevance of commercial speech more narrowly, concluding that the information imparted in advertisements may contribute to the formation of opinions on public issues related to the economic system.

Clearly, the connections between commercial advertising and democratic self-government are tenuous. As Justice Rehnquist in his dissent and Justice Stewart in his concurrence argue, commercial advertising is without conscious ideological content. The influence of an advertisement for a product or service on one's views, even those related to the industry of which the advertised product or service is a part, is indirect at best. The effect of such advertising on the ultimate allocation of resources in society and the relationship of private economic decisions to the public values involved in self-government is similarly indirect. Tenuous relevance to public issues, however, has been of sufficient "importance" to acquire the mantle of First Amendment protection for more traditionally protected forms of speech. It is difficult to argue that commercial advertising is any less "important" than a magazine restaurant review's criticism of a restaurant's food, or than a lurid crime-and-lust magazine. Hence, the Court's holding in *Virginia Board of Pharmacy* that commercial speech falls within the scheme of Constitutionally protected speech appears to conform with the broad outlines of that scheme delineated by the Court. It cures the anomaly by which commercial expression is categorized with forms of speech which are harmful per se. Further, it recognizes that, while commercial expression has aspects of conduct, it is also expression; and to the extent that commercial speech is expression, it should be examined for First Amendment value.

After identifying the societal interests inherent in commercial advertising, the Court sought to circumscribe the range of advertising protected after *Virginia Board of Pharmacy*, expressly carving out false advertising, broadcast advertising, and advertising by the learned professions. Implicitly, the range of protected advertising may be further limited. In particular, the concurrences by Justice Stewart and the Chief Justice suggest that the values the Court discerns in commercial advertising may inhere only in purely factual advertising. If so, the scope of First Amendment protection of commercial advertising might extend only to factual advertising and not to subliminal, image, of "puff" advertising. Moreover, since *Virginia Board of Pharmacy* involved only price advertising, the case could be read on its facts as thus limited.

Other aspects of the majority opinion indicate, however, that the Court does not intend such a distinction. Despite the fact situation of the case, the discussion of the First Amendment values involved was carried on broadly, referring to "commercial information" and "commercial advertising" rather than to "price advertising." In framing the issue in the case, the Court adopted the definition of "commercial speech" set forth in *Pittsburgh Press Co.* v. *Pittsburgh Commission on Human Relations* as speech which does "no more than propose a commercial transaction." Such a definition makes no distinction between factual and promotional advertising, since an advertisement need not be informational in order to offer a commercial transaction. Moreover, any such distinction would be difficult to apply, since even the most generally-laden advertisement is apt to contain information ". . . as to who is producing and selling what product . . . ," if nothing else. Nonfactual advertising is also in the nature of opinion or advocacy; where other forms of speech are involved, advocacy or opinion are generally more protected than factual assertions. Thus, despite the opinions of the concurring Justices, the Court's reasoning in *Virginia Board of Pharmacy* would seem to include nonfactual advertising within the First Amendment orbit.

Since the First Amendment value of commercial advertising stems primarily from society's interest in "the free flow of commercial information," advertising without substantial informational content doubtless has little or no substantial value within the First Amendment orbit. The appropriate approach to such advertising would be to consider it presumptively protected, as is other commercial speech, and to consider the attendant First Amendment interests in relation to the governmental interests in restricting such advertising. To draw any prima facie distinction between commercial advertising which is information and that which is not would require a subject matter test. Yet such tests have been disfavored by the Court as running the risk of censorship. Moreover, while the public interest content standard advanced in *Bigelow* turned on the subject matter of the advertising at issue, in *Virginia Board of Pharmacy* the Court abandoned that standard. Since a distinction between factual and promotional advertising necessitates inquiry into subject matter, a standard of protection based on such a distinction appears inconsistent both with the Court's general disfavor of subject matter tests for First Amendment purposes, as well as with the Court's specific move away from such a test in *Virginia Board of Pharmacy*.

80   Commercial Speech

The Court's examination of the affirmative First Amendment values of commercial expression seemingly indicates that most types of advertising are within the scope of protection. Although the Court took pains to limit its holding to prescription drug price advertising, it based the First Amendment protection of such advertising primarily on the broad societal interests in public and private decision making related to the economic system. These interests may be identified to some degree in virtually all advertising, irrespective of subject matter. *Virginia Board of Pharmacy,* then, can be construed as extending First Amendment protection to all advertising. The extent of this protection, however, requires further examination.

C. Synthesis—Commercial Speech as "Second Class" Speech

1. *The Bases of a Lesser Standard of Protection*

In commenting that commercial speech, while protected speech, is subject to a lesser standard of protection than noncommercial expression, Justice Blackmun stated that this result is justified by "common sense differences" between commercial advertising and other expression. It is unfortunate that the majority opinion leaves this differentiation to "common sense." Like the original exclusion of commercial speech in *Valentine* v. *Chrestensen,* the present differentiation offers a conclusion without a rationalization. An analysis of the Court's discussion of the ways in which commercial advertising may be less protected than other types of speech, and of the reasons for this lesser protection, suggests that the Court implicitly incorporates into its analysis the reasoning which previously supported the nonprotection of commercial speech. First, the Court apparently concluded that although commercial expression cannot be said to have no value, its relationship to the core values of the First Amendment is indirect. Secondly, the court seems to have reasoned that, because it is intimately related to economic behavior, commercial expression is inextricably bound up with conduct whose regulation by the legislature the courts have allowed great discretion.

The Court in *Virginia Board of Pharmacy* drew certain functional distinctions between advertising and other protected speech which further illuminate its lesser standard of protection for commercial speech at least in certain instances.

> The truth of commercial speech . . . may be more easily verifiable by its disseminator than, let us say, news reporting or political commentary, in that ordinarily the advertiser seeks to disseminate information about a specific product or service that he himself provides and presumably knows more about than anyone else. Also, commercial speech may be more durable than other kinds. Since advertising is the sine qua non of commercial profits, there is little likelihood of its being chilled by proper regulation and foregone entirely.
>
>   Attributes such as these, the greater objectivity and hardiness (of commercial speech), may make it less necessary to tolerate inaccurate statements for fear of silencing the speaker.

The "greater objectivity and hardiness" of commercial speech provide, however, only a limited explanation for the lesser protection of such expression. Generally, where speech is regulated, the fear of sanctions may deter legitimate expression. Thus, even restrictions on expression for legitimate purposes may be struck down due to their chilling effect on protected speech. This has been especially so where a line is drawn between protected and unprotected speech according to the truth of the speech, because the burden of determining the truth of his expression may lead the would-be speaker to opt for silence. In *Virginia Board of Pharmacy* the majority asserted that the truth of commercial speech may more easily be ascertained than the truth of other forms of speech, and also that advertisers are impelled to advertise in order to gain profits. This may explain why self-censorship is less likely to result from close regulation of commercial speech, and why, even faced with the burden of hewing to the truth, commercial speakers may be less apt than other speakers to "steer . . . wider of the unlawful zone."[10]

Nevertheless, the *Virginia Board of Pharmacy* majority's functional distinctions do not explain why the "unlawful zone" itself may be wider where commercial speech is involved. According to the Court's opinion in the present case, the lesser protection of commercial speech goes beyond merely reducing the "breathing space"[11] allowed in order to avoid chilling legitimate commercial speech. The Court indicated, for example, that the heavy presumption against prior restraints applicable where other forms of speech are involved does not operate where commercial speech is at issue. Advocacy of illegal conduct, protected in others contexts, is not protected when the conduct advocated is a commercial transaction. Furthermore, the court's functional distinctions between commercial advertising and other speech do not explain why commercial speech that is not factual in content, and therefore not readily susceptible to a test of truth, may be closely regulated. Yet, if commercial advertising may be held to a strict requirement of factual truth, advertising claims tending toward opinion will surely be chilled. As a result, advertising will be less "uninhibited, robust, and wide-open"[12] than it would be absent a strict requirement of truth. The same result follows from permitting prior restraints of commercial speech or from prohibiting the advertisement of illegal transactions. One must assume, absent other justifications for the lesser protection of commercial speech, that in the opinion of the majority in *Virginia Board of Pharmacy,* it simply matters less that advertising becomes inhibited. It follows that advertising is less important in the scheme of First Amendment values than are other, traditionally protected, forms of speech.

Justice Stewart would appear to have spoken for the Court in his concurrence, then, when he distinguished between commercial advertising and ideological communications on the basis that the latter is protected because it "is integrally related to the exposition of thought," whereas the former is protected because it contains " 'information of potential interest and value' . . . rather than because of any direct contribution to the interchange of ideas." Indeed, a plurality of the Court in *Young* v. *American Mini-Theatres, Inc.* cited Justice Stewart's distinction approvingly for the proposition that commercial speech may be regulated in ways "that the First Amendment would not tolerate" with respect to ideological expression.

Understanding of the Court's lesser protection of commercial advertising is further aided by examination of the context in which the Court discusses its lesser standard. Discussion of the lesser protection of commercial advertising appears as a footnote designed to show that various existing forms of regulation are not displaced by the decisions in *Virginia Board of Pharmacy.* The Court's efforts to show that strands of advertising regulation woven into the fabric of state economic regulation will not be unduly affected by its decision suggest that the Court's lesser protection of commercial advertising takes into account the proximate relationship of advertising to economic conduct. A standard of protection which is equivalent to the rigorous scrutiny applied with respect to a noncommercial protected speech would pose serious obstacles to traditionally accepted regulation in the areas cited by the Court. Conceivably, the Court's adoption of a standard of protection which permits numerous forms of state regulation of advertising to stand may be a result-oriented effort to preserve such regulation. Or, more probably, it may reflect a genuine judgment of the theoretical value of commercial advertising. In either case, it necessarily reflects "the fact that commercial advertising is the handmaiden of economic activity . . . ."[13] This fact, coupled with the relatively minimal and indirect relevance of commercial advertising to matters of public concern, appears to underlie the Court's assignment of such speech to a separate category of speech for First Amendment protective purposes. These implicit considerations, which hark back to justifications advanced for the exclusion of commercial advertising from First Amendment protection, appear in the final analysis to explain the Court's special standard of protection better than do the functional distinctions drawn explicitly by the Court.

2. A Lesser Standard of Protection: An Overview

The Court's analysis of the First Amendment value of commercial speech suggests the possibility that the Court is moving toward a new form of two-tiered theory of the First Amendment. Under the Court's traditional First Amendment theory, speech found worthy of protection has been wholly protected, while certain categories of speech deemed of negligible social value are wholly unprotected. In *Virginia Board of Pharmacy,* however, the Court placed traditionally unprotected speech in a new category of limited protection, apparently finding that such speech has some value, but now pressing value. Similarly, in another case decided during the 1975 term, *Young* v. *American Mini-Theatres, Inc.,* a plurality of the Court held that erotic, but not necessarily obscene, films may be placed in a less protected category than films of more general content, reasoning that, while such films cannot be totally suppressed, society's interest in them is less than in films of more conventional subject matter. The Court's special treatment of erotic films in *Young* and commercial advertising in *Virginia Board of Pharmacy* suggests a modification of its traditional two-tiered approach. Under this modified system, the Court appears, at least where commercial advertising or erotic films are involved, to continue differentiation between traditionally protected and traditionally excluded speech, but no longer to exclude the latter entirely from First Amendment protection.

The premise of the traditional two-tiered theory was that wholly excluded categories of speech "are no essential part of any exposition of ideas, and are of such slight social value as a step to truth that any benefit that may be derived from them is clearly outweighed by the social interests in order and morality."[14] In *Virginia Board of Pharmacy,* however, the court found "potential value" in commercial speech, and, at best, value which is indirectly related to the Court's norms of social worth. Yet this marginal value was a sufficient basis for the protection of commercial speech. It would seem therefore, that a two-tiered system of First Amendment protection as it appears to have been modified in *Virginia Board of Pharmacy* and in *Young* reduces the extent to which inquiry into social value determines whether speech is protected. While it is doubtful that the Court would take the position that any speech receives some protection, the natural result of diminished inquiry into the social value of given speech is to move toward protection of expression *qua* expression.

Although inquiry into social value may be diminished, the Court's analysis in *Virginia Board of Pharmacy* nonetheless retains some such inquiry, both as a basis for protection, and, to a greater extent, as a basis for determining what tier of protection is appropriate. This presents a difficulty for future resolution where, as in *Bigelow* v. *Virginia,* advertising which primarily proposes a commercial transaction also does more. Should such advertising be judged in the less protected category put forward in the present case; should it be wholly protected on the same basis as noncommercial speech or should it be judged on a sliding scale between these two categories, according to the degree of social value of its content? A sliding scale seems unduly to risk value-laden judgments. Moreover, as pointed out by Justice Blackmun in *Virginia Board of Pharmacy,* a content-oriented standard applied to commercial advertising may be evaded by injecting material of social value.

It is submitted that the withdrawal from inquiry into social value of expression implied in *Virginia Board of Pharmacy* is a salutary step toward development of a principled basis for determining First Amendment protection. Such a withdrawal reduces the extent to which the Court must play the often difficult and potentially result-oriented role of social critic. In this light, it would seem preferable to rationalize the protection of commercial advertising in terms of its independent subjective value as expression—the expression of advertisers and advertising people, expression that concerns economic behavior, which individuals may use toward their own self-development and definition—rather than on objective social value. Such a rationalization is consistent with a two-tiered approach to commercial speech, because those aspects of commercial advertising that have independent value as expression are limited in comparison to the aspect of commercial advertising as economic conduct.

II. Judicial Review of Restrictions on Commercial Speech

In *Virginia Board of Pharmacy* the Court's two-tiered standard of First Amendment protection stands out in relief when the Court's method of evaluating the challenged statute is examined. The Court's analysis grafts onto the deferential review of legislative purposes applied in economic due process and equal protection cases, the strict scrutiny of legislative means applied in First Amendment cases where regulation of conduct is involved. The result of this hybridization is an intermediate standard of review. This section will examine the analytical method of this standard of review.

A. The Economic Due Process Model

The standard of review in challenges to regulatory legislation based on equal protection and due process grounds where no suspect classification or fundamental interest is at issue is characterized by judicial deference to legislative judgments of policy. Regulatory statutes in those circumstances carry a substantial presumption of constitutionality. To sustain this presumption it is sufficient that there be some conceivable state purpose which is rationally related to the statute at issue; this need not be the purpose-in-fact of the statute, but may be merely the product of judicial supposition. As long as such a rational relationship exists, it is irrelevant that the legislature might have employed means less restrictive of economic freedom or a classification more or less inclusive. The natural result of this deferential standard of review is that regulatory statutes challenged on Fourteenth Amendment grounds are rarely struck down.

Applying this standard of review in *Patterson Drug Co. v. Kingery,* the District Court for the Western District of Virginia upheld in 1969 the same statute struck down in *Virginia Board of Pharmacy.* The district court held summarily that the prohibition against advertising was neither an infringement of an equal protection or a Due Process right, because it was not arbitrary or invidious and "affect(ed) the public health, safety, and welfare."

The district court in *Patterson* relied on three Supreme Court cases in which state prohibitions against professional advertising were upheld in the face of similar challenges. In *Williamson v. Lee Optical Co.,* the Court held that the portion of a statute regulating the professions of optometry, ophthalmology, and opticianry, which prohibited any advertising of the sale of optical appliances, did not violate the Due Process Clause because "(w)e see no constitutional reason why a state may not treat all who deal with the human eye as members of a profession who should use no merchandising methods for obtaining customers." In *Head v. New Mexico Board of Examiners,* the Court summarily held that a New Mexico statute which banned advertising of the prices of optical appliances was not violative of the Fourteenth Amendment. Finally, in *Semler v. Oregon State Board of Dental Examiners,* the Court upheld a statute prohibiting advertising for dental services which made claims of superiority, used large displays, offered discounts, and other promotional devices, on the ground that the state has an especially great interest in preventing "unseemly rivalry" in a health profession.

The *Virginia Board of Pharmacy* Court noted the precedents of the *Williamson* line of cases. With these in mind, the Court concluded that it could not entirely discount the *Virginia Board of Pharmacy's* justifications for Virginia's ban on drug price advertising. The Court, however, did not dispose of the case with the method of analysis applied in these precedents. Instead, the majority reasoned that because prescription drug price advertising is deemed protected speech, closer scrutiny was required than was applied by the Court in the *Williamson* line of Fourteenth Amendment cases and by the district court in *Patterson*.

B. The First Amendment Model

In contrast to the freedom of action protected by the Fourteenth Amendment, freedom of expression protected by the First Amendment is considered a "preferred" freedom. Accordingly, governmental regulation affecting this freedom carries with it a presumption of unconstitutionality, and the burden falls on the state to show that its legitimate interests require restriction of First Amendment freedom. In *United States* v. *O'Brien* the Supreme Court set out its principal method for analysis of such restrictions of freedom of expression, where the regulation of ordinary conduct is also involved:

1. The restrictive measure must be within the Constitutional power of the government.
2. The governmental interest advanced by the restriction must be "important or substantial."
3. The governmental interest must not be related to the suppression of freedom of expression.
4. The restriction of freedom of expression must be no greater than necessary to further the governmental interest.

Once it is determined that the expression at issue is prima facie protected, the analysis developed in *O'Brien* is neutral as to the content of such expression. The analysis focuses instead on the nexus between legitimate governmental ends and the means used to advance these ends.

In 1975 an alternative method of review was applied in *Bigelow* v. *Virginia:* so-called ad hoc balancing. In the "ad hoc balancing" process, the Court engages in a fact-oriented weighing of the interests involved in both the particular expression and particular restriction at issue. In *Bigelow*, the Court reasoned that the First Amendment interests present in the advertisement published by Bigelow outweighed Virginia's relatively insubstantial interest in regulating out-of-state abortion agencies. This form of ad hoc test has been criticized as being "so unstructured that it can hardly be described as a rule of law at all."[15] While the categorical approach of *O'Brien* is largely neutral toward the content of expression under review, and ad hoc balancing of *Bigelow* inquires into the subject matter of expression. Further, where a state interest is found to override the infringement of freedom of expression, ad hoc balancing does not go further to examine the means chosen to advance that state interest. Despite its use of the ad hoc balancing approach in *Bigelow*, the Court in recent years has preferred the more categorical approach set out above in *O'Brien*.[16]

C. Standard of Review Under a Two-tiered System of Speech

The method of analysis in *Virginia Board of Pharmacy* does not conform to traditional First Amendment analysis because it does not carefully weigh the purposes of laws restricting free expression. At the same time the *Virginia Board of Pharmacy* analysis does not conform with the norm in Fourteenth Amendment analysis, because it does closely examine means by which those purposes are affected. In *Virginia Board of Pharmacy,* the Court found the prohibition of prescription drug price advertising within Virginia's constitutional power to regulate the pharmacy profession. Noting its precedents on professional advertising restrictions, the Court conceded that justifications of the type put forward in support of Virginia's prohibition against drug price advertising had been sufficient to sustain similar bans challenged on Fourteenth Amendment grounds. In contrast to Fourteenth Amendment cases, however, these justifications were not put forward on the Court's own suppositions. Rather, they were grounded in evidence brought forward by the state—the necessary result of the shift in the presumption of constitutionality brought about by the First Amendment context of the present case. Furthermore, the identification of a rational and legitimate state purpose in prohibiting pharmacists from advertising, even in fact rather than supposition, was not sufficient to sustain the prohibition. The Court in *Virginia Board of Pharmacy* proceeded to examine the effect of the statutory prohibition on the commercial expression in question. At this point, however, the court appears to have departed from the norm in First Amendment cases. It did not apply the threshold test set out in *O'Brien* and thereby determine whether the interest at issue might be characterized as "compelling." The analysis instead turned on the fourth test in *O'Brien,* whether the Virginia statute was narrowly tailored to meet its legitimate purposes.

Within the framework set out in *O'Brien,*[17] it is possible to interpret the Court's dispositive analysis in *Virginia Board of Pharmacy* in two ways. The first interpretation is that the Court, when it found that the Virginia statute operates ". . . only through the reactions it is assumed people will have to the free flow of drug information," reasoned that the governmental interest in this case is related directly and substantially to the suppression of the expression at issue rather than to the regulation of pharmacists' standards. Accordingly, the ban would become subject to the "comprehensive scrutiny"[18] applied to restrictions entirely directed at expression. Alternatively, the Court may be interpreted to have found the statute substantially related to the legitimate, but not necessarily compelling, purpose of regulation, but that the means employed to effect that purpose were overbroad. Consequently, in this interpretation, means less restrictive of expression might have been employed.

These interpretations differ only in degree, however. In either case, the defect in Virginia's prohibition of drug price advertising lies in its insufficient nexus with its legitimate purposes. The first interpretation amounts to a holding that there is no nexus between these purposes and the statute; the second, that there is no sufficient nexus. Both interpretations are means-focused. Either test implies that, if that were a sufficient nexus between the restriction of advertising and the governmental purposes articulated by the Virginia Board of Pharmacy, the governmental interest in regulation of pharmacy would have sustained the statute. Consequently, the Court's lack of inquiry into the nature of the governmental interests at issue, beyond finding that the state's interests meet the minimum Rationality Standards of the Fourteenth Amendment, suggests that an intermediate standard of review was applied in *Virginia Board of Pharmacy.* Under this standard of review it would seem that restrictions on commercial speech may be upheld so long as the state shows that a rational interest underlies such restrictions, according to Fourteenth Amendment standards of review, and that the restrictive legislation is narrowly drawn and employs the least restrictive means, according to First Amendment standards of review.

The operation of this hybridized standard of review can be illustrated by examining previously decided cases which the Supreme Court has discussed in the light of its subsequent commercial speech decisions. In *Bigelow* v. *Virginia* the Court cited lower court cases whose results, were found consistent with the holding in that case even though their reasoning might no longer be valid. The Court found these cases to have continuing vitality because "there usually existed a clear relationship between the advertising in question and an activity that the government was legitimately regulating." Two of the cases cited by the Court involved speech promoting transactions which were themselves illegal. In *United States v. Bob Lawrence Realty, Inc.*, the Court of Appeals for the Fifth Circuit, in a challenge by realtors who made racial representations in the sale of homes, upheld the constitutionality of the anti-blockbusting provisions of the Fair Housing Act of 1968 on the grounds that these provisions reached only unprotected commercial speech. On the same grounds, the Fourth Circuit Court of Appeals in *United States v. Hunter* upheld the provisions of the Act which prohibit publication of discriminatory notices concerning the sale or rental of housing. In both cases, arguments that the communications were protected by the First Amendment were dismissed summarily by reference to the *Chrestensen* doctrine, an analysis which obviously would be deficient today.

Viewed in terms of their results and not their reasoning, however, both *Bob Lawrence* and *Hunter* are consistent with the results in the Supreme Court's later decision in *Pittsburgh Press Co. v. Pittsburgh Commission on Human Relations*. There, a newspaper's publication of help-wanted advertisements in columns designated by sex preference was found to violate a municipal anti-employment discrimination ordinance. In upholding the ordinance against a First Amendment challenge, the Court found the advertisements to be "classic examples of commercial speech." The Court declined to dispose of the case on those grounds, however, finding it determinative that the advertisements proposed illegal discriminatory hiring transactions. *Pittsburgh Press* was decided before the Court's revision of the commercial speech doctrine in *Bigelow*. It would seem nonetheless that the holding in that case with respect to advertising of an illegal transaction remains valid. In *Virginia Board of Pharmacy*, the Court distinguished drug price advertising from the advertising in *Pittsburgh Press* on the basis that there was no argument that sale of prescription drugs is illegal. Thus, the *Virginia Board of Pharmacy* Court clearly implied that a finding of illegality of the advertised transaction would constitute a basis for upholding the drug price advertising ban.

This line of cases involving speech advertising illegal commercial transactions contrasts with the Court's approach to noncommercial speech proposing illegal conduct. In the latter cases, restriction of expression is not permitted merely if the proposed conduct itself is illegal; the speech itself must present some "clear and present danger"[19] of the proscribed conduct, or must amount to advocacy which ". . . is directed to inciting or producing imminent lawless action and likely to incite or produce such action."[20] In the advertising cases, on the other hand, the illegality of the proposed conduct is determinative in itself without inquiry into the probability or immediacy of such conduct resulting from the advertising. Thus, where commercial expression is involved, restriction of expression is apparently permissible, strictly on the basis that the state has a rational interest in restricting the proposed transaction.

The operation of the Court's hybrid standard of review is also apparent in its reinterpretation of *Valentine v. Chrestensen* as "a reasonable regulation of the manner in which commercial advertising could be distributed." The regulation in *Chrestensen* was a complete ban on distribution of commercial handbills. Where ideological expression is involved, such total bans have been held impermissible because they are unduly restrictive of expression. One must conclude, therefore, that the governmental interests which are "insufficient"[21] to allow highly restrictive time, place, and manner restraints on ideological communication are sufficient to allow a total ban on commercial speech.

The decision in *Virginia Board of Pharmacy* leaves open the permissibility of bans on the advertising of transactions or services which, though legal, are disfavored as a matter of public policy. If, under the hybrid standard of review, the test of advertising ban's permissibility is whether there is "a clear relationship" between the prohibited advertising and a legitimately regulated activity, it would seem that such bans are likely to be upheld. Thus, the result in *Virginia Board of Pharmacy* would presumably be different if, as Justice Rehnquist argued, the ban on prescription drug price advertising existed in order to prevent promotion of drug use, and if, in addition there had been a showing that advertising would in fact have such an effect. Similarly, a decision expressly left open in the present case, *Capital Broadcasting Co.* v. *Mitchell,* in which the District of Columbia Circuit upheld the constitutionality under the First Amendment of the Public Health Cigarette Smoking Act of 1969 ban on broadcast advertising of cigarettes, would appear to remain valid. There is a legitimate state interest in diminishing the demonstrable injury to public health which results from cigarette smoking, and, unlike the interest supporting the advertising ban in *Virginia Board of Pharmacy,* this interest is directly advanced by an advertising ban likely to diminish public demand for cigarettes.

It is submitted that the requirement of a merely rational state interest coupled with close scrutiny of means which the Court apparently has imposed in *Virginia Board of Pharmacy* is the appropriate method for review of challenges to restrictions on commercial speech. This method reconciles the extension of First Amendment protection to commercial speech with the history of judicial restraint within the area of economic regulation. It recognizes that commercial speech has elements of First Amendment value, and should thus be placed in a preferred category, but that it is also "speech plus"[22] because it is bound up with economic conduct. Since few statutes can survive compelling interest scrutiny, a compelling interest threshold in commercial speech cases would bring the commercial speech doctrine into direct conflict with the doctrine of juducial restraint in the economic field.

While according deference to legislative judgments where economic regulation is concerned, the rational interest-narrowly tailored means test avoids any restriction of expression not necessary to further the identified state interest. This places regulation of commercial advertising in a preferrred position in relation to other commercial activities. The method is also preferable to the ad hoc balancing of *Bigelow.* By defining categorically both the type of showing which must be made in order to sustain a restriction on commercial advertising, as well as the method by which a court should examine that showing, the rational basis-narrowly tailored means test applies an analytical balancing analysis less susceptible to subjectivity than is an ad hoc approach. The existing bodies of case law dealing with the identification of "rational interests" and the examination of ends-means relationships in restrictions on expression provide a reference point to enhance the objectivity of the new doctrine and diminish the need for its case-by-case development. It is to be hoped that the Supreme Court will abandon the ad hoc balancing test of *Bigelow* and apply the means test of *Virginia Board of Pharmacy* in future commercial speech cases.

Following the term in which it decided *Virginia Board of Pharmacy,* the Supreme Court decided three commercial speech cases. The tests applied in these decisions varied. As a result, it remains uncertain how the Court intends to apply its lesser standard of protection for commercial speech.

In *Carey* v. *Population Services International,* a mail-order contraceptive company challenged a New York statute which prohibited the sale or distribution of contraceptives to any person if not by a licensed pharmacist and to all minors under sixteen, and also prohibited any advertising or display of contraceptives.

A divided Supreme Court struck down the sale and distribution limitations and held, seven to two, that the ban on contraceptive advertising violates the First Amendment. This decision adds little to the commercial speech doctrine after *Virginia Board of Pharmacy.* The major issue in *Population Services* was the question whether the purchase of contraceptives, including purchase by those under sixteen, is within the zone of personal privacy protected as "liberty" by the Fourteenth Amendment. Once the Court answered this question in the affirmative, reasoning that a state has no legitimate interest in deterring sexual activity among teenagers, the commercial speech question was governed by *Virginia Board of Pharmacy*. At that juncture, the ban on contraceptive advertising amounted to no more than a restriction on advertising of pharmaceutical products. As such, the advertising restraint in *Population Services* was indistinguishable from the one struck down in *Virginia Board of Pharmacy*.

One of the Supreme Court's most noted decisions of the 1976 term, at least for lawyers, was *Bates* v. *State Bar of Arizona*. In *Bates,* the Court addressed the question reserved in *Virginia Board of Pharmacy*: whether advertising by lawyers and other learned professionals is protected commercial speech. In a decision which is inconclusive as a development of the Court's approach to commercial speech questions, the Court held that it is.

Bates was an appeal by two Arizona lawyers who published an advertisement that listed fees for certain routine services at their "legal clinic." Their advertisement violated a provision of the American Bar Association's Code of Professional Responsibility, as adopted by the Arizona Supreme Court, which banned all but highly limited forms of lawyers' advertising. As a result, the Arizona State Bar brought disciplinary proceedings against the two lawyers which resulted in their censure by the state supreme court.

The United States Supreme Court reversed in a five to four decision. As in *Bigelow* v. *Virginia* and *Virginia Board of Pharmacy,* Justice Blackmun was the author of the Court's opinion. In assessing the First Amendment interests at issue in *Bates,* the Court began by noting that the conclusion that Arizona's rule violates the First Amendment arguably flows a fortiori from *Virginia Board of Pharmacy* because ''like the Virginia statute, the disciplinary rule serves to inhibit the free flow of commercial information and to keep the public in ignorance." Nevertheless, acknowledging that in *Virginia Board of Pharmacy* it had left open the First Amendment status of professional advertising, the Court proceeded to examine whether there are justifications for prohibiting attorney advertising.

The Arizona Bar offered six justifications for its advertising ban. In general, these fell into two categories. First, the state bar argued that advertising by attorneys would lower the standards of the legal profession by commercializing it. Thus, lawyers' advertising would cause increased legal fees and standardized "packaging" of legal services unsuited to the needs of individual clients; the machinery of bar regulation would be poorly adapted to the supervision of advertising. In weighing these contentions, the Court concluded that "since the belief that lawyers are 'above' trade has become an anachronism, the historical foundation of the advertising restraint has crumbled." The Court also found that legal fees equally plausibly could be lowered through advertising, that lawyers are unlikely to reduce the quality of their services because they advertise, and that in general lawyers will "uphold the integrity and honor of their profession." Accordingly, the Court rejected this set of justifications.

In its second set of justifications, the State Bar contended that attorney advertising would be inherently misleading because consumers of legal services frequently do not know in advance of a legal consultation what services the need, and because advertising would not reflect the skills of different attorneys. The Court concluded that these arguments do not justify a complete ban on all attorney advertising, at least where advertising of routine legal services is concerned. In the Court's view, the same ends could be achieved by correcting specific cases of misleading advertising. Unpersuaded by either set of justifications, the Court concluded that none of the State Bar's six justifications "rises to the level of an acceptable reason for the suppression of all advertising by attorneys." After determining that neither the term "legal clinic" nor the offer of "reasonable fees" in the specific advertisement at issue were misleading, the Court held the advertisement protected by the First Amendment. The Court also restated without elaboration the view articulated in *Virginia Board of*

Pharmacy that commercial expression is entitled to less First Amendment protection than other expression.

The Court's discussion of lawyers' advertising in *Bates* leaves little in the way of a standard of review for future commercial speech cases. For example, it is not clear by what method the Court reached the conclusion that a view of lawyers as "above trade" is an anachronism, or what empowered the Court to substitute this conclusion for Arizona's evident conclusion to the contrary. To be sure, the presumption of unconstitutionality which arose upon finding that First Amendment interests were at stake required the Court to examine closely the State Bar's justification for its advertising ban. The Court's discussion of the relationship between attorney advertising and professional standards, however, resembled less a factual examination of this relationship than it did a judgment on the wisdom of the advertising ban as a policy. As a result, this portion of the *Bates* decision resembles the ad hoc balancing analysis in *Bigelow* v. *Virginia,* a resemblance reinforced by the language of the Court's conclusion that the State Bar's justifications for its ban did not "rise to a level" sufficient to suppress advertising.

In its discussion of the misleading effect of attorney advertising, on the other hand, the Court acknowledged the validity of the asserted goal of the Arizona ban, but determined that this goal could be advanced as effectively and restrictively of the free flow of information by regulating individual cases of misleading advertising. This discussion in *Bates* resembles the means test apparently applied in *Virginia Board of Pharmacy.* Since the Court applied such shifting methods of analysis in *Bates,* the decision leaves behind no consistently principled methodology.

While the determinative reasoning in *Bates* thus shed little light on the new commercial speech doctrine, a tangential aspect of the decision did provide some illumination. The Court held that the First Amendment Overbreadth Doctrine does not apply where commercial speech is at issue. The First Amendment Overbreadth Doctrine permits a challenge to a statute as violative of the First Amendment in contexts other than those which actually affect the challenger. The rationale for this doctrine is that laws which appear to prohibit protected expression may chill the exercise of such expression. In *Bates,* the Court reasoned that this doctrine should not be extended to commercial speech because the "greater objectivity and hardiness" of commercial speech identified by the *Virginia Board of Pharmacy* Court as the basis of a "lesser degree of protection" for commercial speech make the latter less susceptible to this chilling effect. This aspect of the decision in *Bates* is consistent with the Court's two-tiered treatment of commercial speech, and gives it flesh.

The third commercial speech decision of the 1976 Supreme Court term was less noticed than *Bates,* but more interesting from an analytical standpoint. In *Linmark Associates, Inc.* v. *Township of Willingboro,* the Court held that a municipal ordinance which prohibited the posting of "For Sale" and "Sold" signs in residential neighborhoods violates the First Amendment. The ordinance was enacted as a response to perceived "panic selling" by white homeowners in a racially integrated community. The Court—with Justice Rehnquist absent, unanimous behind Justice Marshall's opinion—did not dwell long on the question whether First Amendment interests were present in the advertising at issue; this question was resolved by brief reference to *Virginia Board of Pharmacy* and *Bigelow* v. *Virginia.* The case thus turned on the Township's efforts to justify its restraint of commercial expression.

The Township offered two justifying arguments. First, it contended that the sign ban was a reasonable restriction on the place—residential neighborhoods—and the manner—signs—of real estate advertising. Second, the Township argued that the ordinance directly advanced the important interest in maintaining stable, racially integrated housing.

The first argument the Court rejected as both inapplicable and wanting on its own terms. Noting that the ordinance did not apply to all signs in residential neighborhoods, the Court determined that it focused on the "For Sale" or "Sold" message. As such, the ordinance was not a genuine restriction on the place or manner of advertising, but direct suppression of communication. Furthermore, even if viewed as a place or manner restraint, the Court found, buyers and sellers of homes had no ways to communicate information as effective as "For Sale" signs. Hence, the restraint on the place or manner of advertising was unreasonable.

The Court then turned to the underlying purpose of the sign ban. Unlike the *Bates* Court, the Court in *Linmark* did not question the validity or importance of the Township's goal in banning signs. It determined, however, that "the record . . . demonstrates that (the Township) failed to establish that this ordinance is necessary to insure that Willingboro remains an integrated community." The Court found insufficient evidence either that panic selling existed in Willingboro or that banning "For Sale" and "Sold" signs would reduce any panic selling. At the same time, the Court distinguished a lower federal court case in which a similar ordinance was upheld. In broad language which echoed *Virginia Board of Pharmacy,* the Court then held the Willingboro ordinance violative of the First Amendment. As it did in *Bates,* the Court also reaffirmed that commercial speech receives "a lesser degree of protection" which permits closer regulation of commercial speech than of other speech.

The sweeping language with which the Court concluded its holding in *Linmark* suggests a high standard of protection for commercial speech which all but prohibits its direct suppression. Nevertheless, the Court's consistent reassertion of its two-tiered approach to commercial speech belies this suggestion. The Court's analysis of the factual nexus between Willingboro's goal of stable, integrated housing and the ordinance banning signs, as well as the Court's express preservation of the lower court case in which such a nexus arguably was found, imply that the Willingboro ordinance would have been upheld if it had been shown to be effective in reducing actual panic selling. If so, then *Linmark* is consistent with the rational interest-narrowly tailored means test which the Court appeared to apply in *Virginia Board of Pharmacy.*

CONCLUSION

In holding that prescription drug price advertising is protected by the First Amendment, the Supreme Court in *Virginia Board of Pharmacy* has extended the scope of First Amendment protection to all purely commercial advertising without regard to extrinsic content, thus abandoning fully the anomalous doctrine whereby commercial speech was wholly excluded from the First Amendment. The Court's approach to commercial expression nonetheless differs from its approach to traditionally protected speech. The Court apparently has concluded that speech which only offers a commercial transaction has less to contribute to public discussion and individual self-fulfillment than does expression which is directly related, even tenuously; to "truth, science, morality, and arts in general . . . (and) administration of government."[23] The Court apparently has further concluded that, because it is closely related to the conduct of economic business, commercial advertising itself is substantially economic conduct. It seems that the result of this approach to commercial speech is a standard of review which permits restrictions on commercial advertising if they are based on a "legitimate," and not necessarily "compelling," interest, but requires that the restrictions meet the traditional standards of First Amendment adjudication in being narrowly tailored to their permissible ends.

The decisions which followed *Virginia Board of Pharmacy* leave undefined both the scope of the new commercial doctrine and the standard of review by which it is to be applied. It is submitted, however, that, under the deferential standard of review which the Court apparently applied in *Virginia Board of Pharmacy,* many of the existing restrictions on commercial advertising will remain intact. The effects of that decision chiefly will be felt by total bans on advertising, except where such bans are applied to advertising of products and services that are illegal or disfavored as a matter of social policy.

NOTES

[1] "Commercial speech" is presently defined as speech which "does no more than propose a commercial transaction." *Virginia Board of Pharmacy,* 425 U.S. at 762, quoting *Pittsburgh Press Co.* v. *Pittsburgh Commission on Human Relations,* 413 U.S. 376, 385 (1973). The Court has clarified that "ommercial speech" does not include otherwise protected speech merely because the latter is communicated in a commercial context. See *New York Times Co.* v. *Sullivan,* 376 U.S. 254, 266 (1964) (advertisment related to matters of great publicc oncern not commercial speech); *Smith* v. *California,* 361 U.S. 147, 150 (1959) (books not commercial speech); *Joseph Burstyn, Inc.* v. *Wilson,* 345 U.S. 495, 501 (1952) (films not commercial speech). "Commercial speech" accordingly appears limited to advertising, and to that advertising which is purely commercial. See *Borough of Collingswood* v. *Ringgold,* 66 N.J. 350, 362 n.2, 331 A.2d 262, 270 n.2 (1975), and cases cited therein. "Commercial speech" should therefore be distinguished from other forms of expression by commercial enterprises, for example, political campaign spending or advertising related to public issues. Cf. *Eastern R.R. Presidents Conference* v. *Noerr Motor Freight, Inc.,* 365 U.S. 127, 138 (1961) (first amendment shields solicitation of government action with intent to monopolize from antitrust liability); see generally Note, Freedom of Expression in a Commercial Contest, 78 HARV. L. REV. 1191 (1965).

[2] See *Valentine* v. *Chrestensen,* 316 U.S. 52 (1942). The *Chrestensen* Court, Justice Roberts writing, stated, without citation:

> This court has unequivocally held that the streets are proper places for the exercise of freedom of communicating information and disseminating opinion and that, though the states and municipalities may appropriately regulate the privilege in the public interest, they may not unduly burden or proscribe its employment in these public thoroughfares. We are equally clear that the Constitution imposes no such restraint on government as respects purely commercial advertising.

Id. at 54, See also *Breard* v. *Alexandria*, 341 U.S. 622–45 (1951) (ordinance prohibiting door-to-door solicitation of orders without request from resident upheld), where the Court distinguished cases striking down prohibitions against similar solicitation, *Marsh* v. *Alabama,* 326 U.S. 501 (1946), and *Tucker* v. *Texas,* 326 U.S. 517 (1946), on the basis that the latter were "more religious than commercial." 341 U.S. at 643; *Martin* v. *Struthers,* 319 U.S. 141, 142 n.1 (1943) (ordinance forbidding door-to-door solicitation not aimed "solely at commercial advertising" found unconstitutional). Although the opinion in *Crestensen* has been described as "casual, almost offhand," *Cammarano* v. *United States,* 358 U.S. 498, 513–14 (1959) (Douglas, J., concurring). *Chrestensen* and its progeny have been followed without significant question by lower courts. *United States* v. *Bob Lawrence Realty, Inc.,* 474 F.2d 115, 121 (5th Cir.), cert. denied, 414 U.S. 826 (1973); *United States* v. *Hunter,* 459 F.2d 205, 211 (4th Cir.), cert. denied, 409 U.S. 934 (1972); *SEC* v. *Texas Gulf Sulphur Co.,* 446 F.2d 1301, 1306 (2d Cir. 1971); *SEC* v. *Wall Street Transcript Corp.,* 422 F.2d 1379 (2d Cir.), cert. denied, 398 U.S. 958 (1970); *Pollak* v. *Public Utilities Commission,* 191 F.2d 450, 457 (D.C. Cir. 1951); reversed on other grounds, 343 U.S. 451 (1952); *Millstone* v. *O'Hanlon Reports, Inc.,* 383 F.Supp. 269, 274 (ED Mo. 1974); *Carpets By The Carload, Inc.* v. *Warren,* 368 F.Supp. 1075, 1078 (ED Wis. 1973); *Boscia* v. *Warren,* 359 F.Supp. 900, 901 (ED Wis. 1973); *Holiday Magic, Inc.* v. *Warren,* 357 F.Supp. 20, 24 (ED Wis. 1973), reversed on other grounds, 497 F.2d 687 (7th Cir. 1974); *Barrick Realty, Inc.* v. *City of Gary,* 354 F.Supp. 126, 132 (ND Ind. 1973); *Jenness* v. *Forbes,* 351 F.Supp. 88, 96 (DRI 1972) (dictum); *Patterson Drug Co.* v. *Kingery,* 305 F.Supp. 821, 825 (WD Va. 1969). *Chrestensen* has been followed by state courts as well, e.g., *Planned Parenthood Comm. of Phoenix, Inc.* v. *Maricopa County,* 92 Ariz. 231, 240, 375, P.2d 719, 725 (1962); *Wirta* v. *Alameda-Contra Costa Transit Dist.,* 68 Cal. 51, 57, 64 Cal. Rptr. 430, 434, 434 2d 982, 986 (1967); *United Advertising Corp.* v. *Borough of Raritan,* 11 N.J. 144, 152, 93 A.2d 362, 366 (1952) (Brennan, J); *HM Distributors of Milwaukee, Inc.* v. *Department of Agriculture,* 55 Wis.2d 261, 272–73, 198 NW 2d 598, 605 (1972). See generally, Redish, "The First Amendment in the Marketplace: Commercial Speech and the Values of Free Expression," 39 GEO. WASH. L. REV. 429, 448–58 (1971); Note, The Commercial Speech Doctrine: The First Amendment at a Discount, supra note 6; Note, Commercial Speech—An End in Sight to *Chrestensen?*, 23 DEPAUL L. REV. 1258, 1261–69 (1974); Comment, The Right to Receive and the Commercial Speech Doctrine: New Constitutional Considerations, 63 GEO. L. J. 775, 794–803 (1975); Note, 61 CORNELL L. REV. 640, 641–44 (1976).

The apparent rationale of this doctrine is discussed in text at notes 78–97 infra.

[3] It is arguable that some categories of speech remain wholly excluded from First Amendment protection. Cf. *Chaplinsky* v. *New Hampshire,* 315 U.S. 568, 572 (1942) ("fighting words," libel and obscenity not protected by First Amendment). If so, then the separate protected categories adopted in *Virginia Board of Pharmacy* for, respectively, commercial speech and other speech would result in a three-tiered First Amendment theory.

This article concludes that the decision in *Virginia Board of Pharmacy* adopts a two-tiered approach to protected speech. The article does not attempt to draw any conclusions as to the vitality of the doctrine that certain speech is wholly unprotected. The possible effects, however, of the present decision on that doctrine are discussed in the text at notes 208–224 infra.

[4] Emerson, Toward a General Theory of the First Amendment 105 n.46 (1966).
[5] *Banzhaf* v. *FCC,* 405 F.2d 1082, 1101–02 (D.C. Cir. 1968), cert. denied, 396 U.S. 842 (1969).
[6] *Chaplinsky* v. *New Hampshire,* 315 U.S. 568, 572 (1942).
[7] Indeed, *Bigelow* is confusing on this point. Although the decision in *Bigelow* changed the method of inquiry in commercial speech cases to require examination of an advertisement's First Amendment value before categorizing it as "purely commercial," this inquiry is similar to that required in determining whether the advertisement does "no more than propose a commercial transaction," *Pittsburgh Press, Co.* v. *Pittsburgh Commission on Human Relations,* 413 U.S. 376, 385 (1973). Thus, were it not for the criticisms of *Chrestensen* in the *Bigelow* opinion, the latter could be reconciled with the prior doctrine as simply a further refinement of the definition of "commercial speech."

Moreover, *Bigelow* could be read narrowly on its facts to leave most examples of commercial advertising within the "purely commercial" category. Since abortion is a highly sensitive and controversial public issue, see *Roe* v. *Wade,* 410 U.S. 113, 116 (1973), *Bigelow* could be construed as requiring a high degree of public interest content in a commercial advertisement in order not to be purely commercial. Furthermore, since the Court in *Bigelow* found the Commonwealth of Virginia's interest in regulating an advertisement for abortion referral agencies in New York to be "entitled to little, if any, weight . . . ,"421 U.S. at 828, a court might also view *Bigelow* as permitting the regulation of commercial speech—even if it contains matters of public interest—on a finding of any more than a minimal state interest. Such an interpretation would place *Bigelow* in a light little different from the decisions in which commercial speech cases were decided on equal protection and due process grounds, (three judge court). In the final analysis, therefore, *Bigelow* is an ambiguous decision, with the result that its application in the lower courts has been confused.

[8] See Redish, "The First Amendment in the Marketplace: Commercial Speech and the Values of Free Expression," 39 GEO. WASH. L. REV. 429, 443–44 (1971):

When the individual is presented with rational grounds for preferring one product or brand over another, he is encouraged to consider the competing information, weigh it mentally in the light of the goals of personal satisfaction he has set for himself, counterbalance his conclusions with possible price differentials, and in doing so exercise his abilities to reason and think; this aids him towards the intangible goal of rational self-fulfillment.

[9] *Thornhill* v. *Alabama,* 310 U.S. 88, 102 (1940).
[10] *Speiser* v. *Randall,* 357 U.S. 513, 526 (1958).
[11] *NAACP* v. *Button,* 371 U.S. 415, 433 (1963).
[12] *New York Times Co.* v. *Sullivan,* 376 U.S. 254, 270 (1964).
[13] Note, "Developments in the Law Deceptive Advertising," 80 HARV. L. REV. 1005, 1027 (1965).
[14] *Chaplinsky* v. *New Hampshire,* 315 U.S. 568, 572 (1942).
[15] Emerson, "The System of Freedom of Expression," 16 (1970).
[16] See *United States* v. *Robel,* 289 U.S. 258, 268 n.20 (1967):

It has been suggested that this case should be decided by "balancing" the governmental interests (at issue) against the First Amendment rights asserted by the appellee. This we decline to do. We recognized that both interests are substantial, but we deem it inappropriate for this Court to label one as being more important or more substantial than the other. Our inquiry is more circumscribed.

See generally, Strong, "Fifty Years of 'Clear and Present Danger': From *Schenk* to *Brandenburg*—And Beyond," 1969 SUP.CT.REV. 41, 59–64.

The ad hoc balancing applied in *Bigelow* appears somewhat anomalous. Among those courts which have applied *Bigelow* to find commercial speech protected, the majority have struck down advertising restrictions on the grounds that governmental ends were advanced by overly restrictive means, a nexus approach akin to the *O'Brien* analysis. See *Terminal-Hudson Electronics, Inc.* v. *Department of Consumer Affairs,* 407 F.Supp. 1075, 1981 (C D.Cal) (three-judge court), vacated for reconsideration in light of *Virginia Board of Pharmacy* sub nom. *Board of Optometry* v. *California Citizen's Action Group,* 426 U.S. 916 (1976); *Anderson, Clayton Co.* v. *Washington State Department of Agriculture,* 402 F.Supp. 1253, 1258 (W.D.Wash. 1975) (three-judge court); *Commonwealth* v. *Sterlace,* 354 A.2d 27, 30 (1976). But see *Millstone* v. *O'Hanlon Reports, Inc.,* 528 F.2d 829, 833 (1976), where former Justice Clark denied a First Amendment challenge to the Fair Credit Reporting Act on the alternative grounds that there is a compelling interest in preventing credit reporting abuses or that this interest outweighs any resulting impingement on freedom of expression. Since a number of courts interpreting *Bigelow* placed the speech at issue categorically outside First Amendment protection, see note 120 supra, they did not reach the question of the appropriate method of review for protected commercial speech.

The analytical approach set out in *O'Brien* nonetheless involves elements of balancing. The requirement of a "compelling" interest involves a balancing judgment at the threshold of the inquiry, although in not inquiring into the speech interests involved, it is a categorical judgment. For a study of the role of balancing in the *O'Brien* model of analysis, see Ely, "Flag Desecration: A Case Study in the Roles of Categorization and Balancing in First Amendment Analysis," 88 HARV. L. REV. 1482 (1975).

Overbreadth analysis, a form of categorical First Amendment analysis, also involves balancing of the degree of overbreadth in relation to the legitimate reach of the challenged statute. Cf. *Broadrick* v. *Oklahoma*, 413 U.S. 601, 615 (1973) (". . . as the otherwise unprotected behavior . . . moves from pure speech toward conduct . . . overbreadth of a statute must not only be real, but substantial as well, judged in relation to the statute's plainly legitimate sweep.") *Broadrick* suggests balancing not only of the extent of overbreadth in a challenged statute, but in the distinction between speech and conduct as well, with overbreadth scrutiny being less rigorously applied as expression moves on the continuum toward conduct.

[17] It is possible that the *O'Brien* model of analysis will not be applied to the commercial speech. Writing for a plurality of the Court in *Young* v. *American Mini-Theatres, Inc.*, 427 U.S. 50 (1976), Justice Stevens suggested that the protection of commercial speech will be judged on a sliding sclae on which "the content of a particular advertisement may determine the extent of its protection" Id. at 68. This method resembles the ad hoc balancing of *Bigelow*.

Given the division of the court in *Young*, however, it seems doubtful that Justice Stevens' approach will prevail: Justice Powell concurred in the result but would have applied the four-step analysis of *O'Brien*, id. at 79–82, and four Justices dissented from the plurality's application of a subject-matter test. Id. at 84–96 (Stewart, J., with Brennan, Marshall, and Blackmun, JJ., dissenting). Since the *O'Brien* model does not involve inquiry into the subject matter of the speech at issue, it would seem that a majority of the Court would favor its application in commercial speech cases over an ad hoc approach.

[18] *Tinker* v. *Des Moines School District*, 393 U.S. 503, 506 (1969).
[19] *Schenk* v. *United States*, 249 U.S. 47, 52 (1917).
[20] *Brandenburg* v. *Ohio*, 395 U.S. 444, 447 (1969).
[21] *Schneider* v. *Town of Irvington*, 308 U.S. 147, 164 (1939); *Lovell* v. *City of Griffin*, 303 U.S. 444, 452 (1938).
[22] *NAACP* v. *Button*, 371 U.S. 415, 455 (1963) (Harlan, J., with Stewart and Clark, JJ., dissenting).
[23] *Roth* v. *United States*, 354 U.S. 476, 484 (1957), I JOURNALS OF THE CONGRESS 108 (1774).

Section 3

The Advertising Challenge: An Alternative to Individual Lawyer Advertising

*John Stewart Geer**

To date, the organized bar has failed to satisfy public informational needs concerning the necessity for and availability of legal services.[1] Despite a recent relaxation of legal advertising constraints,[2] public information remains quantitatively modest and carefully filtered to the citizenry through minimally accessible channels of communication.[3] Consumer consciousness has expanded dramatically over the past ten years. Legislative and judicial responses to consumer problems have evinced a solicitude for the interest of the citizen-purchaser. Inevitably, public attention has focused upon the "marketing" of legal services and, predictably, severe limitations on market information have been found unwarranted. In the context of contemporary consumer awareness, the failure of existing regulatory controls to survive constitutional scrutiny is not surprising.

The Supreme Court's decision in *Bates* v. *State Bar or Arizona*,[4] reflects the conflict between the consumer movement and the Bar's traditional proscription against the overt sale of legal services. The decision, together with other recent Supreme Court opinions in the area of commercial speech,[5] effectively constitutionalizes an important aspect of consumer law, the right of access to information. In *Bates* the Court relies heavily upon its recent pronouncement in *Virginia State Board of Pharmacy* v. *Virginia Citizens Consumer Council, Inc.*[6] In both cases, the Supreme Court's analysis proceeds from the premise that the First Amendment embraces the correlative rights of both speaker and listener, the parties necessary to meaningful commercial communication.[7] In each instance, the Court emphasizes public informational needs. Both cases stress the substantial public interest involved in the dissemination of commercial information.[8] In *Bates*, the Court explicitly recognizes the "individual and societal interests in assuring informed and reliable decision making."[9] In the context of commercial speech, the interests of the consumer-recipient are accorded greater deference than the economic interests of the speaker. The speaker's First Amendment rights are predicated in large part upon the resultant benefit to the audience.

In *Bates* opinion addresses the constitutional dimension of commercial speech in the context of stark alternatives: the availability of commercial information contrasted with a ban on all advertising. The majority opinion in *Bates* draws upon two recent commercial speech decisions: *Bigelow* v. *Virginia*[10] and *Virginia State Board of Pharmacy*.[11] In each case, the Court considered the governmental interest in *prohibiting* commercial speech and found the interest insufficient to justify a total proscription. In *Bigelow*, the Court found no countervailing state interest in prohibiting the dissemination of information concerning the availability of abortions in another state. Similarly, the Court in *Virginia State Board of Pharmacy* found Virginia's statutory proscription against all drug advertising to be constitutionally impermissible. In *Bates* and its predecessors, the Supreme Court concludes that an outright prohibition against public access to commercial information (the availability and prices of

*Stanford Law School, California Law Practice.

goods and services) is constitutionally infirm. Neither in *Bates*, nor its antecedents, does the Supreme Court suggest that advertising may not be regulated. Indeed, the *Bates* Court explicitly qualifies its opinion by recognizing that advertising by attorneys may be regulated. Twice the Court refers to the permissibility of "restrained" professional advertising.[12] The Court suggests, illustratively, certain nonsuspect restraints which may be imposed, including a prohibition against false, deceptive, or misleading advertising.[13] As the Supreme Court has previously stated,[14] and reiterated in *Bates*,[15] reasonable restrictions on the time, place, and manner of advertising may be imposed.

That some constraints upon the advertising of legal services are permissible seems clear. The dimensions of First Amendment tolerances, however, remain uncertain. Regulatory limits may survive constitutional challenge when applied to commercial speech, but perish if applied in a noncommercial context. In *Bates*, the Supreme Court differentiated commercial speech from noncommercial speech in one significant respect. The Court declined to apply the First Amendment Overbreadth Doctrine to professional advertising.[16] Moreover, the Supreme Court has recently recognized that the states have a "compelling interest in the practice of professions within their boundaries"[17] and acknowledged that the "interest of the states in regulating lawyers is especially great since lawyers are essential to the primary governmental function of administering justice, and have historically been 'officers of the court.' "[18] In short, regulatory constraints upon professional advertising may pass constitutional inspection which would be impermissible in other contexts.

Proponents of a continued advertising ban may, however, draw little solace from the availability of regulatory controls. The present disciplinary rules cannot be salvaged with minor renovations; a major reconstruction is necessary. Lawyers have a First Amendment right to advertise their availability and the prices of "routine" services. The public has a correlative right to receipt of that information.

Amid the uncertainty concerning the permissible scope of advertising regulation, the legal profession, largely through the organized bar and the various state supreme courts, must reappraise and revise disciplinary rules governing the advertising of legal services. Although the Supreme Court's decision in *Bates* has limited the options available to the profession, alternative approaches remain to be considered.

Certainly one constitutionally acceptable alternative to the present disciplinary rules is to lift the ban on individual lawyer advertising, restraining attorneys only to the extent that their statements are false, deceptive, or misleading. This alternative, although constitutionally passable (and previously advanced by the American Bar Association Committee on Ethics), is unlikely to fulfill the informational needs which have so concerned the Supreme Court. If the provision of reliable public information concerning the availability and prices of legal services is the constitutional objective of the Court's ruling, one must question minimally restrained individual lawyer advertising as a means of achieving it.

First, individual lawyers and firms are likely to advance information designed solely to increase their own clientele. Although advertising their own services and prices, individual advertisements are unlikely to adequately explain the need for those services and what each service entails. Second, serious questions of misinformation and overreaching will arise. In fact, a substantial law practice may be built on the basis of marketing acumen rather than legal competence. Although the majority opinion in *Bates* assumes the pristine character of the overwhelming majority of attorneys,[19] the reality of professional discipline exposes the majority's perception as overly optimistic. The bustling offices of disciplinary agencies in various states throughout the country suggest that the number of violations of ethical duty is hardly minuscule. A significant minority of practicing attorneys may reasonably be expected to seize the advertising opportunity, capitalizing on a superior bargaining position. Given increased public visibility, a minority of lawyers may further impair public confidence in the Bar. The availability of broad-based advertising will enable the marginal practitioner to shroud a qualitatively deficient product in an attractive and clever marketing package.

Although individual lawyer advertising is the least restrictive solution to the advertising challenge, the Bar must still perform a regulatory function; the profession will remain responsible for enforcement efforts. Effective policing of lawyer advertising which is limited only by proscription against false and misleading statements is at best an ambitious undertaking. Overworked bar disciplinary agencies in many parts of the country are not currently prepared for the task. Further definition of "false" and "misleading" will be necessary, and further dissipation of enforcement efforts will result. As a practical matter, the advertising attorney will be largely self-regulating.

Professional resources ought to be considered. If the conveyance of reliable public information is truly the worthy objective to be pursued, allowing each attorney to advertise individually so diffuses marketing resources as to fail of its purpose.

A carefully directed institutional approach to the advertising of legal services would appear best suited to become the profession's primary informational mechanism. From the standpoint of marketing resources, advertising through an organized bar association or disciplinary agency would provide a focal point to which marketing resources could be directed and most efficiently expended. Moreover, professional advertising could be easily regulated without elaborate policing mechanisms. Perhaps most importantly, the quality of information available to the public would be superior to the self-interested statements of individual practitioners and firms. Disinterested and reliable information could be provided to raise consumer consciousness as to the need for legal services, their availability, and their cost.

A variety of mechanisms could be employed institutionally which would quickly elevate the public image of the profession and fulfill a vital public function which the legal profession is designed to perform. Public information could be disseminated through various media. For example, public service time is most often readily obtainable from radio and television stations. Each FCC licensee must devote a certain quantum of broadcasting time to public service activities. This time, often free of charge, could be utilized to explain the need for the availability of a variety of vital legal services. The necessity for drawing a will and the consequences of dying intestate might be explained. The benefit of legal services in real estate closings could be addressed. Legal considerations involved in divorce litigation could be enumerated. Various means by which lawyers charge fees could be examined. The institutional approach, in short, is potentially the most informative and beneficial approach to the conveyance of legal service information. Public service television and radio announcements might be developed by the American Bar Association or another entity and sold to state bar associations and disciplinary agencies throughout the country. Production costs of such a media enterprise could therefore be efficiently allocated throughout the country.

Although the holding in *Bates* is carefully circumscribed, the Court extends First Amendment protection to newspaper advertisements of basic price information concerning what the Court characterized as "routine" services. Although the release of price information by individual lawyers may not be prohibited, it may be limited, *inter alia,* in the manner in which it is conveyed and otherwise supplemented. If an institutional approach to advertising were undertaken, individual newspaper advertisements could be extensively supplemented by the Bar.

Price information could be submitted by individual lawyers and firms to a single state agency which would compile, and periodically update, brochures which could be made available to the public. This information could be disseminated at various distribution points throughout a state to facilitate public access. Radio and television advertisements could announce the availability of prices and other brochures in each location. Bar sponsored newspaper ads could be utilized to further inform the public of the availability of legal service information.

The dilemma involved in defining "routine" services may be avoided through Bar sponsored advertising activities. A variety of services could be explained in brochures and announcements in order to educate the general public and diminish the possibility that a client may be misled. Although solicitation is not addressed by the Court in *Bates,* individual advertising may be expected to result in an increase in the incidence of solicitation. At least a segment of the Bar is likely to exceed reasonable restraints on advertising if the marketing of legal services is left to individual discretion. The prevention of harassment of the public and overreaching by attorneys is a worthy objective of the disciplinary rule against solicitation. Solicitation is the likely byproduct of minimal constraints on individual advertising.

A logical alternative to minimally restrained individual lawyer advertising is a combination of institutional and individual advertising. Individual lawyers could be permitted to advertise various services and fees in newspapers, while the state bar would remain the primary vehicle for the communication of legal service information. Newspaper ads, perhaps limited in size, could be effectively policed by the profession, while allowing attorneys and firms to communicate directly with the public.

The advertising challenge is truly upon us. Within two weeks of *Bates,* legal advertisements began to appear in local newspapers. Some lawyers have begun to discuss legal services with advertising agencies. State Bars are being pressured to advance a new disciplinary rule governing advertising. The organized bar is the profession's unifying voice and exists in large measure to serve the public interest. If the profession is to retain leadership in the advertising of legal services, the resources of the organized bar must quickly be mounted. A regulatory scheme, capable of withstanding constitutional assaults, must be devised which advances both public and professional interests.

NOTES

[1] In deciding the fate of legal advertising constraints, the Supreme Court observed that the "absence of advertising may be seen to reflect the profession's failure to reach out and serve the community . . ." *Bates v. State Bar of Arizona,* 45 L. W. 4895, 4900 (1977).

[2] In 1974 the American Bar Association amended its disciplinary rules governing advertising to permit the expanded use of law lists. The lists or directories were further permitted to provide information not previously sanctioned by the Code of Professional Responsibility. *See,* American Bar Association, Code of Professional Responsibility, Disciplinary Rule (hereinafter referred to as DR) 2–102(A).

[3] Law lists the legal directories have not been generally available to the consuming public. Moreover, although DR 2-102(A) (6) permits the listing of initial consultation fees in the classified section of telephone company directories, the telephone company does not permit price information to be listed.

[4] 45 L.W. 4895 (1977).

[5] The Supreme Court's decision in *Bates v. State Bar of Arizona* draws substantially upon two recent commercial speech decisions, *Bigelow v. Virginia,* 421 U.S. 809 (1975) and *Virginia State Board of Pharmacy v. Virginia Citizens Consumer Council, Inc.,* 425 U.S. 748 (1976).

[6] 425 U.S. 748 (1976).

[7] *Bates v. State Bar of Arizona,* 45 L.W. 4895, 4899 (1977); *Virginia State Board of Pharmacy v. Virginia Citizens Consumer Council, Inc.,* 425 U.S. 748, 756–57 (1976).

[8] *Bates v. State Bar of Arizona,* 45 L.W. 4895, 4899 (1977); *Virginia State Board of Pharmacy* v. *Virginia Citizens Consumer Council, Inc.,* 425 U.S. 748, 765 (1976).
[9] *Bates v. State Bar of Arizona,* 45 L.W. 4895, 4899 (1977).
[10] 421 U.S. 809 (1975).
[11] 425 U.S. 748 (1976).
[12] 45 L.W. at pp. 4901 and 4902.
[13] 45 L.W. at p. 4904.
[14] *Virginia State Board of Pharmacy* v. *Virginia Citizens Consumer Council, Inc.,* 425 U.S. 748, 771 (1976).
[15] 45 L.W. at p. 4904.
[16] 45 L.W. at p. 4903.
[17] *Goldfarb* v. *Virginia State Bar,* 421 U.S. 773, 792 (1975).
[18] *Id.*
[19] The majority opinion clearly minimizes potential abuse by individual dual lawyers. The Court states in pertinent part:

> We suspect that, with advertising, most lawyers will behave as they always have: they will abide by their solemn oaths to uphold the integrity and honor of their profession and of the legal system. For every attorney who overreaches through advertising, there will be thousands of others who will be candid and honest and straightforward.
>
> 45 L.W. at p. 4903.

Section 4

American Bar Association Recommendations on Lawyer Advertising
Part A
Report to the Board of Governors of the Task Force on Lawyer Advertising

S. Shepherd Tate, Chairman, and Members of the Task Force on Lawyer Advertising, American Bar Association, Aug. 4, 1977*

The Task Force on Lawyer Advertising was established by the Board of Governors June 7, 1977, shortly before the Supreme Court announced its decision in the case of *Bates and O'Steen* v. *State Bar of Arizona* 45 L.W. 4895 (June 27, 1977). The Task Force met promptly after the decision was announced and from time to time thereafter. In the course of its deliberations, it consulted with counsel retained by the Association and considered suggestions received from various committees within the Association, including a recommendation from the Standing Committee on Ethics and Professional Responsibility. That Committee considered the matter at some length at the request of the Task Force and pursuant to its authority under the By-Laws.

On July 25, 1977, the Task Force circulated proposals reflecting its view of two district approaches to the question and requested comments and suggestions from all interested groups. Those proposals were the subject of a public Hearing, August 4, 1977, at which 38 participants, including lawyer, media, and consumer representatives, testified. They have also been widely discussed within the profession and beyond, as reflected by numerous comments and suggestions directed to the Task Force.

It is apparent that substantial difference of opinion exists concerning the implications of *Bates and O'Steen* upon a lawyer's right to advertise. Although many consumer groups urged delay and objected to many provisions of both proposals, a majority of those persons who have communicated to the Task Force seem to favor clarifying the matter by an immediate amendment to the ABA's model Code of Professional Responsibility.

It is also apparent to the Task Force that despite the significant amount of time it has devoted to the subject during the past several weeks, many important questions still need to be answered. It is highly likely that further amendments will be required to clarify such questions as the use of television, the scope of "time, place, and manner" restrictions and the right of a lawyer to indicate a limitation or concentration of practice. Provision should now be made for an ongoing evaluation and also for a program of vigorous consumer education by the organized bar.

---

*Reprinted by permission of the American Bar Association.

LEGAL IMPLICATION OF *BATES AND O'STEEN*

Although the *Bates* decision does not answer all questions concerning lawyer advertising, the following principles were set forth:

1. Advertising regulations adopted by state action are deemed to be a legitimate means of preserving professional integrity, and are exempt from the Sherman Act.
2. The traditional ban against lawyer advertising is contrary to the First Amendment, and the five-member majority noted with "particular interest" the dissenting view in the lower court opinion that the issue should be framed in terms of "the right to the public as consumers and citizens to know about the activities of the legal profession."
3. Appropriate regulations may be established to restrain false, deceptive, or misleading advertising and to some extent control the time, place, and manner of advertising.
4. A lawyer may advertise certain factual and fee information in print media, including the prices at which certain "routine" services will be performed.
5. The First Amendment Overbreadth Doctrine does not apply to commercial speech thereby limiting the holding of the *Bates* decision to the particular facts of that case.
6. Although the facts of the case dealt with newspaper advertising, Mr. Justice Powell notes in footnote 12 to his dissenting opinion, "(I)t is clear that today's decision cannot be confined on a principled basis to price advertisements in newspapers. No distinction can be drawn between newspapers and a rather broad spectrum of other means, for example, magazines, signs in buses and subways, posters, handbills, and mail circulations. But questions remain open as to time, place, and manner restrictions affecting other media, such as radio and television." Similarly, the majority opinion at footnote 26 refers to the fact that certain information is already permitted in legal directories and telephone books, and states, "If the information is not misleading when published in a telephone directory, it is difficult to see why it becomes misleading when published in a newspaper."

PROPOSALS A AND B COMPARED

"Proposal A" may be described as "regulatory." It would specifically authorize certain prescribed forms of lawyer advertising if approved by state authorities. It would seek in advance to channel commercial announcements but would rely on "after the fact" enforcement to discipline persons violating the regulation. It would follow the basic approach of several federal regulatory agencies, such as the Food and Drug Administration and the Securities and Exchange Commission.

In contrast, "Proposal B" may be termed "directive." It would allow publication of all information not "false, fraudulent, misleading, or deceptive," and provides guidelines for the determination of improper advertisements, which would be subject to "after the fact" discipline by state authorities.

Both proposals are constructive responses to the goal recognized by the Supreme Court of providing consumers with needed information about lawyer services and their costs.

"Proposal A" retains many of the present disciplinary rules that specify the categories of information that can be published: name, field of law practice concentration, education, client reference, etc. It adds certain fee information, contingency fees, a range for certain services, hourly rate, and charges for "specific legal services the description of which would not be misunderstood or be deceptive."

(See "Proposal A" DR 2–101(B).) It also provides a procedure for a lawyer to seek to expand information that may be disclosed through application to appropriate state authorities. ("Proposal A" DR 2–101(C).)

"Proposal B" does not list the specific items permitted to be advertised, but adopts a general antifraud standard, and specifies with great particularity the elements of "false, fraudulent, misleading, or deceptive" statements. (See "Proposal B" DR 2–101(B).) As to fees, it would authorize disclosure of the same kind of information permitted under "Proposal A", subject only to the antifraud provision. ("Proposal B" DR 2–101(B) (6).)

Neither proposal would allow one-to-one solicitation, nor would either now permit the use of television in the absence of a determination by the appropriate state authorities that it is necessary to provide adequate information to consumers of legal services. Both provide extensive commentary in ethical considerations to guide regulatory agencies.

Both proposals refer the question of television advertising to the states. Upon consideration of the testimony of several witnesses at the open hearing and a review of the Constitutional considerations involved, the Task Force concludes that certain radio advertising should be permitted now and television advertising should be permitted if, as the Task Force has been assured, safeguards can be developed that will effectively regulate such advertising. However, the Task Force recognizes that it has not had sufficient time and does not have sufficient expertise to identify or fully evaluate all the problems involved or to develop appropriate proposed regulations. The Supreme Court itself recognized that certain electronic advertising might offer special problems. Some observers suggest that print and radio advertising will provide a substantial measure of the legal service information needed by the public, and fear that advertising by television may be apt to emphasize style over substance. On the other hand, it appears that even temporary prohibition against the use of all electronic media might preclude communication to a large segment of the population who are only marginally literate or who do not normally read print media, but who are exposed to electronic media regularly.*

The ABA Code of Professional Responsibility is only a model for review and modification by the states. The Task Force believes that in light of the current lack of experience with professional advertising through television, the ABA should not hastily devise even advisory guidelines but should take advantage of the experience of the several states before developing model standards in this regard.

PROPOSAL TO CREATE A COMMISSION

The Supreme Court has ruled that the Constitution permits lawyers to advertise with certain limitations and recognizes that the bar has an important role to play:

> In sum, we recognize that many of the problems in defining the boundary between deceptive and nondeceptive advertising remain to be resolved, and we expect that the bar will have a special role to play in assuring that advertising by attorneys flows both freely and cleanly. (See slip opinion at page 32.)

---

*A 1975 report by the Department of Health, Education and Welfare indicates that approximately one-fifth of the adults in this nation are functionally incompetent in basic skills, including reading skills. A 1976 Roper Survey indicates that a large majority of the American public obtain information about current affairs from radio and television, rather than newspapers.

Because of the novelty of lawyer advertising, the limitations of the present disciplinary system, and the further fact that advertising is now a possibility for the other professions, the Task Force recommends that a Commission on Professional Advertising be established to monitor developments at the state bar level and within other professions. Such a Commission should evaluate the various systems adopted by states and other professions, and report to the House of Delegates at its midyear and annual meetings, particularly in respect to recommendations to improve the Association's own guidelines on lawyer advertising. Any such Commission should include representation from other professions and interested groups, recognizing that the *Bates* decision emphasizes the need for a close relationship between the professions and the consumers of professional services.

CONSUMER EDUCATION

The Sumpreme Court also noted the legal profession's duty to counsel the public concerning legal services:

> Although, of course, the bar retains the power to correct omissions that have the effect of presenting an inaccurate picture, the preferred remedy is more disclosure, rather than less. If the naivete of the public will cause advertising by attorneys to be misleading, then it is the bar's role to assure that the populace is sufficiently informed as to enable it to place advertising in its proper perspective.

The Code of Professional Responsibility recognizes this obligation of the profession (CPR EC 2-1, 2-2). Both proposals recommend such consumer education programs. (See "Proposal A" ED 2-1, 2-2; "Proposal B" ED 2-1, 2-2.)

It should also be noted that the report of the Special Committee to Survey Legal Needs also cites numerous instances of incorrect consumer perceptions concerning legal services and that the Special Committee on the Delivery of Legal Services on the basis of four years of study contemplates a national workshop on this subject in December as part of the National Conference on Legal Services and the Public in New Orleans. In addition the Special Committee has already begun to circulate to interested sections and committees a resolution for consideration at the 1978 midyear meeting calling for a "public education program designed to increase understanding of basic features of our legal system, to provide sufficient information to make decisions as to when to seek and how to use legal services, and to facilitate the selection of lawyers by the public."

The cost of institutional advertising, particularly for television and national print media, is exceedingly high. If a major consumer education effort is deemed advisable, joint efforts by the Association and state and local bars might produce significant savings. The Task Force recommends that:

> A special committee, to be composed of representatives of the Association and or state bar associations, be established by the Association to study and make recommendations concerning the feasibility, funding, and scope of a national advertising program to educate consumers as to the utility, costs, and availability of legal services, and to report to the House no later than its midyear meeting in February, 1978.

Part B
Advertising: Making the Best of a Good Thing

Remarks delivered by William B. Spann, Jr., President, American Bar Association, to Jacksonville, Florida Bar Association, Oct. 20, 1977*

Ladies and gentlemen, a year ago last month *Business Week* magazine reported to its readers that the professions were in trouble. It cited the malpractice crisis in medicine, increasing demands that accountants assume responsibility for errors in their clients' returns, and burgeoning public distrust of lawyers in the wake of Watergate. "Opinion polls show the public increasingly skeptical of professionals' probity and competence," it said, and it warned of "the gap between what the professions can deliver and what the public expects."

Business Week described a trend or mood that most of us in the professions have recognized. For better or for worse, values are changing. The professions no longer occupy irreproachable positions atop high pedestals. We are still looked up to, I think, but not with the same unreserved reverence and awe as in the past. We are finding that today we must work to earn not only our fees but our clients' respect.

In this same *Business Week* article, I was quoted as saying, "Our biggest problem (in the legal profession) is providing legal services to the great bulk of the people." Nothing in the past year has changed my opinion about that—except to reinforce it. Not only must we work harder for our clients, we must strive to restore public confidence in the legal profession. I can think of no better way than by increasing our capacity to serve more people. For one thing, I have enough confidence in lawyers to feel that the better we are known on a personal level—rather than secondhand through the various media—the better our work will be understood and acknowledged.

Extending services, of course, is easier said than done, not only because the legal community is not unanimous in its support of the idea but also because of the very nature of our profession. In the past, our goals as a profession have inclined more toward quality of service than to its extension. And these goals have been firmly embraced in our Code of Professional Responsibility. For example, under Canon 2 it was said until very recently, "the traditional ban against advertising by lawyers, which is subject to certain limited exceptions, is rooted in the public interest," and the laws of the states reflect this ethical imperative. We adopted limited amendments to the Code in 1976 to permit certain telephone directory advertising but only Pennsylvania amended its code accordingly and then only in May of this year. Even if somehow the membership of the ABA had acted entirely upon its own initiative to modify further this Canon and permit media advertising, that change could not have been implemented until the state Codes or Canons had been altered as well.

I have taken a circuitous route to get to my subject today, but I wanted you to see the *Bates and O'Steen* decision of the Supreme Court in the context of some current problems of our profession. I feel that the decision may provide us with an important shortcut to a necessary broadening of our services—a shortcut that the bar itself could not have taken alone.

But let me back up for a moment and talk about the decision itself and about the action taken at the ABA Annual Meeting concerning that decision. After that I'll have a few more words to say about

---
*Reprinted by permission of the American Bar Association.

the decision's implications upon the legal profession. By the way, since it's now permitted, my offices are on Broad Street in Atlanta and what we lack in diminutive fees we make up for in dedication and good old Southern charm.

It's interesting to note that the *Bates and O'Steen* decision, for all its importance to lawyers, was by and large an extension of an earlier case. In that case, *Virginia Pharmacy Board* v. *Virginia Consumer Council,* the Court held that to prohibit a pharmacist from advertising prescription drug prices was a violation of the First Amendment, disregarding the charge that such a pharmacist was guilty of "unprofessional conduct." In *Bates and O'Steen* v. *The State Bar of Arizona,* the Court arrived at an identical conclusion. It said that the Arizona Supreme Court should have framed its decision, as specified by a dissenting judge, "in terms of 'the right of the public as consumers and citizens to know about the activities of the legal profession.' " The Court added that, where price advertising was concerned, "the State's protectiveness of its citizens rests in large part on the advantages of their being kept in ignorance," and called this practice "highly paternalistic." The Court also observed that the contention that the legal profession would be adversely affected by such advertising had "at its core, the argument . . . that attorneys must conceal from themselves and from their clients the real-life fact that lawyers earn their livelihood at the bar," an argument the Court found unworthy. Moreover, the Court pointed out that bankers and engineers advertise "and yet these professions are not regarded as undignified." Finally, and here we get back to my original subject, Justice Blackmun wrote: "In fact, it has been suggested that the failure of lawyers to advertise creates public disillusionment with the profession."

The Court did not, of course, give a blanket approval to all advertising by lawyers. Quite the contrary, it merely prohibited the states from restricting all advertising. It said, moreover, that "there may well be reasonable restrictions on the time, place, and manner of advertising," noting further that "the special problems of advertising on the electronic broadcast media will warrant special consideration."

Fortunately, we in the ABA were not totally surprised by the Court's decision. In fact, before it was handed down on June 27, a six-member Task Force under now President-Elect Shepherd Tate, had been selected. With only six weeks remaining before the ABA Annual Meeting, they went swiftly to work and, after a full day of hearings in Chicago, brought before the House of Delegates not one but two proposed revisions of Canon 2 of the ABA's model Code of Professional Responsibility.

Proposal A takes the Supreme Court at its word concerning reasonable restrictions. It lists specifically the kinds of advertising a lawyer may use if approved by state authorities and answers definitively questions concerning time and place. It is regulatory in nature and follows the approach of the state regulatory agencies.

The Task Force called Proposal B "directive." It would allow publication of all information not "false, fraudulent, misleading, or deceptive," and provide guidelines for the use of advertising.

Incidentally, Proposal A permits radio advertising, but only if pre-recorded and approved by the lawyer. Neither proposal permits television advertising, but only because the Task Force did not feel qualified, in the brief time it had, to consider all of the ramifications of exposure on that complex medium. I, personally, question this distinction. It seems to me that all we have done is discriminate in favor of the blind and against the deaf.

GIVE EXAMPLE

On August 10 the Task Force recommended to the House of Delegates the adoption of Proposal A, and suggested that Proposal B be sent to the states for their consideration as well. "We firmly believe that this Association should carry but its leadership role and give guidance to the state bar associations and to the regulatory agencies of the states," said Shep Tate. Nevertheless, a motion was made from the floor to postpone a decision until the February meeting. Task Force member Michael Franck then gave a forceful speech on behalf of immediate passage. "The states will have to act," he said. "They do not have the luxury of waiting until 1978, when this situation could get totally out of hand. They will have to draft their own codes, and God knows how good those drafts will be."

A three hour debate ensued. Many of those who spoke on behalf of postponement clearly felt that the Supreme Court's five to four decision was a bad one. Others—and I was among them—simply believe that, rather than run the risk of repeated changes in the Code of Professional Responsibility, specific recommendations should be delayed until a more thorough evaluation of the issue had been completed. Nevertheless, the motion to postpone was defeated and delegates quickly thereafter adopted Proposal A. It seems to me paradoxical actually to amend the Code based on proposal A, and then vote on further resolve to submit both proposals.

Although I did not vote with the majority, neither did I stand with those who suggested delay in the hope that the entire issue would disappear. In a speech on July 14, 1976, I stated my belief that the advertising necessary to enable the public to select an acceptable competent legal counsel should be allowed. As a matter of fact, I must admit to a certain pride in this decision of the House even though I opposed it. For an organization as large and complex as the American Bar Association to move so swiftly on a matter of such importance—especially when that constituted a very substantial change from a previous position—was both a little surprising and encouraging; the House left no doubt that it was willing to accept the mantle of leadership for our profession.

Where do we go from here? The House partly answered that question by authorizing implementation of two further recommendations by the Task Force. One suggested that a commission be formed consisting of both lawyers and interested laymen. This commission would monitor and evaluate the various positions on advertising taken by the states and make recommendations with respect to improving the Association's guidelines on advertising. The other recommendation called for a specific committee to make suggestions concerning the feasibility, funding, and scope of a nationwide institutional advertising program to educate consumers to the utility, cost, and availability of legal services.

EXPLAIN PRESENT STATUS

You may be interested to know, incidentally, that there has been no great rush by lawyers to follow the lead of *Bates and O'Steen*. Reports at the American Bar Association's headquarters in Chicago indicate only a trickle of advertising around the country. And some lawyers who have advertised in their local newspapers have not been entirely delighted with the outcome. One said he spent $800 to get $200 worth of business. Two others, in Harvey, Illinois, revealed an unwillingness to take the whole matter very seriously. They advertised Railroad Reorganizations at $1,500,000.10 each, including costs, providing that the reorganizations are, in the language of the Supreme Court and the *Bates and O'Steen* ad, uncomplicated and uncontested.

It seems obvious to me that both the reticence about using advertising and the facetiousness concerning it will pass. But *Bates and O'Steen* will probably have little overall effect on most lawyers. The challenge remains for our bar associations to find other means of extending legal services to a broader segment of the population.

One suggested means of doing this is by certifying lawyers as specialists in their fields. Four states already have plans to recognize certain specialties in this way, thus enabling these lawyers, in effect, to advertise a certain expertise. In at least one area, Washington, D.C., a directory of lawyers with detailed legal information has been compiled and widely distributed. Tel-Law is another device for disseminating information. A person may phone the local bar association and specify by number any one of 70 tape recordings he would like to hear. One will give advice on how to find an attorney, another on how to get a will, and so forth. And the reluctance of attorneys to use advertising suggests still another task for the bar—providing information about the nature of advertising and how to use it effectively—that is, institutional advertising. This must be done largely on a local basis because of variance between communities.

Many of these topics will be considered at a conference on legal needs to be held in New Orleans in December. Recently, I re-read a report on legal needs circulated to people who will attend that conference. It pointed out that among those less likely to seek counsel when legal problems arise are the following: 1) young adults; 2) members of minority groups, especially females; and 3) the less educated. These are the same people it found, who "show a very strong feeling that the legal system favors the rich and powerful over everyone else." To meet the legal needs of these people and thereby to demonstrate that their point of view is wrong will be an enormously difficult task. The profession as a whole may not like *Bates and O'Steen*. But, the advertising permitted, coupled with appropriate institutional advertising, may help us solve the problem of delivery of legal services to the group of people in the middle which the American Bar Foundation has called "people of moderate means." Let's work to make *Bates and O'Steen* a benefit to the profession and to the public.

Thank you.

Section 5

Cases

VALENTINE v. CHRESTENSEN
316 U.S. 52 (1942)

Mr. Justice Roberts delivered the opinion of the Court.

The respondent, a citizen of Florida, owns a former United States Navy submarine which he exhibits for profit. In 1940 he brought it into New York City and moored it at a State pier in the East River. He prepared and printed a handbill advertising the boat and soliciting visitors for a stated admission fee. On his attempting to distribute the bill in the city streets, he was advised by the petitioner, as Police Commissioner, that this activity would violate Section 318 of the Sanitary Code, which forbids distribution in the streets of commercial and business advertising matter, but was told that he might freely distribute handbills solely devoted to "information or a public protest."

Respondent thereupon prepared and showed to the petitioner, in proof form, a double-faced handbill. On one side was a revision of the original, altered by the removal of the statement as to admission fee but consisting only of commercial advertising. On the other side was a protest against the action of the City Dock Department in refusing the respondent wharfage facilities at a city pier for the exhibition of his submarine, but no commercial advertising. The Police Department advised that distribution of a bill containing only the protest would not violate Section 318, and would not be restrained, but that distribution of the double-faced bill was prohibited. The respondent, nevertheless, proceeded with the printing of his proposed bill and started to distribute it. He was restrained by the police.

Respondent then brought this suit to enjoin the petitioner from interfering with the distribution. In his complaint he alleged diversity of citizenship; an amount in controversy in excess of $3,000; the acts and threats of the petitioner under the purported authority of Section 318; asserted a consequent violation of Section 1 of the Fourteenth Amendment of the Constitution; and prayed an injunction. The District Court granted an interlocutory injunction, and after trial on a stipulation from which the facts appear as above recited, granted a permanent injunction. The Circuit Court of Appeals, by a divided court, affirmed.

The question is whether the application of the ordinance to the respondent's activity was, in the circumstances, an unconstitutional abridgment of the freedom of the press and of speech.

1. This court has unequivocally held that the streets are proper places for the exercise of the freedom of communicating information and disseminating opinion and that, though the states and municipalities may appropriately regulate the privilege in the public interest, they may not unduly burden or proscribe its employment in these public throughfares. We are equally clear that the Constitution imposes no such restraint on government as respects purely commercial advertising. Whether and to what extent one may promote or pursue a gainful occupation in the streets, to what extent such activity shall be adjudged a derogation of the public right of user, are matters for legislative judgment. The question is not whether the legislative body may interfere with the harmless pursuit of a lawful

business, but whether it must permit such pursuit by what it deems an undesirable invasion of, or interference with, the full and free use of the highways by the people in fulfillment of the public use to which streets are dedicated. If the respondent was attempting to use the streets of New York by distributing commercial advertising, the prohibition of the code provision was lawfully invoked against his conduct.

2. The respondent contends that, in truth, he was engaged in the dissemination of matter proper for public information, none the less so because there was inextricably attached to the medium of such dissemination commercial advertising matter. The court below appears to have taken this view, since it adverts to the difficulty of apportioning, in a given case, the contents of the communication as between what is of public interest and what is for private profit. We need not indulge nice appraisal based upon subtle distinctions in the present instance nor assume possible cases not now presented. It is enough for the present purpose that the stipulated facts justify the conclusion that the affixing of the protest against official conduct to the advertising circular was with the intent, and for the purpose, of evading the prohibition of the ordinance. If that evasion were successful, every merchant who desires to broadcast advertising leaflets in the streets need only append a civic appeal, or a moral platitude, to achieve immunity from the law's command.

The decree is *Reversed*.

RAILWAY EXPRESS AGENCY v. NEW YORK
336 U.S. 106 (1949)

The Court upheld a New York ordinance prohibiting advertising on vehicles except "business delivery vehicles . . . engaged in the usual business or regular work of the owner. . . ." The appellant was convicted and fined for violation of a traffic violation of the City of New York.

Mr. Justice Douglas delivered the opinion of the Court.

The Court of Special Sessions concluded that advertising on vehicles using the streets of New York City constitutes a distraction to vehicle drivers and to pedestrians alike and therefore affects the safety of the public in the use of the streets. We do not sit to weigh evidence on the due process issue in order to determine whether the regulation is sound or appropriate; nor is it our function to pass judgment on its wisdom. We would be trespassing on one of the most intensely local and specialized of all municipal problems if we held that this regulation had no relation to the traffic problem of New York City. It is the judgment of the local authorities that it does have such a relation. And nothing has been advanced which shows that to be palpably false.

The question of equal protection of the laws is pressed more strenuously on us. It is pointed out that the regulation draws the line between advertisements of products sold by the owner of the truck and general advertisements. It is argued that unequal treatment on the basis of such a distinction is not justified by the aim and purpose of the regulation. It is said, for example, that one of appellant's trucks carrying the advertisement of a commercial house would not cause any greater distraction of pedestrians and vehicle driver than if the commercial house carried the same advertisement on its own truck. Yet the regulation allows the latter to do what the former is forbidden from doing. It is therefore contended that the classification which the regulation makes has no relation to the traffic problem since a violation turns not on what kind of advertisements are carried on trucks but on whose trucks they are carried.

That, however, is a superficial way of analyzing the problem even if we assume that it is premised on the correct construction of the regulation. The local authorities may well have concluded that those who advertise their own wares on their trucks do not present the same traffic problem in view of the nature or extent of the advertising which they use. It would take a degree of omniscience which we lack to say that such is not the case. If that judgment is correct, the advertising displays that are exempt have less incidence on traffic than those of appellants.

We cannot say that that judgment is not an allowable one. Yet if it is, the classification has relation to the purpose for which it is made and does not contain the kind of discrimination against which the Equal Protection Clause affords protection. It is by such practical considerations based on experience rather than by theoretical inconsistencies that the question of equal protection is to be answered. And the fact that New York City sees fit to eliminate from traffic this kind of distraction but does not touch what may be even greater ones in a different category, such as the vivid displays on Times Square, is immaterial. It is no requirement of equal protection that all evils of the same genus be eradicated or none at all.

It is finally contended that the regulation is a burden on interstate commerce in violation of Article I, Section 8 of the Constitution. Many of these trucks are engaged in delivering goods in interstate commerce from New Jersey to New York. Where traffic control and the use of highways are involved and where there is no conflicting federal regulation, great leeway is allowed local authorities, even though the local regulation materially interferes with interstate commerce.

Mr. Justice Jackson concurring.

The burden should rest heavily upon one who would persuade us to use the due process clause to strike down a substantive law or ordinance. Even its provident use against municipal regulations frequently disables all government—state, municipal, and federal—from dealing with the conduct in question because the requirement of due process is also applicable to state and federal governments. Invalidation of a statute or an ordinance on due process grounds leaves ungoverned and ungovernable conduct which many people find objectionable.

Invocation of the equal protection clause . . . does not disable any governmental body from dealing with the subject at hand. It merely means that the prohibition or regulation must have a broader impact. (T)here is no more effective practical guaranty against arbitrary and unreasonable government than to require that the principles of law which officials would impose upon a minority must be imposed generally. Conversely, nothing opens the door to arbitrary action so effectively as to allow those officials to pick and choose only a few to whom they will apply legislation and thus to escape the political retribution that might be visited upon them if larger numbers were affected. Courts can take no better measure to assure that laws will be just than to require that laws be equal in operation.

This case affords an illustration. Even casual observations from the sidewalks of New York will show that an ordinance which would forbid all advertising on vehicles would run into conflict with many interests, including some, if not all, of the great metropolitan newspapers, which use that advertising extensively. Their blandishment of the latest sensations is not less a cause of diverted attention and traffic hazard than the commonplace cigarette advertisement which this truck-owner is forbidden to display. But any regulation applicable to all such advertising would require much clearer justification in local conditions to enable its enactment than does some regulation applicable to a few.

That the difference between carrying on any business for hire and engaging in the same activity on one's own is a sufficient one to sustain some types of regulations of the one that is not applied to the other, is almost elementary. But it is usual to find such regulations applied to the very incidents wherein the two classes present different problems, such as in charges, liability, and quality of service.

The difference, however, is invoked here to sustain a discrimination in a problem in which the two classes present identical dangers. The courts of New York have declared that the sole nature and purpose of the regulation before us is to reduce traffic hazards. There is not even a pretense here that the traffic hazard created by the advertising which is forbidden is in any manner or degree more hazardous than that which is permitted. It is urged with considerable force that this local regulation does not comply with the equal protection clause because it applies unequally upon classes whose differentiation is in no way relevant to the objects of the regulation.

The question in my mind comes to this. Where individuals contribute to an evil or danger in the same way and to the same degree, may those who do so for hire be prohibited, while those who do so for their own commercial ends but not for hire be allowed to continue? I think the answer has to be that the hireling may be put in a class by himself and may be dealt with differently than those who act on their own. But this is not merely because such a discrimination will enable the lawmaker to diminish the evil. That might be done by many classifications, which I should think wholly unsustainable. It is rather because there is a real difference between doing in self-interest and doing for hire, so that it is one thing to tolerate action from those who act on their own, and it is another thing to permit the same action to be promoted for a price.

Of course, this appellant did not hold itself out to carry or display everybody's advertising, and its rental of space on the sides of its trucks was only incidental to the main business which brought its trucks into the streets. But it is not difficult to see that, in a day of extravagant advertising more or less subsidized by tax deduction, the rental of truck space could become an obnoxious enterprise. While I do not think highly of this type of regulation, that is not my business, and in view of the control I would concede to cities to protect citizens in quiet and orderly use for their proper purposes of the highways and public places . . . , I think the judgment below must be affirmed.

NEW YORK STATE BROADCASTERS ASSOCIATION v. *UNITED STATES*
414 F.2d 990 (CA2 1969)

Feinberg, Circuit Judge.

The New York State Broadcasters Association, Inc. and Metromedia, Inc. have petitioned for review of a declaratory ruling of the Federal Communications Commission on whether certain proposed broadcasts about the New York State Lottery would violate 18 U.S.C. Section 1304, which prohibits broadcasting lottery information, and the Commission's regulations. The Commission specifically ruled as to some types of broadcasts but declined to do so with regard to others, relying instead on general statements of the purpose of the statute and regulations. For reasons set forth below, we hold that the declaratory ruling was incomplete and remand the matter to the Commission.

I

During its 1966 session, the New York State Legislature passed a measure that provided for a vote on a proposed amendment to the state constitution. The amendment authorized the creation of a state lottery and was approved by a substantial majority of New York voters in the November 1966 election. Thereafter, in April 1967, the Legislature passed the New York State Lottery Law, which provided for the sale of lottery tickets with the net proceeds of the sales to be used exclusively for educational purposes by state and local entities.

In June 1967, the Lottery commenced operation and in the meantime has become a familiar feature of the state landscape. Advertisements on billboards, in newspapers, and on public transportation posters proclaim the chance of a lifetime to help education and at the same time win a lottery prize. Despite such promotional efforts, however, the Lottery has been a disappointment to its supporters, and the state has for the most part had to look elsewhere for the revenues to pay the increasing costs of education. Whatever the reasons for the failure of the Lottery to produce the expected revenues, at least some people believe that it would be more successful but for the almost total absence of lottery news, information and advertising on television and radio. As a consequence, the state has sought to increase interest in the Lottery by using radio and television, and this appeal is one result of that effort.

Petitioner, The New York State Broadcasters Association, Inc., is an organization of radio and television broadcasters whose members own 175 broadcast stations, all of which are licensed by the Commission. Petitioner Metromedia, Inc. is one of the licensed broadcaster members of the Association; it owns and operates radio and television stations in New York and elsewhere. According to petitioners' brief, Metromedia and other members of the Association have undertaken to broadcast advertisements and other information about the New York State Lottery if such broadcasts will not result in revocation of or inability to renew their licenses. However, until now thay have refrained from making such broadcasts for fear of violating the antilottery provisions of 18 U.S.C. Section 1304 and the corresponding FCC regulations.

On March 6, 1968, in an attempt to clarify the Commission's position on various types of broadcasts, petitioners filed a request for a declaratory ruling that 18 U.S.C. Section 1304 and the regulations did not apply to broadcasts about the New York State Lottery. More specifically, petitioners requested assurances that no sanction would be applied against a broadcaster who "broadcasts or proposes to broadcast" any of the following:

1. news reports (by aural or visual-and-aural means) of recent events about or relating to the Lottery. The term "news reports" is intended to include accounts suitable for inclusion as news in a newspaper, of events of current interest concerning the Lottery of its operations, or that have some connection with the Lottery. Attached as Appendix II are a number of articles and news items relating to the Lottery that were published in newspapers. The material is included to exemplify material deemed newsworthy by newspaper publishers, and by this inquiry the Association and Metromedia seek to determine if such reports, articles, and news items may be broadcast by radio and television stations;
2. news reports (by aural and visual-and-aural means) about illegal lotteries or other illegal gambling (but not including information tending to aid or facilitate the planning or operation of an illegal lottery);
3. announcements (unpaid) of the places where Lottery tickets may be purchased, where, how, and when winning tickets will be drawn, the amounts of the prizes, and how the proceeds of the sales of Lottery tickets are and will be distributed;
4. advertisements of the Lottery;
5. live broadcasts or simultaneous accounts of public events relating to the Lottery (for example, the broadcast by television of the drawing of the winning Lottery tickets by a prominent actress or by a government official, or the broadcast of a speech given by a public official such as the statement

made by Joseph H. Murphy, New York State Commissioner of Taxation and Finance, before a United States Senate Committee, in which Commissioner Murphy described the operation of the Lottery and its purposes and stated that banks in selling tickets for the Lottery were rendering a public service);
6. interviews with persons holding winning Lottery tickets, relating, among other matters of general interest, to the number of tickets they purchased, their expectation of winning a prize, their reactions upon learning that they held winning tickets, and what they did or intend to do with the prize money;
7. documentary programs on the Lottery, including such material as a) statements by and questioning of public officials, prominent citizens, and religious leaders who favor or oppose the Lottery, b) descriptions (by aural and visual-and-aural means) of the way the Lottery operates and the proceeds are used, and c) reporting the results of opinion polls on the Lottery;
8. documentary programs exposing illegal lotteries, including such material as how and where they operate (and if it is the fact) the knowledge, indifference, or participation of law enforcement officials, and showing effects of such illegal gambling on government, on the attitudes of the public, and on criminal conduct;*
9. editorial comment on the Lottery, on its operation, on its purposes, on the promotion of the Lottery and on the public officials who administer it;
10. panel discussions on various aspects of the Lottery, including those in which proponents and opponents, government officials who administer the Lottery, and others may participate, and in which questions and comments may be received from a studio audience.

Before the Commission, the State of New York supported petitioners' request for a ruling and has filed an amicus brief in this court. In addition, the City of New York, interested both in its governmental and fiscal capacity and as a licensed broadcaster, filed a separate request and was a party before the Commission although it has taken no formal part in these review proceedings.

On September 25, 1968, the Commission issued its declaratory ruling, holding that both the statute and the rules applied to state sponsored lotteries. With regard to the specific types of proposed broadcasts, the Commission rules as follows:

> 7. . . . It remains to be determined, in light of the language of the statute and rules, what, if anything, may properly be broadcast concerning this lottery. What is sought is an interpretation of the phrase "the broadcasting of, any advertisement of or information concerning any lottery," which is found in both the statute and the rules. It is clearly not practicable to attempt to rule on all of the various materials submitted by the parties in the absence of particular factual situations. However, some generalized guidance can be given.
>
> 8. The statute is plainly directed at material which promotes lotteries. This includes any material which, in the generally accepted sense of the terms, is intended to advertise, promote, or encourage the successful conduct of a lottery. In particular, of course, no advertisements of lotteries may be broadcast.
>
> 9. On the other hand, the phrase "any information" about lotteries, should not, on our view, be construed to bar ordinary news reports concerning legislation authorizing the institution of a State lottery, or of public debate on the course State policy should take. Licensee editorials

---

*To exemplify the programs that are the subject of the request for a ruling, there is attached as Appendix III the script of a program broadcast in 1963 entitled "Biography of a Bookie Joint."

on public policy in this area are also not, in our view, proscribed by the statute, and our rules are not to be read as prohibiting them. In the category of news, any material broadcast in normal good faith coverage, which is reasonably related to the audience's right and desire to know and be informed of the day-to-day happenings within the community is permissible.

Thereafter, petitioners filed their request for review of the Commission's declaratory ruling. They argue principally that the ruling is unconstitutional as an infringement of First Amendment rights in several respects. In response, the Government claims that petitioners are precluded from making their constitutional arguments because they did not raise them before the Commission and that the Commission's order was both constitutional and within the scope of the statute. We turn to the procedural question first.

II

The Commission issued the declaratory ruling under review in the exercise of its "sound discretion to terminate a controversy or remove uncertainty." Such rulings are authorized by the Administrative Procedure Act, 5 U.S.C. Section 554 (e); and, when the issues decided could otherwise be adjudicated by the Commission, they are reviewable "as in the case of other orders." The declaratory ruling is thus an order reviewable in this court under 47 U.S.C. Section 402(a). According to the Government, however, petitioners are precluded from making their constitutional arguments to us because they were not presented to the Commission either in the first instance or in a petition for reconsideration. Such a petition is made "a condition precedent to judicial review" by 47 U.S.C. Section 405 "where the party seeking such review . . . relies on questions of fact or law upon which the Commission . . . has been afforded no opportunity to pass."

We do not agree with the Government that petitioners are prevented from seeking judicial review at this time. It is true that the literal words of Section 405 provide for no exception, and two recent court of appeals decisions have applied the statute, or the general doctrine it embodies, in cases involving the scope of the Commission's power and the constitutionality of its action. In those situations, however, there was no attack on the constitutionality of an independent federal criminal statute, the issues involved basic broadcasting policies and the questions would probably have been resolved had they been presented to the Commission in the first instance. Thus, requiring exhaustion of administrative remedies served the usual goals of allowing agency expertise and discretion to be exercised and reducing the likelihood of additional litigation. Here, on the other hand, the Government apparently agrees that the Commission either would not or could not declare that 18 U.S.C. Section 1304 is unconstitutional, as petitioners contend. The Government does not suggest that it would have made any difference at all in the ruling of the Commission had the constitutional arguments been pressed by these petitioners. Indeed, the City of New York did explicitly raise those issues, so that they were before the Commission. Under these circumstances, we agree with petitioners that they were not required by 47 U.S.C. Section 405 to continue to seek administrative relief before petitioning for review.

III

In the Radio Act of 1927 and the Communications Act of 1934, Congress established a system of licensing and regulation to eliminate the chaos that threatened the new radio industry. In addition, Congress exercised to a limited extent the power to regulate and control the content of programming. Thus, in Section 316 of the 1934 Act, Congress enacted a prohibition against broadcasting lottery information which, with changes in phraseology, is now contained in 18 U.S.C. Section 1304:

Whoever broadcasts by means of any radio station for which a license is required by any law of the United States, or whoever, operating any such station, knowingly permits the broadcasting of, any advertisement of or information concerning any lottery, gift enterprise, or similar scheme, offering prizes dependent in whole or in part upon lot or chance, or any list of the prizes drawn or awarded by means of any such lottery, gift enterprise, or scheme, whether said list contains any part or all of such prizes, shall be fined not more than $1,000 or imprisoned not more than one year, or both. Each day's broadcasting shall constitute a separate offense.

In prohibiting the broadcasting of lottery information Congress was not acting in a vacuum; for more than one hundred years a prohibition on conducting a lottery by use of the mail facilities had existed. Similarly, prohibitions on importation and interstate shipment of lottery material also existed when section 1304 was enacted. (See 18 U.S.C. Section 1301.) It is true that Congress has not attempted to prohibit the conduct of lotteries; with narrowly prescribed exceptions the states have done that. But Congress has exercised its power—the existence of which petitioners concede—to inhibit lotteries and to aid the states by denying lottery promoters access to facilities over which the federal government has control.

It is in this light that the Commission's action must be considered—not as an exercise of the power to regulate broadcasting in the public interest necessitated by the nature and technology of broadcasting, but as enforcement of the clear congressional policy embodied in Section 1304. Indeed, the Commission has the duty to enforce that policy in passing on a broadcaster's license, and it has so informed broadcasters by the promulgation of regulations that essentially repeat the language of Section 1304. In its declaratory ruling, the Commission ruled that Section 1304 and the regulations apply to legal state conducted lotteries as well as to lotteries that violate state law. We agree with the Commission. Congress long ago stopped differentiating between legal and illegal lotteries, and as recently as 1067 enacted a law to prevent federally insured banks and savings institutions from selling lottery tickets for state operated lotteries. (See 18 U.S.C. Section 1306.) There can thus be no doubt that Congress intended to prohibit broadcast of lottery information regardless of the legality of the lottery under local law. While petitioners challenge the wisdom of enforcing a policy that runs contrary to state efforts to experiment with a lottery as an alternate device for raising revenue, that issue is for Congress, not us, to resolve.

Petitioners claim, however, that even though Congress has the power and intended to apply some controls on the broadcasting of lottery information, Section 1304, the regulations and the Commission's declaratory ruling violate the First Amendment and deprive them of property without due process of law. The Government responds that the constitutionality of section 1304 is well established.

Petitioners mount their attack in traditional free speech terms, citing well known cases which protect freedom of expression. Thus, they stoutly maintain that there can be no "official government view" which bans lottery information since the market place of ideas must be free to those who support lotteries. But the argument is basically misplaced. Petitioners admit, for example, that the First Amendment does not protect freedom to swindle even though words may be used to accomplish that result, a concession compelled by the Supreme Court's observation that:

> (T)he constitutional guarantees of freedom of speech and freedom of the press (do not) include complete freedom, uncontrollable by Congress, to use the mails for perpetration of swindling schemes.

(*Donaldson* v. *Read Magazine, Inc.*) Moreover, invoking the specter of an official government view does not dispose of the real issues before us. There is an "official" government view as to the sale of narcotics, the offering of fraudulent securities, the interstate transportation of wagering paraphernalia, and the coercion of employees by employers, to name only a few. And the view extends to communications which are designed to—and do—directly effectuate these unwanted results. Clearly an advertisement listing the names and addresses of sellers of narcotics or of fraudulent stock could constitutionally be banned. Of course, we do not suggest that lotteries are a swindle or that lotteries and uncontrolled sale of narcotics are equally deserving of condemnation, but Congress has the power to have a "view" as to these types of conduct and to take steps to inhibit each. Nor do we see a viable distinction here because there is legislative unanimity as to swindling or narcotics but a difference of opinion as to lotteries.

The real point here is that we are not primarily in the realm of ideas at all but are chiefly concerned with speech closely allied with the putting into effect of prohibited conduct. This is not to say that the statute under attack does not raise First Amendment issues. Thus, petitioners contend that Section 1304 is unconstitutional on its face, arguing that its broad terms improperly inhibit "lawful communication unconnected with the operating of a lottery." It is obvious that a literal reading of the statute would support petitioners' challenge, since by its terms it punishes the broadcasting of "any . . . information concerning any lottery." This could include, for example, an editorial for or against continuing the lottery experiment started by New York State in 1967. However, we do not believe—nor did the Commission—that such a broad construction of Section 1304 is warranted. The section obviously prohibits a licensed broadcaster from conducting a lottery on the air. But that prohibition alone would be almost meaningless; by its very nature, a lottery could be promoted by broadcasting information about it with essentially the same effect as conducting it. It is certainly reasonable that Congress acted to prohibit this possibility—the broadcasting of advertisements and information that directly promotes a particular lottery—and we think that the section must be strictly construed to go no further. The language of Section 1304 itself indicates that Congress did not intend that the phrase "information concerning any lottery" be literally construed; otherwise there would have been no need to make certain that lists of winners not be broadcast. Moreover, the words of Section 1304 were patterned after the language of the mail statute which had long been narrowly construed. And when it enacted Section 1304 Congress also directed the Commission to respect First Amendment values. Finally, as the Supreme Court has reminded us, Section 1304 "is a criminal statute" and as such "is to be strictly construed." *(FCC* v. *American Broadcasting Co.)* For all of these reasons, we think that the phrase "information concerning any lottery" refers only to information that directly promotes a particular existing lottery. As we have construed it, Section 1304 neither improperly restricts broadcasters to an official government view nor inhibits the free expression of ideas by reason of its overbreadth. Thus, petitioners' constitutional attacks must fail.

What remains is to consider the validity of the Commission's declaratory ruling in light of the above discussion. Petitioners complain about the order's lack of specificity as well as the Commission's failure to rule on a number of the requests made to it. We think these concerns are to some extent justified. There have apparently never been any prosecutions for violations of Section 1304, and we find no other judicial opinion explicitly interpreting the "information concerning" language of the statute. In view of this, and because of the great interest broadcasters have in not jeopardizing their licenses, we believe that the proper course is to set aside the Commission's declaratory ruling to allow it to reconsider petitioners' requests in light of this opinion.

116 Commercial Speech

A. Advertisements and Announcements

In their specific requests, petitioners sought rulings on whether broadcasts are permitted of (4) advertisements of the New York State Lottery or (3) "announcements (unpaid) of the places where Lottery tickets may be purchased, where, how, and when winning tickets will be drawn, the amounts of the prizes, and how the proceeds of the sales of Lottery tickets are and will be distributed." The Commission answered no as to (4), but its ruling as to (3) is less clear. From the papers before us, we assume that the only difference between items (3) and (4) is that advertisements are paid for and announcements are unpaid. In its ruling, the Commission states that the prohibition of "material which promotes lotteries" includes "any material, which, in the generally accepted sense of the terms, is intended to advertise, promote, or encourage the successful conduct of a lottery." This appears to be broader than our construction of Section 1304, which is that the statute is intended to reach only advertisements or information that directly promote a lottery. Thus, an announcement that a specified number of schools had been built with funds from the lottery might generally "encourage" the conduct of the Lottery, but we would not think that it directly promotes it. However, the contrary would be true if there were coupled with the announcement a plea to buy tickets or information as to when and how to make a purchase. There is a difference between information directly promoting a lottery and information that is simply "news" of a lottery. If a "news" item has the incidental effect of promoting a lottery, it is not banned; but if a lottery advertisement or announcement contains "news," such as the amount a lottery realized for education, it would nonetheless be banned. We are aware that at times the line drawn may be thin, but this will be the usual rather than the common case because advertisements and announcements will ordinarily be more direct and exhortative. We would expect the Commission to apply its expertise to the problem. In any event, although we think that even under our narrow construction of Section 1304 the Commission's ruling as to item (4) would in almost every instance be correct, we believe that petitioners are entitled to more specific guidance as to (3) and the assurance that as to both items and Commission is applying the proper test.

Finally, petitioners complain that the Commission's ban on all advertisements cannot stand in the light of the Supreme Court's decision that paid advertisements "on behalf of a movement whose existence and objectives are matters of highest public interest and concern" are entitled to full constitutional protection. *(New York Times, Co. v. Sullivan.)* While we agree with that statement of the law, petitioners are incorrect in claiming that all Lottery advertisements qualify because they seek public participation in a venture affecting the welfare of New York residents. We believe that petitioners' requests as to items (3) and (4) and the Commission's ruling on them envisioned advertisements or announcements of the usual Lottery promotion type to the extent that the information is incidental and subordinate to the promotion, and thus properly prohibited. Of course, petitioners and others are free to request rulings on material that meets the *Sullivan* test; and, if they do, we believe and the Government agrees that nothing in Section 1304 or the Commission's declaratory ruling prohibits such broadcasts.

B. News Broadcasts

In requests (1), (2), (5), (6), (7), (8), and (10), petitioners described general and specific types of news broadcasts. As far as we can tell, the Commission did not rule precisely on any of them, although it did state that reports on legislation or public debate on "the institution of a State lottery" are not banned. While we agree as to those specific rulings, there exists a possible implication that other types of news reports are not equally outside the scope of Section 1304. This is especially true in the light of a prior letter from the Commission's Secretary, casting doubt on the broadcast of "legitimate news" about the New Hampshire lottery and indicating that Section 1304 permits only news which is *incidentally* connected with a lottery." We believe that any such implication should be disclaimed by the Commission and that Section 1304 prohibits only so-called news that directly promotes the Lottery, e.g., broadcasting lists of winners. As to these, Congress has already made the reasonable determination that such information would be direct promotion of the Lottery. On the other hand, an interview by a television reporter with an excited winner—the counterpart of a newspaper feature story—would seem to us to be legitimate news and an indirect promotion at best. In any event, broadcasters in all fairness should be informed of the scope of the prohibition as specifically as possible. The Commission apparently agrees since it has indicated doubts in another context about imposing liability on a licensee in the absence of prior Commission or judicial decisions. Because of this, we hope that the Commission will take the opportunity to rule specifically on all or most of petitioners' requests—including whether sample newspaper reports or stories submitted to it by petitioners would be permitted on radio and television—with whatever qualifications are appropriate in the light of this opinion.

C. Editorials

The only one of petitioners' specific requests which remains to be discussed, number (9), referred to "editorial comment on the Lottery." Here too the ruling of the Commission specifically covered only editorials regarding a state's lottery policy. However, there should be no implication that other editorials by licensees are affected. In general, we do not believe that Section 1304 was intended to reach fair editorial comment at all and should be read as a ban only if the editorial format is used as a sham to avoid the prohibition on direct promotion of the Lottery.

The declaratory ruling of the Commission is set aside and the case remanded to the Commission for reconsideration and decision in conformity with this opinion.

CAPITAL BROADCASTING COMPANY v. *MITCHELL*
333 F. Supp. 582 (DCDC 1971)

MEMORANDUM OPINION

Gasch, District Judge.

Petitioners, six corporations which operate radio stations under licenses granted by the Federal Communications Commission, seek to enjoin enforcement of Section Six of the Public Health Cigarette Smoking Act of 1969 and to have Section Six declared violative of the First and Fifth Amendments to the Constitution. The National Association of Broadcasters has been permitted to intervene.

This three-judge court was convened pursuant to petitioners' application under 28 U.S.C. 2282 and 2284. We conclude that the Act in question does not conflict with the First or Fifth Amendments.

In 1965, in an attempt to alert the general public to the documented dangers of cigarette smoking, Congress enacted legislation requiring a health warning to be placed on all cigarette packages.[1] By 1969 it was evident that more stringent controls should be required and that both the FCC and the FTC were considering independent action. Under such circumstances Congress enacted the Public Health Cigarette Smoking Act of 1969, (hereafter referred to as the Act) which, as pertinent hereto, provides:

Sec. 6. After January 1, 1971, it shall be unlawful to advertise cigarettes on any medium of electronic communication subject to the jurisdiction of the Federal Commission.

Petitioners allege that the ban on advertising imposed by Section Six prohibits the "dissemination of information with respect to a lawfully sold product . . ." in violation of the First Amendment. It is established that product advertising is less vigorously protected than other forms of speech. The unique characteristics of electronic communication make it especially subject to regulation in the public interest. Whether the Act is viewed as an exercise of the Congress' supervisory role over the federal regulatory agencies or as an exercise of its power to regulate interstate commerce, Congress has the power to prohibit the advertising of cigarettes in any media. The validity of other, similar advertising regulations concerning the federal regulatory agencies has been repeatedly upheld whether the agency be the FCC, the FTC, or the SEC. Petitioners do not dispute the existence of such regulatory power, but urge that its exercise in context of the Act is unconstitutional. In that regard it is dispositive that the Act has no substantial effect on the exercise of petitioners' First Amendment rights. Even assuming that loss of revenue from cigarette advertisements affects petitioners with sufficient First Amendment interest, petitioners, themselves, have lost no right to speak—they have only lost an ability to collect revenue from others for broadcasting their commercial messages. Finding nothing in the Act or its legislative history which precludes a broadcast licensee from airing its own point of view on any aspect of the cigarette smoking question, it is clear that petitioners' speech is not at issue. Thus, contrary to the assertions made by petitioners, Section Six does not prohibit them from disseminating information about cigarettes, and, therefore, does not conflict with the exercise of their First Amendment rights.

The dissent relies upon *Banzhaf* v. *FCC* (1969), for the proposition that since cigarette commercials implicitly state a position on a matter of public importance, such ads are placed within the "core protection" of the First Amendment. As we read this decision, with which we are in full accord, it carefully distinguishes between First Amendment protections as such, and the rather limited extent to which product advertising is tangentially regarded as having some limited indicia of such protection. The fact that cigarette advertising is covered by the FCC's Fairness Doctrine does not require a finding that it is to be given full First Amendment protection, especially in light of contrary existing authority. We do not understand *Banzhaf* or any other decision which the dissent cites to go that far and we are unwilling to blaze that trail in this case.

Petitioners' Fifth Amendment contention raises a more direct constitutional question. Petitioners state their objection "is *not* that any ban upon cigarette advertising would violate the Due Process Clause. Rather, it is Congress' attempt, in Section Six of the Act, to classify media in two categories—those prohibited from carrying cigarette advertisements and those who are not—which contravenes the Fifth Amendment because the Distinctions drawn are 'arbitrary and invidious.' " To withstand due process challenge, a statutory classification must have a reasonable basis, and if such basis exists, the validity of the statute must be upheld without further inquiry. "(T)he law need not be in every respect logically consistent with its aims to be constitutional. It is enough that there is an evil at hand for correction, and that it might be thought that the particular legislative measure was a rational way to correct it." (*Williamson* v. *Lee Optical*.) Finally, Congress is entitled to a presumption "that if any state of facts might be supposed that would support its action, those facts must be presumed to exist." (*International Association of Machinists & Aerospace Workers* v. *National Mediation Board*.)

Under the above criteria there exists a rational basis for placing a ban on cigarette advertisements on broadcast facilities while allowing such advertisements in print. In 1969 Congress had convincing evidence that the labeling Act of 1965 had not materially reduced the incidence of cigarette smoking. Substantial evidence showed that the most persuasive advertising was being conducted on radio and television, and that these broadcasts were particularly effective in reaching a very large audience of young people.[2] Thus, Congress knew of the close relationship between cigarette commercials broadcast on the electronic media and their potential influence on young people, and was no doubt aware that the younger the individual, the greater the reliance on the broadcast message rather than the written word. A pre-school or early elementary school age child can hear and understand a radio commercial or see, hear, and understand a television commercial, while at the same time be substantially unaffected by an advertisement printed in a newspaper, magazine or one appearing on a billboard.

The fact is that there are significant differences between the electronic media and print. As the Court stated in *Banzhaf*:

> Written messages are not communicated unless they are read, and reading requires an affirmative act. Broadcast messages, in contrast are 'in the air.' In an age of omnipresent radio, there scarcely breathes a citizen who does not know some part of a leading jingle by heart. . . . It is difficult to calculate the subliminal impact of this pervasive propaganda, which may be heard even if not listened to, but it may reasonably be thought greater than the impact of the written word.

Moreover, Congress could rationally distinguish radio and television from other media on the basis that the public owns the airwaves and that licensees must operate broadcast facilities in the public interest under the supervision of a federal regulatory agency. Legislation concerning newspapers and magazines must take into account the fact that the printed media are privately owned.

Thus, Congress had information quite sufficient to believe that a proscription covering only the electronic media would be an appropriate response to the problem of cigarette advertising. Petitioners emphasize that much of the revenue formerly allocated to television and radio cigarette advertisements has been diverted to newspapers and magazines. The fact that the Act may create a new and perhaps potentially serious situation in the print media is not sufficient evidence to establish a due process violation. The Fifth Amendment does not compel legislatures "to prohibit all like evils, or none. A legislature may hit at an abuse which it has found, even though it has failed to strike at another." (*United States* v. *Carolene Products*.) Speculation concerning the final impact or success of the classification in question cannot erode the valid factual distinctions upon which such classification was predicated.

The petition for injunctive and declaratory relief is, accordingly, denied.

J. Skelly Wright, Circuit Judge (dissenting):

Cigarette smoking and the danger to health which it poses are among the most controversial and important issues before the American public today. Yet Congress, is passing the Public Health Cigarette Smoking Act of 1969, has suppressed the ventilation of these issues on the country's most pervasive communication vehicle—the electronic media.[3] Under the circumstances, in my judgment, no amount of attempted balancing of alleged compelling state interests against freedom of the press can save this Act from Constitutional condemnation under the First Amendment. The heavy hand of government has destroyed the scales.

It would be difficult to argue that there are many who mourn for the Marlboro Man or miss the ungrammatical Winston jingles. Most television viewers no doubt agree that cigarette advertising represents the carping hucksterism of Madison Avenue at its very worst. Moreover, overwhelming scientific evidence makes plain that the Salem girl was in fact a seductive merchant of death—that the real "Marlboro Country" is the graveyard. But the First Amendment does not protect only speech that is healthy or harmless. The Court of Appeals in this circuit has approved the view that "cigarette advertising implicity states a position on a matter of public controversy." (*Banzhaf* v. *FCC*.) For me, that finding is enough to place such advertising within the core protection of the First Amendment.

I

The *Banzhaf* case, decided three years ago, upheld an FCC determination that, since cigarette advertising was controversial speech on a public issue, the so-called "Fairness Doctrine" applied to it.[4] Stations carrying cigarette advertising were therefore required to "tell both sides of the story" and present a fair number of antismoking messages.

The history of cigarette advertising since *Banzhaf* has been a sad tale of well meaning but misguided paternalism, cynical bargaining, and lost opportunity. In the immediate wake of *Banzhaf*, the broadcast media were flooded with exceedingly effective antismoking commercials. For the first time in years, the statistics began to show a sustained trend toward lesser cigarette consumption. The *Banzhaf* advertising not only cost the cigarette companies customers, present and potential; it also put the industry in a delicate, paradoxical position. While cigarette advertising is apparently quite effective in inducing brand loyalty, it seems to have little impact on whether people in fact smoke. And after *Banzhaf*, these advertisements triggered the antismoking messages which were having a devastating effect on cigarette consumption. Thus the individual tobacco companies could not stop advertising for fear of losing their competitive position; yet for every dollar they spent to advance their product, they forced the airing of more antismoking advertisements and hence lost more customers.

It was against this backdrop that the Consumer Subcommittee of the Senate Committee on Commerce met to consider new cigarette legislation. The legislative prohibition against requiring health warnings in cigarette advertisements had just expired, and the Federal Trade Commission had indicated that it might soon require such warnings if not again stopped by Congress. In addition, the FCC was moving toward rule making which would have removed cigarette advertising from the electronic media. Thus Congress had to decide whether to extend the ban on FTC action and institute a similar restraint against the FCC or, alternatively, to allow the regulatory agencies to move forcefully against cigarette advertisements.

The context in which this decision had to be made shifted dramatically when a representative of the cigarette industry suggested that the Subcommittee draft legislation permitting the companies to remove their advertisements from the air.[5] In retrospect, it is hard to see why this announcement was thought surprising. The *Banzhaf* ruling had clearly made electronic media advertising a losing proposition for the industry, and a voluntary withdrawal would have saved the companies approximately $250,000,000 in advertising costs, relieved political pressure for FTC action,[6] and removed most antismoking messages from the air. At the time, however, the suggestion of voluntary withdrawal was taken by some as a long delayed demonstration of industry altruism. Congress quickly complied with the industry's suggestion by banning the airing of television and radio cigarette commercials. Moreover, the new legislation provided additional rewards for the industry's "altruism" including a delay in pending FTC action against cigarette advertising and a prohibition against stricter state regulation of cigarette advertising and packaging. The result of the legislation was that as both the cigarette advertisements and most antismoking messages left the air, the tobacco companies transferred their advertising budgets to other forms of advertising such as newspapers and magazines where there was no Fairness Doctrine to require a response.

The passage of the Public Health Cigarette Smoking Act of 1969 marked a dramatic legislative *coup* for the tobacco industry. With the cigarette smoking controversy removed from the air, the decline in cigarette smoking was abruptly halted and cigarette consumption almost immediately turned upward again.[7] Thus whereas the *Banzhaf,* which required that both sides of the controversy be aired,[8] significantly depressed cigarette sales, the 1969 legislation which effectively banned the controversy from the air, had the reverse effect. Whereas the *Banzhaf* decision had increased the flow of information by air so that the American people could make an informed judgment on the hazards of cigarette smoking, the 1969 Act cut off the flow of information altogether.[9]

Of course, the fact that the legislation in question may be a product of skillful lobbying or of pressures brought by narrow private interests, or may have been passed by Congress to favor a particular industry, does not necessarily affect its constitutionality. But when the "inevitable effect" of the legislation is the production of an unconstitutional result, the statute cannot be allowed to stand. The legislative history related above shows that the effect of this legislation was to cut off debate on the value of cigarettes just when *Banzhaf* had made such a debate a real possibility. The theory of free speech is grounded on the belief that people will make the right choice if presented with all points of view on a controversial issue. When *Banzhaf* opened the electronic media to different points of view on the desirability of cigarette smoking, this theory was dramatically vindicated. Once viewers saw both sides of the story, they began to stop or cut down on smoking in ever increasing numbers. Indeed, it was presumably the very success of the *Banzhaf* doctrine in allowing people to make an informed choice that frightened the cigarette industry into calling on Congress to silence the debate.

II

This is not an ordinary "free speech" case. It involves expression which is ostensibly apolitical, advocating a particularly noxious habit through a medium which the government has traditionally regulated more extensively than other modes of communication. But the unconventional aspects of the problem should not distract us from the basic First Amendment principles involved. Any statute which suppresses speech over any medium for any purpose begins with a presumption against its validity. If the government is able to come forward with constitutionally valid reasons why this presumption should be overcome, then of course the statute will be allowed to stand. But where, as here, the reasons offered are inconsistent with the purposes of the First Amendment, it becomes the duty of the courts to invalidate the statute.

Thus it may be true, as the government argues, that the special characteristics of the electronic media justify greater governmental regulation than would be permitted for the print media.

Cases such as *Red Lion, Banzhaf,* and *United Church of Christ* are consistent with this approach in that they uphold government power to insure wider access to the means of communication and persuasion. But these decisions in no way serve as precedent for the use of government power to shut off debate on a vital public issue. If the First Amendment means anything at all, it means that Congress lacks this power. There is no constitutional warrant for government censorship of any medium of communication.

Thus the government fails to meet its burden by simply asserting broad regulatory power over the broadcast media. If the statutory ban on cigarette advertising is to withstand constitutional scrutiny, there must be a further showing that either the advertising is not speech within the meaning of the First

Amendment, or it creates a clear and present danger of such substantial magnitude that governmental suppression is justified. While the government in fact makes both of these arguments, I find neither of them persuasive in the context of this case.

Although the status of commercial or "product" advertising under the First Amendment has not been finally resolved, it must be conceded that some cases seem to accord it lesser protection than political or artistic speech. Indeed, as the court in *Banzhaf* stated: "As a rule, (product advertising) does not affect the political process, does not contribute to the exchange of ideas, does not provide information on matters of public importance, and is not, except perhaps for the ad-men, a form of individual self-expression." Commentators too have argued that product advertising is generally unrelated to the values which the First Amendment was designed to preserve, and that broad state regulation should therefore be permitted.

These arguments are no doubt persuasive when applied to most of the activities of Madison Avenue. But it does not follow from their general validity that the words "product advertising" are a magical incantation which, when piously uttered, will automatically decide cases without the benefit of further thought. Thus, when commercial speech has involved matters of public controversy, or artistic expression, or deeply held personal beliefs, the courts have not hesitated to accord it full First Amendment protection.

In my view, this circuit's decisions in *Banzhaf* and *Friends of the Earth* v. *FCC* implicitly recognize this special status which certain forms of product advertising enjoy. Both *Banzhaf* and *Friends of the Earth* suggest that the Fairness Doctrine is not relevant to normal commercial messages. Yet the doctrine was applied in the case of cigarette and automobile advertisements because they, unlike ordinary commercial speech, were controversial statements on important public issues. It can hardly be contended that cigarette commercials are "controversial speech" for purposes of the First Amendment based Fairness Doctrine, yet mere "product advertising" for the purposes of the First Amendment. The *Banzhaf* court recognized that the desirability of cigarette smoking had become a vital question of public concern, and that cigarette advertisements were a part of the debate surrounding that question. The court then went on to hold that "(w)here a controversial issue with potentially grave consequences is left to each individual to decide for himself, the need for an abundant and ready supply of relevant information is too obvious to need belaboring."

Indeed, the desirability of cigarette smoking has become still more controversial since *Banzhaf* was decided. Issues such as whether Congress should end price supports for tobacco, require stricter health warnings, or even outlaw the sale of cigarettes altogether are matters of widespread public debate. The Surgeon General has stated and reiterated his official position that the health hazards of cigarette smoking make it an undesirable habit. The government is, of course, entitled to take that position and to attempt to persuade the American people of its validity. But the government is emphatically not entitled to monopolize the debate or to suppress the expression of opposing points of view on the electronic media by making such expression a criminal offense. Of course, it is true that the courts have on occasion recognized a narrow exception to these general First Amendment principles. Where otherwise protected speech can be shown to present a "clear and present danger" of a severe evil which the state has a right to prevent, suppression of that speech has on occasion been permitted. The argument is made here that the state has an overwhelming interest in the preservation of the health of its citizens and that cigarette advertising poses a clear and present danger to this interest.

Although this argument is superficially attractive, it cannot withstand close scrutiny. The clear and present danger test has always been more or less confined to cases where the state has asserted an overriding interest in its own preservation or in the maintenance of public order. While it cannot be denied that public health is also a vital area of state concern, it is different from the state interest in security in one crucial respect. Whereas there are always innocent victims in riots and revolutions, the only person directly harmed by smoking cigarettes is the person who decides to smoke them. The state can stop speech in order to protect the innocent bystander, but it cannot impose silence merely because it fears that people will be convinced by what they hear and thereby harm themselves. As cases like *Stanley* v. *Georgia* and *Griswold* v. *Connecticut* make clear, the state has no interest at all in what people read, see, hear, or think in the privacy of their own home or in front of their own television set. At the very core of the First Amendment is the notion that people are capable of making up their own minds about what is good for them and that they can think their own thoughts so long as they do not in some manner interfere with the rights of others.

III

This opinion is not intended as a Magna Carta for Madison Avenue. In my view, Congress retains broad power to deal with the evils of cigarette advertising. It can force the removal of deceptive claims, require manufacturers to couple their advertisements with a clear statement of the hazardous nature of their product, and provide for reply time to be awarded to anticigarette groups. But the one thing which Congress may not do is cut off debate altogether.

The only interest which might conceivably justify such a total ban is the state's interest in preventing people from being convinced by what they hear—the very sort of paternalistic interest which the First Amendment precludes the state from asserting. Even if this interest were sufficient in the purely commercial context, the *Banzhaf* decision makes clear that cigarette messages are not ordinary product advertising but rather speech on a controversial issue of public importance, *viz.*, the desirability of cigarette smoking. The government simply cannot have it both ways. Either this is controversial speech in the public arena or it is not. If it is such speech, the Section Six of the Public Health Cigarette Smoking Act is unconstitutional; if it is not, then *Banzhaf* was wrongly decided. Although I respect the opinon of my colleagues in this case, my own view is that the *Banzhaf* decision was correct and that this law is unconstitutional. I come to that position not only because *stare decisis* dictates it, but also because I think that when people are given both sides of the cigarette controversy, they will make the correct decision. That, after all, is what the First Amendment is all about. And our too brief experience with the *Banzhaf* doctrine shows that the theory works in practice.

I respectfully dissent.

NOTES

[1] The required warning states: "Caution: Cigarette Smoking May be Hazardous to Your Health."

[2] The FTC Report of 1967 presented strong evidence of a great attraction on the part of young people to the broadcast media. Typical of the data is the following: Teenage boys surveyed averaged 4.3 hours of radio listening *daily*; teenage girls surveyed averaged 5.3 hours; in every half-hour segment from 8:00 P.M. until 11:00 P.M. radio delivers a minimum (audience) of 24.1 percent of all teenagers; and 87.9 percent of teenage girls hear radio on the average day. The statistics for television were equally impressive. Along with other experts, Congress had the benefit of the testimony of Joseph Cullman, Chairman of Philip Morris, Inc., who stated: . . . I think further that broadcast is quite different from print media. We think that the print media appeals to a more adult person and as such is a more appropriate place for cigarette ads." Hearings on H.R. 6543 before the Consumer Subcommittee of the Committee on Commerce, 91st Cong., 1st Sess. at 115 (1969).

[3] The Act provides: "After January 1, 1971, it shall be unlawful to advertise cigarettes on any medium of electronic communication subject to the jurisdiction of the Federal Communications Commission." In addition, the Act slightly modifies the warning appearing on cigarette packs, prohibits the state from imposing stricter requirements on cigarette advertising and packaging, and extends the ban on Federal Trade Commission action against cigarette advertising.

[4] Because some doubt as to the constitutionality of the Fairness Doctrine existed at that time, the *Banzhaf* court actually rested its decision on the broader "public interest" standard which broadcasters are required to meet. However, *Red Lion Broadcasting Co. v. FCC* has now made clear that the Fairness Doctrine is in fact constitutional. This circuit has thus grounded its subsequent extension of the *Banzhaf* rule squarely on the Fairness Doctrine.

[5] The cigarette companies requested an antitrust exemption so they could reach an agreement among themselves not to advertise on the electronic media without fear of prosecution for restraint of trade.

[6] The Chairman of the FTC had made known his agency's willingness to suspend its proposed requirement of health warnings in all cigarette advertisements if the advertising were removed from the electronic media. *See* Senate Hearing at 172.

[7] The figures on total U.S. cigarette consumption from 1967 to the present are quite striking. U.S. consumption reached a peak of 549.2 billion cigarettes in 1967, the year before the *Banzhaf* ruling. As the *Banzhaf* messages begun to appear on the air in late 1968, consumption began to drop for the first time in two years. It slipped to 545.7 billion in 1968 and 528.9 billion in 1969. Cigarette commercials and most *Banzhaf* messages left the air on January 1, 1970, and their departure was accompanied by an immediate resumption of the upward trend in consumption. In 1970, 536.4 billion cigarettes were consumed in the United States and the projected figure for 1971 is 546.0 billion. The Department of Agriculture has concluded that "U.S. consumption of cigarettes in calendar 1971 likely will gain 2 percent over 1970 . . . . Per capita use is steadying after decline for the past 4 years. With prospects for these factors to continue in 1972, cigarette consumption may again show a small gain." These gains in cigarette consumption are reflected, in turn, in a resumption of prosperous conditions in the cigarette industry.

[8] *Banzhaf* had required broadcasters carrying cigarette messages to carry the antismoking messages free of charge under certain circumstances. With the removal of cigarette advertising, only those antismoking groups who could afford to buy time or who succeeded in persuading broadcasters to donate it remained on the air.

[9] Some of the language in *Banzhaf* makes clear just how far removed the Public Health Cigarette Smoking Act of 1969 is from the spirit which informed that ruling. The *Banzhaf* court argued:

> . . . (I)f we are to adopt petitioners' analysis, we must conclude that Congress legislated to curtail the potential flow of information lest the public learn too much about the hazards of smoking for the good of the tobacco industry and the economy. We are loathe (sic) to impute such a purpose to Congress absent a clear expression. *Where a controversial issue with potentially grave consequences is left to each individual to decide for himself, the need for an abundant and ready supply of relevant information is too obvious to need belaboring.*

HM DISTRIBUTORS v. DEPARTMENT OF AGRICULTURE
55 Wis. 2d 261, 198 NW 2d 598 (1972)

Robert W. Hansen, Justice.

By terms of an action for declaratory relief, the proper procedure, the plaintiff challenges a statute and rules of the state department of agriculture.

THE STATUTE

The statute involved authorizes the state Department of Agriculture to issue orders forbidding methods of competition in business or trade practices in business which are determined by the department to be unfair.[1]

THE RULES

Following a public hearing on the proposed rules, the state Department of Agriculture issued the rules prohibiting the promoting, offering, or granting of participation in a "chain distributor scheme," defining the term as a sales device whereby a person making an investment is granted a license to recruit for profit one or more additional persons who are then granted such license to recruit.[2]

THE TRADE PRACTICE

It is not disputed that one phase of the marketing program of plaintiff-appellant collides head-on with the quoted rules. The challenge is to the validity of the rules and of the statute which authorized them. Not involved in the collision is the general distribution setup for the marketing program for plaintiff-appellant's products. The multilevel structure begins with a door-to-door sales person, who purchases her supplies from an "organizer" who purchases the products from a "master distributor" who receives his materials from the company, but pays for them through a "general distributor." It is at the level of the "general distributor" that the chain distributor scheme is introduced.

A person can work his way up through the organization to become a "general distributor" or can "buy in." In either case, the total payment of $6,500 to $3,500 is for products; $3,000 is an "escrow" payment to be held by the company until the new "general distributor" recruits a "master distributor." Additionally, each time an existing "general distributor" recruits a new "general distributor" it appears that he is to be paid $4,299 and it is specifically represented that ". . . if you did this once each month for the next year . . . you would have earned $51,588 at the end of 12 months . . . ." This is a summarization, but no more is needed where it is conceded that the practice of plaintiff-appellant is prohibited by the rules issued by the Agriculture Department.

THE ISSUES RAISED

In seeking declaratory judgment, the plaintiff-appellant argues that the agriculture department's rules 1) exceed the statutory authority of the department; 2) were not promulgated in accordance with the rule making procedures required; 3) are vague and overbroad; and 4) violate constitutional rights of freedom to make economic investments and freedom of speech. Each issue raised will be dealt with separately.

STATUTORY AUTHORITY EXCEEDED?

Sec. 100.20(1), Stats., prohibits "unfair methods of competition in business" and "unfair trade practices." The plaintiff-appellant finds the use of both terms conjunctively a redundancy. The contention is that the term "unfair trade practices" is contained within and limited to "unfair methods of competition." If accepted, this narrowed interpretation would leave competitors the sole category sought to be protected by the legislative enactment. It would leave investors, purchasers, and others outside the list of those affected by "unfair trade practices." Such construction would hardly give effect to all parts of the statute. When the term "unfair trade practice" was added to "unfair methods of competition in business," the mantle of protection against unfair practices was extended beyond those engaged in making or selling the same or similar products. We hold that the Agriculture Department was entitled to act to protect those, other than business competitors, injured or affected by unfairness in trade practices. As the United States Supreme Court said, quoting the language of the Congress of the United States, in explaining why the words "unfair or deceptive acts or practices" were added to a federal statute which had previously prohibited only "unfair methods of competition:"

> . . . this amendment makes the consumer, who may be injured by an unfair trade practice, of equal concern, before the law, with the merchant or manufacturer injured by the unfair methods of a dishonest competitor . . . .

The trial court in this case held: "Schemes which can cause the loss of money and the victimization of third persons clearly fall within the term 'unfair trade practices' . . . The authority granted to the Department to regulate 'unfair trade practices' was properly exercised within its statutory authority." We agree, and, as a postscript, repeat what this court, many year ago, had to say about the chain letter idea used as a trade practice:

> . . . the real arrangement was a joint scheme to make money by selling similar nominal territorial rights to others who should also, become parties to the scheme and sell similar territorial rights to still others, and so on . . . .it will infallibly leave a greater or less crowd of dupes at the end with no opportunity to recoup their losses because the bubble has at last burst. It contemplates an endless chain of purchasers, or, rather, a series of constantly multiplying endless chains, with nothing but fading rainbows as the reward of those who are unfortuante enough to become purchasers the moment before the collapse of the scheme . . . Such an enterprise we regard as contrary to public policy and void . . . .

PROCEDURE PROPER?

Plaintiff-appellant contends that proper and required rule making procedures were not followed in the adoption of the no chain distributors' rules. Three points are argued:

1. That the required public hearing was held on proposed rules, not adopted rules. The purpose of a public hearing is to give interested parties not only a chance to be heard, but also to have an influence in the final form of the regulations involved. That purpose would not be served if the adopted rules were required to be identical in form to those proposed before the hearing. A question of the need for an additional hearing might well arise where the rules as adopted bore little resemblance to the rules as proposed. Here, where the rules as proposed vary from the rules as adopted only in details of wording and where the scheme prohibited was identical in both, we see no basis for complaint, much less for successful challenge.

2. That the statutory requirement of ". . . a summary of the factual information which its proposal is based . . ."was not met. The trial court specifically found that such summary was presented and that it related to the rules in question. Additionally, the trial court found that: ". . . No evidence was presented which would indicate that the basic procedures were not followed . . . ." The issue involves a question of fact, and the trial court ruling resolves it. On this record, as to this challenge, it is difficult to see how any other finding of fact could have been made.

3. That the department failed to comply with the statutory requirement that ". . . The agency shall keep minutes or a record of the hearing in such manner as it determines to be desirable and feasible." It is conceded that a tape recorded record of the hearing was kept, but plaintiff-appellant contends this does not meet the statutory requirement. The wording of the statute gives the administrative agency wide latitude in determining the means by which a record of the proceedings are to be kept. The trial court's finding that the tape recording was adequate is sustained, particularly because the plaintiff-appellant failed to show that it was in any way denied access to the recording made and record kept.

VOID FOR VAGUENESS?

The focus of attack here is on words used in the rules as promulgated, the claim being that they are inadequately defined. As to some of the words challenged, any standard or law dictionary gives a clear and accepted definition. A "promoter" is a person "who promotes, urges on, encourages, incites, advances, etc.," and "promotion" is the act of doing just that. "Recruiting" is "the raising of recruits," and a "recruit" is "a newcomer to a field of activity." "Recruiting for profit," in the context of these rules, occurs when any person makes money by inducing another to purchase a right or license authorizing the purchaser to also sell such licenses, carrying on the chain of recruitment of license holders. (The label of "stipulated damages" for the asserted economic loss done by the introduction of a new member does not change the realities of the scheme. Whether the person recruited for profit was or was not already somewhere in the distribution system of the plaintiff-appellant would not change the fact that recruitment for profit under the scheme takes place when any nonlicense holder is induced to purchase a license in the chain distributor scheme.)

As to two other words challenged, "investment" and "chain distributor scheme," they are clearly and adequately defined in the Department rules. "Investment" is sufficiently defined as "any acquisition for a consideration other than personal services, of personal property, tangible or intangible, for profit or business purposes . . . ."[3] The key phrase, "chain distributor scheme" is very precisely defined in rules.[4] Clearly stated in the definition are these elements: 1) A person must be granted a license or right, 2) in return for an investment, 3) which gives him the right to recruit for profit, 4) persons to whom similar licenses are granted, 5) in return for an investment. Explicit language in the rules answers plaintiff-appellant's suggestion that its limit of one "general distributor" per ten thousand of population rescues the scheme from illegality. It does not.[5]

In setting the standard for certainty of language in statutes, and certainly the certainty required in administrative rules would be no greater, this court said: "Unless a statute is so vague and uncertain that it is impossible to execute it or to ascertain the legislative intent with reasonable certainty, it is valid . . . ."[6] The rules here challenged meet the test, are not void for vagueness.

CONSTITUTIONAL RIGHTS INVADED?

Plaintiff-appellant finds two Constitutional rights invaded by the Agriculture Department's rules: 1) the right of a person to make the economic investment he chooses; and 2) the right of freedom of speech.

"Upon proper disclosure of information," plaintiff-appellant's brief contends, "a person has the right to make the economic investment he chooses." Every bucket shop operator would applaud the statement, although he might be surprised to have it claimed that the right of his customers to be defrauded is somewhere in the United States Constitution. The proverb stated that "A fool and his money are soon parted," but we did not suspect that accelerating the parting enjoyed Constitutional protection. The plaintiff-appellant does concede to government the right to "protect the public from fraud," but contends "it cannot prevent a citizen from knowledgeably investing in a project he may be aware is speculative" because, as the brief puts it, "Clearly, freedom includes the notion of making one's own economic decisions."

Like the chain distributor scheme which it is invoked to legitimize, the concept is breathtakingly imaginative. However, we do not find anywhere in the United States Constitution or the case cited an authority for denying to the state the right to prohibit "unfair methods of competition" or "unfair trade practices." The right of the sheep to be sheared at a roulette wheel or in a chain distributor scheme is not Consitutionally placed beyond the reach of legislative action and administrative regulations based thereon.

Nor can the proposition that a con man has a Constitutional right to defraud the public so long as he reveals the details of his scheme to the victim be based on the claim that the First Amendment right of freedom of speech is invaded by regulating or prohibiting unfair trade practices or false and misleading advertising of a product or economic opportunity. The United States Supreme Court has held that the Constitutional protection afforded free speech does not apply to commercial advertising, and we find entirely and obviously correct the federal appeals court holding that the nonapplicability extends to the promoting of products.[7] The role of the "spieler" in inducing prospective purchasers to invest their money is not to be underestimated. Whether the proposition is a chance in a carnival shell game or buying a piece of real estate or a share of stock in a legitimate business enterprise, the selling of it involves speaking or writing, almost always. However, the right to regulate or prohibit derives from the nature of the undertaking, what is being done or attempted, not what is said in explaining or selling it. In the record in this case is the script of a sales pitch presentation, termed an "Opportunity Meeting," designed to induce persons to participate in both the legal and now illegal aspects of plaintiff-appellant's marketing and distributor setup. The company-provided script sternly admonishes that "There will be positively no 'ad-libbing' or deviation from this script." Speaking is involved, but the right to prohibit as an unfair trade practice the chain distributor scheme derives from what is being peddled and how it is being peddled. The right to regulate or prohibit derives from the unfairness of what is done and the scheme is not saved by the sales pitch that accompanies it.

Judgment affirmed.

NOTES

[1] Sec. 100.20, Stats., entitled "Methods of competition and trade practices" provides:

1. Methods of competition in business and trade practices in business shall be fair. Unfair methods of competition in business and unfair trade practices in business are hereby prohibited.

2. The department (of agriculture), after public hearing, may issue general orders forbidding methods of competition in busines or trade practices in business which are determined by the department to be unfair. The department, after public hearing, may issue general orders prescribing methods of competition in business or trade practices in business which are determined by the department to be fair.

[2] Ag. 122.03 Prohibition. No person shall promote, offer, or grant participation in a chain distributor scheme.

"Ag. 122.02 Definitions. 1) 'chain distributor scheme' is a sales device whereby a person, upon a condition that he make an investment, is granted a license or right to recruit for profit one or more additional persons who also are granted such license or right upon condition of making an investment and may further perpetuate the chain of persons who are granted such license or right upon such condition . . . .

"Ag. 122.01 Unfair trade practice. The promotional use of a chain distributor scheme in connection with the solicitation of business investments from members of the public is an unfair trade practice under section 100.20. Wis.Stats. When so used, the scheme serves as a lure to improvident uneconomical investment. Many small investors lack commercial expertise and anticipate unrealistic profits through use of the chance to further perpetuate a chain of distributors, without regard to actual market conditions affecting further distribution and sale of the property purchased by them or its market acceptance by final users or consumers. Substantial economic losses to participating distributors have occurred and will inevitably occur by reason of their reliance on perpetuation of the chain distributor scheme as a source of profit."

[3] Ag. 122.02(2) further states: ". . . and includes, without limitation, franchises, business opportunities, and services. It does not include real estate, securities registered under chapter 551. Wis.Stats., or sales demonstration equipment and materials furnished at cost for use in making sales and not for resale."

[4] See: Ag. 122.02(1) quoted in fn. 2, supra.

[5] Ag. 122.02(1) specifically provides: ". . . A limitation as to the number of persons who may participate, or the presence of additional conditions affecting eligibility for the above license or right to recruit or the receipt of profits therefrom, does not change the identity of the scheme as a chain distributor scheme."

[6] *Forest Home Dodge, Inc.* v. *Karns* (1965), 29 Wis. 2d 78, 94 138 NW 2d 214, 222, quoting with approval 50 Am. Jur., Statutes, page 489, sec. 473, stating: " 'A statute is not necessarily void merely because it is vague, indefinite, or uncertain, or contains terms not susceptible of exact meaning, or is stated in general terms, or prescribes a general course of conduct, or does not prescribe precise boundaries, or is imperfect in its details, or contains errors or omissions, or because the intention of the legislature might have been expressed in plainer terms, and questions may arise as to its applicability, and opinions may differ in respect of what falls within its terms, or because the statute is difficult to execute.' "

[7] *Banzhaf* v. *Federal Communications Commission* (1968), 132 U.S. App. DC 14, 405 F.2d 1982, 1101, 1102, holding: ". . . Promoting the sale of a product is not ordinarily associated with any of the interests the First Amendment seeks to protect . . . . It is rather a form of merchandising subject to limitation for public purposes like other business practices . . . ."

HOLIDAY MAGIC, INC. v. *WARREN*
357 F.Supp. 20 (1973)

Reynolds, District Judge.

The question in this litigation is whether Wisconsin may prohibit the promotion of a chain distributor or "pyramid" scheme without running afoul of certain provisions of the federal Constitution. Jurisdiction arises under 28 U.S.C. Sections 1331 and 1343(3). The plaintiff corporations are charged with employing such a scheme. Together with an individual plaintiff they have moved for the convening of a three-judge court to declare unconstitutional Ag. 122, a general order of the Wisconsin Department of Agriculture, and to enjoin its further enforcement. Defendant state officials have opposed that request and have moved to dismiss. The motions for the convening of a three-judge court and to dismiss were briefed and argued together. I have concluded that the federal Constitutional claims are insubstantial. This conclusion prohibits me from requesting the convening of a three-judge court and requires me to dismiss the complaint for want of jurisdiction.

The alleged Constitutional defects in Ag. 122 are that it violates freedom of speech, that it fails to give adequate notice of the conduct prohibited, that it constitutes an undue burden on interstate commerce, that it intrudes into an area pre-empted by the federal government, that it violates plaintiffs' right to work, that it impairs the obligation of contracts, that it bears no rational relation to a valid state purpose, and that it results in discriminatory enforcement. The general order provides:

> "Ag. 122.01 Unfair trade practice. The promotional use of a chain distributor scheme in connection with the solicitation of business investments from members of the public is an unfair trade practice under Section 100.20, Wis.Stats. When so used the scheme serves as a lure to improvident and uneconomical investment. Many small investors lack commercial expertise and anticipate unrealistic profits through use of the chance to further perpetuate a chain of distributors, without regard to actual market conditions affecting further distribution and sale of the property purchased by them or its market acceptance by final users or consumers. Substantial economic losses to participating distributors have occurred and will inevitably occur by reason of their reliance on perpetuation of the chain distributor scheme as a source of profit.

"Ag. 122.02 Definitions. 1) 'Chain distributor scheme' is a sales device whereby a person, upon a condition that he make an investment, is granted a license or right to recruit for profit one or more additional persons who also are granted such license or right upon condition of making an investment and may further perpetuate the chain of persons who are granted such license or right upon such condition. A limitation as to the number of persons who may participate, or the presence of additional conditions affecting eligibility for the above license or right to recruit or the receipt of profits therefrom, does not change the identity of the scheme as a chain distributor scheme.

"2) 'Investment' is any acquisition, for a consideration other than personal services, of personal property, tangible or intangible, for profit or business purposes, and includes, without limitation, franchises, business opportunities, and services. It does not include real estate, securities registered under chapter 551, Wis.Stats., or sales demonstration equipment and materials furnished at cost for use in making sales and not for resale.

"3) 'Person' includes partnerships, corporations, and associations.

"Ag. 122.03 Prohibition. No person shall promote, offer, or grant participation in a chain distributor scheme.

"Ag. 122.04 Statutory exemption. This chapter does not apply to banks, savings and loan associations, insurance companies, and public utilities to the extent exempted from Department regulations under Section 93.01(13), Wis.Stats."

The general order was issued pursuant to authority vested in the Department of Agriculture by Section 100.20 of the Wisconsin Statutes which provides in part:

Methods of competition and trade practices. 1) Methods of competition in business and trade practices in business shall be fair. Unfair methods of competition in business and unfair trade practices in business are hereby prohibited.

2) The Department, after public hearing, may issue general orders forbidding methods of competition in business or trade practices in business which are determined by the department to be unfair.

6) The Department may commence an action in circuit court in the name of the state to restrain by temporary or permanent injunction the violation of any order issued under this section.

Violating an order issued under Section 100.20 subjects a person to a fine of not less than $25 nor more than $5,000 and to imprisonment of not more than one year. (Wis.Stats. Section 100.26(3).) Violating an injunction issued pursuant to Section 100.20(6) subjects a person to a civil forfeiture of not less than $100 nor more than $10,000. (Wis.Stats. Section 100.26(6).)

THE FIRST AMENDMENT

The alleged First Amendment violation lies in prohibiting the mere "promotion" of a chain distributor scheme. Promotion alone, plaintiffs argue, may involve only speech. Consequently, the argument goes, the state may not restrict it without showing that it urges imminent lawless action of an extremely serious nature.

Past opinions of the United States Supreme Court make the decision of the First Amendment claim as easy to reach as it is difficult to justify. In an unbroken line of decisions the Supreme Court, and lower courts as well, have distinguished between the expression protected by the First Amendment and the use of speech, whether truthful or not, in a commercial context like that presented here.[1]

As commentators have noted, the rationale for the distinction is seldom made explicit, and the tests for distinguishing between commercial and noncommercial expression would never survive evenhanded application. For example, the original test implied in *Valentine* v. *Chrestensen,* considered commercial all expression made for the primary purposes of commercial gain. Yet commercial gain is no doubt the primary purpose of many involved in labor disputes and of innumerable authors, journalists, dramatists, and others who earn their livelihood through expression that is unquestionably entitled to First Amendment protection. Even if the expression of professional writers is considered noncommercial, despite the commercial purpose, on the ground that the gain arises from selling the expression itself rather than from using the expression to sell some other product, the expression of those, for example, who advertise to raise funds for a political purpose would still have to be considered commercial under the "primary purpose" test. Yet in *New York Times, Co.* v. *Sullivan* (1964), the Supreme Court granted First Amendment protection to political advertisements, noting that neither the desire to raise funds nor the commercial form of the expression dictated a contrary result. Instead the opinion in *New York Times* implied a new ground for identifying commercial expression and denying it protection; namely, that it dealt exclusively with matters of private rather than public concern. But it is apparent that informative commercial expression dealing with, for example, the safety, cost, and quality of consumer products or, as in this case, the wisdom of possible investments, involves matters of public concern. The concern about the characteristics of products and investments is often more widespread than the concern about labor disputes; individuals will often better develop their capacity to govern themselves and influence their society by evaluating a sales pitch than by reading the crime-oriented magazines and comics granted protection in other cases.

Despite the conceptual difficulties in articulating a test to distinguish commercial from noncommercial expression, the decision to deny protection to commercial expression reflects the Supreme Court's sound judgment about the function of the First Amendment. Put simply, the use of speech to sell products or promote commercial ventures bears little, if any, relation to the discussion of politics, religion, philosophy, art, and other more mundane subjects which the Supreme Court believes the First Amendment was historically designed to protect. Where the government is often barred from interfering with an individual's free choice on those subjects where expression is protected, it has taken an active role in regulating individual behavior in commercial marketplace. That commercial activity takes the form of speech does not necessarily immunize it from regulation.[2] Just as solicitation of murder is regulable, though only speech is involved, so is the promotion of an unlawful commercial activity. In both cases the speech is inseparably related to the particular unlawful activity and not remotely related to the suggested purposes of the First Amendment. By comparison, advocating the social benefits of pyramiding schemes in general in order to change the law is protected. But such advocacy designed to obtain the political support of others is easily distinguishable from the solicitation designed to obtain their immediate financial participation. In this case, the word "promote" is amenable to a construction prohibiting only the expression used in the actual organization, advertisement, or implementation of the prohibited schemes.

VAGUENESS

Fundamental fairness requires that people be given notice of the conduct the law proscribes. But it does not require that regulations proscribe conduct with absolute or mathematical precision, nor does it require that there never be disagreement on the application of the regulation to particular factual situations. Vagueness is not a wooden concept but a flexible one, based on a common sense evaluation of the notice given by a regulation and calling for consideration of the entire text, the subject matter dealt with, and the difficulty in being more precise. The alleged vagueness of Ag 122 lies in the inherent ambiguity of the words "promote" and "scheme" in Section 122.02 and the words "investment," "recruiting for profit," and "additional conditions affecting eligibility" in Section 122.02. Plaintiffs suggest hypothetical factual situations where the application of those words and, hence, of the regulation is uncertain. But, as mentioned above, that does not make the regulation unconstitutionally vague. If it did, statutory interpretation would never be necessary.

Section 122.03, the only prohibitive section, states that no person shall "promote, offer, or grant participation in" indicate that the prohibition extends to any efforts to involve others in the scheme. The scheme itself is defined in Section 122.02(1) as "a sales device whereby a person, upon a condition that they make an investment, is granted a license or right to recruit for profit one or more additional persons who also are granted such license or right . . . upon such condition." The words "investment" and "person" used in defining chain distributor schemes are in turn defined in Sections 122.02(2) and (3). I believe the regulation gives a man of common intelligence a sufficiently definite idea of what is proscribed. Though comparison with other statutes is of dubious value, the regulation is certainly more definite than the Sherman Antitrust Act which prohibits all "contracts . . . in restraint of trade or commerce" and which was held sufficiently definite by Justice Holmes in *Nash* v. *United States*. Plaintiffs' contention that the regulation is unconstitutionally vague is insubstantial.

BURDEN ON INTERSTATE COMMERCE

Though a state has wide-ranging authority under its police power to enact all laws furthering the interests of its citizens, it cannot enact laws which discriminate against or unduly burden interstate commerce. (United States Constitution, Art. I, Section 8.) Plaintiffs cannot contend that Ag 122 discriminates against interstate commerce, for by its terms it is applied evenhandedly to all chain distributor schemes within the state, whether intrastate or interstate in character. Prohibiting the use of commercial schemes, moreover, cannot be compared with burdening the interstate movement of trucks and trains engaged in admittedly lawful commercial activities. Finally, a state's interest in protecting its citizens against fraud or other unlawful business practices has a prominence which would warrant upholding the regulation even if it had a considerable impact on interstate activities. Justice Stewart recently set forth the proper approach in deciding whether regulations like Ag 122 violate the commerce clause:

> . . . Where the statute regulates even-handedly to effectuate a legitimate local public interest, and its effects on interstate commerce are only incidental, it will be upheld unless the burden imposed on such commerce is clearly excessive in relation to the putative local benefits. . . ."

Thus far plaintiffs have not indicated in what way Ag 122 imposes any burden on interstate commerce. Accordingly, plaintiffs' contention that it is unconstitutional on that ground is insubstantial.

PRE-EMPTION

Plaintiff Holiday Magic, Inc., states that it has been charged by the Federal Trade Commission with several counts of violating Section 5 of the Federal Trade Commission Act of 1934, as amended, which provides:

> "Unfair methods of competition in commerce, and unfair or deceptive acts or practices in commerce, are declared unlawful." (U.S.C.A. Section 45(a)(1).)

(See In the Matter of Holiday Magic, Inc. et al., Federal Trade Commission, Docket No. 8834.) Holiday Magic, Inc., then contends that by taking this action the Federal Trade Commission has pre-empted Wisconsin from enforcing Ag. 122 and, it would follow from plaintiffs' argument, from enforcing any general order issue pursuant to Wis.Stats. Section 100.20.

In passing the Federal Trade Commission Act, Congress certainly did not intend to bar states from stopping unfair business practices which might injure their own citizens. Indeed the Act which authorized the Federal Trade Commission to proceed against unfair practices committed in interstate commerce impliedly encouraged states to develop their own laws. Today "little FTC Acts" and other state laws prohibiting unfair practices are in force in more than two-thirds of the states. As Justice Brennan found in *Florida Lime & Avocado Growers, Inc. v. Paul* (1963), where a California statute barred out-of-state avocados which did not meet state standards, there is "neither such actual conflict between the two schemes of regulation that both cannot stand in the same area, or evidence of a congressional design to pre-empt the field."

However, Holiday Magic, Inc., does not claim that the "field" of unfair business practices has been pre-empted. It admits that the state has coordinate authority with the federal government to deal with unfair practices and may generally enforce Ag. 122. But it asserts that when as here the Federal Trade Commission has begun an action against the same company that the state seeks to enjoin, the Federal Trade Commission has exclusive jurisdiction until the action it began is resolved. This assertion is plainly incorrect. Since Congress in enacting the Federal Trade Commission Act left the states free to establish their own standards and penalties for unfair practices, there is no reason why the outcome of the suit brought by the Federal Trade Commission would have any bearing on plaintiffs' liability under state law. It is well settled that when the same act by an individual violates both state and federal law, both the state and the federal government may act without waiting for the other to finish.

In addition, plaintiff has not shown that the Federal Trade Commission is suing it for the same acts that Wisconsin attacks. Being sued by the Federal Trade Commission for certain practices surely does not immunize one during the many months in which the suit is pending from state actions brought to enjoin other practices.

RIGHT TO WORK

Plaintiff Dale Schmidt contends that the regulation deprives him of his Constitutional right to work at his chosen occupation. To illustrate his right to work, plaintiff cites authorities holding that an individual may not be denied the opportunity to work in a lawful vocation because of his beliefs or his exercise of First Amendment rights. But the right not to be barred from a lawful vocation for an unlawful reason does not imply the right to work at what the legislature deems a vocation inimical to the public interest. Plaintiff may respond with Falstaff who met the charge of "purse-taking" with the answer, "But 'tis my vocation Hal, 'tis no sin for a man to labor in his vocation." (*Henry the Fourth*, Part I, Act I, sc. II, lines 116–117.) But sin or not nothing in the Constitution prevents a state from outlawing activities because others have profited from them in the past. Nor must a regulation affecting previous vocations be supported by a more compelling state interest than that supporting any other regulation. Plaintiff's reliance on his right to work does not state a claim on which relief can be granted.

IMPAIRMENT OF CONTRACTS AND DUE PROCESS

The allegations that Ag. 122 impairs the obligations of contracts and bears no reasonable relation to a valid state purpose may be treated together. Historically designed to bar states from arbitrarily relieving debtors from their contracts, the contract clause has long been interpreted to prevent it from being an inflexible barrier to public regulation. In *Home Building & Loan Association v. Blaisdell* (1934), a decision upholding the Minnesota mortgage moratorium law which postponed foreclosure sales and extended the period for redemption of mortgages, Chief Justice Hughes reiterated that state laws reasonably related to a valid state purpose would not be held unlawful because they have incidental effects on contracts created in the past:

> Not only is the (contract clause) qualified by the measure of control which the state retains over remedial processes, but the state also continues to possess authority to safeguard the vital interests of its people. . . . Not only are existing laws read into contracts in order to fix obligations as between the parties, but the reservation of essential attributes of sovereign power is also read into contracts as a postulate of the legal order. The policy of protecting contracts against impairment presupposes the maintenance of a government by virtue of which contractual relations are worth while—a government which retains adequate authority to secure the peace and good order of society. This principle of harmonizing the constitutional prohibition with the necessary residuum of state power has had progressive recognition in the decisions of this Court.
>
> . . . The states retain adequate power to protect the public health against the maintenance of nuisances despite insistence upon existing contracts. . . .

In this case those in the chain who had already paid for the right to recruit others obviously had the value of their contract impaired when Ag. 122 was issued. The question then becomes whether Ag. 122 was reasonably related to a valid state purpose.

To show that Ag. 122 is not reasonably related to a valid state purpose, plaintiffs must overcome the presumption of the constitutionality which all regulations of commercial activity enjoy. Moreover, the ordinary presumption that the regulation bears a reasonable relation to the public interest is buttressed by the regulation's preamble, Section 122.02, in which the Department set forth the facts which led it to believe that prohibiting chain distributor schemes would serve the public interest.

Although plaintiffs state in their brief that at trial they will show that the facts set forth in the preamble are incorrect and that there is no legitimate reason for prohibiting the use of chain distributor schemes, they have not indicated by way of affidavits, detailed allegations in the complaint, assertions of counsel, or otherwise what the nature of these facts would be. Instead they rely upon their conclusory allegations in the complaint that the general order is irrational, but in the context of this case, such allegations alone do not justify requesting a three-judge court.

DENIAL OF EQUAL PROTECTION

Plaintiffs' final contention is that the regulation results in discriminatory enforcement. It is true that if the administrators of a regulation enforce it in bad faith or in a manner which unreasonably discriminates, the defendant may seek to enjoin enforcement on constitutional grounds. But here plaintiffs do not seek to enjoin the mere discriminatory enforcement of a valid regulation. Rather, in asking for a three-judge court they contend that the regulation must necessarily result in discriminatory enforcement, and they seek to enjoin all enforcement. Yet nothing on the face of the regulation indicates that it is more likely to result in discriminatory enforcement than any law. Enforcement of Ag. 122 turns solely on whether a person has attempted to involve another in a chain distributor scheme. No other distinctions are suggested. To distinguish between those who "promote, offer, or grant participation in" the schemes and those who, though otherwise involved in the schemes do not, does not appear to be unreasonable. Plaintiffs' contention does not merit a three-judge court.

For the reasons stated above, it is hereby ordered that plaintiffs' motion for a three-judge court be and it hereby is denied.

It is further ordered that this action be and it hereby is dismissed.

NOTES

[1] Justice Douglas would depart from past authority and afford commercial expression the protection of the First Amendment. See his concurring opinion in *Cammarano v. United States,* 358 U.S. 498, 79 S.Ct. 524, 3 L.Ed.2d 462 (1959), and his dissent in *Dun & Bradstreet, Inc. v. Grove, Trustee et al.,* 404 U.S. 898, 904, 92 S.Ct. 204, 30 L.Ed.2d 175 (1971). On occasion lower courts have implied that constitutional protection hinges on whether the commercial expression is "true." See, e.g., *L.G. Balfour Co. v. Federal Trade Commission,* 442 F.2d 1, 24 (7 Cir., 1971).

[2] By as much as plaintiff overstates the significance of the fact that the unlawful activity takes the form of speech, the often-cited opinion of *Giboney v. Empire Storage & Ice Co.,* 336 U.S. 490, 502, 69 S.Ct. 684, 691, 93 L.Ed. 834 (1949), understates its significance in declaring that:

". . . it has never been deemed an abridgment of freedom of speech or press to make a course of conduct illegal merely because the conduct was in part initiated, evidenced, or carried out by means of language, either spoken, written, or printed. . . ."

Often using speech to carry out an illegal course of conduct will immunize the speaker from arrest. For instance, a speaker at an unruly public demonstration may know that continuing his speech will cause a breach of the peace, yet even if the state shows that he intended that result, he cannot be convicted of breach of the peace or attempted breach of the peace as long as his speech itself qualified for Constitutional protection.

PITTSBURGH PRESS COMPANY v. PITTSBURGH COMMISSION ON HUMAN RIGHTS
413 U.S. 376 (1973)

Mr. Justice Powell delivered the opinion of the Court.

The Human Relations Ordinance of the City of Pittsburgh has been construed below by the courts of Pennsylvania as forbidding newspapers to carry "help wanted" advertisements in sex-designated columns except where the employer or advertiser is free to make hiring or employment referral decisions on the basis of sex. We are called upon to decide whether the Ordinance as so construed violates the freedoms of speech and of the press guaranteed by the First and Fourteenth Amendments.

The Ordinance proscribes discrimination in employment on the basis of race, color, religion, ancestry, national origin, place of birth, or sex. In relevant part, Section 8 of the Ordinance declares (the employment practice unlawful) "except where based upon a bona fide occupational exemption certified by the Commission:"

a. For any employer to refuse to hire any person or otherwise discriminate against any person with respect to hiring because of sex.
e. For any 'employer,' employment agency, or labor organization to publish or circulate, or to cause to be published or circulated, any notice or advertisement relating to 'employment' or membership which indicates any discrimination because of sex.
j. For any person, whether or not an employer, employment agency, or labor organization, to aid in the doing of any act declared to be an unlawful employment practice by this ordinance.

The present proceedings were initiated on October 9, 1969, when the National Organization for Women, Inc. (NOW) filed a complaint with the Pittsburgh Commission on Human Relations (the Commission), which is charged with implementing the Ordinance. The complaint alleged that the Pittsburgh Press Company (Pittsburgh Press) was violating (j) of the Ordinance by "allowing employers to place advertisements in the male or female columns, when the jobs advertised obviously do not have bona fide occupational qualifications or exceptions."

On July 23, 1970, the Commission issued a Decision and Order. It found that during 1969, Pittsburgh Press carried a total of 248,000 help wanted advertisements; that its practice before October, 1969, was to use columns captioned "Male Help Wanted," "Female Help Wanted," "Jobs—Male Interest," "Jobs—Female Interest," and "Male-Female"; and that the advertisements were placed in the respective columns according to the advertiser's wishes, either volunteered by the advertiser or offered in response to inquiry by Pittsburgh Press. The Commission first concluded that (e) of the Ordinance forbade employers, employment agencies, and labor organizations from submitting advertisements for placement in sex-designated columns. It then held that Pittsburgh Press, in violation of (j), aided the advertisers by maintaining a sex-designated classification system. (T)he Commission ordered Pittsburgh Press to cease and desist such violations and to utilize a classification system with no reference to sex. This order was affirmed in all relevant respects by the Court of Common Pleas.

On appeal in the Commonwealth Court, the scope of the order was narrowed to allow Pittsburgh Press to carry advertisements in sex-designated columns for jobs exempt from the antidiscrimination provisions of the Ordinance. The Pennsylvania Supreme Court denied review.

There is little need to reiterate that the freedoms of speech and of the press rank among our most cherished liberties. The repeated emphasis accorded this theme in the decisions of this Court serves to underline the narrowness of the recognized exceptions to the principle that the press may not be regulated by the Government. Our inquiry must therefore be whether the challenged order falls within any of these exceptions.

(S)peech is not rendered commercial by the mere fact that it relates to an advertisement. In *New York Times Co.* v. *Sullivan,* a city official of Montgomery, Alabama, brought a libel action against four clergymen and the *New York Times*. The names of the clergymen had appeared in an advertisement, carried in the *Times,* criticizing police action directed against members of the civil rights movements. In holding that this political advertisement was entitled to the same degree of protection as ordinary speech, the Court stated: "That the *Times* was paid for publishing the advertisement is as immaterial in this connection as is the fact that newspapers and books are sold." If a newspaper's profit motive were determinative, all aspects of its operations—from the selection of news stories to the choice of editorial position—would be subject to regulation if it could be established that they were conducted with a view toward increased sales. Such a basis for regulation clearly would be incompatible with the First Amendment.

The critical feature of the advertisement in *Valentine* v. *Chrestensen* was that, in the Court's view, it did no more than propose a commercial transaction, the sale of admission to a submarine . . . In the crucial respects, the advertisements in the present record resemble the *Chrestensen* rather than the *Sullivan* advertisement. None expresses a position on whether, as a matter of social policy, certain positions ought to be filled by members of one or the other sex, nor does any of them criticize the Ordinance or the Commission's enforcement practices. Each is no more than a proposal of possible employment. The advertisements are thus classic examples of commercial speech.

The Commission made a finding of fact that Pittsburgh Press defers in every case to the advertiser's wishes regarding the column in which a want ad should be placed. It is nonetheless true, however, that the newspaper does make a judgment whether or not to allow the advertiser to select the column.

Under some circumstances, at least, a newspaper's editorial judgments in connection with an advertisement take on the character of the advertisement . . . In the context of a libelous advertisement, for example, this Court has held that the First Amendment does not shield a newspaper from punishment for libel when with actual malice it publishes a falsely defamatory advertisement. *(New York Times Co.* v. *Sullivan.)* The newspaper may not defend a libel suit on the ground that the falsely defamatory statements are not its own.

Similarly, a commercial advertisement remains commercial in the hands of the media, at least under some circumstances. In *Capital Broadcasting Co.* v. *Acting Attorney General,* this Court summarily affirmed a district court decision sustaining the constitutionality of 15 U.S.C. 1335, which prohibits the electronic media from carrying cigarette advertisements. The District Court there found that the advertising should be treated as commercial speech, even though the First Amendment challenge was mounted by radio broadcasters rather than by advertisers. Because of the peculiar characteristics of the electronic media, *Capital Broadcasting* is not dispositive here on the ultimate question of the constitutionality of the Ordinance. Its significance lies, rather, in its recognition that the exercise of this kind of editorial judgment does not necessarily strip commercial advertising of its commercial character.

As for the present case, we are not persuaded that either the decision to accept a commercial advertisement which the advertiser directs to be placed in a sex-designated column or the actual placement there lifts the newspaper's actions from the category of commercial speech. By implication at least, an advertiser whose want ad appears in the "Jobs—Male Interest" column is likely to discriminate against women in his hiring decisions. Nothing in a sex-designated column heading sufficiently dissociates the designation from the want ads placed beneath it to make the placement severable for First Amendment purposes from the want ads themselves. The combination, which conveys essentially the same message as an overtly discriminatory want ad, is in practical effect an integrated commercial statement.

Insisting that the exchange of information is as important in the commercial realm as in any other, the newspaper here would have us abrogate the distinction between commercial and other speech.

Whatever the merits of this contention may be in other contexts, it is unpersuasive in this case. Discrimination in employment is not only commercial activity, it is *illegal* commercial activity under the Ordinance. We have no doubt that a newspaper Constitutionally could be forbidden to publish a want ad proposing a sale of narcotics or soliciting prostitutes. Nor would the result be different if the nature of the transaction were indicated by placement under columns captioned "Narcotics for Sale" and "Prostitutes Wanted" rather than stated within the four corners of the advertisement.

The illegality in this case may be less overt, but we see no difference in principle here. Sex discrimination in nonexempt employment has been declared illegal under 8(a) of the Ordinance, a provision not challenged here. And 8(e) of the Ordinance forbids any employer, employment agency, or labor union to publish or cause to be published any advertisement "indicating" sex discrimination.

Section 8(j) of the Ordinance, the only item which Pittsburgh Press was found to have violated and the only provision under attack here, makes it unlawful for "any person . . . to aid . . . in the doing of any act declared to be an unlawful employment practice by this Ordinance." The Commission and the courts below concluded that the practice of placing want ads for nonexempt employment in sex-designated columns did indeed "aid" employers to indicate illegal sex preferences. The advertisements, as embroidered by their placement, signaled that the advertisers were likely to show an illegal sex preference in their hiring decision. Any First Amendment interest which might be served by advertising an ordinary commercial proposal and which might arguably outweigh the governmental interest supporting the regulation is altogether absent when the commercial activity itself is illegal and the restriction on advertising is incidental to a valid limitation on economic activity.

We emphasize that nothing in our holding allows government at any level to forbid Pittsburgh Press to publish and distribute advertisements commenting on the Ordinance, the enforcement practices of the Commission, or the propriety of sex preferences in employment. Nor, a fortiori, does our decision authorize any restriction whatever, whether of content or layout, on stories or commentary originated by Pittsburgh Press, its columnists, or its contributors. On the contrary, we reaffirm unequivocally the protection afforded to editorial judgment and to the free expression of views on these and other issues, however controversial. We hold only that the Commission's modified order, narrowly drawn to prohibit placement in sex-designated columns of advertisements for nonexempt job opportunities, does not infringe the First Amendment rights of Pittsburgh Press.

Affirmed.

Mr. Chief Justice Burger, dissenting.

Despite the Court's efforts to decide only the narrow question presented in this case, the holding represents, for me, a disturbing enlargement of the "commercial speech" doctrine (*Valentine* v. *Chrestensen* (1942)), and a serious encroachment on the freedom of press guaranteed by the First Amendment. It also launches the courts on what I perceive to be a treacherous path of defining what layout and organizational decisions of newspapers are "sufficiently associated" with the "commercial" parts of the papers as to be Constitutionally unprotected and therefore subject to governmental regulation. Assuming, arguendo, that the First Amendment permits the States to place restrictions on the content of commercial advertisements, I would not enlarge that power to reach the layout and organizational decisions of a newspaper.

Pittsburgh Press claims to have decided to use sex-designated column headings in the classified advertising section of its newspapers to facilitate the use of classified ads by its readers. Not only is this purpose conveyed to the readers in plain terms, but the newspaper also explicitly cautions readers against interpreting the column headings as indicative of sex discrimination. Thus, before each column heading the newspaper prints the following "Notice to Job Seekers":

> Jobs are arranged under Male and Female classifications for the convenience of our readers. This is done because most jobs generally appeal more to persons of one sex than the other, job seekers should assume that the advertiser will consider applicants of either sex in compliance with the laws against discrimination.

To my way of thinking, Pittsburgh Press has clearly acted within its protected journalistic discretion in adopting this arrangement of its classified advertisements. Especially in light of the newspaper's "Notice to Job Seekers," it is unrealistic for the Court to say, as it does, that the sex-designated column headings are not "sufficiently dissociate(d)" from the "want ads placed beneath (them) to make the placement severable for First Amendment purposes from the want ads themselves." In any event, I believe the First Amendment freedom of press includes the right of a newspaper to arrange the content of its paper, whether it be news items, editorials, or advertising, as it sees fit. In the final analysis, the readers are the ultimate "controllers" no matter what excesses are indulged in by even a flamboyant or venal press; that it often takes a long time for these influences to bear fruit is inherent in our system.

The Court's conclusion that the Commission's cease-and-desist order does not constitute a prior restraint gives me little reassurance. That conclusion is assertedly based on the view that the order affects only a "continuing course of repetitive conduct." Even if that were correct, I would still disagree since the Commission's order appears to be in effect an outstanding injunction against certain publications—the essence of a prior restraint. In any event, my understanding of the effects of the Commission's order differs from that of the Court. As noted in the Court's opinion, the Commonwealth Court narrowed the injunction to permit Pittsburgh Press to use sex-designated column headings for want ads dealing with jobs exempt under the Ordinance. The Ordinance does not apply, for example,

> to employers to fewer than five persons, to employers outside the city of Pittsburgh, or to religious, fraternal, charitable, or sectarian organizations, nor does it apply to employment in domestic service or in jobs for which the Commission has certified a bona fide occupational exception.

If Pittsburgh Press chooses to continue using its column headings for advertisements submitted for publication by exempted employers, it may well face difficult legal questions in deciding whether a particular employer is or is not subject to the Ordinance. If it makes the wrong decision and includes a covered advertisement under a sex-designated column heading, it runs the risk of being held in summary contempt for violating the terms of the order.

In practical effect, therefore, the Commission's order in this area may have the same inhibiting effect as the injunction in *Near* v. *Minnesota* (1931), which permanently enjoined the publishers of a newspaper from printing a "malicious, scandalous, or defamatory newspaper, as defined by law." We struck down the injunction in *Near* as a prior restraint. In 1971, we reaffirmed the principle of presumptive unconstitutionality of prior restraint in *Organization for a Better Austin* v. *Keefe* (1971). Indeed, in *New York Times Co.* v. *United States* (1971), every member of the Court, tacitly or explicitly, accepted the *Near* and *Keefe* condemnation of prior restraint as presumptively unconstitutional. In this case, the respondents have, in my view, failed to carry their burden. I would therefore hold the Commission's order to be impermissible prior restraint. At the very least, we ought to make clear that a newspaper may not be subject to summary punishment for contempt for having made an "unlucky" legal guess on a particular advertisement or for having failed to secure advance Commission approval of a decision to run an advertisement under a sex-designated column.

Mr. Justice Douglas, dissenting.

While I join the dissent of Mr. Justice Stewart, I add a few words. As he says, the press, like any other business, can be regulated on business and economic matters. Our leading case on that score is *Associated Press* v. *United States,* which holds that a news gathering agency may be made accountable for violations of the antitrust laws. By like token, a newspaper, periodical, or TV or radio broadcaster may be subjected to labor relations laws. And that regulation could Constitutionally extend to the imposition of penalties or other sanctions if any unit of the press violated laws that barred discrimination in employment based on race or religion or sex.

Pennsylvania has a regulatory regime designed to eliminate discrimination in employment based on sex; and the commission in charge of that program issues cease-and-desist orders against violators. There is no doubt that Pittsburgh Press would have no constitutional defense against such a cease-and-desist order issued against it for discriminatory employment practices.

But I believe that Pittsburgh Press by reason of the First Amendment may publish what it pleases about any law without censorship or restraint by Government. The First Amendment does not require the press to reflect any ideological or political creed reflecting the dominant philosophy, whether transient or fixed. It may use its pages and facilities to denounce a law and urge its repeal or, at the other extreme, denounce those who do not respect its letter and spirit.

Commercial matter, as distinguished from news, was held in *Valentine* v. *Chrestensen,* not to be subject to First Amendment protection. My views on that issue have changed since 1942, the year *Valentine* was decided. As I have stated on earlier occasions, I believe that commercial materials also have First Amendment protection. If Empire Industries Ltd., doing business in Pennsylvania, wanted to run full-page advertisements denouncing or criticizing this Pennsylvania law, I see no way in which Pittsburgh Press could be censored or punished for running the ad, any more than a person could be punished for uttering the contents of the ad in a public address in Independence Hall. The pros and cons of legislative enactments are clearly discussion or dialogue that is highly honored in our First Amendment traditions.

The want ads which gave rise to the present litigation express the preference of one employer for the kind of help he needs. If he carried through to hiring and firing employees on the basis of those preferences, the state commission might issue a remedial order against him, if discrimination in employment was shown. Yet he could denounce that action with impunity and Pittsburgh Press could publish his denunciation or write an editorial taking his side also with impunity.

Where there is a valid law, the Government can enforce it. But there can be no valid law censoring the press or punishing it for publishing its views or the views of subscribers or customers who express their ideas in letters to the editor or in want ads or other commercial space. There comes a time, of course, when speech and action are so closely brigaded that they are really one. Falsely shouting "fire" in a theater, the example given by Mr. Justice Holmes, *Schenck* v. *United States,* is one example. *Giboney* v. *Empire Storage Co.,* written by Mr. Justice Black, is another. There are here, however, no such unusual circumstances.

As Mr. Justice Stewart says, we have witnessed a growing tendency to cut down the literal requirements of First Amendment freedoms so that those in power can squelch someone out of step. Historically, the miscreant has usually been an unpopular minority. Today it is a newspaper that does not bow to the spreading bureaucracy that promises to engulf us. It may be that we have become so stereotyped as to have earned that fate. But the First Amendment presupposes freewheeling, independent people whose vagaries include ideas spread across the entire spectrum of thoughts and beliefs. I would let any expression in that broad spectrum flourish, unrestrained by Government, unless it was an integral part of action—the only point which in the Jeffersonian philosophy marks the permissible point of governmental intrusion.

I therefore dissent from affirmance of this judgment.

Mr. Justice Stewart, with whom Mr. Justice Douglas joins, dissenting.

I have no doubt that it is within the police power of the city of Pittsburgh to prohibit discrimination in private employment on the basis of race, color, religion, ancestry, national origin, place of birth, or sex. I do not doubt, either, that in enforcing such a policy the city may prohibit employers from indicating any such discrimination when they make known the availability of employment opportunities. But neither of those propositions resolves the question before us in this case.

That question, to put it simply, is whether any government agency—local, state, or federal—can tell a newspaper in advance what it can print and what it cannot. Under the First and Fourteenth Amendments I think no government agency in this nation has any such power.

It is true, of course, as the Court points out, that the publisher of a newspaper is amenable to civil and criminal laws of general applicability. For example, a newspaper publisher is subject to nondiscriminatory general taxation, and to restrictions imposed by the National Labor Relations Act, the Fair Labor Standards Act, and the Sherman Act. In short, as businessman or employer, a newspaper publisher is not exempt from laws affecting businessmen and employers generally. Accordingly, I assume that the Pittsburgh Press Company, as an employer, can be and is completely within the coverage of the Human Relations Ordinance of the city of Pittsburgh.

But what the Court approves today is wholly different. It approves a government order dictating to a publisher in advance how he must arrange the layout of pages in his newspaper.

Nothing in *Valentine* v. *Chrestensen,* remotely supports the Court's decision. That case involved the validity of a local sanitary ordinance that prohibited the distribution in the streets of "commercial and business advertising matter." The Court held that the ordinance could be applied to the owner of a commercial tourist attraction who wanted to drum up trade by passing out handbills in the streets. The Court said it was "clear that the Constitution imposes no such restraint on government as respects purely commercial advertising. Whether, and to what extent, one may promote or pursue a gainful occupation in the streets, to what extent such activity shall be adjudged a derogation of the public right of user, are matters for legislative judgment." Whatever validity the *Chrestensen* case may still retain when limited to its own facts, it certainly does not stand for the proposition that the advertising pages of a newspaper are outside the protection given the newspaper by the First and Fourteenth Amendments. Any possible doubt on that score was surely laid to rest in *New York Times Co.* v. *Sullivan.*

So far as I know, this is the first case in this or any other American court that permits a government agency to enter a composing room of a newspaper and dictate to the publisher the layout and makeup of the newspaper's pages. This is the first such case, but I fear it may not be the last. The camel's nose is in the tent. "It may be that it is the obnoxious thing in its mildest and least repulsive form; but illegitimate and unconstitutional practices get their first footing in that way . . ." (*Boyd* v. *United States*.)

So long as members of this Court view the First Amendment as no more than a set of "values" to be balanced against other "values," that Amendment will remain in grave jeopardy. (See *Paris Adult Theatre I* v. *Slaton,* ante, p. 49.) First and Fourteenth Amendment protections outweighed by public interest in "quality of life," "total community environment," "tone of commerce," "public safety,"

(*Branzburg* v. *Hayes*). First Amendment claim asserted by newsman to maintain confidential relationship with his sources outweighed by obligation to give information to grand jury, (*New York Times Co.* v. *United States,* Burger, C.J., dissenting). First Amendment outweighed by judicial problems caused by "unseemly haste," (*Columbia Broadcasting System, Inc.* v. *Democratic National Committee,* Brennan, J., dissenting), (balancing of "the competing First Amendment interests").

It is said that the goal of the Pittsburgh ordinance is a laudable one, and so indeed it is. But, in the words of Mr. Justice Brandeis, "Experience should teach us to be most on our guard to protect liberty when the Government's purposes are beneficent. Men born to freedom are naturally alert to repel invasion of their liberty by evil-minded rulers. The greatest dangers to liberty lurk in insidious encroachment by men of zeal, well-meaning but without understanding." (*Olmstead* v. *United States,* dissenting opinion.) And, as Mr. Justice Black once pointed out, "The motives behind the state law may have been to do good. But . . . (h)istory indicates that urges to do good have led to the burning of books and even to the burning of 'witches.' " (*Beauharnais* v. *Illinois,* dissenting opinion.)

The Court today holds that a government agency can force a newspaper publisher to print his classified advertising pages in a certain way in order to carry out governmental policy. After this decision, I see no reason why government cannot force a newspaper publisher to conform in the same way in order to achieve other goals thought socially desirable. And if government can dictate the layout of a newspaper's classified advertising pages today, what is there to prevent it from dictating the layout of the news pages tomorrow?

Those who think the First Amendment can and should be subordinated to other socially desirable interests will hail today's decision. But I find it frightening. For I believe the Constitutional guarantee of a free press is more than precatory. I believe it is a clear command that government must never be allowed to lay its heavy editorial hand on any newspaper in this country.

Mr. Justice Blackmun, dissenting.

I dissent substantially for the reasons stated by Mr. Justice Stewart in his opinion.

LEHMAN v. *SHAKER HEIGHTS*
418 U.S. 298 (1974)

Mr. Justice Blackmun announced the jugment of the Court and an opinion, in which The Chief Justice, Mr. Justice White and Mr. Justice Rehnquist join.

This case presents the question whether a city which operates a public rapid transit system and sells advertising space for car cards on its vehicles is required by the First and Fourteenth Amendments to accept paid political advertising on behalf of a candidate for public office.

In 1970, petitioner Harry J. Lehman was a candidate for the office of State Representative to the Ohio General Assembly for District 56. The district includes the city of Shaker Heights. On July 3, 1970, petitioner sought to promote his candidacy by purchasing car card space on the Shaker Heights rapid transit system for the months of August, September, and October. The general election was scheduled for November 3. Petitioner's proposed copy contained his picture and read:

"HARRY J. LEHMAN IS OLD-FASHIONED!
ABOUT HONESTY, INTEGRITY AND GOOD GOVERNMENT

"State Representative—District 56 (X) Harry J. Lehman."

Advertising space on the city's transit system is managed by respondent Metromedia, Inc., as exclusive agent under contract with the city. The agreement between the city and Metromedia provides: "The CONTRACTOR shall not place political advertising in or upon any of the said CARS or in, upon, or about any other additional and further space granted hereunder."

When petitioner applied for space, he was informed by Metromedia that, although space was then available, the management agreement with the city did not permit political advertising. The system, however, accepted ads from cigarette companies, banks, savings and loan associations, liquor companies, retail and service establishments, churches, and civic and public service oriented groups. There was uncontradicted testimony at the trial that during the 26 years of public operation, the Shaker Heights system, pursuant to city Council action, had not accepted or permitted *any* political or public issue advertising on its vehicles.

It is urged that the car cards here constitute a public forum protected by the First Amendment, and that there is a guarantee of nondiscriminatory access to such publicly owned and controlled areas of communication "regardless of the primary purpose for which the area is dedicated."

We disagree. In *Packer Corp.* v. *Utah* (the) Court recognized that "there is a difference which justifies the classification between display advertising and that in periodicals or newspapers." In *Packer* the Court upheld a Utah statute that made it a misdemeanor to advertise cigarettes on " 'any bill board, street car sign, street car, placard,' " but exempted dealers' signs on their places of business and cigarette advertising " 'in any newspaper, magazine, or periodical.' " The Court found no equal protection violation. It reasoned that viewers of billboards and streetcar signs had no "choice or volition" to observe such advertising and had the message "thrust upon them by all the arts and devices that skill can produce. . . . The radio can be turned off, but not so the billboard or street car placard." "The streetcar audience is a captive audience. It is there as a matter of necessity, not of choice." In such situations, "(t)he legislature may recognize degrees of evil and adapt its legislation accordingly."

These situations are different from the traditional settings where First Amendment values inalterably prevail. Although American Constitutional jurisprudence, in the light of the First Amendment, has been jealous to preserve access to public places for purposes of free speech, the nature of the forum and the conflicting interests involved have remained important in determining the degree of protection afforded by the Amendment to the speech in question.

Here, we have no open spaces, no meeting hall, park, street corner, or other public thoroughfare. Instead, the city is engaged in commerce. It must provide rapid, convenient, pleasant, and inexpensive service to the commuters of Shaker Heights. The car card space, although incidental to the provision of public transportation, is a part of the commercial venture. In much the same way that a newspaper or periodical, or even a radio or television station, need not accept every proffer of advertising from the general public, a city transit system has discretion to develop and make reasonable choices concerning the type of advertising that may be displayed in its vehicles.

No First Amendment forum is here to be found. The city consciously has limited access to its transit system advertising space in order to minimize chances of abuse, the appearance of favoritism, and the risk of imposing upon a captive audience. These are reasonable legislative objectives advanced by the city in a proprietary capacity. In these circumstances, there is no First or Fourteenth Amendment violation.

Mr. Justice Douglas, concurring.

In asking us to force the system to accept his message as a vindication of his Constitutional rights, the petitioner overlooks the Constitutional rights of the commuters. While petititioner clearly has a right to express his views to those who wish to listen, he has no right to force his message upon an audience incapable of declining to receive it. In my view the right of the commuters to be free from forced intrusions on their privacy precludes the city from transforming its vehicles of public transportation into forums for the dissemination of ideas upon this captive audience.

Buses are not recreational vehicles used for Sunday chautauquas as a public park might be used on holidays for such a purpose; they are a practical necessity for millions in our urban centers. I have already stated this view in my dissent in *Public Utilities Commission* v. *Pollak,* involving the challenge by some passengers to the practice of broadcasting radio programs over loudspeakers in buses and streetcars: "One who tunes in on an offensive program at home can turn it off or tune in another station, as he wishes. One who hears disquieting or unpleasant programs in public places, such as restaurants, can get up and leave. But the man on the streetcar has no choice but to sit and listen, or perhaps to sit and try *not* to listen." There is no difference when the message is visual, nor auricular. In each the viewer or listener is captive.

I do not view the content of the message as relevant either to petitioner's right to express it or to the commuters' right to be free from it. Commercial advertisements may be as offensive and intrusive to captive audiences as any political message. But the validity of the commercial advertising program is not before us since we are not faced with one complaining of an invasion of privacy through forced exposure to commercial ads. Since I do not believe that petitioner has any Constitutional right to spread this message before this captive audience, I concur in the Court's judgment.

Mr. Justice Brennan, with whom Mr. Justice Stewart, Mr. Justice Marshall, and Mr. Justice Powell join, dissenting.

I would reverse. In my view, the city created a forum for the dissemination of information and expression of ideas when it acccepted and displayed commercial and public service advertisements on its rapid transit vehicles. Having opened a forum for communication, the city is barred by the First and Fourteenth Amendments from discriminating among forum users solely on the basis of message content.

The line between ideological and nonideological speech is impossible to draw with accuracy. By accepting commercial and public service advertisements, the city opened the door to "sometimes controversial or unsettling speech" and determined that such speech does not unduly interfere with the rapid transit system's primary purpose of transporting passengers. In the eyes of many passengers, certain commercial or public service messages are as profoundly disturbing as some political advertisements might be to other passengers. There is certainly no evidence in the record of this case indicating that political advertisements, as a class, are so disturbing when displayed that they are more likely than commercial or public service advertisements to impair the rapid transit system's primary function of transportation. In the absence of such evidence, the city's selective exclusion of political advertising constitutes an invidious discrimination on the basis of subject matter, in violation of the First and Fourteenth Amendments.

Moreover, even if it were possible to draw a manageable line between controversial and noncontroversial messages, the city's practice of censorship for the benefit of "captive audiences" still would not be justified. This is not a case where an unwilling or unsuspecting rapid transit rider is powerless to avoid messages he deems unsettling. The advertisements accepted by the city and Metromedia are not broadcast over loudspeakers in the transit cars. The privacy of the passengers is not, therefore, dependent upon their ability "to sit and try *not* to listen." Rather, all advertisements accepted for display are in *written* form. Transit passengers are not forced or compelled to read any of the messages, nor are they "incapable of declining to receive (them)," ante (Douglas, J. concurring). Should passengers chance to glance at advertisements they find offensive, they can "effectively avoid further bombardment of their sensibilities simply by averting their eyes." *Cohen* v. *California*. Surely that minor inconvenience is a small price to pay for the continued preservation of so precious a liberty as free speech.

EISENSTADT v. *BAIRD*
405 U.S. 438 (1972)

Mr. Justice Brennan delivered the opinion of the Court.

Appellee William Baird was convicted . . . under Massachusetts General Laws Ann., c.272, Section 21 . . . for giving a young woman a package of Emko vaginal foam at the close of his address (on contraception to a group of students at Boston University). The Massachusetts Supreme Judicial Court . . . sustained the conviction. Baird subsequently filed a petition for a Federal writ of habeas corpus, which the District Court dismissed. On appeal, however, the Court of Appeals for the First Circuit vacated the dismissal and remanded the action with directions to grant the writ discharging Baird. This appeal . . . followed, and we noted probable jurisdiction. We affirm.

Massachusetts General Laws Ann., c.272, Section 21, under which Baird was convicted, provides a maximum five-year term of imprisonment for "whoever . . . gives away . . . any drug, medicine, instrument, or article whatever for the prevention of conception," except as authorized in Section 21A. Under Section 21A, "(a) registered physician may administer to or prescribe for any married person drugs or articles intended for the prevention of pregnancy or conception. (And a) registered pharmacist actually engaged in the business of pharmacy may furnish such drugs or articles to any married person presenting a prescription from a registered physician." As interpreted by the State Supreme Judicial Court, these provisions make it a felony for anyone, other than a registered physician or pharmacist acting in accordance with the terms of Section 21A, to dispense any article with the intention that it be used for the prevention of conception. The statutory scheme distinguishes among three distinct classes of distributees—first, married persons may obtain contraceptives to prevent pregnancy, but only from doctors or druggists on prescription; second, single persons may not obtain contraceptives from anyone to prevent pregnancy; and third, married or single persons may obtain contraceptives from anyone to prevent not pregnancy, but the spread of disease.

The legislative purposes that the statute is meant to serve are not altogether clear. In *Commonwealth* v. *Baird*, the Supreme Judicial Court noted only the State's interest in protecting the health of its citizens: "(T)he prohibition in Section 21," the court declared, "is directly related to" the State's goal of "preventing the distribution of articles designed to prevent conception which may have undesirable, if not dangerous, physical consequences." In a subsequent decision, *Sturgis* v. *Attorney General,* the court, however, found "a second and more compelling ground for upholding the statute"— namely, to protect morals through "regulating the private sexual lives of single persons."

I

(The Court holds that Baird has standing to assert the interests of unmarried distributees of contraceptives, as well as his own interest as an unauthorized distributor.)

II

The question for our determination in this case is whether there is some ground of difference that rationally explains the different treatment accorded married and unmarried persons under . . . Sections 21 and 21A. For the reasons that follow, we conclude that no such ground exists.

First. (T)he Massachusetts Supreme Court explained that . . . the object of the legislation is to discourage premarital sexual intercourse.

It would be plainly unreasonable to assume that Massachusetts has prescribed pregnancy and the birth of an unwanted child as punishment for fornication, which is a misdemeanor. Aside from the scheme of values that assumption would attribute to the State, it is abundantly clear that the effect of the ban on distribution of contraceptives to unmarried persons has at best a marginal relation to the proffered objective. Like Connecticut's laws (in *Griswold* v. *Connecticut*) Sections 21 and 21A do not at all regulate the distribution of contraceptives when they are to be used to prevent, not pregnancy, but the spread of disease. Nor, in making contraceptives available to married persons without regard to their intended use, does Massachusetts attempt to deter married persons from engaging in illicit sexual relations with unmarried persons. Even on the assumption that the fear of pregnancy operates as a deterrent to fornication, the Massachusetts statute is thus so riddled with exceptions that deterrence of premarital sex cannot reasonably be regarded as its aim.

Moreover, Sections 21 and 21A on their face have a dubious relation to the State's criminal prohibition on fornication. "Fornication is a misdemeanor (in Massachusetts), entailing a thirty dollar fine, or three months in jail. Violation of the present statute is a felony, punishable by five years in prison." (R)ecognizing that the State may seek to deter prohibited conduct by punishing more severely those who facilitate than those who actually engage in its commission, we . . . cannot believe that in this instance Massachusetts has chosen to expose the aider and abetter who simply *gives away* a contraceptive to *20* times the *90-day* sentence of the offender himself.

Second. The Supreme Judicial Court . . . held that the purpose of the amendment was to serve the health needs of the community by regulating the distribution of potentially harmful articles.

If health were the rationale of Section 21A, the statute would be both discriminatory and overbroad. Dissenting in *Commonwealth* v. *Baird* Justices Whittemore and Cutter stated that they saw "in Section 21 and Section 21A, read together, no public health purpose. If there is need to have a physician prescribe (and a pharmacist dispense) contraceptives, that need is as great for unmarried persons as for married persons." The Court of Appeals added: "If the prohibition (on distribution to unmarried persons) . . . is to be taken to mean that the same physician who can prescribe for married patients does not have sufficient skill to protect the health of patients who lack a marriage certificate, or who may be currently divorced, it is illogical to the point of irrationality." Furthermore, we must join the Court of Appeals in noting that not all contraceptives are potentially dangerous. As a result, if the Massachusetts statute were a health measure, it would not only invidiously discriminate against the unmarried, but also be overbroad with respect to the married. We conclude, accordingly, that, despite the statute's superficial earmarks as a health measure, health, on the face of the statute, may no more reasonably be regarded as its purpose than the deterrence of premarital sexual relations.

Third. If the Massachusetts statute cannot be upheld as a deterrent to fornication or as a health measure, may it, nevertheless, be sustained simply as a prohibition on contraception? The Court of

Appeals analysis "led inevitably to the conclusion that, so far as morals are concerned, it is contraceptives per se that are considered immoral to the extent that *Griswold* will permit such a declaration." The Court of Appeals went on to hold:

> To say that contraceptives are immoral as such, and are to be forbidden to unmarried persons who will nevertheless persist in having intercourse, means that such persons must risk for themselves an unwanted pregnancy, for the child, illegitimacy, and for society, a possible obligation of support. Such a view of morality is not only the very mirror image of sensible legislation; we consider that in conflicts with fundamental human rights. In the absence of demonstrated harm, we hold it is beyond the competency of the state.

We need not and do not, however, decide that important question in this case because, whatever the rights of the individual to access to contraceptives may be, the rights must be the same for the unmarried and the married alike.

If under *Griswold* the distribution of contraceptives to married persons cannot be prohibited, a ban on distribution to unmarried persons would be equally impermissible. It is true that in *Griswold* the right of privacy in question inhered in the marital relationship. Yet the marital couple is not an independent entity with a mind and heart of its own, but an association of two individuals each with a separate intellectual and emotional makeup. If the right of privacy means anything, it is the right of the *individual,* married or single, to be free from unwarranted governmental intrusion into matters so fundamentally affecting a person as the decision whether to bear or beget a child.

On the other hand, if *Griswold* is no bar to a prohibition on the distribution of contraceptives, the State could not, consistently with the Equal Protection Clauses, outlaw distribution to unmarried persons, but not to married persons. In each case the evil, as perceived by the State, would be identical, and the underinclusion would be invidious. We hold that by providing dissimilar treatment for married and unmarried persons who are similarly situated, . . . Sections 21 and 21A, violate the Equal Protection Clause.

Mr. Justice White, with whom Mr. Justice Blackmun joins, concurring in the result.

In *Griswold* v. *Connecticut* we reversed criminal convictions for advising married persons with respect to the use of contraceptives. As there applied, the Connecticut law, which forbade using contraceptives or giving advice on the subject, unduly invaded a zone of marital privacy protected by the Bill of Rights. The Connecticut law did not regulate the manufacture or sale of such products and we expressly left open any question concerning the permissible scope of such legislation.

I assume that a State's interest in the health of its citizens empowers it to restrict to medical channels the distribution of products whose use should be accompanied by medical advice. I also do not doubt that various contraceptive medicines and articles are properly available only on prescription, and I therefore have no difficulty with the Massachusetts court's characterization of the statute at issue here as expressing "a legitimate interest in preventing the distribution of articles designed to prevent conception which may have undesirable, if not dangerous, physical consequences." Had Baird distributed a supply of the so-called "pill," I would sustain his conviction under this statute.

Baird, however, was found guilty of giving away vaginal foam. Inquiry into the validity of this conviction does not come to an end merely because some contraceptives are harmful and their distribution may be restricted. Our general reluctance to question a State's judgment on matters of public health must give way where, as here, the restriction at issue burdens the Constitutional rights of married persons to use contraceptives.

Nothing in the record even suggests that the distribution of vaginal foam should be accompanied by medical advice in order to protect the user's health. Nor does the opinion of the Massachusetts court or the State's brief filed here marshal facts demonstrating that the hazards of using vaginal foam are common knowledge or so incontrovertible that they may be noticed judicially. On the contrary, the State acknowledges that Emko is a product widely available without prescription.

Mr. Chief Justice Burger, dissenting.

Mr. Justice White, while acknowledging a valid legislative purpose of protecting health, concludes that the State lacks power to regulate the distribution of the contraceptive involved in this case as a means of protecting health. The opinion grants that appellee's conviction would be valid if he had given away a potentially harmful substance, but rejects the State's placing this particular contraceptive in that category. So far as I am aware, this Court has never before challenged the police power of a State to protect the public from the risks of possibly spurious and deleterious substances sold within its borders. Moreover, a statutory classification is not invalid "simply because more innocent articles or transactions may be found within the proscribed class. The inquiry must be whether, considering the end in view, the statute passes the bounds of reason and assumes the character of a merely arbitrary fiat." (*Purity Extract & Tonic Co.* v. *Lynch.*)

The actual hazards of introducing a particular foreign substance into the human body are frequently controverted. Even assuming no present dispute among medical authorities, we cannot ignore that it has become commonplace for a drug or food additive to be universally regarded as harmless on one day and to be condemned as perilous on the next. It is inappropriate for this Court to overrule a legislative classification by relying on the present consensus among leading authorities. The commands of the Constitution cannot fluctuate with the shifting tides of scientific opinion.

Even if it were conclusively established once and for all that the product dispensed by appellee is not actually or potentially dangerous in the somatic sense, I would still be unable to agree that the restriction on dispensing it falls outside the State's power to regulate in the area of health. The choice of a means of birth control, although a highly personal matter, is also a health matter in a very real sense, and I see nothing arbitrary in a requirement of medical supervision. It is generally acknowledged that contraceptives vary in degree of effectiveness and potential harmfulness. There may be compelling health reasons for certain women to choose the most effective means of birth control available, no matter how harmless the less effective alternatives. Others might be advised not to use a highly effective means of contraception because of their peculiar susceptibility to an adverse side effect. Moreover, there may be information known to the medical profession that a particular brand of contraceptive is to be preferred or avoided, or that it has not been adequately tested. Nonetheless, the concurring opinion would hold, as a Constitutional matter, that a State must allow someone without medical training the same power to distribute this medicinal substance as is enjoyed by a physician.

It is revealing, I think, that those portions of the majority and concurring opinions rejecting the statutory limitation on distributors rely on no particular provision of the Constitution. I see nothing in the Fourteenth Amendment or any other part of the Constitution which even vaguely suggests that these medicinal forms of contraceptives must be available in the open market. I do not challenge *Griswold* v. *Connecticut,* despite its tenuous moorings to the text of the Constitution, but I cannot view it as controlling authority for this case. The Court was there confronted with a statute flatly prohibiting the use of contraceptives, not one regulating their distribution. I simply cannot believe that the limitation on the class of lawful distributors has significantly impaired the right to use contraceptives in Massachusetts. By relying on *Griswold* in the present context, the Court has passed beyond the penumbras of the specific guarantees into the uncircumscribed area of personal predilections.

The need for dissemination of information on birth control is not impinged in the slightest by limiting the distribution of medicinal substances to medical and pharmaceutical channels as Massachusetts has done by statute. The petitioner has succeeded, it seems, in cloaking his activities in some new permutation of the First Amendment although his conviction rests in fact and law on dispensing a medicinal substance without a license. I am constrained to suggest that if the Constitution can be strained to invalidate the Massachusetts statute underlying appellee's conviction, we could quite as well employ it for the protection of a "curbstone quack," reminiscent of the "medicine man" of times past, who attracted a crowd of the curious with a soapbox lecture and then plied them with "free samples" of some unproven remedy. Massachusetts presumably outlawed such activities long ago, but today's holding seems to invite their return.

BIGELOW v. VIRGINIA
421 U.S. 809 (1975)

Mr. Justice Blackmun delivered the opinion of the Court.

An advertisement carried in appellant's newspaper led to his conviction for a violation of a Virginia statute that made it a misdemeanor, by the sale or circulation of any publication, to encourage or prompt the procuring of an abortion. The issue here is whether the editor-appellant's First Amendment rights were unconstitutionally abridged by the statute. The First Amendment, of course, is applicable to the States through the Fourteenth Amendment.

The *Virginia Weekly* was a newspaper published by the Virginia Weekly Associates of Charlottesville. It was issued in that city and circulated in Albemarle County, with particular focus on the campus of the University of Virginia. Appellant, Jeffrey C. Bigelow was a director and the Managing Editor, and responsible officer of the newspaper.

It is to be observed that the advertisement announced that the Women's Pavilion of New York City would help women with unwanted pregnancies to obtain "immediate placement in accredited hospitals and clinics at low cost" and would "make all arrangements" on a "strictly confidential" basis; that it offered "information and counseling"; that it gave the organization's address and telephone numbers; and that it stated that abortions "are now legal in New York" and there "are no residency requirements." Although the advertisement did not contain the name of any licensed physician, the "placement" to which it referred was to "accredited hospitals and clinics."

On May 13 Bigelow was charged with violating (Virginia State law). The statute at that time read:

> If any person by publication, lecture, advertisement, or by the sale or circulation of any publication, or in any other manner encourage or prompt the procuring of abortion or miscarriage, he shall be guilty of a misdemeanor.

The central assumption made by the Supreme Court of Virginia was that the First Amendment guarantees of speech and press are inapplicable to paid commercial advertisements. Our cases, however, clearly establish that speech is not stripped of First Amendment protection merely because it appears in that form.

The fact that the particular advertisement in appellant's newspaper had commercial aspects or reflected the advertiser's commercial interests did not negate all First Amendment guarantees. The State was not free of constitutional restraint merely because the advertisement involved sales or "solicitation," or because appellant was paid for printing it, or because appellant's motive or the motive of the advertiser may have involved financial gain. The existence of "commercial activity in itself, is no justification for narrowing the protection of expression secured by the First Amendment."

Although other categories of speech—such as fighting words, or obscenity, or libel, or incitement—have been held unprotected, no contention has been made that the particular speech embraced in the advertisement in question is within any of these categories.

The advertisement published in appellant's newspaper did more than simply propose a commercial transaction. It contained factual material of clear "public interest." Portions of its message, most prominently the lines, "Abortions are now legal in New York. There are no residency requirements." involve the exercise of the freedom of communicating information and disseminating opinion.

Viewed in its entirety, the advertisement conveyed information of potential interest and value to a diverse audience—not only to readers possibly in need of the services offered, but also to those with a general curiosity about, or genuine interest in, the subject matter or the law of another State and its development, and to readers seeking reform in Virginia. The mere existence of the Women's Pavilion in New York City, with the possibility of its being typical of other organizations there, and the availability of the services offered were not unnewsworthy. Also, the activity advertised pertained to constitutional interests. Thus, in this case, appellant's First Amendment interests coincided with the constitutional interests of the general public.

Moreover, the placement services advertised in appellant's newspaper were legally provided in New York at that time. The Virginia Legislature could not have regulated the advertiser's activity in New York, and obviously could not have proscribed the activity in that State. Neither could Virginia prevent its residents from traveling to New York to obtain those services or, as the State conceded, prosecute them for going there. Virginia possessed no authority to regulate the services provided in New York—the skills and credentials of the New York physicians and of the New York professionals who assisted them, the standards of the New York hospitals and clinics to which patients were referred, or the practices and charges of the New York referral services.

A State does not acquire power or supervision over the internal affairs of another State merely because the welfare and health of its own citizens may be affected when they travel to that State. It may seek to disseminate information so as to enable its citizens to make better informed decisions when they leave. But it may not, under the guise of exercising internal police powers, bar a citizen of another State from disseminating information about an activity that is legal in that State.

We conclude, therefore, that the Virginia courts erred in their assumptions that advertising, as such, was entitled to no First Amendment protection and that appellant Bigelow had no legitimate First Amendment interest. We need not decide in this case the precise extent to which the First Amendment permits regulation of advertising that is related to activites the State may legitimately regulate or even prohibit.

Advertising, like all public expression, may be subject to reasonable regulation that serves a legitimate public interest. To the extent that commercial activity is subject to regulation, the relationship of speech to that activity may be one factor, among others, to be considered in weighing the First Amendment interest against the governmental interest alleged. Advertising is not thereby stripped of all First Amendment protection. The relationship of speech to the marketplace of products or of services does not make it valueless in the marketplace of ideas.

The Court has stated that "a State cannot foreclose the exercise of constitutional rights by mere labels." Regardless of the particular label asserted by the State—whether it calls speech "commercial" or "commercial advertising" or "solicitation"—a court may not escape the task of assessing the First Amendment interest at stake and weighing it against the public interest allegedly served by the regulation. The diverse motives, means, and messages of advertising may make speech "commercial" in widely varying degrees. We need not decide here the extent to which constitutional protection is afforded commercial advertising under all circumstances and in the face of all kinds of regulation.

The task of balancing the interests at stake here was one that should have been undertaken by the Virginia courts before they reached their decision. Virginia is really asserting an interest in regulating what Virginians may *hear* or *read* about the New York services. It is, in effect, advancing an interest in shielding its citizens from information about activities outside Virginia's borders, activities that Virginia's police powers do not reach. This asserted interest, even if understandable, was entitled to little, if any, weight under the circumstances.

No claim has been made, nor could any be supported on this record, that the advertisement was deceptive or fraudulent, or that it related to a commodity or service that was then illegal in either Virginia or in New York, or that it otherwise furthered a criminal scheme in Virginia. There was no possibility that appellant's activity would invade the privacy of other citizens, or infringe on other rights. Observers would not have the advertiser's message thrust upon them as a captive audience.

The strength of appellant's interest was augmented by the fact that the statute was applied against him as publisher and editor of a newspaper, not against the advertiser or a referral agency or a practitioner. The prosecution thus incurred more serious First Amendment overtones.

If application of this statute were upheld under these circumstances, Virginia might exert the power sought here over a wide variety of national publications or interstate newspapers carrying advertisements similar to the one that appeared in Bigelow's newspaper or containing articles on the general subject matter to which the advertisement referred. Other States might do the same. The burdens thereby imposed on publications would impair, perhaps severely, their proper functioning. We know from experience that "liberty of the press is in peril as soon as the government tries to compel what is to go into a newspaper." The policy of the First Amendment favors dissemination of information and opinion, and "(t)he guarantees of freedom of speech and press were not designed to prevent 'the censorship of the press merely, but any action of the government by means of which it might prevent such free and general discussion of public matters as seems absolutely essential . . . ."

We conclude that Virginia could not apply (its state law), as it read in 1971, to appellant's publication of the advertisement in question without unconstitutionally infringing upon his First Amendment rights. The judgment of the Supreme Court of Virginia is therefore reversed.

It is so ordered.

CAREY v. POPULATION SERVICES INTERNATIONAL
431 U.S. 678 (1977)

Mr. Justice Brennan delivered the opinion of the Court (Parts I, II, III, and V), together with an opinion (Part IV), in which Mr. Justice Stewart, Mr. Justice Marshall, and Mr. Justice Blackmun joined.

Under New York Education Law Section 6811 (8) it is a crime 1) for any person to sell or distribute any contraceptive of any kind to a minor under the age of 16 years; 2) for anyone other than a licensed pharmacist to distribute contraceptives to persons over 16; and 3) for anyone, including licensed pharmacists, to advertise or display contraceptives. A three-judge District Court of the Southern District of New York declared Section 6811 (8) unconstitutional in its entirety under the First and Fourteenth Amendments of the Federal Constitution insofar as it applies to nonprescription contraceptives, and enjoined its enforcement as so applied. (398 F. Supp. 321 (1975).) We noted probable jurisdiction, 426 U.S. 918 (1976). We affirm.

I

PPA is a corporation primarily engaged in the mail-order retail sale of nonmedical contraceptive devices from its offices in North Carolina. PPA regularly advertises its products in periodicals published or circulated in New York, accepts orders from New York residents, and fills orders by mailing contraceptives to New York purchasers. Neither the advertisements nor the order forms accompanying them limit availability of PPA's products to persons of any particular age.

Various New York officials have advised PPA that its activities violate New York law. A letter of December 1, 1971, notified PPA that a PPA advertisement in a New York college newspaper violated Section 6811 (8), citing each of the three challenged provisions, and requested "future compliance" with the law. A second letter, dated February 23, 1973, notifying PPA that PPA's magazine advertisements of contraceptives violated the statute, referred particularly to the provisions prohibiting sales to minors and sales by nonpharmacists, and threatened that "In the event you fail to comply, the matter will be referred to our Attorney General for legal action." Finally, PPA was served with a copy of a report of inspectors of the State Board of Pharmacy, dated September 4, 1974, which recorded that PPA advertised male contraceptives, and had been advised to cease selling contraceptives in violation of the state law.

II

Although "(t)he Constitution does not explicitly mention any right of privacy," the Court has recognized that one aspect of the "liberty" protected by the Due Process Clause of the Fourteenth Amendment is "a right of personal privacy, or a guarantee of certain areas or zones of privacy." (*Roe v. Wade*.) This right of personal privacy includes "the interest in independence in making certain kinds of decisions." (*Whalen* v. *Roe*.) While the outer limits of this aspect of privacy have not been marked by the Court, it is clear that among the decisions that an individual may make without unjustified government interference are personal decisions "relating to marriage, *Loving* v. *Virginia*; procreation, *Skinner* v. *Oklahoma*; contraception, *Eisenstadt* v. *Baird* (White, J., concurring in result); family relationships, *Prince* v. *Massachusetts*; and child rearing and education, *Prierce* v. *Society of Sisters*; *Meyer* v. *Nebraska*."

The decision whether or not to beget or bear a child is at the very heart of this cluster of constitutionally protected choices. That decision holds a particularly important place in the history of the right of privacy, a right first explicitly recognized in an opinion holding unconstitutional a statute prohibiting the use of contraceptives, *Griswold* v. *Connecticut,* and most prominently vindicated in recent years in the contexts of contraception, *Griswold* v. *Connecticut; Eisenstadt* v. *Baird,* and abortion, *Roe* v. *Wade*; *Doe* v. *Bolton*; *Planned Parenthood of Central Missouri* v. *Danforth*. This is understandable, for in a field that by definition concerns the most intimate of human activities and relationships, decisions whether to accomplish or to prevent conception are among the most private and sensitive. "If the right of privacy means anything, it is the right of the individual, married or single, to be free of unwarranted governmental intrusion into matters so fundamentally affecting a person as the decision whether to bear or beget a child." (*Eisenstadt* v. *Baird*.)

That the constitutionally protected right of privacy extends to an individual's liberty to make choices regarding contraception does not, however, automatically invalidate every state regulation in this area. The business of manufacturing and selling contraceptives may be regulated in ways that do not infringe protected individual choices. And even a burdensome regulation may be validated by a sufficiently compelling state interest. In *Roe* v. *Wade*, for example, after determining that the "right of privacy . . . encompass(es) a woman's decision whether or not to terminate her pregnancy," we cautioned that the right is not absolute, and that certain state interests (in that case, "interests in safeguarding health, in maintaining medical standards, and in protecting potential life") may at some point "become sufficiently compelling to sustain regulation of the factors that govern the abortion decision." "Compelling" is of course the key word; where a decision as fundamental as that whether to bear or beget a child is involved, regulations imposing a burden on it may be justified only by compelling state interests, and must be narrowly drawn to express only those interests.

III

Restrictions on the distribution of contraceptives clearly burden the freedom to make such decisions. A total prohibition against sale of contraceptives, for example, would intrude upon individual decisions in matters of procreation and contraception as harshly as a direct ban on their use. Indeed, in practice, a prohibition against all sales, since more easily and less offensively enforced, might have an even more devastating effect upon the freedom to choose contraception.

An instructive analogy is found in decisions after *Roe* v. *Wade*, that held unconstitutional statutes that did not prohibit abortions outright but limited in a variety of ways a woman's access to them. The significance of these cases is that they establish that the same test must be applied to state regulations that burden an individual's right to decide to prevent conception or terminate pregnancy by substantially limiting access to the means of effectuating that decision as is applied to state statutes that prohibit the decision entirely. Both types of regulation "may be justified only by a 'compelling state interest' . . . and . . . must be narrowly drawn to express only the legitimate state interests at stake." (*Roe* v. *Wade*.) This is so not because there is an independent fundamental "right of access to contraceptives," but because such access is essential to exercise of the constitutionally protected right of decision in matters of childbearing that is the underlying foundation of the holdings in *Griswold*, *Eisenstadt* v. *Baird*, and *Roe* v. *Wade*.

Limiting the distribution of nonprescription contraceptives to licensed pharmacists clearly imposes a significant burden on the right of the individuals to use contraceptives if they choose to do so. The burden is of course not as great as that under a total ban on distribution. Nevertheless, the restriction of distribution channels to a small fraction of the total number of possible retail outlets renders contraceptive devices considerably less accessible to the public, reduces the opportunity for privacy of selection and purchase, and lessens the possibility of price competition. Of particular relevance here is *Doe* v. *Bolton*, in which the Court struck down, as unconstitutionally burdening the right of a woman to choose abortion, a statute requiring that abortions be performed only in accredited hospitals, in the absence of proof that the requirement was substantially related to the State's interest in protecting the patient's health. (410 U.S., at 193–195.) The same infirmity infuses the limitation in Section 6811 (8). "Just as in *Griswold*, where the right of married persons to use contraceptives was 'diluted or adversely affected' by permitting a conviction for giving advice as to its exercise, so here, to sanction a medical restriction upon distribution of a contraceptive not proved hazardous to health would impair the exercise of the constitutional right." *Eisenstadt* v. *Baird* (White, J., concurring in result).

IV

A

The District Court also held unconstitutional, as applied to nonprescription contraceptives, the provision of Section 6811 (8) prohibiting the distribution of contraceptives to those under 16 years of age. Appellants contend that this provision of the statute is constitutionally permissible as a regulation of the morality of minors, in furtherance of the State's policy against promiscuous sexual intercourse among the young.

The question of the extent of state power to regulate conduct of minors not constitutionally regulable when committed by adults is a vexing one, perhaps not susceptible to precise answer. We have been reluctant to attempt to define "the totality of the relationship of the juvenile and the state." (*In re Gault.*) Certain principles, however, have been recognized. "Minors, as well as adults, are protected by the Constitution and possess Constitutional rights." (*Planned Parenthood of Central Missouri* v. *Danforth*.) "(W)hatever may be their precise impact, neither the Fourteenth Amendment nor the Bill of Rights is for adults alone." (*In re Gault.*) On the other hand, we have held in a variety of contexts that "the power of the state to control the conduct of children reaches beyond the scope of its authority over adults." (*Prince* v. *Massachusetts*.)

Of particular significance to the decision of this case, the right to privacy in connection with decisions affecting procreation extends to minors as well as to adults. *Planned Parenthood of Central Missouri* v. *Danforth* held that a State "may not impose a blanket provision . . . requiring the consent of a parent or person *in loco parentis* as a condition for abortion of an unmarried minor during the first 12 weeks of her pregnancy." As in the case of the spousal consent requirement struck down in the same case, "the State does not have the constitutional authority to give a third party an absolute, and possibly arbitrary, veto, which the state itself is absolutely and totally prohibited from exercising." State restrictions inhibiting privacy rights of minors are valid only if they serve "any significant state interest . . . that is not present in the case of an adult." *Planned Parenthood* found that no such interest justified a state requirement of parental consent.

Since the State may not impose a blanket prohibition, or even a blanket requirement of parental consent, on the choice of a minor to terminate her pregnancy, the constitutionality of a blanket prohibition of the distribution of contraceptives to minors is *a fortiori* foreclosed. The State's interests in protection of the mental and physical health of the pregnant minor, and in protection of potential life are clearly more implicated by the abortion decision than by the decision to use a nonhazardous contraceptive.

Appellants argue, however, that significant state interests are served by restricting minors access to contraceptives, because free availability to minors of contraceptives would lead to increased sexual activity among the young, in violation of the policy of New York to discourage such behavior. The argument is that minors' sexual activity may be deterred by increasing the hazards attendant on it. The same argument, however, would support a ban on abortions for minors, or indeed support a prohibition on abortions, or access to contraceptives, for the unmarried, whose sexual activity is also against the public policy of many States. Yet, in each of these areas, the Court has rejected the argument, noting in *Roe* v. *Wade*, that "no court or commentator has taken the argument seriously." The reason for this unanimous rejection was stated in *Eisenstadt* v. *Baird*: "It would be plainly unreasonable to assume that (the state) has proscribed pregnancy and the birth of an unwanted child (or the physical and psychological dangers of an abortion) as punishment for fornication." We remain reluctant to attribute any such "scheme of values" to the State.

Moreover, there is substantial reason for doubt whether limiting access to contraceptives will in fact substantially discourage early sexual behavior. Appellants themselves conceded in the District Court that "there is no evidence that teenage extramarital sexual activity increases in proportion to the availability of contraceptives," and accordingly offered none, in the District Court or here. Appellees, on the other hand, cite a considerable body of evidence and opinion indicating that there is no such deterrent effect." Although we take judicial notice, as did the District Court, that with or without access to contraceptives, the incidence of sexual activity among minors is high, and the consequences of such activity are frequently devastating, the studies cited by appellees play no part in our decision. It is enough that we again confirm the principle that when a State, as here, burdens the exercise of a fundamental right, its attempt to justify that burden as a rational means for the accomplishment of some significant State policy requires more than a bare assertion, based on a conceded complete absence of supporting evidence, that the burden is connected to such a policy.

V

The District Court's holding that the prohibition of any "advertisement or display" of contraceptives is unconstitutional was clearly correct. Only last term *Virginia State Board of Pharmacy* v. *Virginia Citizens Consumer Council* held that a state may not "completely suppress the dissemination of concededly truthful information about entirely lawful activity," even when that information could be categorized as "commercial speech." Just as in that case, the statute challenged here seeks to suppress completely any information about the availability and price of contraceptives. Nor does the case present any question left open in *Virginia State Board*; here, as there, there can be no contention that the regulation is "a mere time, place, and manner restriction," or that it prohibits only misleading or deceptive advertisement, or "that the transaction proposed in the forbidden advertisements are themselves illegal in any way. Moreover, in addition to the substantial individual and societal interests" in the free flow of commercial information enumerated in *Virginia State Board*, the information suppressed by this statute "related to activity with which, at least in some respects, the State could not interfere."

Appellants contend that advertisements of contraceptive products would be offensive and embarrassing to those exposed to them, and that permitting them would legitimize sexual activity of young people. But these are classically not justifications validating the suppression of expression protected by the First Amendment. At least where obscenity is not involved, we have consistently held that the fact that protected speech may be offensive to some does not justify its suppression. As for the possible "legitimation" of illicit sexual behavior, whatever might be the case if the advertisements directly incited illicit sexual activity among the young, none of the advertisements in this record can even remotely be characterized as "directed to inciting or producing imminent lawless action and . . . likely to incite or produce such action." (*Brandenburg* v. *Ohio*.) They merely state the availability of products and services that are not only entirely legal, but constitutionally protected. These arguments therefore do not justify the total suppression of advertising concerning contraceptives.

Mr. Justice Rehnquist, dissenting.

Those who valiantly but vainly defended the heights of Bunker Hill in 1775 made it possible that men such as James Madison might later sit in the first Congress and draft the Bill of Rights to the

Constitution. The post-Civil War Congresses which drafted the Civil War Amendments to the Constitution could not have accomplished their task without the blood of brave men on both sides which was shed at Shiloh, Gettysburg, and Cold Harbor. If those responsible for these Amendments, by feats of valor or efforts of draftsmanship, could have lived to know that their efforts had enshrined in the Constitution the right of commercial vendors of contraceptives to peddle them to unmarried minors through such means as window displays and vending machines located in the men's room of truck stops, notwithstanding the considered judgment of the New York Legislature to the contrary, it is not difficult to imagine their reaction.

I do not believe that the cases discussed in the Court's opinion require any such result, but to debate the Court's treatment of the question on a case-by-case basis would concede more validity to the result reached by the Court than I am willing to do. There comes a point when endless and ill-considered extension of principles originally formulated in quite different cases produces such an indefensible result that no logic-chopping can possibly make the fallacy of the result more obvious. The Court here in effect holds that the First and Fourteenth Amendments not only guarantee full and free debate *before* a legislative judgment as to the moral dangers to which minors within the jurisdiction of the State should not be subjected, but goes further and absolutely prevents the representatives of the majority from carrying out such a policy *after* the issues have been fully aired.

No questions of religious belief, compelled allegiance to a secular creed, or decisions on the part of married couples as to procreation, are involved here. New York has simply decided that it wishes to discourage unmarried minors in the 14- to 16-year age bracket from having promiscuous sexual intercourse with one another. Even the Court would scarcely go so far as to say that this is not a subject with which the New York Legislature may properly concern itself.

That legislature has not chosen to deny to a pregnant woman, after the *fait accompli* of pregnancy, the one remedy which would enable her to terminate an unwanted pregnancy. It has instead sought to deter the conduct which will produce such *faits accomplis*. The majority of New York's citizens are in effect told that however deeply they may be concerned about the problem of promiscuous sex and intercourse among unmarried teenagers, they may not adopt this means of dealing with it. The Court holds that New York may not use its police power to legislate in the interests of its concept of the public morality as it pertains to minors. The Court's denial of a power so fundamental to self-government must, in the long run, prove to be a temporary departure from a wise and heretofore settled course of adjudication to the contrary. I would reverse the judgment of the District Court.

VIRGINIA STATE BOARD OF PHARMACY v. *VIRGINIA CITIZEN CONSUMER COUNCIL, INC.*
425 U.S. 748 (1976)

Appellees, as consumers of prescription drugs, brought suit against the Virginia State Board of Pharmacy and its individual members, appellants herein, challenging the validity under the First and Fourteenth Amendments of the Virginia statute declaring it unprofessional conduct for a licensed pharmacist to advertise the prices of prescription drugs. A three-judge District Court declared the statute void and enjoined appellants from enforcing it.

Mr. Justice Blackmun delivered the opinion of the Court.

The question first arises whether, even assuming that First Amendment protection attaches to the flow of drug price information, it is a protection enjoyed by the appellees as recipients of the information, and not solely, if at all, by the advertisers themselves who seek to disseminate that information.

Freedom of speech presupposes a willing speaker. But where a speaker exists, as is the case here, the protection afforded is to the communication, to its source, and to its recipients both. This is clear from the decided cases. In *Lamont* v. *Postmaster General,* the Court upheld the First Amendment rights of citizens to receive political publications sent from abroad. More recently, in *Kleindienst* v. *Mandel* we acknowledged that this Court has referred to a First Amendment right to "receive information and ideas," and that freedom of speech " 'necessarily protects the right to receive.' " And in *Procunier* v. *Martinez,* where censorship of prison inmates' mail was under examination, we thought it unnecessary to assess the First Amendment rights of the inmates themselves, for it was reasoned that such censorship equally infringed the rights of noninmates to whom the correspondence was addressed. There are numerous other expressions to the same effect in the Court's decisions. If there is a right to advertise, there is a reciprocal right to receive the advertising, and it may be asserted by these appellees.

The appellants contend that the advertisement of prescription drug prices is outside the protection of the First Amendment because it is "commercial speech." There can be no question that in past decisions the Court has given some indication that commercial speech is unprotected. In *Valentine* v. *Chrestensen,* the Court upheld a New York statute that prohibited the distribution of any "handbill, circular . . . or other advertising matter whatsoever in or upon any street." The Court concluded that, although the First Amendment would forbid the banning of all communication by handbill in the public thoroughfares, it imposed "no such restraint on government as respects purely commercial advertising." Further support for a "commercial speech" exception to the First Amendment may perhaps be found in *Breard* v. *Alexandria,* where the Court upheld a conviction for violation of an ordinance prohibiting door-to-door solicitation of magazine subscriptions. The Court reasoned: "The selling . . . brings into the transaction a commercial feature," and it distinguished *Martin* v. *Struthers,* where it had reversed a conviction for door-to-door distribution of leaflets publicizing a religious meeting, as a case involving "no element of the commercial." Moreover, the Court several times has stressed that communications to which First Amendment protection was given were *not* "purely commercial."

Since the decision in *Breard,* however, the Court has never *denied,* protection on the ground that the speech in issue was "commercial speech." That simplistic approach, which by then had come under criticism or was regarded as of doubtful validity by members of the Court, was avoided in *Pittsburgh Press Co.* v. *Pittsburgh Commission on Human Relations.* There the Court upheld an ordinance prohibiting newspapers from listing employment advertisements in columns according to whether male or female employees were sought to be hired. The Court, to be sure, characterized the advertisements as "classic examples of commercial speech," and a newspaper's printing of the advertisements as of the same character. The Court, however, upheld the ordinance on the ground that the restriction it imposed was permissible because the discriminatory hirings proposed by the advertisements, and by their newspaper layout, were themselves illegal.

Last term, in *Bigelow* v. *Virginia,* the notion of unprotected "commercial speech" all but passed from the scene. We reversed a conviction for violation of a Virginia statute that made the circulation of any publication to encourage or promote the processing of an abortion in Virginia a misdemeanor. The defendant had published in his newspaper the availability of abortions in New York. The advertisement in question, in addition to announcing that abortions were legal in New York, offered the services of a referral agency in that state. We rejected the contention that the publication was unprotected because it was commercial. *Chrestensen's* continued validity was questioned, and its holding was described as "distinctly a limited one" that merely upheld "a reasonable regulation of the manner in which commercial advertising could be distributed." We concluded that "the Virginia courts erred in their assumptions that advertising, as such, was entitled to no First Amendment protection," and we observed that the "relationship of speech to the marketplace of products or of services does not make it valueless in the marketplace of ideas."

Some fragment of hope for the continuing validity of a "commercial speech" exception arguably might have persisted because of the subject matter of the advertisement in *Bigelow*. We noted that in announcing the availability of legal abortions in New York, the advertisement "did more than simply propose a commercial transaction. It contained factual material of clear 'public interest.' " And, of course, the advertisement related to activity with which, at least in some respects, the State could not interfere. Indeed, we observed: "We need not decide in this case the precise extent to which the First Amendment permits regulation of advertising that is related to activities the State may legitimately regulate or even prohibit."

Here, in contrast, the question whether there is a First Amendment exception for "commercial speech" is squarely before us. Our pharmacist does not wish to editorialize on any subject, cultural, philosophical, or political. He does not wish to report any particularly newsworthy fact, or to make generalized observations even about commercial matters. The "idea" he wishes to communicate is simply this: "I will sell you the X prescription drug at the Y price." Our question, then, is whether this communication is wholly outside the protection of the First Amendment.

We begin with several propositions that already are settled or beyond serious dispute. It is clear, for example, that speech does not lose its First Amendment protection because money is spent to project it, as in a paid advertisement of one form or another. Speech likewise is protected even though it is carried in a form that is "sold" for profit, . . . and even though it may involve a solicitation to purchase or otherwise pay or contribute money.

If there is a kind of commercial speech that lacks all First Amendment protection, therefore, it must be distinguished by its content. Yet the speech whose content deprives it of protection cannot simply be speech on a commercial subject. No one would contend that our pharmacist may be prevented from being heard on the subject of whether, in general, pharmaceutical prices should be regulated, or their advertisement forbidden. Nor can it be dispositive that a commercial advertisement is uneditorial, and merely reports a fact. Purely factual matter of public interest may claim protection.

Our question is whether speech which does "no more than propose a commercial transaction," *Pittsburgh Press Co.* v. *Pittsburgh Commission on Human Relations,* is so removed from any "exposition of ideas," and from " 'truth, science, morality, and arts in general, in its diffusion of liberal sentiments on the administration of Government,' " (*Roth* v. *United States*) that it lacks all protection. Our answer is that it is not.

Focusing first on the individual parties to the transaction that is proposed in the commercial advertisement, we may assume that the advertiser's interest is a purely economic one. That hardly disqualifies him for protection under the First Amendment. The interests of the contestants in a labor dispute are primarily economic, but it has long been settled that both the employee and the employer are protected by the First Amendment when they express themselves on the merits of the dispute in order to influence its outcome.

As to the particular consumer's interest in the free flow of commercial information, that interest may be as keen, if not keener by far, than his interest in the day's most urgent political debate.

Appellees' case in this respect is a convincing one. Those whom the suppression of prescription drug price information hits the hardest are the poor, the sick, and particularly the aged. A disproportionate amount of their income tends to be spent on prescription drugs; yet they are the least able to learn by shopping from pharmacist to pharmacist, where their scarce dollars are best spent. When drugs prices vary as strikingly as they do, information as to who is charging what becomes more than a convenience. It could mean the alleviation of physical pain or the enjoyment of basic necessities.

Generalizing, society also may have a strong interest in the free flow of commercial information. Even an individual advertisement, though entirely "commercial," may be of general public interest. Obviously, not all commercial messages contain the same or even a very great public interest element. There are few to which such an element, however, could not be added. Our pharmacist, for example, could cast himself as a commentator on store-to-store disparities in drug prices, giving his own and those of a competitor as proof. We see little point in requiring him to do so, and little difference if he does not.

Moreover, there is another consideration that suggests that no line between publicly "interesting" or "important" commercial advertising and the opposite kind could ever be drawn. Advertising, however tasteless and excessive it sometimes may seem, is nonetheless dissemination of information as to who is producing and selling what product, for what reason, and at what price. So long as we preserve a predominantly free enterprise economy, the allocation of our resources in large measure will be made through numerous private economic decisions. It is a matter of public interest that those decisions, in the aggregate, be intelligent and well informed. To this end, the free flow of commercial information is indispensable. And if it is indispensable to the proper allocation of resources in a free enterprise, it is also indispensable to the formation of intelligent opinions as to how that system ought to be regulated or altered. Therefore, even if the First Amendment were thought to be primarily an instrument to enlighten public decision making in a democracy, we could not say that the free flow of information does not serve that goal.

Arrayed against these substantial individual and societal interests are a number of justifications for the advertising ban. These have to do principally with maintaining a high degree of professionalism on the part of licensed pharmacists.

Price advertising, it is argued, will place in jeopardy the pharmacist's expertise and, with it, the customer's health. It is claimed that the aggressive price competition that will result from unlimited advertising will make it impossible for the pharmacist to supply professional services in the compounding, handling, and dispensing of prescription drugs. Such services are time consuming and expensive; if competitors who economize by eliminating them are permitted to advertise their resulting lower prices, the more painstaking and conscientious pharmacist will be forced either to follow suit or to go out of business. It is also claimed that prices might not necessarily fall as a result of advertising. If one pharmacist advertises, others must, and the resulting expense will inflate the cost of drugs. It is further claimed that advertising will lead people to shop for their prescription drugs among the various pharmacists who offer the lowest prices, and the loss of stable pharmacist-customer relationships will make individual attention—and certainly the practice of monitoring—impossible. Finally, it is argued that damage will be done to the professional image of the pharmacist. This image, that of a skilled and specialized craftsman, attracts talent to the profession and reinforces the better habits of those who are in it. Price advertising, it is said, will reduce the pharmacist's status to that of a mere retailer.

The strength of these proffered justifications is greatly undermined by the fact that high professional standards, to a substantial extent, are guaranteed by the close regulation to which parmacists in

Virginia are subject. And this case concerns the retail sale by the pharmacist more than it does his professional standards. Surely, any pharmacist guilty of professional dereliction that actually endangers his customer will promptly lose his license. At the same time, we cannot discount the Board's justifications entirely. The Court regarded justifications of this type sufficient to sustain the advertising bans challenged on due process and equal protection grounds.

The challenge now made, however, is based on the First Amendment. This casts the Board's justifications in a different light, for on close inspection it is seen that the State's protectiveness of its citizens rests in large measure on the advantages of their being kept in ignorance.

There is, of course, an alternative to this highly paternalistic approach. That alternative is to assume that this information is not in itself harmful, that people will perceive their own best interests if only they are well enough informed, and that the best means to that end is to open the channels of communication rather than to close them. If they are truly open, nothing prevents the "professional" pharmacist from marketing his own assertedly superior product and contrasting it with that of the low-cost, high-volume prescription drug retailer. But the choice among these alternative approaches is not ours to make or the Virginia General Assembly's. It is precisely this kind of choice, between the dangers of suppressing information, and the dangers of its misuse if it is freely available, that the First Amendment makes for us. Virginia is free to require whatever professional standards it wishes of its pharmacists; it may subsidize them or protect them from competition in other ways. But it may not do so by keeping the public in ignorance of the entirely lawful terms that competing pharmacists are offering. In this sense, the justifications Virginia has offered for suppressing the flow of prescription drug price information, far from persuading us that the flow is not protected by the First Amendment, have reinforced our view that it is. We so hold.

In concluding that commercial speech, like other varieties, is protected, we of course do not hold that it can never be regulated in any way. Some forms of commercial speech regulation are surely permissible. We mention a few only to make clear that they are not before us and therefore are not foreclosed by this case.

There is no claim, for example, that the prohibition on prescription drug price advertising is a mere time, place, and manner restriction. We have often approved restrictions of that kind provided that they are justified without reference to the content of the regulated speech, that they serve a significant government interest, and that in so doing they leave open ample alternative channels for communication of the information. Whatever may be the proper bounds of time, place, and manner restrictions on commercial speech, they are plainly exceeded by this Virginia statute, which singles out speech of a particular content and seeks to prevent its dissemination completely.

Nor is there any claim that prescription drug price advertisements are forbidden because they are false or misleading in any way. Untruthful speech, commercial or otherwise, has never been protected for its own sake. Obviously, much commercial speech is not provably false, or even wholly false, but only deceptive or misleading. We foresee no obstacle to a State's dealing effectively with this problem. The First Amendment, as we construe it today, does not prohibit the State from insuring that the stream of commercial information flows cleanly as well as freely.

Also, there is no claim that the transactions proposed in the forbidden advertisements are themselves illegal in any way. Finally, the special problems of the electronic broadcast media are likewise not in this case.

What is at issue is whether a State may completely suppress the dissemination of concededly truthful information about entirely lawful activity, fearful of that information's effect upon its disseminators and its recipients. Reserving other questions* we conclude that the answer to this one is in the negative.

The judgment of the District Court is affirmed.

It is so ordered.

Mr. Justice Stevens took no part in the consideration or decision of this case.

Mr. Chief Justice Burger, concurring.

The Court notes that roughly 95 percent of all prescriptions are filled with dosage units already prepared by the manufacturer and sold to the pharmacy in that form. These are the drugs that have a market large enough to make their preparation profitable to the manufacturer; for the same reason, they are the drugs that it is profitable for the pharmacist to advertise. In dispensing *these* items, the pharmacist performs three tasks: he finds the correct bottle; he counts out the correct number of tablets or measures the right amount of liquid; and he accurately transfers the doctor's dosage instructions to the container. Without minimizing the potential consequences of error in performing these tasks or the importance of the other tasks a professional pharmacist performs, it is clear that in this regard he no more renders a true professional service than does a clerk who sells lawbooks.

Our decision today, therefore, deals largely with the State's power to prohibit pharmacists from advertising the retail price of prepackaged drugs. (Q)uite different factors would govern were we faced with a law regulating or even prohibiting advertising by the traditional learned professions of medicine or law. "The interest of the States in regulating lawyers is especially great since lawyers are essential to the primary governmental function of administering justice, and have historically been 'officers of the courts.' " We have also recognized the State's substantial interest in regulating physicians. Attorneys and physicians are engaged primarily in providing services in which professional judgment is a large component, a matter very different from the retail sale of labeled drugs already prepared by others.

Mr. Justice Stewart aptly observes that the "difference between commercial price and product advertising . . . and ideological communication" allows the state a scope in regulating the former that would be unacceptable under the First Amendment with respect to the latter. I think it important to note also that the advertisement of professional services carries with it quite different risks than the advertisement of standard products. The Court took note of this in *Semler,* in upholding a state statute prohibiting entirely certain types of advertisement by dentists:

> The legislature was not dealing with traders in commodities, but with the vital interest of public health, and with a profession treating bodily ills and demanding different standards of conduct from those which are traditional in the competition of the market place. The community is concerned with the maintenance of professional standards which will insure not only competency in individual practitioners, but protection against those who would prey upon a public peculiarly susceptible to imposition through alluring promises of physical relief. And the community is concerned in providing safeguards not only against deception, but against practices which would tend to demoralize the profession by forcing its members into an unseemly rivalry which would enlarge the opportunities of the least scrupulous.

---

*We stress that we have considered in this case the regulation of commercial advertising by pharmacists. Although we express no opinion as to other professions, the distinctions, historical and functional, between professions, may require consideration of quite different factors. Physicians and lawyers, for example, do not dispense standardized products; they render professional *services* of almost infinite variety and nature, with the consequent enhanced possibility for confusion and deception if they were to undertake certain kinds of advertising.

I doubt that we know enough about evaluating the quality of medical and legal services to know which claims of superiority are "misleading" and which are justifiable. Nor am I sure that even advertising the price of certain professional services is not inherently misleading, since what the professional must do will vary greatly in individual cases. It is important to note that the Court wisely leaves these issues to another day.

Mr. Justice Rehnquist, dissenting.

The logical consequences of the Court's decision in this case, a decision which elevates commercial intercourse between a seller hawking his wares and a buyer seeking to strike a bargain to the same plane as has been previously reserved for the free marketplace of ideas, are far reaching indeed. Under the Court's opinion, the way will be open not only for dissemination of price information but also for active promotion of prescription drugs, liquor, cigarettes and other products the use of which it has previously been thought desirable to discourage. Now, however, such promotion is protected by the First Amendment so long as it is not misleading or does not promote an illegal product or enterprise. In coming to this conclusion, the Court has overruled a legislative determination that such advertising should not be allowed and has done so on behalf of a consumer group which is not directly disadvantaged by the statute in question. This effort to reach a result which the Court obviously considers desirable is a troublesome one, for two reasons. It extends standing to raise First Amendment claims beyond the previous decisions of this Court. It also extends the protection of that Amendment to purely commercial endeavors which its vigorous champions on this Court had thought to be beyond its pale.

BATES AND VAN O'STEEN V. *STATE BAR OF ARIZONA*
433 U.S. 350 (1977)

Mr. Justice Blackmun delivered the opinion of the Court.

As part of its regulation of the Arizona Bar, the Supreme Court of that State has imposed and enforces a disciplinary rule that restricts advertising by attorneys. This case presents two issues: whether Sections 1 and 2 of the Sherman Act, 15 U.S.C. Sections 1 and 2, forbid such state regulation, and whether the operation of the rule violates the First Amendment, made applicable to the States through the Fourteenth. (This edited version of the case will consider only the second issue.)

Appellants John R. Bates and Van O'Steen are attorneys licensed to practice law in the State of Arizona. As such, they are members of the appellee, the State Bar of Arizona. After admission to the bar in 1972, appellants worked as attorneys with the Maricopa County Legal Aid Society.

In March 1974, appellants left the Society and opened a law office, which they call a "legal clinic," in Phoenix. Their aim was to provide legal services at modest fees to persons of moderate income who did not qualify for governmental legal aid. In order to achieve this end, they would accept only routine matters, such as uncontested divorces, uncontested adoptions, simple personal bankruptcies, and changes of name, for which costs could be kept down by extensive use of paralegals, automatic typewriting equipment, and standardized forms and office procedures. More complicated cases, such as contested divorces, would not be accepted. Because appellants set their prices so as to have a relatively low return on each case they handled, they depended on substantial volume.

After conducting their practice in this manner for two years, appellants concluded that their practice and clinical concept could not survive unless the availability of legal services at low cost was advertised and, in particular, fees were advertised. Consequently, in order to generate the necessary flow of business, that is, "to attract clients," appellants on February 22, 1976, placed an advertisement in the *Arizona Republic*, a daily newspaper of general circulation in the Phoenix metropolitan area. As may be seen, the advertisement stated that appellants were offering "legal services at very reasonable fees," and listed their fees for certain services.

(The Court recited the Arizona Supreme Court's conclusion that regulation of professional services by lawyers is constitutionally permissible.)

Of particular interest here is the opinion of Mr. Justice Holohan in dissent. In his view, the case should have been framed in terms of "the right of the public as consumers and citizens to know about the activities of the legal profession," rather than as one involving merely the regulation of a profession. Observed in this light, he felt that the rule performed a substantial disservice to the public:

> Obviously, the information of what lawyers charge is important for private economic decisions by those in need of legal services. Such information is also helpful, perhaps indispensable, to the formation of an intelligent opinion by the public on how well the legal system is working and whether it should be regulated or even altered . . . The rule at issue prevents access to such information by the public."

Although the dissenter acknowledged that some types of advertising might cause confusion and deception, he felt that the remedy was to ban that form, rather than all advertising. Thus, despite his "personal dislike of the concept of advertising by attorneys," he found the ban unconstitutional.

Last term, in *Virginia Pharmacy Board* v. *Virginia Consumer Council,* the Court considered the validity under the First Amendment of a Virginia statute declaring that a pharmacist was guilty of "unprofessional conduct" if he advertised prescription drug prices. The pharmacist would then be subject to a monetary penalty or the suspension or revocation of his license. The statute thus effectively prevented the advertising of prescription drug price information. We recognized that the pharmacist who desired to advertise did not wish to report any particularly newsworthy fact or to comment on any cultural, philosophical, or political subject; his desired communication was characterized simply: " 'I will sell you X prescription drug at the Y price.' " Nonetheless, we held that commercial speech of that kind was entitled to the protection of the First Amendment.

Our analysis began, with the observation that our cases long have protected speech even though it is in the form of a paid advertisement; in a form that is sold for ptofit; or in the form of a solicitation to pay or contribute money. If commercial speech is to be distinguished, it "must be distinguished by its content." But a consideration of competing interests reinforced our view that such speech should not be withdrawn from protection merely because it proposed a mundane commercial transaction. Even though the speaker's interest is largely economic, the Court has protected such speech in certain contexts. The listener's interest is substantial: the consumer's concern for the free flow of commercial speech often may be far keener than his concern for urgent political dialogue. Moreover, significant societal interests are served by such speech. Advertising, though entirely commercial, may often carry information of import to significant issues of the day. And commercial speech serves to inform the public of the availability, nature, and prices of products and services, and thus performs an indispensable role in the allocation of resources in a free enterprise system. In short, such speech serves individual and societal interests in assuring informed and reliable decision making.

Arrayed against these substantial interests in the free flow of commercial speech were a number of proffered justifications for the advertising ban. Central among them were claims that the ban was essential to the maintenance of professionalism among licensed pharmacists. It was asserted that advertising would create price competition that might cause the pharmacist to economize at the customer's expense. He might reduce or eliminate the truly professional portions of his services: the maintenance and packaging of drugs so as to assure their effectiveness, and the supplementation on occasion of the prescribing physician's advice as to use. Moreover, it was said, advertising would cause consumers to price-shop, thereby undermining the pharmacist's effort to monitor the drug use of a regular customer so as to ensure that the prescribed drug would not provoke an allergic reaction or be incompatible with another substance the customer was consuming. Finally, it was argued that advertising would reduce the image of the pharmacist as a skilled and specialized craftsman—an image that was said to attract talent to the profession and to reinforce the good habits of those in it—to that of a mere shopkeeper.

Although acknowledging that the State had a strong interest in maintaining professionalism among pharmacists, this Court concluded that the proffered justifications were inadequate to support the advertising ban. High professional standards were assured in large part by the close regulation to which pharmacists in Virginia were subject. And we observed that "on close inspection it is seen that the State's protectiveness of its citizens rests in large part on the advantages of their being kept in ignorance." But we noted the presence of a potent alternative to this "highly paternalistic" approach: "That alternative is to assume that this information is not in itself harmful, that people will perceive their own best interest if only they are well enough informed, and that the best means to that end is to open the channels of communication rather than to close them." The choice between the dangers of suppressing information and the dangers arising from its free flow was seen as precisely the choice "that the First Amendment makes for us."

We have set out this detailed summary of the *Pharmacy* opinion because the conclusion that Arizona's disciplinary rule is violative of the First Amendment might be said to flow *a fortiori* from it. Like the Virginia statutes, the disciplinary rule serves to inhibit the free flow of commercial information and to keep the public in ignorance. Because of the possibility, however, that the differences among professions might bring different constitutional considerations into play, we specifically reserved judgment as to other professions.

In the instant case we are confronted with the arguments directed explicitly toward the regulation of advertising by licensed attorneys.

The issue presently before us is a narrow one. First, we need not address the peculiar problems associated with advertising claims relating to the quality of legal services. Such claims probably are not susceptible to precise measurement or verification and, under some circumstances, might well be deceptive or misleading to the public, or even false. Appellee does not suggest, nor do we perceive, that appellants' advertisement contained claims, extravagant or otherwise, as to the quality of services. Accordingly, we leave that issue for another day. Second, we also need not resolve the problems associated with in-person solicitation of clients—at the hospital room or the accident site, or in any other situation that breeds undue influence—by attorneys or their agents or "runners." Activity of that kind might well pose dangers of overreaching and misrepresentation not encountered in newspaper announcement advertising. Hence, this issue also is not before us. Third, we note that appellee's criticism of advertising by attorneys does not apply with much force to some of the basic factual content of advertising: information as to the attorney's name, address, and telephone number, office hours, and the like. The American Bar Association itself has a provision in its current Code of Professional Responsibility that would allow the disclosure of such information, and more, in the classified section of the telephone directory. We recognize, however, that an advertising diet limited to such spartan fare would provide scant nourishment.

The heart of the dispute before us today is whether lawyers also may constitutionally advertise the *prices* at which certain routine services will be performed. Numerous justifications are proffered for the restriction of such price advertising. We consider each in turn:

1. The Adverse Effect on Professionalism

Appellee places particular emphasis on the adverse effects that it feels price advertising will have on the legal profession. The key to professionalism, it is argued, is the sense of pride that involvement in the discipline generates. It is claimed that price advertising will bring about commercialization, which will undermine the attorney's sense of dignity and self-worth. The hustle of the marketplace will adversely affect the profession's service orientation, and irreparably damage the delicate balance between the lawyer's need to earn and his obligation selflessly to serve. Advertising is also said to erode the client's trust in his attorney: once the client perceives that the lawyer is motivated by profit, his confidence that the attorney is acting out of commitment to the client's welfare is jeopardized. And advertising is said to tarnish the dignified public image of the profession.

We recognize, of course, and commend the spirit of public service with which the profession of law is practiced and to which it is dedicated. The present Members of this Court, licensed attorneys all, could not feel otherwise. And we would have reason to pause if we felt that our decision today would undercut that spirit. But we find the postulated connection between advertising and the erosion of true professionalism to be severely strained. At its core, the argument presumes that attorneys must conceal from themselves and from their clients the real-life fact that lawyers earn their livelihood at the bar. We suspect that few attorneys engage in such self-deception. And rare is the client, moreover, even one of modest means, who enlists the aid of an attorney with the expectation that his services will be rendered free of charge. In fact, the American Bar Association advises that an attorney should reach "a clear agreement with his client as to the basis of the fee charges to be made," and that this is to be done "(a)s soon as feasible after a lawyer has been employed." Code of Professional Responsibility. If the commercial basis of the relationship is to be promptly disclosed on ethical grounds, once the client is in the office, it seems inconsistent to condemn the candid revelation of the same information before he arrives at that office.

Moreover, the assertion that advertising will diminish the attorney's reputation in the community is open to question. Bankers and engineers advertise, and yet these professions are not regarded as undignified. In fact, it has been suggested that the failure of lawyers to advertise creates public disillusionment with the profession. The absence of advertising may be seen to reflect the profession's failure to reach out and serve the community: studies reveal that many persons do not obtain counsel even when they perceive a need because of the feared price of services or because of an inability to locate a competent attorney. Indeed, cynicism with regard to the profession may be created by the fact that it long has publicly eschewed advertising, while condoning the actions of the attorney who structures his social or civic associations so as to provide contacts with potential clients.

It appears that the ban on advertising originated as a rule of etiquette and not as a rule of ethics. Early lawyers in Britain viewed the law as a form of public service, rather than as a means of earning a living, and they looked down on "trade" as unseemly. Eventually, the attitude toward advertising fostered by this view evolved into an aspect of the ethics of the profession. But habit and tradition are not in themselves an adequate answer to a constitutional challenge. In this day, we do not belittle the person who earns his living by the strength of his arm or the force of his mind. Since the belief that lawyers are somehow "above" trade has become an anachronism the historical foundation for the advertising restraint has crumbled.

2. The Inherently Misleading Nature of Attorney Advertising

It is argued that advertising of legal services inevitably will be misleading a) because such services are so individualized with regard to content and quality as to prevent informed comparison on the basis of an advertisement, b) because the consumer of legal services is unable to determine in advance just what services he needs, and c) because advertising by attorneys will highlight irrelevant factors and fail to show the relevant factor of skill.

We are not persuaded that restrained professional advertising by lawyers inevitably will be misleading. Although many services performed by attorneys are indeed unique, it is doubtful that any attorney would or could advertise fixed prices for services of that type. The only services that lend themselves to advertising are the routine ones: the uncontested divorce, the simple adoption, the uncontested personal bankruptcy, the change of name, and the like—the very services advertised by appellants. Although the precise service demanded in each task may vary slightly, and although legal services are not fungible, these facts do not make advertising misleading so long as the attorney does the necessary work at the advertised price. The argument that legal services are so unique that fixed rates cannot meaningfully be established is refuted by the record in this case: the appellee State Bar itself sponsors a Legal Services Program in which the participating attorneys agree to perform services like those advertised by the appellants at standardized rates. Indeed, until the decision of this Court in *Goldfarb* v. *Virginia State Bar,* the Maricopa County Bar Association apparently had a schedule of suggested minimum fees for standard legal tasks. We thus find of little force the assertion that advertising is misleading because of an inherent lack of standardization in legal services.

The second component of the argument—that advertising ignores the diagnostic role—fares little better. It is unlikely that many people go to an attorney merely to ascertain if they have a clean bill of legal health. Rather, attorneys are likely to be employed to perform specific tasks. Although the client may not know the detail involved in performing the task, he no doubt is able to identify the service he desires at the level of generality to which advertising lends itself.

The third component is not without merit: advertising does not provide a complete foundation on which to select an attorney. But it seems peculiar to deny the consumer, on the ground that the information is incomplete, at least some of the relevant information needed to reach an informed decision. The alternative—the prohibition of advertising—serves only to restrict the information that flows to consumers. Moreover, the argument assumes that the public is not sophisticated enough to realize the limitations of advertising, and that the public is better kept in ignorance than trusted with correct but incomplete information. We suspect the argument rests on an underestimation of the public. In any event, we view as dubious any justification that is based on the benefits of public ignorance. Although, of course, the bar retains the power to correct omissions that have the effect of presenting an inaccurate picture, the preferred remedy is more disclosure, rather than less. If the naivete of the public will cause advertising by attorneys to be misleading, then it is the bar's role to assure that the populace is sufficiently informed as to enable it to place advertising in its proper perspective.

3. **The Adverse Effect on the Administration of Justice**

Advertising is said to have the undesirable effect of stirring up litigation. The judicial machinery is designed to serve those who feel sufficiently aggrieved to bring forward their claims. Advertising, it is argued, serves to encourage the assertion of legal rights in the courts, thereby unsettling societal repose. There is even a suggestion of barratry.

But advertising by attorneys is not an unmitigated source of harm to the administration of justice. It may offer great benefits. Although advertising might increase the use of the judicial machinery, we cannot accept the notion that it is always better for a person to suffer a wrong silently than to redress it by legal action. As the bar acknowledges, "the middle 70 percent of our population is not being reached or served adequately by the legal profession." (*American Bar Association, Revised Handbook on Prepaid Legal Services: Papers and Documents Assembled by the Special Committee on Prepaid Legal Services,* 2 (1972). Among the reasons for this underutilization is fear of the cost, and an inability to locate a suitable lawyer. Advertising can help to solve this acknowledged problem: advertising is the traditional mechanism in a free-market economy for a supplier to inform a potential purchaser of the availability and terms of exchange. The disciplinary rule at issue likely has served to burden access to legal services, particularly for the not-quite-poor and the unknowledgeable. A rule allowing restrained advertising would be in accord with the bar's obligation to "facilitate the process of intelligent selection of lawyers, and to assist in making legal services fully available." (American Bar Association, Code of Professional Responsibility.)

4. **The Undesirable Economic Effects of Advertising**

It is claimed that advertising will increase the overhead costs of the profession, and that these costs then will be passed along to consumers in the form of increased fees. Moreover, it is claimed that the additional cost of practice will create a substantial entry barrier, deterring or preventing young attorneys from penetrating the market and entrenching the position of the bar's established members.

These two arguments seem dubious at best. Neither distinguishes lawyers from others, and neither appears relevant to the First Amendment. The ban on advertising serves to increase the difficulty of discovering the lowest-cost seller of acceptable ability. As a result, to this extent attorneys are isolated from competition, and the incentive to price competitively is reduced. Although it is true that the effect of advertising on the price of services has not been demonstrated, there is revealing evidence with regard to products; where consumers have the benefit of price advertising, retail prices often are dramatically lower than they would be without advertising. It is entirely possible that advertising will serve to reduce, not advance, the cost of legal services to the consumer.

The entry barrier argument is equally unpersuasive. In the absence of advertising, an attorney must rely on his contacts with the community to generate a flow of business. In view of the time necessary to develop such contacts, the ban in fact serves to perpetuate the market position of established attorneys. Consideration of entry-barrier problems would urge that advertising be allowed so as to aid the new competitor in penetrating the market.

5. **The Adverse Effect of Advertising on the Quality of Service**

It is argued that the attorney may advertise a given "package" of service at a set price, and will be inclined to provide, by indiscriminate use, the standard package regardless of whether it fits the client's needs.

Restraints on advertising, however, are an ineffective way of deterring shoddy work. An attorney who is inclined to cut quality will do so regardless of the rule on advertising. And the advertisement of a standardized fee does not necessarily mean that the services offered are undesirably standardized. Indeed, the assertion that an attorney who advertises a standard fee will cut quality is substantially undermined by the fixed fee schedule of appellee's own prepaid Legal Services Program. Even if advertising leads to the creation of "legal clinics" like that of appellants—clinics that emphasize standardized procedures for routine problems—it is possible that such clinics will improve service by reducing the likelihood of error.

6. The Difficulties of Enforcement

Finally, it is argued that the wholesale restriction is justified by the problems of enforcement if any other course is taken. Because the public lacks sophistication in legal matters, it may be particularly susceptible to misleading or deceptive advertising by lawyers. After-the-fact action by the consumer lured by such advertising may not provide a realistic restraint because of the inability of the layman to assess whether the service he has received meets professional standards. Thus, the vigilance of a regulatory agency will be required. But because of the numerous purveyors of services, the overseeing of advertising will be burdensome.

It is at least somewhat incongruous for the opponents of advertising to extol the virtues and altruism of the legal profession at one point, and, at another, to assert that its members will seize the opportunity to mislead and distort. We suspect that, with advertising, most lawyers will behave as they always have: they will abide by their solemn oaths to uphold the integrity and honor of their profession and of the legal system. For every attorney who overreaches through advertising, there will be thousands of others who will be candid and honest and straightforward. And, of course, it will be in the latters' interest, as in other cases of misconduct at the bar, to assist in weeding out those few who abuse their trust.

In sum, we are not persuaded that any of the proffered justifications rises to the level of an acceptable reason for the suppression of all advertising by attorneys.

In the usual case involving a restraint on speech, a showing that the challenged rule served unconstitutionally to suppress speech would end our analysis. In the First Amendment context, the Court has permitted attacks on overly broad statutes without requiring that the person making the attack demonstrate that in fact his specific conduct was protected. Having shown that the disciplinary rule interferes with protected speech, appellants ordinarily could expect to benefit regardless of the nature of their acts.

The First Amendment overbreadth doctrine, however, represents a departure from the traditional rule that a person may not challenge a statute on the ground that it might be applied unconstitutionally in circumstances other than those before the court. The reason for the special rule in First Amendment cases is apparent: an overbroad statute might serve to chill protected speech. First Amendment interests are fragile interests, and a person who contemplates protected activity might be discouraged by the *in terrorem* effect of the statute. Indeed, such a person might choose not to speak because of uncertainty whether his claim of privilege would prevail if challenged. The use of overbreadth analysis reflects the conclusion that the possible harm to society from allowing unprotected speech to go unpunished is outweighed by the possibility that protected speech will be muted.

But the justification for the application of overbreadth analysis applies weakly, if at all, in the ordinary commercial context. As was acknowledged in *Virginia Pharmacy Board* v. *Virginia Consumer Council,* there are "common sense differences" between commercial speech and other varieties. Since advertising is linked to commercial well-being, it seems unlikely that such speech is particularly susceptible to being crushed by overbroad regulation. Moreover, concerns for uncertainty in determining the scope of protection are reduced; the advertiser seeks to disseminate information about a product or service that he provides, and presumably he can determine more readily than others whether his speech is truthful and protected. Since overbreadth has been described by this Court as "strong medicine," which "has been employed . . . sparingly and only as a last resort," *(Broadrick v. Oklahoma)* we decline to apply it to professional advertising, a context where it is not necessary to further its intended objective.

Is, then, appellants' advertisement outside the scope of basic First Amendment protection? Aside from general claims as to the undesirability of any advertising by attorneys, a matter considered above, appellee argues that appellants' advertisement is misleading, and hence unprotected, in three particulars: a) the advertisement makes reference to a "legal clinic," an allegedly undefined term; b) the advertisement claims that appellants offer services at "very reasonable" prices, and, at least with regard to an uncontested divorce, the advertised price is not a bargain; and c) the advertisement does not inform the consumer that he may obtain a name change without the services of an attorney. On this record, these assertions are unpersuasive. We suspect that the public could readily understand the term "legal clinic"—if, indeed, it focused on the term at all—to refer to an operation like that of appellants' that is geared to provide standardized and multiple services. In fact, in his deposition the President of the State Bar of Arizona observed that there was a committee of the Bar "exploring the ways in which the legal clinic concept can be properly developed." And the clinical concept in the sister profession of medicine surely by now is publicly acknowledged and understood.

As to the cost of an uncontested divorce, appellee stated at oral argument that this runs from $150 to $300 in the area. Appellants advertised a fee of $175 plus a $20 court filing fee, a rate that seems "very reasonable" in light of the customery charge. Appellee's own Legal Services Program sets the rate for an uncontested divorce at $250. Of course, advertising will permit the comparison of rates among competitors, thus exposing if the rates are reasonable.

As to the final argument—the failure to disclose that a name change might be accomplished by the client without the aid of an attorney—we need only note that most legal services may be performed legally by the citizen for himself. The record does not unambiguously reveal some of the relevant facts in determining whether the nondisclosure is misleading, such as how complicated the procedure is and whether the State provides assistance for laymen. The deposition of one appellant, however, reflects that when he ascertained that a name change required only the correction of a record or the like, he frequently would send the client to effect the change himself. (App. 112.)

We conclude that it has not been demonstrated that the advertisement at issue could be suppressed.

In holding that advertising by attorneys may not be subjected to blanket suppression, and that the advertisement at issue is protected, we, of course, do not hold that advertising by attorneys may not be regulated in any way. We mention some of the clearly permissible limitations on advertising not foreclosed by our holding.

Advertising that is false, deceptive, or misleading of course is subject to restraint. Since the advertiser knows his product and has a commercial interest in its dissemination, we have little worry that regulation to assure truthfulness will discourage protected speech. And any concern that strict requirements for truthfulness will undesirably inhibit spontaneity seems inapplicable because commercial speech generally is calculated. Indeed, the public and private benefits from commercial speech derive from confidence in its accuracy and reliability. Thus, the leeway for untruthful or misleading expression that has been allowed in other contexts has little force in the commercial arena. In fact, because the public lacks sophistication concerning legal services, misstatements that might be overlooked or deemed unimportant in other advertising may be found quite inappropriate in legal advertising. For example, advertising claims as to the quality of services—a matter we do not address today—are not susceptible to measurement or verification; accordingly, such claims may be so likely to be misleading as to warrant restriction. Similar objections might justify restraints on in-person solicitation. We do not foreclose the possibility that some limited supplementation, by way of warning or disclaimer or the like, might be required of even an advertisement of the kind ruled upon today so as to assure that the consumer is not misled. In sum, we recognize that many of the problems in defining the boundary between deceptive and nondeceptive advertising remain to be resolved, and we expect that the bar will have a special role to play in assuring that advertising by attorneys flows both freely and cleanly.

As with other varieties of speech, it follows as well that there may be reasonable restrictions on the time, place, and manner of advertising. Advertising concerning transactions that are themselves illegal obviously may be suppressed. And the special problems of advertising on the electronic broadcast media will warrant special consideration.

The constitutional issue in this case is only whether the State may prevent publication in a newspaper of appellants' truthful advertisement concerning the availability and terms of routine legal services. We rule simply that the flow of such information may not be restrained, and we therefore hold the present application of the disciplinary rule against appellants to be violative of the First Amendment.

The judgment of the Supreme Court of Arizona is therefore affirmed in part and reversed in part.

It is so ordered.

Mr. Chief Justice Burger, concurring in part and dissenting in part.

I am in general agreement with Mr. Justice Powell's analysis and with Part II of the Court's opinion. I particularly agree with Mr. Justice Powell's statement that "today's decision will effect profound changes in the practice of law." Although the exact effect of those changes cannot now be known, I fear that they will be injurious to those whom the ban on legal advertising was designed to protect—the members of the general public in need of legal services.

Some Members of the Court apparently believe that the present case is controlled by our holding one year ago in *Virginia Board of Pharmacy*. However, I had thought that we made most explicit that our holding there rested on the fact that the advertisement of standardized, prepackaged, name-brand drugs was at issue. In that context, the prohibition on price advertising, which had served a useful function in the days of individually compounded medicines, was no longer tied to the conditions which had given it birth. The same cannot be said with respect to legal services which, by necessity, must vary greatly from case to case. Indeed, I find it difficult, if not impossible, to identify categories of legal problems or services which are fungible in nature. For example, Justice Powell persuasively demonstrates the fallacy of any notion that even a noncontested divorce can be "standard." A "reasonable charge" for such a divorce could be $195, as the appellants wish to advertise, or it could reasonably be a great deal more, depending on such variables as child custody, alimony, support, or any property settlement. Because legal services can rarely, if ever, be "standardized," and because potential clients rarely know in advance what services they do in fact need, price advertising can never give the public an accurate picture on which to base its selection of an attorney. Indeed, in the context of legal services, such incomplete information could be worse than no information at all. It could become a trap for the unwary.

The Court's opinion largely disregards these facts on the unsupported assumption that attorneys will not advertise anything but "routine" services—which the Court totally fails to identify or define—or, if they do advertise, that the bar and the courts will be able to protect the public from those few practitioners who abuse their trust. The former notion is highly speculative and, of course, does nothing to solve the problems that this decision will create; as to the latter, the existing administrative machinery of both the profession and the courts has proved wholly inadequate to police the profession effectively. (See ABA Special Committee On Evaluation of Disciplinary Enforcement: Problems and Recommendations in Disciplinary Enforcement.) To impose the enormous new regulatory burdens called for by the Court's decision on the presently deficient machinery of the bar and courts is unrealistic; it is almost predictable that it will create problems of unmanageable proportions. The Court thus takes a "great leap" into an unexplored, sensitive regulatory area where the legal profession and the courts have not yet learned to crawl, let alone stand up or walk. In my view, there is no need for this hasty plunge into a problem where not even the wisest of experts—if such experts exist—can move with sure steps.

To be sure, the public needs information concerning attorneys, their word and their fees. At the same time, the public needs protection from the unscrupulous or the incompetent practitioner anxious to prey on the uninformed. It seems to me that these twin goals can best be served by permitting the organized bar to experiment with, and perfect programs which would announce to the public the probable *range* of fees for specifically defined services and thus give putative clients some idea of potential cost liability when seeking out legal assistance. However, even such programs should be confined to the known and knowable, e.g., the truly "routine" uncontested divorce which is defined to exclude any dispute over alimony, property rights, child custody, or support, and should make clear

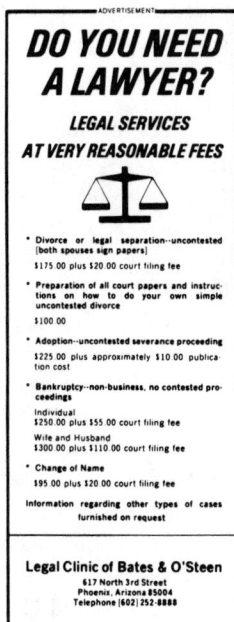

Courtesy of Bates and O'Steen.

Figure 6

to the public that the actual fee charged in any given case will vary according to the individual circumstances involved, in order to insure that the expectations of clients are not unduly inflated. Accompanying any reform of this nature must be some type of *effective* administrative procedure to hear and resolve the grievances and complaints of disappointed clients.

Unfortunately, the legal profession in the past has approached solutions for the protection of the public with too much caution, and, as a result, too little progress has been made. However, as Justice Powell points out, the organized bar has recently made some reforms in this sensitive area and more appear to have been in the offing. Rather than allowing these efforts to bear fruit, the Court today opts for a draconian "solution" which I believe will only breed more problems than it can conceivably resolve.

OHRALIK v. OHIO STATE BAR ASSOCIATION
436 U.S. 447 (1978)

Mr. Justice Powell delivered the opinion of the Court.

In *Bates* v. *State Bar of Arizona,* this Court held that truthful advertising of "routine" legal services is protected by the First and Fourteenth Amendments against blanket prohibition by a state. The Court expressly reserved the question of the permissible scope of regulation of "in-person solicitation of clients—at the hospital room or the accident site, or in any other situation that breeds undue influence—by attorneys or their agents or 'runners.'" Today we answer part of the question so reserved, and hold that the Bar—acting with state authorization—constitutionally may discipline a lawyer for soliciting clients in person, for pecuniary gain, under circumstances likely to pose dangers that the State has a right to prevent.

I

Appellant, a member of the Ohio Bar, lives in Montville, Ohio. Until recently he practiced law in Montville and Cleveland. On February 13, 1974, while picking up his mail at the Montville Post Office, appellant learned from the postmaster's brother about an automobile accident that had taken place on February 2 in which Carol McClintock, a young woman with whom appellant was casually acquainted, had been injured. Appellant made a telephone call to Ms. McClintock's parents, who informed him that their daughter was in the hospital. Appellant suggested that he might visit Carol in the hospital. Mrs. McClintock assented to the idea, but requested that appellant first stop by at her home.

During appellant's visit with the McClintocks, they explained that their daughter had been driving the family automobile on a local road when she was hit by an uninsured motorist. Both Carol and her passenger, Wanda Lou Holbert, were injured and hospitalized. In response to the McClintocks' expression of apprehension that they might be sued by Holbert, appellant explained that Ohio's guest statute would preclude such a suit. When appellant suggested to the McClintocks that they hire a lawyer, Mrs. McClintock retorted that such a decision would be up to Carol, who was 18 years old and would be the beneficiary of a successful claim.

Appellant proceeded to the hospital, where he found Carol lying in traction in her room. After a brief conversation about her condition, appellant told Carol he would represent her and asked her to sign an agreement. Carol said she would have to discuss the matter with her parents. She did not sign the agreement, but asked appellant to have her parents come to see her. Appellant also attempted to see Wanda Lou Holbert, but learned that she had just been released from the hospital. He then departed for another visit with the McClintocks.

On his way appellant detoured to the scene of the accident, where he took a set of photographs. He also picked up a tape recorder, which he concealed under his raincoat before arriving at the McClintocks' residence. Once there, he re-examined their automobile insurance policy, discussed with them the law applicable to passengers, and explained the consequences of the fact that the driver who struck Carol's car was an uninsured motorist. Appellant discovered that the McClintocks' insurance policy would provide benefits of up to $12,500 each for Carol and Wanda Lou under an uninsured motorist clause. Mrs. McClintock acknowledged that both Carol and Wanda Lou could sue for their injuries, but recounted to appellant that "Wanda swore up and down she would not do it." The McClintocks also told appellant that Carol had phoned to say that appellant could "go ahead" with her representation. Two days later appellant returned to Carol's hospital room to have her sign a contract, which provided that he would receive one-third of her recovery.

In the meantime, appellant obtained Wanda Lou's name and address from the McClintocks after telling them he wanted to ask her some questions about the accident. He then visited Wanda Lou at her home, without having been invited. He again concealed his tape recorder and recorded most of the conversation with Wanda Lou. After a brief unproductive inquiry about the facts of the accident, appellant told Wanda Lou that he was representing Carol and that he had a "little tip" for Wanda Lou: the McClintocks' insurance policy contained an uninsured motorist clause which might provide her with a recovery of up to $12,500. The young woman, who was 18 years of age and not a high school graduate at the time, replied to appellant's query about whether she was going to file a claim by stating that she really did not understand what was going on. Appellant offered to represent her, also, for a contingent fee of one-third of any recovery, and Wanda Lou stated "Okay."

Wanda's mother attempted to repudiate her daughter's oral assent the following day, when appellant called on the telephone to speak to Wanda. Mrs. Holbert informed appellant that she and her daughter did not want to sue anyone or to have appellant represent them, and that if they decided to sue they would consult their own lawyer. Appellant insisted that Wanda had entered into a binding agreement. A month later Wanda confirmed in writing that she wanted neither to sue nor to be represented by appellant. She requested that appellant notify the insurance company that he was not her lawyer, as the company would not release a check to her until he did so. Carol also eventually discharged appellant. Although another lawyer represented her in concluding a settlement with the insurance company, she paid appellant one-third of her recovery in settlement of his lawsuit against her for breach of contract.

Both Carol McClintock and Wanda Lou Holbert filed complaints against appellant with the Grievance Committee of the Geauga County Bar Association. The County Bar Association filed a formal complaint with the Board of Commissioners on Grievance and Discipline of the Supreme Court of Ohio. After a hearing, the Board found that appellant had violated Disciplinary Rules (DR) 2–103(A) and 2–104(A) of the Ohio Code of Professional Responsibility. The Board rejected appellant's defense that his conduct was protected under the First and Fourteenth Amendments. The Supreme Court of Ohio adopted the findings of the Board, reiterated that appellant's conduct was not constitutionally protected, and increased the sanction of a public reprimand recommended by the Board to indefinite suspension.

The decision in *Bates* was handed down after the conclusion of proceedings in the Ohio Supreme Court. We noted probable jurisdiction in this case to consider the scope of protection of a form of commercial speech, and an aspect of the State's authority to regulate and discipline members of the bar, not considered in *Bates.* We now affirm the judgment of the Supreme Court of Ohio.

II

The solicitation of business by a lawyer through direct, in-person communication with the prospective client has long been viewed as inconsistent with the profession's ideal of the attorney-client relationship and as posing a significant potential for harm to the prospective client. It has been proscribed by the organized Bar for many years. Last term the Court ruled that the justifications for prohibiting truthful, "restrained" advertising concerning "the availability and terms of routine legal services" are insufficient to override society's interest, safeguarded by the First and Fourteenth Amendments, in assuring the free flow of commercial information. *(Bates,* supra; see *Virginia Pharmacy Board* v. *Virginia Consumer Council.)* The balance struck in *Bates* does not predetermine the outcome in this case. The entitlement of in-person solicitation of clients to the protection of the First Amendment differs from that of the kind of advertising approved in Bates, as does the strength of the State's countervailing interest in prohibition.

A

Appellant contends that his solicitation of the two young women as clients is indistinguishable, for purposes of constitutional analysis, from the advertisement in *Bates.* Like that advertisement, his meetings with the prospective clients apprised them of their legal rights and of the availability of a lawyer to pursue their claims. According to appellant, such conduct is "presumptively an exercise of his free speech rights" which cannot be curtailed in the absence of proof that it actually caused a specific harm that the State has a compelling interest in preventing. But in-person solicitation of professional employment by a lawyer does not stand on a par with truthful advertising about the availability and terms of routine legal services, let alone with forms of speech more traditionally within the concern of the First Amendment.

Expression concerning purely commercial transactions has come within the ambit of the Amendment's protection only recently. In rejecting the notion that such speech "is wholly outside the protection of the First Amendment," we were careful not to hold "that it is wholly undifferentiable from other forms" of speech. We have not discarded the "common sense" distinction between speech proposing a commercial transaction, which occurs in an area traditionally subject to government regulation, and other varieties of speech. To require a parity of constitutional protection for commercial and noncommercial speech alike could invite dilution, simply by a leveling process, of the force of the Amendment's guarantee with respect to the latter kind of speech. Rather than subject the First Amendment to such a devitalization, we instead have afforded commercial speech a limited measure of protection, commensurate with its subordinate position in the scale of First Amendment values, while allowing modes of regulation that might be impermissible in the realm of noncommercial expression.

Moreover, "it has never been deemed an abridgment of freedom of speech or press to make a course of conduct illegal merely because the conduct was in part initiated, evidenced, or carried out by means of language, either spoken, written, or printed." Numerous examples could be cited of communications that are regulated without offending the First Amendment, such as the exchange of information about securities, corporate proxy statements, the exchange of price and production information among competitors, and employers' threats of retaliation for the labor activities of employees. Each of these examples illustrates that the State does not lose its power to regulate commercial activity deemed harmful to the public whenever speech is a component of that activity. Neither *Virginia Pharmacy* nor *Bates* purported to cause doubt on the permissibility of these kinds of commercial regulation.

In-person solicitation by a lawyer of remunerative employment is a business transaction in which speech is an essential but subordinate component. While this does not remove the speech from the protection of the First Amendment, as was held in *Bates* and *Virginia Pharmacy,* it lowers the level of appropriate judicial scrutiny.

As applied in this case, the disciplinary rules are said to have limited the communication of two kinds of information. First, appellant's solicitation imparted to Carol McClintock and Wanda Lou Holbert certain information about his availability and the terms of his proposed legal services. In this respect, in-person solicitation serves much the same function as the advertisement at issue in *Bates*. But there are significant differences as well. Unlike a public advertisement, which simply provides information and leaves the recipient free to act upon it or not, in-person solicitation may exert pressure and often demands an immediate response, without providing an opportunity for comparison or reflection. The aim and effect of in-person solicitation may be to provide a one-sided presentation and to encourage speedy and perhaps uninformed decision making; there is no opportunity for intervention or countereducation by agencies of the Bar, supervisory authorities, or persons close to the solicited individual. The admonition that "the fitting remedy for evil counsels is good ones" is of little value when the circumstances provide no opportunity for any remedy at all. In-person solicitation is as likely as not to discourage persons needing counsel from engaging in a critical comparison of the "availability, nature, and prices" of legal services, it actually may disserve the individual and societal interest, identified in *Bates,* in facilitating "informed and reliable decision making."

It also is argued that in-person solicitation may provide the solicited individual with information about his or her legal rights and remedies. In this case, appellant gave Wanda Lou a "tip" about the prospect of recovery based on the uninsured motorist clause in the McClintocks' insurance policy, and he explained that clause and Ohio's guest statute to Carol McClintock's parents. But neither of the disciplinary rules here at issue prohibited appellant from communicating information to these young women about their legal rights and the prospects of obtaining a monetary recovery, or from recommending that they obtain counsel. DR 2–104(A) merely prohibited him from using the information as bait with which to obtain an agreement to represent them for a fee. The rule does not prohibit a lawyer from giving unsolicited legal advice; it proscribes the acceptance of employment resulting from such advice.

Appellant does not contend, and on the facts of this case could not contend, that his approaches to the two young women involved political expression or an exercise of associational freedom, "employing constitutionally privileged means of expression to secure constitutionally guaranteed civil rights." Nor can he compare his solicitation to the mutual assistance in asserting legal rights that was at issue in *United Transportation Union* v. *Michigan Bar.* A lawyer's procurement of remunerative employment is a subject only marginally affected with First Amendment concerns. It falls within the State's proper sphere of economic and professional regulation. While entitled to some constitutional protection appellant's conduct is subject to regulation in furtherance of important state interests.

B

The state interests implicated in this case are particularly strong. In addition to its general interest in protecting consumers and regulating commercial transactions, the State bears a special responsibility for maintaining standards among members of the licensed professions. "The interest of the States in regulating lawyers is especially great since lawyers are essential to the primary governmental function of administering justice, and have historically been 'officers of the courts.' " While lawyers act in part as "self-employed businessmen," they also act "as trusted agents of their clients, and as assistants to the court in search of a just solution to disputes."

As is true with respect to advertising, it appears that the ban on solicitation by lawyers originated as a rule of professional etiquette rather than as a strictly ethical rule. "(T)he rules are based in part on deeply ingrained feelings of tradition, honor, and service. Lawyers have for centuries emphasized that the promotion of justice, rather than the earning of fees, is the goal of the profession." But the fact that the original motivation behind the ban on solicitation today might be considered an insufficient justification for its perpetuation does not detract from the force of the other interests the ban continues to serve. While the Court in *Bates* determined that truthful restrained advertising of the prices of "routine" legal services would not have an adverse effect on the professionalism of lawyers, this was only because it found "the postulated connection between advertising and the erosion of true professionalism to be severely strained." (emphasis supplied). The *Bates* Court did not question a State's interest in maintaining high standards among licensed professionals. Indeed, to the extent that the ethical standards of lawyers are linked to the service and protection of clients, they do further the goals of "true professionalism."

The substantive evils of solicitation have been stated over the years in sweeping terms; stirring up litigation, assertion of fraudulent claims, debasing the legal profession, and potential harm to the solicited client in the form of overreaching, overcharging, underrepresentation, and misrepresentation. The American Bar Association, as amicus curiae, defends the rule against solicitation primarily on three broad grounds: it is said that the prohibitions embodied in Disciplinary Rules 2–103(A) and 2–104(A) serve to reduce the likelihood of overreaching and the exertion of undue influence on lay persons; to protect the privacy of individuals; and to avoid situations where the lawyer's exercise of judgment on behalf of the client will be clouded by his own pecuniary self-interest.

We need not discuss or evaluate each of these interests in detail as appellant has conceded that the State has a legitimate and indeed "compelling" interest in preventing those aspects of solicitation that involve fraud, undue influence, intimidation, overreaching, and other forms of "vexatious conduct." We agree that protection of the public from these aspects of solicitation is a legitimate and important state interest.

III

Appellant's concession that strong state interests justify regulation to prevent the evils he enumerates would end this case but for his insistence that none of those evils was found to be present in his acts of solicitation. He challenges what he characterizes as the "indiscriminate application" of the rules to him and thus attacks the validity of DR 2–103(A) and DR 2–104(A) not facially, but as applied to his acts of solicitation. And because no allegations or findings were made of the specific wrongs appellant concedes would justify disciplinary action, appellant terms his solicitation "pure," meaning "soliciting and obtaining agreements from Carol McClintock and Wanda Lou Holbert to represent each of them," without more. Appellant therefore argues that we must decide whether a State may discipline him for solicitation per se without offending the First and Fourteenth Amendments.

We agree that the appropriate focus is on appellant's conduct. And, as appellant urges, we must undertake an independent review of the record to determine whether that conduct was constitutionally protected. But appellant errs in assuming that the constitutional validity of the judgment below depends on proof that his conduct constituted actual overreaching or inflicted some specific injury on Wanda Holbert or Carol McClintock. His assumption flows from the premise that nothing less than actual proven harm to the solicited individual would be a sufficiently important state interest to justify disciplining the attorney who solicits employment in person for pecuniary gain.

Appellant's argument misconceives the nature of the State's interest. The rules prohibiting solicitation are prophylactic measures whose objective is the prevention of harm before it occurs. The rules were applied in this case to discipline a lawyer for soliciting employment for pecuniary gain under circumstances likely to result in the adverse consequences the State seeks to avert. In such a situation, which is inherently conducive to overreaching and other forms of misconduct, the State has a strong interest in adopting and enforcing rules of conduct designed to protect the public from harmful solicitation by lawyers whom it has licensed.

The State's perception of the potential for harm in circumstances such as those presented in this case is well-founded. The detrimental aspects of face-to-face selling even of ordinary consumer products have been recognized and addressed by the Federal Trade Commission, and it hardly need be said that the potential for overreaching is significantly greater when a lawyer, a professional trained in the art of persuasion, personally solicits an unsophisticated, injured, or distressed lay person. Such an individual may place his or her trust in a lawyer, regardless of the latter's qualifications or the individual's actual need for legal representation, simply in response to persuasion under circumstances conducive to uninformed acquiescence. Although it is argued that personal solicitation is valuable because it may apprise a victim of misfortune of his or her legal rights, the very plight of that person not only makes him or her more vulnerable to influence but also may make advice all the more intrusive. Thus, under these adverse conditions the overtures of an uninvited lawyer may distress the solicited individual simply because of their obtrusiveness and the invasion of the individual's privacy, even when no other harm materializes. Under such circumstances, it is not unreasonable for the State to presume that in-person solicitation by lawyers more often than not will be injurious to the person solicited.

The efficacy of the State's effort to prevent such harm to prospective clients would be substantially diminished if, having proved a solicitation in circumstances like those of this case, the State were required in addition to prove actual injury. Unlike the advertising in *Bates,* in-person solicitation is not visible or otherwise open to public scrutiny. Often there is no witness other than the lawyer and the lay person whom he has solicited, rendering it difficult or impossible to obtain reliable proof of what actually took place. This would be especially true if the lay person were so distressed at the time of the solicitation that he or she could not recall specific details at a later date. If appellant's view were sustained, in-person solicitation would be virtually immune to effective oversight and regulation by the State or by the legal profession, in contravention of the State's strong interest in regulating members of the Bar in an effective, objective, and self-enforcing manner. It therefore is not unreasonable, or violative of the Constitution, for a State to respond with what in effect is a prophylactic rule.

On the basis of the undisputed facts of record, we conclude that the disciplinary rules constitutionally could be applied to appellant. He approached two young accident victims at a time when they were especially incapable of making informed judgments or of assessing and protecting their own interests. He solicited Carol McClintock in a hospital room where she lay in traction and sought out Wanda Lou Holbert on the day she came home from the hospital, knowing from his prior inquiries that she had just been released. Appellant urged his services upon the young women and used the information he had obtained from the McClintocks, and the fact of his agreement with Carol, to induce Wanda to say "Okay" in response to his solicitation. He employed a concealed tape recorder, seemingly to insure that he would have evidence of Wanda's oral assent to the representation. He emphasized that his fee would come out of the recovery, thereby tempting the young women with what sounded like a cost-free and therefore irresistible offer. He refused to withdraw when Mrs. Holbert requested him to do so only a day after the initial meeting between appellant and Wanda Lou, and continued to represent himself to the insurance company as Wanda Holbert's lawyer.

The court below did not hold that these or other facts were proof of actual harm to Wanda Holbert or Carol McClintock but rested on the conclusion that appellant had engaged in the general misconduct proscribed by the disciplinary rules. Under our view of the State's interest in averting harm by prohibiting solicitation in circumstances where it is likely to occur, the absence of explicit proof or findings of harm or injury is immaterial. The facts in this case present a striking example of the potential for overreaching that is inherent in a lawyer's in-person solicitation of professional employment. They also demonstrate the need for prophylactic regulation in furtherance of the State's interest in protecting the lay public. We hold that the application of Disciplinary Rules 2–103(A) and 2–104 (A) to appellant does not offend the Constitution.

Accordingly, the judgment of the Supreme Court of Ohio is
Affirmed

IN RE EDNA SMITH PRIMUS
436 U.S. 412 (1978)

Mr. Justice Powell delivered the opinion of the Court.

We consider on this appeal whether a State may punish a member of its Bar who, seeking to further political and ideological goals through associational activity, including litigation, advises a lay person of her legal rights, and discloses in a subsequent letter that free legal assistance is available from a nonprofit organization with which the lawyer and her associates are affiliated. Appellant, a member of the Bar of South Carolina, received a public reprimand for writing such a letter. The appeal is opposed by the State Attorney General, on behalf of the Board of Commissioners on Grievances and Discipline of the Supreme Court of South Carolina. As this appeal presents a substantial question under the First and Fourteenth Amendments, we noted probable jurisdiction.

I

Appellant, Edna Smith Primus, is a lawyer practicing in Columbia, South Carolina. During the period in question, she was associated with the "Carolina Community Law Firm," and an officer of and cooperating lawyer with the Columbia branch of the American Civil Liberties Union (ACLU). She received no compensation for her work on behalf of the ACLU, but was paid a retainer as a legal consultant for the South Carolina Council on Human Relations (Council), a nonprofit organization with offices in Columbia.

During the summer of 1973, local and national newspapers reported that pregnant mothers on public assistance in Aiken County, S.C. were being sterilized or threatened with sterilization as a condition of the continued receipt of medical assistance under the "Medicaid" program. Concerned by this development, Gary Allen, an Aiken businessman and officer of a local organization serving indigents, called the Council, requesting that one of its representatives come to Aiken to address some of the women who had been sterilized. At the Council's behest, appellant, who had not known Allen previously, called him and arranged a meeting in his office in July 1973. Among those attending was Mary Etta Williams, who had been sterilized by Dr. Clovis H. Pierce after the birth of her third child. Williams and her grandmother attended the meeting because Allen, an old family friend, had invited them and because Williams wanted "(t)o see what it was all about . . . ." At the meeting, appellant advised those present, including Williams and the other women who had been sterilized by Dr. Pierce, of their legal rights and suggested the possibility of a lawsuit.

Early in August 1973 the ACLU informed appellant that it was willing to provide representation for Aiken mothers who had been sterilized. Appellant testified that after being advised by Allen that Williams wished to institute suit against Dr. Pierce, she decided to inform Williams of the ACLU's offer of free legal representation. Shortly after receiving appellant's letter dated August 30, 1973—the centerpiece of this litigation—Williams visited Dr. Pierce to discuss the progress of her third child who was ill. At the doctor's office, she encountered his lawyer and at the latter's request signed a release of liability in the doctor's favor. Williams showed appellant's letter to the doctor and his lawyer, and they retained a copy. She then called appellant from the doctor's office and announced her intention not to sue. There was no further communication between appellant and Williams.

On October 9, 1974, the Secretary of the Board of Commissioners on Grievances and Discipline of the Supreme Court of South Carolina (Board) filed a formal complaint with the Board, charging that appellant had engaged in "solicitation in violation of the Canons of Ethics" by sending the August 30, 1973 letter to Williams. Appellant denied any unethical solicitation and asserted, *inter alia,* that her conduct was protected by the First and Fourteenth Amendments and by Canon 2 of the Code of Professional Responsibility of the American Bar Association (ABA). The complaint was heard by a panel of the Board on March 20, 1975. The State's evidence consisted of the letter, the testimony of Williams, and a copy of the summons and complaint in the action instituted against Dr. Pierce and various state officials. Following denial of appellant's motion to dismiss, she testified in her own behalf and called Allen, a number of ACLU representatives, and several character witnesses.

The panel filed a report recommending that appellant be found guilty of soliciting a client on behalf of the ACLU, in violation of Disciplinary Rules (DR) 2–103(D)(5)(a) and (c) and 2–194(A)(5) of the Supreme Court of South Carolina, and that a private reprimand be issued. It noted that "(t)he evidence is inconclusive as to whether (appellant) solicited Mrs. Williams on her own behalf, but she did solicit Mrs. Williams on behalf of the ACLU, which would benefit financially in the event of successful prosecution of the suit for money damages." The panel determined that appellant violated DR 2–103(D)(5) "by attempting to solicit a client for a nonprofit organization which, as its primary purpose, renders legal services, where respondent's associate is a staff counsel for the nonprofit organization." Appellant also was found to have violated DR 2–104(A)(5) because she solicited Williams, after providing unsolicited legal advice, to join in a prospective class action for damages and other relief that was to be brought by the ACLU.

After a hearing on January 9, 1976, the full Board approved the panel report and administered a private reprimand. On March 17, 1977, the Supreme Court of South Carolina entered an order which adopted verbatim the findings and conclusions of the panel report and increased the sanction, *sua sponte,* to a public reprimand.

On July 9, 1977, appellant filed a jurisdictional statement and docketed this appeal. We noted probable jurisdiction on October 3, 1977. We now reverse.

II

This appeal concerns the tension between contending values of considerable moment to the legal profession and to society. Relying upon *NACCP* v. *Button,* and its progeny, appellant maintains that her activity involved Constitutionally protected expression and association. In her view, South Carolina has not shown that the discipline meted out to her advances a subordinating state interest in a manner that avoids unnecessary abridgment of First Amendment freedoms. Appellee counters that appellant's letter to Williams falls outside of the protection of *Button,* and that South Carolina acted lawfully in punishing a member of its Bar for solicitation.

The States enjoy broad power to regulate "the practice of professions within their boundaries," and "(t)he interest of the States in regulating lawyers is especially great since lawyers are essential to the primary governmental function of administering justice, and have historically been 'officers of the courts.' " For example, we decide today in *Ohralik* v. *Ohio State Bar Association,* that the States may vindicate legitimate regulatory interests through proscription, in certain circumstances, of in-person solicitation by lawyers who seek to communicate purely commercial offers of legal assistance to lay persons.

Unlike the situation in *Ohralik,* however, appellant's act of solicitation took the form of a letter to a woman with whom appellant had discussed the possibility of seeking redress for an allegedly unconstitutional sterilization. This was not in-person solicitation for pecuniary gain. Appellant was communicating an offer of free assistance by attorneys associated with the ACLU, not an offer predicated on entitlement to a share of any monetary recovery. And her actions were undertaken to express personal political beliefs and to advance the civil liberties objectives of the ACLU, rather than to derive financial gain. The question presented in this case is whether, in light of the values protected by the First and Fourteenth Amendments, these differences materially affect the scope of state regulation of the conduct of lawyers.

III

In *NAACP* v. *Button,* the Supreme Court of Appeals of Virginia had held that the activities of members and staff attorneys of the National Association for the Advancement of Colored People (NAACP) and its affiliate, the Virginia State Conference of NAACP Branches (Conference), constituted "solicitation of legal business" in violation of state law. Although the NAACP representatives and staff attorneys had "a right to peaceably assemble with members of the branches and other groups to discuss with them and advise them relative to their legal rights in matters concerning racial segregation," the court found no constitutional protection for efforts to "solicit prospective litigants to authorize the filing of suits" by NAACP-compensated attorneys.

This Court reversed: "We hold that the activities of the NAACP, its affiliates, and legal staff shown on this record are modes of expression and association protected by the First and Fourteenth Amendments which Virginia may not prohibit, under its power to regulate the legal profession, as improper solicitation of legal business violative of (state law) and the Canons of Professional Ethics." The solicitation of prospective litigants, many of whom were not members of the NAACP, or the Conference, for the purpose of furthering the civil rights objectives of the organization and its members was held to come within the right " 'to engage in association for the advancement of beliefs and ideas.' "

Since the Virginia statute sought to regulate expressive and associational conduct at the core of the First Amendment's protective ambit, the *Button* Court insisted that "government may regulate in the area only with narrow specificity." The Attorney General of Virginia had argued that the law merely (i) proscribed control of the actual litigation by the NAACP after it was instituted, and (ii) sought to prevent the evils traditionally associated with common-law maintenance, champerty, and barratry. The Court found inadequate the first justification because of an absence of evidence of NAACP interference with the actual conduct of litigation, or neglect, or harassment of clients, and because the statute, as construed, was not drawn narrowly to advance the asserted goal. It rejected the analogy to the common-law offenses because of an absence of proof that malicious intent or the prospect of pecuniary gain inspired the NAACP-sponsored litigation. It also found a lack of proof that a serious danger of conflicts of interest marked the relationship between the NAACP and its member and nonmember Negro litigants. The Court concluded that "although the (NAACP) has amply shown that its activities fall within the First Amendment's protections, the State has failed to advance any substantial regulatory interest, in the form of substantive evils flowing from (the NAACP's) activities, which can justify the broad prohibitions which it has imposed."

Subsequent decisions have interpreted *Button* as establishing the principle that "collective activity undertaken to obtain meaningful access to the courts is a fundamental right within the protection of the First Amendment." The Court has held that the First and Fourteenth Amendments prevent state proscription or a range of solicitation activities by labor unions seeking to provide low-cost, effective legal representation to their members. And "lawyers accepting employment under (such plans) have a like protection which the State cannot abridge." (*Railroad Trainmen,* supra, at 8.) Without denying the power of the State to take measures to correct the substantive evils of undue influence, overreaching, misrepresentation, invasion of privacy, conflict of interest, and lay interference that potentially are present in solicitation of prospective clients by lawyers, this Court has required that "broad rules framed to protect the public and to preserve respect for the administration of justice" must not work a significant impairment of "the value of associational freedoms."

IV

We turn now to the question whether appellant's conduct implicates interests of free expression and association sufficient to justify the level of protection recognized in *Button* and subsequent cases. The Supreme Court of South Carolina found appellant to have engaged in unethical conduct because she " 'solicit(ed) a client for a nonprofit organization, which, as its primary purpose, renders legal services, where respondent's associate is a staff counsel for the nonprofit organization.' " It rejected appellant's First Amendment defenses by distinguishing *Button* from the case before it. Whereas the NAACP in that case was primarily a " 'political' " organization that used " 'litigation as an adjunct to the overriding political aims of the organization' " the ACLU " 'has as one of its primary purposes, the rendition of legal services.' " The court also intimated that the ACLU's policy of requesting an award of counsel fees indicated that the organization might " 'benefit financially in the event of successful prosecution of the suit for money damages.' "

Although the disciplinary panel did not permit full factual development of the aims and practices of the ACLU, supra, the record does not support the state court's effort to draw a meaningful distinction between the ACLU and the NAACP. From all that appears, the ACLU and its local chapters, much like the NAACP and its local affiliates in *Button,* "engage . . . in extensive educational and lobbying activities" and "also devote . . . much of (their) funds and energies to an extensive program of assisting certain kinds of litigation on behalf of (their) declared purposes." The court below acknowledged that " 'the ACLU has only entered cases in which substantial civil liberties questions are involved . . . .' " It has engaged in the defense of unpopular cases and unpopular defendants and has represented individuals in litigation that has defined the scope of constitutional protection in areas such as political dissent, juvenile rights, prisoners' rights, military law, amnesty, and privacy. For the ACLU, as for the NAACP, "litigation is not a technique of resolving private differences"; it is "a form of political expression" and "political association."

We find equally unpersuasive any suggestion that the level of constitutional scrutiny in this case should be lowered because of a possible benefit to the ACLU. The discipline administered to appellant was premised solely on the possibility of financial benefit to the organization, rather than any possibility of pecuniary gain to herself, her associates, or the lawyers representing the plaintiffs in the *Doe* v. *Pierce* litigation. It is conceded that appellant received no compensation for any of the activities in question. It is also undisputed that neither the ACLU nor any lawyer associated with it would have shared in any monetary recovery by the plaintiffs in *Doe* v. *Pierce*. If Williams had elected to bring suit, and had been represented by staff lawyers for the ACLU, the situation would have been similar to that in *Button,* where the lawyers for the NAACP were "organized as a staff and paid by" that organization.

Contrary to appellee's suggestion, the ACLU's policy of requesting an award of counsel fees does not take this case outside of the protection of *Button*. Although the Court in *Button* did not consider whether the NAACP seeks counsel fees, such requests are often made both by that organization, and by the NAACP Legal Defense Fund, Inc. In any event, in a case of this kind there are differences between counsel fees awarded by a court and traditional fee-paying arrangements which militate against a presumption that ACLU sponsorship of litigation is motivated by considerations of pecuniary gain rather than by its widely recognized goal of vindicating civil liberties. Counsel fees are awarded in the discretion of the court; awards are not drawn from the plaintiff's recovery, and are usually premised on a successful outcome; and the amounts awarded often may not correspond to fees generally obtainable in private litigation. Moreover, under prevailing law during the events in question, an award of counsel fees in federal litigation was available only in limited circumstances. And even if there had been an award during the period in question, it would have gone to the central fund of the ACLU. Although such benefit to the organization may increase with the maintenance of successful litigation, the same situation obtains with voluntary contributions and foundation support, which also may rise with ACLU victories in important areas of the law. That possibility, standing alone, offers no basis for equating the work of lawyers associated with the ACLU or the NAACP with that of a group that exists for the primary purpose of financial gain through the recovery of counsel fees.

Appellant's letter of August 30, 1973 to Mrs. Williams thus comes within the generous zone of First Amendment protection reserved for associational freedoms. The ACLU engages in litigation as a vehicle for effective political expression and association, as well as a means of communicating useful information to the public. As *Button* indicates, and as appellant offered to prove at the disciplinary hearing (see n.9, supra), the efficacy of litigation as a means of advancing the cause of civil liberties often depends on the ability to make legal assistance available to suitable litigants. " 'Free trade in ideas' means free trade in the opportunity to persuade to action not merely to describe facts." The First and Fourteenth Amendments require a measure of protection for "advocating lawful means of vindicating legal rights," including "advis(ing) another that his legal rights have been infringed and refer(ing) him to a particular attorney or group of attorneys . . . for assistance."

V

South Carolina's action in punishing appellant for soliciting a prospective litigant by mail, on behalf of the ACLU, must withstand the "exacting scrutiny applicable to limitations on core First Amendment rights. . . ." South Carolina must demonstrate "subordinating interest which is compelling,'' and that the means employed in furtherance of that interest are ''closely drawn to avoid unnecessary abridgement of associational freedoms.''

Appellee contends that the disciplinary action taken in this case is part of a regulatory program aimed at the prevention of undue influence, overreaching, misrepresentation, invasion of privacy, conflict of interest, lay interference, and other evils that are thought to inhere generally in solicitation by lawyers of prospective clients, and to be present on the record before us. We do not dispute the importance of these interests. This Court's decision in *Button* makes clear, however, that ''(b)road prophylactic rules in the area of free expression are suspect,'' and that ''(p)recision of regulation must be the touchstone in an area so closely touching our most precious freedoms.'' Because of the danger of censorship through selective enforcement of broad prohibitions, and ''(b)ecause First Amendment freedoms need breathing space to survive, government may regulate in (this) area only with narrow specificity.''

A

The disciplinary rules in question sweep broadly. Under DR 2–103(D)(5), a lawyer employed by the ACLU or a similar organization may never give unsolicited advice to a lay person that he or she retains for the organization's free services, and it would seem that one who merely assists or maintains a cooperative relationship with the organization also must suppress the giving of such advice if he or anyone associated with the organization will be involved in the ultimate litigation. Notwithstanding appellee's consession in this Court, it is far from clear that a lawyer may communicate the organization's offer of legal assistance at an informational gathering such as the July 1973 meeting in Aiken without breaching the literal terms of the rule. Moreover, the disciplinary rules in question permit punishment for mere solicitation unaccompanied by proof of any of the substantive evils that appellee maintains were present in this case. In sum, the rules in their present form have a distinct potential for dampening the kind of ''cooperative activity that would make advocacy of litigation meaningful,'' as well as for permitting discretionary enforcement against unpopular cases.

B

Even if we ignore the breadth of the disciplinary rules, and the absence of findings in the decision below that support the justifications advanced by appellee in this Court, we think it clear from the record—which appellee does not suggest is inadequately developed—that findings compatible with the First Amendment could not have been made in this case. As in *New York Times Co.* v. *Sullivan,* ''considerations of effective judicial administration require us to review the evidence in the present record to determine whether it could constitutionally support a judgment (against appellant). This Court's duty is not limited to the elaboration of constitutional principles; we must also in proper cases review the evidence to make certain that those principles (can be) constitutionally applied.''

Where political expression or association is at issue, this Court has not tolerated the degree of imprecision that often characterizes government regulation of the conduct of commercial affairs. The approach we adopt today in *Ohralik,* that the State may proscribe in-person solicitation for pecuniary gain under circumstances likely to result in adverse consequences, cannot be applied to appellant's activity on behalf of the ACLU. Although a showing of potential danger may suffice in the former context, appellant may not be disciplined unless her activity in fact involved the type of misconduct at which South Carolina's broad prohibition is said to be directed.

The record does not support appellee's contention that undue influence, overreaching, misrepresentation, or invasion of privacy actually occurred in this case. Appellant's letter of August 30, 1973, followed up the earlier meeting—one concededly protected by the First and Fourteenth Amendments—by notifying Williams that the ACLU would be interested in supporting possible litigation. The letter imparted additional information material to making an informed decision about whether to authorize litigation, and permitted Williams an opportunity, which she exercised, for arriving at a deliberate decision. The letter was not facially misleading; indeed, it offered "to explain what is involved so you can understand what is going on." The transmittal of this letter—as contrasted with in-person solicitation—involved no appreciable invasion of privacy; nor did it afford any significant opportunity for overreaching or coercion. Moreover, the fact that there was a written communication lessens substantially the difficulty of policing solicitation practices that do offend valid rules of professional conduct. The manner of solicitation in this case certainly was no more likely to cause harmful consequences than the activity considered in *Button*.

Nor does the record permit a finding of a serious likelihood of conflict of interest or injurious lay interference with the attorney-client relationship. Admittedly, there is some potential for such conflict or interference whenever a lay organization supports any litigation. That potential was present in *Button*, in the NAACP's solicitation of nonmembers and its disavowal of any relief short of full integration. But the Court found that potential insufficient in the absence of proof of a "serious danger" of conflict of interest, (*id.,* at 443), or of organizational interference with the actual conduct of the litigation. As in *Button,* "(n)othing that this record shows as to the nature and purpose of (ACLU) activities permits an inference of any injurious intervention in or control of litigation which would constitutionally authorize the application," of the disciplinary rules to appellant's activity. A "very distant possibility of harm," cannot justify proscription of the activity of appellant revealed by this record.

The State's interests in preventing the "stirring up" of frivolous or vexatious litigation and minimizing commercialization of the legal profession offer no further justification for the discipline administered in this case. The *Button* Court declined to accept the proffered analogy to the common-law offenses of maintenance, champerty, and barratry, where the record would not support a finding that the litigant was solicited for a malicious purpose of "for private gain, serving no public interest." The same result follows from the facts of this case. And considerations of undue commercialization of the legal profession are of marginal force where, as here, a nonprofit organization offers its services free of charge to individuals who may be in need of legal assistance and may lack the financial means and sophistication necessary to tap alternative sources of such aid.

At bottom, the case against appellant rests on the proposition that a State may regulate in a prophylactic fashion all solicitation activities of lawyers because there may be some potential for overreaching, conflict of interest, or other substantive evils whenever a lawyer gives unsolicited advice and communicates an offer of representation to a layman. Under certain circumstances, that approach is appropriate in the case of speech that simply "propose(s) a commercial transaction." In the context of political expression and association, however, a State must regulate with significantly greater precision.

VI

The State is free to fashion reasonable restrictions with respect to the time, place, and manner of solicitation by members of its Bar. The State's special interest in regulating members of a profession it licenses, and who serve as officers of its courts, amply justifies the application of narrowly drawn rules to proscribe solicitation that in fact is misleading, overbearing, or involves other features of deception or improper influence. A State also may forbid in-person solicitation for pecuniary gain under circumstances likely to result in these evils. And a State may insist that lawyers not solicit on behalf of lay organizations that exert control over the actual conduct of any ensuing litigation. Accordingly, nothing in this opinion should be read to foreclose carefully tailored regulation that does not abridge unnecessarily the associational freedom of nonprofit organizations, or their members, having characteristics like those of the NAACP or the ACLU.

We conclude that South Carolina's application of its Disciplinary Rules 2–103 (D) (5) (a) and (c) and 2–104(A)(5) to appellant's solicitation by letter on behalf of the ACLU violates the First and Fourteenth Amendments. The judgment of the Supreme Court of South Carolina is

Reversed.

Mr. Justice Brennan took no part in the consideration or decision of this case.

Mr. Justice Blackmun, concurred.

NOTE

FTC Issues Rule on Advertising of Ophthalmic Goods and Services, May 24, 1978

The FTC has by unanimous vote issued a final rule removing public and private restraints on the advertising of the price and availability of prescription eyeglasses, contact lenses, and eye examinations.

The rule goes into effect 30 days after publication in the Federal Register and—

- preempts most state laws which either prohibit or burden the advertising of prescription eyewear or eye examinations;
- prohibits restrictions on advertising of this type imposed by private groups such as trade associations; and
- requires that consumers be provided with copies of their prescriptions after they have had their eyes examined.

Where a state or local regulation requires that all retail advertising contain certain disclosures, its application to ophthalmic advertising will not be prevented. Across-the-board regulations of this type (e.g., a requirement that all advertisements offering a special price disclose the price normally charged) would not be preempted.

The rule also permits the states to require that advertisements affirmatively disclose whether an advertised price for eyeglasses 1) includes single vision and/or multifocal lenses, 2) refers to soft and/or hard contact lenses, 3) includes an eye examination, 4) includes all dispensing fees, and 5) includes both frames and lenses.

"Restrictions on the advertising of ophthalmic goods and services emanate from a complex web of state and private regulation of the providers of eye care: ophthalmologists, optometrists, and opticians," the Commission said. "Professional associations, through their codes of ethics, rules of practice, membership requirements, and informal pressures, reinforce existing legal restraints and often suppress advertising even where it is legally permitted."

Finding that these advertising bans are unfair, the Commission said: "By providing the consumer information concerning product, price, and performance characteristics, advertising helps the consumer to assess product differences and make a rational purchase decision. And for some groups, such as the aged, the absence of advertising imposes virtually insurmountable obstacles to effective search in the ophthalmic market.

". . . The economic losses being borne by consumers as the result of advertising bans do not represent the full extent of the consumer injury associated with these restraints. Advertising bans and the attendant higher prices have resulted in a significant decrease in consumption of vision care products and services among the less affluent. The problem is perhaps greatest with respect to the elderly. Approximately 93 percent of those over age 65 use some form of corrective eyeware. Since many elderly consumers have relatively low income levels but need corrective eyeware much more frequently than other groups, any decline in consumption attributable to high prices is especially serious for the elderly.

". . . And just as many of the elderly and poor are doing without needed eyeglasses because of high prices and lack of information and affordable alternatives, they are also doing without eye examinations. Evidence in the record indicates that more people could get eye examinations more often if prices were lower."

The Commission said that the rule requirement that a copy of the eyeglass prescription be given to the buyer "is necessary to make the price disclosure provision fully effective. Without the right to their prescriptions, the Commission's efforts to insure maximum useful information in the market will have little effect on consumers where these practices prevail. Thus, it is the Commission's finding that . . . (this requirement) is justified both as a specific delineation of an unfair act or a practice as well as a remedy to implement the right to advertise."

No additional fee may be charged for releasing the prescription to a consumer.

TALSKY v. DEPARTMENT OF REGISTRATION AND EDUCATION
12 Ill. Dec. 550, 68 Ill.2d 579, 370 N.E.2d 173 (1977)

Underwood, Justice, delivered the opinion of the court.

Plaintiff, Richard J. Talsky, filed an action in the circuit court of Cook County for administrative review of an order issued by the defendant Ronald E. Stackler, Director of the Department of Registration and Education, suspending plaintiff's license to practice as a chiropractor for 90 days on the grounds that he had engaged in advertising to solicit professional business in violation of Subsections 4 and 13 of Section 16 of the Medical Practice Act. The suspension was stayed by the circuit court pending administrative review. On review, the circuit court reversed the Department's decision on the basis that the restrictions on advertising contained in Section 16(13) of the Medical Practice Act were overly broad and impermissibly restricted freedom of speech in contravention of the First Amendment to the United States Constitution. The Department appeals directly to this court.

At the conclusion of an administrative hearing before the Medical Examining Committee of the Department of Registration and Education, the plaintiff was found to have violated Section 16(4) of the Medical Practice Act for "(e)ngaging in dishonorable, unethical, or unprofessional conduct of a character likely to deceive, defraud, or harm the public" as well as Section 16(13) of the Act, which prohibits advertising. It was the latter section which the circuit court held unconstitutional, and our review is accordingly limited to a consideration of that section, which provided for revocation or suspension of plaintiff's license on the following grounds:

"13. Except as otherwise provided in Section 16.01, advertising or soliciting, by himself or through another, by means of handbills, posters, circulars, steropticon slides, motion pictures, radio, newspapers, or in any other manner for professional business."

The exceptions to the advertising ban are described as follows in section 16.01:

Any person licensed under this Act may list his name, title, office hours, address, telephone number, and any specialty in professional and telephone directories; may announce, by way of a professional card not larger than 3½ inches by 2 inches, only his name, title, degree, office location, office hours, phone number, residence address and phone number, and any specialty; may list his name, title, address and telephone number, and any specialty in public print limited to the number of lines necessary to state that information; may announce his change of place of business, absence from, or return to business in the same manner; or may issue appointment cards to his patients, when the information thereon is limited to the time and place of appointment and that information permitted on the professional card. Listings in public print, in professional and telephone directories, or announcements of change of place of business, absence from, or return to business, may not be made in bold faced type."

The facts are not in substantial dispute. On August 30, 1972, plaintiff caused to be published in the *Berwyn Life* newspaper the one-half page advertisement which is reproduced in Appendix 1 to this opinion (omitted). Copies of the advertisement were also affixed to a substantial portion of the exterior window of the plaintiff's office in Cicero. As can be seen, the ads offered "Free Chicken," "Free Refreshments" and "Free Spinal X-Ray," and contained a section condemning reliance on drugs while extolling the virtues of the drugless chiropractic profession. On about August 13, 1974, plaintiff, individually or through another, attached advertising circulars similar to the ones reproduced in appendix 2 (omitted) to certain traffic light posts, a traffic control box, and a United States mail box located at the intersection of 57th Avenue and Cermak Road in Cicero, together with other circulars which identified the location of the Talsky chiropractic offices in the Chicago area. These circulars remained at that location until the end of September 1974. Plaintiff also attached circulars of the same type to the exterior of his office window in Cicero in addition to business cards which would be torn off and removed by passersby. The cards contained the words "Chiropractic TLC Office," plaintiff's name, address and telephone number with the words "Talsky Life Center" and "Tender Loving Care" appearing in small hearts.

It is apparent that we are here concerned with the extent to which the State may exercise its police power to restrict advertising by members of the health-related professions without impermissibly infringing upon those members' First Amendment rights to freedom of speech. In order to place the questions involved in this appeal in their proper context, it is appropriate to trace the development of these concepts in the decisions of the United States Supreme Court and this court.

In *Semler v. Oregon State Board of Dental Examiners* (1935), the Court considered a statute which prohibited dentists from advertising their professional superiority and their prices; from using certain types of advertising displays; from employing solicitors or publicity agents; and from advertising free dental work, free examinations, guaranteed work or painless dental operations. The question before the court was whether the restrictions were arbitrary and invalid under the Due Process Clause of the Fourteenth Amendment. In upholding the validity of the regulation, the Court stated:

The legislature was not dealing with traders in commodities, but with the vital interest of public health, and with a profession treating bodily ills and demanding different standards of conduct from those which are traditional in the competition of the market place. The community is concerned with the maintenance of professional standards which will insure not only competency in individual practitioners, but protection against those who would prey upon a public peculiarly susceptible to imposition through alluring promises of physical relief . . .

. . . The legislature was entitled to consider the general effects of the practices which it described, and if these effects were injurious in facilitating unwarranted and misleading claims, to counteract them by a general rule even though in particular instances there might be no actual deception or misstatement.

The rationale of the *Semler* decision was adopted by this Court in a number of cases upholding the right of the State to regulate advertising by those engaged in medical and related professions. In *Lasdon,* it was observed: "In the exercise of police power the practice of the professions has been subjected to licensing and regulation for the reason that the services customarily rendered by those engaged in such professions are so closely related to the public health, welfare, and general good of the people, that regulation is deemed necessary to protect such interests. It has been held a proper exercise of police power to legislate and protect the professions performing such services against commercialization and exploitation." In upholding the statute which prohibited advertising by those engaged in the business of making dental plates, we further stated in that case: "It is well known that masses of the public do not comprehend or understand the skill that is necessary to the making of proper dentures and the proper charges to be made for such services. Such persons are often attracted by the advertisements of the quack and charletan and seek his services."

The foregoing cases were decided primarily on due process grounds and were not concerned with First Amendment questions. This undoubtedly resulted from the fact that at the time those cases were decided the advertising of products and services was considered "purely commercial" speech which the United States Supreme Court had held was not entitled to First Amendment protection. The viability of the "commercial speech" exception to First Amendment protection as enunciated in *Valentine* was seriously questioned by the court in *Pittsburgh Press Co.* v. *Pittsburgh Commission on Human Relations* (1973), and was subsequently terminated in *Bigelow* v. *Virginia* (1975), *Virginia State Board of Pharmacy* v. *Virginia Citizens Consumer Council, Inc.* (1976), and *Bates* v. *State Bar of Arizona* (1977). The latter two decisions, while not precisely on point, are highly significant in any consideration of the First Amendment questions here.

In *Virginia Citizens,* the court struck down a Virginia statute which labelled it unprofessional conduct for a pharmacist to advertise prices of prescription drugs. No specific advertisement was at issue in the case, but the court hypothesized one reading as follows: "I will sell you the X prescription at the Y price." The Court first unequivocally held that such pure commercial speech does have some First Amendment protections. The Court also noted that the adverse effect of the suppression of prescription drug price information was greatest upon the poor, the sick, and the aged, who must spend a disproportionate amount of their income on prescription drugs. "When drug prices vary as strikingly as they do, information as to who is charging what becomes more than a convenience. It could mean the alleviation of physical pain or the enjoyment of basic necessities." The Court was of the opinion that information as to who is producing and selling what product, for what reason, and at what price plays an important role in the preservation of a predominantly free-enterprise economy in which the allocation of resources is in large measure made through numerous private economic decisions. "It is a matter of public interest that those decisions, in the aggregate, be intelligent and well informed. To this end, the free flow of commercial information is indispensable." The Court found the restrictions unconvincing, largely because high professional standards were already guaranteed to a substantial extent by the strict regulation to which pharmacists were subject in Virginia. The Court further stated that "the State's protectiveness of its citizens rests in large measure on the advantages of their being kept in ignorance. The advertising ban does not directly affect professional standards one way or the other. It affects them only through the reactions it is assumed people will have to the free flow of drug price information." The Court also suggested the following alternative to what it considered the "highly paternalistic approach" of the State: "That alternative is to assume that this information is not in itself harmful, that people will perceive their own best interests if only they are well enough informed, and that the best means to that end is to open the channels of communication rather than to close them." *Virginia Citizens* clearly does not, however, mean that a State can never regulate commercial speech. The Court said: "Some forms of commercial speech regulation are surely permissible. We mention a few (time, place, and manner restriction; false, deceptive, or misleading speech; and speech which proposes an illegal transaction) only to make clear that they are not before us and therefore are not foreclosed by this case."

Virginia Citizens also left open the question whether advertisement of professional services was entitled to First Amendment protection, similar to that given to advertisement of retail prices of prepackaged prescription drugs. The Court in *Bates* has quite recently answered this question affirmatively with respect to the advertisement of routine professional (legal) services. There, the Court struck down a disciplinary rule of the Arizona Supreme Court prohibiting a lawyer from advertising. Two Arizona lawyers operating a legal clinic had advertised: "Do you need a lawyer? Legal services at very reasonable fees," and had specified fees for several routine uncontested matters.

In defining the issue before it, the Court pointed out that no questions were raised relative to advertising the quality of legal services, nor was it concerned with problems associated with in-person solicitation of clients. Instead, the narrow question was whether lawyers could constitutionally advertise the prices at which certain "routine" services would be performed. Various arguments were proffered by the State bar in support of the restriction on price advertising, including an alleged adverse effect on professionalism, and contentions that professional advertising by lawyers inevitably would be misleading, that advertising would have an adverse effect on the administration of justice as well as on the quality of services provided by the legal profession, and that a wholesale restriction on advertising by lawyers is justified by the enforcement problems which would result if any other course was taken. While these arguments were not considered sufficient to justify a ban upon all advertising, the Court apparently considered them sufficient to warrant the narrow restriction or regulation of advertising which the opinion indicated would be permissible. The Court stated: "The disciplinary rule at issue likely has served to burden access to legal services, particularly for the not-quite-poor and the unknowledgeable. A rule allowing restrained advertising would be in accord with the Bar's obligation to 'facilitate the process of intelligent selection of lawyers, and to assist in making legal services fully available.' " (American Bar Association, Code of Professional Responsibility EC 2–1 (1976).) The Court concluded that the publication in a newspaper of a truthful advertisement concerning the availability and prices of routine legal services was entitled to First Amendment protection, and that application of the disciplinary rule was violative of the First Amendment. As it did in the *Virginia Citizens* case, however, the Court emphasized that its holding did not mean that advertising by attorneys could not be regulated in any manner. The court again specifically stated that advertising which is false, deceptive, or misleading is subject to restraint and pointed out that "the leeway for untruthful or misleading expression that has been allowed in other contexts has little force in the commercial arena." The Court also reiterated the view expressed earlier in the *Virginia Citizens* case that the State may impose reasonable restrictions on the time, place, and manner of advertising and could suppress advertising concerning illegal transactions.

It is entirely clear that the advertisements before us violate Section 16(13). However, under the authority of *Virginia Citizens* and *Bates,* we must conclude that the restrictions therein are overly broad and may operate in some cases to suppress commercial speech in violation of the First Amendment. We commend to the General Assembly the reconsideration of these restrictions in the light of current constitutional interpretations.

Ordinarily a litigant is permitted to bring First Amendment overbreadth attacks against a statute without demonstrating that his particular conduct is protected. The rationale is to fully protect permissible speech which might otherwise be inhibited by an overbroad statute. But the Sumpreme Court in *Bates* ruled that this rationale is inapplicable to commercial speech such as in this case. "(I)t seems unlikely that such speech is particularly susceptible to being crushed by overbroad regulation. . . . Since overbreadth has been described by this Court as 'strong medicine,' which 'as a last resort,' we decline to apply it to professional advertising, a context where it is not necessary to further its intended objective." Accordingly, we must specifically examine plaintiff's advertisements to determine whether they are entitled to First Amendment protection under the criteria set forth in *Virginia Citizens* and *Bates.*

There can be no question about the fact that advertising by those engaged in the profession of treating bodily ills involves different considerations and risks than are involved in advertising by others. The availability of proper medical attention at the right time and from the right source obviously is of critical importance to every person. The natural and compelling urge to maintain good health and to find a cure for disease renders people particularly susceptible to advertising which suggests a means to accomplish these objectives. The potential to mislead is great, and it is apparent that the State has a very real and compelling interest in restricting the advertising of health care services to those which are truthful, informative, and helpful to the potential consumer in making an intelligent decision.

It is evident that Dr. Talsky's advertisements are significantly different from those in the *Virginia Citizens* and *Bates* cases, which were described by the Supreme Court as "restrained professional advertising." We note in particular the portion of the newspaper ad (omitted) entitled "Do You Feel Like This Fellow Looks?" which asks the questions "Wouldn't you like to feel better? Think about this . . . If you feel as bad as you do now, how will you feel in 10, 20, 30 years from now? Can you afford to continue patching up symptoms when health is within reach through chiropractic. It's not true to say . . . 'We are doing everything possible' *unless chiropractic is included*." "How about a *chiropractic* spinal *'Back' to school check-up*." The posted circulars and cards contained a before/after type set of pictures showing one healthy and one apparently sick, starving child and stating "*Sadness* to *Sunshine*" and "*Sickness* to *Health*"; the business cards play upon the letters TLC—"Talsky Life Center" and "Tender Loving Care"—both phrases being contained in little hearts. The advertisements assure the reader that "health is in reach through chiropractic" and "elimination of the *need* for drugs . . . is not a far fetched idea, but an accomplished fact!! The answer to most health problems is found in chiropractic—the world's largest and finest drugless healing profession. That's right: drugless. Chiropractic eliminates the need for drugs which treat symptoms by eliminating the true cause of most chronic health problems—displacement of spinal vertebrae." The advertisements offer free chicken and refreshments, identify with a well known celebrity (the newspaper advertisement quotes

Art Linkletter on drug abuse), and picture a man on his knees praying and asking, "Why didn't someone tell me about chiropractic care sooner" while relaying the message, "Others get well, so can you."

We include the foregoing lengthy recitation of plaintiff's advertisements and techniques to emphasize the differences between this case and the *Virginia Citizens/Bates* tandem. Plaintiff does not advertise "X product or X service at Y price." Plaintiff's advertisements do not concern a uniform product or a routine standardized service, nor do they convey information which is susceptible of precise measurement or empirical testing in order to determine whether it is false, deceptive, or misleading.

In *Bates,* citing *Virginia Citizens,* the Court emphasized the importance of not restricting the dissemination of information which assures "informed and reliable decision making" by the public. The thinly veiled, alluring promises of physical relief contained in Dr. Talsky's advertisements clearly do not serve that function. Little, if any, information is given which would be helpful to intelligent decision making, and it cannot, in our judgment, fairly be said that prohibiting advertising of the type before us denies useful information to any segment of society as in *Virginia Citizens* or inhibits access to needed professional services as in *Bates.* This case simply does not involve "restrained professional advertising."

The potential for abuse in advertising by professionals, especially in the health care field, where persons are peculiarly susceptible to alluring promises of relief, has long been recognized. The recent Supreme Court decisions do not require that our concern for such problems be discarded. On the contrary, *Bates* recognized the need for close regulation and tight restrictions on misleading and untruthful professional advertising, and its rationale is applicable here: "Thus, the leeway for untruthful or misleading expression that has been allowed in other contexts has little force in the commercial arena. (Citations.) In fact, because the public lacks sophistication concerning legal services, misstatements that might be overlooked or deemed unimportant in other advertising may be found quite inappropriate in legal advertising. For example, advertising claims as to the quality of services—a matter we do not address today—are not susceptible to measurement or verification; accordingly, such claims may be so likely to be misleading as to warrant restriction. Similar objections might justify restraints on in-person solicitation. We do not foreclose the possibility that some limited supplementation, by way of warning or disclaimer or the like, might be required of even an advertisement of the kind ruled upon today so as to assure that the consumer is not misled."

We emphasize that this opinion should not be construed as indicating our blanket approval of the statutory restrictions as applied to "restrained professional advertising" by those professionals subject to the Medical Practice Act.

Since, in our view, plaintiff's advertisements were uninformative and misleading, they were not entitled to First Amendment protection within the purview of the *Virginia Citizens* and *Bates* decisions. We believe it is further evident that the attachment of even protected advertising material to traffic light posts, traffic control boxes, and United States mail boxes would constitute an improper time, place, and manner for the advertising of professional services under those cases. We therefore conclude that the trial court erred in holding Section 16(13) of the Medical Practice Act unconstitutional and violative of plaintiff's First Amendment right of freedom of speech with regard to the advertising here in question.

Plaintiff also argues that the statute must be held invalid since the terms "advertising" and "solicitation" are unconstitutionally vague and because review of the Department's decision under the Administrative Review Act does not provide a sufficiently prompt resolution of the matter. We find no merit to these contentions. Likewise, we do not agree with plaintiff's argument that he has been denied equal protection of the law by a statute which singles out medical practioners for restrictions on advertising. The justification and necessity for regulation of those engaged in professions which are closely related to public health, welfare, and the general good of the public are too well established to require discussion.

The judgment of the circuit court of Cook County is reversed, and the order of the Department of Registration and Education suspending plaintiff's license for 90 days is affirmed.

Judgment reversed; order affirmed.

Mr. Justice Dooley, dissenting.

LINMARK ASSOCIATES, INC. and *WILLIAM MELLMAN* v. *TOWNSHIP OF WILLINGBORO* and *GERALD DALY*
431 U.S. 85 (1977)

Mr. Justice Marshall delivered the opinion of the Court.

This case presents the question whether the First Amendment permits a municipality to prohibit the posting of "For Sale" or "Sold" signs when the municipality acts to stem what it perceives as the flight of white homeowners from a racially integrated community.

Petitioner Linmark Associates, a New Jersey corporation, owned a piece of realty in the Township of Willingboro, New Jersey. Petitioner decided to sell its property, and on March 26, 1974, listed it with petitioner Mellman, a real estate agent. To attract interest in the property, petitioners desired to place a "For Sale" sign on the lawn. Willingboro, however, narrowly limits the types of signs that can be erected on land in the township. Although prior to March of 1974 "For Sale" and "Sold" signs were permitted, subject to certain restrictions not at issue here, on March 18, 1974, the Township Council enacted Ordinance 5–1974, repealing the statutory authorization for such signs on all but model homes. Petitioners brought this action against both the township and the building inspector charged with enforcing the ban on "For Sale" signs, seeking declaratory and injunctive relief. The District Court granted a declaration of unconstitutionality, but a divided court of appeals reversed (*Linmark Associates, Inc.* v. *Township of Willingboro,* 535 F. 2d 786 (CA3 1976)). We granted certiorari and reverse the judgment of the Court of Appeals.

I

The Township of Willingboro is a residential community located in southern New Jersey near Fort Dix, McGuire Air Force Base, and offices of several national corporations. The township was developed as a middle income community by Levitt and Sons, beginning in the late 1950s. It is served by over 80 realtors.

During the 1960s Willingboro underwent rapid growth. The white population increased by almost 350 percent, and the nonwhite population rose from 60 to over 5,000, or from .005 percent of the population to 11.7 percent. As of the 1970 census, almost 44,000 people resided in Willingboro. In the 1970s however, the population growth slowed; from 1970 to 1973, the latest year for which figures were available at the time of trial, Willingboro's population rose by only 3 percent. More significantly, the white population actually declined by almost 2,000 in this interval, a drop of over 5 percent, while the nonwhite population grew by more than 3,000, an increase of approximately 60 percent. By 1973, nonwhites constituted 18.2 percent of the township's population.

At the trial in this case, respondent presented testimony from two realtors, two members of the Township Council, and three members of the Human Relations Commission, all of whom agreed that a major cause in the decline in the white population was "panic selling"—that is, selling by whites who feared that the township was becoming all black, and that property values would decline. One realtor estimated that the reason 80 percent of the sellers gave for their decision to sell was that "the whole town was for sale, and they didn't want to be caught in any bind." Respondents' witnesses also testified that in their view "For Sale" and "Sold" signs were a major catalyst of these fears.

William Kearns, the Mayor of Willingboro during the year preceding enactment of the ordinance and a member of the Council when the ordinance was enacted, testified concerning the events leading up to its passage. According to Kearns, beginning at least in 1973 the community became concerned about the changing population. At a town meeting in February 1973, called to discuss "Willingboro, to sell or not to sell," a member of the community suggested that real estate signs be banned. The suggestion received the overwhelming support of those attending the meeting. Kearns brought the proposal to the Township Council, which requested the Township Solicitor to study it. The Council also contacted National Neighbors, a nationwide organization promoting integrated housing, and obtained the names of other communities that had prohibited "For Sale" signs. After obtaining a favorable report from Shaker Heights, Ohio, on its ordinance, and after receiving an endorsement of the proposed ban from the Willingboro Human Relations Commission, the Council began drafting legislation.

Rather than following its usual procedure of conducting a public hearing only after the proposed law had received preliminary Council approval, the Council scheduled two public meetings on Ordinance 5–1974. The first took place in February 1974, before the initial Council vote, and the second in March 1974, after the vote. At the conclusion of the second hearing, the Ordinance was approved unanimously.

The transcripts of the Council hearings were introduced into evidence at trial. They reveal that at the hearings the Council received important information bearing on the need for and likely impact of the ordinance. With respect to the justification for the ordinance, the Council was told (a) that a study of Willingboro home sales in 1973 revealed that the turnover rate was roughly 11 percent; J.A. 89 (b) that in February 1974, a typical month, 230 "For Sale" signs were posted among the 11,000 houses in the community, and (c) that the Willingboro Tax Assessor had reported that "by and large the increased value of Willingboro properties was way ahead of . . . comparable communities." With respect to the projected effect of the ordinance, several realtors reported that 30 to 35 percent of their purchaser-clients came to them because they had seen one of the realtor's "For Sale" or "Sold" signs, and one realtor estimated, based on his experience in a neighboring community that already had banned signs, that selling realty without signs takes twice as long as selling with signs.

The transcripts of the Council hearings also reveal that the hearings provided useful barometers of public sentiment towards the proposed ordinance. The council was told, for example, that surveys in two areas of the township found overwhelming support for the law. In addition, at least at the second meeting, the nonrealtor citizens who spoke favored the proposed ordinance by a sizable margin. Interestingly, however, at both meetings those defending the ordinance focused primarily on aesthetic considerations and on the effect of signs, and transiency generally, on property values. Few speakers directly referred to the changing racial composition of Willingboro in supporting the proposed law.

Although the ordinance had been in effect for nine months prior to trial, no statistical data was presented concerning its impact. Respondent's witnesses all agreed, however, that the number of persons selling or considering selling their houses because of racial fears had declined sharply. But several of these witnesses also testified that the number of sales in Willingboro had not declined since the ordinance was enacted. Moreover, respondents' realtor-witnesses both stated that their business had increased by 25 percent since the ordinance was enacted, and one of these realtors reported that the racial composition of his clientele remained unchanged.

The District Court did not make specific findings of fact. In the course of its opinion, however, the court stated that Willingboro "is to a large extent a transient community partly due to its proximity to the military facility at Fort Dix and in part due to the numerous transfers of real estate." The court also stated that there was "no evidence" that whites were leaving Willingboro *en masse* as "For Sale" signs appeared, but "merely an indication that its residents are concerned that there may be a large influx of minority groups moving in to the town with the resultant effect being a reduction in property values." The Court of Appeals essentially accepted these "findings," although it found that Willingboro was experiencing "incipient" panic selling, and that a "fear psychology (had) developed."

II

A

The starting point for analysis of petitioners' First Amendment claim must be the two recent decisions in which this Court has eroded the "commercial speech" exception to the First Amendment. In *Bigelow* v. *Virginia*, decided just two years ago, this Court for the first time expressed its dissatisfaction with the then prevalent approach of resolving a class of First Amendment claims simply by categorizing the speech as "commercial." "Regardless of the particular label," we stated, "a court may not escape the task of assessing the First Amendment interest at stake and weighing it against the public interest allegedly served by the regulation." After conducting such an analysis in *Bigelow*, we concluded that Virginia could not constitutionally punish the publisher of a newspaper for printing an abortion referral agency's paid advertisement which not only promoted the agency's services but also contained information about the availability of abortions.

One year later, in *Virginia State Board of Pharmacy* v. *Virginia Citizens Consumer Council, Inc.*, we went further. Conceding that "(s)ome fragment of hope for the continuing validity of a 'commercial speech' exception arguably might have persisted because of the subject matter in the advertisement in *Bigelow*," we held quite simply, that commercial speech is not "wholly outside the protection of the First Amendment." Although recognizing that "(s)ome forms of commercial speech regulation"—such as regulation of false or misleading speech—"are surely permissible," we had little difficulty in finding that Virginia's ban on the advertising of prescription drug prices by pharmacists was unconstitutional.[1]

Respondents contend, as they must, that the "For Sale" signs banned in Willingboro are constitutionally distinguishable from the abortion and drug advertisements we have previously considered. It is to the distinctions respondents advance that we now turn.

B

If the Willingboro law is to be treated differently from those invalidated in *Bigelow* and *Virginia Pharmacy*, it cannot be because the speakers or listeners have a lesser First Amendment interest in the subject matter of the speech that is regulated here. Persons desiring to sell their homes are just as interested in communicating that fact as are sellers of other goods and services. Similarly, would-be purchasers of realty are no less interested in receiving information about available property than are purchasers of other commodities in receiving like information about those commodities. And the societal interest in "the free flow of commercial information," *Virginia State Board of Pharmacy* v. *Virginia Citizens Consumer Council, Inc.*, is in no way lessened by the fact that the subject of the commercial information here is realty rather than abortions or drugs.

Respondents nevertheless argue that First Amendment concerns are less directly implicated by Willingboro's ordinance because it restricts only one method of communication. This distinction is not without significance to First Amendment analysis, since laws regulating the time, place, or manner of speech stand on a different footing than laws prohibiting speech altogether. Respondents effort to defend the ordinance on this ground is unpersuasive, however, for two reasons.

First, serious questions exist as to whether the ordinance "leave(s) open ample alternative channels for communication," (*Virginia Pharmacy*). Although in theory sellers remain free to employ a number of different alternatives, in practice realty is not marketed through leaflets, sound tracks, demonstrations, or the like. The options to which sellers realistically are relegated—primarily newspaper advertising and listing with realtors—involve more cost and less autonomy than "For Sale" signs; are less likely to reach persons not deliberately seeking sales information; and may be a less effective media for communicating the message that is conveyed by a "For Sale" sign in front of the house to be sold. The alternatives, then, are far from satisfactory.

Second, the Willingboro ordinance is not genuinely concerned with the place of the speech—front lawns—or the manner of the speech—signs. The township has not prohibited all lawn signs—or all lawn signs of a particular size or shape—in order to promote aesthetic values or any other value "unrelated to the suppression of free expression," (*United States* v. *O'Brien*).[2] Nor has it acted to restrict a mode of communication that "intrudes on the privacy of the home, . . . makes it impractical for the unwilling viewer or auditor to avoid exposure," (*Erznoznik* v. *City of Jacksonville*) or otherwise reaches a group the township has a right to protect. And respondents have not demonstrated that the place or manner of the speech produces a detrimental "secondary effect" on society. Rather, Willingboro has proscribed particular types of signs based on their content because it fears their "primary" effect—that they will cause those receiving the information to act upon it. That the proscription applies only to one mode of communication, therefore, does not transform this into a "time, place, or manner" case. If the ordinance is to be sustained, it must be on the basis of the township's interest in regulating the content of the communication, and not on any interest in regulating the form.

C

Respondents do seek to distinguish *Bigelow* and *Virginia Pharmacy* by relying on the vital goal this ordinance serves: namely, promoting stable, racially integrated housing. There can be no question about the importance of achieving this goal. This Court has expressly recognized that substantial benefits flow to both whites and blacks from interracial association and that Congress has made a strong national commitment to promoting integrated housing.

That this ordinance was enacted to achieve an important governmental objective, however, does not distinguish the case from *Virginia Pharmacy*. In *Virginia Pharmacy*, the State argued that its prohibition on prescription drug price advertising furthered the health and safety of state residents by preventing low cost, low quality pharmacists from driving reputable pharmacists out of business. We expressly recognized the "strong interest" of a State in maintaining "professionalism on the part of licensed pharmacists." But we nevertheless found the Virginia law unconstitutional because we were unpersuaded that the law was necessary to achieve this objective, and were convinced that in any event, the First Amendment disabled the State from achieving its goal by restricting the free flow of truthful information. For the same reasons we conclude that the Willingboro ordinance at issue here is also constitutionally infirm.

The record here demonstrates that respondents failed to establish that this ordinance is needed to assure that Willingboro remains an integrated community. As the District Court concluded, the evidence does not support the Council's apparent fears that Willingboro was experiencing a substantial incidence of panic selling by white homeowners. *A fortiore*, the evidence does not establish that "For Sale" signs in front of 2 percent of Willingboro homes were a major cause of panic selling. And the record does not confirm the township's assumption that proscribing such signs will reduce public awareness of realty sales and thereby decrease public concern over selling.[3]

The constitutional defect in this ordinance, however, is far more basic. The Township Council here like the Virginia Assembly in *Virginia Pharmacy*, acted to prevent its residents from obtaining certain information. That information, which pertains to sales activity in Willingboro, is of vital interest to Willingboro residents, since it may bear on one of the most important decisions they have a right to make: where to live and raise their families. The Council has sought to restrict the free flow of this data because it fears that otherwise, homeowners will make decisions inimical to what the Council view's as the homeowners' self-interest and the corporate interest of the township: they will choose to leave town. The Council's concern, then, was not with any commercial aspect of "For Sale" signs—with offerors communicating offers to offerees—but with the substance of the information communicated to Willingboro citizens. If dissemination of this information can be restricted, then every locality in the country can suppress any facts that reflect poorly on the locality, so long as a plausible claim can be made that disclosure would cause the recipients of the information to act "irrationally." *Virginia Pharmacy* denies government such sweeping powers. As we said there in rejecting Virginia's claim that the only way it could enable its citizens to find their self-interest was to deny them information that is neither false nor misleading:

> There is . . . an alternative to this highly paternalistic approach. That alternative is to assume that information is not in itself harmful, that people will perceive their own best interest if only they are well enough informed, and that the best means to that end is to open the channels of communication rather than to close them . . . But the choice among these alternative approaches is not ours to make or the Virginia General Assembly's. It is precisely this kind of choice, between the dangers of suppressing information, and the dangers of its misuse if it is freely available, that the First Amendment makes for us. (425 U.S., at 770.)

Or as Mr. Justice Brandeis put it, "If there be time to expose through discussion the falsehood and fallacies, to avert the evil by the process of education, the remedy to be applied is more speech, not enforced silence. Only an emergency can justify repression."

Since we can find no meaningful distinction between Ordinance 5–1974 and the statute overturned in *Virginia Pharmacy*, we must conclude this ordinance violates The First Amendment.

III

In invalidating this law, we by no means leave Willingboro defenseless in its effort to promote integrated housing. The township obviously remains free to continue "the process of education" it has already begun. It can give widespread publicity—through "Not for Sale" signs or other methods—to the number of whites remaining in Willingboro. And it surely can endeavor to create inducements to retain individuals who are considering selling their homes.

Beyond this, we reaffirm our statement in *Virginia Pharmacy* that the "common sense differences between speech that 'does no more than propose a commercial transaction' (*Pittsburgh Press Co.* v. *Human Relations Commission*), and other varieties . . . suggest that a different degree of protection is necessary to insure that the flow of truthful and legitimate commercial information is unimpaired." Laws dealing with false or misleading signs, and laws requiring such signs to "appear in such a form, or include such additional information . . . as (is) necessary to prevent (their) being deceptive," (ibid.), therefore, would raise very different constitutional questions. We leave those questions for another day, and simply hold that the ordinance under review here, which impairs "the flow of truthful and legitimate commercial information" is constitutionally infirm.

Reversed.

Mr. Justice Rehnquist took no part in the consideration or decision of this case.

NOTES

[1] The Court of Appeals did not have the benefit of *Virginia Pharmacy* when it issued its decision in this case. To some extent the court anticipated that decision, recognizing that the fact that "a communication is commercial in nature does not *ipso facto* strip the communication of its First Amendment protections." But the court premised its analysis on a sharp dichotomy between commercial and "pure" or noncommercial speech, and concluded that commercial speech may be restricted if its "impact be found detrimental" by a municipality, and if "the limitation on any pure speech element (is) minimal." After *Virginia Pharmacy* it is clear that commercial speech cannot be banned because of an unsubstantiated belief that its impact is "detrimental."

[2] Accordingly, we do not decide whether a ban on signs or a limitation on the number of signs could survive constitutional scrutiny if it were unrelated to the suppression of free expression.

[3] While this assumption is certainly plausible, it is also possible that eliminating signs will cause homeowners to turn to other sources for information, so that their awareness of, and concern over, selling will be unaffected. Indeed, banning signs actually may fuel public anxiety over sales activity by increasing homeowners' dependence on rumor and surmise.

The fact that sales volume remained unchanged in Willingboro in the first nine months after the ordinance was enacted suggests that it did not affect public conern over selling, if that concern was a significant cause of housing turnover.

ZACCHINI v. SCRIPPS-HOWARD BROADCASTING COMPANY
433 U.S. 562 (1977)

Mr. Justice White delivered the opinion of the Court.

Petitioner, Hugo Zacchini, is an entertainer. He performs a "human cannonball" act in which he is shot from a cannon into a net some 200 feet away. Each performance occupies some 15 seconds. In August and September, petitioner was engaged to perform his act on a regular basis at the Geauga County Fair in Burton, Ohio. He performed in a fenced area, surrounded by grandstands, at the fair grounds. Members of the public attending the fair were not charged a separate admission fee to observe his act.

On August 30, a freelance reporter for Scripps-Howard Broadcasting Company, the operator of a television broadcasting station and respondent in this case, attended the fair. He carried a small movie camera. Petitioner noticed the reporter and asked him not to film the performance. The reporter did not do so on that day; but on the instructions of the producer of respondent's daily newscast, he returned the following day and videotaped the entire act. This film clip, approximately 15 seconds in length, was shown on the 11 o'clock news program that night, together with favorable commentary.

Like the concurring judge in the Court of Appeals, the Supreme Court of Ohio rested petitioner's cause of action under state law on his "right to the publicity value of his performance." The opinion Syllabus, to which we are to look for the rule of law used to decide the case, declared first, that one may not use for his own benefit the name or likeness of another, whether or not the use or benefit is a commercial one; and second, that respondent would be liable for the appropriation, over petitioner's objection and in the absence of license or privilege, of petitioner's right to the publicity value of his performance. The court nevertheless gave judgment for respondent because, in the words of the Syllabus,

> (a) TV station has a privilege to report in its newscasts matters of legitimate public interest which would otherwise be protected by an individual's right of publicity, unless the actual intent of the TV station was to appropriate the benefit of the publicity for some nonprivileged private use, or unless the actual intent was to injure the individual.

(T)he court placed principal reliance on *Time, Inc.* v. *Hill,* a case involving First Amendment limitations on state tort actions. It construed the principle of that case, along with that of *New York Times v.* Sullivan, to be that "the press has a privilege to report matters of legitimate public interest even though such reports might intrude on matters otherwise private," and concluded, therefore, that the press is also "privileged when an individual seeks to publicly exploit his talents while keeping the benefits private." The privilege thus exists in cases "where the appropriation of the right of publicity is claimed." The court's opinion also referred to Draft 21 of the relevant portion of *Restatement of Torts,* 2d., which was understood to make room for reasonable press appropriations by limiting the reach of the right of privacy rather than by creating a privileged invasion. The court preferred the notion of privilege over the Restatement's formulation, however, reasoning that "since the gravamen of the issue in this case is not whether the degree of intrusion is reasonable, but whether *First Amendment principles* require that the right of privacy give way to the public right to be informed of matters of public interest and concern, the concept of privilege seems the more useful and appropriate one." (Emphasis added.)

The Ohio Supreme Court relied heavily on *Time, Inc.* v. *Hill,* but that case does not mandate a media privilege to televise a performer's entire act without his consent. Involved in *Time, Inc.* v. *Hill* was a claim under the New York "Right of Privacy" statute that *Life* magazine, in the course of reviewing a new play, had connected the play with a long-past incident involving petitioner and his family and had falsely described their experience and conduct at that time. The complaint sought damages for humiliation and suffering flowing from these nondefamatory falsehoods that allegedly invaded Hill's privacy. The Court held, however, that the opening of a new play linked to an actual incident was a matter of public interest and that Hill could not recover without showing that the *Life* report was knowingly false or was published with reckless disregard for the truth—the same rigorous standard that had been applied in *New York Times* v. *Sullivan*.

Time, Inc. v. *Hill,* which was hotly contested and decided by a divided court, involved an entirely different tort than the "right of publicity" recognized by the Ohio Supreme Court. As the opinion reveals in *Time, Inc.* v. *Hill,* the Court was steeped in the literature of privacy law and was aware of the developing distinctions and nuances in this branch of the law. The Court, for example, cited Prosser, *Handbook of the Law of Torts* (3d ed. 1964), and the same author's well known article, "Privacy" (48 *Calif. L. Rev.* 383 (1960)), both of which divided privacy into four distinct branches. The Court was aware that it was adjudicating a "false light" privacy case involving a matter of public interest, not a case involving "intrusion," "appropriation" of a name or likeness for the purposes of trade, or "private details" about a nonnewsworthy person or event. It is also abundantly clear that *Time, Inc.* v. *Hill* did not involve a performer, a person with a name having commercial value, or any claim to a "right of publicity." This discrete kind of "appropriation" case was plainly identified in the literature cited by the Court and had been adjudicated in the reported cases.

The differences between these two torts are important. First, the State's interests in providing a cause of action in each instance are different. "The interest protected" in permitting recovery for placing the plaintiff in a false light "is clearly that of reputation, with the same overtones of mental distress as in defamation." (Prosser, *supra,* 48 *Calif.L.Rev.,* at 400.) By contrast, the State's interest in permitting a "right of publicity" is in protecting the proprietary interest of the individual in his act in part to encourage such entertainment. As we later note, the State's interest is closely analogous to the goals of patent and copyright law, focusing on the right of the individual to reap the reward of his endeavors, and having little to do with protecting feelings or reputation. Second, the two torts differ in the degree to which they intrude on dissemination of information to the public. In "false light" cases the only way to protect the interests involved is to attempt to minimize publication of the damaging matter, which in "right of publicity" cases the only question is who gets to do the publishing. An entertainer such as petitioner usually has no objection to the widespread publication of his act as long as he gets the commercial benefit of such publication. Indeed, in the present case petitioner did not seek to enjoin the broadcast of his act; he simply sought compensation for the broadcast in the form of damages.

Nor does it appear that our later cases, such as *Rosenbloom* v. *Metromedia, Inc., Gertz* v. *Robert Welch, Inc.,* and *Time, Inc.* v. *Firestone,* require or furnish substantial support for the Ohio court's privilege ruling. These cases, like *New York Times,* emphasize the protection extended to the press by the First Amendment in defamation cases, particularly when suit is brought by a public official or a public figure. None of them involve an alleged appropriation by the press of a right of publicity existing under state law.

Moreover, *Time, Inc.* v. *Hill, New York Times, Metromedia, Gertz,* and *Firestone* all involved the reporting of events; in none of them was there an attempt to broadcast or publish an entire act for which the performer ordinarily gets paid. It is evident, and there is no claim here to the contrary, that petitioner's state law right of publicity would not serve to prevent respondent from reporting the newsworthy facts about petitioner's act. Wherever the line in particular situations is to be drawn between media reports that are protected and those that are not, we are quite sure that the First and Fourteenth Amendments do not immunize the media when they broadcast a performer's entire act without his consent. The Constitution no more prevents a State from requiring respondent to compensate petitioner for broadcasting his act on television than it would privilege respondent to film and broadcast a copyrighted dramatic work liability to the copyright owner.

The broadcast of a film of petitioner's entire act poses a substantial threat to the economic value of that performance. As the Ohio court recognized, this act is the product of petitioner's own talents and energy, the end result of much time, effort, and expense. Much of its economic value lies in the "right of exclusive control over the publicity given to his performance;" if the public can see the act for free on television, they will be less willing to pay to see it at the fair. The effect of a public broadcast of the performance is similar to preventing petitioner from charging an admission fee. "The rationale for (protecting the right of publicity) is the straightforward one of preventing unjust enrichment by the theft of good will. No social purpose is served by having the defendant get for free some aspect of the plaintiff that would have market value and for which he would normally pay." (Kalven, "Privacy in Tort Law: Were Warren and Brandeis Wrong?" 31 *Law and Contemporary Problems* 326, 331 (1966).) Moreover, the broadcast of petitioner's entire performance, unlike the unauthorized use of another's name for purposes of trade or the incidental use of a name or picture by the press, goes to the heart of petitioner's ability to earn a living as an entertainer. Thus, in this case, Ohio has recognized what may be the strongest case for a "right of publicity," involving not the appropriation of an entertainer's reputation to enhance the attractiveness of a commercial product, but the appropriation of the very activity by which the entertainer acquired his reputation in the first place.

Of course, Ohio's decision to protect petitioner's right of publicity here rests on more than a desire to compensate the performer for the time and effort invested in his act; the protection provides an economic incentive for him to make the investment required to produce a performance of interest to the public. This same consideration underlies the patent and copyright laws long enforced by this Court. As the Court stated in *Mazer* v. *Stein* (1954),

> The economic philosophy behind the clause empowering Congress to grant patents and copyrights is the conviction that encouragement of individual effort by personal gain is the best way to advance public welfare through the talents of authors and inventors in "science and useful arts." Sacrificial days devoted to such creative activities deserve rewards commensurate with the services rendered.

These laws perhaps regard the "reward to the owner (as) a secondary consideration," but they were "intended definitely to grant valuable, enforceable rights" in order to afford greater encouragement to the production of works of benefit to the public. The Constitution does not prevent Ohio from making a similar choice here in deciding to protect the entertainer's incentive in order to encourage the production of this type of work.

There is no doubt that entertainment, as well as news, enjoys First Amendment protection. It is also true that entertainment itself can be important news. But it is important to note that neither the public nor respondent will be deprived of the benefit of petitioner's performance as long as his commercial stake in his act is appropriately recognized. Petitioner does not seek to enjoin the broadcast of his performance; he simply wants to be paid for it. Nor do we think that a state law damages remedy against respondent would represent a species of liability without fault contrary to the letter or spirit of *Gertz*. Respondent knew exactly that petitioner objected to televising his act, but nevertheless displayed the entire film.

We conclude that although the State of Ohio may as a matter of its own law privilege the press in the circumstances of this case, the First and Fourteenth Amendments do not require it to do so.

Reversed.

Mr. Justice Powell, with whom Mr. Justice Brennan and Mr. Justice Marshall join, dissenting.

Disclaiming any attempt to do more than decide the narrow case before us, the Court reverses the decision of the Supreme Court of Ohio, based on repeated incantation of a single formula: "a performer's entire act." The holding today is summed up in one sentence:

> Wherever the line in particular situations is to be drawn between media reports that are protected and those that are not, we are quite sure that the First and Fourteenth Amendments do

not immunize the media when they broadcast a performer's entire act without his consent. (*Ante*, at 12.)

I doubt that this formula provides a standard clear enough even for resolution of this case. In any event, I am not persuaded that the Court's opinion is appropriately sensitive to the First Amendment value at stake, and I therefore dissent.

Although the Court would draw no distinction, I do not view respondent's action as comparable to unauthorized commercial broadcasts of sporting events, theatrical performances, and the like where the broadcaster keeps the profits. There is no suggestion here that respondent made any such use of the film. Instead, it simply reported on what petitioner concedes to be a newsworthy event, in a way hardly surprising for a television station—by means of film coverage. The report was part of an ordinary daily news program, consuming a total of 15 seconds. It is a routine example of the press fulfilling the informing function so vital to our system.

The Court's holding that the station's ordinary news report may give rise to substantial liability has disturbing implications, for the decision could lead to a degree of media self-censorship. Hereafter, whenever a television news editor is unsure whether certain film footage received from a camera crew might be held to portray an "entire act," he may decline coverage—even of clearly newsworthy events—or confine the broadcast to watered-down verbal reporting, perhaps with an occasional still picture. The public is then the loser. This is hardly the kind of news reportage that the First Amendment is meant to foster.

In my view the First Amendment commands a different analytical starting point from the one selected by the Court. Rather than begin with a quantitative analysis of the performer's behavior—is this or is this not his entire act?—we should direct initial attention to the actions of the news media: what use did the station make of the film footage? When a film is used, as here, for a routine portion of a regular news program, I would hold that the First Amendment protects the station from a "right of publicity" or "appropriation" suit, absent a strong showing by the plaintiff that the news broadcast was a subterfuge or cover for private or commercial exploitation.

I emphasize that this is an "reappropriation" suit, rather than one of the other varieties of "right of privacy" tort suits identified by Dean Prosser in his classic article. (Prosser, "Privacy," 48 *Calif. L.Rev.* 383 (1960).) In those other causes of action the competing interests are considerably different. The plaintiff generally seeks to avoid any sort of public exposure, and the existence of constitutional privilege is therefore less likely to turn on whether the publication occurred in a news broadcast or in some other fashion. In a suit like the one before us, however, the plaintiff does not complain about the fact of exposure to the public, but rather about its timing or manner. He welcomes some publicity, but seeks to retain control over means and manner as a way to maximize for himself the monetary benefits that flow from such publication. But having made the matter public—having chosen in essence, to make it newsworthy—he cannot, consistently with the First Amendment, complain of routine news reportage.

Since the film clip here was undeniably treated as news, and since there is no claim that the use was subterfuge, respondent's actions were constitutionally privileged. I would affirm.

Mr. Justice Stevens, dissenting.

The Ohio Supreme Court held that respondent's telecast of the "human cannonball" was a privileged invasion of petitioner's common law "right of publicity" because respondent's actual intent was neither (a) to appropriate the benefit of the publicity for a private use, nor (b) to injure petitioner.

As I read the state court's explanation of the limits on the concept of privilege, they define the substantive reach of a common law tort rather than anything I recognize as a limit on a federal Constitutional right. The decision was unquestionably influenced by the Ohio court's proper sensitivity to First Amendment principles, and to this Court's cases construing the First Amendment; indeed, I must confess that the opinion can be read as resting entirely on federal Constitutional grounds. Nevertheless, the basis of the state court's action is sufficiently doubtful that I would remand the case to that court for clarification of its holding before deciding the federal Constitutional issue.

FIRST NATIONAL BANK OF BOSTON V. BELLOTTI
98 S.Ct. 1407 (1978)

Mr. Justice Powell delivered the opinion of the Court.

In sustaining a state criminal statute that forbids certain expenditures by banks and business corporations for the purpose of influencing the vote on referendum proposals, the Massachusetts Supreme Judicial Court held that the First Amendment rights of a corporation are limited to issues that materially affect its business, property, or assets. The court rejected appellants' claim that the statute abridges freedom of speech in violation of the First and Fourteenth Amendments. The issue presented in this context is one of first impression in this Court. We postponed the question of jurisdiction to our consideration of the merits. We now reverse.

I

The statute at issue, Massachusetts General Laws ch. 55, Section 8, prohibits appellants, two national banking associations and three business corporations, from making contributions or expenditures "for the purpose of . . . influencing or affecting the vote on any question submitted to the voters, other than one materially affecting any of the property, business, or assets of the corporation." The statute further specifies that "(n)o question submitted to the voters solely concerning the taxation of the income, property, or transactions of individuals shall be deemed materially to affect the property, business, or assets of the corporation." A corporation that violates Section 8 may receive a maximum fine of $50,000; a corporate officer, director, or agent who violates the section may receive a maximum fine of $10,000 or imprisonment for up to one year, or both.

Appellants wanted to spend money to publicize their views on a proposed constitutional amendment that was to be submitted to the voters as a ballot question at a general election on November 2, 1976. The amendment would have permitted the legislature to impose a graduated tax on the income of individuals. After appellee, the Attorney General of Massachusetts, informed appellants that he intended to enforce Section 8 against them, they brought this action seeking to have the statute declared unconstitutional. On April 26, 1976, the case was submitted to a single Justice of the Supreme Judicial Court on an expedited basis and upon agreed facts, in order to settle the question before the upcoming election. Judgment was reserved and the case referred to the full court that same day.

Appellants argued that Section 8 violates the First Amendment, the Due Process and Equal Protection Clauses of the Fourteenth Amendment, and similar provisions of the Massachusetts Constitution. They prayed that the statute be declared unconstitutional on its face and as it would be applied to their proposed expenditures. The parties' statement of agreed facts reflected their disagreement as to the effect that the adoption of a personal income tax would have on appellants' business; it noted that "(t)here is a division of opinion among economists as to whether and to what extent a graduated income tax imposed solely on individuals would affect the business and assets of corporations." (App.17.) Appellee did not dispute that appellants' management believed that the tax would have a significant effect on their businesses.

On September 22, 1976, the full bench directed the single justice to enter judgment upholding the Constitutionality of Section 8. An opinion followed on February 1, 1977. In addressing appellants' Constitutional contentions, the court acknowledged that Section 8 "operate(s) in an area of the most fundamental First Amendment activities," and viewed the principal question as "whether business corporations, such as (appellants), have First Amendment rights coextensive with those of natural persons or associations of natural persons." The court found its answer in the contours of a corporation's Constitutional right, as a "person" under the Fourteenth Amendment, not to be deprived of property without due process of law. Distinguishing the First Amendment rights of a natural person from the more limited rights of a corporation, the court concluded that "whether its rights are designated 'liberty' rights or 'property' rights, a corporation's property and business interests are entitled to Fourteenth Amendment protection. . . . (A)s an incident of such protection, corporations also possess certain rights of speech and expression under the Fourteenth Amendment." Accordingly, the court held "that only when a general political issue materially affects a corporation's business, property or assets may that corporation claim First Amendment protection for its speech or other activities entitling it to communicate its position on that issue to the general public." Since this limitation is "identical to the legislative command in the first sentence of (Section 8)," the court concluded that the legislature "has clearly identified in the challenged statute the parameters of corporate free speech."

The court also declined to say that there was "no rational basis for (the) legislative determination," embodied in the second sentence of Section 8, that a ballot question concerning the taxation of individuals could not materially affect the interests of a corporation. In rejecting appellants' argument that this second sentence established a conclusive presumption in violation of the Due Process Clause, the court construed Section 8 to embody two distinct crimes: The first prohibits a corporation from spending money to influence the vote on a ballot question not materially affecting its business interests; the second, and more specific prohibition, makes it criminal per se for a corporation to spend money to influence the vote on a ballot question solely concerning individual taxation. While acknowledging that the second crime is "related to the general crime" stated in the first sentence of Section 8, the court intimated that the second sentence was intended to make criminal an expenditure of the type proposed by appellants without regard to specific proof of the materiality of the question to the corporation's business interests. The court nevertheless seems to have reintroduced the "materially affecting" concept into its interpretation of the second sentence of Section 8, as a limitation on the scope of the so-called "second crime" imposed by the Federal Constitution rather than the Massachusetts Legislature. But because the court thought appellants had not made a sufficient showing of material effect, their challenge to the statutory prohibition as applied to them also failed.

Appellants' other arguments fared no better. Adopting a narrowing construction of the statute, the Supreme Judicial Court rejected the contention that Section 8 is overbroad. It also found no merit in appellants' vagueness argument because the specific prohibition against corporate expenditures on a referendum solely concerning individual taxation is "both precise and definite." Finally, the court held that appellants were not denied the equal protection of the laws.

II

Because 1976 referendum has been held, and the proposed constitutional amendment defeated, we face at the outset a question of mootness. As the case falls within the class of controversies "capable of repetition, yet evading review," we conclude that it is not moot. Present here are both elements identified in *Weinstein v. Bradford* (1975), as precluding a finding of mootness in the absence of a class action: "1) the challenged action was in its duration too short to be fully litigated prior to its cessation or expiration, and 2) there (is) a reasonable expectation that the same complaining party (will) be subjected to the same action again."

Under no reasonably foreseeable circumstances could appellants obtain plenary review by this Court of the issue here presented in advance of a referendum on a similar constitutional amendment. In each of the legislature's four attempts to obtain constitutional authorization to enact a graduated income tax, including this most recent one, the period of time between legislative authorization of the proposal and its submission to the voters was approximately 18 months. This proved too short a period of time for appellants to obtain complete judicial review, and there is every reason to believe that any future suit would take at least as long. Furthermore, a decision allowing the desired expenditures would be an empty gesture unless it afforded appellants sufficient opportunity prior to the election date to communicate their views effectively.

Nor can there be any serious doubt that there is a "reasonable expectation" (*Weinstein v. Bradford,* supra), that appellants again will be subject to the threat of prosecution under Section 8. The 1976 election marked the fourth time in recent years that a proposed graduated income tax amendment has been submitted to the Massachusetts voters. Appellee's suggestion that the legislature may abandon its quest for a constitutional amendment is purely speculative. Appellants insist that they will continue to oppose the constitutional amendment, and there is no reason to believe that the Attorney General will refrain from prosecuting violations of Section 8.

Meanwhile, Section 8 remains on the books as a complete prohibition of corporate expenditures related to individual tax referenda, and as a restraining influence on corporate expenditures concerning other ballot questions. The criminal penalties of Section 8 discourage challenge by violation, and the effect of the statute on arguably protected speech will persist. Accordingly, we conclude that this case is not moot and proceed to address the merits.

III

The court below framed the principal question in this case as whether and to what extent corporations have First Amendment rights. We believe that the court posed the wrong question. The Constitution often protects interests broader than those of the party seeking their vindication. The First Amendment, in particular, serves significant societal interests. The proper question therefore is not whether corporations "have" First Amendment rights and, if so, whether they are coextensive with those of natural persons. Instead, the question must be whether Section 8 abridges expression that the First Amendment was meant to protect. We hold that it does.

A

The speech proposed by appellants is at the heart of the First Amendment's protection.

> The freedom of speech and of the press guaranteed by the Constitution embraces at the least the liberty to discuss publicly and truthfully all matters of public concern without previous restraint or fear of subsequent punishment. . . . Freedom of discussion, if it would fulfill its his-

toric function in this nation, must embrace all issues about which information is needed or appropriate to enable the members of society to cope with the exigencies of their period.

The referendum issue that appellants wish to address falls squarely within this description. In appellants' view, the enactment of a graduated personal income tax, as proposed to be authorized by constitutional amendment, would have a seriously adverse effect on the economy of the State. The importance of the referendum issue to the people and government of Massachusetts is not disputed. Its merits, however, are the subject of sharp disagreement.

As the Court said in *Mills* v. *Alabama* (1966), "there is practically universal agreement that a major purpose of (the First) Amendment was to protect the free discussion of governmental affairs." If the speakers here were not corporations, no one would suggest that the State could silence their proposed speech. It is the type of speech indispensable to decision making in a democracy, and this is no less true because the speech comes from a corporation rather than an individual. The inherent worth of the speech in terms of its capacity for informing the public does not depend upon the identity of its source, whether corporation, association, union, or individual.

The court below nevertheless held that corporate speech is protected by the First Amendment only when it pertains directly to the corporation's business interests. In deciding whether this novel and restrictive gloss on the First Amendment comports with the Constitution and the precedents of this Court, we need not survey the outer boundaries of the Amendment's protection of corporate speech, or address the abstract question whether corporations have the full measure of rights that individuals enjoy under the First Amendment. The question in this case, simply put, is whether the corporate identity of the speaker deprives this proposed speech of what otherwise would be its clear entitlement to protection. We turn now to that question.

B

The court below found confirmation of the legislature's definition of the scope of a corporation's First Amendment rights in the language of the Fourteenth Amendment. Noting that the First Amendment is applicable to the States through the Fourteenth, and seizing upon the observation that corporations "cannot claim for themselves the liberty which the Fourteenth Amendment guarantees," the court concluded that a corporation's First Amendment rights must derive from its property rights under the Fourteenth.

This is an artificial mode of analysis, untenable under decisions of this Court.

> In a series of decisions beginning with *Gitlow* v. *New York* (1925), this Court held that the liberty of speech and of the press which the First Amendment guarantees against abridgment by the federal government is within the liberty safeguarded by the Due Process Clause of the Fourteenth Amendment from invasion by state action. That principle has been followed and reaffirmed to the present day.

Freedom of speech and the other freedoms encompassed by the First Amendment always have been viewed as fundamental components of the liberty safeguarded by the Due Process Clause, and the Court has not identified a separate source for the right when it has been asserted by corporations. In *Grosjean* v. *American Press Co.* (1936), the Court rejected the very reasoning adopted by the Supreme Judicial Court and did not rely on the corporation's property rights under the Fourteenth Amendment in sustaining its freedom of speech.

Yet appellee suggests that First Amendment rights generally have been afforded only to corporations engaged in the communications business or through which individuals express themselves, and the court below apparently accepted the "materially affecting" theory as the conceptual common denominator between appellee's position and the precedents of this Court. It is true that the "materially affecting" requirement would have been satisfied in the Court's decisions affording protection to the speech of media corporations and corporations otherwise in the business of communication or entertainment, and to the commercial speech of business corporations. In such cases, the speech would be connected to the corporation's business almost by definition. But the effect on the business of the corporation was not the governing rationale in any of these decisions. None of them mentions, let alone attributes significance to the fact, that the subject of the challenged communication materially affected the corporation's business.

The press cases emphasize the special and Constitutionally recognized role of that institution in informing and educating the public, offering criticism, and providing a forum for discussion and debate. But the press does not have a monopoly on either the First Amendment or the ability to enlighten. Similarly, the Court's decisions involving corporations in the business of communication or entertainment are based not only on the role of the First Amendment in fostering individual self-expression, but also on its role in affording the public access to discussion, debate, and the dissemination of information and ideas. Even decisions seemingly based exclusively on the individual's right to express himself acknowledge that the expression may contribute to society's edification.

Nor do our recent commercial speech cases lend support to appellee's business interest theory. They illustrate that the First Amendment goes beyond protection of the press and the self-expression of individuals to prohibit government from limiting the stock of information from which members of the public may draw. A commercial advertisement is Constitutionally protected not so much because it pertains to the seller's business as because it furthers the societal interest in the "free flow of commercial information."

C

We thus find no support in the First or Fourteenth Amendments, or in the decisions of this Court, for the proposition that speech that otherwise would be within the protection of the First Amendment loses that protection simply because its source is a corporation that cannot prove, to the satisfaction of a court, a material effect on its business or property. The "materially affecting" requirement is not an identification of the boundaries of corporate speech etched by the Constitution itself. Rather, it amounts to an impermissible legislative prohibition of speech based on the identity of the interests that spokesmen may represent in public debate over controversial issues and a requirement that the speaker have a sufficiently great interest in the subject to justify communication.

Section 8 permits a corporation to communicate to the public its views on certain referendum subjects—those materially affecting its business—but not others. It also singles out one kind of ballot question—individual taxation—as a subject about which corporations may never make their ideas public. The legislature has drawn the line between permissible and impermissible speech according to whether there is a sufficient nexus, as defined by the legislature, between the issue presented to the voters and the business interests of the speaker.

In the realm of protected speech, the legislature is constitutionally disqualified from dictating the subjects about which persons may speak and the speakers who may address a public issue. If a legislature may direct business corporations to "stick to business," it also may limit other corporations—religious, charitable, or civic—to their respective "business" when addressing the public. Such power in government to channel the expression of views is unacceptable under the First Amendment. Especially where, as here, the legislature's suppression of speech suggests an attempt to give one side of a debatable public question an advantage in expressing its views to the people, the First Amendment is plainly offended. Yet the State contends that its action is necessitated by governmental interests of the highest order. We next consider these asserted interests.

IV

The constitutionality of Section 8's prohibition of the "exposition of ideas" by corporations turns on whether it can survive the exacting scrutiny necessitated by a state-imposed restriction of freedom of speech. Especially where, as here, a prohibition is directed at speech itself, and the speech is intimately related to the process of governing, "the State may prevail only upon showing a subordinating interest which is compelling, and the burden is on the government to show the existence of such an interest." Even then, the State must employ means "closely drawn to avoid unnecessary abridgment. . . ."

The Supreme Judicial Court did not subject Section 8 to "the critical scrutiny demanded under accepted First Amendment and equal protection principles," because of its view that the First Amendment does not apply to appellants' proposed speech. For this reason the court did not even discuss the State's interests in considering appellants' First Amendment argument. The court adverted to the conceivable interests served by Section 8 only in rejecting appellants' equal protection claim. Appellee nevertheless advances two principal justifications for the prohibition of corporate speech. The first is the State's interest in sustaining the active role of the individual citizen in the electoral process and thereby preventing diminution of the citizen's confidence in government. The second is the interest in protecting the rights of shareholders whose views differ from those expressed by management on behalf of the corporation. However weighty these interests may be in the context of partisan candidate elections, they either are not implicated in this case or are not served at all, or in other than a random manner, by the prohibition in Section 8.

A

Preserving the integrity of the electoral process, preventing corruption, and "sustain(ing) the active, alert responsibility of the individual citizen in a democracy for the wise conduct of government" are interests of the highest importance. Preservation of the individual citizen's confidence in government is equally important.

Appellee advances a number of arguments in support of his view that these interests are endangered by corporate participation in discussion of a referendum issue. They hinge upon the assumption that such participation would exert an undue influence on the outcome of a referendum vote, and—in the end—destroy the confidence of the people in the democratic process and the integrity of government. According to appellee, corporations are wealthy and powerful and their views may drown out other points of view. If appellee's arguments were supported by record or legislative findings that corporate advocacy threatened imminently to undermine democratic processes, thereby denigrating rather than serving First Amendment interests, these arguments would merit our consideration. But there has been no showing that the relative voice of corporations has been overwhelming or even significant in influencing referenda in Massachusetts, or that there has been any threat to the confidence of the citizenry in government.

Nor are appellee's arguments inherently persuasive or supported by the precedents of this Court. Referenda are held on issues, not candidates for public office. The risk of corruption perceived in cases involving candidate elections simply is not present in a popular vote on a public issue. To be sure, corporate advertising may influence the outcome of the vote; this would be its purpose. But the fact that advocacy may persuade the electorate is hardly a reason to suppress it: The Constitution "protects expression which is eloquent no less than that which is unconvincing." We noted only recently that "the concept that government may restrict the speech of some elements of our society in order to enhance the relative voice of others is wholly foreign to the First Amendment. . . ." Moreover, the people in our democracy are entrusted with the responsibility for judging and evaluating the relative merits of conflicting arguments. They may consider, in making their judgment, the source and credibility of the advocate. But if there be any danger that the people cannot evaluate the information and arguments advanced by appellants, it is a danger contemplated by the Framers of the First Amendment. In sum, "(a) restriction so destructive of the right of public discussion (as Section 8), without greater or more imminent danger to the public interest than existed in this case, is incompatible with the freedoms secured by the First Amendment."

B

Finally, the State argues that Section 8 protects corporate shareholders, an interest that is both legitimate and traditionally within the province of state law. The statute is said to serve this interest by preventing the use of corporate resources in furtherance of views with which some shareholders may disagree. This purpose is belied, however, by the provisions of the statute, which are both under- and over-inclusive.

The under-inclusiveness of the statute is self-evident. Corporate expenditures with respect to a referendum are prohibited, while corporate activity with respect to the passage or defeat of legislation is permitted, though corporations may engage in lobbying more often than they take positions on ballot questions submitted to the voters. Nor does Section 8 prohibit a corporation from expressing its views, by the expenditure of corporate funds, on any public issue until it becomes the subject of a referendum, though the displeasure of disapproving shareholders is unlikely to be any less.

The fact that a particular kind of ballot question has been singled out for special treatment undermines the likelihood of a genuine state interest in protecting shareholders. It suggests instead that the legislature may have been concerned with silencing corporations on a particular subject. Indeed, appellee has conceded that "the legislative and judicial history of the statute indicates . . . that the second crime was 'tailor made' to prohibit corporate campaign contributions to oppose a graduated income tax amendment." (Brief for Appellee 6.)

Nor is the fact that Section 8 is limited to bands and business corporations without relevance. Excluded from its provisions and criminal sanctions are entities or organized groups in which numbers of persons may hold an interest or membership, and which often have resources comparable to those of large corporations. Minorities in such groups or entities may have interests with respect to institutional speech quite comparable to those of minority shareholders in a corporation. Thus the exclusion of Massachusetts business trusts, real estate investment trusts, labor unions, and other associations undermines the plausibility of the State's purported concern for the persons who happen to be shareholders in the banks and corporations covered by Section 8.

The over-inclusiveness of the statute is demonstrated by the fact that Section 8 would prohibit a corporation from supporting or opposing a referendum proposal even if its shareholders unanimously authorized the contribution or expenditure. Ultimately shareholders may decide, through the procedures of corporate democracy, whether their corporation should engage in debate on public issues. Acting through their power to elect the board of directors or to insist upon protective provisions in the corporation's charter, shareholders normally are presumed competent to protect their own interests. In addition to intra-corporate remedies, minority shareholders generally have access to the judicial remedy of a derivative suit to challenge corporate disbursements alleged to have been made for improper corporate purposes or merely to further the personal interests of management.

Assuming, arguendo, that protection of shareholders is a "compelling" interest under the circumstances of this case, we find "no substantially relevant correlation between the governmental interest asserted and the State's effort" to prohibit appellants from speaking.

V

Because Section 8 prohibits protected speech in a manner unjustified by a compelling state interest, it must be invalidated. The judgment of the Supreme Judicial Court is

Reversed.

Mr. Chief Justice Burger, concurring.

I join the opinion and judgment of the Court but write separately to raise some questions likely to arise in this area in the future.

A disquieting aspect of Massachusetts' position is that it may carry the risk of impinging on the First Amendment rights of those who employ the corporate form—as most do—to carry on the business of mass communications, particularly the large media conglomerates. This is so because of the difficulty, and perhaps impossibility, of distinguishing, either as a matter of fact or constitutional law, media corporations from corporations such as the appellants in this case.

Making traditional use of the corporate form, some media enterprises have amassed vast wealth and power and conduct many activities, some directly related—and some not—to their publishing and broadcasting activities. Today, a corporation might own the dominant newspaper in one or more large metropolitan centers, television and radio stations in those same centers and others, a newspaper chain, news magazines with nationwide circulation, national or world-wide wire news services, and substantial interests in book publishing and distribution enterprises. Corporate ownership may extend, vertically, to pulp mills and pulp timber lands to insure an adequate, continuing supply of newsprint and to trucking and steamship lines for the purpose of transporting the newsprint to the presses. Such activities would be logical economic auxiliaries to a publishing conglomerate. Ownership also may extend beyond to business activities unrelated to the task of publishing newspapers and magazines or broadcasting radio and television programs. Obviously, such far-reaching ownership would not be possible without the state-provided corporate form and its "special rules relating to such matters as limited liability, perpetual life, and the accumulation, distribution, and taxation of assets. . . ."

In terms of "unfair advantage in the political process" and "corporate domination of the electoral process," it could be argued that such media conglomerates as I described pose a much more realistic threat to valid interests than do appellants and similar entities not regularly concerned with shaping popular opinion on public issues. In *Tornillo,* for example, we noted the serious contentions advanced that a result of the growth of modern media empires "has been to place in a few hands the power to inform the American people and shape public opinion."

In terms of Massachusetts' other concern, the interests of minority shareholders, I perceive no basis for saying that the managers and directors of the media conglomerates are more or less sensitive to the views and desires of minority shareholders than are corporate officers generally. Nor can it be said, even if relevant to First Amendment analysis—which it is not—that the former are more virtuous, wise, or restrained in the exercise of corporate power than are the latter. Thus, no factual distinction has been identified as yet that would justify government restraints on the right of appellants to express their views without, at the same time, opening the door to similar restraints on media conglomerates with their vastly greater influence.

Despite these factual similarities between media and nonmedia corporations, those who view the Press Clause as somehow conferring special and extraordinary privileges or status on the "institutional press"—which are not extended to those who wish to express ideas other than by publishing a newspaper—might perceive no danger to institutional media corporations flowing from the position asserted by Massachusetts. Under this narrow reading of the Press Clause, government could perhaps impose on nonmedia corporations restrictions not permissible with respect to "media" enterprises. The Court has not yet squarely resolved whether the Press Clause confers upon the "institutional press" any freedom from government restraint not enjoyed by all others.

I perceive two fundamental difficulties with a narrow reading of the Press Clause. First, although certainty on this point is not possible, the history of the Clause does not suggest that the authors contemplated a "special" or "institutional" privilege. The common 18th Century understanding of freedom of the press is suggested by Andrew Bradford, a colonial American newspaperman. In defining the nature of the liberty, he did not limit it to a particular group:

> But, by the Freedom of the Press, I mean a Liberty, within the Bounds of Law, for any Man to communicate to the Public, his sentiments on the Important Points of Religion and Government; of proposing any Laws, which he apprehends may be for the Good of his Country, and of applying for the Repeal of such, as he Judges pernicious . . . .
> This is the Liberty of the Press, the great Palladium of all our other Liberties, which I hope the good People of this Province, will forever enjoy . . . ."

Indeed most pre-First Amendment commentators "who employed the term 'freedom of speech' with great frequency, used it synonymously with freedom of the press."

Those interpreting the Press Clause as extending protection only to, or creating a special role for, the "institutional press" must either a) assert such an intention on the part of the Framers for which no supporting evidence is available, b) argue that events after 1791 somehow operated to "constitutionalize" this interpretation, or c) candidly acknowledging the absence of historical support suggest that the intent of the Framers is not important today.

To conclude that the Framers did not intend to limit the freedom of the press to one select group is not necessarily to suggest that the Press Clause is redundant. The Speech Clause standing alone may be viewed as a protection of the liberty to express ideas and beliefs, while the Press Clause focuses specifically on the liberty to disseminate expression broadly and "comprehends every sort of publication which affords a vehicle of information and opinion." Yet there is no fundamental distinction between expression and dissemination. The liberty encompassed by the Press Clause, although complementary to and a natural extension of Speech Clause liberty, merited special mention simply because it had been more often the object of official restraints. Soon after the invention of the printing press, English and continental monarchs, fearful of the power implicit in its use and the threat to Establishment thought and order—political and religious—devised restraints, such as licensing, censors, indices of prohibited books, and prosecutions for seditious libel, which generally were unknown in the pre-printing press era. Official restrictions were the official response to the new, disquieting idea that this invention would provide a means for mass communication.

The second fundamental difficulty with interpreting the Press Clause as conferring special status on a limited group is one of definition. The very task of including some entities within the "institutional press'' while excluding others, whether undertaken by legislature, court, or administrative agency, is reminiscent of the abhorred licensing system of Tudor and Stuart England—a system the First Amendment was intended to ban from this country. Further, the officials undertaking that task would be required to distinguish the protected from the unprotected on the basis of such variables as content of expression, frequency or fervor of expression, or ownership of the technological means of dissemination. Yet nothing in this Court's opinions supports such a confining approach to the scope of Press Clause protection. Indeed, the Court has plainly intimated the contrary view:

> Freedom of the press is a "fundamental personal right" which "is not confined to newspapers and periodicals. It necessarily embraces pamphlets and leaflets. . . . The press in its historic connotation comprehends every sort of publication which affords a vehicle of information and opinion.'' . . . The information function asserted by representatives of the organized press . . . is also performed by lecturers, political pollsters, novelists, academic researchers, and dramatists. Almost any author may quite accurately assert that he is contributing to the flow of information to the public. . . .''

The meaning of the Press Clause, as a provision separate and apart from the Speech Clause, is implicated only indirectly by this case. Yet Massachusetts' position poses serious questions. The evolution of traditional newspapers into modern corporate conglomerates in which the daily dissemination of news by print is no longer the major part of the whole enterprise suggests the need for caution in limiting the First Amendment rights of corporations as such. Thus, the tentative probings of this brief inquiry are wholly consistent, I think, with the Court's refusal to sustain Section 8's serious and potentially dangerous restriction on the freedom of political speech.

Because the First Amendment was meant to guarantee freedom to express and communicate ideas, I can see no difference between the right of those who seek to disseminate ideas by way of a newspaper and those who give lectures or speeches and seek to enlarge the audience by publication and wide dissemination. "(T)he purpose of the Constitution was not to erect the press into a privileged institution but to protect all persons in their right to print what they will as well as to utter it. '. . . The liberty of the press is no greater and no less . . .' than the liberty of every citizen of the Republic.''

In short, the First Amendment does not "belong" to any definable category of persons or entities: it belongs to all who exercise its freedoms.

Mr. Justice White, with whom Mr. Justice Brennan and Mr. Justice Marshall join, dissenting.

The Massachusetts statute challenged here forbids the use of corporate funds to publish views about referenda issues having no material effect on the business, property, or assets of the corporation. The legislative judgment that the personal income tax issue, which is the subject of the referendum out of which this case arose, has no such effect was sustained by the Supreme Court of Massachusetts and is not disapproved by this Court today. Hence, as this case comes to us, the issue is whether a State may prevent corporate management from using the corporate treasury to propagate views having no connection with the corporate business. The Court commendably enough squarely faces the issue but unfortunately errs in deciding it. The Court invalidates the Massachusetts statute and holds that the First Amendment guarantees corporate managers the right to use not only their personal funds, but also those of the corporation, to circulate fact and opinion irrelevant to the business placed in their charge and necessarily representing their own personal or collective views about political and social questions. I do not suggest for a moment that the First Amendment requires a State to forbid such use of corporate funds, but I do strongly disagree that the First Amendment forbids state interference with managerial decisions of this kind.

By holding that Massachusetts may not prohibit corporate expenditures or contributions made in connection with referenda involving issues having no material connection with the corporate business, the Court not only invalidates a statute which has been on the books in one form or another for many years, but also casts considerable doubt upon the Constitutionality of legislation passed by some 31 States restricting corporate political activity, as well as upon the Federal Corrupt Practices Act, 2 U.S.C. Section 441(b). The Court's fundamental error is its failure to realize that the state regulatory interests in terms of which the alleged curtailment of First Amendment rights accomplished by the statute must be evaluated are themselves derived from the First Amendment. The question posed by this case, as approached by the Court, is whether the State has struck the best possible balance, i.e., the one which it would have chosen, between competing First Amendment interests. Although in my view the choice made by the State would survive even the most exacting scrutiny, perhaps a rational argument might be made to the contrary. What is inexplicable, is for the Court to substitute its judgment as to the proper balance for that of Massachusetts where the State has passed legislation reasonably designed to further First Amendment interests in the context of the political arena where the expertise of legislators is at its peak and that of judges is at its very lowest. Moreover, the result reached today in critical respects marks a drastic departure from the Court's prior decisions which have protected against governmental infringement the very First Amendment interests which the Court now deems inadequate to justify the Massachusetts statute.

I

There is now little doubt that corporate communications come within the scope of the First Amendment. This, however, is merely the starting point of analysis, because an examination of the First Amendment values corporate expression further and the threat to the functioning of a free society it is capable of posing reveals that it is not fungible with communications emanating from individuals and is subject to restrictions which individual expression is not. Indeed, what some have considered to be the principal function of the First Amendment, the use of communication as a means of self-expression, self-realization and self-fulfillment, is not at all furthered by corporate speech. It is clear that the communications of profit making corporations are not "an integral part of the development of ideas, of mental exploration, and of the affirmation of self." They do not represent a manifestation of individual freedom or choice. Undoubtedly, as this Court has recognized, there are some corporations formed for the express purpose of advancing certain ideological causes shared by all their members, or, as in the case of the press, of disseminating information and ideas. Under such circumstances, association in a corporate form may be viewed as merely a means of achieving effective self-expression. But this is hardly the case generally with corporations operated for the purpose of making profits. Shareholders in such entities do not share a common set of political or social views, and they certainly have not invested their money for the purpose of advancing political or social causes or in an enterprise engaged in the business of disseminating news and opinion. In fact, the government has a strong interest in assuring that investment decisions are not predicated upon agreement or disagreement with the activities of corporations in the political arena.

Of course, it may be assumed that corporate investors are united by a desire to make money, for the value of their investment to increase. Since even communications which have no purpose other than that of enriching the communicator have some First Amendment protection, activities such as advertising and other communications integrally related to the operation of the corporation's business may be viewed as a means of furthering the desires of individual shareholders. This unanimity of purpose breaks down, however, when corporations make expenditures or undertake activities designed to influence the opinion or votes of the general public on political and social issues that have no material connection with or effect upon their business, property, or assets. Although it is arguable that corporations make such expenditures because their managers believe that it is in the corporations' economic interest to do so, there is no basis whatsoever for concluding that these views are expressive of the heterogeneous beliefs of their shareholders whose convictions on many political issues are undoubtedly shaped by considerations other than a desire to endorse any electoral or ideological cause which would tend to increase the value of a particular corporate investment. This is particularly true where, as in this case, whatever the belief of the corporate managers may be, they have not been able to demonstrate that the issue involved has any material connection with the corporate business. Thus when a profit making corporation contributes to a political candidate this does not further the self-expression or self-fulfillment of its shareholders in the way that expenditures from them as individuals would.

The self-expression of the communicator is not the only value encompassed by the First Amendment. One of its functions, often referred to as the right to hear or receive information, is to protect the interchange of ideas. Any communication of ideas, and consequently any expenditure of funds which makes the communication of ideas possible, it can be argued, furthers the purposes of the First Amendment. This proposition does not establish, however, that the right of the general public to receive communications financed by means of corporate expenditures is of the same dimension as that to hear other forms of expression. In the first place, as discussed supra, corporate expenditures designed to further political causes lack the connection with individual self-expression which is one of the principal justifications for the Constitutional protection of speech provided by the First Amendment. Ideas which are not a product of individual choice are entitled to less First Amendment protection. Secondly, the restriction of corporate speech concerned with political matters impinges much less severely upon the availability of ideas to the general public than do restrictions upon individual speech. Even the complete curtailment of corporate communications concerning political or ideological questions not integral to day-to-day business functions would leave individuals, including corporate shareholders, employees, and customers, free to communicate their thoughts. Moreover, it is unlikely that any significant communication would be lost by such a prohibition. These individuals would remain perfectly free to communicate any ideas which could be conveyed by means of the corporate form. Indeed, such individuals could even form associations for the very purpose of promoting political or ideological causes.

I recognize that there may be certain communications undertaken by corporations which could not be restricted without impinging seriously upon the right to receive information. In the absence of advertising and similar promotional activities for example, the ability of consumers to obtain information relating to products manufactured by corporations would be significantly impeded. There is also a need for employees, customers, and shareholders of corporations to be able to receive communications about matters relating to the functioning of corporations. Such communications are clearly desired by all investors and may well be viewed as an associational form of self-expression. Moreover, it is unlikely that such information would be disseminated by sources other than corporations. It is for such reasons that the Court has extended a certain degree of First Amendment protection to activities of this kind. None of these considerations, however, are implicated by a prohibition upon corporate expenditures relating to referenda concerning questions of general public concern having no connection with corporate business affairs.

It bears emphasis here that the Massachusetts statute forbids the expenditure of corporate funds in connection with referenda but in no way forbids the board of directors of a corporation from formulating and making public what it represents as the views of the corporation even though the subject addressed has no material effect whatsoever on the business of the corporation. These views could be publicized at the individual expense of the officers, directors, stockholder, or anyone else interested in circulating the corporate view on matters irrelevant to its business.

The governmental interest in regulating corporate political communications, especially those relating to electoral matters, also raises considerations which differ significantly from those governing the regulation of individual speech. Corporations are artificial entities created by law for the purpose of furthering certain economic goals. In order to facilitate the achievement of such ends, special rules relating to such matters as limited liability, perpetual life, and the accumulation, distribution, and taxation of assets are normally applied to them. States have provided corporations with such attributes in order to increase their economic viability and thus strengthen the economy generally. It has long been recognized, however, that the special status of corporations has placed them in a position to control vast amounts of economic power which may, if not regulated, dominate not only the economy but also the very heart of our democracy, the electoral process. Although *Buckley* v. *Valeo* (1976) provides support for the position that the desire to equalize the financial resources available to candidates does not justify the limitation upon the expression of support which a restriction upon individual contributions entails, the interest of Massachusetts and the many other States which have restricted corporate political activity is quite different. It is not one of equalizing the resources of opposing candidates or opposing positions, but rather of preventing institutions which have been permitted to amass wealth as a result of special advantages extended by the State for certain economic purposes from using that wealth to acquire an unfair advantage in the political process, especially where, as here, the issue involved has no material connection with the business of the corporation. The State need not permit its own creation to consume it. Massachusetts could permissibly conclude that not to impose limits upon the political activities of corporations would have placed it in a position of departing from neutrality and indirectly assisting the propagation of corporate views because of the advantages its laws give to the corporate acquisition of funds to finance such activities. Such expenditures may be viewed as seriously threatening the role of the First Amendment as a guarantor of a free marketplace of ideas. Ordinarily, the expenditure of funds to promote political causes may be assumed to bear some relation to the fervency with which they are held. Corporate political expression, however, it not only divorced from the convictions of individual corporate shareholders, but also, because of the case with which corporations are permitted to accumulate capital, bears no relation to the conviction with which the ideas expressed are held by the communicator.

The Court's opinion appears to recognize at least the possibility that fear of corporate domination of the electoral process would justify restrictions upon corporate expenditures and contributions in connection with referenda, but brushes this interest aside by asserting that "there has been no showing that the relative voice of corporations has been overwhelming or even significant in influencing referenda in Massachusetts" (ante, at 22–23), and by suggesting that the statute in issue represents an attempt to give an unfair advantage to those who hold views in opposition to positions which would otherwise be financed by corporations (Ante, at 18–19). It fails even to allude to the fact, however, that Massachusetts' most recent experience with unrestrained corporate expenditures in connection with ballot questions establishes precisely the contrary. In 1972, a proposed amendment to the Massachusetts Constitution which would have authorized the imposition of a graduated income tax on both individuals and corporations was put to the voters. The Committee for Jobs and Government

Economy, an organized political committee, raised and expended approximately $120,000 to oppose the proposed amendment, the bulk of it raised through large corporate contributions. Three of the present appellant corporations each contributed $3,000 to this committee. In contrast, the Coalition for Tax Reform, Inc., the only political committee organized to support the 1972 amendment, was able to raise and expend only approximately $7,000. Perhaps these figures reflect the Court's view of the appropriate role which corporations should play in the Massachusetts electoral process, but it nowhere explains why it is entitled to substitute its judgment for that of Massachusetts and other States, as well as the United States, which have acted to correct or prevent similar domination of the electoral process by corporate wealth.

This Nation has for many years recognized the need for measures designed to prevent corporate domination of the political process. The Corrupt Practices Act, first enacted in 1907, has consistently barred corporate contributions in connection with federal elections. This Court has repeatedly recognized that one of the principal purposes of this prohibition is "to avoid the deleterious influences on federal elections resulting from the use of money by those who exercise control over large aggregations of capital." Although this Court has never adjudicated the constitutionality of the Act, there is no suggestion in its cases construing it, cited supra, that this purpose is in any sense illegitimate or deserving of other than the utmost respect; indeed, the thrust of its opinions, until today, has been to the contrary.

II

There is an additional overriding interest related to the prevention of corporate domination which is substantially advanced by Massachusetts' restrictions upon corporate contributions: assuring that shareholders are not compelled to support and financially further beliefs with which they disagree where, as is the case here, the issue involved does not materially affect the business, property, or other affairs of the corporation. The State has not interfered with the prerogatives of corporate management to communicate about matters that have material impact on the business affairs entrusted to them, however much individual stockholders may disagree on economic or ideological grounds. Nor has the State forbidden management from formulating and circulating its views at its own expense or at the expense of others, even where the subject at issue is irrelevant to corporate business affairs. But Massachusetts has chosen to forbid corporate management from spending corporate funds in referenda elections absent some demonstrable effect of the issue on the economic life of the company. In short, corporate management may not use corporate monies to promote what does not further corporate affairs but in the last analysis are the purely personal views of the management, individually or as a group.

This is not only a policy which a State may adopt consistent with the First Amendment but also one which protects the very freedoms that this Court has held to be guaranteed by the First Amendment. In *Board of Education* v. *Barnette* (1943), the Court struck down a West Virginia statute which compelled children enrolled in public school to salute the flag and pledge allegiance to it on the ground that the First Amendment prohibits public authorities from requiring an individual to express support for or agreement with a cause with which he disagrees or concerning which he prefers to remain silent. Subsequent cases have applied this principle to prohibit organizations to which individuals are compelled to belong as a condition of employment from using compulsory dues to support candidates, political parties, or other forms of political expression with which members disagree or do not wish to support. In *Machinists* v. *Street* (1961), the Court was presented with allegations that a union shop authorized by the Railway Labor Act, had used the union treasury to which all employees were compelled to contribute "to finance the campaigns of candidates for federal and state offices whom (the petitioners) opposed, and to promote the propagation of political and economic doctrines, concepts, and ideologies with which (they) disagreed." The Court recognized that compelling contributions for such purposes presented constitutional "questions of the utmost gravity" and consequently construed the Act to prohibit the use of compulsory union dues for political purposes. Last term, in *Abood* v. *Detroit Board of Education* (1977), we confronted these Constitutional questions and held that, a State may not, even indirectly, require an individual to contribute to the support of an ideological cause he may oppose as a condition of employment. At issue were political expenditures made by a public employees union. Michigan law provided that unions and local government employers might agree to an agency shop arrangement pursuant to which every employee—even those not union members—must pay to the union, as a condition of employment, union dues or a service fee equivalent in amount to union dues. The legislation itself was not coercive; it did not command that local governments employ only those workers who were willing to pay union dues but left it to a bargaining representative democratically elected by a majority of the employees to enter or not enter into such a contractual arrangement through collective bargaining. In addition, of course, no one was compelled to work at a job covered by an agency shop arrangement. Nevertheless, the Court ruled that under such circumstances the use of funds contributed by dissenting employees for political purposes impermissibly infringed their First Amendment right to adhere to their own beliefs and to refuse to defer to or support the beliefs of others.

Presumably, unlike the situations presented by *Street* and *Abood,* the use of funds invested by shareholders with opposing views by Massachusetts corporations in connection with referenda or elections would not constitute state action and, consequently, not violate the First Amendment. Until now, however, the States have always been free to adopt measures designed to further rights protected by the Constitution even when not compelled to do so. It would hardly be plausibly contended that just because Massachusetts' regulation of corporations is less extensive than Michigan's regulation of labor-management relations, Massachusetts may not constitutionally prohibit the very evil which Michigan may not constitutionally permit. Yet this is precisely what the Court today holds. Although the Court places great stress upon the alleged infringement of the right to receive information produced by Massachusetts' ban on corporate expenditures which, for the reasons stated supra, I believe to be misconceived, it fails to explain why such an interest was not sufficient to compel a different weighing of First Amendment interests and, consequently, a different result in *Abood*. After all, even contributions for political causes coerced by labor unions would, under the Court's analysis, increase unions' ability to disseminate their views and, consequently, increase the amount of information available to the general public.

The Court assumes that the interest in preventing the use of corporate resources in furtherance of views which are irrelevant to the corporate business and with which some shareholders may disagree is a compelling one, but concludes that the Massachusetts statute is nevertheless invalid because the State has failed to adopt the means best suited, in its opinion, for achieving this end. It proposes that the aggrieved shareholder assert his interest in preventing the expenditure of funds for nonbusiness causes he finds unconscionable through the channels provided by "corporate democracy" and purports to be mystified as to "why the dissenting shareholder's wishes are entitled to such greater solicitude in this context than in many others where equally important corporate decisions are made by management or by a predetermined percentage of the shareholder." It should be obvious that the alternative means upon the adequacy of which the majority is willing to predicate a constitutional adjudication is no more able to satisfy the State's interest than a ruling in *Street* and *Abood* leaving aggrieved employees to the remedies provided by union democracy would have satisfied the demands of the First Amendment. The interest which the State wishes to protect here is identical to that which the Court has previously held to be protected by the First Amendment: the right to adhere to one's own beliefs and to refuse to support the dissemination of the personal and political views of others, regardless of how large a majority they may compose. In most contexts, of course, the views of the dissenting shareholder have little, if any First Amendment significance. By purchasing interests in corporations shareholders accept the fact that corporations are going to make decisions concerning matters such as advertising integrally related to their business operations according to the procedures set forth in their charters and bylaws. Otherwise, corporations could not function. First Amendment concerns of stockholders are directly implicated, however, when a corporation chooses to use its privileged status to finance ideological crusades which are unconnected with the corporate business or property and which some shareholders might not wish to support. Once again, we are provided no explanation whatsoever by the Court as to why the State's interest is of less constitutional weight than that of corporations to participate financially in the electoral process and as to why the balance between two First Amendment interests should be struck by this Court. Moreover, the Court offers no reason whatsoever for Constitutionally imposing its choice of means to achieve a legitimate goal and invalidating those chosen by the State.

Abood cannot be distinguished, as the present Court attempts to do, on the ground that the Court there did not Constitutionally prohibit expenditures by unions for the election of political candidates or for ideological causes so long as they are financed from assessments paid by employees who are not coerced into doing so against their will. In the first place, the Court did not purport to hold that all political or ideological expenditures not Constitutionally prohibited were Constitutionally protected. A State might well conclude that the most and perhaps, in its view, the only effective way of preventing unions or corporations from using funds contributed by differing members of shareholders to support political causes having no connection with the business of the organization is to absolutely ban such expenditures. Secondly, unlike the remedies available to the Court in *Street* and *Abood* which required unions to refund the exacted funds in the proportion that union political expenditures with which a member disagreed bore to total union expenditures, no such alternative is readily available which would enable a corporate shareholder to maintain his investment in a corporation without supporting its electoral or political ventures other than prohibiting corporations from participating in such activities. There is no apparent way of segregating one shareholder's ownership interest in a corporation from another's. It is no answer to respond, as the Court does, that the dissenting "shareholder is free to withdraw his investment at any time and for any reason." The employees in *Street* and *Abood* were also free to seek other jobs where they would not be compelled to finance causes with which they disagreed, but we held in *Abood* that First Amendment rights could not be so burdened. Clearly the State has a strong interest in assuring that its citizens are not forced to choose between supporting the propagation of views with which they disagree and passing up investment opportunities.

Finally, even if corporations developed an effective mechanism for rebating to shareholders that portion of their investment used to finance political activities with which they disagreed, a State may still choose to restrict corporate political activity irrelevant to business functions on the grounds that many investors would be deterred from investing in corporations because of a wish not to associate with corporations propagating certain views. The State has an interest not only in enabling individuals to exercise freedom of conscience without penalty, but also in eliminating the danger that investment decisions will be significantly influenced by the ideological views of corporations. While the latter concern may not be of the same Constitutional magnitude as the former, it is far from trivial. Corporations, as previously noted, are created by the State as a means of furthering the public welfare. One of their functions is to determine, by their success in obtaining funds, the uses to which society's resources are to be put. A State may legitimately conclude that corporations would not serve as economically efficient vehicles for such decisions if the investment preferences of the public were significantly affected by their ideological or political activities. It has long been recognized that such pursuits are not the proper business of corporations. The common law was generally interpreted as prohibiting corporate political participation. Indeed, the Securities and Exchange Commission's rules permit corporations to refuse to submit for shareholder vote any proposal which concerns a general economic, political, racial, religious, or social cause that is not significantly related to the business of the corporation or is not within its control.

The necessity of prohibiting corporate political expenditures in order to prevent the use of corporate funds for purposes with which shareholders may disagree is not a unique perception of Massachusetts. This Court has repeatedly recognized that one of the purposes of the Corrupt Practices Act was to prevent the use of corporate or union funds for political purposes without the consent of the shareholders or union members and to protect minority interests from domination by corporate or union leadership. Although the Court has never, as noted supra, adjudicated the Constitutionality of the Act, it has consistently treated this objective with deference. Indeed, in *United States* v. *CIO* (1948), the Court construed a previous version of the Corrupt Practices Act so as to conform its prohibitions to those activities to which the Court believed union members or shareholders might object. After noting that if the statute "were construed to prohibit the publication, by corporations and unions in the regular course of conducting their affairs, of periodicals advising their members, stockholders, or customers of danger or advantage to their interests from the adoption of measures, or the election to office of men espousing such measures, the gravest doubt would arise in our minds as to its Constitutionality," the Court held that the statute did not prohibit such in-house publications. It was persuaded that the purposes of the Act would not be impeded by such an interpretation, because it "is unduly stretching language to say that the members of stockholders are unwilling participants in such normal organizational activities, including the advocacy thereby of governmental policies affecting their interests, and the support thereby of candidates thought to be favorable to their interests."

The Court today purports not to foreclose the possibility that the Corrupt Practices Act and state statutes which prohibit corporate expenditures only in the context of elections to public office may survive Constitutional scrutiny because of the interest in preventing the corruption of elected representatives through the creation of political debts. It does not choose to explain or even suggest, however, why the state interests which it so cursorily dismisses are less worthy than the interest in preventing corruption or the appearance of it. More importantly, the analytical framework employed by the Court clearly raises great doubt about the Corrupt Practices Act. The question in the present case, as viewed by the Court, "is whether the corporate identity of the speaker deprives this proposed speech of what otherwise would be its clear entitlement to protection," which it answers in the negative. But the Court has previously held in *Buckley* v. *Valeo,* that the interest in preventing corruption is insufficient to justify restrictions upon individual expenditures relative to candidates for political office. If the corporate identity of the speaker makes no difference, all the Court has done is to reserve the formal interment of the Corrupt Practices Act and similar state statutes for another day. As I understand the view that has now become part of First Amendment jurisprudence, the use of corporate funds, even for causes irrelevant to the corporation's business, may be no more limited than that of individual funds. Hence, corporate contributions to and expenditures on behalf of political candidates may be no more limited than those of individuals. Individual contributions under federal law are limited but not entirely forbidden, and under *Buckley* v. *Valeo*, expenditures may not Constitutionally be limited at all. Most state corrupt practices acts, like the federal Act, forbid any contributions or expenditures by corporations to or for a political candidate.

In my view, the interests in protecting a system of freedom of expression are sufficient to justify any incremental curtailment in the volume of expression which the Massachusetts statute might produce. I would hold that apart from corporate activities, such as those discussed in Part I, and exempted from regulation in CIO, which are integrally related to corporate business operations, a State may prohibit corporate expenditures for political or ideological purposes. There can be no doubt that corporate expenditures in connection with referenda immaterial to corporate business affairs fall clearly into the category of corporate activities essence of our democracy. It is an arena in which the public interest in preventing corporate domination and the coerced support by shareholders of causes with which they disagree is at its strongest and any claim that corporate expenditures are integral to the economic functioning of the corporation is at its weakest.

I would affirm the judgment of the Supreme Judicial Court for the Commonwealth of Massachusetts.

Mr. Justice Rehnquist, dissenting.

This Court decided at an early date, with neither argument nor discussion, that a business corporation is a "person" entitled to the protection of the Equal Protection Clause of the Fourteenth Amendment. Likewise, it soon became accepted that the property of a corporation was protected under the Due Process Clause of that same amendment. Nevertheless, we concluded soon thereafter that the liberty protected by that amendment "is the liberty of natural, not artificial persons." Before today, our only considered and explicit departures from that holding have been that a corporation engaged in the business of publishing or broadcasting enjoys the same liberty of the press as is enjoyed by natural persons, and that a nonprofit membership corporation organized for the purpose of "achieving . . . equality of treatment by all government, federal, state, and local, for the members of the Negro community" enjoys certain liberties of political expression.

The question presented today, whether business corporations have a Constitutionally protected liberty to engage in political activities, has never been squarely addressed by any previous decision of this Court. However, the General Court of the Commonwealth of Massachusetts, the Congress of the United States, and the legislatures of 30 other States of this Republic have considered the matter, and have concluded that restrictions upon the political activity of business corporations are both politically desirable and Constitutionally permissible. The judgment of such a broad consensus of governmental bodies expressed over a period of many decades is entitled to considerable deference from this Court. I think it quite probable that their judgment may properly be reconciled with our controlling precedents, but I am certain that under my views of the limited application of the First Amendment to the States, which I share with the two immediately preceding occupants of my seat on the Court, but not with my present colleagues, the judgment of the Supreme Judicial Court of Massachusetts should be affirmed.

Early in our history, Mr. Chief Justice Marshall described the status of a corporation in the eyes of federal law:

> A corporation is an artificial being, invisible, intangible, and existing only in contemplation of law. Being the mere creature of law, it possesses only those properties which the charter of creation confers upon it, either expressly, or as incidental to its very existence. These are such as

are supposed best calculated to effect the object for which it was created. (*Dartmouth College* v. *Woodward* (1819).)

The appellants herein either were created by the Commonwealth or were admitted into the Commonwealth only for the limited purposes described in their charters and regulated by state law. Since it cannot be disputed that the mere creation of a corporation does not invest it with all the liberties enjoyed by natural persons (corporations do not enjoy the privilege against self-incrimination), our inquiry must seek to determine which Constitutional protections are "incidental to its very existence."

There can be little doubt that when a State creates a corporation with the power to acquire and utilize property, it necessarily and implicitly guarantees that the corporation will not be deprived of that property absent due process of law. Likewise, when a State charters a corporation for the purpose of publishing a newspaper, it necessarily assumes that the corporation is entitled to the liberty of the press essential to the conduct of its business. *Grosjean* so held, and our subsequent cases have so assumed. Until recently, it was not thought that any persons, natural or artificial, had any protected right to engage in commercial speech. Although the Court has never explicitly recognized a corporations' right of commercial speech, such a right might be considered necessarily incidental to the business of a commercial corporation.

It cannot be so readily concluded that the right of political expression is equally necessary to carry out the functions of a corporation organized for commercial purposes. A State grants to a business corporation the blessings of potentially perpetual life and limited liability to enhance its efficiency as an economic entity. It might reasonably be concluded that those properties, so beneficial in the economic sphere, pose special dangers in the political sphere. Furthermore, it might be argued that liberties of political expression are not at all necessary to effectuate the purposes for which States permit commercial corporations to exist. So long as the Judicial Branches of the State and Federal Governments remain open to protect the corporation's interest in its property, it has no need, though it may have the desire, to petition the political branches for similar protection. Indeed, the States might reasonably fear that the corporation would use its economic power to obtain further benefits beyond those already bestowed. I would think that any particular form of organization upon which the State confers special privileges or immunities different from those of natural persons would be subject to like regulation, whether the organization is a labor union, a partnership, a trade association, or a corporation.

One need not adopt such a restrictive view of the political liberties of business corporations to affirm the judgment of the Supreme Judicial Court in this case. That court reasoned that this Court's decisions entitling the property of a corporation to Constitutional protection should be construed as recognizing the liberty of a corporation to express itself on political matters concerning that property. Thus, the Court construed the statute in question not to forbid political expression by a corporation "when a general political issue materially affects a corporation's business, property, or assets."

I can see no basis for concluding that the liberty of a corporation to engage in political activity with regard to matters having no material effect on its business is necessarily incidental to the purposes for which the Commonwealth permitted these corporations to be organized or admitted within its boundaries. Nor can I disagree with the Supreme Judicial Court's factual finding that no such effect has been shown by these appellants. Because the statute as construed provides at least as much protection as the Fourteenth Amendment requires, I believe it is Constitutionally valid.

It is true, as the Court points out, decisions of this Court have emphasized the interest of the public in receiving the information offered by the speaker seeking protection. The free flow of information is in no way diminished by the Commonwealth's decision to permit the operation of business corporations with limited rights of political expression. All natural persons, who owe their existence to a higher sovereign than the Commonwealth, remain as free as before to engage in political activity.

I would affirm the judgment of the Supreme Judicial Court.

NOTE

On February 6, 1978 William F. Buckley, Jr. completed an article entitled "The Court Has Ruled: Long Live Chaos." It contains a few observations concerning the Supreme Court's complicated decision entitled *First National Bank of Boston* v. *Bellotti*. Apparently Mr. Buckley was informed of the Court's decision four months before it was announced. According to Buckley:

> It is really a can of worms. . . . Much of the Court's meandering had really to do with the preferences of individual members of the Court facing questions faced by Congress, notably: What should we do about the mess we're in?
>
> They say it is a Rich Man's Bill. Well, in a way it is, in a way it isn't. . . . The current decision of the Court says that anyone can devote as much money as he wants to furthering his own political candidacy. . . .
>
> (T)he very rich people in America who spend a lot of money on their candidacies tend to be on the left side of their parties. I recall with special amusement the race for governor of New York in 1958. The candidates were leading members of three of the wealthiest families in New York. Corliss Lamont was running as a left-socialist. Averell Harriman, the incumbent, as a left-Democrat. And Nelson Rockefeller as a left-Republican. (*National Review,* vol. XXVIII (Mar. 5, 1976), pp. 230–231.)

FCC v. *NATIONAL CITIZENS COMMITTEE FOR BROADCASTING*

CHANNEL TWO TELEVISION COMPANY v. *NATIONAL CITIZENS COMMITTEE FOR BROADCASTING*

NATIONAL ASSOCIATION OF BROADCASTERS v. *FCC*

AMERICAN NEWSPAPER PUBLISHERS ASSOCIATION v. *NATIONAL CITIZENS COMMITTEE FOR BROADCASTING*

ILLINOIS BROADCASTING COMPANY, INC. v. *NATIONAL CITIZENS COMMITTEE FOR BROADCASTING*

POST COMPANY v. *NATIONAL CITIZENS COMMITTEE FOR BROADCASTING*

98 S.Ct. 2096 (1978)

Mr. Justice Marshall delivered the opinion of the Court.

At issue in these cases are Federal Communications Commission regulations governing the permissibility of common ownership of a radio or television broadcast station and a daily newspaper located in the same community. Second Report and Order (is) hereinafter cited as Order, as amended upon reconsideration. The regulations, adopted after a lengthy rulemaking proceeding, prospectively bar formation or transfer of co-located newspaper-broadcast combinations. Existing combinations are generally permitted to continue in operation. However, in communities in which there is common ownership of the only daily newspaper and the only broadcast station, or (where there is more than one broadcast station) of the only daily newspaper and the only television station, divestiture of either the newspaper or the broadcast station is required within five years, unless grounds for waiver are demonstrated.

The questions for decision are whether these regulations either exceed the Commission's authority under the Communications Act of 1934, or violate the First or Fifth Amendment rights of newspaper owners; and whether the lines drawn by the Commission between new and existing newspaper-broadcast combinations, and between existing combinations subject to divestiture and those allowed to continue in operation, are arbitrary or capricious within the meaning of Section 10(e) of the Administrative Procedure Act. 5 U.S.C. Section 706(2)(A). For the reasons set forth below, we sustain the regulations in their entirety.

I

A

Under the regulatory scheme established by the Radio Act of 1927, and continued in the Communications Act of 1934, no television or radio broadcast station may operate without a license granted by the Federal Communications Commission. Licensees who wish to continue broadcasting must apply for renewal of their licenses every three years, and the Commission may grant an initial license or a renewal only if it finds that the public interest, convenience, and necessity will be served thereby.

In setting its licensing policies, the Commission has long acted on the theory that diversification of mass media ownership serves the public interest by promoting diversity of program and service viewpoints, as well as by preventing undue concentration of economic power. This preception of the public interest has been implemented over the years by a series of regulations imposing increasingly stringent restrictions of multiple ownership of broadcast stations. In the early 1940s, the Commission promulgated rules prohibiting ownership or control of more than one station in the same broadcast service (AM radio, FM radio, or television) in the same community. In 1953, limitations were placed on the total number of stations in each service a person or entity may own or control. And in 1970, the Commission adopted regulations prohibiting, on a prospective basis, common ownership of a VHF television station and any radio station serving the same market.

More generally, "(d)iversification of control of the media of mass communications" has been viewed by the Commission as "a factor of primary significance" in determining who, among competing applicants in a comparative proceeding, should receive the initial license for a particular broadcast facility. Thus, prior to adoption of the regulations at issue here, the fact that an applicant for an initial incense published a newspaper in the community to be served by the broadcast station was taken into account on a case-by-case basis, and resulted in some instances in awards of licenses to competing applicants.

Diversification of ownership has not been the sole consideration thought relevant to the public interest, however. The Commission's other, and sometimes conflicting, goal has been to ensure "the best practicable service to the public." To achieve this goal, the Commission has weighed factors such as the anticipated contribution of the owner to station operations, the proposed program service, and the past broadcast record of the applicant—in addition to diversification of ownership—in making initial comparative licensing decisions. Moreover, the Commission has given considerable weight to a policy of avoiding undue disruption of existing service. As a result, newspaper owners in many instances have been able to acquire broadcast licenses for stations serving the same communities as their newspapers, and the Commission has repeatedly renewed such licenses on findings that continuation of the service offered by the common owner would serve the public interest.

B

Against this background, the Commission began the instant rulemaking proceeding in 1970 to consider the need for a more restrictive policy toward newspaper ownership of radio and television broadcast stations. Citing studies showing the dominant role of television stations and daily newspapers as sources of local news and other information, the notice of rulemaking proposed adoption of regulations that would eliminate all newspaper-broadcast combinations serving the same market, by prospectively banning formation or transfer of such combinations and requiring dissolution of all existing combinations within five years. The Commission suggested that the proposed regulations would serve "the purpose of promoting competition among the mass media involved, and maximizing diversification of service sources and viewpoints." At the same time, however, the Commission expressed "substantial concern" about the disruption of service that might result from divestiture of existing combinations. Comments were invited on all aspects of the proposed rules.

The notice of rulemaking generated a consideration response. The Commission concluded, first, that it had statutory authority to issue the regulations under the Communications Act, and that the regulations were valid under the First and Fifth Amendments to the Constitution. It observed that "(t)he term public interest encompasses many factors including 'the widest possible dissemination of information from diverse and antagonistic sources,' " and that "ownership carries with it the power to select, to edit, and to choose the methods, manner and emphasis of presentation." The Order further explained that the prospective ban on creation of co-located newspaper-broadcast combinations was grounded primarily in First Amendment concerns, while the divestiture regulations were based on both First Amendment and antitrust policies. In addition, the Commission rejected the suggestion that it lacked the power to order divestiture, reasoning that the statutory requirement of license renewal every three years necessarily implied authority to order divestiture over a five-year period.

After reviewing the comments and studies submitted by the various parties during the course of the proceeding, the Commission then turned to an explanation of the regulations and the justifications for their adoption. The prospective rules, barring formation of new broadcast-newspaper combinations in the same market, as well as transfers of existing combinations to new owners, were adopted without change from the proposal set forth in the notice of rulemaking. While recognizing the pioneering contributions of newspaper owners to the broadcast industry, the Commission concluded that changed circumstances made it possible, and necessary, for all new licensing of broadcast stations to "be expected to add to local diversity." In reaching this conclusion, the Commission did not find that existing co-located newspaper-broadcast combinations had not served the public interest, or that such combinations necessarily "speak ( ) with one voice" or are harmful to competition. In the Commission's view, the conflicting studies submitted by the parties concerning the effects of newspaper ownership on competition and station performance were inconclusive, and no pattern of specific abuses by existing cross-owners was demonstrated. The prospective rules were justified, instead, by reference to the Commission's policy of promoting diversification of ownership: increases in diversification of ownership would possibly result in enhanced diversity of viewpoints and, given the absence of persuasive countervailing considerations, "even a small gain in diversity" was "worth pursuing."

With respect to the proposed across-the-board divestiture requirement, however, the Commission concluded that "a mere hoped for gain in diversity" was not a sufficient justification. Characterizing the divestiture issues as "the most difficult" presented in the proceeding, the Order explained that the proposed rules, while correctly recognizing the central importance of diversity considerations, "may have given too little weight to the consequences which could be expected to attend a focus on the abstract goal alone." Forced dissolution would promote diversity, but it would also cause "disruption for the industry and hardship for individual owners," "resulting in losses or diminution of service to the public."

The Commission concluded that in light of these countervailing considerations divestiture was warranted only in "the most egregious cases," which it identified as those in which a newspaper-broadcast combination has an "effective monopoly" in the local "marketplace of ideas as well as economically." The Commission recognized that any standards for defining which combinations fell within that category would necessarily be arbitrary to some degree, but "(a) choice had to be made." It thus decided to require divestiture only where there was common ownership of the sole daily newspaper published in a community and either 1) the sole broadcast station providing that entire community with a clear signal, or 2) the sole television station encompassing the entire community with a clear signal.

The Order identified eight television-newspaper and 10 radio-newspaper combinations meeting the divestiture criteria. Waivers of the divestiture requirement were granted *sua sponte* to one television and one radio combination, leaving a total of 16 stations subject to divestiture. The Commission explained that waiver requests would be entertained in the latter cases, but, absent waiver, either the newspaper or the broadcast station would have to be divested by January 1, 1980.

On petitions for reconsideration, the Commission reaffirmed the rules in all material respects.

C

Various parties—including the National Citizens Committee for Broadcasting (NCCB), the National Association of Broadcasters (NAB), the American Newspaper Publishers Association (ANPA), and several broadcast licensees subject to the divestiture requirement—petitioned for review of the regulations in the United States Court of Appeals for the District of Columbia Circuit. Numerous other parties intervened, and the United States—represented by the Justice Department—was made a respondent. (T)he broadcast licensees subject to divestiture argued that the regulations went too far in restricting cross-ownership of newspapers and broadcast stations; NCCB and the Justice Department contended that the regulations did not go far enough and that the Commission inadequately justified its decision not to order divestiture on a more widespread basis.

Agreeing substantially with NCCB and the Justice Department, the Court of Appeals affirmed the prospective ban on new licensing of co-located newspaper-broadcast combinations, but vacated the limited divestiture rules, and ordered the Commission to adopt regulations requiring dissolution of all existing combinations that did not qualify for a waiver under the procedure outlined in the Order. The court held, first, that the prospective ban was a reasonable means of furthering "the highly valued goal of diversity" in the mass media, and was therefore not without a rational basis. The court concluded further that, since the Commission "explained why it considers diversity to be a factor of exceptional importance," and since the Commission's goal of promotion diversification of mass media ownership was strongly supported by First Amendment and antitrust policies, it was not arbitrary for the prospective rules to be "based on (the diversity) factor to the exclusion of others customarily relied on by the Commission."

The court also held that the prospective rules did not exceed the Commission's authority under the Communications Act. The court reasoned that the public interest standard of the Act permitted, and indeed required, the Commission to consider diversification of mass media ownership in making its licensing decisions, and that the Commission's general rulemaking authority under 47 U.S.C. allowed the Commission to adopt reasonable license qualifications implementing the public interest standard. The court concluded, moreover, that since the prospective ban was designed to "increase(e) the number of media voices in the community," and not to restrict or control the content of free speech, the ban would not violate the First Amendment rights of newspaper owners.

After affirming the prospective rules, the Court of Appeals invalidated the limited divestiture requirement as arbitrary and capricious within the meaning of Section 10(e) of the Administrative Procedure Act, 5 U.S.C. Section 706 (2)(A). The court's primary holding was that the Commission lacked a rational basis for "grandfathering" most existing combinations while banning all new combinations. The court reasoned that the Commission's own diversification policy, as reinforced by First Amendment policies and the Commission's statutory obligation to "encourage the larger and more effective use of radio in the public interest," 47 U.S.C. Section 303(g), required the Commission to adopt a "presumption" that stations owned by co-located newspapers "do not serve the public interest." The court observed that, in the absence of countervailing policies, this "presumption" would have dictated adoption of an across-the-board divestiture requirement, subject only to waiver "in those cases where the evidence early discloses that cross-ownership is in the public interest." The countervailing policies relied on by the Commission in its decision were, in the court's view, "lesser policies" which had not been given as much weight in the past as its diversification policy. And "the record (did) not disclose the extent to which divestiture would actually threaten these (other policies)." The court concluded, therefore, that it was irrational for the Commission not to give controlling weight to its diversification policy and thus to extend the divestiture requirement to all existing combinations.

The Court of Appeals held further that, even assuming a difference in treatment between new and existing combinations was justifiable, the Commission lacked a rational basis for requiring divestiture in the 16 "egregious" cases while allowing the remainder of the existing combinations to continue in operation. The court suggested that "limiting divestiture to small markets of 'absolute monopoly' squanders the opportunity where divestiture might do the most good," since "(d)ivestiture . . . may be more useful in the larger markets." The court further observed that the record "(did) not support the conclusion that divestiture would be more harmful in the grandfathered markets than in the 16 affected markets," nor did it demonstrate that the need for divestiture was stronger in those 16 markets. On the latter point, the court noted that, "(a)lthough the affected markets contain fewer voices, the amount of diversity in communities with additional independent voices may in fact be no greater."

The Commission, NAB, ANPA, and several cross-owners who had been intervenors below, and whose licenses had been grandfathered under the Commission's rules but were subject to divestiture under the Court of Appeals' decision, petitioned this Court for review. We granted certiorari, and we now affirm the judgment of the Court of Appeals insofar as it upholds the prospective ban and reverse the judgment insofar as it vacates the limited divestiture requirement.

II

Petitioners NAB and ANPA contend that the regulations promulgated by the Commission exceed its statutory rule-making authority and violate the constitutional rights of newspaper owners. We turn first to the statutory, and then to the constitutional, issues.

Petitioners NAB and ANPA also argue that the regulations, though designed to further the First Amendment goal of achieving "the widest possible dissemination of information from diverse and antagonistic sources," nevertheless violate the First Amendment rights of newspaper owners. We cannot agree, for this argument ignores the fundamental proposition that there is no "unabridgeable First Amendment right to broadcast comparable to the right of every individual to speak, write, or publish."

The physical limitations of the broadcast spectrum are well known. Because of problems of interference between broadcast signals, a finite number of frequencies can be used productively; this number is far exceeded by the number of persons wishing to broadcast to the public. In light of this physical scarcity, government allocation and regulation of broadcast frequencies are essential, as we have often recognized. No one here questions the need for such allocation and regulation, and, given that need, we see nothing in the First Amendment to prevent the Commission from allocating licenses so as to promote the "public interest" in diversification of the mass communications media.

NAB and ANPA contend, however, that it is inconsistent with the First Amendment to promote diversification by barring a newspaper owner from owning certain broadcasting stations. Requiring those who wish to obtain a broadcast license to demonstrate that such would serve the "public interest" does not restrict the speech of those who are denied licenses; rather, it preserves the interests of the "people as a whole . . . in free speech." As we stated in *Red Lion,* "to deny a station license because 'the public interest' requires it 'is not a denial of free speech.'"

Relying on cases such as *Speiser* v. *Randall,* and *Elrod* v. *Burns,* NAB and ANPA also argue that the regulations unconstitutionally condition receipt of a broadcast license upon forfeiture of the right to publish a newspaper. Under the regulations, however, a newspaper owner need not forfeit anything in order to acquire a license for a station located in another community. More importantly, in the cases relied on by petitioners, unlike the instant case, denial of a benefit had the effect of abridging freedom of expression, since the denial was based solely on the content of constitutionally protected speech; in *Speiser* veterans were deprived of a special property-tax exemption if they declined to subscribe to a loyalty oath, while in *Elrod* certain public employees were discharged or threatened with discharge because of their political affiliation. As we wrote in *National Broadcasting,* "the issue before us would be wholly different" if "the Commission (were) to choose among applicants upon the basis of their political, economic or social views." Here the regulations are not content-related; moreover, their purpose and effect is to promote free speech, not to restrict it.

Finally, petitioners argue that the Commission has unfairly "singled out" newspaper owners for more stringent treatment than other license applicants. But the regulations treat newspaper owners in essentially the same fashion as other owners of the major media of mass communications were already treated under the Commission's multiple ownership rules; owners of radio stations, television stations, and newspapers alike are now restricted in their ability to acquire licenses for co-located broadcast stations. *Grosjean* v. *American Press Co.,* in which this Court struck down a state tax imposed only on newspapers, is thus distinguishable in the degree to which newspapers were singled out for special treatment. In addition, the effect of the tax in *Grosjean* was "to limit the circulation of information to which the public is entitled," an effect inconsistent with the protection conferred on the press by the First Amendment.

In the instant case, far from seeking to limit the flow of information, the Commission has acted, in the Court of Appeals' words, "to enhance the diversity of information heard by the public without on-going government surveillance of the content of speech." The regulations are a reasonable means of promoting the public interest in diversified mass communications; thus they do not violate the First Amendment rights of those who will be denied broadcast licenses pursuant to them. Being forced to "choose among applicants for the same facilities," the Commission has chosen on a "sensible basis," one designed to further, rather than contravene, "the system of freedom of expression."

III

After upholding the prospective aspect of the Commission's regulations, the Court of Appeals concluded that the Commission's decision to limit divestiture to 16 "egregious cases" of "effective monopoly" was arbitrary and capricious within the meaning of the Administrative Procedure Act (APA). We agree with the Court of Appeals that regulations promulgated after informal rulemaking, while not subject to review under the "substantial evidence" test of the APA, may be invalidated by a reviewing court under the "arbitrary or capricious" standard if they are not rational and based on consideration of the relevant factors. Although this review "is to be searching and careful," "(t)he court is not empowered to substitute its judgment for that of the agency."

In the view of the Court of Appeals, the Commission lacked a rational basis, first, for treating existing newspaper-broadcast combinations more leniently than combinations that might seek licenses in the future; and, second, even assuming a distinction between existing and new combinations had been justified, for requiring divestiture in the "egregious cases" while allowing all other existing combinations to continue in operation. We believe that the limited divestiture requirement reflects a rational weighing of competing policies, and we therefore reinstate the portion of the Commission's order that was invalidated by the Court of Appeals.

A

(1)

The Commission was well aware that separating existing newspaper-broadcast combinations would promote diversification of ownership. It concluded, however, that ordering widespread divestiture would not result in "the best practicable service to the American public." Order, at 1074, a goal that the Commission has always taken into account and that has been specifically approved by this Court. In particular, the Commission expressed concern that divestiture would cause "disruption for the industry" and "hardship to individual owners," both of which would result in harm to the public interest. Especially in light of the fact that the number of co-located newspaper-broadcast combinations was already on the decline as a result of natural market forces, and would decline further as a result of the prospective rules, the Commission decided that across-the-board divestiture was not warranted.

The Order identified several specific respects in which the public interest would or might be harmed if a sweeping divestiture requirement were imposed: the stability and continuity of meritorious service provided by the newspaper owners as a group would be lost; owners who had provided meritorious service would unfairly be denied the opportunity to continue in operation; "economic dislocations" might prevent new owners from obtaining sufficient working capital to maintain the quality of local programming; and local ownership of broadcast stations would probably decrease. We cannot say that the Commission acted irrationally in concluding that these public interest harms outweighed the potential gains that would follow from increasing diversification of ownership.

In the past, the Commission has consistently acted on the theory that preserving continuity of meritorius service furthers the public interest, both in its direct consequence of bringing proven broadcast service to the public, and in its indirect consequence of rewarding—and avoiding losses to—licensees who have invested the money and effort necessary to produce quality performance. Thus, although a broadcast license must be renewed every three years, and the licensee must satisfy the Commission that renewal will serve the public interest, both the Commission and the courts have recognized that a licensee who has given meritorious service has a "legitimate renewal expectanc(y)" that is "implicit in the structure of the Act" and should not be destroyed absent good cause. Accordingly, while diversification of ownership is a relevant factor in the context of license renewal as well as initial licensing, the Commission has long considered the past performance of the incumbent as the most important factor in deciding whether to grant license renewal and thereby to allow the existing owner to continue in operation. Even where an incumbent is challenged by a competing applicant who offers greater potential in terms of diversification, the Commission's general practice has been to go with the "proven product" and grant renewal if the incumbent has rendered meritorious service.

In the instant proceeding, the Commission specifically noted that the existing newspaper-broadcast cross-owners as a group had a "long record of service" in the public interest; many were pioneers in the broadcasting industry and had established and continued "(t)raditions of service" from the outset. Notwithstanding the Commission's diversification policy, all were granted initial licenses upon findings that the public interest would be served thereby, and those that had been in existence for more than three years had also had their licenses renewed on the ground that the public interest would be furthered. The Commission noted, moreover, that its own study of existing co-located newspaper-television combinations showed that in terms of percentage of time devoted to several categories of local programming, these stations had displayed "an undramatic but nonetheless statistically significant superiority" over other television stations. An across-the-board divestiture requirement would result in loss of the services of these superior licensees, and—whether divestiture caused actual losses to existing owners, or just denial of reasonably anticipated gains—the result would be that future licensees would be discouraged from investing the resources necessary to produce quality service.

At the same time, there was no guarantee that the licensees who replaced the existing cross-owners would be able to provide the same level of service or demonstrate the same long-term commitment to broadcasting. And even if the new owners were able in the long run to provide similar or better service, the Commission found that divestiture would cause serious disruption in the transition period. Thus, the Commission observed that new owners "would lack the long knowledge of the community and would have to begin raw," and—because of high interest rates—might not be able to obtain sufficient working capital to maintain the quality of local programming.

The Commission's fear that local ownership would decline was grounded in a rational prediction, based on its knowledge of the broadcasting industry and supported by comments in the record, see Order, at 1068–1069, that many of the existing newspaper-broadcast combinations owned by local interests would respond to the divestiture requirement by trading stations with out-of-town owners. It is undisputed that roughly 75 percent of the existing co-located newspaper-television combinations are locally owned, and these owners' knowledge of their local communities and concern for local affairs, built over a period of years, would be lost if they were replaced with outside interests. Local ownership in and of itself has been recognized to be a factor of some—if relatively slight—significance even in the context of initial licensing decisions. It was not unreasonable, therefore, for the Commission to consider it as one of several factors militating against divestiture of combinations that have been in existence for many years.

In light of these countervailing considerations, we cannot agree with the Court of Appeals that it was arbitrary and capricious for the Commission to "grandfather" most existing combinations, and to leave opponents of these combinations to their remedies in individual renewal proceedings. In the latter connection we note that, while individual renewal proceedings are unlikely to accomplish any "overall restructuring" of the existing ownership patterns, the Order does make clear that existing combinations will be subject to challenge by competing applicants in renewal proceedings, to the same extent as they were prior to the instant rulemaking proceedings. That is, diversification of ownership will be a relevant but somewhat secondary factor. And, even in the absence of a competing applicant, license renewal may be denied if, *inter alia,* a challenger can show that a common owner has engaged in specific economic or programming abuses.

(2)

In concluding that the Commission acted unreasonably in not extending its divestiture requirement across-the-board, the Court of Appeals apparently placed heavy reliance on a "presumption" that existing newspaper-broadcast combinations "do not serve the public interest." The Court derived this presumption primarily from the Commission's own diversification policy, as "reaffirmed" by adoption of the prospective rules in this proceeding, and secondarily from "(t)he policies of the First Amendment," and the Commission's statutory duty to "encourage the larger and more effective use of radio in the public interest." As explained in Part II above, we agree that diversification of ownership furthers statutory and constitutional policies, and, as the Commission recognized, separating existing newspaper-broadcast combinations would promote diversification. But the weighing of policies under the "public interest" standard is a task that Congress has delegated to the Commission in the first instance, and we are unable to find anything in the Communications Act, the First Amendment, or the Commission's past or present practices that would require the Commission to "presume" that its diversification policy should be given controlling weight in all circumstances.

Such a "presumption" would seem to be inconsistent with the Commission's longstanding and judicially approved practice of giving controlling weight in some circumstances to its more general goal of achieving "the best practicable service to the public." Certainly, as discussed in Part III-A(1) above, the Commission through its license renewal policy has made clear that it considers diversification of ownership to be a factor of less significance when deciding whether to allow any existing licensee to continue in operation than when evaluating applicants seeking initial licensing. Nothing in the language or the legislative history of Section 303(g) indicates that Congress intended to foreclose all differences in treatment between new and existing licensees, and indeed, in amending Section 307(d) of the Act in 1952, Congress appears to have lent its approval to the Commission's policy of evaluating existing licensees on a somewhat different basis than new applicants. Moreover, if enactment of the prospective rules in this proceeding itself were deemed to create a "presumption" in favor of divestiture, the Commission's ability to experiment with new policies would be severely hampered. One of the most significant advantages of the administrative process is its ability to adapt to new circumstances in a flexible manner, and we are unwilling to presume that the Commission acts unreasonably when it decides to try out a change in licensing policy primarily on a prospective basis.

The Court of Appeals also relied on its perception that the policies militating against divestiture were "lesser policies" to which the Commission had not given as much weight in the past as its divestiture policy. This perception is subject to much the same criticism as the "presumption" that existing co-located newspaper-broadcasting combinations do not serve the public interest. The Commission's past concern with avoiding disruption of existing service is amply illustrated by its license renewal policies. In addition, it is worth noting that in the past when the Commission has changed its multiple ownership rules it has almost invariably tailored the changes so as to operate wholly or primarily on a prospective basis. For example, the regulations adopted in 1970 prohibiting common ownership of a VHF television station and a radio station serving the same market were made to apply only to new licensing decisions; no divestiture of existing combinations was required. The limits set in 1953 on the total numbers of stations a person could own, upheld by this Court in *United States* v. *Storer Broadcasting Co.*, were intentionally set at levels that would not require extensive divestiture of existing combinations. And, while the rules adopted in the early 1940s prohibiting ownership or control of more than one station in the same broadcast service in the same community required divestiture of approximately 20 AM radio combinations, the Commission afforded an opportunity for case-by-case review. Moreover, television and FM radio had not yet developed, so that application of the rules to these media was wholly prospective.

The Court of Appeals apparently reasoned that the Commission's concerns with respect to disruption of existing service, economic dislocations, and decreases in local ownership necessarily could not be very weighty since the Commission has a practice of routinely approving voluntary transfers and assignments of licenses. But the question of whether the Commission should compel proven licensees to divest their stations is a different question from whether the public interest is served by allowing transfers by licensees who no longer wish to continue in the business. As the Commission's brief explains:

(I)f the Commission were to force broadcasters to stay in business against their will, the service provided under such circumstances, albeit continuous, might well not be worth preserving. Thus, the fact that the Commission approves assignments and transfers in no way undermines its decision to place a premium on the continuation of proven past service by those licensees who wish to remain in business.

The Court of Appeals' final basis for concluding that the Commission acted arbitrarily in not giving controlling weight to its divestiture policy was the Court's finding that the rulemaking record did not adequately "disclose the extent to which divestiture would actually threaten" the competing policies relied upon by the Commission. However, to the extent that factual determinations were involved in the Commision's decision to grandfather most existing combinations, they were primarily of a judgmental or predictive nature—*e.g.*, whether a divestiture requirement would result in trading of stations with out-of-town owners; whether new owners would perform as well as existing crossowners, either in the short run or in the long run; whether losses to existing owners would result from forced sales; whether such losses would discourage future investment in quality programming; and whether new owners would have sufficient working capital to finance local programming. In such circumstances complete factual support in the record for the Commission's judgment or prediction is not possible or required; "a forecast of the direction in which future public interest lies necessarily involves deductions based on the expert knowledge of the agency."

B

We also must conclude that the Court of Appeals erred in holding that it was arbitrary to order divestiture in the 16 "egregious cases" while allowing other existing combinations to continue in operation. The Commission's decision was based not—as the Court of Appeals may have believed—on a conclusion that divestiture would be more harmful in the grandfathered markets than in the 16 affected markets, but rather on a judgment that the need for diversification was especially great in cases of local monopoly, and indeed was founded on the very same assumption that underpinned the diversification policy itself and the prospective rules upheld by the Court of Appeals and now by this Court—that the greater the number of owners in a market, the greater the possibility of achieving diversity of program and service viewpoints.

As to the Commission's criteria for determining which existing newspaper-broadcast combinations have all "effective monopoly" in the "local marketplace of ideas as well as economically," we think the standards settled upon by the Commission reflect a rational legislative-type judgment. Some line had to be drawn, and it was hardly unreasonable for the Commission to confine divestiture to communities in which there is common ownership of the only daily newspaper and either the only television station or the only broadcast station of any kind encompassing the entire community with a clear signal. It was not irrational, moreover, for the Commission to disregard media sources other than newspapers and broadcast stations in setting its divestiture standards. The studies cited by the Commission in its notice of rulemaking unanimously concluded that newspapers and television are the two most widely utilized media sources for local news and discussion of public affairs; and, as the Commission noted in its Order, "aside from the fact that (magazines and other periodicals) often had only a tiny fraction in the market, they were not given real weight since they often dealt exclusively with regional or national issues and ignored local issues." Moreover, the differences in treatment between radio and television stations, were certainly justified in light of the far greater influence of television than radio as a source for local news.

The judgment of the Court of Appeals is affirmed in part and reversed in part.
It is so ordered.
Mr. Justice Brennan took no part in the consideration or decision of these cases.

ACTION FOR CHILDREN'S TELEVISION v. *FCC*
564 F2d 458 (1977)

Before Tamm, MacKinnon and Wilkey, Circuit Judges.
Opinion for the court filed by Tamm, Circuit Judge.
Tamm, Circuit Judge:
This appeal comes to us upon a petition for review of a decision by the Federal Communications Commission (Commission or FCC) not to adopt certain rules proposed by a public-interest organization to improve children's television. We affirm the Commission because we find that it substantially complied with the applicable procedures, provided a reasoned analysis for its action, did not depart from established policies, and did not otherwise abuse its discretion.

REVIEW OF THE MERITS

ACT challenges the Commission's interpretation of the Communications Act's public interest standard in light of the record compiled during the notice and comment proceedings in Docket 19142. In all cases of reviewable administrative action, "(i)t is the necessary and proper task of this court to undertake a careful and deliberate scrutiny of an agency's decisions to insure compliance with law and the legislative mandate." In this case, however, we need not determine whether the Commission's action is supported by substantial evidence in the record for neither the Act nor any agency regulation requires an evidentiary hearing as a condition precedent to Commission rulemaking. Rather the proper standard of review for informal rulemaking action is the far less demanding one specified, which requires a reviewing court to set aside agency action deemed to be "arbitrary, capricious, an abuse of discretion, or otherwise not in accordance with law." In applying this standard we ought not to be either pusillanimous or overbearing. We cannot substitute our judgment for the agency's, and our review is confined to a determination of whether the challenged action was based on "consideration of the relevant factors" and is supported by a reasoned opinion. In other words, we can only fault the agency's decision if it manifests a clear error of judgment. In sum, we must sustain the Commission's decision that the public interest does not require the promulgation of specific rules for the time being, if it violates no law, is blessed with an articulated justification that makes a "rational connection between the facts found and the choice made," and follows upon a "hard look" by the agency at the relevant issues.

We agree with the Commission that its decision not to adopt specific regulations governing advertising and programming practices for children's television was a reasoned exercise of its broad discretion. The Supreme Court has emphasized that the Commission's construction of its own governing statute "should be followed unless there are compelling indications that it is wrong . . . ," and we have recognized that

> in a statutory scheme in which Congress has given an agency various tools with which to protect the public interest, the agency is entitled to some leeway in choosing which jurisdictional base and which regulatory tools will be most effective in advancing the Congressional objective.

As a corollary of this broad general discretion, the Commission has considerable latitude in responding to requests to institute proceedings or to promulgate rules, even though it possesses the authority to do so should it see fit. "Administrative rule making does not ordinarily comprehend any rights in private parties to compel an agency to institute such proceedings or promulgate rules." There may be situations in which exceptions to this general rule governing the promulgation of rules are warranted, but this case is not one.

ACT concedes that we must exercise restraint in reviewing policymaking action by the Commission, but argues that "(t)he deference owed to an expert tribunal cannot be allowed to slip into a judicial inertia . . . ." We, of course, have no quarrel with this proposition; we simply are not persuaded that the Commission's decision not to issue rules at this time was arbitrary, irrational or biased in favor of industry interests. While we believe that the Commission may well have adequate authority to regulate in this area, and even perhaps to the extent proposed by ACT, we see no compelling reason why the Commission should not be allowed to give the industry's self-regulatory efforts a reasonable period of time to demonstrate that they will be successful in rectifying the inadequacies of children's television identified in the *Report*.

The Commission's decision was not an abrupt departure from the past policies. Its *Report* has simply clarified the efforts expected of broadcast licensees in fulfilling their public interest obligations to the child audience. Furthermore, the Commission has detailed the significant first amendment and policy problems that inhere in regulation of programming and advertising practices and militate against an immediate adoption of rules, such as urged by ACT, and we cannot say that it erred in concluding that they counselled a more cautious approach. Heeding that counsel, the Commission has chosen to accord licensees a substantial measure of their customary discretion in the areas of programming and advertising decisions, and yet it has made it quite clear that general improvements must be forthcoming in the time devoted to advertisements, in separation of advertisements from program content, and in increased educational or informative programming.

ACT argues that attempts to substitute industry self-regulation for specific rules or standards against which licensee performance may be accurately tested have been historically ineffective. Referring us to experience with the Commission's *Blue Book* and *Editorializing Report,* ACT predicts that the *Report* "is likely to fall between the same regulatory cracks to become another ineffective, unenforced policy statement." Whether or not this prediction ultimately proves accurate, we do not consider the results flowing from these far more general statements of Commission policy, irrespective of how one interprets them, to be an adequate basis for judicial nullification of the self-regulatory efforts underwritten by the *Report*. It is true that self-regulation has not always worked out as desired, but this does not mean that self-regulation has never worked or that it cannot work in this case. Much, we suppose, depends on the degree to which such efforts are focused on specific problems and the extent to which the Commission and the public monitor the level of actual performance. We believe that the *Report* promises reasonable success from both standpoints.

ACT also argues that Commission reliance on action by the NAB and INTV is presumptively ineffective because these associations have only limited participation and no real enforcement power. We believe that this misses the point, however. The Commission is not relying on these industry groups, with whatever enforcement mechanisms may be at their disposal to rehabilitate errant members, as "chosen agents(s)" to vivify and sustain the policies established in the *Report*. Rather, the Commission emphasized the public interest obligation of *every licensee* to respond in good faith to these policies. The Commission's emphasis on the self-regulatory actions taken by the NAB and the INTV during these rulemaking proceedings was hardly a recognition on its part that they sufficed to resolve all the concerns raised during the public comment stage and later addressed in the *Report*. That emphasis was placed to demonstrate that industry self-regulation was not a mere will-o-the-wisp, but rather an encouraging sign that it would be sufficiently responsive to obviate the need for substantial governmental intrusion into areas in which, for good reasons, licensees traditionally have exercised considerable discretion.

The Commission did not act arbitrarily or otherwise abuse its broad discretion in declining to adopt ACT's proposed rules as its own, or, for that matter, in declining to adopt any rules whatsoever for the time being. It has set forth its views in this area in a thorough and detailed manner. Its *Report* manifests a reasoned consideration of the issues raised during these proceedings and contains clearly stated conclusions which justify the approach taken. Our review may take us no further.

CONCLUSION

We might occasionally wish that judges were imbued with legislative powers as well, but we know that under our constitutional system of government we are not. Our authority is limited, both constitutionally and by statute, and this is no less true when we sit in review of the orders of administrative agencies. The Commission, as the expert agency entrusted by Congress with the administration and regulation of the crucial, dynamic communications field, requires and deserves some latitude in carrying out its substantial responsibilities. It may not be the sole guardian of the public's interest in broadcasting—licensees, the courts and the general public in varying ways share responsibility with it for defining and advancing that interest—but, in the formulation of broadcast policy, the Commission nevertheless must continue to play a leading role.

If our relationship with the Commission and other federal agencies is to remain a partnership, we may not succumb to the temptation of casting ourselves in the unsuited role of *primus inter pares*. Rather, our function in passing upon these particular proceedings must come to an end once we have concluded that the Commission's action was a reasoned exercise of its discretion. Having so concluded upon a careful review of the record before us, the order of the Commission challenged by ACT herein is

Affirmed.

FCC v. PACIFICA FOUNDATION
98 S.Ct. 3026 (1978)

Mr. Justice Stevens delivered the opinion of the Court (Parts I, II, III, and IV–C) and an opinion in which The Chief Justice and Mr. Justice Rehnquist joined (Parts IV–A and IV–B).

This case requires that we decide whether the Federal Communications Commission has any power to regulate a radio broadcast that is indecent but not obscene.

A satiric humorist named George Carlin recorded a 12-minute monologue entitled "Filthy Words" before a live audience in a California theater. He began by referring to his thoughts about "the words you couldn't say on the public, ah, airwaves, um, the ones you definitely wouldn't say, ever." He proceeded to list those words and repeat them over and over again in a variety of colloquialisms. The transcript of the recording, which is appended to this opinion, indicates frequent laughter from the audience.

At about 2 o'clock in the afternoon on Tuesday, October 30, 1973, a New York radio station owned by respondent, Pacifica Foundation, broadcast the "Filthy Words" monologue. A few weeks later a man, who stated that he had heard the broadcast while driving with his young son, wrote a letter complaining to the Commission. He stated that, although he could perhaps understand the "record's being sold for private use, I certainly cannot understand the broadcast of same over the air that, supposedly, you control."

The complaint was forwarded to the station for comment. In its response, Pacifica explained that the monologue had been played during a program about contemporary society's attitude toward language and that immediately before its broadcast listeners had been advised that it included "sensitive language which might be regarded as offensive to some." Pacifica characterized George Carlin as "a significant social satirist" who "like Twain and Sahl before him, examines the language of ordinary people. . . . Carlin is not mouthing obscenities, he is merely using words to satirize as harmless and essentially silly our attitudes towards those words." Pacifica stated that it was not aware of any other complaints about the broadcast.

On February 21, 1975, the Commission issued a Declaration Order granting the complaint and holding that Pacifica "could have been the subject of administrative sanctions." The Commission did not impose formal sanctions, but it did state that the order would be "associated with the station's license file, and in the event that subsequent complaints are received, the Commission will then decide whether it should utilize any of the available sanctions it has been granted by Congress."

In its Memorandum Opinion the Commission stated that it intended to "clarify the standards which will be utilized in considering" the growing number of complaints about indecent speech on the airwaves. Advancing several reasons for treating broadcast speech differently from other forms of expression, the Commission found a power to regulate indecent broadcasting in two statutes: 18 U.S.C. Section 1464, which forbids the use of "any obscene, indecent, or profane language by means of radio communications," and 47 U.S.C. Section 303(g), which requires the Commission to "encourage the larger and more effective use of radio in the public interest."

The Commission characterized the language used in the Carlin monologue as "patently offensive," though not necessarily obscene, and expressed the opinion that it should be regulated by principles analogous to those found in the law of nuisance where the "law generally speaks to channeling behavior more than actually prohibiting it . . . . (T)he concept of 'indecent' is intimately connected with the exposure of children to language the describes, in terms patently offensive as measured by contemporary community standards for the broadcast medium, sexual or excretory activities and organs, at times of the day when there is a reasonable risk that children may be in the audience." 56 F.C.C.2d, at 98.

Applying these considerations to the language used in the monologue as broadcast by respondent, the Commission concluded that certain words depicted sexual and excretory activities in a patently offensive manner, noted that they "were broadcast at a time when children were undoubtedly in the audience (i.e., in the early afternoon)," and that the prerecorded language, with these offensive words "repeated over and over," was "deliberately broadcast." In summary, the Commission stated: "We therefore hold that the language as broadcast was indecent and prohibited by 18 U.S.C. 1464."

After the order issued, the Commission was asked to clarify its opinion by ruling that the broadcast of indecent words as part of a live newscast would not be prohibited. The Commission issued another opinion in which it pointed out that it "never intended to place an absolute prohibition on the broadcast of this type of language, but rather sought to channel it to times of day when children most likely would not be exposed to it." The Commission noted that its "declaratory order was issued in a specific factual context," and declined to comment on various hypothetical situations presented by the petition. It relied on its "long standing policy of refusing to issue interpretive rulings of advisory opinions when the critical facts are not explicitly stated or there is a possibility that subsequent events will alter them."

The United States Court of Appeals for the District of Columbia reversed, with each of the three judges on the panel writing separately. Judge Tamm concluded that the order represented censorship and was expressly prohibited by Section 326 of the Communications Act. Alternatively, Judge Tamm read the Commission opinion as the functional equivalent of a rule and concluded that it was "overbroad." Chief Judge Bazelon's concurrence rested on the Constitution. He was persuaded that Section 326's prohibition against censorship is inapplicable to broadcasts forbidden by Section 1464. However, he concluded that Section 1464 must be narrowly construed to cover only language that is obscene or otherwise unprotected by the First Amendment. Judge Leventhal, in dissent, stated that the only issue was whether the Commission could regulate the language "as broadcast." Emphasizing the interest in protecting children, not only from exposure to indecent language, but also from exposure to the idea that such language has official approval, he concluded that the Commission had correctly condemned the daytime broadcast as indecent.

Having granted the Commission's petition for certiorari, —U.S.—, we must decide: 1) whether the scope of judicial review encompasses more than the Commission's determination that the monologue was indecent "as broadcast"; 2) whether the Commission's order was a form of censorship forbidden by Section 326; 3) whether the broadcast was indecent within the meaning of Section 1464; and 4) whether the order violates the First Amendment of the United States Constitution.

I

The general statements in the Commission's memorandum opinion do not change the character of its order. Its action was an adjudication under 5 U.S.C. Section 554(e) (1976 ed.); it did not purport to engage in formal rulemaking or in the promulgation of any regulations. The order "was issued in a special factual context;" questions concerning possible action in other contexts were expressly reserved for the future. The specific holding was carefully confined to the monologue "as broadcast."

"This Court . . . reviews judgments, not statements in opinions." That admonition has special force when the statements raise constitutional questions, for it is our settled practice to avoid the unnecessary decision of such issues. However appropriate it may be for an administrative agency to write broadly in an adjudicatory proceeding, federal courts have never been empowered to issue advisory opinions. Accordingly, the focus of our review must be on the Commission's determination that the Carlin monologue was indecent as broadcast.

II

The relevant statutory questions are whether the Commission's action is forbidden "censorship" within the meaning of 47 U.S.C. Section 326 and whether speech that concededly is not obscene may be restricted as "indecent" under the authority of 18 U.S.C. Section 1464. The questions are not unrelated, for the two statutory provisions have a common origin. Nevertheless, we analyze them separately.

Section 29 of the Radio Act of 1927 provided:

> "Nothing in this Act shall be understood or construed to give the licensing authority the power of censorship over the radio communications or signals transmitted by any radio station, and no regulation or condition shall be promulgated or fixed by the licensing authority which shall interfere with the right of free speech by means of radio communications. No person within the jurisdiction of the United States shall utter any obscene, indecent, or profane language by means of radio communication."

The prohibition against censorship unequivocally denies the Commission any power to edit proposed broadcasts in advance and to excise material considered inappropriate for the airwaves. The prohibition, however, has never been construed to deny the Commission the power to review the content of completed broadcasts in the performance of its regulatory duties.

During the period between the original enactment of the provision in 1927 and its re-enactment in the Communications Act of 1934, the courts and the Federal Radio Commission held that the section deprived the Commission of the power to subject "broadcasting matter to scrutiny prior to its release," but they concluded that the Commission's "undoubted right" to take note of past program content when considering a licensee's renewal application "is not censorship."

Not only did the Federal Radio Commission so construe the statute prior to 1934; its successor, the Federal Communications Commission, has consistently interpreted the provision in the same way ever since. And, until this case, the Court of Appeals for the District of Columbia has consistently agreed with this construction. Judge Wright forcefully pointed out that the Commission is not prevented from canceling the license of a broadcaster who persists in a course of improper programming.

Entirely apart from the fact that the subsequent review of program content is not the sort of censorship at which the statute was directed, its history makes it perfectly clear that it was not intended to limit the Commission's power to regulate the broadcast of obscene, indecent, or profane language.

A single section of the 1927 Act is the source of both the anticensorship provision and the Commission's authority to impose sanctions for the broadcast of indecent or obscene language. Quite plainly, Congress intended to give meaning to both provisions. Respect for that intent requires that the censorship language be read as inapplicable to the prohibition on broadcasting obscene, indecent, or profane language.

There is nothing in the legislative history to contradict this conclusion. The provision was discussed only in generalities when it was first enacted. In 1934, the anticensorship provision and the prohibition against indecent broadcasts were re-enacted in the same section, just as in the 1927 Act. In 1948, when the Criminal Code was revised to include provisions that had previously been located in other titles of the United States Code, the prohibition against obscene, indecent, and profane broadcasts was removed from the Communications Act and re-enacted as Section 1464 of Title 18. That rearrangement of the Code cannot reasonably be interpreted as having been intended to change the meaning of the anticensorship provision.

We conclude, therefore, that Section 326 does not limit the Commission's authority to impose sanctions on licensees who engage in obscene, indecent, or profane broadcasting.

III

The only other statutory question presented by this case is whether the afternoon broadcast of the "Filthy Words" monologue was indecent within the meaning of Section 1464. Even that question is narrowly confined by the arguments of the parties.

The Commission identified several words that referred to excretory or sexual activities or organs, stated that the repetitive, deliberate use of those words in an afternoon broadcast when children are in the audience was patently offensive, and held that the broadcast was indecent. Pacifica takes issue with the Commission's definition of indecency, but does not dispute the Commission's preliminary determination that each of the components of its definition was present. Specifically, Pacifica does not quarrel with the conclusion that this afternoon broadcast was patently offensive. Pacifica's claim that the broadcast was not indecent within the meaning of the statute rests entirely on the absence of prurient appeal.

The plain language of the statute does not support Pacifica's argument. The words "obscene, indecent, profane" are written in the disjunctive, implying that each has a separate meaning. Prurient appeal is an element of the obscene, but the normal definition of "indecent" merely refers to nonconformance with accepted standards of morality.

IV

Pacifica makes two constitutional attacks on the Commission's order. First, it argues that the Commission's construction of the statutory language broadly encompasses so much constitutionally protected speech that reversal is required even if Pacifica's broadcast of the "Filthy Words" monologue is not itself protected by the First Amendment. Second, Pacifica argues that inasmuch as the recording is not obscene, the Constitution forbids any abridgment of the right to broadcast it on the radio.

A

The first argument fails because our review is limited to the question whether the Commission has the authority to proscribe this particular broadcast. As the Commission itself emphasized, its order was "issued in a specific factual context." That approach is appropriate for courts as well as the

Commission when regulation of indecency is at stake, for indecency is largely a function of context—it cannot be adequately judged in the abstract.

The approach is also consistent with *Red Lion Broadcasting Co., Inc. v. FCC*. In that case the Court rejected an argument that the Commission's regulations defining the fairness doctrine were so vague that they would inevitably abridge the broadcasters' freedom of speech. The Court of Appeals had invalidated the regulations because their vagueness might lead to self-censorship of controversial program content. This Court reversed. After noting that the Commission had indicated, as it has in this case, that it would not impose sanctions without warning in cases in which the applicability of the law was unclear, the Court stated:

> "We need not approve every aspect of the Fairness Doctrine to decide these cases, and we will not now pass upon the constitutionality of these regulations by envisioning the most extreme applications conceivable, but will deal with those problems if and when they arise."

It is true that the Commission's order may lead some broadcasters to censor themselves. At most, however, the Commission's definition of indecency will deter only the broadcasting of patently offensive references to excretory and sexual organs and activities. While some of these references may be protected, they surely lie at the periphery of First Amendment concern. The danger dismissed so summarily in *Red Lion,* in contrast, was that broadcasters would respond to the vagueness of the regulations by refusing to present programs dealing with important social and political controversies. Invalidating any rule on the basis of its hypothetical application to situations not before the Court is "strong medicine" to be applied "sparingly and only as a last resort." We decline to administer that medicine to preserve the vigor of patently offensive sexual and excretory speech.

B

When the issue is narrowed to the facts of this case, the question is whether the First Amendment denies government any power to restrict the public broadcast of indecent language in any circumstances. For if the government has any such power, this was an appropriate occasion for its exercise.

The words of the Carlin monologue are unquestionably "speech" within the meaning of the First Amendment. It is equally clear that the Commission's objections to the broadcast were based in part on its content. The order must therefore fall if, as Pacifica argues, the First Amendment prohibits all governmental regulation that depends on the content of speech. Our past cases demonstrate, however, that no such absolute rule is mandated by the Constitution.

The classic exposition of the proposition that both the content and the context of speech are critical elements of First Amendment analysis is Mr. Justice Holmes' statement for the Court in *Schenck v. United States*:

> "We admit that in many places and in ordinary times the defendants in saying all that was said in the circular would have been within their constitutional rights. But the character of every act depends upon the circumstances in which it is done . . . . The most stringent protection of free speech would not protect a man in falsely shouting fire in a theatre and causing a panic. It does not even protect a man from an injunction against uttering words that may have all the effect of force . . . . The question in every case is whether the words used are used in such circumstances and are of such a nature as to create a clear and present danger that they will bring about the substantive evils that Congress has a right to prevent."

Other distinctions based on content have been approved in the years since *Schenck*. The government may forbid speech calculated to provoke a fight. It may pay heed to the " 'commonsense differences' between commercial speech and other varieties." It may treat libels against private citizens more severely than libels against public officials. See *Gertz* v. *Robert Welch, Inc.*, 418 U.S. 323. Obscenity may be wholly prohibited. *Miller* v. *California*, 413 U.S. 15. And only two Terms ago we refused to hold that a "statutory classification is unconstitutional because it is based on the content of communication protected by the First Amendment." *Young* v. *American Mini Theatres*, 427 U.S. 50, 52.

The question in this case is whether a broadcast of patently offensive words dealing with sex and excretion may be regulated because of its content. Obscene materials have been denied the protection of the First Amendment because their content is so offensive to contemporary moral standards. But the fact that society may find speech offensive is not a sufficient reason for suppressing it. Indeed, if it is the speaker's opinion that gives offense, that consequence is a reason for according it constitutional protection. For it is a central tenet of the First Amendment that the government must remain neutral in the marketplace of ideas. If there were any reason to believe that the Commission's characterization of the Carlin monologue as offensive could be traced to its political content—or even to the fact that it satirized contemporary attitudes about four letter words—First Amendment protection might be required. But that is simply not this case. These words offend for the same reasons that obscenity offends. Their place in the hierarchy of First Amendment values are aptly sketched by Mr. Justice Murphy when he said, "such utterances are no essential part of any exposition of ideas, and are of such slight social value as a step to truth that any benefit that may be derived from them is clearly outweighed by the social interest in order and morality."

Although these words ordinarily lack literary, political, or scientific value, they are not entirely outside the protection of the First Amendment. Some uses of even the most offensive words are unquestionably protected. Indeed, we may assume, *arguendo,* that this monologue would be protected in other contexts. Nonetheless, the constitutional protection accorded to a communication containing such patently offensive sexual and excretory language need not be the same in every context. It is a characteristic of speech such as this that both its capacity to offend and its "social value", to use Mr. Justice Murphy's term, vary with the circumstances. Words that are commonplace in one setting are shocking in another. To paraphrase Mr. Justice Harlan, one occasion's lyric is another's vulgarity.

In this case it is undisputed that the content of Pacifica's broadcast was "vulgar," "offensive," and "shocking." Because content of that character is not entitled to absolute constitutional protection under all circumstances, we must consider its context in order to determine whether the Commission's action was constitutionally permissible.

C

We have long recognized that each medium of expression presents special First Amendment problems. And of all forms of communication, it is broadcasting that has received the most limited First Amendment protection. Thus, although other speakers cannot be licensed except under laws that carefully define and narrow official discretion, a broadcaster may be deprived of his license and his forum if the Commission decides that such an action would serve "the public interest, convenience, and necessity." Similarly, although the First Amendment protects newspaper publishers from being required to print the replies of those whom they criticize, it affords no such protection to broadcasters; on the contrary, they must give free time to the victims of their criticism.

The reasons for these distinctions are complex, but two have relevance to the present case. First, the broadcast media have established a uniquely pervasive presence in the lives of all Americans.

Patently offensive, indecent material presented over the airwaves confronts the citizen, not only in public, but also in the privacy of the home, where the individual's right to be let alone plainly outweighs the First Amendment rights of an intruder. Because the broadcast audience is constantly tuning in and out, prior warnings cannot completely protect the listener or viewer from unexpected program content. To say that one may avoid further offense by turning off the radio when he hears indecent language is like saying that the remedy for an assault is to run away after the first blow. One may hang up on an indecent phone call, but that option does not give the caller a constitutional immunity or avoid a harm that has already taken place.

Second, broadcasting is uniquely accessible to children, even those too young to read. Although Cohen's written message might have been incomprehensible to a first grader, Pacifica's broadcast could have enlarged a child's vocabulary in an instant. Other forms of offensive expression may be withheld from the young without restricting the expression at its source. Bookstores and motion picture theatres, for example, may be prohibited from making indecent material available to children. We held in *Ginsberg* v. *New York,* that the government's interest in the "well being of its youth" and in supporting "parents' claim to authority in their own household" justified the regulation of otherwise protected expression. The ease with which children may obtain access to broadcast material, coupled with the concerns recognized in *Ginsberg,* amply justify special treatment of indecent broadcasting.

It is appropriate, in conclusion, to emphasize the narrowness of our holding. This case does not involve a two-way radio conversation between a cab driver and a dispatcher, or a telecast of an Elizabethan comedy. We have not decided that an occasional expletive in either setting would justify any sanction or, indeed, that this broadcast would justify a criminal prosecution. The Commission's decision rested entirely on a nuisance rationale under which context is all-important. The concept requires consideration of a host of variables. The time of day was emphasized by the Commission. The content of the composition of the audience, and differences between radio, television, and perhaps closed-circuit transmissions, may also be relevant. As Mr. Justice Sutherland wrote, a "nuisance may be merely a right thing in the wrong place—like a pig in the parlor instead of the barnyard." We simply hold that when the Commission finds that a pig has entered the parlor, the exercise of its regulatory power does not depend on proof that the pig is obscene.

The judgment of the Court of Appeals is reversed.

APPENDIX

The following is a verbatim transcript of "Filthy Words" prepared by the Federal Communications Commission.

"Aruda-du, ruba-tu. I was thinking about the curse words and the swear words, the cuss words and the words that you can't say, that you're not supposed to say all the time, cause words or people into words want to hear your words. Some guys like to record your words and sell them back to you if they can, (laughter) listen in on the telephone, write down what words you say. A guy who used to be in Washington knew that his phone was tapped, used to answer, Fuck Hoover, yes, go ahead. (laughter) Okay, I was thinking one night about the words you couldn't say on the public, ah, airwaves, um, the ones you definitely wouldn't say, ever cause I heard a lady say bitch one night on television, and it was cool like she was talking about, you know, ah, well, the bitch is the first one to notice that in the litter Johnie right (murmur) Right. And, uh, bastard you can say, and hell and damn so I have to figure out which ones you couldn't and ever and it came down to seven but the list is open to amendment, and in fact, has been changed, uh, by now, ha, a lot of people pointed things out to me, and I noticed some myself. The original seven words were, shit, piss, fuck, cunt, cocksucker, motherfucker, and tits. Those are the ones that will curve your spine, grow hair on your hands and (laughter) maybe, even bring us, God help us, peace without honor (laughter) um, and a bourbon. (laughter) And now the first thing that we noticed was that word fuck was really repeated in there because the word motherfucker is a compound word and it's another form of the word fuck. (laughter) You want to be a purist it doesn't really—it can't be on the list of basic words. Also, cocksucker is a compound word and neither half of that is really dirty. The word—the half sucker that's merely suggestive (laughter) and the word cock is a half-way dirty word, 50 percent dirty-dirty half the time, depending on what you mean by it. (laughter) Uh, remember when you first heard it, like in 6th grade, you used to giggle. And the cock crowed three times, heh (laughter) the cock—three times. It's in the Bible, about a cock-fight, remember—What? Huh? Naw. It ain't that, are you stupid? man. (laughter) It's chickens, you know. (laughter) Then you have the four letter words from the old Anglo-Saxon fame. Uh, shit and fuck. The word, shit, uh, is an interesting kind of word in that the middle class has never really accepted it and approved it. They use it like crazy but it's not really okay. It's still a rude, dirty, old kind of gushy word. (laughter) They don't like that, but they say it, like they say it like, a lady now in a middle-class home, you'll hear most of the time she says it as an expletive, you know, it's out of her mouth before she knows. She says, Oh shit oh shit, (laughter) oh shit. If she drops something, Oh, the shit hurt the broccoli. Shit. Thank you. (footsteps fading away) (papers ruffling)

Read it! (from audience)

Shit! (laughter) I won the Grammy, man, for the comedy album. Isn't that groovy? (clapping, whistling) (murmur) That's true. Thank you. Thank you man. Yeah. (murmur) (continuous clapping) Thank you man. Thank you. Thank you very much, man. Thank, no. (end of continuous clapping) for that and for the Grammy, man, cause (laughter) that's based on people liking it man, yeh, that's ah, that's okay man. (laughter) Let's let that go, man. I got ma Grammy. I can let my hair hang down now, shit. (laughter) Ha! So! Now the word shit is okay for the man. At work you can say it like crazy. Mostly figuratively. Get that shit out of here, will ya? I don't want to see that shit anymore. I can't cut that shit, buddy. I've had that shit up to here. I think you're full of shit myself. (laughter) He don't know shit from Shinola. (laughter) you know that? (laughter) Always wondered how the Shinola people felt about that (laughter) Hi, I'm the new man from Shinola. (laughter) Hi, how are ya? Nice to see ya. (laughter) How are ya? (laughter) Boy, I don't know whether to shit or wind my watch. (laughter) Guess, I'll shit on my watch. (laughter) Oh, the shit is going to hit de fan. (laughter) Built like a brick shit-house. (laughter) Up, he's up shit's creek. (laughter) He's had it. (laughter) He hit me, I'm sorry. (laughter) Hot shit, holy shit, tough shit, eat shit. (laughter) shit-eating grin. Uh, whoever thought of that was ill. (murmur laughter) He had a shit-eating! He had a what? (laughter) Shit on a stick. (laughter) Shit in a handbag. I always like that. He ain't worth shit in a handbag. (laughter) Shitty. He acted real shitty. (laughter) Wow! Shit-fit. Whew! Glad I wasn't there. (murmur, laughter) All the animals—Bull shit, horse shit, cow shit, rat shit, bat shit. (laughter) First time I heard bat shit, I really came apart. A guy in Oklahoma, Boggs, said it, man. Aw! Bat shit. (laughter) Vera reminded me of that last night, ah (murmur). Snake shit, slicker than owl shit. (laughter) Get your shit together. Shit or get off the pot. (laughter) I got a shit-load full of them. (laughter) I got a shit-pot full, all right. Shit-head, shit-heel, shit in your heart, shit for brains, (laughter) shit-face, heh (laughter) I always try to think how that could have originated; the first guy that said that. Somebody got drunk and fell in some shit, you know. (laughter) Hey, I'm shit-face. (laughter) Shit-face, today. (laughter) Anyway, enough of that shit. (laughter) The big one, the word fuck that's the one that hangs them up the most. Cause in a lot of cases that's the very act that hangs them up the most. So, it's natural that the word would, uh, have the same effect. It's a great word, fuck, nice word, easy word, cute word, kind of. Easy word to say. One syllable, short u. (laughter) Fuck. (Murmur) You know, it's easy. Starts with a nice soft sound fuh ends with a kuh. Right? (laughter) A little something for everyone. Fuck (laughter) Good word. Kind of a proud word, too. Who are you? I am FUCK. (laughter) FUCK OF THE MOUNTAIN. (laughter) Tune in again next week to FUCK OF THE MOUNTAIN. (laughter) It's an interesting word too, cause it's got a double kind of a life—personality—dual, you know, whatever the right phrase is. It leads a double life, the word fuck. First of all, it means, sometimes, most of the time, fuck. What does it mean? It means to make love. Right? We're going to make love, yeh, we're going to fuck, yeh, we're going to fuck, yeh, we're going to make love. (laughter) we're really going to fuck, yeh, we're going to make love. Right? And it also means the beginning of life, it's the act that begins life, so there's the word hanging around with words like love, and life, and yet on the other hand, it's also a word that we really use to hurt each other with, man. It's a heavy. It's one that you save toward the end of the argument. (laughter) Right? (laughter) You finally can't make out. Oh, fuck you man. I said, fuck you. (laughter, murmur) Stupid fuck. (laughter) Fuck you and everybody that looks like you. (laughter) man. It would be nice to change the movies that we already have and substitute the word fuck for the word kill, wherever we could, and some of those movie cliches would change a little bit. Madfuckers still on the loose. Stop me before I fuck again. Fuck the ump, fuck the ump, fuck the ump, fuck the ump, fuck the ump. Easy on the clutch Bill, you'll fuck the engine again. (laughter) The other shit one was, I don't give a shit. Like its worth something, you know? (laughter) I don't give a shit. Hey, well, I don't take no shit, (laughter) you know what I mean? You know why I don't take no shit? (laughter) Cause I don't give a shit. (laughter) If I give a shit, I would have to pack shit. (laughter) But I don't pack no shit cause I don't give a shit. (laughter) You wouldn't shit me, would you? (laughter) That's a joke when you're a kid with a worm looking out the bird's ass. You wouldn't shit me, would you? (laughter) It's an eight-year old joke but a good one. (laughter) The additions to the list. I found three more words that had to be put on the list of words you could never say on television, and they were fart, turd and twat, those three. (laughter) Fart, we talked about, it's harmless. It's like tits, it's a cutie word, no problem, Turd, you can't say but who wants to, you know? (laughter) The subject never comes up on the panel so I'm not worried about that one. Now the word twat is an interesting word. Twat! Yeh, right in the twat. (laughter) Twat is an interesting word because it's the only one I know of, the only slang word another meaning to it. Like, ah, snatch, box and pussy all have other meanings, man. Even in a Walt Disney movie, you can say, We're going to snatch that pussy and put him in a box and bring him on the airplane. (murmur, laughter) Everybody loves it. The twat stands alone, man, as it should. And two-way words. Ah, ass is okay providing you're riding into town on a religious feast day. (laughter) You can't say, up your ass. (laughter) You can say, stuff it! (murmur) There are certain things you can say its weird but you can just come so close. Before I cut, I, uh, want to, ah, thank you for listening to my words, man, fellow, uh, space travelers. Thank you man for tonight and thank you also. (clapping, whistling)"

NBC v. NIEMI
98 S.Ct. 705 (1978)

Mr. Justice Rehnquist, Circuit Justice.

Applicants have requested that I stay the commencement of a civil trial in the Superior Court of the City and County of San Francisco in which they are defendants in order that they may have an opportunity to apply for and obtain a writ of certiorari from this Court to review the judgment of the Court of Appeal of the State of California filed October 26, 1977. That court reversed the judgment of dismissal rendered by the Superior Court in a case wherein respondent sought damages from petitioners for injuries allegedly inflicted upon her by persons who were acting under the stimulus of observing a scene of brutality which had been broadcast in a television drama entitled "Born Innocent." Applicants contend that the First and Fourteenth Amendments to the United States Constitution prevent their being subjected to liability and damages in an action such as this, and intend to petition this Court for certiorari to review the judgment of the Court of Appeal remanding the case for trial.

I find it unnecessary to determine whether four Justices of this Court would vote to grant a petition for certiorari by these applicants to review a California judgment sustaining a judgment for damages against them on the basis described above in the face of their claim that the First and Fourteenth Amendments prohibit the rendering of such a judgment. The only question before me is whether those same Constitutional provisions would be thought by at least four Justices of this Court to call for the granting of a writ of certiorari to review the interlocutory judgment of the state Court of Appeal which did no more than remand the case for a trial on the issues joined. I am quite prepared to assume that the Court would find the decision of the Court of Appeal sought to be stayed a "final judgment" for purposes of 28 U.S.C. Section 1257(2) pursuant to its holding in *Cox Broadcasting Corp. v. Cohn* (1975). But the mere fact that the Court would have jurisdiction to grant a stay does not dispose of all the prudential considerations which, to my mind, militate against the grant of the application in this case. Every year we grant petitions for certiorari or note probable jurisdiction in cases in which we ultimately conclude that a state or federal court has failed to give sufficient recognition to a federal Constitutional claim, and have as a consequence reversed the judgment of such Court rendered upon the merits of the action. But this is a far cry from saying that this Court would have stayed further proceedings in the same cases at an interlocutory stage comparable to the case now before me.

True, in the case of double jeopardy, we have held that the subjecting of the defendant to the second trial itself is a violation of the Constitutional right secured by the Sixth Amendment, even though any judgment of conviction rendered in that trial would be subject to ultimate reversal on appeal. The same doctrine is found in cases more closely resembling this such as *Miami Herald Publishing Co. v. Tornillo* (1974), and *Cox*. But in both *Tornillo* and in *Cox* the First and Fourteenth Amendment claims were far more precisely drawn as a result of the decisions of the state courts than is the case here. A reading of the opinion of the Court of Appeal indicates that it might have been based on a state procedural ground, by reason of the fact that the trial judge after denial of a motion for summary judgment but before the empanelment of a jury himself viewed the entire film and rendered judgment for applicants because he found that it did not "advocate or encourage violent and depraved acts and thus did not constitute an 'incitement.' " The Court of Appeal held that this was a violation of respondent's right to trial by jury guaranteed her by the California Constitution, and went on to state that:

> It is appropriate to acknowledge that, if the case had proceeded properly to trial before a jury and a verdict awarding damages to appellant had been the result, it would have been the responsibility of the trial court, or perhaps of this Court on appeal, to determine upon a re-evaluation of the evidence whether the jury's fact determination could be sustained against a First Amendment challenge to the jury's determination of a 'Constitutional fact.' "

The contours of California tort law are regulated by the California courts and the California Legislature, subject only to the limitations imposed on those bodies by the United States Constitution and laws and treaties enacted pursuant thereto. In the principal case relied upon by applicants in support of their stay, according to applicants "a sheriff allowed appellant to be lynched pending appeal to this Court of his conviction." A requirement to defend an action such as respondent's are now required to defend in the Superior Court, and if unsuccessful there to post supersedeas bond and prosecute their Constitutional claims through the normal appellate process to this Court, is scarcely a comparable example of irreparable injury. Since I find that applicants' claims of irreparable injury resulting from the judgment of the Court of Appeal in this case are not sufficient to warrant my granting their application, I accordingly deny the stay.

NOTE I

During the last days of July 1978 the trial began in San Francisco Superior Court. After hearing the arguments on both sides, the judge threw out the $11 million "Born Innocent" damage suit. The jury never received the opportunity to decide the issue, NBC having persuaded the court to dismiss the complaint on First Amendment grounds.

NBC said the rape scene that graphically portrayed a girl, aided by three other girls using a wooden handle of a plumber's plunger to rape the star Linda Blair, in a reformatory shower-room, was essential to the film's artistic integrity, although the network sanitized the scene after the furor created by the initial showing. According to the *Manchester Guardian,* "(f)or more than a decade, top NBC executives publicly have recognized as valid the warnings by growing numbers of behavioral experts that, in some latently aggressive children and early adolescents, TV violence predictably will stimulate anti-social conduct or even modeling of such conduct." (August 27, 1978).

Mrs. Neimi's suit was initially dismissed in 1976 by a state trial judge who ruled the litigation was barred by constitutional guarantees of free speech and free press. The state Court of Appeals overturned that decision, saying it violated the Niemi girl's right to a trial on the question. NBC then went to the United States Supreme Court which refused to hear the appeal.

By refusing to hear the appeal, the Supreme Court cleared the way for jury trial of the $11 million damage suit based on charges that broadcasters are liable when an episode of violence on television leads to a real-life crime. When the San Francisco Superior Court failed to respond by sending the case to a jury for a determination as to whether NBC should be liable for a sexual assault that mirrored a program it had presented, this trial court seemed to at least imply that the First Amendment right of expression and free speech outweighed any consideration as to whether there was a causal connection between the fictional program and the real-life tragedy that followed.

NOTE II

In the Matter of The American Medical Association, a corporation,

The Connecticut State Medical Society, a corporation,

The New Haven County Medical Association, Inc.

AMA's Ban on Advertising by Doctors is Illegal, FTC Judge Rules

The AMA, the nation's largest association of physicians, has hindered, restricted, restrained, foreclosed and frustrated competition in the provision of physicians' services throughout the U.S. and caused substantial injury to the public. This is one of the primary conclusions of a Federal Trade Commission administrative law judge in an initial decision announced today.

In his decision in the matter of American Medical Association (AMA), Connecticut State Medical Society, and New Haven County Medical Association, Inc., FTC Administrative Law Judge Ernest G. Barnes found that the respondents have "conspired, combined and agreed to adopt, disseminate and enforce ethical standards which ban physician solicitation of business, severely restrict physician advertising and prohibit certain contractual arrangements between physicians and health care delivery organizations and between physicians and nonphysicians." These acts and practices, Barnes concluded, constitute unfair methods of competition and unfair acts or practices in violation of Section 5 of the FTC Act.

Barnes noted that the result of the challenged practices has been the "placement of a formidable impediment to competition in the delivery of health care services by physicians in this country. That barrier has served to deprive consumers of the free flow of information about the availability of health care services, to deter the offering of innovative forms of health care and to stifle the rise of almost every type of health care delivery that could potentially pose a threat to the income of fee-for-service physicians in private practice. The costs to the public in terms of less expensive or even perhaps, more improved forms of medical services, are great."

This is not a final decision of the Commission and may be appealed, stayed, or docketed for review.

The initial decision is based on the FTC's complaint issued against respondents on December 19, 1975. That complaint charged the associations with violations of Section 5 of the FTC Act by restricting the ability of their members to advertise for and solicit patients and to enter into various contractual arrangements in connection with the offering of their services to the public. Specifically, the complaint charges that respondents have agreed with others to prevent or hinder their physician members from:

- soliciting business, by advertising or otherwise.
- engaging in price competition; and
- otherwise engaging in competitive practices.

The complaint further alleges that, as a result of those acts and practices:

- prices of physician services have been stabilized, fixed or otherwise interfered with;
- competition between medical doctors in the provision of such services has been hindered, restrained, foreclosed and frustrated;
- consumers have been deprived of information pertinent to the selection of a physician and of the benefits of competition.

The FTC's complaint and the initial decision announced today deal with the associations' ethics restrictions. Those restrictions do not, according to Barnes, deal with medical or therapeutic aspects of a physician's practice but with restrictions on economic activities.

Barnes noted that respondents challenged the FTC's jurisdiction over them. In dealing with the jurisdictional question, Barnes found that the respondents were a "company . . . or association . . . organized to carry on business for its own profit or that of its members," as required under Section 4 of the FTC Act. He further found that respondents' acts and practices were "in or affecting commerce," as required by Section 5 of the FTC Act. Thus, he concluded that the FTC has jurisdiction over the respondents.

Barnes noted that the main body of evidence against AMA consists of the Principles of Medical Ethics, official interpretations of the Principles, and letter after letter from AMA officials explaining the Principles and urging compliance with them.

Barnes found that the ethical restrictions on advertising and solicitation seek to prevent any doctor from presenting his name or information about his practice to the public in any way that "sets him apart from other physicians." These restrictions, according to Barnes, "affect all facets of competition among physicians." Specifically cited in the initial decision were restrictive ethics actions taken by respondents against advertising and solicitation efforts of Health Maintenance Organizations (HMOs) and their physicians.

Barnes further found that the ". . . organization of each of the respondents, their interrelationships and the mutuality manifest throughout their application and enforcement of ethics proscriptions attest to the logical conclusion that the respondents and others have acted in concert to restrain competition among physicians."

The effect of the conspiracy, according to Barnes, has been to "deprive consumers of the free flow of commercial information that is indispensable in making informed economic decisions, and to interfere with the freedom of physicians to make their own decisions as to their employment conditions."

He further noted that AMA's restrictions have discouraged, restricted and in some instances, eliminated new methods of health care.

Barnes noted that the remedy must be one which "will open the channels of communication and prevent obstruction to physicians and . . . HMOs in their contractual arrangements."

Barnes order will require that respondents:

- Cease and desist from engaging in the challenged practices.
- Revoke and rescind any existing ethical principles or guidelines which restrict physicians' advertising, solicitation, or contractual relations.
- Provide adequate notification to its members and affiliated societies of the terms of the order.
- Deny affiliation to any society that engages in any practices that violate the terms of the order.

The order will permit respondents, beginning two years after the order becomes final, to issue ethical guidelines and affecting advertising and solicitation with the permission and approval of the FTC.

Each of the respondents is comprised primarily of physicians engaged in the private practice, fee-for-service, delivery of medical care. AMA is a national organization, with its basic make-up that of a federacy of state medical societies and local medical societies. A substantial majority of all physicians retain membership in the AMA and in the state and local medical societies.

AMA consists of 170,000 physicians. Its offices are located in Chicago, Ill. Respondent Connecticut State Medical Society has 4400 physician members. Respondent New Haven County Medical Association, Inc. has approximately 1200 physician members. Both associations have their offices in New Haven, Conn.

In 1974, physician members of the respondents received in excess of $1 billion in fees for medical services. (Ernest G. Barnes, Administrative Law Judge, United States of America before Federal Trade Commission, filed November 13, 1978, initial decision, FTC summary of 312 page, single-spaced decision and opinion of the Judge, November 29, 1978.)

NOTE III

In the case of *United States* v. *CBS and ABC* (459 F.Supp. 832 (1978)), the government brought action against two television networks charging violation of the Sherman Act. On the defendants' motion to dismiss, the district judge held that (1) two networks' individual possession of 33 per cent of the primary market of the national commercial television network prime time entertainment programs was insufficient to establish their possession of monopoly power prohibited under the Sherman Act, and that (2) each network's prime time entertainment programs constituted a relevant submarket for antitrust purposes. The motion was thus granted in part and denied in part.

Judge Kelleher delivered the opinion of the court.

In the instant case, the individual defendant's competitors are the other networks. Each competitor—and each individual defendant—controls approximately 33 percent of the relevant primary market. It cannot be said that each of defendant's competitors is "relatively small." Nor has the government shown, in its pleading or in its recital of evidence required by order of the Court, or in oral argument, the alleged presence of any other factors sufficient to give each individual defendant monopoly power in the relevant primary market. The government has, in fact, been obscure to the point of evasion with respect to each individual defendant's Section 2 liability in the primary market. In an effort to aid the Court in refining the issues and to enable defense counsel to fashion their response and discovery, the Court ordered the government to set forth in refining the issues its claims with respect to the relevant market with some particularity. The government has not done so, for the obvious reason that it cannot do so.

Because possession of monopoly power in the relevant market is essential to Section 2 liability, the Court dismisses the Section 2 charge with respect, and only with respect to, the so-called "relevant primary market."

It has long been recognized that "there may be an outer market and one or more inner submarkets within which competitive effects are to be appraised, i.e., a relevant submarket may constitute the product market for antitrust purposes." The problem is whether submarkets exist, for the purposes of antitrust law, containing, respectively, only CBS or ABC prime time television entertainment programs.

The ancient formula for determining the relevant market, set forth in *du Pont* (Cellophane), was interchangeability of products. However, the reasonable interchangeability test "has been refined and modified in subsequent cases." Interchangeability is not and should not be the sole test because

> (a) monopolist always sells in the elastic region of his demand schedule . . . (O)ne reason that most demand schedules have an elastic region is that the higher the price of a product, the more attractive substitute products become to the consumer. Hence it is not surprising to find a high cross-elasticity

of demand between a monopolized product and other products at the monopoly price-output level, meaning that at that level the demand for the substitute products is highly responsive to a change in the price of the monopolized product.

Thus, in determining the parameters of relevant submarkets for antitrust purposes, several other factors have been brought into play. The submarkets must be "sufficiently distinct in commercial reality to permit a company that dominated these submarkets to exclude competition and control prices. . . . This depends upon whether efforts to exclude competition or control prices in the submarkets in question would be negated by a shift of buyers to other portions of the market."

Given the law to this point, a further issue arises as to whether an antitrust defendant can be found to be monopolizing a submarket consisting entirely of its own products.

Although the defendants hint that it is otherwise, the government's allegations and evidence show that the three predominant buyers of prime time television entertainment programs are the three networks. Because the three possess approximately equal shares of prime time airspace (i. e., 33 percent), they cannot be accused of monopolizing the "primary" market, at least in the absence of some kind of "shared monopoly" allegation, a theory expressly rejected by governmental counsel in oral argument. However, because there are but three dominant buyers in the relevant primary market, that is, in technical terms, an oligopsony (i. e., many sellers, few buyers), the answer may be different in the submarket.

The government's recital of its evidence would be more than sufficient, if adduced at trial, to enable a jury to reasonably find against the defendants on a Section 2 charge, at least on the issue of the existence of a viable submarket composed only of CBS (or ABC) prime time television network entertainment programs.

In summary, the government maintains that "CBS television entertainment programs are not reasonably interchangeable with programs considered by ABC and NBC, because CBS insulates itself from competition from the other two national . . . networks by imposing an elaborate structure of contractual restraints on independent television program producers and others. These contractual restraints create a separate and distinct submarket. . . . Proof . . . will include evidence of contractual restraints on the interchangeability of programs among the networks and the monopsonistic effects of those restraints."

The Court concludes that the government's definition of and recital of evidence concerning the relevant markets in the context of its non-per se claims is sufficient, and hence in compliance with its June 20 order. The Court is satisfied that the government has alleged sufficient facts upon which relief could be granted as to all these theories, and will entertain no further motions to dismiss at this pre-trial stage.

Chapter III

False and Deceptive Advertising

Section 1

Deceptive Business Practices: Federal Regulations

*Daniel M. Rohrer**

INTRODUCTION

The art of advertising arises from production and distribution. Thus, to the extent that the free enterprise system is a justified means to a better standard of living, advertising serves as an equally honorable end in the search for a better world in which to live.

As was stated in the landmark decision of *Bates and Van O'Steen* v. *State Bar of Arizona,* 433 U.S. 350 (1977): "(T)he consumer's concern for the free flow of commercial speech often may be far keener than his concern for urgent political dialogue. Moreover, significant societal interests are served by such speech. Advertising, though entirely commercial, may often carry information of import to significant issues of the day. (See *Bigelow* v. *Virginia, supra.*) And commercial speech serves to inform the public of the availability, nature, and prices of products and services, and thus performs an indispensable role in the allocation of resources in a free enterprise system. (See *FTC* v. *Procter & Gamble Co.,* 386 U.S. 568, 603–604 (1967).) In short, such speech serves individual and societal interests in assuring informed and reliable decisionmaking. 425 U.S. at 761–765."

An effort upon which tens of billions of dollars are spent annually deserves some attention in terms of the methods which are employed in its advancement. Such methods may involve both acceptable and unacceptable, legal and illegal means. The purpose of this chapter is to demonstrate additional areas in which various advertising techniques have become subject to criticism, and to consider whether present controls upon such techniques are adequate.

It goes without saying that false advertising or untrue claims in behalf of a service or product are illegal, and the Federal Trade Commission has done much to curtail such abuses, as will be shown under the description of deceptive advertising practices.

A second form of advertising which has raised some concern involves omissions—presenting half the truth, partial truth, or incomplete information. The high court responded to this complaint again in the case of *Bates and Van O'Steen* v. *State Bar of Arizona*: "But it seems peculiar to deny the consumer, on the ground that the information is incomplete, at least some of the relevant information needed to reach an informed decision. The alternative—the prohibition of advertising—serves only to restrict the information that flows to consumers," *supra.*

---

*My thanks to Jane Baker of Los Angeles for assistance on this section.

The third area of concern is that of misleading or deceptive advertising. The Supreme Court responded to this issue in the following words: "Obviously, much commercial speech is not provably false, or even wholly false, but only deceptive or misleading. We foresee no obstacle to a State's dealing effectively with this problem. The First Amendment, as we construe it today, does not prohibit the State from insuring that the stream of commercial information flows cleanly as well as freely (*Virginia State Board of Pharmacy* v. *Virginia Citizens Consumer Council, Inc.*, 425 U.S. 748 (1976)).

Furthermore, the Supreme Court has ruled that a practice which was unfair only to consumers was an illegal act under Section 5 of the Federal Communications Act (*FTC* v. *Sperry and Hutchinson and Co.*, 405 U.S. 233 (1972); *Wisc. LR* 1071–1072 (1972)). While the FTC lost this case on a technicality, the court ruling clarified and reiterated the authority of the FTC to regulate false and deceptive advertising practices.

Previously, "the business community was still arguing that 'unfair' acts were limited to acts which were unfair to competitors and that there could be no such thing as an unfair act which was unfair only to consumers."[1]

THE FEDERAL TRADE COMMISSION

The FTC was established by Congress in 1914 under the Federal Trade Commission Act. Section 5 of the act held that: "Unfair methods of competition in commerce are hereby declared unlawful; the Commission is hereby empowered and directed to prevent persons, partnerships, or corporations from using unfair methods of competition in commerce."[2]

The first case in which the FTC's right to regulate this particular business practice was sustained in *FTC* v. *Winsted Hosiery Co.* in 1922. It was held that false advertising was an unfair method of competition. The reasoning behind this is obvious. What was surprising was that competitors did not need to show actual business losses in order to collect damages. Deception of the public was simply not an issue at the time, and was dismissed further in *FTC* v. *Raladam*, 283 U.S. 643 (1931). Here the court held that the only valid ground for advertising regulation was adversely-affected competition.

However, the Wheeler-Lea Amendments of 1938 added the phrase "deceptive acts or practices" to Section 15 U.S.C. 45 (FTC Act) and established the protection of consumers from unfair advertising. Special emphasis was also placed on food, drug, cosmetic, and device advertisements as they were "misleading in a material respect."

Jurisdiction of the FTC was expanded to contemporary limits in the case of *Mueller* v. *United States*, 262 F.2d 443 (CA5 1958). Here the district court decided that interstate sales need not be a prerequisite to FTC action so long as there were interstate advertisements.

The courts have given unusually broad latitude to the FTC to determine which advertisements are deceptive and which are in the public interest. They normally go along with the FTC's decision unless there is some "abuse of discretion." Indeed, the FTC's broad powers of interpretation of advertisements caused one industry representative to remark that "an ad means what the FTC determines it to mean."[3] The FTC has, however, developed guidelines to determine if an advertisement is deceptive.[4]

First, misrepresentation of fact in an advertisement is considered deceptive. Thus, in the case where Rapid Shave claimed to soften sandpaper, it was found that the substance was, in fact, a mixture of plexiglass and sand. Rapid Shave could be shown to shave sandpaper, but only after a soaking period of 80 minutes (*FTC* v. *Colgate-Palmolive Co.*, 380 U.S. 374 (1965)).

Secondly, if an advertisement is susceptible to being read in a way which distorts the function of the product, it may be controlled. For example, in the case of *Savitch* v. *FTC* a product for the treatment of delayed menstruation which used the headlines "At last—IT CAN BE SOLD!" and "Don't risk disaster" was found to be deceptive in that it deceives women into purchasing what they thought was an abortifacient (218 F.2d 817 (CA2 1955)).

Much later the FTC ordered the Hudson Pharmaceutical Corporation to stop advertising its Spider-Man brand vitamins in comic books or on television programs aimed at children.

The FTC said that "such use of Spider-Man can lead significant numbers of children to believe that the endorsed product has qualities and characteristics it doesn't have . . . and induce children to take excessive amounts of vitamins which can be dangerous to their health."

The Federal agency also said that the pharmaceutical company "agreed to the order without admitting or denying the charges." The company had introduced the product a year earlier.[5]

Finally, if valid statistical evidence is presented out of context, the advertisement is considered unacceptable. Thus, an Old Gold cigarettes advertisement which quoted the results of a study in which they had the lowest tar and nicotine levels, without pointing out that the variations among brands were so small as to be insignificant, was found to be deceptive (*P. Lorillard Co.* v. *FTC*, 186 F.2d 52 (CA4 1956)).

Thus, the FTC has primary jurisdiction for the actual determination of unfair or deceptive advertising in all media, and for the regulation of such advertising.[6]

METHODS OF REGULATION

The FTC has several remedies available in actions against advertisers. The first is the traditional cease and desist order. This is the typical method of enforcement, but has its obvious drawbacks. It amounts simply to an admonishment to "go forth and sin no more."[7] But it has little punitive or deterrent effect except as an alert that if such practices are continued, at least one of the following consequences may occur:

1. The FTC also relies on a mechanism known as affirmative disclosure. Rather than enforcing against those who misrepresent their product through its positive depiction in the advertisement, the Commission attempts to force producers to include any or all information which would induce a consumer not to buy the product. Thus, Geritol was forced in its advertisements to admit that it could do nothing in cases of pernicious anemia and that few of the persons who had anemia had that type (*J.B. Williams Co.* v. *FTC*, 381 F.2d 884 (CA6 1967)).

Similarly, the court found in *Heller and Son, Inc.* v. *FTC* that: "We commence our study of the instant case with the knowledge that the Commission may require affirmative disclosures where necessary to prevent deception, and that failure to disclose by mark or label material facts concerning merchandise, which, if known to prospective purchasers, would influence their decisions of whether or not to purchase, is an unfair trade practice" (191 F.2d 954 (CA7 1951)).

2. A more recent and much criticized method of relief is that of corrective advertising. This is based on the sleeper theory and others which contend that the advertisement continues to do its work after it is seen. Corrective advertisements help to prevent the influencing of consumer purchasing once the deceptive material is blocked from the media. Their function is two-fold: 1) They help consumers "re-think" their attitudes towards the product or brand in question and 2) they attempt to make up for losses to competitors who were the victims of the misconceptions.[8]

The usual procedure is to force the industry to devote 25 percent of his advertising budget for one year to advertisements which bring to light the contested facts. These are usually written by or based upon drafts by the FTC. One example of this is action taken by the Commission against Bufferin—on the ground that it does not "work twice as fast as aspirin." The sample drawn up by the FTC to replace such advertisements reads as follows:

> In the case of the product Bufferin it has not been established that Bufferin relieves pain faster than aspirin; it has not been established that Bufferin will cause gastric discomfort less frequently than aspirin, and that Bufferin will relieve nervous tension, irritability, or enable persons to cope with ordinary stresses to everyday life.[9]

Several other companies promoting pain relievers and analgesics were also found guilty of misrepresentation. Examples of claims cited were:

Excedrin—"relieves tension and anxiety"
Bayer—"more effective for the relief of minor pain than aspirin"
Anacin—"more effective for pain relief than aspirin"

All were required to spend 25 percent of their advertisement budgets for two years to correct consumer misconception. However, the FTC has modified its corrective advertisement policy in one respect. Should the company be able to present evidence that the advertisements have achieved their goal before the two-year period ends, they may resume normal advertising.[10]

Profile Bread has also been required to declare that their product (which simply reduces the width of a slice of bread) is not an effective means of weight reduction (*ITT Continental Baking Company*, 36 Fed. Reg. 18, 522 (1971)). A similar requirement has been placed upon the Coca-Cola Co. to demonstrate that their Hi-C fruit drinks are indeed not fruit juices, thereby repudiating the previously false nutritional claims connoted with that term (*Coca-Cola Co., Inc. et al.*, 3 CCH Trade Reg. Rep. 19, 351 (1970)).

More recently it was determined that neither legislative revision of the Federal Trade Commission Act nor the First Amendment affects the power of the FTC in cease and desist proceedings. For example, in the case of *Warner-Lambert Co.* v. *FTC*, the agency ordered the manufacturer of Listerine mouthwash to insert corrective statements in future advertisements to remedy mistaken consumer belief resulting from past advertisements (562 F.2d 749 (CADC, 1977)).

The Commission's order, in the first corrective advertising case to face court review, requires Warner-Lambert to run language in $10 million worth of advertisements stating that: "Listerine will not help prevent colds or sore throat or lessen their severity," *supra*. The court eliminated the FTC's lead-in phrase, "Contrary to previous advertising." The corrective disclosure is to be made until the manufacturer spends an amount equaling the average annual Listerine advertisement budget during the period from April 1962 to March 1972—approximately $10 million according to FTC estimates.

The Federal Court made a similar decision in the case of *United States* v. *STP*, _____ Fed. Supp. _____ (1978). The STP Corporation was fined half a million dollars in the second false advertising settlement involving corrective advertising to be decided in court. The FTC announced that under a settlement approved by a Federal Court in New York, STP will publish notices in newspapers and magazines informing the public that it based its advertising claims on unreliable road tests.

The company had been claiming that its oil treatment reduced oil consumption by up to 20 percent. The settlement resulted from an FTC complaint alleging that STP violated a 1976 Commission order. As a result of these two court decisions, there is less uncertainty over whether the FTC may Constitutionally require corrective advertising.

Indeed a major barrier has been lifted for it is a matter of procedural problems rather than lack of interest or resources that have served as major obstacles to more vigorous prosecutions by the FTC in cases of false and deceptive advertising. The FTC is now devoting more of its time and resources to this problem.

In 1976 the FTC had issued a consent order requiring the Fort Lauderdale manufacturer of oil and gasoline additives and oil filters, and its Chicago advertising agency, among other things, to cease making false and misleading effectiveness claims and representation for its products. (*In the Matter of STP Corporation, et al.*, 87 FTC 55 (1976).)

As a final example, a FTC administrative law judge ruled on September 16, 1978 that the manufacturers of the headache remedy Anacin falsely advertised their product as a tension reliever and should be ordered to correct that false impression. Judge Montgomery K. Hyun ruled in the false-advertising case brought by the FTC in 1973 that: "Anacin does not relieve nervousness, tension, stress, fatigue or depression, nor will it enable persons to cope with the ordinary stresses of everyday life." He recommended that the maker, American Home Products Corporation of New York City, be required to say "Anacin is not a tension reliever" in its next $24 million of advertising, approximately one year's advertising budget.

The tension-relief claim was dropped from advertisements in 1973 after the FTC first challenged the claim. However the judge argued that the false claim was made so many times that an incorrect image of the product remains in the minds of many consumers. Nevertheless the judge's decision can be reviewed and changed by the five-member Commission before it takes effect.

The judge further found other parts of advertisements for Anacin and Arthritis Pain Formula, another American Home product, to be false. He recommended against corrective advertising for these other claims and instead recommended prohibiting the claims unless they were established scientifically. Hyun found to be false or unfair:

> Advertisements that say Anacin is stronger than aspirin. "Anacin's analgesic ingredient is not unusual, special or stronger than aspirin, since it is nothing other than aspirin. . . . Anacin's only other ingredient, caffeine, is not an analgesic."
>
> Claims that a person who takes Anacin can expect relief within 22 seconds. "Relief from Anacin is not obtained within that period of time."
>
> References to a "doctor's survey" used in promoting Anacin. These are deceptive because the survey "does not provide a reasonable basis for the representations."
>
> Claims that Anacin is more effective for relieving pain than any other analgesic available without a prescription have "not been scientifically established."
>
> Advertising that it has been established that Arthritis Pain Formula will cause gastric discomfort less frequently than any other nonprescription analgesic. "There existed a substantial question, recognized by experts, . . . as to the validity of the representation."

Consumer sales of Anacin totaled approximately $41 million during the first half of 1977 and were approximately $7 million for Arthritis Pain Formula.

3. The final alternative to the cease and desist order is the advertisement substantiation program. Established by the FTC regulation in 1971, it requires:

> All advertisers to submit, on demand, documentation, to support their claims regarding the safety, performance, efficacy, quality, or comparative price of the product.[11]

Failure to provide substantiation, or the provision of inadequate substantiation is considered a violation. This was the Commission's first attempt to provide a pre-facto solution to the problem. Their resolution was further developed a year later in the *Charles Pfizer & Co.* case when the Commission promulgated the reasonable basis standard as a test of substantiation. The court found that since there were no controlled scientific studies testing the validity of product claims (in this case, the aerosol anesthetic, UNBURN) the manufacturers should bear the economic risk that the product might not perform as advertised, in the absence of prior reasonable basis.[12] Without relevant assurances, the court said, a consumer would be incapable of making a rational consumption decision.

There is some indication that the advertisement substantiation program may not achieve its goal. So far, two-thirds of the data submitted is either questionable or too technical to understand. The cold remedy companies sought a delay of one year, figuring that the Commission would not attempt to investigate year-old commercials.[13]

Another criticism has been that the public, for whom the program was designed, is ignoring the submitted reports. There has, however, been considerable interest expressed by journalists, academicians, and public interest groups.[14]

PSYCHOLOGICAL ADVERTISING

The Commission has not, however, taken any definitive steps against advertisements which play upon our psyches. Yet there may be some evidence that the FTC is beginning to recognize advertisements in this latter category as being potentially deceptive.[15]

While little research has been done to determine the effects of such advertising, recent research by Richard Harris of Kansas State University confirms that people do not discriminate between what is directly stated and what is implied. He gives several examples of ways in which consumers are misled by linguistic manipulation:

> The use of hedge words that weaken the statement, such as "knock-out capsules may relieve tension."
>
> Using comparison adjectives that give no comparison, such as "Chore gives you whiter wash." The statement is undeniably true because it could be completed with any phrase, such as, "than washing with coal dust."
>
> Inadequate or incomplete reporting of survey or test results.
>
> Using a negative question, which implies an affirmative answer: "Isn't quality the most important thing to consider in buying aspirin?" The answer might very well be no, but the assumption is yes.
>
> The use of expressions such as "hospital-tested" or "doctor-tested" that give little information but lend an air of scientific respectability.[16]

It should be noted in reference to this study that the FTC, which regulates advertising on radio and television, has not defined a clear legal status for implied claims. "What constitutes deceptive advertising is complex, and though the intent to deceive is clearly prohibited, it is difficult to substantiate."[17]

THE FEDERAL COMMUNICATION COMMISSION

The area of false, misleading, and deceptive advertising and its regulation has provided a profound challenge to both the Federal Communication Commission and the Federal Trade Commission. These two agencies have established a working liaison to handle abuses of advertising, but the precise lines of authority and responsibility have not been fully clarified.[18]

It is generally the policy of the FCC to 1) avoid content review of alleged deceptive advertising; 2) to refer all complaints on the subject to the FTC;[19] and 3) to act only in clear, flagrant cases (*Consumers Association of District of Columbia* v. *CBS and WTOP-TV*, 32 FCC 2d 405 (1971)).

However, the broadcaster does have a continuing obligation to "take reasonable steps to satisfy himself as to the reliability and reputation of prospective advertisers" (*Neckritz and Ordower* v. *KGO-TV, KRON-TV, KPIX, KNBC, and KNXT*, 29 FCC 2d 813 (1971)).

Where the licensee is unfamiliar with the advertiser or his product, he may either contact the local Better Business Bureau or other similar organizations, or he may request a statement or documentation of product claims from the advertising agency's counsel.

NATIONAL ASSOCIATION OF BROADCASTER'S CODES

Since 1937 commercial broadcasters have voluntarily devised general standards of practice for evaluating programming and advertising content. To that end the effort toward self-regulation has become increasingly sophisticated as the issues confronting broadcasters have become more complex. The industry is now served by the NAB Radio Code and Television Code.[20]

One function of the Code Authority is to assist subscribing stations in the review of commercials for Code compliance. Action results from inquiry or complaint of station managers, advertisers, advertising agencies, or the public. In addition, a few categories of advertising, including children's toy commercials, are subject to a Code "pre-clearance". The Code has a built-in appeal process whereby staff rulings may be reviewed, upon request, by the appropriate Code Board committees and, ultimately, by the Code Boards themselves.[21]

CONCLUSION

In light of the wide range of laws, rules, and regulations enforced by the FTC and the FCC, as well as the code of ethics which is guided by the National Association of Broadcasters, it is difficult to see what more could reasonably be done to further control false and deceptive advertising.

Puffery in advertising and selling has been highly criticized,[22] yet it is difficult to distinguish between puffery and deceptive advertising. One of the best known critics of puffery in advertising and selling, Ivan L. Preston of The University of Wisconsin at Madison, himself refers to this form of advertising and selling as "the purest baloney,"[23] an offense hardly worth curtailing.

In fairness to Preston, however, it should be noted that the intent of his statement is probably to the effect that puffery is worthless, yet should be controlled. Preston has made probably the most thorough legal study of this subject. His research is rigorous and his analysis is sound.

An equally energetic empirical study on the effectiveness of puffery has been conducted by Herbert Rotfeld. Some of his work is discussed and summarized in the third section of this chapter.[24] This work should be helpful in determining whether there is any relationship between puffery and the Least Reasonable Man Standard, and in determining whether puffery in advertising has any effect on anyone, regardless of intelligence or education. Several related studies have been done on this subject as well.[25]

In this regard it might also be useful to consider the "Final and Proposed Guides Concerning Use of Endorsements and Testimonials in Advertising."[26] When puffery is involved in the use of advertising, whether in the form of endorsements or other more common forms, it is important to know whether such methods have any tangible effect upon the buying patterns of consumers. If empirical studies, such as those cited above, demonstrate that such advertising methods do have a substantial impact upon the consumer, it is likely that the FTC will take action to curtail such abuse. If such action involves an attempt to accommodate the Least Reasonable Man Standard, however, it is quite possible that the court may strike down the respective FTC orders for in most areas of the law the court rests its judgment on the basis of how the reasonable person is likely to react under a given set of circumstances.

The merits of such a legal position were reinforced at least in part by the conclusions drawn, and by the empirical data upon which the conclusions are based, in the PhD dissertation of Herbert J. Rotfeld.[27] Here the investigator found that there is no way you can determine by looking at what an advertisement says what people will believe on the basis of viewing it.

Rotfeld also found that with puffery it is assumed that even if the claims are communicated, they cannot possess a tendency or capacity to deceive since "no one would rely on its patently exaggerated claims. . . . To puff is to blow up, exaggerate, over-state or state superlatives concerning matters of subjective judgement and opinion of taste, beauty, pleasure, popularity, durability and similar qualities."[28]

It is suggested, furthermore, that in practice, a determination of puffery is made by looking at what the advertisement says literally. Based on certain legal and historical assumptions concerning how consumers will interpret and/or rely on literal advertising content that may be labelled as puffery, it is acceptable on the assumption that it is so exaggerated that it is patently unbelievable. Logically, if the claim is unbelievable, it cannot be deceptive.[29]

The Federal Communication Commission is, nevertheless, expanding its consumer protection staff in an effort to strengthen its ability to evaluate both puffery and deceptive advertising in the electronic media. The question remains, however, whether this Commission will expand its role in the control and regulation of the advertising media.

One area in which the regulation of advertising and "puffery" might be expanded and encouraged is that of children's advertising. For example, the Federal Trade Commission has been urged by President Jimmy Carter's consumer adviser and a private Washington-based consumer group for a federal investigation of advertising for Total breakfast cereal. The Center for Science in the Public Interest (CPSI) asked the FTC to investigate Total's television commercials that it said simply the General Mills cereal is "16 times as nutritious as other cereals." Michael Jacobson, CSPI executive director, claimed that: Wheaties, another General Mills cereal, is nearly identical to Total, except that it is fortified with smaller amounts of vitamins and minerals."[30]

On February 28, 1978 the FTC decided to hold public hearings on whether to order a curtailment of television advertisements directed at children. The commission ordered the hearings because of its staff's concern that the ads might lead to poor nutrition and dental cavities. The staff, in a proposal made public the previous week, recommended a ban on all advertisements directed at very young children.

In this action it was acknowledged that millions of advertising dollars are at stake. The Television Bureau of Advertising said, for example, that 1977 expenditures for confections and soft drinks, two groups most likely to be seriously affected by any FTC action, were $487 million.[31]

Washington United States District Court Judge Gerhard A. Gesell set for hearing on October 30, 1978, the case in which five advertising and industry groups were seeking the disqualification of FTC Chairman Michael Pertschuk from the children's advertising proceeding.[32] Soon thereafter the Association of National Advertisers, American Association of Advertising Agencies and American Advertising Federation filed in the FTC inquiry into children's advertising a 64-page document. On November 27, 1978 it noted that advertising to children was not "an insidious, corrosive force preying on young innocents," but "a productive and constructive enterprise which is of genuine benefit to children themselves, their families and society at large."[33]

Other countries appear to have curtailed children's advertising more than has the United States. For example, cartoon characters like Tony the Tiger, created specifically to promote products like Sugar Frosted Flakes, have been banned from Canadian television shows for youngsters.[34] Throughout Europe, furthermore, there are various advertising restrictions on how children can be portrayed in ads as well as limits on the nature of advertisers' appeals and even on the kinds of television programming which can carry ads oriented to children.[35]

Perhaps the United States is more hesitant to engage in such restrictive measures as a result of empirical studies as well as industrial pressure. For example, Dr. Seymour Banks, vice-president in charge of Media Research, Leo Burnett U.S.A., Chicago, found that "a considerable body of methodologically acceptable research provides no empirical substantiation of the charges of broad negative social effects arising from advertising to children."[36]

Likewise, in the view of others: "It's highly debatable whether commercials per se harm children. Take high-sugar food. The chief problem comes when parents allow themselves to be pressured into buying too many unhealthful goodies. Parental common sense and fortitude remain the best protection for children."[37]

Further study on this subject is made available by Gerald Thain in an article published in the *Boston University Law Review*.[38]

In the meantime the FCC will in all probability continue deferring most cases of false and deceptive advertising to the FTC: "We therefore normally have not made, and do not intend to make, judgments whether particular broadcast advertisements are false and misleading. While we may indeed act in a clear, flagrant case, we shall continue our practice of generally deferring on these matters to the FTC." (*Consumers Association of D.C. v. CBS and WTOP-TV,* 32 FCC 2d 400, 405 (1971).)

NOTES

[1] Gerald J. Thain, "Preface," Ivan L. Preston, *The Great American Blow-Up* (Madison: The University of Wisconsin Press, 1975), p. xii.
[2] 15 U.S. Code 45, Sect. 5 (a) 1 (1970).
[3] Davis, "False Advertising and The Federal Trade Commission," 25 *Baylor LR* (1973), 650–659.
[4] "Guides Against Deceptive Pricing," (Washington, D.C.: The Federal Trade Commission, 1964).
[5] William D. Smith, *New York Times* (September 7, 1976), p. 52.
[6] *Legal Guide to FCC Broadcast Regulations and Policies* (Washington, D.C.: National Association of Broadcasters, 1977), pp. iv–1.
[7] Gerald Thain, "Advertising Regulation and the Contemporary FTC Approach," *Fordham Urban LJ* (Spring 1973), p. 353.

[8] Thain, *Op. Cit.*, p. 352.
[9] Rex Davis, "False Advertising: The Expanding Presence of the FTC," 25 *Baylor LR* (1973), 650–659.
[10] Ibid.
[11] Willard F. Meueller, "Advertising, Monopoly and the FTC's Breakfast Cereal Case: An Attack on Advertising?" 6 *Antitrust Law and Economics Law Review* (1973), 73–82.
[12] "The Pfizer Reasonable Basis Test—A Fast Relief for Consumers but a Headache for Advertisers," *Duke LJ* (1973), p. 563.
[13] Ibid.
[14] Ibid.
[15] "Psychological Advertising: A New Area of FTC Regulation," *Wisconsin LR* (1972), p. 1097.
[16] Sherida Bush, "The Art of Implying More Than You Say," 10 *Psychology Today* (1977), pp. 36.
[17] Ibid, p. 90.
[18] *Legal Guide to FCC Broadcast Regulations and Policies,* ibid.
[19] Ibid.
[20] Ibid, p. iv-2.
[21] Ibid.
[22] Preston, *The Great American Blow-Up, op. cit.*
[23] *Ibid*, p. 3.
[24] Also see the following studies which have been done by Herbert Rotfeld: "Advertising and Product Quality: Are Heavily Advertised Products Better?" *Journal of Consumer Affairs*, vol. 10 (summer 1976), pp. 33–47 (with Kim B. Rotzoll); "Toward an Associative Model of Advertising Creativity: The Relationship of Associative Ability, Attitude, and Creative Ability," *Journal of Advertising*, vol. 5 (Fall 1976), pp. 24–29 (with Leonard N. Reid); "Advertiser Supplied Message Research: Extending the Advertising Substantiation Program," *Journal of Consumer Affairs*, vol. 11 (Summer 1977), pp. 128–134 (with Leonard N. Ried).
[25] See for example, Isabella C. M. Cummingham and William H. Cunningham, "Standards for Advertising Regulation," *Journal of Marketing*, vol. 41 (Oct. 1977), pp. 92–97; Terence A. Shimp, "The Misleading Potential of Incomplete Comparison Advertising," *Journal of Advertising Research* (1977–78); E. John Kottman, "Toward an Understanding of Truth in Advertising," *Journalism Quarterly*, vol. 47 (Spring 1970), pp. 81–86).
[26] 39,038 *Trade Regulation Reporter* (Chicago: Commerce Clearing House, Inc., 1977).
[27] Herbert J. Rotfeld, "Advertising Deception, Consumer Research and Puffery: An Inquiry into Puffery's Power and Potential to Mislead Consumers," PhD dissertation, University of Illinois at Urbana-Champaign, College of Communications (October 1978); see also Herbert J. Rotfeld, "Advertising Puffery as Deception: Evidence and Arguments," Working Paper, Boston College School of Management, Management Institute, 79–50 (Fall 1978).
[28] *Ibid.*, Ch. 4, p. 669, Ch. 14, p. 558; see also Herbert J. Rotfeld and Janette M. Racicot, "Puffery and Advertising Deception—Do Consumers Believe Puffs and Their Implications?" Paper presented to the American Academy of Advertising National Conference in East Lansing, Michigan (April 1979).
[29] *Ibid.*, Ch. 7, p. 136.
[30] "FTC Urged to Probe Breakfast Cereal Ads," *Boston Evening Globe* (October 16, 1978), p. 5.
[31] "Ban on Children's TV Ads Weighed," *New York Times* (March 1, 1978), p. C26.
[32] "FTC Entangled in Courtroom," *Broadcasting* (October 30, 1978), p. 40.
[33] "Three Industry Groups are Unequivocal in Support of Children's Ads," *Broadcasting* (November 27, 1978), p. 21.
[34] Robert A. McLean, "Chasing Sugar off TV North of the Border," *Boston Globe* (February 15, 1978), p. 24.
[35] "Kid Ad Restrictions in Europe Tighter Than U.S.," *Advertising Age* (February 27, 1978), p. 93.
[36] "Banks Says His Kids TV Ad Research Summary was Different Than What Was Reported by Cohen," *Advertising Age* (October 24, 1977), p. 92.
[37] *Milwaukee Journal* (March 31, 1978).
[38] Gerald Thain, "Suffer the Hucksters to Come unto the Little Children? Possible Restrictions of Television Advertising to Children Under Section 5 of the Federal Trade Commission Act," 56 *Boston University Law Review* 651 (1976).

Section 2

Deceptive Business Practices: State Regulations

*Daniel M. Rohrer**

INTRODUCTION

The power to regulate advertising and promotional practices for purposes of interstate trade is derived from the Federal Trade Commission Act of 1914.[1] This law directs the Federal Trade Commission to prevent persons subject to the act from using "unfair methods of competition in commerce and unfair or deceptive acts or practices in commerce."[2] The phrase, "unfair or deceptive acts or practices in commerce," was amended in 1938 as a result of the Wheeler-Lea Act.[3]

The regulatory power of the Commission may be exercised whenever it "shall have reason to believe" that someone is engaged in practices forbidden by the Act and that a proceeding by the Commission "would be to the interest of the public."[4] This would include either injury to a competitor or injury to consumers themselves.

The FTC has acted against a number of types of false, misleading, or deceptive business practices. For example, use of various labels or tradenames which create the impression that the product advertised is something other than it actually is, has frequently been held to constitute an unfair method of competition or deceptive practice.[5]

Furthermore, doing business under a name which has a tendency to create an erroneous impression as to the nature of the business carried on has been held in some cases to constitute a deceptive practice subject to corrective action by the FTC.[6] And advertising which falsely represents the type of business done or the extent of such business has on occasion been restrained by the FTC.[7]

Misrepresentations as to the going price of articles advertised, and various schemes under which a prospective buyer is induced to believe that he is getting something for nothing, or that he has been specially selected as one to receive a particular article at a greatly reduced price, have been restrained by the FTC as well.[8]

Moreover, the courts have generally upheld FTC action barring use of fictitious testimonials and unauthorized indorsements.[9] And extravagant claims as to the content, makeup, performance, or characteristics of a product have frequently been held sufficiently misleading to merit action by the FTC.[10]

Although state statutes excuse the time-honored custom of "puffing,"[11] such advertising methods have been rejected by federal law where the exaggeration was too extreme.[12] And orders of the FTC restraining advertising claims in regard to the curative value of various preparations and devices have been upheld in a wide variety of cases.[13]

Advertising or labeling which creates an erroneous impression as to the origin of the product advertised has occasionally been found by the FTC to be misleading or deceptive, and cease and desist orders in such cases have been upheld by the courts.[14]

*My thanks to Professor Sanford Fox of Boston College Law School for recommendations and assistance on this section.

260 False and Deceptive Advertising

While the FTC Act makes no specific mention of disparaging remarks about competing products, upon occasion the agency has ruled that such remarks may constitute an unfair method of competition, and its orders to refrain from such activities have been upheld.[15] It has generally been however, that expressions of opinion, as distinguished from statements of fact, may not be made the basis for a cease and desist order of the FTC.[16]

Nevertheless, advertisements, even though technically true, have been held misleading and subject to restraint if they demonstrate a tendency to mislead the casual reader.[17] Yet, while the body of federal regulation concerning false, misleading, and deceptive advertising is far more comprehensive than that embodied in most state statutes, it is also highly restricted in that it must be confined to interstate commerce.

State law, on the other hand, is intended to regulate advertising within the limits of each respective state. Many states have no criminal laws designed to regulate advertising, and several states have repealed such laws recently.[18] Still other states have adopted laws concerning deceptive business practices similar to those proposed by The American Law Institute in its Model Penal Code of 1962.[19] These unacceptable practices include mislabeling or adulterating products; making false or misleading statements in any advertisement addressed to the public, or for the purpose of obtaining property or credit, or for the purpose of promoting the sale of property or securities.[20]

The behavior which will be discussed in this section ". . . involves restraints upon the free operation of business without at the same time denying commitment to a free enterprise system."[21] Here an assumption is being made that "(t)he demarcation of the line between the legitimate, indeed the affirmatively desirable, and the illegitimate in business conduct is continually in flux and subject to wide controversy in the community."[22]

ELEMENTS OF DECEPTION

By state law, the term "deception" has been described in regard to five elements:

1. The first element involves ". . . creating or reinforcing a false impression, including false impressions of fact, law, value, or intention or other state of mind that the actor does not believe to be true."[23] The term "creation," as employed in this section, ". . . contemplates both verbal misrepresentation and conduct having that effect. Whether mere conduct, as a general matter, will suffice to support a false pretense conviction under present law in unclear, although there is authority indicating that an affirmative misrepresentation is necessary."[24]

By imposing liability for a false representation as to a state of mind, Arkansas state law ". . . precludes a successful prosecution grounded on evidence merely showing a default with respect to promised future action. The state must show that the actor did not intend at the time the promise was made to carry it out."[25] "Finally, it should be observed that the actor must believe his representation to be false or have no belief either way if his conduct is to fall within the provision. An honest but unreasonable belief in the truth of a false representation does not create liability."[26]

In other words, "(d)eception as to a person's intention to perform a promise shall not be inferred solely from the fact that he did not subsequently perform the promise. Deception does not include falsity as to matters having no pecuniary significance or puffing by statements unlikely to deceive ordinary persons in the group addressed."[27] Thus, the latter statement, ". . . in addition to precluding any inferences of deception based solely on the failure to perform a promise, excludes from the subsection's coverage those types of misleading statements that are ordinarily tolerated in the context of commercial dealings. Exaggerating the qualities of one's goods or services is to a certain extent expected by the public and should not deceive the ordinary person. Statements as to matters without pecuniary significance are likewise beyond the statute's ambit."[28] For example, a false representation that a certain person patronized a particular hotel was held not to have defrauded a guest who stayed at the hotel as a result of the representation. (*Morgan* v. *State*, 42 Ark. 131 (1883).)

It should be noted that: "Criminal intent is not as easily inferred from a taking executed through a market transaction, as it is from a taking by force."[29] In affirming a mail fraud conviction, the difficulty in establishing fraudulent intent has been described in the following way:

> Fraudulent intent, as a mental element of crime, . . . is too often difficult to prove by direct and convincing evidence. In many cases it must be inferred from a series of seemingly isolated acts and instances which have been rather aptly designated as badges of fraud. When these are sufficiently numerous they may in their totality properly justify an inference of a fraudulent intent; and this is true even though each act or instance, standing by itself, may seem rather unimportant. (*Aiken* v. *United States*, 108 F.2d 182 (CA4, 1939).)

Furthermore, in order to demonstrate intent, it is not only necessary to establish some kind of cumulative effect in most instances, but "(u)nlike most street crimes, economic offenses require proof of the involvement and intent of 'higher-up,' " if the criminal sanction is not to be confined to hirelings. This will often necessitate obtaining the tesimony of those less culpable, and corroboration of their testimony.[30] This challenge was stated well in the following words:

> The trial judge in his charge recognized that there was no general rule in law which makes a principal criminally responsible for the *unauthorized* acts of his agents, employees, or even his salesmen, and very emphatically told the jury that it "would have to be convinced beyond a reasonable doubt that the proof shows that the defendant himself dominated and controlled his salesmen, and also knew and was participating in the scheme to defraud or sell (the securities) by means of fraudulent misstatements or statements". . . . (*United States* v. *Hayutin*, 398 F.2d 944 (CA2, 1968).)

2. The second element of the term "deception" involves ". . . preventing another from acquiring information which would affect his judgment of a transaction."[31] This aspect of deception ". . . applies only if a party to a transaction actively hinders the discovery of facts that might influence the willingness of the other party to enter the transaction."[32] As is the case under the first element, ". . . there is no affirmative duty to disclose such facts."[33]

3. The third element of the term "deception" entails ". . . failing to correct a false impression that the actor knows to be false and a) that he created or reinforced, or b) that he knows to be influencing another to whom he stands in a fiduciary or confidential relationship."[34] This element of deception ". . . describes two situations in which the actor is under an affirmative duty to correct misinformation. The actor must be aware that the other party to the transactions is laboring under a false impression and must either be partially responsible for that false impression or stand in a fiduciary or confidential relationship to the other party. Imposing liability in the first situation is probably redundant since the actor who creates or reinforces a false impression has already engaged in 'deception' under (the first element). Imposing criminal liability for failure to disclose facts to one

with whom the actor has a confidential or fiduciary relationship probably departs from existing law although it is clear that such conduct will suffice to establish fraud in a civil case."[35]

4. The fourth element of deception involves ". . . failing to disclose a lien, adverse claim, or other legal impediment to the enjoyment of property which the actor transfers or encumbers in consideration for the property or service obtained, or in order to continue to deprive another of his property, whether such impediment is or is not valid, or is or is not a matter of official record."[36]

Under this condition, "(r)einforcement contemplates an affirmative contribution to the false impression. Mere failure to correct a false impression is 'deception" only under the circumstances set out in (elements 3 and 4)."[37]

Furthermore, it remains established that: "A false representation as an inducement to pay money that something thereafter was to be or was not to be done is not a false pretense. It is well settled that in this state and elsewhere that the false pretense relied upon to constitute an offense under the statute must relate to a past event, or to some present existing fact, and not to something to happen in the future." (*Conner* v. *State*, 137 Ark. 123 at 126, 206 SW 747 at 748 (1918).)

Consequently, element 4 of the term deception ". . . imposes on the seller of property an affirmative duty to disclose liens or other legal impediments to the purchaser. Under current law, the seller must expressly represent that the property is free of other claims before he is guilty of obtaining property by false pretense; the mere failure to disclose liens or legal impediments are subject at most to misdemeanor liability under (Arkansas state law)."[38]

It might be concluded, therefore, that the seller is under no affirmative obligation to reveal future encumbrances upon the land, even if they are known certainly, such as required sewage installation or road pavement. Moreover, the Supreme Court has held that the current false pretense statute is not violated if the encumbrances are in fact invalid since the seller's representations were true. (*State* v. *Asher*, 50 Ark. 427, 8 SW 177 (1887); *Fox* v. *State*, 102 Ark. 451, 145 SW 228 (1912).)

5. The fifth element of deception involves ". . . employing any other scheme to defraud, under Arkansas state law. This condition would include a wide variety of offenses, including many of those specified in the Model Penal Code of 1962. And in some states this element would also include "chain distributor schemes." While this deceptive business practice constitutes a civil offense in a great many states, it is also a criminal offense in a few states, such as Montana and Florida.[39]

The term "chain distributor scheme" has been defined to mean ". . . a sales device whereby a person, under a condition that he make an investment, is granted a license or right to recruit for consideration one or more additional persons who are also granted such license or right upon condition of making an investment, and may further perpetuate the chain of persons who are granted such license or right upon such condition."[40]

STATE LAW AND THE MODEL PENAL CODE

Section 224.7 of the Model Penal Code of 1962 sets forth explicitly seven deceptive business practices, any violation of which constitutes a misdemeanor.[41] Under this Code: "It is an affirmative defense to prosecution . . . if the defendant proves by a preponderance of the evidence that his conduct was not knowingly or recklessly deceptive."[42]

1. According to the first provision of the deceptive business practices section: "A person commits a misdemeanor if in the course of business he . . . uses or possesses for use a false weight or measure, or any other device for falsely determining or recording any quality or quantity."[43] Statutes

in the states of Montana, Maine, South Dakota, and Kentucky all employ language similar to that explicated in the Model Code.[44] Yet many states omit this provision altogether.

A false weight or measure has been defined as ". . . one which does not conform to the standard established by the laws of the United States of America."[45] All states employing this provision in their statutes specify "purposely," "knowingly," or "intentionally" in the language of their respective laws.

2. The second provision of the Model Penal Code stipulates that: "A person commits a misdemeanor if in the course of business he . . . sells, offers, or exposes for sale, or delivers less than the represented quantity of any commodity or service."[46] Statutes in the states of Montana, Maine, and Kentucky have adopted this section of the Code verbatim. Nevertheless, as was the previous case, many states ignore this provision entirely.

3. The third section of the Model Penal Code provides that: "A person commits a misdemeanor if in the course of business he . . . takes or attempts to take more than the represented quantity of any commodity or service when as buyer he furnishes the weight or measure."[47] Again, Montana, Maine, and Kentucky have reflected in their criminal statutes the essence of the Code with respect to this section. Most other states have ignored it as was the case in the previous sections.

4. The fourth section of the Model Penal Code becomes more complicated, and more philosophical. Here a person commits a misdemeanor if in the course of business he ". . . sells, offers, or exposes for sale adulterated or mislabeled commodities. 'Adulterated' means varying from the standard of composition or quality prescribed by or pursuant to any statute providing criminal penalties for such variance, or set by established commercial usage. 'Mislabeled' means varying from the standard of truth or disclosure in labeling prescribed by or pursuant to any statute providing criminal penalties for such variance, or set by established commercial usage."[48]

Again, the states of Maine, Montana, Kentucky, and South Dakota demonstrate the closest semblance of the Model Penal Code with regard to laws prohibiting deceptive business practices. The Maine statute defines "adulterated" and "mislabeled" in precisely the same way as the Model Penal Code.[49] Montana law defines "adulterated" as ". . . varying from the standard of composition or quality prescribed by statute or lawfully promulgated administrative regulation, or if none, as set by established commercial usage."[50]

Furthermore, according to Montana law, "mislabeled" means, ". . . varying from the standard of truth or disclosure in labeling prescribed by statute or lawfully promulgated administrative regulation, or if none, as set by established commercial usage; or . . . represented as being another person's produce, though otherwise labeled accurately as to quality and quantity."[51]

Combining provisions 1–4 of the Model Penal Code along with both enforcement and penalty mechanisms, South Dakota criminal law has provided that: "Any person engaged in the production, manufacture, selling, or distribution of any metallic commodity in general use, who intentionally and for the purpose of deceiving any customer or purchaser, misbrands or misrepresents the kind, gauge, analysis, weight, quantity, or quality of the metallic commodity offered for sale, or if it be an imitation, sells or offers it for sale under the distinctive name of another article, shall be deemed guilty of a misdemeanor, and if the violator is a corporation its charter shall be forfeited upon action commenced by the attorney general upon complaint of any person aggrieved, and the penalties and remedies herein provided shall be cumulative to any others prescribed by statute."[52]

5. Section 5 of the Model Penal Code makes a misdemeanor ". . . a false or misleading statement in any advertisement addressed to the public or to a substantial segment thereof for the purpose

of promoting the purchase or sale of property or services."[53] Again, three state laws have responded to the American Law Institute recommendations in regard to this need. They are Maine, Montana, and Kentucky.

6. Making a false or misleading written statement for the purpose of obtaining property or credit is another limitation placed upon acceptable business practices as a result of the Model Penal Code.[54] Such offenses have been legislated against in terms of "bait advertising" in Kentucky,[55] and "wholesale" and "below cost sale" in Florida.[56]

There is a rebuttable presumption that the person named in or obtaining the benefits of any misleading advertisement or any such sale is responsible for such misleading advertisement or unlawful sale, according to Florida law.[57] Furthermore, announcing that a sale or an offer is being made by a private party rather than a business firm, corporation, or association, when such statement is not true is in violation of Arkansas criminal law.[58] Such a claim is also in violation of Oklahoma law if it is intended to affect the market price of any kind of property.[59] Finally, in terms of misnaming the actual seller, Utah law stipulates that: "It is unlawful for any person, whether acting on his own behalf or on behalf of another, who is engaged in the business of buying and selling or dealing in property, real or personal, or who is engaged in the business of performing or furnishing service of any kind to the public, to advertise, call attention to, or give publicity to any sale to the public of any such property or any such service, thereby representing that such sale is being made or service furnished by a person not in fact making such sales or furnishing such service."[60]

Utah law further qualifies the unauthorized use of the name or picture of an individual for purposes of promotion. In the following words it provides that: "Any person who uses for advertising purposes or for purposes of trade, or upon any postal card, the name, portrait, or picture of any person, if such person is living, without first having obtained the written consent of such person, or, if a minor, of his parent or guardian, or, if such person is dead, without the written consent of his heirs or personal representatives, is guilty of a misdemeanor."[61]

The state of Utah has legislated one of the most thorough provisions adopting the fifth and sixth parts of the Code. It has placed a comprehensive and specific ban upon falsely representing sales to be made or service furnished:

> Every person, whether acting on his own behalf or on behalf of another, who, with intent to sell or in any way dispose of real or personal property, choses in action, merchandise, service, or anything of any nature whatsoever offered by such person, directly or indirectly, to the public for sale, use or distribution, or with intent to increase the consumption thereof, or to induce any member of the public to enter into any obligation relating thereto, or to acquire title thereto, or any interest therein, publishes, disseminates, circulates, or causes to be published, disseminated or circulated, or who in any manner places, or causes to be placed, before the public in this state, by any newspaper, magazine, book, pamphlet, circular, letter, handbill, placard, poster, or other publication, or by any billboard, sign, card, label, or window sign, showcase or window display, or by any other advertising device, or by public outcry or proclamation, or by telephone or radio, or in any other manner whatever, an advertisement regarding such property or service so offered to the public, which advertisement shall contain any statement, representation or assertion concerning such property or service, or concerning any circumstance or matter of fact connected in any way, directly or indirectly, with the proposed sale, performance or disposition thereof, which statement, representation or assertion is false in any respect, or which is deceptive or misleading, and which is known, or by the exercise of reasonable care could be known to be false, deceptive,

or misleading, to the person publishing, disseminating, circulating, or placing before the public such advertisement, is guilty of a misdemeanor.[62]

Still another element of provision five and six of the Model Penal Code is the intent not to sell merchandise offered or advertised. Kentucky has adopted one of the most descriptive clauses prohibiting this offense. Entitled "bait advertising," this law provides that: "A person is guilty of bait advertising when in any manner, including advertising or other means of communication, he offers to the public or a substantial number of persons property or services as part of a scheme or plan with the intent not to sell or provide the advertised property or services: a) at the price at which he offered them; or b) in a quantity sufficient to meet the reasonably expected public demand, unless the quantity is specifically stated in the advertisement; or c) at all."[63]

Similar statutes have been adopted in the states of Maine, Florida, and South Dakota.[64] Florida has further specified a presumption of violation in the following terms: "The failure to sell any article or a class of articles advertised, or the refusal to sell at the price at which it was advertised to be available for purchase, shall create a rebuttable presumption of an intent to violate this section."[65]

Finally, advertising false former or comparative prices has been banned in at least one criminal statute. Florida law states this restriction in the following way: "No price shall be advertised as a former or comparative price of the thing advertised unless the alleged former price was the prevailing price for not less than thirty consecutive days within the four months next immediately preceding the date of the advertisement, or unless the date when the alleged former price did prevail is clearly and conspicuously stated in the advertisement, and on any price listing otherwise used, which must be available to customers and police officers."[66]

7. The seventh and final provision of the Model Penal Code states that: "A person commits a misdemeanor if in the course of business he . . . makes a false or misleading written statement for the purpose of promoting the sale of securities, or omits information required by law to be disclosed in written documents relating to securities."[67] States having adopted this provision include Arkansas, Florida, South Dakota, and Washington.[68]

CONCLUSION

It has been noted in both the Model Penal Code and in state statute that intent with regard to publicity for purposes of advertising or promoting trade, whether it be a product, commodity, or service, must occur in either a knowingly or recklessly deceptive manner in order for there to be a finding of fault. If nonexistent or unavailable products or services are advertised, there is a rebuttable presumption of guilt in at least one state. A deceptive or fraudulent business practice may range anywhere from misleading rhetoric to scratching out the serial number of an automobile on sale.

Arnold H. Loewy, Professor of Law at the University of North Carolina, holds the view that in the case of adulterated food there is liability without fault:

(C)ulpability, though normally present, is difficult to prove. For example, a defendant who sells adulterated food is usually careless, but to prove negligence in a particular case is difficult. There are instances . . . where an honest and reasonable mistake will not be available as a defense. The most obvious are strict liability crimes. Since no intent is required in the first place (e.g., for selling adulterated foods . . .), obviously an honest and reasonable mistake will not negate *mens rea*.[69]

Consequently legislatures have the power to dispense entirely with the requirement of a criminal state of mind and to punish particular acts without regard to the mental attitude of the doer. Nevertheless this power is limited to so-called "public welfare offenses," and it does not extend to common law crimes. Thus nearly all statutory "public welfare offenses," such as the sale of adulterated foodstuffs or mislabeled goods, do not require *mens rea* or criminal intent, and as a result mistake of fact is no defense (*People* v. *Wilson,* 106 Colo. 437, 106 Pac.2d 352 (1940), 115 ALR 1230).

Intent with regard to deception for civil action in tort is not the same, however. Here the defendant is to be held liable only if he knows that he is not speaking the truth (see *Irvine* v. *Gibson,* 117 Ky. 306, 77 SW 1106 (1904); *Chaddock* v. *Chaddock,* 130 Misc. 900, 226 N.Y.S. 152 (1927); *Beaubeauf* v. *Reed,* 4 La. App. 344 (1926).

Statutes in the states of Montana, Kentucky, and Maine reproduce the Model Penal Code almost verbatim in regard to the first four provisions; whereas several other states emphasize the final three provisions as embodied in their laws. In all cases, action to restrain and prevent false, misleading, and deceptive advertising in violation of state law is undertaken by the state attorney general or the prosecuting attorneys of the several counties.[70]

While penalties for such offenses range from a fine in the amount of $500 to imprisonment in the county jail for a term of ninety days to six months, it should be observed that ". . . strong ideological differences separate the proponents and opponents of economic regulation. Judgments about the effect of penal sanctions in achieving compliance tend to turn upon judgments about the merits of the substantive regulation. Liberally oriented social scientists, otherwise critical of the case made for the deterrent and vindicatory uses of punishing of ordinary offenders, may be found supporting stern penal enforcement against economic violators."[71]

In this context, Sutherland and Cressey have pointed out that: "This change in the economic system from free competition to private collectivism has been produced largely by the efforts of businessmen. Although they have not acted en masse with a definite intention of undermining the traditional American institutions, their behavior has actually produced this result."[72] It should be concluded, nevertheless, that there is ". . . a real difference between prosecuting one who takes money by fraud and one who takes it at the point of a gun, notwithstanding the argument that it is conceptually difficult to distinguish between the two cases. Criminal intent is not as easily inferred from a taking executed through a market transaction, as it is from a taking by force."[73]

Deceptive business practices have been known to involve longer prison sentences and larger fines, however. For example, in Montana the penalty for involvement in promoting a chain distributor scheme, a felony crime, is, upon conviction, imprisonment in the state prison for a period not to exceed one year, or punishment by a fine not to exceed one thousand dollars, or both such fine and imprisonment. Any person convicted of a second offense under this law shall be imprisoned in the state prison for a period not to exceed five years or punished by a fine not to exceed five thousand dollars or both such fine and imprisonment.[74]

In lieu of punishment, however, states have also been known to accept an assurance of discontinuance of unlawful business practices.[75] If such is the case after the commencement of any action by a prosecuting attorney, the attorney general may not accept an assurance of discontinuance without the consent of the prosecuting attorney.[76]

Two additional exemptions for violation of deceptive business practices laws should be mentioned as well. They involve the media and insurance companies. In the states of Arkansas, Maine, South Dakota, Florida, and Washington, the fact of the publishing or printing of deceptive advertising does not constitute prima facie evidence of actual knowledge of falsity. Unless the electronic or print media are aware of such falsity, they are exempt from prosecution and/or conviction for the violation of any deceptive business practice based upon the laws of the respective states.

Where advertising in connection with the sale of insurance is regulated under the insurance laws of the state, any offense is exempt from prosecution and/or conviction as a violation of any deceptive business practice law.[77] In the states where such deceptive business practice laws exist, the traditional "let the consumer beware" philosophy may no longer hold true, and some care should be taken as to the accuracy of advertising and promotional claims.

NOTES

[1] 15 U.S.C. Section 41 *et seq.*
[2] 15 U.S.C. Section 45(a)(6).
[3] 52 Stat. Ill. Ch. 49.
[4] 15 U.S.C. Section 45.
[5] "What Constitutes False, Misleading, or Deceptive Advertising or Promotional Practices Subject to Action by Federal Trade Commission," 65 *ALR* 2d 225 at 253 (1959).
[6] Id. at 263.
[7] Id. at 268.
[8] Id. at 270.
[9] Id. at 276.
[10] Id. at 278.
[11] Explicitly acknowledging this fact is *Ark. Crim. Code,* Ann. Ed., Title 41, Ch. 22, Section 41–2201, 154, 157.
[12] Op. cit., 65 *ALR* 2d 225 at 283.
[13] Id at 285.
[14] Id at 297.
[15] Id. at 299.
[16] Id. at 301–302.
[17] Id. at 303.
[18] 5–A *NH Rev. Stat. Ann.,* Ch. 580, Sections 1–30, 79–85; *Burns Ind. Stat. Ann.,* Cum. Pocket Supp, Ch. 5, Section 35–17–5–13 (10–3040), Section 35–17–5–10 (10–3037); 39–41; 4 Ind. Code, Cum. Pocket Supp., Ch. 31, Section 18–3112, 82.
[19] Model Penal Code, Section 224.7, 179–180.
[20] Id.
[21] Sanford H. Kadish, "Some Observations on the Use of Criminal Sanctions in Enforcing Economic Regulations," 30 U Chgo. LR 423 at 435–440 (1963), in Sanford H. Kadish and Monrad G. Paulsen, *Crim. Law and Its Proceeses,* 3 (Boston: Little, Brown, 1975), p. 57.
[22] Id.
[23] *Ark. Crim Code,* op. cit. at 154.
[24] Id. at 156. See *McCorkle* v. *State,* 170 Ark. 105, 278 SW 965 (1926).
[25] Id.
[26] Id. at 157.
[27] Id. at 154.
[28] Id. at 157.
[29] Kadish, op. cit., at 60. See *Holland* v. *United States,* 348 U.S. 121 at 139–140 (1954); *United States* v. *Woodner,* 317 F.2d 649 at 651 (CA2, 1963).
[30] Id.
[31] *Ark. Crim. Code,* op. cit., at 154.
[32] Id. at 156.
[33] Id.
[34] Id. at 154.
[35] Id. at 156. See *Johnson* v. *Johnson,* 237 Ark. 311, 372 SW 2d 598 (1963).
[36] Id. at 154.
[37] Id. at 156.

[38] Id. at 154.
[39] *Mon. Crim. Code of 1973,* Title 94, Ch. 6, Part 3, Section 94–6–308.1, 98–99; 22 *Fl. Stat. Ann.,* Title XLIV, Section 817.416, 283–284.
[40] *Mon. Crim. Code,* id. at 98.
[41] Model Penal Code, op. cit.
[42] Id. at 180.
[43] Id.
[44] *Mon. Crim. Code of 1973,* op. cit. at 97; 8 *Rev. Codes of Mon. Ann.,* Ch. 19, Section 94–1901, 115; Ma. Rev. Stat. Ann., Title 17–18, Ch. 37, Section 901, 157; *So. Dak. Cod. Laws Rev.,* Title 22, Ch. 22, Section 22–41–10, 108; 16 *Ky. Rev. Stat. Ann.,* Ch. 516, Section 517.010, 571.
[45] 8 *Rev. Codes of Mon. Ann.,* id. at 115.
[46] Model Penal Code, op. cit.
[47] Id.
[48] Id.
[49] *Ma. Rev. Stat. Ann.,* op. cit. at 158.
[50] *Mon. Crim. Code of 1973,* op. cit. at 98.
[51] Id.
[52] 8 *So. Dak. Compiled Laws Ann.,* op. cit., 181–182.
[53] Model Penal Code, op. cit.
[54] Id.
[55] *Ky. Rev. Stat. Ann.,* op. cit. at 573.
[56] 22 *Fl. Stat. Ann.,* op. cit., at 521–522.
[57] Id.
[58] *Ark. Crim. Code,* Ann. Ed., Ch. 23, Section 41–2365, 180.
[59] 21 *Okl. Stat. Ann.,* Section 851, Section 1200, 243.
[60] *Utah Code Ann.,* Ch. 4, Section 76–4–2, 254.
[61] Id. at 255.
[62] Id. at 253.
[63] 16 *Ky. Rev. Stat. Ann.,* op. cit. at 573.
[64] 9 *Ma. Rev. Stat. Ann.,* op. cit., at 199; 22 *Fl. Stat. Ann.,* op. cit. at 524; 8 *So. Dak. Comp. Laws Ann.,* Title 22, Ch. 22 Section 22–41–11, 181.
[65] Id.
[66] Id. at 523.
[67] Model Penal Code, op. cit.
[68] *Ark. Crim. Code Ann.,* op. cit. at 180; 22 *Fl. Stat. Ann.,* op. cit.; 8 *So. Dak. Comp. Laws Ann.,* op. cit. at 180; *Rev. Code of Wash. Ann.,* op. cit. at 27.
[69] Arnold H. Loewy, *Criminal Law* (St. Paul: West, 1975), 121.
[70] See, for example, *Rev. Code of Wash. Ann.,* op. cit. at 33.
[71] Kadish, op. cit. at 55.
[72] Sutherland and Cressey, *Principles of Criminology,* V (1955), 40–47, in Kadish, Id.
[73] Kadish, id. at 60; see also, *Holland* v. *United States,* op. cit. at 139–140; *United States* v. *Woodner,* op. cit. at 651.
[74] *Mon. Crim. Code of 1973,* op. cit. at 98–99.
[75] See *Rev. Code of Wash. Ann.,* op. cit. at 34.
[76] Id.
[77] See 22 *Fl. Stat. Ann.,* op. cit. at 525.

Section 3

The Law, Consumer Research, and the Question of Puffery

Herbert J. Rotfeld*

A popular college textbook on copyrighting begins its discussion of legal problems by stating that any discussion of legal concerns with product claims would almost necessarily read like a list of prohibitions. A few paragraphs later, though, the author points out that:[1]

> To show that the law is not completely arbitrary, there is another recognized category known as "puffery" or "puffing." Under this heading come the harmless exaggerations that are expressions of opinion rather than claims of some objective quality or characteristic for the product. For example, even the most gullible consumer is considered capable of grappling with the fact that such statements as "the best of its kind," "the most beautiful" or "the finest" might not be literally true.

As such, the broad category of advertising puffery is an area of claims considered not deceptive though not really true. Puffery claims are legally regarded as opinions rather than factual claims, which, though not proved true, are not proved false. The law has permitted such advertised statements on the grounds that they have no precise meaning, and, since no reasonable consumer would seriously rely on them, no one would be deceived. However, some authors feel there exists evidence that consumers do rely on puffery claims as facts, that these people are deceived by such advertising, and that the "puffery exemption" remains as a lone remnant of the tradition of *caveat emptor*.[2]

In his recent book, *The Great American Blow-Up,* Ivan Preston draws the reader through a detailed analysis of history and the law, pointing out what can be seen as a logical inconsistency: while puffery is legally acceptable because it does not influence sales, it is used because it does. In sum, he argues that puffery's special status in the eyes of the law is really an anachronism of the American marketplace, a "throw-back" to earlier attitudes towards business regulation. Preston feels that in today's clime of *caveat venditor,* where the desire is that consumers be able to rely on seller's claims, the advertiser's puffery defense against charges of deceptive advertising should be terminated.[3] Such a view is indirectly supported by former copywriter Carl P. Wrighter's book that seems to express an intuitive belief in the persuasive power of the advertiser's half statements and "weasel words,"[4] as well as Preston's own research in a related area, finding that people may perceive "more" in ads than what is actually stated, possibly looking beyond the content to what they feel the advertiser might have "liked to say."[5] Preston's arguments, though, are basically jurisprudential in nature, based on an analysis of legal history, market practices, Federal Trade Commission (FTC) decisions, and logic. Thus far, there has been virtually no research specifically addressed to questions of what puffery communicates to consumers, asking whether consumers are actually deceived by puffery.

*Assistant Professor of Marketing, Bowling Green State University.

CONSUMER RESEARCH AND ADVERTISING REGULATION

Before conducting any research on questions of puffery's power and potential to deceive consumers, a more basic problem must first be addressed, namely, how to combine the legal and behavioral perspectives so research results can best be included in court decisions. While formulated in terms of advertising and communication concerns, such research revolves around a legal question or issue and must therefore keep the legal perspective in mind.

There exists a growing body of literature which calls for the Federal Trade Commission, the main government body involved with the regulation of advertising claims, to integrate consumer research and behavioral perspectives into its programs and policies of advertising regulation. Some authors have addressed themselves to the broad issue of a basic need for more consumer research inputs in public policy planning,[6] while others have discussed the more specific problems and issues surrounding the use of consumer research as evidence for deception in FTC proceedings.[7] The conventional wisdom in legal and marketing literature is that the FTC tends to scorn consumer research evidence and concentrates on its own intuitive understanding of an advertising message's potential for deception.[8] (In fact, one article presents evidence that marketing researchers may be alienating public policy makers with their general tendency to "attack" the basis for public policy decisions that are felt to have been formulated without aid of research.[9]) The fact is, though, that the Commission's use of "external" research evidence has been increasing in recent years, prompting a recommendation that marketers retain lawyers who are well trained "in interpreting and introducing behavioral data and in contracting for the research needed to produce such data."[10]

It must be pointed out that the mere increased use of external survey evidence does not mean FTC policies and procedures have evolved into academic discussions on possible interpretations of research data. While possibly trying to show a growing awareness of actual marketplace conditions and behaviors, the Commission's orientation remains jurisprudential in nature, utilizing recognizable legal procedures. Researchers cannot demand the FTC adopt their standards and definitions of deception, but rather, they need to understand the regulatory-legal process in order to best formulate research that would aid the FTC's planning and decision making. A researcher lacking knowledge and understanding of the legal process can only attempt (and probably unsuccessfully) to impose his perspective on the Commissioners.[11]

An example of legal perspective can be seen in the logic behind the current FTC and court attitude towards advertising puffery. Legal rules and guides under which puffery is not considered deceptive are, for the most part, addressed to the literal form and content of advertising, making certain assumptions on how consumers will interpret and/or utilize such content. It can be seen that every ad or commercial contains two possible types of claims—fact claims and puffery claims. Fact claims are based on facts and are substantiable, and puffery claims are statements of opinion, and so while not substantiable as true, they cannot be proved false. These two labels are obvious on the face of the ad such that an advertiser, lawyer, or young student of advertising should be able to look at the literal statements of an ad and say, "This is a puffery claim; this other statement is a fact claim." Deception, however, is in the mind of the audience. Any statement or claim is legally referred to as having a tendency to deceive and can be proscribed if it can be seen to communicate, by literal statement or implication, a fact that is not true.

Of course, literally stated falsehoods are easily seen as misleading. The FTC has in recent years also been finding advertising's factual claims implying more and more kinds of potentially deceptive statements to the public, thus increasing regulation of fact claim implied falsehoods having been thoroughly documented elsewhere.[12] It is felt, though, that puffery claims are not deceptive, the legal logic assuming that puffery claims and the facts such claims might imply are not believed nor relied upon by consumers and that such claims do not influence purchase decisions. Admittedly, some weaknesses might be noted in the above mentioned fact-puffery dichotomy of literal advertising claims. There are some "grey areas," such as testimonials or certain demonstrations, which might be labelled as either fact or puffery claims, depending on how they are utilized by the advertiser. For purposes of advertising regulation case decisions, though, the important considerations are in terms of what the ad can be labelled as literally stating—puffery or facts—and what consumers can be seen to take away from the ad. Any case in which there are allegations of deceptive or misleading advertising claims is based on certain knowledge *or assumptions* about consumer perceptions and/or behavior. With puffery, Preston and others are now questioning the validity of current legal assumptions about its potential for misleading consumers. To researchers, there is the problem of how to best conduct research addressing those questions.

When the research addresses a legal issue of question, the procedures utilized should be in a format that can be understood by Commission lawyers and a form oriented to legal procedures and evidence-information needs. With the FTC, as with any business or organization, the "best" research must be aimed toward aiding in making a final decision. However, with public policy research there exists the added constraint that the study and its results must fit existing formal decision making procedures.

In recent years, a few proposals for behavior definitions of deception have appeared in the literature, such as those by Gardner,[13] Armstrong and Russ,[14] and Haefner.[15] There exists a degree of conceptual agreement among these perspectives which, in turn, are somewhat compatable with legal definitions. Marketers and advertisers generally recognize that the important legal inquiry with advertising deception is in terms of the impression the ad makes on consumers,[16] so conceptualizing research in this area involves operationalizing legal perspectives, and not telling lawyers how to redefine their terms. While even law journal articles decry FTC determinations of deception without use of behavioral evidence,[17] one author points out:[18]

> (It) would be more precise to say that the agency has characterized deception quite properly as a behavioral concept but has failed in the methodology it has used to determine existence of deception.

DEFINITIONS OF DECEPTION

As outlined above, both legal and behavioral definitions apparently agree that determinations of advertising deception should consider the impact or impression of the ad on its audience. Simply speaking, when considered from either a legal or marketing perspective, it is a question of comparing what is communicated to consumers with what is factually true and untrue. Such a definition was proposed by Gardner[19] and revised:[20]

> If an advertisement (or advertising campaign) leaves the average consumer within some reasonable market segment with an impression(s) and/or belief(s) different from what would normally be expected if the average consumer within that market segment had reasonable knowledge and that impression(s) and/or belief(s) is factually untrue or potentially misleading, then deception is said to exist.

There are some important elements in Gardner's definition that should be pointed out and expanded upon.

Gardner's definition refers to deception, in part, in terms of the relationship between facts and what the consumer audience believes of an ad's statements. Such a comparison forms a major part of both the aforementioned Armstrong-Russ and Haefner perspectives, and is quite logical in terms of the marketing research literature in this area. It is generally felt that an ad cannot be considered deceptive unless it influences purchases, what is referred to in legal terms as the claims "materiality," and it is therefore seen as important to many that references to deception deal with questions of attitudes and behavioral intentions.

Either directly or indirectly, these operational definitions of deception look to the various models relating attitudes, behavioral intentions, and actual behavior, most notably the concepts and constructs found in the work of Fishbein.[21] Based on such work, it is argued that behavioral intentions and attitudes towards purchase behavior are a function of beliefs about that product and evaluations of those beliefs. From these attitude theories, the various models posit that beyond communication of false claims, they must also be believed, for a change in beliefs is seen as necessary for the ad to alter attitudes, behavior intentions, and eventually, influence purchasers. Thus, deception is seen to occur when a consumer believes a false claim.

Unlike Armstrong-Russ, Gardner does not refer to deception solely in terms of comparing beliefs and false claims, but rather, in terms of "impression(s) *and/or* belief(s)" (emphasis added). This brings up an important point: while what consumers believe is important, it is important to ask what they believe apart from what the ad says to them. First and foremost, this refers to the Commission's need to argue only that the ad or commercial message has "capacity to deceive" in that it merely communicates false claims. For example, in the *Profile Bread* case, the ads possessed a capacity to deceive by merely communicating the false claim that Profile is significantly lower in calories than ordinary bread, while actual deception would refer to consumer belief of such claims. In short, deceptive *capacity* may exist prior to actual deception. Along these lines, the legal questions and/or issues in many FTC cases have been merely addressed to what claims were made and not whether consumers believed such claims.

Furthermore, when conceptualizing deception and sales influences, some feel that, especially in the case of television advertising, more must be considered than just attitude change or claim-belief and fact comparisons. When considering situations of low audience involvement, such as television advertising, Krugman posits that:[22]

> (P)ersuasion as such, i.e., overcoming a resistant attitude, is not involved at all and that it is a mistake to look for it in our personal lives as a test of television's advertising impact. Instead, as trivia are repeatedly learned and repeatedly forgotten and then repeatedly learned a little more, it is possible that two things happen: 1) more simply, that so-called "overlearning" will move some information out of short-term and into long-term memory systems, and 2) more complexly, that we will permit significant alterations in the *structure* of our perception of a brand or product, but in ways which may fall short of persuasion or of attitude change.

In other words, such a view says that it may be necessary to reject as incomplete a model of television advertising's influence that requires changes in attitude *prior* to changes in behavior. Advertising may be seen as a cumulative influence affecting what Gardner referred to as "vertical perception,"[23] with the purchase setting acting as a catalyst that brings out all potential shifts in perspective that the consumer has accumulated to that point.

> (T)he public lets down its guard to the repetitive commercial use of the television medium and . . . it easily changes its ways of perceiving products and brands and its purchasing behavior without thinking very much about it at the time of TV exposure or at any time prior to purchase, and without up to then changing verbalized attitudes.[24]

Television advertsing, therefore, can be said to not always produce sales by changing attitudes, but rather, by working over time on broad consumer perceptions and brand salience (for example: "Coke adds life," "You can be sure if it's Westinghouse"). This could be a major reason why so much television advertising could be seen to not be involved in attempts to influence consumers' factual beliefs about products. This is evidenced by a recent study in which less than half the sampled commercials met a liberal criteria of possessing useful consumer information cues.[25]

At this point, an apparent inconsistency in FTC and court logic in this area becomes evident: the Commission need only find a "tendency to deceive" and therefore, in many cases, only looks at what an ad says and not what consumers believe. Yet to conclude a claim is legally acceptable puffery, it is assumed that the communicated claim is not believed nor relied upon by consumers. The goal of a study on puffery would attempt to present research and information which the FTC could understand and might wish to adopt in *refining* its own definitions and approaches to labelling certain advertised claims deceptive. From the foregoing analysis, it would appear to be necessary to distinguish between a "potential for deception," and actual "deception" for purposes of research definitions. The former, following from the Commission's legal need to merely find a "tendency to deceive," consists of the commercial communicating false claims, while the latter entails consumers believing such claims.

On the basis of the above discussion, the following are possible operational definitions of tendency to deceive and deception:

> If an advertisement leaves a consumer within some reasonable market segment with an impression (it communicates a claim) that is factually untrue, then there exists a tendency (or potential) for that consumer being deceived.
>
> If an advertisement leaves a consumer within some reasonable market segment with a belief that is factually untrue, then that consumer has been deceived.

With any definition utilized, the consumer's perception is the matter of interest, not what the ad either intends or says literally. This is clearly compatable with the legal aim or interest of the regulatory process, which, as Preston notes, operates on the advertising and not the advertiser.[26] However, the main thrust or researcher concerns of these definitions are in terms of the perceptual processes of individual consumers. To relate these behavioral definitions to the FTC and court terminology, it can be said that: an ad will legally be labelled as having a tendency to deceive (and be proscribed) if there exists a tendency or potential for it to deceive n percent of a reasonable market segment; the ad can be legally labelled as deceptive if it deceives n percent of a reasonable market segment.

What is the relevant "n percent" is a legal determination, not a researcher's. It is the court's rules and regulations; the investigator can only speculate. Some recent FTC cases have started working in such a direction, but no clear and consistent guides have as yet evolved from these decisions. Gellhorn has suggested that for mere inaccurate product descriptions, 10 to 15 percent deception would be "allowable," but if the product involves consumer health and safety, almost any deception (and "certainly not more than 5 percent") would justify issuance of a cease and desist order.[27] Gerlach has also suggested variable guidelines based on different standards, such as: in cases where the product directly involves public health and safety, 1 to 5 percent of deception would be enough for a cease and desist order; with ads aimed solely at children and the elderly, 10 percent; economic harm, such as a dancing school that does not live up to its promises, 15 to 20 percent; commercial harm, hurting only competition and not the general public, about 30 to 40 percent.[28]

The point, though, is that such standards must be arrived at by legal determinations, and for a researcher to presume to be able to attempt such decisions in his definitions would entail a degree of unwarranted arbitrariness. The researcher can only suggest possible standards based on his data. Even standards of a consumer "type" for such guidelines, be it "average," "reasonable," or "ignorant," can be seen as in the legal providence. A historical study of FTC decisions reveals that such standards have varied over time, possibly in relation to the consumerist's claim of the period and type of public harm feared.[29]

CONCLUSIONS

This section described a possible basis for blending communication research methods and the law, looking toward studies that will provide some research guidance as to puffery's proper status before the law. Not only is this area of research new, but so are the perspectives and definitions that will finally be utilized. When reading the literature on advertising regulation, one begins to realize the degree of difference between marketers' and lawyers' concepts, ideas, and perspectives. Even their professional languages are vastly different. Any conceptualization of research in this area will probably have to walk a middle ground, hopefully keeping in close touch with both worlds.

NOTES

[1] Philip Ward Burton, *Advertising Copywriting,* 3rd edition, (Columbis, Ohio: Grid, Inc., 1974), p. 379.
[2] Ivan L. Preston and Ralph G. Johnson, "Puffery—A Problem the FTC Didn't Want (And May Try to Eliminate)," *Journalism Quarterly,* vol. 49 (Autumn 1972), pp. 558–68.
[3] Ivan L. Preston, *The Great American Blow-Up* (Madison: University of Wisconsin Press, 1975).
[4] Carl P. Wrighter, *I Can Sell You Anything* (New York: Ballantine Books, 1972).
[5] Ivan L. Preston, "Logic and Illogic in the Advertising Process," *Journalism Quarterly,* vol. 44 (#2), pp. 231–9;
  Ivan L. Preston and Steven E. Scharbach, "Advertising: More than Meets the Eye?" *Journal of Advertising Research,* vol. 11 (June 1971), pp. 19–24.
[6] For example, see: Mary Gardiner Jones and Murray Silverman, "Is There A Role for Research in the Federal Trade Commission," address presented at American Marketing Association Conference, Northwestern University, June, 1972;
  William L. Wilkie, Stephen A. Greyser, "Consumer Research Inputs into Public Policy and Legal Decisions," unpublished workshop report for Marketing Science Institute, April, 1974;
  David M. Gardner, "Dynamic Homeostasis: Behavioral Research and the FTC," *Advances in Consumer Research,* Volume I, Association for Consumer Research, 1973 Proceedings, Scott Ward and Peter Wright, eds.;
  William L. Wilkie and David M. Gardner, "The Rolle of Marketing Research in Public Policy Decision Making," *Journal of Marketing,* vol. 38 (January 1974), pp. 38–47.
[7] For example, see: Joseph G. Smith, "My Day in Court," *Journal of Advertising Research,* vol. 13 (October 1973), pp. 9–22;
  Richard W. Pollay, "Deceptive Advertising and Consumer Behavior: A Case For Legislation and Judicial Reform," *Kansas Law Review,* vol. 17 (1969), pp. 625–39;
  Gary G. Gerlach, "The Consumer's Mind: A Preliminary Inquiry into the Emerging Problems of Consumer Evidence and the Law," Marketing Science Institute Working Paper, December, 1972.
  Herbert J. Rotfeld and Leonard N. Reid, "Advertiser Supplied Message Research: Extending the Advertising Substantiation Program," *Journal of Consumer Affairs,* vol. 11 (summer 1977), pp. 128–34.

[8] Michael T. Brandt and Ivan L. Preston, "The Federal Trade Commission's Use of Evidence to Determine Deception," *Journal of Marketing,* vol. 41 (January 1977), p. 54.

[9] Robert F. Dver and Terence A. Shimp, "Enhancing the Role of Marketing Research in Public Policy Decision Making," *Journal of Marketing,* vol. 41 (January 1977), p. 63.

[10] Brandt and Preston, op. cit., pp. 60–1.

[11] Ivan L. Preston, "A Comment on 'Defining Misleading Advertising' and 'Deception in Advertising,' " Marketing Notes and Communications section, *Journal of Marketing,* vol. 40 (July 1976), p. 54.

[12] Ivan L. Preston, "The FTC's Handling of Puffery and Other Selling Claims Made 'By Implication,' " paper presented to the Advertising Division, Association for Education in Journalism National Conference, University of Maryland, 1976.

[13] David M. Gardner, "Deception in Advertising: A Conceptual Approach," *Journal of Marketing,* vol. 39 (January 1975), pp. 40–6;
   This same basic definition was later revised in David M. Gardner, "Deception in Advertising: A Receiver Oriented Approach to Understanding," *Journal of Advertising,* vol. 5 (Fall 1976), pp. 5–11, 19.

[14] Gary M. Armstrong and Frederick A. Russ, "Detecting Deception in Advertising," *MSU Business Topics,* vol. 23 (Spring 1975), pp. 21–31.

[15] James E. Haefner, Working paper, University of Illinois, Department of Advertising, 1978.

[16] C.H. Sandage and Vernon Fryburger, *Advertising Theory and Practice,* ninth edition (Homewood, Ill.: Richard D. Irwin, Inc., 1975), pp. 76–8.

[17] For example, see: Ira M. Millstein, "The Federal Trade Commission and False Advertising," *Columbia Law Review,* vol. 64 (1964), pp. 439–99; and
   Ernest Gellhorn, "Proof of Consumer Deception Before the FTC," *Kansas Law Review,* vol. 17 (1969), pp. 559–72.

[18] Preston, "Comment on Defining Misleading Advertising and Deception," p. 55.

[19] Gardner, op. cit., p. 42.

[20] Gardner, op. cit., p. 7.

[21] Martin Fishbein "A Behavior Theory Approach to Relations Between Beliefs about an Object and the Attitude Toward the Object," in Martin Fishbein, ed. *Readings in Attitude Theory and Measurement* (New York: John Wiley and Sons, 1967), pp. 389–99;
   See also M. Fishbein and I. Afzen, *Belief, Attitude, Intention, and Behavior: An Introduction to Theory and Research* (Reading, Mass.: Addison-Wesley Publishing Co., 1975).

[22] Herbert E. Krugman, "The Impact of Television Advertising: Learning Without Involvement," *Public Opinion Quarterly,* vol. 29 (Fall 1965), pp. 349–50 at 353.

[23] Gardner, op. cit., p. 6–7.

[24] Krugman, op. cit., p. 354.

[25] Alan Resnik and Bruce L. Stein, "An Analysis of Information Content of Television Advertising," *Journal of Marketing,* vol. 41 (January 1977), pp. 50–3.

[26] Preston, *Great American Blow-Up,* Chapter 9.

[27] Gellhorn, op. cit., pp. 571–2.

[28] Gerlach, op. cit., pp. 44–5.

[29] Ivan L. Preston, "Reasonable Consumer or Ignorant Consumer? How the FTC Decides," *Journal of Consumer Affairs,* vol. 8 (Winter 1974), pp. 131–43; see also *The Great American Blow-up,* Chapter 10, pp. 162–74.

Section 4

Adult-Oriented Businesses: A Case Study of Deceptive Advertising

*Richard A. Kallan**

Massage parlors, escort services, and other businesses whose implicit products merchandised are of a sexual nature have proliferated in cities across the country—much to the dismay of local officials. Several cities have battled these "adult-oriented" businesses in an attempt to ban or restrict their operations. Las Vegas, Nevada is no exception. The legal maneuvers Las Vegas employed to curtail such enterprises, however, were unique when compared to the efforts of other cities.

Rather than advancing charges of sexual prostitution or resorting to stricter business ordinances and/or property rezonings, Las Vegas, through its City Attorney, wished to argue that local adult-oriented businesses were guilty of *deceptive advertising*—that is, they promised sexual favors when, in fact, favors were not forthcoming. In hopes of gathering data that might support their argument, the city authorized five University of Nevada, Las Vegas professors to study adult-oriented advertisements appearing in the Las Vegas *Panorama* (a weekly, promotional newspaper given free to tourists) for a six-month period, May 31, 1975, to December 19, 1975. As a result of the report, "Possible Deception in Adult-Oriented Advertising: A Rhetorical, Linguistic, and Sociological Analysis,"[1] and testimony by deceived customers, the City Commission revoked the licenses of two massage parlors. These businesses, the Commission and City Attorney agreed, were guilty of deceptive advertising.

The study by the University of Nevada professors was comprised of four reports, each embracing a different methodological perspective. Three *qualitative* criticisms maintained that most of the advertisements scrutinized were misleading. The fourth report, a *quantitative* survey by two sociologists, confirmed the conclusions rendered in the earlier analyses: readers were likely to be deceived by adult-oriented advertisements.

The present essay is based on the report I authored. As a rhetorical critic, I was concerned with the interaction of message and audience and how each functioned to shape and influence the other.[2] In this particular investigation, my interest was in determining the probable inferences to be drawn from reading adult-oriented advertisements. My starting point was basic communication theory.

Teachers of communication often discuss the differences among fact, inference, and judgment. Students are taught that facts are empirically verifiable: John is 8 feet, 8 inches tall. An inference, on the other hand, is based on fact but represents an extension of fact—"a guess about the unknown on the basis of the known:"[3] (because he is 8′ 8″) John must have difficulty purchasing clothes. Judgments are pronouncements of value and say more about the describer than the described; they are opinions influenced by fact and inference: Anyone who is 8′ 8″ looks grotesque.

While all statements are expressions of fact, inference, or judgment, it is the inferential process that is of concern here. Continually, we make and act on inference; indeed, often what is viewed as

---

*Chairman, Department of Communication Studies, University of Nevada, Las Vegas.

fact actually is inference. "The New York Yankees and Boston Red Sox are playing today . . . ," the story reads. Because both the Yankees and Red Sox are professional baseball teams, one infers they are playing baseball. But where is it stated that baseball—and not basketball or football—is being played? Inferential reasoning of the former is typical of our everyday behavior.

Certainly, the meaning any advertisement has for its reader/viewer is determined considerably by inference. To know the popular experiences (linguistic denotations and connotations, for example) shared culturally by an audience is to know the inferential-drawing "character" of that audience. Put another way, the exercise of inferential thought assumes that from any single word or statement others naturally entail; with one truth there correspond other truths. Although the following analysis focuses primarily on individual verbal tokens found in massage and escort advertisements, the conclusion posited is that these tokens, viewed collectively, produce a whole rhetoric inferring the availability of sexual services.

Finally, one last introductory note. The state of Nevada does not prohibit prostitution; rather each county may exercise individual prerogative in this matter. In Clark County, which incorporates Las Vegas, prostitution is illegal. Hence, adult-oriented advertisers face a double bind: if they supply sexual prostitution, they break the law; if they do not supply sexual prostitution but imply they do, they illegally deceive their audiences. Assuming that prostitution is not peddled in the businesses discussed (as their owners maintain), I viewed any advertisement which appeared to offer prostitution as deceptive.

"It's Legal in Nevada." In most of the advertisements surveyed, there appears either the statement, "It's legal in Nevada," or some semblance thereof—e.g., "Come where it's legal," or "We are definitely legal." The statement beckons the reader's attention and may well represent the most salient verbal portion of adult-oriented advertisements.

"It," of course, suggests the presence of some antecedent—that is, a previously noted referent. Yet in the advertisements considered, "it" is never verbally denoted; no clear linguistic equivalent prevails. The absence of a verbal antecedent draws the reader inexorably to the presence of any visual referent. The reader ultimately settles upon photographs of naked or seminaked women. "It" becomes synonymous with an eager-to-please, sexual profiteer whose services are available to any paying customer.

Environmental contexts color and shade this visual referent. For example, why note that "It's legal in Nevada," if there were not some presumption that "it's" refers to prostitution. After all, one would never see an advertisement to the effect that automobiles or supermarkets are legal in Nevada. Then, too, there is the naive tourist who knows that prostitution is legal in Nevada but whose legal worldliness does not extend to the specifics of the law.

Thus, because of a) the visual referent for "it" and its overt sexual overtones, b) the presumptive posture communicated in advertising "It's legal in Nevada," and c) the popular misconception regarding the legality of prostitution in Las Vegas, the reader is likely to conclude that massage parlors and escort services provide sexual prostitution.

"I want to satisfy you." Several massage parlors and escort services employ some variation of the phrase, "I want to satisfy you." One declares, "Satisfy your every need with one of our pros;" another offers, "Let our pros satisfy you." Such statements when combined with a picture of a nude or seminude model create a deceptive advertisement.

Saying "I want to satisfy you" suggests that certain devotions will be shown completely and unhesitatingly. In the context of a restaurant advertisement, one might expect the finest in culinary services and would be justified in ethically questioning any restaurant whose services were incon-

Figure 7. This advertisement is representative of massage parlor and escort service appeals once found in the *Panorama*.

gruent with promises of complete satisfaction. And so when it is advertised that sensuous women eagerly desire to satisfy, does it not follow that the satisfaction referenced is sexual? Popular experience—the culturally shared connotations of a naked woman declaring her willingness to satisfy—encourages the inference that sexual procurement transpires. But given that prostitution is illegal, the advertisement must be deceptive.

"No need to leave your hotel room." In everyday usage, "escort" denotes accompanying someone, usually from one place to another—"A number of persons, or often a single person, accompanying anyone on a journey for the purpose of protection or guidance, or for courtesy's sake."[4] One would never say to another, "Come over to my house and *escort* me for a cup of coffee . . . ," or "Drop by and *escort* me as I watch television." Similarly, there is intrinsic contradiction in an escort service advertising that the customer need never leave his room: escort service cannot be provided in a hotel room. The obvious inference is that "escort" symbolizes something beyond conventional denotation.

Other statements further suggest contextually that sexual favors are pandered. For instance, several escort services combine the phrases, "no need to leave your hotel room" and "for a short time or all night." What does one do in a hotel room for a short time or all night with a seductive nude model? What does popular experience suggest?

Subtle and not so subtle clues abound. "Sweet loving" is promised by one escort service, while others remind the reader to "Ask for a quickie," or "Ask about the all niter!" Interspersed are the subtleties, as in, "All legally licensed *escorts.*" The emphasis on "girls" seems motivated by the desire to equate "licensed girls" with "licensed prostitutes." Such juxtapositioning is misleading since one *can be* a licensed prostitute in Nevada but never a licensed "girl."

Especially clever is the escort service that enlightens, "Just maybe a professional knows something you don't." A professional escort has knowledge of people and places of visitational interest. But this knowledge can have little relevance or applicability if "escorting" remains confined to a hotel room. One wonders what the suite-bound client possibly could learn from the escort's professionalism if the experience and excellence connotated supposedly are unrelated to activities performed in hotel rooms. Ordinarily, "professional" is not equated necessarily with prostitution, but when describing the body bountiful, "professional" implies a mercenary instructor of sexual schooling. After all, what professional services does a woman usually render in the buff? Patently, "professional" is not to be perceived as having anything to do with escorting.

Certain massage parlors and escort services alluded to are no longer in business. The City Commission, however, could exercise jurisdiction only over the city of Las Vegas proper; massage parlors and escort services in the surrounding area of Clark County were not brought to hearing. Yet, even in businesses operating outside city limits the trend is towards tamer advertisements (note the progressive asexuality in Figures 7–10). Found absent today are the statements, "It's legal in Nevada," "I want to satisfy you," and "No need to leave your hotel room."

Some have gone yet further. Shrewd to recognize that it is perhaps only a matter of time before the County Commissioners take their turn in investigating adult-oriented businesses, Joey Richards, the owner of three escort services, has led the field in laundering his advertisements. Gradually, he has eliminated the nude model and the suggestive comment; no sexual favors are promised—in fact, little of anything is pledged the customer. Indeed, it appears unlikely that massage parlors and escort

Figure 8. In a slightly more subdued advertisement for V.O.T.D. Escort Service, note that the model is shown fully-clothed and that there does not appear the statement, "Come where it's legal."

Adult-Oriented Business 281

Figure 9. In promoting his Valley of the Dolls, Joey Richards, also owner of the V.O.T.D., continued the trend towards sexually milder adult-oriented advertisements.

Figure 10. Completing the revolution from risque to antiseptic is this advertisement for Vegas Touch Escorts, owned by Joey Richards.

services will ever resort to past deceptions. The city's success in license-revocation hearings and its willingness to apply state and local statutes against deception may check effectively adult-oriented advertising.

It should be emphasized that the issue raised here is not sexual freedom, but deceptive advertising: what is "acceptable" exaggeration and what is outright falsehood? The massage parlors and escort services studied herein, I maintain, were guilty of misleading advertising and their licenses revoked deservingly. Deception, whether in the form of blatant lie or misleading inference, is neither guaranteed nor protected by the First Amendment. To be sure, the right of freedom of speech is not the right to deceive. The case of Las Vegas and its adult-oriented businesses once more documents this fundamental conviction of our democratic society.

NOTES

[1] Evan Blythin, Thomas L. Clark, Richard A. Kallan, Frederick W. Preston, and Ronald W. Smith, "Possible Deception in Adult-Oriented Advertising: A Rhetorical, Linguistic, and Sociological Analysis, unpublished manuscript, Las Vegas, Nevada, 1976.

[2] I adhere to Donald Bryant's classic definition: rhetoric "is the *function of adjusting ideas to people and of people to ideas.*" "Rhetoric: Its Functions and Its Scope," *Quart. Jour. of Speech,* 39 (1953), p. 413.

[3] William D. Brooks, *Speech Communication,* 2nd ed. (Dubuque, Iowa: William C. Brown, 1974), p. 77. For a good discussion of fact, inference, and judgment, see pp. 75–83.

[4] *The Oxford English Dictionary* (Oxford: Clarendon Press, 1933).

Section 5

Improbable Claiming

*Evan Blythin**

INTRODUCTION

Las Vegas has been the scene of perennial legal skirmish between law enforcement agencies and enterprises of "adult" entertainment. Recently, the battleground shifted from the issue of obscenity to that of deceptive advertising.

In the spring of 1975, two sociologists, one linguist and two rhetorical critics from the University of Nevada at Las Vegas[1] were approached by a representative[2] of the City of Las Vegas with the task of examining the advertising claim, "Oral Love Is a Beautiful Thing." Tourists who responded to this and other ads from the Palace of Love found that the service rendered was a reading of literature; because their expectations had been thwarted, a number of them left town feeling they had been deceived.

Proof of deception was difficult to establish. Those who had responded to the advertisment were not acceptable witnesses because they could be accused of intending participation in an illegal act. Further, for the city to send its representatives to check the "validity" of the advertisement would be to risk the claims of biased auditors, entrapment, invasion of privacy, illegal search, and so forth. The question the city presented to us was whether or not deception could be demonstrated by some form of objective analysis of the advertisement.

We undertook the analysis, but the case for or against the Palace of Love never reached the courtroom; no one is sure why. Perhaps the number of complaints, perhaps the analyses of five independent researchers, or perhaps the financial exigencies of the time pre-empted further battle. The business decided to close its doors rather than pursue its case in court.

In December of 1975, the city again approached us with essentially the same problem. For the new study, the city requested examination of a body of advertisements found over a six-month period in the adult section of *Panorama,* a local publication designed for tourist consumption. The City Attorney was convinced that many of the advertisements in the adult section of *Panorama* were of the same nature as those previously used by the Palace of Love. As with the advertisements for the Palace of Love, many of the adult-oriented advertisements in *Panorama* had elicited complaints from tourists.

We accepted the task of analysis on the condition that the function of our examination was not to determine (that a given body of advertisements was deceptive); rather, our task was to determine whether or not a given body of advertisements were deceptive. This report 1) outlines our general approach to the task, 2) specifies my particular approach to the problem, 3) summarizes the results of the overall study, 4) discusses the significance of the studies, and 5) suggests possible areas of meaningful review.

---

*Mr. Blythin is an Associate Professor of Communication Studies at the University of Nevada, Las Vegas. Reprinted by permission from *Journal of Speech Communication* (Fall 1977).

GENERAL APPROACH

We independently focused on these variables we each believed to be particularly significant in the communication process; audience, context, and message. We specifically avoided analysis of source intent, feeling it to be the business of a judge and jury. The sociologists focused on auditors. They administered questionnaires to both local and out-of-town populations in an effort to determine what a general auditor would see as promised in the advertisements. If the general auditor thought that something was offered that could not, in reality, be offered, the examined advertisements were considered to be deceptive—at least, potentially. The linguist examined the contexts of the advertisements in an attempt to determine whether they promised more or less than might be legally or probably expected from the advertising business. One rhetorical critic examined the enthymematic form of the advertisements and their context to determine whether or not the unstated premises could be misleading. I examined the stated claims of the messages.

Our hope was that, at some point, a comparison of the independent results would lead to a consensus judgment. If, for example, a general receiver thought that the advertisements promised something a judge would know to be illegal, then the claim might be made that the communication process was potentially deceptive. If the context of the messages examined was also determined to be deceptive, then the claim that the communication process was deceptive would gain certainty. Finally, if the message structure and claims were determined to be deceptive, the claim of deception would have greater certainty. Conversely, if the variables examined in this particular study were revealed to be not deceptive, then the claim of general deception would lose certainty.

CLAIMS ANALYSIS

It would be impossible to detail in one brief report the claims of all the advertisements found in the *Panorama*. Analysis of the advertisements for the Palace of Love, however, represents how I established and utilized the criterion of judgment. The advertisements for the Palace of Love revealed three kinds of claims: 1) the claim without referent, 2) the arguable claim, and 3) the definite claim.

The claim without referent was always considered deceptive. The reader cannot know, for example, in reading the advertisements for the Palace of Love, if "It's legal in Nevada," because the "It" is never explicitly related to anything. The claim that "It's legal in Nevada" may indicate that the source of the message has some interest in the establishment of integrity, but the "It" of the claim is vague. "This is the real thing" is another example of the indefinite claim; "This" can never, from the text, be affixed to a specific reality. Lack of referent in a claim is considered deceptive in this work because what appears to be a warrantable claim is not; there is only the illusion of some reality.

The second form of claim found in the advertisements for the Palace of Love was considered as only sometimes deceptive. For example, in the March 1, 1974 edition of *Panorama,* the Palace advanced the claim that "Oral Love is a Beautiful Thing." This is an arguable claim and may or may not be deceptive. Because no universal standard for beauty has yet been established, any claim that a particular thing is beautiful is a matter of debate.

Definite claims found in the advertisements for the Palace of Love did not seem deceptive. Definite claims, like "Open 24 hours," have specific referent and did not seem value-oriented.

In analyzing the May 30 to December 19, 1975 advertisements found in the adult section of *Panorama,* those ads engaging primarily in definite claims were not dealt with. Those ads which

286 False and Deceptive Advertising

Courtesy of Evan Blythin.

Figure 11

appeared to present indefinite or value-claiming were focused upon. Each advertisement was then described and juxtaposed to its description. Finally, judgments were made about the indefinite and value claims.

SUMMARY STUDIES

The combined efforts of the researchers in this study did not always lead to clear consensus, perhaps because we sometimes focused on different advertisements or different elements within them. For example, several studies focused on major advertisements (those with full page documentation) while others examined both small and large ads. Some studies focused on those businesses which operated within the city of Las Vegas; another dealt with advertisements from both the city and the county. Finally, one study did not summarize, but gave guidelines and suggestions for how judgment concerning the context might be made. Four out of the five studies agreed upon five of the same businesses as deceptive (the remaining study offered guidelines which encompassed the same five businesses).

The two sociologists surveyed residents and tourists in the Las Vegas area and residents of a large Southern California city. The survey revealed that 79.9 percent of the auditors of three massage parlor advertisements thought that the businesses were "offering sexual intercourse and/or favors."[3] Ninety-two percent of the auditors viewing the advertisements from three escort services believed that sexual services or favors were being offered.[4]

The linguist argued in his study that the context definitely cast the advertisements of eight businesses in a shady light. The form and content of the examined advertisements were, the linguist argued, in close proximity, and stylistically similar, to the advertisements for the legal brothels located outside of Clark County, Nevada. The linguist testified that such visuals as bananas, whips, etc., lent many of the advertisements sexual overtones.[5]

The other rhetorical critic involved thought that the average viewer would be deceived by the enthymematic structure of the advertisements. He argued, for example, that the "it's" in "it's legal in Nevada" referred to prostitution and that the auditor would then fill in the premise that Las Vegas was part of Nevada, hence, prostitution was the sold service.[6]

Utilization of a claims analysis led to the belief that seven escort services, three massage parlors, and one wrestling service were deceptive in their advertisements.[7]

Of the businesses which the studies indicted for deceptive advertising, two found themselves immediately facing a show-cause hearing. In Las Vegas, certain legal matters concerning the licensing of businesses are heard before the City Commissioners and are then subject to review by a District Court. Through a legal tangle, it turned out that escort services could not be reviewed under the statutes assumed by the city. The two massage parlors first reviewed by the City Commissioners had their licenses revoked and appealed their case to District Court, arguing violation of legal procedure. The District Court, at this writing, is reviewing the case. It is generally believed that, should the District Court uphold the revocation of the licenses, the defendants will appeal to a higher court. In the meantime, the city of Las Vegas continues its war on deceptive advertising, using the commissioned studies wherever applicable.

SIGNIFICANCE

The studies commissioned by the city of Las Vegas were popular. Interested spectators and representatives of every major televison network attended the hearings. The City Commissioners, lawyers, and expert witnesses enjoyed about three weeks of rapt local attention. The studies were utilized. Whether the months of preparation, weeks of public attention, and utilization will translate to lasting significance can only be determined by further judicial and academic review.

Judicial review will be the first test of lasting significance for the studies. If they are accepted by a higher court, then a method for determining deception will have been legally sanctioned, perhaps to be utilized in determining deception in other human interchanges.

Academic review is a second possible test of significance for the reported studies. Such review would be particularly important if judicial hearings do not focus on the methods employed in Las Vegas. Since the defense lawyers did not, in the local hearings, deal extensively with the methodologies employed by the expert witnesses, and since the District Court will only review the material presented at the hearings, scholarly review may be necessary if the significant liabilities and assets of the approach taken by the expert witnesses are to be revealed.[8]

AREAS SUGGESTED FOR REVIEW

Scholarly review might well begin with the omissions of the studies. For example, a review of literature concerning ethics and persuasion in general and deceptive advertising in particular was not part of the studies. Such a review would do a great deal toward placing the commissioned studies in perspective.

Another significant omission in the studies was the lack of full discussion concerning the means of judging certainty and uncertainty. As mentioned in this report, the expert witnesses functioned with the hope that comparison assumed that when there was discrepancy in judgments, a claim of general deception lost certainty. The degrees of certainty and uncertainty obtained with the studies need fuller explication.

Consideration of degrees of certainty might begin with the question of whether or not three communication variables (audience, context, message) uncertainty might begin with the fact that, in one of the first hearings, one expert witness did not agree that the business discussed had engaged in deception. The commissioners disregarded the discrepancy and the business was adjudged to be engaging in deceptive advertising. The acceptance of discrepancy leads to the conclusion that a communication event may be both deceptive and not-deceptive. How much agreement is necessary for certainty? Ultimately, it seems, further review must come to grips with what appears to be a fine line between probable truth and improbable claiming.

Further review might also focus on the lack of discussion concerning the interrelationship(s) of the methodologies used. There were critical and empirical studies, each prefaced with a discussion of methods, but the studies were not methodologically juxtaposed. Further review would reveal whether or not the empirical data obtained by the social scientists supported the theoretic standards assumed by the linguist and rhetorical critics.

The substance, degree of certainty, and degree of methodological mix in the studies may, upon review, be found to be impeccable. I like to think they will. It is also possible, however, that the omissions in the studies are not significantly different from the omissions found in an indefinite claim. Judicial review will be one test of the studies. Academic review might be another.

NOTES

[1] Drs. Frederick W. Preston and Ronald W. Smith from the Department of Sociology; Dr. Thomas L. Clark from the Department of English; and Drs. Richard Kallan and Evan Blythin from the Department of Communication Studies.

[2] The representative, Mr. Dale Haley, was a paralegal assistant to the City Attorney and a graduate of the University. He reported to two Assistant City Attorneys, Leonard P. Smith and Daniel E. Ahlstrom (they were later replaced on the case by Richard Koch). The City Attorney was Carl E. Lovell Jr., who has since retired from public service.

[3] Frederick W. Preston and Ronald W. Smith, "Receiver's Perception and Probability of Deception," in *Possible Deception in Adult-Oriented Advertising: A Rhetorical, Linguistic, and Sociological Analysis*, unpublished manuscript submitted to the city of Las Vegas in April, 1976.

[4] Ibid.

[5] Thomas L. Clark, "The Role of Context in Advertising," in *Possible Deception in Adult-Oriented Advertising: A Rhetorical, Linguistic, and Sociological Analysis*.

[6] Richard A. Kallan, "A Logical Analysis of Advertising Deception in *Panorama's* Adult Section," in *Possible Deception in Adult-Oriented Advertising: A Rhetorical, Linguistic, and Sociological Analysis*.

[7] Evan Blythin, "Improbable Claiming," *Possible Deception in Adult-Oriented Advertising: A Rhetorical, Linguistic, and Sociological Analysis*.

[8] The defense lawyer for the first business was Mr. Jeffrey Shanner; defense for the second business was handled by Mr. George Spizziri.

Section 6

Cases

FEDERAL COMMUNICATIONS COMMISSION v.
AMERICAN BROADCASTING CO., INC.

FEDERAL COMMUNICATIONS COMMISSION v.
NATIONAL BROADCASTING CO., INC.

FEDERAL COMMUNICATIONS COMMISSION v.
COLUMBIA BROADCASTING SYSTEM, INC.

347 U.S. 284, (1954)

Mr. Chief Justice Warren delivered the opinion of the Court.

These cases are before us on direct appeal from the decision of a three-judge District of New York, enjoining the Federal Communications Commission from enforcing certain provisions in its rules relating to the broadcasting of so-called "give-away" programs. The question presented is whether the enjoined provisions correctly interpret (a statute prohibiting) the broadcasting of ". . . any lottery, gift enterprise, or similar scheme, offering prizes dependent in whole or in part upon lot or chance."

The appellees are national radio and television broadcasting companies. They are, in addition, the operators of radio and television stations licensed by the Commission. Each of the appellees broadcasts, over its own and affiliated stations, certain programs popularly known as "give-away" programs. Generally characteristic of this type of program is the distribution of prizes to home listeners, selected wholly or in part on the basis of chance, as an award for correctly solving a given problem or answering a question.

All the parties agree that there are three essential elements of a "lottery, gift enterprise, or similar scheme:" 1) the distribution of prizes; 2) according to chance; 3) for a consideration. They also agree that prizes on the programs under review are distributed according to chance, but they fall out on the question of whether the home contestant furnishes the necessary consideration.

Section 1304 itself does not define the type of consideration needed for a "lottery, gift enterprise, or similar scheme," nor do the postal lottery statutes from which this language was taken. The legislative history of Section 1304 and the postal statutes is similarly unilluminating. For guidance, therefore, we must look primarily to American decisions, both judicial and administrative, construing comparable antilottery legislation.

Enforcing such legislation has long been a difficult task. Law enforcement officers, federal and state, have been plagued with as many types of lotteries as the seemingly inexhaustible ingenuity of their promoters could devise in their efforts to circumvent the law. When their schemes reached the courts, the decision, of necessity, usually turned on whether the scheme, on its own peculiar facts, constituted a lottery. So varied have been the techniques used by promoters to conceal the joint factors of prize, chance, and consideration, and so clever have they been in applying these techniques to feigned as well as legitimate business activities, that it has often been difficult to apply the decision of one case to the facts of another.

And so it is here. We find no decisions precisely in point on the facts of the cases before us. The courts have defined consideration in various ways, but so far as we are aware none has ever held that a contestant's listening at home to a radio or television program satisfies the consideration requirement. Some courts—with vigorous protest from others—have held that the requirement is satisfied by a "raffle" scheme giving free chances to persons who go to a store to register in order to participate in the drawing of a prize, and similarly by a "bank night" scheme giving free chances to persons who gather in front of a motion picture theatre in order to participate in a drawing held for the primary benefit of the paid patrons of the theatre. But such cases differ substantially from the cases before us. To be eligible for a prize on the "give-away" programs involved here, not a single home contestant is required to purchase anything or pay an admission price or leave his home to visit the promoter's place of business; the only effort required for participation is listening.

We believe that it would be stretching the statute to the breaking point to give it an interpretation that would make such programs a crime. Particularly is this true when through the years the Post Office Department and the Department of Justice have consistently given the words "lottery, gift enterprise, or similar scheme" a contrary administrative interpretation. Thus the Solicitor of the Post Office Department has repeatedly ruled that the postal lottery laws do not preclude the mailing of circulars advertising the type of "give-away" program here under attack. Similarly, the Attorney General—charged with the enforcement of federal criminal laws—refused to bring criminal action against broadcasters of such programs. And in this very action, it is noteworthy that the Department of Justice has not joined the Commission in appealing the decision below.

It is true, as contended by the Commission, that these are not criminal cases, but it is a criminal statute that we must interpret. There cannot be one construction for the Federal Communications Commission and another for the Department of Justice. If we should give Section 1304 the broad construction urged by the Commission, the same construction would likewise apply in criminal cases. We do not believe this construction can be sustained. Not only does it lack support in the decided cases, judicial and administrative, but also it would do violence to the well-established principle that penal statutes are to be construed strictly.

It is apparent that these so-called "give-away" programs have long been a matter of concern to the Federal Communications Commission; that it believes these programs to be the old lottery evil under a new guise, and that they should be struck down as illegal devices appealing to cupidity and the gambling spirit. It unsuccessfully sought to have the Department of Justice take criminal action against them. Likewise, without success, it urged Congress to amend the law to specifically prohibit them. The Commission now seeks to accomplish the same result through agency regulations. In doing so, the Commission has overstepped the boundaries of interpretation and hence has exceeded its rule-making power. Regardless of the doubts held by the Commission and others as to the social value of the programs here under consideration, such administrative expansion of Section 1304 does not provide the remedy.

The judgments are Affirmed.

TESTING SYSTEMS, INC. v. MAGNAFLUX CORP.
251 F.Supp. 286 (1966)

John W. Lord, Jr., District Judge.

This is an action for trade libel or disparagement of property. The matter is now before this Court on defendant's motion to dismiss for failure to state a claim upon which relief can be granted.

Essentially the facts are these. Both plaintiff, Testing Systems, Inc., and the defendant, Magnaflux Corp., are engaged in the manufacture and sale of equipment, devices, and systems, including chemical products, for use in the nondestructive testing of commercial and industrial materials. The allegedly actionable statements concern similar chemical products of the parties; that of the plaintiff being known as "Flaw Finder," and that of the defendant identified as "Spotcheck." The complaint contains allegations that both written and oral statements disparaging plaintiff's product were circulated by the defendant's agents to plaintiff's current and prospective customers. Specifically, in the former category, it is alleged that the defendant did on or about May 6, 1965, through its agents, publish an allegedly false report to the effect that the United States Government had tested plaintiff's product, and found it to be about only 40 percent as effective as that of the defendant.

It appears further from the complaint that on or about May 23, 1965, while in attendance at a manufacturer's convention in Philadelphia, defendant's agent, in the presence of plaintiff's current and prospective customers, "did in a loud voice state that . . . (plaintiff's) . . . stuff is no good," and that "the government is throwing them out."

For the purposes of this motion, defendant admits the truth of the allegation, but asserts that the action must nevertheless be dismissed because 1) the defendant did no more than make an unfavorable comparison of plaintiff's product with its own; and 2) even assuming that the statements were actionable, plaintiff has failed to allege his damages with the required specificity.

UNFAVORABLE COMPARISON

It would serve no useful purpose to dwell at length on the issue of unfavorable comparison. Suffice it to say, as the defendant properly points out, that a statement which takes the form of an unfavorable comparison of products, or which "puffs" or exaggerates the quality of one's own product is not ordinarily actionable. This has long been the rule in England, where the action originated, and is now well established in the vast majority of United States jurisdictions.

However, this Court is not convinced by the defendant's arguments that his comments amounted to mere unfavorable comparison. The modern history of the doctrine of unfavorable comparison and its permissible use in the conduct of business traces its origin to the leading English case of *White* v. *Mellin*. There the defendant had advertised his product as being far more healthful than plaintiff's. In refusing relief the Court established the precedent that irrespective of their truth or falsity, statements by one competitor which compare his product with that of another are not actionable.

It does not follow from this, however, that every trade disparagement is protectible under the guise of unfavorable comparison merely because the perpetrator was canny enough to mention not only the product of his competitor but also his own. The decision in *White* v. *Mellin* was founded on the near impossibility of ascertaining the truth or falsity of general allegations respecting the superiority of one product over another. To decide otherwise, explained Lord Herschell, would turn the courts "into a machinery for advertising rival productions by obtaining a judicial determination (as to) which of the two was better." One is expected to believe in the superiority of his wares, and he may properly declare his belief to interested parties. It has even been said that he may "boast untruthfully of his wares." (B)ut see the Lanham Trademark Act, which gives a civil action to anyone injured or damaged by false advertising of goods involved in interstate commerce.

The fine line that separates healthy competitive effort from underhanded business tactics is frequently difficult to determine. Apart from the tradesman's right of free speech, which must be vigorously safeguarded, the public has a genuine interest in learning the relative merits of particular products, however that may come about. To advance these interests, the law of the market place gives the competitor a wide berth in the conduct of his business.

Nonetheless, there is an outer perimeter to permissible conduct. The tradesman must be assured that his competitors will not be suffered to engage in conduct which falls below the minimum standard of fair dealing. "(I)t is no answer that they can defend themselves by also resorting to disparagement. A self-respecting businessman will not voluntarily adopt, and should not be driven to adopt, a selling method which he regards as undignified, unfair, and repulsive. A competitor should not, by pursuing an unethical practice, force his rival to choose between its adoption and the loss of his trade."

The defendant's comments in the case presently before this Court do not entitle him to the protection accorded to "unfavorable comparison." There is a readily observable difference between saying that one's product is, in general, better than another's . . . and asserting, as here, that such other's is only 40 percent as effective as one's own. The former, arguably, merely expresses an opinion, the truth or falsity of which is difficult or impossible of ascertainment. The latter, however, is an assertion of fact, not subject to the same frailties of proof, implying that the party making the statement is fortified with the substantive facts necessary to make it. This distinction has never been seriously questioned. The defendant in this case admittedly circulated to plaintiff's present and prospective customers false statements to the effect that the government had tested both products and found the defendant's to be 60 percent more effective than plaintiff's. This is not the sort of "comparison" that courts will protect.

Apart from this, there is at least one additional factor which withdraws the defendant's comments from the category of unfavorable comparison. Not content with making the admittedly false statements and allowing them to be evaluated independently of any extraneous influence, the defendant here gave added authenticity to its assertions, by invoking the reputation of a third party, the United States Government. It is unnecessary to speculate on the additional force the defendant's remarks must have had when coupled with the purported approval of so highly credible a source. This, of course, is to say nothing of the statements to the effect that plaintiff had been "thrown out," which by no stretch of the imagination could be termed mere comparison.

For all of the above reasons, it is the judgment of this Court that the defendant's remarks are actionable.

DAMAGES

However, there remains for consideration the equally important matter of damages. In his complaint, plaintiff states merely that as a result of the defendant's disparagement, he has suffered a loss of customers, current and prospective. No attempt is made to specify which customers, nor is there any effort to even approximate their value to him. He asserts merely that the amount of his loss exceeds the minimum jurisdictional requirements of this Court.

After careful examination of the authorities on the question, it is apparent that plaintiff has failed to set forth his damages with the required particularity. The necessity of pleading and proving special damages has been an integral part of the action of disparagement of property since it first developed as an extension of slander of title. It arose as a result of the friction between the ecclesiastical and common law courts of England when the common law courts sought to assume jurisdiction over actions for defamation. "Since slander of any kind was a sin, church courts alone could punish unless temporal damage could be shown to have resulted from the defamatory words."

Until the 19th Century the requirement did not impose any untoward burden on the litigant. The early business community was devoid of the complexities that characterize the modern marketplace, and it was the rule, rather than the exception, that tradesmen knew their customers well. It was not too difficult, therefore, to determine just when and why one's customers began to favor a competitor.

As is so often the case, however, the rule respecting special damages continued in force long after its raison d'etre had passed. Today, in the vast majority of States, including Pennsylvania, a plaintiff in a disparagement of property action must both plead and prove special damages. (*Smith, Disparagement of Property,* supra.) The inflexibility of most courts in demanding strict compliance with the rule has hampered the effectiveness of the action and contributed to its unpopularity. One can appreciate the plight of the small metropolitan retailer whose patrons are, for the most part, unknown to him by name. Here, however, we are not dealing with small retailers. Both the defendant and the plaintiff in this action are business organizations of some substance who are well aware of their present and potential sources of business. The rule requiring some showing of damage, while perhaps harsh in some cases, is entirely reasonable under the circumstances as presented here.

But even if this were not so, this Court is not at liberty to disregard the law of the State and to substitute therefore its own conception of what the law ought to be. The Pennsylvania cases in this area, although few in number, leave little doubt as to how the State courts would receive plaintiff's claim. "(H)e," the plaintiff, "must in his complaint set out the names of his lost customers and show by figures how much he has lost financially."

As recently as 1962 the Pennsylvania Supreme Court had occasion to reconsider its position, although indirectly. In *Cosgrove,* supra, the objectionable comments imputed a lack of integrity to the plaintiff. The lower court dismissed the action because the plaintiff had failed to set forth his damages specially. On appeal the decision of the lower court was reversed, with the court concluding that the comments were libelous per se in which case damages need not be specially pleaded or proved, since they are implied. The absence of any reference in the court's opinion to pleading requirements when the statements are not libelous per se, coupled with Pennsylvania lower court decisions on the matter, leave this Court no alternative but to conclude that the requirement still exists in Pennsylvania.

Thus to avoid the necessity of specially pleading his damages, the plaintiff must show that the defendant's statements constituted libel per se. Although some argument to this effect appears in plaintiff's brief, it clearly falls short of the mark. It is possible in most disparagement cases to infer some criticism of the tradesman personally. However, where the comments fail to directly or by reasonable inference impugn the personal character of business conduct of the plaintiff, courts will not extend the range of judicial inventiveness to find libel per se where obviously none exists. Here the defendant falsely reported that the United States Government had found plaintiff's product to be so ineffective in comparison with defendant's that it chose to discontinue dealing with plaintiff. However unethical this may be from a business standpoint, it does not amount to libel per se. It does not accuse the plaintiff of fraud or otherwise attack his character personally, nor does it by reasonable inference draw into question the solvency of his business. Under these circumstances libel per se did not materialize, and this argument must be dismissed accordingly.

Finally, even if the more liberal federal rules of pleading are applied, plaintiff's allegation of damages still fails to satisfy our requirements. Although, in general, all that is required is that the defendant be put on notice as to the general nature of the claim, the facts and information must be sufficient to form the basis of reasonably fruitful discovery proceedings. The defendant had called to the attention of this Court a case that appears to be peculiarly applicable here. In *Fowler* v. *Curtis Publishing Co.*, the plaintiffs sought damages for personal defamation and trade libel. The following quotation appears in the opinion of the Circuit Court which affirmed the District Court's dismissal of the action.

" '(I)t was . . . necessary for the plaintiff to allege either the loss of particular customers by name, or a general diminution in its business, and extrinsic facts showing that such special damages were the natural and direct result of the false publication. If the plaintiff desired to predicate its right to recover damages upon general loss of custom, it should have alleged facts showing an established business, the amount of sales for a substantial period preceding the publication, the amount of sales subsequent to the publication, facts showing that such loss in sales were the natural and probable result of such publication, and facts showing the plaintiff could not allege the names of particular customers who withdrew or withheld their custom.' "

The complaint in this action was filed almost immediately after the disparagement occurred. Nine months have expired since the cause of action arose. It may now be possible for plaintiff to plead over with the requisite degree of specificity. For this reason, the complaint will not be dismissed unless the plaintiff fails to so plead within the period specified below.

ORDER

And now, to wit, this 2nd day of March, A.D. 1966, it is ordered that the complaint in this action be dismissed unless the plaintiff, within thirty (30) days hereof, amends his complaint to properly reflect his special damages.

FEDERAL TRADE COMMISSION v. *COLGATE-PALMOLIVE CO.*
380 U.S. 374 (1965)

Mr. Chief Justice Warren delivered the opinion of the Court.

The basic question before us is whether it is a deceptive trade practice, prohibited by Section 5 of the Federal Trade Commission Act, to represent falsely that a televised test, experiment, or demonstration provides a viewer with visual proof of a product claim, regardless of whether the product claim is itself true.

The case arises out of an attempt by respondent, Colgate-Palmolive Company, to prove to the television public that its shaving cream, "Rapid Shave," outshaves them all. Respondent Ted Bates & Company, Inc., an advertising agency, prepared for Colgate three one-minute commercials designed to show that Rapid Shave could soften even the toughnesss of sandpaper. Each of the commercials contained the same "sandpaper test." The announcer informed the audience that, "To prove Rapid Shave's super-moisturizing power, we put it right from the can onto this tough, dry sandpaper. It was apply . . . soak . . . and off in a stroke." While the announcer was speaking, Rapid Shave was applied to a substance that appeared to be sandpaper, and immediately thereafter a razor was shown shaving the substance clean.

The Federal Trade Commission issued a complaint against respondents Colgate and Bates charging that the commercials were false and deceptive. The evidence before the hearing examiner disclosed that sandpaper of the type depicted in the commercials could not be shaved immediately following the application of Rapid Shave, but required a substantial period of approximately 80 minutes. The evidence also showed that the substance resembling sandpaper was in fact a simulated prop, or "mock-up," made of plexiglass to which sand had been applied.

In reviewing the substantive issues in the case, it is well to remember the respective roles of the Commission and the courts in the administration of the Federal Trade Commission Act. When the Commission was created by Congress in 1914, it was directed by Section 5 to prevent "(u)nfair methods of competition in commerce." Congress amended the Act in 1938 to extend the Commission's jurisdiction to include "unfair or deceptive acts or practices in commerce"—a significant amendment showing Congress' concern for consumers as well as for competitors. It is important to note the generality of these standards of illegality; the prescriptions in Section 5 are flexible, "to be defined with particularity by the myriad of cases from the field of business."

This statutory scheme necessarily gives the Commission an influential role in interpreting Section 5 and in applying it to the facts of particular cases arising out of unprecedented situations. Moreover, as an administrative agency which deals continually with cases in the area, the Commission is often in a better position than are courts to determine when a practice is "deceptive" within the meaning of the Act. This Court has frequently stated that the Commission's judgment is to be given great weight by reviewing courts. This admonition is especially true with respect to allegedly deceptive advertising since the finding of a Section 5 violation in this field rests so heavily on inference and pragmatic judgment. Nevertheless, while informed judicial determination is dependent upon enlightenment gained from administrative experience, in the last analysis the words "deceptive practices" set forth a legal standard and they must get their final meaning from judicial construction.

We are not concerned in this case with the clear misrepresentation in the commercials concerning the speed with which Rapid Shave could shave sandpaper, since the Court of Appeals upheld the Commission's finding on that matter and the respondents have not challenged the finding here. We granted certiorari to consider the Commission's conclusion that even if an advertiser has himself conducted a test, experiment, or demonstration which he honestly believes will prove a certain product claim, he may not convey to television viewers the false impression that they are seeing the test, experiment, or demonstration for themselves, when they are not because of the undisclosed use of mock-ups.

We accept the Commission's determination that the commercials involved in this case contained three representations to the public: 1) that sandpaper could be shaved by Rapid Shave; 2) that an experiment had been conducted which verified this claim; and 3) that the viewer was seeing this experiment for himself. Respondents admit that the first two representations were made, but deny that the third was. The Commission, however, found to the contrary, and since this is a matter of fact resting on an inference that could reasonably be drawn from the commercials themselves the Commission's finding should be sustained. For the purposes of our review, we can assume that the first two representations were true; the focus of our consideration is on the third which was clearly false. The parties agree that Section 5 prohibits the intentional misrepresentation of any fact which would constitute a material factor in a purchaser's decision whether to buy. They differ, however, in their conception of what "facts" constitute a "material factor" in a purchaser's decision to buy. Respondents submit, in effect, that the only material facts are those which deal with the substantive qualities of a product. The Commission, on the other hand, submits that the misrepresentation of *any* fact so long as it materially induces a purchaser's decision to buy is a deception prohibited by Section 5.

The Commission's interpretation of what is a deceptive practice seems more in line with the decided cases than that of respondents. It has long been considered a deceptive practice to state falsely that a product ordinarily sells for an inflated price but that it is being offered at a special reduced price, even if the offered price represents the actual value of the product and the purchaser is receiving his money's worth. Applying respondents' arguments to these cases, it would appear that so long as buyers paid no more than the product was actually worth and the product contained the qualities advertised, the misstatement of an inflated original price was immaterial. It had also been held a violation of Section 5 for a seller to misrepresent to the public that he is in a certain line of business, even though the misstatement in no way affects the qualities of the product.

The courts of appeals have applied this reasoning to the merchandising of reprocessed products that are as good as new, without a disclosure that they are in fact reprocessed. And it has also been held that it is a deceptive practice to misappropriate the trade name of another.

Respondents claim that all these cases are irrelevant to our decision because they involve misrepresentations related to the product itself and not merely to the manner in which an advertising message is communicated. This distinction misses the mark for two reasons. In the first place, the present case is not concerned with a mode of communication, but with a misrepresentation that viewers have objective proof of a seller's product claim over and above the seller's word. Secondly, all of the above cases, like the present case, deal with methods designed to get a consumer to purchase a product, not with whether the product, when purchased, will perform up to expectations. We find an especially strong similarity between the present case and those cases in which a seller induces the public to purchase an arguably good product by misrepresenting his line of business, by concealing the fact that the product is reprocessed, or by misappropriating another's trademark. In each the seller has used a misrepresentation to break down what he regards to be an annoying or irrational habit of the buying public—the preference for particular manufacturers or known brands regardless of a product's actual qualities, the prejudice against reprocessed goods, and the desire for verification of a product claim. In each case the seller reasons that when the habit is broken the buyer will be satisifed with the performance of the product he receives. Yet, a misrepresentation has been used to break the habit and, as was stated in *Algoma Lumber,* a misrepresentation for such an end is not permitted.

We need not limit ourselves to the cases already mentioned because there are other situations which also illustrate the correctness of the Commission's finding in the present case. It is generally accepted that it is a deceptive practice to state falsely that a product has received a testimonial from a respected source. In addition, the Commission has consistently acted to prevent sellers from falsely stating that their product claims have been "certified." We find these situations to be indistinguishable from the present case. We can assume that in each the underlying product claim is true and in each the seller actually conducted an experiment sufficient to prove to himself the truth of the claim. But in each the seller has told the public that it could rely on something other than his word concerning both the truth of the claim and the validity of his experiment. We find it an immaterial difference that in one case the viewer is told to rely on the word of a celebrity or authority he respects, in another on the word of a testing agency, and in the present case on his own perception of an undisclosed simulation.

Respondents again insist that the present case is not like any of the above, but is more like a case in which a celebrity or independent testing agency has in fact submitted a written verification of an experiment actually observed, but, because of the inability of the camera to transmit accurately an impression of the paper on which the testimonial is written, the seller reproduces it on another substance so that it can be seen by the viewing audience. This analogy ignores the finding of the Commission that in the present case the seller misrepresented to the public that it was being given objective proof of a product claim. In respondents' hypothetical, the objective proof of the product claim that is offered, the word of the celebrity or agency that the experiment was actually conducted, does exist; while in the case before us the objective proof offered, the viewer's own perception of an actual experiment, does not exist. Thus, in respondents' hypothetical, unlike the present case, the use of the undisclosed mock-up does not conflict with the seller's claim that there is objective proof.

We agree with the Commission, therefore, that the undisclosed use of plexiglass in the present commercials, was a material deceptive practice, independent and separate from the other misrepresentation found. We find unpersuasive respondents' other objections to this conclusion. Respondents claim that it will be impractical to inform the viewing public that it is not seeing an actual test, experiment, or demonstration, but we think it inconceivable that the ingenious advertising world will be unable, if it so desires, to conform to the Commission's insistence that the public be not misinformed. If, however, it becomes impossible or impractical to show simulated demonstrations on television in a truthful manner, this indicates that television is not a medium that lends itself to this type of commercial, not that the commercial must survive at all costs. Similarly unpersuasive is respondents' objection that the Commission's decision discriminates against sellers whose product claims cannot be "verified" on television without the use of simulations. All methods of advertising do not equally favor every seller. If the inherent limitations of a method do not permit its use in the way a seller desires, the seller cannot by material misrepresentation compensate for those limitations.

We turn our attention now to the order issued by the Commission. It has been repeatedly held that the Commission has wide discretion in determining the type of order that is necessary to cope with the unfair practices found, and that Congress has placed the primary responsibility for fashioning orders upon the Commission. For these reasons the courts should not "lightly modify" the Commission's orders. However, this Court has also warned that an order's prohibitions "should be clear and precise in order that they may be understood by those against whom they are directed," and that "(t)he severity of possible penalties proscribed . . . for violations of orders which have become final underlines the necessity for fashioning orders which are, at the outset, sufficiently clear and precise to avoid raising serious questions as to their meaning and application."

The Court of Appeals has criticized the reference in the Commission's order to "test, experiment, or demonstration" as not capable of practical interpretation. It could find no difference between the Rapid Shave commercial and a commercial which extolled the goodness of ice cream while giving viewers a picture of a scoop of mashed potatoes appearing to be ice cream. We do not understand this difficulty. In the ice cream case the mashed potato prop is not being used for additional proof of the product claim, while the purpose of the Rapid Shave commercial is to give the viewer objective proof of the claims made. If in the ice cream hypothetical the focus of the commercial becomes the undisclosed potato prop and the viewer is invited, explicitly or by implication, to see for himself the truth of the claims about the ice cream's rich texture and full color, and perhaps compare it to a "rival product," then the commercial has become similar to the one now before us. Clearly, however, a commercial which depicts happy actors delightedly eating ice cream that is in fact mashed potatoes or drinking a product appearing to be coffee but which is in fact some other substance is not covered by the present order.

The crucial terms of the present order—"test, experiment, or demonstration . . . represented . . . as actual proof of a claim"—are as specific as the circumstances will permit. If respondents in their subsequent commercials attempt to come as close to the line of misrepresentation as the Commission's order permits, they may without specifically intending to do so cross into the area proscribed by this order. However, it does not seem "unfair to require that one who deliberately goes perilously close to an area of proscribed conduct shall take the risk that he may cross the line." In commercials where the emphasis is on the seller's word, and not on the viewer's own perception, the respondents need not fear that an undisclosed use of props is prohibited by the present order. On the other hand, when the commercial not only makes a claim, but also invites the viewer to rely on his own perception for demonstrative proof of the claim, the respondents will be aware that the use of undisclosed props in strategic places might be a material deception.

We believe that respondents will have no difficulty applying the Commission's order to the vast majority of their contemplated future commercials. If, however, a situation arises in which respondents are sincerely unable to determine whether a proposed course of action would violate the present order, they can, by complying with the Commission's rules, oblige the Commission to give them definitive advice as to whether their proposed action, if pursued, would constitute compliance with the order.

Finally, we find no defect in the provision of the order which prohibits respondents from engaging in similar practices with respect to "any product" they advertise. The propriety of a broad order depends upon the specific circumstances of the case, but the courts will not interfere except where the remedy selected has no practices found to exist. In this case the respondents produced three different commercials which employed the same deceptive practice. This we believe gave the Commission a sufficient basis for believing that the respondents would be inclined to use similar commercials with respect to the other products they advertise. We think it reasonable for the Commission to frame its order broadly enough to prevent respondents from engaging in similarly illegal practices in future advertisements.

The judgment of the Court of Appeals is reversed and the case remanded for the entry of a judgment enforcing the Commission's order.

Reversed and remanded.

J.B. WILLIAMS (GERITOL)
68 FTC 481 (1965)

This case involves an order requiring a New York City manufacturer of drug preparations and its advertising agency, to cease misrepresenting the effectiveness of its "Geritol" liquid and tablets by falsely representing in television commercials and newspaper advertising that all cases of tiredness, loss of strength, run-down feeling, nervousness, and irritability indicate a deficiency of iron. They further represent that the common effective remedy for these symptoms is "Geritol." Finally they state affirmatively that in the great majority of cases of tiredness the symptoms are not caused by such iron or vitamin deficiency.

Pursuant to the provisions of the Federal Trade Commission Act, and by virtue of the authority vested in it by said Act, the (FTC), having reason to believe that The J.B. Williams Company, Inc., a corporation, and Parkson Advertising Agency, Inc., a corporation, hereinafter referred to as respondents, have violated the provisions of said Act, and it appearing to the Commission that a proceeding by it in respect thereof would be in the public interest, hereby issues its complaints stating its charges.

Through the use of the statements in the aforesaid advertisements, and others similar thereto not specifically set out herein, respondents have represented, and are now representing, directly and by implication:

1. That the use of Geritol Liquid and Geritol Tablets will be of benefit, safe and effective in the treatment and relief of an established or existing deficiency of iron and iron deficency anemia, and tiredness, loss of strength, run-down feeling, nervousness, and irritability.
2. That Geritol Liquid and Geritol Tablets, and each of them, will increase the strength and energy of every part of the body within 24 hours.
3. That Geritol Liquid and Geritol Tablets, and each of them, will promote convalescence from a cold, flu, fever, virus infection, sore throat, and other winter illnesses.
4. That the vitamins contained in both Geritol Liquid and Geritol Tablets contribute to the effectiveness of these preparations in the treatment or relief of an established or existing deficiency of iron or iron deficiency anemia.
5. That the purchase price of Geritol Liquid and Geritol Tablets will be refunded unconditionally if the purchaser is not satisifed with the product.

In truth and in fact:

1. Neither Geritol Liquid nor Geritol Tablets will be of benefit in the treatment of tiredness, loss of strength, run-down feeling, nervousness, or irritability except in a small minority of persons whose tiredness, loss of strength, run-down feeling, nervousness, or irritability is due to an established or existing deficiency of one or more of the vitamins provided by these preparations or to an established or existing deficiency of iron or to iron deficiency anemia.

Furthermore, the statements and representations in said advertisements have the capacity and tendency to suggest, and do suggest, to persons viewing or hearing such advertisements that in cases of person of both sexes and all ages who experience tiredness, loss of strength, run-down feeling, nervousness, or irritability there is a reasonable probability that these symptoms in such cases will respond to treatment by the use of these preparations; and have the capacity and tendency to suggest, and do suggest, that in cases of persons of both sexes and all ages who have an established or existing deficiency of iron or who have iron deficiency anemia the preparations can be used safely and effectively in the treatment and relief of an established or existing deficiency of iron or of iron deficiency anemia and their symptoms. In the light of such statements and representations, said advertisements are misleading in a material respect and therefore constitute "false advertisements," as that term is defined in the Federal Trade Commission Act, because they fail to reveal the material facts that in the great majority of persons, or of any age, sex, or other group or class thereof, who experience tiredness, loss of strength, run-down feeling, nervousness, or irritability, these symptoms are not caused by an established or existing deficiency of one or more of the vitamins provided by Geritol Liquid or Geritol Tablets or by an established or existing deficiency of iron or iron deficiency anemia, and that in such persons the said preparations will be of no benefit; and they are additionally misleading in a material respect because they fail to reveal the material fact, when representing that the preparations will be effective in the treatment and relief of an established or existing deficiency of iron or of iron deficiency anemia in adults, and when ascribing symptoms of tiredness, loss of strength, run-down feeling, nervousness, or irritability in adults, to an established or existing deficiency of iron or to iron deficiency anemia, that in women of any age beyond the usual childbearing age and in men of all ages, an established or existing deficiency of iron or iron deficiency anemia is almost invariably due to bleeding and the use of the preparations may mask the signs and symptoms and thereby permit the progression of such disease or disorder.

2. Neither Geritol Liquid nor Geritol Tablets will increase the strength or energy of any part of the body within 24 hours.

3. Neither Geritol Liquid nor Geritol Tablets will be of benefit in promoting convalescence from a cold, flu, fever, virus infection, sore throat, or other winter illnesses.

4. The vitamins supplied in neither Geritol Liquid nor Geritol Tablets are of any benefit in the treatment or relief of an established or existing deficiency of iron or iron deficiency anemia.

5. The purchase price of Geritol Liquid or Geritol Tablets is not refunded unconditionally, but there are terms and conditions which must be complied with by a purchaser in order for him to secure a refund, which terms and conditions are not disclosed in the advertising.

The aforesaid advertisements set forth and referred to in Paragraph Five above were, and are, misleading in material respects and constitute "false advertisements," as that term is defined in the Federal Trade Commission Act.

The dissemination by the respondents of the false advertisements, as aforesaid, constituted, and now constitutes, unfair and deceptive acts and practices in commerce, in violation of Sections 5 and 12 of the Federal Trade Commission Act.

CONCLUSIONS

1. The Federal Trade Commission has jurisdiction of the subject matter of this proceeding and of the respondents.
2. The complaint herein states a cause of action and this proceeding is in the public interest.
3. The dissemination by the respondents of the false advertisements as herein found constituted, and now constitutes, unfair and deceptive acts and practices in commerce, in violation of Sections 5 and 12 of the Federal Trade Commission Act.

ORDER

It is ordered, that respondents, the J.B. Williams Company, Inc., a corporation, and Parkson Advertising Agency, Inc., a corporation, and their officers, and respondents' representatives, agents, and employees, directly or through any corporate or other device, in connection with the offering for sale, of substantially similar composition or possessing substantially similar properties, under whatever name or names sold, do forthwith cease and desist from, directly or indirectly:

1. Disseminating or causing to be disseminated by means of the United States mails or by any means in commerce, as "commerce" is defined in the Federal Trade Commission Act, any advertisement which represents directly or by implication:

a. That the use of such preparation will be of benefit in the treatment or relief of tiredness, loss of strength, run-down feeling, nervousness, or irritability unless such advertisement expressly limits the effectiveness of the preparation to those persons whose symptoms are due to an established or existing deficiency of one or more of the vitamins provided by the preparation, or to an established or existing deficiency of iron or to iron deficiency anemia, and, further, unless the advertisement clearly and conspicuously reveals the fact that in the great majority of persons, of any age, sex, or other group or class thereof, who experience such symptoms, these symptoms are due to conditions other than those which may respond to treatment by the use of the preparation, and that in such persons the preparation will not be of benefit.

b. That the use of such preparation will be of benefit in the treatment or relief of tiredness, loss of strength, run-down feeling, nervousness, or irritability due to an established or existing deficiency of iron, or to iron deficiency anemia, in adults other than women in the usual childbearing age group, unless such advertisement, in addition to the requirements of paragraph (a) hereof, clearly and conspicuously reveals the fact that an established or existing deficiency of iron, or iron deficiency anemia, in such adults, or in any age, sex, or other group or class thereof, is almost invariably due to bleeding from some serious disease or disorder, and that in the absence of adequate treatment of the underlying cause the use of the preparation in such adults may mask the signs and symptoms and thereby permit the progression of such disease or disorder.

c. That the use of such preparation will be of benefit in the treatment or relief of an established or existing deficiency of iron, or of iron deficiency anemia, in adults other than women in the usual childbearing age group, unless such advertisement clearly and conspicuously reveals the fact that an established or existing deficiency of iron, or iron deficiency anemia, in such adults, or in any age, sex, or other group or class thereof, is almost invariably due to bleeding from some serious disease or disorder and that, in the absence of adequate treatment of the underlying cause, the use of the preparation in such adults may mask the signs and symptoms and thereby permit the progression of such disease or disorder.

d. That the use of such preparation will increase the strength or energy of any part of the body within 24 hours.

e. That the use of such preparation will promote convalescence from a cold, flu, fever, virus infection, sore throat, or other winter illnesses.

f. That the vitamins supplied in such preparation are of any benefit in the treatment or relief of an established or existing deficiency of iron or iron deficiency anemia.

2. Disseminating, or causing to be disseminated, by any means, for the purpose of inducing, or which is likely to induce, directly or indirectly, the purchase of any such preparation, in commerce, as "commerce" is defined in the Federal Trade Commission Act, any advertisement which contains any of the representations prohibited in, or which fails to comply with the affirmative requirements of, Paragraph 1, hereof.

It is further ordered, that so much of the complaint as charged that the purchase price of Geritol or Geritol Tablets is not refunded unconditionally if the purchaser is not satisifed with the product be, and the same hereby is, dismissed.

LIBBEY-OWENS-FORD GLASS COMPANY v. FEDERAL TRADE COMMISSION
325 F.2d 415 (1965)

Before Weick, Chief Judge, Phillips, Circuit Judge, and Taylor, District Judge.*
Per Curiam.

These two cases are before the Court on petitions to review cease and desist orders of the Federal Trade Commission issued upon complaint charging Libbey-Owens-Ford Glass Company (LOF), a manufacturer and sole supplier of automobile glass for General Motors cars, and General Motors Corporation (GM) with unfair and deceptive acts and practices and unfair methods of competition in violation of Section 5 of the Federal Trade Commission Act, 15 U.S.C. Section 45.

Specifically, the facts as to LOF involved twenty-two television commercials purporting to show the superiority of safety plate glass used in all of the windows of GM cars over safety sheet glass used in the side and rear windows of non-GM cars. The facts as to GM involved the televising of one commercial on two separate occasions purporting to show the same superiority.

The Commission found in both cases that the commercials contained false representations that the plate glass used in the side and rear windows of GM cars was the same grade and quality as the plate glass used in the windshields of GM cars, and that the sheet glass used in the side and rear windows of non-GM cars was the same grade and quality as sheet glass used in home windows. The Commission also found that the commercials in both cases contained false demonstrations achieved through the use of undisclosed "mock-ups" or "props." In respect to LOF, it was found that the commercials exaggerated the distortion in sheet glass by using different camera lens in filming, more acute angles, and other techniques, including taking a photograph through an open window instead of through the plate glass window as the viewer was led to believe. As to GM, the same exaggeration was achieved by the use of streaks of vaseline applied to the glass being photographed and panning the camera from side to side as though the viewer were walking past a home window. Based on these findings the Commission ordered LOF and GM to cease and desist from such practices.

Both LOF and GM contended that there was no basis for the inferences drawn by the Commission that the commercials misrepresented that the grade and quality of plate glass used in the side and rear windows of GM cars was the same as plate glass used in the windshields of GM cars, and that the sheet glass used in the side and rear windows of non-GM cars was the same grade and quality as sheet glass used in home windows.

1. We think that it was within the discretion of the Commission to interpret and determine the meaning of the commercials and the impressions they would likely make upon the viewing public. The weight to be given the facts as well as inferences reasonably to be drawn therefrom was for the Commission.

2. The decision of the Supreme Court in *Federal Trade Commission* v. *Colgate-Palmolive Co.* disposed of the "mock-up" issue here. There, the Court held that the undisclosed use of mock-ups was a deceptive practice even though the test, experiment, or demonstration actually proved the product claim.

3., 4. On the authority of *Colgate* we sustain the Commission's order barring LOF and GM from using undisclosed mock-ups in advertising automotive glass products. We find no merit in LOF's

---

*Robert L. Taylor, Chief Judge, United States District Court for the Eastern District of Tennessee, sitting by designation.

contention that it should not be held liable for the use of props by the film producer who, it claims, was an independent contractor. It asserted that in good faith it directed the advertising agency to present a fair commercial and it was unaware of the use of the open window. In our opinion LOF may not delegate its advertising to an independent contractor and escape liability for the acts of its advertising agency and film producer in advertising LOF products.

We find no merit in GM's contention that *Colgate* does not apply to it because the kind of misrepresentation presented by the Colgate commercials was not contained in the GM commercial.

In our judgment, upon consideration of the record as a whole there was substantial evidence to support the findings of facts of the Commission and they are binding on us.

5. GM claimed that the order was improper as to it because it abandoned its single commercial eighteen months prior to the Commission's complaint and, as found by the Commission, had no intention of using the commercial again. It also argued on the same grounds that there is no public interest. It was within the Commission's discretion to determine if the public interest was affected, and to frame an order to protect against related and similar practices in the future, some of which were not embraced in GM's assurances. We find no abuse of discretion.

6. The only remaining questions go to the scope of the orders which both petitioners claimed were too broad. We think the order entered against LOF was not too broad and was authorized by *Colgate*. The Commission had authority to stop misrepresentations as to other glass products in other advertisements. The order against GM was also authorized except the following language contained in paragraph 1(a) therein: "or otherwise misrepresenting the grade or quality of glass used in any window." We believe this portion of the order was too vague and indefinite to warrant enforcement. It is therefore ordered that the quoted language be stricken from the order.

The order of the Commission is No. 15,663 is affirmed and enforced.

The order of the Commission is No. 15,664, is affirmed and enforced as modified.

ON PETITION FOR REHEARING

Upon consideration of the Petition for Rehearing, it is ordered that there be deleted from Paragraph 1(a) of the Commission's final order entered against Libbey-Owens-Ford Glass Company, the words "or otherwise misrepresenting the grade or quality of glass used in any window."

It is further ordered that the Petition for Rehearing be and it is hereby denied.

J.B. WILLIAMS COMPANY, INC. v. *FEDERAL TRADE COMMISSION*
381 F.2d 884 (CA5 1967)

Celebrezze, Circuit Judge.

The question presented by this appeal is whether Petitioners' advertising of a product, Geritol, for relief of iron deficiency anemia, is false and misleading so as to violate Sections 5 and 12 of the Federal Trade Commission Act.[1] At the conclusion of an administrative proceeding upon a complaint which charged Petitioners with engaging in unfair and deceptive acts, the Federal Trade Commission affirmed in part the findings of the Hearing Examiner that the Petitioners had violated Sections 5 and

12 of the Federal Trade Commission Act. Petitioners seek review to set aside the Order to cease and desist, issued by the Commission.

The J.B. Williams Company, Inc. is a New York corporation engaged in the sale and distribution of two products known as Geritol Liquid and Geritol Tablets. Geritol Liquid was first marketed in August, 1950; Geritol Tablets in February, 1952. Geritol is sold throughout the United States and advertisements for Geritol have appeared in newspapers and or television in all the States of the United States.

Parkson Advertising Agency, Inc. has been the advertising agency for Williams since 1957. Most of the advertising money for Geritol is spent on television advertising.

The Commission's Order requires that not only must the Geritol advertisements be expressly limited to those persons whose symptoms are due to an existing deficiency of one or more of the vitamins contained in the preparation, or due to an existing deficiency of iron, but also the Geritol advertisements must affirmatively disclose the negative fact that a great majority of persons who experience these symptoms do not experience them because they have a vitamin or iron deficiency; that for the great majority of people experiencing these symptoms, Geritol will be of no benefit. Closely related to this requirement is the further requirement of the Order that the Geritol advertisements refrain from representing that the symptoms are generally reliable indications of iron deficiency.

An understanding of the function of iron in the human body and how it is lost is essential to an understanding of the issues in this case and the medical testimony relating to these issues.

Noted specialists in hematology, and obstretrics and gynecology testified for both sides. Their testimony was not all in agreement. Doctors Dameshek, Goldsmith, McGanity, Tein, Moore, and Arrowsmith testified that the symptoms presented in the Geritol advertising are common symptoms of many diseases and are not specific to iron deficiency anemia. These symptoms occur in most diseases, and most commonly occur in neurosis or nervous tension. Only in severe or perhaps moderately severe cases of iron deficiency anemia are these symptoms present. The Commission's finding that the Geritol advertisements create a false and misleading impression on the public by taking common or universal symptoms and representing these symptoms as generally reliable indications of iron deficiency or iron deficiency anemia, is supported by substantial evidence.

The main thrust of the Commission's Order is that the Geritol advertising must affirmatively disclose the negative fact that a great majority of persons who experience these symptoms do not experience them because there is a vitamin or iron deficiency.

The medical evidence on this issue is conflicting and the question is not one which is susceptible to precise statistical analysis. The evidence presented a range estimated by the doctors to be from one percent to ten percent of the people in this country with iron deficiency or iron deficiency anemia. It is clear that the incidence of iron deficiency anemia is higher in women than in men. Doctors Dameshek, Adelson, and McGanity testified that a majority of pregnant women do not develop iron deficiency anemia. Doctor Wintrobe and Doctor Bentler testified that iron deficiency anemia is the most common and most important nutritional deficiency.

Since the symptoms of tiredness, loss of strength, nervousness, or irritability are universal, nonspecific complaints, there was naturally a disagreement as to whether these symptoms are usually due to iron deficiency anemia, or are present when a person has iron deficiency anemia.

Not all of the approximate ten percent of the population who have iron deficiency anemia have moderate to severe anemia, and consequently exhibit mild or no symptoms. While there are no statistics available as to the number of people who are tired and run-down, or the number of people who are tired and run-down due to iron deficiency anemia, there is direct testimony that only a minority of people with these symptoms have the symptoms because of iron deficiency anemia. Considering this evidence along with the fact that these symptoms are common and nonspecific, the Commission could reasonably infer, and there was substantial evidence to support the finding, that the majority of the people who have these symptoms, have them because of causes other than iron deficiency anemia.

There was testimony that in severe or moderately severe cases the symptoms occurred as a result of iron deficiency anemia. The highest incidence of iron deficiency anemia was found to be in women in the childbearing age group. Doctor Dameshek said the presence of these symptoms was hardly ever due to iron deficiency anemia; Doctor Moore said the presence of these symptoms could be explained on a basis other than iron deficiency anemia, and that only in a minority of women were these symptoms due to iron deficiency anemia; Doctor Reznikoff did not accept these symptoms as being caused by iron deficiency.

Not all of the approximate ten percent of the population who have iron deficiency anemia have moderate to severe anemia, and consequently exhibit mild or no symptoms. While there are no statistics available as to the number of people who are tired and run-down, or the number of people who are tired and run-down due to iron deficiency anemia, there is direct testimony that only a minority of people with these symptoms exhibit these symptoms because of iron deficiency anemia. Considering this evidence along with the fact that these symptoms are common and nonspecific, the Commission could reasonably infer, and there was substantial evidence to support the finding, that the majority of the people who have these symptoms, have them because of causes other than iron deficiency anemia.

While the advertising does not make the affirmative representation that the majority of people who are tired and run-down are so because of iron deficiency anemia and the product Geritol will be an effective cure, there is substantial evidence to support the finding of the Commission that most tired people are not so because or iron deficiency anemia, and the failure to disclose this fact is false and misleading, because the advertisement creates the impression that the tired feeling is caused by something which Geritol can cure.

Here the advertisements emphasize the fact that if you are often tired and run-down, you will feel stronger fast by taking Geritol. The Commission, in looking at the overall impression created by the advertisements on the general public, could reasonably find these advertisements were false and misleading. The finding that the advertisements link common, nonspecific symptoms with iron deficiency anemia, and thereby create a false impression because most people with these symptoms are not suffering from iron deficiency anemia is both reasonable and supported by substantial evidence. The Commission is not bound to the literal meaning of words, nor must the Commission take a random sample to determine the meaning and impact of the advertisements.

Petitioners argue vigorously that the Commission does not have the legal power to require them to state the negative fact that "in the great majority of persons who experience such symptoms, these symptoms are not caused by a deficiency of one or more of the vitamins contained in the preparation or by iron deficiency or iron deficiency anemia;" and "for such persons the preparation will be of no benefit."

We believe the evidence is clear that Geritol is of no benefit in the treatment of tiredness except in those cases where tiredness has been caused by a deficiency of the ingredients contained in Geritol. The fact that the great majority of people who experience tiredness symptoms do not suffer from any deficiency of the ingredients in Geritol is a "material fact" under the meaning of that term as used in Section 15[2] of the Federal Trade Commission Act, and Petitioners' failure to reveal this fact in this day when the consumer is influenced by mass advertising utilizing highly developed arts of persuasion, renders it difficult for the typical consumer to know whether the product will in fact meet his needs unless he is told what the product will or will not do. This does not fall within the sphere of negative advertising, it merely presents to the consumer an opportunity to make an intelligent choice.

Under the facts of this case, the disclosure requirement of 1(d)(1) is both proper and justified.

The Commission also found that Petitioners' advertisements represent that Geritol is generally an effective cure for tiredness because of its iron and vitamin content. The Petitioners concede that their Geritol advertisements must be limited to those persons whose symptoms are due to iron deficiency anemia. Petitioners contend their advertisements are so limited.

The advertisements say that the condition of tiredness and run-down feeling may be caused by iron deficiency, and, if it is, Geritol will give fast relief. Geritol, then, is good for iron deficiency anemia. The Commission has found, and we have agreed, that the advertisements create the impression that iron deficiency anemia causes most tiredness. The Commission's conclusion is reasonable when it completed the syllogism by finding that the advertisements represent that Geritol is good for most tiredness. It is this representation, that Geritol is good for most tiredness, which is the inherent vice of the advertisements.

The Commission forbids the Petitioners' representation that the presence of iron deficiency anemia can be self-diagnosed or can be determined without a medical test. The danger to be remedied here has been fully and adequately taken care of in the other requirements of the Order. We can find no Congressional policy against self-medication on a trial and error basis where the consumer is fully informed and the product is safe as Geritol is conceded to be. In fact Congressional policy is to encourage such self-help. In effect the Commission's Order 1(f) tends to place Geritol in the prescription drug field. We do not consider it within the power of the Federal Trade Commission to remove Geritol from the area of proprietary drugs and place it in the area of prescription drugs. This requirement of the Order will not be enforced. We also find this Order is not unduly vague and fairly apprises the Petitioners of what is required of them. Petition denied and, except for 1(f) of the Commission's Order, enforcement of the Order will be granted.

NOTES

[1] Section 5(a)(1), 52 State. 111, 15 U.S.C. Section 45(a)(1):

"Unfair methods of competition in commerce, and unfair or deceptive acts or practices in commerce, are declared unlawful."

"Section 12, 52 Stat. 114, 15 U.S.C. 52:

"(a) It shall be unlawful for any person, partnership, or corporation to disseminate, or cause to be disseminated, any false advertisement—

(1) By United States mails, or in commerce by any means, for the purpose of inducing, or which is likely to induce, directly or indirectly the purchase of food, drugs, devices, or cosmetics; or

(2) By any means, for the purpose of inducing, or which is likely to induce, directly or indirectly, the purchase in commerce of food, drugs, devices, or cosmetics.

(b) The dissemination or the causing to be disseminated of any false advertisement within the provisions of subsection (a) of this section shall be an unfair or deceptive act or practice in commerce within the meaning of Section 45 of this title."

[2] 15 USCA Section 55. "(a)(1) The term 'false advertisement' means an advertisement, other than labeling, which is misleading in a material respect; and in determining, there shall be taken into account (among other things) not only representations made or suggested by statement, word, design, device, sound, or any combination thereof, but also the extent to which the advertisement fails to reveal facts material in the light of such representations or material with respect to consequences which may result from the use of commodity to which the advertisement relates under the conditions prescribed in said advertisement, under such conditions as are customary or usual.

J.B. WILLIAMS (VIVARIN)
81 F.T.C. 238 (1972)

This case involves a consent order requiring a New York City seller and distributor of a stimulant type product, and its advertising agencies, among other things, to cease disseminating any advertisement which represents the use of any such products will solve an individual's sexual, marital, or personality problems; advertising as a stimulant, any product which contains caffeine unless the caffeine content is expressed in terms of the number of average cups of ordinary coffee, clearly and conspicuously, in immediate conjunction with a statement of active ingredients; representing any nonprescription drug as new when such product has been distributed for six months or more.

ORDER

I

It is ordered, that respondents, the J.B. Williams Company, Inc., a corporation, Della Femina, Travisano & Partners, Inc., a corporation, and Parkson Advertising Agency, Inc., a corporation, their successors and assigns and respondents' representatives, agents, and employees, directly or through any corporation, subsidiary, division, or other device, in connection with the advertising, offering for sale, or distribution of the product designated "Vivarin" or any other stimulant drug product or any calmative drug product, including sleep-inducers, do forthwith cease and desist from:

    1. Disseminating, or causing to be disseminated, by means of the United States mails or by any means in commerce, as "commerce" is defined in the Federal Trade Commission Act, any advertisement which represents directly or by implication that:

    a. The use of any such product will solve an individual's marital, sexual, or personality problems.

    b. The use of any such product will improve an individual's personality or make it more exciting or will improve an individual's physical appearance, marriage, or sex life.

Provided however, that in advertisements of sleep inducers this paragraph shall not prohibit representations that, by providing the user with a good night's sleep, such products can help the user to feel rested and look better. This paragraph shall not preclude the Commission from challenging these representations as unlawful in a future proceeding under Section 5(b) of the Federal Trade Commission Act.

    2. Disseminating, or causing the dissemination of, any advertisement by any means, for the purpose of inducing, or which is likely to induce, directly or indirectly, the purchase of any such product, in commerce, as "commerce" is defined in the Federal Trade Commission Act, which contains any of the representations prohibited in Paragraph 1 above.

II

It is further ordered, that respondents, the J.B. Williams Company, Inc., a corporation, Della Femina, Travisano & Partners, Inc., a corporation, and Parkson Advertising Agency, Inc., a corporation, their successors and assigns, and respondents' officers, representatives, agents, and employees, directly or through any corporation, subsidiary, division, or other device, do forthwith cease and desist from:

1. Advertising, as a stimulant, "Vivarin" or any other drug product which contains caffeine unless the caffeine content, expressed in terms of the number of average size cups of ordinary coffee, is clearly and conspicuously disclosed with a statement in immediate conjunction therewith that caffeine is the primary active ingredient, or one of the primary active ingredients if such product contains more than one active ingredient.

2. Disseminating, or causing the dissemination of, any advertisement by means of the United States mails or by any means in commerce, as "commerce" is defined in the Federal Trade Commission Act, which contained statements which are inconsistent with, negate, or contradict the affirmative disclosure required by Paragraph 1 above, or which in any way obscures the meaning of such disclosure.

III

It is further ordered, that respondents, the J.B. Williams Company, Inc., a corporation, and Parkson Advertising Agency, Inc., a corporation, their successors and assigns, and respondents' officers, agents, representatives, and employees, directly or through any corporation, subsidiary, division, or other device, do forthwith cease and desist from representing, directly or by implication, that any nonprescription drug product is new, has new ingredients, or is new in its therapeutic effectiveness when such product has been distributed for six months or more or when it is substantially similar in composition and therapeutic effectiveness to another product advertised for the same therapeutic effect which has been distributed for at least six months. (For the purpose of this provision "distributed" shall not include distribution in areas representing not more than 15 percent of the population.)

Provided however, respondents may represent that any such product has not been previously sold, advertised, or manufactured by respondent the J.B. Williams Company, Inc., if such is the case.

IV

It is further ordered, that respondents shall forthwith distribute a copy of this order to each of their operating divisions.

It is further ordered, that respondents notify the Commission at least thirty (30) days prior to any proposed change in the corporate respondents such as dissolution, assignment, or sale resulting in the emergence of a successor corporation, the creation or dissolution of subsidiaries or any other change in the corporation which may affect compliance obligations arising out of the order.

It is further ordered, that respondents shall, within sixty (60) days after service of this order upon them, each file with the Commission a report in writing setting forth in detail the manner and form of their compliance with this order.

CONSUMERS ASSOCIATION OF DISTRICT OF COLUMBIA v. CBS AND WTOP-TV
32 FCC 2d 405 (1971)

By Direction of the commission, Ben F. Waple, *Secretary.*

This refers to the complaint filed on behalf of the Consumers Association of the District of Columbia against the Columbia Broadcasting System, Inc., and the licensee of Station WTOP-TV, Washington, D.C., alleging failure on their part to fulfill the obligation to protect the public from false, misleading, or deceptive advertising.

IV. Discussion

A. General

In treating this complaint, we shall first discuss the issues raised generally and then turn to the specific advertisements. We think it important initially to delineate the role of this agency vis-a-vis other governmental entities.

As we have previously made clear, the main thrust in the field of deceptive advertising must continue to come from the Federal Trade Commission, the agency specifically created by Congress to deal with that problem. That agency, unlike this Commission, has the capacity to formulate standards of deceptive advertising which are applicable to the various media. It thus has the scientific and related expertise which we lack in this area. Further, FTC action applies to the advertiser (and often the agency), and this has the advantage of running against the party who instigates the deception, and who knows the facts as to tests, surveys, etc., in relation to the claims made. In view of these considerations and the further factor of great problems confronting this agency, with its limited staff resources, in its own areas of exclusive jurisdiction (e.g., licensing, renewal, transfers, fairness, equal time, etc.), it would make no sense for us to undertake to duplicate the work of the FTC by ourselves determining the scientific validity of claims or the precise application of subtle principles in an evolving field.

We therefore normally have not made, and do not intend to make, judgments whether particular broadcast advertisements are false and misleading. While we may indeed act in a clear, flagrant case, we shall continue our practice of generally deferring on these matters to the course upon us since it recognizes that "the Commission may be reluctant to get into the business of determining whether particular advertisements are deceptive."

But that does not mean that this Commission has no role to play in this important area. It clearly has. That role stems from the responsibility of its broadcast licensees in this field.

Our Public Notice dated November 7, 1961, entitled "Licensee Responsibility with Respect to the Broadcast of False, Misleading, or Deceptive Advertising," indicated that "a licensee's duty to protect the public from false, misleading, or deceptive advertising is an important ingredient of his operation in the public interest." We stated that when an advertisement becomes the subject of an FTC complaint a licensee "should . . . exercise particular care in deciding whether to accept it for broadcast;" that the broadcast of an advertisement subject to a final order by the FTC indicating that it is false or misleading would raise a serious question of whether the licensee was operating his station in the public interest: that prior to acceptance of any advertising material the licensee should "take reasonable steps to satisfy himself as to the reliability and reputation of every prospective advertiser and as to his ability to fulfill promises made to the public over the licensed facilities" and that when an advertisement is deemed inappropriate for broadcast it should be brought to the attention of the FTC. In a recent case, *Alan F. Neckritz,* 1971 (the *Chevron* decision), we recognized that most licensees lack the expertise and resources to determine whether certain advertisements are false or misleading. However, we stated that when an advertisement is the subject of an FTC complaint, "(t)he licensee should acquaint itself with the charges recited in the FTC complaint and the advertiser's response," and that "(t)his should assist the licensee in making a responsible determination as to whether continuing to carry the advertisement would be in the public interest."

The foregoing is a summary of policies enunciated to date. Our role is to take all appropriate actions to insure reasonable, good faith discharge by the licensee of its responsibilities. This brings us to the heart of the present complaint. What should our policies be? What specific burdens or responsibilities should be imposed upon the licensee in this field?

The complaint here focuses its attention largely upon the claimed inadequacy of the staffs of both WTOP-TV and the CBS network to deal with the numerous deceptive advertisements which it contends have been carried by WTOP-TV, through either local or network origination. The complaint urges in this connection that the station, which understandably must rely upon the network to a great extent, has a duty to determine that the network's staff is adequate to the performance of the screening function. It is urged that WTOP-TV has failed to make an adequate assessment in this regard, and that the Commission should act to insure that both network and local personnel are adequate in numbers and training to deal with all attempts at deceptive advertising. For example, it is suggested that the CBS medical advisor cannot devote adequate time to his assignment because he is also a practicing physician who is a member of the teaching staff of a medical school, and that the network's Research Department is not, as it should be, composed of chemists, biologists, and/or engineers.

First, we do not believe it to be either reasonable or feasible to impose upon the industry requirements for medical or other scientific testing procedures. Such requirements would, we believe, go beyond what can reasonably be demanded. It is simply not reasonable to try to make networks or licensees into a kind of mini-FTC. Without wide-ranging scientific expertise, it is not feasible to resolve a host of issues that can and do arise. Nor, in any event, do we consider ourselves sufficiently well advised in this area to specify the composition of a scientifically trained staff which we could definitively find to be adequate to perform the functions apparently contemplated by the complainant. Lacking particular expertise concerning the substance of the law of deceptive advertising, we also lack the expertise to lay down prescriptions concerning the type of specialized training which is adequate to make determinations in this area.

Furthermore, even if we felt competent to prescribe appropriate staffing, we would have to take account of the wide variations in station size (and perhaps advertising revenue), and would be required to specify the size and composition, for each category of station, of the staff required to review advertising generally. In our view, this is simply not a feasible undertaking for this Commission.

What then is the appropriate role of the licensee here? The fundamental, bedrock duty which we expect of licensees, in performing their responsibilities under our previous policy statements, is the assiduous attention which can be expected of intelligent and informed individuals. This means that when a matter not involving scientific judgment comes before a broadcaster, either on his own recognition or a complaint, he must make a common sense judgment—since there is no question of scientific expertise. Of course, that judgment may be a difficult one, in light of the facts or FTC principles; the licensee's good faith, reasonable assessment may eventually be proven wrong in an FTC proceeding. He simply must make it as best he can.

Reasonable diligence here clearly calls for the licensee to be alert to obvious areas of concern, in light of his own past experience or of established policies and past rulings of the Federal Trade Commission. (For example, the FTC has taken action many times with respect to fraudulent claims in the area of baldness or the alleged great profits to be made by the purchase of a pair of chinchillas.) Such rulings have been well-publicized over a period of many years. The licensee can, and should, check initially into the reliability of the local advertiser based on his past actions; the Better Business Bureau may be able to provide such information, and a local station owner or manager obviously will have other sources. Where, in his judgment, there are grounds for doubt or a significant complaint, he clearly should call for the subject of reasonable diligence in the discharge of the licensee's responsibilities under the above stated policies.

Licensees may appropriately turn to certain other sources for assistance in the field of national advertising. First, the NAB can and does maintain considerable staff and resources which can be of aid to its members with respect to national spot advertising; while the licensee may give great weight to NAB Code Authority advice, he remains responsible for the ultimate common sense judgment to be made. Second, just as in the case of fairness or equal time complaints, licensees, if they so choose, can rely upon the network in the case of network advertising. While, as we have noted, the networks cannot feasibly have a complete scientific staff, they do and should have considerable personnel on their staff who possess expertise in judging whether advertising is false or deceptive (e.g., a substantial knowledge of the applicable laws and FTC decisions in this field, as well as education and training in advertising practices and techniques). Of course, it is also reasonable for a network to consult outside sources such as the FTC, the NAB Code Authority, and consultants in specialized fields. Further, licensees should maintain continuing contact with their networks because network advertisements are being disseminated over the network facilities to all affiliates. A complaint received by an affiliate concerning a network commercial should therefore be forwarded to the network with a request that it be given appropriate consideration and that the affiliate be notified of its disposition. Instead of relying on the network, the licensee may of course make its own judgment: if a licensee reaches the conclusion that a network advertisement is false or deceptive, it should so notify the network, along with its cessation of carriage of the advertisement.

In short, every station must have a program to protect the public in this area. The extent of its program will, of course, depend upon the size and resources of the station, with the larger stations making a correspondingly greater effort in this field. However, somewhere in every station operation (whether it be owner, manager, or staff) there must be cognizance of problems regarding deceptive or misleading advertising, familiarity with the important policies and developments in this area, and the responsibility for determining the acceptability of advertising offered to the station. While reasonable diligence thus varies with the station and with each factual situation, what is called for is a commitment by the licensee to be as vigilant as is feasible in his circumstances to protect the public.

While we have rejected the approaches put forth by the Association, we believe it appropriate to issue a new Public Notice in the near future restating the 1961 policy statement, so as to include the pronouncements in this and the recent *Chevron* case. This notice will be sent to all licensees, in order to underscore again the licensee's obligation in this area. We will also explore with the FTC the possibility of developing an "advertising primer" similar to the Fairness Doctrine primer. We have also fully considered the desirability of instituting formal rule making such as requested by TUBE to codify the requirement of reasonable diligence on the part of licensees. However, such a rule would be essentially a restatement of existing principles and would present formidable difficulties of formulation if it is to be any more precise than a general statement of principle. While adoption of a rule would facilitate the imposition of forfeitures, they could be used only in the rare, clear-cut flagrant case. We do not believe much would be gained by a new, time consuming rule making proceeding at this time. If the present efforts of the FTC and our own renewed attention to this problem discussed herein prove to be inadequate, we can again review the question of additional rule making.

It has been suggested that we amend the renewal and other application forms to require licensees to describe specifically their procedures for detecting and preventing deceptive advertising, and for handling complaints received on this subject. Part VI of Section IV of the renewal and other broadcast application forms have general questions to be answered concerning station operating procedures, including policies with respect to advertising standards and procedures used to keep the applicant familiar with the Communications Act and Commission rules, and to insure compliance. While these questions could be more specifically pointed to advertising problems, in practice, many licensees describe their operational arrangements with respect to deceptive advertising. We have sought to pare the application forms as much as possible, and we do not believe that we should now move to add questions such as the one in question. However, we do believe it desirable that the applicant set out his procedures and staff responsibility in the area of deceptive advertising, and that he keep this information at the station with his proposed public file on complaints. We shall consider implementing this in Docket No. 19153.

We recognize that our discussion up to this point does not deal with a number of crucial issues in this area. Most important are the twin issues of delay and deterrence. Since it presently may take years for the FTC to adjudicate finally whether a particular advertisement is false and misleading, relief can come far too late; indeed, the advertisement may no longer be in use. In such circumstances, there is little real deterrence to the use of the false and misleading. But here again we are back to the consideration noted at the outset—that we can act only in the broadcast field, and with little expertise, whereas FTC action is across-the-board. There appear to be promising, *overall* developments in this area. The FTC is seeking authority to request injunctive relief when it issues a complaint. Finally, we note also that in the area of substantiating claims (with public disclosure thereof), there are FTC programs and Congressional bills.

In all these areas, we believe that we should await further industry-wide developments before considering whether we should act on a piecemeal basis.

We recognize that our contribution along the lines set forth is limited; indeed, as stated, it would be misleading on our part if we were to give the impression that we are going to take over from the FTC a substantial role with respect to false advertising in the broadcast field. We are not. But we do have a duty to "promote the larger and more effective use of radio in the public interest" (Section 303(g) of the Communications Act). That duty includes promoting a strong commitment by our licensees to discharge as fully and effectively as feasible their responsibility in the area of false and misleading advertising. That is the purpose of the actions contemplated by us—to create a strengthened, indeed, hopefully, a new mood of heightened awareness on the part of licensees to the importance of the matter.

This is consistent with the recent FTC actions, Congressional developments, and responses by the advertising industry itself (see, e.g., the National Advertising Review Board). Broadcasters are also called upon to make their contribution. For, commercial broadcasting, by definition, is based on carriage of commercials, and its own integrity thus depends on the integrity of the commercial message. The false and misleading advertisement disserves the broadcasting industry as well as the public, for it acts as a kind of Gresham's Law.

Finally, what has been said above does not reflect the end of our concern. We shall continue to study the problems in light of emerging developments either at the FTC or in the Congress, and the comments received in Dockets Nos. 19260 and 19142. We intend to strengthen our liaison with the FTC so that we may be more assured that we are taking all actions appropriate to promote our joint goal.

B. Specific matters in the complaint

As we have noted, the Association has asked the Commission to examine "what appears to be a pattern or practice rather than to evaluate any particular advertisement," and it is further stated with respect to specific advertisements cited in the complaint that, "(t)he Association does not expect the Commission to make an independent examination of the honesty or deceptiveness of each of those commercials. Rather, the complaint was designed to set forth some of the respects in which the commercials violated the standards of deception which have clearly been recognized and adopted by WTOP-TV, CBS and/or the FTC."

With the foregoing as general background, we have examined the specific commercials primarily relied upon, to determine whether they indicate a practice of carrying misleading advertisements. Without undertaking the actual inspection of these commercials—something which the complainant has not asked us to do and we would not do in light of the general principles discussed—we cannot find that they are indicative of the alleged course of conduct. For example, the Dancerina Doll commercial carried on December 19, 1970 is alleged to be misleading in that it indicated that the doll performs all by itself, whereas in fact the doll must be manipulated manually. We could not evaluate this commercial without viewing it, since the claim of deception rests upon the visual presentation of the doll in the commercial. We also note the CBS representation that it approved the commercial only after it gave specific consideration to this aspect and reached the conclusion that the commercial was not misleading in this regard. CBS also states that it reviewed the commercials after the issuance of a Federal Trade Commission Proposed Complaint. (It further claims that the commercials described in the Proposed Complaint appeared to differ in several respects from those which had been cleared and broadcast.) It is thus clear that the network did exercise its responsibility to review the content of the commercials, and we have no basis upon this record for finding that a deceptive commercial was broadcast.

As another example, we note the claim in the complaint that a commercial for Sugar Frosted Flakes indicates that the cereal is an extremely good source of energy, strength, and endurance which will last throughout the day. But, here again, since the alleged claim that the cereal will give energy throughout the day appears to depend largely upon the visual presentation of an animated cartoon tiger working at various activities with members of a family who have eaten the cereal, we could not adequately determine the extent of the claim made in the commercial without viewing it. Thus, CBS denies that nutritional claims are made in the commercial except, by implication, that the food will provide energy, and that there is an implication that the energy will last all day. We are thus faced with a factual dispute which we cannot resolve upon this record.

In the area of local commercials carried by WTOP-TV, the complaint cites commercials for Chevron F-310 gasoline, and commercials for Patio Mexican Food which stated that it has "a little more." With respect to the latter commercial, and in line with our discussion above, we do not deem it our proper role to determine the dividing line between harmless puffing and deception, at least in the absence of some definitive guidelines laid down by those with more authority in this area. The complaint cites us to no decision of the Federal Trade Commission or a court which could assist us here. The only cited case, *P. Lorillard Co.* v. *F.T.C.*, dealt with a clear claim of superiority based upon a direct perversion of a technical study relied upon on the commercial. With respect to the Chevron F-310 commercial, WTOP-TV states that "the substantial publicity concerning the commercial, both pro and con, on the merits of an FTC complaint challenging the technical claim made provided sufficient information to enable the stations to reach an informed, independent judgment on the commercial."

In light of our decision in *Alan F. Neckritz,* we do not believe that this was an adequate exercise of its responsibilities by the station. As stated in that case, where there is a Federal Trade Commission complaint, the licensee should acquaint itself with the charges recited in the complaint and the advertiser's response. We recognize that the commercial was carried prior to our ruling, but we believe it important to point out again that requirement.

For the reasons given above, and in view of the disclaimers by the complainant of any intent to make particularized complaints requiring individual examination by the Commission, we have reviewed the material before us on an overall basis, without attempting to resolve every factual dispute, to determine whether the record demonstrates any consistent practice by WTOP-TV of carrying deceptive advertising. We do not find that it does. Therefore, no further action on this basis is warranted. In view of the foregoing discussion, the requests for relief of complainant as to WTOP-TV and CBS (i.e., issuance of a forfeiture; use of cease and desist procedures, an order requiring the broadcast of remedial announcements) are not being granted.

Accordingly, the complaint of the Consumers Association of the District of Columbia is denied.

Commissioner Johnson dissenting for the reasons expressed in his dissenting opinion in the TUBE matter; Commissioner Reid not participating.

FEDERAL TRADE COMMISSION v. SPERRY & HUTCHINSON CO.
405 U.S. 233 (1972)

"S & H" has been issuing trading stamps—small pieces of gummed paper about the size of postage stamps—since 1896. In 1964, the year from which data in this litigation are derived, the company had about 40 percent of the business in an industry that annually issues 400 billion stamps to more than 200,000 retail establishments for distribution in connection with retail sales of some 40 billion dollars. In 1964, more than 60 percent of all American consumers saved S & H Green Stamps.

In the normal course, the trading stamp business operates as follows. S & H sells its stamps to retailers, primarily to supermarkets and gas stations, at a cost of about $2.65 per 1200 stamps; retailers give the stamps to consumers (typically at a rate of one for each 10¢ worth of purchases) as a bonus for their patronage; consumers paste the stamps in books of 1,200 and exchange the books for "gifts" at any of 850 S & H Redemption Centers maintained around the country. Each book typically buys between $2.86 and $3.31 worth of merchandise, depending on the location of the redemption center and type of goods purchased. Since its development of this cycle 75 years ago, S & H has sold over one trillion stamps and redeemed approximately 86 percent of them.

A cluster of factors relevant to this litigation tends to disrupt this cycle and, in S & H's view, to threaten its business. An incomplete book has no redemption value. Even a complete book is of limited value because most "gifts" may be obtained only on submission of more than one book. For these reasons a collector of another type of stamps who has acquired a small number of green stamps may benefit by exchanging with a green stamp collector who has opposite holdings and preferences. Similarly, because of the seasonal usefulness or immediate utility of an object sought, a collector may want to buy stamps outright and thus put himself in a position to secure redemption merchandise immediately though it is "priced" beyond his current stamp holdings. Or a collector may seek to sell his stamps in order to use the resulting cash to make more basic purchases (food, shoes, etc.) than redemption centers normally provide.

Periodically over the past 70 years, professional exchanges have arisen to service this demand. Motivated by the prospect of profit realizable as a result of serving as middlemen in swaps, the exchanges will sell books of S & H stamps previously acquired from consumers, or, for a fee, will give a consumer another company's stamps for S & H's or vice versa. Further, some regular merchants have offered discounts on their own goods in return for S & H stamps. Retailers do this as a means of competing with merchants in the area who issue stamps. By offering a price break in return for stamps, the redeeming merchant replaces the incentive to return to the issuing merchant (to secure more stamps so as to be able to obtain a gift at a redemption center) with the attraction of securing immediate benefit from the stamps by exchanging them for a discount at his store.

S & H fears these activities because they are believed to reduce consumer proclivity to return to Green Stamp-issuing stores and thus lower a store's incentive to buy and distribute stamps. The company attempts to pre-empt "trafficking" in its stamps by contractual provisions reflected in a notice on the inside cover of every S & H stamp book. The notice reads:

> Neither the stamps nor the books are sold to merchants, collectors or any other persons, at all times the title thereto being expressly reserved in the Company . . . . The stamps are issued to you as evidence of cash payment to the merchants issuing the same. The only right which you acquire in said stamps is to paste them in books like this and present them to us for redemption. You must not dispose of them or make any further use of them without our consent in writing. We will in every case where application is made to us give you permission to turn over your stamps to any other bona fide collector of S & H Green . . . Stamps; but if the stamps or the books are transferred without our consent, we reserve the right to restrain their use by, or take them from other parties. It is to your interest that you fill the book, and personally derive the benefits and advantages of redeeming it." (Reproduced at 2 App. 230.)

S & H makes no effort to enforce this condition when consumers casually exchange stamps with each other, though reportedly some 20 percent of all the company's stamps change hands in this manner. But S & H vigorously moves against unauthorized commercial exchanges and redeemers. Between 1957 and 1965, by its own account, the company filed for 43 injunctions against merchants who redeemed or exchanged its stamps without authorization, and it sent letters threatening legal action to 140 stamp exchanges and 175 businesses that redeemed S & H stamps. In almost all instances the threat or the reality of suit forced the businessmen to abandon their unauthorized practices.

". . . We believe this is an unfair method of competition and an unfair act and practice in violation of Section 5 of the Federal Trade Commission Act and so hold," (1 App. 178); its observation that:

> Respondent's individual acts and its acts with others taken to suppress trading stamp exchanges and other stamp redemption activity are all part of a clearly defined restrictive policy pursued by the respondent. In the circumstances surrounding this particular practice it is difficult to wholly separate the individual acts from the collective acts for the purpose of making an analysis of the consequences under the antitrust laws (1 App. 179).

and like statements throughout the opinion.

There is no indication in the Commission's opinion that it found S & H's conduct to be unfair in its effect on competitors because of considerations other than those at the root of the antitrust laws. For its part, the theory that the FTC's decision is derived from its concern for consumers finds support in only one line of the Commission's opinion. The Commission's observation that S & H's conduct limited "stamp collecting consumers' . . . freedom of choice in the disposition of trading stamps" (1 App. 176) will not alone support a conclusion that the FTC has found S & H guilty of unfair practices because of damage to consumers.

Arguably, the Commission's findings, in contrast to its opinion, go beyond concern with competition and address themselves to noncompetitive and consumer injury as well. It may also be that such findings would have evidentiary support in the record. But even if the findings were considered to be adequate foundation for an opinion and order resting on unfair consequences to consumer interests, they still fail to sustain the Commission action; for the Commission has not rendered an opinion which, by the route suggested, links its findings and its conclusions. The opinion is barren of any attempt to rest the order on its assessment of particular competitive practices or considerations of consumer interests independent of possible or actual effects on competition. Nor were any standards for doing so referred to or developed.

Our view is that "the considerations urged here in support of the Commission's order were not those upon which its action was based." At the least, the Commission has failed to "articulate any rational connection between the facts found and the choice made."

The Commission's action being flawed in this respect, we cannot sustain its order.

AMERICAN HOME PRODUCTS v. JOHNSON AND JOHNSON
3 Med. L. Rptr. 1097 (1977)

Stewart, J.

Plaintiff, American Home Products Corporation (AHP), manufactures and distributes the brand name drug Anacin through its marketing subsidiary Whitehall Laboratories. The defendant, McNeil Laboratories, Inc. (McNeil), a subsidiary of defendant Johnson and Johnson, manufactures and distributes the brand name drug Tylenol. Both Anacin and Tylenol are mild internal analgesics which are sold over-the-counter, or "OTC", without a prescription. Anacin is a compound of aspirin (ASA), which gives it its analgesic property, and caffeine. Tylenol's analgesic ingredient is acetominophen (APAP). The two drugs are in direct competition and, while Anacin is still the largest selling aspirin-compound, not only is Tylenol the leading non-aspirin analgesic, but since July and August of 1976, its tablet sales have surpassed Anacin's.

This lawsuit concerns two Anacin advertisements. The first is a 30-second television commercial which was initially aired by AHP on November 29, 1976. A storyboard of this ad (hereafter "Your Body Knows" or "the commercial") which includes the full text and some of the accompanying visual presentation follows. (omitted)

The advertising theme introduced by the "Your Body Knows" commercial was carried into the print media when the second advertisement in issue began appearing in national magazines in late January, 1977 (advertisement omitted).

After the "Your Body Knows" commercial began running, McNeil wrote to all three television networks protesting the ad on the ground that it was deceptive and misleading because 1) its sole purpose was to persuade consumers that Anacin is a more effective analgesic when the medical evidence shows that ASA and APAP are equipotent, 2) it sought to convince consumers that Anacin is a superior analgesic for the conditions mentioned in the ad due to Anacin's ability to reduce inflammation, and this alleged property is unsupported by the medical evidence and 3) it invidiously sought to convey the message, for which there is no medical support, that Anacin works faster than Tylenol. (PX 14, 15 and 16.) McNeil also protested to the print media (PX 18) and filed a complaint with the National Advertising Division of the Better Business Bureau. (PX 13.) Despite these products, CBS and NBC and the print media continued to carry the two ads in the form printed above. ABC, however, required AHP to change the statements "Anacin reduces that inflammation as Anacin relieves pain fast. These do not." to "Anacin relieves both pain and its inflammation fast. These do nothing for inflammation."

As a consequence of the McNeil protests to the media, AHP commenced the instant action on March 21, 1977 seeking declaratory relief pursuant to 28, U.S.C. Section 2201. AHP claimed that McNeil's complaints to the media concerning the TV commercial constituted charges that AHP had violated Section 43(a) of the Lanham Trademark Act, 15 U.S.C. Section 1125(a) by making false and misleading advertising claims. AHP alleged that McNeil's charges had had, and would continue to have, an adverse effect on AHP's business, and thus that there was a live controversy between the parties requiring adjudication. AHP requested the court to declare that the commercial violated no rights of McNeil and to enjoin McNeil from interfering with the broadcasting of the commercial or publishing of the analogous print ad. AHP also asserted a pendant claim of trade libel and unfair competition.

McNeil counterclaimed alleging that AHP violated the Lanham Act by publishing and airing advertisements and commercials which contain the false claims that Anacin 1) is a superior analgesic to Tylenol, 2) is an efficacious anti-inflammatory drug for the conditions listed in the ads, and 3) provides faster analgesia than Tylenol. McNeil also claimed that AHP misbranded Anacin in violation of Sections 331 and 352(f), because there are no labeling directions for Anacin's use as a therapeutic agent for the reduction of inflammation. In addition, it asserted a pendant claim of unfair competition. McNeil sought declaratory and injunctive relief prohibiting AHP from continuing to make false claims for Anacin which falsely disparaged Tylenol.

Section 1125(a) provides in pertinent part that

> . . . any person who shall . . . use in connection with any goods . . . any false description or representation, including words or symbols, tending to falsely describe or represent the same, and shall cause such goods . . . to enter into commerce, and any person who shall with knowledge of the falsity of such . . . description or representation cause or procure the same to be transported or used in commerce . . . shall be liable to a civil action by any person who believes that he is or is likely to be damaged by the use of any such false description or representation.

The statute prohibits the use of

> . . . any false description or representation, including words or other symbols, tending falsely to describe or represent the same . . .

Although the parties' positions have shifted somewhat over the course of the litigation, it appears that some disagreement remains as to exactly what representations have been made in the ads concerning Anacin.

McNeil alleged that four statements in the ad were false:

> 1. TV version: "Your body knows the difference between these pain relievers (Tylenol and Datril) and Adult Strength Anacin."
>
> Print version: "With these pains (referring to the enumerated conditions), your body knows the difference between the pain relievers in Adult Strength Anacin and other pain relievers like Tylenol."

McNeil claimed that these statements conveyed the false message that Anacin is a superior analgesic. AHP contended that any analgesic superiority claim was limited to inflammatory conditions.

> 2. TV version: "For pain other than headache, Anacin reduces the inflammation that comes with pain. These (Tylenol and Datril) do not. Specifically, inflammation of tooth extraction, muscle strain, backache, or if your doctor diagnoses tendonitis, neuritis."
>
> Print version: "Anacin can reduce inflammation that comes with most pain . . . Anacin can reduce the inflammation that often comes with these pains (referring to 'sinusitis, tooth extraction, muscular backache, muscle strain, sprains,' and 'doctor diagnosed tendonitis and neuritis.') Tylenol cannot."

McNeil contended that these statements conveyed the general false message that Anacin is a more effective or superior analgesic than Tylenol. McNeil also asserted that these statements falsely claimed that Anacin is effective drug therapy for the reduction of inflammation that is associated with the listed conditions, and thus conveyed the false message that Anacin will cure the inflammation.

AHP contended that these statements made no claim that Anacin is effective drug therapy for the treatment and cure of inflammation associated with the conditions listed. It contended that the message is that as a pain reliever, Anacin has an anti-inflammatory effect which Tylenol lacks and thus is a more effective analgesic for inflammatory conditions.

> 3. TV (CBS and NBC) version only: "Anacin reduces that inflammation as Anacin relieves pain fast. These (Tylenol and Datril) do not."

McNeil alleged that these statements imply that Anacin gives faster relief than Tylenol and thus that the consumer receives the false message that Anacin is faster.

AHP contended that the statements do not make any claim of competitive superiority with respect to speed of relief and that the consumer does not receive a message of "faster relief" from the commercial.

> 4. Print version only: "Millions take Anacin with no upset stomach."

Although McNeil did not specifically refer to this sentence in its counterclaims, it argued later that not only is this statement literally false, but it also falsely implies to consumers that Anacin will not cause any stomach upset.

AHP contended that this statement conveyed the truthful message that millions of people use ASA without stomach upset although others may suffer from this side effect.

While the Federal Trade Commission (FTC) may rely on its own expertise in interpreting the language of an advertisement in order to discover what message has been conveyed for purposes of determining whether or not an ad was false and thus an unfair or deceptive practice in violation of 15 U.S.C. Sections 45 and 52, it is the reaction of the consumer that is critical when determining whether an ad made false representations or used words tending to falsely represent the product in violation of 15 U.S.C. Sections 1125(a). As Judge Lasker indicated in *American Brands,*

A court may, of course, construe and parse the language of the advertisement. It may have personal reactions as to the defensibility or indefensibility of the deliberately manipulated words. It may conclude that the language is far from candid and would never pass muster under tests otherwise applied—for example, the Securities Act's injunction that "thou shalt disclose;" but the courts' reaction is at best not determinative, and at worst irrelevant. The question in such cases is—what does the person to whom the advertisement is addressed find to be the message?

Both parties have presented evidence of consumer reactions to the ad consisting of opinion research conducted by organizations which both parties recognize as the major advertisement testing organizations in the country. In addition, each side presented expert witness testimony concerning the interpretation of the ads.

Both Mr. Albert Shepard and Dr. Donald Payne, the expert witnesses who testified as to the meaning of the ad and commercial, are concededly highly qualified in the field of market research, especially with respect to advertising. And under some circumstances, we would be inclined to afford their opinions as to the message of the advertising substantial weight. We have not done so here for a number of reasons.

First, and most importantly, we have actual tests of consumer reactions which are recognized as the best evidence of what meaning consumers take from advertising. And second, we did not find the testimony of either expert particularly enlightening or helpful to understanding the test data. Mr. Shepard's testimony was based largely on his personal review of the ad and commercial in question plus an additional promotional flyer and another, different Anacin commercial. Some of the material he considered is not involved in this action and, although he referred to some of the test data to support his opinions, he was not able to accommodate the data which did not support his position in a satisfactory way. Dr. Payne's testimony rebutting Mr. Shepard's was more closely tied to the data, but we found illogical and ill-considered his suggestion that in evaluating the data the proper interviewee base to use was all those who had been surveyed, and not just those who claimed or were proven to have recalled the advertisement. In short, we found neither expert's opinions to be very reliable and have concluded that they are significant only to the extent that they corroborate, or were corroborated by, the test data itself. Since this data was presented in full at trial and was self-explanatory to a great extent, we think it preferable to consider the data directly and not through the testimony of either expert.

The consumer testing was conducted in two different ways. (The court summarizes the methodology and results).

With this comparison of the reliability of the tests for our purposes in mind, we will consider the conclusions of the ASI and G & R tests. It appears from both studies that the principal message was that Anacin provided symptom relief. This relief appeared to be for pain generally and not, by and large, for only particular kinds of pain such as in those conditions listed in the ad. Specifically, the statement concerning reduction of inflammation was not played back as substantially modifying the message as to the kind of pain relief Anacin could give.

Next, the studies both supported the claim that competitive superiority was a message taken by the consumer. There was no evidence that the superiority claim was limited to pain associated with inflammation as AHP claimed and thus we think the preponderance of the evidence supports the claim that the commercial made the broad representation that Anacin gives superior pain relief.

The tests made it equally clear that the consumer did not think that the ad was making a claim that Anacin cures inflammation. The tests reported divergent findings, however, on the issue of whether the language of the ad conveyed a claim of "faster" relief.

Turning to the print version of the ad, we have one study of consumer reaction done by G&R. (CCX 108.) (The court summarizes the methodology and results).

Thus we find that the preponderance of the evidence of consumer reaction demonstrates that the competitive superiority message conveyed in the print ad was a qualified one, that Anacin is better for relieving pain for some conditions because it reduces inflammation.

Thus we find that the evidence did not show that the print ad makes a representation that Anacin can be taken without any stomach upset.

In sum, we find that the evidence of consumer reaction showed that the message which the consumers took from the first statements, which McNeil claimed to be false in the TV commercial, was that Anacin is a superior analgesic generally, and not only with reference to particular conditions such as those enumerated in the ad or to Anacin's alleged ability to reduce inflammation. However, the evidence of consumer reaction showed that the message from the print ad was a more limited superiority claim, that Anacin is a superior analgesic for certain kinds of pain because Anacin can reduce inflammation. There was no disagreement that the commercial and ad both represent that Anacin can reduce inflammation associated with the conditions listed which was McNeil's second claimed falsity.

We find that the evidence is not sufficient to sustain McNeil's claim that the language of the CBS and NBC version of the commercial conveyed the message that Anacin works faster or its fourth claim that the print ad conveyed the message that Anacin can be taken without any stomach upset. While it appeared at trial that McNeil was contending that the literal language "millions take Anacin with no stomach upset" was false, i.e., that everyone who takes aspirin, and therefore Anacin, suffers stomach upset, their final position was that the statement is literally true.

We can now consider the question as to whether these messages 1) Anacin is a superior analgesic, 2) Anacin is a superior analgesic for certain conditions because it reduces inflammation, and 3) Anacin reduces inflammation for the conditions listed in the advertisement, are "false representations" or tend to falsely represent Anacin.

McNeil contended that the burden was on AHP to substantiate its claims by reliable scientific evidence. It suggested that AHP had to prove the truthfulness of its claim either by a preponderance of the evidence, the normal burden in a civil action, and the standard required of the FTC in actions brought by the commission under 15 U.S.C. Sections 45 and 52, or by "substantial evidence," the standard set by the Food and Drug Administration (FDA) for approving new drug applications. Although it would appear that the FDA standard is lower, the FDA has defined "substantial evidence" very strictly as

> evidence consisting of adequate and well-controlled investigations, including clinical investigations, by experts qualified by scientific training and experience to evaluate the effectiveness of the drug involved, on the basis of which it could fairly and reasonably be concluded by such experts that the drug will have the effect it purports or is represented to have under the conditions of use prescribed, recommended, or suggested in the labeling or proposed labeling thereof. (21 U.S.C. Section 355(d).)

Under its regulations, the FDA has further indicated that in order to be an "adequate and well-controlled clinical investigation," the study must include:

1. A clear statement of the objectives of the study;
2. A method of subject selection which minimizes bias, assures suitability, and assures that the subjects are comparable;
3. An explanation of observation and recording methods, including steps taken to minimize bias on the part of the subject or observer;
4. A comparison of results with a control, in such a way as to permit quantitative evaluation; and
5. A summary of methods of analysis and data.

By contrast, the FTC has stated that the exact nature of the evidence that will constitute a reasonable basis for a product claim

> is essentially a factual issue which will be affected by the interplay of overlapping considerations such as 1) the type and specificity of the claim made—e.g., safety, efficacy, dietary, health, medical; 2) the type of product—e.g., food, drug, potentially hazardous consumer product, other consumer product; 3) the possible consequences of a false claim—e.g., personal injury, property damage; 4) the degree of reliance by consumers on the claims; 5) the type, and accessibility, of evidence adequate to form a reasonable basis for making the particular claims. More specifically, there may be some types of claims for some types of products for which the only reasonable basis, in fairness and in the expectations of consumers, would be a valid scientific or medical basis. The precise formulation of the "reasonable basis" standard, however, is an issue to be determined at this time on a case-by-case basis.

McNeil has asserted that the FTC "expressly adopted and applied (the FDA standard and regulations) as the minimal criteria for substantiation of advertising claims" in Warner-Lambert. We find no such indication in that case. Although the Commission stated that even the "substantial evidence" standard had not been met there, it reaffirmed its "preponderance of the evidence test" and its position that, although it would take into account determinations by the FDA, it would not "automatically defer" to that agency. While determinations of neither the FDA nor FTC are controlling in the instant case, we think that a private action for false advertising under the Lanham Act is more analagous to an FTC proceeding under 15 U.S.C. Sections 45 and 52 than an FDA proceeding for approving a new drug. Accordingly, the FDA's standard of proof and definition of what evidence it will consider probative is not applicable here.

However, we do not agree that the sole burden is on AHP in order for McNeil to prevail on its counterclaims and obtain the injunctive relief it seeks. McNeil has the burden of proving that AHP violated Section 1125 by a preponderance of the evidence just as AHP has the burden of proving that it did not violate the statute in order to obtain the injunctive relief it seeks, as well as any damages.

Before considering the medical and scientific evidence on the claims, we think it appropriate to comment briefly on what we see the role of this court to be. What is before us is a private cause of action between two competitors in which the advertising claims of one, AHP, have been challenged on the grounds that they contain false representations about Anacin, and that they unfairly disparage

Tylenol. While we are mindful that the products involved are drugs and that the advertising is aimed at the general consuming public, not informed professionals, an action under the Lanham Act and state unfair competition laws is not the proper legal vehicle in which to vindicate the public's interest in health and safety. These concerns have been primarily entrusted to the care and guardianship of the FTC which is empowered to bring actions to enjoin deceptive and unfair trade practices under 15 U.S.C. Sections 45 and 52, and the FDA which is empowered initially to pass on the safety and efficacy of all new drugs and to promulgate regulations concerning the conditions under which various categories of OTC drugs, including analgesics and antirheumatic products, are safe, effective, and not misbranded.

Thus we do not think that it is within the province of this court to go beyond the issue of the falsity of the advertisement's representations and consider whether the public interest is well served by allowing such representations to be made. In addition to arguing that ASA will cause many serious side effects, McNeil has sought to impress on this court the dangers to the public of the Anacin ad on the grounds that it encourages consumers to self-diagnose their ailments and self-prescribe the drug with which to treat their condition. We agree that these are undesirable practices and we note that it was to discourage them that the "IAP" has recommended that the labeling of internal analgesics be limited to general claims of pain relief and not enumerate the conditions for which they may be used.

However, even if the IAP's recommendations are adopted by the FDA, that agency does not have authority over advertising claims. Thus the IAP recognized that all it could do was request that the agency responsible for regulating advertising, the FTC,

> . . . more effectively regulate commercial advertising of internal analgesic, antipyretic, and antirheumatic preparations on the basis of the labeling recommendations contained in (the IAP Report). Further, the Panel strongly urges the Federal Trade Commission to require that the cautionary language and warnings developed by the Panel be given emphasis in commercial advertising more so than is currently being done.

We think the record here supports the view that FTC regulation of OTC drug advertising in conformity with the IAP's labeling recommendations would have a salutary effect, but we do not think these considerations should enter into our determination of this action.

Before considering the first two claims (supra) concerning Anacin's efficacy as an analgesic, we will evaluate the claim that Anacin reduces the inflammation that often comes with pain—specifically the inflammation accompanying the conditions listed in the advertisements—because this is the general medical premise upon which the possibility of superior analgesia rests.

The parties, the experts, general medical opinion, and the medical studies are in substantial agreement concerning several aspects of ASA's anti-inflammatory properties. It is generally recognized in the medical community that ASA has anti-inflammatory properties, and there is complete agreement that ASA has an anti-inflammatory effect specifically in the treatment of rheumatoid arthritis (RA). (The court summarizes the medical.)

Considering all these factors, we think that the clinical test evidence suggests that ASA may have some anti-inflammatory effect in OTC dosages for conditions associated with inflammation other than RA, but goes no further than this.

The advertising is not limited, however, to a general claim concerning ASA's efficacy in reducing inflammation, but lists specific conditions in which it is asserted that Anacin does reduce inflammation.

The expert witnesses were not in agreement as to what diseases were meant by the terms used with the exception of "tooth extraction." They also disagreed as to the nature of the diseases which they understood the ad to encompass, particularly as to whether or not the disease was associated with inflammation. And they disagreed concerning whether ASA is, or should properly be, used for these diseases, and whether ASA, if used, would have a clinically significant anti-inflammatory effect on the disease at OTC dosages.

While Dr. Derby contended that several of the conditions listed would not have inflammation associated with them, the evidence from the medical literature and the testimony of the other expert witnesses established that at least some forms of all the diseases listed have inflammatory components. (The court summarizes reports from medical literature.)

On all the other conditions, we have only the testimony of mainly Drs. Weissmann and Sheldon Blau, and some general comments in medical texts concerning the use of ASA and its possible anti-inflammatory effect. On the other hand, we have Dr. Derby's carefully considered testimony, evidence from some other texts and concessions by some of AHP's witnesses that ASA is not recommended therapy for some forms of the conditions listed.

In light of the confusion that the terms have caused among trained medical persons, the fact that an anti-inflammatory response is very hard to distinguish from an analgesic one, and the inherent unreliability of clinical observation (Tr. 561), we have concluded that clinical observation of efficacy is unacceptable as evidence to support the claims made for the conditions listed except as corroboration of results obtained from well-conducted studies.

While Dr. Weissmann may be correct that clinical studies for each and every condition listed might not be necessary to support the claims made (Tr. 730), we have concluded that some substantial clinical testing of the conditions is required. The clinical materials on tendonitis, discussed above, are not studies or tests at all. The actual tests with tooth extraction did not focus on the anti-inflammatory, as opposed to the analgesic, effect of ASA clearly enough to enable us to draw any conclusions concerning ASA's anti-inflammatory properties from them. Thus the clinical reports and tests do not lend any certainty or greater reliability to the very tentative extrapolation which we think may be made from the RA tests, and the informed speculations and clinical observations expressed by AHP's witnesses.

Accordingly, we find that there is no reliable evidence showing that ASA reduces inflammation to a clinically significant extent in the conditions listed in the advertisements at OTC dosages. On the other hand, we think that McNeil has not proved by a preponderance of the evidence that this claim is, or tends to be, false. It appears that the state of medical and scientific knowledge is not such as to allow anyone to make a definitive conclusion either way on this issue. Were this, then, the only representation made in the ad, we would have to grapple with the question of whether a competitor could succeed on a Lanham Act claim by showing that there was no reliable evidence to support the representation, even though the competitor could not itself affirmatively prove that the claim was false or tended to misrepresent the product. However, two other claims concerning Anacin's relative efficacy as an analgesic, which are integral to and inseparable from this representation, are susceptible of more definitive proof.

We have found that the first allegedly false representation, that Anacin is a superior analgesic, reached the television viewer without qualifications limiting the claimed superior efficacy to conditions accompanied by inflammation. While the actual comparison made in the TV commercial was between Anacin and Tylenol and Datril, many viewers thought the comparison was between Anacin and other aspirin products. A claim of superior analgesia for Anacin compared to ASA would be nonsensical since the only analgesic ingredient in Anacin is ASA. We will consider, therefore, what evidence there is of the relative analgesic efficacy of ASA and APAP.

While AHP has not actually conceded that ASA and APAP are generally considered to be equally effective pain relievers, it has pressed its argument for ASA as a superior analgesic only in conditions in which inflammation is present. We find that the overwhelming weight of the evidence—from medical studies and the clinical experience and impressions of both AHP's and McNeil's experts—indicates that ASA and APAP are equally effective as general, mild, internal analgesic.

In all but one of a number of controlled double-blind clinical studies comparing the analgesic effectiveness of ASA and APAP, the data revealed no statistically significant differences between the two drugs, although in several cases ASA scored better than APAP.

That ASA and APAP are roughly equivalent and effective as analgesics is generally recognized in the medical community. And the expert witnesses presented by both AHP and McNeil agreed that simply as analgesics, the two drugs were equally effective.

Thus we find that the overwhelming weight of the evidence indicates that ASA and APAP are equally effective as general mild, internal analgesics.

The second allegedly false representation is a modified claim of analgesic for conditions which are associated with inflammation or have an inflammatory component. We have evaluated the medical studies cited in Footnote 10, with respect to this modified superiority claim and find that they offer no real support for it either. Two of the studies were of the analgesic effects of ASA and APAP in RA patients. In the more recent study, PX 88, although ASA scored better, there was no statistical difference between its analgesic efficacy and APAP's. PX 93 reported a significant difference in ASA over APAP, but we found this not as methodologically sound as PX 88 and some of the other tests reported. Thus, the strongest conclusion that we are willing to draw from these two studies is that they suggest that ASA may be a more effective analgesic in a condition (there, RA) with an inflammatory component.

Weighing against this "suggestion" is the fact that in many of the other studies in which no statistically different analgesic effect between ASA and APAP was reported, the conditions involved were accompanied by inflammation. These include post partum pain, post-operative pain, tonsillectomy, and oral surgery. Thus, we think that the weight of the medical studies indicates that ASA and APAP are equally effective analgesics in conditions associated with inflammation.

However, there was considerable evidence of the opinion in the medical community that ASA is, or may be, a more useful or effective analgesic than APAP in conditions with inflammatory components.

The expert witnesses presented by AHP also testified that ASA is a more effective analgesic than APAP for conditions accompanied by inflammation. Dr. Weismann, whom we found to be a knowledgeable, careful, and credible witness, testified that on the basis of ASA's anti-inflammatory properties, in conditions where "substantial inflammation" was present, the pain relief provided by ASA "would be greater" than that provided by APAP.

Dr. Koelle, whom we also found to be a knowledgeable and credible witness, although recognizing that "according to most all of the double-blind clinical pharmacological trails in patients, at a given moment, both APAP and ASA have the same amount of analgesic potency," testified that

> if a patient is treated for a week, say, following a sprained ankle, he should have relief of the pain several days sooner by an anti-inflammatory agent that is also an analgesic, because it would

reduce the inflammation of the sprained ankle, and he should be free of pain in a shorter period of time.

He also stated that he thought the patient might get more relief from ASA over a period of time because ASA attacks the site of pain. Dr. Koelle's reasoning was that ASA achieved its analgesic effect primarily through peripheral, rather than central nervous system ("CNS") action. He thought the predominantly peripheral action of ASA has been demonstrated by the research concerning ASA's ability to reduce inflammation which is achieved by peripheral action at the site of the pain. There is evidence that APAP acts both peripherally and on the CNS, but Dr. Koelle was not prepared to say which action predominates with APAP. He has concluded, though, that APAP acts peripherally to a lesser extent than ASA, and thus would have less of an effect in reducing pain at the site.

Dr. Blau, a practicing rheumatologist, also testified that ASA was a superior analgesic for patients suffering from rheumatic disorders accompanied by inflammation.

We found Dr. Weissmann's and Dr. Koelle's hypotheses and expectations as to the superior analgesic effect of ASA for conditions with an inflammatory component reasonable. However, we note that neither of these prominent, knowledgeable, and careful medical researchers pressed the claim of superior analgesia for these conditions beyond the point of informed expectation. Thus, we conclude that there is reputable evidence in the medical literature and in the well-considered opinions of experts in the field, that ASA may be a more effective analgesic for conditions which have an inflammatory component. However, in evaluating whether there has been "any false description or representation, including words or symbols tending falsely to describe or represent the same" (15 U.S.C. Section 1125(a)), we cannot give much weight to these expectations and opinions which after all are basically speculations. The data from well-conducted tests of the comparative analgesic effects of ASA and APAP demonstrate that they are equally effective as analgesics for conditions which are associated with inflammation and for those which are not. Thus we conclude that the preponderance of the reliable evidence indicates that ASA and APAP are equally effective analgesics at OTC levels for conditions which are associated with inflammation or have inflammatory components.

In light of the foregoing findings, we conclude that AHP has made false representations concerning the properties of its product Anacin by claiming 1) that Anacin is a superior analgesic to Tylenol generally, and 2) that Anacin is a superior analgesic to Tylenol for conditions which are associated with inflammation or have inflammatory components. As to the third representation, that Anacin at OTC dosages reduces inflammation in the conditions listed in the advertisements to a clinically significant extent, the state of medical knowledge and research is not such as to allow us to reach a definitive conclusion as to the falsity of this claim. But since we find that the three claims are integral and inseparable, we find that the advertisements as a whole make false representations for Anacin and falsely disparages Tylenol in violation of the Lanham Act.

There is substantial evidence that consumers have been and will continue to be deceived as to the relative efficacy of the two products, and that this deception is injuring, and will continue to injure, Tylenol's reputation among customers. Accordingly, McNeil is entitled to a permanent injunction restraining plaintiff AHP, its agents, servants, officers, and all those in privity with it from publishing or inducing any television or radio network or local station, newspaper, magazine, trade periodical, or other periodical to publish or from using in connection with any other promotional activity, the "Your Body Knows" advertisement or any other advertising or promotional material which contains, in the context of a representation as to any anti-inflammatory property of Anacin, the representation that

Anacin is a superior analgesic generally or a superior analgesic for conditions which are associated with inflammation or have inflammatory components.

In light of these conclusions, we deny AHP's request for injunctive relief and damages and dismiss the complaint.

This memorandum opinion constitutes the court's findings of fact and conclusions of law pursuant to Rule 52(a) of the Federal Rules of Civil Procedure. Costs and attorneys' fees to neither party.

Settle order on notice within ten days.

(An appendix to the Court's opinion is omitted.)

WARNER-LAMBERT CO. v. FEDERAL TRADE COMMISSION
562 F.2d 749 (CADC 1977)

J. Skelly Wright, Circuit Judge.

The Warner-Lambert Company petitions for review of an order of the Federal Trade Commission requiring it to cease and desist from advertising that its product, Listerine Antiseptic mouthwash, prevents, cures, or alleviates the common cold. The FTC order further requires Warner-Lambert to disclose in future Listerine advertisements that: "Contrary to prior advertising, Listerine will not help prevent colds or sore throats or lessen their severity." We affirm but modify the order to delete from the required disclosure the phrase "Contrary to prior advertising."

I. Background

The order under review represents the culmination of a proceeding begun in 1972, when the FTC issued a complaint charging petitioner with violation of Section 5(a)(1) of the Federal Trade Commission Act by misrepresenting the efficacy of Listerine against the common cold.

Listerine has been on the market since 1879. Its formula has never changed. Ever since its introduction, it has been represented as being beneficial in certain respects for colds, cold symptoms, and sore throats. Direct advertising to the consumer, including the cold claims as well as others, began in 1921.

Following the 1972 complaint, hearings were held before an administrative law judge (ALJ). The hearings consumed over four months and produced an evidentiary record consisting of approximately 4,000 pages of documentary exhibits and the testimony of 46 witnesses. In 1974, the ALJ issued an initial decision sustaining the allegations of the complaint. Petitioner appealed this decision to the Commission. On December 9, 1975 the Commission issued its decision essentially affirming the ALJ's findings. It concluded that petitioner had made the challenged representations that Listerine will ameliorate, prevent, and cure colds and sore throats, and that these representations were false. Therefore the Commission ordered petitioner to:

1. cease and desist from representing that Listerine will cure colds or sore throats, prevent colds or sore throats, or that users of Listerine will have fewer colds than nonusers;
2. cease and desist from representing that Listerine is a treatment for, or will lessen the severity of, colds or sore throats; that it will have any significant beneficial effect on the symptoms of sore throats or any beneficial effect on symptoms of colds; or that the ability of Listerine to

kill germs is of medical significance in the treatment of colds or sore throats or their symptoms;

3. cease and desist from disseminating any advertisement for Listerine unless it is clearly and conspicuously disclosed in each such advertisement, in the exact langauge below, that: "Contrary to prior advertising, Listerine will not help prevent colds or sore throats or lessen their severity." This requirement extends only to the next ten million dollars of Listerine advertising.

II. *Substantial Evidence*

The first issue on appeal is whether the Commission's conclusion that Listerine is not beneficial for colds or sore throats is supported by the evidence. The Commission's findings must be sustained if they are supported by substantial evidence on the record viewed as a whole. We conclude that they are.

Both the ALJ and the Commission carefully analyzed the evidence. They gave full consideration to the studies submitted by petitioner. The ultimate conclusion that Listerine is not an effective cold remedy was based on six specific findings of fact.

First, the Commission found that the ingredients of Listerine are not present in sufficient quantities to have any therapeutic effect. This was the testimony of two leading pharmacologists called by Commission counsel. The Commission was justified in concluding that the testimony of Listerine's experts was not sufficiently persuasive to counter this testimony.

Second, the Commission found that in the process of gargling it is impossible for Listerine to reach the critical areas of the body in medically significant concentration. The liquid is confined to the mouth chamber. Such vapors as might reach the nasal passage would not be in thereapeutic concentration. Petitioner did not offer any evidence that vapors reached the affected areas in significant concentration.

Third, the Commission found that even if significant quantities of the active ingredients of Listerine were to reach the critical sites where cold viruses enter and infect the body, they could not interfere with the activities of the virus because they could not penetrate the tissue cells.

Fourth, the Commission discounted the results of a clinical study conducted by petitioner on which petitioner heavily relies. Petitioner contends that in a four-year study, school children who gargled with Listerine had fewer colds and cold symptoms than those who did not gargle with Listerine. The Commission found that the design and execution of the "St. Barnabas study" made its results unreliable. For the first two years of the four-year test no placebo was given to the control group. For the last two years the placebo was inadequate: the control group was given colored water which did not resemble Listerine in smell or taste. There was also evidence that the physician who examined the test subjects was not blinded from knowing which children were using Listerine and which were not, that his evaluation of the cold symptoms of each child each day may have been imprecise, and that he necessarily relied on the nonblinded child's subjective reporting. Both the ALJ and the Commission analyzed the St. Barnabas study and the expert testimony about it in depth and were justified in concluding that its results are unreliable.

Fifth, the Commission found that the ability of Listerine to kill germs by millions on contact is of no medical significance in the treatment of colds or sore throats. Expert testimony showed that bacteria in the oral cavity, the "germs" which Listerine purports to kill, do not cause colds and play no role in cold symptoms. Colds are caused by viruses. Further, "while Listerine kills millions of bacteria in the mouth, it also leaves millions. It is impossible to sterilize any area of the mouth, let alone the entire mouth.

Sixth, the Commission found that Listerine has no significant beneficial effect on the symptoms of sore throat. The Commission recognized that gargling with Listerine could provide temporary relief from a sore throat by removing accumulated debris irritating the throat. But this type of relief can also be obtained by gargling with salt water or even warm water. The Commission found that this is not the significant relief promised by petitioner's advertisements. It was reasonable to conclude that "such temporary relief does not 'lessen the severity' of a sore throat any more than expectorating or blowing one's nose 'lessens the severity' of a cold."

In its attack on the Commission's findings, petitioner relies heavily on a recent study of over-the-counter cold remedies by the Food and Drug Administration which petitioner alleges found Listerine "likely to be effective." Its argument is two-pronged: first, that the fact that the Commission's findings differ from the FDA's proves that the Commission's findings are wrong; and second, that it was error for the Commission to refuse to reopen its proceedings when the FDA study was released. We conclude that both of these arguments are without merit for the simple reason that the FDA study does not, to any significant degree, contradict the Commission's findings.

The FDA study is the product of an expert panel appointed in 1972 to study all over-the-counter cold, cough, allergy, bronchodilator, and anti-asthmatic drug products—some 180 ingredients used in as many as 50,000 products. The panel's draft report was issued in February 1976, two months after the FTC issued its order against Listerine. The FTC refused to reopen its proceedings to consider the draft report. In September 1976 the expert panel's report was published, but it has not yet been adopted by the Commissioner of the FDA.

The only evidence pertinent to the effectiveness of Listerine that the FDA panel considered was the St. Barnabas study, and it appears that reference to it was included in the report only as an afterthought. More importantly, the reference which does appear does not endorse or adopt the St. Barnabas study; the FDA report merely describes it and recounts the results. The panel's own conclusions are reflected in the operative language repeated for each ingredient of Listerine:

> There are no well-controlled studies documenting the effectiveness of (eucalyptol/eucalyptus oil, menthol, thymol) as an (antitussive, expectorant, nasal decongestant).
>
> For use as a mouthwash: Data to demonstrate effectiveness will be required . . . .

Each ingredient of Listerine was placed in Categroy III, defined as "the available data are insufficient to classify such condition under either (Category I, generally recognized as safe and effective) or (Category II, not generally recognized as safe and effective) and for which further testing is therefore required." Petitioner's assertion that this is equivalent to finding the product "likely to be effective" is not supported by the facts.

In sum, the FDA study does not reflect any new data not considered by the FTC. Since the FDA did not consider the extensive record compiled in the FTC proceedings, its conclusion that there is insufficient data about the ingredients of Listerine to justify classifying it as effective or ineffective is not necessarily inconsistent with the FTC's conclusion that Listerine's advertising claims are deceptive. The FTC did not err in refusing to reopen its proceedings to consider the draft FDA study, and the FDA findings do not establish that the FTC's conclusions are wrong.

III. The Commission's Power

Petitioner contends that even if its advertising claims in the past were false, the portion of the Commission's order requiring "corrective advertising" exceeds the Commission's statutory power. The argument is based upon a literal reading of Section 5 of the Federal Trade Commission Act, which authorizes the Commission to issue cease and desist orders against violators and does not expressly mention any other remedies. The Commission's position, on the other hand, is that the affirmative disclosure that Listerine will not prevent colds or lessen their severity is absolutely necessary to give effect to the prospective cease and desist order; a hundred years of false cold claims have built up a large reservoir of erroneous consumer belief which would persist, unless corrected, long after petitioner ceased making the claims.

The need for the corrective advertising remedy and its appropriateness in this case are important issues which we will explore. But the threshold question is whether the Commission has the authority to issue such an order. We hold that it does.

Petitioner's narrow reading of Section 5 was at one time shared by the Supreme Court. In *FTC v. Eastman Kodak Co.* the Court held that the Commission's authority did not exceed that expressly conferred by statute. The Commission has not, the Court said, "been delegated the authority of a court of equity."

But the modern view is very different. In 1963 the Court ruled that the Civil Aeronautics Board has authority to order divestiture in addition to ordering cessation of unfair methods of competition by air carriers. The CAB statute, like Section 5, spoke only of the authority to issue cease and desist orders, but the Court said, "We do not read the Act so restrictively . . . . (W)here the problem lies within the purview of the Board, . . . Congress must have intended to give it authority that was ample to deal with the evil at hand." The Court continued, "Authority to mold administrative decrees is indeed like the authority of courts to frame injunctive decrees . . . . (The) power to order divestiture need not be explicitly included in the powers of an administrative agency to be part of its arsenal of authority . . . ."

Later, in *FTC v. Dean Foods Co.*, the Court applied Pan American to the Federal Trade Commission. In upholding the Commission's power to seek a preliminary injunction against a proposed merger, the Court held that it was not necessary to find express statutory authority for the power. Rather, the Court concluded, "It would stultify congressional purpose to say that the Commission did not have the . . . power . . . . Such ancillary powers have always been treated as essential to the effective discharge of the Commission's responsibilities."

Thus it is clear that the Commission has the power to shape remedies which go beyond the simple cease and desist order. Our next inquiry must be whether a corrective advertising order is for any reason outside the range of permissible remedies. Petitioner and amici curiae argue that it is because 1) legislative history precludes it, 2) it impinges on the First Amendment, and 3) it has never been approved by any court.

The First Amendment

Petitioner and amici further contend that corrective advertising is not a permissible remedy because it trenches on the First Amendment. Petitioner is correct that this triggers a special responsibility on the Commission to order corrective advertising only if the restriction inherent in its order is no greater than necessary to serve the interest involved. But this goes to the appropriateness of the order in this case, an issue we reach in Part IV of this opinion. Amici curiae go further, arguing that, since the Supreme Court has recently extended First Amendment protection to commercial advertising, mandatory corrective advertising is unconstitutional.

A careful reading of *Virginia State Board of Pharmacy* v. *Virginia Citizens Consumer Council* compels rejection of this argument. For the Supreme Court expressly noted that the First Amendment presents "no obstacle" to government regulation of false or misleading advertising. The First Amendment, the Court said,

> as we construe it today, does not prohibit the State from insuring that the stream of commercial information flow(s) cleanly as well as freely.

In a footnote, the Court went on the delineate several differences between commercial speech and other forms which may suggest "that a different degree of protection is necessary . . . ." For example, the Court said, they may

> make it appropriate to require that a commercial message appear in such a form, or include such additional information, warnings, and disclaimers, as are necessary to prevent its being deceptive.

The Supreme Court clearly foresaw the very question before us, and its statement is dispositive of amici's contention.

Precedents

According to petitioner, "The first reference to corrective advertising in Commission decisions occurred in 1970, nearly fifty years and untold numbers of false advertising cases after passage of the Act." In petitioner's view, the late emergence of this "newly discovered" remedy is itself evidence that it is beyond the Commission's authority. This argument fails on two counts. First, the fact that an agency has not asserted a power over a period of years is not proof that the agency lacks such power. Second, and more importantly, we are not convinced that the corrective advertising remedy is really such an innovation. The label may be newly coined, but the concept is well established. It is simply that under certain circumstances an advertiser may be required to make affirmative disclosure of unfavorable facts.

One such circumstance is when an advertisement that did not contain the disclosure would be misleading. For example, the Commission has ordered the sellers of treatments for baldness to disclose that the vast majority of cases of thinning hair and baldness are attributable to heredity, age, and endocrine balance (so-called "male pattern baldness") and that their treatment would have no effect whatever on this type of baldness. It has ordered the promoters of a device for stopping bedwetting to disclose that the device would not be of value in cases caused by organic defects or diseases. And it has ordered the makers of Geritol, an iron supplement, to disclose that Geritol will relieve symptoms of tiredness only in persons who suffer from iron deficiency anemia, and that the vast majority of people who experience such symptoms do not have such a deficiency.

Each of these orders was approved on appeal over objections that it exceeded the Commission's statutory authority. The decisions reflect a recognition that, as the Supreme Court has stated,

If the Commission is to attain the objectives Congress envisioned, it cannot be required to confine its road block to the narrow lane the transgressor has traveled; it must be allowed effectively to close all roads to the prohibited goal, so that its order may not be bypassed with impunity.

Affirmative disclosure has also been required when an advertisement, although not misleading if taken alone, becomes misleading considered in light of past advertisements. For example, for 60 years Royal Baking Powder Company had stressed in its advertising that its product was superior because it was made with cream of tartar, not phosphate. But, faced with rising costs of cream of tartar, the time came when it changed its ingredients and became a phosphate baking powder. It carefully removed from all labels and advertisements any reference to cream of tartar and corrected the list of ingredients. But the new labels used the familiar arrangement of lettering, coloration, and design, so that they looked exactly like the old ones. A new advertising campaign stressed the new low cost of the product and dropped all reference to cream of tartar. But the advertisements were also silent on the subject of phosphate and did not disclose the change in the product.

The Commission held, and the Second Circuit agreed, that the new advertisements were deceptive, since they did not advise consumers that their reasons for buying the powder in the past no longer applied. The court held that it was proper to require the company to take affirmative steps to advise the public. To continue to sell the new powder

> on the strength of the reputation attained through 60 years of its manufacture and sale and wide advertising of its superior powder, under an impression induced by its advertisements that the product purchased was the same in kind and as superior as that which had been so long manufactured by it, was unfair alike to the public and to the competitors in the baking powder business.

In another case the Waltham Watch Company of Massachusetts had become renowned for the manufacture of fine clocks since 1849. Soon after it stopped manufacturing clocks in the 1950s, it transferred its trademarks, good will, and the trade name "Waltham" to a successor corporation which began importing clocks from Europe for resale in the United States. The imported clocks were advertised as "product of Waltham Watch Company since 1850, a famous 150-year-old company."

The Commission found that the advertisements caused consumers to believe they were buying the same fine Massachusetts clocks of which they had heard for many years. To correct this impression the Commission ordered the company to disclose in all advertisements and on the product that the clock was not made by the old Waltham company and that it was imported. The Seventh Circuit affirmed, relying on "the well-established general principle that the Commission may require affirmative disclosure for the purpose of preventing future deception."

It appears to us that the order in *Royal* and *Waltham* were the same kind of remedy the Commission has ordered here. Like Royal and Waltham, Listerine has built up over a period of many years a widespread reputation. When it was ascertained that that reputation no longer applied to the product, it was necessary to take action to correct it. Here, as in *Royal* and *Waltham,* it is the accumulated impact of past advertising that necessitates disclosure in future advertising. To allow consumers to continue to buy the product on the strength of the impression built up by prior advertising—an impression which is now known to be false—would be unfair and deceptive.

IV. The Remedy

Having established that the Commission does have the power to order corrective advertising in appropriate cases, it remains to consider whether use of the remedy against Listerine is warranted and equitable. We have concluded that Part 3 of the order should be modified to delete the phrase "Contrary to prior advertising." With that modification, we approve the order.

Our role in reviewing the remedy is limited. The Supreme Court has set forth the standard:

> The Commission is the expert body to determine what remedy is necessary to eliminate the unfair or deceptive trade practices which have been disclosed. It has wide latitude for judgment and the courts will not interfere except where the remedy selected has no reasonable relation to the unlawful practices found to exist.

The Commission has adopted the following standard for the imposition of corrective advertising:

> (I)f a deceptive advertisement has played a substantial role in creating or reinforcing in the public's mind a false and material belief which lives on after the false advertising ceases, there is clear and continuing injury to competition and to the consuming public as consumers continue to make purchasing decisions based on the false belief. Since this injury cannot be averted by merely requiring respondent to cease disseminating the advertisement, we may appropriately order respondent to take affirmative action designed to terminate the otherwise continuing ill effects of the advertisement.

We think this standard is entirely reasonable. It dictates two factual inquiries: 1) did Listerine's advertisements play a substantial role in creating or reinforcing in the public's mind a false belief about the product? and 2) would this belief linger on after the false advertising ceases? It strikes us that if the answer to both questions is not yes, companies everywhere may be wasting their massive advertising budgets. Indeed, it is more than a little peculiar to hear petitioner assert that its commercials really have no effect on consumer belief.

For these reasons it might be appropriate in some cases to presume the existence of the two factual predicates for corrective advertising. But we need not decide that question, or rely on presumptions here, because the Commission adduced survey evidence to support both propositions. We find that the "Product Q" survey data and the expert testimony interpreting them constitute substantial evidence in support of the need for corrective advertising in this case.

We turn next to the specific disclosure required: "Contrary to prior advertising, Listerine will not help prevent colds or sore throats or lessen their severity." Petitioner is ordered to include this statement in every future advertisement for Listerine for a defined period. In printed advertisements it must be displayed in type size at least as large as that in which the principal portion of the text of the advertisement appears, and it must be separated from the text so that it can be readily noticed. In television commercials the disclosure must be presented simultaneously in both audio and visual portions. During the audio portion of the disclosure in television and radio advertisements, no other sounds, including music, may occur.

These specifications are well calculated to assure that the disclosure will reach the public. It will necessarily attract the notice of readers, viewers, and listeners, and be plainly conveyed. Given these safeguards, we believe the preamble "Contrary to prior advertising" is not necessary. It can serve only two purposes: either to attract attention that a correction follows or to humiliate the advertiser. The Commission claims only the first purpose for it, and this we think is obviated by the other terms of the order. The second purpose, if it were intended, might be called for in an egregious case of deliberate deception, but this is not one. While we do not decide whether petitioner proffered its cold claims in good faith or bad, the record compiled could support a finding of good faith. On these facts, the confessional preamble to the disclosure is not warranted.

Finally, petitioner challenges the duration of the disclosure requirement. By its terms it continues until respondent has expended on Listerine advertising a sum equal to the average annual Listerine advertising budget for the period April 1962 to March 1972. That is approximately ten million dollars. Thus, if petitioner continues to advertise normally, the corrective advertising will be required for about one year. We cannot say that is an unreasonably long time in which to correct a hundred years of cold claims. But, to petitioner's distress, the requirement will not expire by mere passage of time. If petitioner cuts back its Listerine advertising, or ceases it altogether, it can only postpone the duty to disclose. The Commission concluded that correction was required and that a duration of a fixed period of time might not accomplish that task, since petitioner could evade the order by choosing not to advertise at all. The formula settled upon the Commission is reasonably related to the violation it found.

Accordingly, the order, as modified, is

Affirmed.

Robb, Circuit Judge, dissenting in part:

I agree with the majority that there is substantial evidence in the record to support an order requiring Warner-Lambert to cease and desist from advertising Listerine as a remedy for colds and sore throats. I therefore agree that Parts I, II, IV and V of the Commission's order must be affirmed.

I dissent from the affirmance of Section III of the order which 1) forbids Warner-Lambert to disseminate any advertisement for Listerine unless accompanied by a corrective statement relating to past advertising, and 2) provides that this "duty to disclose the corrective statement shall continue until respondent has expended on Listerine advertising a sum equal to the average annual Listerine advertising budget for the period of April 1962 to March 1972 "—a sum of approximately ten million dollars. In my judgment this requirement of corrective advertising is beyond the statutory authority of the Federal Trade Commission. The Commission's authority to enter cease and desist orders is prospective in nature; the purpose of cease and desist orders is "to prevent illegal practices in the future" not "to punish or to fasten liability on respondents for past conduct." The cases that have construed the Commission's remedial power, stand only for the proposition that the Commission has broad discretion in determining what conduct of a respondent shall be forbidden prospectively. I think this authority does not encompass the power to employ the retrospective remedy of corrective advertising; and I find no other basis for that asserted power.

NOTE

In an article entitled "Is FTC Action in *Listerine* Case Legal?", Joseph Furth, Vice President, Kelly-Furth Division of Frank L. Beam Company in Chicago, suggests that the FTC and Court decisions in the case of *Warner-Lambert* "was a bleak day for American business and for the advertising industy. But it was a much sadder day for America." Furth agrees with Judge Roger Robb, who dissented in the review which upheld the FTC order requring Warner-Lambert to correct and admit in $10 million worth of future advertising that past claims in their Listerine advertising were untrue.

Furth and Robb agree that the FTC and the Courts lack the authority to make such a decision. Furth explains that:

> A careful study of the parent statutes enacted by Congress to regulate advertising not only denies the Commission any such authority to impose penalities, but actually prohibits the agency from exercising any sort of right for punitive power.
>
> The concessions for the enactment of the FTC Act relating to advertising did not go over without a great deal of argument, debate, and compromise. The legislative intent was obvious . . . .
>
> Congress reduced FTC's legal requirements for determining liability . . . . The penalty clauses became, and still are, that the seller must STOP THE MESSAGE. To CEASE AND DESIST. That's all . . . . The law specifically prohibits FTC regulatory punitive authority."
> (*Advertising Age,* vol. 49 (June 5, 1978), pp. 56–58.)

UNITED STATES v. *STP*
United States District Court
Southern District of New York (1978)

This action having been commenced by the filing of a complaint; service of the complaint having been acknowledged by the defendant; and the parties having been represented by the attorneys whose names appear hereafter; the parties agree to the settlement of all claims against defendant upon the terms and conditions set forth below.

1. Without admitting liability for the offenses charged in the complaint, and for settlement purposes only defendant agrees to pay the plaintiff, pursuant to 15 U.S.C. Section 5(1), a civil penalty in the amount of $500,000 due and payable within fifteen days from the date of the entry of this judgment, such payment to be made by certified check payable to the Treasurer of the United States and delivered to the United States Attorney for the Southern District of New York;

2. In the event of default in payment which default continues for 10 days beyond the due date of the payment, interest at the rate of nine percent per annum shall accrue thereon from the date of default to the date of payment and upon filing of an affidavit by plaintiff certifying that defendant is in default and without further notice to defendant, the clerk of the Court shall enter judgment for the full amount against defendant and/or its successors and assigns;

3. Defendant, its successors and assigns, and its officers, agents, representatives, and employees, directly or through any corporation, subsidiary, division, or other device, is enjoined from engaging in any act of practice which is prohibited by the Federal Trade Commission's Order in Docket Number C–2777, a copy of which is attached as Appendix A and made a part of this Consent Judgment;

4. Defendant agrees to cause the dissemination through SFM Media Services Corporation, 6 East 43rd Street, New York, New York 10017, of the notice set forth in Appendix B and to pay SFM Media Services Corporation within 10 days of demand $200,000 for costs and fees of preparation and placement of the notice. The notice will be placed by SFM Media Services Corporation independently in each periodical, identified in Appendix C in the page size specified therein for publication at the earliest possible time on or after February 13, 1978;

5. Nothing contained in this consent judgment or in the notice attached as Appendix B shall be considered an admission or agreement by the plaintiff with the statements made by the defendant in the notice attached as Appendix B;

6. This consent judgment resolves all disputes between the parties with respect to advertisements submitted to the Federal Trade Commission in denfendant's compliance report of February 25, 1976, and supplemental materials submitted prior to December 31, 1977.

7. Jurisdiction is retained for the purpose of enabling any of the parties to this final judgment to apply to the Court at any time for such further orders and directions as may be necessary or appropriate for the interpretation or modification of this final judgment, for the enforcement of compliance therewith, or for the punishments of violations thereof;

It appearing that this Court has jurisdiction pursuant to 15 U.S.C. Sections 45(1) and 49;

It is hereby ordered, adjudged, and decreed that judgment be entered in favor of the plaintiff, United States of America, and against the defendant, STP Corporation, under the terms and conditions recited above. Defendant shall pay the costs of this suit.

ORDER

A

It is ordered that respondents STP Corporation, and Stern, Walters & Simmons, Inc., corporations, and their officers, successors, assigns, representatives, agents, and employees, directly or through any corporation, subsidiary, division, or other device:

1. In connection with the advertising, offering for sale, sale, or distribution of STP Oil Treatment, or any other product the customary or usual use of which is as an additive to motor oil, in or affecting commerce, as "commerce" is defined in the Federal Trade Commission Act, do forthwith cease and desist from representing, directly or by implication, that any such product:
    a. Prevents cars which use it from experiencing mechanical breakdowns or from requiring repairs;
    b. Cures or remedies mechanical malfunctions;
    c. Eliminates friction or wear or is required to protect against friction or wear;
    d. Acts or performs like or has the effect of antifreeze in the oil; or will enable cars to start, or to start more easily, in cold weather;
    e. Is required in order to obtain lubrication from motor oil;
    f. Is slipperier than motor oil alone.
2. In connection with the advertising, offering for sale, sale, or distribution of STP Oil Treatment, or any other product the customary or usual use of which is as an additive to motor oil, or which is advertised for such use, in or affecting commerce, as "commerce" is defined in the Federal Trade Commission Act, do forthwith cease and desist from misrepresenting the capacities, characteristics, or qualities of motor oil or of any grade or weight of motor oil.

B

It is further ordered that respondents STP Corporation, and Stern, Walters & Simmons, Inc., corporations, and their officers, successors, assigns, representatives, agents, and employees, directly or through any corporation, subsidiary, division, or other device in connection with the advertising, offering for sale, sale, or distribution of STP Gas Treatment, or any other product the customary or usual use of which is as defined in the Federal Trade Commission Act, do forthwith cease and desist from representing, directly or by implication, that any such product:

1. Tunes an engine, or will provide the equivalent of a complete engine tune-up, or makes engine tune-ups unnecessary;
2. Provides any portion of an engine tune-up unless, in immediate conjunction therewith, respondents disclose, clearly and conspicuously, that the advertised product does not provide all of the features of a mechanical engine tune-up;
3. Cleans or helps to clean an entire engine without clearly designating the component or components or functional areas of the engine or other portions of the motor vehicle which are affected.

C

It is further ordered that respondents STP Corporation, and Stern Walters & Simmons, Inc., corporations, and their officers, successors, assigns, agents, representatives, and employees, directly or through any corporation, subsidiary, division, or other device in connection with the advertising, offering for sale, sale, or distribution of oil filters in or affecting commerce, as "commerce" is defined in the Federal Trade Commission Act, do cease and desist from:

1. Representing, directly or by implication, that any such product:
   a. Meets, conforms with, or exceeds any automotive manufacturers' specifications, or is approved by any automobile manufacturer for use in connection with any vehicle or engine, when such is not the fact;
   b. "Double cleans" motor oil, or representing in any other manner that any such product filters motor oil more than once each time the oil flows through the filter cannister, except as provided in paragraph 2, immediately below, unless the motor oil flows through two or more filtering elements in series each time the motor oil flows through the filter cannister.
2. Using the words "dual," "double," "double stage," "two filters in one," "two stage," "filter within a filter," or any other terminology which suggests the presence of more than one filtering element, to describe any automotive oil filter without clearly disclosing that the motor oil is filtered only once each time it flows through the filter cannister, unless the motor oil flows through two or more filtering elements in series each time the motor oil flows through the filter cannister. In television advertising, the disclosure that motor oil may be filtered only once each time it flows through the filter cannister when such is the fact shall be made in such a manner that it is clearly disclosed.

D

It is further ordered that respondents STP Corporation and Stern, Walters & Simmons, Inc., corporations, and their officers, successors, assigns, agents, representatives, and employees, directly or through any corporation, subsidiary, division, or other device, in connection with the advertising, offering for sale, sale, or distribution of STP Oil Treatment, or any other product the customary or usual use of which is as an additive to motor oil, in or affecting commerce, as "commerce" is defined in the Federal Trade Commission Act, do forthwith cease and desist from disseminating any advertisement in which a representation of benefit is made as to such product when used as an additive to motor oil unless 1) such representation is true; 2) respondent STP Corporation possesses and relies upon, prior to the time such representation is first made, a competent and reliable scientific test or tests, or other objective data which substantiate such representation; or 3) with respect to respondent

Stern, Walters & Simmons, Inc., respondent possesses and relies upon, prior to the time such representation which shall consist of an opinion in writing signed by a person qualified by education and experience to render such an opinion (who, if qualified by education and experience, may be a person retained or employed by respondent's client) that a competent and reliable scientific test or tests or other objective data exist to substantiate such representation, provided that any such opinion also discloses the nature of such test or tests or other objective data and provided further that respondent neither knows, nor has known, that such test or tests or other objective data do not in fact substantiate such representation or that any such opinion does not constitute a reasonable basis for such representation.

E

It is further ordered that respondents STP Corporation and Stern, Walters & Simmons, Inc., corporations, and their officers, successors, assigns, agents, representatives, and employees, directly or through any corporation, subsidiary, division, or other device in connection with the advertising, offering for sale, sale, or distribution of STP Oil Treatment, STP Gas Treatment, STP Oil Filters, or any other product manufactured, sold or distributed by STP Corporation the customary or usual use of which is as an additive to motor oil or gasoline or as an oil filter, in or affecting commerce, as "commerce" is defined in the Federal Trade Commission Act, do cease and desist from:

1. Advertising by or through the use of or in conjunction with any test, experiment, or demonstration or the result thereof, or any other information or evidence that appears or purports to confirm or prove, or is offered as confirmation, evidence, or proof of any fact, product characteristic of the truth of any representation, which does not accurately demonstrate, prove, or confirm such fact, product characteristic, or representation.
2. Using any pictorial or other visual means of communication with or without an accompanying verbal text which directly or by implication creates a misleading impression in the minds of viewers as to the true state of material facts which are the subject of said pictures or other visual means of communication.
3. Misrepresenting in any manner or by any means any characteristic, property, quality, or the result of use of any such product.

It is further ordered that respondents STP Corporation and Stern, Walters & Simmons, Inc., shall forthwith distribute a copy of this Order to each of their operating divisions and to each of their officers, agents, representatives, or employees engaged in the creation or approval of advertisements.

It is further ordered that respondents STP Corporation and Stern, Walters & Simmons, Inc., notify the Commission at least thirty (30) days prior to any proposed change in said corporate respondent such as dissolution, assignment, or sale resulting in the emergence of a successor corporation, the creation or dissolution of subsidiaries, or any other change in the corporation which may affect compliance obligations arising out of this Order.

It is further ordered that respondents STP Corporation and Stern, Walters & Simmons, Inc., shall, within sixty (60) days after service of this Order upon them, file with the Commission, in writing, a report setting forth in detail the manner and form in which they have complied with this Order.

By the Commission. Commissioner Hanford dissented on the grounds that the Order is too weak and that STP should be explicitly required to qualify its future claims.

NOTE I

On December 11, 1978 the following Interstate Commerce Commission Rules and Regulations were amended to allow price competition among ICC practitioners through use of advertising and soliciting for employment:

Public communication and solicitation. A practitioner shall not in any way use or participate in the use of any form of public communication or solicitation for employment containing a false, fraudulent, misleading, or deceptive statement or claim. Such prohibition includes, but is not limited to, the use of statements containing a material misrepresentation of fact or omitting a material fact necessary to keep the statement from being misleading; statements intended or likely to create an unjustified expectation; statements that are not objectively verifiable; statements of fee information which are not complete and accurate; statements containing information on past performance or prediction of future success; statements of prior commission employment outside the context of biographical information; statements containing a testimonial about or endorsement of a practitioner; statements containing an opinion as to the quality of a practitioner's services; or statements intended or likely to attract clients by the use of showmanship, puffery, or self-laudation, including the use of slogans, jingles, or sensational language or format. A practitioner shall not solicit a potential client who has given the practitioner adequate notice that he or she does not want to receive communications from the practitioner, nor shall a practitioner make a solicitation which involves the use of undue influence. A practitioner shall not solicit a potential client who is apparently in a physical or mental condition which would make it unlikely that he or she could exercise reasonable, considered judgment as to the selection of a lawyer. A practitioner shall not pay or otherwise assist any other person who is not also a practitioner and a member or associate of the same firm to solicit employment for the practitioner. If a public communication is to be made through use of radio or television, it must be prerecorded and approved for broadcast by the practitioner. A recording of the actual transmission must be retained by the practitioner for a period of 1 year after the date of the final transmission. A paid advertisement must be identified as such unless it is apparent from the context that it is a paid advertisement. A practitioner shall not compensate or give anything of value to a representative of any communication medium in anticipation of or in return for professional publicity in a news item. (47 LW 2409–2410.)

NOTE II

Under approved Federal Trade Commission rules and regulations, which take effect on January 1, 1980, vocational and trade school deceptive advertising should be curtailed in the following ways based upon the condition that a school offering classroom or correspondence courses must:

1. Refund tuition payments in full to students who drop out of a course or program during a 14-day "cooling-off period" after they enroll or sign a contract.
2. Give students a prorated refund of the tuition they paid for the unused portion of their courses if they drop out any time after the first 14 days. The school could keep up to $75 as a registration fee.
3. Provide students with information about graduation and dropout rates.
4. Provide students with data about the school's record of placing graduates in jobs and about graduates' earnings—if the school has "made express claims concerning the availability of jobs or earnings potential for . . . graduates."

Explicitly excluded from the rules, the commission said, are "highschool equivalency and self-improvement courses and courses leading to standard college-level degrees."

The rules on tuition refunds "can have a shattering impact on private, non-profit schools, many of which are now 80 per cent or more dependent on tuition revenues for survival," said the National Association of Independent Colleges and Schools. (See Cheryl M. Fields, "FTC Adopts Stiff Rules to Regulate Advertising by Vocational Institutions," XVII *Chronicle of Higher Education* (January 8, 1979), 16.)

Although 53 per cent of the four million students in two-year institutions are enrolled in occupational programs, the large majority will not be affected by the proposed guidelines, said John E. Tirrell, government-affairs officer for the American Association of Community and Junior Colleges. ("U.S. Bars Bias in Vocational Education; Little Impact on Colleges is Expected," *ibid.,* 18.)

Chapter IV

Censorship and the Media

Section 1

The Promotion of Obscenity and Pornography

Daniel M. Rohrer

INTRODUCTION

In February 1970, Jerry Garcia, the Grateful Dead's leading exponent of freedom of speech, uttered a four-letter word while being interviewed on Philadelphia's noncommercial educational radio station, WUHY. Someone complained to the FCC and eventually that station was forced to pay a $100 fine.

Seven years later the Federal Appeals Court of Washington, D.C. reversed a similar FCC decision, ruling that such language should receive First Amendment protection even on the air waves when children might be listening. In March 1977, U.S. circuit Judge Edward A. Tamm said the FCC order was too broad and carried the agency into the "forbidden realm of censorship." In this case words, ranging from three to 12 letters in length and describing various sexual activities and portions of the female anatomy or excretory functions of the human body were aired in December 1973 on a New York radio station when it broadcast a record of a comedy routine by comedian George Carlin, (*Pacifica Foundation* v. *FCC*, (556 F.2d 9 (CADC 1977)). In the summer of 1978 the United States Supreme Court upheld the original FCC ruling banning the broadcast of Carlin's "offensive" words over the air waves where they might be heard involuntarily by America's unwitting youth.

HISTORY

All levels of government in the United States have promulgated laws designed to protect the public from the dissemination of immoral or depraved matter. These acts encompass both administrative regulation and criminal prohibition. In reviewing cases arising out of such anti-obscenity statutes, the courts (with few exceptions) were long guided by the British precedent in *Queen* v. *Hicklin*. Lord Chief Justice Cockburn noted in that case that the test for obscenity was "whether the tendency of the matter charged as obscenity is to deprave and corrupt those whose minds are open to such immoral influences, and into whose hands a publication of this sort might fall." This standard, basing societal guidelines upon the most corruptible, is so broad that it renders First Amendment rights virtually inapplicable in obscenity cases.[1]

It was not until 1957, in *Roth* v. *United States* (354 U.S. 476 (1957)), that the Supreme Court began to establish more sophisticated criteria for identifying obscenity. In that case Justice Brennan articulated for the majority that expression is obscene if "to the average person, applying contemporary community standards, the dominant theme of the material taken as a whole appeals to prurient interests."[2] Thus obscenity was no longer to be appraised with respect to the most susceptible, but rather to the average, member of society.

The guideline, however, remained vague, and in later years the Court sought to explicate it. In *Manual Enterprises* v. *Day* (370 U.S. 478 (1962)), it held that obscene matter must not only cater to prurient interests, it must be "patently offensive" as well. In *Jocabellis* v. *Ohio* (378 U.S. 184 (1964)), it further ruled that expression which has literary or scientific or any other form of social importance may not be branded as obscene. An additional criterion for determining obscenity was announced in *Ginzburg* v. *United States* (383 U.S. 463 (1966)). In evaluating the claims of the publisher of *Eros* and other erotic literature to First Amendment protection, the Court introduced the notion of intent, stating that "where the purveyors' sole emphasis is on the sexually provocative aspects of his publications, that fact may be decisive in the determination of obscenity."

Although the Court has sought properly to confine the scope of anti-obscenity legislation, current efforts are unsuccessful in clarifying poetic license; they compel jurists to enter the thicket of literary criticism. Judges are asked to consider questions of taste and artistic merit that have baffled critics for centuries. The most profound philosophers of art have foundered whenever they attempted to abstract the essence of good art. The contribution of the Supreme Court to this endeavor has been a collection of empty generalities that offer scant guidance in difficult cases. Once sex is recognized as a valid aspect of artistic expression, it becomes virtually impossible to draw lines. Other nations have eliminated censorship legislation for adults, and the United States should do the same.

In its obscenity discussions the Supreme Court has also acted to shield the individual from the actions of administrative censorship agencies. In *Freedman* v. *Maryland* (380 U.S. 51 (1965)), it held that only a judicial tribunal has the power to exercise final restraint on free expression. Thus provision must be made for judicial review of administrative decisions in First Amendment cases.[3]

The extent of such judicial review can be seen in the decision of the U.S. Supreme Court to hear a case that could once and for all answer the question of whether the government is permitted to bar indecent language on the public airwaves. It is the case involving New York City's radio station WBAI which broadcast indecent language when it carried comedian George Carlin's monologue on "The seven words you can't say on television." As was indicated above, the U.S. Court of Appeals overruled the FCC in the Spring of 1977, claiming that the agency's anti-indecency guidelines were unclear, and that the FCC had improperly engaged in censorship.

In order to better understand the dilemma faced by the high Court on this issue, perhaps it would be helpful to trace the circle drawn by the Court between 1966 and 1977 on the question of the advertising and promotion of obscenity and pornography.

In 1966 the so-called liberal and progressive Warren Court upheld the obscenity conviction of Ralph Ginzburg. The court analyzed the advertising and promotion for Mr. Ginzburg's publications and ruled that in "close cases" evidence of "pandering," or appealing to prurient interests, could determine whether doubtful material was obscene or not (*Ginzburg* v. *United States,* 383 U.S. 463 (1966)).

This decision evoked much criticism. Mr. Ginzburg was something of a celebrity, his sentence was severe, and by the time it was finally confirmed, many people had concluded that his wares were not terribly offensive.[4] Indeed, for the following eleven years there is little sign of a similar reaction on the part of the Court which would parallel such an aphorism. Indeed, quite the opposite was the case.[5]

After the Warren Court became the Burger Court, a majority of five Supreme Court Justices, including the Court's four Nixon appointees, changed the definition of obscenity. Prior to their new ruling in *Miller* v. *California* on June 21, 1973, obscene material was held protected by First Amendment guarantees unless the work, taken as a whole, was found to 1) appeal to the prurient interest, 2) exceed the standards of candor in the representation of sexual matters, and 3) be "utterly without redeeming social value," (*Roth* v. *United States/Alberts* v. *California,* 354 U.S. 476 (1957); *Memoirs* v. *Massachusetts,* 383 U.S. 413 (1966)).

This test of obscenity was established in *Roth* v. *United States, supra.* Under this definition, as elaborated in subsequent cases, the three elements must coalesce. For example, "a book cannot be proscribed unless it is found to be utterly without redeeming social value. This is so even though the book is found to possess the requisite prurient appeal and to be patently offensive. Each of the three federal Constitutional criteria is to be applied independently; the social value of the book can neither be weighed against nor cancelled by its prurient appeal or patent offensiveness" (Memoirs v. *Massachusetts, supra).* "Roth was convicted of mailing obscene circulars and advertising, and an obscene book, in violation of a federal obscenity statute" (*Stanley* v. *Georgia,* 394 U.S. 557 (1969)).

Between 1973 and 1977, however, to be defined as obscene, the work, taken as a whole, had to 1) appeal to the prurient interests, 2) portray sexual conduct in a patently offensive manner, and 3) be lacking in any serious literary, artistic, political, or scientific value (*Miller* v. *California,* 413 U.S. 15 (1973)). Although questions of appeal to the "prurient interest" or of patent offensiveness are "essentially questions of fact," "it would be a serious misreading of *Miller* to conclude that juries have unbridled discretion in determining what is 'patently offensive' " (*Jenkins* v. *Georgia,* 418 U.S. 153 (1974)).

Indeed, the justices were quite specific about what they meant by "patently offensive:" ultimate sexual acts, masturbation, excretion, and lewd exhibition of genitalia. The other two criteria they left open to interpretation. They also ruled in *Miller* that obscene materials would have to be assessed in terms of "community standards." This innocuous term concealed a trap, for the Court failed to specify whether "community" meant the judicial district from which the jurors were selected and in which the trial was held, or an abstract concept encompassing what was morally acceptable to the average American.[6]

Lower courts have attempted to make such a distinction nevertheless. For example the case of *United States* v. *Various Articles of Obscene Merchandise* (3 Med.L.Rptr. 1116, 562 F.2d 185 (CA2, 1977)) resulted in a federal court determination that material must be found obscene within local community standards of the district in which the material was seized, rather than within community standards of the district in which the addressee of the material resides.

The case of *Smith* v. *United States* (a partial text of which is reprinted in the following section of this chapter), clarifies further that whether the work depicts or describes, in a patently offensive way, sexual conduct, must be determined on the basis of specific definitions within applicable state law.

It is on this basis that the Supreme Court applied the protection of the First Amendment to topless dancing. The Court felt that since there was no proof that the petitioner's dance, in the context of contemporary community standards, appealed to the prurient interest of the audience and exceeded customary limits of candor, the conviction for indecent exposure and dissolute conduct should be reversed. (*In re Gianinni,* 69 Cal. 2d 563, 446 P.2d 535, 72 Cal. Rptr. 655 (1968).)

At the conclusion of the prosecution's case, the defense moved for a directed verdict because no evidence of the "community standard" had been introduced. The trial court judge denied the motion, apparently on the grounds that the jury represented the community's standards adequately. The defendants introduced evidence that bare breasts and topless dancing were widely accepted in California, but they were found guilty nonetheless. (*Ibid*, 565–67, 446 P.2d 536–38, 72 Cal. Rptr. 657–58; see also 58 *California Law Review* 175 (1970).)

The Supreme Court found the performance of a dance for an audience to be comparable to other forms of expression or communication which enjoy protection under the First Amendment until shown to be obscene. Since the lower court had made no attempt to test the defendants' conduct by the obscenity standards laid down by the United States Supreme Court in *Roth* as modified by *Memoirs* v. *Massachusetts,* the Supreme Court held that the conviction was an invasion of First Amendment freedom. (*Ibid.;* see 69 Cal. 2d 577, 446 P.2d 545, 72 Cal. Rptr. 665.)

If the effect of this California decision was to elevate state standards above local standards, at least two subsequent decisions did otherwise. In the case of *Utah* v. *International Amusements* (565 P.2d 1112 (1977)), the court held that contemporary community standards by which the jury was to evaluate allegedly pornographic material were local standards as opposed to statewide standards. Here the court concluded that "the trial court properly determined that the same did not require the application of a statewide standard. The wording of the statute clearly establishes a local standard as opposed to a statewide standard by adopting the following language: '. . . those current standards in the vicinage where an offense alleged under this act has occurred, is occurring, or will occur.'

"Although the geographic area is not specifically described, the use of the term 'vicinage' is clearly lesser in area than the total confines of the State of Utah." (*Ibid,* 1113.)

In like manner the court in *Movie World, Inc*. v. *Sloane* (458 F.Supp. 863 (1978)) held that where licensing provisions of the ordinance appeared to be guided by narrow, objective and definite standards, where enforcement of the ordinance did not appear to be in bad faith or for the purpose of harassment, and where the ordinance did not flagrantly or patently violate constitutional guarantees, the city and others would not be restrained from enforcing its provisions. The injunction restraining the defendant from enforcing the ordinance was thus denied.

A different interpretation was made in the state court of Michigan. Here it was decided that where there is a conflict between local ordinances and state statutes, the latter are dispositive in defining community standards for obscene material (*People* v. *Llewellyn,* a partial text of which is reprinted in the following section of this chapter).

In cases where neither state law nor local ordinances may define specifically all obscene matter which is found by the court to violate community standards, past court precedent within the state may serve as an equally valid mechanism for defining material that will be prohibited (*Ward* v. *Illinois,* a partial text of which is reprinted in the following section of this chapter).

Despite such distinctions drawn by the lower courts, government attorneys have gone venue-shopping by selecting a location where obtaining a conviction is likely. It is thus that Al Goldstein, who publishes *Screw* magazine in New York, found he was going to be tried in Wichita, and Harry Reems, a New York actor, came to be on trial in Memphis.

In the spring of 1976 the publisher of *Screw* magazine was found guilty of distributing obscene materials through the mails. The star of "Deep Throat," however, was more fortunate. After his conviction early in 1976 on charges of conspiring to transport obscene material across state lines, a federal district court judge wrote an eight-page order in April 1877 claiming that Mr. Reems deserved another chance in court because his activities in the sexually explicit film had taken place prior to the

Supreme Court ruling on obscenity in 1973. Such a condition was insufficient to save *Ward,* however, *supra.*

The standards set forth in that ruling were followed by the jury that convicted Reems on May 1, 1976, of conspiring to distribute the film nationally. He was acquitted of charges that he actually took part in transporting the film across state lines from Fort Lauderdale, Florida, to Memphis, where the trial was held.

However, Larry C. Flynt, publisher and editor of *Hustler* magazine, was convicted in Cincinnati on February 8, 1977 on charges of pandering obscenity and participating in organized crime. This case, was expected to provide a major test of whether communities may dictate their own obscenity standards and indirectly set standards which are nationwide.

The problem is that in Memphis, Wichita, and Cincinnati the court attempted to superimpose its own local, community standard on the nation as a whole, precisely the effect the Supreme Court had attempted to circumvent in its 1973 *Miller* v. *California* decision. In the *Miller* case the high Court put aside a national standard for determining what is obscene and recognized that community standards of a small town in upstate New York were no more similar to the standards of New York City than the standards of Maine were to those of Las Vegas.

Having already been victimized by uncertainty over the *Miller* community standard, Larry Flynt announced on December 3, 1977, in a Speech Communication Association of America convention program (see figure 12), that he intended to return to Cincinnati to sell personally one more copy of *Hustler* magazine before the nature and character of the publication changed. Flynt's intent was to test the First Amendment on the merits of his original publication so that no one could argue validly that his religious conversion and the proposed changes in his publication constituted an effort to stay out of prison.[7]

Although Flynt acknowledged that he had not changed into a traditional Christian, speaking of his *Hustler* magazine he claimed that : "We will try to do what God would approve of in our stories and pictures."[8] Five days later he was shot and wounded critically while on trial in Lawrenceville, Georgia.[9] The judge declared a mistrial.

In many ways a case of socially redeeming value can be made for Flynt and his publiction. The pornography publisher explained during his SCA convention program that he had gone to the White House and offered President Carter one million dollars to implement a national study on the effects of obscenity and pornography.

Flynt further explained in his SCA convention program that he felt so-called obscene and pornographic publications are a symptom rather than a cause of man's inability to cope with sex. Futhermore, he argued that *Hustler* magazine is the "poor man's art." It is intended for the uneducated and uncultured person who has a First Amendment right to media entertainment becoming to his taste, whatever it may be.

The publisher of *Hustler* has engaged in other "morality" campaigns ranging from an attempt to reopen the Warren Commission Study on the assassination of President John F. Kennedy to full page advertisements in major newspapers promoting world peace, an end to hunger, and a tribute to Hubert Humphrey for his position on civil rights, peace, and human dignity. Entitled "You Taught Us Not to Hide Our Feelings," one such public service advertisement appeared in the *Boston Sunday Globe* on December 18, 1977 (see figure 13).[10]

(photo by author)

Figure 12. Permission by all three participants of the SCA panel discussions. From left to right: Larry Flint, Publisher and Editor, *Hustler Magazine;* Michael Geltner, Georgetown University Law Center; Gerald R. Miller, Michigan State University; Dec. 3, 1977, Washington, D.C.

Numerous attempts to achieve some form of socially redeeming value have appeared in *Hustler* magazine. On one occasion a public service advertisement was printed for the purpose of defining Larry Flynt's concept of obscenity. It was an emotion packed picture of a defigured GI, something perfectly acceptable in a newspaper or news magazine.

The November 1977 issue of *Hustler* provides a lucid example of a lack of pandering combined with worthwhile social service. The front cover (see figure 14) is an excellent illustration of the former, and the back cover (see figure 15) constitutes a still more impressive sample of the latter.

Unfortunately for Flynt, because the cases against him may now be moot, the courts may find some difficulty equating socially redeeming value with the new serious literary, artistic, political, or scientific value criteria established as one of the *Miller* standards. Indeed it may very well be that there is no clearly definable, permissible limits on obscenity and pornography.

Perhaps it is for this reason that the Supreme Court turned another somersault in 1977 when it handed down several more decisions on the subject. In the case of *Marks* v. *United States,* a new

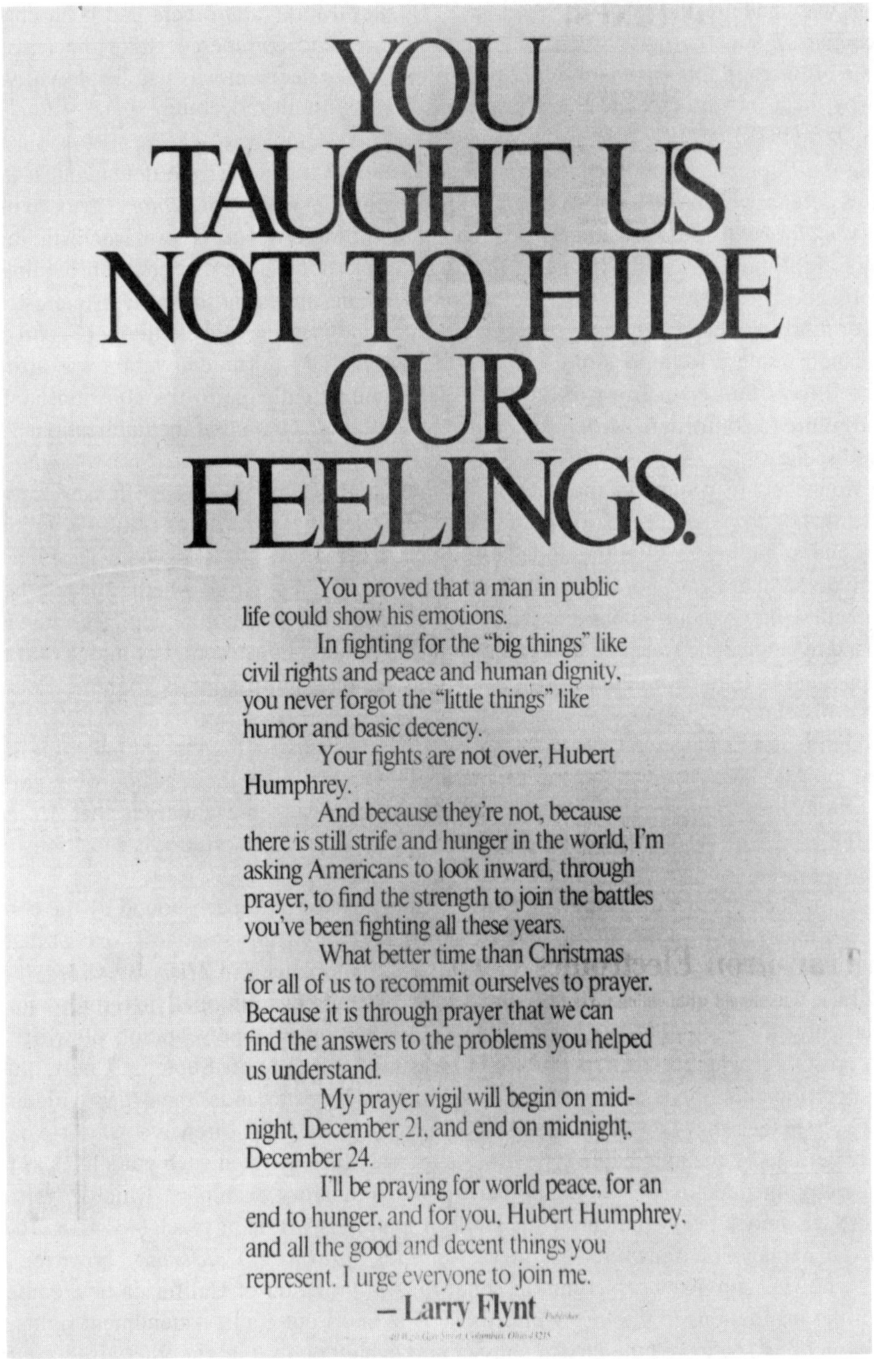

The Promotion of Obscenity and Pornography 347

YOU TAUGHT US NOT TO HIDE OUR FEELINGS.

You proved that a man in public life could show his emotions.

In fighting for the "big things" like civil rights and peace and human dignity, you never forgot the "little things" like humor and basic decency.

Your fights are not over, Hubert Humphrey.

And because they're not, because there is still strife and hunger in the world, I'm asking Americans to look inward, through prayer, to find the strength to join the battles you've been fighting all these years.

What better time than Christmas for all of us to recommit ourselves to prayer. Because it is through prayer that we can find the answers to the problems you helped us understand.

My prayer vigil will begin on midnight, December 21, and end on midnight, December 24.

I'll be praying for world peace, for an end to hunger, and for you, Hubert Humphrey, and all the good and decent things you represent. I urge everyone to join me.

— **Larry Flynt** *Publisher*

Figure 13

Reprinted with permission from *Hustler* Magazine.

application was made to the "*Miller* Standards." Stanley Marks and others had been charged with several counts of transporting obscene materials in interstate commerce. Like the case of Harry Reems, the offenses in this case took place before the *Miller* decision was handed down, which may explain why the Court returned to the *Memoirs* "utterly without redeeming social value" criterion. (430 U.S. 188 (1977).)

While the Supreme Court found retroactivity sufficient to rule for the defendant in the case of *Marks,* this defense was insufficient in the similar case of *Ward* v. *State of Illinois.* Prior to the decison in *Miller* v. *California,* Wesley Ward was convicted of selling obscene sado-masochistic materials in violation of the Illinois obscenity statute forbidding the sale of obscene matter and providing that "(a) thing is obscene if, considered as a whole, its predominant appeal is to prurient interest, that is, a shameful or morbid interest in nudity, sex, or excretion, and if it goes substantially beyond customary limits of candor in description or representation of such matters." The conviction was affirmed after *Miller,* the Illinois Supreme Court rejecting the appellant's challenge to the constitutionality of the statute for failure to conform to *Miller* standards, as well as his claim that the publications in question were not obscene.

The Court held its ground in applying pre-*Miller* standards to pre-*Miller* offenses, notwithstanding the fact that *Miller* standards also apply. The Court ruled that the Illinois statute is not unconstitutionally vague as failing to give the appellant notice that materials dealing with the kind of sexual conduct involved here could not be legally sold in the state. This is true whether or not the state has complied with *Miller's* requirement that the sexual conduct that may not be depicted must be specifically defined by applicable state law as written or authoritatively construed. The high Court concluded that the appellant had ample guidance from a previous decision of the Illinois Supreme Court, making it clear that his conduct did not conform to Illinois law.

The high Court further ruled that sado-masochistic materials are the kind of materials that may be proscribed by state law, *Mishkin* v. *New York* (383 U.S. 502), even though they were not expressly included within the examples of the kinds of sexually explicit representations that *Miller* used to explicate the aspect of its obscenity definition dealing with patently offensive depictions of specifically defined sexual conduct.

The court also concluded that the materials in question were properly found by the courts below to be obscene under the Illinois statute, which conforms to the *Miller* standards, except that it retains the stricter "redeeming social value" obscenity criterion announced in *Memoirs* v. *Massachusetts.*

Finally, it was determined that the Illinois statute is not unconstitutionally overbroad for failure to state specifically the kinds of sexual conduct the description or representation of which the state intends to proscribe, where it appears that in prior decisions the Illinois Supreme Court, although not expressly describing the kinds of conduct intended to be referred to under the *Miller* guideline requiring inquiry "whether the work depicts or describes, in a patently offensive way, sexual conduct specifically defined by the applicable state law," expressly incorporated such guidelines as part of the law and thereby intended as well to adopt the *Miller* explanatory examples, which gave substantive meaning to such guidelines by indicating the kinds of materials within its reach (431 U.S. 767 (1977)).

Such an explanation fails to exist in the case of *Splawn* v. *California,* however. Here the petitioner, who was convicted of selling obscene films in violation of California law, contended that protions of the instructions to the jury violated his First and Fourteenth Amendment rights, claiming that the instructions 1) allowed the jury to convict him even though it might otherwise have found that the film was protected under the standards of *Miller* v. *California* because the instructions permitted

The Promotion of Obscenity and Pornography 349

Figure 14

Reprinted with permission from *Hustler* Magazine, November 1977.

Censorship and the Media

The Original Flip-top Box for Smokers

A PUBLIC SERVICE ADVERTISEMENT FROM HUSTLER MAGAZINE

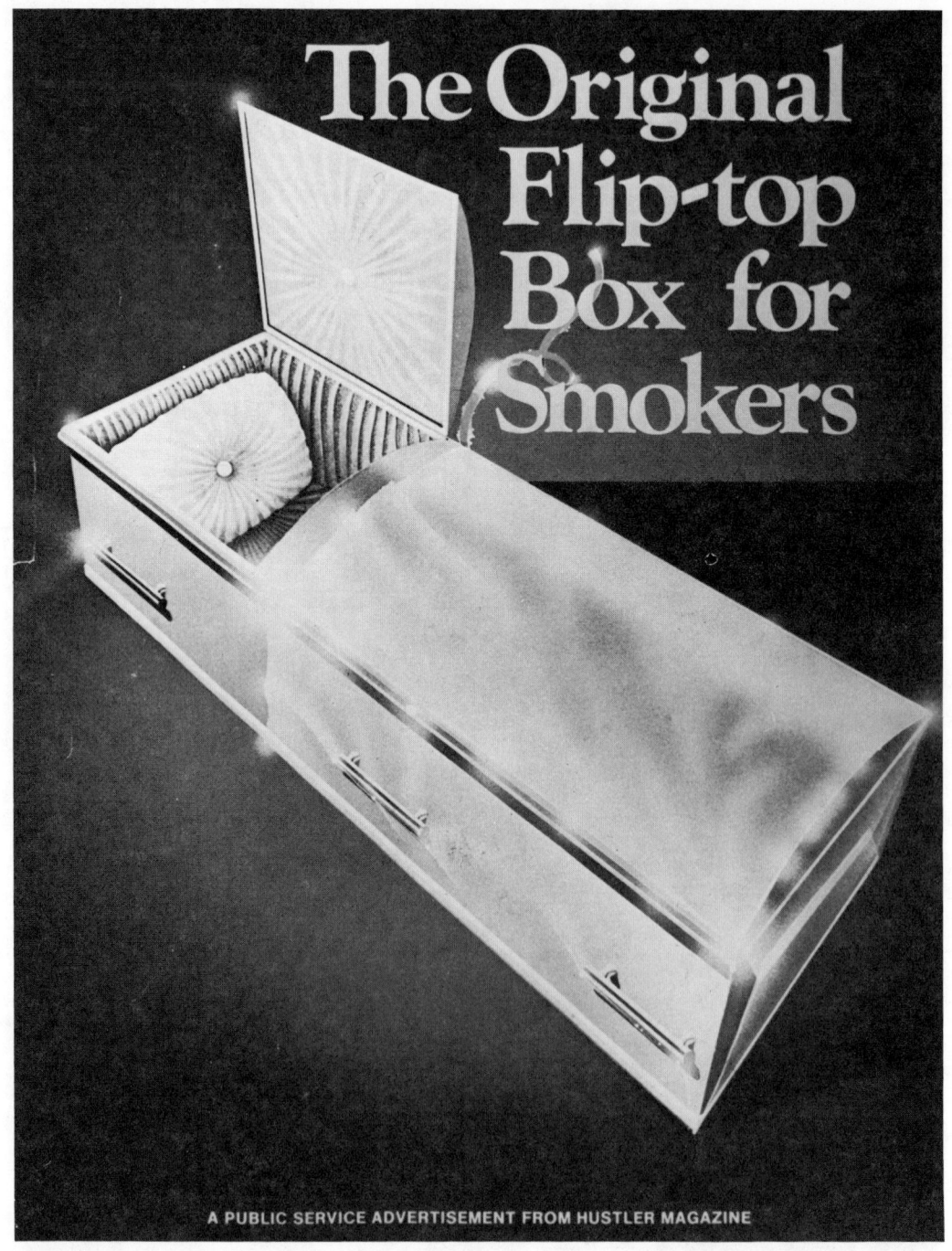

Figure 15

Reprinted with permission from *Hustler* Magazine, November 1977.

the jury to consider motives of commercial exploitation on the part of persons in the chain of distribution other than the petitioner himself, and 2) violated the prohibition against *ex post facto* laws, and the fair-warning requirement of *Bouie* v. *Columbia* (378 U.S. 347). The challenged instruction permitted the jury, in determining whether the film was utterly without redeeming social importance, to consider the circumstances of the sale and distribution, particularly whether such circumstances indicated that the film was being commercially exploited for the sake of its prurient appeal.

The high Court held that the instruction violated no First Amendment rights of the petitioner. The circumstances of distribution of the material are relevant from the standpoint of whether public confrontation with potentially offensive aspects of the material is being forced and are "equally relevant to determining whether social importance claimed for the material in the courtroom was, in the circumstances, pretense or reality—whether it was the basis upon which it was traded in the marketplace or a spurious claim for litigation purposes . . ." (431 U.S. 595 (1977)). The Court based this reason on the *Ginzburg* v. *United States* decison which had been handed down eleven years earlier as a shocking and unexpected exception, and in so doing returned to the same shocking and unexpected exception.

In this decision the Court completed its eleven year circle on the same note. Justice Stevens, with whom Justice Brennan, Justice Stewart and Justice Marshall joined in dissenting, stated the significance of the majority decision well when he wrote: "I would not send Mr. Splawn to jail for telling the truth about his shabby business." In a footnote these justices further recorded their dissent from the Court's disposition of the petitioner's *ex post facto* argument (*ibid.*).

While the 1973 *Miller* decision was intended to relieve the United States Supreme Court from the painful and difficult burden of making subjective and inconsistent judgments, at least one survey found that the *Miller* decision has failed to spur convictions on "smut." Based on 542 responses to 1,320 questionnaires sent to federal and local prosecutors across the country, nearly 80 percent of the prosecutors who responded felt that obscenity had adverse and harmful effects on society. Yet nearly 30 percent said that they placed a lower priority on obscenity prosecutions now than their offices had in 1971—two years before the Supreme Court's decision. Only 13 percent said they were giving obscenity prosecutions a higher priority, and the rest said there had been no change.[11]

The question thus arises as to whether some kind of harm derives from so-called obscene publications or picture shows. This issue has been addressed from time to time in various reports and investigations. *The Report of the Commission on Obscenity and Pornography* provides the reader with conclusions based upon a national survey of American adults and youth which involved face-to-face interviews with a random probability sample of 2,486 adults and 769 young persons between the ages of 15 and 20 in the continental United States.

Based upon results of this study, it was found that the effects of sexual materials upon sexual behavior had little effect or no change "in these behaviors:" "In general, established patterns of sexual behavior were found to be very stable and not altered substantially by exposure to erotica. When sexual activity occurred following the viewing or reading or these materials, it constituted a temporary activation of individuals' preexisting patterns of sexual behavior."[12]

In terms of criminal and delinquent behavior, "statistical studies of the relationship between availability of erotic materials and the rates of sex crimes in Denmark indicate that the increased availability of explicit sexual materials has been accompanied by a decrease in the incidence of sexual crime."[13]

Statistical studies of the relationship described above in the United States presents a more complex picture: "During the period in which there has been a marked increase in the availability of erotic materials, some specific rates of arrest for sex crimes have increased (e.g., forcible rape) and others have declined (e.g., overall juvenile rapes)."[14]

The Commission makes the point that: "In discussions about obscenity and pornography, the fact is often overlooked that legal control on the availability of explicit sexual materials is not the only, or necessarily the most effective, method of dealing with these materials."[15]

Nevertheless, this view should be considered in light of specific instances which occur from time to time. For example, a young man who saw "Violated," a sex movie at the local theatre, left it determined to "get a girl," and slugged a Lakeland girl with a wrapped brick a block from her home.[16] When she screamed, he darted behind the Lakewood Police Station where he was arrested and made a confession before the victim had notified police of the assault.[17]

" 'This picture at the Lower Mall,' he told police, 'excited me. It showed a man who had stabbed a woman to death because she rebuffed him. I intended to rape the girl but her screams scared me off. I don't know what came over me.' "[18]

A more relevant question is by what means should the general problem of how to control the promotion of obscenity and pornography be approached. It seems clear that these controversial publications serve to increase sales by virtue of the controversy they create. The problem to be resolved is whether there should be greater control upon the direct advertising of obscene or pornographic materials, or whether greater controls should be placed upon the content of such publications, or upon the electronic media.

RADIO AND TELEVISION

In answering the question as to whether there should be a change in the regulation of obscenity and pornography, or of offensive speech, as the case may be, it might be worthwhile to consider the extent to which self-regulation of media takes place presently, and then consider where the need of government regulation may be most critical.

The need for regulation may be greater in the electronic media than in the print media simply because it is more difficult to censor children's access to radio and television than to adult literature. The National Association of Broadcasters has recognized this problem, but, like the FCC, was previously unable to enforce any regulation of it as a result of the U.S. Court of Appeals decision in the WBAI case involving George Carlin and the seven words banned by the FCC.

Although this Court decision prevented any enforcement, the NAB guidelines take into account local standards and mores. The NAB Television Board of Directors, at its September 16 meeting in Washington, unanimously approved revised language for Television Code IV–8. Generally, the new language states that Code subscribers "shall not broadcast any material which they determine to be obscene, profane, or indecent." That language replaces the existing provision which prohibits material that is obscene, indecent, or profane as proscribed by law. The Television Board took note of the fact that because of last year's family viewing Court decision, guidelines in the area of programming cannot be enforced.

Board Chairperson Kathryn F. Broman, Springfield (Mass.) Television Corporation, commented: "I believe this language represents a step forward especially in view of the fact that we do have a Code that is strictly voluntary. This language does not prohibit television from treating adult themes in programming, but it does place the responsibility for what goes out over-the-air squarely on the shoulders of the individual subscribers."[19]

The new Code language reads:

- Subscribers shall not broadcast any material which they determine to be obscene, profane, or indecent.
- Above and beyond the requirements of law, broadcasters must consider the family atmosphere in which many of their programs are viewed.
- There shall be no graphic portrayal of sexual acts by sight or sound. The portrayal of implied sexual acts must be essential to the plot and presented in a responsible and tasteful manner.
- Subscribers are obligated to bring positive responsibility and reasoned judgment to bear upon all those involved in the development, production, and selection of programs."[20]

In addition to the NAB regulation above, which, for a time, the courts would not permit it to enforce against networks and local broadcast stations, there is also a 1948 federal statute against broadcasting obscene language, which can once again be enforced on the basis of the U.S. Supreme Court decision on the *Pacifica Foundation* v. *FCC* case. This law, which remains on the books, provides that: "Whoever utters any obscene, indecent, or profane language by means of radio communication shall be fined not more than $10,000 or imprisoned not more than two years, or both." (Section 1464 Communications Act of 1934, Ch. 645, 62 Stat. 769.)[21]

Since the Supreme Court reversed the *Pacifica Foundation* decision, presumably the seven-word prohibition would apply to television as well. Indeed the case of *Al Hanf* v. *State of Oklahoma* (560 P.2d 207 (1977)) underlines the fact that some acts which are permitted in print are by state statute ruled a felony crime in the electronic media.

BILLBOARDS

No less important, though perhaps less pervasive, is the problem of obscenity and pornography on billboards. Many states have laws which limit the content and degree of pandering possible in outdoor advertising, especially near highways. For example, in the state of Washington, any billboard must comply with its statute regulating public nuisances or be removed. (*Wash. Leg. Svc.*, Ch. 55.)

A recent example of a billboard which might fall into a similar category is an attractive suntan lotion advertisement entitled: "The Tan You Want to Touch." It appeared in various locations during the year 1977. (It was modified in 1978). When the New York City advertising agency responsible was asked in the summer of 1977 for permission to reprint a picture of the billboard in this book, the writer was asked in turn whether it would be published in a favorable or negative context. The writer responded that it would be in a favorable and definitely not a negative context.

The representative of the advertising agency then explained that it was the policy of the advertising agency to grant permission under such circumstances, and that there should not be any problem. The agency preferred, however, to consult its client on the matter before making a final decision. The final answer was in the negative. No explanation was given.

CHILD PORNOGRAPHY

Like regulation of the air waves and transportation public ways, there is no First Amendment barrier to the control on sale or distribution of obscene or pornographic material. Such regulation can take place on the federal or state level, or on the local level through ordinances relating to zoning, licensing, public nuisances, or relating to a specific type of business such as adult bookstores or drive-in movies. Many states have laws prohibiting pornographic materials or materials harmful to minors, although some publications are also protected from child pornography laws.

One such case reached the U.S. Supreme Court earlier in 1978. In May of that year the Court distinguished children from a definition of the "average person" within the community by whose standards obscenity should be judged. The Court declared that it might very well reach a much lower "average" when children are part of the equation than it would if it restricted its consideration to the effect of allegedly obscene materials on adults. (*William Pinkus, DBA "Rosslyn News Company* v. *United States,* (1978).)

In the same case the Court reinforced its decison in *Ginzburg* v. *United States, supra,* with its pandering instruction to the jury. The lower court had permitted correctly the jury to consider the touting descriptions in the advertising brochures, along with the materials themselves, to determine whether the materials were intended to appeal to the recipient's prurient interest in sex. The jury was thus allowed to consider whether the pornographic material constituted commercial exploitation of erotica, solely for the sake of their prurient appeal, as was the case in *Ginzburg* v. *United States, supra.*

While child pornography is classified in a category by itself, and precluded from consideration of the character of a community, there are still qualifications on the censorship, especially prior restraint, of child pornography. For example, late in 1977, New York officials were preliminarily enjoined by a federal district court from enforcing the state's new child pornography law against the publisher and sellers of *Show Me,* a book designed for use by parents in educating their children about sex. (*St. Martin's Press* v. *Carey,* 3 Med. L. Rptr. 1598 (1977).)

The statute, New York Penal Law Section 263.15, prohibits the promotion of a "sexual performance by a child" under the age of sixteen. The book, which contains nude photographs of children under 16 years of age and which is explicit in its depiction of human sexuality, comes within the "clear language" of the statute, according to the court, *supra.*

However, the court noted that St. Martin's has not yet been investigated, arrested, or prosecuted for violating the statute which prohibits the promotion of a sexual performance by a child. Not only was the preliminary injunction prohibiting the sale and distribution of the book a case of unconstitutional prior restraint, but the case raises substantive due process questions, since the photographs in the book were taken outside the U.S. and prior to the effective date of the statute, *supra.*

A film which has come under attack as a case of child pornography is entitled "Pretty Baby." Its star, well known model Brooke Shields, was twelve years of age at the time the film was made. Brooke explains: "It's only a role . . . I'm not going to grow up and become a prostitute." Brooke's "nude" scenes were shot with her wearing a body stocking, with one exception. When Violet (the role Brooke plays) chastely poses naked for the photographer Bellocq (Keith Carradine), the French director closed the set to everyone but himself and the cinematographer. The R-rated film has been banned outright in the Canadian provinces of Ontario and Saskatchewan.[22]

Hearings have been held in the Senate Subcommittee on Juvenile Delinquency on the subject of "Protection of Children Against Sexual Exploitation,"[23] and the Senate Committee on the Judiciary has issued a report on the "Protection of Children Against Sexual Exploitation Act of 1977."[24]

CONCLUSION

In the *Roth* case of 1957 and the *Miller* case of 1973, the Supreme Court twice established three criteria for determining permissible limits of obscenity and pornography. In each case the first criterion, that of appealing to the prurient interest, remained the same. The second criterion changed from exceeding the standards of candor in the representation of sexual matters in *Roth* to portraying sexual conduct in a patently offensive manner in *Miller*. The third criterion changed from being utterly without redeeming social value in *Roth* to lacking any serious literary, artistic, political, or scientific value in *Miller*.

On the basis of court precedent, it is reasonable to conclude that there can be greater regulation of time, place, and manner, than of content, where questions are raised as to the legality of publishing or broadcasting certain controversial matter considered to be obscene or pornographic. Furthermore there is more limited First Amendment protection of pornographic materials when they involve use of advertising, air waves, billboards in public places, obscenity for children or by children, or any form of commercialization intended to increase the circulation of the publication.

Government regulation of radio and television, billboards, and child pornography does not violate the First Amendment. In each case these activities involve captive audiences to some extent, and they constitute acts by virtue of the fact that they are staged for the media.

Consequently, regulation of such activities meets the most rigid of all First Amendment standards—the Absolute Standard. Major proponents of the Absolute Standard, such as Justices Black and Douglas, would agree to such limitations on the First Amendment when they involve conduct or commercialization, lacking in the expression of individual ideas.

Taking these acts in reverse order, though in equally important order, child pornography may be regulated by the government without violating the First Amendment because children are viewed as lacking in adult ability to make choices. Portrayal of child pornography is conduct, not speech. Such conduct is unrelated to the expression of ideas, and therefore it is undeserving of First Amendment protection. In cases such as this, First Amendment protection is considered a privilege rather than a right.

Government regulation of billboards, furthermore, poses no constitutional problems of any kind. In the case of *Lehman v. City of Shaker Heights,* for example (a partial text of which can be found in Chapter 2 on Commercial Speech), the Court pointed out specifically that the prohibition of a certain class of advertisements on billboards results in no equal protection violation, but rather that it involves the protection of a captive audience. (418 U.S. 298, 302 (1974).) Moreover it was emphasized in *Railway Express Agency, Inc.* v. *New York* (a text of which may also be found in Chapter 2), that billboard displays in Times Square constitute serious traffic hazards. ((336 U.S. 106, 110 (1949).)

Finally, however, it should be noted that a case can be made for the government regulation of worthless and objectionable commentary on radio, and of any obscene or pornographic conduct which may be shown on television. In neither case would restrictions on the activity or conduct violate the First Amendment. Again it is simply a matter of justifying the regulation. Once that task is accomplished, there is no intrusion on the First Amendment by virtue of implementing the regulation under consideration.

Indeed the Court has listed censorship among the areas whereby even prior restraint may be imposed Constitutionally when conditions serve such governmental restraint and interest. (See *Near* v. *Minnesota,* 283 U.S. 697 (1931); *Brandywine-Main Line Radio* v. *FCC* (see Chapter 5).) The Court places severe restrictions upon censorship in the form of prior restraint, however. (See *Bantam Books, Inc.* v. *Sullivan,* 372 U.S. 58 (1963).)

The airwaves are limited, obviously. Consequently, to some extent a captive audience is involved. Once this fact is accepted, there is no absolute value to be considered, unless it is the protection of the privacy rights of a captive audience and some consideration for the interests of the people in the captive audience. This limitation would not be true of cable television, however.

While it is possible to turn to another channel if one objects to the programming on the one viewed at the time, there remain a limited number of changes possible. These limited options raise questions concerning the needs and interests of the viewer and listener. Again, such conditions may very well be changed by cable television which increases substantially the number of options available.

Furthermore, when it can be demonstrated that there is a causal relationship between anti-social conduct displayed or portrayed in the programming, and similar conduct emulated by the viewers, a case for regulation can be made in the form of individual tort action. Such an inducement for self-regulation occurred in the case of *NBC* v. *Niemi* (a partial text of which may also be found in Chapter 2), where self-regulation was found to provide insufficient protection for the consumer. Here a television network's failure to show irreparable injury caused by a California court of appeal decision requiring trial in damages action brought against the network for its broadcast of a movie, "Born Innocent," that allegedly provoked an assault on the plaintiff was found to warrant the Circuit Justice's denial of the network's application for a stay of appeal of the court decision. Upon retrial, however, a San Francisco judge dismissed the case in August 1978.

This case, like the one involving Ronney A. Zamora in Florida, is centered around negligence action seeking damages for the television network's broadcast of a movie that allegedly inspired the assault upon the plaintiff. Thus the assumption has been made that at least violence and rape seen on television may induce violence and rape on the part of some viewers. 98 S.Ct. 705 (1978). The high Court upheld the stay.

In the case of *First National Bank of Boston* v. *Bellotti* (a partial text of which appears in Chapter 2), Chief Justice Burger explains that newspapers and broadcasting stations could be said to represent a larger threat to what he calls "valid interests in the electoral process than other corporations." (1978). Burger further expresses his personal view on the power of the press by pointing out that "large media conglomerates" had no special claim on Constitutional liberties, including First Amendment rights of free expression. (*Ibid.*)

Media conglomerates, however, have been broken up by the courts in the past, and this practice continues to occur. Furthermore, when private tort action may be brought against television network stations for damages resulting from violent or criminal acts committed, surely the FTC and FCC have the power, initiative, and First Amendment support in regulating obscene expressions, both actions and words.

Billboards can be regulated easily on the state and local level, and even child pornography could be controlled at that level as well. But when advertising or the airwaves is involved, there may be an obligation for the government to curtail more than child pornography and other public displays, such as billboards.

A strong case, nevertheless, can be made and has been made for deregulation of the airwaves. For example, House communications subcommittee leaders proposed in June 1978 granting permanent licenses to radio and television owners, banning any censorship of program content, and eliminating the review process that forces stations to air news and public service programs. In the form of a 217-page bill, the proposal constitutes the most dramatic example in many years of a serious effort to return to "free market" economic competition in place of regulation in "the public interest." (HR 13015, 95th Cong.2d Session).

The subcommittee had negotiated the bill for three years with the broadcasting industry, the American Telephone and Telegraph Co. (AT&T), and the FCC, the agency which oversees both. Under such a proposal, the FCC would be restructured, and would lose much of its power. Although the bill may not reach the House floor before 1979, or the Senate before 1980, most of the major elements have the consent of the industries affected.

It has been estimated that deregulation would save the broadcast and telephone industries, which are the most powerful lobbies on FCC issues, hundreds of millions of dollars in administration, record-keeping, and legal costs. Furthermore, while one barrier to the intrusion of cable television upon networks and local stations would be removed, removal of one restrictive regulation would not leave broadcasters vulnerable to cable television. Indeed sufficient protection has been and can be provided by enforceable state laws which deny cable television the use of network and station productions without their consent.

Finally, the security of having permanent licenses would give station owners a windfall increase in the resale value of their stations because new stations are technically impossible in most markets. Consequently, new entrants would have to buy from present owners.

Among other things, this bill would ban any censorship or other regulation or program content. It would also eliminate any power to censor or punish stations for airing sex or violence or racial, ethnic, or other stereotypes. In light of the newly approved alternative of private tort actions against such offenses, efforts on the part of a federal regulatory agency may be duplicative and unnecessary.

In at least one respect limitations which may be placed constitutionally on the public display of billboards may be correlated to the limitations which may be placed constitutionally on the use of "indecent language" over the public airwaves. In both instances Justice Douglas' concurring opinion in *Lehman* v. *Shaker Heights* (418 U.S. 298 (1974)) may apply rational limits with both authority and clarity: "While petitioner clearly has a right to express his views to those who wish to listen, he has no right to force his message upon an audience incapable of declining to receive it." The same principle may apply to the constitutionality of restricting child pornography, as well as the advertising and promotion of any obscene or pornographic material.

It is thus that the case of *Pacifica* v. *FCC* clarifies the meaning of Section 1464 of Title 18 of the United States Code in the form of a law that makes it a criminal offense, punishable by imprisonment and/or a fine, to "utter any obscene, indecent or profane language by means of radio communications." According to Abbott Washburn, FCC Commissioner, this case provides the first clear legal definition of "indecent language." Washburn emphasized that the Court properly stressed that broadcasters have a special responsibility to the public because of the "uniquely pervasive presence" of radio and television in the home.[25]

NOTES

[1] Milton R. Konvitz, *Fundamantal Liberties of a Free People* (1957), pp. 163–169.
[2] *Roth* v. *United States,* 354 U.S. 476 (1957).
[3] Henry P. Monaghan, "First Amendment Due Process," 83 *Harvard Law Review (1969), pp. 520–524.*
[4] *New York Times* (June 12, 1977).
[5] For a concise history of obscenity and pornography, see *Paris Adult Theatre I* v. *Slaton,* 413 U.S. 49 (1973). Also see Daniel M. Rohrer, *Justice Before the Law* (Skokie, Ill.: National Textbook Co., 1971), pp. 215–217, for an earlier history.
[6] Ted Morgan, "United States Versus the Princess of Porn," *New York Times Magazine* (Mar. 6, 1977), p. 16.
[7] Larry Flynt, "The *Hustler* Hassle," Speech Communication Association of America Convention Program sponsored by the Communication and Law Committee and Commission of Freedom of Speech (Dec. 3, 1977), Washington, D.C.
[8] George Vecsey, "A Pornography Publisher Says He Has Changed, But Not Into a Traditional Christian," *New York Times* (Feb. 2, 1978), p. A16.

[9] Wayne King, "Larry Flynt, Owner of *Hustler,* Is Shot Near Georgia Court," *New York Times* (Feb. 7, 1978), p. 1.
[10] Ibid., p. 73.
[11] Tom Goldstein, "Survey Finds High Court Decision Fails to Spur Convictions on Smut," *New York Times* (Mar. 20, 1977).
[12] *The Report of the Commission on Obscenity and Pornography* (New York: Bantam Books, 1970), pp. 26–29.
[13] Ibid., p. 30.
[14] Ibid., p. 31.
[15] Ibid., p. 32.
[16] Charles Lucy, Scripps-Howard Writer, *Cleveland Press* (Sept. 28, 1954), p. 1.
[17] Ibid.
[18] Ibid.
[19] "New TV Code Obscenity Language Approved By NAB Television Board of Directors," *Code News* (Oct. 10, 1977).
[20] Ibid.
[21] "Appendix C," *Communications Act of 1934* (Washington, D.C.: U.S. Government Printing Office, 1971), p. 131.
[22] Kristin McMurran, *People* (May 29, 1978), p. 42.
[23] Hearings Before the Subcommittee to Investigate Juvenile Delinquency of the Committee on the Judiciary, U.S. Senate, 95th Congress, 1st Session, Chicago, Ill., May 27, 1977, June 16, 1977 (Washington, D.C.: U.S. Government Printing Office, 1978).
[24] Report of the Committee on the Judiciary, U.S. Senate on S. 1585, Report No. 95–438, 95th Congress, 1st Session, Sept. 15–16, 1977 (Washington, D.C.: U.S. Government Printing Office, 1977); for further consideration of child pornography see "Sexual Exploitation of Children," Hearings Before the Subcommittee on Crime of the Committee on the Judiciary, U.S. House of Representatives, 95th Congress, 1st Session, May 23, 25, June 10, and September 20, 1977 (Washington, D.C.: U.S. Government Printing Office, 1977).
[25] Abbott Washburn, " 'Seven Dirty Words' and the Court," *New York Times* (November 16, 1978), p. A26.
*For a United Kingdom Case of child obscenity and pornography, which was appealed to and conviction upheld by the European Court of Human Rights in Strasbourg, see *Richard Handyside* v. *United Kingdom* in *Freedom of Speech and Human Rights: An International Perspective* (1979), by the same author and publisher as this text.

Section 2

Cases

ROTH v. UNITED STATES

ALBERTS v. CALIFORNIA

354 U.S. 476 (1957)

Mr. Justice Brennan delivered the opinion of the Court.

The Constitutionality of a criminal obscenity statute is the question in each of these cases. In *Roth*, the primary Constitutional question is whether the federal obscenity statute violates the provision of the First Amendment that "Congress shall make no law . . . abridging the freedom of spech, or of the press . . . ." In *Alberts,* the primary Constitutional question is whether the obscenity provisions of the California Penal Code invade the freedoms of speech and press as they may be incorporated in the liberty protected from state action by the Due Process Clause of the Fourteeenth Amendment.

Other Constitutional questions are: whether these statutes violate due process, because they are too vague to support conviction for crime; whether power to punish speech and press offensive to decency and morality is in the States alone, so that the federal obscenity statutes violates the Ninth and Tenth Amendments (raised in *Roth*); and whether Congress, by enacting the federal obscenity statute, under the power . . . to establish post offices and post roads, pre-empted the regulation of the subject matter (raised in *Alberts*).

Roth conducted a business in New York in the publication and sale of books, photographs, and magazines. He used circulars and advertising matter to solicit sales. He was convicted by a jury in the District Court for the Southern District of New York upon 4 counts of a 26-count indictment charging him with mailing obscene circulars and advertising, and an obscene book, in violation of the federal obscenity statute. His conviction was affirmed by the Court of Appeals for the Second Circuit. We granted certiorari.

Alberts conducted a mail-order business from Los Angeles. He was convicted by the Judge of the Municipal Court of the Beveraly Hills Judicial District (having waived a jury trial) under a misdemeanor complaint which charged him with lewdly keeping for sale obscene and indecent books, and with writing, composing, and publishing an obscene advertisement of them, in violation of the California Penal Code. The conviction was affirmed by the Appellate Department of the Superior Court of the State of California in and for the County of Los Angeles. We noted the probable jurisdiction.

The dispositive question is whether obscenity is utterance within the area of protected speech and press. Although this is the first time the question has been squarely presented to this Court, either under the First Amendment or under the Fourteenth Amendment, expressions found in numerous opinions indicate that this Court has always assumed that obscenity is not protected by the freedoms of speech and press.

The guarantees of freedom of expression in effect in 10 of the 14 States which by 1792 had ratified the Constitution, gave no absolute protection for every utterance. Thirteen of the 14 States provided for the prosecution of libel, and all of those States made either blasphemy or profanity, or both, statutory crimes. As early as 1712, Massachusetts made it criminal to publish "any filthy, obscene, or profane song, pamphlet, libel, or mock sermon" in imitation or mimicking of religious services. Thus, profanity and obscenity were related offenses.

In light of this history it is apparent that the unconditional phrasing of the First Amendment was not intended to protect every utterance. This phrasing did not prevent this Court from concluding that libelous utterances are not within the area of Constitutionally protected speech. (*Beauharnais* v. *Illinois*.) At the time of the adoption of the First Amendment, obscenity law was not as fully developed as libel law, but there is sufficiently contemporaneous evidence to show that obscenity, too, was outside the protection intended for speech and press.

The protection given speech and press was fashioned to assure unfettered interchange of ideas for the bringing about of political and social changes desired by the people.

All ideas having even the slightest redeeming social importance—unorthodox ideas, controversial ideas, even ideas hateful to the prevailing climate of opinion—have the full protection of the guarantees, unless excludable because they encroach upon the limited area of more important interests. But implicit in the history of the First Amendment is the rejection of obscenity as utterly without redeeming social importance. This rejection for that reason is mirrored in the universal judgment that obscenity should be restrained, reflected in the international agreement of over 50 nations, in the obscenity laws of all of the 48 States, and in the 20 obscenity laws enacted by the Congress from 1842 to 1956. This is the same judgment expressed by this Court in *Chaplinsky* v. *New Hampshire:*

> . . . There are certain well-defined and narrowly limited classes of speech, the prevention and punishment of which have never been thought to raise any Constitutional problem. *These include the lewd and obscene* . . . . *It has been well observed that such utterances are no essential part of any exposition of ideas, and are of such slight social value as a step to truth that any benefit that may be derived from them is clearly outweighed by the social interest in order and morality* . . . . (Emphasis added.)

We hold that obscenity is not within the area of Constitutionally protected speech or press.

It is strenuously urged that these obscenity statutes offend the Constitutional guarantees because they punish incitation to impure sexual thoughts, not shown to be related to any overt antisocial conduct which is or may be incited in the persons stimulated to such thoughts. It is insisted that the Constitutional guarantees are violated because convictions may be had without proof either that obscene material will perceptibly create a clear and present danger of antisocial conduct, or will probably induce its recipients to such conduct. But, in light of our holding that obscenity is not protected speech, the complete answer to this argument is in the holding of this Court in *Beauharnais* v. *Illinois:*

> Libelous utterances not being within the area of Constitutionally protected speech, it is unnecessary, either for us or for the State courts, to consider the issues behind the phrase 'clear

and present danger.' Certainly no one would contend that obscene speech, for example, may be punished only upon a showing of such circumstances. Libel, as we have seen, is in the same class.

However, sex and obscenity are not synonymous. Obscene material is material which deals with sex in a manner appealing to prurient interest. The portrayal of sex, e.g., in art, literature, and scientific works, is not itself sufficient reason to deny material the Constitutional protection of freedom of speech and press. Sex, a great and mysterious motive force in human life, has indisputably been a subject of absorbing interest to mankind through the ages; it is one of the vital problems of human interest and public concern. As to all such problems, this Court said in *Thornhill v. Alabama*:

> The freedom of speech and of the press guaranteed by the Constitution embraces at the least the liberty to discuss publicly and truthfully *all matters of public concern* without previous restraint or fear of subsequent punishment. The exigencies of the Colonial Period and the efforts to secure freedom from oppressive administration developed a broadened conception of these liberties as adequate to supply the public need for *information and education with respect to the significant issues of the times* . . . . Freedom of discussion, if it would fulfill its historic function in this nation, must embrace *all issues about which information is needed or appropriate to enable the members of society to cope with the exigencies of their period.* (Emphasis added.)

The fundamental freedoms of speech and press have contributed greatly to the development and well being of our free society and are indispensable to its continued growth. Ceaseless vigilance is the watchword to prevent their erosion by Congress or by the States. The door barring federal and state intrusion into this area cannot be left ajar; it must be kept tightly closed and opened only the slightest crack necessary to prevent encroachment upon more important interests. It is therefore vital that the standards for judging obscenity safeguard the protection of freedom of speech and press for material which does not treat sex in a manner appealing to prurient interest.

The early leading standard of obscenity allowed material to be judged merely by the effect of an isolated excerpt upon particularly susceptible persons. Some American courts adopted this standard but later decisions have rejected it and substituted this test: whether to the average person, applying contemporary community standards, the dominant theme of the material taken as a whole appeals to prurient interest. The *Hicklin* test, judging obscenity by the effect of isolated passages upon the most susceptible persons, might well encompass material legitimately treating with sex, and so it must be rejected as unconstitutionally restrictive of the freedoms of speech and press. On the other hand, the substituted standard provides safeguards adequate to withstand the charge of Constitutional infirmity.

Mr. Chief Justice Warren, concurring in the result.

I agree with the result reached by the Court in these cases, but because we are operating in a field of expression and because broad language used here may eventually be applied to the arts and sciences and freedom of communication generally, I would limit our decison to the facts before us and to the validity of the statutes in question as applied.

That there is a social problem presented by obscenity is attested by the expression of the legislatures of the 48 states as well as the Congress. To recognize the existence of a problem, however, does not require that we sustain any and all measures adopted to meet that problem. The history of the application of laws designed to suppress the obscene demonstrates convincingly that the power of government can be invoked under them against great art or literature, scientific treatises, or works exciting social controversy. Mistakes of the past prove that there is a strong countervailing interest to be considered in the freedoms guaranteed by the First and Fourteenth Amendments.

The line dividing the salacious or pornographic from literature or science is not straight and unwavering. Present laws depend largely upon the effect that the materials may have upon those who receive them. It is manifest that the same object may have a different impact, varying according to the part of the community it reached. But there is more to these cases. It is not the book that is on trial; it is a person. The conduct of the defendant is the central issue, not the obscenity of a book or picture. The nature of the materials is, of course, relevant as an attribute of the defendant's conduct, but the materials are thus placed in context from which they draw color and character. A wholly different result might be reached in a different setting.

The personal element in these cases is seen most strongly in the requirement of scienter. Under the California law, the prohibited activity must be done "willfully and lewdly." The federal statute limits the crime to acts done "knowingly." In his charge to the jury, the district judge stated that the matter must be "calculated" to corrupt or debauch. The defendants in both these cases were engaged in the business of purveying textual or graphic matter openly advertised to appeal to erotic interest of their customers. They were plainly engaged in the commercial exploitation of the morbid and shameful craving for materials with prurient effect. I believe that the State and Federal Governments can Constitutionally punish such conduct. That is all that these cases present to us, and that is all we need to decide.

Mr. Justice Harlan, concurring in the result in (*Alberts*) and dissenting in (*Roth*).

I regret not to be able to join the Court's opinion. I cannot do so because I find lurking beneath its disarming generalizations a number of problems which not only leave me with serious misgivings as to the future effect of today's decisions, but which also, in my view, call for different results in these two cases.

My basic difficulties with the Court's opinion are threefold. First, the opinion paints with such a broad brush that I fear it may result in a loosening of the tight reins which state and federal courts should hold upon the enforcement of obscenity statutes. Second, the Court fails to discriminate between the different factors which, in my opinion, are involved in the Constitutional adjudication of state and federal obscenity cases. Third, relevant distinctions between the two obscenity statutes here involved, and the Court's own definition of "obscenity," are ignored.

In final analysis, the problem presented by these cases is how far, and on what terms, the state and federal governments have power to punish individuals for disseminating books considered to be undesirable because of their nature or supposed deleterious effect upon human conduct. The Court seems to assume that "obscenity" is a peculiar genus of "speech and press," which is as distinct, recognizable, and classifiable as poison ivy is among other plants. On this basis the Constitutional question before us simply becomes, as the Court says, whether "obscenity," as an abstraction, is protected by the First and Fourteenth Amendments, and the question whether a particular book may be suppressed becomes a mere matter of classification, of "fact," to be entrusted to a fact-finder and insulated from independent Constitutional judgment. But surely the problem cannot be solved in such a generalized fashion. Every communication has an individuality and "value" of its own. The suppression of a particular writing or other tangible form of expression is, therefore, an individual matter, and in the nature of things every such suppression raises an individual Constitutional problem, in which a reviewing court must determine for itself whether the attacked expression is suppressible within Constitutional standards. Since those standards do not readily lend themselves to generalized definitions, the Constitutional problem in the last analysis becomes one of particularized judgments which appellate courts must make for themselves.

Many juries might find that Joyce's *Ulysses* or Boccaccio's *De cameron* are obscene, and yet the conviction of a defendant for selling either book would raise, for me, the gravest Constitutional problems, for no such verdict could convince me, without more, that these books are "utterly without redeeming social importance." In short, I do not understand how the Court can resolve the Constitutional problems now before it without making its own independent judgment upon the character of the material upon which these convictions are based. I am very much afraid that the broad manner in which the Court has decided these cases will tend to obscure the peculiar responsibilities resting on state and federal courts in this field and encourage them to rely on easy labeling and jury verdicts as a substitute for facing up to the tough individual problems of Constitutional judgment involved in every obscenity case.

Quite a different situation is presented . . . where the federal government imposes the ban. The danger is perhaps not great if people of one State, through their legislature, decide that *Lady Chatterley's Lover* goes so far beyond the acceptable standards of candor that it will be deemed offensive and nonsellable, for the State next door is still free to make its own choice. At least we do not have one uniform standard. But the dangers to free thought and expression are truly great if the federal government imposes a blanket ban over the nation on such a book. The prerogative of the States to differ on their ideas of morality will be destroyed, the ability of States to experiment will be stunted. The fact that the people of one State cannot read some of the works of D.H. Lawrence seems to me, if not wise or desirable, at least acceptable. But that no person in the United States should be allowed to do so seems to me to be intolerable, and violative of both the letter and spirit of the First Amendment.

I judge this case, then, in view of what I think is the attenuated federal interest in this field, in view of the very real danger of deadening uniformity which can result from nationwide federal censorship, and in view of the fact that the Constitutionality of this conviction must be weighed against the First and not the Fourteenth Amendment. So viewed, I do not think that this conviction can be upheld. The petitioner was convicted under a statute which, under the judge's charge, makes it criminal to sell books which "tend to stir sexual impulses and lead to sexually impure thoughts." I cannot agree that any book which tends to stir sexual impulses and lead to sexually impure thoughts necessarily is "utterly without redeeming social importance." Not only did this charge fail to measure up to the standards which I understand the Court to approve, but as far as I can see, much of the great literature of the world could lead to conviction under such a view of the statute. Moreover, in no event do I think that the limited federal interest in this area can extend to mere "thoughts." The federal government has no business, whether under the postal or commerce power, to bar the sale of books because they might lead to any kind of "thoughts."

It is no answer to say, as the Court does, that obscenity is not protected speech. The point is that this statute, as here construed, defines obscenity so widely that it encompasses matters which might very well be protected speech. I do not think that the federal statute can be Constitutionally construed to reach other than what the government has termed as "hard-core" pornography. Nor do I think the statute can fairly be read as directed only at persons who are engaged in the business of catering to the prurient minded, even though their wares fall short of hard-core pornography. Such a statute would raise Constitutional questions of a different order. That being so, and since in my opinion the material here involved cannot be said to be hard-core pornography, I would reverse this case with instructions to dismiss the indictment.

Mr. Justice Douglas, with whom Mr. Justice Black concurs, dissenting.

When we sustain these convictions, we make the legality of a publication turn on the purity of thought which a book or tract instills in the mind of the reader. I do not think we can approve that standard and be faithful to the command of the First Amendment, which by its terms is a restraint on Congress and which by the Fourteenth is a restraint on the States.

By these standards punishment is inflicted for thoughts provoked, not for overt acts nor antisocial conduct. This test cannot be squared with our decisions under the First Amendment. Even the ill-starred *Dennis* case conceded that speech to be punishable must have some relation to action which could be penalized by government. (*Dennis* v. *United States*.) This issue cannot be avoided by saying that obscenity is not protected by the First Amendment. The question remains, what is the Constitutional test of obscenity?

The tests by which these convictions were obtained required only the arousing of sexual thoughts. Yet the arousing of sexual thoughts, and desires, happens every day in normal life in dozens of ways. Nearly 30 years ago a questionnaire sent to college and normal school women graduates asked what things were most stimulating sexually. Of 409 replies, 9 said "music;" 18 said "pictures;" 29 said "dancing;" 40 said "drama;" 95 said "books;" and 218 said "man." (Alpert, "Judicial Censorship of Obscene Literature," 52 *Harv. L. Rev.* 40, 73.)

If we are certain that impurity of sexual thoughts impelled to action, we would be on less dangerous ground in punishing the distributors of this sex literature. But it is by no means clear that obscene literature, as so defined, is a significant factor in influencing substantial deviations from the community standards.

There are a number of reasons for real and substantial doubts as to the soundness of that hypothesis. 1) Scientific studies of juvenile delinquency demonstrate that those who get into trouble, and are the greatest concern of the advocates of censorship, are far less inclined to read than those who do not become delinquent. The delinquents are generally the adventurous type, who have little use for reading and other nonactive entertainment. Thus, even assuming that reading sometimes has an adverse effect upon moral conduct, the effect is not likely to be substantial, for those who are susceptible seldom read. 2) Sheldon and Eleanor Glueck, who are among the country's leading authorities on the treatment and causes of juvenile delinquency, have recently published the results of a ten-year study of its causes. They exhaustively studied approximately 90 factors and influences that might lead to or explain juvenile delinquency, but the Gluecks gave no consideration to the type of reading material, if any, read by the delinquents. This is, of course, consistent with their finding that delinquents read very little. When those who know so much about the problem of delinquency among youth—the very group about whom the advocates of censorship are most concerned—conclude that what delinquents read has so little effect upon their conduct that it is not worth investigating in an exhaustive study of causes, there is good reason for serious doubt concerning the basic hypothesis on which obscenity censorship is defended. 3) The many other influences in society that stimulate sexual desire are so much more frequent in their influence, and so much more potent in their effect, that the influence of reading is likely, at most, to be relatively insignificant in the composite of forces that lead an individual into conduct deviating from the community sex standards. The Kinsey studies show the minor degree to which literature serves as a potent sexual stimulant.

The absence of dependable information of the effect of obscene literature on human conduct should make us wary. It should put us on the side of protecting society's interest in literature, except and unless it can be said that the particular publication has an impact on action that the government can control.

As noted, the trial judge in the *Roth* case charged the jury in the alternative that the federal obscenity statute outlaws literature dealing with sex which offends "the common conscience of the community." That standard is, in my view, more inimical still to freedom of expression.

The standard of what offends "the common conscience of the community" conflicts, in my judgment, with the command of the First Amendment that "Congress shall make no law . . . abridging the freedom of speech, or of the press." Certainly that standard would not be an acceptable one if religion, economics, politics, or philosophy were involved. How does it become a Constitutional standard when literature treating with sex is concerned?

Any test that turns on what is offensive to the community's standards is too loose, too capricious, too destructive of freedom of expression to be squared with the First Amendment. Under that test, juries can censor, suppress, and punish what they don't like, provided the matter relates to "sexual impurity" or has a tendency "to excite lustful thought." This is community censorship in one of its worst forms. It creates a regime where, in the battle between the literati and the Philistines, the Philistines are certain to win. If experience in this field teaches anything, it is that "censorship of obscenity has almost always been both irrational and indiscriminate."

I can understand (and at times even sympathize) with programs of civic groups and church groups to protect and defend the existing moral standards of the community. I can understand the motives of the Anthony Comstocks who would impose Victorian standards on the community. When speech alone is involved, I do not think that government, consistently with the First Amendment, can become the sponsor of any of these movements. I do not think that government, consistently with the First Amendment, can throw its weight behind one school or another. Government should be concerned with antisocial conduct, not with utterances. Thus, if the First Amendment guarantee of freedom of speech and press is to mean anything in this field, it must allow protests even against the moral code that the standard of the day sets for the community. In other words, literature should not be suppressed merely because it offends the moral code of the censor.

I do not think that the problem can be resolved by the Court's statement that "obscenity is not expression protected by the First Amendment." With the exception of *Beauharnais* v. *Illinois,* none of our cases has resolved problems of free speech and free press by placing any form of expression beyond the pale of the absolute prohibition of the First Amendment. Unlike the law of libel, wrongfullly relied on in *Beauharnais,* there is no special historical evidence that literature dealing with sex was intended to be treated in a special manner by those who drafted the First Amendment. I reject too the implication that problems of freedom of speech and of the press are to be resolved by weighing against the values of free expression, the judgment of the Court that a particular form of the expression has "no redeeming social importance." The First Amendment, its prohibition in terms absolute, was designed to preclude courts as well as legislatures from weighing the values of speech against silence. The First Amendment puts free speech in the preferred position.

I would give the broad sweep of the First Amendment full support. I have the same confidence in the ability of our people to reject noxious literature as I have in their capacity to sort out the true from the false in theology, economics, politics, or any other field.

MEMOIRS v. MASSACHUSETTS
383 U.S. 413 (1966)

Mr. Justice Brennan announced the judgment of the Court and delivered an opinion in which The Chief Justice and Mr. Justice Fortas join.

(T)he sole question before the state courts was whether *Memoirs* satisfies the test of obscenity established in *Roth v. United States*.

Under this definition, as elaborated in subsequent cases, three elements must coalesce: it must be established that a) the dominant theme of the material taken as a whole appeals to a prurient interest in sex; b) the material is patently offensive because it affronts contemporary community standards relating to the description or representation of sexual matters; and c) the material is utterly without redeeming social value.

The (Massachusetts) Supreme Judicial Court erred in holding that a book need not be "unqualifiedly worthless before it can be deemed obscene." A book cannot be proscribed unless it is found to be utterly without redeeming social value. This is so even though the book is found to possess the requisite prurient appeal and to be patently offensive. Each of the three federal Constitutional criteria is to be applied independently; the social value of the book can neither be weighted against nor canceled by its prurient appeal or patent offensiveness. Hence, even on the view of the court below that *Memoirs* possessed only a modicum of social value, its judgment must be reversed as being founded on an erroneous interpretation of federal Constitutional standard.

It does not necessarily follow from this reversal that a determination that *Memoirs* is obscene in the Constitutional sense would be improper under all circumstances. On the premise, which we have no occasion to assess, that *Memoirs* has the requisite prurient appeal and is patently offensive, but has only a minimum of social value, the circumstances of production, sale, and publicity are relevant in determining whether or not the publication or distribution of the book is Constitutionally protected. Evidence that the book was commercially exploited for the sake of prurient appeal, to the exclusion of all other values, might justify the conclusion that the book was utterly without redeeming social importance. In this proceeding the courts were asked to judge the obscenity of *Memoirs* in the abstract, and the declaration of obscenity was neither aided nor limited by a specific set of circumstances of production, sale, and publicity. All possible uses of the book must therefore be considered, and the mere risk that the book might be exploited by panderers because it so pervasively treats sexual matters cannot alter the fact—given the view of the Massachusetts court attributing to *Memoirs* a modicum of literary and historical value—that the book will have redeeming social importance in the hands of those who publish or distribute it on the basis of that value.

Reversed.

Mr. Justice Black and Mr. Justice Stewart concur in the reversal for the reasons stated in their respective dissenting opinions in *Ginzburg v. United States* and *Mishkin v. New York*.

Mr. Justice Douglas, concurring.

The Constitution forbids abridgement of "freedom of speech, or of the press." Censorship is the most notorious form of abridgment. It substitutes majority rule where minority tastes or viewpoints were to be tolerated.

It is to me inexplicable how a book that concededly has social worth can nonetheless be banned because of the manner in which it is advertised and sold. However florid its cover, whatever the pitch of its advertisements, the contents remain the same.

Every time an obscenity case is to be argued here, my office is flooded with letters and postal cards urging me to protect the community or the nation by striking down the publication. The messages are often identical even down to commas and semicolons. The inference is irresistible that they were all copied from a school or church blackboard. Dozens of postal cards often are mailed from the same precinct. The drives are incessant and the pressures are great. Happily we do not bow to them. I mention them only to emphasize the lack of popular understanding of our Constitutional system. Publications and utterances were made immune from majoritarian control by the First Amendment, applicable to the States by reason of the Fourteenth. No exceptions were made, not even for obscenity. The Court's contrary conclusion in *Roth,* where obscenity was found to be "outside" the First Amendment, is without justification.

Mr. Justice Clark, dissenting.

It is with regret that I write this dissenting opinion. However, the public should know of the continuous flow of pornographic material reaching this Court and the increasing problem States have in controlling it. *Memoirs of a Woman of Pleasure,* the book involved here, is typical. I have "stomached" past cases for almost 10 years without much outcry. Though I am not known to be a purist—or a shrinking violet—this book is too much even for me. It is important that the Court has refused to declare it obscene and thus gives it further circulation. In order to give my remarks the proper setting I have been obliged to portray the book's contents, which gives me embarrassment. However, quotations from typical episodes would so debase our reports that I will not follow that course.

In my view, evidence of social importance is relevant to the determination of the ultimate question of obscenity. But social importance does not constitute a separate and distinct Constitutional test. Such evidence must be considered together with evidence that the material in question appeals to prurient interest and is patently offensive. Accordingly, we must first turn to the book here under attack.

Memoirs is nothing more than a series of minutely and vividly described sexual episodes. This is presented to the reader through an uninterrupted succession of descriptions by Fanny, either as an observer or participant, of sexual adventures so vile that one of the male expert witnesses in the case was hesitant to repeat any one of them in the courtroom. These scenes run the gamut of possible sexual experience such as lesbianism, female masturbation, homosexuality between young boys, the destruction of a maidenhead with consequent gory descriptions, the seduction of a young virgin boy, the flagellation of male by female, and vice versa, followed by fervid sexual engagement, and other abhorent acts, including over two dozen separate bizarre descriptions of different sexual intercourses between male and female characters.

In my view, the book's repeated and unrelieved appeals to the prurient interest of the average person leave it utterly without redeeming social importance.

Mr. Justice Harlan, dissenting.

The central development that emerges from the aftermath of *Roth* v. *United States* is that no stable approach to the obscenity problem has yet been devised by this Court. Two Justices believe that the First and Fourteenth Amendments absolutely protect obscene and nonobscene material alike. Another Justice believes that neither the States nor the federal government may suppress any material save for "hard-core pornography."

My premise is that in the area of obscenity the Constitution does not bind the States and the federal government in precisely the same fashion.

Federal suppression of allegedly obscene matter should, in my view, be Constitutionally limited to that often described as "hard-core pornography."

To me it is plain, for instance, that *Fanny Hill* does not fall within this class and could not be barred from the federal mails.

State obscenity laws present problems of quite a different order. The varying conditions across the country, the range of views on the need and reasons for curbing obscenity, and the traditions of local self-government in matters of public welfare all favor a far more flexible attitude in defining the bounds for the States. From my standpoint, the Fourteenth Amendment requires of a State only that it apply criteria rationally related to the accepted notion of obscenity and that it reach results not wholly out of step with current American standards.

Mr. Justice White, dissenting.

If "social importance" is to be used as the prevailing opinion uses it today, obscene material, however far beyond customary limits of candor, is immune if it has any literary style, if it contains any historical references or language characteristic of a bygone day, or even if it is printed or bound in an interesting way. Well written, especially effective obscenity is protected; the poorly written is vulnerable. And why shouldn't the fact that some people buy and read such material prove its "social value?"

In my view, "social importance" is not an independent test of obscenity but is relevant only to determining the predominant prurient interest of the material, a determination which the court or the jury will make based on the material itself and all the evidence in the case, expert or otherwise.

Application of the *Roth* test, as I understand it, necessarily involves the exercise of judgment by legislatures, courts, and juries.

Finally, it should be remembered that if the publication and sale of *Fanny Hill* and like books are proscribed, it is not the Constitution that imposes the ban. Censure stems from a legislative act, and legislatures are Constitutionally free to embrace such books whenever they wish to do so. But if a State insists on treating *Fanny Hill* as obscene and forbidding its sale, the First Amendment does not prevent it from doing so.

I would affirm the judgment below.

GINZBURG v. UNITED STATES
383 U.S. 463 (1966)

Mr. Justice Brennan delivered the opinion of the Court.

In the cases in which this Court has decided obscenity questions since *Roth,* it has regarded the materials as sufficient in themselves for the determination of the question. In the present case, however, the prosecution charged the offense in the context of the circumstances of production, sale, and publicity and assumed that, standing alone, the publications themselves might not be obscene. We agree that the question of obscenity may include consideration of the setting in which the publications were presented as an aid to determining the question of obscenity, and assume without deciding that the prosecution could not have succeeded otherwise. We view the publications against a background of commercial exploitation of erotica solely for the sake of their prurient appeal. The record in that regard amply supports the decision of the trial judge that the mailing of all three publications offended the statute.

The three publications were *Eros,* a hard-cover magazine of expensive format; *Liaison,* a bi-weekly newsletter; and *The Housewife's Handbook on Selective Promiscuity* (hereinafter the *Handbook*), a short book. The issue of *Eros* specified in the indictment, Vol. 1, No. 4, contains 15 articles and photo-essays on the subject of love, sex, and sexual relations. The specified issue of *Liaison,* Vol. 1, contains a prefatory "Letter from the Editors" announcing its dedication to "keeping sex an art and preventing it from becoming a science." The remainder of the issue consists of digests of two articles concerning sex and sexual relations which had earlier appeared in professional journals and a report of an interview with a psychotherapist who favors the broadest license in sexual relationships. As the trial judge noted, "(w)hile the treatment is largely superficial, it is presented entirely without restraint of any kind. According to defendants' own expert, it is entirely without literary merit." The *Handbook* purports to be a sexual autobiography detailing with complete candor the author's sexual experiences from age 3 to age 36. The text includes, and prefatory and concluding sections of the book elaborate, her views on such subjects as sex education of children, laws regulating private consensual adult sexual practices, and the equality of women in sexual relationships. It was claimed at trial that women would find the book valuable, for example as a marriage manual or as an aid to the sex education of their children.

Besides testimony as to the merit of the material, there was abundant evidence to show that each of the accused publications was originated or sold as stock in trade of the sordid business of pandering—"the business of purveying textual or graphic matter openly advertised to appeal to the erotic interest of their customers." *Eros* early sought mailing privilege from the postmasters of Intercourse and Blue Ball, Pennsylvania. The trial court found the obvious, that these hamlets were chosen only for the value their names would have in furthering petitioners' effort to sell their publications on the basis of salacious appeal; the facilities of the post offices were inadequate to handle the anticipated volume of mail, and the privileges were denied. Mailing privileges were then obtained from the postmaster of Middlesex, New Jersey. *Eros* and *Liaison* thereafter mailed several million circulars soliciting subscriptions from that post office; over 5,500 copies of the *Handbook* were mailed.

The *"leer of the sensualist"* also permeates the advertising for the three publications. The circulars sent for *Eros* and *Liaison* stressed the sexual candor of the respective publications, and openly boasted that the publishers would take full advantage of what they regarded as an unrestricted license allowed by law in the expression of sex and sexual matters. The advertising for the *Handbook,* apparently mailed from New York, consisted almost entirely of a reproduction of the introduction of the book, written by one Dr. Albert Ellis. Although he alludes to the book's informational value and its putative therapeutic usefulness, his remarks are preoccupied with the book's sexual imagery. The solicitation was indiscriminate, not limited to those, such as physicians or psychiatrists, who might independently discern the book's therapeutic worth. Inserted in each advertisement was a slip labeled "Guarantee" and reading, "Documentary Books, Inc., unconditionally guarantees full refund of the price of *The Housewife's Handbook on Selective Promiscuity* if the book fails to reach you because of U.S. Post Office censorship interference." Similar slips appeared in the advertising for *Eros* and *Liaison;* they highlighted the gloss petitioners put on the publications, eliminating any doubt what the purchaser was being asked to buy.

The evidence, in our view, was relevant in determining the ultimate question of "obscenity" and, in the context of this record, serves to resolve all ambiguity and doubt. The deliberate representation of petitioners' publications as erotically arousing, for example, stimulated the reader to accept them as prurient; he looks to titillation not for saving intellectual content. Similarly, such representation would tend to force public confrontation with the potentially offensive aspects of the work; the brazenness of such an appeal heightens the offensiveness of the publications to those who are offended by such material. And the circumstances of presentation and dissemination of material are equally relevant to determining whether social importance claimed for material in the courtroom was, in the circumstances, pretense or reality—whether it was the basis upon which it was traded in the marketplace or a spurious claim for litigation purposes. Where the purveyor's sole emphasis is on the sexually provocative aspects of his publications, that fact may be decisive in the determination of obscenity. Certainly in a prosecution which, as here, does not necessarily imply suppression of the materials involved, the fact that they originate or are used as a subject of pandering is relevant to the application of the *Roth* test.

A proposition argued as to *Eros,* for example, is that the trial judge improperly found the magazine to be obscene as a whole, since he concluded that only four of the 15 articles predominantly appealed to prurient interest and substantially exceeded community standards of candor, while the other articles were admittedly nonoffensive. But the trial judge found that "(t)he deliberate and studied arrangement of *Eros* is editorialized for the purpose of appealing predominantly to prurient interest and to insulate through the inclusion of nonoffensive material." However erroneous such a conclusion might be if unsupported by the evidence of pandering, the record here supports it. *Eros* was created, represented and sold solely as a claimed instrument of the sexual stimulation it would bring. Like the other publications, its pervasive treatment of sex and sexual matters rendered it available to exploitation by those who would make a business of pandering to "the widespread weakness for titillation by pornography." Petitioners' own expert agreed, correctly we think, that "(i)f the object (of a work) is material gain for the creator through an appeal to the sexual curiosity and appetite," the work is pornographic. In other words, by animating sensual detail to give the publication a salacious cast, petitioners reinforced what is conceded by the government to be an otherwise debatable conclusion.

It is important to stress that this analysis simply elaborates the test by which the obscenity *vel non* of the material must be judged. Where an exploitation of interests in titillation by pornography is shown with respect to material lending itself to such exploitation through pervasive treatment or description of sexual matters, such evidence may support the determination that the material is obscene even though in other contexts the material would escape such condemnation.

Mr. Justice Black, dissenting.

Only one stark fact emerges with clarity out of the confusing welter of opinions and thousands of words written in this and two other cases today. That fact is that Ginzburg, petitioner here, is now finally and authoritatively condemned to serve five years in prison for distributing printed matter about sex which neither Ginzburg nor anyone else could possibly have known to be criminal. Since, as I have said many times, I believe the federal government is without any power whatever under the Constitution to put any type of burden on speech and expression of ideas of any kind (as distinguished from conduct), I agree with Part II of the dissent of my Brother Douglas in this case, and I would reverse Ginzburg's conviction on this ground alone. Even assuming, however, that the Court is correct in holding today that Congress does have power to clamp official censorship on some subjects selected by the Court in some ways approved by it, I believe that the federal obscenity statute as enacted by Congress and as enforced by the Court against Ginzburg in this case should be held invalid on two other grounds.

Criminal punishment by government, although universally recognized as a necessity in limited areas of conduct, is an exercise of one of government's most awesome and dangerous powers. Consequently, wise and good governments make all possible efforts to hedge this dangerous power by restricting it within easily identifiable boundaries.

I agree with my Brother Harlan that the Court has in effect rewritten the federal obscenity statute and thereby imposed on Ginzburg standards and criteria that Congress never thought about, or if it did think about them, certainly did not adopt them. Consequently, Ginzburg is, as I see it, having his conviction and sentence affirmed upon the basis of a statute amended by this Court for violation of which amended statute he was not charged in the courts below. Such an affirmance we have said violates due process.

My conclusion is that certainly after the fourteen separate opinions handed down in these three cases today no person, not even the most learned judge much less a layman, is capable of knowing in advance of an ultimate decision in his particular case by this Court whether certain material comes within the area of "obscenity" as that term is confused by the Court today. For this reason even if as appears from the result of the three cases today, this country is far along the way to a censorship of the subjects about which the people can talk or write, we need not commit further Constitutional transgressions by leaving people in the dark as to what literature or what words or what symbols if distributed through the mails make a man a criminal. As bad and obnoxious as I believe governmental censorship is in a Nation that has accepted the First Amendment as its basic ideal for freedom, I am compelled to say that censorship that would stamp certain books and literature as illegal in advance of publication or conviction would in some ways be preferable to the unpredictable book-by-book censorship into which we have now drifted.

Mr. Justice Douglas, dissenting.

The use of sex symbols to sell literature, today condemned by the Court, engrafts another exception on First Amendment rights that is as unwarranted as the judge-made exception concerning obscenity. This new exception condemns an advertising technique as old as history. The advertisements of our best magazines are chock-full of thighs, ankles, calves, bosoms, eyes, and hair, to draw the potential buyers' attention to lotions, tires, food, liquor, clothing, autos, and even insurance policies. The sexy advertisement neither adds nor detracts from the quality of the merchandise being offered for sale. And I do not see how it adds to or detracts one whit from the legality of the book being distributed. A book should stand on its own, irrespective of the reasons why it was written or the wiles used in selling it. I cannot imagine any promotional effort that would make chapters 7 and 8 of the *Song of Solomon* any the less or any more worthy of First Amendment protection than does its unostentatious inclusion in the average edition of the *Bible*.

Mr. Justice Harlan, dissenting.

The First Amendment, in the obscenity area, no longer fully protects material on its face nonobscene, for such material must now also be examined in the light of the defendant's conduct, attitude, motives. This seems to me a mere euphemism for allowing punishment of a person who mails otherwise Constitutionally protected material just because a jury or a judge may not find him or his business agreeable. Were a State to enact a "panderer" statute under its police power, I have little doubt that—subject to clear drafting to avoid attacks on vagueness and equal protection grounds—such a statute would be Constitutional. Possibly the same might be true of the federal government acting under its postal or commerce powers. What I fear the Court has done today is in effect to write a new statute, but without the sharply focused definitions and standards necessary in such a sensitive area. Casting such a dubious gloss over a straightforward 101-year-old statute is for me an astonishing piece of judicial improvisation.

If there is anything to this new pandering dimension to the mailing statute, the Court should return the case for a new trial, for petitioners are at least entitled to a day in court on the question on which their guilt has ultimately come to depend. Compare the action of the Court in a book named *"John Cleland's Memoirs"* v. *Attorney General,* where the Court affords the State an opportunity to prove in a subsequent prosecution that an accused purveyor of *Fanny Hill* in fact used pandering methods to secure distribution of the book.

Mr. Justice Stewart, dissenting.

The petitioner has been sentenced to five years in prison for sending through the mail copies of a magazine, a pamphlet, and a book. There was testimony at his trial that these publications possess artistic and social merit. Personally, I have a hard time discerning any. Most of the material strikes me as both vulgar and unedifying. But if the First Amendment means anything, it means that a man cannot be sent to prison merely for distributing publications which offend a judge's esthetic sensibilities, mine or any other's.

Censorship reflects a society's lack of confidence in itself. It is a hallmark of an authoritarian regime. Long ago those who wrote our First Amendment charted a different course. They believed a society can be truly strong only when it is truly free. In the realm of expression they put their faith, for better or for worse, in the enlightened choice of the people, free from the interference of a policeman's intrusive thumb or a judge's heavy hand. So it is that the Constitution protects coarse expression as well as refined, and vulgarity no less than elegance. A book worthless to me may convey something of value to my neighbor. In the free society to which our Constitution has committed us, it is for each to choose for himself.

There does exist a distinct and easily identifiable class of material in which all of these elements coalesce. It is that, and that alone, which I think government may Constitutionally suppress, whether by criminal or civil sanctions. I have referred to such material before as hard-core pornography, without trying further to define it. *(Jacobellis* v. *Ohio.)*

The Court today appears to concede that the materials Ginzburg mailed were themselves protected by the First Amendment. But, the Court says, Ginzburg can still be sentenced to five years in prison for mailing them. Why? Because, says the Court, he was guilty of "commercial exploitation," of "pandering," and of "titillation." But Ginzburg was not charged with "commercial exploitation;" he was not charged with "pandering;" he was not charged with "titillation." Therefore, to affirm his conviction now on any of those grounds, even if otherwise valid, is to deny him due process of law. But those grounds are not, of course, otherwise valid. Neither the statute under which Ginzburg was convicted, nor any other federal statute I know of, makes "commercial exploitation" or "pandering" or "titillation" a criminal offense. And any criminal law that sought to do so in the terms so elusively defined by the Court would, of course, be unconstitutionally vague and therefore void. All of these matters are developed in the dissenting opinions of my Brethren, and I simply note here that I fully agree with them.

For me, however, there is another aspect of the Court's opinion in this case that is even more regrettable. Today the Court assumes the power to deny Ralph Ginzburg the protection of the First Amendment because it disapproves of his "sordid business." That is a power the Court does not possess. For the First Amendment protects us all with an even hand. It applies to Ralph Ginzburg with no less completeness and force than to G. P. Putnam's Sons. In upholding and enforcing the Bill of Rights, this Court has no power to pick or to choose. When we lose sight of that fixed star of Constitutional adjudication, we lose our way. For then we forsake a government of law and are left with government by Big Brother.

PARIS ADULT THEATRE I v. SLATON
413 U.S. 49 (1973)

Mr. Chief Justice Burger delivered the opinion of the Court.

Petitioners are two Atlanta, Georgia, movie theatres and their owners and managers, operating in the style of "adult" theatres. On December 28, 1970, respondents, the local state district attorney, and the solicitor for the local state trial court, filed civil complaints in that court alleging that petitioners were exhibiting to the public for paid admission two allegedly obscene films, contrary to Georgia Code Sec 2.6–2101.

It should be clear from the outset that we do not undertake to tell the States what they must do, but rather to define the area in which they may chart their own course in dealing with obscene material. This Court has consistently held that obscene material is not protected by the First Amendment as a limitation on the state police power by virtue of the Fourteenth Amendment.

We categorically disapprove the theory, apparently adopted by the trial judge, that obscene, pornographic films acquire Constitutional immunity from state regulation simply because they are exhibited for consenting adults only. This holding was properly rejected by the Georgia Supreme Court. Although we have often pointedly recognized the high importance of the state interest in regulating the exposure of obscene materials to juveniles and unconsenting adults, this Court has never declared these to be the only legitimate state interests permitting regulation of obscene material. The States have a long-recognized legitimate interest in regulating the use of obscene material in local commerce and in all places of public accommodation.

The sum of experience, including that of the past two decades, affords an ample basis for legislatures to conclude that a sensitive, key relationship of human existence, central to family life, community welfare, and the development of human personality, can be debased and distorted by crass commercial exploitation of sex. Nothing in the Constitution prohibits a State from reaching such a conclusion and acting on it legislatively simply because there is no conclusive evidence or empirical data.

Even assuming that petitioners have vicarious standing to assert potential customers' rights, it is unavailing to compare a theatre, open to the public for a fee, with the private home of *Stanley* v. *Georgia* and the marital bedroom of *Griswold* v. *Connecticut*. This Court has, on numerous occasions, refused to hold that commercial ventures such as a motion picture house are "private" for the purpose of civil rights litigation and civil rights statutes. The Civil Rights Act of 1964 specifically defines motion picture houses and theatres as places of "public accommodation" covered by the Act as operations affecting commerce.

Our prior decisions recognizing a right to privacy guaranteed by the Fourteenth Amendment included "only those personal rights that can be deemed 'fundamental' or 'implicit in the concept of ordered liberty.'" (*Palko* v. *Connecticut, Roe* v. *Wade.*) This privacy right encompasses and protects the personal intimacies of the home, the family, marriage, motherhood, procreation, and child rearing. Nothing, however, in this Court's decisions intimates that there is any "fundamental" privacy right "implicit in the concept of ordered liberty" to watch obscene movies in places of public accommodation.

If obscene material unprotected by the First Amendment in itself carried with it a "penumbra" of Constitutionally protected privacy, this Court would not have found it necessary to decide *Stanley* on the narrow basis of the "privacy of the home," which was hardly more than a reaffirmation that "a man's home is his castle." The idea of a "privacy" right and a place of public accommodation are, in this context, mutually exclusive. Conduct or depictions of conduct that the state police power can prohibit on a public street does not become automatically protected by the Constitution merely because the conduct is moved to a bar or a "live" theatre stage, any more than a "live" performance of a man and woman locked in a sexual embrace at high noon in Times Square is protected by the Constitution because they simultaneously engage in a valid political dialogue.

Finally, petitioners argue that conduct which directly involves "consenting adults" only has, for that sole reason, a special claim to Constitutional protection. Our Constitution establishes a broad range of conditions on the exercise of power by the States, but for us to say that our Constitution incorporates the proposition that conduct involving consenting adults only is always beyond state regulation, that is a step we are unable to take. Commercial exploitation of depictions, descriptions, or exhibitions of obscene conduct on commercial premises open to the adult public falls within a State's broad power to regulate commerce and protect the public environment. The issue in this context goes beyond whether someone, or even the majority, considers the conduct depicted as "wrong" or "sinful." The States have the power to make a morally neutral judgment that public exhibition of obscene material, or commerce in such material, has a tendency to injure the community as a whole, to endanger the public safety, or to jeopardize, in Chief Justice Warren's words, the States' right . . . to maintain a decent society." (*Jacobellis* v. *Ohio* (dissenting opinion).)

Mr. Justice Douglas, dissenting.

People are, of course, offended by many offerings made by merchants in this area. They are offended by political pronouncements, sociological themes, and by stories of official misconduct. The list of activities and publications and pronouncements that offend someone is endless. Some of it goes on in private; some of it is inescapably public, as when a government official generates crime, becomes a blatant offender of the moral sensibilities of the people, engages in burglary, or breaches the privacy of the telephone, the conference room, or the home. Life in this crowded modern technological world creates many offensive statements and many offensive deeds. There is no protection against offensive ideas, only against offensive conduct.

"Obscenity" at most is the expression of offensive ideas. There are regimes in the world where ideas "offensive" to the majority (or at least to those who control the majority) are suppressed. There life proceeds at a monotonous speed. Most of us would find that world offensive. One of the most offensive experiences in my life was a visit to a nation where bookstalls were filled only with books on mathematics and books on religion.

I am sure I would find offensive most of the books and movies charged with being obscene. But in a life that has not been short, I have yet to be trapped into seeing or reading something that would offend me. I never read or see the materials coming to the Court under charges of "obscenity," because I have thought the First Amendment made it unconstitutional for me to act as a censor. I see ads in bookstores and neon lights over theatres that resemble bait for those who seek vicarious exhilaration. As a parent or a priest or as a teacher, I would have no compulsion in edging my children or wards away from the books and movies that did no more than excite man's base instincts. But I never supposed that government was permitted to sit in judgment on one's tastes or beliefs—save as they involved action within the reach of the police power of government.

Mr. Justice Brennan, with whom Mr. Justice Stewart and Mr. Justice Marshall join, dissenting.

This case requires the Court to confront once again the vexing problem of reconciling state efforts to suppress sexually oriented expression with the protections of the First Amendment, as applied to the States through the Fourteenth Amendment. No other aspect of the First Amendment has, in recent years, demanded so substantial a commitment of our time, generated such disharmony of views, and remained so resistant to the formulation of stable and manageable standards. I am convinced that the approach initiated 15 years ago in *Roth* v. *United States* and culminating in the Court's decision today, cannot bring stability to this area of the law without jeopardizing fundamental First Amendment values, and I have concluded that the time has come to make a significant departure from that approach.

I need hardly point out that the factors which must be taken into account are judgmental and can only be applied on "a case-by-case, sight-by-sight" basis. (*Mishkin* v. *New York* (Black, J., dissenting).) These considerations suggest that no one definition, no matter how precisely or narrowly drawn, can possibly suffice for all situations, or carve out fully suppressable expression from all media without also creating a substantial risk of encroachment upon the guarantees of the Due Process Clause and the First Amendment.

As a result of our failure to define standards with predictable application to any given piece of material, there is no probability of regularity in obscenity decisions by state and lower federal courts. That is not to say that these courts have performed badly in this area or paid insufficient attention to the principles we have established. The problem is, rather, that one cannot say with certainty that material is obscene until at least five members of this Court, applying inevitably obscure standards, have pronounced it so. The number of obscenity cases on our docket gives ample testimony to the burden that has been placed upon this Court.

Our experience since *Roth* requires us not only to abandon the effort to pick out obscene materials on a case-by-case basis, but also to reconsider a fundamental postulate of *Roth*: that there exists a definable class of sexually oriented expression that may be totally suppressed by the federal and state governments. Assuming that such a class of expression does in fact exist, I am forced to conclude that the concept of "obscenity" cannot be defined with sufficient specificity and clarity to provide fair notice to persons who create and distribute sexually oriented materials, to prevent substantial erosion of protected speech as a byproduct of the attempt to suppress unprotected speech, and to avoid very costly institutional harms. Given these inevitable side effects of state efforts to suppress what is assumed to be *unprotected* speech, we must scrutinize with care the state interest that is asserted to justify the suppression. For in the absence of some very substantial interest in suppressing such speech, we can hardly condone the ill-effects that seem to flow inevitably from the effort.

Obscenity laws have a long history in this country. Most of the States that had ratified the Constitution by 1792 punished the related crime of blasphemy or profanity despite the guarantees of free expression in their constitutions, and Massachusetts expressly prohibited the "composing, writing, printing, or publishing of any filthy, obscene, or profane song, pamphlet, libel, or mock-sermon, in imitation of preaching, or any other part of divine worship." In 1815, the first reported obscenity conviction was obtained under the common law of Pennsylvania. A conviction in Massachusetts under its common law and colonial statute followed six years later. Although the number of early obscenity laws was small and their enforcement exceedingly lax, the situation significantly changed after about 1870 when federal and state governments, mainly as a result of the efforts of Anthony Comstock, took an active interest in the suppression of obscenity. By the end of the 19th Century, at least 30 States had some type of general prohibition on the dissemination of obscene materials, and by the time of our decision in *Roth*, no State was without some provision on the subject. The federal government meanwhile had enacted no fewer than 20 obscenity laws between 1842 and 1956.

This history caused us to conclude in *Roth* "that the unconditional phrasing of the First Amendment (that "Congress shall make no law . . . abridging the freedom of speech, or of the press . . .")

was not intended to protect every utterance." It also caused us to hold, as numerous prior decisions of this Court had assumed, that obscenity could be denied the protection of the First Amendment and hence suppressed because it is a form of expression "utterly without redeeming social importance" as "mirrored in the universal judgment that (it) should be restrained . . . ."

Because we assumed—incorrectly, as experience has proven—that obscenity could be separated from other sexually oriented expression without significant costs either to the First Amendment or to the judicial machinery charged with the task of safeguarding First Amendment freedoms, we had no occasion in *Roth* to probe the asserted state interest in curtailing unprotected, sexually oriented speech. Yet as we have increasingly come to appreciate the vagueness of the concept of obscenity, we have begun to recognize and articulate the state interest at stake. Significantly, in *Redrup* v. *New York,* where we set aside findings of obscenity with regard to three sets of material, we pointed out that

> (i)n none of the cases was there a claim that the statute in question reflected a specific and limited state concern for juveniles. In none was there any suggestion of an assault upon individual privacy by publication in a manner so obtrusive as to make it impossible for an unwilling individual to avoid exposure to it. And in none was there evidence of the sort of "pandering" which the Court found significant in *Ginzburg* v. *United States.*

The opinions in *Redrup* and *Stanley* v. *Georgia* reflected our emerging view that the state interests in protecting children and in protecting unconsenting adults may stand on a different footing from the other asserted state interests. It may well be, as one commentator has argued, that "exposure to (erotic material) is for some persons an intense emotional experience. A communication of this nature, imposed upon a person contrary to his wishes, has all the characteristics of a physical assault . . . . (And it) constitutes an invasion of his privacy . . . ." Similarly, if children are "not possessed of that full capacity for individual choice which is the presupposition of the First Amendment guarantees," then the State may have a substantial interest in precluding the flow of obscene materials even to consenting juveniles.

But whatever the strength of the state interests in protecting juveniles and unconsenting adults from exposure to sexually oriented materials, those interests cannot be asserted in defense of the holding of the Georgia Supreme Court in this case. That court assumed for the purposes of its decison that the films in issue were exhibited only to persons over the age of 21 who viewed them willingly and with prior knowledge of the nature of their contents. And on that assumption, the state court held that the films could still be suppressed. The justification for the suppression must be found, therefore, in some independent interest in regulating the reading and viewing habits of consenting adults.

At the outset it should be noted that virtually all of the interests that might be asserted in defense of suppression, laying aside the special interests associated with distribution to juveniles and unconsenting adults, were also posited in *Stanley* v. *Georgia,* where we held that the State could not make the "mere private possession of obscene material a crime." That decision presages the conclusions I reach here today.

If, as the Court today assumes, "a state legislature may . . . act on the . . . assumption that . . . commerce in obscene books, or public exhibitions focused on obscene conduct, have a tendency to exert a corrupting and debasing impact leading to antisocial behavior," (*Paris Adult Theatre* v. *Slaton, ante,*) then it is hard to see how state-ordered regimentation of our minds can ever be forestalled. For if a State may, in an effort to maintain or create a particular moral tone, prescribe what its citizens cannot read or cannot see, then it would seem to follow that in pursuit of that same objective a State could decree that its citizens must read certain books or must view certain films. However laudable its goal—and that is obviously a question on which reasonable minds may differ—the State cannot proceed by means that violate the Constitution. The precise point was established a half century ago in *Meyer* v. *Nebraska*.

Recognizing these principles, we have held that so-called thematic obscenity—obscenity which might persuade the viewer or reader to engage in "obscene" conduct—is not outside the protection of the First Amendment.

MILLER v. CALIFORNIA
413 U.S. 15 (1973)

Mr. Chief Justice Burger delivered the opinion of the Court.

This is one of a group of "obscenity-pornography" cases being reviewed by the Court in a re-examination of standards enunciated in earlier cases involving what Mr. Justice Harlan called "the intractable obscenity problem."

Appellant conducted a mass mailing campaign to advertise the sale of illustrated books, euphemistically called "adult" material. After a jury trial, he was convicted of violating California Penal Code Sec. 311,2(a), a misdemeanor, by knowingly distributing obscene matter, and the Appellate Department, Superior Court of California, County of Orange, summarily affirmed the judgment without opinion. Appellant's conviction was specifically based on his conduct in causing five unsolicited advertising brochures to be sent through the mail in an envelope addressed to a restaurant in Newport Beach, California. The envelope was opened by the manager of the restaurant and his mother. They had not requested the brochures; they complained to the police.

The brochures advertise four books entitled *Intercourse, Man-Woman, Sex Orgies Illustrated,* and *An Illustrated History of Pornography,* and a film entitled "Marital Intercourse." While the brochures contain some descriptive printed material, primarily they consist of pictures and drawings very explicitly depicting men and women in groups of two or more engaging in a variety of sexual activities, with genitals often prominently displayed.

This case involves the application of a State's criminal obscenity statute to a situation in which sexually explicit materials have been thrust by aggressive sales action upon unwilling recipients who had in no way indicated any desire to receive such materials. This Court has recognized that the States have a legitimate interest in prohibiting dissemination or exhibition of obscene material when the mode of dissemination carries with it a significant danger of offending the sensibilities of unwilling recipients or of exposure to juveniles. It is in this context that we are called on to define the standards which must be used to identify obscene material that a State may regulate without infringing the First Amendment as applicable to the States through the Fourteenth Amendment.

In *Roth* the Court sustained a conviction under a federal statute punishing the mailing of "obscene, lewd, lacivious, or filthy . . ." materials. The key to that holding was the Court's rejection of the claim that obscene materials were protected by the First Amendment.

Nine years later in *Memoirs* v. *Massachusetts,* the Court veered sharply away from the *Roth* concept and, with only three Justices in the plurality opinion, articulated a new test of obscenity. The plurality held that under the *Roth* definition:

... as elaborated in subsequent cases, three elements must coalesce: it must be established that a) the dominant theme of the material taken as a whole appeals to a prurient interest in sex; b) the material is patently offensive because it affronts contemporary community standards relating to the description or representation of sexual matters; and c) the material is utterly without redeeming social value.

(T)he *Memoirs* plurality went on to state:

The Supreme Judicial Court erred in holding that a book need not be "unqualifiedly worthless before it can be deemed obscene." A book cannot be proscribed unless it is found to be *utterly* without redeeming social value.

While *Roth* presumed "obscenity" to be "utterly without redeeming social value," *Memoirs* required that to prove obscenity it must be affirmatively established that the material is *"utterly without redeeming social value."* Thus, even as they repeated the words of *Roth,* the *Memoirs* plurality produced a drastically altered test that called on the prosecution to prove a negative, *i.e.,* that the material was *"utterly* without redeeming social value"—a burden virtually impossible to discharge under our criminal standards of proof. Such considerations caused Justice Harlan to wonder if the *"utterly* without redeeming social value" test had any meaning at all.

Apart from the initial formulation in the *Roth* case, no majority of the Court has at any given time been able to agree on a standard to determine what constitutes obscene, pornographic material subject to regulation under the States' police power.

This much has been categorically settled by the Court, that obscene material is unprotected by the First Amendment. We acknowledge, however, the inherent dangers of undertaking to regulate any form of expression. State statutes designed to regulate obscene materials must be carefully limited. As a result, we now confine the permissible scope of such regulation to works which depict or describe sexual conduct. That conduct must be specifically defined by the applicable state law, as written or authoritatively construed. A state offense must also be limited to works which, taken as a whole, appeal to the prurient interest in sex, which portray sexual conduct in a patently offensive way, and which, taken as a whole, do not have serious literary, artistic, political, or scientific value.

The basic guidelines for the trier of fact must be: a) whether "the average person, applying contemporary community standards" would find that the work, taken as a whole, appeals to the prurient interest, b) whether the work depicts or describes, in a patently offensive way, sexual conduct specifically defined by the applicable state law, and c) whether the work, taken as a whole, lacks serious literary, artistic, political, or scientific value. We do not adopt as a Constitutional standard the *"utterly* without redeeming social value" test of *Memoirs* v. *Massachusetts;* that concept has never commanded the adherence of more than three Justices at one time. If a state law that regulates obscene material is thus limited, as written or construed, the First Amendment values applicable to the States through the Fourteenth Amendment are adequately protected by the ultimate power of appellate courts to conduct an independent review of Constitutional claims when necessary.

We emphasize that it is not our function to propose regulatory schemes for the States. That must await their concrete legislative efforts. It is possible, however, to give a few plain examples of what a state statute could define for regulation under the second part (b) of the standard announced in this opinion:

a. Patently offensive representations or descriptions of ultimate sexual acts, normal or perverted, actual or simulated.
b. Patently offensive representations or descriptions of masturbation, excretory functions, and lewd exhibition of the genitals.

Sex and nudity may not be exploited without limit by films or pictures exhibited or sold in places of public accommodation any more than live sex and nudity can be exhibited or sold without limit in such public places. At minimum, prurient, patently offensive depiction or description of sexual conduct must have serious literary, artistic, political, or scientific value to merit First Amendment protection. For example, medical books for the education of physicians and related personnel necessarily use graphic illustrations and descriptions of human anatomy. In resolving the inevitably sensitive questions of fact and law, we must continue to rely on the jury system, accompanied by the safeguards that judges, rules of evidence, presumption of innocence, and other protective features provide, as we do with rape, murder, and a host of other offenses against society and its individual members.

Under the holdings announced today, no one will be subject to prosecution for the sale or exposure of obscene materials unless these materials depict or describe patently offensive "hard core" sexual conduct specifically defined by the regulating state law, as written or construed. We are satisfied that these specific prerequisites will provide fair notice to a dealer in such materials that his public and commercial activities may bring prosecution. If the inability to define regulated materials with ultimate, god-like precision altogether removes the power of the States or the Congress to regulate, then "hard core" pornography may be exposed without limit to the juvenile, the passerby, and the consenting adult alike, as, indeed, Mr. Justice Douglas contends. In this belief, however, Mr. Justice Douglas now stands alone.

It is certainly true that the absence, since *Roth,* of a single majority view of this Court as to proper standards for testing obscenity has placed a strain on both state and federal courts. But today, for the first time since *Roth* was decided in 1957, a majority of this Court has agreed on concrete guidelines to isolate "hard core" pornography from expression protected by the First Amendment. Now we may abandon the casual practice of *Redrup* v. *New York,* and attempt to provide positive guidance to the federal and state courts alike.

This may not be an easy road, free from difficulty. But no amount of "fatigue" should lead us to adopt a convenient "institutional" rationale—an absolutist, "anything goes" view of the First Amendment—because it will lighten our burdens. "Such an abnegation of judicial supervision in this field would be inconsistent with our duty to uphold the Constitutional guarantees." Nor should we remedy "tension between state and federal courts" by arbitrarily depriving the States of a power reserved to them under the Constitution, a power which they have enjoyed and exercised continuously from before the adoption of the First Amendment to this day.

Under a national Constitution, fundamental First Amendment limitations on the powers of the States do not vary from community to community, but this does not mean that there are, or should or can be, fixed, uniform national standards of precisely what appeals to the "prurient interest" or is "patently offensive." These are essentially questions of fact, and our nation is simply too big and too diverse for this Court to reasonably expect that such standards could be articulated for all 50 States in a single formulation, even assuming the prerequisite consensus exists. When triers of fact are asked to decide whether "the average person, applying contemporary community standards," would consider certain materials "prurient," it would be unrealistic to require that the answer be based on some abstract formulation. The adversary system, with lay jurors as the usual ultimate factfinders in criminal prosecutions, has historically permitted triers-of-fact to draw on the standards of their community, guided always by limiting instructions on the law. To require a State to structure obscenity proceedings around evidence of a *national* "community standard" would be an exercise in futility.

It is neither realistic nor Constitutionally sound to read the First Amendment as requiring that the people of Maine or Mississippi accept public depiction of conduct found tolerable in Las Vegas, or New York City. As the Court made clear in *Mishkin* v. *New York,* the primary concern with requiring a jury to apply the standard of "the average person, applying contemporary community standards" is to be certain that, so far as material is not aimed at a deviant group, it will be judged by its impact on an average person, rather than a particularly susceptible or sensitive person—or indeed a totally insensitive one.

One can concede that the "sexual revolution" of recent years may have had useful byproducts in striking layers of prudery from a subject long irrationally kept from needed ventilation. But it does not follow that no regulation of patently offensive "hard core" materials is needed or permissible; civilized people do not allow unregulated access to heroin because it is a derivative of medicinal morphine.

In sum we a) reaffirm the *Roth* holding that obscene material is not protected by the First Amendment, b) hold that such material can be regulated by the States, subject to the specific safeguards enunciated above, without a showing that the material is "*utterly* without redeeming social value," and c) hold that obscenity is to be determined by applying "contemporary community standards," not "'national standards."

Mr. Justice Douglas, dissenting.

Today the Court retreats from the earlier formulations of the Constitutional test and undertakes to make new definitions. This effort, like the earlier ones, is earnest and well-intentioned. The difficulty is that we do not deal with Constitutional terms, since "obscenity" is not mentioned in the Constitution or Bill of Rights. And the First Amendment makes no such exception from "the press" which it undertakes to protect nor, as I have said on other occasions, is an exception necessarily implied, for there was no recognized exception to the free press at the time the Bill of Rights was adopted which treated "obscene" publications differently from other types of papers, magazines, and books. So there are no Constitutional guidelines for deciding what is and what is not "obscene." The Court is at large because we deal with tastes and standards of literature.

Obscenity cases usually generate tremendous emotional outbursts. They have no business being in the courts. If a Constitutional amendment authorized censorship, the censor would probably be an administrative agency. Then criminal prosecutions could follow if and when publishers defied the censor and sold their literature. Under that regime a publisher would know when he was on dangerous ground. Under the present regime—whether the old standards or the new ones are used—the criminal law becomes a trap.

Obscenity—which even we cannot define with precision—is a hodge-podge. To send men to jail for violating standards they cannot understand, construe, and apply is a monstrous thing to do in a nation dedicated to fair trials and due process.

If there are to be restraints on what is obscene, then a Constitutional amendment should be the way of achieving the end. There are societies where religion and mathematics are the only free segments. It would be a dark day for America if that were our destiny. But the people can make it such if they choose to write obscenity into the Constitution and define it.

We deal with highly emotional, not rational, questions. To many the *Song of Solomon* is obscene. I do not think we, the judges, were even given the Constitutional power to make definitions of obscenity. If it is to be defined, let the people debate and decide by a Constitutional amendment what they want to ban as obscene and what standards they want the legislatures and the courts to apply. Perhaps the people will decide that the path towards a mature, integrated society requires that all ideas competing for acceptance must have no censor. Perhaps they will decide otherwise. Whatever the choice, the courts will have some guidelines. Now we have none except our own predilections.

Mr. Justice Brennan, with whom Mr. Justice Stewart and Mr. Justice Marshall join, dissenting.

(T)he statute under which the prosecution was brought is unconstitutionally overbroad, and therefore invalid on its face. "(T)he transcendent value to all society of Constitutionally protected expression is deemed to justify allowing 'attacks on overly broad statutes with no requirement that the person making the attack demonstrate that his own conduct could not be regulated by a statute drawn with the requisite narrow specificity.' "

Since my view in *Paris Adult Theatre* represents a substantial departure from the course of our prior decisions, and since the state courts have as yet had no opportunity to consider whether a "readily apparent construction suggests itself as a vehicle for rehabilitating the (statute) in a single prosecution," I would reverse the judgment of the Appellate Department of the Superior Court and remand the case for proceedings not inconsistent with this opinion.

JENKINS v. GEORGIA
418 U.S. 153 (1974)

Mr. Justice Rehnquist delivered the opinion of the Court.

Appellant was convicted in Georgia of the crime of distributing obscene material. His conviction, in March 1972, was for showing the film "Carnal Knowledge" in a movie theater in Albany, Georgia. The jury that found appellant guilty was instructed on obscenity pursuant to the Georgia statute, which defines obscene material in language similar to that of the definition of obscenity set forth in this Court's plurality opinion in *Memoirs* v. *Massachusetts* (the Court summarizes the three criteria which actually stem from *Roth*.)

We conclude here that the film "Carnal Knowledge" is not obscene under the constitutional standards announced in *Miller* v. *California,* and that the First and Fourteenth Amendments therefore require that the judgment of the Supreme Court of Georgia affirming appellant's conviction be reversed.

We agree with the Supreme Court of Georgia's implicit ruling that the Constitution does not require that juries be instructed in state obscenity cases to apply the standards of a hypothetical statewide community. *Miller* approved the use of such instructions; it did not mandate their use. What *Miller* makes clear is that state juries need not be instructed to apply "national standards." We also agree with the Supreme Court of Georgia's implicit approval of the trial court's instructions directing jurors to apply "community standards" without specifying what "community."

But all of this does not lead us to agree with the Supreme Court of Georgia's apparent conclusion that the jury's verdict against appellant virtually precluded all further appellate review of appellant's assertion that this exhibition of the film was protected by the First and Fourteenth Amendments. Even though questions of appeal to the "prurient interest" or of patent offensiveness are "essentially questions of fact," it would be a serious misreading of *Miller* to conclude that juries have unbridled discretion in determining what is "patently offensive." Not only did we there say that "the First

Amendment values applicable to the States through the Fourteenth Amendment are adequately protected by the ultimate power of appellate courts to conduct an independent review of Constitutional claims when necessary," but we made it plain that under that holding "no one will be subject to prosecution for the sale or exposure of obscene materials unless these materials depict or describe patently offensive 'hard core' sexual conduct."

We also took pains in *Miller* to "give a few plain examples of what a state statute could define for regulation under . . ." the requirement of patent offensiveness. These examples included "representations or description of ultimate sexual acts, normal or perverted, actual or simulated," and "representations or descriptions of masturbation, excretory functions, and lewd exhibition of the genitals." While this did not purport to be an exhaustive catalog of what juries might find patently offensive, it was certainly intended to fix substantive Constitutional limitations, deriving from the First Amendment, on the type of material subject to such a determination. It would be wholly at odds with this aspect of *Miller* to uphold an obscenity conviction based upon a defendant's depiction of a woman with a bare midriff, even though a properly charged jury unanimously agreed on a verdict of guilty.

Our own view of the film satisfies us that "Carnal Knowledge" could not be found under the *Miller* standards to depict sexual conduct in a patently offensive way. Nothing in the movie falls within either of the two examples given in *Miller* of material which may Constitutionally be found to meet the "patently offensive" element of those standards, nor is there anything sufficiently similar to such material to justify similar treatment. While the subject matter of the picture is, in a broader sense, sex, and these are scenes in which sexual conduct including "ultimate sexual acts" is to be understood to be taking place, the camera does not focus on the bodies of the actors at such times. There is no exhibition whatever of the actors' genitals, lewd or otherwise, during these scenes. There are occasional scenes of nudity, but nudity alone is not enough to make material legally obscene under the *Miller* standards.

Appellant's showing of the film "Carnal Knowledge" is simply not the "public portrayal of hard core sexual conduct for its own sake, and for ensuing commercial gain" which we said was punishable in *Miller*. We hold that the film could not, as a matter of Constitutional law, be found to depict sexual conduct in a patently offensive way, and therefore is not outside the protection of the First and Fourteenth Amendment.

Mr. Justice Brennan, with whom Mr. Justice Stewart and Mr. Justice Marshall join, concurring in result.

It is my view that the Court's reformulation hardly represented a solution to what Mr. Justice Harlan called "the intractable obscenity problem." Today's decision confirms my observation that the Court's new formulation does not extricate us from the mire of case-by-case determinations of obscenity.

After the Court's decision today, there can be no doubt that *Miller* requires appellate courts—including this Court—to review independently the Constitutional fact of obscenity.

In order to make the review mandated by *Miller,* the Court was required to screen the film "Carnal Knowledge" and make an independent determination of obscenity *vel non*. Following that review, the Court holds that "Carnal Knowledge" "could not, as a matter of Constitutional law, be found to depict sexual conduct in a patently offensive way, and that therefore it is not outside the protection of the First and Fourteenth Amendments because it is obscene."

Thus, it is clear that as long as the *Miller* test remains in effect "one cannot say with certainty that material is obscene until at least five members of this Court, applying inevitably obscure standards, have pronounced it so." (*Paris Adult Theater I* v. *Slaton,* Brennan, J., dissenting.) Because of the attendant uncertainty of such a process and its inevitable institutional stress upon the judiciary, I continue to adhere to my view that, "at least in the absence of distribution to juveniles or obtrusive exposure to unconsenting adults, the First and Fourteenth Amendments prohibit the state and federal governments from attempting wholly to suppress sexually oriented materials on the basis of their allegedly 'obscene' contents." It is clear that, tested by that Constitutional standard, the Georgia obscenity statutes under which appellant Jenkins was convicted are Constitutionally overbroad and therefore facially invalid. I therefore concur in the result in the Court's reversal of Jenkins' conviction.

WARD v. ILLINOIS
431 U.S. 767 (1977)

Mr. Justice White delivered the opinion of the Court.

The principal issue in this case is the validity of the Illinois obscenity statute, considered in light of *Miller v. California*. There we reaffirmed numerous prior decisions declaring that "obscene material is unprotected by the First Amendment," by acknowledging "the inherent dangers of undertaking to regulate any form of expression," we recognized that official regulation must be limited to "works which depict or describe sexual conduct" and that such conduct "must be specifically defined by the applicable state law, as written or authoritatively construed." Basic guidelines for the trier of fact, along with more specific suggestions, were then offered:

> The basic guidelines for the trier of fact must be: a) whether "the average person, applying contemporary community standards" would find that the work, taken as a whole, appeals to the prurient interest, *Kois* v. *Wisconsin, supra,* at 230, quoting *Roth* v. *United States, supra,* at 489; b) whether the work depicts or describes, in a patently offensive way, sexual conduct specifically defined by the applicable state law; and c) whether the work, taken as a whole, lacks serious literary, artistic, political, or scientific value. We do not adopt as a constitutional standard the *'utterly* without redeeming social value' test of *Memoirs* v. *Massachusetts,* 383 U.S., at 419; the concept has never commanded the adherence of more than three Justices at one time. See *supra,* at 21. If a state law that regulates obscene material is thus limited, as written or construed, the First Amendment values applicable to the States through the Fourteenth Amendment are adequately protected by the ultimate power of appellate courts to conduct an independent review of constitutional claims when necessary. See *Kois* v. *Wisconsin, supra* at 232; *Memoirs* v. *Massachusetts, supra,* at 459–460 (Harlan, J., dissenting); *Jacobellis* v. *Ohio,* 378 U.S., at 204 (Harlan, J., dissenting); *New York Times Co.* v. *Sullivan,* 376 U.S. 254, 284–285 (1964); *Roth* v. *United States, supra,* at 497–498 (Harlan, J., concurring and dissenting).
>
> We emphasize that it is not our function to propose regulatory schemes for the States. That must await their concrete legislative efforts. It is possible, however, to give a few plain examples of what a state statute could define for regulation under part (b) of the standard announced in this opinion, *supra:*
>
> a) Patently offensive representations or descriptions of ultimate sexual acts, normal or perverted, actual or simulated.
>
> b) Patently offensive representations or descriptions of masturbation, excretory functions, and lewd exhibition of the genitals. *Id.,* at 24–25. (Footnotes omitted.)

Ill Rev. Stat. c. 38, Section 11–20(a)(1) forbids the sale of obscene matter. Section 11–20(b) defines "obscene" as follows:

> A thing is obscene if, considered as whole, its predominant appeal is to prurient interest, that is, a shameful or morbid interest in nudity, sex, or excretion, and if it goes substantially beyond customary limits of candor in description or representation of such matters. A thing is obscene even though the obscenity is latent, as in the case of undeveloped photographs.

In October 1971 appellant Ward was charged in the State of Illinois with having sold two obscene publications in violation of Section 11–20(a)(1). A jury was waived. At the bench trial the State's evidence consisted solely of the two publications—"Bizarre World" and "Illustrated Case Histories: A Study of Sado-Masochism"—and the testimony of the police officer who purchased them in Ward's store. Ward was found guilty, and in April 1972, he was sentenced to one day in jail and fined $200. His conviction was affirmed in the state appellate courts after this Court's decision in *Miller*. The Illinois Supreme Court expressly rejected his challenge to the Constitutionality of the Illinois obscenity statute for failure to conform to the standards of *Miller*, as well as a claim that the two publications were not obscene. Ward appealed to resolve a conflict with a decision of a three-judge District Court for the Northern District of Illinois. We affirm.

As we read the questions presented by Ward, they fairly subsume four issues. First is the claim that Illinois has failed to comply with *Miller*'s requirement that the sexual conduct that may not be depicted in a patently offensive way must be "specifically defined by applicable state law as written or authoritatively construed" (see *supra*, at 1), and that absent such compliance the Illinois law is unconstitutionally vague because it failed to give him notice that materials dealing with the kind of sexual conduct involved here could not legally be sold in the State. The claim is wholly without merit. As we shall see below, the State has complied with *Miller*, but even if this were not the case, appellant had ample guidance from the Illinois Supreme Court that his conduct did not conform to the Illinois law. Materials such as these, which by title or content may fairly be described as sado-masochistic, had been expressly held to violate the Illinois statute, long before *Miller* and prior to the sales for which Ward was prosecuted.

In *People* v. *Sekara* there are detailed recitations of the kind of sexual conduct depicted in the materials found to be obscene under the Illinois statute. These recitations included "sadism and masochism." The construction of the statute is *Sekara* gives detailed meaning to the Illinois law, is binding on us, and makes plain that Section 11–20 reaches the kind of sexual materials which we now have before us. If Ward cannot be convicted for selling those materials, it is for other reasons and not because the Illinois statute is vague and gave him no notice that the statute purports to ban the kind of materials he sold. The statute is not vague as applied to Ward's conduct.

Second, Ward appears to assert that sado-masochistic materials may not be Constitutionally proscribed because they are not expressly included within the examples of the kinds of sexually explicit representations that *Miller* used to explicate the aspect of its obscenity definition dealing with patently offensive depictions of specifically defined sexual conduct. But those specifics were offered merely as "examples," and, as later pointed out in *Hamling* v. *United States,* they "were not intended to be exhaustive." Furthermore, there was no suggestion in *Miller* that we intended to extend Constitutional protection to the kind of flagellatory materials that were among those held obscene in *Mishkin* v. *New York*. If the *Mishkin* publications remain unprotected, surely those before us today deal with a category of sexual conduct which, if obscenely described, may be proscribed by state law.

The third claim is simply that these materials are not obscene when examined under the three-part test of Miller. This argument is also foreclosed by *Mishkin* v. *New York,* which came down the same day as *Memoirs* v. *Massachusetts,* and which employed the obscenity criteria announced by the latter case. The courts below examined the materials and found them obscene under the Illinois statute, which conforms to the standards set out in *Miller,* except that it retains the stricter *Memoirs* formulation of the "redeeming social value" factor. We have found no reason to differ with the Illinois courts.

Fourth, even assuming that the Illinois statute had been construed to overcome the vagueness challenge in this case, and even assuming that the materials at issue here are not protected under *Miller,* there remains the claim that Illinois has failed to conform to the *Miller* requirement that a state obscenity law, as written or authoritatively construed, must state specifically the kinds of sexual conduct the description or representation of which the State intends to proscribe by its obscenity law. If Illinois has not complied with this requirement, its statute is arguably overbroad, unconstitutional on its face, and an invalid predicate for Ward's conviction.

As we see it, Illinois has not failed to comply with *Miller,* and its statute is not overbroad. *People* v. *Ridens* involved a conviction under this same Illinois obscenity law. It was pending on our docket when our judgment and opinion in *Miller* issued. We vacated the *Ridens* judgment and remanded the case for further consideration in the light of *Miller.* On remand, the Illinois Supreme Court explained that originally Section 11–20 had provided the tests for obscenity found in *Roth* v. *United States,* and that it subsequently had been construed to incorporate the tripartite standard found in *Memoirs* v. *Massachusetts,* including the requirement that the materials prohibited be "utterly without redeeming social value." (*People* v. *Ridens.*) The Illinois court then proceeded to "construe Section 11–20 of the Criminal Code . . . to incorporated parts (a) and (b) of the *Miller* standards," but to retain the "utterly without redeeming social value" standard of *Memoirs* in preference to the more relaxed criterion contained in part (c) of the *Miller* guidelines. Ridens' conviction was affirmed, and we denied certiorari.

Because the Illinois court did not go further and expressly describe the kinds of sexual conduct intended to be referred to under part (b) of the *Miller* guidelines, the issue is whether the Illinois obscenity law is open-ended and overbroad. As we understand the Illinois Supreme Court, however, the statute is not vulnerable in this respect. That court expressly incorporated into the statute part (b) of the guidelines, which requires inquiry "whether the work depicts or describes, in a patently offensive way, sexual conduct specifically defined by the applicable state law." The Illinois court thus must have been aware of the need for specificity and of the *Miller* Court's examples explaining the reach of part (b). The Illinois court plainly intended to conform the Illinois law to part (b) of *Miller,* and there is no reason to doubt that, in incorporating the guideline as part of the law, the Illinois court intended as well to adopt the *Miller* examples, which gave substantive meaning to part (b) by indicating the kinds of materials within its reach. The alternative reading of the decision would lead us to the untenable conclusion that the Illinois Supreme Court chose to create a fatal flaw in its statute by refusing to take cognizance of the specificity requirement set down in *Miller.*

Furthermore, in a later case, *People* v. *Gould,* the Illinois Supreme Court quoted at length from *Miller* v. *California,* including the entire passage set out at the beginning of this opinion, a passage that contains the explanatory examples as well as the guidelines. It then stated that *Ridens* had construed the Illinois statute to include parts (a) and (b) of the *Miller* guidelines, and it expressly referred to the standards set out in the immediately preceding quotation from *Miller.* Because the quotation contained not only part (b) but the examples given to explain that part, it would be a needlessly technical and wholly unwarranted reading of the Illinois opinions to conclude that the state court did not adopt these explanatory examples as well as the guidelines themselves.

It might be argued that, whether or not the Illinois court adopted the *Miller* examples as part of its law, Section 11–20 nevertheless remains overbroad because the State has not provided an exhaustive list of the sexual conduct the patently offensive description of which may be held obscene under the statute. We agree with the Illinois Supreme Court, however, that "in order that a statute be held overbroad, the overbreadth 'must not only be real, but substantial as well, judged in relation to the statute's plainly legitimate sweep.' " (*People* v. *Ridens*.) Since it is plain enough from its prior cases and from its response to *Miller* that the Illinois court recognizes the limitations on the *kinds* of sexual conduct which may not be represented or depicted under the obscenity laws, we cannot hold the Illinois statute to be unconstitutionally overbroad.

Given that Illinois has adopted *Miller*'s explanatory examples, what the State has done in attempting to bring its statute in conformity with *Miller* is surely as much as this Court did in its post-*Miller* construction of federal obscenity statutes. In *Hamling* v. *United States* we construed 18 U.S.C. Section 1461, which prohibits the mailing of obscene matter, to be limited to "the sort of" patently offensive representations or descriptions of that specific hard core sexual conduct given as examples in *Miller*. We have also indicated our approval of an identical approach with respect to the companion provisions of 18 U.S.C. Section 1462, which prohibits importation or transportation of obscene matter.

Finding all four of Ward's claims to be without merit, we affirm the judgment of the Illinois Supreme Court.

So ordered.

Mr. Justice Brennan, with whom Mr. Justice Stewart joins, dissenting.

Petitioner was convicted of selling allegedly obscene publications in violation of the Illinois Obscenity Statute, Ill. Rev. Stat. 1969, c. 38, Section 11–20. The Illinois Supreme Court affirmed the conviction. Although I have joined my Brother Stevens' dissent, I could also reverse the conviction on the ground I have previously relied upon, namely that this statute is "clearly overbroad and unconstitutional on its face."

Mr. Justice Stevens, with whom Mr. Justice Brennan, Mr. Justice Stewart, and Mr. Justice Marshall join, dissenting.

The decision in this case confirms the statement in *Miller* v. *California* that "(t)his is an area in which there are few eternal verities." Today, the Court silently abandons one of the cornerstones of the *Miller* test announced so forcefully just five years ago.

The *Miller* Court stated:

> Under the holdings announced today, no one will be subject to prosecution for the sale or exposure of obscene materials unless these materials depict or describe patently offensive "hard core" sexual conduct specifically defined by the regulating state law, as written or construed. We are satisfied that these specific prerequisites will provide fair notice to a dealer in such materials that his public and commercial activities may bring prosecution. (*Id.*, at 27.)

The specificity requirement is stressed elsewhere in the opinion. More than 50 cases were remanded for further consideration to give the defendants the "benefit" of this aspect of *Miller*.

Many state courts, taking *Miller* at face value, invalidated or substantially limited their obscenity laws. Others, like Illinois, did "little more than pay lip service to the specificity requirement in

Miller." (Schauer, The Law of Obscenity 167.) Like most pre-*Miller* obscenity statutes, the Illinois statute contained open-ended terms broad enough to prohibit the distribution of any material making an "appeal . . . to prurient interest." In its post-*Miller* opinions, the Illinois Supreme Court has made it clear that the statute covers all of the Miller examples. It has not, however, stated that the statute is limited to those examples, or to any other specifically defined category.

Nevertheless, this Court affirms the conviction in this Illinois case on two theories. The first is that this particular defendant had notice that the State considered these materials obscene, because prior Illinois cases had upheld obscenity convictions concerning similar material. But, if such notice is all that is required, it is difficult to understand why the *Miller* case itself was remanded for consideration of the specificity issue. For the description of the materials involved in *Miller* leaves no room for doubt that they were similar to materials which had often been the subject of prosecutions in the past; there clearly was no question of fair notice.

The Court's second theory is that, in any event, the Illinois statute is sufficiently specific to satisfy *Miller.* Although the statute does not contain an "exhaustive list" of specific examples, it passes muster because it contains a generic reference to "the *kinds* of sexual conduct which may not be represented or depicted under the obscenity laws . . . ." To hold that the list need not be exhaustive is to hold that a person can be prosecuted although the materials he sells are not specifically described in the list. Only five years ago, the Court promised that "no one" could be so prosecuted. And if the statute need only describe the "kinds" of proscribed sexual conduct, it adds no protection to what the Constitution itself creates. For in *Jenkins* v. *Georgia* this Court held that the Constitution protected all expression which is not "within either of the two examples given in *Miller*" or "sufficiently similar to such material to justify similar treatment."

One of the strongest arguments against regulating obscenity through criminal law is the inherent vagueness of the obscenity concept. The specificity requirement as described in *Miller* held out the promise of a principled effort to respond to that argument. By abandoning that effort today, the Court withdraws the cornerstone of the *Miller* structure and, undoubtedly, hastens its ultimate downfall. Although the decision is therefore a mixed blessing, I nevertheless respectfully dissent.

SPLAWN v. *CALIFORNIA*
431 U.S. 595 (1977)

Mr. Justice Rehnquist delivered the opinion of the Court.

Petitioner Splawn was convicted in 1971 of the sale of two reels of obscene film, a misdemeanor violation of California Penal Code Section 311.2. After the conviction was affirmed on appeal by the California First District Court of Appeals and the State Supreme Court denied review, this Court granted certiorari, vacated the judgment, and remanded for consideration in light of our decision in *Miller* v. *California,* which had set forth the standards by which the constitutionality of Section 311.2 was to be determined. After the State Supreme Court ruled that the statute satisfied the requirements articulated in *Miller,* the Court of Appeals again affirmed the conviction and the California Supreme Court denied petitioner's motion for a hearing.

We again granted certiorari to consider petitioner's assorted contentions that his conviction must be reversed because portions of the instructions given to the jury during his trial render his conviction violative of the First and Fourteenth Amendments. He claims that the instruction allowed the jury to convict him even though it might otherwise have found the material in question to have been protected under the *Miller* standards. He also contends that the same portions of the instructions render his conviction invalid by reason of the constitutional prohibition against *ex post facto* laws and the requirement of fair warning in the construction of a criminal statute enunciated in *Bouie* v. *Columbia*. We consider these contentions in light of the fact that petitioner has abandoned any claim that the material of which he was convicted of selling could not be found to be obscene consistently with the First and Fourteenth Amendments, and any claim that the California statute under which he was convicted does not satisfy the requirements articulated in *Miller*.

As it was understood by the California Court of Appeals, petitioner's challenge is leveled against the following portion of the instructions:

> In determining the question of whether the allegedly obscene matter is utterly without redeeming social importance, you may consider the circumstances of sale and distribution, and particularly whether such circumstances indicate that the matter was being commercially exploited by the defendants for the sake of its prurient appeal. Such evidence is probative with respect to the nature of the matter and can justify the conclusion that the matter is utterly without redeeming social importance. The weight, if any, such evidence is entitled is a matter for you, the Jury, to determine.
>
> Circumstances of production and dissemination are relevant to determining whether social importance claimed for material was in the circumstances pretense or reality. If you conclude that the purveyor's sole emphasis is in the sexually provocative aspect of the publication, that fact can justify the conclusion that the matter is utterly without redeeming social importance.

There is no doubt that as a matter of First Amendment obscenity law, evidence of pandering to prurient interests in the creation, promotion, or dissemination of material is relevant in determining whether the material is obscene. This is so partly because, as the Court has pointed out before, the fact that the accused made such an appeal has a bearing on the ultimate constitutional tests for obscenity:

> . . . The deliberate representation of petitioners' publications as erotically arousing, for example, stimulated the reader to accept them as prurient; he looks for titillation, not for saving intellectual content. Similarly, such representation would tend to force public confrontation with the potentially offensive aspects of the work; the brazenness of such an appeal heightens the offensiveness of the publications to those who are offended by such material. And the circumstances of presentation and dissemination of material are equally relevant to determining whether social importance claimed for material in the courtroom was, in the circumstances, pretense or reality—whether it was the basis upon which it was traded in the marketplace or a spurious claim for litigation purpose . . . . (*Ginzburg* v. *United States,* 383 U.S., at 470.)

Petitioner's interpretation of the challenged portion of the instructions in his case is that it permitted the jury to consider motives of commercial exploitation on the part of persons in the chain of distribution of the material other than himself. We upheld a similar instruction in *Hamling,* however, wherein the jury was told that it could consider "whether the materials had been pandered, by looking to their '(m)anner of distribution, circumstances or production, sale, . . . adversiting, . . . (and) editorial intent . . . .' This instruction was given with respect to both the "Illustrated Report" and the brochure which advertised it, both of which were at issue in the trial."

Both *Hamling* and *Ginzburg* were prosecutions under federal obscenity statutes in federal courts, where our authority to review jury instructions is a good deal broader than is our power to upset state court convictions by reason of instructions given during the course of a trial. We can exercise the latter authority only if the instruction renders the subsequent conviction violative of the U.S. Constitution. Questions of what categories of evidence may be admissible and probative are otherwise for the courts of the States to decide. We think *Hamling,* and *Ginzburg* rather clearly show that the instruction in question abridges no rights of petitioner under the First Amendment as made applicable to the States by the Fourteenth Amendment.

Mr. Justice Brennan, with whom Mr. Justice Stewart and Mr. Justice Marshall join, dissenting.

The California courts, in response to our remand for reconsideration in light of *Miller* v. *California,* reaffirmed petitioner's 1971 conviction for selling obscene films in violation of California Penal Code Section 311.2. I would reverse the conviction. I adhere to my view expressed in *Miller* that this statute is "unconstitutionally overbroad, and therefore invalid on its face."

Mr. Justice Stewart, with whom Mr. Justice Brennan and Mr. Justice Marshall join, dissenting.

In my view the statute under which the petitioner was convicted is constitutionally invalid on its face. Accordingly, I have joined Mr. Justice Brennan's dissent.

But even if, as the Court believes, the statute itself is not invalid, Mr. Justice Stevens has surely demonstrated that this petitioner was unconstitutionally convicted under it. On that basis, I also join the dissenting opinion of Mr. Justice Stevens.

Mr. Justice Stevens, with whom Mr. Justice Brennan, Mr. Justice Stewart, and Mr. Justice Marshall, join, dissenting.

Under the trial court's instructions, the jury may have determined that the films sold by the petitioner had some social significance and therefore were not in themselves obscene, but nevertheless found him guilty because they were advertised and sold as "sexually provocative." A conviction pursuant to such an instruction should not be allowed to stand.

Truthful statements which are neither misleading nor offensive are protected by the First Amendment even though made for a commercial purpose. Nothing said on petitioner's behalf in connection with the marketing of these films was false, misleading, or even arguably offensive either to the person who bought them or to an average member of the community. The statements did make it clear that the films were "sexually provocative," but that is hardly a confession that they were obscene. And, if they were not otherwise obscene, I cannot understand how these films lost their protected status by being truthfully described.

Even if the social importance of the films themselves is dubious, there is a definite social interest in permitting them to be accurately described. Only an accurate description can enable a potential viewer to decide whether or not he wants to see them. Signs which identify the "adult" character of a motion picture theater or of a bookstore convey the message that sexually provocative entertainment is to be found within; under the jury instructions which the Court today finds acceptable, these signs may deprive otherwise nonobscene matter of its constitutional protection. Such signs, however, also provide a warning to those who find erotic materials offensive that they should shop elsewhere for other kinds of books, magazines, or entertainment. Under any sensible regulatory scheme, truthful description of subject matter that is pleasing to some and offensive to others ought to be encouraged, not punished.

I would not send Mr. Splawn to jail for telling the truth about his shabby business.

JERRY LEE SMITH v. UNITED STATES
431 U.S. 291 (1977)

Mr. Justice Blackmun delivered the opinion of the court.

In *Miller v. California,* this Court rejected a plea for a uniform national standard as to what is patently offensive; the Court held, instead, that these essentially were questions of fact to be measured by contemporary standards of the community. The instant case presents the issue of the Constitutional effect of state law, that leaves unregulated the distribution of obscene material to adults, on the determination of contemporary community standards in a prosecution for a mailing that is wholly intrastate. The case also raises the question whether (the federal law) is unconstitutionally vague as applied in these circumstances, and the question whether the trial court, during the voir dire of prospective jurors, correctly refused to ask proffered questions relating to community standards.

I

Between February and October 1974 petitioner, Jerry Lee Smith, knowingly caused to be mailed various materials from Des Moines, Iowa, to post office box addresses in Mount Ayr and Guthrie Center, two communities in southern Iowa. This was done at the written request of postal inspectors using fictitious names. The materials so mailed were delivered through the United States postal system to the respective postmasters serving the addresses. The mailings consisted of 1) issues of *Intrigue* magazine, depicting nude males and females engaged in masturbation, fellatio, cunnilingus, and sexual intercourse; 2) a film entitled "Lovelace," depicting a nude male and a nude female engaged in masturbation and simulated acts of fellatio, cunnilingus, and sexual intercourse; and 3) a film entitled "Terrorized Virgin," depicting two nude males and a nude female engaged in fellatio, cunnilingus, and sexual intercourse.

II

For many years prior to 1974 the statutes of Iowa made it a misdemeanor to sell or offer to sell or to give away "any obscene, lewd, indecent, lascivious, or filthy book, pamphlet, paper, . . . picture, photograph, writing . . ." or to deposit in any post office within Iowa any article of that kind.

In 1973, however, the Supreme Court of Iowa, in response to the standards enunciated in *Miller v. California,* unanimously held that a related and companion Iowa statute, prohibiting the presentation of any obscene or immoral drama, play, exhibition, or entertainment, was unconstitutionally vague and overbroad. *(State v. Wedelstedt.)*

On July 1, 1974, Laws of Iowa became effective. These specifically repealed Sections 725.3, 725.5, and 725.6 of the 1973 Code. In addition, however, c. 1267 (thereafter codified as the first 10 sections of c. 725 of the 1975 Iowa Code) defined, among other things, "obscene material," and made it "a public offense" to disseminate obscene material to *minors* (defined as persons "under the age of eighteen"). Dissemination of obscene material to adults was not made criminal or even proscribed. Section 9 of c. 1267 (now Section 725.9 of the 1975 Code) insured that the law would be applied uniformly throughout the State, and that no lesser governmental unit would impose more stringent regulations on obscene material.

In 1976, the Iowa Legislature enacted a "complete revision" of the State's "substantive criminal laws." This is entitled the "Iowa Criminal Code" and is generally effective January 1, 1978. The existing definition of "obscene material" remains unchanged, but a new provision, Section 2804 of the Criminal Code, although limited in scope, applies by its terms to adults. It reads:

Any person who knowingly sells or offers for sale material depicting a sex act involving sadomasochistic abuse, excretory functions, a child, or bestiality which the average adult taking the material as a whole in applying contemporary community standards would find that it appeals to the prurient interest and is patently offensive; and the material, taken as a whole, lacks serious literary, scientific, political, or artistic value shall, upon conviction be guilty of a simple misdemeanor.

In summary, therefore, we have in Iowa 1) until 1973 state statutes that proscribed generally the dissemination of obscene writings and pictures; 2) the judicial nullification of some of those statutory provisions in that year for reasons of overbreadth and vagueness; 3) the enactment, effective July 1, 1974, of replacement obscenity statutes restricted in their application to dissemination to minors; and 4) the enactment in 1976 of a new Code, effective in 1978, with obscenity provisions, somewhat limited in scope, but not restricted in application to dissemination to minors.

Petitioner's mailings, described above and forming the basis of his federal prosecution, took place in 1974, after the theretofore existing Iowa statutes relating to obscene material had been nullified by *Wedelstedt,* but obviously before the 1976 legislation imposing misdemeanor liability with respect to certain transactions with adults becomes effective. Because there is no contention that the materials petitioner mailed went to any minor, the 1974 legislation has no application to his case. And the 1976 legislation, of course, has no effect on petitioner's criminal liability.

Thus, what petitioner did clearly was not a violation of state law at the time he did it. It is to be observed, also, that there is no suggestion that petitioner's mailings went to any nonconsenting adult or that they were interstate.

III

Petitioner was indicted on seven counts of violating 18 U.S.C. Section 1461, which prohibits the mailing of obscene materials. He pleaded not guilty. At the start of his trial petitioner proposed and submitted six questions for voir dire. The court accepted in substance and utilized the first question; this was designed to reveal whether any juror was connected with an organization devoted to regulating or banning obscene materials. The court declined to ask the other five. One of the questions made inquiry as to whether the jurors had any knowledge of contemporary community standards in the Southern District of Iowa with regard to the depiction of sex and nudity. Two sought to isolate the source of the jurors' knowledge and their understanding of those standards. The remaining two would have explored the jurors' knowledge of Iowa law on the subject.

At the trial, the government introduced into evidence the actual materials covered by the indictment. It offered nothing else on the issue of obscenity *vel non*. Petitioner did not testify. Instead, in defense, he introduced numerous sexually explicit materials that were available for purchase at "adult" bookstores in Des Moines and Davenport, Iowa, several advertisements from the *Des Moines Register and Tribune,* and a copy of what was then c. 725 of the Iowa Code, prohibiting the dissemination of "obscene material" only to minors. At the close of the government's case, and again at the close of all the evidence, petitioner moved for a directed verdict of acquittal on the grounds, *inter alia,* that the Iowa obscenity statute, proscribing only the dissemination of obscene materials to minors, set forth the applicable community standard, and that the prosecution had not proved that the materials at issue offended that standard.

The District Court denied those motions and submitted the case of the jury. The court instructed the jury that contemporary community standards were set by what is in fact accepted in the community as a whole. In making that determination, the jurors were entitled to draw on their own knowledge of the views of the average person in the community as well as the evidence presented as to the state law on obscenity and as to materials available for purchase.

The jury found petitioner guilty on all seven counts. He was sentenced to concurrent three-year terms of imprisonment, all but three months of which were suspended, and three years' probation.

In his motion for a new trial, petitioner again asserted that Iowa law defined the community standard. In denying this motion, the District Court held that Section 1461 was "a federal law which neither incorporates nor depends upon the laws of the states." (T)he federal policy was simply different in this area. Furthermore, the court observed, Iowa's decision not to regulate distribution of obscene material did not mean that the people of Iowa necessarily "approved of the permitted conduct." (W)hether they did was a question of fact for the jury. The court rejected petitioner's argument that it was in error not to ask the jurors the question about the extent of their knowledge of contemporary community standards. It held that the jurors were entitled to draw on their own knowledge; voir dire on community standards would be no more appropriate than voir dire on the jurors' concept of "reasonableness." The court refused to hold that the government was required to introduce evidence on a community standard in order to sustain its burden of proof. The materials introduced "can and do speak for themselves." The court did not address petitioner's vagueness point.

The United States Court of Appeals for the Eighth Circuit agreed with the District Court that the questions submitted by petitioner on community standards, except for the first, were impermissible, since they concerned the ultimate question of guilt or innocence rather than juror qualification. The court noted, however, that it was not holding that no questions whatsoever could be asked in that area. With respect to the effect of state law, the court held that the issue of offense to contemporary community standards was a federal question, and was to be determined by the jury in a federal prosecution. The court noted the admission of Iowa's obscenity statute into evidence but stated that this was designed to give the jury knowledge of the State's policy on obscenity when it determined the contemporary community standard. The state policy was not controlling, since the determination was for the jury. The conviction, therefore, was affirmed.

We granted certiorari in order to review the relationship between state legislation regulating or refusing to regulate the distribution of obscene material, and the determination of contemporary community standards in a federal prosecution.

IV

The "basic guidelines" for the trier of fact in a state obscenity prosecution were set out in *Miller v. California* in the form of a three-part test:

a) whether "the average person, applying contemporary community standards" would find that the work, taken as a whole, appeals to the prurient interest . . . ; b) whether the work depicts or describes, in a patently offensive way, sexual conduct specifically defined by the applicable state law; and c) whether the work, taken as a whole, lacks serious literary, artistic, political, or scientific value.

In two companion cases, the Court held that the *Miller* standards were equally applicable to federal legislation. (*United States* v. *12 200-ft. Reels of Film* (importation of obscene materials); *United States* v. *Orito* (movement of obscene material in interstate commerce).) In *Hamling* v. *United States*

(1974), it held specifically that the *Miller* standards applied in a (federal) prosecution (such as this one).

The phrasing of the *Miller* test makes clear that contemporary community standards take on meaning only when they are considered with reference to the underlying questions of fact that must be resolved in an obscenity case. The test itself shows that appeal to the prurient interest is one such question of fact for the jury to resolve. The *Miller* opinion indicates that patent offensiveness is to be treated in the same way. The fact that the jury must measure patent offensiveness against contemporary community standards does not mean, however, that juror discretion in this area is to go unchecked. Both in *Hamling* and in *Jenkins* v. *Georgia,* the Court noted that part (b) of the *Miller* test contained a substantive component as well. The kinds of conduct that a jury would be permitted to label as "patently offensive" in a Section 1461 prosecution are the "hard core" types of conduct suggested by the examples given in *Miller.* Literary, artistic, political, or scientific value, on the other hand, is not discussed in *Miller* in terms of contemporary community standards.

The issue we must resolve is whether the jury's discretion to determine what appeals to the prurient interest and what is patently offensive is circumscribed in any way by a state statute such as c. 725 of the Iowa Code. Put another way, we must decide whether the jury is entitled to rely on its own knowledge of community standards, or whether a state legislature (or a smaller legislative body) may declare what the community standards shall be, and, if such a declaration has been made, whether it is binding in a federal prosecution of Section 1461.

Obviously, a state legislature would not be able to define contemporary community standards in a vacuum. Rather, community standards simply provide the measure against which the jury decides the questions of appeal to prurient interest and patent offensiveness. In *Hamling* v. *United States,* the Court recognized the close analogy between the function of "contemporary community standards" in obscenity cases and "reasonableness" in other cases:

> A juror is entitled to draw on his own knowledge of the views of the average person in the community of vicinage from which he comes for making the required determination, just as he is entitled to draw on his knowledge of the propensities of a "reasonable" person in other areas of the law.

It would be just as inappropriate for a legislature to attempt to freeze a jury to one definition of reasonableness as it would be for a legislature to try to define the contemporary community standard of appeal to prurient interest or patent offensiveness, if it were even possible for such a definition to be formulated.

This is not to say that state legislatures are completely foreclosed from enacting laws setting substantive limitations for obscenity cases. On the contrary, we have indicated on several occasions that legislation of this kind is permissible. State legislation must still define the kinds of conduct that will be regulated by the State. For example, the Iowa law in effect at the time this prosecution was instituted was to the effect that no conduct aimed at adults was regulated. At the other extreme, a State might seek to regulate all the hard core pornography that it Constitutionally could. The new Iowa law, which will regulate only material "depicting a sex act involving sado-masochistic abuse, excretory functions, a child, or bestiality," provides an example of an intermediate approach.

If a State wished to adopt a slightly different approach to obscenity regulation, it might impose a geographic limit on the determination of community standards by defining the area from which the jury could be selected in an obscenity case, or by legislating with respect to the instructions that must be given to the jurors in such cases. In addition, the State might add a geographic dimension to its regulation of obscenity through the device of zoning laws. It is evident that ample room is left for state legislation even though the question of the community standard to apply, when appeal to prurient interest and patent offensiveness are considered, is not one that can be defined legislatively.

An even stronger reason for holding that a state law regulating distribution of obscene material cannot define contemporary community standards in the case before us is the simple fact that this is a *federal* prosecution. The Court already has held, in *Hamling,* that (such) substantive conduct is confined to "the sort of 'patently offensive representations or descriptions of that specific 'hard core' sexual conduct given as examples in *Miller* v. *California.'"* The community standards aspects likewise present issues of federal law, upon which a state statute such as Iowa's cannot have conclusive effect. The kinds of instructions that should be given to the jury are likewise a federal question. For example, the Court has held that Section 1461 embodies a requirement that local rather than national standards should be applied. Similarly, obscenity is to be judged according to the average person in the community, rather than the most prudish or the most tolerant. Both of these substantive limitations are passed on to the jury in the form of instructions.

The fact that the mailings in this case were wholly intrastate is immaterial for a prosecution under Section 1461. That statute was one enacted under Congress' postal power, granted in Art. I, Section 8, cl 7, of the Constitution, and the postal power clause does not distinguish between interstate and intrastate matters. This Court consistently has upheld Congress' exercise of that power to exclude from the mails materials that are judged to be obscene. See *Ex parte Jackson* (1904) (power to exclude from the mail "information of a character calculated to debauch the public morality").

Our decision that contemporary community standards must be applied by juries in accordance with their own understanding of the tolerance of the average person in their community does not mean, as has been suggested, that obscenity convictions will be virtually unreviewable. We have stressed before that juries must be instructed properly, so that they consider the entire community and not simply their own subjective reactions, or the reactions of a sensitive or of a callous minority. The type of conduct depicted must fall within the substantive limitations suggested in *Miller* and adopted in *Hamling* with respect to Section 1461. The work also must lack serious literary, artistic, political, or scientific value before a conviction will be upheld; this determination is particularly amenable to appellate review. Finally, it is always appropriate for the appellate court to review the sufficiency of the evidence.

Petitioner argues that a decision to ignore the Iowa law will have the practical effect of nullifying that law. We do not agree. In the first place, the significance of Iowa's decision in 1974 not to regulate the distribution of obscene materials to adults is open to question. Iowa may have decided that the resources of its prosecutors' offices should be devoted to matters deemed to have greater priority than the enforcement of obscenity statutes. Such a decision would not mean that Iowa affirmatively desired free distribution of those materials; on the State's part that the federal government's prosecutions under statutes such as Section 1461 would be sufficient for the State's purposes. The State might also view distribution over the counter as different from distribution through the mails. It might conclude that it is easier to keep obscene materials out of the hands of minors and unconsenting adults in retail establishments than it is when a letter or package arrives at a private residence. Furthermore, the history of the Iowa law suggests that the State may have left distribution to consenting adults unregulated simply because it was not then able to arrive at a compromise statute for the regulation of obscenity.

Arguments similar to petitioner's "nullification" thesis were made in cases that followed *Stanley* v. *Georgia*. In *United States* v. *12 200-ft. Reels of Film,* the question was whether the United States Constitutionally might prohibit the importation of obscene material that was intended solely for private, personal use and possession. *Stanley* had upheld the individual's right to possess obscene material in the home, and the argument was made that this right would be virtually meaningless if the government could prevent importation of, and hence access to, the obscene material. The Court held that *Stanley* had been based on the privacy of the home, and that it represented a considered line of demarcation in obscenity area. Consequently, despite the incidental effect that the importation prohibition had on the privacy right to possess obscene material in the home, the Court upheld the statute. A similar result was reached, in the face of similar argument, in *United States* v. *Orito*. There, the statute prohibiting knowing transportation of obscene material in interstate commerce, was at issue. The Court held that *Stanley* did not create a right to receive, transport, or distribute obscene material, even though it had established the right to possess the material in the privacy of the home.

In this case, petitioner argues that the Court has recognized the right of States to adopt a laissez-faire attitude toward regulation of pornography, and that a holding that section 1461 permits a federal prosecution will render the States' right meaningless. Just as the individual's right to possess obscene material in the privacy of his home, however, did not create a correlative right to receive, transport, or distribute the material, the State's right to abolish all regulation of obscene material does not create a correlative right to force the federal government to allow the mails or the channels of interstate or foreign commerce to be used for the purpose of sending obscene material into the permissive State.

Even though the State's law is not conclusive with regard to the attitudes of the local community on obscenity, nothing we have said is designed to imply that the Iowa statute should not have been introduced into evidence at petitioner's trial. On the contrary, the local statute on obscenity provides relevant evidence of the mores of the community whose legislative body enacted the law. It is quite appropriate, therefore, for the jury to be told of the law and to give such weight to the expression of the State's policy on distribution as the jury feels it deserves. We hold only that the Iowa statute is not conclusive as to the issue of contemporary community standards for appeal to the prurient interest and patent offensiveness. Those are questions for the jury to decide, in its traditional role as factfinder.

V

A. We also reject petitioner's arguments that the prospective jurors should have been asked about their understanding of Iowa's community standards and Iowa law, and that Section 1461 was unconstitutionally vague as applied to him. The particular inquiries requested by petitioner would not have elicited useful information about the jurors' qualifications to apply contemporary community standards in an objective way. A request for the jurors' description of their understanding of community standards would have been no more appropriate than a request for a description of the meaning of "reasonableness." Neither term lends itself to precise definition. This is not to preclude other more specific and less conclusory questions for voir dire. For example, it might be helpful to know how long a juror has been a member of the community, how heavily the juror has been involved in the community, and with what organizations having an interest in the regulation of obscenity the juror has been affiliated. The propriety of a particular question is a decision for the trial court to make in the first instance. In this case, however, we cannot say that the District Court abused its discretion in refusing to ask the specific questions tendered by petitioner.

B. Neither do we find Section 1461 unconstitutionally vague as applied here. Our construction of the statute flows directly from the decisions in *Hamling, Miller, Reidel,* and *Roth*. As construed in

Hamling, the type of conduct covered by the statute can be ascertained with sufficient ease to avoid due process pitfalls. Similarly, the possibility that different juries might reach different conclusions as to the same material does not render the statute unconstitutional. We find no vagueness defect in the statute attributable to the fact that federal policy with regard to distribution of obscene material through the mail was different from Iowa policy with regard to the intrastate sale of like material.

VI

Since the Iowa law on obscenity was introduced into evidence, and the jurors were told that they could consider it as evidence of the community standard, petitioner received everything to which he was entitled. To go further, and to make the state law conclusive on the issues of appeal to prurient interest and patent offensiveness, in a federal prosecution under Section 1461, would be inconsistent with our prior cases. We hold that those issues are fact questions for the jury, to be judged in light of the jurors' understanding of contemporary community standards. We also hold that Section 1461 is not unconstitutionally vague as so applied, and that petitioner's proposed voir dire questions were not improperly refused. The judgment of the Court of Appeals is affirmed.

It is so ordered.

PEOPLE v. LLEWELLYN
257 NW2d 902, 401 Mich. 314, 3 Med. L. Rptr. 1649 (1977)

Defendants Llewellyn and Las Vegas Cinema, Inc., appeal their convictions for exhibition of two allegedly obscene films under an East Detroit anti-obscenity ordinance. Defendants argue that their conviction must be reversed. The question in this case is whether the legislature has pre-empted the anti-obscenity ordinance by the existing state statutory scheme governing criminal obscenity offenses, and whether such pre-emption is unconstitutional under Const. 1963, Art. 7, Section 22.

State pre-emption may be found first in an express statement of intent to pre-empt, or second implied from an examination of legislative history. Third, the pervasiveness of the state regulatory scheme may support a finding of pre-emption, although pervasiveness is not generally sufficient by itself. Pervasiveness is a factor which should be considered as evidence of pre-emption. Fourth, the nature of the regulated subject matter may demand exclusive state regulation to achieve the uniformity necessary to serve the state's purpose or interest.

This case instructs us that a Michigan obscenity statute defining both obscenity and criminal obscenity offenses is pre-emptive of the field and precludes localities from enacting ordinances dealing with the same subject matter.

Per Curiam

(E)xamination of relevant Michigan cases indicates that where the nature of the regulated subject matter calls for regulation adapted to local conditions, and the local regulation does not interfere with the state regulatory scheme, supplementary local regulation has generally been upheld.

However, where the Court has found that the nature of the subject matter regulated called for a uniform state regulatory scheme, supplementary local regulation has been held pre-empted. Especially pertinent to the instant case in this regard is *Walsh* v. *City of River Rouge,* where this Court held pre-empted a municipal ordinance granting certain emergency powers to the mayor. The subject matter of the ordinance in *Walsh* involved the potential restriction of important civil liberties of the people, as does the case before us. The Court apparently concluded that the protection of these important civil liberties demanded that the state retain sole control of the circumstances under which the emergency powers would be exercised.

(See also *Noey* v. *City of Saginaw,* (the state was held to have exclusive authority to control alcoholic beverage traffic, with specific reference to the need for uniformity); *City of Grand Haven* v. *Grocer's Cooperative Dairy Co.,* (the state was held to have exclusive control over the pasteurization of milk).)

The four guidelines outlined above lead us to conclude that the state, in its criminal obscenity statutory scheme, has pre-empted the field of regulation which East Detroit seeks to enter with its anti-obscenity ordinance.

We have no express statutory language nor legislative history which indicates one way or the other whether the state statutory scheme pre-empts an ordinance such as the one before us.

However, the two other factors to be considered indicate that an ordinance such as the one before us has been pre-empted because the comprehensiveness of the statutory scheme established by the state shows a pre-emptive intent, and because the nature of the regulated subject matter demands uniform, statewide treatment.

As to the comprehensiveness issue, an examination of the state statutory scheme reveals a broad, detailed, and multifaceted attack on the sale, distribution, and exhibition of obscenity.

In enacting the present statutory scheme, the legislature replaced its much simpler predecessor, a detailed five-section statutory framework intended to define and regulate obscenity.

The breadth and detail of this statutory scheme provides an indication that the legislature has pre-empted the definition and deterence of criminal obscenity, at least to the exclusion of a supplementary ordinance such as the one before us, which seeks to establish its own definition and test for obscenity, to modify the state standards for a prima facie case of the prohibited conduct, and to alter the state prescribed punishment upon conviction.

This conclusion is buttressed by the fact that, for reasons discussed below, the definition and prohibition of obscenity offenses is clearly an area of the law which demands uniform statewide treatment.

First, it seems clear that if each locality in the state of Michigan were allowed to establish its own definition of obscenity, a great deal of uncertainty and confusion would be created. We observe that no less than the United States Supreme Court has had over a period of decades considerable difficulty in defining the line between obscenity and protected speech and determining what material constituted obscenity under such a definition. To allow each of the multitude of Michigan localities to establish its own definition of obscenity would be to invite the cultivation of a legal thicket which would make both the scope of the individual right to free expression and the permissible prohibition of obscenity well-nigh impossible to determine.

Second, a balkanized system of obscenity definition and prohibition would, through the resultant confusion and provocation of endless appeals, both threaten important individual rights and undermine efficiency in the control of obscenity.

On the one hand, the uncertainty created by local definitions of obscenity would effectively chill the right to free expression, and raise serious due process problems in that an unwary national or statewide distributor of books or films may be subject to criminal prosecution and incarceration although there was little opportunity to discover the nature of the prohibited conduct. It is a longstanding rule in this state that criminal offenses must establish with reasonable certainty the elements of the offenses so that all persons subject to their penalities may know what acts it is their duty to avoid. The unfairness which is at the root of this rule is also present where local definition of obscenity in municipalities of all sizes across the state make it extremely difficult for a national or statewide distributor to determine what acts it is his or her duty to avoid.

On the other hand, a uniform statewide system of obscenity regulation provides not only the fairest, but also the most effective means of combating obscenity. A balkanized system of obscenity regulation undoubtedly would cause criminal prosecutions under local ordinances to be considerably delayed in the appellate system. Such would be the case because of holding of an appellate court that a particular obscenity conviction was valid would not necessarily be dispositive of other convictions, even those involving the very same allegedly obscene materials, if the conviction were obtained under different local standards for obscenity. We note also that such a situation would put a heavy burden of a state appellate system already confronted with an ever-increasing caseload, and thus further slow appellate review of all cases.

For all the above reasons, we hold that the state has pre-empted the field which the municipality in this case seeks to enter.

We note that New Jersey and California have reached the same conclusion.

(W)e do not mean to suggest in this opinion that a municipality is pre-empted from enacting ordinances outside the field of regulation occupied by the state statutory scheme governing criminal obscenity. For example, there is not the slightest indication that the state legislature acted in MCLA 750.343a et seq.; MSA 28.575(1) et seq. to preclude local zoning ordinances governing the location of establishments featuring "adult entertainment" such as that recently approved by the United States Supreme Court in *Young* v. *American Mini Theatres, Inc*.

The Detroit ordinance challenged in *Young* involved zoning, not criminal prohibition, and "adult establishments" featuring erotica not defined in terms of obscenity. Clearly, then, such municipal regulation is outside of the state's present statutory scheme governing criminal obscenity.

Ryan, J., dissenting.

The majority concedes that there is "no express statutory language nor legislative history which indicates one way or the other whether the state statutory scheme pre-empts an ordinance such as the one before us." The Court thus appears to overlook our precedential requirement that an express showing of a legislative expression of intent to pre-empt the field be made before we will invalidate a local ordinance.

The language of the statute itself in no sense expresses or even infers an intent to occupy the field of obscenity regulation to the exclusion of local communities.

The first of the two reasons assigned by the majority for finding pre-emption is that "the comprehensiveness of the statutory scheme established by the state shows a pre-emptive intent." That the statute in question is not sufficiently comprehensive to suggest such a legislative intent is evident from a line by line comparison of it with the ordinance. The ordinance forbids nothing the statute permits and permits nothing the statute forbids, criteria we approved in *Miller*. Further evidence that the statute lacks the pre-emptive comprehensiveness claimed for it by the majority is this Court's on-the-record declaration in *People* v. *Bloss*, while speaking of the statute here in question, that:

> We are divided as to whether such statutes can properly be construed by us without further legislative expression as proscribing the dissemination of "obscene" material to consenting adults. (Emphasis added.)

Absent such construction or subsequent legislation, local ordinances proscribing such conduct can hardly be said to be inconsistent with the general law or the general law be held so comprehensive as to pre-empt local ordinances.

Because the state law has neither expressly nor by reasonable inference permitted the dissemination of obscene material to consenting adults, on that point alone it is unquestionably within the province of local authorities to further protect their legitimate interests in the field of obscenity legislation through the enactment of local ordinances prohibiting such conduct.

The second reason relied upon by the Court in concluding that the ordinance before us is pre-empted is ". . . because the nature of the regulated subject matter demands uniform, statewide treatment."

The fact that a subject is one which logically lends itself to statewide uniform regulation or even demands it is hardly justification for the conclusion that such legislation has been enacted, or if enacted is in conflict with local ordinances on the subject. More significantly, whether the regulation of obscenity "demands uniform statewide treatment" is a judgment for the legislature to make, not the judiciary. It has given no indication to date, despite this Court's invitation in *Bloss,* of an intent to pre-emptively provide the comprehensive, uniform statewide regulation my colleagues say the subject demands.

The considerations advanced by the majority in favor of pre-emption are factors to be weighed by our state legislature in deliberations concerning future obscenity legislation.

Should the legislature deem it appropriate, it may choose to completely occupy the field at that time. Under the present statutory scheme, however, local governments are not prohibited from legislating in the interest of furthering a valid "municipal concern" by regulating obscenity within their respective communities in a manner that does not conflict with the state's nonexclusive regulation in this field.

The prevailing opinion does violence to the legitimate interests of our municipalities in locally regulating a subject of vital concern to them by striking down virtually every ordinance in Michigan proscribing obscenity, despite the fact that the state has not adequately legislated in the field.

WESTERN CORPORATION v. KENTUCKY
558 SW 2d 605 (1977)

Reed, J., delivered the opinion of the Court.

Appellant, The Western Corporation, and two of its employees, were charged with four counts of exhibiting an allegedly obscene motion picture entitled "Deep Throat." The jury convicted The Western Corporation on all counts and fixed as penalty a fine of $1,000 on each count. The jury was unable to agree concerning the guilt of the two employees, the manager of the theatre and the projectionist, and the charges against them were subsequently dismissed on motion of the prosecution.

The Western Corporation filed a motion for appeal under KRS 21.140(2). We have delayed disposition because of the pendency of several federal cases posing federal Constitutional issues before the Supreme Court of the United States. Those cases have now been decided. We have agreed to grant the motion for an appeal, but we affirm the judgment for the reasons later stated.

Western, the corporate operator of a motion picture theatre in Paducah, Kentucky, was tried and convicted for violation of KRS 436.101, the state obscenity statute in effect at the time of the exhibition of the motion picture. This statute has undergone legislative revision and has now been succeeded by KRS 531.010, a part of the Kentucky Penal Code.

The evidence for the prosecution established that on April 12, 1974, the Judge of the Paducah Police Court, accompanied by two police officers, an attorney for the City of Paducah, and an assistant Commonwealth's Attorney, went to the Fourth Street Cinema, operated by Western, and watched the showing of the film "Deep Throat" in its entirety. At the conclusion of the showing of the film, Police Officer Eberhardt signed and swore to an affidavit for a warrant which was forthwith executed by the officer.

The next day, April 13, Officer Eberhardt went again to the Fourth Street theatre where another print or copy of "Deep Throat" was being shown, and after viewing the entire picture, made an arrest, and seized another copy of the film. On April 22, Officer Eberhardt entered the theatre and viewed approximately 15 minutes of the film "Deep Throat." He determined that it was identical to a 15-minute portion of the film he had seen on April 12 and April 13, 1974, and made an arrest. Later in the day, on April 22, 1974, Eberhardt again went to the theatre. This time he saw approximately 18 minutes of the subject film which he determined was identical to portions of the film he had seen on April 12 and 13 in its entirety. Eberhardt again made an arrest.

The movie "Deep Throat" was introduced in evidence and has been viewed by this court. It contains repeated scenes of actual sexual intercourse, anal sodomy, fellatio, and cunnilingus. The story line consists entirely of the sexual activities of Miss Linda Lovelace. We failed to find any serious literary, artistic, political, or scientific value in this motion picture. We, therefore, agree with the jury's conclusion that this exhibited material was obscene and violative of contemporary community standards under the tests prescribed in *Miller* v. *California*.

Western argues that KRS 436.101 was unconstitutional under the First and Fourteenth Amendments to the Constitution of the United States. This argument is based on the assertion that KRS 436.101 did not comply with the standards prescribed in *Miller* v. *California*. Although Western asserts that the Supreme Court of the United States did not intend the Miller standards to be prospective only, that contention has been rejected by the Supreme Court in an appeal concerning the same motion picture, which was the subject of a federal prosecution in Kentucky. In *Marks* v. *United States*, the Supreme Court held that part (c) of the *Miller* test was not retroactive, but that part (b) of the same test, wherein the Court enumerated specific categories of material, did not purport to make criminal, for the purpose of the federal statute proscribing the exhibition of obscene material, conduct which had not previously been thought criminal. We have no difficulty in concluding that our previous decisions concerning the Constitutionality of KRS 436.101 in light of the decision in *Miller* were correct. In *Hall* v. *Commonwealth ex rel Schroering*, we construed our statute as consistent with the explications in *Miller*: "The hard core pornography with which we are here concerned has consistently been held by this court to constitute obscene material within the proscription of the statute prior to our decision in *Hall*."

In *Smith* v. *United States*, the Supreme Court rejected a contention that the federal obscenity statute, 18 U.S.C. Section 1461, was unconstitutionally vague. The court held that the judicial constructions of the statute flowed directly from its decisions in *Hamling* v. *United States, Miller* v. *California, United States* v. *Reidel*, and *Roth* v. *United States*.

Our decisions cited herein make it quite clear that appellant was forewarned in sufficiently specific terms that the depiction in this film of the actual sexual conduct under the circumstances presented was proscribed because it was hard core pornography.

Certainly, we were more specific than was the concerned state court in *Ward* v. *Illinois*, which was decided by the Supreme Court of the United States on June 9, 1977. In that case the Supreme Court's majority opinion declared: "We agree with the Illinois Supreme Court, however, that 'in order that a statute be held overbroad the overbreadth must not only be real, but substantial as well, judged in relation to the statute's plainly legitimate sweep.' " The Supreme Court of the United States held that since it was plain enough from prior cases decided by the Illinois court and from its response to *Miller* that the state court recognized the limitations on the kinds of sexual conduct which could not be represented or depicted under the obscenity laws, the Illinois statute could not be held to be unconstitutionally overbroad. We, therefore, again reject the contention that KRS 436.101, as it was construed by the decisions of this court prior to the time of the commission of the offenses by Western, was unconstitutional under either the First or Fourteenth Amendments to the Constitution of the United States.

Western's next complaint is that the procedure used for seizure of the film was unlawful. The same procedure was approved and recommended in *Heller* v. *New York*. A neutral magistrate viewed a public showing of the film and then issued written authority to a police officer to seize the film as evidence of a violation of the obscenity statute. We are not impressed with Western's argument that the seizure violated the requirements of Section 10 of the Constitution of Kentucky. Although we entertain a real doubt that public exhibitions of films where admission is charged and there is no legitimate expectation of privacy are within the ambit of the protection of privacy policy of Section 10 of our state constitution, we hold that the specific affidavit of Officer Eberhardt met the requirements of Section 10, if it be conceded, arguendo, that Western's operation was within the scope of protection at the time of the seizure.

Western asserts that there was not sufficient evidence from which the jury could conclude that the film seen by Officer Eberhardt on April 13 and twice on April 22 was identical to the film seen and seized on April 12, 1974. Eberhardt testified that the film seen on April 13, 1974, in its entirety was identical to that seen on April 12, 1974, and the film segments seen on April 22 were identical to those segments of the film introduced in evidence at the trial. The evidence was established that the marquee or billboard in front of the theatre on each of these occasions showed that the film "Deep Throat" would be shown. We think this evidence was sufficient to withstand a motion for directed verdict. In common human experience, an advertised motion picture film generally is shown as advertised as is usual with things of that nature. It would appear that the widely advertised motion picture film given the circumstances presented here was shown in this theatre on these occassions, and there is no claim to the contrary.

Western also complains that the instructions were erroneous. The first contention concerning the inadequacy of the instructions is bottomed on the proposition that the trial court should not have permitted separate convictions on the second, third, and fourth counts for violation of the obscenity statute. Western indicates that while a $1,000 fine for the first count might be sustainable upon a conviction, nevertheless, for the second, third, and fourth proven instances of violation of the statute, he should have been fined only $500 instead of $1,000. KRS 436.101(2) related to punishment and provided that violations of the statutes are punishable by fine of not more than $1,000 or imprisonment for not more than six months, or both, for the first offense, "plus $5.00 for each additional unit of material coming within the provisions of this chapter, which is involved in the offense, not to exceed $10,000 . . . plus one day for each additional unit of material coming within the provisions of this chapter, and which is involved in the offense, such basic maximum and additional days not to exceed 360 days in the county jail, or by both such fine and imprisonment."

A reading of the statute makes it abundantly clear that each proven occurrence of the showing of an obscene motion picture was a separate violation of law and was punishable as such. If, on the occasion of the exhibition of "Deep Throat," Western has scheduled a double or triple feature, a different question might be presented; but these were entirely separate exhibitions of this motion picture for which admission was charged. These exhibitions clearly are separate offenses under KRS 436.101(2).

The second claimed error in the instructions is so devoid of merit as not to warrant discussion. The instructions as given clearly and specifically followed the *Miller* standards and the standards delineated by this court at the time the offenses were committed.

Western's final complaint is addressed to a provision of the final judgment entered in which the trial court adjudged that if there was no successful appeal the film was ordered to be destroyed. This provision is plainly consistent with KRS 436.101(9) which provided that upon conviction of the accused the court could, when the conviction becomes final, order the obscene matter destroyed. There was an additional provision in the order that recited that the movie "Deep Throat" "should not be shown any further in this county." Western does not seriously argue that this prohibition is inappropriate as it relates to it, assuming, of course, the conviction was proper. The complaint Western makes is that the prohibition is overbroad in that it apparently applies to all persons and not merely those who were parties to the case.

The jury not only convicted Western as required by the statute, it found the film obscene. The only party to this appeal was properly convicted, as we have determined. We will not indulge in speculation concerning the overbreadth of the provision against showing the film and the parties to whom that prohibition applies. Certainly, Western has no standing to question the operation and validity of the questioned portion of the final order.

The judgment is affirmed.

All concur.

PUSSYCAT THEATRE v. STATE OF FLORIDA
355 So. 2d 829 (1978)

Per Curiam

This is an appeal by the defendants, Gayety Theatres, Inc., d/b/a Pussycat Theatre, and Leroy Griffith, from an order adjudicating them to be in contempt of court

> . . . for their willful failure to comply with this Court's February 14, 1975 order by failing to advertise the film "Deep Throat" with the legends "Revised Version" or "Edited Version" in type at least one-half as large as the largest type in their advertisements.

The defendants were sentenced to pay a fine of $3,000.00. In default of payment of the fine, defendant Griffith is to serve 5 days in the Dade County jail.

The record reflects that these proceedings were commenced in 1973, culminating in a restraining order on March 15, 1974, enjoining the showing of the motion picture "Deep Throat" at any of the defendants' places of business in Dade County, Florida. Subsequently, it was brought to the attention of the trial court that the defendants were, in fact, showing the film. Upon the representation of defendants' counsel that the film being shown was a simulated version and that the explicit sexual scenes had been deleted, an agreed order was entered on February 14, 1975, and signed by counsel for the defense and for the prosecution. That order provided:

> Upon such representation and with consent of counsel, accordingly, it is ordered that on all advertisements, bill boards, placards, marquees, and all other advertising matter that there be included therein the legend "Revised Version" or "Edited Version" and that the letters of said legend be at least one-half as high as the highest print in any such advertising material.

In September of 1976, the State filed a petition for rule to show cause alleging that the defendants' advertisements were in violation of the February 14, 1975, order in that:

> a) From August 4 to August 9; August 11 to August 17; and August 20 to September 3, 1976, advertisements appeared in the *Miami Herald* for the Pussycat Theater (sic) for the showing of the film "Deep Throat" with no legends in the advertisements indicating either "Revised Edition" or "Edited Edition."
>
> b) From September 5 to September 11, 1976, advertisements appeared in the *Miami Herald* for the Pussycat Theater (sic) for the showing of the film "Deep Throat" with the legend "Revised" appearing at the bottom of the advertisements, below the title of a second film, and in letters less than one-half as high as the highest print in the advertisements.

The court issued a rule to show cause. Following an evidentiary hearing, the defendants were adjudicated to be in contempt of the order of the court, and were sentenced. This appeal ensued.

1. As their first point on appeal, the defendants contend that the court erred in finding them in contempt in the absence of evidence showing a willful or intentional violation of the court order. Our review of the record indicates that there was evidence that on numerous occasions during the months of August and September, 1976, defendants' advertisements appeared in the *Miami Herald,* a newspaper of general circulation in the community, with only the word "revised" added, or without any reference at all to the legends "revised version" or "edited version" as specifically required by the court order.

2. In our opinion, the defendants' argument that there was no showing of willful disregard for the order is without merit. They claim that they instructed the *Miami Herald* to include the word "revised" in their advertisements, and that they were unaware that the *Herald* was printing their advertisements without the addition of the word "revised", and further, that as soon as they were put on notice of the noncompliance by the office of the State Attorney, that they again instructed the *Miami Herald* to correct the advertisements by inserting the word "revised." The addition of the word "revised" is not what the order requires. Moreover, the defendants were under an obligation to continuously check their advertisements to be certain that the required language had been omitted, the advertisement should have been corrected immediately or else discontinued. Therefore, the trial court did not err in finding that the defendants did willfully disobey the order of February 14, 1975, and in entering an adjudication of contempt.

3. From the record in this case, the defendants were guilty of an indirect criminal contempt. However, it does appear that the fine imposed on the defendants is excessive and must be reduced.

The maximum penalty for criminal contempt is one year imprisonment and a fine of $500.00 (*Aaron v. State,* 284 So.2d 673 (Fla. 1973); *Miami Health Studios, Inc.* v. *State ex rel. Gerstein,* 294 So.2d 365 (Fla. 3rd DCA 1974); Section 775.02, Florida Statutes (1975).) Therefore, the adjudication of contempt is affirmed and the cause is remanded to the trial court to modify the sentence, reducing the fine to no more than $500.00.

The remaining points on appeal are without merit and will not be discussed.
Affirmed and remanded for modification.

ST. MARTIN'S PRESS v. CAREY
3 Med. L. Rptr. 1598 (1977)

Ward, J.

Plaintiff St. Martin's Press, Incorporated ("St. Martin's") is the publisher of a book entitled *Show Me!,* and plaintiffs Crutcher and Newman Book Sellers, Inc., and Patricia Ince ("booksellers") are in the business of selling books at retail, including the book *Show Me!* They instituted this action on October 28, 1977, seeking declaratory and injunctive relief. On the same date, they brought on an order to show cause why the defendants should not be preliminarily enjoined from enforcing newly enacted Section 263.15 of the Penal Law of New York against them or their employees with respect to the book *Show Me!*

Claiming violation of 42 U.S.C. Section 1983 and the First and Fourteenth Amendments to the United States Constitution, plaintiffs allege that Section 263.15, which is entitled "Promoting a sexual performance by a child," prohibits the publication, distribution, advertisement, or sale of the book *Show Me!* by imposing up to seven years imprisonment upon any person who publishes, distributes, advertises, or sells *Show Me!* in the State of New York.

Defendants are the Governor of New York, the District Attorney of New York County, where St. Martin's has its principal place of business, and the District Attorneys of Westchester and Suffolk Counties, where the booksellers have their principal places of business, or reside, own and operate their respective bookstores.

Defendant Carl A. Vergari, District Attorney of Westchester County, joined by the other defendants, has cross-moved to dismiss for lack of a justiciable controversy. Argument on the motions was held by the Court on November 3, 1977. For the reasons hereinafter stated, plaintiffs' motion for a preliminary injunction is granted and defendants' cross-motion to dismiss is denied.

FACTS

Section 263.15 which became effective on November 9, 1977 provides in part:

A person is guilty of promoting a sexual performance by a child when, knowing the character and content thereof, he produces, directs, or promotes any performance which includes sexual conduct by a child less than sixteen years of age.

Plaintiffs assert that Section 262.15 is unconstitutionally overbroad on its face because it applies to motion pictures or photographs whether or not they are obscene in violation of the principle that where first amendment interests are involved, regulations which proscribe both protected and unprotected expression are invalid. In addition, plaintiffs assert that Section 263.15 is unconstitutional as applied to this book for three reasons. First, plaintiffs argue that Section 263.15 is unconstitutional as applied to *Show Me!* because *Show Me!* is not obscene, but is a serious, artistic, educational, and scientific book designed for parents to use in educating their children about the emotional and physical aspects of sex. Second, insofar as the statute's purpose is to prevent New York children from being exploited or otherwise affected by their unwitting involvement in sexual enterprises, it can have no rational application to *Show Me!*, which was photographed entirely in Munich, Germany between 1969 and 1973, where the book was first published. Therefore, in making criminal the sale or distribution of such a book New York has exceeded its police powers and thereby denied plaintiffs substantive due process. Third, plaintiffs contend that Section 263.15 is unconstitutional as applied to *Show Me!* because it is violative of the right of parents to receive and distribute such information. Therefore, the statute infringes the Constitutionally protected right of privacy of parents to teach their children about such personal matters as sex.

RIPENESS

Defendants contend that this case is not ripe for adjudication. It is undisputed that defendants have not prosecuted, charged, arrested, or investigated plaintiffs' activities with respect to *Show Me!* This is not surprising since Section 263.15 had not taken effect at the time suit was brought and argument was held on the preliminary injunction motion. Yet, if plaintiffs' injuries are only "imaginary," or amount to "nothing more than speculation about the future," the case is not ripe. The problem, then, is to determine whether there is a genuine risk of prosecution notwithstanding the lack of activity on the part of the defendants.

Analysis of the ripeness cases involving attacks on criminal laws reveals three types of fact patterns. In the first category, state officials have taken some kind of action against the plaintiffs, ranging from, for example, ongoing prosecution in *Younger* v. *Harris* (1971), to arrest and seizures of materials deemed obscene, but no prosecution in *Black Jack Distributors, Inc.* v. *Beame* (1977), to threat of arrest and prosecution, coupled with the prosecution of the federal plaintiff's companion in *Steffel* v. *Thompson* (1974). Further, a mere threat to enforce a law against the federal plaintiff sufficed to make *Police Department of Chicago* v. *Mosley* (1972), ripe. Moreover, a prosecuting official's affirmative response to an individual's inquiry regarding the prospect of prosecution has been held to constitute a threat sufficient to make a federal challenge ripe. Finally, an individual's general inquiry of prosecutors regarding the Constitutionality of a law and whether the state would enforce it, and the prosecutors' general response that public officials must obey the law and are duty bound to enforce the law, were held sufficient to make a federal court challenge ripe.

In the second category of cases, no action of any kind had been taken against the federal plaintiffs by state officials; rather, other persons had been the subject of some prosecutorial action under the challenged, or similar law, (e.g., *Doe* v. *Bolton* (1973) history of enforcement of the predecessor to the statute under attack was sufficient to permit federal plaintiffs to challenge the new law even though it had not yet been enforced against anyone; *Naprstek* v. *City of Norwich* (1976) 56-year history of enforcement of the city's curfew ordinance against other persons sufficed to make plaintiffs' suit ripe).

The final category of cases involves challenges to statutes which have not been enforced nor threatened to be enforced. In *Pierce* v. *Society of Sisters* (1925), where the injury with which plaintiffs were imminently threatened was the withdrawal of pupils from their schools as a result of an Oregon law making it a crime for parents to send their children to private schools, the Supreme Court affirmed a federal court grant of a preliminary injunction restraining enforcement of the statute even though it was not to take effect, and there clearly would be no prosecutions thereunder, until more than one year after the Supreme Court's decision. Further, in *Epperson* v. *Arkansas* (1968), a high school teacher was permitted to attack Arkansas' anti-evolution law even though there had been no recorded prosecutions since the law's adoption in 1928, and it was therefore "possible that the statute (was) presently more of a curiosity than a vital fact of life."

In determining whether a genuine risk of prosecution exists, one indicium of a concrete controversy is the clarity of the application of the challenged statute to the plaintiff's conduct. Where it is unclear if the law covers that conduct, as in *Steffel* v. *Thompson,* supra, it is more essential for there to be overt action by the prosecution officials towards the plaintiffs; conversely, where the statute clearly applies to plaintiffs' conduct, as this Court finds infra, no prosecutorial action is necessary.

As to the applicability of Section 263.15 to these plaintiffs, it is undisputed that plaintiffs have published, distributed, sold, or advertised *Show Me!* in the past and desire to do so in the future. Therefore, if the content of *Show Me!* comes within the statute's definitions of sexual conduct, etc., Section 263.15 would be applicable to plaintiffs. Plaintiffs concede that *Show Me!* contains nude photographs of children under the age of sixteen, is explicit in its depiction, through children, of certain aspects of human sexuality, and at least one of the photographs meets the statutory definition of sexual conduct. Therefore they assert that *Show Me!* comes within the clear language of Section 263.15 and so that section is plainly applicable. Moreover, plaintiffs contend that the legislative history confirms that Section 263.15 was intended to apply to *Show Me!* and even suggests that that section may in part have been specifically directed against *Show Me!* Without relying on the sketchy and inconclusive legislative history, the Court is in a position to conclude that *Show Me!* does come within the language of Section 263.15 and therefore the absence of affirmative conduct on the part of defendant prosecutors is not dispositive.

Although Section 263.15 is clearly applicable to *Show Me!,* if there were a state policy of nonenforcement of the statute, preliminary injunctive relief would not be granted. However, because Section 263.15 is "recent and not moribund," (*Doe* v. *Bolton,* 410 U.S. at 188) there is neither a policy of nonenforcement nor a pattern of enforcement. Moreover, Section 263.15 appears to be a unique attempt to control child abuse, and therefore there is no history of enforcement or nonenforcement of similar statutes upon which to gauge the likelihood of prosecution. Accordingly, it is necessary to evaluate the general reaction *Show Me!* has evoked historically and in light of that history to assess defendants' position with respect to *Show Me!*

Show Me! would appear to be a controversial, and to some, an offensive book. Obscenity prosecutions, all unsuccessful, have been brought in Massachusetts, Oklahoma, and New Hampshire, as well as Toronto, Canada; under Section 263.15 a prosecution could be brought notwithstanding lack of obscenity.

Defendant prosecutors would have the Court ignore the coercive nature of this statute: that the clearly applicable serious penal sanctions necessarily have externally induced plaintiffs to take reasonable responsive conduct, as the legislature apparently has intended. Instead, they accuse plaintiffs of legal paranoia, contending that plaintiffs' fears are unjustified inasmuch as there are no investigations pending in their respective offices with respect to *Show Me!* They characterize plaintiffs' termination of activities with respect to *Show Me!* rather than risk prosecution for violating Section 263.15 as "unilateral cessation" of activities, and "a self-imposed Hobson's choice," induced by "nothing more than speculation about the future." However, at oral argument, none could tell the Court whether photographs taken in Germany between 1969 and 1973 would be outside the scope of Section 263.15; more importantly, none could or would dismiss out of hand the possibility of a prosecution being brought against plaintiffs. This noncommittal posture stemmed in part from the policy some of the defendants have against rendering advisory opinions; in addition, some of the defendant prosecutors pointed out that although their office may not be planning a prosecution, they could not foreclose the possibility of a private citizen initiating a complaint. Under these circumstances, it cannot be said "that the state maintains a policy of non-prosecution." Rather, defendants' responses are essentially equivalent to those given by the prosecutors in the *Love* case, supra, i.e., prosecuting authorities have a duty to enforce the law as written. Therefore, as in *Love,* although defendant prosecutors have not themselves threatened prosecution, their inability to obviate the threat indicates that the threat is not chimerical. Moreover, this threat seems even greater when gauged in light of the climate in which the statute takes effect and in light of the reactions previously provoked by *Show Me!* In view of these circumstances, the Court finds that there is at least a concrete risk of a prosecution resulting from a private citizen's initiating a complaint.

Of perhaps most importance in assessing the ripeness of a case is "the actual hardship to the litigants of denying them the relief sought." The Court is not presented solely with a subjective chill of First Amendment rights, but with a "present and very real" injury, inasmuch as Section 263.15 has the effect of abridging First and Fourteenth Amendment rights and preventing St. Martin's, and to a lesser extent the booksellers, from "engaging in activities that could be an important source of their livelihood."

For the foregoing reasons the Court concludes that the controversy is ripe for adjudication and denies defendants' cross-motion for dismissal.

PRELIMINARY INJUNCTION STANDARD

The standard that plaintiffs must meet to obtain a preliminary injunction is: 1) a clear showing of possible irreparable harm and probable success on the merits; or 2) a clear showing of possible irreparable harm and sufficiently serious questions going to the merits to make them a fair ground for litigation and a balance of hardships tipping decidedly in favor of the plaintiffs.

1. Irreparable Injury

In view of the applicability of Section 263.15 to *Show Me!*, plaintiffs contend that they face two equally undesirable options: cease publication and sale of *Show Me!* or risk a felony prosecution and potential incarceration of up to seven years for continuing their activities with respect to the book. As a result, pending a final decision on the merits, St. Martin's has determined to cease distribution and sale of the book in New York and advise its distributors and bookstore customers of the risk of prosecution under Section 263.15. Similarly, the booksellers have determined to stop selling or carrying the book absent preliminary injunctive relief. One of the distributors of *Show Me!*, Doubleday & Company, Inc., has advised St. Martin's that in the absence of preliminary injunctive relief, it will cease distribution of the book to Doubleday bookstores throughout New York State and will return the copies on hand to St. Martin's. St. Martin's states that all New York booksellers with whom it has discussed the matter have said they will refuse to display or sell the book once Section 263.15 has taken effect.

Plaintiffs assert that the losses occasioned by their decisions to cease all activities with respect to *Show Me!* are infringement of the First Amendment rights of the authors of the book, booksellers, parents, educators, and other customers: substantial economic injury to plaintiffs, particularly St. Martin's; and infringement of Fourteenth Amendment substantive due process rights.

With respect to the first of these, corporations are not guaranteed rights of free speech under the First and Fourteenth Amendments. However, corporate plaintiffs have standing to raise the First Amendment rights of persons not before the Court, otherwise those rights would, in all probability, never be protected.

The Second Circuit has recognized the dilemma facing plaintiffs who must choose between giving up their First Amendment rights and violating the law. The former option "involves a deprivation of (plaintiff's) and the public's First Amendment rights to show and to view films, and in itself constitutes irreparable injury justifying injunctive relief, because there is no means to make up the irretrievable loss of that which would have been expressed." On the other hand, the latter option "may cause, as it is alleged to cause, irreparable injury both economic . . . and personal (the freedom to exercise First Amendment rights without genuine fear of prosecution)." Due to the clear applicability of Section 263.15 and its severe penal sanctions, plaintiffs face the same dilemma. As noted above, had they chosen to violate Section 263.15 and await prosecution, they and their employees would have risked substantial prison terms of up to seven years. Thus, they effectively were forced to cease publication and sale of *Show Me!* The consequence of their decisions is the irretrievable loss of the First Amendment rights of the authors, booksellers, and readers. "The loss of First Amendment freedoms, for even minimal periods of time, unquestionably constitutes irreparable injury." Thus, assuming a violation of the First Amendment, plaintiff Ince has suffered and continues to suffer irreparable injury by virtue of the deprivation of her First Amendment rights.

The corporate plaintiffs cannot rely on the deprivation of the First Amendment rights of their parties to make their showing of irreparable harm. However, that does not mean that they cannot suffer irreparable injury of their own. St. Martin's asserts that as a consequence of being forced not to publish, distribute, or sell *Show Me!*, it will lose the profits it would have received had it continued to sell the book, and this loss will be irreparable due to the unlikelihood of ever recouping the lost sales even if the statute is invalidated at some later date. In addition, St. Martin's will incur the cost of buying back the copies of *Show Me!* currently in the bookstores. The booksellers assert that they anticipate some economic loss as a result of the removal of *Show Me!* from their shelves. The Court finds that plaintiff St. Martin's has suffered and will continue to suffer substantial economic injury. This injury coupled with the loss of First Amendment rights of others constitutes irreparable harm.

Furthermore, all three plaintiffs assert a deprivation of their rights to substantive due process. Both individuals and corporations are protected by that clause of the Fourteenth Amendment, and therefore all plaintiffs appear to have standing to assert this alleged deprivation. Assuming such a deprivation, the infringement of plaintiffs' property rights and Ince's First Amendment rights would constitute irreparable injury to their due process rights.

2. Merits

In their facial attack on Section 263.15 plaintiffs claim that it is overbroad since it forbids the publication, sale, etc. of photographs or moving pictures without regard to whether they are obscene. Since plays, motion pictures, and photographs are protected forms of expression, any restriction upon their dissemination must be carefully tailored in order to ensure full protection of First Amendment rights. Although some regulation of nonobscene motion pictures and photographs of the sexual conduct of children might be permissible, the use of felony statutes to prohibit dissemination of such material is Constitutionally suspect. Therefore there is a serious question as to the facial Constitutionality of Section 263.15.

3. Balance of Hardships

Assuming that plaintiffs have demonstrated only serious questions going to the merits, the Court will weigh the balance of hardships. The immediate and permanent harm to plaintiffs which would result from denial of an injunction has already been discussed. The temporary harm to defendants which would result from enjoining future state prosecutions during the pendency of this action was described by Justice Rehnquist:

> Although only temporary, the injunction does prohibit state and local enforcement activities against the federal plaintiff pending final resolution of his case in the federal court. Such a result seriously impairs the State's interest in enforcing its criminal laws, and implicates the concerns for federalism which lie at the heart of *Younger.*

It is important to note that notwithstanding the quoted language, *Doran* upheld the grant of a preliminary injunction.

Plaintiffs in *Doran* attacked an ordinance which prohibited topless dancers in their bars under penalty of a $500 fine for each violation. They alleged that absent preliminary relief they would suffer economically and perhaps go bankrupt. Except for the degree of economic hardship, the plaintiffs before this Court risk more of a hardship than those in *Doran.* Violation of Section 263.15 subjects the violator to a felony prosecution and potential incarceration of up to seven years, rather than a fine. Therefore, the consequences of continuing to exercise First Amendment rights are in some ways more severe. Moreover, *Show Me!* appears to be a book fully protected under the First Amendment, while "the customary 'barroom' type of nude dancing may involve only the barest minimum of protected expression." Accordingly, if the balance of hardships favored plaintiffs in *Doran a fortiori* it favors plaintiffs here.

Furthermore, the grant of temporary relief to plaintiffs will not unduly hamper the state, for the scope of relief is limited in that it will apply solely to Section 263.15, leaving the book open to prosecution under Section 263.10. In addition, temporary relief will not preclude prosecutions under Section 263.15 against books other than *Show Me!*

Accordingly, the Court finds that the balance of hardships tips decidedly in plaintiffs' favor.

COMITY

Steffel v. *Thompson* (1974), made it clear that the principles of *Younger* v. *Harris,* requiring federal courts to refrain in most circumstances from interfering with state laws when a state proceeding is pending, do not apply in the absence of state proceedings. "Requiring the federal courts totally to step aside when no state criminal prosecution is pending . . . would turn federalism on its head."

The reason why *Younger* did not apply is because the *Younger* concern with avoiding disruption and duplication of state proceedings and calling into question the state judiciary's ability and willingness to deal with Constitutional issues has no application when no state judicial proceeding is pending. Therefore, although the *Steffel* exception to *Younger* applied only to declaratory relief, it extended *Steffel* to permit the grant of a preliminary injunction against the enforcement of a state law when no state proceeding is pending. Thus, the Court need not stay its hand under *Younger* principles.

Nor must the Court abstain under the Pullman abstention doctrine, for when the meaning and applicability of the statute is clear it is not necessary to give the state courts the first chance to declare their state statutes unconstitutional. This is particularly true where, as here, a facial attack is made on First Amendment grounds. "When such important national rights as First Amendment freedoms are at stake, there 'should not be the slightest risk of nullification by state process; . . . at least where the individual has chosen a federal forum to protect them.'" Moreover, should the Court refrain from acting now plaintiffs may be precluded from seeking federal relief under *Hicks* v. *Miranda* (1975), should a state prosecution be brought before substantial progress is made on the merits of this case. Accordingly, the Court believes that principles of comity do not require this Court to refrain from granting preliminary injunctive relief.

CONCLUSION

Having made "a realistic appraisal of the total circumstances to determine whether the prospect of enforcement of the statute is 'chimerical' . . . 'concrete'," and determined that they are concrete, the Court will not place the plaintiffs "between the Scylla of intentionally flouting state law and the Charybdis of forgoing what (they believe) to be Constitutionally protected activity in order to avoid becoming enmeshed in a criminal proceeding." To require plaintiffs to await overt prosecutorial action against them is contrary to the teachings of *Epperson* v. *Arkansas,* supra, and *Pierce* v. *Society of Sisters,* which hold that where the clear terms of a statute unmistakably threaten First Amendment rights, an attack on the statute is ripe.

The Court recognizes the gravity of injunctive relief, even temporary, directed at state officials responsible for enforcing the law, and that such relief can be justified only where "exceptional circumstances" exist. Given the apparent overbreadth problems of Section 263.15 in its coverage of nonobscene expression, the fact that *Show Me!* may be fully protected by the First Amendment, the irreparable harm to First and Fourteenth Amendment rights by the removal of *Show Me!* from the marketplace, and the concrete economic injury to the plaintiffs, the Court finds the "circumstances" of this case to be "exceptional."

Defendants are, therefore, enjoined *pendente lite* from enforcing Section 263.15 of the Penal Law of New York against plaintiffs, their officers, employees, agents, customers, distributors, or customers of distributors, with respect to the publication, promotion, advertising, display, sale, or distribution of the book entitled *Show Me!* published by St. Martin's Press, Inc.

Settle order on Notice.
Dated: November 28, 1977.

WILLIAM PINKUS, DBA ROSSLYN NEWS COMPANY v. UNITED STATES
436 U.S. 293 (1978)

Mr. Chief Justice Burger delivered the opinion of the court.

We granted certiorari in this case to decide whether the court's instructions in a trial for mailing obscene materials prior to 1973, and therefore tried under the *Roth-Memoirs* standards, could properly include children and sensitive persons within the definition of the community by whose standards obscenity is to be judged. We are also asked to determine whether the evidence supported a charge that members of deviant sexual groups may be considered in determining whether the materials appealed to prurient interest in sex; whether a charge of pandering was proper in light of the evidence; and whether comparison evidence proffered by petitioner should have been admitted on the issue of contemporary community standards.

Petitioner was convicted after a jury trial in United States District Court on 11 counts, charging that he had mailed obscene materials and advertising brochures for obscene materials in violation of 18 U.S.C. Section 1461. On appeal, his conviction was reversed on the grounds that the instructions to the jury defining obscenity had been cast under the standards established in *Miller v. California*, although the offenses charged occurred in 1971 when the standards announced in *Roth v. United States*, and particularized in *Memoirs v. Massachusetts*, were applicable. Accordingly, the case was remanded to the District Court for a new trial under the standards controlling in 1971.

On retrial in 1976, petitioner was again convicted on the same 11 counts. He was sentenced to terms of four years imprisonment on each count, the terms to be served concurrently, and fined $500 on each count, for a total fine of $5,500. The Court of Appeals affirmed.

I

The evidence presented by the government in its case in chief consisted of materials mailed by the petitioner accompanied by a stipulation of facts which, among other things, recited that petitioner, knowing the contents of the mailings, had "voluntarily and intentionally" used the mails on 11 occasions to deliver brochures illustrating sex books, magazines, and films, and to deliver a sex magazine (one count) and a sex film (one count), with the intention that these were for the personal use of the recipients. From the stipulation and the record, it appears undisputed that the recipients were adults who resided both within and without the State of California. Because of the basis of our disposition of this case, it is unneccessary for us to review the contents of the exhibits in detail.

The defense consisted of expert testimony and surveys offered to demonstrate that the materials did not appeal to prurient interest, were not in conflict with community standards, and had redeeming social value. Two films were proffered by the defense for the stated purpose of demonstrating that comparable material had received wide box office acceptance, thus demonstrating the indicted materials were not obscene and complied with community standards.

As a rebuttal witness, the government presented an expert who testified as to what some of the exhibits depicted and that in his opinion they appealed to the prurient interest of the average person and to that of members of particular deviant groups.

II

In this Court as in the Court of Appeals, petitioner challenges four parts of the jury instructions and the trial court's rejection of the comparison films.

A. Instruction as to Children

Petitioner challenges that part of the jury instruction which read:

> "In determining community standards, you are to consider the community as a whole, young and old, educated and uneducated, the religious and the irreligious, men, women, and children, from all walks of life."

The Court of Appeals concluded that the inclusion of children was "unneccessary" and that it would "prefer that children be excluded from the court's (jury) instruction until the Supreme Court clearly indicates that inclusion is proper." It correctly noted that this Court had been ambivalent on this point, having sustained the conviction in *Roth,* where the instruction included children, and having intimated later in *Ginzburg* v. *United States,* that it did not necessarily approve the inclusion of "children" as part of the community instruction.

Reviewing the charge as a whole under the traditional standard of review, cogent arguments can be made that the inclusion of children was harmless error, see *Hamling* v. *United states;* however, the courts, the bar, and the public are entitled to greater clarity than is offered by the ambiguous comment in *Ginzburg* on this score. Since this is a federal prosecution under an Act of Congress, we elect to take this occasion to make clear that children are not to be included for these purposes as part of the "community" as that term related to the "obscene materials" proscribed by 18 U.S.C. Section 1461.

Earlier in the same term in which *Roth* was decided, the Court had reversed a conviction under a state statute which made criminal the dissemination of a book "found to have a potentially deleterious effect on youth." (*Butler* v. *Michigan.*) The statute was invalidated because it's "incidence . . . is to reduce the adult population . . . to reading only what is fit for children. The instruction given here, when read as a whole, did not have an effect so drastic as the *Butler* statute. But it may well be that a jury conscientiously striving to define the relevant community of persons, the "average person," (*Smith* v. *United States*) by whose standards obscenity is to be judged would reach a much lower "average" when children are part of the equation than they would if they restricted their consideration to the effect of allegedly obscene materials on adults. There was no evidence that children were the intended recipients of the materials at issue here, or that petitioner had reason to know children were likely to receive the materials. Indeed, an affirmative representation was made that children were not involved in this case. We therefore conclude it was in error to instruct the jury that they were a part of the relevant community, and accordingly the conviction cannot stand.

B. Instruction as to Sensitive Persons

It does not follow, however, as petitioner contends, that the inclusion of "sensitive persons" in the charge advising the jury of whom the community consists was in error. The District Court's charge was:

> Thus the brochures, magazines, and film are not to be judged on the basis of your personal opinion. Nor are they to be judged by their effect on a particularly sensitive or insensitive person or group in the community. You are to judge these materials by the standard of the hypothetical average person in the community, but in determining this average standard you must include the sensitive and the insensitive, in other words, you must include everyone in the community."

Petitioner's reliance on passages from *Miller,* and *Smith* v. *United States,* for the proposition that inclusion of sensitive persons in the relevant community was in error is misplaced. In *Miller* we said,

> (T)he primary concern with requiring a jury to apply the standard of the "average person, applying contemporary community standards" is to be certain that, so far as material is not aimed at a deviant group, it will be judged by its impact on an average person, rather than a particularly susceptible or sensitive person—or indeed a totally insensitive one.

This statement was essentially repeated in *Smith.*

> (T)he Court has held that section 1461 embodies a requirement that local rather than national standards should be applied. *(Hamling* v. *United States.)* Similarly, obscenity is to be judged according to the average person in the community, rather than the most prudish or the most tolerant. *(Hamling* v. *United States, supra; Miller* v. *California, supra; Roth* v. *United States,* 354 U.S. 476 (1957).) Both of these substantive limitations are passed on to the jury in the form of instructions.

The point of these passages was to emphasize what was an issue central to *Roth,* that "judging obscenity by the effect of isolated passages upon the most susceptible persons, might well encompass material legitimately treating with sex, and so it must be rejected as unconstitutionally restrictive of the freedom of speech and press." But nothing in those opinions suggests that "sensitive" and "insensitive" persons, however defined, are to be excluded from the community as a whole for the purpose of deciding if materials are obscene. In the narrow and limited context of this case, the community includes all adults who comprise it, and a jury can consider them all in determining relevant community standards. The vice is in focusing upon the most susceptible or sensitive members when judging the obscenity of materials, not in including them alone with all others in the community.

Petitioner relies also on *Hamling* v. *United States,* to support his argument. Like *Miller* and *Smith, supra,* though, *Hamling* merely restated the by now familiar rule that jurors are not to base their decision about the materials on their "personal opinion, nor by its effect on a particularly sensitive or insensitive person or group." It is clear the trial court did not instruct the jury to focus on sensitive persons or groups. It explicitly said the jury should not use sensitive persons as a standard, and emphasized that in determining the "average person" standard the jury "must include the sensitive and the insensitive, in other words . . . everyone in the community."

The difficulty of framing charges in this area is well recognized. But the term "average" person as used in this charge means what it usually means, and is no less clear than "reasonable" person used for generations in other contexts. Cautionary instructions to avoid subjective personal and private views in determining community standards can do no more than tell the individual juror that in evaluating the hypothetical "average person" he is to determine the collective view of the community, as best as it can be done.

Simon E. Sobeloff, then Solicitor General, later Chief Judge of the United States Court of Appeals for the Fourth Circuit, very aptly stated the dilemma:

> Is the so-called definition of negligence really a definition? What could be fuzzier than the instruction to the jury that negligence is a failure to observe that care which would be observed by

a "reasonable man"—a chimerical creature conjured up to give an aura of definiteness where definiteness is not possible.

* * * * *

Every man is likely to think of himself as the happy exemplification of "the reasonable man;" and so the standard he adopts in order to fulfill the law's prescription will resemble himself, or what he thinks he is, or what he thinks he should be, even if he is not. All these shifts and variations of his personal norm will find reflection in the verdict. The whole business is necessarily equivocal. This we recognize, but we are reconciled to the impossibility of discovering any form of words that will ring with perfect clarity and be automatically self-executing. Alas, there is no magic push-button in this or in other branches of the law.

However one defines "sensitive" or "insensitive" persons, they are part of the community. The contention that the instruction was erroneous because it included sensitive persons is therefore without merit.

C. Instruction as to Deviant Groups

Challenge is made to the inclusion of "members of a deviant sexual group" in the charge which recited:

The first test to be applied in determining whether a given picture is obscene, is whether the predominant theme or purpose of the picture, when viewed as a whole and not part by part, and when considered in relation to the intended and probable recipients, is an appeal to the prurient interest of the average person of the community as a whole or the prurient interest of members of a deviant sexual group at the time of mailing.

* * * * *

In applying this test, the question involved is not how the picture now impresses the individual juror, but rather, considering the intended and probable recipients, how the picture would have impressed the average person, or a member of a deviant sexual group at the time they received the picture.

Examination of some of the materials could lead to the reasonable conclusion that their prurient appeal would be more acute to persons of deviant persuasions, but it is equally clear they were intended to arouse the prurient interest of any reader or observer. Nothing prevents a court from giving an instruction on prurient appeal to deviant sexual groups as part of an instruction pertaining to appeal to the average person when the evidence, as here, would support such a charge. Many of the exhibits depicted aberrant sexual activities. These depictions were generally provided along with or as a part of the materials which apparently were thought likely to appeal to the prurient interest in sex of non-deviant persons. One of the mailings even provided a list of deviant sexual groups which the recipient was asked to mark to indicate interest in receiving the type of materials thought appealing to that particular group.

Whether materials are obscene generally can be decided by viewing them; expert testimony is not necessary. But petitioner claims that to support an instruction on appeal to the prurient interest of deviants, the prosecution must come forward with evidence to guide the jury in its deliberations, since jurors cannot be presumed to know the reaction of such groups to stimuli as they would that of the average person. Concededly, in the past we have "reserve(d) judgment . . . on the extreme case . . . where contested materials are directed at such a bizarre deviant group that the experience of the trier of fact would be plainly inadequate to judge whether the material appeals to the (particular) prurient interest." But here we are not presented with that "extreme" case because the government did in fact present expert testimony on rebuttal which, when combined with the exhibits themselves, sufficiently guided the jury. This instruction, therefore, was acceptable.

D. Instruction on Pandering

Pandering is "the business of purveying texual or graphic matter openly advertised to appeal to the erotic interest of their customers." (*Ginzburg* v. *United States, supra,* at 467.) We have held, and reaffirmed, that to aid a jury in its determination of whether materials are obscene, the methods of their creation, promotion, or dissemination are relevant. In essence, the Court has considered motivation relevant to the ultimate evaluation if the prosecution offers evidence of motivation.

In this case the trial judge gave a pandering instruction to which the jury could advert if it found "this to be a close case" under the three part *Roth-Memoirs* test. This was not a so-called finding instruction which removed the jury's discretion; rather it permitted the jury to consider the touting descriptions along with the materials themselves to determine whether they were intended to appeal to the recipient's prurient interest in sex, whether they were "commercial exploitation of erotica—solely for the sake of their prurient appeal," (*Ginzburg,* supra, at 466) if indeed the evidence admitted of any other purpose. And while it is true the government offered no extensive evidence of the methods of production, editorial goals, if any, methods of operation, or means of delivery other than the mailings and the names, locations, and occupations of the recipients, the evidence was sufficient to trigger the *Ginzburg* pandering instruction.

E. Exclusion of Comparison Evidence

At trial petitioner proffered, and the trial judge rejected, two films which were said to have had considerable popular and commercial success when displayed in Los Angeles and elsewhere around the country. He proffered this assertedly comparable material as evidence that materials as explicit as his had secured community tolerance. Apparently the theory was that display of such movies had altered the level of community tolerance.

On appeal the Court of Appeals began an inquiry into whether the comparison evidence should have been admitted. It held that exclusion of the evidence was proper as to the printed materials; but it abandoned the inquiry when, in reliance on the so-called concurrent sentence doctrine, it concluded that even if the comparison evidence had been improperly excluded as to the count involving petitioner's film, the sentence would not be affected. It therefore exercised its discretion not to pass on the admissibility of the comparison evidence and hence did not review the conviction on the film count.

However, the sentences on the 11 counts were not in fact fully concurrent; petitioner's 11 prison terms of four years each were concurrent but the $500 fines on each of the counts were cumulative, totalling $5,500, so that a separate fine of $500 was imposed on the film count. Petitioner thus had at least a pecuniary interest in securing review of his conviction on each of the counts.

In light of our disposition of the case, the issue of admissibility of the comparison evidence is not before us and we leave it to the Court of Appeals to decide whether or to what extent such evidence is relevant to a jury's evaluation of community standards.

Accordingly, the case is remanded to the Court of Appeals for further consideration consistent with this opinion.

Reversed and remanded.

Mr. Justice Brennan, with whom Mr. Justice Stewart and Mr. Justice Marshall join.

I concur in the judgment reversing petitioner's conviction. However, because I adhere to the view that this statute is "clearly overbroad and unconstitutional on its face," I would not remand for further consideration, but rather with direction to dismiss the indictment.

Mr. Justice Stevens, concurring.

If the Court were prepared to re-examine this area of the law, I would vote to reverse this conviction with instruction to dismiss the indictment. But my views are not now the law. The opinion that the Chief Justice has written is faithful to the cases on which it relies. For that reason, and because a fifth vote is necessary to dispose this case, I join his opinion.

Mr. Justice Powell, dissenting.

Although I agree with the Court that in a federal prosecution the instruction as to children should not have been given, on the facts of this case I view the error as harmless beyond a reasonable doubt. I therefore would affirm the judgment of the Court of Appeals.

NOTE I

On remand from the decision of the United States Supreme Court immediately above, reversing conviction, the United States Court of Appeals, Ninth Circuit, heard the case of *United States* v. *Pinkus* and decided on August 11, 1978 that an obscenity defendant seeking to admit, as probative of community standards, materials comparable to that which is charged with being obscene must demonstrate reasonable resemblance between proffered evidence and allegedly obscene material, and must establish a reasonable degree of community acceptance of proffered materials. It concluded further that the trial judge has wide discretion in determining whether the defendant has satisfied this test. (4 Med. L. Rptr. 1349.)

Before Wright and Wallace, Circuit Judges, and Orrick, District Judge, Eugene A. Wright, Circuit Judge delivered the following opinion of the court.

The Supreme Court reversed and remanded, holding the jury instructions improper insofar as they permitted children to be included in the community by whose standards obscenity was to be judged. Portions of the charge relating to sensitive persons, deviant groups and pandering were approved.

The Supreme Court held also that we improperly invoked the concurrent sentence doctrine in declining to address the trial court's rejection of the defendant's offers of sexually explicit films, allegedly "comparable" to the charged film "No. 613," as evidence of community standards. Because there may be a new trial, and because this issue is likely to be raised again, we offer the following guidelines for the district court.

The admissibility of "comparables" in obscenity prosecutions has been a subject of confusion. "The defendant in an obscenity prosecution, just as a defendant in any other prosecution, is entitled to an opportunity to adduce relevant, competent evidence bearing on the issues to be tried." But there are foundational requirements for admissibility of such evidence that have evolved as logical indicia of its materiality and relevance.

We earlier explained that a defendant must meet a two-pronged test to establish that the proffered comparable materials are admissible as probative of community standards. First, there must be a reasonable resemblance between the proffered comparables and the allegedly obscene materials. Second, the proponent must establish a reasonable degree of community acceptance of the proffered comparables.

We held that the assertedly comparable films, "Deep Throat" and "The Devil in Miss Jones," satisfied the first prong of the *Jacobs* test because they bore resemblance to the film "No. 613." We did not decide whether the second prong had been satisfied, but that is another question.

Whether a foundational showing is sufficient to meet the second prong of the *Jacobs/Womack* test is a matter for the trial judge to determine as he has "wide discretion whether to permit the introduction" of comparable materials. We express no opinion as to whether the foundational showing made does or does not suffice.

Admittedly, this is a difficult area and the standards are ill-defined. "Decisions regarding admissibility require application of the balancing formula in the (Federal Rules of Evidence) an undertaking unmistakably committed to the discretion of the trial judge." On remand the trial court will exercise its discretion in deciding whether to admit the evidence as well as in deciding how much each comparable need be displayed to the jury.

Should the defendant be retried, he should be given opportunity to make the necessary showing. Preferably that could be done in a separate hearing outside the presence of the jury. The record should reflect with clarity the grounds for the trial court's ruling on the evidence.

The opinion is withdrawn and the cause is remanded to the district court. The mandate will issue now. (579 F.2d 1175 (CA9 1978).)

NOTE II

In a Tenth Circuit decision of the United States Court of Appeals on May 1, 1978, it was determined that evidence was ample for the jury to conclude that photographs in the case, portraying 10-and 11-year-old nude girls in suggestive poses and engaging in a variety of lewd acts, were obscene. The court concluded that the trial court did not err in instructing the jury that it could consider evidence of "pandering" in making a finding of obscenity, even though pandering was not charged in the indictment. The defendant's other contentions were held to be lacking in merit.

In a petition for ceriorari filed on May 26, 1978, questions presented were: 1. At the time of the defendant's alleged offense, did the law treat the photographs of the children differently from photographs of adults, assuming that the content of the photographs is otherwise similar? 2. Are materials in this case obscene or unlawful when considered against proper constitutional standards? 3. Was the defendant denied due process by the judge's "pandering" instruction, and was evidence sufficient to justify invocation of that doctrine? (*Dost* v. *U.S.*, 47 USLW 3053 (August 8, 1978)).

NOTE III

In contrast to the obscenity decision discussed above, the United States District Court in Massachusetts held that the First Amendment precludes public school boards from removing properly selected, non-obscene books from high school libraries because the board considers the theme and language to be offensive.

At issue in this case is the school board's decision to remove from the high school library an anthology of writings by adolescents entitled *Male and Female Under 18*. The action was prompted by a parent's objection to the language of one selection entitled "The City to a Young Girl." It was a poem written by a 15-year-old New York City high school student.

A group of high school students, parents, teachers, and librarians brought this suit seeking a court order requiring the anthology returned to the library. The school board defended its action by claiming an unconstrained authority to remove books from the shelves of the school library. This authority derives from various state statutes giving it "general charge" over the public schools within its jurisdiction and directing it to purchase textbooks and other supplies for the schools. The board argued further that it was not required to purchase *Male and Female* for the library and therefore could remove it at will.

The court observed that because of the important interplay between First Amendment goals and the function of our schools, courts have occasionally found it necessary to intervene in the administration of school affairs. Nevertheless despite such intervention, local authorities are, and must continue to be, the principle policymakers in the public schools. It is the tension between these necessary administrative powers and the First Amendment rights of those within the school system that underlies the conflict in this case. (*Right to Read Defense Committee of Chelsea* v. *School Committee of Chelsea*, 47 USLW 2053 (August 1, 1978)).

Tauro, District Judge, delivered the following opinion of the court.

At issue is the decision by a majority of the Chelsea School Committee (Committee) to bar from the High School Library an anthology of writings by adolescents entitled "Male and Female Under 18." The Committee's action was prompted by a Chelsea parent's objection to the language in one selection, "The City to a Young Girl" (City), a poem written by a fifteen year old New York City high school student.

The Supreme Court has commented that "(t)he vigilant protection of constitutional freedoms is nowhere more vital than in the community of American schools." The fundamental notion underlying the First Amendment is that citizens, free to speak and hear, will be able to form judgments concerning matters affecting their lives, independent of any governmental suasion or propaganda. Consistent with that noble purpose, a school should be a readily accessible warehouse of ideas.

Recognizing the important interplay between First Amendment goals and the function of our schools, courts have occasionally found it necessary to intervene in the administration of school affairs. It has been declared unconstitutional for a state to forbid instruction, other than in the English language, to students below the eighth grade, and to prohibit the teaching of evolution in public schools.

It is clear despite such intervention, however, that local authorities are, and must continue to be, the principal policy makers in the public schools. School committees require a flexible and comprehensive set of powers to discharge the challenging tasks that confront them.

It is the tension between these necessary administrative powers and the First Amendment rights of those within the school system that underlies the conflict in this case. Clearly, a school committee can determine what books will go into a library and, indeed, if there will be a library at all. But the question presented here is whether a school committee has the same degree of discretion to order a book removed from a library.

Here, there is no evidence that the challenged anthology is obsolete. Indeed, there was ample evidence to support the plaintiffs' assertion that the work is relevant to a number of courses taught at Chelsea High School. No contention has been made that the book was improperly selected, insofar as

Chelsea procurement regulations were concerned. Despite their continuing objection to the language employed, defendants do not now contend the work is obscene. Limitations of resources such as money and shelf space are not factors here. The book has already been purchased and paid for.

The library is "a mighty resource in the marketplace of ideas." There a student can literally explore the unknown, and discover areas of interest and thought not covered by the prescribed curriculum. The student who discovers the magic of the library is on the way to a life-long experience of self-education and enrichment. That student learns that a library is a place to test or expand upon ideas presented to him, in or out of the classroom.

The most effective antidote to the poison of mindless orthodoxy is ready access to a broad sweep of ideas and philosophies. There is no danger of such exposure. The danger is in mind control. The Committee's ban of the anthology *Male & Female* is enjoined.

An order will issue. *(Right to Read Defense Com. v. School Com.,* 454 F. Supp. 703 (1978).)

Chapter V

Public Access to the Media

Section 1

The Fairness Doctrine and Equal Protection

Daniel M. Rohrer

INTRODUCTION

The question of whether broadcasting stations are to be considered common carriers has been resolved by the courts in the negative. Consequently they are not required to "permit broadcasting by whoever comes to (their) microphones" (*McIntire* v. *Wm. Penn Broadcasting Co.*, 151 F.2d 597 (1945)). It is for this reason that a licensee may refuse to sell time for products or services it finds objectionable or for copy it considers in poor taste. Furthermore, a licensee may refuse to do business with parties whose credit is unacceptable or who otherwise fails to measure up to reasonable business standards.[1]

It was not until 1973 that a court decision made the final determination as to whether stations would be allowed to refuse to sell time for opinion or editorial advertising. That issue was decided in favor of the broadcasters in the U.S. Supreme Court decision: *CBS* v. *DNC*, 412 U.S. 94 (1973).

This decision does not comprise a blanket rule, however, for stations may not refuse to sell time to a political candidate in response to a valid equal opportunities request arising from Section 315 of the Communications Act of 1934. This section provides facilities for candidates for public office. It states that: "If any licensee shall permit any person who is a legally qualified candidate for any public office to use a broadcasting station, he shall afford equal opportunities to all other such candidates for that office in the use of such broadcasting station: *provided*, that such licensee shall have no power of censorship over the material broadcast under the provisions of this section. No obligation is hereby imposed upon any licensee to allow the use of its station by any such candidate."[2]

Secondly, antitrust laws create a legal ban on station refusal to advertise if the refusal is part of a conspiracy to restrain or monopolize trade. According to the Communications Act of 1934: "All laws of the United States relating to unlawful restraints and monopolies and to combinations, contracts, or agreements in restraint of trade are hereby declared to be applicable to the manufacture and sale of and to trade in radio apparatus and devices entering into or affecting interstate or foreign commerce and to interstate or foreign radio communications."[3]

In this respect stations may place geographical limits upon the advertisements and commercials they sell, but such limits may not be placed under any agreement or understanding with other stations or local advertisers. Stations may not participate in any actions or decisions which may tend "to restrain and inhibit trade and competition."[4]

422 Public Access to the Media

At the outset this section will attempt a brief overview of the Fairness Doctrine, and then distinguish it from both the advertising and print media.

FAIRNESS DOCTRINE

The FCC is charged with ensuring that holders of its broadcast licenses operate "in the public interest."[5] Consequently: "The Commission's interpretation of this provision requires these licensees to devote a reasonable amount of broadcast time to contrasting viewpoints on controversial issues of public importance."[6] The Commission is prohibited by Section 326 of the Communications Act from censoring broadcast material, and it does not attempt to direct broadcasters in the selection or presentation of specific programming.

However, under the Fairness Doctrine, if a station presents one side of a controversial issue of public importance it must afford reasonable opportunity for the presentation of contrasting views. This policy does not require that "equal time" be afforded for each side, as would be the case if a political candidate appeared on the air during his campaign. Instead, the broadcast licensee has an affirmative duty to encourage and implement the broadcast of contrasting views in its overall programming which includes statements or actions reported on news programs.

This objective is based upon the principle that: "Freedom of speech on the radio must be broad enough to provide . . . equal opportunity for the presentation to the public of all sides . . . of important public questions, fairly, objectively, and without bias." (*Mayflower Broadcasting Co.*, 8 FCC 333, 340 (1940).)

Therefore, if anyone licensed to operate a radio broadcasting station shall permit any person who is a legally qualified candidate for public office to broadcast over such station, he shall "afford equal opportunities" to all other such candidates for that office and "shall have no power of censorship" over the material broadcast under this section. Under these conditions such a licensee may not delete material from a candidate's radio speech on the ground that such material may be defamatory because, regardless of state law, such a licensee is not liable for defamatory statements made in a speech broadcast over his station by a candidate for public office. (*Farmers Educational & Cooperative Union of America, North Dakota Division* v. *WDAY, Inc.*, 360 U.S. 525 (1959).)

The FCC has for many years imposed on broadcasters a Fairness Doctrine requiring that public issues be presented by broadcasters and that each side of those issues be given fair coverage. The Fairness Doctrine began shortly after the Federal Radio Commission was established to allocate frequencies among competing applicants in the public interest, and insofar as there is an affirmative obligation of the broadcaster to see that both sides are presented, the personal attack doctrine and regulations do not differ from the Fairness Doctrine. (*Red Lion Broadcasting Co., et al.* v. *FCC et al.*, 395 U.S. 367 (1969).)

NEWSPAPER EXCEPTION

The limitation on air waves is a crucial element in this decision for no such requirement is placed upon the publishers of printed materials. (Poughkeepsie Buying Service, Inc. v. *Poughkeepsie Newspaper, Inc.*, 205 Misc. 982, 131 NYS2d 515 (1954): *Miami Herald Publishing Company* v. *Tornillo*, 418 U.S. 241 (1974).)

In the *Poughkeepsie* case, the court concluded that the refusal to maintain trade relations with any individual is an inherent right which every person may exercise lawfully, for reasons he feels are sufficient, or for no reasons whatever. It is immaterial whether such refusal is based upon reason or is a result of mere caprice (emotion), prejudices, or malice. The court decided that the publication and distribution of newspapers is a private business and newspaper publishers lawfully conducting their business have the right to determine the policy they will pursue and the persons with whom they will deal (*op. cit.*).

Because newspaper publishers are private and limited air waves are public, the court has distinguished between the opportunities that must be made available by each. Broadcasters must provide equal time and newspaper publishers are not required to do so. In keeping with this principle the court pointed out in *Miami Herald* that even if a newspaper would face no additional costs to comply with the statute and would not be forced to forgo publication of news or opinion by the inclusion of a reply, the statute still fails to clear the First Amendment's barriers because of its intrusion into the function of editors in choosing what material goes into a newspaper and in deciding on the size and content of the paper and the treatment of public issues and officials (*op. cit.*). There are, however, exceptions to this rule.

The first instance in which a newspaper may be obligated to provide advertising space involves the question of equal protection which it may impose upon itself. For example, a corporation owning and publishing a newspaper is considered a quasi public corporation which must treat all advertisers fairly and without discrimination. Furthermore, fraudulent conspiracy or furthering an unlawful monopoly are considered impermissible infringements upon the intent of the First Amendment. (*Poughkeepsie, op. cit.*)

A second exception to the right of the press to deny differing points of view lies in the area of responses to defamation on the part of the publication. For example, Benno C. Schmidt, Jr., Professor of Law at Columbia Law School, suggests that the *Miami Herald* decision should not be a bar to the "mandatory publication of retractions where defamation has been established."[7]

A third exception to the immunity of the press from government regulation has further been suggested by Schmidt. He goes on to suggest that the application of access obligations to "commercial advertising where a medium has accepted other ads dealing with the same activity," where the newspaper cannot claim that its refusal to take an advertisement reflects disapproval of the advertisement or the underlying activity, should likewise not be barred by the *Miami Herald* decision.[8]

ADVERTISING EXCEPTION

In order for the advertising exception of the Fairness Doctrine requirements to take effect, it is necessary to demonstrate that a commercial rather than a political issue is at stake. This dichotomy is clarified in the case of *Georgia Power Project* v. *FCC*, 3 Med. L. Rptr. 1299, 559 F.2d 237 (CA 5, 1977). In this case the court found that the Federal Communications Commission did not act arbitrarily and capriciously in ruling that a television broadcast licensee was not unreasonable in determining that its presentation of an electric power company advertisement did not advocate directly and specifically a rate increase, and thus did not trigger the Fairness Doctrine requirement of affording reasonable opportunity for the presentation of opposing viewpoints.

This case involves a petition to review the FCC decision which held that a broadcast licensee acted reasonably in determining that the electric power company advertisements did not present arguments on one side of a rate increase controversy. Thus it did not require Fairness Doctrine obligations. The petition for review is denied, and the FCC action is affirmed in this appeal.

A second case which distinguishes advertising from the Fairness Doctrine is that of *National Citizens Committee for Broadcasting* v. *FCC* (3 Med. L. Rptr. 1273, 567 F.2d 1095 (CADC, 1977)). In this case it is evident that the FCC did not act arbitrarily and capriciously in deciding to exclude broadcast of standard product commercials from the scope of the Fairness Doctrine. Indeed, far from denying equal protection under the law, it is understood, recognized, and accepted that FCC determination that application of the Fairness Doctrine to such commercials does not enhance presentation of all viewpoints on controversial issues of public importance. Furthermore it is evident that FCC enforcement of Fairness Doctrine obligations for commercial advertisements only decreases broadcasters' attention to other aspects of the doctrine. This principle will become axiomatic upon a reading of the text of the case in the section which follows.

Advertisement exceptions are not limited to the area of the print media alone for Judge Bazelon has held that the Cigarette Labeling Act of 1965 does not constitute congressional pre-emption of the field of regulation addressed to the health problem posed by cigarette smoking, and therefore does not deny FCC authority to require radio and television stations which carry cigarette advertising to devote significant amounts of broadcast time to presenting a case against cigarette smoking. The Court also held that the cigarette ruling did not violate the First Amendment. (*Banzhaf, III* v. *FCC*, 405 F.2d 1082 (CA 2, 1968).)

It would seem reasonable to conclude from the distinguished decision and opinion in this case that when the limited air waves make use of commercials and advertisements which are against public policy, there is a greater burden to redeem themselves by making available through whatever means possible an equal representation of the other side of whatever position is being presented.

CONCLUSION

It is likewise possible that a given class of commercials will be banned from television and radio altogether, as has been the case with alcohol. The advertising of hard liquor on television and radio does not appear to justify the detriment its consumption seems to have on the individual and society. As a result the National Association of Broadcasters has determined that restricting its promotion on television does not violate the First Amendment.

Consequently, commercials may be curtailed or compensated for by an order from the Federal Trade Commission or the FCC respectively, the National Association of Broadcasters, the courts, Congress, and ultimately public opinion, when such protection of the public appears justified.

In the end, it comes down to what seems beneficial to society and the individual. When it is perceived that both are being harmed, there is no question that the First Amendment can withstand the application of the Balancng Standard in order to compensate for the deleterious effects that may result from advertising harmful products.

In other words, the First Amendment is asked to consider the merits of the harm that is being felt on both sides. There is a strong presumption in American society to place considerable weight upon utilitarian values, upon aesthetic appeal, and upon religious and cultural mores as well. There is also a conflicting presumption in favor of capitalism and free enterprise.

When any of these interests come into conflict with each other, the First Amendment finds itself in a dilemma. The only answer to this dilemma is a universal standard which will be flexible enough to adapt to changing circumstances, yet substantial enough to be delimited clearly. Such a standard can be neither vague nor broad, and it must remain consistent with the ideals of the American public.

Forty-five years after the passage of the Federal Communications Act of 1934, it is possible that a single, uniform standard of regulation may be found. It is one of deregulation. It was learned in *National Citizens Committee for Broadcasting* v. *FCC, supra*, that the FCC had decided to withdraw from applying the Fairness Doctrine to the broadcast of commercial advertisements, and that such a decision did not violate the First Amendment. Indeed the Court said that invoking the First Amendment in this context may even have the opposite effect from encouraging speech. The Court noted that broadcasters are discouraged from presenting messages which trigger Fairness Doctrine obligations. The Court upheld the FCC decision to reverse its prior policy, and to withhold application of the Fairness Doctrine to the broadcast of commercials.

A second example of self-regulation rather than FCC regulation is found in the decision of *Kuczo* v. *Western Connecticut Broadcasting*, 566 F.2d 384 (CA 2, 1977). Consistent with the case of *Lehman* v. *Shaker Heights* (see Chapter 2), the Court held that radio stations' censorship of mayoral candidates' political advertisements, in violation of Section 315(a) of the Communications Act and for which the FCC initiated license revocation proceedings and ultimately imposed $10,000 forfeiture against the stations' licensee, is not governmental action subject to the First Amendment. Thus two candidates who were unsuccessful in their efforts to become mayor of Stamford, Connecticut, were just as unsuccessful on the legal front as well. The U.S. Court of Appeals for the Second Circuit rejects their argument that a radio station's censorship of their paid political advertisements violated their First Amendment rights. The Court concluded that Western's action was not governmental, and that its holding is a narrow one.

One way of broadening the Court's decision, while at the same time adopting a single, uniform standard for regulation of the electronic media, would be to eliminate the FCC altogether. Such an action would substantially reduce federal independent regulatory agency control over the private domestic economy in the U.S. Apparently the House communications subcommittee is serious about taking such action.

In a 217-page bill, which the subcommittee completed and proposed in June, 1978, it recommended replacing the seven-member FCC with a five-member agency called the Communications Regulatory Commission, with each member to serve a single ten-year term rather than the present renewable seven-year term. (HR 13015.)

Until now, Congress and the FCC have opposed deregulation due to the scarcity of television licenses, which virtually guaranteed a limited number of viewpoints being heard, and almost ensured profit to the broadcasters holding such licenses. Thus the FCC felt the public was entitled to rules requiring certain types of programs.

This bill, however, would free all radio stations from having to offer news and public affairs programs; reduce considerably the amount of public affairs coverage required of TV stations; eliminate the "equal time" and "Fairness Doctrine" rights to reply; create a lottery for assigning any new TV and radio frequencies, rather than judging applicants on broadcast experience and financial backing; extend all radio and television licenses, which currently run for three years, to five years, renewable for another five, and then make the owner's license permanent unless he has repeatedly violated the minimal remaining laws; and let market forces solve problems arising from stations offending a substantial number of people through blatant disregard of their interests.

Such market forces would also have to solve any problem of ensuring balanced discussions of controversial issues that the Fairness Doctrine has served to protect in the past. Thus, as it once did, the First Amendment would reflect a limitation upon federal power, leaving the right to enforce restrictions of speech to the states. (See *Dennis v. United States*, 341 U.S. 494, 521–522 (1951).)

NOTES

[1] *Guide to FCC Broadcast Rules, Regulations, and Policies* (Washington, D.C.: National Association of Broadcasters, 1977), p. 4–17.
[2] *Communications Act of 1934* (Washington, D.C.: U.S. Government Printing Office, 1971), . 51.
[3] Ibid. p. 50, Section 313.
[4] *Legal Guide to FCC Rules, op. cit.*
[5] *Communications Act of 1934*, 47 U.S.C. Section 307(a) (1970).
[6] Ira Mark Ellman, "And Now a Word Against Our Sponsor: Extending the FCC's Fairness Doctrine to Advertising," 60 *Cal.LR* 1416 (1972).
[7] Benno C. Schmidt, Jr., *Freedom of the Press v. Public Access* (New York: Praeger, 1976), p. 13.
[8] Ibid.

Section 2

Cases and Hearings

POUGHKEEPSIE BUYING SERVICE, INC. v. POUGHKEEPSIE
NEWSPAPERS, INC.

205 Misc. 982, 131 N.Y.S.2d 515 (1954)

Eager, J.

This is a motion to dismiss the complaint herein upon the ground that it fails to state facts sufficient to constitute a cause of action. The action is by a merchant, who alleges he conducts two retail stores in the city of Poughkeepsie, N.Y., and is brought against a publisher of a Poughkeepsie daily newspaper. The complaint alleges that the newspaper in Poughkeepsie and is known as the *Poughkeepsie New Yorker,* and that, by reason of its large circulation and high reputation, it is "the dominant advertising medium in the entire area of its publication." It is further alleged that the defendant refuses, because of the persuasion and coercion of local merchants in competition with plaintiff, to publish advertising of the plaintiff in the defendant's newspaper and that, as a result, the plaintiff's business has been seriously reduced and such refusal has caused and will continue to cause irreparable damage to plaintiff's business. Further alleging that plaintiff has no adequate remedy at law, injunctive relief is demanded, namely, judgment directing the defendant to accept and publish plaintiff's advertising on payment of the usual charges of the defendant.

To dispose of the motion, the court must decide whether a newspaper publisher may be required to publish proper advertising matter upon the tender of the usual charge therefore or whether such publisher is free to contract and deal with whom he pleases. There are no New York decisions in point. The holding of courts in other States is summarized in a note in Volume 87 of *American Law Reports* at page 979 as follows:—"With the exception of one case, *Uhlman* v. *Sherman,* it has been uniformly held in the few cases which have considered the question that the business of publishing a newspaper is a strictly private enterprise, as distinguished from a business affected with a public interest, and that its publisher is under no legal obligation to sell advertising to all who may apply for it."

The plaintiff contends that this court should reject the majority view and adopt the reasoning laid down by the Ohio decision of *Uhlman* v. *Sherman.* It was there held that the newspaper business was clothed with a public interest and that a corporation owning and publishing a newspaper was in the class of a quasi-public corporation bound to treat all advertisers fairly and without discrimination. It was further there specifically held that a newspaper publisher, having advertising space to sell, had no right to discriminate against a local merchant, who, in his application for advertising, complies with the law and all reasonable rules of the publisher, and tenders the regular and ordinary fee charged therefore by the paper. Courts in other States have, however, expressly refused to follow this Ohio decision.

This court has also reached the conclusion that the rationale of said Ohio decision is not to be followed in this State in that it is contrary to general and fundamental doctrine laid down in our decisional law. For instance, we find decisions here, though not in point, in which it has been generally held that the publication and distribution of newspapers is a private business and that newspaper publishers lawfully conducting their business have the right to determine the policy they will pursue therein and the persons with whom they will deal. And it is said to be "the well-settled law of this

State the refusal to maintain trade relations with any individual is an inherent right which every person may exercise lawfully, for reasons he deems sufficient or for no reasons whatever, and it is immaterial whether such refusal is based upon reason or is the result of mere caprice, prejudice, or malice. It is a part of the liberty of action which the Constitutions, state and federal, guarantee to the citizen." *(Locker v. American Tobacco Co.)* There are limitations to this inherent right, but such limitations must be found either in firmly established common law principles or in statutory regulations enacted pursuant to the police power for the public good. It has been ably pointed out that there was no rule at common law, similar to the rules applicable to common carriers and inns, whereby a newspaper was forbidden to discriminate between customers. And there are no pertinent statutory regulations in this State. It may be that the legislature has the right to reasonably regulate the newspaper business, but the fact that it has not seen fit to do so does not confer power upon the courts to impose rules for the conduct of such business.

This court holds, therefore, that, in this State, the newspaper business is in the nature of a private enterprise and that, in the absence of valid statutory regulation to the contrary, the publishers of a newspaper have the general right either to publish or reject a commercial advertisement tendered to them. Their reasons for rejecting a proposed advertisement are immaterial, assuming, of course, there are absent factual allegations connecting them with a duly pleaded fraudulent conspiracy or with furthering an unlawful monopoly. There are no such allegations in this case.

The complaint is dismissed. Submit order on notice.

MIAMI HERALD PUBLISHING CO. v. *TORNILLO*
418 U.S. 241 (1974)

After the appellant newspaper had refused to print the appellee's replies to editorials critical of the appellee's candidacy for state office, action was brought for declaratory and injunction relief and for damages arising from the newspaper's refusal, based on Florida's "right of reply" statute that grants a political candidate a right to equal space to answer criticism and attacks on his record by a newspaper, and making it a misdemeanor for the newspaper to fail to comply. The Circuit Court, Dade County, entered judgment holding the statute unconstitutional and the plaintiff appealed. The Florida Supreme Court, reversed and remanded, holding that the statute did not violate constitutional guarantees, and that civil remedies, including damages, were available. Upon appeal by the newspaper, the U.S. Supreme Court held that the Florida statute, requiring newspapers which assail the character of political candidates to afford free space to a candidate for reply, is unconstitutional as a violation of the First Amendment's guarantee of a free press.

Mr. Chief Justice Burger delivered the opinion of the Court.

The issue in this case is whether a state statute granting a political candidate a right to equal space to reply to criticism and attacks on his record by a newspaper, violates the guarantees of a free press.

The challenged statute creates a right to reply to press criticism of a candidate for nomination or election. The statute was enacted in 1913 and this is only the second recorded case decided under its provisions.

Appellant contends that statute is void on its face because it purports to regulate the content of a newspaper in violation of the First Amendment. Alternatively it is urged that the statute is void for vagueness since no editor could know exactly what words would call the statute into operation. It is also contended that the statute fails to distinguish between critical comment which is and is not defamatory.

The appellee and supporting advocates of an enforceable right of access to the press vigorously contend that government has an obligation to ensure that a wide variety of views reach the public. The contentions of access proponents will be set out in some detail. It is urged that at the time the First Amendment to the Constitution was enacted, in 1791, as part of our Bill of Rights, the press was broadly representative of the people it was serving. While many of the newspapers were intensely partisan and narrow in their views, the press collectively presented a broad range of opinions to readers. Entry into publishing was inexpensive; pamphlets and books provided meaningful alternatives to the organized press for the expression of unpopular ideas and often treated events and expressed views not covered by conventional newspapers. A true marketplace of ideas existed in which there was relatively easy access to the channels of communication.

Access advocates submit that although newspapers of the present are superficially similar to those of 1791, the press of today is in reality very different from that known in the early years of our national existence. In the past half century a communications revolution has seen the introduction of radio and television into our lives, the promise of a global community through the use of communications satellites, and the spectre of a "wired" nation by means of an expanding cable television network with two-way capabilities. The printed press, it is said, has not escaped the effects of this revolution. Newspapers have become big business and there are far fewer of them to serve a larger literate population. Chains of newspapers, national newspapers, national wire and news services, and one-newspaper towns, are the dominant features of a press that has become noncompetitive and enormously powerful and influential in its capacity to manipulate popular opinion and change the course of events. Major metropolitan newspapers have collaborated to establish news services national in scope. Such national news organization provide syndicated "interpretative reporting" as well as syndicated features and commentary, all of which can serve as part of the new school of "advocacy journalism."

The elimination of competing newspapers in most of our large cities, and the concentration of control of media that results from the only newspaper being owned by the same interests which own a television station and a radio station, are important components of this trend toward concentration of control of outlets to inform the public.

The result of these vast changes has been to place in a few hands the power to inform the American people and shape public opinion. Much of the editorial opinion and commentary that is printed is that of syndicated columnists distributed nationwide and, as a result, we are told, on national and world issues there tends to be a homogeneity of editorial opinion, commentary, and interpretative analysis. The abuses of bias and manipulative reportage are, likewise, said to be the result of the vast accumulations of unreviewable power in the modern media empires. In effect, it is claimed, the public has lost any ability to respond or to contribute in a meaningful way to the debate on issues. The monopoly of the means of communication allows for little or no critical analysis of the media except in professional journals of very limited readership.

> This concentration of nationwide news organizations—like other large institutions—has grown increasingly remote from and unresponsive to the popular constituencies on which they depend and which depend on them."

The obvious solution, which was available to dissidents at an earlier time when entry into publishing was relatively inexpensive, today would be to have additional newspapers. But the same economic factors which have caused the disappearance of vast numbers of metropolitan newspapers, have made entry into the marketplace of ideas served by the print media almost impossible. It is urged that the claim of newspapers to be "surrogates for the public" carries with it a concomitant fiduciary obligation to account for that stewardship. From this premise it is reasoned that the only effective way to insure fairness and accuracy and to provide for some accountability is for government to take affirmative action. The First Amendment interest of the public in being informed is said to be in peril because the "marketplace of ideas" is today a monopoly controlled by the owners of the market.

Proponents of enforced access to the press take comfort from language in several of this Court's decisions which suggests that the First Amendment acts as a sword as well as a shield, that it imposes obligations on the owners of the press in addition to protecting the press from government regulation. In *Associated Press* v. *United States,* the Court, in rejecting the argument that the press is immune from the antitrust laws by virtue of the First Amendment, stated:

> The First Amendment, far from providing an argument against application of the Sherman Act, here provides powerful reasons to the contrary. That amendment rests on the assumption that the widest possible dissemination of information from diverse and antagonistic sources is essential to the welfare of the public, that a free press is a condition of free society. Surely a command that the government itself shall not impede the free flow of ideas does not afford nongovernmental combinations a refuge if they impose restraints upon that Constitutionally guaranteed freedom. Freedom to publish means freedom for all and not for some. Freedom to publish is guaranteed by the Constitution, but freedom to combine to keep others from publishing is not. Freedom of the press from governmental interference under the First Amendment does not sanction repression of that freedom by private interests. (Footnote omitted.)

In *New York Times Co.* v. *Sullivan*, the Court spoke of "a profound national commitment to the principle that debate on public issues should be uninhibited, robust, and wide-open." It is argued that the "uninhibited, robust" debate is not "wide-open" but open only to a monopoly in control of the press. Appellee cites the plurality opinion in *Rosenbloom* v. *Metromedia, Inc.*, which he suggests seemed to invite experimentation by the States in right to access regulation of the press.

Access advocates note that Mr. Justice Douglas a decade ago expressed his deep concern regarding the effects of newspaper monopolies:

> Where one paper has a monopoly in an area, it seldom presents two sides of an issue. It too often hammers away on one ideological and political line using its monopoly position not to educate people, not to promote debate, but to inculcate its readers with one philosophy, one attitude—and to make money . . . The newspaper that gives a variety of views and news that is not slanted or contrived are few indeed. And the problem promises to get worse . . . .

They also claim the qualified support of Professor Thomas I. Emerson, who has written that "(a) limited right of access to the press can be safely enforced," although he believes that "(g)overnment measures to encourage a multiplicity of outlets, rather than compelling a few outlets to represent everybody, seems a preferable course of action."

However much validity may be found in these arguments, at each point the implementation of a remedy such as an enforceable right of access necessarily calls for some mechanism either governmental or consensual. If it is governmental coercion, this at once brings about a confrontation with the express provisions of the First Amendment and the judicial gloss on that amendment developed over the year.

The Court foresaw the problems relating to government enforced access as early as its decision in *Associated Press v. United States.* There it carefully contrasted the private "compulsion to print" called for by the Association's bylaws with the provisions of the District Court decree against appellants which "does not compel AP or its members to permit publication of anything which their 'reason' tells them should not be published." In *Branzburg v. Hayes* we emphasized that the case then before us "involves no intrusions upon speech and assembly, no prior restraint or restriction on what the press may publish, and no express or implied command that the press publish what it prefers to withhold." In *Columbia Broadcasting System, Inc. v. Democratic National Committee* the plurality opinion noted:

> The power of a privately owned newspaper to advance its own political, social, and economic views is bounded by only two factors: first, the acceptance of a sufficient number of readers—and hence advertisers—to assure financial success; and, second, the journalistic integrity of its editors and publishers.

An attitude strongly adverse to any attempt to extend a right of access to newspapers was echoed by several members of this Court in their separate opinions in that case. Recently, while approving a bar against employment advertising specifying "male" or "female" preference, the Court's opinion in *Pittsburgh Press Co. v. Pittsburgh Commission on Human Relations* took pains to limit its holding within narrow bounds:

> Nor, a *fortiori,* does our decision authorize any restriction whatever, whether of content or layout, on stories or commentary originated by Pittsburgh Press, its columnists, or its contributors. On the contrary, we reaffirm unequivocally the protection afforded to editorial judgment and to the free expression of views on these and other issues, however controversial.

Dissenting in *Pittsburgh Press,* Mr. Justice Stewart joined by Mr. Justice Douglas expressed the view that no "government agency—local, state, or federal—can tell a newspaper in advance what it can print and what it cannot."

We see that beginning with *Associated Press,* the Court has expressed sensitivity as to whether a restriction or requirement constituted the compulsion exerted by government on a newspaper to print that which it would not otherwise print. The clear implication has been that any such compulsion to publish that which " 'reason' tells them should not be published" is unconstitutional. A responsible press is an undoubtedly desirable goal, but press responsibility is not mandated by the Constitution and, like many other virtues, it cannot be legislated.

Appellee's argument that the Florida statute does not amount to a restriction of appellant's right to speak because "the statute in question here has not prevented the *Miami Herald* from saying anything it wished" begs the core question. Compelling editors or publishers to publish that which " 'reason' tells them should not be published" is what is at issue in this case. The Florida statute operates as a command in the same sense as a statute or regulation forbidding appellant from publishing specified matter. Governmental restraint on publishing need not fall into familiar or traditional patterns to be subject to Constitutional limitations on governmental powers. The Florida statute exacts a penalty on the basis of the content of a newspaper. The first phase of the penalty resulting from the compelled printing of a reply is exacted in terms of the cost in printing and composing time and materials and in taking up space that could be devoted to other material the newspaper may have preferred to print. It is correct, as appellee contends, that a newspaper is not subject to the finite technological limitations of time that confront a broadcaster but it is not correct to say that, as an economic reality, a newspaper can proceed to infinite expansion of its column space to accommodate the replies that a government agency determines or a statute commands the readers should have available.

Faced with the penalties that would accrue to any newspaper that published news or commentary arguably within the reach of the right of access statute, editors might well conclude that the safe course is to avoid controversy and that, under the operation of the Florida statute, political and electoral coverage would be blunted or reduced. Government enforced right of access inescapably "dampens the vigor and limits the variety of public debate." The Court, in *Mills* v. *Alabama,* stated:

> (T)here is practically universal agreement that a major purpose of (the First) Amendment was to protect the free discussion of governmental affairs. This of course includes discussion of candidates . . . .

Even if a newspaper would face no additional costs to comply with a compulsory access law and would not be forced to forego publication of news or opinion by the inclusion of a reply, the Florida statute fails to clear the barriers of the First Amendment because of its passive receptacle or conduit for news, comment, and advertising. The choice of material to go into a newspaper, and the decisions made as to limitations on the size of the paper, and content, and treatment of public issues and public officials—whether fair or unfair—constitutes the exercise of editorial control and judgment. It has yet to be demonstrated how governmental regulation of this crucial process can be exercised consistent with First Amendment guarantees of a free press as they have evolved to this time. Accordingly, the judgment of the Supreme Court of Florida is reversed.

It is so ordered.

Mr. Justice White, concurring.

The Court today holds that the First Amendment bars a State from requiring a newspaper to print the reply of a candidate for public office whose personal character has been criticized by that newspaper's editorials. According to our accepted jurisprudence, the First Amendment erects a virtually insurmountable barrier between government and the print media so far as government tampering, in advance of publication, with news and editorial content is concerned. A newspaper or magazine is not a public utility subject to "reasonable" governmental regulation in matters affecting the exercise of journalistic judgment as to what shall be printed. We have learned, and continue to learn, from what we view as the unhappy experiences of other nations where government has been allowed to meddle in the internal editorial affairs of newspapers. Regardless of how beneficient-sounding the purposes of controlling the press might be, we prefer "the power of reason as applied through public discussion" and remain intensely skeptical about those measures that would allow government to insinuate itself into the editorial rooms of this nation's press.

Whatever differences may exist about interpretations of the First Amendment, there is practically universal agreement that a major purpose of that Amendment was to protect the free discussion of governmental affairs. This of course includes discussions of candidates, structures, and forms of government, the manner in which government is operated or should be operated, and all such matters relating to political processes. The Constitution specifically selected the press . . . to play an important role in the discussion of public affairs. Thus the press serves and was designed to serve as a powerful antidote to any abuses of power by governmental officials and as a Constitutionally chosen means for keeping officials elected by the people responsible to all the people whom they were selected to serve. Suppression of the right of the press to praise or criticize governmental agents and to clamor and contend for or against change . . . muzzles one of the very agencies the Framers of our Constitution thoughtfully and deliberately selected to improve our society and keep it free.

Of course, the press is not always accurate, or even responsible, and may not present full and fair debate on important public issues. But the balance struck by the First Amendment with respect to the press is that society must take the risk that occasionally debate on vital matters will not be comprehensive and that all viewpoints may not be expressed. The press would be unlicensed because, in Jefferson's words, "(w)here the press is free, and every man able to read, all is safe." Any other accommodation—any other system that would supplant private control of the press with the heavy hand of government intrusion—would make the government the censor of what the people may read and know.

To justify this statute, Florida advances a concededly important interest of ensuring free and fair elections by means of an electorate informed about the issues. But prior compulsion by government in matters going to the very nerve center of a newspaper—the decision as to what copy will or will not be included in any given edition—collides with the First Amendment. Woven into the fabric of the First Amendment is the unexceptionable, but nonetheless timeless, sentiment that "liberty of the press is in peril as soon as the government tries to compel what is to go into a newspaper."

The Constitutionally obnoxious feature of Section 104.38 is not that the Florida legislature may also have placed a high premium on the protection of individual reputational interests; for, government certainly has "a pervasive and strong interest in preventing and redressing attacks upon reputation." Quite the contrary, this law runs afoul of the elementary First Amendment proposition that government may not force a newspaper to print copy which, in its journalistic discretion, it chooses to leave on the newsroom floor. Whatever power may reside in government to influence the publishing of certain narrowly circumscribed categories of material, we have never thought that the First Amendment permitted public officials to dictate to the press the contents of its news columns or the slant of its editorials.

But though a newspaper may publish without government censorship, it has never been entirely free from liability for what it chooses to print. Among other things, the press has not been wholly at liberty to publish falsehoods damaging to individual reputation. At least until today, we have cherished the average citizen's reputation interest enough to afford him a fair chance to vindicate himself in an action for libel characteristically provided by state law. He has been unable to force the press to tell his side of the story or to print a retraction, but he has had at least the opportunity to win a judgment if he can prove the falsity of the damaging publication, as well as a fair chance to recover reasonable damages for his injury.

Reaffirming the rule that the press cannot be forced to print an answer to a personal attack made by it, however, throws into stark relief the consequences of the new balance forged by the Court in the companion case also announced today. *Gertz* v. *Robert Welch, Inc.* goes far towards eviscertating the effectiveness of the ordinary libel action, which has long been the only potent response available to the private citizen libeled by the press. Under *Gertz,* the burden of proving liability is immeasurably increased, proving damages is made exceedingly more difficult, and vindicating reputation by merely proving falsehood and winning a judgment to that effect are wholly foreclosed. Needlessly, in my view, the Court trivializes and denigrates the interest in reputation the law has always afforded.

Of course, these two decisions do not mean that because government may not dictate what the press is to print, neither can it afford a remedy for libel in any form. *Gertz* itself leaves a putative remedy for libel intact, albeit in severely emaciated form; and the press certainly remains liable for knowing or reckless falsehoods under *New York Times* and its progeny, however improper an injunction against publication might be.

One need not think less of the First Amendment to sustain reasonable methods for allowing the average citizen to redeem a falsely tarnished reputation. Nor does one have to doubt the genuine decency, integrity, and good sense of the vast majority of professional journalists to support the right of any individual to have his day in court when he has been falsely maligned in the public press. The press is the servant, not the master, of the citizenry, and its freedom does not carry with it an unrestricted hunting license to prey on the ordinary citizen.

> In plain English, freedom carries with it responsibility even for the press; freedom of the press is not a freedom from responsibility for its exercise.
>
> . . . Without . . . a lively sense of responsibility a free press may readily become a powerful instrument of injustice.

To me it is a near absurdity to so deprecate individual dignity, as the Court does in *Gertz,* and to leave the people at the complete mercy of the press, at least in this stage of our history when the press, as the majority in this case so well documents, is steadily becoming more powerful and much less likely to be deterred by threats of libel suits.

Mr. Justice Brennan, with whom Mr. Justice Rehnquist joint, concurring.

I join the Court's opinion which, as I understand it, addresses only "right of reply" statutes and implies no view upon the Constitutionality of "retraction" statutes affording plaintiffs able to prove defamatory falsehoods a statutory action to require publication of a retraction.

NOTE

In 1978 the California Superior Court reaffirmed the position of earlier decisions which held more generally that newspapers are exempt from any obligation to accept advertisements for publication when they would prefer, for any reason, to reject them. Here it was determined that newspapers have no common law or statutory obligation to accept advertisements from producers and distributors of sexually explicit motion pictures, and failure of producers and distributors to allege or show that a given newspaper persuaded, or exerted pressure on, other newspapers to refuse to accept such advertisements warranted dismissal of their complaint, alleging the newspaper's tortious interference with prospective economic benefits.

The complaint was filed on behalf of two distributors, six producers, and an association of producers, distributors, and exhibitors of sexually explicit motion pictures. They have charged that for a period of 17 years they had contracted with the defendant, Times Mirror Company, to publish advertising by the plaintiffs. The plaintiffs allege that this refusal was malicious and for the sole purpose of interfering with their prospective economic benefits that would accrue from the anticipated patronage of persons attracted by the advertising. (*Adult Film Association of America* v. *Times Mirror Company*, — Cal. — (1978).)

BANZHAF, III v. *FEDERAL COMMUNICATIONS COMMISSION*
405 F.2d 1082 (1968)

Bazelon, Chief Judge.

In these appeals, we affirm a ruling of the Federal Communications Commission requiring radio and television stations which carry cigarette advertising to devote a significant amount of broadcast time to presenting the case against cigarette smoking. This holding rests on negative answers to the following principal questions:

I. whether in the Cigarette Labeling Act of 1965 Congress preempted the field of regulation addressed to the health problem posed by cigarette smoking so as to deny the FCC any authority it otherwise had to issue its cigarette ruling
II. if not so forbidden, whether the ruling is nonetheless unauthorized, either
   A. because the Commission has no authority to regulate broadcast content, or
   B. because any authority over program content which the Commission may have cannot support a ruling of this kind; and
III. if neither forbidden nor unauthorized, whether the ruling is unconstitutional, either
   A. because the First Amendment permits no regulation of program content, or
   B. because the cigarette ruling in particular violates the First Amendment.

The history of the cigarette ruling dates to December 1966, when citizen John F. Banzhaf, III asked WCBS-TV to provide free time in which anti-smokers might respond to the pro-smoking views he said were implicit in the cigarette commercials it broadcast. Although he cited several specific commercial messages, Banzhaf's target included

> all cigarette advertisements which, by their portrayals of youthful or virile looking or sophisticated persons enjoying cigarettes in interesting and exciting situations, deliberately seek to create the impression and present the point of view that smoking is socially acceptable and desirable, manly, and a necessary part of a rich full life.

He said this point of view raised one side of a "controversial issue of public importance" and concluded that under the FCC's Fairness Doctrine, WCBS was under obligation to "affirmatively endeavor to make (its) . . . facilities available for the expression of contrasting viewpoints held by responsible elements . . . ."

WCBS replied that it had broadcast several news and information programs presenting the facts about the smoking-health controversy, as well as five public service announcements of the American Cancer Society aired free of charge during recent months. On the basis of these broadcasts it was confident that "its coverage of the health ramifications of smoking has been fully consistent with the Fairness Doctrine." But it doubted in any event that "the Fairness Doctrine can properly be applied to commercial announcements solely and clearly aimed at selling products and services . . . ."

Thereupon, Banzhaf forwarded the correspondence to the Federal Communications Commission under cover of a complaint that the station was violating the Fairness Doctrine. And thereby hangs the following legal tale.

The Commission sustained the Banzhaf complaint. In a letter dated June 2, 1967, it agreed that the cited cigarette commercials "present the point of view that smoking is 'socially acceptable and desirable, manly, and a necessary part of a rich full life,' " and, as such, invoke the Fairness Doctrine. It said in part:

> We stress that our holding is limited to this product—cigarettes. Governmental and private reports and congressional action assert that normal use of this product can be a hazard to the health of millions of persons. The advertisements in question clearly promotes the use of a particular cigarette as attractive and enjoyable. Indeed, they understandably have no other purpose. We believe that a station which presents such advertisements has the duty of informing its audience of the other side of this controversial issue of public importance—that, however enjoyable, such smoking may be a hazard to the smoker's health.

The Commission refused, however, to require "equal time" for the anti-smoking position and emphasized that "the type of programming and the amount and nature of time to be afforded is a matter for the good faith, reasonable judgment of the licensee . . . ." But it directed stations which carry cigarette commercials to provide "a significant amount of time for the other viewpoint . . . ." And by way of illustration it suggested they might discharge their responsibilities by presenting "each week . . . a number of the public service announcements of the Amercian Cancer Society or HEW in this field."

In response to numerous petitions and requests for reconsideration, the Commission affirmed its ruling in a lengthy Memorandum Opinion. It rejected contentions that the Fairness Doctrine is unconstitutional and that the cigarette ruling is precluded by the Cigarette Labeling and Advertising Act of 1965. The opinion did make clear that cigarette advertising in general, not any particular commercials, necessarily conveys the controversial view that smoking is a good thing. But the Commission stressed again that its ruling was "limited to this product—cigarettes" and disclaimed any intention "to imply that any appeal to the Commission by a vocal minority will suffice to classify advertising of a product as controversial and of public importance." While defending its failure to provide interested persons an opportunity to be heard before issuing its ruling, the Commission emphasized that any procedural lapse was cured by its exhaustive consideration of the many petitions for review. Finally, it concluded that, "the specifics of the Fairness Doctrine" aside, its ruling was required by the public interest.

Subsequently, in response to a request for clarification, the Commission ruled that stations which carry cigarette advertising are under no obligation to provide the cigarette companies free time in which to respond to broadcast claims that smoking endangers health.

In this review proceeding, the Commission is challenged at virtually every point. Mr. Banzhaf complains that the anti-smoking forces should have been granted equal time. Petitioners Station WTRF-TV, the National Association of Broadcasters, The Tobacco Institute, and eight cigarette manufacturers (hereinafter "petitioners"), all of whose appeals have been consolidated, complain of almost everything else. They are supported by Intervenors CBS and NBC-ABC-WLLE, Inc. The Commission is supported by the interventions of the American Tuberculosis Association and the ubiquitous Mr. Banzhaf.

We turn now to the issues these legal armies present for our consideration.

I. *The Cigarette Labeling Act*

We are confronted at the outset by the contention that the Commission's action is precluded by the Federal Cigarette Labeling and Advertising Act of 1965. That Act requires cigarette manufacturers and importers to print on each pack the warning "Caution: Cigarette Smoking May Be Hazardous to Your Health" and provides that

> no statement relating to smoking and health shall be required in the advertising of any cigarettes the packages of which are labeled in conformity with the provisions of this Act.

Since the Commission's ruling does not require the inclusion of any "statement . . . in the advertising of any cigarettes," but rather directs stations which advertise cigarettes to present "the other side" each week, it does not violate the letter of the Act.

But petitioners contend that, though Congress said only "no statement shall be required- . . . in . . . advertising," it meant to forbid any regulation addressed to the smoking-health problem except the Federal Trade Commission's specifically exempted power to police false and misleading advertising. In support of this proposition, they refer us primarily to the Act's Declaration of Policy, in which Congress asserts a purpose to

> establish a comprehensive Federal program to deal with cigarette labeling and advertising with respect to any relationship between smoking and health, whereby—1) the public may be adequately informed that cigarette smoking may be hazardous to health by inclusion of a warning to that effect on each package of cigarettes; and 2) commerce and the national economy may be a) protected to the maximum extent consistent with this declared policy, and b) not impeded by diverse, nonuniform, and confusing cigarette labeling and advertising regulations with respect to any relationship between smoking and health.

From this declaration and from assorted snippets of legislative history, they conclude that Congress has definitively balanced the conflicting interests of the health of the public and the health of the economy and determined—in effect as a matter of law—that the public will be "adequately informed" on the smoking-and-health issue until July, 1969, without any further governmental requirements.

The Commission, on the other hand, thought its ruling implemented a congressional policy of promoting intensive smoker education during the life of the Act as an alternative to the "drastic step" of requiring warnings in every cigarette advertisement. Its opinion cites the express reliance in both House and Senate Reports on the anti-smoking campaigns of public and private groups as a reason for deferring stronger congressional action. And it notes that Congress itself appropriated $2 million to fund the extensive informational activities in this area of the Department of Health, Education, and Welfare.

This evidence does not establish unequivocally that Congress did not intend to rely exclusively on such noncoercive educational efforts to inform the public. Congress expressed no purpose in the Act of informing the public of anything except the bare fact that "cigarette smoking may be hazardous to health." Its prescribed warnings do that much and no more. They merely flash danger signals without either particularizing the danger of providing facts on which it may be appraised.

But the anti-smoking campaigns are scarcely so pervasive or so well-funded that additional information could be regarded as mere surfeit. Accordingly, if we are to adopt petitioners' analysis, we must conclude that Congress legislated to curtail the potential flow of information lest the public learn too much about the hazards of smoking for the good of the tobacco industry and the economy. We are loathe to impute such a purpose to Congress absent a clear expression. Where a controversial issue with potentially grave consequences is left to each individual to decide for himself, the need for an abundant and ready supply of relevant information is too obvious to need belaboring.

In the present case, we find no such clear expression of restrictive intent. On the contrary, there are positive indications that Congress's "comprehensive program" was directed at the relatively narrow specific issue of regulation of "cigarette labeling and advertising." The Act was in fact passed in response to a pending Federal Trade Commission rule which would have required warnings both on packages and in all advertising. Subjected to competing pressures and uncertain of the full extent of the health hazard, Congress apparently settled on half of the FTC's proposed loaf, shelved the other half for four years, and expressly disclaimed any intent to affect other FTC policies or powers. Nothing in the Act indicates that Congress had any intent at all with respect to other types of regulation by other agencies—much less that it specifically meant to foreclose all such regulation. If it meant to do anything so dramatic, it might reasonably be expected to have said so directly—especially where it was careful to include a section entitled "Pre-emption" specifically forbidding designated types of regulatory action.

In short, we think the Cigarette Labeling Act represents the balance drawn between the narrow purpose of warning the public "that cigarette smoking may be hazardous to health" and the interests of the economy. In that reckoning, the question of the public's need for information about the nature, extent, and certainty of the danger was left out of the scales, and so is left unaffected, except incidentally, by the result. Congress may reasonably have concluded that a warning on each pack was adequate warning. It surely did not think the warnings were themselves adequate information. And we find no sufficiently persuasive evidence that Congress hoped to impede the flow of adequate information for fear that, if the public knew all the facts, too many of them would stop smoking.

This relatively narrow reading of the Act is not in conflict with its declared objective of protecting commerce and the national economy against "diverse, nonuniform, and confusing cigarette labeling and advertising regulations with respect to any relationship between smoking and health. Congress patently did not want cigarette manufacturers harassed by conflicting affirmative requirements with respect to the content of their advertising. In addition, it evidently decided that the case against smoking was not yet so overwhelming as to warrant compelling the cigarette companies to dig their own graves by neutralizing their own advertising messages. Even if these policies implicitly pre-empt regulations of advertising substantially equivalent to the FTC's proposed required warnings, they do not exclude a single, uniform regulation of broadcasters designed to inform the public.

II. The Commission's Authority Under the Public Interest Standard of the Communications Act

A fundamental question, of course, is whether the Commission's ruling, though not expressly forbidden by statute, is within the scope of its delegated authority. The ruling originated in response to a "Fairness Doctrine" complaint and held that the Fairness Doctrine applied to cigarette advertising. But in its opinion affirming the ruling, the Commission also asserted that it "clearly has the authority to make this public interest ruling" under the public interest standard of the Communications Act and relied upon "the licensee's statutory obligation to operate in the public interest."

Last year in *Red Lion Broadcasting Co.* v. *FCC,* we upheld the Fairness Doctrine in the face of arguments that it was unauthorized and unconstitutional. Since then, in *Radio Television News Directors* v. *FCC,* the Seventh Circuit has held that the Commission's personal attack rules violate the First Amendment and, in so doing, has cast some doubt on the Constitutionality of the underlying Fairness Doctrine. These issues are not to be resolved by the Supreme Court.

In part for this reason, we do not think protracted discussion of the Fairness Doctrine will materially advance our inquiry. It is clear to us that, even if incorporated into the Fairness Doctrine, the ruling before us is to all intents a novel application. In only one instance has the Commission previously held the advertising of a consumer product subject to the rule that broadcasters' presentation of controversial public issues must be fair and balanced. The narrow issue presented by the facts of that case was whether a station in the temperance belt which advertised alcoholic beverages could, consistently with the principles now known as the Fairness Doctrine, refuse to accept antiliquor advertising from temperance groups. The case has not been followed in the 20 years since it was decided. It is not in any event a clear precedent for a ruling which instructs stations to broadcast opposition to their paid commercials regardless of whether opponents buy—or even request—such broadcast time. In addition, except for the personal attack rules struck down by the Seventh Circuit, we know of no case in which the Commission has so specifically defined the stations' duties under the Fairness Doctrine.

We also note that elsewhere the Commission has been hesitant to invoke the Fairness Doctrine where a controversial issue is raised only by implication. Finally, the Commission itself concluded that its main point would be lost if the legal debate concentrated too intensely on the "specifics of the Fairness Doctrine."

None of the novel aspects of the ruling, of course, precludes an extension of the Fairness Doctrine at this time. But the extension must, like the doctrine itself, find its authority in the public interest standard. Thus, whether the ruling is viewed as a new application of the Fairness Doctrine or as an independent public interest ruling, the ultimate question is the same. Moreover, in view of the Constitutional attack on the doctrine, the specific question of greatest long term importance may be whether the cigarette ruling can stand on its own feet.

In fact, we think the best statement of the Commission's holding and rationale is contained in the summary paragraph introducing the "Conclusions" section of its opinion.

There is, we believe, some tendency to miss the main point at issue by concentration on labels such as the specifics of the Fairness Doctrine or by conjuring up a parade of "horrible" extensions of the ruling. The ruling is really a simple and practical one, required by the public interest. The licensee, who has a duty "to operate in the public interest" is presenting commercials urging the consumption of a product whose normal use has been found by the Congress and the Government to represent a serious potential hazard to public health. Ordinarily the question presented would be how the carriage of such commercials is consistent with the obligation to operate in the public interest. In view of the legislative history of the Cigarette Labeling Act, that question is one reserved for judgment of the

Congress upon the basis of the studies and reports submitted to it . . . . But there is, we think, no question of the continuing obligation of a licensee who presents such commercials to devote a significant amount of time to informing his listeners of the other side of the matter—that however enjoyable smoking may be, it represents a habit which may cause or contribute to the earlier death of the user. This obligation stems not from any esoteric requirements of a particular doctrine but from the simple fact that the public interest means nothing if it does not include such a responsibility.

The Fairness Doctrine, we think, serves chiefly to put flesh on these policy bones by providing a familiar mold to define the general contours of the obligation imposed.

The attack on the alleged statutory authority for this "public interest" ruling takes two forms: 1) a general denial that the Commission has any authority to supervise the content of broadcasting under the public interest standard; and 2) an argument that any delegation of the power to make ad hoc public interest determinations of this kind is invalid for want of adequate limiting standards.

A. The Commission's Authority Over Broadcast Content in General

Nothing in the Communications Act of 1934 expressly grants the Commission any general authority over programming. The most relevant provisions go no further than to authorize it to grant and renew broadcast licenses according to the dictates of the "public interest, convenience, and necessity." A case could be made, as an abstract proposition, that this licensing power is limited to policing the traffic over the airwaves to prevent interference between stations and perhaps to assure a minimum level of technical competence. If the question were *res nova,* that case would receive substantial support from the Supreme Court decisions requiring a clear mandate for regulatory activity which brushes closely against sensitive Constitutional areas.

But the argument was in fact made and rejected long ago in *National Broadcasting Company* v. *United States.* Justice Frankfurter, speaking for the Court, said in part:

> An important element of public interest and convenience affecting the issue of a license is the ability of the licensee to render the best practicable service to the community reached by his broadcasts.

The Commission's licensing function cannot be discharged, therefore, merely by finding that there are no technological objections to the granting of a license. If the criterion of "public interest" were limited to such matters, how could the commission choose between two applicants for the same facilities, each of whom is financially and technically qualified to operate a station? Since the very inception of federal regulation by radio (sic), comparative considerations as to the services to be rendered have governed the application of the standard of "public interest, convenience, or necessity."

The avowed aim of the Communications Act of 1934 was to secure the maximum benefits of radio to all the people of the United States. To that end Congress endowed the Communications Commission with comprehensive powers to promote and realize the vast potentialities of radio.

These provisions, individually and in the aggregate, preclude the notion that the Commission is empowered to deal only with technical and engineering impediments to the "larger and more effective use of radio in the public interest."

In fact, neither the courts nor the Commission have thought it had to make its decisions among competing applicants blindfolded to the content of their programs. Both the old Radio Commission and the FCC have likewise refused to renew licenses on the basis of past programming not in the public interest, and this Court affirmed such a refusal as long ago as 1931. If agency power to designate programming "not in the public interest" is a slippery slope, the Commission and the courts started down it too long ago to go back to the top now unless Congress or the Constitution sends them. But Congress has apparently specifically endorsed this understanding of the public interest. And whatever the limits imposed by the First Amendment, we do not think it requires eradicating every trace of a programming component from the public interest standard.

The power to refuse a license on grounds of past or proposed programming necessarily entails some power to define the stations' public interest obligations with respect to programming. It is this power to specify material which the public interest requires or forbids to be broadcast that carries the seeds of the general authority to censor denied by the Communications Act and the First Amendment alike. But elementary canons of administrative and constitutional law prevent the Commission from terminating a license without giving reasons or from condemning a station's overall programming as inimical to the public interest without identifying the offending material and particularizing the public interest. And if the Commission must explain its view of the public interest when it denies or revokes a license, it may surely give advance notice of its views by way of an official ruling which is subject to judicial review. Indeed, in some cases fairness to the stations may require some advance warning of their responsibilities.

Thus, in applying the public interest standard to programming, the Commission walks a tightrope between saying too much and saying too little. In most areas it has resolved this dilemma by imposing only general affirmative duties—e.g., to strike a balance between the various interests of the community, or to provide a reasonable amount of time for the presentation of programs devoted to the discussion of public issues. The licensee has broad discretion in giving specific content to these duties, and on application for renewal of a license it is understood the Commission will focus on his overall performance and good faith rather than on specific errors it may find him to have made. In practice, the Commission rarely denies licenses for breaches of these duties. Given its long established authority to consider program content, this general approach probably minimizes dangers of censorship or pervasive supervision.

In other areas, however, the Commission has on occasion imposed more specific duties or found specific programs or advertisements to be contrary to the public interest. Such rulings must be closely scrutinized lest they carry the Commission too far in the direction of the forbidden censorship. But particularity is not in itself a vice; indeed, in some circumstances it may serve to limit an otherwise impermissibly broad intrusion upon a licensee's individual responsibility for programming.

B. The Authority for the Cigarette Ruling in Particular

Thus, in the context of the Communications Act as it has long been understood, we do not think that public interest rulings relating to specific program content invariably amount to "censorship" within the meaning of the Act. However, there is high risk that such rulings will reflect the Commission's selection among tastes, opinions, and value judgments, rather than a recognizable public interest. Especially with First Amendment issues lurking in the near background, the "public interest" is too vague a criterion for administrative action unless it is narrowed by definable standards.

The ruling before us neither forbids nor requires the publication of any specific material. But as an extension of the Fairness Doctrine it is an unusual limitation of the licensee's discretion. And as an independent public interest ruling it requires independent support. We cannot uphold it merely on the ground that it may reasonably be thought to serve the public interest.

Whatever else it may mean, however, we think the public interest indisputably include the public health. There is perhaps a broader public consensus on that value, and also on its core meaning, than on any other likely component of the public interest. The power to protect the public health lies at the heart of the states' police power. It has sustained many of the most drastic exercises of that power, including quarantines, condemnations, civil commitments, and compulsory vaccinations. Likewise, public health concerns now support a sizable portion of the civilian federal bureaucracy. The public health has in effect become a kind of basic law, both justifying new extensions of old powers and evoking the legitimate concern of government wherever its regulatory power otherwise extends.

But the ruling on cigarette advertising is vulnerable to none of these objections against a broad mandate to the Commission to consider the public health. The danger cigarettes may pose to health is, among others, a danger to life itself. As the Commission emphasized, it is a danger inherent in the normal use of the product, not one merely associated with its abuse or dependent on intervening fortuitous events. It threatens a substantial body of the population, not merely a peculiarly susceptible fringe group. Moreover, the danger, though not established beyond all doubt, is documented by a compelling cumulation of statistical evidence. The only member of the Commission to express doubts about the validity of its ruling had no doubts about the validity of its premise that, in all probability, cigarettes are dangerous to health:

> Cigarette smoking is a substantial hazard to the health of those who smoke which increases both with the number of cigarettes smoked and with the youthfulness when smoking is started. Cigarette smoking increases both the likelihood of the occurrence and the seriousness of the consequences of various types of cancer, of cardiovascular failures, and of numerous other pathologies of smokers. These conclusions are established by overwhelming scientific evidence, by the findings of government agencies, and by congressional reports and statute . . . . The evidence on this subject is not conclusive, but scientific evidence is never conclusive. All scientific conclusions are probablistic (sic) . . . . Furthermore, law does not and cannot demand conclusive proof. Even in a capital case, the law requires only proof beyond a reasonable doubt . . . . The evidence as to the dangers of cigarette smoking to the smoker is clearly beyond a mere preponderance and approaches proof beyond a reasonable doubt.

Finally, the Commission expressly refused to rely on any scientific expertise of its own. Instead, it took the word of the Surgeon General's Advisory Committee, whose findings had already been adopted in substance by the Department of Health, Education, and Welfare, the Federal Trade Commission, and the Senate Commerce Committee, and had in addition been recognized and acted upon by Congress itself in the Cigarette Labeling Act.

In these circumstances, the Commission could reasonably determine that news broadcasts, private and governmental educational programs, the information provided by other media, and the prescribed warnings on each cigarette pack, inadequately inform the public of the extent to which its life and health are most probably in jeopardy. The mere fact that information is available, or even that it is actually heard or read, does not mean that it is effectively understood. A man who hears a hundred "yeses" for each "no," when the actual odds lie heavily the other way, cannot be realistically deemed adequately informed. Moreover, since cigarette smoking is psychologically addicting, the confirmed smoker is likely to be relatively unreceptive to information about its dangers; his hearing is dulled by his appetite. And since it is so much harder to stop than not to start, it is crucial that an accurate picture be communicated to those who have not yet begun.

Thus, as a public health measure addressed to a unique danger authenticated by official and congressional action, the cigarette ruling is not invalid on account of its unusual particularity. It is in fact the product singled out for special treatment which justifies the action taken. In view of the potentially grave consequences of a decision to continue—or above all to start—smoking, we think it was not an abuse of discretion for the Commission to attempt to insure not only that the negative view be heard, but that it be heard repeatedly. The Commission has made no effort to dictate the content of the required anti-cigarette broadcasts. It has emphasized that the responsibility for content, source, specific volume, and precise timing rests with the good faith discretion of the licensee.

The cigarette ruling does not convert the Commission into either a censor or a big brother. But we emphasize that our cautious approval of this particular decision does not license the Commission to scan the airwaves for offensive material with no more discriminating a lens than the "public interest" or even the "public health."

III. The First Amendment

It is difficult to separate the First Amendment question from the question of the Commission's authority. Section 326 of the Communications Act expressly provides that "no regulation or condition shall be promulgated or fixed by the Commission which shall interfere with the right of free speech by means of radio communication." It might reasonably be thought that "the right of free speech," is shorthand for the First Amendment. But since constructions of the First Amendment have broadened since 1934, and inasmuch as the First Amendment argument advanced in this case challenges a long settled construction of the Act, we treat the Constitutional question separately for purposes of analysis.

A. Regulation of Broadcast Content Under the First Amendment in General

Intervenors NBC, et al. argue cogently that the public interest standard cannot Constitutionally now include any component of program content. They say the First Amendment obviously would not tolerate administrative supervision of the material published by the newspaper press. The radio press was initially treated differently only because 1) peculiar technical factors require a policeman to prevent interference between different stations, and 2) the then available broadcasting channels were so limited in number that the Commission could hardly ignore all considerations of the nature and quality of programming in choosing among applicants. The first reason does not justify supervision of content, they say, and the second, if ever sufficient, is an anachronism now that the available channels often outnumber the applicants and the broadcasting stations serving most areas far outnumber the newspapers. Accordingly, in their view the First Amendment now limits the Commission's licensing discretion to technological considerations; the content of broadcasting, like that of the publishing press, must be left entirely to the licensees and ultimately to the market.

This argument has considerable force. First Amendment complaints against FCC regulation of content are not adequately answered by mere recitation of the technically imposed necessity for some regulation of broadcasting and the conclusory propositions that "the public owns the airwaves" and that a broadcast license is a "revocable privilege." It may well be that some venerable FCC policies cannot withstand Constitutional scrutiny in the light of contemporary understanding of the First Amendment and the modern proliferation of broadcasting outlets.

On the other hand, we cannot solve such complex questions by replacing one set of shibboleths with another. The First Amendment is unmistakably hostile to governmental controls over the content of the press, but that is not to say that it necessarily bars every regulation which in any way affects what the newspapers publish. Even if it does, there may still be a meaningful distinction between the two media justifying different treatment under the First Amendment. Unlike broadcasting, the written press includes a rich variety of outlets for expression and persuasion, including journals, pamphlets, leaflets, and circular letters, which are available to those without technical skills or deep pockets. Moreover, the broadcasting medium may be different in kind from publishing in a way which has particular relevance to the case at hand. Written messages are not communicated unless they are read, and reading requires an affirmative act. Broadcast messages, in contrast, are "in the air." In an age of omnipresent radio, there scarcely breathes a citizen who does not know some part of a leading cigarette jingle by heart. Similarly, an ordinary habitual television watcher can avoid these commercials only by frequently leaving the room, changing the channels, or doing some other such affirmative act. It is difficult to calculate the subliminal impact of this pervasive propaganda, which may be heard even if not listened to, but it may reasonably be thought greater than the impact of the written word.

B. Constitutionality of the Cigarette Ruling in Particular

These considerations are at least sufficient to convince us that we are not obliged simply to "invalidate the entire course of broadcasting development" with no inquiry into the particulars of the ruling before us. Rather, we think the proper approach to the difficult First Amendment issues petitioners raise is to consider them in the context of individual regulatory policies and practices on a case-by-case basis. On this approach, since the narrow public health power which supports the cigarette ruling does not "sweep . . . widely and . . . indiscriminately" across protected freedoms, the Constitutional question before us is only whether the Communications Act, construed to authorize a public health ruling in the circumstances of this case, offends the First Amendment. And whatever the Constitutional infirmities of other regulations of programming, we are satisfied that the cigarette ruling does not abridge the First Amendment freedoms of speech or press. We reach this conclusion in the light of the following considerations:

1. The cigarette ruling does not ban any speech. In traditional doctrinal terms, the Constitutional argument against it is only that it may have a "chilling effect" on the exercise of First Amendment freedoms by making broadcasters more reluctant to carry cigarette advertising.

2. The speech which might conceivably be "chilled" by this ruling barely qualifies as Constitutionally protected "speech." It is established that some utterances fall outside the pale of First Amendment concern. Many cases indicate that product advertising is at least less rigorously protected than other forms of speech. Promoting the sale of a product is not ordinarily associated with any of the interests the First Amendment seeks to protect. As a rule, it does not affect the political process, does not contribute to the exchange of ideas, does not provide information on matters of public importance, and is not, except perhaps for the ad-men, a form of individual self-expression. It is rather a form of merchandising subject to limitation for public purposes like other business practices. In the instant case, this argument is not dispositive because the cigarette ruling was premised on the fact that cigarette advertising implicitly states a position on a matter of public controversy. But though this advertising strongly implies that cigarette smoking is a desirable habit, petitioners have correctly insisted that the advertisements in question present no information or arguments in favor of smoking which might contribute to the public debate. Accordingly, even if cigarette commercials are protected speech, we think they are at best a negligible "part of any exposition of ideas, and are of . . . slight social value as a step to truth . . . ."

3. In any event, the danger that even this marginal "speech" will be significantly chilled as a result of the ruling is probably itself marginal. We cannot, of course, undertake an economic analysis to determine the probability that the volume of cigarette advertising over radio and television will decline. We can say with fair certainty, however, that the cigarette manufacturers' interest in selling their product guarantees a continued resourceful effort to reach the public. We note also that cigarette advertising accounts for a sizable portion of broadcasting revenues, and we think it at best doubtful that many stations will refuse to carry cigarette commercials in order to avoid the obligations imposed by the ruling.

4. Even if some valued speech is inhibited by the ruling, the First Amendment gain is greater than the loss. A primary First Amendment policy has been to foster the widest possible debate and dissemination of information on matters of public importance. That policy has been pursued by a general hostility toward any deterrents to free expression. The difficulty with this negative approach is that not all free speakers have equally loud voices, and success in the marketplace of ideas may go to the advocate who can shout loudest or most often. Debate is not primarily an end in itself, and a debate in which only one party has the financial resources and interest to purchase sustained access to the mass communications media is not a fair test of either an argument's truth or its innate popular appeal.

Countervailing power on the opposite sides of many issues of public concern often neutralizes this defect. In many other cases, the courts must act as if such an inherent balancing mechanism were at work in order to avoid either weighing the worth of conflicting views or emasculating the robust debate they seek to promote. If the fairness doctrine cannot withstand First Amendment scrutiny, the reason is that to insure a balanced presentation of controversial issues may be to insure no presentation, or no vigorous presentation, at all. But where, as here, one party to a debate has a financial clout and a compelling economic interest in the presentation of one side unmatched by its opponent, and where the public stake in the argument is no less than life itself—we think the purpose of rugged debate is served, not hindered, by an attempt to repress the balance.

5. Finally, not only does the cigarette ruling not repress any information, it serves affirmatively to provide information. We do not doubt that official prescription in detail or in quantity of what the press must say can be as offensive to the principle of a free press as official prohibition. But the cigarette ruling does not dictate specific content and, in view of its special context, it is not a precedent for converting broadcasting into a mouthpiece for government propaganda. And the provision of information is no small part of what the First Amendment is about. A political system which assigns vital decisions to individual free choice assumes a well-informed citizenry. We do not think the principle of free speech stands as a barrier to required broadcasting of facts and information vital to an informed decision to smoke or not to smoke.

IV. *Other Contentions*

The resolution of these basic questions leaves a residue of unanswered contentions. Mr. Banzhaf's complaint that the anti-smokers should have been granted equal time need not detain us. Even if it had authority to specify equal time, the Commission could reasonably find such a specific requirement an unnecessary intrusion upon the licensees' discretion. Likewise, the Commission did not abuse its discretion in refusing to require rebuttal time for the cigarette manufacturers. The public health rationale which supports the principal ruling would hardly justify compelling broadcasters to inform the public that smoking might not be dangerous. And an issue of "fairness" arises principally because the cigarette manufacturers are deterred from making health claims in their advertisements by the FTC's warning that such claims would be "unfair and deceptive." If the FTC's determination is in error, the remedy does not lie in a further particularization of the FCC's Fairness Doctrine.

Finally, The Tobacco Institute contends that the Commission's ruling is void on account of procedural irregularities. The initial ruling was made without providing interested parties either notice or an opportunity to be heard. But since the Commission subsequently entertained numerous petitions for review, wrote a thorough opinion affirming its ruling, and made the ruling prospective from the date of the affirming order, we find no prejudice to substantial rights. The Tobacco Institute also intimates that the Commission should have held an oral hearing, should have made factual investigations of its own, or should have instituted a full-fledged rule-making proceeding, before issuing its ruling. As a general rule, we agree that more careful procedures are required to support innovation by an administrative agency. But the essential premises of the instant ruling are only 1) that cigarette advertising inherently promotes cigarette smoking as a desirable habit, 2) that very substantial medical and scientific authority regards this habit as highly dangerous to health and therefore undesirable, and 3) that in view of the volume of cigarette advertising, existing sources were inadequate to inform the public of the nature and extent of the danger. These premises are supported by the record. We do not see, and The Tobacco Institute has never suggested, what evidence a more extensive proceeding might have produced to refute them.

Affirmed.

RED LION BROADCASTING CO. v. FEDERAL COMMUNICATIONS COMMISSION

UNITED STATES v. RADIO TELEVISION NEWS DIRECTORS ASSN.

395 U.S. 367 (1969)

Mr. Justice White delivered the opinion of the Court.

The Federal Communications Commission has for many years imposed on radio and television broadcasters the requirement that discussion of public issues be presented on broadcast stations, and that each side of those issues must be given fair coverage. This is known as the Fairness Doctrine, which originated very early in the history of broadcasting and has maintained its present outlines for some time. It is an obligation whose content has been defined in a long series of FCC rulings in particular cases, and which is distinct from the statutory requirement of Section 315 of the Communications Act that equal time be allotted all qualified candidates for public office. Two aspects of the Fairness Doctrine, relating to personal attacks in the context of controversial public issues and to political editorializing, were codified more precisely in the form of FCC regulations in 1967. The two cases before us now, which were decided separately below, challenge the Constitutional and statutory bases of the doctrine and component rules. *Red Lion* involves the application of the Fairness Doctrine to a particular broadcast, and RTNDA arises as an action to review the FCC's 1967 promulgation of the personal attack and political editorializing regulations, which were laid down after the *Red Lion* litigation had begun.

The Red Lion Broadcasting Company is licensed to operate a Pennsylvania radio station, WGCB. On November 27, 1964, WGCB carried a 15-minute broadcast by Reverend Billy James Hargis as part of a "Christian Crusade" series. A book by Fred J. Cook entitled *Goldwater: Extremist on the Right* was discussed by Hargis, who said that Cook had been fired by a newspaper for fabricating false charges against city officials; that Cook had then worked for a Communist-affiliated publication; that he had defended Alger Hiss and attacked J. Edgar Hoover and the Central Intelligence Agency; and that he had now written a "book to smear and destroy Barry Goldwater." When Cook heard of the broadcast he concluded that he had been personally attacked and demanded free reply time, which the station refused. After an exchange of letters among Cook, Red Lion, and the FCC, the FCC declared that the Hargis broadcast constituted a personal attack on Cook; that Red Lion had failed to meet its obligation under the Fairness Doctrine.

When a broadcaster grants time to a political candidate, Congress itself requires that equal time be offered to his opponents. It would exceed our competence to hold that the Commission is unauthorized by the statute to employ a similar device where personal attacks or political editorials are broadcast by a radio or television station.

In light of the fact that the "public interest" in broadcasting clearly encompasses the presentation of vigorous debate of controversial issues of importance and concern to the public; the fact that the FCC has rested upon that language from its very inception a doctrine that these issues must be discussed, and fairly; and the fact that Congress has acknowledged that the analogous provisions of Section 315 are not preclusive in this area, and knowingly preserved the FCC's complementary efforts, we think the Fairness Doctrine and its component personal attack and political editorializing regulations are a legitimate exercise of congressionally delegated authority. The Communications Act is not notable for the precision of its substantive standards and in this respect the explicit provisions of Section 315, and the doctrine and rules at issue here which are closely modeled upon that section, are far more explicit than the generalized "public interest" standard in which the Commission ordinarily finds its sole guidance, and which we have held a broad but adequate standard before. We cannot say that the FCC's declaratory ruling in *Red Lion,* or the regulations at issue in RTNDA, are beyond the scope of the congressionally conferred power to assure that stations are operated by those whose possession of a license serves "the public interest."

The (RTNDA) broadcasters challenge the Fairness Doctrine and its specific manifestations in the personal attack and political editorial rules on conventional First Amendment grounds, alleging that the rules abridge their freedom of speech and press. Their contention is that the First Amendment protects their desire to use their allotted frequencies continuously to broadcast whatever they choose, and to exclude whomever they choose from ever using that frequency. No man may be prevented from saying or publishing what he thinks, or from refusing in his speech or other utterances to give equal weight to the views of his opponents. This right, they say, applies equally to broadcasters.

Although broadcasting is clearly a medium affected by a First Amendment interest, differences in the characteristics of new media justify differences in the First Amendment standards applied to them. For example, the ability of new technology to produce sounds more raucous than those of the human voice justifies restrictions on the sound level, and on the hours and places of use, of sound trucks so long as the restrictions are reasonable and applied without discrimination.

Just as the government may limit the use of sound amplifying equipment potentially so noisy that it drowns out civilized private speech, so may the government limit the use of broadcast equipment. The right of free speech of a broadcaster, the user of a sound truck, or any other individual does not embrace a right to snuff out the free speech of others.

Because of the scarcity of radio frequencies, the government is permitted to put restraints on licensees in favor of others whose views should be expressed on this unique medium. But the people as a whole retain their interest in free speech by radio and their collective right to have the medium function consistently with the ends and purposes of the First Amendment. It is the right of the viewers and listeners, not the right of the broadcasters, which is paramount. It is the purpose of the First Amendment to preserve an uninhibited marketplace of ideas in which truth will ultimately prevail, rather than to countenance monopolization of that market, whether it be by the government itself or a private licensee. It is the right of the public to receive suitable access to social, political, esthetic, moral, and other ideas and experiences which is crucial here.

In terms of Constitutional principle, and as enforced sharing of a scarce resource, the personal attack and political editorial rules are indistinguishable from the equal time provisions of Section 315, a specific enactment of Congress requiring stations to set aside reply time under specified circumstances and to which the Fairness Doctrine and these constituent regulations are important complements. That provision, which has been part of the law since 1927 (Radio Act of 1927), has been held valid by this Court as an obligation of the licensee relieving him of any power in any way to prevent or censor the broadcast, and thus insulating him from liability for defamation. The Constitutionality of the statute under the First Amendment was unquestioned.

Nor can we say that it is inconsistent with the First Amendment goal of producing an informed public capable of conducting its own affairs to require a broadcaster to permit answers to personal attacks occurring in the course of discussing controversial issues, or to require that the political opponents of those endorsed by the station be given a chance to communicate with the public. Otherwise, station owners and a few networks would have unfettered power to make time available only to the highest bidders, to communicate only their own views on public issues, people, and candidates, and to permit on the air only those with whom they agreed. There is no sanctuary in the First Amendment for unlimited private censorship operating in a medium not open to all.

In view of the prevalence of scarcity of broadcast frequencies, the government's role in allocating those frequencies, and the legitimate claims of those unable without governmental assistance to gain access to those frequencies for expression of their views, we hold the regulations and ruling at issue here are both authorized by statute and Constitutional. The judgment of the Court of Appeals in *Red Lion* is affirmed and that in *RTNDA* reversed and the causes remanded for proceedings consistent with this opinion.

RETAIL STORE EMPLOYEES UNION, LOCAL 880, RETAIL CLERKS INTERNATIONAL ASSOCIATION, AFL-CIO v. FEDERAL COMMUNICATIONS COMMISSION
436 F.2d 248 (CADC, 1970)

Before Bazelon, Chief Judge, and Robinson and Robb, Circuit Judges.
Bazelon, Chief Judge.

This is an appeal from a memorandum opinion and order of the Federal Communications Commission renewing without hearing the broadcasting license of Radio Station WREO of Ashtabula, Ohio, over the protest of Retail Store Employees Local 880 (Union). We conclude that the Commission has failed to demonstrate adequate consideration of issues of substantial importance, and accordingly remand the case to the Commission for further proceedings.

This case arises out of a labor-management dispute not involving WREO. Hill's Department Store of Ashtabula, Ohio (Hill's Ashtabula) is one of a chain of such stores in Ohio and Pennsylvania. (A)ppellant Union was certified by the National Labor Relations Board as the bargaining agent for employees of Hill's Ashtabula. (A)fter some months of bargaining, the Union determined to seek its objectives by going on strike. Hill's Ashtabula was struck, and a boycott beginning there spread to other Hill's stores in the area.

During this period, Hill's regularly purchased radio air time for advertising. Although no samples of Hill's advertisements are before us, the parties are agreed that the advertising was standard commercial copy, extolling the virtues of Hill's stock, bargains, and service, and on that basis urging listeners to patronize the various Hill's outlets. Seventy such announcements were run by WREO between January 10 and February 22, 1966. Similar copy was carried by stations WFMJ of Youngstown, WHHH of Warren, and WLEC of Sandusky. Beginning in February, 1966, the Union undertook to support its boycott by purchasing time for one-minute spot announcements stating that a strike was in progress against Hill's Ashtabula, and urging listeners to respect the picket lines at that and other Hill's Department Stores. Three hundred and twenty-two such announcements were carried by WREO between February 16 and April 7, 1966. In addition, WFMJ of Youngstown carried two such spot announcements (both on March 22), and WLEC of Sandusky carried 170 such announcements from February 23 through March 28. WHHH of Warren, Ohio, although approached by the Union, refused to accept any of the Union's advertisements upon the advice of its counsel that "no fairness question was presented" and that the station was therefore not compelled to run the proferred advertisements.

As the spring wore on, however, the Union experienced more and more difficulty in purchasing air time for its advertisements. Despite continuing attempts by the Union, through an advertising agency, to purchase further time, by early April of 1966 it could find no station serving the area around Ashtabula willing to run its advertisements. Apparently the last of the stations to cancel was WREO of Ashtabula, which on April 5 wrote the advertising agencies representing the Union and Hill's Ashtabula to inform them that WREO "would accept no further commercial copy from either party concerning the strike between Hill's and the Union." Subsequently, after counsel for the Union informed WREO that he had filed a complaint regarding this action with the FCC, the station on April 22 offered free time to both parties for a single "round table discussion" of the issues presented by the strike. This offer was never accepted by either party.

In the meantime, WREO continued to broadcast advertisements for Hill's Ashtabula. One hundred and twenty-three announcements and six sponsored programs were run during the month of April, and from April 1 to the end of the year, the station broadcast 1,088 spot announcements, 176 sponsored programs, and 14 sponsored one-third segments of football games on behalf of the store. Similarly, it appears that advertising on behalf of Hill's continued to be broadcast by WFMJ, WHHH, and WLEC.

The FCC wrote each of the affected stations inquiring why Union advertising had been rejected. After receiving replies to its inquiry, the Commission in a memorandum opinion and order denied the

Union's petitions regarding WFMJ, WHHH, and WLEC. The Commission, apparently relying upon its letter to the Union of April 29, 1966, found no fairness question presented.

But the Supreme Court, this court, and the Commission itself have all recognized that the Fairness Doctrine is not an island whole unto itself. It is merely one aspect of the Commission's implementation of the requirement that broadcast stations serve the public "interest, convenience, and necessity." Accordingly, although as a general matter equal time is not required so long as a reasonable opportunity is afforded for the presentation of opposing viewpoints, the Commission has upon occasion recognized that time, rather than information, is of the essence. Thus, in regard to broadcast spot announcements soliciting campaign contributions, the Commission has recognized that at least with regard to two major party candidates, "fairness would obviously require that these two be treated roughly the same with respect to the announcements." Presumably, the additional *information* presented to the public by repeated announcements would be minimal; the value of repetition would be solely in the additional coverage obtained. Similarly, in *Times-Mirror,* a station had aired more than 20 broadcasts by commentators favoring one major-party candidate for governor, and 2 broadcasts by commentators favoring his opponent. Summarizing its ruling, the Commission stated that "(t)he continuous, repetitive opportunity afforded for the expression of the commentators' viewpoints on the gubernatorial campaign, in contrast to the minimal opportunity afforded to opposing viewpoints, violated the right of the public to a fair presentation of views." Most recently, in the Commission's landmark ruling on cigarette advertising, the Commission stated:

> We think that the frequency of the presentation of one side of the controversy is a factor appropriately to be considered in our administration of the Fairness Doctrine. For, while the Fairness Doctrine does not contemplate "equal time," if the presentation of one side of the issue is on a regular continual basis, fairness and the right of the public adequately to be informed compels the conclusion that there must be some regularity in the presentation of the other side of the issue.

In the present case, it seems clear to us that the strike and the Union boycott were controversial issues of substantial public importance within Ashtabula, the locality primarily served by WREO. The ultimate issue with regard to the boycott was simple: whether or not the public should patronize Hill's Ashtabula. From April through December, Hill's broadcast over WREO more than a thousand spot announcements and more than a hundred sponsored programs explaining why in its opinion the public should patronize its store. During that same period, the Union was denied any opportunity beyond a single roundtable broadcast to explain why, in its opinion, the public should not patronize the store. We need not now decide whether, as the Union would have us hold, these facts make out a *per se* claim of a violation of the Fairness Doctrine. We do believe, however, that the question deserves fuller analysis than the Commission has seen fit to give it.

Central to the Union's argument on this point is the proposition that, in urging listeners to patronize Hill's Ashtabula Department Store, Hill's advertisements presented one side of a controversial issue of public importance. Hill's copy, of course, made no mention of the strike or boycott, or of the unresolved issues between the Union and the store. But the advertisements did urge the listening public to take one of the two competing sides on the boycott question—they urged the public to patronize the store, i.e., not to boycott it. It seems to us an inadequate answer to this argument merely to point out that Hill's copy made no specific mention of the boycott. In dealing with cigarette advertising, the Commission has recognized that a position represented by an advertisement may be implicit rather than explicit. And although the Commission repeatedly emphasized that its holding in that case—that stations broadcasting cigarette advertisements must regularly provide free time if necessary for the presentation of arguments opposing cigarette advertising, the reasons advanced by the Commission to support that limitation seem to us not to imply that other advertisements may not carry an implicit as well as an explicit message, but rather that the implicit and explicit messages normally carried by advertising do not concern controversial issues of public importance.

The Commission's ruling with regard to cigarette advertising relied heavily upon the judgment of other branches of government that, in light of the possible dangers of smoking "to the health of millions of persons," the question whether or not to smoke cigarettes was one of substantial importance to the public. In its regulation of labor-management relations, Congress has indicated substantial concern with equalizing the bargaining power of employees and their employers. Stripped to its essentials, this dispute is one facet of the economic warfare that is a recognized part of labor-management relations: the Union, in urging a boycott of Hill's Department Stores, was seeking to put economic pressure upon management to accede to its demands; management on the other hand, was seeking to resist the Union's pressure by continuing profitable operations. Part of the Union's campaign was publicity for its boycott; part of management's arsenal was advertising to persuade the public to patronize its stores.

If viewed in this light, it could well be argued that the traditional purposes of the Fairness Doctrine are not substantially served by presentation of advertisements intended less to inform than to serve merely as a weapon in a labor-management dispute. But the Fairness Doctrine, as we have pointed out, is only one aspect of the FCC's implementation of the statutory requirement that broadcast stations operate to serve the public interest. The public policy of the United States has been declared by Congress as favoring the equalization of economic bargaining power between workers and their employers. It is at the very least a fair question whether a radio station properly serves the public interest by making available to an employer broadcast time for the purpose of urging the public to patronize his store, while denying the employees any remotely comparable opportunity to urge the public to join their side of the strife and boycott the employer. If the Union's claim is to be rejected, we believe this question should be dealt with by the Commission.

In summary, we believe that the Union's evidence of denial of access to radio air time raised questions regarding possible improper influence by Hill's that were not adequately answered by Hill's bare denial and the station's letter of denial and explanation. With regard to the Union's fairness question, we recognize the primary responsibility of the FCC in assuring that radio broadcasters operate their stations in the public interest. We have not here attempted a full canvas of the issues raised by even a good-faith denial to the Union of access to broadcast time; we have merely sought to indicate some of the questions that must be answered. We do believe, however, that these issues deserve far more comprehensive treatment than was afforded them by the FCC. Accordingly, we remand the case to the Commission for further proceedings consistent with this opinion.

So ordered.

Robb, Circuit Judge (dissenting).

BRANDYWINE-MAINE LINE RADIO, INC. v. FEDERAL COMMUNICATIONS COMMISSION
473 F.2d 16 (CADC 1972)

Tamm, Circuit Judge.

FACTUAL BACKGROUND

Brandywine was licensed to operate WXUR in 1962 by the Commission after a determination that such license would be beneficial in serving the public interest. (In 1964 Faith Theological) Seminary filed an application with the Commission seeking approval for the proposed purchase of Brandywine's stock and for Commission approval for the Seminary's proposed operation of WXUR.

The major concern of the opponents to the transfer was that the station would be incapable of providing for a balanced presentation of opposing views in light of McIntire's* connection with the Seminary and in view of his radio programs and publications. (It was pointed out in *In Re Application of George E. Borst* that) "(t)he main thrust of the complaints concerning Rev. McIntire, is that in his radio programs and publications, he has made false and misleading statements and deliberate distortions of the facts relating to various public issues such as race relations, religious unity, foreign aid, etc.; that he has made "intemperate" attacks on other religious denominations and leaders, various organizations, governmental agencies, political figures, and international organizations; and that such expressions are irresponsible and a derisive force in the community and help create a climate of fear, prejudice, and distrust of democratic institutions.

The Commission refused to adopt the Hearing Examiner's *Initial Opinion* and adopted its own opinion on July 7, 1970 in which it denied the licensee's application for renewal after an independent review of the record. In its review the Commission drew adverse conclusions with reference to Brandywine's compliance with the Fairness Doctrine, compliance with the personal attack principle, and also to the manner in which Brandywine misrepresented its program plans to the Commission.

THE FAIRNESS DOCTRINE

The Fairness Doctrine was, in the Commission's view, the central aspect of the litigation. The reason for this is axiomatic—prior to issuing Brandywine's initial license a tremendous amount of concern was expressed to the Commission by numerous parties, each featuring that WXUR would fail to comply with the doctrine. Brandywine's response to these fears was clear and apparently forthright—it had promised at the time of the transfer application to fully comply with the doctrine. In point of fact, the decision of the Commission had "reiterated the necessity that a licensee serve the public interest by adherence to the Fairness Doctrine, including the personal attack principle."

The Commission proceeded to review the record, including 15 days of monitored broadcasts, and concluded "that Brandywine under its new ownership did not make reasonable efforts to comply with the Fairness Doctrine during the license period." The Commission discovered, as a result of studying the submissions based on the monitored periods, that WXUR had failed to comply in a number of instances in which one side of an issue was broadcast

---

*Reverend Carl McIntire was President of the Board of Directors of Faith Theological Seminary, Inc., and sponsor for the program *20th Century Reformation Hour,* which had been terminated recently at nearby station WVCH.

during these periods without presenting any opposing viewpoints on any but one of these issues, and with an insignificant presentation on that issue, despite the fact that such controversial issue programming was a substantial part of WXUR's total programming.

Additionally, the Commission found that WXUR had failed to affirmatively come forth with the requisite responsive evidence necessary to illustrate Brandywine's efforts to assure compliance with both the Fairness Doctrine and the personal attack principles, as promised in the initial transfer application. The Commission found that:

Brandywine failed to establish any regular procedure for previewing, monitoring, or reviewing its broadcasts; and thus did not regularly know what views were being presented on controversial issues of public importance. Despite the *prima facie* evidence presented by the other parties on this issue, Brandywine did not respond with any further review of its treatment of such controversial issues, either for the full license period or any smaller reasonable segment of time. Furthermore it made no showing of public announcement inviting the presentation of contrasting views at the times the issues in Appendix A (or others) were discussed, nor of any other adequate action to encourage the presentation of contrasting viewpoints on these issues. Brandywine relies upon certain call-in and interview programs as meeting its fairness obligations. However, our review of the record shows that these programs were inadequate to this purpose because they either were not directed at obtaining opposing views on the issues (i.e., speakers were not secured or presented in connection with these issues), or were so conducted as to discourage the presentation of views not shared by their moderators.

WXUR contended that Rev. McIntire had undertaken substantive efforts to assure compliance with the Fairness Doctrine. This submission took the form of letters which evidenced unaccepted invitations to appear on the *20th Century Reformation Hour.* The Commission rejected this would-be indicia of compliance since "these were not invitations by the licensee and, more important, they do not constitute adequate invitations to present contrasting views on the issues set forth in Appendix A." Similarly, the Commission rejected the suggestion that the licensee's fairness obligations could be met by the existence of a daily one-hour call-in program, entitled *Freedom of Speech,* on which a listener could comment briefly on any topic he wished. "On the contrary," the Commission stated, "its operation demonstrates a failure to provide a fair forum by a licensee specifically on notice of its responsibilities in the fairness area." This was especially true since the program "was conducted so as to discourage viewpoints with which (the moderator) disagreed. From the outset he both cut off and insulated callers who did not share his views. This conduct, for which Brandywine is of course responsible, is patently inconsistent with the requirement of fairness."

The Commission closed its 23-page opinion by stating:

We conclude upon an evaluation of all the relevant and material evidence contained in the hearing record, that renewals of the WXUR and WXUR-FM licenses should not be granted. The record demonstrates that Brandywine failed to provide reasonable opportunities for the presentation of contrasting views on controversial issues of public importance, that it ignored the personal attack principle of the Fairness Doctrine, that the applicant's representations as to the manner in which the station would be operated were not adhered to, that no adequate efforts were made to keep the station attuned to the community's or area's needs and interests, and that no showing has been made that it was, in fact, so attuned. *Any one of these violations would alone be sufficient to require denying the renewals here, and the violations are rendered even more serious by the fact that we carefully drew the Seminary's attention to a licensee's responsibilities before we approved transfer of the stations to its ownership and control.*

In its petition for reconsideration Brandywine in no way challenged the Commission's earlier finding that despite Brandywine's initial representation and despite the Commission's strong warnings in the transfer decision, "Brandywine had taken no steps to encourage the presentation of contrasting views on several issues of public importance where it had presented one side of each of these issues. Brandywine contended that it had broadcast material on certain news, interview, and call-in shows which, although never considered by the Commission, did satisfy the Fairness Doctrine requirements as to these issues.

BRANDYWINE'S PROGRAM REPRESENTATIONS

This aspect of the case, while not the most troublesome, is clearly the most disturbing to the Court.

The changes which took place on WXUR within the very first days following the transfer show a common design on the part of the licensee to engage in deceit and trickery in obtaining a broadcast license. Within nine days, a totally unexpected group of seven programs, each of a nature different than those on the typical program schedule, were on the air. These programs, . . . characterized as the "Hate Clubs of the Air," replaced programs which were predominantly entertainment oriented. The speed with which these changes took place can lead the Court to one conclusion, and one conclusion only—Brandywine intended to place these controversial programs on the air from the first but feared to so inform the Commission lest the transfer application be denied. This approach was foolish.

FIRST AMENDMENT CONSIDERATIONS

The most serious aspect of this case relates to the basic freedoms of speech and press which are essential guarantees of the First Amendment. This is the area of greatest concern to the Court. Any shortcomings in this area would necessitate our reversing the decision of the Commission.

(T)he concept of censorship (is) an implicit issue in this case. (T)hose cases which have sanctioned previous restraints of the utterances of specific individuals have not involved restraints by administrative action, but rather by judicial restraint. It was a prime objective of those seeking to ban previous restraints to outlaw censorship which could be accomplished through licensing. It was in this setting that John Milton directed his offensive in his *Appeal for the Liberty of Unlicensed Printing*.

(T)here are areas where the federal government has, at one time or another, placed restraints on both freedoms of speech and press. Those areas include, or have included, censorship of the mails, e.g., fraud orders and obscenity; regulation of business and labor activities; regulation of political activities by federal employees; legislation to protect the armed forces and the war power; loyalty regulations; the Smith Act; and the registration of subversive organizations.

Broadcasting's freedom has been curtailed by fiat through rulings of the Supreme Court. The Court has stated that as long as we are licensed by the government, we are not as free as the printed press and therefore not eligible in the same manner for the First Amendment guarantees. The father of all such restrictive rulings is the decision in *National Broadcasting Co. v. United States,* where the Court found that freedom of utterance was abridged to anyone who wanted to use the limited facilities of the radio. The Court went on to find that radio was unlike other modes of expression in that it was not available to all. It was this unique characteristic that distinguished the radio from other forms of expression and made it a subject of government regulation. More recently, the Supreme Court's ruling in *Red Lion Broadcasting Co. v. FCC* upheld the "personal attack rule" and found that where substantially more individuals wish to broadcast than there are frequencies available to allocate, it is idle to attempt to establish an unabridgeable First Amendment right to broadcast comparable to the right of each individual to speak, write, or publish.

Journalists and broadcasters have no monopoly over concern with censorship. The courts, and indeed the American public as a whole, have a tremendous stake in a free press and an informed citizenry. Yet, how can the citizenry remain informed if broadcasters are permitted to espouse their own views only without attempting to fully inform the public? This is the issue of good faith which, unfortunately, a small number of broadcasters refuse to exercise.

BRANDYWINE AND THE FIRST AMENDMENT

The Commission has made no attempt to influence WXUR's programming or censor its programming in general or specifically. Had the licensee met the obligations required of it, we have no reason to believe that Brandywine would have met with any difficulty. The law places requirements on licensees as fiduciaries. Failure to live up to the trust placed in the hands of the fiduciary requires that a more responsible trustee be found. This is not the public's attempt to silence the trustee—it is the trustee's attempt to silence the public. This is not the public censoring the trustee—it is the trustee censoring the public. Attempting, to impose the blame on the Commission for its own shortcomings can only be likened to the spoiled child's tantrum at being refused a request by an otherwise overly benevolent parent.

As in the *Red Lion* case, we note that other questions in this area could pose more serious First Amendment problems. Since such questions are not at issue here, there is no need to hypothecate upon them.

SANCTIONS

In light of the extensive violations found by the Commission in the areas of the Fairness Doctrine, the personal attack rules, and misrepresentation of program plans, the Commission refused to renew Brandywine's license. The Commission, while finding that its action would have been justified when based on any of these areas, chose to base its opinion on a consideration of Brandywine's total performance.

CONCLUSION

Appellants have blazed a trail marked by empty promises and valueless verbiage. They have attempted to prevail by wearing down both Commission and court. However, those charged with protecting the precious rights of the public will not, and cannot, be exhausted by a group of recalcitrants who attempt to cajole and bully. Freedom of speech is not an empty slogan or a rallying cry—nor can it be snatched from the hands of the American people by an outpouring of emotional indignation. Freedom of speech is a truth that we have long held to be self-evident; we refuse to sit by idly and watch that truth snuffed out by a group of overly zealous men whose sole interest is filling the airwaves with their own views to the exclusion of the views of all others. Dr. McIntire and his followers have every right to air their views; but so do the balance of our 210 million people.

Brandywine was given every opportunity to succeed in the broadcast endeavor on which it set out. The Commission fulfilled its duty in granting the initial license although it may have proven more popular and expedient to bow to the protestations of Brandywine's detractors. The Commission forewarned Brandywine about its Fairness Doctrine and its personal attack rules and made every effort to explain them. Despite the Commission's sanguine outlook it was soon evidence that Brandywine refused to comply with those requirements, which are designed to serve the public interest and the broadcast audience. Commission good faith was interpreted as an act of weakness.

The First Amendment was never intended to protect the few while providing them with a sacrosanct sword and shield with which they could injure the many. Censorship and press inhibition do not sit well with this Court when engaged in by either the Commission or by a defiant licensee. The most serious wrong in this case was the denial of an open and free airwave to the people of Philadelphia and its environs.

Consequently, the opinion of the Federal Communications Commission is
Affirmed.

COLUMBIA BROADCASTING SYSTEM, INC. v. DEMOCRATIC NATIONAL COMMITTEE

BUSINESS EXECUTIVES' MOVE FOR A VIETNAM PEACE v. FEDERAL COMMUNICATIONS COMMISSION

412 U.S. 94 (1973)

Mr. Chief Justice Burger delivered the opinion of the Court.

We granted the writ in these cases to consider whether a broadcast licensee's general policy of not selling advertising time to individuals or groups wishing to speak out on issues they consider important violates the Federal Communications Act of 1934 or the First Amendment.

In two orders announced the same day; the Federal Communications Commission ruled that a broadcaster who meets his public obligation to provide full and fair coverage of public issues is not required to accept editorial advertisements. A divided Court of Appeals reversed the Commission, holding that a broadcaster's fixed policy of refusing editorial advertisements violates the First Amendment; the court remanded the cases to the Commission to develop procedures and guidelines for administering a First Amendment right of access.

Balancing the various First Amendment interests involved in the broadcast media and determining what best serves the public's right to be informed is a task of a great delicacy and difficulty. The process must necessarily be undertaken within the framework of the regulatory scheme that has evolved over the course of the past half-century. For during that time, Congress and its chosen administrative agency have established a delicately balanced system of regulation intended to serve the interests of all concerned. The problems of regulation are rendered more difficult because the broadcast industry is dynamic in terms of technological change; solutions adequate a decade ago are not necessarily so now, and those acceptable today may well be outmoded 10 years hence. The judgment of the legislative branch cannot be ignored or undervalued simply because one segment of the broadcast constitutency casts its claims under the umbrella of the First Amendment. That is not to say we "defer" to the judgment of the Congress and the Commission on a Constitutional question, nor that we would hesitate to invoke the Constitution should we determine that the Commission has not fulfilled its task with appropriate sensitivity to the interests in free expression. The point is, rather, that when we face a complex problem with many questions and few easy answers, we do well to pay careful attention to how the other branches of government have addressed the same problem.

Of particular importance, in light of Congress' flat refusal to impose a "common carrier" right of access for all persons wishing to speak out on public issues, is the Commission's "Fairness Doctrine," which evolved gradually over the years spanning federal regulation of the broadcast media. Formulated under the Commission's power to issue regulations consistent with the "public interest," the doctrine imposes two affirmative responsibilities on the broadcaster: coverage of issues of public importance must be adequate and must fairly reflect differing veiwpoints. In fulfilling its Fairness Doctrine obligations, the broadcaster must provide free time for the presentation of opposing views if a paid sponsor is unavailable, and it must initiate programming on public issues if no one else seeks to do so.

Since it is physically impossible to provide time for all viewpoints, however, the right to exercise editorial judgment is granted to the broadcaster. The broadcaster, therefore, is allowed significant journalistic discretion in deciding how best to fulfill its Fairness Doctrine obligations, although that discretion is bounded by rules designed to assure that the public interest in fairness is furthered.

Thus, under the Fairness Doctrine, broadcasters are responsible for providing the listening and viewing public with access to a balanced presentation of information on issues of public importance. The basic principle underlying that responsibility is "the right of the public to be informed, rather than any right on the part of the government, any broadcast licensee, or any individual member of the public to broadcast his own particular views on any matter." (*Report on Editorializing,* 13 F.C.C. 1246, 1249 (1949).) Consistent with that philosophy, the Commission on several occasions has ruled that no private individual or group has a right to command the use of broadcast facilities.

As we have seen, with the advent of radio a half-century ago, Congress was faced with a fundamental choice between total government ownership and control of the new medium—the choice of most other countries—or some other alternative long before the impact and potential of the medium was realized. Congress opted for a system of private broadcasters licensed and regulated by government. The legislative history suggests that this choice was influenced not only by traditional attitudes toward private enterprise but by a desire to maintain for licensees, so far as consistent with necessary regulation, a traditional journalistic role.

The tensions inherent in such a regulatory structure emerge more clearly when we compare a private newspaper with a broadcast licensee. The power of a privately owned newspaper to advance its own political, social, and economic views is bounded by only two factors: first, the acceptance of a sufficient number of readers—and hence advertisers—to assure financial success; and, second, the journalistic integrity of its editors and publishers. A broadcast licensee has a large measure of journalistic freedom but not as large as that exercised by a newspaper. A licensee must balance what it might prefer to do as a private entrepreneur with what it is required to do as a "public trustee." To perform its statutory duties, the Commission must oversee without censoring. This suggests something of the difficulty and delicacy of administering the Communications Act—a function calling for flexibility and the capacity to adjust and readjust the regulatory mechanism to meet changing problems and needs.

The licensee policy challenged in this case is intimately related to the journalistic role of a licensee for which it has been given initial and primary responsibility by Congress. The licensee's policy against accepting editorial advertising cannot be examined as an abstract proposition, but must be viewed in the context of its journalistic role. It does not help to press on us the idea that editorial ads are "like" commercial ads for the licensee's policy against editorial spot ads is expressly based on a journalistic judgment that 10- to 60-second spot announcements are ill suited to intelligible and intelligent treatment of public issues; the broadcaster has chosen to provide a balanced treatment of controversial questions in a more comprehensive form. Obviously, the licensee's evaluation is based on its own journalistic judgment of priorities and news worthiness.

Moreover, the Commission has not fostered the licensee policy challenged here; it has simply declined to command particular action because it fell within the area of journalistic discretion. The Commission explicitly emphasized that "there is of course no Commission policy thwarting the sale of time to comment on public issues." The Commission's reasoning, consistent with nearly 40 years of precedent, is that so long as a licensee meets its "public trustee" obligation to provide balanced coverage of issues and events, it has broad discretion to decide how that obligation will be met.

There remains for consideration the question whether the "public interest" standard of the Communications Act requires broadcasters to accept editorial advertisements or, whether, assuming governmental action, broadcasters are required to do so by reason of the First Amendment. In resolving those issues, we are guided by the "venerable principle that the construction of a statute by those charged with its execution should be followed unless there are compelling indications that it is wrong."

The Commission was justified in concluding that the public interest in providing access to the marketplace of "ideas and experiences" would scarcely be served by a system so heavily weighted in favor of the financially affluent, or those with access to wealth. Even under a first-come-first-served system, proposed by the dissenting Commissioner in these cases, the views of the affluent could well prevail over those of others, since they would have it within their power to purchase time more frequently. Moreover, there is the substantial danger, as the Court of Appeals acknowledged, that the time allotted for editorial advertising could be monopolized by those of one political persuasion.

If the Fairness Doctrine were applied to editorial advertising, there is also the substantial danger that the effective operation of that doctrine would be jeopardized. To minimize financial hardship and to comply fully with its public responsibilities a broadcaster might well be forced to make regular programming time available to those holding a view different from that expressed in an editorial advertisement; indeed, BEM has suggested as much in its brief. The result would be a further erosion of the journalistic discretion of broadcasters in the coverage of public issues, and a transfer of control over the treatment of public issues from the licensees who are accountable to private individuals who are not. The public interest would no longer be "paramount" but rather subordinate to private whim especially since, under the Court of Appeals' decision, a broadcaster would be largely precluded from rejecting editorial advertisements that dealt with matters trivial or insignificant or already fairly covered by the broadcaster.

Nor can we accept the Court of Appeals' view that every potential speaker is "the best judge" of what the listening public ought to hear or indeed the best judge of the merits of his or her views. All journalistic tradition and experience is to the contrary. For better or worse, editing is what editors are for; and editing is selection and choice of material. That editors—newspaper or broadcast—can and do abuse this power is beyond doubt, but that is not reason to deny the discretion Congress provided. Calculated risks of abuse are taken in order to preserve higher values. The presence of these risks is nothing new; the authors of the Bill of Rights accepted the reality that these risks were evils for which there was no acceptable remedy other than a spirit of moderation and a sense of responsibility—and civility—on the part of those who exercise the guaranteed freedoms of expression.

Under a Constitutionally commanded and government supervised right-of-access system urged by respondents and mandated by the Court of Appeals, the Commission would be required to oversee far more of the day-to-day operations of broadcasters' conduct, deciding such questions as whether a particular individual or group has had sufficient opportunity to present its viewpoint and whether a particular viewpoint has already been sufficiently aired. Regimenting broadcasters is too radical a therapy for the ailment respondents complain of.

Under the Fairness Doctrine, the commission's responsibility is to judge whether a licensee's overall performance indicates a sustained good faith effort to meet the public interest in being fully and fairly informed. The Commission's responsibilities under a right-of-access system would tend to draw it into a continuing case-by-case determination of who should be heard and when.

The Commission is also entitled to take into account the reality that in a very real sense listeners and viewers constitute a "captive audience." The "captive" nature of the broadcast audience was recognized as early as 1924, when Commerce Secretary Hoover remarked at the Fourth National Radio Conference that "the radio listener does not have the same opinion that the reader of publications has—to ignore advertising in which he is not interested—and he may resent its invasion on his set." As the broadcast media became more prevasive in our society, the problem has become more acute.

Conceivably at some future date Congress or the Commission—or the broadcasters—may devise some kind of limited right of access that is both practicable and desirable. Indeed, the Commission noted in these proceedings that the advent of cable television will afford increased opportunities for the discussion of public issues.

For the present the Commission is conducting a wide-ranging study into the effectiveness of the Fairness Doctrine to see what needs to be done to improve the coverage and presentation of public issues on the broadcast media.

Mr. Justice Douglas.

While I join the Court in reversing the judgment below, I do so for quite different reasons.

My conclusion is that the TV and radio stand in the same protected position under the First Amendment as do newspapers and magazines. The philosophy of the First Amendment requires that result, for the fear that Madison and Jefferson had of government intrusion is perhaps even more relevant to TV and radio than it is to newspapers and other like publications.

If a broadcast licensee is not engaged in governmental action for purposes of the First Amendment, I fail to see how Constitutionally we can treat TV and the radio differently than we treat newspapers. It would come as a surprise to the public as well as to publishers and editors of newspapers to be informed that a newly created federal bureau would hereafter provide "guidelines" for newspapers or promulgate rules that would give a federal agency power to ride herd on the publishing business to make sure that fair comment on all current issues was made. In 1970 Congressman Farbstein introduced a bill, never reported out of the Committee, which provided that any newspaper of general circulation published in a city with a population greater than 25,000 and in which fewer than two separately owned newspapers of general circulation are published "shall provide a reasonable opportunity for a balanced presentation of conflicting views on issues of public importance" and giving the Federal Communications Commission power to enforce the requirement.

Thomas I. Emerson, our leading First Amendment scholar has stated that " . . . effort to solve the broader problems of a monopoly by forcing newspapers to cover all 'newsworthy' events and print all viewpoints, under the watchful eyes of petty public officials, is likely to undermine such independence as the press now shows without achieving any real diversity." (The System of Freedom of Expression (1970), p. 671.)

Red Lion Broadcasting Co. v. *FCC,* in a carefully written opinion that was built upon predecessor cases put the TV and the radio under a different regime. I did not participate in that decision and, with all respect, would not support it. The Fairness Doctrine has no place in our First Amendment regime. It puts the head of the camel inside the tent and enables administration after administration to toy with TV or radio in order to serve its sordid or its benevolent ends. In 1973—as in other years—there is clamoring to make the TV and radio emit the messages that console certain groups. There are charges that these mass media are too slanted, too partisan, too hostile in their approach to candidates and the issues.

Government has no business in collating, dispensing, and enforcing, subtly or otherwise, any set of ideas on the press. Beliefs, proposals for change, clamor for controls, protests against any governmental regime are protected by the First Amendment against governmental ban or control.

Mr. Justice Brennan, with whom Mr. Justice Marshall concurs, dissenting.

As a practical matter, the Court's reliance on the Fairness Doctrine as an "adequate" alternative to editorial advertising seriously overestimates the ability—or willingness—of broadcasters to expose the public to the "widest possible dissemination of information from diverse and antagonistic sources." As Professor Jaffe has noted, "there is considerable possibility that the broadcaster will exercise a large amount of self-censorship and try to avoid as much controversy as he safely can." Indeed, in light of the strong interest of broadcasters in maximizing their audience, and therefore their profits, it seems almost naive to expect the majority of broadcasters to produce the variety and controversiality of material necessary to reflect a full spectrum of viewpoints. Stated simply, angry customers are not good customers and, in the commercial world of mass communications, it is simply "bad business" to espouse—or even to allow others to espouse—the heterodox or the controversial. As a result, even under the Fairness Doctrine, broadcasters generally tend to permit only established—or at least moderated—views to enter the broadcast world's "marketplace of ideas."

Moreover, the Court's reliance on the Fairness Doctrine as the *sole* means of informing the public seriously misconceives and underestimates the public's interest in receiving ideas and information directly from the advocates of those ideas without the interposition of journalistic middlemen. Under the Fairness Doctrine, broadcasters decide what issues are "important," how "fully" to cover them, and what format, time, and style of coverage are "appropriate." The retention of such *absolute* control in the hands of a few government licensees is inimical to the First Amendment, for vigorous, free debate can be attained only when members of the public have at least *some* opportunity to take the initiative and editorial control into their own hands.

Our legal system reflects a belief that truth is best illuminated by a collision of genuine advocates. Under the Fairness Doctrine, however, accompanied by an absolute ban on editorial advertising, the public is compelled to rely *exclusively* on the "journalistic discretion" of broadcasters, who serve in theory as surrogate spokesmen for all sides of all issues. This separation of the advocate from the expression of his views can serve only to diminish the effectiveness of that expression.

Nor is this case concerned solely with the adequacy of coverage of those views and issues which generally are recognized as "newsworthy." For also at stake is the right of the public to receive suitable access to new and generally unperceived ideas and opinions. Under the Fairness Doctrine, the broadcaster is required to present only *"representative* community views and voices on controversial issues" of public importance. Thus, by definition, the Fairness Doctrine tends to perpetuate coverage of those "views and voices" that are already established, while failing to provide for exposure of the public to those "views and voices" that are novel, unorthodox, or unrepresentative of prevailing opinion.

Finally, it should be noted that the Fairness Doctrine permits, indeed *requires,* broadcasters to determine for themselves which views and issues are sufficiently "important" to warrant discussion. The briefs of the broadcaster-petitioners in this case illustrate the type of "journalistic discretion" licensees now exercise in this regard. Thus, ABC suggests that it would refuse to air those views which *it* considers "scandalous" or "crackpot," while CBS would exclude those issues or opinions that are "insignificant" or "trivial." Similarly, NBC would bar speech that strays "beyond the bounds of normally accepted taste," and WTOP would protect the public from subjects that are "slight, parochial, or inappropriate."

The genius of the First Amendment, however, is that it has always defined what the public ought to hear by permitting speakers to say what they wish.

(T)he *absolute* ban on editorial advertising seems particularly offensive because, although broadcasters refuse to sell any airtime whatever to groups or individuals wishing to speak out on controversial issues of public importance, they make such airtime readily available to those "commercial" advertisers who seek to peddle their goods and services to the public. Thus, as the system now operates, any person wishing to market a particular brand of beer, soap, toothpaste, or deodorant has direct, personal, and instantaneous access to the electronic media. He can present his own message, in his own words, in any format he selects and at a time of his own choosing. Yet a similar individual seeking to discuss war, peace, pollution, or the suffering of the poor is denied this right to speak. Instead, he is compelled to rely on the beneficence of a corporate "trustee" appointed by the government to argue his case for him.

COUNCIL FOR EMPLOYMENT AND ECONOMIC ENERGY USE v. *FCC*
575 F.2d 311 (1978)

Before Coffin, Chief Judge, Campbell and Bownes, Circuit Judges.
Levin H. Campbell, Circuit Judge.
We are asked to disapprove a Federal Communications Commission ruling made under its "Fairness Doctrine". On October 26, 1976, one week before the general election in November, the Council for Employment and Economic Energy Use (the "Council") petitioned the Commission for a declaratory ruling with respect to application of the "Fairness Doctrine" to radio advertisements concerning a referendum question on the Massachusetts ballot. Two days later, the Commission's Broad-

cast Bureau responded by ruling that the practices about which the Council complained were permissible. After the election, the Council applied for review by the full Commission, which upheld the Broadcast Bureau. The Council then sought review in this court. Before argument the Commission filed a motion to dismiss the appeal for lack of jurisdiction, arguing that the Council is not a "party aggrieved" by a Commission order within the meaning of 28 U.S.C. 2344.

The Council is a political organization formed under Mass. Gen. Laws ch. 55 and 6. It had opposed a proposed law which, if approved in the November 1976, referendum, would have prohibited utilities from selling electricity at discount to large consumers. Commencing October 4, 1976, the Council advertised its views by means of paid radio advertising. Fair Share, Inc., an organization with views opposing those of the Council, thereafter demanded and received from three Massachusetts stations free time to respond to the Council's advertisements. The Council's petition alleged that Fair Share received one free minute of radio time from these stations for every two purchased by the Council. The Council claimed that Fair Share had had adequate resources to pay for the radio time and in fact purchased $30,000 of television time after it had received the free radio time. The petition requested the FCC to rule

> that it is unreasonable for stations to offer free time to (Fair Share) solely because the Council purchased time on the stations and that stations carrying the Council's announcements are not required to offer free time to FSI.

The Broadcast Bureau upheld the reasonableness of the particular stations' actions on the ground of the wide range of discretion accorded broadcasters in meeting their Fairness Doctrine responsibilities. The Bureau observed,

> It is . . . the responsibility of the licensees within their good faith discretion to determine how to present contrasting views on the issue in question. They may choose to provide free spot or program time or choose any other format in any reasonable manner to discharge their Fairness Doctrine obligation in their overall programming. The Commission will review the licensees' actions only to determine whether the licensees have acted reasonably and in good faith.

Although the voters decided the referendum in accordance with the Council's wishes, the Council pressed an appeal to the Commission. The Council contended that the Bureau had failed to address the question of whether the Fairness Doctrine compelled the action taken by the three radio stations.

> The question presented for review is whether radio stations are required under the 'Cullman rule'* to provide a fixed ratio of free spot announcements to an organization seeking to express views on a ballot proposition different from views expressed in paid spot announcements broadcast on the stations when the organization is fully able to pay for the time it requests.

The application did not directly challenge the determination that the radio stations had acted reasonably, and in its reply to comments on the application made by other parties, the Council declared,

---

*Cullman Broadcasting Company, Inc., 40 FCC 576 (1963).

(The central issue of this case) is not, as the Bureau suggests, whether 'the licensees abused their discretion in offering free time to (Fair Share),' but, rather, whether the Commission should have imposed any Fairness Doctrine obligations on the stations under the particular facts of this case. It is the Commission's requirement and not the licensees' response to that requirement that is at issue here.

In spite of the way the Council cast the question for review, the Commission chose to delve into the appropriateness of the response by the three radio stations to their perceived obligations. As the Commission put it,

It appears that the Council is requesting the Commission to hold that the stations, by donating time to (Fair Share), did more than was necessary to discharge the Fairness Doctrine obligations they felt had been incurred by broadcasting the Council's paid spot announcements. As indicated more fully herein, the question, in effect, is not whether the licensees were required to give time to (Fair Share) to broadcast a contrasting view on the electric rate ballot proposition, but whether the stations acted reasonably in determining to discharge their fairness obligations in this particular manner.

The Commission ruled that "the Council is correct in its assertion that the stations were not required to give time" to Fair Share. The stations' Fairness Doctrine obligations could have been met in a number of ways, including paid advertisements, increased news coverage, or debate broadcasts. But considering the totality of the circumstances, the Commission declined to rule that the action taken by the three radio stations was unreasonable or in bad faith. It noted its past refusal to insist upon substantiation of a plea of poverty before an interest group obtained free time pursuant to the Fairness Doctrine, and instead relied on the sound discretion and financial self-interest of broadcasters to assure that groups that could pay for air time would be charged.

The Commission argues that we lack jurisdiction to entertain this appeal because the dispute between the Council and the radio stations is moot and therefore no longer constitutes a justiciable case or controversy. Supporting this contention are the facts that the referendum over which this conflict arose is over, that the Council's position prevailed, and that the Commission could not now meaningfully order increased broadcasting directed to either side of the issue. The Council responds by pointing out that the question addressed in the 1976 election—whether electric utilities may be allowed to sell power at a discount to large consumers—remains a live issue in Massachusetts. Further efforts are underway to prohibit these discounts, which the Council will oppose. It is therefore possible that the issue presented in this proceeding will arise once more, leaving the Commission's present declaratory ruling as dispositive unless reversed by this court. The Commission replies that the Council failed to disclose any ongoing political interest past the 1976 election, but under Massachusetts law a political organization such as the Council does not come to an end automatically upon the passing of the particular election for which it was organized. See Mass. Gen. Laws ch. 55 and 6. The very fact that the Council continues to seek a decision after the election is some indication that its concern is real and continuing. We do not think the case is moot.

The FCC contends that the Council was not aggrieved by the Commission's decision, and thereby lacks standing under 28 U.S.C. and 2344. The Commission argues that in deciding whether radio stations were required to give free time to the Council's opponents, it resolved in the Council as the only issue on review. But the Commission also ruled that the manner in which the three radio stations satisifed their fairness obligations in the 1976 campaign was reasonable, a conclusion which the Council has disputed throughout these proceedings. We think the Council is aggrieved.

The narrow issue before us is whether the Commission could properly allow a radio station to allot free time to a political organization to rebut advertisements paid for by another, where subsequent events indicate that the rebutting organization might have been able to pay for the time received. Significantly, the Council has not alleged that the radio stations deliberately chose to ignore the ability of Fair Share to pay or acted in bad faith. Rather the thrust of its contention seems to be that the radio stations acted unreasonably even if they believed in good faith that Fair Share could not, or perhaps for some good reason, would not, pay. So stated, the Council's position is unsupportable. The Fairness Doctrine has been upheld as constitutional by the Supreme Court. The Court has said "that the Congress and the Commission do not violate the First Amendment when they require a radio or television station to give reply time to answer personal attacks and political editorials." The focus of the Fairness Doctrine is upon the public dissemination of both sides of an issue rather than protection of particular advertisers. While, with respect to payment for time, there may be a point at which a calculated inequality of treatment by broadcasters among advertisers would raise a litigable issue, we see nothing arbitrary about the Commission's hands-off policy here. The Commission has done no more than rule that the donating of reply time is one acceptable means of meeting a licensee's obligations under the Communications Act, at least where there is no showing that the licensee had deliberately and discriminatorily disregarded a respondent's ability to pay. The Commission may well believe that for it to try to instruct broadcasters when to offer free time and when not would deprive them of flexibility needed to apply the Fairness Doctrine in the varied situations that arise. Broadcasters may normally be expected to charge for time when feasible, but circumstances may arise where the public interest is better served by an allotment of free time. In any event, we see nothing unreasonable, unconstitutional or otherwise illegal in the Commission's policies in this regard.

The Council argues that a fixed ratio of reply time to paid political advertising time constitutes an unconstitutional quota in derogation of its First Amendment and equal protection rights and cites a variety of race discrimination cases to support its claim. The argument is patently absurd: these ratios, even if they were as rigidly imposed as the Council represents, in no way restricted the amount of time available to the Council. The Council's only complaint is that its opponents also had an opportunity to communicate their views. It would be a novel interpretation of the first amendment to find within its strictures a right not to be controverted in public political debate.

Petition dismissed. Costs for Commission.

NOTE I

In the case of *Council for Employment and Economic Energy Use* v. *FCC,* the court held that the Fairness Doctrine permits radio stations to donate time for the purpose of rebutting paid political advertisements to groups that the station in good faith believes is unable to buy air time.

As a result of this decision, a petition for certiorari was filed on August 2, 1978 raising the following questions: 1) Was the petitioner's right to equal protection under law violated by the FCC rule, upheld by the court of appeals, allowing radio stations to give free advertising time to the political opponent of the petitioner where such opponent was financially able to pay for that time? 2) Was the holding of the FCC, upheld in the court of appeals, that certain radio stations had acted reasonably in meeting their "Fairness Doctrine" obligations, supported by substantial evidence? 3) Is application of the Fairness Doctrine in terms of the method that the radio stations employed to comply with its requirements in the present case consistent with public interest? (47 USLW 3111 (August 29, 1978).)

NOTE II

In the case of *Office of Communication of the United Church of Christ v. FCC,* the United States Circuit Court of Appeals of Washington, D.C. decided that the FCC, in its interpretation of the Communications Act's "equal time" requirement, did not err by including, within the section's exemption for "on-the-spot" coverage of bona-fide news events, delayed broadcast of a taped political debate, based upon the Commission's finding that broadcasters need substantial discretion in determining "on-the-spot" political coverage.

In 1976 the Commission ruled that broadcasters would not incur equal time obligations by providing live broadcasts of newsworthy political events. Now the Commission has lifted the equal time requirement for delayed broadcasts of "bona fide" news events involving political candidates. In so doing, the Commission stressed the need to preserve "considerable discretion in the presentation of news programming," and also emphasized the broadcaster's responsibility to judge whether delayed broadcast would be justified by the event's "current newsworthiness." The FCC noted that length of delay would be a factor in determining the broadcaster's reasonableness and good faith, adding that "absent unusual circumstances, a delay of more than a day would raise questions" as to a broadcast's eligibility for an exemption. (47 USLW 2161 (September 19, 1978).)

FIRST AMENDMENT IMPLEMENTATION ACT OF 1975
Congressional Record, H 1351–H 1353 (March 4, 1975)

Statement of Congressman Robert Drinan[*]

The Speaker pro tempore. Under a previous order of the House, the gentleman from Massachusetts (Mr. Drinan) is recognized for 15 minutes.

Mr. Drinan. Mr. Speaker, I would like to bring to the Members' attention a bill which I recently introduced, the First Amendment Implementation Act of 1975, H.R. 2189. This legislation is designed to strengthen the objectives of the First Amendment as applied to radio and television broadcasting stations. Under its provisions, the Federal Communications Commission (FCC) would no longer have control over the content of broadcasts over the public airways.

Our guaranteed freedom of speech and expression is a unique highlight of the American Constitutional system. The press receives favored treatment under the Constitution due to its importance in providing information vital to a rational process of decision making, both on public and private issues. The First Amendment directs that the Congress "make no law abridging the freedom of speech, or of the press," and among these freedoms is the editorial right of a newspaper to determine what may or may not be published. There is no compulsion that a paper must include everything

[*]Former Dean of Boston College Law School.

submitted to it as news. Indeed, as Benjamin Franklin, a one time managing editor of a newspaper, declared, "my publication is not a stagecoach with seats for everyone."

Radio and television serve the same function as newspapers—they inform and entertain. The same First Amendment rights adhere to broadcasters as well as the press. And yet since 1940, the federal government has attempted to control the content of programing through the FCC's so-called "Fairness Doctrine." Our Founding Fathers did not attempt to limit the First Amendment freedoms to one particular aspect of the press, and neither should their descendants. Just as newspapers are free to determine broadcasting content, unfettered by governmental intervention (*sic*).

Mr. Speaker, the "Fairness Doctrine" supposedly enhances the public's "right to know," but I submit that the doctrine threatens that right. Rather than encouraging the expression of differing viewpoints, it chills their expression. In attempting to comply with the FCC's regulations, broadcasters are sidestepping many of the current issues of the day. The result is that the Fairness Doctrine defeats the purpose of its existence. For these reasons and others, it is now time to abolish the doctrine and give way to true First Amendment freedoms.

FAIRNESS DOCTRINE SUSPECT UNDER FIRST AMENDMENT

The Supreme Court, on numerous occasions, has indicated that the broadcast media comes under the protection of the First Amendment. It has also indicated the dangers to that protection when government attempts to intervene too actively in this area.

Chief Justice Burger, in *Columbia Broadcasting System, Inc.* v. *Democratic National Committee*, 412 U.S. 94 (1973) spoke of the editorial freedom of newspapers and broadcast media:

> That editors—newspaper and broadcast—can and do abuse this power is beyond doubt, but that is no reason to deny the discretion that Congress provided. Calculated risks of abuse are taken in order to preserve higher values. The presence of these risks is nothing new; the authors of the Bill of Rights accepted the reality that these risks were evils for which there was no acceptable remedy other than a spirit of moderation and a sense of responsibility . . . on the part of those who exercise the guaranteed freedom of expression.

The Court itself states:

> Any approach whereby a government agency would undertake to govern day-to-day editorial decision of broadcast licensees endangers the loss of journalistic discretion and First Amendment values. (412 U.S. at 120–121)

In *Miami Herald Publishing Co.* v. *Tornillo* (94 S.Ct. 2831 (1974)), the Supreme Court held unconstitutional a Florida statute enforcing a "right of reply" to newspaper articles critical of public persons or policies. Chief Justice Burger stated that treatment of public issues, fairly or unfairly, comprises exercise of editorial content and judgment; Government regulation of this process is irreconcilable with the guarantees of a free press.

Recently, the U.S. District Court of Appeals for the District of Columbia in *National Broadcasting Company, Inc.* v. *Federal Communications Commission* (43 L.W.2133 (CADC 1974)) used the

Supreme Court's comments in overturning an FCC application of the Fairness Doctrine to a television documentary:

> The First Amendment is broadly staked on the view that our country and our people . . . is best served by widest latitude to the press, as broadening input and outlook, through a robust and uninhibited debate that is subject only to minimum controls necessary for the vitality of our democratic society . . . the evils of communications controlled by a nerve center of government looms larger than the evils of editorial abuse by multiple licensees who are not only governed by the standards of their profession but aware that their interest lies in long term confidence.

The strongest indictment of the FCC's Fairness Doctrine's effect on First Amendment freedoms comes from Judge David L. Bazelon, of the U.S. District Court of Appeals for the District of Columbia. In dissenting in *Brandywine-Main Line Radio, Inc. v. Federal Communications Commission* (973 F.2d 16 (D.C. Cir. 1972)), Judge Bazelon stated that the FCC's licensee revocation of WXUR, a small Pennsylvania radio station was "a prima facie violation of the First Amendment." He said the Commission should reconsider whether "time and technology have so eroded the necessity of governmental imposition of fairness obligations that the doctrine has come to defeat its purpose"; perhaps "more freedom for the individual broadcasters would enhance rather than retard the press's right to a marketplace of ideas."

Even FCC members have commented on the potential irreconciliation between First Amendment rights and the Fairness Doctrine. According to Henry Geller, former FCC General Counsel, the resulting series of ad hoc fairness rulings "have led the Commission ever deeper into the journalistic process, and have raised serious problems." He maintained that the Supreme Court's decision in *Columbia Broadcasting System, Inc. v. Democratic National Committee* (412 U.S. 94 (1973)) rejected the idea of a Constitutional right of access as involving the FCC in too much of the daily editorial decisions of broadcasters. Significantly, Mr. Geller presented this view in an amicus brief in *National Broadcasting Company, Inc. v. Federal Communications Commission* (43 L.W. 2133 (CADC 1974)).

Mr. Speaker, there is general agreement that the broadcast media shares the benefits of the First Amendment with newspapers. There is also agreement that needless governmental regulation in these areas is detrimental to the development of a free press.

NO VALID CRITERIA FOR GOVERNMENTAL INTERVENTION

Reasonable limitations on Constitutional rights can be employed by government, given overriding public interests. These interests must be definable and immediate. Supporters of the Fairness Doctrine argue that, given the limited physical nature of the airwaves, and the broadcast monopoly which arises from this fact, government intervention is necessary to insure the public's exposure to a diversity of viewpoints.

The basic premises upon which this argument rests, limited nature of the airwaves and the resulting limitation of broadcast competition, are false. A present member of the FCC, Mr. Glen O. Robinson, questioned these premises in a November 1967 article in the *Minnesota Law Review*.

According to Mr. Robinson, the "broadcast spectrum" is not an irreversible aspect of nature. He states:

> The "spectrum" is a purely artificial construct of the Commission itself. To give this construct an independent nature and thus attempt to justify the regulation itself in those terms is entirely circular.

The broadcast spectrum is not now, and may never be, saturated. Therefore government intervention to protect a limited resource must fall if it is used to restrict First Amendment rights. Yet even if scarcity were a factor, the Supreme Court in *Columbia Broadcasting System, Inc.* v. *Democratic National Committee* (412 U.S. 94 (1973)) stated that not all regulation can be jusified in the name of scarcity.

There is an economic barrier to broadcast media—one less restrictive however, than in the case of newspapers, "which lie essentially beyond public control." This fact, however, discourages enforcement of a Fairness Doctrine, since radio and TV are more competitive outlets for expression than newspapers, or other published media combined. This disparity is increasing. There are roughly 1,750 daily newspapers. There are nearly 7,400 radio stations and 1,000 TV stations. The effects of this disparity on a local scale are even more distinct. In New York City, there are 10 TV stations, not counting cable TV systems, while there are only 3 major daily English language newspapers in the city's limits. Milwaukee, Wisconsin has 6 TV stations and 20 radio stations—but only 2 daily newspapers, both of which are owned by the same individual. A smaller city presents even more contrast: Wassau, Wisconsin—population 35,000—has two TV stations and five radio stations—but only one daily newspaper.

These stations prove the fallacy in the broadcast monopoly premise. They show the exact opposite to be true: competition among broadcasters is more diverse and varied than among newspapers, which are unregulated. The average community is more likely to get diverse viewpoints from broadcasters, who compete for a viewer's time, than from the one major newspaper that most towns possess. The Fairness Doctrine is not needed to encourage this process.

Finally, Mr. Robinson hits the nub of the problem when he states:

> The mere fact that there are barriers to entry into the communications media, be it newspapers or radio and television, does not in itself resolve the problem of the kinds of control that are permissible and how narrow the focus of restraint of free speech may be.

Mr. Speaker, both newspapers and the broadcast media are protected by the First Amendment. Government restraint of newspapers on the basis of monopoly or limited facilities is unconstitutional. Permitting government restraint of broadcast media on similar grounds, especially when no adequate basis for such restraint is found to exist, is also unconstitutional.

FAIRNESS DOCTRINE SELF-DEFEATING

Laws require the performance of specific functions beneficial to the community. When the law no longer brings about the specific function for which it was created, or its performance is detrimental to the community, it should be abolished.

The Fairness Doctrine is a case in point. It was enacted to enhance the presentation of conflicting views by encouraging—or rather demanding—broadcasters to afford reasonable opportunity for comments by parties with opposing viewpoints. In operation, the Fairness Doctrine discourages the presentation of conflicting views and encourages uniformity of expression. It "protects" the viewer with a diet of blandness.

Here are several examples:

Numerous radio stations refused to broadcast the song, "Unborn Child," a recording by the singing team of Seals and Croft. It presented an argument against abortion. Station executives argued that, under the Fairness Doctrine, they would have to rearrange their broadcast schedules to provide equal time to proabortion people.

ABC's "Dick Cavett Show," featuring an FCC complaint, postponed the airing of one segment with some radical leaders; during this time, it deleted 12 minutes of the segment and added another spokesman to achieve "balance."

WXUR, a Pennsylvania radio station controlled by fundamentalist preacher Dr. Carl McIntire, had its license revoked by the FCC for lack of compliance with the Fairness Doctrine. If it had decreased the number of issues discussed or the intensity of discussion, it could have kept its license.

Knowledgeable FCC officials have long lamented the inequity of the Fairness Doctrine. Mr. Robinson, in the 1967 *Minnesota Law Review* article states:

> The Commission's insistence on the licensees' presenting "balanced" programming, although done in the name of promoting diversity, has had largely the opposite effect. Notwithstanding repreated criticism by various commissioners . . . the Commission's own policies do little to encourage diversity or originality either in the style or content of individual programs or in the overall format of a station's program operations. Indeed its policies have, if anything, added to the inherent tendency of broadcasters to conform to safe, established patterns of operation and programming.

Mr. Geller, in his amicus brief in *National Broadcasting Company, Inc. v. Federal Communications Commission* (43 L.W. 2133 (CADC 1974)), commented on the effect of the fairness rulings:

> The effect, particularly on the small broadcaster, has been to inhibit the promotion of robust, wide open debate.

This effect derives not merely from rulings adverse to the broadcaster, but also in the strain, time, and resources involved in coping with particular challenges, even if they are unsuccessful.

A case in point: KREM-TV, a Spokane, Washington station, was accused of violating the Fairness Doctrine. The FCC ruled in favor of KREM-TV after the station spent 21 months in proceedings, 480 man-hours of executive and supervisory time, and at a cost of $20,000 in legal expenses alone, discounting any amount spent for travel expenses. Other examples can be cited.

CBS's "Pensions: The Broken Promise," winner of the Peabody Award was ruled in violation of the Fairness Doctrine by the FCC, due to lack of balanced presentation. It required two years of manpower and expense in the U.S. Court of Appeals for the District of Columbia before the Commission's ruling was overturned.

The president of WCOJ, a 5,000-watt radio station in West Chester, Pennslvania acknowledged that the Fairness Doctrine prevented the station from airing a series produced by the Anti-Defamation League of the B'nai B'rith on "The Radical Right." "Why?" the president asked:

> Simply because airing these programs would open the floodgates to . . . a response . . . from the "nut" group . . . . True, we could refuse to air the programs on the basis of their patent untruth, but this would cost us a $10,000 lawsuit up to the Supreme Court of the United States and even then there would be a possibility of losing . . . . This station is not small but it is not that large. We have neither the time nor the money to devote to such Joan-of-Arcian causes.

Implicit in Mr. Geller's brief and the above examples is the fact that the Fairness Doctrine, established to prevent monpolistic broadcasters from only giving one point of view, encourages the creation of monopoly. Only a large well-financed station can hope to continually challenge the FCC rulings. Smaller stations must make certain that their programming arouses no controversy—or go bankrupt trying to correct FCC rulings.

The potential chilling effect of the Fairness Doctrine is best stated by Richard Salant, an executive of ABC:

> When one's very survival in one's business—broadcasting—depends on licensing by the government, when the penalty for error and for government disagreement is not a fine but the loss of your operating license, does anybody think for a moment that there are not those who have said, "Let us skip this one, let us not make waves, let us stay out of trouble?"

Mr. Salant's argument is by no means an exaggerated claim:

- Since 1934, the FCC has put off or kept off the air a total of 105 broadcasters;
- Since January 1, 1970, the FCC has revoked or denied renewal of 21 broadcast licenses;
- Since January 1, 1970, there have been 511 fines totaling $638,275 levied by the FCC.

Lawyer's fees alone for handling "small" fairness complaints are rarely less than $3000 to $5000.

Rather than promoting diverse ideas, the Fairness Doctrine has stifled creative programming through the use of the fine and the power of license revocation. Rather than encouraging a large number of broadcasting stations, the Fairness Doctrine has required the development of large, well-financed stations as an entrance fee for freedom of expression.

The First Amendment was enacted to protect people's right to know. Its protection extends to broadcast media and newspapers alike. Only reasons of overriding public interest can modify these rights. The Fairness Doctrine itself has subverted the very purpose for which it was created—the enhancement of the public's right to know. It is in the public's overriding interest to continue a doctrine that stifles the development of a free press? I think not. It should be abolished.

FIRST AMENDMENT IMPLEMENTATION ACT OF 1975

Mr. Speaker, I have introduced legislation which would implement the First Amendment for the broadcasting industry. For the benefit of my colleagues, I would like to explain the provisions of the bill.

Section One delineates the purpose of the act, which is to strengthen the objectives of the First Amendment by removing needless statutory and regulatory restrictions on broadcasters operating under the Communications Act of 1934.

Section 2 defines "public interest, convenience, and necessity" so as to exclude FCC jurisdiction in matters relating to the expression of any views by any persons. The Commission would not be able to control, supervise, review, or comment upon the content or scheduling of any programs or broadcasts. The FCC would, on the other hand, retain its license renewal and revocation powers, with the exceptions provided for in the bill. It should also be mentioned that the language of the bill does not repeal federal laws presently in effect which prohibit the broadcasting of obscenities and lottery information.

Section 3 repeals Section 312(a) of the 1934 Communications Act, which permits licensee revocation of any station willfully refusing or failing to allow a candidate for federal office to buy reasonable amounts of broadcast time.

Section 4 repeals Section 315 of the 1934 Communications Act, containing the equal time and Fairness Doctrine provisions. This repeal could give greater freedom to political candidates. A reminder of this is the temporary repeal of Section 315 in 1960, allowing the Kennedy-Nixon debates—certainly one of broadcasting's most effective presentations of political candidates and their views.

Section 5 amends Section 326 of the 1934 Communications Act, by clarifying the broadcaster's rights to determine the scheduling, content, and personal appearances by individuals on their programs.

Finally, Section 6 repeals the prohibition of political editorializing by noncommercial educational broadcasting stations.

Mr. Speaker, I do want to make it clear that H.R. 2189 by no means makes the Federal Communications Commission an obsolete agency. The FCC still retains wide discretion in determining the resolution of technical matters associated with broadcasting, a primary reason for its existence. Only the FCC's power to determine the content of a program is curbed. Neither are issues affected which are not associated with the FCC and the Fairness Doctrine, such as public service announcements.

For the information of the members, I would now like to insert the actual text of my bill, H.R. 2189 (The First Amendment Implementation Act of 1975):

H.R. 2189

Be it enacted by the Senate and House of Representatives of the United States of America in Congress assembled.

SHORT TITLE AND STATEMENT OF PURPOSE

SECTION 1. (a) This Act may be cited as the "First Amendment Implementation Act of 1975."

(b) It is the purpose of this Act to recognize and confirm the applicability of and to strengthen and further the objectives of the First Amendment of the Constitution of the United States by removing statutory and regulatory restrictions on broadcasters operating under the Communications Act of 1934.

DEFINITION OF PUBLIC INTEREST, CONVENIENCE, AND NECESSITY

SECTION 2. Section 309 of the Communications Act of 1934 is amended by inserting at the end thereof the following:

"(1) Notwithstanding any other provision of this part, effective on and after the date of the enactment of this subsection for the purposes of this part, the terms 'public interest, convenience, and necessity' shall not be construed to give the commission jurisdiction to require the provision of broadcast time to any person or persons or for the expression of any viewpoint or viewpoints or otherwise to exercise any power, supervision, control, influence, comment, or review, either directly or indirectly, over the content or schedule of any program or any other material broadcast by licensees, except where the broadcast of such material is otherwise prohibited by law."

REPEAL OF LICENSE OR CONSTRUCTION PERMIT REVOCATION POWER RELATING TO FACILITIES FOR CANDIDATES FOR FEDERAL OFFICE

SECTION 3. Section 312(a) of the Communications Act of 1934 is amended by inserting "or" at the end of clause (5), striking out the semicolon and "or" at the end of clause (6) and inserting in lieu thereof a period, and striking out clause (7).

REPEAL OF SECTION 315 RELATING TO FACILITIES FOR CANDIDATES FOR PUBLIC OFFICE

SECTION 4. Section 315 of the Communications Act of 1934 is repealed.

RECOGNITION OF APPLICATION OF RIGHT OF FREE PRESS

SECTION 5. Section 326 of the Communications Act of 1934 is amended by inserting after "speech" the following: "or the right of free press" and by striking the period after "communication" and inserting in lieu thereof a comma and "including the right of a radio station to determine the schedule of its programs and the content of its programs. Nothing in this Act shall be construed to require the provision of broadcasting time to any person or persons."

REPEAL OF PROHIBITION OF POLITICAL EDITORIALS

SECTION 6. Section 399 of the Communications Act of 1934 is repealed.

THE FIRST AMENDMENT IMPLEMENTATION ACT OF 1975 AND THE FAIRNESS DOCTRINE

Congressional Record, H 4646–H 4648 (May 22, 1975)

Statement of Congressman Robert Drinan*

The speaker pro tempore. Under a previous order of the House, the gentleman from Massachusetts (Mr. Drinan) is recognized for 10 minutes.

*Former Dean of Boston College Law School.

Mr. Drinan. Mr. Speaker, I have reintroduced the First Amendment Implementation Act of 1975, H.R. 7227 a bill which would strengthen the objectives of the First Amendment insofar as radio and television broadcasting. Under its provisions, the Fairness Doctrine would be repealed so that the Federal Communications Commission would no longer have control over the content of media broadcasting. In addition, the equal time regulations of the FCC would be eliminated.

I am pleased to announce, Mr. Speaker, that 10 cosponsors have joined me in filing the First Amendment Implementation Act. They include Mr. Eilberg of Pennsylvania, Mr. Fraser of Minnesota, Mr. Hicks of Washington, Mr. McDonald of Georgia, Mrs. Meyner of New Jersey, Mr. Mitchell of Maryland, Mr. Mosher of Ohio, Mr. Stark of California, Mr. Symms of Idaho, and Mr. Won Pat of Guam.

In recent years, this country's First Amendment rights have been seriously abridged by what is known as the Fairness Doctrine, a Federal Communications Commission regulation calling for the balanced presentation of issues in television and radio broadcasting. Despite the doctrine's praiseworthy rationale, however, the Fairness Doctrine cannot be justified under the dictates of the First Amendment. It is repealed in my bill because it represents an unconstitutional incursion into the rights of the press.

The Fairness Doctrine was not formally enunciated by the FCC until 1949. At that time it was adopted as part of an FCC report upholding the right of broadcast licensees to editorialize. The new policy was not designed to repress the expression of differing views, but to stimulate the multiplicity of opinions. In 1959, the doctrine was further expanded statutorily when Congress amended the 1934 Communications Act. The amendment required broadcast licensees "to afford reasonable opportunity for the discussion of conflicting views on issues of public importance." The reasoning behind the legislation was that the air is public, and the public should have access to broadcast facilities using its airways.

Mr. Speaker, I think it is significant to note that Senator Proxmire was one of the leading proponents of the amendment which statutorily enacted the Fairness Doctrine. He, like many others, sincerely believed that the public was in need of such protection. Yet Senator Proxmire is now one of the prime sponsors in the Senate of legislation to repeal the doctrine. The Senator understands the danger of tampering with the First Amendment, as this sort of action can only serve to lead to a diminution of an individual's personal liberties.

THE FAIRNESS DOCTRINE AND THE FIRST AMENDMENT

Over the years this country has witnessed the fragility of our First Amendment traditions. In the Constitution there is no question as to the meaning and intent of the First Amendment. It rings out clearly, directing that the Congress "make no law abridging the freedom of speech, or of the press."

The enactment of the Fairness Doctrine is an excellent example of the subtle abridgement process which all too often takes place. Our governmental leaders often come to believe that the interests of government and those of the First Amendment are in conflict. From the standpoint of the Fairness Doctrine, there is a feeling that the broadcast media may be too powerful, too irresponsible, or too controlled by special interests to exercise First Amendment rights.

The fairness and balance rationale of the doctrine has such great appeal on the surface that even the Supreme Court has upheld its existence. In its *Red Lion* decision, the Court proclaimed that—

> The licensee has no Constitutional right . . . to monopolize a radio frequency of his fellow citizens.

Red Lion has become the enabling act of the Fairness Doctrine, transforming an ethic of fairness into a rigid law supported by the Judiciary.

The *Red Lion* decision is in distinct contrast with a later decision by the Supreme Court in the *Miami Herald* case. There, the Supreme Court ruled in 1974 that a Florida statute enforcing a right of reply to newspaper articles critical of public persons or policies was unconstitutional. Chief Justice Burger held that government regulation in this area was irreconcilable with the guarantees of a free press. Consequently, Mr. Speaker, what we have is a situation in which the newspapers need grant no right of reply to editorial policies, while the broadcast media must provide such a forum.

The fiction of distinguishing the newspaper press and the broadcast media is now recognized by the courts. But even the Supreme Court in *Red Lion* recognized that the distinction might be a false one. The Court stated in *Red Lion:*

> If experience with the administration of these doctrines indicates that they have the net effect of reducing rather than enhancing the volume and quality of coverage, there will be time enough to reconsider the Constitutional implications.

I submit that that time has now come. In his concurring opinion in *CBS* v. *Democratic National Committee,* Justice William Douglas clearly indicated that no distinction is permissible between newspapers and the media. Justice Douglas wrote:

> My conclusion is that the TV and radio stand in the same protected position under the First Amendment as do newspapers and magazines. The philosophy of the First Amendment requires that result, for the fear that Madison and Jefferson had of government intrusion is perhaps even more relevant to TV and radio than it is to newspapers and other like publications.

Justice Douglas went on to say that the Fairness Doctrine has no place in our First Amendment law.

What kind of First Amendment would best serve our needs as we approach the 21st Century may be an open question. But the old fashioned First Amendment that we have is the Court's only guideline; and one hard and fast principle which it announces is that government shall keep its hands off the press. That principle has served us through days of calm and eras of strife and I would abide by it until a new First Amendment is adopted. That means, as I view it, that TV and radio, as well as the more conventional methods for disseminating news, are all included in the concept of "press" as used in the First Amendment and therefore are entitled to live under the laissez-faire regime which the First Amendment sanctions.

As Justice Douglas has indicated, there is no justifiable basis for distinguishing the newspapers from the media insofar as the application of the First Amendment is concerned. While technical arguments have been made over the years to justify the distinction, they can no longer justify this serious abridgment of First Amendment rights.

THE PERVASIVE CHILLING EFFECT OF THE DOCTRINE

The application of the Fairness Doctrine to the broadcast media does not raise mere academic questions or discussion. The effect of the doctrine has a pervasive chilling effect which is felt throughout radio and television journalism, hindering the true exercise of First Amendment rights. Because of their prior experience with the Fairness Doctrine, the media is often unwilling to take risks in airing a program or documentary which might bring the Fairness Doctrine into play.

Unfortunately, this means that not only are broadcasters hindered, but the American public is prevented from being exposed to a true diversity of viewpoints. Rather than guaranteeing fairness, the doctrine is most often responsible for guaranteeing blandness to the viewers or listeners in their exposure to radio and television.

Mr. Speaker, perhaps the most famous example of the Fairness Doctrine in action is found in the FCC's refusal to renew the license of radio station WXUR in Media, Pennsylvania. This station was under the control of the Rev. Carl McIntire, a fundamentalist preacher who insisted on devoting a substantial amount of time to the teaching of his religious beliefs. The FCC claimed that WXUR failed to adhere to the Fairness Doctrine in its fundamentalist orientation, and therefore revoked its license to operate. Although I may not be a follower of Reverend McIntire's, I strongly support his right to operate WXUR and the programming which he wants to offer. To hold otherwise represents a serious incursion into the area of thoughts and ideas where the government may not inject itself.

The revocation of WXUR's license is an egregious case, but many other examples can be pointed to in indicating a need for the doctrine's repeal. A television station in Spokane, Washington, KREM, was accused of violating the Fairness Doctrine by failing to provide sufficient air time to Spokane citizens who proposed a local bond issue. The complaint was eventually decided in KREM's favor, but in the meantime, the station had to spend some 480 work hours of executive and supervisory time satisfying the FCC that it had indeed been fair on the bond issue. The legal bill of $20,000 presented a heavy burden to the station.

The NBC television network was also involved in a protracted legal struggle with the FCC after the airing of its documentary "Pensions: The Broken Promise." The documentary won four awards, including the prestigious Peabody Award for Public Service in Television and a certificate of merit presented by the American Bar Association. The FCC, however, cited the program for its lack of a balanced presentation, and the ensuing legal struggle required two years of manpower and expense culminating in the U.S. Court of Appeals for the District of Columbia. There, NBC finally won its case, and the Commission's decision was overturned.

One final example which I would like to cite involved a CBS series entitled "The Loyal Opposition." The program was contemplated as a periodic series featuring leaders of the party out of power presenting views contrasting with those of the President. After the first broadcast, however, featuring Democratic National Committee Chairman Larry O'Brien, the Republican National Committee filed a fairness complaint. The FCC upheld the complaint and ordered CBS to provide free time to the Republicans. CBS appealed, and the result was 14 months and tens of thousands of dollars in legal expenses expended before the Court of Appeals finally reversed the FCC and vindicated the network. In view of the difficulties which resulted, however, CBS abandoned "The Loyal Opposition" program.

The chilling effect which these examples present, Mr. Speaker, represents a basic threat to network broadcasting. As one official at WCBS-TV in New York has said, "There are enough pressures in the business; who needs troubles from the FCC?" The profit motive still underlies the operations of media broadcasting, and network executives can be easily led to feel, "Let's skip this one, let's not make waves, let's stay out of trouble." An NBC reporter summed up the current situation quite well:

> Even if we win, you can be sure that the next time someone comes up with an idea for a tough expose, the brass is going to think quite a while before it gives us the go-ahead, and then they'll probably impose their own "Fairness Doctrine" on us.

Even if the broadcast executives decide to throw caution to the winds and to proceed with a controversial program, the chilling effect also extends down to the reporters who are involved in the particular piece. Richard Salant, president of CBS News, described—

> A constant fear that somebody down the line—reporters or producers or somebody—will think "Gee, we've caused such headaches to management, or to ourselves, in having to dig out all this stuff, when the lawyers come around, I'll play it easy."

Salant has even sent a memorandum to his news staff telling them that he considered self-censorship a "high crime." But even aside from the threat which the Fairness Doctrine imposes, Salant also indicated that it serves as a shield for some broadcasters who want to duck hard investigative reporting. "I am persuaded, but obviously cannot yet prove, that the brooding on the presence of the fairness doctrine does indeed affect the state of mind of some reporters, some editors, some news executives," because they realize that their stories, no matter how truthful or valid, may bring on FCC complaints. For reporters as well as broadcasting executives, the chilling effect is omnipresent.

Serious disclosures within recent months with regard to White House involvement in the FCC's operations give pause for further worries and strengthen my feeling that the Fairness Doctrine must be abolished. In a taped statement of President Nixon speaking to H.R. Haldeman and John Dean, dated September 15, 1970, Nixon said:

> The main, main thing is the *Post* is going to have damnable, damnable problems out of this one. They have a television station . . . and they're going to have to get it renewed.

The use of White House pressure in the Federal Communications Commission's operations was not unique to the Nixon Presidency. It has just been revealed that both President Kennedy and President Johnson used the Fairness Doctrine as well in attempting to bring about certain ends. President Kennedy used the Fairness Doctrine to require equal time for his side of the story on the ratification of the Nuclear Test Ban Treaty with the Soviet Union. It was felt by Kennedy that the treaty was being jeopardized by right-wing commentators who denounced it and argued against its ratification. Kennedy and the Democratic National Committee also used the Fairness Doctrine to counter right-wing critics who were backing the candidacy of Barry Goldwater for President. As one Kennedy lieutenant disclosed:

Our massive strategy was to use the Fairness Doctrine to challenge and harass the right-wing broadcasters and hope that the challenges would be so costly to them that they would be inhibited, and decide it was too expensive to continue.

Political involvement in the Fairness Doctrine cannot be ignored when we consider the chilling effect and the possible dangers involved in the Fairness Doctrine. The government influence should not be present so as to encourage or discourage broadcasters from the probing, hard-hitting journalism which is in the public interest, but possibly conflicts with the doctrine. In view of the many hair-splitting decisions which must be made to implement the regulations, there is no alternative other than simply eliminating the doctrine.

THE FALLACY OF THE SCARCITY THEORY

The most widely accepted justification today for the Fairness Doctrine is the scarcity of tele-communications outlets, and therefore, the scarcity of frequency bands available to the citizenry. The key to the scarcity theory is that with the limited number of frequencies the government must carefully regulate those broadcasters who are granted licenses. Today, however, there is serious doubt as to whether the scarcity of broadcast frequencies exists. The emergence of cable TV, the perfection of UHF technology, and the more efficient usage of the VHF broadcast spectrum promise an end to the scarcity of broadcast frequencies.

When one considers the actual facts insofar as the number of radio and TV stations as opposed to newspapers, the fallacy of the scarcity theory is clearly revealed. The FCC speaks in terms of scarcity, and yet there are far more broadcasting stations than newspapers, although newspapers are not regulated in the least. As of December 31, 1974, there were 7,785 radio stations on the air and 952 TV stations, serving nearly every part of the country. Yet as of January 1, 1971 daily newspapers totaled only 1,749. To this fact must be added our current technological capability which allows even more stations to be added to the broadcast spectrum.

In the future, we can look forward to fewer rather than more daily newspapers. On the other hand, just speaking in terms of the television market, it is predicted that in perhaps ten years it will be possible to provide to the televison viewer 400 channels. With the possibilities for cable television, the scarcity theory surely must fall.

Under the scarcity rationale, the government argues that the broadcast media must be regulated to encourage a diversity of ideas to counteract the scarcity of frequencies. But from the above statistics and our own common knowledge, it can readily be seen that there is no evidence of a deficiency of diversity in the media—unless we consider the deficiencies which the Fairness Doctrine creates. Radio and television stations are much more competitive than newspapers in terms of numbers and accessibility insofar as ownership. It is markedly easier to start a radio or television station than a newspaper. In view of these quantitative and qualitative differences, the scarcity theory can no longer be upheld.

CONCLUSION: THE FAIRNESS DOCTRINE MUST BE ABOLISHED

The Fairness Doctrine is inappropriately named. Its regulations do not maximize fairness, but rather, the abridgement of the First Amendment. As Judge David L. Bazelon has stated, the exercise of power over speech has led the Government knee-deep into the regulation of expression. And that, we have always assumed, is forbidden by the First Amendment. The Supreme Court has so held, time and time again.

At present, the Fairness Doctrine is leading to a diminution of the press's role as an information provider. The free flow of information is absolutely essential to self-government and to a democracy as a whole. A government which can dictate what is fair reporting can largely control information to the public in a manner which subverts this self-government. As we have learned, in order to keep our government alive and vibrant, the press must be available to criticize the government, to make its views freely know, and to publish its opinions in a forthright manner. The Fairness Doctrine is a hindrance to all of these pursuits. It is for this reason, Mr. Speaker, that I have filed the First Amendment Implementation Act of 1975. I feel that this legislation is needed to correct an artificial distinction which has been promulgated by the Federal Communications Commission and erroneously endorsed by the Congress.

It is true that the repeal of the doctrine could result in some abuses. But then again, such abuses can be tolerated when we are defending the principles of an axiom as important as the First Amendment. Chief Justice Warren Burger has conceded that both newspaper and broadcast editors can and do abuse the powers which are accorded to them through the Constitution, yet he argues that this is no reason to deny this discretion. As Burger says:

Calculated risks of abuse are taken in order to preserve higher values.

Here we clearly do have a case of higher values, and it is for this reason that I so strongly urge the Congress to take action to repeal the Fairness Doctrine.

GEORGIA POWER PROJECT v. *FEDERAL COMMUNICATIONS COMMISSION*
3 Med. L. Rptr. 1299, 559 F.2d 237 (CA 5, 1977)

Before Wisdom, Simpson, and Tjoflat, Circuit Judges.

Per Curiam:

This case arises under the Federal Communication Commission's (FCC or "Commission") Fairness Doctrine. Under this doctrine when a broadcast station presents programming on one side of a controversial issue of public importance, a reasonable opportunity for the presentation of opposing views must be provided. The controversy arose when the petitioner complained to the FCC that a series of spots sponsored by the Georgia Power Company and repeatedly broadcast by the licensees of WJBF-TV and WQXI-TV (now WXIA-TV) gave rise to Fairness Doctrine obligations. The petitioner, Georgia Power Project, contended that these broadcasts presented one side of a controversial issue of public importance, namely the power company's rate increase requests then pending before the Georgia Public Service Commission (PSC).

Over a period of two and one-half years, the FCC issued three separate decisions concerning petitioner's Fairness Doctrine complaint. With respect to the advertisements at issue in this petition for review, (ads A-2 through A-5[1]) the FCC in its initial decision, *Media Access Project* (1973), stated that it would not rule on the applicability of the Fairness Doctrine. The Commission noted, however, that the advertisements arguably asserted the need for an increase in generating capacity and thus also advocated one side of the rate increase issue. The Commission did find that two additional advertisements sponsored by the power company, A–1 and A–10, had directly and specifically advocated the rate increase and that the licensees had not afforded a reasonable opportunity for the presentation of opposing viewpoints. The Commission therefore directed the licensees to submit, within seven days of the decision, a statement indicating what additional material they had broadcast or intended to broadcast in the near future that would afford opportunity for the presentation of contrasting views on the rate increase issue. In response to the initial FCC decision, both licensees submitted descriptions of the broadcasting which they contended was sufficient to satisfy the Fairness Doctrine obligations found by the FCC in its initial decision.

After evaluating these responses, the FCC issued its second decision, *Fuqua Television, Inc.* (1974), in which it concluded that the licensees had afforded a reasonable opportunity for the presentation of viewpoints contrasting with those contained in announcements A–1 and A–10. With regard to ads A–2 through A–5, however, the FCC concluded that WJBF and WQXI were not unreasonable in concluding that the advertisements did not present arguments on one side of the rate increase controversy. The FCC's determination—that the ads were not "devoted in an obvious and meaningful way to the discussion of the rate increase issue—was based on an interpretation of the Fairness Doctrine which had been adopted by the FCC three months earlier.

Subsequently, on December 16, 1974, the petitioner filed the instant petition for review and simultaneously moved this Court for leave to present newly discovered evidence before the FCC.

The Court, on January 28, 1975, granted petitioner's motion solely with respect to one item of evidence described as a report of a telephone conversation between a representative of Georgia Power Company and a representative of WJBF. Thereafter, in a third decision, *Fuqua Television, Inc.* (July 30, 1976), the Commission considered the additional evidence which the petitioner was permitted to present by virtue of an order of this Court. After reviewing the report adduced by petitioner, the Commission reaffirmed its second decision.

II

The petitioner argues[2] that the failure on the part of the FCC to find that advertisements A–2 through A–5 presented only one side of a controversial issue of public importance was arbitrary and capricious. We disagree and affirm the Commission's finding.

As the Commission did not have a definite standard by which to gauge broadcasts that treated issues implicitly, rather than explicitly, the Commission refined its policy in the context of an extensive, open policy inquiry. In this report, the Commission made clear that:

> . . . what we are really concerned with is an obvious participation in public debate and not a subjective judgment as to the advertiser's actual intentions. Accordingly, we expect our licensees to do nothing more than to make a reasonable, common sense judgment as to whether the "advertisement" presents a meaningful statement which obviously addresses, and advocates a point of view on, a controversial issue of public importance.

As the Commission pointed out, this judgment may be a difficult one on which individual licensees might well differ. Consequently, the Commission declared it would "not rule against the licensee unless the facts are so clear that the only reasonable conclusion would be to view the 'advertisement' as a presentation on one side of a specific public issue."

Furthermore our review of the Commission's determination is limited. Thus in the present context, where the Commission upholds the licensee's judgment, it will be a rare case indeed when reversal is warranted. We cannot, in the instant case, say that the Commission's determination that a reasonable licensee could find that advertisements A–2 through A–5 did not advocate one side of a controversial issue of public importance was arbitrary and capricious.

We might note in conclusion, however, that the procedure by which the Commission ruled on advertisements A–2 through A–5, is improper and, we trust, will not be repeated. The purpose of the second decision, *Fuqua Television,* or *Fuqua I,* was to evaluate whether the licensees had afforded a reasonable opportunity for the presentation of viewpoints contrasting with those contained in advertisements A–1 and A–10. The gratuitous ruling on advertisements A–2 through A–5, coming without advance notice to the parties that this issue was still alive, is improper although in these circumstances the error was harmless.

The Petition for Review is Denied.

NOTES

[1] Ads A–2 through A–5 read as follows:

A–2

(Audio)—Chris is one year old. In his lifetime he'll experience love, independence, and morning gold with sunshine.

In that lifetime Chris may need a million kilo-watt-hours of electricity. Along with more than 90,000 babies born in Georgia last year he'll continue using it, needing it, in ever increasing amounts. That's why Georgia Power must double its generating capacity by the year 1978 . . . and it took us over 40 years to build the system we have today. This year we'll have to spend near two million dollars every working day for construction.

A–3

(Audio)—You're feeling the pulse beat of a modern electric hospital. People struggling for life with the help of . . . Electrocardiograms . . . Electric Fluoroscopes . . . Electric Iron Lungs . . . Electric Operating Lights . . . (Sound; Baby crying) . . . Electric Incubators.

As the population grows, so does the need for hospital facilities. That's another reason Georgia Power must spend nearly $2 million every working day, just for construction. To serve your growing needs.

A–4

(Video)—Water glass with one straw. Straws are added one by one. Last straw is added as glass almost empties.

(Audio)—Funny thing about electricity. Just when you think you've got enough for everybody. Everybody wants more. For new schools, new hospitals, new office buildings, new shopping centers, new air and water purification equipment, better lighting for our street. And for the thousands of new homes and apartments built in Georgia every year.

That's why Georgia Power must build today to provide the kinds of generating facility necessary to satisfy your growing demands. Otherwise, there just might not be enough power to go around.

And that would really be the last straw. The Georgia Power Company.

A–5

(Audio)
(Sound: Typing)
Do you know what your son saw in school today? A herd of charging elephants.
Through a motion picture projector.
He saw a living cell divide. Through an electric microscope.
He watched a computer . . . . estimate world population changes.
(Sound: Typing)
He printed a newspaper.
He heard a Spaniard reciting from *Don Quixote* . . . with the help of a tape recorder.

[2] We have also considered the FCC's claim of mootness and petitioner's additional claims that the FCC departed from prior pronouncements on the fairness doctrine's application to editorial advertising and that the FCC improperly interpreted the Court's order concerning supplementary evidence and find these claims are without merit.

NATIONAL CITIZENS COMMITTEE FOR BROADCASTING v. FEDERAL COMMUNICATIONS COMMISSION
3 Med. L. Rptr. 1273, 567 F.2d 1095 (CADC, 1977)

Before Wright, McGowan and Tamm, Circuit Judges.

Opinion for the Court filed by Circuit Judge McGowan.

McGowan, Circuit Judge.

These three consolidated petitions for review challenge various aspects of the Federal Communications Commission's Fairness Report. That Report was the product of an inquiry by the FCC, extending five years from its initiation in 1971, the issuance of the Report in 1974, and the denial of reconsideration in 1976, into the policies underlying the Fairness Doctrine and their implementation. It was the first such sustained review since the doctrine was originally articulated by the Commission nearly 30 years ago; and it was a proceeding in which written comments were received from over 120 persons or organizations, with 80 participants in a week-long series of panel discussions and oral arguments held by the FCC in 1972.

For the reasons hereinafter appearing, we leave undisturbed the Report itself, including its central determination to withhold application of the Fairness Doctrine to broadcast communications promoting the sale of commercial products. Our remand to the FCC, however, is with directions to pursue further inquiry into two of the alternative courses of action proposed by some of the petitioners as ways by which the general objectives giving rise to the Fairness Doctrine can be realized.

The Fairness Doctrine, which is not identified in terms in the statutes administered by the FCC, had its inception in 1949. The Notice of Inquiry initiating the reexamination (1971), stated that the ensuing investigation would center around four major topics:

1. The Fairness Doctrine generally;
2. Application of the Fairness Doctrine to broadcast of paid announcements;
3. Access to broadcast media for discussion of public issues; and
4. Application of the Fairness Doctrine to political broadcasts.

The issues considered on this appeal relate to all but the last of these topics, which was the subject of a separate report issued in 1972.

(P)etitioners National Citizens Committee for Broadcasting (NCCB) and Friends of the Earth, and petitioner Council of Economic Priorities (CEP), object to the decision in the Fairness Report not to apply the Fairness Doctrine to ordinary product advertisements, and further contend that the National Environmental Policy Act of 1969 (NEPA), requires the Commission to apply the Fairness Doctrine to advertisements for environmentally dangerous products.

(P)etitioner Committee for Open Media (COM) challenges the Commission's failure, on reconsideration of the Fairness Report, to adopt, or order further inquiry into, its access proposal as an alternative to current Fairness Doctrine enforcement. (I)ntervenor Henry Geller challenges the Commission's decisions to continue case-by-case consideration of Fairness Doctrine complaints, and its failure to consider and adopt his "10-issue" proposal relating to the Fairness Doctrine requirement that a broadcaster devote a reasonable amount of time to coverage of public issues.

Because the Fairness Doctrine and its application have been the subject of extensive commentary in prior decisions of both this court and the Supreme Court, we do not consider it necessary in this opinion to delve into these matters beyond the extent to which they directly impinge on the issues now before us. Similarly, we shall not comment upon those parts of the Fairness Report and order denying reconsideration which are not challenged on these appeals except to the extent they cannot be disentangled from the particular questions we confront.

Accordingly, we shall first consider, in Part II hereof, the challenges to the reach of the Fairness Doctrine. Part III of the opinion will address the specific contentions concerning the manner of enforcement of the Fairness Doctrine.

II

The Fairness Report concludes that the Fairness Doctrine should not be applied to broadcast advertisements promoting the sale of a commercial product. This decision was made with a conscious awareness that it represents a marked shift from previous FCC policy. That previous policy, which was developed in a series of ad hoc decisions by the Commission and the courts, was never subject to precise articulation or definition, leading to uncertainty and difficulties in achieving full and fair enforcement. While we are under no illusion that the new policy, described more fully below, will solve all or perhaps even most of the implementation problems encountered heretofore, we believe that we are without warrant to deny the Commission the opportunity to attempt a new resolution of those difficulties provided that its action is consistent with Constitutional and statutory commands and is otherwise in accordance with standards governing such an exercise of agency discretion. Our function in reviewing the validity of the Commission's decision to reverse its previous course of action is to ensure that it has

> provide(d) an opinion or analysis indicating that the (previous) standard is being changed and not ignored, and assuring that it is faithful and not indifferent to the rule of law.

This standard is a distillation of the general criteria governing judicial review of an exercise of agency discretion in the context of informal rulemaking such as that before us. Our

> responsibility is to assure that the agency has not abused or exceeded its authority, that every essential element of the order is supported by substantial evidence, and that the agency has given reasoned consideration to the pertinent factors.

A. Background

The basic principles of the Fairness Doctrine were established long before the doctrine was given a label: broadcast licensees are obliged both to cover controversial issues of public importance and to broadcast opposing points of view on them. The Commission and petitioners disagree as to when it became FCC policy to apply these obligations to ordinary commercial advertising. In a decision rendered in 1946, the Commission noted that fairness principles could be applicable to produce advertisements if the latter involved controversial public issues. The FCC's first comprehensive statement of the Fairness Doctrine in 1949 did not mention its applicability to product commercials, although the statement did refer approvingly to the FCC's 1946 decision.

Whether or not these statements nearly three decades ago can be said to have established a policy of subjecting commercial advertisements to fairness requirements, it is undeniable that any such policy lay practically dormant until 1967. In that year the Commission held in *WCBS-TV,* upon reconsideration, that cigarette commercials raised the controversial and publicly important issue of whether smoking is desirable, and thus gave rise to the second obligation of the Fairness Doctrine. In *Banzhaf* v. *FCC*, this court affirmed the Commission's authority to apply the Fairness Doctrine to cigarette advertisements. In so doing, we recognized the unique danger to health posed by cigarettes but did not in terms foreclose the possibility that the Commission would be obliged to follow the cigarette precedent with respect to other product advertisements raising controversial issues of public importance.

In *Friends of the Earth* v. *FCC* (1971), we held that, under the approach taken by the Commission with respect to cigarettes in *Banzhaf*, advertisements for high powered automobiles and leaded gasoline also gave rise to the fairness obligation to broadcast opposing points of view. Just as cigarette advertisements were thought to have raised the issue of the desirability of smoking, so also the advertisements at issue in *Friends of the Earth* posed the question of the desirability of motorist preferences which increased air pollution. Moreover, as had been true in the cigarette controversy, there existed uncontroverted evidence of the hazards to health caused by air pollution; and this was unquestionably a controversial issue of public importance. We thus found it impossible to ignore the analogy between the *Banzhaf* cigarette advertisements and the advertisements for cars and gasoline challenged in *Friends of the Earth*, and held that the FCC was obliged to follow the cigarette advertising precedent until and unless the Commission reformulated the policy that it had articulated in *WCBS-TV.*

We noted in *Friends of the Earth* that

(i)t is obvious that the Commission is faced with great difficulties in tracing a coherent pattern for the accommodation of product advertising to the Fairness Doctrine. (449 F.2d at 1170.) This may, if anything, have understated the problem. Once the Commission determined in *WCBS-TV* that implicit advocacy gave rise to the Fairness Doctrine obligation to broadcast opposing points of view, it inevitably became necessary to draw a line between messages so opaque that it could not fairly be said a controversial issue was adumbrated, and messages which have the clear effect of advocacy, albeit in a subtle and nonexplicit manner.

In *Neckritz* v. *FCC* (1974), this court refused to find that an advertisement for a gasoline additive purportedly helpful in reducing automobile emissions raised the controversial issue of auto pollution. Under the approach taken in *Banzhaf* and *Friends of the Earth,* the court could have reached a different conclusion under the following chain of reasoning: 1) the gasoline additive can be used only in conjunction with gasoline, and, indeed, the challenged advertisements promoted the sale of gasoline with the additive; 2) advocating the use of gasoline raises the desirability of such use; 3) gasoline use causes air pollution, which is a controversial issue of public importance; 4) thus, the advertisements raised a controversial issue of public importance. An advertisement with the theme of reducing air pollution would have been held to give rise to the fairness obligation to present the point of view that the product promoted would not reduce air pollution.

This is different from the situation in *Banzhaf, Retail Store Employees Union,* and *Friends of the Earth,* where the advertisements implicitly took a position on the ultimate public issue, rather than a position on ways to solve the ultimate matter in controversy. The court in *Neckritz* thus limited the reach of the approach stated in *Banzhaf* for application of the Fairness Doctrine to product commercials; debate over the efficacy of a product in solving an issue of public concern does not raise that issue. The basic policy choice underlying the *Neckritz* holding is that the Fairness Doctrine should not be transformed into a vehicle for correction of allegedly false advertising. However, it is understandable that some confusion was caused by the holding in *Neckritz,* on the one hand, that a commercial explicitly mentioning a matter of public concern does not give rise to fairness obligations, and the holding in *Friends of the Earth,* on the other, that a commercial only implicitly raising that same issue does give rise to fairness obligations.

The difficulty of defining issues "implicitly" raised by product promotions is only one source of the confusion which resulted from the decision in *WCBS-TV* to apply the Fairness Doctrine to commercial advertisements. It has also proven difficult to apply the Fairness Doctrine to advertisements which do not directly promote a product. Thus, in *Green* v. *FCC,* this court affirmed the FCC conclusion (1970), that armed forces recruitment messages did not raise the issues of the military draft and the Vietnam war, which at the time were significant and controversial issues. While we admitted that the issue of voluntary military recruitment was "implicit" in the challenged announcements, we were not prepared to conclude that the broader issue of the desirability of military service generally was thereby also raised.

On the other hand, this court expressed agreement with the Commission's decision in *National Broadcasting* (1971), that advertisements by Esso advocating oil exploration and drilling in Alaska raised the then-controversial issue of whether the Alaska pipeline should be built, even though the advertisements under challenge did not refer to this issue or state explicitly that the pipeline should be built.

Both *Green* and *National Broadcasting* involved a type of advertisement close to what has been called "institutional advertising"—that is "advertising that promotes the overall image of its sponsor and (only) indirectly its product." In at least one important respect, it is even more difficult to articulate a workable standard for what constitutes an issue "implicitly raised" in the institutional advertising context than it is in the context of advertisements promoting a product or service, such as those in *Banzhaf, Retail Store Employees Union,* and *Friends of the Earth.* The latter explicitly advocate patronizing a product. In most cases, only one clear inference need be drawn in order to state the issue implicitly raised; the desirability of engaging in such purchases. Where the advertisement at issue merely presents the sponsor, it could be concluded that every issue affecting the viability of the enterprise promoted is thereby "implicitly" raised. The Commission refused to take such an approach with respect to institutional advertising, but, as was true with respect to ordinary product commercials, neither the Commission nor the courts were able to articulate clear criteria for ascertaining which issues are and are not "implicitly" raised by institutional advertisements.

B. New FCC Policy with Respect to Commercial Advertisements

The failure of either the courts or the Commission to delineate clearly in the foregoing decisions the contours of the *Banzhaf* approach to commercial advertising and the Fairness Doctrine may be ascribed in part to the very proceeding now under review. Aware that a thorough inquiry into the Fairness Doctrine was pending, neither the agency conducting that inquiry nor the courts reviewing agency execution of current Fairness Doctrine policy were eager to use specific fairness complaints as a vehicle for comprehensive analysis of the efficacy and contours of the *Banzhaf* approach.

The Report divides advertisements into three general categories: editorial advertisements; standard product commercials; and advertisements making product efficacy claims about which there is dispute. Henceforth, only those advertisements in the first of these categories will give rise to Fairness Doctrine obligations. While petitioners raise objection only to the Report's treatment of standard product commercials, we believe that, to be adequately analyzed and understood, this portion of the Report must be considered in the context of FCC policy generally concerning application of the Fairness Doctrine to advertisements. Therefore, we shall briefly examine the Report's conclusions with respect to each of the categories of advertisements listed above.

Editorial advertisements consist of "direct and substantial commentary" on controversial issues of public importance. The classic example of such an announcement is an "overt" editorial, referred to at another point in the Report as an advertisement "that explicitly raise(s) (a) controversial issue." However, the Report recognizes that certain advertisements which do not explicitly or overtly discuss a controversial issue nevertheless should be considered editorial advertisements because they present "a meaningful statement which obviously addresses, and advocates a point of view on," controversial issues of public importance.

The Report concludes that one type of announcement which may give rise to Fairness Doctrine obligations even though it is not an overt editorial is institutional advertising "designed to present a favorable public image of a particular corporation or industry rather than to sell a product," (Id.) Although institutional advertising "ordinarily does not involve debate on public issues," if the advertiser "seek(s) to play an obvious and meaningful role in public debate(,) . . . the Fairness Doctrine . . . applies." The Commission has attempted to provide some guidance for determining whether Fairness Doctrine obligations apply to advertisements that are not "explicitly controversial." Licensees are advised that when the relationship of an advertisement to ongoing debate in the community is substantial and obvious, the ad is likely to represent "obvious participation in public debate." In such circumstances, the Fairness Doctrine should be applied.

We interpret the foregoing pronouncements concerning overt editorials and institutional advertising as reaffirmations of previous FCC policy in these areas. That portion of the Report dealing with standard product commercials, on the other hand, is an explicit departure from previous policy. The Report announces that advertisements for commercial products or services, such as the cigarette advertisements in *Banzhaf* and the automobile and gasoline advertisements in *Friends of the Earth,* henceforth will not give rise to fairness obligations because they "make no meaningful contribution to informing the public on any side of any issue," even though "the business, product, or service advertised is itself controversial." The Commission thus explicitly rejects the chain of reasoning first enunciated in *WCBS-TV:* that because promoting a product raises the issue of the desirability of its use, such promotion triggers application of the Fairness Doctrine if use of the product is a controversial issue of public importance.

Under the policy announced in the Fairness Report, promotion of controversial products will not require presentation of points of view opposing use or sale of the products. This does not mean that all product advertisements are exempt from fairness obligations, however. If in the course of promotion of a product there is "obvious and meaningful . . . discussion" on one side of a controversial issue impinging on the desirability of the product, fairness obligations attach because such advocacy qualifies as an editorial advertisement.

The third and final category of advertisements discussed in the Fairness Report are product claims alleged to be false or misleading, such as the claims for a gasoline additive at issue in *Neckritz,* discussed above. The Report essentially takes the position enunciated by this court in that case. In refusing to apply the Fairness Doctrine to those claims, the court in *Neckritz* distinguished between raising the issue of the effect of a product on a problem which is a controversial issue of public importance and directly raising the controversial issue itself. The opinion went on to suggest that a Federal Trade Commission action for false advertising was the appropriate way to resolve disputes over the truthfulness of efficacy claims. Likewise, the Report concludes that product efficacy claims "play no meaningful or significant role in the debate of controversial issues." Under the policy announced in the Report, the FCC will forego application of the Fairness Doctrine to product claims, however controversial those claims may be and however controversial the public issue to which they relate. The Report concludes that there exists an alternative and preferable "congressionally-mandated remedy for deceptive advertising . . . in the form of various FTC sanctions."

C. Constitutionality of the New FCC Policy

As already mentioned, petitioners and intervenors in this case have not made specific objections to those portions of the Fairness Report that, in effect, reaffirm previous policy with respect to editorial advertisements and product efficacy claims. Nor does this court find any cause to upset these portions of the Report, which seem to us well reasoned and fully consistent with constitutional and statutory commands.

The Report's treatment of commercial advertising is vigorously challenged on both statutory and Constitutional grounds. We believe that the challenges invoking the First Amendment are based on a fundamental misunderstanding of the relationship between Constitutional protection of commercial, or any other type of, speech and the functioning of the Fairness Doctrine. As best we can determine, petitioners make two First Amendment arguments. The first proceeds as follows:

a. commercial speech is protected under the First Amendment because the public has an interest in the free flow of such information;
b. statements which oppose views presented in commercial advertisements are a form of commercial speech;
c. thus, the public has an interest in the free flow of such statements;
d. thus, the FCC must require its licensees to broadcast such statements.

But surely there is no right to broadcast a particular point of view simply because that point of view is protected by the First Amendment. This was clearly established in *Columbia Broadcasting System, Inc. v. Democratic National Committee* (1973), which held that a network need not sell time to persons wishing to present their views on important public issues. Of course, this court has also recognized that speech protected by the First Amendment need not necessarily be broadcast under the second obligation of the Fairness Doctrine.

Petitioners' other First Amendment argument begins with a slightly different application of *Virginia State Board*:

a. to the individual, commercial information may be of more interest than is "the day's most urgent political debate," and such advertisements "may be of general public interest;"
b. thus, commercial advertisements contribute meaningfully to public debate;
c. the Commission's decision not to subject commercial advertisements to the Fairness Doctrine is therefore unconstitutional because it is based on the denial of (b).

The last proposition is a nonsequitur. There is a missing link in the argument, which is that all speech which contributes meaningfully to public debate must be subject to the Fairness Doctrine. We reject the suggestion that any speech protected by the First Amendment must, as a matter of Constitutional law, trigger application of the Fairness Doctrine. While an ultimate function of both the First Amendment and the Fairness Doctrine may be to encourage the dissemination of viewpoints and information, this does not mean that the two principles cover exactly the same ground. There is an obvious difference between the standard employed by the Commission for determining whether the Fairness Doctrine applies to advertisements—that is, whether the advertisement advocates one side of a controversial public issue—and the holding in *Virginia State Board* that advertising is protected by the First Amendment because it represents dissemination of valuable information important to the functioning of a free enterprise system. Nothing in the Supreme Court's decision in *Red Lion Broadcasting Co. v. FCC* (1969), upholding the Constitutionality of the political editorializing and personal attack rules promulgated under the Fairness Doctrine, suggests that the obligation to present opposing points of view must be applied to all Constitutionally protected speech. Indeed, in most instances in which the Fairness Doctrine has been held not to apply, the speech which it was contended triggered application of the obligation was clearly protected by the First Amendment.

We recognize that petitioners' confusion between the standard for First Amendment protection and the standard for application of the Fairness Doctrine may result from misplaced reliance in the Fairness Report itself on the scope of First Amendment protection. Issued before either *Virginia State Board* or *Bigelow v. Virginia,* the Report appeared to equate its conclusion that standard product commercials "make no meaningful contribution toward informing the public on any side of any issue" with the statement by this court in *Banzhaf* (also decided prior to *Virginia State Board* and *Bigelow*), that "(p)romoting the sale of a product is not ordinarily associated with any of the interests the First Amendment seeks to protect." The conclusion reached by the Commission is stated overbroadly; clearly, standard product promotions inform the public about many matters, such as price and efficacy. However, the correctness of the conclusion is not dependent upon whether or not advertisements are associated with First Amendment values. The persuasiveness—or lack thereof—of the Commission's essential finding, that standard commercials do not present "a meaningful discussion of a controversial issue of public importance," is not altered by the recent expansion of First Amendment protection in the area of commercial speech.

Indeed, it can be argued that the First Amendment protection afforded commercial speech cuts precisely contrarily from the manner urged by petitioners. It has been contended by commentators, although viewed skeptically by the Supreme Court, that broadcasters are discouraged from presenting messages which trigger Fairness Doctrine obligations. If the Fairness Doctrine does have this chilling effect, then First Amendment protection of commercial speech would make application of the Fairness Doctrine to such speech less, rather than more, desirable. This was certainly the context in which the *Banzhaf* court—upholding the Commission's decision to subject cigarette advertisements to the Fairness Doctrine—discussed the relevance of First Amendment consideration.

D. Statutory Challenges to the New Commission Policy

It is alleged that the Commission's decision to withdraw standard product commercials from the purview of the Fairness Doctrine violates the standards of the Communications Act and was arbitrary, capricious, and an abuse of discretion.

In the 1959 amendments to the Communication Act, Congress made clear that the already existing statutory requirement that broadcasters operate in the "public interest" included the obligation "to discuss both sides of controversial issues." Petitioners contend tht under this obligation, which the Supreme Court has said gave "statutory approval to the Fairness Doctrine," the Commission must apply the Fairness Doctrine "to advertisements for products whose effects have engendered important controversies over the sale and use of the products." This contention is based on the view that at the time of the 1959 amendments, it was Commission policy to apply the *WCBS-TV* approach to fairness obligations and commercial advertisements; that Congress recognized this policy; and that the 1959 amendments were intended to put the policy in statutory form. We believe that there is no persuasive evidence supporting the basic premise upon which this view is based. It was not clear Commission policy in 1959 to require broadcast of opposing views in response to the advertisements for controversial products.

The 1946 decision concerning commercial advertisements so heavily relied on by petitioners merely stated that debate over the "relative merits of one product or another" could raise "basic and important social, economic, or political issues." The *WCBS-TV* approach extended upon this principle in determining that the promotion of a controversial product was an important and controversial issue. The Fairness Report contracts the potential scope of the principle in requiring that the controversial issue be directly and obviously raised in the debate. But neither the *WCBS-TV* approach nor the Fairness Report is inconsistent with the principle announced in the 1946 Commission decision. Thus, while the 1959 amendments to the Communications Act "codifi(ed) the standards of fairness," we are not convinced that the *WCBS-TV* standard was one of the standards referred to.

There still remains the possibility that the *WCBS-TV* approach inheres in the public interest standard of the Communications Act regardless of whether Congress recognized this in 1959. We think that this view is unwarranted, and realize that both the Commission and this court used stronger language than was necessary in stating that the decision in *WCBS-TV* was "required by the public interest." As this court and the Supreme Court have emphasized, the public interest would not be served by taking away from the FCC all discretion in its administration of the general principles of the Fairness Doctrine. Clearly, application of Fairness Doctrine requirements to commercial advertisements has been fraught with difficulties; remaining faithful to the general principles of the doctrine, the Commission should be allowed to alter the precise contours of the doctrine in a manner it reasonably believes will help resolve these difficulties. As we have demonstrated, two of the greatest uncertainties in administration of the *WCBS-TV* approach were 1) ascertaining that issues were "implicitly" raised by standard product commercials and institutional advertising, and 2) determining when a view on a controversial issue of public importance was expressed so elliptically that it could not be said to have been "raised" for purposes of the Fairness Doctrine. The policies announced in the Fairness Report seem to us to be a straightforward attempt to remove these uncertainties by all-but-completely removing "implicit" advocacy from the confines of the Fairness Doctrine. As long as the Commission strictly enforces the core part two, fairness obligation to present opposing points of view whenever there is direct, obvious, or explicit advocacy on one side of a controversial issue of public importance, it will be acting consistently with the public interest standard.

Nor do we believe that the Commission has acted arbitrarily or that it has abused its discretion in withdrawing most commercial advertisements from application of the Fairness Doctrine. Of course, the mere fact that the approach spelled out in the Fairness Report represents a definite change of policy does not require that it be struck down. We further conclude that the Commission has "given reasoned consideration to each of the pertinent factors" and that its policy choices with respect to the scope of the Fairness Doctrine are supported by substantial, though not necessarily conclusive, evidence.

It is important to track the exact reasoning employed by the Commission in its decision to overrule *WCBS-TV*. The Commission did not contend that standard product promotions do not implicitly raise the issues of the product's desirability. Rather, it concludes that mere promotion of a controversial product (that is, a product the use or purchase of which is controversial) does not constitute "meaningful" advocacy with respect to the merits of a "controversial issue of public importance." Petitioners contend that the Commission has thus arbitrarily excluded from the operation of the Fairness Doctrine one type of controversial issue: product desirability.

Given the reasons that the Commission puts forth for its new policy, such an outright Fairness Doctrine exemption for product commercials would not be arbitrary or an abuse of discretion. However, we are not convinced that petitioners' contention even correctly states what the Commission has done. When read in conjunction with that portion of the Report dealing with overt editorial and institutional advertising, the Commission's conclusion with respect to standard product commercials is more aptly characterized as being based on the view that the ultimate controversial issue of public importance is not the desirability of the product but the issues raised in the debate over desirability. Merely advocating the use of a product does not present information or involve discussion of these underlying issues; that is, promotional presentations are not "meaningful discussion(s) of . . . controversial issues of public importance." When read in this manner, the Fairness Report has not arbitrarily excluded one class of issues from operation of the Fairness Doctrine; it has rather stated one standard for Fairness Doctrine application, quoted above, and refined and reformulated the definition of a controversial issue of public importance.

In any event, we think that the Commission has adequately supported its decision to exclude standard product commercials from the scope of the Fairness Doctrine. Three major arguments are presented by the Commission. First, the Commission made the judgment that the *WCBS-TV* approach to the Fairness Doctrine and standard product commercials at most informed the public about only one side of a controversial issue. Since the underlying purpose of the Fairness Doctrine is to contribute to an informed public opinion, the Commission determined that a change from the *WCBS-TV* approach was called for.

Certainly it must be admitted that counter-commercials are of a very different genre than are the product commercials themselves. They do not simply state, "Do not buy X; it is not desirable," but rather argue one side of the issues underlying the debate over desirability. Given this fundamental asymmetry, we do not think it was unreasonable for the Commission to conclude that application of the Fairness Doctrine to standard product commercials does not further the objective of presenting all viewpoints on controversial issues of public importance.

The second major argument put forth by the Commission is that application of the Fairness Doctrine to noneditorial advertisements would "divert the attention of broadcasters from their public trustee responsibilities in aiding the development of an informed public opinion." This argument is of course premised to some extent on the first. We understand the Commission to be indicating that even if enforcement of Fairness Doctrine obligations with respect to commercial advertisements might marginally contribute to an informed public opinion, these benefits are outweighed by the reduction in public information which results from the decreased attention that broadcasters will afford to other aspects of the Fairness Doctrine. Given the wide range of controversial products to which the *WCBS-TV* approach could be applied and the difficulties, discussed above, in determining which issues implicitly addressed give rise to fairness obligations, it is indeed quite possible that the effort broadcasters would have to devote to enforcing the Fairness Doctrine with respect to commercial advertisements would contribute relatively little to the overall objectives of the doctrine. We caution, however, that it is doubtful that the new FCC policy will substantially lessen the difficulties of drawing the line between advertisements which do and those which do not incur fairness obligations. The difference between obvious and unobvious advocacy is not obvious.

Finally, the Commission suggested in the Fairness Report, though not in its arguments to this court, that application of the Fairness Doctrine to commercial advertisements could undermine the economic base of commercial broadcasting. It is possible that sponsors would be discouraged from broadcasting advertisements subject to mandatory counter-commercials, and that broadcasters could suffer additional losses through operation of the *Cullman* principle under which they must bear the cost of presenting opposing views where paid sponsorship is not available. Yet no evidence has been presented which indicates that the *WCBS-TV* policy had an adverse effect on commercial broadcasters, though admittedly this may be due to the rather unvigorous and confused enforcement of that policy. While we do not think this economic argument is conclusive standing alone, the other two arguments put forth by the Commission provide adequate and substantial support for its decision.

III

The FCC's decision to limit the applicability of the Fairness Doctrine lays upon it some obligation to consider carefully other serious suggestions that have been made to ensure sufficient and balanced coverage of important public issues. We conclude that two of the proposals rejected by the Commission in its Fairness Report and Reconsideration Order deserve further considerations at the agency level.

Both the Commission and reviewing courts have been acutely sensitive to the multiple dilemmas posed by government regulation of the broadcast media. First, there is the recognition that given the scarcity of broadcast channels, it is not possible that all who desire to speak through these media will be able to do so. A limitation both on the number of broadcast licensees and on the number of viewpoints and topics covered is unavoidable. It is further recognized that these limitations should be fashioned in a way that best furthers the interest of the public in receiving various viewpoints on important issues. Inevitably this requires at least some government oversight of broadcasters' decisions as to which issues are covered. Enunciation and enforcement of the Fairness Doctrine is of course the primary mechanism employed by the FCC to accomplish this oversight. The Commission has chosen to rely primarily on third-party complaints and limited review of Fairness Doctrine decisions by individual broadcasters in order to avoid excessive governmental supervision of licensee operations.

Yet case-by-case, issue-by-issue enforcement of the second obligation of the Fairness Doctrine still requires considerable Commission intrusion into the licensee decision making process. At the same time, reliance on third party complaints means that many fairness violations will not be called to account with respect to both part one and part two obligations.

The Commission procedures with respect to part two complaints are spelled out in the Fairness Report. The complainant must describe the station, issue, and program involved, and must also "state his reasons for concluding that in its other programming the station has not presented contrasting views on the issue." An unavoidable consequence of these procedures is that complaints will not be received, or will not be acted upon, unless there exist persons or organizations who are simultaneously "regular" viewers or listeners of the relevant station, aware that there exist opposing points of view to that presented by the station, are interested enough in having those opposing views aired that they are willing to initiate a Commission inquiry into the matter.

The potential for less than full enforcement of the first obligation under the Fairness Doctrine—provision of "a reasonable amount of time for the presentation . . . of programs devoted to the discussion and consideration of public issues"—is even greater. Given the Commission's view that it is rare that a particular issue is "of such great public importance that it would be unreasonable for a licensee to ignore (it) completely," there exists very little incentive for members of the public, whom we may conclude are vitally concerned with a limited number of public issues, to initiate complaints relating to the first fairness obligation. A citizen would almost have to consider himself a guardian of the general public interest in being informed in order successfully to initiate such a complaint. Thus, it is not surprising that the usual fairness complaint relates to the part two obligation.

The Commission received three major proposals designed to overcome these difficulties of current Fairness Doctrine enforcement. Petitioner COM urged that the Commission adopt as an optional substitute for the current Fairness Doctrine a system whereby licensees devote a specified percentage of their broadcast time to what COM labeled "free speech messages" and other public issue programming. Intervenor Geller requested the Commission to adopt a requirement "that the licensee list annually the ten controversial issues of public importance, local and national, which it chose for coverage in the prior year." Geller also proposed that the Commission confine review of Fairness Doctrine complaints to the time of license renewal.

A. The COM Access Proposal

The Fairness Report stated that the fairness inquiry did not disclose "any scheme of government-dictated access which we consider 'both practicable and desirable.'" The Commission concluded that 1) a system of paid access would favor wealthy spokesmen, 2) a system of first-come, first-served free access would "give no assurance that the most important issues would be discussed on a timely basis," and 3) any alternative system of free access would inevitably require the FCC to determine who should be allowed on the air.

After the Report was issued, COM petitioned the Commission to reconsider or clarify its position with respect to right-to-access policies voluntarily adopted by licensees. In its petition, COM proposed a specific access scheme, not presented to the Commission during the fairness inquiry itself, which could be deemed presumptive compliance with the Fairness Doctrine. Under the scheme suggested by COM:

1. a licensee would set aside one hour per week for spot announcements and lengthier programming which would be available for presentation of messages by members of the public;
2. half of this time would be allocated on a first-come, first-served basis on any topic whatsoever; the other half would be apportioned "on a representative spokesperson system;"

3. both parts of the allocation scheme would be "nondiscretionary as to content with the licensee;"
4. however, the broadcaster would still be required to ensure that spot messages or other forms of response to "editorial advertisements" are broadcast.

The Commision addressed COM's proposal in its order denying reconsideration, stating that while the proposal was "the first serious attempt to meet" what the Commission deemed the essential requirements of any access scheme, "(i)t is as a rule or policy." The Commission also expressed the view that the COM system could be a supplement to, but not a substitute for, the current Fairness Doctrine requirements.

We recognize that the Commission is not required in informal rule making to consider exhaustively every idea put forth or to explain in detail the reasons that certain alternatives were rejected. Nevertheless, we think that the COM proposal has desirable aspects that the Commission may have overlooked, and indeed that the Commission may not have correctly understood the true nature of the proposal. In these circumstances, we conclude that the Commission should give further consideration to the proposal, including the solicitation of comments thereon.

Our conclusions are prompted by the Commission's own criteria for what would constitute an acceptable "optional access system to be administered by the licensee, and supplemented by the Fairness Doctrine:"

The essential requirements for any such system would be that 1) licensee discretion be preserved, and 2) no right of access accrue to particular persons or groups. Furthermore, 3) the access system would not be permitted to allow important issues to escape timely public discussion. Most importantly, 4) the system must not draw the government into the role of deciding who should be allowed on the air and when.

First, it seems to us that the Commission has not explained adequately why the COM proposal does not meet most of these requirements. The fourth requirement would be furthered even more than it is under present Fairness Doctrine enforcement, since under the COM proposal the licensee would be subject to fairness complaints only with respect to "editorial advertisements." The nondiscretionary apportionment system in the COM proposal would appear to be responsive to the second requirement listed above. COM vigorously argues that the third requirement would be met because spokesmen will inevitably come forth to speak on important issues.

The first FCC requirement is that "licensee discretion be preserved." COM argues that its proposal assures licensee discretion in that the licensee can decide not to adopt the access system and instead continue to operate under current Fairness Doctrine procedures. (COM Brief at 43.) But of course the discretion to which the Commission is referring is with respect to deciding which issues should be covered initially and which initial coverage requires the presentation of opposing points of view.

The Commission evidently bases this requirement on language in *CBS* v. *DNC*, that "the allocation of journalistic priorities should be concentrated in the licensee rather than diffused among many." However, while the Court did state that " 'public trustee' broadcasting" should not be exchanged "for a system of self-appointed editorial commentators," it also stated that there might be devised "some kind of limited right of access that is both practicable and desirable." We cannot read *CBS* v. *DNC*—which held that broadcasters were not statutorily or Constitutionally required to accept paid editorial messages—as indicating that voluntarily licensee adoption of a system of limited access such as that proposed by COM would violate the public interest standard of the Communications Act. The COM proposal is of course not aptly characterized as solely "a system of self-appointed editorial commentators," because it would retain the broadcaster's present responsibility to present opposing points of view in response to editorial advertisements.

Moreover, in stating its "essential requirements" for an access system as a substitute for the current Fairness Doctrine, the Commission appears to want to have its cake and eat it too. If the preservation of journalistic "discretion" under the first requirement is meant to mandate that all decisions with respect to which issues are covered be left to the licensee, then substantial government involvement in the form of agency oversight, contrary to the spirit if not the letter of the fourth requirement, cannot be avoided. We do not think that the Commission has demonstrated in the Fairness Report, in the Reconsideration Order, or in its written and oral arguments to this court that the COM proposal retains insufficient licensee discretion.

Nor do the Commission's stated requirements take into account all crucial elements of an access scheme, or indeed any other mechanism of Fairness Doctrine enforcement. Certainly, the "essential requirements" must include some consideration of the scheme's likely success in meeting the first obligation of the Fairness Doctrine: the coverage of controversial issues. We have already described the limited extent to which current enforcement procedures can assure that this obligation is fulfilled, and we understand the reluctance of the Commission to become more involved in dictating which issues must be covered under the obligation. COM's proposal will involve the Commission even less than do present procedures in overseeing compliance with the first obligation. At the same time, the proposal would ensure a minimum amount of coverage of public issues.

Similarly, we think that the Commission cannot ignore the advantage of an access system in providing information to the public which would not be provided under even full compliance with both obligations of the Fairness Doctrine as currently implemented. For instance, we have sustained the Commission's decision to exclude standard product commercials from the part two fairness obligation. Although we have determined that presentation of counter-commercials is not required by the public interest standard of the Communications Act, neither the Commission's decision nor our affirmance of it was based on the view that the information contained in counter-commercials is useless or harmful. Allowing presentation of these messages would certainly not be inconsistent with the Commission's statutory obligations. The only reservation about the utility of counter-commercials stated in the Fairness Report and Reconsideration Order was that they would present only one side of controversial issues of public importance. But an access system could result in presentation of information opposing the purchase of certain products and messages opposing these counter-commercials.

We recognize, of course, that there may be significant difficulties with the COM access proposal. For instance, there is no absolute assurance that the issues addressed during access time will be the most important or controversial issues facing the licensee's community, and even less assurance of balance in presentation of opposing viewpoints. In its further inquiry into the COM proposal, we expect the Commission to ascertain how serious these potential defects are and to examine whether they can be overcome. Throughout this process, it is especially important that the nature and scope of issue coverage under the proposed access scheme be compared to the degree of coverage actually achieved under the current system of Fairness Doctrine implementation, not to the coverage that would be achieved were both fairness obligations currently complied with and enforced.

B. Other Proposals Relating to the First Fairness Obligation

In conducting further inquiry on the COM proposal, the Commission will have to examine how best to ensure that licensees devote a reasonable amount of time to programming on public issues, as is required under the first obligation under the Fairness Doctrine. We do not think that this examination should be limited to comparison of only two alternatives: present procedures for implementing this obligation, on the one hand, and the COM proposal, on the other. There may well exist other ways of achieving compliance with the first obligation that deserve critical consideration, either in conjunction with, or as alternatives to, the procedures referred to above.

One of the proposals submitted to the Commission during the fairness inquiry seems especially promising as one step toward fuller compliance with the first fairness obligation. Intervenor Geller suggests that

> the licensee list annually the ten controversial issues of public importance, local and national, which it chose for the most coverage in the prior year, set out the offers for response made; and note representative programming that was presented on each issue.

Mr. Geller made this proposal both during the Fairness Doctrine inquiry and in his petition for reconsideration of the Fairness Report. There is no indication that this rather modest proposal has received the serious consideration it deserves. Although the Commission alluded to the proposal in its order denying reconsideration, it failed to state even in conclusory terms why the proposal was being rejected. Therefore, we conclude that further inquiry into the Geller proposal would be appropriate as part of, or as a supplement to, additional examination of the COM access scheme.

Mr. Geller failed to state exactly what he believed the Commission should do with the issue reports that it receives, and it is not our role to flesh out the details of this proposal. It does seem to us, however, that issue reports could be useful to the Commission in one or more ways. For instance, the Commission initially could review each annual list to determine whether it appears that the licensee fulfilled his part one obligation. If this is not obvious from the list, or if the Commission had received complaints concerning the overall issue coverage afforded by the licensee, the Commission might take no immediate action with respect to the annual reports, but instead examine them at the time of license renewal. We leave it to the Commission's further examination to consider whether these or other uses of annual reports such as those proposed by Mr. Geller would be appropriate in enforcement of the Fairness Doctrine. The Commission may find it necessary to consider also under what standard the annual reports might be reviewed. We likewise leave how best to conduct further inquiry into Mr. Geller's proposal, including whether this inquiry should be conducted separately from or as part of the further inquiry into the COM proposal.

C. Review at Renewal Only

Under a wholly separate proposal put forth by Intervenor Geller, both during the fairness inquiry and in his petition for reconsideration, the FCC would abandon its current case-by-case consideration of Fairness Doctrine complaints, and return to its pre-1962 practice of ascertaining at renewal time whether or not the licensee has complied with the Fairness Doctrine. The proposal further suggests that the standard of review at renewal time be limited to whether there is "an indicated pattern of a flagrant nature, akin to 'malice' or bad faith, or 'reckless disregard' of fairness obligations."

This proposal is directed at reducing the amount of government interference in the everyday editorial decisions of licensees. This objective was a major consideration in the decision in *CBS* v.

DNC, which held that there exists no statutorily or Constitutionally mandated right of access for paid editorial broadcasts. But we think that Intervenor errors in inferring from isolated language in that decision that the case-by-case determinations made by the FCC under current procedures for Fairness Doctrine enforcement are invalid under the Communications Act and under the Constitution. If the Court in *CBS* v. *DNC* had intended to invalidate all case-by-case procedures employed by the FCC, it is unlikely that it would have reaffirmed *Red Lion*, decided by the Commission in just this manner, without at least mentioning its disapproval of the manner in which that case had come before it.

We therefore conclude that the Commission is neither Constitutionally nor statutorily required to return to its pre-1962 method of Fairness Doctrine enforcement. Nor do we think that its rejection of the proposal that it do so was unreasonable or arbitrary. It is not contended that the Commission failed to give the proposal serious consideration. The Commission concluded that the proposed renewal assessment could not be made without inquiring into individual complaints, inquiries which would often be made on the basis of stale records. The Commission also argued—we believe convincingly—that review only at the time of renewal would discourage the filing of specific complaints from persons who sought to present opposing views in a timely fashion, and would deny the Commission the ability "to remedy violations before a flagrant pattern of abuse develops." In light of these considerations, we think the Commission correctly concluded that the specific renewal-only approach set forth by Intervenor is not practicable at this time.

IV

In summary, we reject the challenges to the Commission's decision to exempt product commercials which do not "obviously and meaningfully address a controversial issue of public importance" from Fairness Doctrine obligations, and find no merit in the contentions that the Commission has violated the substantive and procedural requirements of NEPA. We also affirm the Commission's decisions to continue its policy of case-by-case consideration of fairness complaints and its policies relating to licensee consideration of editorial advertisements, news slanting, and political editorializing. However, we remand the orders reviewed on this appeal with instructions that the Commission undertake further inquiry into petitioner COM's access proposal and Intervenor Geller's "10-issue" proposal in accordance with this opinion.

It is so ordered.

THE COMMUNICATIONS ACT OF 1934 WITH AMENDMENTS RECAPPED TO 1969

Facilities for Candidates for Public Office

Section 315
   a.   If any licensee shall permit any person who is a legally qualified candidate for any public office to use a broadcasting station, he shall afford equal opportunities to all other such candidates for that office in the use of such broadcasting station: provided, that such licensee shall have no power of censorship over the material broadcast under the provisions of this section. No obligation is hereby imposed upon any licensee to allow the use of its station by any such candidate. Appearance by a legally qualified candidate on any—
   1. bona fide newscast,

2. bona fide news interview,

3. bona fide news documentary (if the appearance of the candidate is incidental to the presentation of the subject or subjects covered by the news documentary), or

4. on-the-spot coverage of bona fide news events (including but not limited to political conventions and activities incidental thereto), shall not be deemed to be use of a broadcasting station within the meaning of this subsection. Nothing in the foregoing sentence shall be construed as relieving broadcasters, in connection with the presentation of newscasts, news interviews, news documentaries, and on-the-spot coverage of news events, from the obligation imposed upon them under this Act to operate in the public interest and to afford reasonable opportunity for the discussion of conflicting views on issues of public importance.

b. The charges made for the use of any broadcasting station for any of the purposes set forth in this section shall not exceed the charges made for comparable use of such station for other purposes.

c. The Commission shall prescribe appropriate rules and regulations to carry out the provisions of this section.

NOTE I

The question of a partnership which operated a public service and legal advertising business dealing with notices of sales by trustees under deeds of trust arose in the case of *Corwin v. Los Angeles Newspaper Service Bureau, Inc.* (583 P.2d 777 (1978)). Here action was brought charging that the bureau was organized to enable the county newspapers to acquire a share of the legal advertising market and member newspapers with violation of antitrust laws.

The Supreme Court of California held that: (1) The trial court's finding that the paragraph of agreement between the bureau and member newspapers whereby a member's withdrawal of any class of legal advertising from the terms of the agreement constituted a waiver of its right to participate in distribution of the bureau's profits was not a restraint of trade in that no member had ever been penalized for withdrawing advertising. (2) The trial court's findings that the paragraph of agreement between bureau and member newspapers whereby each member agreed to pay the bureau 15 per cent commission on each legal notice published whether or not the particular advertisement was placed by the bureau was not a restraint of trade in that the members were free at any time to withdraw the class of advertisements from the agreement.

NOTE II

The United States Supreme Court ruled on October 16, 1978, that three Massachusetts radio stations did not violate government regulations by giving free air time to one group favoring a 1976 ballot referendum while taking payments from another group opposing the ballot question.

Chapter VI

Warranty Limits on Free Speech and Advertising

Section 1

From Advertising to Warranties

Daniel M. Rohrer*

INTRODUCTION

The bargaining process employed in making a deal may be lengthy or brief, involving a variety of methods and techniques. At some point along the way it becomes reasonable to conclude that an agreement has been reached. When this occurs the legal consequences of an enforceable contract come into existence, and neither party may withdraw from the negotiation.

A contract is an agreement which the law will enforce in some way. It must contain at least one promise or a commitment to do something in the future. It may take the form of a formal written document or an informal oral acknowledgment.

Mutual assent, in the nature of an offer and an acceptance, is necessary for the formation of a contract. Thus one party proposes a bargain and the other agrees to it. In most cases, the offer will contain a conditional promise, and will ask the other party to accept the proposal by making a promise in return.

In some instances, however, rather than proposing an exchange of promises, the offer will propose an exchange of a promise for an act. Such an agreement is known as a unilateral contract.

A bilateral contract, on the other hand, consists of an exchange of promises. Most contracts are bilateral since both parties usually promise to do something.

The legal effect of an offer is to create a power in the offeree to enter into a contract. The offeree completes the formation of the contract by making his acceptance. Normally the offer alone is insufficient to bring the contract into being. The contract is created when the offer is accepted.

Ordinarily advertisements appearing in the mass media, on billboards, in store windows, etc., do not constitute offers to sell because words of commitment to sell are insufficient. Rather they comprise an invitation to the public for an offer to buy.

REQUEST FOR AN OFFER

Preliminary negotiations are explained by *Restatement* in the following terms: "A manifestation of willingness to enter into a bargain is not an offer if the person to whom it is addressed knows or has reason to know that the person making it does not intend to conclude a bargain until he has made a

---

*My thanks to Professor William Willier of Boston College Law School for suggestions and recommendations which were followed in this book.

further manifestation of assent." (Section 25.) Under such circumstances the actor may intend to make a bargain in the future, but only if he makes some further manifestation of assent. If the addressee of a proposal has reason to know that no offer is intended, there is no offer, even though he understands it to be an offer. "Reason to know" depends not only on the words or other conduct, but also on the circumstances, including previous communications of the parties and the usages of their community or line of business. (Section 25a.)

For example, governmental agencies and private individuals often advertise for bids from construction contractors prepared to undertake the building of a building or other structure, or from persons prepared to supply goods or services. It may be customary or required by law that the contract be awarded to the lowest responsible bidder whose bid conforms to published specifications. A bidder in such a case may seek bids from subcontractors for part of the work. The rule in such cases is much like that governing auctions—unless a contrary intention is manifested, the advertisement is not an offer but a request for offers; bidders on both prime contract and subcontract make offers when they submit bids. (Section 27c3.) All bids may be rejected because the bid is the offer.

At the beginning of the bargaining process one party may request the other to make an offer; or the seller may offer specific goods for immediate delivery and on advertised terms of cash or credit. The advertisement is not an offer; it is a request for offers. (*Leskie* v. *Haseltine*, 155 Pa. 98, 25 A 886 (1893).)

This is true even if it may be common practice to accept the best bid made, or where the advertisement may not even request an offer. In the latter case the advertisement may request no more than a reply that will further the negotiation in the direction of an offer. Nevertheless, if the advertisement requests an offer, it may not generate one.[1]

For example an invitation to prospective buyers to negotiate for a license, and to trade, even when confined to a definite class, does not bind the sender to accept any offer thereafter received. The order of the prospective buyer does not ripen into a contract, which is an agreement that creates an obligation until the defendant's acceptance, and then only as to goods specifically ordered. (*Montgomery Ward & Co.* v. *Johnson*, 209 Mass. 89, 95 NE 290 (1911).)

Nevertheless it is possible to make an offer by an advertisement directed to the general public (see *Restatement* Section 28), but when this occurs, there will normally be some language of commitment or some invitation to take action without further communication. (Section 25.)

OFFER BY ADVERTISEMENT

However a notice that funds had been provided for the purchase of certain county bonds at par and interest to a specified date, and that the holders could send their bonds to a certain bank for surrender on such terms, could be found to be an offer to purchase and not merely a solicitation for offers to sell. (*R.E. Crummer & Co.* v. *Nuveen et al.*, 147 F.2d 3 (CA7 1945).)

Therefore a contract may originate in an advertisement or offer addressed to the public generally, and, if the offer is accepted by anyone in good faith, without qualifications or conditions, the acceptance will be sufficient to convert the offer into a binding obligation or a completed contract. (*Seymour* v. *Armstrong et al.*, 62 Kan. 720, 64 Pac 612 (1901).)

Before a binding contract can be made with one advertising an offer, the person acting under the offer must know of it, and it is immaterial whether or not the advertiser knows that work has been done by any one under any offer at any time. A binding contract with an advertiser comes into being when work is performed by one taking advantage of the offer. At this point it merely remains necessary for the one who has done the work to bring his claim to the attention of the advertiser, when he is entitled to the rewards offered by the advertisement. (*Payne* v. *Lautz Bros. & Co.*, 166 NYS 844 (1916).)

It is possible to make a definite and operative offer to buy or to sell goods by advertisement in a newspaper, by a handbill, or on a placard in a store window. (*Carlill* v. *Carbolic Smoke Ball Co.*, 1 QB 256 (1893).) For example an offer of specified compensation to the person obtaining the highest vote based on paid subscriptions to a newspaper, after acceptance and part performance of the terms of the offer, becomes an executory contract between the person making and the person so accepting the terms of the offer. (*Mooney* v. *Daily News Co. of Minneapolis*, 116 Minn. 212, 133, NW 573 (1911).)

Such procedure is not customary, however, and the presumption is the other way. Neither the advertiser nor the reader of his notice understands that an agreement will be reached before further clarification is made on the part of the advertiser. The typical advertisement is understood to be no more than a request to consider, examine, and negotiate. No one may reasonably regard them otherwise unless the words used are unusually specific and thorough.[2]

Although a seller's advertisements of his goods, in circulars and periodicals, or on radio and television, are seldom interpreted as offers which create the power of acceptance, any statements describing the quality of the products may formulate warranties that become a part of a contract, that is subsequently entered into with a buyer, for the sale of such products. Such results do not occur, however, if the advertised statements would be interpreted by a reasonable person to be mere "puffing" or expressions of opinion. "The question depends upon the usual principles of interpretation and upon the expressions of the parties in their negotiations subsequent to the advertisement."[3]

A *warranty* is a promise that a proposition of fact is true, and a *contract* is an undertaking or stipulation, either in writing or verbally, to the effect that a certain fact in relation to the subject of a contract is or shall be as it is stated or promised to be.[4] *Agreement* means the bargain of the parties in fact as found in their language or by implication from other circumstances, including course of dealing, usage of trade, or course of performance.[5]

REVOCATION OF GENERAL OFFER BY ADVERTISEMENT

When an offer has been made by an advertisement, a power of acceptance is created in all those who read it. This power may be terminated by personal notice or revocation, but it is often impracticable for the offerer to find and notify everyone who has seen his offer.[6] Nevertheless an offer by publication may be revoked by publication, and the power of acceptance is terminated despite the fact that some offeree never hears of the revocation and completes the acceptance as originally intended. (*Shuey* v. *United States*, 92 U.S. 73 (1875).)

ACCEPTANCE BY PROMISE OR PERFORMANCE

After the offeror has created the power, the legal consequences which may result are beyond his control and he may be brought into numerous consequential relations of which he may have neither been aware nor provided his consent. For example, the manufacturer, producer, and advertiser may be subject to strict liability for fault or cause of a defect in the product. They may be held liable either for knowledge of the defect or for the responsibility to know of the defect.

Under modern conditions of manufacture and distribution, it has become acceptable practice to give the ultimate consumer injured by a defective commodity a direct cause of action against the dominant figure in the marketing chain. The dominant figure, usually the manufacturer,[7] is the party best able to control and distribute such risks of injury as part of his enterprise cost.[8]

The case of *Winterbottom* v. *Wright*, for example, involved an action in contract for failure to keep a commitment, and an expansion of tort policy into action of contract by reason of negligence for failure to fulfill the obligation of a contract. Here the defendant failed to meet his commitment to the Postmaster to keep a stagecoach maintained. (10 M & W 109, 152 Eng. Rep. 402 (1842).)

In the related case of *MacPherson* v. *Buick Motor Co.*, an action in tort for failure to inspect a vehicle resulted in a similar expansion of tort policy into action for contract. The court paid more attention to duty in care than to whether there is a contract in this case. (217 N.Y. 382, 111 NE 1050 (1916).)

MacPherson is a case of negligence rather than strict liability. The user or buyer of a product could maintain an action despite lack of privity (relationship or connection) between the plaintiff and defendant. The plaintiff is not required to purchase the product from the manufacturer directly, despite the fact that an implied warranty and contract is the essence of the case. Thus in negligence cases, the buyer, user or passenger in an automobile could recover against the manufacturer for negligence in manufacturing the vehicle.

Several advertising cases demonstrate much the same point, as does the Uniform Commercial Code.[9] One of the most prominent cases on the subject is *Henningsen* v. *Bloomfield Motors, Inc.*, a partial text of which is reprinted in the following section of this chapter. It is also discussed in the section under basic definitions and unconscionability. Before the definitions, however, implied and express warranties will be explained and distinguished in the context of tort liability.

IMPLIED AND EXPRESS WARRANTIES DISTINGUISHED

Before continuing this discussion, it would be useful to distinguish between implied warranty of merchantability and express warranty. An express warranty is defined by the UCC in the following terms:

1. Express warranties by the seller are created as follows:
   a. Any affirmation of fact or promise made by the seller to the buyer which relates to the goods and becomes part of the basis of the bargain creates an express warranty that the goods shall conform to the affirmation or promise.
   b. Any description of the goods which is made part of the basis of the bargain creates an express warranty that the goods shall conform to the description.
   c. Any sample or model which is made part of the basis of the bargain creates an express warranty that the whole of the goods shall conform to the sample or model.
2. It is not necessary to the creation of an express warranty that the seller use formal words such as "warrant" or "guarantee," or that he have a specific intention to make a warranty, but an affirmation merely of the value of the goods or a statement purporting to be merely the seller's opinion or commendation of the goods does not create a warranty.[10]

An implied warranty, on the other hand, comes into existence when the law derives it by implication or inference from the nature of the transaction or the relative situation or circumstances of the parties. (*Great Atlantic and Pacific Tea Co.* v. *Walker*, 104 SW 2d 627, 632 (1937).)

The most common implied warranty is the warranty of *merchantability*. This means that the seller promises that the product purchased by the consumer is fit for the ordinary uses of the product. For example, a reclining chair must recline, and a toaster must toast. If something on that order fails to do so, the purchaser has a legal right to recover his investment.

Applying the Uniform Commercial Code, a recent court ruling suggested that the implied warranty of merchantability does not render the retail bookseller liable for injuries allegedly caused by improper instructions contained in a cookbook sold, without knowledge of the alleged defect on the part of the bookseller. (*Cardoza v. True,* 342 S.2d 1053 (1977).)

In this decision the court explained that "even publishers have not been held liable where injuries have occurred through the use of products advertised in their publications (*id.*). The court seemed to feel that liability without fault must relieve newsdealers as well as advertisers from tort liability arising from contracts for the same reason they are relieved from liability in defamation of character "where the dealer did not know and reasonably could not have known that the publication contained defamatory material." Thus liability without fault has long been held inappropriate in an action against one passing on printed words without an opportunity to investigate them (*id.*).

Not only is the intent or knowledge of the defect critical in some instances, but the cause of the problem is equally important. In the case of *Crocker v. Sears, Roebuck and Co.* (22 UCC Rep. 349, 346 So.2d 921 (1977)), the court found that the plaintiff could not recover on either implied warranty of merchantability or express warranty through failure to introduce evidence from which the jury could reasonably conclude that a defect in a stove purchased from the defendant caused the fire which destroyed her house. In light of the facts that the house was in the process of being remodeled and had been completely rewired, that the defendant failed to install the stove but had merely delivered it, and that the fire might well have arisen from negligent installation rather than from defective manufacture, the jury would have had to engage in pure speculation to conclude that the fire was caused by the defective manufacture of the stove.

Additional cases which may be of assistance in gaining a better understanding of the relationship between warranties and tort liability are as follows: *Jacob E. Decker and Sons, Inc. v. Capps; Lasky v. Economy Grocery Stores* (partial texts of both cases are reprinted in the next section of this chapter); *Cox Motor Car Co. v. Castle,* 3 UCC Rep. 397, 402 SW 2d 429 (Ky., 1966); *Ford Motor Co. v. Gunn,* 8 UCC Rep. 1180, 123 Ga. App. 550, 181 SE 2d 694 (1971); *Courtesy Motor Sales, Inc. v. Farrior,* 15 UCC Rep. 85, 298 So.2d 26 (Ala. App., 1974); *Stream v. Sportscar Salon, LTD.,* 22 UCC Rep. 631, 397 NYS 2d 677 (1977); *Bichler v. Willing,* 22 UCC Rep. 49 (1977); *Dunham-Bush, Inc. v. Thermo-Air Service, Inc.,* 22 UCC 347 (1977); *Holdridge v. Heyer-Schulte Corp. of Santa Barbara,* 22 UCC Rep. 978 (1977).

It can be seen from the examples above that both the express and implied aspects of a warranty may create a pre-existing duty on the part of the vendor, owner, manufacturer, etc. In cases such as these, questions will arise as to whether the capabilities of the product have been represented accurately. Before considering these facets of a contract, it may be helpful to consider the following definitions.

Specific Performance

There are some circumstances in which monetary damages provide inadequate compensation for the aggrieved party. The damages may be too speculative or uncertain to be determined in a reasonable way, or the goods may be so unique that damages may not be a sufficient substitute for the defendant's performance of the contract. Under such circumstances the court may, at its discretion, order the defendant to perform the contract itself rather than to pay damages.

As a result of the fact that specific performance is an equitable remedy, it is available only where the plaintiff can show that legal damages are inadequate. The decree for specific performance may include such terms and conditions as to payment of the price, damages, or other relief as the court may deem just.[11]

Consideration

In order to arrive at a reasonable balance between the power of state and independence of man, not all contracts are enforced. As a condition to enforceability, the common law usually requires that informal promises be made for something in return. Judges and legal scholars have identified three elements which must concur before a promise is supported by consideration. They are as follows:

1. The promisee must suffer legal detriment; that is, do or promise to do what he is not legally obligated to do; or refrain from doing or promise to refrain from doing what he is legally privileged to do.
2. The detriment must induce the promise. In other words, the promisor must have made the promise because he wishes to exchange it at least in part for the detriment to be suffered by the promisee.
3. The promise must induce the detriment. This means in effect . . . that the promisee must know of the offer and intend to accept.

"The essence of consideration . . . is legal detriment that has been bargained for and exchanged for the promise."[12] The orthodox view of consideration is that of an agreed upon exchange or price in return for a promise.

Detrimental Reliance

One form of consideration in return for a promise is detrimental reliance. For example, if the promisee has suffered a substantial economic loss, as well as a legal detriment, in reliance upon the promise, the promise is enforceable, even though it was intended to be gratuitous. Where one has led another to act in reasonable reliance upon his promise so as to worsen his position, a substitute to the ordinary requirements for consideration is found in detrimental reliance.

Condition Precedent

Any provision in a contract, whether express or implied, may contain an act or event which must occur or be legally excused. Whether express or implied in fact or law, a condition precedent must actually occur or be legally excused before the other party's duty of performance arises.

Unconscionable Contracts

Unconscionability is one form of inadequacy of consideration. Contracts that, as a result of superior bargaining power on the part of one party or the other, are so one-sided as to be unfair and oppressive are not legally enforceable at least in terms of their unconscionable provisions. For example the case of *Henningsen* v. *Bloomfield Motors, Inc.* (a partial text of which is reprinted in the following section) involves an action to recover damages for breach of an implied warranty. Henningsen's wife, the plaintiff, was injured by a steering failure in a new car purchased from Bloomfield Motors, the defendant, under a contract in which the dealer purported to disclaim all implied warranties of merchantability. She was injured only ten days after the car had been delivered. Bloomfield Motors contends that any implied warranty of merchantability was disclaimed by a provision on the back of the purchase contract (among eight and one-half inches of fine print) which limited liability for breach of warranty to replacement of defective parts.

The court was called upon to decide whether an automobile dealer's (or manufacturer's) disclaimer of all warranties of merchantability (beyond replacement of parts) is effective in insulating that automobile dealer from liability for breach of a warranty of merchantability which would otherwise be implied. This decision involves a concise rule of law to the effect that an attempt by an automobile dealer (or manufacturer) to disclaim an otherwise implied warranty of merchantability will be declared void as against public policy.

The court held that the seller's fine print was no defense when its provisions are conducive to injury of the public, despite the fact that "freedom of contract" is an important and guiding principle of law. The court felt that due to the size and power of the automobile industry, where similar disclaimer clauses predominate, the consumer was placed in the position of taking the contract as he finds it or foregoing the purchase of a reasonable means of transportation.

In this landmark case, for the first time the court ruled against an exculpatory clause in an "adhesive" contract solely on the ground that it violated public policy. Courts have previously denied seemingly "unfair" clauses and their intended effects by various processes of strained interpretation, which resulted in confused and inconsistent doctrine.

This trend has been reinforced by UCC 2-302 concerning "unconscionable" clauses. It states that:

1. If the court as a matter of law finds the contract or any clause of the contract to have been unconscionable at the time it was made, the court may refuse to enforce the contact, or it may enforce the remainder of the contract without the unconscionable clause, or it may so limit the application of any unconscionable clause as to avoid any unconscionable result.

2. When it is claimed or appears to the court that the contract or any clause thereof may be unconscionable, the parties shall be afforded a reasonable opportunity to present evidence as to its commercial setting, purpose, and effect to aid the court in making the determination.[13]

Pre-Existing Duty

Pre-existing duty is the opposite of legal detriment. Legal detriment involves doing something which one is not already legally bound to do or refraining from doing something one has the legal right to do. However, if one has a pre-existing duty or a legal duty to act or refrain from acting, which existed prior to the agreement in question, the agreement is not legally enforceable. However, if the promisee has given something in addition to what he already owes in return for the promise he now seeks to enforce, or has in some way agreed to vary his pre-existing duty, such as by accelerating performance, there is consideration. It is usually immaterial how slight the change is. Furthermore, the UCC states that any agreement modifying a contract subject to the UCC needs no consideration to be binding. This rule operates only where both parties are acting in good faith, however.[14]

PRE-EXISTING DUTY RULE AND WAIVER OF WARRANTIES

Under common law warranties, especially in the sale of appliances and automobiles, there is an implied warranty unless anything is written to limit the warranty. Therefore the seller is liable unless the contract states otherwise.

As in the case of *Hull-Dobbs, Inc.* v. *Mallicoat* (415 SW 2d 344 (1966)), on the surface it may not necessarily be clear whether the contract states otherwise. In such instances, the use of parol evidence (such as conversations and oral discussions between buyer and seller relevant to the agreement, or testimony related to a car inspection on the part of a mechanic), may be used to clarify a term or to interpret what might be an ambiguous term.

The case of *Hull-Dobbs* demonstrates that words in a contract, such as "accepted in its present condition," may refer to acceptance and not necessarily be taken as synonymous with "as is" or "with all fault," which are phrases tending to exclude warranties. Here the plaintiff-buyer of an automobile signed a "security agreement" saying he examined and accepted the auto "in its present condition" and a "retail buyer's order" which excludes warranties and parol representations.

Nevertheless, the court concluded it cannot be said the parties intended the "security agreement" to be the final statement of the terms of the sale. While as a rule of law parol evidence cannot contradict the written terms of an agreement, it can contradict representations made as an inducement to the contract and form the basis or consideration of it.

Representations that are considered an inducement are not expected to be included by the parties in the written terms, and they were not in this case. Therefore, while the buyer's examination of the auto failed to reveal its defects, an auto mechanic was permitted to testify that a defect discovered after the purchase would cause the driver to have little control over the car.

Thus, while the "security agreement" stated that it was the entire agreement between the parties, the court decided that the seller's warranties, representations, and promises are not binding on the buyer.

Recently warranties have been used to lure customers. Hence the critical issue becomes whether warranties constitute an integral part of a contract, or whether they lie outside. This question will be confronted and illustrated in the context of warranties and deceptive advertising.

WARRANTIES AND DECEPTIVE ADVERTISING

Cases involving warranties and misrepresentation in advertising matter have become increasingly more common. In fact there have been so many instances of the problem recently that this discussion will concentrate on the latest period. A cross section of earlier cases will also be cited.

In an action for breach of warranty, the court determined as early as 1965 that some connection or relationship need not exist between the contracting parties where the purchaser of an automobile relies upon representations made in advertising by the manufacturer of the automobile in the mass communications media to the effect that its automobiles are trouble-free, economical in operation and built and manufactured with a high quality of workmanship. In this case, the purchaser suffered damage in the form of diminution of value of the automobile attributable to latent defects not readily ascertainable at the time of purchase. (*Inglis* v. *American Motors Corp.*, 2 UCC Rep. 961, 3 Ohio St 2d 132, 2 Ohio Op 2d 136, 209 NE 2d 583 (1965).)

Similarly the court decided a year later that where a warranty had been communicated to all claimants who had relied upon it, no connection or relationship between the contracting parties was required. The liability of the manufacturer remains the same where his product has been misrepresented. In this case, pedigreed seed was advertised, and rogue seed was sold. (*Klein v. Asgrow Seed Co.*, 3 UCC Rep. 934, 246 Cal. App 2d 87, 54 Cal. Rptr. 609 (1966).)

On the other hand, no express warranty existed where representations were made in an advertising pamphlet to the effect that a manufacturer's fastener gun eliminated the possibility of an overdriven stud or a ricochet of the stud. While the purchaser's employee was injured by the ricochet of the stud shank which separated from the lead while the fastener gun was being used by a fellow workman, the representations in the pamphlet referred to the fastener gun rather than to the studs. (*Speed Fastners, Inc. v. Newsom*, 4 UCC Rep. 681, 382 F.2d 395 (CA 10, 1967).)

In an earlier case, where the manufacturer's breach of its express and implied warranties was a proximate cause of the injuries sustained by the plaintiff, a cause of action was stated for breach of warranty against the manufacturer despite the fact that no specific information was alleged as constituting a sale of goods to the plaintiff. This case involved allegations that the defendant manufacturer of hair dye, by means of extensive advertising through radio, television, and other mass media, implied and/or expressly warranted to the plaintiff as a user of the product that it was safe and fit for its intended use. Acting in reliance upon these representations, a beauty parlor purchased the product from the manufacturer and the plaintiff accepted the beauty parlor's use of it on her hair. (*Garthwait v. Burgio*, 3 UCC Rep. 171, 153 Conn. 284, 216 A.2d 189 (1965).)

As is true in the case above, affirmations of fact give rise to an express warranty where the record shows the buyer had no knowledge of any of the facts. For example, statements in the seller's advertising material for panels for a greenhouse roofing to the effect that 1) "tests" showed no deterioration in five years of normal use, 2) the paneling would not turn black or discolor even after years of exposure, and 3) the paneling would not burn, rot, rust, or mildew, are examples of such affirmations of fact. (*General Supply and Equipment Co., Inc. v. Phillips*, 12 UCC Rep. 35, 490 SW 2d 913 (Tex. Civ. App., 1972).)

Furthermore, in an action involving an alleged motor vehicle products liability claim, interrogatories inquiring whether the defendant manufacturer had contracts with any advertising agency concerning the advertisement of its pickup trucks were relevant since advertisements by the manufacturers of widely distributed products sold in the stream of commerce may, in proper instances, be treated as warranties of the merchandise. (*Neel v. Ford Motor Co.*, 7 UCC Rep. 1311, 49 Pa. D & C.2d 243 (Pa. Ct. Com. Pl., 1970).)

In 1969, a jury found a new set of circumstances which were sufficient to create warranty liability. In an action against the seller of a used crane, based on alleged breach of express warranties as to the crane's condition and lifting power, the seller's advertisement and its letter to the buyer stating that the crane was of 30-ton capacity and in good condition, combined with the language of the purchase order describing the crane as of 30-ton capacity and the statement of the seller's foreman at the time the buyer's president inspected the crane to the effect that it could lift 30 tons and was in "very good condition," was sufficient to support the jury finding that a warranty existed and must be honored. (*Capital Equipment Enterprises, Inc. v. North Pier Terminal Co.*, 7 UCC Rep. 290, 117 App. 2d 264, 254 NE 2d 542 (1969).)

Soon thereafter, however, an express warranty was denied in the case of an advertisement for defendant's seed corn which was based upon his past performance while using it, rather than upon any offer guaranteeing its effectiveness. The advertisement for seed corn purchased by the plaintiffs was merely a statement of the seller's opinion and not a warranty that such a quality of seed corn would produce a crop meeting the standards and expectations of the purchaser. (*Bickett* v. *W.R. Grace and Co.*, 12 UCC Rep. 629 (DCWD Ky, 1972).).

Nevertheless, the court soon decided the other way in cases concerned with specific performance capabilities and advertisements shedding enlightenment upon the intent of expressed warranties. In the first case, the defendant manufacturer sent an advertising brochure to the plaintiff constituting an express warranty even though there was no connection or relationship between the manufacturer and the plaintiff. Here statements were made in the brochure as to the degree of utility that should be expected from the produce rather than the degree of past performance as was illustrated in the preceding example. (*Hawkins Construction Co.* v. *Matthews Co., Inc.*, 12 UCC Rep. 1013, 209 NW 2d 643 (1973).).

Specific performance is no less important than the intent of a written warranty which the defendant has given to the purchaser. Such was the case in an action for breach of express warranty to recover damages for the death of the plaintiff's decedent when a tire manufactured by the defendant failed causing death. An advertisement was used to demonstrate the scope of protection intended for the buyer and user. (*Collins* v. *Uniroyal, Inc.*, 14 UCC Rep. 306, 126 NJ Super. 401, 315 A.2d 30 (1973), affd. 14 UCC Rep. 294, 64 NJ 260, 315 A.2d 16 (1974).).

A more recent example of breach of warranty, both express and implied, can be found in the case of *Auto-Teria, Inc.*, v. *Ahern* (352 NE 2d 774 (1976)). Here a seller of automatic car wash equipment brought an action against buyers of that equipment for the balance due on the equipment. The purchaser counterclaimed on the ground that the seller's advertising brochure represented that the brush unit could be automatically operated by a consumer's deposit of coins in a meter. Thus a bargain between the buyer and seller had come into existence. This bargain was broken when the equipment failed to function in keeping with its description.

Still more recently, the role of detrimental reliance created by the advertising of merchandise was illustrated in the case of *Whitaker* v. *Farmhand, Inc.* (22 UCC Rep. 375 (1977)). Here a remote manufacturer, having no connection with or relation to the buyer may be liable for breach of express warranty by advertising on radio and television, in newspapers and magazines, and in brochures made available to perspective buyers if they rely on such advertising to their detriment. In this case, the court found that under such circumstances an irrigation system had been manufactured in such a reckless, careless, and negligent manner, and designed and installed by the defendants in such a way that it never operated for the purpose for which it was sold, that the seller was liable for breach of warranty. Most courts now follow the rule set forth in *Henningsen* v. *Bloomfield Motors, Inc.*, a partial text of which may be found in the next section of this book, which holds the remote manufacturer liable for implied warranties. In the *Whitaker* case the court found that such implied warranties of merchantability and fitness for a particular purpose did exist and were breached. (*Id.* at 381.)

Moreover, if a bargain resulting from the representation of products or services is to be retracted, such revocation must occur within a reasonable time after the buyer discovers or should have discovered the ground for it, and before any substantial change in condition of the goods, which is not caused by their own defects, occurs. Under these circumstances the buyer must take reasonable care of the goods for which he has revoked acceptance. (*Durfee* v. *Rod Baxter Imports, Inc.*, 22 UCC Rep. 945 (1977).) If a buyer intends to revoke his part of the bargain, however, he must be especially careful that conversion does not occur.

In breach of warranty cases punitive damages, on the other hand, are not even conditional for they are not considered to be an extension of contract law. The court decided in the case of *Novosel* v.

Northway Motor Corporation (47 L.W. 2311 (1978)) that a disgruntled buyer of an automobile, who, under state law, is precluded from recovering punitive damages for the seller's alleged breach of warranty, is not entitled to recover punitive damages for the alleged violation of the Magnuson-Moss Warranty Act.

The question of punitive damages depends upon state law which tends to reflect the firmly established rule that punitive damages are generally not recoverable in contract actions. From the allegations in the complaint, the *Novosel* court concluded that the sole purpose of the plaintiff's claim for punitive damages was to obtain the necessary minimum amount in controversy under the Magnuson-Moss Act. These allegations "amount to nothing more than an ordinary breach of warranty which is unquestionably remediable under the appropriate provisions of the Uniform Commercial Code."

The issue in this case is not merely a formal defect in the complaint—a failure to allege some sort of wanton or willful act for which punitive damages are recoverable—but rather the primary concern which "is not to permit unwarranted access to the federal courts in situations of this kind by the simple device of pleading punitive damages when the remedies in (s)tate court are available to fully and fairly compensate for the alleged breaches." (Judge Foley, United States District Court, N.N.Y.)

The similarity or close relationship between warranties and advertising and tort liability is underlined in the case of *Shaffer* v. *Victoria Station, Inc.* (47 L.W. 2427 (1978).) Here a restaurant patron was injured by the breakage of a glass containing wine he had ordered. The court held that the patron had a cause of action against the restaurant for breach of implied warranty under U.C.C. 2-314, even though the restaurant is not a merchant with respect to the glass and title to the glass did not pass. (Judge Dolliver, Washington Sup. Court.)

CONVERSION

An advertisement for the sale of a chattel by one who has no right to it, while the owner's possession remains undisturbed, does not make the defendant a converter. For example, where a mortgagee wrongfully advertised an automobile for sale under mortgage, the sale was not legally valid and the mortgagor was not authorized to remove it from another location. (*Carroll* v. *M. & J. Finance Corporation*, 233 SC 200, 104 SE 2d 171 (1958).)

In the earlier case of *Brandburg* v. *Northwestern Jobbers' Credit Bureau et al.*, the court held that the advertising of goods for sale through a mistake does not amount to conversion so long as there is no sale or loss or misappropriation (128 Minn. 411, 151 NW 134 (1915)).

CONCLUSION

According to UCC Section 2-313, an express warranty is created by any affirmation of fact or promise made by the seller to the buyer which relates to the goods and becomes part of the basis of the bargain. (*A.A. Baxter Corp.* v. *Colt Industries, Inc.*, 7 UCC Rep. 1312, 10 CA 3d 144 (Cal. App., 1970); *Werner* v. *Montana*, 22 UCC Rep. 894 (1977).) Representations in regard to goods that do not relate to their quality may come within the definition of express warranty. (*Elanco Products Co.* v. *Akin-Tunnell*, 10 UCC Rep. 30, 474 SW 2d 789 (Tex. Civ. App., 1971).)

The Warranty Act provides that all warranties must be easy to read and understandable, written in ordinary language but not in fine print. Every term and condition of the warranty must be spelled out in writing. Anything that is not there is not part of the warranty.

The more specific the manufacturer, producer, distributor, or seller becomes in advertising the conditions of the sale and purchase of a product or service, the more likely it is to be a firm offer rather than an invitation for a potential customer or consumer to make an offer. Even when there is no connection with or relationship (privity of contract) between the parties to the bargain, an implied or express contract may come into being accordingly if the media is used for the purpose of advertising the seller's product or service.

Once an express or implied contract has been created, and its conditions have been specified in oral and/or written form, it is likely to be enforced on the basis of some pre-existing duty rule, specific performance, detrimental reliance, or past performance if there have been continuing transactions between buyer and seller. Courts place a presumption in favor of enforcing contracts. However, any fraud or deception involved in the formation of a contract, bargain, agreement, or warranty, or in the advertising of its conditions, may lead to its nullification or revocation.

NOTES

[1] Arthur L. Corbin, *Contracts,* I (St. Paul, Minn.: West Publishing Co., 1952), § 24, pp. 41–42.
[2] Ibid. § 25, p. 43.
[3] Ibid. pp. 43–44.
[4] *Black's Law Dictionary,* IV (St. Paul, Minn.: West Publishing Co., 1968), pp. 1757–58.
[5] "General Definitions," *Uniform Commercial Code,* §1–201 (3) (Philadelphia: The American Law Institute, 1972), p. 12.
[6] Corbin, *op cit.,* § 41, p. 68.
[7] Note 37, *Col LR* 77 (1937).
[8] Friedrich Kessler and Grant Gilmore, *Contracts,* II (Boston: Little, Brown and Co., 1974), p. 70.
[9] "Unconscionable Contract or Clause," *Uniform Commercial Code,* §2–302 (Philadelphia: The American Law Institute, 1972), pp. 61–62.
[10] "Express Warranties by Affirmation, Promise, Description, Sample," UCC, id., pp. 79–80.
[11] "Buyer's Right to Specific Performance or Replevin," UCC, id., §2–716, p. 198.
[12] John D. Calamari and Joseph M. Perillo, *The Law of Contracts* 2ed. (St. Paul, Minn.: West Publishing Co., 1977), p. 134.
[13] See footnote 9.
[14] "Modification, Rescission, and Waiver," UCC, id., §2–209(1), p. 57.

Section 2

Cases

Part A: Offer

CRAFT v. ELDER & JOHNSTON CO.
38 NE 2d 416 (1941)

Ordinarily a store lacks sufficient items to satisfy the theoretical demand that an advertisement for its products might produce. By this rule, the advertisement favors the store owner over the customer. This case involves an action to recover damages for breach of contract for the sale of goods. From a judgment for dismissal the plaintiff appeals.

Here Elder, the defendant business, refused to sell to Craft, the plaintiff, a $175 sewing machine for $26 as advertised as a "Thursday Only Special" in the local newspaper. The court was called upon to decide whether an advertisement constitutes an offer which can be accepted by any member of the public. It decided in the negative for an advertisement is not an offer to sell but rather an invitation to the public to come and purchase or an invitation to bargain. Advertisements, circulars, and trade bills are merely expressions of a willingness to negotiate.

In the same sense that an unsolicited price quotation is not considered an offer, an advertisement is likewise not an offer. Furthermore price lists are not binding since quantities are not listed. This protects the seller should his stock run out.

Barnes, Judge.

On or about January 31, 1940, the defendant, the Elder & Johnson Company, carried an advertisement in the *Dayton Shopping News,* an offer for sale of a certain all electric sewing machine for the sum of $26 as a "Thursday Only Special." Plaintiff in her petition, after certain formal allegations, sets out the substance of the above advertisement carried by defendant in the *Dayton Shopping News.* She further alleges that the above publication is an advertising paper distributed in Montgomery County and throughout the city of Dayton; that on Thursday, February 1, 1940, she tendered to the defendant company $26 in payment for one of the machines offered in the advertisement, but that defendant refused to fulfill the offer and has continued to so refuse. The petition further alleges that the value of the machine offered was $175 and she asks damages in the sum of $149 plus interest from February 1, 1940.

The particular advertisement set forth on page 9 of the publication cannot be reproduced in this opinion, but may be described as containing a cut of the machine and other printed matter including the price of $26 and all conforming substantially to the allegations of the petition.

The trial court dismissed plaintiff's petition as evidenced by a journal entry, the pertinent portion of which reads as follows: "Upon consideration the court finds that said advertisement was not an offer which could be accepted by plaintiff to form a contract, and this case is therefore dismissed with prejudice to a new action, at costs of plaintiff."

It seems to us that this case may easily be determined on well-recognized elementary principles. The first question to be determined is the proper characterization to be given to defendant's advertisement in the *Shopping News*. It was not an offer made to any specific person but was made to the public generally. Thereby it would be properly designated as a unilateral offer and not being supported by any consideration could be withdrawn at will and without notice. This would be true because no contractural relations of any character existed between the defendant company and any other person. Plaintiff's tendering of the money and demanding the article advertised would not create a contractural relation. Defendant's refusal to deliver the electric sewing machine would constitute in law a withdrawal of a unilateral offer.

It is argued that an offer can only be withdrawn where notice is given prior to the acceptance. This is true where the negotiations have advanced to the status of at least, a unilateral contract. We distinguish between a unilateral offer and a unilateral contract.

There are instances where unilateral offers through advertisements may create contractual relations with members of the public, but these instances involve special circumstances.

"The most frequent case in which an advertisement has been construed as an offer in the technical sense, involves a published offer of a reward for the furnishing of certain information, the return of particular property, or the doing of a certain act. In such case all that is necessary to confer the benefit demanded by the offeror is performance of the required act. Such offers, of course, are unilateral contracts, and principles of unjust enrichment alone would prevent the offeror from refusing to perform his promise upon the doing of the act."

Furthermore, conditions sometimes arise where the offer is made through an advertisement and a customer procures the articles without notice of the withdrawal of the offer and in such instances the advertiser will be held to his offer, but it must be noted that in these cases the relations of the parties have progressed to a consummated deal.

"It is clear that in the absence of special circumstances an ordinary newspaper advertisement is not an offer, but is an offer to negotiate—an offer to receive offers—or, as it is sometimes called, an offer to chaffer." (Restatement of the Law of Contracts.)

Under the above paragraph the following illustration is given, " 'A', a clothing merchant, advertises overcoats of a certain kind for sale at $50. This is not an offer but an invitation to the public to come and purchase."

"Thus, if goods are advertised for sale at a certain price, it is not an offer and no contract is formed by the statement of an intending purchaser that he will take a specified quantity of the goods at that price. The construction is rather favored that such an advertisement is a mere invitation to enter into a bargain rather than an offer. So a published price list is not an offer to sell the goods listed at the published price." (Williston on Contracts.)

"The commonest example of offers meant to open negotiations and to call forth offers in the technical sense are advertisements, circulars, and trade letters sent out by business houses. While it is possible that the offers made by such means may be in such form as to become contracts, they are often merely expressions of a willingness to negotiate."

"Business advertisements published in newspapers and circulars sent out by mail or distributed by hand stating that the advertiser has a certain quantity or quality of goods which he wants to dispose of at certain prices, are not offers which become contracts as soon as any person to whose notice they may come signifies his acceptance by notifying the other that he will take a certain quantity of them. They are merely invitations to all persons who may read them that the advertiser is ready to receive offers for the goods at the price stated."

We are constrained to the view that the trial court committed no prejudicial error in dismissing plaintiff's petition.

The judgment of the trial court will be affirmed and costs adjudged against the plaintiff-appellant.

STEINBERG v. CHICAGO MEDICAL SCHOOL
41 Ill. App. 3d 804, 354 NE 2d 586 (1976)

Dempsey, Justice.

In December 1973 the plaintiff, Robert Steinberg, applied for admission to the defendant, the Chicago Medical School, as a first-year student for the academic year 1974–75 and paid an application fee of $15. The Chicago Medical School is a private, not-for-profit educational institution, incorporated in the State of Illinois. His application for admission was rejected and Steinberg filed a class action against the school, claiming that it had failed to evaluate his application and those of other applicants according to the academic entrance criteria printed in the school's bulletin. Specifically, his complaint alleged that the school's decision to accept or reject a particular applicant for the first-year class was primarily based on such nonacademic considerations as the prospective student's familial relationship to members of the school's faculty and to members of its board of trustees, and the ability of the applicant or his family to pledge or make payment of large sums of money to the school. The complaint further alleged that by using such unpublished criteria to evaluate applicants the school had breached the contract, which Steinberg contended was created when the school accepted his application fee.

In his prayer for relief Steinberg sought an injunction against the school prohibiting the continuation of such admission practices, and an accounting of all application fees, donations, contributions, and other sums of money collected by the school from its applicants during a ten-year period prior to the filing of his suit. He did not ask the court to direct the school to admit him, to review his application, or to return his fee.

The defendant filed a motion to dismiss, arguing that the complaint failed to state a cause of action because no contract came into existence during its transaction with Steinberg inasmuch as the school's informational publication did not constitute a valid offer. The trial court sustained the motion to dismiss and Steinberg appeals from this order.

The 1974–75 bulletin of the school, which was distributed to prospective students, represented that the following criteria would be used by the school in determining whether applicants would be accepted as first-year medical students:

> Students are selected on the basis of scholarship, character, and motivation without regard to race, creed, or sex. The student's potential for the study and practice of medicine will be evaluated on the basis of academic achievement, Medical College Admission Test results, personal appraisals by a pre-professional advisory committee or individual instructors, and the personal interview, if requested by the Committee on Admissions.

In his four-count complaint, Steinberg alleged, in addition to his claim that the school breached its contract (Count I), that the school's practice of using selection standards which were not disclosed in the school's informational brochure, constituted a violation of the Consumer Fraud and Deceptive Business Practices Act and of the Uniform Deceptive Trade Practices Act (Count II); fraud (Count III), and unjust enrichment (Count IV).

Since we are in accord with the trial court's decision that the complaint did not state a cause of action under Counts II, III and IV, we shall limit our discussion to Count I.

A contract is an agreement between competent parties, based upon a consideration sufficient in law, to do or not do a particular thing. It is a promise or a set of promises for the breach of which the law gives a remedy, or the performance of which the law in some way recognizes as a duty. A contract's essential requirements are: Competent parties, valid subject matter, legal consideration, mutuality of obligation, and mutuality of agreement. Generally, parties may contract in any situation where there is no legal prohibition, since the law acts by restraint and not by conferring rights. However, it is basic contract law that in order for a contract to be binding the terms of the contract must be reasonably certain and definite.

A contract, in order to be legally binding, must be based on consideration. Consideration has been defined to consist of some right, interest, profit, or benefit accruing to one party or some forbearance, disadvantage, detriment, loss, or responsibility given, suffered, or undertaken by the other. Money is valuable consideration and its transfer or payment or promises to pay it or the benefit from the right to its use, will support a contract.

In forming a contract, it is required that both parties assent to the same thing in the same sense and that their minds meet on the essential terms and conditions. Furthermore, the mutual consent essential to the formation of a contract, must be gathered from the language employed by the parties or manifested by their words or acts. The intention of the parties gives character to the transaction and if either party contracts in good faith he is entitled to the benefit of his contract no matter what may have been the secret purpose or intention of the other party.

Steinberg contends that the Chicago Medical School's informational brochure constituted an invitation to make an offer that his subsequent application and the submission of his $15 fee to the school amounted to an offer; that the school's voluntary reception of his fee constituted an acceptance and because of these events a contract was created between the school and himself. He contends that the school was duty bound under the terms of the contract to evaluate his application according to its stated standards and that the deviation from these standards not only breached the contract, but amounted to an arbitrary selection which constituted a violation of due process and equal protection. He concludes that such a breach did in fact take place each and every time during the past ten years that the school evaluated applicants according to their relationship to the school's faculty members or members of its board of trustees, or in accordance with their ability to make or pledge large sums of money to the school. Finally, he asserts that he is a member and a proper representative of the class that has been damaged by the school's practice.

The school counters that no contract came into being because information brochures, such as its bulletin, do not constitute offers, but are construed by the courts to be general proposals to consider, examine, and negotiate. The school points out that this doctrine has been specifically applied in Illinois to university informational publications.

(However), Steinberg is not claiming that his submission of the application and the $15 constituted an acceptance by him; he is merely maintaining that it was an offer, which required the subsequent acceptance of the school to create a contract. Also, it is obvious that his assertion that the bulletin of the school only amounted to an invitation to make an offer, is consistent with the prevailing law and the school's own position.

More importantly, Steinberg is not requesting that the school be ordered to admit him as a student, pursuant to the contract, but only that the school be prohibited from misleading prospective students by stating in its informational literature, evaluation standards that are not subsequently used in the selection of students. Furthermore, the school does not allege, nor did it demonstrate by way of its bulletin or its charter that it had reserved the right to reject any applicant for any reason. It only stated certain narrow standards by which each and every applicant was to be evaluated.

In relation to the preceding argument, the school also maintains that the $15 application fee did not amount to a legal consideration but only constituted a pre-contracting expense. Consequently, the school argues that as a matter of law the $15 is not recoverable as damage even if a contract was eventually entered into and breached.

(Nevertheless), (a)lthough (there is a leading precedent) for the proposition that expenses incurred during preliminary negotiations to procure a contract are not recoverable as damages, it has no relevance to the allegations of Steinberg's complaint. He does not claim that the brochure was an offer and his submission of a fee an acceptance of that offer. To repeat, what he does claim is that the brochure was an invitation to make an offer; that his response was an offer, and that the school's retention of his fee was an acceptance of that offer.

We agree with Steinberg's position. We believe that he and the school entered into an enforceable contract; that the school's obligation under the contract was stated in the school's bulletin in a definitive manner and that by accepting his application fee—a valuable consideration—the school bound itself to fulfill its promises. Steinberg accepted the school's promises in good faith and he was entitled to have his application judged according to the school's stated criteria.

The school argues that he should not be allowed to recover because his complaint did not state a causal connection between the rejection of his application and the school's alleged use of unpublished evaluation criteria. It points out that there is an equal probability that his application was rejected for failing to meet the stated standards, and since the cause of his damages is left to conjecture they may be attributed as easily to a condition for which there is no liability as to one for which there is.

This argument focuses on the wrong point. Once again, Steinberg did not allege that he was damaged when the school rejected his application. He alleged that he was damaged when the school used evaluation criteria other than those published in the school's bulletin. This ultimate, well-pleaded allegation was admitted by the school's motion to dismiss.

The primary purpose of pleadings is to inform the opposite party and the court of the nature of the action and the facts on which it is based. The Civil Practice Act of Illinois provides that pleadings shall be liberally construed to the end that controversies may be settled on their merits. Therefore, a cause of action should not be dismissed unless it clearly appears that no set of facts can be proven under the pleadings which will entitle the plaintiff to recover.

Additionally, a complaint will not be dismissed for failure to state a cause of action if the facts essential to its claim appear by reasonable implication. A complaint is not required to make out a case which will entitle the plaintiff to all of the sought-after relief, but it need only raise a fair question as to the existence of the right.

Count I of Steinberg's complaint stated a valid cause of action, and the portion of the trial court's order dismissing that count will be reversed and remanded.

Alternatively, the school asserts that if Steinberg is entitled to recover, the recovery should be limited to $15 because he is not a proper representative of the class of applicants that was supposed to be damaged by the school's use of unpublished entrance standards. Fundamentally, it argues that it had no contract with Steinberg and since he does not have a cause of action, he cannot represent a class of people who may have similar claims. We have found, however, that he does have a cause of action.

The primary test for the validity of a class action is whether the members of the class have a community of interest in the subject matter and the remedy. Even if the wrongs were suffered in unrelated transactions, a class action may stand as long as there are common factual and legal issues. The legal issue in this case would be the same as to each member of the class, and the factual issue—the amount payed by each member, an application fee of $15—identical.

Steinberg alleged that in applying for admission to the school, each member of the class assumed that the school would use the selection factors set out in its 1974–75 bulletin, and that admission fees were paid and contracts created, but that each contract was breached in the same manner as his. This allegation established a community of interest between him and the other members of the class in terms of subject matter and remedy, and since he has a valid cause of action against the school the class has also. He is a proper representative of the class and his suit is a proper vehicle to resolve the common factual and legal issues involved even though the members of the class suffered damage in separate transactions.

However, the class action cannot be as extensive as Steinberg's complaint requested. Recovery cannot be had by everyone who applied to the medical school during the ten years prior to the filing of his complaint. His action was predicated on standards described in the school's 1974–75 brochure; therefore, the class to be represented is restricted to those applicants who sought admission in reliance on the standards in that brochure.

We agree with the school's contention that a state through its courts does not have the authority to interfere with the power of the trustees of a private medical school to make rules concerning the admission of students. The requirement in the case of public schools, applicable because they belong to the public, that admission regulations must be reasonable is not pertinent in the case of a private school or university. We also agree that using unpublished entrance requirements would not violate an applicant's right to due process and equal protection of law. The provisions of the due process clause of the federal Constitution are inhibitions upon the power of government and not upon the freedom of action of private individuals. The equal protection clause of the Fourteenth Amendment does not prohibit the individual invasion of individual rights.

The order dismissing Counts II, III and IV is affirmed. The order dismissing Count I is reversed. The cause is remanded for further proceedings not inconsistent with the views expressed in this opinion.

Affirmed in part; reversed in part and remanded with directions.

Mejda, P.J., and M Gloon, J., concur.

STEINBERG v. CHICAGO MEDICAL SCHOOL
371 NE 2d 634, 69 Ill. 2d 320, 13 Ill. Dec. 699 (1977)

Dooley, Justice:

Robert Steinberg received a catalog, applied for admission to defendant, Chicago Medical School, for the academic year 1974–75, and paid a $15 fee. He was rejected. Steinberg filed a class action against the school claiming it had failed to evaluate his application and those of other applicants according to the academic criteria in the school's bulletin. According to the complaint, defendant used nonacademic criteria, primarily the ability of the applicant or his family to pledge or make payment of large sums of money to the school.

The 1974–75 bulletin distributed to prospective students contained this statement of standards by which applicants were to be evaluated:

Students are selected on the basis of scholarship, character, and motivation without regard to race, creed, or sex. The student's potential for the study and practice of medicine will be evaluated on the basis of academic achievement, Medical College Admission Test results, personal appraisals by a pre-professional advisory committee or individual instructors, and the personal interview, if requested by the Committee on Admissions.

Count I of the complaint alleged breach of contract; count II was predicated on the Consumer Fraud and Deceptive Business Practices Act and the Uniform Deceptive Trade Practices Act; count III charged fraud; and count IV alleged unjust enrichment. This was sought to be brought as a class action. Accordingly, there were the customary allegations common to such an action.

The trial court dismissed the complaint for failure to state a cause of action. The appellate court reversed as to count I, the contract action, and permitted it to be maintained as a limited class action. It affirmed the circuit court's dismissal of the remaining counts II, III, and IV.

That the Consumer Fraud and Deceptive Business Practices Act is inapplicable is patent from the title of the Act: "An Act to protect consumers and borrowers and businessmen against fraud, unfair methods of competition and unfair or deceptive acts or practices in the conduct of any trade or commerce . . . ." A "consumer" is "any person who purchases or contracts for the purchase of merchandise . . . ." Obviously, plaintiff and those whom he represents were not consumers.

In equity a constructive trust may be imposed to redress unjust enrichment where there is either actual fraud or implied fraud resulting from a fiduciary relationship. Here there is no fiduciary relationship to support a constructive trust and the fraud charges are subsumed in count III. Accordingly, we affirm the appellate court's dismissal of counts II and IV.

The real questions on this appeal are: Can the facts support a charge of breach of contract? Is an action predicated on fraud maintainable? Is this a proper class action situation?

On motion to dismiss we accept as true all well-pleaded facts. Count I alleges Steinberg and members of the class to which he belongs applied to defendant and paid the $15 fee, and that defendant, through its brochure, described the criteria to be employed in evaluating applications, but failed to appraise the applications on the stated criteria. On the contrary, defendant evaluated such applications according to monetary contributions made on behalf of those seeking admission.

A contract, by ancient definition, is "an agreement between competent parties, upon a consideration sufficient in law, to do or not to do a particular thing."

An offer, an acceptance, and consideration are basic ingredients of a contract. Steinberg alleges that he and others similarly situated received a brochure describing the criteria that defendant would employ in evaluating applications. He urges that such constituted an invitation for an offer to apply, that the filing of the applications constituted an offer to have their credentials appraised under the terms described by defendant, and that defendant's voluntary reception of the application and fee constituted an acceptance, the final act necessary for the creation of a binding contract.

This situation is similar to that wherein a merchant advertises goods for sale at a fixed price. While the advertisement itself is not an offer to contract, it constitutes an invitation to deal on the terms described in the advertisement. Although in some cases the advertisement itself may be an offer, usually it constitutes only an invitation to deal on the advertised terms. Only when the merchant takes the money is there an acceptance of the offer to purchase.

Here the description in the brochure containing the terms under which an application will be appraised constituted an invitation for an offer. The tender of the application, as well as the payment of the fee pursuant to the terms of the brochure, was an offer to apply. Acceptance of the application and fee constituted acceptance of an offer to apply under the criteria defendant had established.

Consideration is a basic element for the existence of a contract. Any act or promise which is of benefit to one party or disadvantage to the other is a sufficient consideration to support a contract. The application fee was sufficient consideration to support the agreement between the applicant and the school.

Defendant contends that a further requisite for contract formation is a meeting of the minds. But a subjective understanding is not requisite. It suffices that the conduct of the contracting parties indicates an agreement to the terms of the alleged contract. Williston, in his work on contracts, states:

> In the formation of contracts it was long ago settled that secret intent was immaterial, only overt acts being considered in the determination of such mutual assent as that branch of the law requires. During the first half of the nineteenth century there were many expressions which seemed to indicate the contrary. Chief of these was the familiar cliche, still reechoing in judicial dicta, that a contract requires the 'meeting of the minds' of the parties.

Here it would appear from the complaint that the conduct of the parties amounted to an agreement that the application would be evaluated according to the criteria described by defendant in its literature.

Defendant urges *People ex rel. Tinkoff* v. *Northwestern University* (1947) controls. There the plaintiff alleged that since he met the stated requirement for admission, it was the obligation of the university to accept him. Plaintiff was first rejected because he was 14 years of age. He then filed a *mandamus* action, and subsequently the university denied his admission, apparently because of the court action. That decision turned on the fact that Northwestern University, a private educational institution, had reserved in its charter the right to reject any applicant for any reason it saw fit. Here, of course, defendant had no such provision in its charter or in the brochure in question. But, more important, Steinberg does not seek to compel the school to admit him. The substance of his action is that under the circumstances it was defendant's duty to appraise his application and those of the others on the terms defendant represented.

A medical school is an institution so important to life in society that its conduct cannot be justified by merely stating that one who does not wish to deal with it on its own terms may simply refrain from dealing with it at all.

As the appellate court noted in a recent case in which this defendant was a party: "A contract between a private institution and a student confers duties upon both parties which cannot be arbitrarily disregarded and may be judicially enforced."

Here our scope of review is exceedingly narrow. Does the complaint set forth facts which could mean that defendant contracted, under the circumstances, to appraise applicants and their applications according to the criteria it described? This is the sole inquiry on this motion to dismiss. We believe the allegations suffice and affirm the appellate court in holding count I stated a cause of action.

Count III alleges that, with intent to deceive and defraud plaintiffs, defendant stated in its catalogs it would use certain criteria to evaluate applications; that these representations were false in that applicants were selected primarily for monetary considerations; that plaintiffs relied on said representations and were each thereby induced to submit their applications and pay $15 to their damage.

These allegations support a cause of action for fraud. Misrepresentation of an existing material fact coupled with scienter, deception, and injury are more than adequate. *Roth* v. *Roth* (1970), succinctly stated when a misrepresentation may constitute fraud:

A misrepresentation in order to constitute a fraud must consist of a statement of material fact, false and known to be so by the party making it, made to induce the other party to act, and, in acting, the other party must rely on the truth of the statement.

Plaintiff's allegations meet the test of common law fraud.

Not to be ignored is defendant's *modus operandi* as described in *DeMarco* v. *University of Health Sciences* (1976):

> An analysis of those exhibits shows that in 1970, at least 64 out of 83 entering students had pledges made in their behalves totalling $1,927,900. The pledges varied in amounts from $1400 to $100,000 and averaged $30,123. In 1971, at least 55 out of 83 students had pledges made in their behalves totalling $1,893,000. The pledges varied in amounts from $3000 to $100,000 and averaged $34,418. In 1972, at least 73 out of an entering class of 92 had contributions made in their behalves totalling $3,111,000. The pledges varied in amounts from $20,000 to $100,000 and averaged $42,603. In 1973, at least 78 out of 91 students had contributions made in their behalves totalling $3,749,000. The pledges varied in amounts from $10,000 to $100,000 and averaged $48,064. In addition, there were amounts pledged and partial payments made for students who did not enter or dropped out shortly after entering.

It is immaterial here that the misrepresentation consisted of a statement in the medical school catalog, referring to future conduct, that "the student's potential for the study and practice of medicine will be evaluated on the basis of academic achievement, Medical College Admission Test results, personal appraisals by a pre-professional advisory committee or individual instructors, and the personal interview, if requested by the Committee on Admissions." We concede the general rule denies recovery for fraud based on a false representation of intention or future conduct, but there is a recognized exception where the false promise or representation of future conduct is alleged to be the scheme employed to accomplish the fraud. Such is the situation here.

Here an action for fraud is consistent with the recognition of a contract action. The law creates obligations "on the ground that they are dictated by reason and justice." The right to recover on a "constructive contract," although phrased in contract terminology, is not based on an agreement between parties but is an obligation created by law. "Such contracts are contracts merely in the sense that (they) . . . are created and governed by the principles of equity." So here the facts of this situation mandate that equity implies an obligation by the defendant. We note this since the circumstances before us justify a contract action, as well as a fraud action, or, in the event no contract in fact can be proven, an action on an implied-in-law obligation of the defendant.

What about the propriety of a class action here? A class action is a potent procedural vehicle. Under its terms claims by multiple persons can be decided without the necessity of the appearance of each. A vindication of the rights of numerous persons is possible in a single action when for many reasons individual actions would be impracticable. The origins of this invention of equity, according to Professor Chafee (Some Problems of Equity 157 *et seq.*), go back almost 300 years. Its purpose has been described as "to enable it (equity) to proceed to a decree in suits where the number of those interested in the subject of the litigation is so great that their joinder as parties in conformity to the usual rules of procedure is impracticable."

Notwithstanding the importance of this litigation tool, until the very recent enactment of a law, Illinois had no statute or rule of procedure pertaining to class actions other than a provision of the Civil Practice Act relating to compromise or dismissal of class actions. Hence, all class action questions were determined by case law. According to one law review Illinois, as of 1974, was one of but seven States relying on the common law to determine class actions.

In *Korn v. Franchard Corp.* (2d Cir. 1972), where multiple cases are collected it is said:

> In fraud or 10b–5 cases decided in recent years, various rules, mechanisms, or presumptions have been put forward for mitigating the problem of showing reliance: Split trials for individual proof on reliance; inferring from the materiality of the misstatement that a reasonable investor would have relied; stressing general reliance on a common course of conduct over a period of time; dispensing with or minimizing the need to prove individual reliance in cases of nondisclosure; using the test, in instances of omission, of whether the claimant would have been influenced to act differently, if the undisclosed fact had been made known, than he in fact did.

> We do not cite these formulations to tell the District Court that it should or must follow any of them. Our purpose is only to show that, though many paths have been taken, the federal courts have concurred in adopting procedures and rules which can reduce the difficulties of showing individual reliance. More specifically, in several of these decisions the courts, faced with our problem, have agreed in comparable class suit situations that the common questions predominate and the requirement of Rule 23(b)(3) is satisfied.

An Illinois court determining that an essential element of the proof is common to only certain members of the class could order separate trials on that particular issue. Or the class could be broken into various subclasses, as the Federal decisions point out. The class action, however, is not to be dismissed because of these differences in elements of proof between members of the class.

Who constitutes the class Steinberg represents? The appellate court limited the class to those who applied to the medical school in the same year as Steinberg on the basis that the complaint was predicated on the standards described in the 1974–75 catalog. However, the complaint makes allegations broad enough to state a cause of action for all who applied and paid a fee predicated on a brochure containing the alleged misrepresentations. We hold that each of these can be members of this class. The commencement of the class action suspends the applicable statute of limitations as to all asserted members of the class who would have been parties had the suit continued as a class action.

On remand the trial court should, by a preliminary hearing, determine the following: a) the proper members of the class; b) whether the plaintiff will be able to adequately represent the class so that there will be no denial of due process; c) whether notice is required to other members of the class and the character of such notice; and d) other such pretrial findings proper to class action litigation.

Part B: Acceptance

CARLILL v. CARBOLIC SMOKE BALL CO.
(1893) 1 Q.B. 256 (C.A. 1892)

This case involves an action for damages for breach of contract. Here Carbolic, the defendant, offered a 100 pound reward to anyone who used their product as directed and still contracted influenza. When Carlill, the plaintiff, contracted influenza after using the smoke ball as directed, she sued for 100 pounds in damages. The court considered whether there was an acceptance of Carbolic's offer, and decided in the affirmative. It concluded that while ordinarily a meeting of the minds is required for a contract to come into existence, the person making the offer can dispense with the need for notification of acceptance, if he wishes to do so. This can be done by intimating that a certain type of performance is all that is required for acceptance, an action sufficient to replace notification. To determine if the offer requires only a type of performance for acceptance, the court must look to the offer itself in order to observe the types of words used (words of promise) which infer that performance will dispense with the condition of acceptance.

Appeal from a decision of Hawkins, J. (1892) 2 Q.B. 484.

The defendants, who were the proprietors and vendors of a medical preparation called "The Carbolic Smoke Ball," inserted in the *Pall Mall Gazette* of November 13, 1891, and in other newspapers, the following advertisement:

£100 reward will be paid by the Carbolic Smoke Ball Company to any person who contracts the increasing epidemic influenza, colds, or any disease caused by taking cold, after having used the ball three times daily for two weeks according to the printed directions supplied with each ball. £1000 is deposited with the Alliance Bank, Regent Street showing our sincerity in the matter.

During the last epidemic of influenza many thousand carbolic smoke balls were sold as preventives against this disease, and in no ascertained case was the disease contracted by those using the carbolic smoke ball.

One carbolic smoke ball will last a family several months, making it the cheapest remedy in the world at the price, 10s., post free. The ball can be refilled at a cost of 5s. Address, Carbolic Smoke Ball Company, 27 Princes Street, Hanover Square, London.

The plaintiff, a lady, on the faith of this advertisement, bought one of the balls at a chemist's and used it as directed, three times a day, from November 20, 1891, to January 17, 1892, when she was attacked by influenza. Hawkins, J., held that she was entitled to recover the £100. The defendants appealed.

Lindley, L.J. We must first consider whether this was intended to be a promise at all, or whether it was a puff which meant nothing. Was it a mere puff? My answer to that question is "No," and I base my answer upon this passage: "£1000 is deposited with the Alliance Bank, showing our sincerity in the matter." Now, for what was that money deposited or that statement made except to negative the suggestion that this was a mere puff and meant nothing at all? The deposit is called in aid by the advertiser as a proof of his sincerity in the matter—that is, the sincerity of his promise to pay this £100 in the event which he has specified. I say that for the purpose of giving point to the observation that we are not inferring a promise; there is the promise, as plain as words can make it.

Then it is contended that it is not binding. In the first place, it is said that it is not made with anybody in particular. Now that point is common to the words of this advertisement and to the words of all other advertisements offering rewards. They are offers to anybody who performs the conditions named in the advertisement, and anybody who does perform the condition accepts the offer. In point of law this advertisement is an offer to pay £100 to anybody who will perform these conditions, and the performance of the conditions, is the acceptance of the offer. That rests upon a string of authorities, the earliest of which is *Williams* v. *Carwardine* (4 Barn. & Adol. 621), which has been followed by many other decisions upon advertisements offering rewards.

But then it is said, "Supposing that the performance of the conditions is an acceptance of the offer, that acceptance ought to have been notified." Unquestionably, as a general proposition, when an offer is made, it is necessary in order to make a binding contract, not only that it should be accepted, but that the acceptance should be notified. But is that so in cases of this kind? I apprehend that they are an exception to that rule, or, if not an exception, they are open to the observation that the notification of the acceptance need not precede the performance. This offer is a continuing offer. It was never revoked, and if notice of acceptance is required—which was expressed and explained by Lord Blackburn in the case of *Brogden* v. *Railway Co.*—if notice of acceptance is required, the person who makes the offer gets the notice of acceptance contemporaneously with his notice of the performance of the condition. If he gets notice of the acceptance before his offer is revoked, that in principle is all you want. I, however, think that the true view, in a case of this kind, is that the person who makes the offer shows by his language and from the nature of the transaction that he does not expect and does not require notice of the acceptance apart from notice of the performance.

I come now to the last point which I think requires attention: that is, the consideration. It has been argued that his is nudum pactum—that there is no consideration. We must apply to that argument the usual legal tests. Let us see whether there is no advantage to the defendants. It is said that the use of the ball is no advantage to them, and that what benefits them is the sale; and the case is put that a lot of these balls might be stolen, and that it would be no advantage to the defendants if the thief or other people used them. The answer to that, I think, is as follows: It is quite obvious that in view of the advertisers, a use by the public of their remedy, if they can only get the public to have confidence enough to use it, will react and produce a sale which is directly beneficial to them. Therefore, the advertisers get out of the use an advantage which is enough to constitute a consideration.

But there is another view. Does not the person who acts upon this advertisement and accepts the offer put himself to some inconvenience at the request of the defendants? Is it nothing to use this ball three times daily for two weeks according to the directions at the request of the advertiser? Is that to go for nothing? It appears to me that there is a distinct inconvenience, not to say a detriment, to any person who so uses the smoke ball. I am of opinion, therefore, that there is ample consideration for the promise.

Bowen, L.J. I am of the same opinion. (I)t was said that there was no notification of the acceptance of the contract. One cannot doubt that, as an ordinary rule of law, an acceptance of an offer made ought to be notified to the person who makes the offer, in order that the two minds may come together. Unless this is done, the two minds may be apart, and there is not that consensus which is necessary according to the English law—I say nothing about the laws of other countries—to make a contract. But there is this clear gloss to be made upon that doctrine, that as notification of acceptance is required for the benefit of the person who makes the offer, the person who makes the offer may dispense with notice of himself if he thinks it desirable to do so, and I suppose there can be no doubt that where a person in an offer made by him to another person, expressly or impliedly intimates a particular mode of acceptance as sufficient to make the bargain binding, it is only necessary for the other person to whom such offer is made to follow the indicated method of acceptance; and if the person making the offer, expressly or impliedly intimates in his offer that it will be sufficient to act on the proposal without communicating acceptance of it to himself, performance of the condition is a sufficient acceptance without notification.

Now, if that is the law, how are we to find out whether the person who makes the offer does intimate that notification of acceptance will not be necessary in order to constitute a binding bargain? In many cases you look to the offer itself. In many cases you extract from the character of the transaction that notification is not required, and in the advertisement cases it seems to me to follow as an inference to be drawn from the transaction itself that a person is not to notify his acceptance of the offer before he performs the condition, but that if he performs the condition notification is dispensed with. It seems to me that from the point of view of common sense no other idea could be entertained. If I advertise to the world that my dog is lost, and that anybody who brings the dog to a particular place will be paid some money, are all the police or other persons whose business it is to find lost dogs to be expected to sit down and write a note saying that they have accepted my proposal? Why, of course, they at once look after the dog, and as soon as they find the dog they have performed the condition. The essence of the transaction is that the dog should be found, and it is not necessary under such circumstances, as it seems to me, that in order to make the contract binding there should be any notification of acceptance. It follows from the nature of the thing that the performance of the condition is sufficient acceptance without the notification of it, and a person who makes an offer in an advertisement of that kind makes an offer which must be read by the light of that common sense reflection. He does, therefore, in his offer impliedly indicate that he does not require notification of the acceptance of the offer.

Appeal Dismissed.

GEORGIAN CO. v. BLOOM
27 Ga. App. 468, 108 SE 813 (1921)

Action by the Georgian Company against Jennie Bloom for the price of certain advertisements. The defendant asserted a counterclaim on these facts: The defendant, being in ladies' ready-to-wear business, requested the plaintiff to insert the following advertisement: "Special in furs. Large animal scarfs, taupe, brown, and black, satin lined into brush. For three days only. Special price $15.00." This advertisement was run in the plaintiff's newspaper, but with the price stated $5.00.

The defendant alleged that in consequence she was obliged to sell 48 of the scarfs at a loss of $10 each, incurring a total loss of $480.00. The counterclaim was held invalid by the trial court, but the Superior Court ordered a new trial, and the case now comes up on exceptions to this order of the judge of the superior court.

The court decided on appeal that a general advertisement in a newspaper for the sale of goods is a mere invitation to enter into a bargain, and not an offer.

Hill, J.

A general advertisement in a newspaper for the sale of an indefinite quantity of goods is a mere invitation to enter into a bargain, rather than an offer. "A business advertisement published in newspapers and circulars sent out by mail or distributed by hand, stating that the advertiser has a certain quantity or quality of goods which he wants to dispose of at certain prices, are not offers which become contracts as soon as any person to whose notice they might come signifies his acceptance by notifying the other that he will take a certain quantity of them. They are mere invitations to all persons who may read them that the advertiser is ready to receive offers for the goods at the price stated . . . . If goods are advertised for sale at a certain price . . . the construction is rather favored that such advertisement is a mere invitation to enter into a bargain, rather than an offer."

In the instant case the advertisement, which is the basis of the counterclaim, specified no definite quantity of the furs for sale, though there was a more or less indefinite description of the qualities of the goods. The first essential of a sale is that there must be "an identification of the thing sold." To consummate a contract there must be "a meeting of minds." There was no merit in the counterclaim filed by the defendant in the municipal court, and the judge of that court committed no error in striking it, and entering up judgment for the plaintiff. He had a right to do so at the trial term of the court, and the judge of the superior court erred in sustaining the certiorari and ordering a new trial.

Judgment reversed.

Part C: Consideration

COLE-McINTYRE-NORFLEET CO. v. HOLLOWAY
141 Tenn. 679, 214 SW 817 (1919)

Mr. Chief Justice Lansden delivered the opinion of the Court.

This case presents a question of law, which so far as we are advised, has not been decided by this court in its exact phases. March 26, 1917, a traveling salesman of plaintiff in error solicited and received from defendant in error, at his country store in Shelby County, Tennessee, an order for certain goods, which he was authorized to sell. Among these goods were fifty barrels of meal. The meal was to be ordered out by defendant by the 31st day of July, and afterwards five cents per barrel per month was to be charged him for storage.

After the order was given, the defendant heard nothing from it until the 26th of May, 1917, when he was in the place of business of plaintiff in error and told it to begin shipment of the meal on his contract. He was informed by plaintiff in error that it did not accept the order of March 26, and for that reason the defendant had no contract for meal.

The defendant in error never received confirmation or rejection from plaintiff in error, or other refusal to fill the order. The same traveling salesman of plaintiff in error called on defendant as often as once each week, and this order was not mentioned to defendant, either by him or by his principles, in any way. Between the day of the order and the 26th of May, the day of its alleged rejection, prices on all of the articles in the contract greatly advanced. All of the goods advanced about 50 percent, in value.

Some jobbers at Memphis received orders from their drummers, and filled the orders or notified the purchaser that the orders were rejected; but this method was not followed by plaintiff in error.

The contract provided that it was not binding until accepted by the seller at its office in Memphis, and that the salesman had no authority to sign the contract for either the seller or buyer. It was further stipulated that the order should not be subject to countermand.

It will be observed that plaintiff in error was silent upon both the acceptance and rejection of the contract. It sent forth its salesman to solicit this and other orders. The defendant in error did not have the right to countermand orders and the contract was closed, if and when it was accepted by plaintiff in error. The proof that some jobbers in Memphis uniformly filled such orders unless the purchaser was notified to the contrary is of no value because it does not amount to a custom.

The case, therefore, must be decided upon its facts. The circuit court and the court of civil appeals were both of opinion that the contract was completed because of the lapse of time before plaintiff in error rejected it. The time intervening between the giving of the order by defendant and its alleged repudiation by plaintiff in error was about 60 days. Weekly opportunities were afforded the salesman of plaintiff in error to notify the defendant in error of the rejection of the contract, and, of course daily occasions were afforded plaintiff in error to notify him by mail or wire. The defendant believed the contract was in force on the 26th of May, because he directed plaintiff in error to begin shipment of the meal on that day. Such shipments were to have been completed by July 31st, or defendant to pay storage charges. From this evidence the circuit court found as an inference of fact that plaintiff in error had not acted within a reasonable time, and therefore its silence would be construed as an acceptance of the contract. The question of whether the delay of plaintiff in error was reasonable or unreasonable was one of fact, and the circuit court was justified from the evidence in finding that the delay was unreasonable. Hence the case, as it comes to us, is whether delay upon the part of plaintiff in error for an unreasonable time in notifying the defendant in error of its action upon the contract is an acceptance of its terms.

We think such delay was unreasonable, and effected an acceptance of the contract. It should not be forgotten that this is not the case of an agent exceeding this authority, or acting without authority. Even in such cases the principal must accept or reject the benefits of the contract promptly and within a reasonable time.

Plaintiff's agent in this case was authorized to do precisely that which he did do, both as to time and substance. The only thing which was left open by the contract was the acceptance or rejection of its terms by plaintiff in error. It will not do to say that a seller of goods like these could wait indefinitely to decide whether or not he will accept the offer of the proposed buyer. This was all done in the usual course of business, and the articles embraced with the contract were consumable in the use, and some of them would become unfitted for the market within a short time.

It is undoubtedly true that an offer to buy or sell is not binding until its acceptance is communicated to the other party. The acceptance, however, of such an offer may be communicated by the other party either by a formal acceptance, or acts amounting to an acceptance. Delay in communicating action as to the acceptance may amount to an acceptance itself. When the subject of a contract, either in its nature or by virtue of conditions of the market, will become unmarketable by delay, delay in notifying the other party of his decision will amount to an acceptance by the offerer. Otherwise, the offerer could place his goods upon the market, and solicit orders, and yet hold the other party to the contract, while he reserves time to himself to see if the contract will be profitable.

Writ denied.

RESPONSE TO PETITION TO REHEAR

An earnest petition to rehear has been filed, and we have reexamined the question with great care. The petition quotes the text of 13 Corpus Juris. p. 276 as follows:

> An offer made to another, either orally or in writing, cannot be turned into an agreement because the person to whom it is made or sent makes no reply, even though the offer states that silence will be taken as consent, for the offerer cannot prescribe conditions of rejection, so as to turn silence on the part of the offeree into acceptance.

And further: "In like manner mere delay in accepting or rejecting an offer cannot make an agreement."

It is also said that diligent research reveals only one case holding in accord with the court's decision of this case, and that case is *Blue Grass Cordage Co.* v. *Luthy,* and it is said this case was overruled by the later case of *L.A. Becker Co.* v. *Alvey.* We have examined both of these cases, and we do not think either is authority on the question at issue. In the first case, the contract was admittedly executed, and the suit was for damages for its breach. The second case does not refer to the first, and is upon another branch of contracts. The quotation from Corpus Juris contemplates the case of an original offer, unaccompanied by other circumstances, and does not apply to this case, where the parties had been dealing with each other before the contract, and were dealing in due course at the time.

It is a general principle of the law of contracts that, while an assent to an offer is requisite to the formation of an agreement, yet such assent is a condition of the mind, and may be either express or evidence by circumstances from which the assent may be inferred. And see the cases cited in the notes of these authorities. They all agree that acceptance of an offer may be inferred from silence. This is only where the circumstances surrounding the parties afford a basis from which an inference may be drawn from silence. There must be the right and the duty to speak, before the failure to do so can prevent a person from afterwards setting up the truth. We think it is the duty of a wholesale merchant, who sends out his drummers to solicit orders for perishable articles, and articles consumable in the use, to notify his customers within a reasonable time that the orders are not accepted; and if he fails to do so, and the proof shows that he had ample opportunity, silence for an unreasonable length of time will amount to an acceptance, if the offerer is relying upon him for the goods.

The petition to rehear is denied.

MORRIS LEFKOWITZ v. GREAT MINNEAPOLIS SURPLUS STORE, INC.

251 Minn. 188, 86 NW 2d 689 (1957)

Contracts are unable to solve every legal dispute. A contract is a relationship between two or more parties in which one promises to do something, and the other accepts the promise for the undertaking—a promisory transaction. Every advertisement in the newspaper making an offer for which anyone can accept would place too great a burden upon the offeror to potentially be obligated to serve the whole world. As a result under normal circumstances an advertisement for the sale of an article, if it is clear, definite, and explicit, and leaves nothing open for negotiation, constitutes an offer which will create a binding contract upon acceptance.

In this case, the court recognizes advertising limitations. If the ad comprises an offer, no new limitations may be added when the customer responds. The offer or advertisement should be read to see what is expected. This case involves an action to recover damages for breach of contract. Here a surplus store, the defendant, advertised one fur stole on a "first-come-first-served" basis but would not sell the stole to Lefkowitz, the plaintiff, who accepted the alleged offer.

In considering the question whether a newspaper advertisement constitutes an offer such that acceptance will complete the contract, the court decided that it would. The test of whether a binding obligation may originate in advertisements addressed to the public is "whether the facts show that some performance was promised in positive terms in return for something requested." The performance sometimes calls for an act, a promise, or an exchange. The exchange could be a promise for a promise, a promise for an act, or an act for a promise. Money may be offered in return for any of these exchanges.

Whether an advertisement constitutes an offer or merely an invitation for offers depends on the legal intention of the parties and the surrounding circumstances. In this case, the defendant's advertisement comprises an offer, the acceptance of which created a binding contract. Nevertheless, while an advertiser has the right at any time before acceptance to modify his offer, he does not have the right, after acceptance to impose new or arbitrary conditions not contained in the published offer.

Murphy, Justice.

This is an appeal from an order of the Municipal Court of Minneapolis denying the motion of the defendant for amended findings of fact, or, in the alternative, for a new trial. The order for judgment awarded the plaintiff the sum of $138.50 as damages for breach of contract.

This case grows out of the alleged refusal of the defendant to sell to the plaintiff a certain fur piece which it had offered for sale in a newspaper advertisement. It appears from the record that on April 6, 1956, the defendant published the following advertisement in a Minneapolis newspaper.:

SATURDAY 9 A.M. SHARP

3 BRAND NEW

FUR COATS

Worth to $100.00

First Come

First Served

$1

EACH

On April 13, the defendant again published an advertisement in the same newspaper as follows:

SATURDAY 9 A.M.

2 BRAND NEW PASTEL

MINK 3-SKIN SCARFS

Selling for $89.50

Out they go

Saturday. Each $1.00

1 BLACK LAPIN STOLE

Beautiful,

Worth $139.50 . . . . . . $1.00

FIRST COME, FIRST SERVED

The record supports the findings of the court that on each of the Saturdays following the publication of the above-described ads the plaintiff was the first to present himself at the appropriate counter in the defendant's store and on each occasion demanded the coat and the stole so advertised and indicated his readiness to pay the sale price of $1. On both occasions, the defendant refused to sell the merchandise to the plaintiff, stating on the first occasion that by a "house rule" the offer was intended for women only and sales would not be made to men, and on the second visit that plaintiff knew defendant's house rules.

The trial court properly disallowed plaintiff's claim for the value of the fur coats since the value of these articles was speculative and uncertain. The only evidence of value was the advertisement itself to the effect that the coats were "Worth to $100.00," how much less being speculative especially in view of the price for which they were offered for sale. With reference to the offer of the defendant on April 13, 1956, to sell the "1 Black Lapin Stole . . . worth $139.50 . . ." the trial court held that the value of this article was established and granted judgment in favor of the plaintiff for that amount less the $1 quoted purchase price.

The defendant contends that a newspaper advertisement offering items of merchandise for sale at a named price is a "unilateral offer" which may be withdrawn without notice. He relies upon authorities which hold that, where an advertiser publishes in a newspaper that he has a certain quantity or quality of goods which he wants to dispose of at certain prices and on certain terms, such advertisements are not offers which become contracts as soon as any person to whose notice they may come signifies his acceptance by notifying the other that he will take a certain quantity of them. Such advertisements have been construed as an invitation for an offer sale on the terms stated, which offer, when received, may be accepted or rejected and which therefore does not become a contract of sale until accepted by the seller; and until a contract has been so made, the seller may modify or revoke such prices or terms.

The defendant relies principally on *Craft* v. *Elder & Johnston Co.* In that case, the court discussed the legal effect of an advertisement offering for sale, as a one-day special, an electric sewing machine at a named price. The view was expressed that the advertisement was "not an offer made to any specific person but was made to the public generally. Thereby it would be properly designated as a unilateral offer and not being supported by any consideration could be withdrawn at will and without notice." It is true that such an offer may be withdrawn before acceptance. Since all offers are by their nature unilateral because they are necessarily made by one party or on one side in the negotiation of a contract, the distinction made in that decision between a unilateral offer and a unilateral contract is not clear. On the facts before us we are concerned with whether the advertisement constituted an offer, and, if so, whether the plaintiff's conduct constituted an acceptance.

There are numerous authorities which hold that a particular advertisement in a newspaper or circular letter relating to a sale of articles may be construed by the court as constituting an offer, acceptance of which would complete a contract.

The test of whether a binding obligation may originate in advertisements addressed to the general public is "whether the facts show that some performance was promised in positive terms in return for something requested."

The authorities above cited emphasize that, where the offer is clear, definite, and explicit, and leaves nothing open for negotiation, it constitutes an offer, acceptance of which will complete the contract.

Whether in any individual instance a newspaper advertisement is an offer rather than an invitation to make an offer depends on the legal intention of the parties and the surrounding circumstances. We are of the view on the facts before us that the offer by the defendant of the sale of the Lapin fur was clear, definite, and explicit, and left nothing open for negotiation. The plaintiff having successfully managed to be the first one to appear at the seller's place of business to be served, as requested by the advertisement, and having offered the stated purchase price of the article, he was entitled to performance on the part of the defendant. We think the trial court was correct in holding that there was in the conduct of the parties a sufficient mutuality of obligation to constitute a contract of sale.

The defendant contends that the offer was modified by a "house rule" to the effect that only women were qualified to receive the bargains advertised. The advertisement contained no such restriction. This objection may be disposed of briefly by stating that, while an advertiser has the right at any time before acceptance to modify his offer, he does not have the right, after acceptance, to impose new or arbitrary conditions not contained in the published offer.

Affirmed.

JENKINS TOWEL SERVICE, INC. v. FIDELITY-PHILADELPHIA TRUST CO.
400 Pa. 98, 161 A2d 334 (1960)

The Trust Company, after many unsuccessful attempts to sell a piece of real estate owned as trustee, on June 18, 1959 circulated a letter in which it requested interested parties to submit sealed bids for the property. The letter provided that on June 24, 1959 the bids were to be opened and that an Agreement of Sale would be tendered "to the highest acceptable bidder whose offer is in excess of $92,000 cash, free and clear of any and all brokerage commissions." The Trust Company reserved to itself the right to "approve or disapprove of any or all offers, or to withdraw the properties from the market." It also emphasized its fiduciary duty to recommend "the most advantageous offer." Plaintiff submitted a bid for said properties of $95,600 cash, accompanied by a treasurer's check in the amount of $10,000.

The only other bid was made by the Esso Standard Oil Corporation for the same amount conditioned however on a change in zoning to permit the use of those properties as a gasoline station, and subject to approval by its home office in New York. When the Trust Company refused to effect an agreement of sale with plaintiff, preferring Esso to plaintiff, the latter sued for specific performance. The Court of Common Pleas dismissed the bill and plaintiff appealed.

The Supreme Court of Pennsylvania reversed, holding that where the trustee as owner of properties sent a letter stating that it would accept sealed bids and sell properties to the party submitting the highest acceptable cash bid in excess of a certain sum, notwithstanding the fact that the letter stated that the trustee reserved the right to approve or disapprove any or all offers or to withdraw properties from the market, the letter constituted an offer of sale subject to terms and conditions set forth therein.

Since the plaintiffs were the only ones who duly and unconditionally accepted the offer, they were entitled to specific performance. The courts reasons for its decision are as follows:

Bell, J.

The rights of the parties depend upon the proper construction of Fidelity's letter of June 18, 1959. Plaintiff claims the letter was an offer which it unconditionally accepted. Defendants claim that the letter was merely "preliminary negotiations" and "an invitation to bid."

Fidelity's letter of June 18 is ambiguous and therefore it must be interpreted most strongly against the Fidelity, which drew it.

Plaintiff's sealed bid of $95,600 was unequivocal, unconditional, and in full compliance with all the terms and conditions set forth by the Fidelity in its letter-offer dated June 18, 1959. On the other hand, the bid of Esso Standard Oil Company was conditional and qualified. Esso's bid was not an acceptance of the offer made by Fideltiy; on the contrary it was a rejection of this offer and a counter-offer. It is clear that plaintiff was the only party which accepted the Fidelity's offer.

If, as defendants contend, Fidelity's letter of June 18 was merely an invitation to prospective purchasers who had been negotiating unsuccessfully for several years to submit a higher bid or offer which it could accept or reject in its sole and arbitrary descretion, why did Fidelity ask for "sealed bids" from all interested parties on or before June 24, 1959, and further state "at the time the bids will be opened and an *Agreement of Sale* tendered to the highest acceptable bidder, provided the offer is in excess of $92,000 cash, free and clear of all brokerage commissions," and then specify in detail the other provisions which were to be incorporated in the Agreement of Sale? On its face, and especially in the light of the prior negotiations, the surrounding circumstances and the objects which the parties apparently had in view, the contention of defendants that this was merely an invitation to bid, which Fidelity could reject in its unfettered discretion, is unreasonable.

In an attempt to support Fidelity's construction and position, defendants have overlooked not only the law as to the interpretation of a contract which must be considered in its entirety, but also the most important provision, viz. that after the bids are opened it will tender to the highest acceptable bidder* an Agreement of Sale, the details of which are set forth in Fidelity's letter of June. 18.

Defendants rely upon the statement in Fidelity's letter that it was acting as fiduciary and was "obligated to recommend the offer which it believed most advantageous to its estate." This contention is devoid of merit. Plaintiff unconditionally and unqualifiedly accepted all the terms and conditions of Fidelity's offer, and no other party did; and there was no higher or more advantageous offer. Defendants also rely upon the following sentence—"The Trustees, of course, reserve the right to approve or disapprove of any and all offers, or to withdraw the properties from the market." This sentence standing alone is what creates a possible ambiguity. This sentence must be interpreted, we repeat, by considering the surrounding circumstances, the objects Fidelity apparently had in view, and the contract in its entirety, and if there is any ambiguity which is reasonably susceptible of two interpretations, the ambiguity must be resolved against the Fideltiy which drew the letter-offer. So interpreted, we believe the sentence means that Fidelity can withdraw the properties from the market at any time before the opening of the sealed bids, and can approve or disapprove any offer which does not *fully* comply with all the conditions set forth by the Fidelity, or which complies but adds unsatisfactory terms.

We are convinced that the letter of Fidelity Trust Company dated June 18, 1959, was an offer of sale of the properties in question by Fidelity, subject to the terms and conditions therein set forth and that the offer was duly and unconditionally accepted by plaintiff alone. The Court below therefore erred in sustaining the defendant's preliminary objections and in dismissing plaintiff's amended bill of complaint. If the defendants are unable to controvert the facts set forth in the amended complaint, the plaintiff should be awarded specific performance of the contract.

Decree reversed with a procedendo at the cost of the trust estate of which Fidelity-Philadelphia Trust Company is trustee or co-trustee.

Benjamin R. Jones, Justice, dissenting.

---

*There is no contention that plaintiff was not acceptable.

The crux of my disagreement with the majority of this court lies in the interpretation of the letter of June 18, 1959 from Fidelity to Jenkins. The majority construes this letter as a firm *offer* on the part of Fidelity to sell this real estate to the highest bidder, whereas I construe this letter as an *invitation for an offer* to be submitted to purchase this real estate.

Fidelity held title to this property as a fiduciary: such fact, known to Jenkins, required that in the disposal of such property Fidelity exercise a high degree of care, (*Herbert Estate*, 356 Pa. 107, 110, 51 A.2d 753). In recognition of its fiduciary duty, Fidelity warned Jenkins that, as a fiduciary, it was "obligated to recommend the offer which it believes most advantageous to its Estate."

Four different times the letter employs the words "offer" or "offers" to describe that which Jenkins is to submit. The letter requests the addressee to "forward your highest offer;" it states that all "*offers*" were to be made on a cash basis; it directs that a check should accompany the offer "in the amount of at least 10 percent of the *offer*;" lastly, Fidelity reserved the right to approve or disapprove of "any or all *offers*."

The majority bases its interpretation of the letter as an "offer" on two facets of its language: first, the letter asks for "sealed bids," and second, the letter states that "at that time (June 24, 1959) the bids will be opened and an Agreement of Sale tendered." A "sealed bid" is simply an "offer" or a "bid" submitted in such form that its contents are concealed until the time of opening, a cautionary measure which insures to bidders an equality of treatment at the hands of the person who invites such offers or bids. The mere fact that a "bid" is sealed does not determine whether the bid is an "offer" of "an acceptance or an offer." The employment of the word "sealed" adds no magic to the situation.

Had the letter stated an "Agreement of Sale (will be) tendered to the highest bidder" the majority view *might* be supportable, but the majority overlooks an all-important word in the phrase actually employed, i.e., the word "acceptable." An Agreement of Sale was not to be tendered to "the *highest* bidder," but to "the *highest acceptable* bidder." The word "acceptable" certainly and clearly modifies the word "highest" and reveals a clear intent on the part of Fidelity that an Agreement of Sale will be tendered to the highest bidder *only if such bidder is* "*acceptable*." This phrase does support not the majority, but my view that *Fidelity* reserved the right of rejection of any bid that was not *acceptable* to it.

Finally, Fidelity's letter expressly states: "The Trustees, of course, reserve the right to approve or disapprove of any or all offers, or to withdraw the properties from the market." The majority states that this "sentence means that Fidelity can withdraw the properties from the market at any time before the opening of the sealed bids, and can approve or disapprove any offer which does not *fully* comply with all the conditions set forth by Fideltiy, or which complies but adds unsatisfactory terms." Such a construction is absolutely unjustified under the clear language employed by Fidelity. If a bid did not *fully* comply with the terms of the letter, or, if it complied, but added any terms, whether satisfactory or unsatisfactory, such a bid, even if called an "acceptance," would not constitute an acceptance to any offer contained in the letter. As to the interpretation by the majority that Fidelity's right to withdraw ceased at the time the sealed bids were opened, such a construction rewrites the language of the letter and imposes on Fidelity's part a condition judge-created, and not Fidelity intended and expressed.

If the English language ever was effectively employed to express a fiduciary's reservation of the right to reject any and all bids, it appears in this letter. Fundamental concepts inherent in the law of contracts should not be lightly cast aside for the sake of expediency in the determination of a particular case. Instead of construing this letter as written, the majority, under the guise of a supposed ambiguity of language, now undertakes to rewrite the letter and to create a contract where no contract exists.

I, accordingly, dissent.

Part D: Contract and Tort

JACOB E. DECKER & SONS, INC. v. *CAPPS*
139 Tex. 609, 164 SW 2d 828 (1942)

Alexander, Chief Justice.

This suit involves the question of the liability of a manufacturer of food products to the consumer thereof for damages for personal injuries sustained by him as the result of the unwholesomeness of such food.

Jacob E. Decker & Sons, Inc., manufactured and sold certain sausage, advertised as being suitable for human consumption in the summertime, under the trade name of "Cervalet", which sausage was wrapped in a cellophane package. The sausage in question was sold on March 16, 1939, by Jacob E. Decker & Sons, Inc., to a retail merchant in Texas for resale, and was purchased by C.K. Capps on March 19, 1939. It was consumed immediately by members of Capps' family, and as a result one of the children died and other members of the family were made seriously ill. Mrs. Capps, after the death of her husband from other causes, brought suit for herself for damages for the injuries sustained by her as a result of the eating of the contaminated sausage. She also brought two other suits as next friend for her two surviving minor children for damages for the injuries suffered by them. The three suits were tried together. The jury found that at the time the sausage in question was processed and manufactured it was contaminated and poisonous to such an extent as to be unfit for human consumption; and that the eating thereof by the members of Capps' family proximately resulted in their serious illness. The jury further found, however, that Decker & Sons did not fail to properly inspect the sausage, and that the contaminated and poisonous condition of the sausage at the time it was manufactured was not due to negligence of Decker & Sons in the manufacture and processing thereof, and that the illness suffered by Capps' family from the eating of the sausage was the result of an unavoidable accident. Judgments in favor of the plaintiffs for damages sustained by them were affirmed by the Courts of Civil Appeals.

The jury's verdict, as we understand it, amounts to a finding that the sausage, at the time it was processed and manufactured by Decker & Sons, was so contaminated and poisonous as to be unfit for human consumption and the members of Capps' family were seriously injured by the eating thereof; but Decker & Sons was not negligent in the manufacture of the sausage. The finding of the jury that the injuries suffered by plaintiffs were the result of an unavoidable accident amounted to nothing more than a finding that there was no negligence on the part of either the plaintiff or the defendant.

Under the foregoing facts, the question to be determined is whether a nonnegligent manufacturer, who processes and sells contaminated food to a retailer for resale for human consumption, is liable to the consumer for the injuries sustained by him as a result of the eating of such food. So far as we have been able to ascertain, this exact question has not heretofore been before this Court. While there is quite a contrariety of opinion on the subject in other jurisdictions, there is no dearth of authorities.

After having considered the matter most carefully, we have reached the conclusion that the manufacturer is liable for the injuries sustained by the consumers of the products in question. We think the manufacturer is liable in such a case under an implied warranty imposed by operation of law as a matter of public policy. We recognize that the authorities are by no means uniform, but we believe the better reasoning supports the rule which holds the manufacturer liable. Liability in such case is not based on negligence, nor on a breach of the usual implied contractual warranty, but on the broad principle of the public policy to protect human health and life. It is a well known fact that articles of food are manufactured and placed in the channels of commerce, with the intention that they shall pass from hand to hand until they are finally used by some remote consumer. It is usually impracticable, if not impossible, for the ultimate consumer to analyze the food and ascertain whether or not it is suitable for human consumption. Since it has been packed and placed on the market as a food for human consumption, and marked as such, the purchaser usually eats without the precaution of having it analyzed by a technician to ascertain whether or not it is suitable for human consumption. In fact, in most instances the only satisfactory examination that could be made would be only at the time and place of the processing of the food. It seems to be the rule that where food products sold for human consumption are unfit for that purpose, there is such an utter failure of the purpose for which the food is sold, and the consequences of eating unsound food are so disastrous to human health and life, that the law imposes a warranty of purity in favor of the ultimate consumer as a matter of public policy.

Since very early times the common law has applied more stringent rules to sales of food than to sales of other merchandise. It has long been a well established rule that in sales of food for domestic use there is an implied warranty that it is wholesome and fit for human consumption. A majority of the American courts that have followed this holding have not based such warranty upon an implied term in the contract between buyer and seller, nor upon reliance by the buyer on the representation of the seller, but have imposed it as a matter of public policy in order to discourage the sale of unwholesome food.

The rule has been adhered to by (many court) decisions in this country and has been recognized as a distinct implied warranty peculiar to sales of food, although the obligation existed long before implied warranties were recognized. This implied warranty was not based on any reliance by the buyer upon the representations of the seller, or upon his skill and judgment, but was grounded squarely upon the public policy of protecting the public health.

The implied warranty of wholesomeness has been recognized and applied in Texas by the Court of Civil Appeals. A similar holding was made by the Court of Civil Appeals in the instant case.

While a right of action in such a case is said to spring from a "warranty," it should be noted that the warranty here referred to is not the more modern contractual warranty, but is an obligation imposed by law to protect public health. According to Professor Williston, the law of warranty is older by a century than the action of special assumpsit, from which the modern law of contracts developed. The action on a warranty sounded in tort was in the nature of an action on the case for deceit, although it was not necessary to plead or prove scienter. It is believed that much of the confusion among the courts on this question is due to the failure to note the difference in the use of the term "warranty." It had led many courts to believe that in order to sustain an action under such a warranty there must be privity of contract and reliance on the representation. The doctrine of privity of contract and of the necessity therefore in order to sustain an action grew out of the later action of assumpsit. It applies only when one is seeking to enforce a contract. Here the liability of the manufacturer and vendor is imposed by operation of law as a matter of public policy for the protection of the public, and is not dependent on any provision of the contract, either expressed or implied.

It must be conceded that many courts have denied recovery against the manufacturer and have insisted strictly on the requirement of privity.

There is a growing tendency, however, to discard the requirement of privity and to hold the manufacturer liable directly to the ultimate consumer.

It is also true that there are many cases in which liability has been sustained on the ground of contractual warranty. Where there is privity of contract and there is a breach of warranty, either expressed or implied, liability can be sustained thereon, as in the case of the sale of commodities other than food. The fact, however, that liability may be sustained does not argue against the sustaining of liability on the ground herein adhered to—warranty imposed by law as a matter of public policy. The two remedies may coexist, and liability may be sustained under either one of them that is available.

Many of the courts which have allowed a recovery where there was no direct contractual relationship between plaintiff and defendant have done so by indulging in fictions, such as presumed negligence, fraud, assignment of cause of action from dealer to consumer, third party beneficiary contract, and agency of the buyer for the consumer. Such authorities but evidence the efforts made by the courts to place absolute liability on the manufacturer and vendor of food products to the consumer for damages caused by impurities therein. Such fictions are indulged merely because it is thought necessary to do so in order to get away from the rule which requires privity of contract where recovery is sought on an implied warranty growing out of a contract. We believe the better and sounder rule places liability solidly on the ground of a warranty not in contract, but law as a matter of public policy.

Some courts have imposed upon the manufacturer and vendor an implied warranty which is said to "run with the article." While this appears to be based on sound logic, it is more a reason for the imposition of warranty by operation of law than it is an independent ground of liability on itself. There certainly is justification for indulging a presumption of a warranty that runs with the article in the sale of food products. A party who processes a product and gives it the appearance of being suitable for human consumption, and places it in the channels of commerce, expects someone to consume the food in reliance on its appearance that it is suitable for human consumption. He expects the appearance of suitableness to continue with the product until someone is induced to consume it as food. But a modern manufacturer or vendor does even more than this under modern practices. He not only processes the food and dresses it up so as to make it appear appetizing, but he uses the newspapers, magazines, billboards, and the radio to build up the phycology to buy and consume his products. The invitation extended by him is not only to the housewife to buy and serve his product, but to the members of the family and guest to eat it. In fact, the manufacturer's interest in the product is not terminated when he has sold it to the wholesaler. He must get it off the wholesaler's shelves before the wholesaler will buy a new supply. The same is not only true of the retailer, but of the housewife, for the housewife will not buy more until the family has consumed that which she has in her pantry. Thus the manufacturer or other vendor intends that this appearance of suitability of the article for human consumption should continue and be effective until someone is induced thereby to consume the goods. It would be but to acknowledge a weakness in the law to say that he could thus create a demand for his products by inducing a belief that they are suitable for human consumption when, as a matter of fact, they are not, and reap the benefits of the public confidence thus created, and then avoid liability for the injuries caused thereby merely because there was no privity of contract between him and the one whom he induced to consume the food. The mere fact that a manufacturer of other vendor may thus induce the public to consume unwholesome food evidences the soundness of the rule, which imposes a warranty, as a matter of public policy on the sale of food or other products intended for human consumption.

Or course, ordinarily, in the absence of a representation or contract to the contrary, a manufacturer or vendor should not be held liable for defects caused by contamination or deterioration which occur after the commodity has left his hands. In this case, however, the jury found that the food was contaminated at the time it was processed.

The policy of the law to protect the health and life of the public would only be half served if we were to make liability depend on the ordinary contractual warranty. Privity of contract and reliance on the skill and judgment of the manufacturer or other vendor would be necessary to a recovery in such a case. Under this rule, although a guest should go with the host and aid in selecting the food, the host alone could recover for the injuries caused by the eating thereof, because there would be no contractual relation between the guest and the manufacturer of other vendor. The same would be true with reference to the rule which requires proof of reliance on the skill and judgment of the manufacturer or vendor. Only those who could swear that they relied on the skill and judgment of the manufacturer as to the purity of the food before eating it could recover, when, as a matter of fact, the very eating of the food evidences a reliance on its appearance as being suitable for human consumption. If the main purpose of the rule is to protect the health and life of the public, there is no merit in denying relief to a consumer against the manufacturer on the ground of lack of direct contractual relation. If a man buys food and his whole family and guest eat it and all become ill, it would be arbitrary and unreasonable to say that only the man who bought the food would have a remedy for his sufferings. As said in *Keterer v. Armour & Co.*: "The remedies of injured consumers ought not to be made to depend upon the intricacies of the law of sales. The obligation of the manufacturer should not be based alone upon privity of contract. It should rest, as was once said, upon the demands of social justice."

It will also be noted that in many cases liability is placed on negligence in the processing of the food, and this has led some courts to conclude that proof of negligence was essential to a recovery. But it must be borne in mind that liability could be based on negligence, independent of the rule which imposes a warranty as a matter of public policy, and therefore those authorities which allow a recovery on proof of negligence are not authority for holding that a recovery cannot be had under the doctrine of a warranty imposed by an operation of law, even though there is no negligence. Since the warranty of suitableness is imposed by law as a matter of public policy, there is no need for proof of negligence. In the case of *Coca-Cola Bottling Works* v. *Simpson* it is said:

> Appellant introduced the witness Curtis for the purpose of proving that its machinery and methods, by means of which it bottled the Coca-Cola, were modern and of the best and not obsolete. On appellee's objection this evidence was excluded; and appellant argues that this action of the court was error. If error, it was without any harm whatever, because appellant, by its evidence, absolutely demonstrated that its machiney and methods rendered it all but impossible for any foreign substance to get into the bottles during the process of manufacture. But the evidence failed to show that it was impossible. Negligence is not the basis of this action. Appellant is liable to appellee if the foreign substances got into the bottle of Coca-Cola in question during the process of manufacture, regardless of the efficiency of appellant's machinery and methods used in its plant. As stated above in this opinion, the basis of this suit is breach of an implied warranty, and not negligence on the part of appellant.

In fact, a rule which would require proof of negligence as a basis of recovery would, in most instances, by reason of the difficulty of making such proof, be equivalent to a denial of recovery. It is well known that in many instances the product is processed in a distant state or in a foreign country many months prior to a discovery of the defect. It would be impracticable, if not impossible, for the consumer to prove the circumstances under which a particular can of beans or meat eaten by him had been processed. This can be very well illustrated by the facts involved in the case of *Burkhardt* v. *Armour & Co.* In that case a resident of Connecticut purchased a can of meat from a local merchant. The merchant had purchased it from Armour & Company, of Illinois, who in turn had purchased it from Frigorifico Armour de la Plata, of Argentina. The latter company had purchased it from a packer in Argentina. It would have been impracticable, if not impossible, for the consumer to have proved the conditions under which the food had been packed in Argentina many months prior to the date of the injury suffered by the consumer. All this furnished proof of the soundness of the rule herein quoted from *Van Bracklin* v. *Fonda*, wherein it was held that in the sale of food for human consumption "the vendor is bound to know that they are sound and wholesome, at his peril." Such a rule would seem to be more desirable because it permits the placing of the ultimate loss upon the manufacturer, who is in the best position to prevent the production and sale of unwholesome food. It stimulates and induces a greater degree of precaution for the protection of human health and life than does the rule of ordinary care.

There is no doubt about the public policy of this state with regard to the sale of impure foods. Article 706 of the Penal Code expressly provides that no person shall manufacture or offer for sale in this state any adulterated food. Article 707 of the Penal Code, Section (b)(5) and (6), defines adulterated food as any food containing any added poisonous or deleterious ingredients which may render such food injurious to health, or consists in whole or in part of a filthy, decomposed, or putrid animal or vegetable substance.

We hold that the defendant, as the manufacturer and vendor of the sausage in question, was liable to the plaintiffs, as the consumers thereof, for the injuries caused to them by the contaminated and poisonous substances in the sausage at the time the defendant manufactured and sold the same, even though the defendant was not negligent in the processing thereof.

The judgments of the Court of Civil Appeals and of the trial court in each of the three cases are affirmed.

Critz, Justice, concurring.

I agree to the judgment in this case. In doing so I agree to the holding expressed in the opinion of this Court that the manufacturer or processor of food intended for human consumption impliedly warrants that it is free from contamination and fit for human consumption. I think this rule is universal in its application, and applies even to food put up in sealed containers, with or without the name of the manufacturer or processor indicated thereon. I do not believe that the above rule applies to retailers of food put up in sealed containers, with the name of the manufacturer or processor indicated on such containers.

HENNINGSEN v. BLOOMFIELD MOTORS, INC.
32 N.J. 358, 161 A2d 69 (1960)

Plaintiff, Claus Henningsen purchased a new Plymouth automobile from Bloomfield Motors and gave it to his wife, the co-plaintiff, as a present. The automobile was manufactured by the defendant, Chrysler Corporation, and sold by it to the other defendant, Bloomfield Motors, a retail dealer. When he purchased the car, Henningsen signed a purchase order without reading two paragraphs in fine print on its front referring to the back of the purchase order which contained 8½ inches again of fine *print.** *The purchase order was a printed form of one page. Included here was a clause which provided for an explicit agreement stating that the manufacturer and the dealer would give no warranties, express or implied, "made by either the dealer or the manufacturer on the motor vehicle or chassis," except that they would make good at the factory any parts which became defective within ninety days of delivery of the car to the original purchaser, or before the car had been driven 4,000 miles, which ever event should occur first.*

This warranty was expressly in lieu of all other warranties expressed or implied, and all other obligations or liabilities on its part and it neither assumes nor authorizes any other person to assume for it any other liability in connection with the sale of its vehicles.

Mrs. Henningsen was injured seriously and the car demolished when she was driving the car ten days after it had been delivered. The steering mechanism failed and the car turned into a wall. It had no servicing and no mishaps before the event of May 19. The Henningsens sued Bloomfield Motors and Chrysler for negligence and for breach of an implied warranty of merchantability imposed by the Uniform Sales Act. The negligence count was dismissed by the trial court and the cause was submitted to the jury solely on the issues of implied warranty and merchantability, with results favorable to the plaintiffs against both defendants. The trial court felt that the proof was insufficient to make out a prima facie case as to the negligence of either the manufacturer or the dealer.

Francis, J.

I. The Claim of Implied Warranty Against the Manufacturer

In the ordinary case of sale of goods by description, an implied warranty of merchantability is an integral part of the transaction. If the buyer, expressly or by implication, makes known to the seller the particular purpose for which the article is required and it appears that he has relied on the seller's skill or judgment, an implied warranty arises of reasonable fitness for that purpose. The former type of warranty simply means that the thing sold is reasonably fit for the general purpose for which it is manufactured and sold. As Judge (later Justice) Cardozo remarked in *Ryan,* the distinction between a warranty of fitness for a particular purpose and of merchantability in many instances is practically meaningless. In that particular case, he was concerned with food for human consumption in a sealed container. Perhaps no more apt illustration of the notion can be thought of than the instance of the ordinary purchaser who informs the automobile dealer that he desires a car for the purpose of business and pleasure driving on the public highway.

In this connection, it is appropriate to note that sale of an article by a trade name does not negate the warranty of merchantability. An informative statement of the rule (said to be supported by overwhelming authority) was made by the Supreme Court of Pennsylvania:

> It is perfectly clear that even if the sale be under a trade name there is implied an obligation on the part of the seller that the article delivered will be of the same quality, material, workmanship, and availability for use as articles generally sold under such name. It would be wholly

---

*The two paragraphs read as follows:

"The front and back of this Order comprise the entire agreement effecting this purchase and no other agreement or understanding of any nature concerning same has been made or entered into, or will be recognized. I hereby certify that no credit has been extended to me for the purchase of this motor vehicle except as appears in writing on the face of this agreement.

"I have read the matter printed on the back hereof and agree to it as a part of this order the same as if it were printed above my signature. I certify that I am 21 years of age, or older, and hereby acknowledge receipt of a copy of this order."

unreasonable to hold that, if one were to purchase, for example, an automobile under the trade name of "Ford" or "Buick" or "Cadillac" or the like, no implied warranty of merchantable quality could be asserted by the purchaser even though the particular car delivered was in such bad condition, so gravely defective in materials and construction, that it could not be operated at all and was wholly useless for the ordinary purpose which an automobile is designed to serve.

Of course such sales, whether oral or written, may be accompanied by an express warranty. Under the broad terms of the Uniform Sale of Goods Law, any affirmation of fact relating to the goods is an express warranty if the natural tendency of the statement is to induce the buyer to make the purchase. And over the years since the almost universal adoption of the act, a growing awareness of the tremendous development of modern business methods has prompted the courts to administer that provision with a liberal hand. Solicitude toward the buyer plainly harmonizes with the intention of the Legislature. That fact is manifested further by the later section of the act which preserved and continues any permissible implied warranty, despite an express warranty, unless the two are inconsistent.

The uniform act codified, extended, and liberalized the common law of sales. The motivation in part was to ameliorate the harsh doctrine of caveat emptor, and in some measure to impose a reciprocal obligation on the seller to beware. The transcendent value of the legislation, particularly with respect to implied warranties, rests in the fact that obligations on the part of the seller were imposed by operation of law, and did not depend for their existence upon agreement of the parties. And of tremendous significance in a rapidly expanding commercial society was the recognition of the right to recover damages on account of personal injuries arising from a breach of warranty. The particular importance of this advance resides in the fact that under such circumstances strict liability is imposed upon the maker or seller of the product. Recovery of damages does not depend upon proof of negligence or knowledge of the defect.

As the Sales Act and its liberal interpretation by the courts threw this protective cloak about the buyer, the decisions in various jurisdictions revealed beyond doubt that many manufacturers took steps to avoid these ever increasing warranty obligations. Realizing that the act governed the relationship of buyer and seller, they undertook to withdraw from actual and direct contractual contact with the buyer. They ceased selling products to the consuming public through their own employees and making contracts of sale in their own names. Instead, a system of independent dealers was established; their products were to dealers who in turn dealt with the buying public, obstensibly solely in their own personal capacity as sellers. In the past, in many instances, manufacturers were able to transfer to the dealers burdens imposed by the act and thus achieved a large measure of immunity for themselves. But, as will be noted in more detail hereafter, such marketing practices, coupled with the advent of large scale advertising by manufacturers to promote the purchase of these goods from dealers by members of the public, provided a basis upon which the existence of express or implied warranties was predicated, even though the manufacturer was not a party to the contract of sale.

The general observations that have been made are important largely for purposes of perspective. They are helpful in achieving a point from which to evaluate the situation now presented for solution. Primarily, they reveal a trend and a design in legislative and judicial thinking toward providing protection for the buyer. It must be noted, however, that the sections of the Sales Act, to which reference has been made, do not impose warranties in terms of unalterable absolutes. R.S. 46:30–3 (Uniform Sales Act Section 71) provides in general terms that an applicable warranty may be negated or varied by express agreement. As to disclaimers or limitations of the obligations that normally attend a sale, it seems sufficient at this juncture to say they are not favored, and that they are strictly construed against the seller.

With these considerations in mind, we come to a study of the express warranty on the reverse side of the purchase order signed by Claus Henningsen. At the outset we take notice that it was made only by the manufacturer and that by its terms it runs directly to Claus Henningsen. On the facts detailed above, it was to be extended to him by the dealer as the agent of Chrysler Corporation. The consideration for this warranty is the purchase of the manufacturer's product from the dealer by the ultimate buyer.

Although the franchise agreement between the defendants recites that the relationship of principal and agent is not created, in particular transactions involving third persons, the law will look at their conduct and not to their intent or their words as between themselves but to their factual relation. The normal pattern that the manufacturer-dealer relationship follows relegates the position of the dealer to the status of a way station along the car's route from maker to consumer. This is indicated by the language of the warranty. Obviously the parties knew and so intended that the dealer would not use the automobile for 90 days or drive it 4,000 miles. And the words "original purchaser," taken in their context, signify the purchasing member of the public. Moreover, the language of this warranty is that of the uniform warranty of the Automobile Manufacturers Association, of which Chrysler is a member. And it is the form appearing in the Plymouth Owner Service Certificate mentioned in the serving instruction guide sent with the new car from the factory. The evidence is overwhelming that the dealer acted for Chrysler in including the warranty in the purchase contract.

The terms of the warranty are a sad commentary upon the automobile manufacturers' marketing practices. Warranties developed in the law in the interest of and to protect the ordinary consumer who cannot be expected to have the knowledge or capacity or even the opportunity to make adequate inspection of mechanical instrumentalities, like automobiles, and to decide for himself whether they are reasonably fit for the designed purpose. But the ingenuity of the Automobile Manufacturers Association, by means of its standardized form, has metamorphosed the warranty into a device to limit the maker's liability. To call it an "equivocal" agreement, as the Minnesota Supreme Court did, is the least that can be said in criticism of it.

The manufacturer agrees to replace defective parts for 90 days after the sale or until the car has been driven 4,000 miles, whichever is first to occur, *if the part is sent to the factory, transportation charges prepaid, and if examination discloses to its satisfaction that the part is defective*. It is difficult to imagine a greater burden on the consumer, or less satisfactory remedy. Aside from imposing on the buyer the trouble of removing and shipping the part, the maker has sought to retain the uncontrolled discretion to decide the issue of defectiveness. Some courts have removed much of the force of that reservation by declaring that the purchaser is not bound by the manufacturer's decision. In (one) case, the court said:

> It would nevertheless be repugnant to every conception of justice to hold that, if the parts thus returned for examination were, in point of fact, so defective as to constitute a breach of warranty, the appellee's right of action could be defeated by the appellant's arbitrary refusal to recognize that fact. Such an interpretation would substitute the appellant for the courts in passing upon the question of fact, and would be unreasonable.

Also, suppose, as in this case, a defective part or parts caused an accident and that the car was so damaged as to render it impossible to discover the precise part or parts responsible, although the circumstances clearly pointed to such fact as the cause of the mishap. Can it be said that the impossibility of performance deprived the buyer of the benefit of the warranty?

Moreover, the guaranty is against defective workmanship. That condition may arise from good parts improperly assembled. There being no defective parts to return to the maker, is all remedy to be denied? One court met that type of problem by holding that where the purchaser does not know the precise cause of inoperability, calling a car a "vibrator" would be sufficient to state a claim for relief. It said that such a car is not an uncommon one in the industry. The general cause of the vibration is not known. Some part or parts have been either defectively manufactured or improperly assembled in the construction and manufacture of the automobile. In the operation of the car, these parts give rise to vibrations. The difficulty lies in locating the precise spot and cause. But the warranty does not specify what the purchaser must do to obtain relief in such case, if a remedy is intended to be provided. Must the purchaser return the car, transportation charges prepaid, over a great distance to the factory? It may be said that in the usual case the dealer also gives the same warranty and that as a matter of expediency the purchaser should turn to him. But under the law, the buyer is entitled to proceed against the manufacturer. Further, dealers' franchises are precarious. For example, Bloomfield Motors' franchise may be cancelled by Chrysler on 90 days' notice. And obviously dealers' facilities and capacity, financial and otherwise, are not as sufficient as those of the primarily responsible manufacturer in his distant factory.

The matters referred to represent only a small part of the illusory character of the security presented by the warranty. Thus far the analysis has dealt only with the remedy provided in the case of a defective part. What relief is provided when the breach of the warranty results in personal injury to the buyer? (Injury to third persons using the car in the purchaser's right will be treated hereafter.) As we have said above, the law is clear that such damages are recoverable under an ordinary warranty. The right exists whether the warranty sued on is express or implied. And of course, it has long since been settled that where the buyer or a member of his family driving with his permission suffers injuries because of negligent manufacture or construction of the vehicle, the manufacturer's liability exists. But in this instance, after reciting that defective parts will be replaced at the factory, the alleged agreement relied upon by Chrysler provides that the manufacturer's "obligation under this warranty" is limited to that undertaking; further, that such remedy is "in lieu of all other warranties, express or implied, and all other obligations or liabilities on its part." The contention has been raised that such language bars any claim for personal injuries which may emanate from a breach of the warranty. Although not urged in this case, it has been successfully maintained that the exclusion "of all other obligations and liabilities on its part" precludes a cause of action for injuries based on negligence. Another Federal Circuit Court of Appeals holds to the contrary. There can be little doubt that justice is served only by the latter ruling.

Putting aside for the time being the problem of the efficacy of the disclaimer provisions contained in the express warranty, a question of first importance to be decided is whether an implied warranty of merchantability by Chrysler Corporation accompanied the sale of the automobile to Claus Henningsen.

Preliminarily, it may be said that the express warranty against defective parts and workmanship is not inconsistent with an implied warranty of merchantability. Such warranty cannot be excluded for that reason.

Chrysler points out that an implied warranty of merchantability is an incident of a contract of sale. It concedes, of course, the making of the original sale to Bloomfield Motors, Inc., but maintains that this transaction marked the terminal point of its contractual connection with the car. Then

Chrysler urges that since it was not a party to the sale by the dealer to Henningsen, there is no privity of contract between it and the plaintiffs, and the absence of this privity eliminates any such implied warranty.

There is no doubt that under early common law concepts on contractual liability only those persons who were parties to the bargain could sue for a breach of it. In more recent times a noticeable disposition has appeared in a number of jurisdictions to break through the narrow barrier of privity when dealing with sales of goods in order to give realistic recognition to a universally accepted fact. The fact is that the dealer and the ordinary buyer do not, and are not expected to buy goods, whether they be foodstuffs or automobiles, exclusively for their own consumption or use. Makers and manufacturers know this and advertise and market their products on that assumption; witness, the "family" car, the baby foods, etc. The limitations of privity in contracts for the sale of goods developed their place in the law when marketing conditions were simple, when maker and buyer frequently met face to face on an equal bargaining plane and when many of the products were relatively uncomplicated and conducive to inspection by a buyer competent to evaluate their quality. With the advent of mass marketing, the manufacturer became remote from the purchaser, sales were accomplished through intermediaries, and the demand for the product was created by advertising media. In such an economy it became obvious that the consumer was the person being cultivated. Manifestly, the connotation of "consumer" was broader than that of "buyer." He signified such a person who, in the reasonable contemplation of the parties to the sale, might be expected to use the product. Thus, where the commodities sold are such that if defectively manufactured they will be dangerous to life or limb, then society's interests can only be protected by eliminating the requirement of privity between the maker and his dealers and the reasonably expected ultimate consumer. In that way the burden of losses consequent upon use of defective articles is borne by those who are in a position to either control the danger or make an equitable distribution of the losses when they do occur. As Harper and James put it, "The interest in consumer protection calls for warranties by the maker that *do* run with the goods, to reach all who are likely to be hurt by the use of the unfit commodity for a purpose ordinarily to be expected." As far back as 1932, in the well known case of *Baxter v. Ford Motor Co.,* the Supreme Court of Washington gave recognition to the impact of then existing commercial practices on the strait jacket of privity, saying:

> It would be unjust to recognize a rule that would permit manufacturers of goods to create a demand for their products by representing that they possess qualities which they, in fact, do not possess, and then, because there is no privity of contract existing between the consumer and the manufacturer, deny the consumer the right to recover if damages result from the absence of those qualities, when such absence is not readily noticeable.

Although only a minority of jurisdictions have thus far departed from the requirement of privity, the movement in that direction is most certainly gathering momentum. Liability to the ultimate consumer in the absence of direct contractual connection has been predicated upon a variety of theories. Some courts hold that the warranty runs with the article like a covenant running with land; others recognize a third party beneficiary thesis; still others rest their decision on the ground that public policy requires recognition of a warranty made directly to the consumer.

Most of the cases where lack of privity has not been permitted to interfere with recovery have involved food and drugs. In fact, the rule as to such products has been characterized as an exception to the general doctrine. But more recently courts, sensing the inequity of such limitation, have moved into broader fields.

We see no rational doctrinal basis for differentiating between a fly in a bottle of beverage and a defective automobile. The unwholesome beverage may bring illness to one person, the defective car, with its great potentiality for harm to the driver, occupants, and others, demands even less adherence to the narrow barrier of privity.

Under modern conditions, the ordinary layman, on responding to the importuning of colorful advertising, has neither the opportunity nor the capacity to inspect or to determine the fitness of an automobile for use; he must rely on the manufacturer who has control of its construction, and to some degree on the dealer who, to the limited extent called for by the manufacturer's instructions, inspects and services it before delivery. In such a marketing milieu, his remedies and those of persons who properly claim through him should not depend "upon the intricacies of the law of sales. The obligation of the manufacturer should not be based alone on privity of contract. It should rest, as was once said, upon 'the demands of social justice.' " "If privity of contract is required," then, under the circumstances of modern merchandising, "privity of contract exists in the consciousness and understanding of all right-thinking persons."

Accordingly, we hold that under modern marketing conditions, when a manufacturer puts a new automobile in the stream of trade and promotes its purchase by the public, an implied warranty that it is reasonably suitable for use as such accompanies it into the hands of the ultimate purchaser. Absence of agency between the manufacturer and the dealer who makes the ultimate sale is immaterial.

II. The Effect of the Disclaimer and Limitation of Liability Clauses on the Implied Warranty of Merchantability

(This part of the opinion has been omitted.)

III. The Dealer's Implied Warranty

The principles that have been expounded as to the obligation of the manufacturer apply with equal force to the separate express warranty of the dealer. This is so, irrespective of the absence of the relationship of principal and agent between these defendants, because the manufacturer and the Association establish the warranty policy for the industry. The bargaining position of the dealer is inextricably bound by practice to that of the maker and the purchaser must take or leave the automobile, accompanied and encumbered as it is by the uniform warranty.

Moreover, it must be remembered that the actual contract was between Bloomfield Motors, Inc., and Claus Henningsen, and that the description of the car sold was included in the purchase order. Therefore, R.S. 46:30–31(2) (Uniform Sales Act, Section 15(2)) annexed an implied warranty of merchantability to the agreement. It remains operative unless the disclaimer and liability limitation clauses were competent to exclude it and the ordinary remedy for its breach. It has been said that this doctrine is harsh on retailers who generally have only a limited opportunity for inspection of the car. But, as Chief Judge Chardozo said in *Ryan*:

> The burden may be heavy. It is one of the hazards of the business.
> . . . In such circumstances, the law casts the burden on the seller, who may vouch in the manufacturer, if the latter was to blame. The loss in its final incidence will be borne where it is placed by the initial wrong.

For the reasons set forth in Part I hereof, we conclude that the disclaimer of an implied warranty of merchantability by the dealer, as well as the attempted elimination of all obligations other than replacement of defective parts, are violation of public policy and void.

V. The Defense of Lack of Privity Against Mr. Henningsen

Both defendants contend that since there was no privity of contract between them and Mrs. Henningsen, she cannot recover for breach of any warranty made by either of them. On the facts, as they were developed, we agree that she was not a party to the purchase agreement. Her right to maintain the action, therefore, depends upon whether she occupies such legal status thereunder as to permit her to take advantage of a breach of defendants' implied warranties.

For the most part the cases that have been considered dealt with the right of the buyer or consumer to maintain an action against the manufacturer where the contract of sale was with a dealer and the buyer had no contractual relationship with the manufacturer. In the present matter, the basic contractual relationship is between Claus Henningsen, and Bloomfield Motors, Inc. The precise issue presented is whether Mrs. Henningsen, who is not a party to their respective warranties, may claim under them. In our judgment, the principles of those cases and the supporting texts are just as proximately applicable to her situation. We are convinced that the cause of justice in this area of the law can be served only by recognizing that she is such a person who, in the reasonable contemplation of the parties to the warranty, might be expected to become a user of the automobile. Accordingly, her lack of privity does not stand in the way of prosecution of the injury suit against the defendant Chrysler.

The context in which the problem of privity with respect to the dealer must be considered, is much the same. Defendant Bloomfield Motors is chargeable with an implied warranty of merchantability to Claus Henningsen. There is no need to engage in separate or extended discussion of the question. The legal principles which control are the same in quality. The manufacturer establishes the network of trade and the dealer is a unit utilized in that network to accomplish sales. He is the beneficiary of the same express and implied warranties from the manufacturer as he extends to the buyer of the automobile. If he is sued alone, he may implead the manufacturer. His understanding of the expected use of the car by persons other than the buyer is the same as that of the manufacturer. And, so, his claim to the doctrine of privity should rise no higher than that of the manufacturer.

It is important to express the right of Mrs. Henningsen to maintain her action in terms of a general principle. To what extent may lack of privity be disregarded in suits on such warranties? In that regard, the *Faber* case points the way. By a parity of reasoning, it is our opinion that an implied warranty of merchantability chargeable to either an automobile manufacturer or dealer extends to the purchaser of the car, members of his family, and to other persons occupying or using it with his consent. It would be wholly opposed to reality to say that use by such persons is not within the anticipation of parties to such a warranty of reasonable suitability of an automobile for ordinary highway operation. Those persons must be considered within the distribution chain.

Harper and James suggest that this remedy ought to run to members of the public, bystanders, for example, who are in the path of harm from a defective automobile. Section 2–318 of the Uniform Commercial Code proposes that the warranty be extended to "any natural person who is in the family or household of his buyer or who is a guest in his home if it is reasonable to expect that such person may use, consume, or be affected by the goods and who is injured in person by breach of the warranty." And the section provides also that "A seller may not exclude or limit the operation" of the extension. A footnote thereto says that beyond this provision "the section is neutral and is not intended to enlarge or restrict the developing case law on whether the seller's warranties, given to his buyer, who resells, extend to other persons in the distributive chain." (Uniform Commercial Code.)

It is not necessary in this case to establish the outside limits of the warranty protection. For present purposes, with respect to automobiles, it suffices to promulgate the principle set forth above.

In his charge as to Mrs. Henningsen's right to recover on the implied warranty, the trial court referred to her husband's testimony that he was buying the car for her use, and then instructed the jury that on such facts the warranty extended to her. In view of our holding, obviously the protection of the warranty runs to her as an incident of the sale without regard to such testimony. Accordingly, the contention that the instruction was reversible error must be rejected.

The final argument on this point relates to the damage claim of Claus Henningsen. That claim has two aspects: one for property damage to the automobile and the other for medical and hospital expenses and loss of his wife's society and services. As to the first, he being an actual party to the contract of sale, and the owner of the automobile, clearly the property damage is recoverable. The second claim is a derivative one, stemming from his wife's right. But it is universally known that in family relations husbands and fathers are ordinarily responsible for such expenses of spouses and children. It would be illogical to accept the right of a wife to recover in contract for breach of warranty and to hold that the husband's derivative claim was not within the contemplation of the parties when the agreement of sale was made. For this reason it was proper to submit Henningsen's consequential losses to the jury as an element of damage.

VI.

Plaintiffs contend on cross-appeal that the negligence claim against the defendants should not have been dismissed. Their position is that on the facts developed, the issue should have been submitted to the jury for determination. The result we have reached on the other aspects of the case makes it unnecessary to consider the problem. For that reason we express no opinion thereon.

VII. Conclusion

Under all of the circumstances outlined above, the judgments in favor of the plaintiffs and against defendants are affirmed.

For affirmance—Chief Justice Weintraub, and Justices Burling, Jacobs, Francis, Proctor and Schettino—6.

For reversal—None.

LASKY v. ECONOMY GROCERY STORES
319 Mass. 224, 65 NE 2d 305 (1946)

Ronan, A. Justice.

This is an action of tort to recover damages for personal injuries sustained by Mary F. Lasky, hereinafter called the plaintiff, from the explosion of a bottle of carbonated beverage described as "tonic" that she had taken from one of several wooden cases which had been set up in the defendant's store for the purpose of sale to customers who were willing to serve themselves by selecting the bottles they wished to purchase and by paying for them as they left the store. The plaintiff had a verdict upon a count in the declaration alleging a breach of an implied warranty of fitness of a bottle of tonic supplied to her by the defendant under a contract of sale, and upon another count alleging a breach of an implied warranty of merchantability of a bottle of tonic furnished to her by the defendant in accordance with a contract of purchase and sale of the said bottle. The defendant excepted to the denial of its motion for a direct verdict on each count.

The jury could find the facts herein recited. A customer enters the defendants' store through a turnstile, where he obtains a carrier equipped with a basket in which he places the articles he selects as he pushes the carrier along by the counters. The goods are displayed with the prices on them. Signs are posted advising the customers to serve themselves. A customer, as he goes through the store, selects whatever articles he desires, and he is free to return any article he has selected to the place from which he took it. After he has finally selected the goods that he wishes to purchase, he pushes the carrier to the cashier's counter where the goods are taken out of the basket, inspected, checked, and put in bags. The total price is ascertained by the cashier, and is paid by the customer. The plaintiff was familiar with the method of purchasing goods at the defendant's store. She had never been told by a cashier that she could not have as many articles as she wanted, but "it had been her experience in going in these stores to have gone around and seen something she liked and put it in the carrier and then later to go back and put it on the shelves; " . . . until a customer got up to the cashier's cage, with the exception of the meat department, you were on your own so to speak." She knew that it was necessary to pay for the goods before she left the store, and she intended to pay when she arrived at the cashier's desk. The plaintiff desired to purchase six bottles of tonic, and after she had put some of the bottles in the basket, and while she was taking another bottle from the case but before she had an opportunity to place this bottle in the basket, it exploded, severely injuring her.

The plaintiff in order to recover must prove that at the time of the injury, she had entered into a contract with the defendant for the sale of tonic to her, and that under the contract to sell the defendant had assumed an obligation to see that the goods were reasonably fit for the use intended to be made of them by the plaintiff or had assumed an obligation to see that the goods were of merchantable quality for goods of that description. The question here is whether the evidence is sufficient to prove that either obligation had been undertaken by the defendant.

The defendant's method of doing business differs from that usually employed in retail stores, where a clerk furnishes the customer with the goods requested and the latter completes the transaction by paying the price. In these sales over the counter, the delivery of the goods, the passing of the title and the payment of the price all occur at substantially the same time. No executory contract is involved in the transaction. The defendant makes only cash sales, but all these sales must be made at the cashier's counter. The system in vogue at the defendant's store requires the customer to select and collect the goods he desires to purchase and to convey them to the only person who can sell them to him. This system, undoubtedly, requires the performance by the customer of certain acts before he can complete the purchase of the goods. It is urged by the plaintiff that the operation of the defendant's system of merchandising contemplates the making of an executory contract of sale, which arises as soon as the customer begins the performance of any of these preliminary acts and terminates upon the completion of the sale. She contends that such a contract came into existence as soon as she took possession of the bottle of tonic for the purpose of purchasing it; that the display of the tonic with the signs advising her to serve herself constituted an offer to sell, which she accepted by taking the bottle; and that the title to the bottle passed to her when she took it from the case. We assume in favor of the plaintiff that a warranty in a contract for the sale of a specific article survives the destruction of the article before the sale is completed. It is true that customers were invited to take possession of the goods that they intended to purchase and, if such possession may be considered the equivalent of a delivery of the bottle of tonic, such delivery was conditional and was made only for the purpose of permitting the customer to take it to the cashier. Possession alone was not in these circumstances sufficient to pass title to the bottle. Title did not pass until the delivery became absolute upon the payment of the price to the cashier. The defendant did not intend to part with the title until the price was paid, and the plaintiff knew that she was making a purchase for cash which she intended to pay to the cashier.

It is plain upon the plaintiff's own testimony that it was optional with her to return the article she had selected or to keep it and later become the purchaser, and there is nothing to show that the defendant could compel her to purchase the bottle as soon as she selected it, or could have prevented her from returning it to the case or that it became bound as soon as she selected it to sell it to her. The plaintiff has failed to show that, just before the time she was injured, she had become bound to purchase the bottle and that the defendant had become bound to sell it to her.

An examination of all the evidence would not warrant a finding that the defendant did anything more than to make an offer to the plaintiff to sell for cash, at the prices marked on the goods, such articles as the plaintiff might wish to purchase and might take to the cashier. Until there was an acceptance by her of this offer in accordance with its term, no contractual relation arose between the parties in reference to the sale of the tonic. The offer could not be considered as accepted before the goods reached the cashier, and the defendant before that time arrived had not assumed any contractual obligation with the plaintiff to sell the tonic.

The explosion of the bottle does not appear to have been due to any fault or negligence of the defendant, but we need not decide, if an executory contract of sale had been proved, whether the contract would have been avoided by the destruction of the bottle. The plaintiff has based her case entirely upon a breach of warranty, but there could be no warranty in the absence of a sale or a contract of sale.

Exceptions sustained.

Judgment for the defendant.

IMPERIAL ICE CO. v. *ROSSIER*
112 P.2d 631 (1941)

Traynor, Justice.

The California Consumers Company purchased from S.L. Coker an ice distributing business, inclusive of good will located in territory comprising the city of Santa Monica and the former city of Sawtelle. In the purchase agreement, Coker contracted as follows: "I do further agree in consideration of said purchase and in connection therewith, that I will not engage in the business of selling and or distributing ice, either directly or indirectly, in the above described territory so long as the purchasers, or anyone deriving title to the goodwill of said business from said purchasers, shall be engaged in a like business therein." Plaintiff, the Imperial Ice Company, acquired from the successor in interest of the California Consumers Company full title to this ice distributing business, including the right to enforce the covenant not to compete. Coker subsequently began selling, in the same territory in violation of the contract, ice supplied to him by a company owned by W. Rossier, J.A. Matheson, and Fred Matheson. Plaintiff thereupon brought this action in the superior court for an injunction to restrain Coker from violating the contract and to restrain Rossier and the Mathesons from inducing Coker to violate the contract. The complaint alleges that Rossier and the Mathesons induced Coker to violate this contract so that they might sell ice to him at a profit.

The question thus presented to this court is under what circumstances may an action be maintained against a defendant who has induced a third party to violate a contract with the plaintiff.

It is universally recognized that an action will lie for inducing breach of contract by a resort to means in themselves unlawful such as libel, slander, fraud, physical violence, or threats of such action. Most jurisdictions also hold that an action will lie for inducing a breach of contract by the use of moral, social, or economic pressures, in themselves lawful, unless there is sufficient justification for such inducement.

Such justification exists when a person induces a breach of contract to protect an interest which has greater social value than insuring the stability of the contract. Thus, a person is justified in inducing the breach of a contract the enforcement of which would be injurious to health, safety, or good morals. The interest of labor in improving working conditions is of sufficient social importance to justify peaceful labor tactics otherwise lawful, though they have the effect of inducing breaches of contracts between employer and employee or employer and customer. The presence or absence of ill-will, sometimes referred to as "malice," is immaterial, except as it indicates whether or not an interest is actually being protected.

It is well established, however, that a person is not justified in inducing a breach of contract simply because he is in competition with one of the parties to the contract and seeks to further his own economic advantage at the expense of the other. Whatever interest society has in encouraging free and open competition by means not in themselves unlawful, contractual stability is generally accepted as of greater importance than competitive freedom. Competitive freedom, however, is of sufficient importance to justify one competitor in inducing a third party to forsake another competitor if no contractual relationship exists between the latter two. A person is likewise free to carry on his business, including reduction of prices, advertising, and solicitation in the usual lawful manner although some third party may be induced thereby to breach his contract with a competitor in favor of dealing with the advertiser. Again, if two parties have separate contracts with a third, each may resort to any legitimate means at his disposal to secure performance of his contract even though the necessary result will be to cause a breach of the other contract. A party may not, however, under the guise of competition, actively and affirmatively induce the breach of a competitor's contract in order to secure an economic advantage over the competitor. The act of inducing the breach must be an intentional one. If the actor had no knowledge of the existence of the contract or his actions were not intended to induce a breach he cannot be held liable though an actual breach results from his lawful and proper acts.

In California (a) case (is of sufficient consequence that it) has been considered by many as establishing the proposition that no action will lie for inducing breach of contract by means which are not otherwise unlawful.

The complaint in the present case alleges that defendants actively induced Coker to violate his contract with plaintiffs so that they might sell ice to him.

The contract gave to plaintiff the right to sell ice in the stated territory free from the competition of Coker. The defendants, by virtue of their interest in the sale of ice in that territory, were in effect competing with plaintiff. By inducing Coker to violate his contract, as alleged in complaint, they sought to further their own economic advantage at plaintiff's expense. Such conduct is not justified. Had defendants merely sold ice to Coker without actively inducing him to violate his contract, his distribution of the ice in the forbidden territory in violation of his contract would not then have rendered defendants liable. They may carry on their business of selling ice as usual without incurring liability for breaches of contract by their customers. It is necessary to prove that they intentionally and actively induced the breach. Since the complaint alleges that they did so and asks for an injunction on the grounds that damages would be inadequate, it states a cause of action, and the demurrer should therefore have been overruled.

The judgment is reversed.

Part E: Warranties and the Pre-Existing Duty Rule

WOOD v. LUCY, LADY DUFF-GORDON
222 NY 88, 118 NE 214 (1917)

Warranties limit rather than expand contractural obligations. They are an advertising gimmick, and a limitation of liability on the manufacturer. Common law warranties might give consumers greater protection if manufacturer's warranties did not exist.

This case involves an action by Otis F. Wood against Lucy, Lady Duff-Gordon, from a judgment of the Appellate Division, which reversed an order denying the defendant's motion for judgment on the pleading, and which dismissed the complaint. Here the plaintiff appeals, and succeeds in obtaining a reversal.

The court decided that where the plaintiff, who possessed a business organization adapted to the placing of such designs and indorsements as the plaintiff might make or approve, entered into an agreement for the exclusive right to handle and sell all such or license others to market them, and take out copyrights to protect them, and where in return the defendant was to have one-half of "all profits and revenues" to be accounted for monthly, the assumption of the exclusive agency was an assumption of its duties.

Although not stated in the contract, it is furthermore implied that the plaintiff must use all reasonable efforts to market such indorsements and designs. Hence the contract is not void for lack of mutuality and consideration.

Cardozo, J.

The defendant styles herself "a creator of fashions." Her favor helps a sale. Manufacturers of dresses, millinery, and like articles are glad to pay for a certificate of her approval. The things which she designs, fabrics, parasols, and what not, have a new value in the public mind when issued in her name. She employed the plaintiff to help her to turn this vogue into money. He was to have the exclusive right, subject always to her approval, to place her indorsement on the designs of others. He was also to have the exclusive right, to place her own designs on sale, or to license others to market them. In return she was to have one-half of "all profits and revenues" derived from any contracts he might make. The exclusive right was to last at least one year from April 1, 1915, and thereafter from year to year, unless terminated by notice of 90 days. The plaintiff says that he kept the contract on his part, and that the defendant broke it. She placed her indorsement on fabrics, dresses, and millinery without his knowledge, and withheld the profits. He sues her for the damages, and the case comes here on demurrer.

The agreement of employment is signed by both parties. It has a wealth of recitals. The defendant insists, however, that it lacks the elements of a contract. She says that the plaintiff does not bind himself to anything. It is true that he does not promise in so many words that he will use reasonable efforts to place the defendant's indorsements and market her designs. We think, however, that such a promise is fairly to be implied. The law has outgrown its primitive stage of formalism when the precise word was the sovereign talisman, and every slip was fatal. It takes a broader view today. A promise may be lacking, and yet the whole writing may be "instinct with an obligation," imperfectly expressed. If that is so, there is a contract.

The implication of a promise here finds support in many circumstances. The defendant gave an exclusive privilege. She was to have no right for at least a year to place her own indorsement or market her own designs except through the agency of the plaintiff. The acceptance of the exclusive agency was an assumption of its duties. We are not to suppose that one party was to be placed at the mercy of the other. Many other terms of the agreement point the same way. We are told at the outset by way of recital that:

"The said Otis F. Wood possesses a business organization adapted to the placing of such indorsements as the said Lucy, Lady Duff-Gordon, has approved."

The implication is that the plaintiff's business organization will be used for the purpose for which it is adapted. But the terms of the defendant's compensation are even more significant. Her sole compensation for the grant of an exclusive agency is to be one-half of all the profits resulting from the plaintiff's efforts. Unless he gave his efforts, she could never get anything. Without an implied promise, the transaction cannot have such business "efficacy, as both parties must have intended that at all events it should have." But the contract does not stop there. The plaintiff goes on to promise that he will account monthly for all moneys received by him, and that he will take out all such patents and copyrights and trademarks as may in his judgment be necessary to protect the rights and articles affected by the agreement. It is true, of course, as the Appellate Division has said, that if he was under no duty to try to market designs or to place certificates of indorsement, his promise to account for profits or take out copyrights would be valueless. But in determining the intention of the parties the promise has a value. It helps to enforce the conclusion that the plaintiff had some duties. His promise to pay the defendant one-half of the profits and revenues resulting from the exclusive agency and to render accounts monthly was a promise to use reasonable efforts to bring profits and revenues into existence. For this conclusion the authorities are ample.

The judgment of the Appellate Division should be reversed, and the order of the Special Term affirmed, with costs in the Appellate Division and in this court.

Part F: Warranties and Deceptive Advertising

AUTO-TERIA, INC. v. *AHERN*
352 NE2d 774 (1976)

Lowdermilk, Judge.

CASE SUMMARY

The instant case was transferred from the Second District to this office on July 1, 1976, in order to lessen the disparity in caseloads between the Districts.

Plaintiff-appellant Auto-Teria, Inc., appeals from a judgment of $10,220.27 on the counterclaim of defendants-appellees Jack E. Ahern and Stephen M. Suhre (buyers) and $2,000 on the counterclaim of Suhre individually.

We affirm.

FACTS

The facts most favorable to the appellees reveal that in 1969 buyers, certified public accountants, were interested in a self-service car wash business. They contacted Del. O. Amy, President of Auto-Teria, an Indianapolis manufacturer of automatic carwash equipment, because they felt buying locally would facilitate repair and the acquisition of spare parts, and because Auto-Teria sold one of the few coin-operated systems on the market.

They communicated to Amy their desire to invest in a business that would require little of their time; they specifically wanted a unit which would not require the presence of an operator-repairman.

During the course of negotiations Amy gave them Auto-Teria's newsletter and an advertising brochure and sent them a letter—all describing Auto-Teria's brush-type coin-operated carwash.

The "President's Report" in the newsletter concluded:

> The coin car wash industry has graduated to a new level with many installations totaling $150,000 or more. With the perpetual ideas and equipment improvements, I foresee a market for the investor that will be unsurpassed in: 1. LABOR PROBLEMS; 2. OWNER TIE-DOWN REQUIREMENTS; 3. RETURN OF THE INVESTED DOLLAR. (Original emphasis.)

The front page of the three-color illustrated brochure depicted a "talking coin-meter" and emphasized: "Automatic-Coin-Operated-No Hand-Wash Labor." At the bottom of the back page—in the smallest type used on that page—appeared the statement:

> Inasmuch as the quality of car wash is contingent upon so many factors beyond the control of Auto-Teria, Auto-Teria cannot guarantee such or rectify damage to car, such being the responsibility of attendant.
>
> Manufacturer reserves right to substitute equal or superior components for equipment mentioned.
>
> Quality and quantity of equipment vary according to model ordered. (Original emphasis.)

The letter from Amy stated, omitting pleasantries:

> I believe you will agree that the coin-operated carwash business is one of the most profitable investments on the market today, with the least amount of hired help requirements.
>
> I have experienced the sale of many types of equipment all over the world and for this reason feel you should compare equipment very closely because maintenance can become a major problem with piston pumps and poor design. Purchasing the right car washing facility is merely COMMON SENSE, like so many other facets of life.
>
> THERE IS NO MAGIC implied by AUTO-TERIA except that we usually offer more capacity in the component parts than any other equipment on the market today. If you will compare AUTO-TERIA's gear capacity, electric motor horse power ratings, and brush sizes, you will quickly see that the reason Auto-Teria facilities give you a greater return on your investment is a better wash and a more satisfied customer.
>
> REMEMBER, the customer only sees the end results . . . .
>
> AUTO-TERIA'S QUALITY DOES PAY . . . (Original emphasis.)

Amy took the buyers to the factory where the brush units were being assembled and showed them a model unit. He then took them to a four-day installation in Nobelville where, he said, the operator had generated business of $700 to $800 a month with only self-service equipment which customers must hold to operate.

Buyers and Auto-Teria executed an "Order Form and Sales Agreement" for an automatic brush unit installed in one of the bays of the Noblesville facility plus the used self-service equipment which was to be "completely checked out and put in working order."

Buyers received a photocopy of the form—but no written warranty until later. The buyers drew two notes payable to Auto-Teria, the face amount of one being $64,789.20 and the other $2,527.20.

After the brush unit was installed, buyers could not get the coin meter to work properly and therefore disconnected it—so that an attendant had to be present to operate the unit.

Buyers then discovered that the brushes were working too fast and were ripping mirrors and antennaes off customers' cars, and that the various phases of the wash cycle were out of time.

Inasmuch as repeated calls to Amy failed to produce any repair response, buyers turned to Byford Thompson, who owned and operated an Auto-Teria installation in Anderson and who had worked for the manufacturer in the assembly and installation of buyers' unit. Thompson added mechanisms to slow the brushes, got the system back "in cycle," and alleviated the breakage problem by moving the brushes out—in which position they did not effectively wash autos.

Thompson had to repair the automatic unit two to five times per month inasmuch as it would not perform for any extended period of time.

Buyers moved the brush unit to a Nora gas station, where they hoped, the station personnel could operate it and repair it. However, it worked no better.

While Suhre was operating the unit at the Nora station, the top brush unaccountably began falling toward an auto being washed. To prevent the brush from damaging the car, Suhre reached up to push a button which stopped the brush. As he did so a finger on his left hand was broken in three places when it was caught between the unit and the doorway through which it was passing.

As a result of this "painful" injury the left-handed accountant was treated at a hospital and was unable to work for a period of time.

When winter struck, buyers learned that the system to keep water flowing through the self-service units at Noblesville had not been put in working order by Auto-Teria. As a result, the water froze in the pipes and hoses—bursting them.

Only in two months did the carwash produce the business reported by Amy.

In the summer of 1970 buyers returned the brush unit to Noblesville, from where Auto-Teria took possession of it.

Of all the equipment purchased by buyers, Auto-Teria was able to resell only the brush unit. It was sold for $5,500 or $5,600—after Auto-Teria spent $2,599 to $3,500 to put it into saleable condition.

Buyers paid only $9,720.27 on the notes, upon which Auto-Teria sued. Buyers jointly counterclaimed for damages as a result of the transaction; Suhre also counterclaimed for damages for his personal injury.

Following the post-trial entry of judgment for buyers on their counterclaims, present counsel for Auto-Teria entered his appearance between 3:30 and 4:00 P.M., June 4, 1973, and filed a "Motion to Correct Errors." He personally applied to the pleadings the file stamp located in the trial court's office. Later he learned that the stamp read: "FILED June 5, 1973."

On June 4, 1973, it was the everyday practice of the room clerk assigned to the trial court to leave at 3:30 P.M., which was before the trial court closed. It was also her practice to move the file stamp ahead to the next business day before leaving.

ISSUES

1. Whether the trial court erred in not changing its records to show a filing date of June 4, 1973, for Auto-Teria's "Motion to Correct Errors."
2. Whether the trial court erred in its handling of Auto-Teria's Exhibits D and E.
3. Whether the trial court erred in rendering judgment for buyers, jointly.
4. Whether the trial court erred in rendering judgment for Suhre individually.
5. Whether the trial court denied Auto-Teria a fair trial by conducting a portion of the proceedings outside the regular courtroom.

DECISION

Issue One

Before discussing the merits of Auto-Teria's appeal, we must resolve whether the trial court erred in denying Auto-Teria's "Petition for Correction of Error," which sought to have the record altered to show that Auto-Teria's "Motion to Correct Errors" was filed on June 4, 1973, rather than on June 5, 1973.

The trial court entered its judgment in favor of buyers on April 4, 1973. The sixtieth day following that entry was Sunday, June 3, 1973.

Therefore, the latest date on which Auto-Teria could file a timely motion to correct errors—and thereby preserve its right to appeal—was June 4, 1973. (Ind. Rules of Procedure, Trial Rule 6(A), Trial Rule 59(C), and Trial Rule 59(G).)

"Clerical mistakes" in all parts of the record may be corrected at any time by the trial court—sua sponte or upon the motion of any party. (Ind. Rules of Procedure, Trial Rule 60(A).)

This provision is analyzed at 4 Harvey and Townsend, Indiana Practice 205–206 (1969):

> The types of 'clerical mistakes' . . . which may be corrected under Rule 60(A) will be controlled in a large measure by prior Indiana case law—law which is no haven for the lawyer seeking precise rules and answers. Prior case law distinguished between a motion to correct clerical errors and the procedure for correcting inconsistencies between the verdict or finding and the judgment, and between the evidence and the verdict, findings or judgment . . . .
>
> . . . (C)lerical errors or mechanical mistakes involved in the process of making computations, spelling, transcribing, or making entries into the records of the court by the judge or other court officer could be corrected at any time. It is this type of error or mistake within the ambit of Rule 60(A). Prior Indiana case law allowing the correction at any time of mistakes in the mathematical calculation of damages, in spelling, or omission of names, misdescriptions of real estate and the like appearing in the judgment or other records of the court will remain important under Rule 60(A) . . . "(Citations omitted.)

Our Supreme Court in *Jenkins v. Long* (1864) (23 Ind. 460, 461–462) dealt with a clerk's computation error which was entered in the record at 23 Ind. 461–462:

> Two questions only are presented for our consideration by the argument of the appellant: 1) Could the correction be made after the expiration of one year from the rendition of the judgment? 2) Was the extrinsic evidence admissible? . . .
>
> 1) The statute relied on by the appellants we suppose to be Section 99 of the code, which authorizes the court, within a year, to relieve a party from a judgment taken against him, . . . and supply an omission in any proceedings. But we do not think this statute at all applicable to the question. It was not sought to supply any 'omission' in the proceedings, for on their face they were regular and complete, but simply to correct a clerical error of commission. The inherent power of the court was invoked—a power much older than the code—to make its record speak the truth as to what it had done, upon the suggestion that its ministerial officer, by mistake, had not correctly recorded its judgment actually rendered . . .
>
> 2) Was any evidence admissible, upon the hearing of the motion, outside of the judgment sought to be amended? This question can receive only an affirmative answer. It would be in vain to seek relief against a clerical error, unless such error may be shown to exist; and the instances would be rare indeed in which the error would be apparent upon the fact of the record itself . . . .

It is clear that the error in the case at bar was "clerical" although counsel for Auto-Teria was involved in making it.

Buyers, of course, seek to short circuit Auto-Teria's appeal by asserting the propriety of the trial court's refusal to grant relief under TR. 60(A). They argue that changing the date of filing of Auto-Teria's "Motion to Correct Errors" would have been an improper *nunc pro tunc* entry by the trial court.

The purpose of a *nunc pro tunc* entry is to insert into the record some court action which was mistakenly omitted from the record. There generally must be some writing upon which to base the amendment, so that "entries may not be entered *nunc pro tunc* from thin air." Our Supreme Court held that where the written memorial relied upon does not on its face disclose an error in the record, the court cannot consider extrinsic evidence in making a *nunc pro tunc* entry. (*Cook v. State* (1911).)

In the case at bar, the record contains a written entry that could have been corrected. It is uncontroverted that on June 4, 1973, Auto-Teria's "Motion to Correct Errors" did exist and had been filed with the trial court.

Therefore the trial court, by granting the relief requested under TR. 60(A), would not have entered in its record a fact that did not exist at the time specified in the entry. *Jenkins v. Long* establishes that the rule in *Cook v. State* does not apply where there is a clerical error of commission rather than an omission.

Although relief under TR. 60(A) is clearly within the discretion of the trial court, we conclude that the trial court should have corrected its record to make it speak the truth where the only evidence before it indicated that a clerical error had been committed and where a refusal of relief deprived Auto-Teria of its right to appeal.

Issues Two, Three, and Four

We shall deal with several of appellant's assertions of error in one discussion, pursuant to Ind. Rules of Procedure, Appellate Rule 8.3(A)(7). Inasmuch as the transaction between the parties came within the scope of the Uniform Commercial Code, we shall refer to that statute as the UCC and cite it by UCC section number for the sake of brevity.

Auto-Teria contends that buyers' actions with respect to the goods in question constituted an acceptance rather than an effective rejection—so that buyers became obligated to pay the agreed price.

Assuming without deciding that Auto-Teria's argument is correct, buyers' remedy for breach of warranty by Auto-Teria remained viable.

A prerequisite to this post-acceptance remedy is notice of breach to the seller within a reasonable time after the buyer discovers or should have discovered said breach. Inasmuch as buyers complained to Auto-Teria about the brush unit immediately after its installation and about the self-service equipment after it burst, the trial court could have concluded that the notice requirement was satisfied.

By making any promise or affirmation of fact relating to the goods, or by giving any description of the goods, or by showing any sample or model, a seller creates an express warranty that the goods shall conform to the promise, affirmation, description, sample, or model—so long as these acts go to "the basis of the bargain" with the buyer. No specific intent or formal words are necessary for a seller to create an express warranty.

By model, by description in the advertising brochure, and by affirmation of fact in Amy's letter, spoken words, and printed words in the newsletter, the trial court could have found that Auto-Teria created an express warranty that its brush unit could be automatically operated by a customer's deposit of coins in the meter, rather than by an attendant. Inasmuch as buyers entered the transaction with just such a system in mind, the trial court could have found that Auto-Teria's acts went to the basis of the parties' bargain.

Auto-Teria's promise to put the used self-service equipment into working order so as to prevent freezing and bursting could have been found to create another express warranty going to the basis of the bargain, inasmuch as the parties added the promise to the written document of sale.

We turn now to the UCC implied warranties which this court discussed in *Woodruff* v. *Clark County Farm Bureau Cooperative Assoc., Inc.* (1972).

> These implied warranties of merchantability and fitness for a particular purpose do not arise out of an agreement between the parties; they may even exist when no specific promise has been made by the seller to the buyer . . . . Thus, they are imposed by operation of law for the protection of the buyer, and they must be liberally construed in favor of the buyer . . . ." (Original emphasis; citations omitted.)

A merchant-seller impliedly warrants that his goods are, inter alia, "fit for the ordinary purposes for which such goods are used"—unless he takes action to modify or exclude the warranty.

Therefore the trial court could have held Auto-Teria to an implied warranty of merchantability that the brush unit would effectively wash automobiles without knocking off their exterior accessories.

Section 2–315 provides:

> Implied warranty—Fitness for particular purpose—Where the seller at the time of contracting has reason to know any particular purpose for which the goods are required and that the buyer is relying on the seller's skill or judgment to select or furnish suitable goods, there is unless excluded or modified . . . an implied warranty that the goods shall be fit for such purpose.

Where a buyer communicated to a seller the particular purpose for which the sellers' goods were to be used, this court found an implied warranty of fitness for that particular purpose.

An Indiana user of goods benefited from an implied warranty of fitness for a particular purpose where the goods had been advertised expressly for the use to which they were put.

Therefore the court could have found—based either on the discussions between the parties or on the advertising brochure—an implied warranty that the brush unit would be fit for automatic coin operation by customers.

This warranty could have been cumulative with the first express warranty.

For the disclaimer in fine print at the bottom of the back page of the advertising brochure to exclude or modify the implied warranties, it must be conspicuous, e.g., in larger type, or contrasting in type or color. Therefore the court could have found that this statement did not affect Auto-Teria's implied warranties.

Although the declaration in Amy's letter—that Auto-Teria implied no "magic"—could have been held to be conspicuous, it does not mute or destroy the implied warranties. It must mention merchantability to affect the implied warranty of merchantability. To exclude the warranty of fitness for a particular purpose it must state, "for example, that 'There are no warranties which extend beyond the description on the face hereof.'" Nor is there any "as is" or "with all faults" language which would exclude either implied warranty. This court will not favor disclaimers of implied warranties, but will construe them against a seller for reasons of public policy.

Neither statement affects Auto-Teria's express warranties, for "if it is unreasonable or impossible to construe the language of the express . . . warranty and the language of the disclaimers as consistent, the disclaimer becomes inoperative."

The trial court could have held Auto-Teria's written warranty (Exhibit E, infra) to be outside the contract between the parties inasmuch as it was not given to buyers until after the purchase was completed.

Inasmuch as the brush unit could not be automatically operated by a customer's deposit of coins and would not effectively wash cars without damaging them, the trial court could have found a breach of Auto-Teria's express and implied warranties. And the trial court could have held Auto-Teria in breach of its other express warranty inasmuch as the self-service equipment froze and burst as a result of Auto-Teria's failure to put it into proper working condition.

Auto-Teria argues that it cannot be held accountable for Suhre's injury in that Suhre produced no evidence showing that Auto-Teria sold the brush unit in a defective condition—as required by Section 402A, Restatement, 2d of Torts, which is the Indiana standard for strict products liability, adopted by our Supreme Court in *Ayr-Way Stores, Inc.* v. *Chitwood* (1973).

Auto-Teria overlooks the extension of the UCC breach of warranty remedy to personal injury of a buyer.

Auto-Teria attacks the judgment of $10,220.27 for the buyers jointly and $2,000 for Suhre on the ground that neither amount appears in the record. This court will not require breach of warranty damages to be proved by mathematical precision; any reasonable manner of proof is permitted. And where doubt exists as to the exact proof of damages, we will resolve the uncertainty against the wrongdoer.

The UCC provides the traditional measure of damages for breach of warranty: the value of the goods as warranted less the value as accepted.

The price paid for the goods is competent evidence of their value as warranted.

The consideration given by buyers totaled $67,716.40; Auto-Teria's evidence showed that the workable goods were resold for approximately $5,500—after another $2,500 to $3,500 was expended to make them saleable. Thus the amount of judgment in favor of the buyers jointly fits comfortably within the boundaries of the evidence. In addition, the UCC allows for the recovery of incidental and foreseeable consequential damages for breach of warranty. Buyers have therefore recovered for lost profits, repairs, and costs of pacifying dissatisfied patrons.

Suhre testified as to the pain and lost working time attributable to his injury.

Therefore we conclude that the trial court determined the damages in this case in a reasonable manner.

We turn now to Auto-Teria's assignment of error relating to the trial court's handling of Auto-Teria's Exhibits D and E.

Exhibit D consisted of two documents. The first was a completion certificate—signed by buyers—which states that the goods were furnished in accordance with the sales agreement and that the goods properly functioned. It was conditional upon the second document, an attached letter setting forth various items which had not been performed.

Exhibit E was Auto-Teria's written warranty.

Trial counsel for Auto-Teria offered the writings during his case in chief. The trial court "withheld ruling" on them when offered, but sustained buyers' objection to them when trial counsel for Auto-Teria requested a ruling at the end of his case in chief.

Trial counsel for Auto-Teria renewed his offer of the completion certificate after eliciting admissions of its contents and execution from Ahern on cross-examination. The trial court again refused to rule.

When Suhre was cross-examined, the trial court noted that both exhibits were "still under advisement." No one mentioned the exhibits thereafter.

The tenor of the record leads us to conclude that the trial court provisionally excluded the exhibits. This was far from the best course to follow upon the offer of evidence of debatable admissibility in a trial to the court.

Inasmuch as trial counsel for Auto-Teria re-offered the exhibits and resumed a line of questioning directed toward getting them admitted into evidence, this issue was preserved for our review.

This court will reverse a trial court for excluding evidence only where there was an erroneous exclusion of evidence vital to an appellant's case; any valid theory of exclusion will suffice to sustain the trial court's ruling.

The trial court's exclusion of the completion certificate was within its discretion inasmuch as the contents of the exhibit were put into evidence through the testimony of Ahern. (*Killion v. Updike* (1974), Ind. App., 316 N.E. 2d 837.) The admissions by Ahern were primary evidence of the contents of the certificate.

Inasmuch as Auto-Teria's warranty was not part of the parties' contract (*Zoss v. Royal Chevrolet, Inc.*), the exhibit tended to prove only nonmaterial facts. Therefore, the trial court committed no error in excluding the warranty, for "only evidence which is pertinent to the issues presented by the case is admissible."

We conclude that Auto-Teria has shown no error in the trial court's handling of its Exhibits D and E.

Issue Five

Auto-Teria finally claims that it was denied a fair trial in that the trial court commenced the trial in a room other than the regular courtroom where the court reporter was unable to understand and record several questions of counsel and responses from the stand.

The record reveals that this problem was corrected before the first witness' testimony was concluded. The record also discloses no objection was made by Auto-Teria's trial counsel to the bad accoustics which are now claimed to be responsible for the "inaudibles."

Therefore, Auto-Teria will not be heard to complain about the conduct of the trial upon appeal.

This cause is remanded with the instruction to the trial court to make its records reflect the filing of Auto-Teria's "Motion to Correct Errors" on June 4, 1973; and after the record is corrected the trial court's judgment is in all matters affirmed.

Robertson, C.J. and Lybrook, J., concur.

LANTNER v. CARSON
373 N.E.2d 973 (1978)

Hennessey, C.J.

In March, 1977, the plaintiffs commenced an action under G.L. c. 93A, inserted by St. 1967, c. 813, Section One, commonly known as the Consumer Protection Act, against the defendants who as private individuals sold them their home. The complaint sought treble damages, attorneys' fees, and other relief in connection with the repair of several defects discovered by the plaintiffs after they took occupancy.

The defendants filed a motion to dismiss the complaint under Mass. R. Civ. P. 12(b)(6), which motion was allowed. Judgment was entered accordingly, and the case was dismissed. Thereafter, the plaintiffs appealed asserting that the remedial provisions of G.L. c. 93A apply, even where the consumer transaction at issue is the isolated sale of a private home. We granted direct appellate review.

It is well established that in proscribing "unfair or deceptive acts or practices in the conduct of any trade or commerce" the consumer protection statute reaches "(a) wide range of activities," including the "sale . . . of any . . . property, . . . real, personal, or mixed." We conclude, however, that as broadly and expansively as the statute applies to the regulation of business practices, G.L. c. 93A is not available where the transaction is strictly private in nature, and is in no way undertaken in the ordinary course of a trade or business. Accordingly, we affirm the dismissal of the plaintiffs' complaint.

For the purposes of our ruling on the motion to dismiss, we accept as true the factual allegations in the complaint. They are as follows. Under an agreement dated April 12, 1976, the plaintiffs agreed to buy and the defendants agreed to sell the premises at 48 Georgetown Road, Boxford, which property was the private residence of the defendants. The purchase and sale agreement, drawn by Wini McDuff as the broker, provided in part that: "This agreement is made . . . subject to the following: Water turned on, well functional, and water quality tests acceptable." Prior to this written agreement, the defendants had made other representations, namely that 1) the evident damage to second floor ceilings was a result of a defective roof which had since been repaired; and that 2) the second floor fireplace was stuffed with paper to avoid drafts, but was otherwise in complete working order.

The sale was consummated on or about May 19, 1976. The plaintiffs took occupancy on June 8, 1976. Almost immediately thereafter, difficulties developed.

First, on June 10, 1976, the water pump failed. Inspection and repair work revealed that the plaintiffs had been informed incorrectly as to the type of well on the property, and that its pump apparatus was inadequate and defective.

Second, in August, 1976, the well almost ran dry. During that time, the plaintiffs experienced several problems, including lack of water. As a result the pipes sucked in sand. A professional investigation disclosed that the functioning of the well was "marginal."

Third, in December, 1976, the plaintiffs replastered the damaged second floor ceilings. After several snowfalls it became apparent that, contrary to the defendants' representations, the roofing leaks which caused the original damage had not been repaired. As a result, water penetrated both the second and first floors.

Finally, after contracting for the cleaning of the second floor fireplace, the plaintiffs discovered that the fireplace was not merely "stuffed with paper to avoid drafts," but in fact was partially reconstructed from newspaper "bricks." The newspaper had been covered with a one-eighth inch coat of plaster and painted black.

The plaintiffs repaired these defects. On January 17, and February 10, 1977, the plaintiffs sent to the defendants a written demand for relief. Having received no tender of settlement from the defendants within thirty days of the demand, the plaintiffs commenced the instant action.

1. For the purpose of our subsequent analysis, it is useful at this time to review briefly the applicable sections of G.L. c. 93A. Through Section 9(1), as amended through St. 1971, c. 241, G.L. c. 93A provides a private right of action to "(a)ny person who purchases . . . property . . . primarily for personal, family, or household purposes and thereby suffers any loss of money or property . . . as a result of the use . . . by another person of an unfair or deceptive act or practice declared unlawful by Section 2." Section 2 proscribes "unfair or deceptive acts or practices in the conduct or any trade or commerce," and Section One states that "trade" and "commerce" shall include "the advertising, the offering for sale, . . . (or) sale . . . of any . . . property . . . real, personal, or mixed."

The plaintiffs argue that the terms of Sections 1 and 2 are broad enough to reach *any* type of commercial exchange, regardless of the nature of the transaction or the character of the parties involved. According to the plaintiffs, the Legislature made no distinction in the statute between the professional salesperson or business person, and the amateur, the individual who may sell a consumer item only on an isolated basis. Therefore, they argue, the remedial provisions of Section 9 should be available to the consumer who purchases from an individual homeowner, regardless of the fact the transaction is not in pursuit of the seller's ordinary course of business. We do not agree with this expansive reading.

First, the statute does not specifically define the phrase "in the conduct of any trade or commerce." Nevertheless, we may infer its meaning from reading the statute as a whole. In so doing, we observe that, contrary to the plaintiffs' assertion, G.L. c. 93A creates a sharp distinction between a business person and an individual who participates in commercial transactions on a private, nonprofessional basis.

For example, where Section 9 affords a private remedy to the individual consumer who suffers a loss as a result of the use of an unfair or deceptive act or practice, an entirely different section, Section 11, extends the same remedy to "(a)ny person who engages in the conduct of any trade or commerce." In *Slaney* v. *Westwood Auto, Inc.,* we concluded that by these terms, Section 11 extends the consumer protection remedies of G.L. c. 93A to the "businessman." Indeed, this construction is a necessary one. Were we to interpret the phrase "in the conduct of any trade or commerce" as the plaintiffs suggest, to apply to any commercial transaction whatsoever, the "persons" covered by Sections 1 and 11 would be identical. Section 11 would thus be superfluous—merely a repetition of Section One. We have stated that "(a)n intention to enact a barren and ineffective provision is not lightly to be imputed to the Legislature." Therefore, we conclude that with respect to G.L. c. 93A, where the Legislature employed the terms "persons engaged in the conduct of any trade of commerce," it intended to refer specifically to individuals acting in a business context.

These considerations are helpful in determining the meaning of Section 2, which employs the phrase "in the conduct of any trade or commerce." Following the rule of statutory construction which suggests that words used in one place within a statute be given the same meaning when found in other parts of the statute, and cases cited, we conclude that the terms of Section 2 must be construed similarly to those in Section 11. Thus, the proscription in Section 2 of "unfair or deceptive acts or practices in the conduct of any trade or commerce" must be read to apply to those acts or practices which are perpetrated in a business context.

Contrary to the plaintiffs' assertions, this conclusion is entirely consistent with *Slaney* v. *Westwood Auto, Inc.,* where we described G.L. c. 93A as "a statute of broad impact" with "far-reaching effects." At the same time, however, we stated that the statute's private remedies "are available to the individual consumer . . . who suffers a loss . . . as a result of the employment of an unfair or deceptive act or practice by a *businessman*" (emphasis added). Thus at no time did we intimate in *Slaney* that the remedial provisions of c. 93A were available to a consumer as against an individual, nonprofessional seller.

Finally, we note that our conclusions with respect to the scope of G.L. c. 93A are not inconsistent with the statute's broadly protective legislative purpose. In *Dodd* v. *Commercial Union Ins. Co.,* we stated that the basic policy of G.L. c. 93A was "to regulate business activities with the view to providing . . . a more equitable balance in the relationship of consumers to persons conducting business activities." An individual homeowner who decides to sell his residence stands in no better bargaining position than the individual consumer. Both parties have rights and liabilities established under common law principles of contract, tort, and property law. Thus, arming the "consumer" in this circumstance does not serve to equalize the positions of buyer and seller. Rather, it serves to give superior rights to only one of the parties, even though as nonprofessionals both stand on an equal footing.

Judgment affirmed.

Chapter VII

Defamation and Advertising

Section 1

The Role of Advertising in Defamation of Character

Daniel M. Rohrer with Martin P. LoMonaco*

USE OF NAME OR LIKENESS AS DEFAMATION OF CHARACTER

Introduction

Despite individual claims and public concern for the preservation of private rights to protection of one's character, for many years, the legislatively progressive state of New York had no specific statute to protect against defamation. The New York antidefamation statute was not passed until the common law protection against libel and slander was practiced widely throughout the United States. Indeed, this was a curious situation for a state characterized by highly visible performers, businessmen, and politicians. Defamation cases, however, were brought before the courts, under the New York Civil Rights Law, Sections 50–51. Within the last decade, the state legislature of the Empire State has remedied this oversight with the passage of Sections 75–78 of the Civil Rights Law.

For these reasons, our concentration will be placed on consideration of defamation precedents set by mostly non-New York courts, although New York is traditionally considered a leader in the area of individual rights and liberties and their protection.

Basis of Liability

William Prosser explains that "a defamatory communication usually has been defined as one that tends to hold the plaintiff up to hatred, contempt, or ridicule, or to cause him to be shunned or avoided." The case of *Flake* v. *Greensboro News Co.* divides libel into three classes. These subdivisions include publications which are obviously defamatory, statements susceptible to more than one interpretation, one of which is defamatory, and publications which are not obviously defamatory, "but which become so, when considered in connection with innuendo, colloquim, and explanatory circumstances," (*infra*).

Libels per quod

While the first two examples of defamation are evident in *Flake,* the third requires further development. This issue "concerns cases of libel in which the defamatory meaning, or innuendo, is not apparent on the face of the publication, but must be made out by proof of extrinsic facts; and the

---

*Our thanks to John McGivney of Boston College Law School for editing this section.

question is whether in such a case the libel is actionable without proof of special damages, where the same words would not be so actionable if they were slander," (Prosser, 79 Harvard Law Review 1629, 1630–1631 (1966)).

Professor Prosser's view is that "libel per quod" should require the pleading of special damages, thus subjecting it to the same proof of damages as is the case in slander actions. However, in Massachusetts, the distinction between meaning on "face," and meaning in "context," is "irrelevant to the issue of pleading special damages," (*Sharratt* v. *Housing Innovations,* 310 NE 2d 343 (1974)). This is the case in most of the states, whereby requirements for proof of damages in *libels per quod* are the same as they are in libel in general and in slander *per se,* rather than in slander in general.

In *Sharratt,* a registered architect and the corporation of which he was the principal stockholder brought a defamation action against the publisher of a promotional stockholder brought a defamation action against the publisher of a promotional brochure, which stated the associate architect rather than the plaintiff had been awarded an architectural contract for a development project. The defendants argued that on their face, the words could not be construed as defamatory. The plaintiff, of course, argued that within their context, the background and circumstances, and the audience's sophistication, they could well be understood as defamatory, and to have defamatory effect. On subsequent appeal, the Supreme Judicial Court of Massachusetts held that each party was correct. Thus, the issue here is whether the determination of libel is to be made viz. the words alone, or their context in extrinsic facts pleaded. The court concluded that all libel is actionable, *per se,* (*ibid.*).

This decision establishes *libel per quod* as any libel, separating it from the slander standard. In *Lynch* v. *Lyons,* (303 Mass. 116, 118–119, 20 NE 2d 953, 955 (1939)), it was settled that words spoken orally are not actionable *per se,* unless they charge a plaintiff with a crime, claim he suffers from some disease, or creates prejudice against him, professionally. In these instances of slander, it would not be necessary to demonstrate damages to the plaintiff for recovery, although in other types of slander action it would be necessary for the plaintiff to do so, in order to obtain relief from a jury.

In cases of libel *per quod,* the damages would be assumed and automatic in Massachusetts, though in a few states the slander standard would be applied to libels *per quod* and damages would only be assumed or automatic in the instances isolated in *Lynch.*

Mitigating Circumstances in Action for Libel or Slander

According to Section 78 of the Act, the mitigating circumstances which the defendant may attempt to prove include the sources of his information and the grounds for his belief, regardless of whether he has pleaded or attempted to prove any defense (*Goodrow* v. *Press Co.,* 233 App. Div. 41, 251 NYS. 364 (1931)). Such circumstances include a number of factors which will be described below.

"Absolute Privilege" is a complete defense against defamation. Whether privilege exists at all is a question for the court, not for the jury (*Follendorf* v. *Brei,* 51 Misc. 2d 363, 273 NYS 2d 128 (1968)). Government reports are an example of this privilege (*Pauling* v. *News Syndicate Co.,* 335 F.2d 659 (CANY, 1964), cert den 379 U.S. 968 (1964)).

"Fair Comment" includes any honest statement of actual facts relating to public acts which have been commented upon in a reasonable and justifiable way. It may involve criticism short of attacks upon private character or defamatory statements concerning an official which are considered improper and unjustified (*Cheatum* v. *Wehle,* 5 NY 2d 585, 186 NYS 2d 606, 159 NE 2d 166 (1959); *Danziger* v. *Hearst Corp.,* 304 NY 244, 107 NE 2d 62 (1952); *Kelly* v. *Hearst Corp.,* 2 AD 2d 480, 157 NYS 2d 498, 3 AD 2d 610, 158 NYS 2d 781, app den 3 AD 2d 963, 163 NYS 2d 937 (1956)).

Both public officials and private citizens speak on "matters of public interest," whether speaking in performance of their public duties or for general circulation of the press, are protected by freedom of speech guarantees, even if a citizen is defamed in the process (*Follendorf* v. *Brei, supra; Paul* v. *Davis, Ill.,* 424 U.S. 693 (1976); *Time, Inc.* v. *Firestone,* 424 U.S. 448 (1976)).

The vacating of a lower court conviction in the case of *Time, Inc.* v. *Firestone* represents a classic case in which the defamatory remarks of a private citizen may be printed with immunity. After Mary Alice Firestone had filed a separate action for divorce, her husband, the scion of a wealthy industrial family, filed a counterclaim for divorce on grounds of extreme cruelty and adultery. The lower court granted the counterclaim, stating that "neither party is domesticated, within the meaning of that term as used by the Supreme Court of Florida," and that "the marriage should be dissolved" (*supra*).

On the basis of newspaper and wire service reports and information from a bureau chief and a "stringer," *Time* Magazine published an item reporting that the divorce was granted "on grounds of extreme cruelty and adultery." After *Time* had declined to retract, Mary Alice Firestone brought a libel action in state court, which granted a jury verdict for damages against *Time* (*supra*).

While the Florida Supreme Court upheld this decision, the U.S. Supreme Court overturned it despite the fact that no finding was ever made by the divorce court that Firestone was guilty of adultery as *Time* had reported. The final court decision was based upon its conclusion that there was no finding of fault on the part of *Time* in its publication of the defamatory material, a Constitutional limitation imposed by *Gertz* v. *Robert Welch, Inc.* (418 U.S. 323 (1974)).

The case of *Paul* v. *Davis* represents a major instance whereby a matter of public interest and official information provided by a government agency is privileged despite its defamatory use. Here a photograph of the respondent bearing his name was included in a flyer of "active shoplifters" after the respondent had been arrested on a shoplifting charge. After that charge had been dismissed, the respondent brought an action under 42 U.S.C. Section 1983 against the police chiefs who had distributed the flyer to area merchants, alleging that the petitioner's action, under color of law, had deprived him of his Constitutional rights (*supra*).

In the dissenting opinion of Mr. Justice Brennan, with whom Mr. Justice White and Mr. Justice Marshall concur, it was argued that it is a regrettable abdication of the Bill of Rights "when the Court tolerates arbitrary and capricious official conduct branding an individual as a criminal without compliance with Constitutional procedures designed to ensure the fair and impartial ascertainment of criminal culpability. Today's decision must surely be a shortlived aberration" (*supra*).

More recent cases have cast further light specifically on what constitutes a public figure for purposes of defamation of character. For example, in the case of *Wolston* v. *Reader's Digest Association,* the plaintiff, who pleaded guilty in 1958 to criminal contempt charges brought after he failed to appear before a special grand jury investigating activities of Soviet intelligence agents in the U.S., and who now has brought libel action against the author and publisher of a book on Soviet agents, is a public figure for limited purposes of comment on his connection with Soviet espionage in the 1950s, since espionage is public controversy and the plaintiff, through his refusal to appear before a grand jury, voluntarily injected himself into that controversy. "He cannot now be heard to complain that someone noticed him, unless he can prove actual malice." (429 F. Supp. 167 (DCDC 1977).)

Likewise, a Californian corporation identified in a Federal Trade Commission press release as the target of proposed FTC enforcement proceedings for unfair and deceptive practices is a public figure for purposes of defamation action brought against the newspapers and national wire services that published erroneous reports about the FTC complaint. Thus, it must prove that media defendants published reports with knowledge or reckless disregard of their falsity. *Trans World Accounts, Inc.* v. *Associated Press* (2 Med. L. Rptr. 1334 (ND Cal. 1977)).

In a similar manner, a publishing company was held not libel for unflattering and allegedly libelous characterizations concerning the public figure plaintiff that appeared in a book on Ernest Hemingway, even though the book's author, contrary to the impression conveyed by the book, apparently had no first hand knowledge of the plaintiff, since the publication of statements that are not demonstrably unreliable and that cannot be independently verified does not constitute reckless disregard for the truth (*Hotchner* v. *Castillo-Puche,* 551 F.2d 910 (CA2 1977)).

Furthermore, the Speech and Debate Clause barred a scientist's suit against a U.S. Senator and his administrative assistant for damages suffered as a result of investigation into the Federal funding of the scientist's research. In a speech on the Senate floor, the Senator bestowed a "golden fleece" award on research for wasting tax dollars, and he issued a press release reciting the substance of the Senate speech, *Hutchinson* v. *Proximire* (U.S. DC, W. Wisc. 1977)).

Newspapers cannot be held liable in defamation action brought against them by public figure scientists for an article that fairly and accurately reported on charges made in an environmental group's magazine that scientists were "paid to lie," since accurate reporting by the press of newsworthy accusations is privileged under the First Amendment's right of "neutral reporting" (*Edwards* v. *National Audubon Society,* 556 F.2d 113 (CA 1977)).

In a case where a prosecutor, who sent an allegedly defamatory letter to the state legislature protesting proposed reimbursement of an inmate for wrongful conviction, the court found that he acted within the scope of his official duties and that the prosecutor's "good faith" is a defense to state law libel action. The cause was remanded to the district court for determination of whether the prosecutor acted with malice. The questions presented are: "1) Did court of appeals err in holding that prosecutor under Michigan law did not enjoy absolute privilege for defamation arising out of exercise of official duties of his public office, but instead was clothed only with qualified privilege defensible by showing common law malice? 2) Did court of appeals err in applying 'actual malice' rule of *New York Times Co.* v. *Sullivan* (376 U.S. 254 (1964)) only to media defendant and not to public prosecutor where plaintiff is conceded 'public figure'?" *Cahalan* v. *Walker* (542 F.2d 681 (CA6)).

In the appeal of *Laredo Newspapers, Inc.* v. *Foster* the high Court ruled that the trial court properly held that an elected county surveyor was a public official within the meaning of *New York Times Co.* v. *Sullivan,* but remanded his case for determination of whether allegedly libelous statements contained in the newspaper article clearly related to the surveyor's official conduct. The Court advised that a county surveyor who also worked as a consulting engineer and performed subdivision drainage studies is not a public figure for purposes of controversy involving the flooding of a subdivision, and that a private individual may recover damages from a publisher of defamatory falsehoods as compensation for actual injury upon showing that the publisher knew or should have known that the defamatory statement was false (541 SW 2d 809).

More important than whether the issue involves a matter of public interest is whether the individual involved will be considered a public figure. In answering this question the following cases may also be consulted: *Exner* v. *American Medical Association* (12 Wash. App. 215, 529 P2d 863 (1974)); *Maheu* v. *Hughes Tool Co.* (384 F. Supp. 166 (CD Cal. 1974)); *Kapiloff* v. *Dunn.* (275 Md 598, 343 A 2d 251 (1975)); *Bandelin* v. *Pietch et al.,* (2 Med. L. Rptr. 1600 (Ida 1977)).

Publications which rely on "government information," or which may defame an individual by truthful statements of fact, or believing a trustworthy source have falsely defamed an individual are found as not liable.

Probably the classic case which sets the "malice standard" for civil libel action is that of *New York Times Company* v. *Sullivan*. Here the defendant published a full page, ten-paragraph advertisement in its daily newspaper describing events which had taken place in Montgomery, Alabama, in connection with the Civil Rights movement. Some of the statements in the advertisement were not accurate. The plaintiff was the Montgomery Commissioner of Police. He brought an action against the defendant on the claim that some of the statements published referred to him in his official capacity as Police Commissioner. Prior to bringing suit the plaintiff sought a retraction from the defendant, but the request was denied. The denial gave him the right as a public official to seek punitive damages. The trial judge instructed the jury that the statements under consideration were libelous per se and that the defendant was liable if they found that he had both published the statements and if the statements referred to the plaintiff. The jury was also instructed that if they found malice on the part of the defendant they might award punitive damages. The plaintiff was awarded $500,000. The award was upheld on appeal by the Supreme Court of Alabama in rejecting the defendant's contention that the verdict and award abridged the freedoms of speech and press that are guaranteed by the First and Fourteenth Amendments (376 U.S. 255 (1964)).

On appeal the U.S. Supreme Court reversed the judgment, holding that: 1) the Constitution delimits a state's power to award damages for libel in actions brought by public officials against critics of their official conduct. 2) A public official is prohibited from recovering damages for a defamatory falsehood relating to his official conduct unless he proves that the statement is made with actual malice—that is, knowledge that it is false or with reckless disregard of whether it is false or not. 3) In this case the evidence did not support a finding of malice (ibid.).

This is a leading and landmark case in modern constitutional law. It establishes a special Constitutional rule for libel actions by public officials in their official capacity. The rule allows recovery only upon proof of actual malice. The only prior defense to such actions was that of truth. It is now truth or lack of malice. The rule is based on the First Amendment, with special reference to the history of the Sedition Act and applicable to the states through the Fourteenth Amendment. It establishes the right to criticize official conduct, granting citizens a fair equivalent of the immunity granted to officials themselves. Three of the nine judges felt the rule ought to be one of absolute immunity, making recovery impossible under any conditions.

In summary, Prosser attached absolute immunity to judicial proceedings, legislative proceedings, executive communications, consent of the plaintiff, communications between husband and wife, and political broadcasts; and qualified privilege to interest of publisher, interest of others, common interest, communications to one who may act in the public interest, fair comment on matters of public concern, and reports of public proceedings.

Finally, the truth is a defense against defamation. According to Prosser: "The defense that the defamatory statement is true has been given the technical name of justification . . . (T)he law presumes in the first instance that all defamation is false, and the defendant has the burden of pleading and proving its truth."

Retraction

Since a retraction is the withdrawal of the accusation or charge, absent a statute in the jurisdiction that establishes retraction as a defense to an action for defamation, the retractor would only have the effect of reducing the damages for which the author of the defamation would be liable. One reason for this principle is that although the retraction may be conveyed in precisely the same fashion as the original defamation, not everyone who learned of the defamation would learn of the retraction or believe it and therefore the retraction is not a complete defense. The retraction does undo some of the damage done to the victim of the defamation, and it does evidence a willingness on the part of the author of the defamation to undo part of the harm that was caused. For these reasons the victim, less injured, deserves less compensation and the defamer deserves less punishment. Consequently, compensatory and punitive damages are reduced.

In a number of states' statutes ordinarily referring to newspapers and periodicals, but sometimes including radio and television broadcasting stations, have been enacted to limit the victim of defamation when there has been a timely retraction to compensate for only those damages they can specifically prove. Some statutes allow punitive damages only where malice is shown.

An example of a retraction resulted from the following statement, among others: "Bizarre stories are not limited to the Cambridge Food Coop. There was the time that Deleo, according to several sources, apparently 'punched out' Hill,'' who on another occasion as health inspection supervisor refused, allegedly, access to public records when faced with charges that a food inspector had apparently solicited and accepted bribes. (*Real Paper* (June 30, 1976).)

On July 7, 1976, the *Real Paper* printed the following correction:

> In an article in last week's *Real Paper* on Cambridge health inspectors, Senior Code Enforcement inspector Bernard Hill was incorrectly described as also working at Libby's Liquor Market in Central Square. It was an unfortunate case of mistaken identity. There are two Bernard Hill's in Cambridge. The man who helps run the liquor store also serves as the captain of Cambridge's Auxiliary Police Force and has no connection with the city's health department. We apologize to both men for the confusion.

Another example of an actual retraction may be noted as follows:

Correction

At 46 LW 1162 it was incorrectly reported that the New York Times refuses to accept advertising for x-rated movies. It is the policy of the Times to accept advertising for films which may be x-rated so long as the advertising is in compliance with the Times' acceptability standards.

One of the most recent specific instances of a court decision based upon retraction is that of *Davidson v. Rogers*, (281 Or. 219, 574 P.2d 624 (1978)). Here the Oregon Supreme Court considered a libel action brought against a magazine on the basis of an article which it had published. From a decision of the Oregon Circuit Court, Lane County, sustaining the defendants' demurrer to the complaint, the plaintiff appealed. Only general damages were requested. The defendants' demurrer to the complaint was sustained upon the basis that the facts stated were insufficient to constitute a cause of action for general damages because it was not alleged that a retraction had been requested of the defendants and refused by them as required by ORS 30.160:

> 1. In an action for damages on account of a defamatory statement published or broadcast in a newspaper, magazine, other printed periodical, or by radio, television or motion pictures, the plaintiff shall not recover *general damages* unless:

a. A correction or retraction is demanded but not published as provided in ORS 30.165; or

b. The plaintiff proves by a preponderance of the evidence that the defendant actually intended to defame the plaintiff.

2. Where the plaintiff is entitled to recover general damages, the publication of a correction or retraction may be considered in mitigation of damages.

The plaintiff appealed, conceding that under Oregon's present decision in *Holden* v. *Pioneer Broadcasting Co.* (1961), he cannot maintain his action. However, he urges the court to reconsider that decision and to hold that the statute is unconstitutional as being in violation of that part of Article I, Section 10, of the Oregon Constitution which provides that " . . . every man shall have remedy by due course of law for injury done him in his person, property or reputation."

The Oregon Supreme Court saw no reason to depart from its prior decision upon the subject. The language of the constitution does not specify that the remedy need be the same as was available at common law at the time of the adoption of the constitution; and the statute, while restricting the remedy, does not abolish the cause of action. Even though a retraction is not requested, the right of action still exists for an intentional defamation and, in any event, for recovery of specific demonstrable economic loss. Such a limitation is not violative of Article I, Section 10, for the reason that it does not wholly deny the injured party a remedy for the wrong suffered.

In addition, the legislature has made available a retraction as a substitute for the remedy which the law would otherwise have provided. As a practical matter, retraction can come nearer to restoring an injured reputation than can money, although neither can completely restore it.

If the specific remedies available at common law were frozen at the adoption of Oregon's Constitution, the legislature would have been helpless to enact limitations upon actions such as those provided by the Workmen's Compensation Law and the guest passenger statute, or to concern itself with other similar matters about which it is usual for legislatures to take action.

The judgment of the trial court is affirmed.

The Montana Supreme Court, on the other hand, took a different view. Rather than maintaining that a retraction, while perhaps an insufficient means of eradicating damages, is at least a necessary recourse for the libeled plaintiff to pursue, held that its state retraction statute, which requires allegedly libeled individuals to give notice and opportunity for correction to the publisher of an alleged libel prior to commencing any civil action, violates the Montana constitutional requirement that a remedy be afforded for every injury to character, since the "right" of libeled individuals to obtain a retraction is not in itself a remedy. (*Madison* v. *Yunker,* 4 Med L. Rptr. 1337 (1978).) Both courts agreed that in itself retraction is not necessarily a remedy, but the Utah court required the libeled plaintiff to request a retraction before filing a claim in damages against libel while the Montana court held the requirement unconstitutional.

In the Montana case, Mr. Justice Gene B. Daly delivered the opinion of the court.

Plaintiff appeals from the order of the District Court, Missoula County, granting defendants' motion to dismiss plaintiff's cause of action for libel and from the entry of judgment for defendants.

The District Court in this case dismissed Madison's complaint because Madison failed to give the required notice for retraction. It must be said that the District Court was simply following the statute.

We do not find that the "right" of a libeled individual to obtain a retraction under section 64-207.1 is in itself a remedy. Remedies for "injury of . . . character" are found in "courts of justice" which "shall be open to every person". In all suits for libel, "the truth thereof may be given in evidence, and the jury, under the direction of the court, shall determine the law and the facts". (Article II, Section 7 and 16, 1972 Montana Constitution.) Thus, the state constitution fixes the right to a remedy and where it may be sought. The legislature is without power to provide otherwise.

We therefore hold section 64-207.1, R.C.M. 1947, unconstitutional in that it is in violation of the provisions which we have noted of Article II, Sections 7 and 16, 1972 Montana Constitution. (Ibid.) The Montana decision should not be interpreted, however, as providing any basis for minimizing the potential of the retraction as a viable means of demonstrating lack of malice and mitigation of damages.

On the contrary, the defendant may introduce evidence of a retraction in mitigation of damages, but the degree of the mitigation, if any, is for the jury to determine. (*Stone* v. *Essex County Newspapers*, 330 N.E.2d 161 (1975).) This case involved a newspaper article which had printed the father's name rather than the son's name, thus defaming the father.

To the effect that the *Tornillo* case on right-of-reply statutes does not indicate the unconstitutionality of retraction statutes, William Prosser suggests considering Justice Brennan's concurring opinion in *Miami Herald Pub. Co.* v. *Tornillo* (418 U.S. 241, 258 (1974)). Also see (Morris, "Inadvertent Newspaper Libel and Retraction, 32 *Illinois Law Review* 36 (1937)), and (80 *Harvard Law Review* 1730 (1967)). Recall that the *Tornillo* case appears in Chapter V Section II on this text.

Action for Libel: Evidence and Separate Verdicts

At the trial for any civil action for libel, the defendant may attempt to prove that the plaintiff has already recovered damages, thus providing a retroactive effect for consideration by the jury in fixing the amount of the verdict (Section 76, *Campbell* v. *New York Evening Post,* 245 NY 320, 157 NE 153 (1927)).

Actions by one plaintiff against several defendants may be consolidated (Section 76, *Goodrow* v. *New York Times Co.*, 241 App. Div. 190, 271 NYS 855, affd. 266 NY 531, 195 NE (1934)), but the measure of damages against each defendant shall be determined separately (Section 76 *ibid.*). Nevertheless, a cause of action in slander may not be united with one in libel (*Brown* v. *Reed*, 10 Misc 2d 8, 167 NYS 2d 41 (1957)).

Defamation by Radio or Television

The newer defamation sections of the law provide more specific protection for the licensed owners and operators of radio and television broadcasting stations against liability "for any legally qualified candidate for public office whose utterances under rules and regulations of the Federal Communications Commission may not be subject to censorship by such owner, licensee, or operator . . . or their agents or employees" (Section 75). According to the statute, a legally qualified candidate "means any person who has publicly announced that he is a candidate for nomination by a convention of a political party or for nomination or election in a primary, special, or general election; municipal, county, state, or national; and one who meets the qualifications prescribed by the applicable laws to hold the office for which he is a candidate . . ." (Section 75). In order to be absolved from liability for damages for any utterance by a legally qualified candidate, the owner, licensee, or employee of a broadcasting station, or a network of stations, shall announce, in substance, at the beginning and end of each political broadcast to more than five minutes duration or less, that the remarks about to be made, or which have been made, by the speaker are not to be construed as reflecting the opinions or beliefs of the station, its ownership or management" (Section 75).

Libel and Slander in the Electronic Media

While libel is generally considered written defamation, and slander oral defamation, of character, with a greater burden for showing damages in cases of slander than in cases of libel, it is not always easy to distinguish between libel and slander.

For example, in the case of *Charles Parker Company v. Silver City Crystal Company,* a manufacturer brought action against a candidate for mayor and a radio broadcasting company for defamation because of a prepared statement read over radio by the candidate during an election campaign. He falsely stated that because of the neglect and indifference of the incumbent mayor the manufacturer was 90 percent out of production and was up for sale and that 1,000 jobs would disappear. The Supreme Court of Errors of Connecticut held that the law of libel rather than the law of slander was applicable, that the statement was not libelous *per se* and would not support an action for libel without proof of special damage, and that the statement was privileged in the absence of showing animosity or ill will, (142 Conn 605, 116 A 2d 440 (1955)).

Likewise in the case of *Shor v. Billingsley,* the court determined that a defamatory broadcast or telecast will be treated as libel, rather than as slander, even though no prepared script was used. Here the use of the plaintiff's name and picture for the defendant's alleged advantage was solely in connection with alleged defamatory statements made on a telecast. The plaintiff alleged that his name and picture were used without his consent as a part of the program; that this was done for the purpose of increasing the value of the program to the sponsors and to the telecasters, of enhancing the reputation and commercial value of Billingsley as a performer, for the purpose of advertising "The Stork Club" and increasing its trade at the expense of the plaintiff, its competitor (158 NYS 2d 476 (1956)).

The case of *American Broadcasting—Paramount Theatres, Inc. v. EL Simpson* involved an action against television companies for defamation in the dramatic presentation of an event in which a well known prisoner was transported by railway train. The courts of Georgia held that the presentation was actionable *per se* as defamacast, and that the plaintiff, who had been one of two guards who attended the prisoner inside the car, could maintain action in light of the presentation indicating that one of the two guards accepted a bribe, either by showing by extrinsic facts that he was the guard referred to, or as a member of a two-man group (106 Ga App 230, 126 SE 2d 873 (1962)).

Defamation and Appropriation Through Cable Television

The presentation of likeness by cable television raises many of the same problems which are present in broadcast communities (viz. radio and television); however, the technological control of cable television presents unique legal questions in three areas: 1) defamation, 2) copyright and related issues, and 3) program privacy.

Defamation of character takes two forms: slander and libel. Slander is the unjust and malicious injury to one's reputation using spoken words; libel is the unjust and malicious injury to one's reputation using written or printed words and pictures. In practice, the legal distinction is at best vague. In reference to injuries committed via television and radio, the distinction is even more confounding. The distinction based upon a New York state court decision, *Shor v. Billingsley, et al.,* is that all defamatory broadcast statements, whether read from a script or spoken extemporaneously, be considered libel (*supra*). In other jurisdictions, remarks broadcast on the radio have been considered slander; whereas those on television have been considered libel. This distinction is based upon the definitions given above, and there is, however, no consensus on either of these decisions. However, recent legal opinion seems to indicate that the distinction between libel and slander should be based upon potential for harm and not the performance of form.

If the criteria of potential harm is invoked, then defamatory remarks on the local origination channel of a cable television system may be considered slander because of the relatively limited distribution of that signal over a geographic area. This is exclusive of the form taken. The complicating factor is that in particular communities there are particular problems involved. If, for instance, a cable television system has 90 percent saturation, and defamatory remarks are made relative to a prominent citizen in a well-viewed locally originated television newscast, then the potential for harm is much greater and the defamation can be considered libel. In the case of political candidates, there are different rules applicable. The Federal Communications Commission regulations now seem to indicate that since a station cannot censor a political candidate when he or she is making a campaign speech, the station is relieved of responsibility for defamatory statements. The same holds true for cable television local origination.

Clearly however, laws relating to defamation via television and radio vary from state to state and from judicial jurisdiction to judicial jurisdiction. Until such time that there is a high level federal decision relative to this point, one should be advised to be familiar with applicable state regulations.

Copyright

Even before passage of the 1976 Copyright Law Revision, the issue of copyright and cable television had been well established by judicial decision. Early threads of what became copyright related cases can be found in the *Intermountain Broadcasting* v. *Idaho Microwave* case where a district court rejected restrictions upon a cable television system carrying programs as unfair competition (196 F. Supp. 315 (DC Id 1961)); and the *Cable-Vision* v. *KUTV* case in which a circuit court rejected the right of a broadcaster to restrict cable television carriage on the basis of an exclusive contract (335 F.2d 348 (CA9), cert den 379 U.S. 989 (1965)).

The judicial precedent for the *Cable-Vision* case came by analogy to patent cases heard by the U.S. Supreme Court, namely the *Sears-Roebuck* and the *Compco* cases. The first case which dealt with copyright as a specific issue was the *Fortnightly Corp.* v. *United Artists* case (392 U.S. 390 (1968)). Here it was decided that cable carriage of copyrighted broadcast programming was not an infringement of copyright. The legal reasoning is that distribution via a cable system is not considered a performance. It should be noted that this seems to have been a reversal in judicial thinking set forth in the *Buck* v. *Jewel-LaSalle-Realty Co.* decision (283 U.S. 202 (1931)). In this case, a hotel owner who piped radio music into each guest room in his hotel did constitute a performance. More recently the *Teleprompter* v. *CBS* case has clarified the question of cable television constituting a performance (415 U.S. 394 (1974)). The *Teleprompter* v. *CBS* case made a distinction between off-the-air reception of television signals and importation of distant signals by microwave. The court decided that neither of these functions infringes upon copyright because the court argued, "neither method of signal distribution alters the function the cable system provides for its subscribers." The court decided that "the reception and rechanneling of these signals for simultaneous viewing is essentially a viewer function, irrespective of the distance between the broadcasting station and the ultimate viewer.

While it might be noted that causes of action for libel and invasion of privacy often overlap, and that program privacy is considered in the next chapter as part of Section I, it might be pointed out here that even though a derivative work may be in the public domain, "to the extent that it partakes of (an) original work it cannot be used without the consent of the proprietor of the underlying copyright." Having so decided, the United States District Court for Central California awarded summary judgment to the owners of the play "Pygmalion" in their copyright infringement action against the distributors of a derivative film which has entered the public domain. (*Russell* v. *Price,* 387 PTCJ A-2 (1977).)

The example above is given for the purpose of comparing the results of this case with the application of the traditional "Fair Use Exception Doctrine" and the implementation of the 1978 "Fair Use Exception Clause" as an amendment to the Copyright Law. (Title 17 USCA Section 107 (1978).) A new copyright law took effect January 1, 1978, bringing the 1909 statutes up to date with technological advancements in communication and setting standards of fair use for educators.

The Copyright Revision Act of 1976 (Public Law 94-553, 94th Congress, 90 Stat. 2541), brings under the statutes for the first time the doctrine of "fair use" to cover the duplication and use of copyrighted material by educators. Section 107 of the law says use of copyrighted works is not an infringement if used for "purposes such as criticism, comment, news reporting, teaching (including multiple copies for classroom use), scholarship, or research. In determining whether the use made of a work in any particular case is a fair use the factors to be considered shall include—

1. the purpose and character of the use, including whether such use is of a commercial nature or is for nonprofit educational purposes;
2. the nature of the copyrighted work;
3. the amount and substantiality of the portion used in relation to the copyrighted work as a whole; and
4. the effect of the use upon the potential market for or value of the copyrighted work.

The limitations are on exclusive rights, reproduction by libraries and archives. (Title 17 USCA Section 107 (1978).)

To the extent that the courts have clarified what is meant by this law, and in the process determine its standards, the guidelines seem to suggest that for classroom use or citicizing anything that has thrust itself into the public domain would both fall within the fair use exception. For more information on the new law, request the "General Guide to the Copyright Act of 1976," available from the Copyright Office, Library of Congress, Washington, D.C. 20559. The Copyright Law Revision of the Committee on the Judiciary, House of Representatives, Report No. 94-1476, 94th Congress, 2nd Session, 1976, would also be useful in suggesting the following possibilities.

Like many laws, this new provision of the copyright law is subject to a variety of meanings, interpretations, and varying decisions of different courts. And in this case the scholar, writer and publisher may be confronted with the dilemma of determining whether the "fair use exception clause" will continue to be applied as it was on the basis of common law, or whether it will be applied in another way. One of the first test cases involves a difficult controversy in which a political committee brought action against another political committee for engaging in the reproduction of the plaintiff's likeness in an unfair context produced by defendant committee. It involved the use of 15 seconds of the plaintiff's committee recording, the restraining order denied on the basis of it not appearing that the plaintiff had suffered or would suffer any monetary damage, that the possibility of prejudice to the plaintiff was outweighed by public interest in full and free discussion of issues relative to election campaign, and that the defendant would probably not succeed on the merits of its claim of violation of copyright and unfair competition. As a result petitions for injunctive relief were denied. (*Keep Thomson Governor Committee* v. *Citizens for Gallen Committee,* 457 F.Supp. 957 (1978).)

Courts will probably continue interpreting what is meant by "criticism," "comment," "scholarship or research," and especially "the amount and substantiality of the portion used in relation to the copyrighted work as a whole; and the effect of the use upon the potential market for or value of the copyrighted work."

The plaintiff must be concerned with the possibility of an injunction issued against him or with liability and possible damages after use of copyrighted material on a limited basis without consent. Prior restraint is seldom imposed by the courts when freedom of speech, press or association is involved. For example, the Pennsylvania Supreme Court has ruled that an injunction issued against a client restraining her from demonstrating by carrying a "sandwich-board" sign denouncing her former lawyers was an invalid prior restraint on speech. The client carried the sign, which stated that the named law firm had "stole money from me and sold me out to the insurance company," in a pedestrian plaza in downtown Philadelphia. (*Willing v. Mazzocone,* 393 A.2d 1155 (1978).)

Uncertainty over whether the court will approve limited appropriation of copyrighted materials under the fair use exception clause will either inhibit freedom of speech and press or place the potential plaintiff in a position of personal risk. In order for the plaintiff to avoid possible violation of the Copyright Act, he must either avoid any reproduction of copyrighted material without permission or inject himself into unknown areas because the: "Declaratory Judgment Act applies only to controversies of justiciable nature, thus excluding advisory decree." (*Ashwander v. Tennessee Valley Authority,* 297 US 288, 80 L.Ed. 688, 56 S.Ct. 466, reh. den. 297 US 728, 80 L.Ed. 1011, 56 S.Ct. 588 (1936).)

Nevertheless, the difference between abstract question and "controversy" contemplated by the Declaratory Judgment Act is necessarily one of decree. (*Maryland Casualty Co. v. Pacific Coal and Oil Co.,* 312 US 270, 85 L.Ed. 826, 61 S.Ct. 510 (1941); *Evers v. Dwyer,* 358 US 202, 3 L.Ed.2d 222, 79 S.Ct. 178 (1958).)

For it would be difficult, if it would be possible, to fashion a precise test for determining in every case whether there was such a controversy; basically, the question in each case is whether the facts alleged, under all circumstances, show that there is substantial controversy, between parties having adverse legal interests, of sufficient immediacy and reality to warrant issuance of a declaratory judgment. (*Rozelle v. Quinn,* 47 F.Supp. 740 (DC Cal. 1942); *Cornelius v. Parma* 374 F.Supp. 730 (DC Ohio 1974), vacated without op 506 F.2d 1400 (CA6 Ohio), vacated on other grounds 422 US 1052, 45 L.Ed.2d 705, 95 S.Ct. 2673 and remanded without op 521 F.2d 1401 (CA6 Ohio), cert. den. 424 US 955, 47 L.Ed.2d 360, 96 S.Ct. 1430.)

The Declaratory Judgment Act only permits federal courts to entertain actual, concrete controversies, and not hypothetical questions, and the distinction between the former and the latter, is one of degree to be determined on a case by case basis. (*Blessings Corp. v. Altman,* 373 F.Supp. 802 (DCNY 1974).)

It would indeed seem that if permission to reprint an advertisement or picture accompanying a news item, for example, in a book about to be published, were denied, a concrete controversy rather than an abstract or academic question would exist. Such was the case when an alleged infringer of a patent, once he was threatened by the patentee, had a remedy by complaint for a declaratory judgment. (*Grip Nut Co. v. Sharp,* 124 F.2d 814 (CA7 Ill. 1941).)

Furthermore, action to have a patent declared invalid was determined to be within 28 USCS § 2201 where the defendant threatened an infringement suit. (*Zenie Bros. v. Miskend,* 10 F.Supp. 779 (DCNY 1935).) The court has jurisdiction under 28 USCS § 2201 where a complaint alleged that the defendant claimed infringement of a patent and threatened suit thereon. (*Derman v. Gersten,* 22 F.Supp. 877 (DCNY 1938); *B. F. Goodrich Co. v. American Lakes Paper Co.,* 23 F.Supp. 682 (DC Del. 1938).)

Moreover, the requirements of a direct or an indirect threat as a prerequisite to finding an actual controversy in patent cases is given very liberal interpretation and is applied pragmatically in light of business realities that are involved. (*Mine Safety Appliance Co. v. Energetics Science, Inc.*, 416 F.Supp. 530 (DCNY 1976).)

The right to a declaratory judgment of the validity of a patent arises when a potential infringer is threatened with litigation and cannot compel the patentee to proceed. (*Uniroyal, Inc. v. Sperberg*, 63 FRD 55 (DCNY 1973).)

An actual controversy existed when a patent owner's attorney wrote the plaintiff expressing the attorney's opinion that the plaintiff had infringed patents despite the fact that the attorney later stated that the letter was merely an expression of his own opinion as distinguished from that of the patent owner, and that he had no authority to write the letter. (*Telechron, Inc. v. Parissi*, 97 F.Supp. 355 (DCNY 1951).)

Most relevant to the instant case is a court finding that an actual justiciable controversy exists where a declaratory judgment complaint alleges that the defendant has threatened the plaintiff and its customers with infringement suits under patent of which the defendant is the exclusive licensee. (*Pennsalt Chemicals Corp. v. Dravo Corp.*, 240 F.Supp. 837 (DC Pa. 1965).)

Indeed, under 28 USCS § 2201, an actual controversy exists if there has been a charge of infringement, and such charge need not be expressed but can be found in any conduct or course of action of the patentee which would lead reasonable men to fear that he or his customers face an infringement suit or threat of one if he continues or commences activity in question. (*Electro Medical Systems, Inc. v. Medical Plastics, Inc.*, 393 F.Supp. 617 (DC Minn. 1975).)

While the cases of patent law described above provide a close analogy to the instant case of copyright law, there is still more analogous precedent in the area of copyright law itself. For example, the court found that where a defendant has refused the plaintiff the right to publish his speeches, and has threatened suit should the plaintiff attempt to do so, there is no obligation on the plaintiff to infringe the copyright he challenges before he may maintain declaratory judgment action. Here Justiciable controversy exists since a conflict exists between the defendant's right to copyright his speeches and the plaintiff's right to publish materials allegedly in the public domain. (*Public Affairs Associates, Inc. v. Rickover*, 268 F.Supp. 444 (DCDC 1967).)

Not only do many more precedents exist in the area of copyright and patent law, but in the related area of trademarks as well. (See, for example, *Lee v. Park Lane Togs, Inc.*, 81 F.Supp. 853 (DCNY 1948).)

The final requirement of the Declaratory Judgment Act is that the case in controversy be of a constitutional nature. Most cases bringing the fair use exception clause into question would almost inevitably involve constitutional, political or advertising issues, all or most of which seem to have merged to some extent.

Nevertheless, when advertising is involved, the limitation is greater. The use of a name as a title is a form of advertising for its purpose is to increase the circulation of the publication.

This limitation may be observed in the case of *WGBH v. Penthouse International* (453 F.Supp. 1347 (1978)). Here there was evidence, in a suit by the producers of a public television program entitled "Nova," against a magazine publisher planning to print a science fiction and occult issue entitled "Nova." Furthermore, there was evidence that the magazine was published for the purpose of catering to its audience's desire for titillation, thus threatening the plaintiff's image of seriousness and integrity, imperiling the program's funding and audience, and warranting the federal district court's preliminary injunction halting publication of the magazine and requiring the defendant to withdraw its patent office application for registration of "Nova" as its mark of identity. This case involved the appropriation of a name and an identity for commercial purposes. Thus such use justified not only the suppression of the appropriation, but in the form of prior restraint.

Use of copyrighted material for the purpose of critical commentary and illustration, however, is another matter. Limited use in this sense is protected by the fair use exception clause, as was demonstrated in the *Committee* v. *Committee* case cited above. Here the political committee's use of a portion of the opposing candidate's copyrighted theme song in commercials criticizing the candidate's program was found by the Federal District Court to constitute "fair use" and thus does not infringe on the opponent's copyright.

There are other ways that a copyrighted work may be thrust into the public domain, thus facilitating its fair use by another interest under the protection of both the amended Copyright Law and the traditional fair use exception doctrine created by common law. For example, in Maine, the expiration of a movie company's statutory copyright in the 1937 film entitled, "A Star Is Born," and the dedication of its use for public interest, created the fair use of the company's common law copyright in the film's dialogue, script, and musical score. (*Classic Film Museum* v. *Warner Brothers*, 453 F.Supp. 852 (1978).)

Conclusion

During the period from 1967 to 1974, private individuals involved in matters of public interest were often faced with the burden of proving the *New York Times* v. *Sullivan* malice standard in their libel suits, regardless of whether they may have been unwilling participants in public events (*supra*). In 1967 the reasoning of Justice Douglas was applied to invasion of privacy in the form of the *Time, Inc.* v. *Hill* decision (*infra*).

Having borrowed the malice standard from libel in order to apply it to privacy, the Court adopted the broadest possible interpretation of the new public principle and began applying it in cases of libel. The private individual who believed he had been defamed was now required to prove actual malice if the damaging news story concerned any matter of public interest (*United Medical Laboratories, Inc.* v. *Columbia Broadcasting System, Inc.*, 404 F.2d 706 (CA9 1968), cert den 394 U.S. 921 (1969); *Davis* v. *National Broadcasting Co.*, 487 P.2d 1304 (Ala 1971); *Time, Inc.* v. *Johnston*, 448 F.2d 378 (CA4 1971)).

This trend was highlighted in the case of *Rosenbloom* v. *Metromedia, Inc.* when the high Court approved extending the actual malice rule in libel whenever the statement was considered a matter of public interest. Here Justice Brennan joined the Chief Justice and Justice Blackmun in concluding that the *New York Times* standard of knowing or reckless falsity applies in a state civil libel action brought by a private individual for a defamatory falsehood uttered in a radio news broadcast about the individual's involvement in an event of public or general interest. Justice Black concluded that the First Amendment protects the news media from libel judgments even when statements are made with knowledge that they are false. Justice White concluded that, in the absence of actual malice as defined in *New York Times*, the First Amendment gives the news media a privilege to report and comment upon the official actions of public servants in full detail, without sparing from public view the reputation or privacy of an individual involved in or affected by any official action (403 U.S. 29 (1971)).

In the case of *Gertz* v. *Robert Welch, Inc.*, however, the high Court rejected the requirement that private individuals libeled in stories that were matters of public interest must prove the stringent *Times-Sullivan* test of actual malice. Instead they need to establish only negligence on the part of the publisher or broadcaster. Nevertheless, these private individuals are required to show damages, a significant departure from the historic concept of the presumption of injury in questions of libel *per se*. The Court concluded that private individuals are more vulnerable to injury, have less access to the media for rebuttal, and are more deserving of recovery because they had not voluntarily entered the public spotlight. With this reasoning and decision, the Court ended its traditional requirement of strict liability *(supra)*.

Justice Brennan, who had written the plurality opinion in *Rosenbloom,* joined Justice Douglas to dissent in the *Gertz* case. Again relying on *Time, Inc.* v. *Hill (supra),* Brennan addressed himself to the assumption that private people deserve special treatment because they do not assume the risk of defamation by freely entering the public arena. He reiterated the reasoning which had been developed in *Time-Hill* that " . . . voluntarily or not, we are all 'public' men to some degree" *(Gertz, supra).*

Quickly discarding the possibility that Gertz might be a public figure, it became necessary for a long series of cases to determine the notion of how a public figure might be defined. One of the first cases to make such an attempt is that of *Meeropol* v. *Nizer,* which announced that the children of famous parents had achieved general fame or notoriety in the community. Here the Court failed to acknowledge that the children of Julius and Ethel Rosenberg may have renounced the public spotlight by changing their name to Meeropol. Perhaps this was because they had re-entered the spotlight in an effort to vindicate their parents alleged wrongful conviction and execution in 1953. Thus the Meeropols, as public figures, would have the burden of proving actual malice on the part of Attorney Louis Nizer in a libel action against his use of letters written by their parents in his book, *The Implosion Conspiracy (Meeropol* v. *Nizer,* 381 F.Supp. 29 (SDNY 1974)).

Subsequent cases have ranged from those who have thrust themselves into the public eye to those who have been drawn into the public limelight, and from those who have achieved public recognition for purposes of a single or limited range of issues to those who have become universal public figures. Examples of thrusting oneself into the public eye include accepting the position of a highschool principalship, *Kapiloff* v. *Dunn* (275 Md 598, 343 A 2d 251 (1975)) and serving as an accountant for the Finance Committee to Re-elect the President just prior to the Watergate episode *(Buchanan* v. *Associated Press,* 398 F.Supp. 1196 (DCDC 1975)).

In a similar case, a longstanding flouridation advocate was held to be a public figure for purposes of that issue by having assumed leadership and by having attempted to influence the outcome of the controversy *(supra).*

The case of *Gertz* opened the door for individuals to be drawn into a public controversy, thus becoming public figures with no intention or awareness that such would become the outcome. Here the court suggested that " . . . it may be possible for someone to become a public figure through no purposeful action of his own, but the instances of truly involuntary public figures must be exceedingly rare" *(supra).*

Based upon this interpretation, the Court found that even a corporation could be drawn into a particular public controversy by virtue of being investigated by the Federal Trade Commission for potentially harmful activities on the part of the firm. The Court held that by means of its own conduct and activities, Trans World Accounts had become a public figure for the limited range of issues relating to the FTC complaint, *Trans World Accounts, Inc.* v. *Associated Press et al. (supra).*

In the case of *Wolston* v. *Reader's Digest Association,* also discussed earlier, the Court was not concerned whether the plaintiff had been "thrust" or "drawn" into the public eye since his failure to respond to the subpoena "invited attention and comment" *(supra).*

Nevertheless, the act of defamation itself is not sufficient to draw the plaintiff into the public eye. For example, when a newspaper implied that Mrs. Mary Troman conducted her home as a gang headquarters, an untrue accusation, the court ruled that she was a private, not a public figure (*Troman v. Wood,* 340 NE 2d 292 (1976)).

It is well established that in defamation, once a person has become a public figure, he remains a public figure (*Sidis, supra; Bandelin* v. *Pietsch et al.,* 2 Med L Rptr. 1600 (1977); *Richard J. Ryder* v. *Time, Inc.,* 2 Med Rptr. 1221 (CADC 1976)).

The critical and remaining question is when and under what conditions will the court utilize the public official, public figure, private figure, and the newsworthy, public or general interest standard, and how are these criteria defined and distinguished under similar and differing circumstances. In light of the fact that the *Gertz* case involved a media defendant, application of its principles in non-media cases remained a still more open question.

Soon to follow the Gertz decision, the case of *Jacron Sales* v. *Sindorf* (276 Md. 580, 350 A.2d 688 (1976)) applied the *Gertz* standard to a non-media defendant as a matter of state law. In the words of the court:

> Nor do we discern any persuasive basis for distinguishing media and non-media cases. The rationale for the application of a constitutional privilege in *New York Times* and *Gertz* is that the defense of truth is not alone sufficient to assure free and open discussion of important issues. Issues of public interest may equally be discussed in media and non-media contexts. And the need for a constitutional privilege, therefore, obtains in either case. The proposition that the press enjoys greater rights than members of the public generally was rejected by the Supreme Court in *Pell* v. *Procunier,* where a newspaper argued that it had a constitutional right to interview inmates of a state correctional system despite a regulation prohibiting such contacts.
>
> Wholly apart from any possible Supreme Court holding in the future based on constitutional grounds, we conclude as a matter of state law that the Gertz holding should apply to media and non-media defendants alike, and to both libel and slander. (*Ibid.,* 695.)

It was because the *Rosenbloom* approach did not afford sufficient recognition of the state interest in protecting private persons who have been defamed that the *Gertz* Court found it unacceptable and "sounded the death knell" for the "public or general interest" test as a constitutional requirement. (*Ibid.,* 693.) And in another case decided after *Gertz,* in which a private plaintiff alleged a defamation by a media defendant, a negligence standard was adopted "even though the libel occurred in the reporting of an event of public or general concern." (*Ibid.,* 697; *Stone* v. *Essex County Newspapers, supra.*)

The public interest standard may not have died a complete death, however, for subsequent cases have been mixed in their application of the public interest, public figure, and public official standards. The case of *Mechner* v. *Dow Jones* (4 Med. L. Rptr. 1239 (1978)), for example, involved evidence, in a libel and invasion of privacy action brought against a financial newspaper for its front-page article concerning the plaintiff's attempt to raise $25 million in venture capital, showing that the plaintiff's activity falls within the sphere of legitimate public concern and showing that the author conducted competent and responsible research in writing and verifying the article warrants the New York trial court's grant of summary judgment for the defendants.

The case of *Jet Asphalt v. New York Post* (4 Med. L. Rptr. 1156, 405 N.Y.S.2d 1014 (memorandum decision, 1978)) also based its decision in an action in libel at least in part on the immense public interest in the subject matter of the article published by the defendant newspaper. The court was explicit in its reasons for application of the public interest standard:

> While no stretch of the imagination can characterize the plaintiff as a public figure, there is a useful analogy to be found. For by contracting with the City of New York, the plaintiff is in point of fact contracting with the people of the City of New York who have a cognizable interest in the contractual relationship between Jet and the City. Accordingly, it is to be expected, or it should be expected, that such a business relationship would be subject to closer scrutiny than a business transaction that was "strictly private". A party dealing with the government, with the representative of the people, should expect closer inspection of its activities insofar as they deal with the City, and it cannot expect that when its activities are called into question that it will remain a private affair.

Nevertheless, the court will utilize the public official or public figure standard whenever possible as a defense against libel. This principle can be seen readily in the case of *Malerba v. Newsday* (406 N.Y.S.2d 552 (1978)), whereby a police patrolman was found to be a public official for purposes of his New York libel action against the defendant newspaper for publishing an article that he claims falsely identified him as being involved in an alleged police brutality incident.

The issue to be resolved in *Twohig v. Boston Herald-Traveler* (291 N.E.2d 398 (1973)) was whether to apply the "public official," "public figure," or "public interest" standard since it had been "confused" by the case of *Rosenbloom v. Metromedia,* "which lived a short life." There the United States Supreme Court expressly rejected the "public figure" doctrine, where it applied the *New York Times* standard of actual malice to a state civil libel action brought by a private citizen against a radio station which had reported his arrest for his involvement in the "smut literature racket." The court held that the determinant whether the First Amendment applies to state libel actions is whether the utterance involved concerns an issue of public or general concern.

Thus it was necessary in *Twohig* for the court to reinstate the public figure standard as a rule of law before the jury could be presented with the question of making a malice determination based upon the evidence presented in the trial.

In a related case evidence in a libel action was brought against a defendent magazine for an article it published referring to the plaintiff as "mobster," it subjected the plaintiff to the dissemination of printed reports to the effect that he had been involved in activities concerning organized crime. The plaintiff was thus thrust into the public eye for he was an unwilling public figure who asserted that he never sought such status. The court held that he was a public figure despite his contention that such status was neither by his design nor of his own choice of creation. (*Rosanova v. Playboy Enterprises,* 411 F.Supp. 440 (1976).)

The public figure criterion was reaffirmed by the Tennessee Supreme Court when it considered the case of a social worker who had investigated child abuse charges, removed children from their home, and counseled their parents on conditions for the children's return. The court found that, despite her low ranking in the state government hierarchy, the plaintiff was not only a public figure but a public official for purposes of her Tennessee libel action against a newspaper for a series of articles charging that she coerced the mother into submitting to sterilization in order to procure return of her children. (*Press* v. *Verran,* 569 S.W.2d 435 (1978).)

On the public figure question, the case of *St. Amant* v. *Thompson* (390 U.S. 727, 88 S.Ct. 1323, 20 L.Ed.2d 262 (1968)) is one of the most prominent. In this decision the Court required proof by public figure plaintiffs that the press entertained "serious doubts" as to the truth of the publication. In a related case the "serious doubts" criterion is modified in favor of a more widesweeping criterion which would claim a constitutional privilege for an accurate publication regardless of the press's belief concerning the truth of the statements. (*Dickey* v. *CBS,* 583 F.2d 1221 (CA3 1978).) Again, the standard for a public figure is the same, for again a public official is involved.

Both of the cases discussed above involved a broadcast of televised political speeches. Likewise, in the case of *Sims* v. *KIRO, Inc.* (580 P.2d 642 (1978)), the plaintiff's failure, in his libel action against the defendent television station for its allegedly defamatory news feature, appearing to show with convincing clarity that the statement was directed toward him, warranted a Washington trial court's grant of summary judgment for the defendant. The Court concluded, on the question of costs, that:

> As the judgment obtained by the plaintiff was less favorable than the defendant's offer of judgment, the defendant is entitled to costs incurred after the making of the offer. The trial court refused to allow attorney's fees and expert witness fees as costs pursuant to the rule, indicating that he did not have authority to include expenses in such an award beyond the statutory costs allowable.
>
> The term "costs" has been interpreted as not including attorney's fees and expert witness fees. In the event that the rule is to be expanded to include attorney's fees and expert witness fees as "costs," it should be expanded by statute or by amendment. We decline to assume to ourselves the prerogative to do so.
>
> The summary judgment of dismissal is affirmed.

In the classic divorce case of Mary Alice Firestone, a Palm Beach, Florida socialite, a *Time* Magazine article claimed that adultery was a part of the judge's findings, an untrue accusation. Adultery had been charged during litigation, but it had not been ruled upon by the judge. The Florida Supreme Court claimed that since alimony was awarded, the reporter should have known that adultery was not part of the finding because Florida law denies alimony to those who are found to have committed adultery. The high Court disagreed, however, ruling that this burden might be too much to expect of the average reporter. If Mrs. Firestone had been ruled a "public figure" by this court, she would have been required to demonstrate actual malice under *Times-Sullivan* and *Gertz* in order to collect damages. But since the Supreme Court decided that she was a "private person," despite the fact that she had invited attention and comment in her press conferences, which she had called, she was required to demonstrate only negligence plus damages in order to win a judgment, *Time, Inc.* v. *Firestone (supra).*

The often difficult decision as to whether libel plaintiffs are public or private individuals is a critical one which has been considered by the courts in a variety of cases. Several such instances worthy of investigation are as follows: *Washington Post Co.* v. *Keogh,* 365 F.2d 965 (1964); *Thomas H. Maloney and Sons, Inc.* v. *EW Scripps Co.,* 334 NE 2d 494 (Ohio 1974); *Chapadeau* v. *Utica Observer-Dispatch, Inc.,* 38 NY 2d 196, 341 NE 2d 569 (1975); *Walker* v. *Colorado Springs Sun Inc.,* 538 P.2d 450 (1975); *Troman* v. *Wood,* 340 NE 2d 292 (Ill 1975); *Gobin* v. *Globe Pub. Co.* 531 P.2d 76, 216 Kan. 223 (1975); *Rosanova* v. *Playboy Enterprises, Inc.,* 411 F. Supp. 440 (SD Ga 1976); *Walters* v. *Sanford Herald, Inc.,* 228 SE 2d 776 (NC 1976); *Jacron Sales Co., Inc.* v. *Sindorf,*

350 A.2d 688 (Md. 1976); *Taskett v. King Broadcasting Co.,* 546 P.2d 81 (Wash. 1976); *Martin Marieta Corp. v. Evening Star Newspaper Co.,* 417 F. Supp. 947 (1976); *Afco Heating & Air Conditioning Co. v. Northwest Publications, Inc.,* 321 NE 2d 580 (Ind 1975), cert. den. 424 U.S. 913 (1976); *Paegler v. Phoenix Newspaper Inc.,* 560 P.2d 1216 (Ariz 1977)).

It is clear that the states, which have a strong interest in protecting the reputations of their citizens, may set negligence or any other standard they wish, so long as they do not impose liability without fault. By the beginning of 1977, it had been demonstrated in the cases indicated above that nine states had adopted the standard of negligence for private individual libel plaintiffs to plead and prove against their alleged defamers. One state had adopted the more difficult to prove "gross irresponsibility" standard, and two others adopted the *New York Times* actual malice fault standard. Here the private person as well as the public official or public figure would be required to prove knowing or reckless falsehood by the publisher. Furthermore, it has been ruled in the District of Columbia that when a corporation, as distinct from a "natural person," brings a libel suit, it shall be subject to the same rigid actual malice standard.

Thus, it is well recognized that one who publishes a false and defamatory communication concerning a private individual is subject to liability if, and only if, the defaming person, institution, or organization is aware that the statement is false and that it defames the other, acts in reckless disregard of these matters, or acts negligently in failing to ascertain them. The latter least restrictive standard is the failure to use the amount of care which a reasonably prudent individual would use under these circumstances. It is for the jury to decide whether the defendant acted reasonably in attempting to discover the truth or falsity of the defamatory character of the publication. The judge must decide whether the statement is capable of a defamatory meaning or interpretation, and the jury must decide whether such an interpretation has been made by at least one third party.

In general it is important to note that words may be libellous unless they cannot be reasonably understood in a defamatory sense, or, to express it in another way, unless they are incapable of a defamatory meaning. The test is whether, in the circumstances, the writing discredits the plaintiff in the minds of any considerable and respectable class of the community. Here, the question is whether the words in the letter would tend to injure the plaintiff's reputation in the community and expose her to hatred, ridicule, and contempt. A publication may be libellous even if no wrongdoing or bad character is imputed to the plaintiff. If a publication is susceptible to both defamatory and harmless meanings, it presents a question for the trier of fact and cannot be ruled non-libellous as a matter of law. Inferences which might be drawn by a considerable and respectable segment of the community can make a publication actionable. Words may be actionable even if they do not tend to damage a plaintiff's reputation or hold him up to ridicule in the community at large or among all reasonable people; it is enough to do so among a considerable and respectable class of people. (*Smith v. Suburban Restaurants,* 373 N.E.2d 215 (1978).)

In another case an admittedly false newspaper article stating that the plaintiff prison inmate was to be given a new identity through the government's witness protection program did not hold the inmate up to scorn or ridicule in the eyes of a significant element of the community and, as a matter of law, was not libelous. (*Burrascano v. Levi,* 452 F.Supp. 1066 (1978).)

Under Maryland law, the question of whether a communication is defamatory is a legal question, within the province of the court rather than the jury. Although there is no Maryland authority directly on point, it is evident as a matter of law that a communication is not libellous if it merely accuses one of being a criminal informant. This result is compelled by the rule that, in order to be libellous, a false communication must hold the plaintiff up to scorn or ridicule in the eyes of a significant element of the community. The criminal element, albeit the milieu within which the plaintiff's misdeeds have placed him, is simply not such an element.

> A communication to be defamatory need not tend to prejudice the other in the eyes of everyone in the community or all of his associates, nor even in the eyes of a majority of them. It is enough that the communication would tend to prejudice him in the eyes of a substantial and respectable minority of them. The fact that a communication tends to prejudice another in the eyes of even a substantial group is not enough if the group is one whose standards are so anti-social that it is not proper for the courts to recognize them. (*Ibid.*)

In the case of *Denny* v. *Mertz* (267 N.W.2d 304 (1978)), the attorney's allegation, in his Wisconsin libel action against the defendant magazine, claiming that the publication had libeled him in its article falsely stating, without explanation, that he was "fired" as company's general counsel, was found by the Wisconsin Supreme Court to be sufficient to state a claim upon which relief can be granted, since such a statement is capable of being understood in a defamatory sense by reasonable people in the community.

In cases such as this one and most others in the same class, the court must initially decide whether a communication is capable of a defamatory meaning. Defamation has been defined as that which tends to injure reputation in the popular sense; to diminish the esteem, respect, goodwill or confidence in which the plaintiff is held, or to excite adverse, derogatory or unpleasant feelings or opinions against him. (Ibid.)

In the case of *Shofield* v. *Milwaukee Free Press Co.* (126 Wis. 81, 85, 105 N.W. 227 (1905)), the court held that for a newspaper article to be libelous it need only tend to degrade or disgrace the plaintiff generally or to subject him to public distrust, ridicule, or contempt in the community.

The words alleged to be libelous are to be construed and taken in their plain and popular sense. (*Pandow* v. *Eichstad*, 90 Wis. 298, 300, 63 N.W. 284 (1895).)

Words or elements in an article may not be considered in isolation, but must be viewed in the context of the whole article to determine if they are defamatory. (*Westby* v. *Madison Newspapers, Inc.*, 81 Wis. 2d 1, 259 N.W. 2d 707 (1977); *Waldo* v. *Journal Co.*, 45 Wis. 2d 203, 208, 209, 172 N.W. 2d 680 (1969).)

The question concerning when to apply the negligence and malice standards has been clarified in *Gertz* and in several other cases. For example, in *Gobin* v. *Globe Publishing Co.* (supra.), a negligence standard was adopted in the case of a private plaintiff and media defendant for the defendant in reporting judicial proceedings. In this case the court held that a newspaper is privileged with respect to its reporting of trials of non-public figures only if the reporting is fair and accurate. If a paper negligently reports on the trial of a non-public figure it is liable for the actual damage done to his reputation. The privilege is conditional and does not cover false, inaccurate, mistaken or malicious statements. The privilege here is called the "reporter's privilege," or "record libel." It has been extended to the reporting of public, but not private, meetings.

Consequently, it has been held that a standard of negligence must be applied in cases of purely private defamation. (*Jacron, supra.*, 697.) It should be noted that under the negligence standard adopted here, truth is no longer an affirmative defense to be established by the defendant, but instead the burden of proving falsity rests upon the plaintiff, since, under this standard, he is already required to establish negligence with respect to such falsity.

The court held in this case that proof of fault in cases of purely private defamation must meet the standard of the preponderance of the evidence. This is the quantum of proof ordinarily required in other types of actions for negligence, and is apt to be more readily understood by juries. (*Ibid.*, 698.)

It has been suggested that adoption of the negligence standard of fault in defamation cases would have the practical effect of rendering obsolete the common law defense of conditional privilege. The reasoning which underlies this position is that many jurisdictions follow the rule that one of the means by which a conditional privilege may be defeated is by proving negligence on the part of the defendant. (Ibid.)

The fault required by *Gertz* to be proved to establish liability would amount to an abuse of, and thereby defeat, a conditional privilege. (*Ibid.*, 699.) In Maryland, however, the courts have never held that negligence is among the grounds on which a conditional privilege may be forfeited. (*Ibid.*)

Malice was variously defined in the cases as a lack of good faith, ill-will, hostility, or hatred. Excessive publication and unnecessarily abusive language were held to be evidence of malice. Express or actual malice represents something more than conduct that is merely negligent. (*Ibid.*)

Were the plaintiff, who is confronted with a conditional privilege, is incapable of proving the malice necessary to overcome that hurdle, it would be of no consequence that he might have met the lesser standard of negligence.

Unless a conditional privilege is found to have existed, the plaintiff would be required at the new trial of this case to establish the liability of the defendant through proof of negligence by the preponderance of the evidence, and may recover compensation for actual injury, as defined in *Gertz,* but neither presumed nor punitive damages, unless he establishes liability under the more demanding *New York Times* standard of knowing falsity or reckless disregard for the truth. Should the court determine that a common law conditional privilege existed, the question of its forfeiture vel non shall be governed by the views expressed in this case. (*Ibid.*, 700.)

Upheld was the trial court's directed verdict for Jacron on the ground that Sindorf had failed to present sufficient evidence of "actual malice" to defeat the common law privilege protecting Jacron. As a result the court held that the question of malice was properly for the jury, a decision upheld after the second appeal. (*Ibid.*, 700.)

In more detail the case of *Stone v. Essex County Newspapers (supra.)* clarifies the conditions which will apply to the use of the negligence and malice standards. Here the court held that a plaintiff who is not a public officer or a public figure may recover damages in an action for libel by proof of negligence in publishing libel by the defendant, its agents or servants, even though libel occurred in reporting of an event of public or general concern, but that a plaintiff who is a public officer or a public figure may recover only on proof of "actual malice," that is, a reckless disregard of truth in the publishing of libel, that punitive damages may not be awarded in a defamation action, that damages may be assessed only for actual injury and only on a compensatory basis, subject to a searching judicial scrutiny at trial and appellate levels, and that, in the event the plaintiff must show knowledge of falsity or reckless disregard of the truth, he must establish his proof, not merely by a fair preponderance of evidence, but by proof that it is clear and convincing.

This case rejected the allowance of punitive damages, whether based on negligence or reckless or wilful conduct. The court based its decision on the possibility of excessive and unbridled jury verdicts, grounded on punitive assessments, impermissibly chilling the exercise of First Amendment rights by promoting apprehensive self-censorship.

The court reaffirmed the following controlling principles: In a case of defamation, the plaintiff's recovery is limited to actual damages, which are compensatory for the wrong done by the defendant. Where specific harm is alleged to have resulted from the defendant's tortious conduct, such harm may be pleaded and damages recovered. Otherwise the plaintiff is limited to compensatory damages for actual injury, which include mental suffering, and harm to reputation. Punitive damages are prohibited, even on proof of actual malice.

REFERENCES

The Consolidated Laws of New York Annotated (New York: Edward Thompson Company, 1948), p. 67.

William L. Prosser, "More Libel Per Quod," 79 Harv LR 1629, 1630–1631 (1966). His views on both policy and law are disputed in Eldridge, "The Spurious Rule of Libel Per Quod," 79 *Harv LR* 733 (1966).

For further reading on the subject of defamation and cable television see Walter B. Emery, *Broadcasting and Government: Responsibilities and Regulation* (East Lansing, Mich.: Michigan State University Press, 1961); Ron R. LeDuc, *Cable Television and the FCC: A Crisis in Media Control* (Philadelphia: Temple University Press, 1973); Paul W. MacAvoy, *Deregulation of Cable Television* (Washington, D.C.: American Enterprise Institute for Policy Research, 1977).

See 37 *BU LR* 378 (1957); 32 *Tul LR* 136 (Dec 1957); 71 *Harv LR* 384 (Dec 1957); 31 *St. John's LR* 314 (May 1957).

Harry Kalven, Jr. "Privacy in Tort Law—Were Warren and Brandeis Wrong?" 31 *Law and Contemporary Problems* 326 (1966). The concept of merging privacy and defamation in one tort is developed further in Wade, "Defamation and the Right of Privacy," 15 *Vand LR* 1093 (1962).

Section 2

First Amendment Restrictions on the Public Disclosure Tort

*Joyce Rechtschaffen**

INTRODUCTION

The notion of a common law right to privacy was first articulated by Lewis Brandeis and Samuel Warren in a famous law review article published in 1890.[1] One aspect of that privacy[2] centered on the publication of true but private and embarrassing facts about an individual.[3] Warren and Brandeis acknowledged, however, that the individual's right to privacy did not extend to matters of public interest; today, all states that grant recovery under the public disclosure tort allow the defense of "newsworthy"[4] or "legitimate public interest." While California has limited this defense based on a determination of "social value,"[5] most states have established a broad definition of newsworthy.[6]

These common law privileges available to the press in public disclosure cases recognized the potential conflict between the state's protection of an individual's privacy interests and the press' First Amendment right to publish truthful information. Until recently, however, the First Amendment restrictions on the state's right to grant recovery for disclosure of private, embarrassing facts has not been framed in explicit Constitutional terms.[7]

During the 1960s, the Warren Court strengthened the First Amendment protections of free speech and free press. On the other hand, by the mid-20th Century, a majority of jurisdictions had upheld a cause of action for disclosure of private facts.[8] Further, Constitutional restrictions on governmental interference with the individual's privacy rights[9] increased the demand for protecting these interests against invasion by the press. Justice Brennan, in a footnote to his opinion in *Time, Inc.* v. *Hill*,[10] noted the conflicting interests at stake:

> The limitation to newsworthy persons and events does not of course foreclose an interpretation of the statute to allow damages where "Revelations may be so intimate and so unwarranted in view of the victim's position as to outrage the community's notion of decency." *This case presents no question whether truthful publication of such matter could be constitutionally proscribed.* (Emphasis added.)[11]

It was not until 1974–1975, however, that the Supreme Court was presented with a case involving the publication of true, but private and embarrassing facts. In *Cox Broadcasting Corp.* v. *Cohn*,[12] appellant published the name of appellee's daughter, who had died as a victim of a rape incident. The publication followed the trial of several of the youths arrested in the incident; publication had been prevented until then partly because of a Georgia statute proscribing publication of a rape victim's name. The Georgia Supreme Court held that defendant invaded plaintiff's common law right of privacy and the Court relied on the Georgia statute[13] as a declaration of state policy that the name of a

---

*Ms. Rechtschaffen, a graduate of Harvard Law School, JD 1978, represents the Law Firm of Fried, Frank, Harris, Shriver and Kampelman in Washington, DC.

rape victim was not privileged as a matter of public concern. Further, the Court upheld the Constitutionality of the statute against appellant's claim that it violated the First and Fourteenth Amendments. The Court could discern "no public interest or general concern about the identity of the victim of such crime as will make the right to disclose the identity give rise to the level of First Amendment protection."[14]

The United States Supreme Court reversed, but decided the case on the narrow grounds that the First and Fourteenth amendments will not allow the state to impose sanctions for the publication of truthful information available to the public in official court documents. The Court avoided the larger question presented by the case:

> Whether truthful publications may ever be subjected to civil or criminal liability consistently with the First and Fourteenth Amendments, or to put it another way, whether the State may ever define and protect an area of privacy free from unwarranted publicity in the press.[15]

This section focuses on the broader issue left open by the Supreme Court in *Cox Broadcasting*. Does the press' Constitutional right under the First Amendment extend to the publication of all truthful information, no matter how private? Can the state Constitutionally provide any protection against public disclosure of true facts, found to be private and offensive? If the First Amendment does not guarantee truth as a complete Constitutional defense, what are the boundaries of the press' First Amendment rights? Is it Constitutional for the state to award damages for disclosure of private facts that are also newsworthy? What accommodation can be developed between the individual's privacy interests, protected under state law, and the press' right to publish, guaranteed by the First Amendment? Dean Prosser's warning in 1960 is still applicable today. Noting the "jealous safeguards thrown about freedom of speech and the press" in the field of defamation, he observed that the courts have accepted a power of censorship over what the public may be permitted to read in public disclosure cases.

> This is not to say the developments are wrong . . . It is to say that it is high time we realize what we are doing, and give some consideration to where, if anywhere, we are to call a halt.[16]

The tensions between the First Amendment and the state's protection of privacy interests will be discussed in the context of three groups of plaintiffs:

1. the "involuntary public figure" who becomes involved in an event through no pre-planned action. One recent example is Oliver Sipple, a man thrust into the public limelight by his actions in deflecting the gun during an attempted assassination of President Ford. Sipple filed a $2.5 million action for invasion of privacy against twelve defendant newspapers for publishing the admittedly true fact that he was a "prominent figure in the gay community."[17]

2. The individual who had received public attention in the distant past but now maintains a private existence. In *Briscoe v. Reader's Digest Association*[18] plaintiff, rehabilitated and leading an exemplary life, had participated 11 years ago in a hijacking. Defendants, as part of an article dealing with the effects of hijacking on business profits, discussed the details of the hijacking episode, including mention of plaintiff's name. The Court described the general subject matter as newsworthy, but held that the report was not privileged because mention of plaintiff's name "serves little independent

purpose."[19] Similarly, in *Melvin v. Reed*,[20] plaintiff, remarried and rehabilitated, was a former prostitute who had been tried and acquitted in a sensational murder trial. Defendant produced a movie of the trial—"The Red Kimono"—referring to plaintiff's maiden name. The Court ruled that the movie was not protected as newsworthy because the producers used the plaintiff's original name. On the other hand, in *Sidis v. F.R. Publishing Corp.*,[21] the Court denied recovery to a former child protegé who now lived an obscure life. *Sidis* involved publicizing the subsequent history of an individual who had once been subject to close public attention; the Court stated that the current whereabouts of plaintiff remained a matter of public concern. "Regrettably or not, the misfortunes and frailities of neighbors and 'public figures' are subjects of considerable interest and discussion to the rest of the population."[22]

3. The private individual who, without any contributory conduct on his part, is involved in a situation, trend, or lifestyle which the newspaper deems a matter of public interest. For example, in *Smith et al. v. Goro et al.*,[23] plaintiffs were poor and underprivileged slum dwellers in the South Bronx. Defendants claimed that the discussion of plaintiffs lives, as part of a book and magazine article, constituted a newsworthy account of a social condition—the conditions of life in a slum—which should be of interest to every citizen.[24] In denying defendants' motion for summary judgment and motion to dismiss, the Court observed:

> Undoubtedly the lives and the plight of the poor are, and of right ought to be of public interest . . . The issue is whether it necessarily follows that said people being natural subjects for study, have no right of privacy . . . No case has been cited or found which supports the view that a writer may seek out such people and write about them and by that fact alone make them public figures or persons of public interest debarred from claiming an invasion of their privacy.[25]

INTERPRETING COX BROADCASTING

To date the Ninth Circuit is the only court of appeals that has interpreted the Supreme Court's opinion in *Cox Broadcasting*. In *Virgil v. Time*,[26] *Sports Illustrated* (owned by *Time*), wrote an article entitled, "The Closest Thing to Being Born," depicting the spirit of body surfing as practiced at the Wedge, the world's most dangerous site for body surfing. The article focused on the character of the unique breed of man who enjoys meeting the hazards of body surfing. Virgil was well known as a constant frequenter of the Wedge, and other body surfers labeled him the most daredevil of them all. To some degree, Virgil fits into the category of a private individual involved in a matter of public interest. His exploits, however, would unavoidably attract public attention; in this respect he differed from the completely private individuals in *Smith v. Goro*.[27]

Sports Illustrated interviewed Virgil extensively; the article quoted episodes from his younger days, intending to help explain his carefree style at the Wedge. These escapades included extinguishing lighted cigarettes in his mouth, eating insects, and diving headlong down a flight of steps to impress women.[28] Virgil filed an action for invasion of privacy, seeking $2,000,000 in compensatory damages and $10,000,000 in punitive damages. The complaint requested damages only under the public disclosure tort; plaintiff did not contest either the truth of the facts or the manner in which they had been obtained.

The district court denied *Time*'s motion for summary judgment. However, emphasizing the important First Amendment issues at stake, the court granted *Time* permission to appeal from the denial of summary judgment.[29] In its brief to the Ninth Circuit, *Time* argued that since appellee did not dispute the truth of the facts published, the publication was privileged under the First Amendment.

The Ninth Circuit failed to reverse and dismiss as plaintiff had requested;[30] instead it vacated the denial of summary judgment and remanded the case to the district court for further consideration concerning factual questions to be decided by a jury. Writing for the Ninth Circuit, Judge Merrill first observed that the Supreme Court in *Cox Broadcasting* had refused to decide *Time*'s contention that truth is an absolute defense in privacy actions:

> The law has not yet gone so far . . . . The Supreme Court has not held in accordance with the contentions of appellant. Instead, it has expressly declined to reach the issue presented.[31]

The court then ruled that in the Ninth Circuit, Constitutional protection does not extend to all true facts. The First Amendment does not require that the press "be free to pry into the unnewsworthy private affairs of individuals."[32] The Court based its conclusion on the theory that the press' right to publish information extends only as far as the public's right to know. "It is because the public has a right to know that the press has a function to inquire and to inform." And the public's right to know is "subject to reasonable limitation so far as concerns the private facts of its individual members."[33]

In its holding, the court limited First Amendment protection to that which is newsworthy. The court defined newsworthy as set out in the *Restatement* (Second) *of Torts*:

> In determining what is a matter of legitimate public interest, account must be taken of the customs and conventions of the community; and in the last analysis what is proper becomes a matter of community mores. The line is to be drawn when the publicity ceases to be the giving of information to which the public is entitled and becomes a morbid and sensational prying into lives for its own sake, with which a reasonable member of the public, with decent standards, would say he had no concern.[34]

The Ninth Circuit thus adopted a standard that based Constitutional protection upon a determination of the mores of individual communities. Having defined the standard, the court refused to decide the case as a matter of law and remanded to the district court to decide if a jury could reasonably find that the facts were privileged under the *Restatement* test.[35]

On remand, in a decision dated Dec. 20, 1976,[36] the district court granted *Time*'s motion for summary judgment, holding that the private facts and the identity of Virgil were privileged as newsworthy under the First Amendment. District Judge Thompson interpreted the Ninth Circuit standard as allowing for a broad definition of newsworthy. He divided the *Restatement* test into two levels. First, all facts which do not reach a very high level of offensiveness—offensive to a degree of morbidity or sensationalism—receive absolute Constitutional protection. Importantly, Judge Thompson found that if the facts do not fall within the highly offensive zone, the state cannot Constitutionally grant recovery for invasion of privacy. The First Amendment protects publication of these facts regardless of whether they are newsworthy. Secondly, the court denied Constitutional protection to highly offensive facts only if the revelation is "for its own sake"—defined as that which is not newsworthy. In sum, the district court required a court evaluation of public interest only with respect to highly offensive facts.

TRUTH AS A COMPLETE DEFENSE—A CONSTITUTIONAL REQUIREMENT

As noted earlier, in *Virgil*, the court of appeals ruled on the broad issue not yet decided by the Supreme Court: in the Ninth Circuit, Constitutional protection does not extend to publication of all true facts. In evaluating this holding, it is first necessary to delineate the interests the state seeks to protect under the public disclosure tort. For the Supreme Court decision in *Gertz* v. *Robert Welch, Inc.*[37] implies that if the interests are identical to those at stake in a defamation suit, truth *must* be recognized as a complete defense. In effect, the tort of public disclosure would no longer exist.

In *Gertz*, the Court held that the states could establish any standard of liability other than strict liability for a publisher or broadcaster of defamatory falsehoods injurious to a private individual. As Justice Powell, the author of *Gertz*, notes in his concurring opinion in *Cox Broadcasting*: "It is fair to say that if the statements are true, the standard contemplated by *Gertz* cannot be satisfied." Powell then discusses the impact of *Gertz* on cases involving only the reputation interest. "In cases in which the interests sought to be protected are similar to those considered in *Gertz*, I view that opinion as requiring that truth be recognized as a complete defense."[38]

Both the defamation and public disclosure torts protect the individual's reputation interest; publication of defamatory statements and private, embarrassing facts affect the public's perception of an individual.[39] But the public disclosure tort safeguards interests distinct from reputation. Rutgers law professor Edward Bloustein stresses that the individual has an important interest is controlling the release of private information about himself; if the press violates that interest, the individual suffers intense emotional anguish. The control over release of information is essential to an individual's dignity and sense of self-worth.

> What is really at issue when, for instance, a magazine gives an account of the emotional crisis that a man faced in leaving his wife and children is not merely the distress the individual suffers as a result of the reawakening of this agony, but the debasement of his sense of himself as a person that results because his life has become a public spectacle against his will. There is anguish and mortification, a blow to human dignity, in having the world intrude as an unwanted witness to private tragedy. The wrong is to be found in the fact that a private life has been transformed into a public spectacle.[40]

Bloustein also identifies the individual's desire to determine for himself the type of life he wishes to lead and the nature of his relationship with others. As the court noted in *Briscoe* v. *Reader's Digest:*

> The claim is not so much one of total secrecy as it is of the right to define one's circle of intimates—of the right to choose who shall see beneath the quotidian mask. Loss of control over which "face" one puts on may result in literal loss of self-identity.[41]

For example, Oliver Sipple alleges that as a result of disclosure of his homosexual status, certain members of his family "heard for the first time of his homosexual sexual orientation, causing plaintiff great mental anguish, embarrassment, and humiliation."[42] Similarly, in *Briscoe,* publication of plaintiff's past criminal record disrupted his relationship with his daughter, who had not known about the episode.

Thus, the interests at stake in the public disclosure tort extend beyond the reputation interest protected in defamation suits, and *Gertz* does not mandate that truth be an absolute Constitutional defense. Truth is a complete defense in a defamation action in part because the impact of a true defamatory statement—although potentially harmful—remains far less serious than the effect of a false defamatory statement. In public disclosure cases, on the other hand, the truth of the statements does not reduce the extent of damages to the interests, other than reputation, protected by the tort.

SHOULD TRUTH BE A COMPLETE DEFENSE?

Supreme Court decisions discussing the important values guarded by the First Amendment indicate that the Court does not view protection of truth *in itself* as an absolute. Rather, the Court has leaned strongly toward the Meiklejohn theory of the First Amendment.[43] For Meiklejohn, the First Amendment protects a narrower category of values—those related to "governing importance."

> The First Amendment does not protect a "freedom to speak." It protects the freedom of those activities of thought and communication by which we "govern." It is concerned, not with a private right, but with public power, a governmental responsibility. . . . There are many forms of thought and expression within the range of human communications from which the voter derives the knowledge, intelligence, sensitivity to human values, the capacity for sane and objective judgment which, so far as possible, a ballot should express. These too must suffer no abridgment of their freedom.[44]

It is important to note, however, that previous Supreme Court cases adopting Meikeljohn's analysis have dealt with false facts. Perhaps Meiklejohn's notion of governing importance should place no limits on the publication of *true* facts.

The argument for recognizing truth as a complete Constitutional defense rests on a conception of the First Amendment that extends beyond the Meikeljohn theory and the Ninth Circuit court's view in *Virgil* that "it is because the public has a right to know that the press has a function to inquire and to inform."[45] Yale law professor Thomas Emerson has developed a broad outline of the First Amendment stressing the role of freedom of expression in assuring individual self-fulfillment. Above all, Emerson emphasizes the inherent value to the individual in expressing the truth, regardless of content.

> The proper end of man is the realization of his character and potentialities as a human being. For the achievement of his self-realization, the mind must be free. Hence, suppression of belief, opinion, or other expression is an affront to the dignity of man, a negation of man's essential nature.[46]

Emerson rejects limiting the ambit of First Amendment protection to newsworthy facts.

> A classification that bases the right to First Amendment protection or some estimate of how much general interest there is in the communication is surely in conflict with the whole idea of the First Amendment.[47]

Even Emerson, however, would not extend First Amendment protection to publication of all truthful facts. He identifies an area of inner privacy interests in which the press receives no Constitutional protection: "the most inner core of the personality, involving the kind of intimate details that were the Court's concern in *Griswold.*"[48] Thus, according to Emerson, the state can Constitutionally grant recovery for publication of facts which fall within a very narrow sphere of privacy. Complete First Amendment protection extends to publication of all other truthful facts.

TOWARDS A RECOGNITION OF PRIVACY INTERESTS

In *Gertz* v. *Welch,* the Supreme Court indicates the importance of providing some protection for an individual's privacy interests. Although the effect of *Gertz* on privacy actions has not yet been determined, the Court's reasoning implies the need for a compromise between First Amendment rights and privacy interests in public disclosure cases.[49]

The Court allowed recovery in *Gertz* by a private plaintiff for false, defamatory statements without proof of actual malice. *Gertz* overruled the Supreme Court's holding in *Rosenbloom* v. *Metromedia*[50] that based the level of Constitutional protection on the presence of public interest. Instead, the Court determined Constitutional protection using a balancing test between the First Amendment and the individual's interests being protected by the state—in Gertz' case, reputation.

In performing the Balancing Test, the Court ruled that the state had a greater need to consider the individual's reputation interest, and thus limit First Amendment protection, with respect to private persons than public figures. Justice Harlan stressed that the first remedy of defamation—self-help through publicizing the truth—was unavailable to the private plaintiff who had limited access to the press. Secondly, Harlan notes that private individuals, unlike public figures, do not deliberately invite public attention to their actions.

The factors discussed by Justice Harlan also apply to public disclosure cases. The remedy of self-help is ineffective in disclosure cases—more publicity adds to the injury suffered. Further, the private plaintiff such as the indigents in *Smith* v. *Goro* have done nothing to ask for attention. Similarly, if the involuntary plaintiff can be regarded as having "invited attention," it is only to the limited situation in which he participated.

In sum, the reasoning in *Gertz* indicates that the Supreme Court will recognize some accommodation between the First Amendment and the individual's privacy interest. Arguing that all true facts should receive complete Constitutional protection ignores the Court's move towards a balancing approach.

Concern for reconciling privacy interests and First Amendment rights has also been evident in the newsgathering area. While the First Amendment extends to a reporter's pursuit of news,[51] the protection does not include certain physical invasions by the press.[52] In *Dietemann* v. *Time, Inc.,*[53] two *Life* journalists were doing an investigative study on "medical quacks." Using a ruse, they gained entry into the home of Dietemann and secretly photographed and recorded an episode involving advice by a "medical quack." When *Life* published the articles and photographs, Dietemann sued for invasion of privacy. The Ninth Circuit divided the action into intrusion and publication and held that while the publication might be privileged as newsworthy, the manner in which they were obtained was not. "The First Amendment has never been construed to accord newsmen immunity from torts or crimes committed during the course of newsgathering."[54]

Further, in cases involving protection of individuals against government disclosure of information, the Supreme Court has given Constitutional recognition to the same privacy interests involved in public disclosure cases.[55] In *Doe* v. *McMillan,*[56] a congressional committee investigating disciplinary problems in schools ordered the publication of its report, which included the absenteeism, failing grades, and disciplinary problems of individual students. The Supreme Court held that government officials, other than members of Congress, could be enjoined from further publication on the ground that it was beyond the need of the legislative process. Importantly, in a concurring opinion, Justices Douglas, Brennan, and Marshall concluded that such disclosure "for the sake of exposure" which exceeded the "sphere of legitimate legislative activity" violated the students' Constitutional rights.[57] Although the individual's privacy interests against the press are protected under state law, the government disclosure case indicates that the interest in keeping information private was considered to be of Constitutional dimension where direct government infringement was involved.

Some commentators have asserted that the right to privacy in public disclosure cases is Constitutionally protected, based on the right against governmental intrusion recognized in *Griswold* v. *Connecticut*[58] and *Roe* v. *Wade*.[59] But subsequent Supreme Court decisions have interpreted this right solely as a governmental restriction on invading the lives of citizens;[60] no state action is present in a case against private publishers.

Moreover, the type of interests at stake in public disclosure cases may, to some extent, be regarded as closer to those interests involved in the Supreme Court's recent decision in *Paul* v. *Davis*.[61] In that case, petitioner had unjustifiably distributed to local merchants a flyer containing the names and pictures of "active shoplifters."[62] Accepting as true the damage caused to plaintiff, the Supreme Court held that a person's interest in his good name and reputation does not constitute deprivation of an interest protected by the Fourteenth Amendment. The majority conceeded that Davis probably would have a cause of action for defamation under state law. However, Justice Rehnquist warned that if a state cause of action was converted into a Constitutional claim every time state action was present, "it is hard to perceive any logical stopping place to such a line of reasoning."[63] The reasoning in *Paul* v. *Davis* suggests that in public disclosure cases, even if state action can be established, the federal courts might view the interests as similar to those in *Paul* v. *Davis*; following the holding in that case, the federal courts would require plaintiffs to pursue their remedies under the state public disclosure tort.

Another interesting theory seeking a Constitutional basis for a right to privacy in public disclosure cases asserts that the right has First Amendment underpinnings.[64] According to this thesis, the First Amendment consists of two stages: transmission of information from speaker to listener and application of that information—in the mind of the person who receives it—to the individual decisions of self-governance. If the second stage is to operate effectively, the individual must be uninhibited in his actions, and control of information about oneself is essential to that goal.

> He who performs his listening and deciding in a glass house is coerced by public opinion . . . . If every magazine he reads, every rally he attends, every person he speaks to might somehow become a matter of public knowledge, he would feel inhibiting pressure.[65]

Again, however, lack of state action proves a major obstacle to this theory.

Recent Supreme Court cases thus indicate that the First Amendment does not completely bar state protection of the individual's most compelling privacy interests and that some balancing test must be developed. It is important to remember, however, that the individual's privacy *interests* in public disclosure cases do not qualify as Constitutionally protected *rights*.

WHAT LEVEL OF CONSTITUTIONAL PROTECTION?

Even if truth does not provide a complete Constitutional defense for the press in privacy actions, the Ninth Circuit in *Virgil* unduly restricts the level of protection extended to publication of true private facts. Under the *Virgil* test, if a judge or jury finds facts highly offensive according to a community more standard, the only Constitutional defense available to the press is legitimate public interest or newsworthiness. The circuit court, in effect, establishes the same level of Constitutional protection for the press as in *Time* v. *Hill*. But *Time* involved false facts of "no Constitutional value."[66] The inherent value in safeguarding expressions of truth requires that a broader ambit of Constitutional rights be available to the press in public disclosure cases than in false light privacy actions.

An accommodation between privacy interests and this broad First Amendment protection must reject the Ninth Circuit's emphasis on legitimate public interest and community mores. Instead, it is necessary to delineate an independent area in which the privacy interests at stake are most compelling—a zone of innermost privacy. This area must be identified as a matter of law, and should not depend on an elusive notion of community mores. *Truth* would serve as *an absolute Constitutional defense* for publication of all facts outside this zone, even though a judge or jury might find the facts morbid or sensational according to the mores of an individual community. First Amendment protection should be compromised only when the press infringes on the individual's most compelling privacy interests; a determination that facts are highly offensive according to proper community mores does not necessarily meet this requirement.

As the district court recognized in *Virgil,* if the facts do not violate the innermost zone of privacy, the judge or jury has no discretion to determine newsworthiness. First Amendment rights can be limited by an evaluation of legitimate public concern only when the state's justification is most compelling—i.e., protection of the individual's strongest privacy interests. For example, Virgil's escapades may be sensational according to a community mores standard, but the descriptions do not fall within the innermost zone; thus the facts receive absolute Constitutional protection without any consideration of newsworthiness.

The standard seeks to safeguard serious privacy interests while avoiding the chilling effect on the press resulting from judicial censorship. Unless the privacy interests fit within the narrow area mentioned above, judges and juries retain no power to identify "fine details as to whether the communication has great or small social value or is important or unimportant to the exposition of ideas."[67]

That the test provides a fair accommodation between the First Amendment and privacy interests can be seen in *Virgil*. The description of Virgil's extinguishing cigarettes in his mouth at parties does not intrude on the fundamental privacy interests previously listed. On the other hand. lack of a Constitutional protection for publishing these facts might create a serious chilling effect on the press; an editor would struggle to predict whether a judge or jury could find these facts offensive according to a vague community mores standard.

IDENTIFYING THE ZONE

Thomas Emerson identifies the area which falls outside the absolute protection of the First Amendment as:

The inner core of personality involving the kind of intimate details of personal life that were the Court's concern in *Griswold* . . . Descriptions or photographs of women in childbirth, of sexual intercourse, and of similar personal and intimate details of one's life would receive similar protection.[68]

Other commentators[69] have noted the existence of a "societal consensus" concerning the most private areas, including publication of the details of one's sexual experience,[70] health,[71] and distant past.[72] This consensus places an editor on notice regarding which facts might lead to liability and reduces the potential chilling effect on the press.[73] On the other hand, without a Constitutional privilege to publish true defamatory statements, an editor would be uncertain as to those facts that would result in liability; the chilling effect might prove significant.[74]

The tests developed in this paper thus far may provide a remedy for the involuntary plaintiff and the public plaintiff who has resumed a private life; Oliver Sipple's homosexual status and Briscoe's distant past fall within the zone of innermost privacy. No relief, however, will be granted to private plaintiffs, such as those in *Smith v. Goro*. In that case, the press coverage dealt mainly with the everyday lifestyle and habits of a number of poor families—facts which do not fall within the zone. Under the analysis formulated above, the press would possess an absolute First Amendment right to publish these facts, regardless of whether they were newsworthy. (The facts in *Smith v. Goro* present the strongest case because the living conditions of the poor constitute a matter of public interest.)

It is important that the state should not be permitted to award damages to the plaintiff in *Smith v. Goro* under the public disclosure tort. As discussed earlier, the press' First Amendment rights can be limited only when confronted with the most compelling privacy interests. The state advances a strong claim for protecting the private plaintiff, who takes no action to invite attention (either voluntarily or involuntarily), against any disclosures about his life. But if these disclosures do not fall within the innermost zone, the state's interest is not compelling enough to justify a significant encroachment on First Amendment rights. A contrary conclusion would result in a dangerous chilling effect; editors would have great difficulty in identifying a "private individual."

Instead, the plaintiffs in *Smith v. Goro* should rely on protection under the tort of intrusion of privacy. Plaintiffs can maintain a cause of action when the press physically invades any area in which the individual has a reasonable expectation of privacy; similarly, the individual is protected from such invasion by the government under the Fourth Amendment. The press may be liable for intrusion regardless of any public interest in the information obtained through the invasion.

Protection against intrusion by the press does not pose as direct a conflict with the First Amendment as liability under the public disclosure tort. First Amendment protection for the newsgathering process has been established more recently than protection for that which has been published; the coverage has never included crimes and torts committed during the process.[75] Moreover, the tort of intrusion bears close resemblance to the Constitutional right to privacy against governmental intrusion.

Thus in *Smith v. Goro*, the state Constitutionally could protect the individual against publication of the number of children that slept in each bedroom; the individual clearly has a reasonable expectation of privacy within his home. On the other hand, the press has an absolute Constitutional right to publish descriptions of clothing worn by children to school, or the conditions of the exterior of the house.

COMPELLING PRIVACY INTERESTS vs. NEWSWORTHY FACTS

Emerson's definition of the innermost core of privacy provides adequate protection for the individual's most serious privacy interests; he would grant *no constitutional protection* to the press within this area. Rather, the zone is "protected by rules which cut across any opposing rules of the collectivity."[76] The privacy rules should be dedicated to establish a "sphere of space that has not been dedicated to public use or control."[77] Does Emerson's balancing of First Amendment rights and the individual's privacy interests provide sufficient protection for the press? Can the individual's interest in his core of privacy rights override the press' right to publish all true information, including newsworthy facts? Does the Supreme Court's opinion in *Gertz* mandate that within the area of compelling privacy interests there can be no Constitutional protection for matters of public interest?

In *Gertz*, the Court rejected a test of Constitutional protection based on the presence of public interest. The effect of this holding on privacy cases has not been determined; in fact, the majority in *Gertz* specifically declined to decide whether the public interest test set forth in *Time* v. *Hill* still applies in false light privacy cases.[78]

> Our inquiry would involve considerations somewhat different from those discussed above if a state purported to condition civil liability on a factual misstatement whose content did not warn a reasonably prudent editor or broadcaster of its defamatory potential. Cf. *Time* v. *Hill*. Such a case is not now before us, and we intimate no view as to its proper resolution.[79]

Justice Powell, however, in a footnote to his concurring opinion in *Cox Broadcasting*, noted that *Gertz* "at least calls for a re-examination of *Time*'s public interest test."[80]

Whatever the impact of *Gertz* on false light cases, in truthful public disclosure actions, the press should always retain the Constitutional protection to publish matters of legitimate public interest. This protection must exist even when the press publishes facts that fall within the innermost privacy zone.

Unlike *Gertz* and *Hill*, in which the facts were false and of "no constitutional value," public disclosure cases deal with true facts possessing intrinsic value. A conflict between the individual's core privacy interests and the press' right to publish newsworthy facts involves the basis of the First Amendment as discussed by Meiklejohn. In allowing the state to protect core privacy interests at the expense of facts that are *not newsworthy*, we sacrifice the interest in expression of all truth; this First Amendment infringement appears limited when compared to the privacy interests at stake. But *any* restriction on the right to publish true facts of legitimate public interest directly threatens the functioning of a democracy and the ability of individuals to participate in the governing process. The *Restatement* (Second) *of Torts* acknowledges these considerations and eliminates any liability for publication of true, newsworthy facts, regardless of how embarrassing the facts may be.

> There has been a question for some time as to whether the Supreme Court will find Sec. 652D (publicity for embarrassing details of private life) to be reconcilable with the First Amendment . . . . This Section has therefore been retained with the utilization of the phrase "of legitimate concern to the public."[81]

Several examples may serve to illustrate the importance of guaranteeing First Amendment protection to all newsworthy facts, even those which invade the inner core of privacy interests. Oliver Sipple's homosexual status falls within this zone. But publication was of legitimate and immediate public concern; President Ford's failure to send a thank you note was allegedly liked to this fact. The public's right to be informed about the President's attitude towards homosexuals seems essential. Further, the gay community in San Francisco had been pressing for more publicity. "In this instance such news would have the effect of dispelling stereotypes respecting those in the gay community as being weak or ineffectual."[82] If these factors had not been present, the analysis presented would allow Sipple to recover for publication of the fact that he was a homosexual.

Events in an individual's distant past also fall within the zone of innermost privacy, but recovery should not be allowed if the events are newsworthy. In *Barbieri* v. *News Journal Publishing Co.*,[83] during a series of 1961 debates in the state senate over whether whipping should be mandatory punishment for certain crimes, the press mentioned that plaintiff had been the last person to feel the lash after conviction for breaking and entering in 1952. The court rejected Barbieri's argument that his criminal record was no longer newsworthy; the facts were of public concern because of the interest in whipping. All the details of the whipping, including Barbieri's history, were potentially important factors in evaluating the continued use of the punishment; therefore, they should receive Constitutional protection.

In *Briscoe* v. *Reader's Digest*, all facts of the hijacking, although dealing with plaintiff's distant past, merited First Amendment protection. In that case, the California court balanced "social values" and concluded that the identity of rehabilitated criminals did not qualify as newsworthy. In fact, however, the court seemed more concerned with factors unrelated to any determination of legitimate public interests: rehabilitation of the defendant and efficiency of the penal system. Under an analysis restricted to public interest considerations, the episode provided a useful example of the effect of hijacking on business, and should have been Constitutionally protected.

Similarly, in *Melvin* v. *Reed* the court based its decision that use of Mrs. Melvin's name was improper on factors unrelated to legitimate public interest in the information published.

> One of the major objectives of society . . . and of the administration of our penal system, is the rehabilitation of the fallen and the reformation of the criminal . . . . Where a person . . . has rehabilitated himself, we, as right-thinking members of society, should permit him to continue in the path of rectitude rather than throw him back into a life of shame or crime.[84]

While the facts concerning Mrs. Melvin's past history fall within the zone of innermost privacy, re-enactment of all the details of a sensational murder trial—including the name and background of defendant—receives protection as newsworthy.[85]

In both *Briscoe* and *Melvin*, the courts attempted to distinguish between publishing the facts of the episode and mentioning the plaintiff's name. "The use of appellant's true name in connection with the incidents of her former life . . . was unnecessary and indelicate and a willful and wanton disregard of that charity which should activate us in our social intercourse."[86] In effect, these decisions seek to limit First Amendment protection of true, newsworthy facts by an elusive test of good taste or "charity." The need to provide breathing space for the press, essential to the First Amendment, does not permit any distinction between publication of true, newsworthy events and publication of the name of the individual involved in that event.

DEFINING NEWSWORTHY

The theory presented in this section extends First Amendment protection to publication of facts within the innermost zone of privacy which qualify as newsworthy; at this point, it is necessary to define the scope of newsworthy or legitimate public interest.

Stanford law professor Marc Franklin[87] argues for an absolutist approach to the scope of public interest: that which the press publishes becomes by definition, newsworthy. Similarly, some commentators have defined newsworthy as anything of "widespread" public interest. As in the absolutist approach, the court virtually withdraws from the process:

> The publisher has almost certainly published any given report because he judged it to be of interest to his audience . . . . The difficulties of proving that a public item, distributed widely, was not really very interesting to a greater part of the audience, seems considerable.[88]

Professor Harry Kalven,[89] in his analysis of *Time* v. *Hill*, asserts that any standard based on an evaluation of newsworthiness will inevitably give the press broad discretion. In tort law, the privilege of public interest has been virtually defined by the press; Constitutional protection will yield the same result.

> In brief, the press will be the arbiters of it and the Court will be forced to yield to the argument that whatever the press prints is by virtue of that fact newsworthy . . . . The upshot, and it is an important one, is that the logic of *New York Times* and *Hill* taken together grants the press some measure of Constitutional protection for anything the press thinks is a matter of public interest.[90]

Other determinations of newsworthy attempt to avoid granting the press absolute control. The standards described by Kalven and Franklin result in "swallowing"[91] the tort of public disclosure; the court will simply find that anything published within the zone of innermost privacy qualifies as newsworthy because the press chose to print it. Instead, the courts should develop guidelines for judging whether legitimate public interest exists. Professor Bloustein, adopting a Meiklejohn approach, defines the scope as that which relates to the essentials of a democracy. Bloustein grants protection as newsworthy if the facts about a private life appear relevant to the public understanding necessary to self-government.[92] The Supreme Court in *Time* v. *Hill* defined legitimate public interest as extending beyond subjects related to governance. Matters of public interest

> . . . are not the preserve of political expression or comment upon public affairs . . . . We have no doubt that the subject of the *Life* article, the opening of a new play linked to the actual incident, is a matter of public interest. The line between the informing and entertaining is too elusive for protection of (freedom of the press).[93]

These tests of legitimate public interest, however, grant the courts broad discretion in evaluating facts; such discretion creates potential for abuse through judicial censorship. In *Cantrell* v. *Forest City Publishing Co.*,[94] on the other hand, the Sixth Circuit articulates a standard which narrows the court's role without abdicating all responsibility to the press.

The judgment of what is newsworthy must remain primarily a function of the publisher .... Only in cases of flagrant breach of privacy which has not been waived or obvious exploitation of public curiosity where no legitimate public interest exists should a court substitute its judgment for that of the publisher.[95]

Under the *Cantrell* standard, the court would deny Constitutional protection as newsworthy only in cases involving "clear abuse" of editor's discretion. The Sixth Circuit's standard is especially appealing in allowing "breathing space" for the press.[96] One of the Supreme Court's most important concerns in the First Amendment area has been to prevent any chilling effect on the press. For this reason, the Court has extended Constitutional protection to false defamatory statements "of no constitutional value." Similarly, an editor's judgment regarding legitimate public interest must not be completely subject to the Monday morning discretion of a judge or jury.[97]

AS A MATTER OF LAW

Both steps of the constitutional test developed in this section—determining if the facts are within the zone of innermost privacy and, if so, considering whether they are matters of legitimate public interest—must be decided as a matter of law by the judge. In *Virgil*, instead of reaching its own determination, the court of appeals entrusted First Amendment protection to the jury, instructing the district court to retain only the "veto" power of summary judgment and judgment n.o.v.

We cannot agree that the First Amendment requires that the question must be confined to one of law to be decided by the judge. Courts have not yet gone so far in other areas of the law involving First Amendment problems, such as libel and obscenity.[98]

In ruling that the First Amendment protection should be determined by a jury, the Ninth Circuit ignored Supreme Court decisions holding that the courts must decide, as a matter of law, the application of a Constitutional standard to the content of a publication.[99] First Amendment protection should not be subject to the passions of juries. For example, in *Rosenblatt v. Baer*,[100] the Court stated that it was the judge's responsibility to determine whether respondent was a public official:

Such a course will both lessen the possibility that a jury will use the cloak of a general verdict to punish unpopular ideas and assure an appellant court the record and findings required for review of constitutional decisions.[101]

In *Monitor Patriot Co. v. Roy*,[102] a determination of "relevance" was for the court, since a jury

... is unlikely to be neutral with respect to the content of speech and holds real danger of becoming an instrument for suppression of those "vehement, caustic, and sometimes, unpleasantly sharp attacks," which must be protected if the guarantees of the First and Fourteenth Amendments are to prevail.[103]

In *Pape v. Time, Inc.*,[104] the question of "rational relevance" was for the Court so that the publisher would not be "virtually at the mercy of an unguided discretion of a jury." The Supreme Court has also ruled as a matter of law regarding whether the content of publications met the standard of "actual malice," including falsity, defamatory content, failure to retract, and investigatory failure in *New York Times* v. *Sullivan*,[105] falsity in *Curtis Publishing Co.* v. *Butts*,[106] and ill will and negligence in *Garrison* v. *Louisiana*.[107]

Further, the Ninth Circuit in *Virgil* erred in refusing to recognize that even if a jury can determine First Amendment protection, the court must be particularly vigilant in exercising its power of summary judgment. The *Virgil* court states that "the *manner* in which the evidence is to be examined in light of that standard is the same as in all other cases in which it is claimed that a case should not go to the jury."[108] Other circuit court opinions, however, have stressed that the court must be extremely wary of failure to grant summary judgment in cases involving the First Amendment. As Judge Skelley Wright observes in *Washington Post* v. *Koegh*:[109]

> For the stake here, if harassment succeeds, is free debate . . . . The threat of being put to the defense of a lawsuit brought by a popular public official, may be as chilling to the exercise of First Amendment freedoms as fear of the outcome of the lawsuit itself . . . . Unless persons, including newspapers, desiring to exercise their First Amendment rights, are assured freedom from the harassment of lawsuits, they will tend to become self-censors.[110]

CONCLUSION

The section has attempted to reach an accommodation between the state's needs to protect the individual's compelling privacy interests and the press' right under the First Amendment to publish true facts. The tests developed place restrictions on the press *only* when the innermost zone of privacy is at stake; further, the state can *never* prohibit publication of true newsworthy facts, regardless of their privacy content. In sum, this analysis advises that the Supreme Court answer the broad question left open in *Cox Broadcasting* by concluding that the state can Constitutionally grant recovery under the public disclosure tort for publication of true facts—but only in the most narrow circumstances.

NOTES

[1] Warren and Brandeis, "The Right of Privacy," 4 Harv. L. Rev. 193 (1890).

[2] Prosser, "Privacy," 48 Calif. L. Rev. 383 (1960) has analyzed the law of privacy as comprising four distinct elements. In addition to the public disclosure tort, Prosser lists: 1) Intrusion upon plaintiff's physical solitude or seclusion by physical interference, eavesdropping, etc.; 2) publicity which places the plaintiff in a false light in the public eye; and 3) appropriation for defendant's benefit or advantage of plaintiff's name or likeness.

[3] According to Prosser, *id.*, the public disclosure tort has three elements: 1) The disclosure must be to the public at large; 2) The facts disclosed must be private at the time; and 3) The facts must be offensive to a reasonable man of ordinary sensibilities. The *Restatement* (Second) *of Torts*, Sec. 652D of Tentative Draft No. 21 also requires that the plaintiff prove as one of the elements of the tort, that the facts are "not of legitimate concern to the public."

[4] See *Jenkins* v. *Dell Publishing Co.*, 251 F.2d 447, 451 (3rd Cir. 1958):

> For present purposes, news need be defined as comprehending events such as in common experience are likely to be of public interest . . . . It is clear that information and entertainment are not mutually exclusive categories. A large part of the matter which appears in newspapers and news magazines today is not published or read for the value or importance of the information it conveys. Some readers are attracted by shocking news. Others are titillated by sex in the news. Still others are entertained by news which has an incongruous or ironic aspect.

[5] The California test includes balancing: 1) The social value of the facts published; 2) The depth of the article's intrusion into ostensibly private affairs; and 3) The extent to which the party voluntarily acceded to a position of public notoriety. *Briscoe* v. *Reader's Digest Association*, 4 Cal. 3d 529, 483 P.2d 34, 93 Cal.Rpt. 865 (1971). See also *Melvin* v. *Reed*, 112 Cal. App. 285, 297 P. 91 (1931).

596   Defamation and Advertising

[6] See *Mertze* v. *Associated Press*, 230 S.C. 330, 95 S.E.2d 606 (1952), holding that the birth of a son to a 12 year old girl was privileged as newsworthy. *Sweeneke* v. *Pathe News*, 16 F.Supp. 746, 749 (E.D. N.Y. 1936), Motion pictures of women exercising in a gymnasium had public interest "so long as a large portion of the female population continues its present concern about any increase in poundage"; *Jones* v. *Herald Post Co.*, 230 Ky. 227, 18 S.W.2d 972 (1929), action for invasion of privacy barred in case where newspaper printed an identifiable shocked wife after she had witnessed the murder of her husband on the grounds that the murder was an event of public interest.

But see *Barber* v. *Time*, 348 Mo. 1199, 159 S.W.2d 291 (1942)—Recovery awarded against *Time* for publication of an article and picture of a woman labeled the starving glutton. The court agreed that the illness was newsworthy but said that the name and picture conveyed no medical information and was not essential to the story.

[7] Note, "First Amendment and Public Disclosure," 124 U. of Pa. L. Rev. 1385, 1387 (1976).

[8] "In one form or another, the right of privacy is by this time recognized and accepted in all but a very few jurisdictions." Only four states have explicitly rejected the tort. Prosser, *Handbook of the Law of Torts*, Sec. 117 p. 801 (1971).

[9] See *Griswold* v. *Connecticut*, 381 U.S. 479 (1965).

[10] 385 U.S. 374 (1967).

[11] *Id.* at 383, n.7.

[12] 420 U.S. 469 (1975).

[13] Ga. Code Ann. Sec. 26-9001 (1972):

It shall be unlawful for any news media or any other person to print and publish, broadcast, televise, or disseminate through any other medium of public dissemination or cause to be printed and published, broadcast, televised, or disseminated in any newspaper, magazine, periodical, or other publication published in this State or through any radio or television broadcast originating in the State the name or identity of any female who may have been raped or upon whom an assault with intent to commit rape may have been made. Any person or corporation violating the provisions of this section shall upon conviction, be punished as for a misdemeanor.

[14] *Cox Broadcasting Corp.* v. *Cohn*, 231 Ga. 60, 68, 200 S.E.2d 133, 134 (1973), rehearing denied, 231 Ga. 67, 200 S.E.2d 133 (1973), rev'd, 420 U.S. 469 (1975).

[15] 420 U.S. 469, 491.

[16] Prosser, *supra* note 2, at 422-23.

[17] The information about Sipple first appeared in a column in the *San Francisco Chronicle* on September 24, 1975. The article in the *Los Angeles Times* on September 25, 1975, indicated that Sipple was "active among San Francisco gays," was "a prominent figure in the gay community," and conceded himself to be a member of the "court" of Mike Caringi, who was elected "emperor of San Francisco" by the gay community. The article also reported that President Ford had refused thus far to thank Sipple because of his activities and that the performance of a heroic act by one associated with the community would have "enormous national ramifications" for improving the image of homosexuals. The *Los Angeles Times* moved for summary judgment, on the grounds that the material published was Constitutionally protected as newsworthy. The *Times* also filed a motion to dismiss on the grounds that the facts were not "private" since they had been published previously in *The Chronicle* and had been freely revealed to a *Times* reporter by plaintiff.

The California Superior Court on June 14, 1976, denied the motion for summary judgment, motion to strike and demurrer of The Chronicle Publishing Company and denied the motion for summary judgment, motion to strike, and demurrers of The Times Mirror Company. Discovery is currently being conducted.

[18] 4 Cal. 3d 529, 483 P.2d 34, 93 Cal.Rpt. 866 (1971).

[19] *Id.* at 537, 483 P.2d at 39-40, 93 Cal.Rpt. at 871-73.

[20] 112 Cal. App. 285, 297 P. 91 (1931).

[21] 113 F.2d 806 (2d Cir.), *cert. denied*, 311 U.S. 711 (1940).

[22] *Id.* at 809.

[23] 66 Misc.2d 1011 (1970).

[24] Memorandum in Behalf of Defendant *New York Magazine*, p. 16.

[25] 66 Misc.2d 1011, 1014, 1015. The court also refused to dismiss on grounds that there were issues of fact to be decided at trial as to whether the publications were truthful and whether releases for use of pictures had been properly obtained. At the same time, the court denied plaintiff's motion for a preliminary injunction against Random House. The case was settled before trial.

[26] 527 F.2d 1122 (9th Cir. 1975), *cert. denied*. 96 S.Ct. 2215 (1976).

[27] Plaintiff admitted that he willingly gave interviews but alleged that he "revoked consent" upon being informed that the article was not confined to testimonials to his physical prowess. *Id.* at 1124.

[28] For example:

Virgil's carefree style at the Wedge appears to have emanated from some escapades in his younger days, such as the time at a party when a young lady approached him and asked him where she might find an ashtray. "Why my dear, right here," said Virgil, taking here lighted cigarette and extinguishing it in his mouth. He also won a small bet one time by burning a hole in a dollar bill that was resting on the back of his hand. In the process he also burned two holes in his wrist . . . "Every summer I'd work construction and dive off billboards to hurt myself or drop loads of lumber on myself to collect unemployment so I could surf at the Wedge . . . I guess I used to live a pretty reckless life. I think I might have been drunk most of the time. I fought a bull in Mexico and got knocked down, destroyed . . . . I worked on a tuna boat and got down in the nets to throw out the sharks that we had collected with the tuna . . . I do what feels good . . . If it makes me feel good, whether it's against the law or not, I do it."

Thomas Kirkpatrick, "The Closest Thing to Being Born," *Sports Illustrated*, February 22, 1971, pp. 71–72.
[29]28 U.S.C. 1292(b).
[30]On April 10, 1974, the Ninth Circuit withheld further consideration of the appeal pending the Supreme Court's decision in *Cox Broadcasting*, which presented the possibility that the questions involved in Virgil would be decided in that case. When the Supreme Court specifically declined to pass on those issues, the Ninth Circuit resumed consideration.
[31]527 F.2d at 1127.
[32]*Id.* at 1128.
[33]*Id.* at 1128.
[34]*Restatement* (Second) *of Torts*, Sec. 652F (Tentative Draft No. 13, 1967).
[35]527 F.2d at 1131.
[36]*Virgil* v. *Time*, Civil No. 71–179–GJ, (S.D. Cal. 1976).
[37]418 U.S. 323 (1974).
[38]420 U.S. at 500 (Powell, J. concurring). The majority in *Cox Broadcasting* disagreed with Powell's analysis. "The Court has nevertheless carefully left open the question whether the First and Fourteenth Amendments require that truth be recognized as a defense in a defamation action brought by a private person as distinguished from a public official or public figure." 420 U.S. at 490, Justice Powell, who wrote *Gertz* presents a more convincing argument.
[39]But see Bloustein, "Privacy as an Aspect of Human Dignity: An Answer to Dean Prosser," 39 N.Y.U. L. Rev. 962 (1964). Bloustein argues that loss of reputation is only incidental to the real wrong "which is made out even if the public takes a sympathetic, rather than a hostile view of the facts." The real complaint is that some aspect of an individual's life has been held up to public scrutiny at all.
[40]Bloustein, "Privacy, Tort Law, and the Constitution: Is Warren and Bradeis' Tort Petty and Unconstitutional as Well?" 46 Texas L. Rev. 611, 619 (1968).
[41]483 P.2d at 37.
[42]Complaint filed in *Oliver Sipple* v. *The Chronicle Publishing Co. et al.*, Superior Court of San Francisco, California Paragraph XII. Motion for summary judgment and motion to dismiss denied June 11, 1976. See *supra* note 17.
[43]See Brennan, "The Supreme Court and the Meiklejohn Interpretation of the First Amendment," 79 Harv. L. Rev. 1 (1965).
[44]Meiklejohn, "The First Amendment is an Absolute," 1961 Sup. Ct. Rev. 245, 255, 256.
[45]527 F.2d at 1128.
[46]Emerson, *The System of Freedom of Expression* 6 (1970).
[47]*Id.* at 554.
[48]*Id.* at 556.
[49]See Beytagh, "Privacy and A Free Press: A Contemporary Conflict in Values," 20 N.Y.L.F. 453, 482 (1975).
[50]403 U.S. 30 (1971).
[51]See *Branzburg* v. *Hayes*, 408 U.S. 665, 681 (1972).
[52]See Note, "First Amendment and Public Disclosure," *supra*, note 7 at 1407.
[53]284 F.Supp. 925 (C.D. Cal. 1968), *aff'd*, 449 F.2d 245 (9th Cir. 1971).
[54]*Id.* at 249.
[55]See Note, "First Amendment and Public Disclosure," *supra*, note 7.
[56]412 U.S. 306 (1973).
[57]*Id.* at 328 (Douglas, J., concurring).
[58]381 U.S. 479 (1965).
[59]410 U.S. 113 (1973).
[60]Comment, "The First Amendment Privilege and Public Disclosure of Private Facts," 25 Cath. L. Rev. 271, 292 (1976).
[61]96 S.Ct. 1155 (1976).
[62]Respondent had been arrested on a charge of shoplifting, but upon his plea of not guilty, the charge had been "filed away with leave (to reinstate)." Shortly after circulation of the flyer the charge was dismissed.
[63]*Id.* at 1157.
[64]Note, "Privacy in the First Amendment," 82 Yale L.J. 1462 (1973).
[65]*Id.* at 1466.
[66]*Gertz* v. *Robert Welch, Inc.*, 418 U.S. 323, 340 (1974).
[67]Emerson, *supra*, note 46 at 556.
[68]*Id.* at 557.

[69] See Note, "First Amendment and Public Disclosure," *supra*, note 7 at 1411.
[70] See *Garner v. Triangle Publications*, 97 F. Supp. 546 (S.D. N.Y. 1951).
[71] See *Barber v. Time, Inc.*, 348 Mo. 1199, 159 S.W.2d 291 (1942).
[72] See text, p. 4.
[73] See Note, "First Amendment and Public Disclosure," *supra*, note 7 at 1411.
[74] Miller, *Assault on Privacy* 193 (1971).
[75] See *Dietemann v. Time, Inc.*, 284 F.Supp. 925 (C.D. Cal. 1968), *aff'd*, 449 F.2d 245 (9th Cir. 1971).
[76] Emerson, *supra*, note 46 at 556.
[77] *Id*. at 556.
[78] After *Gertz*, it seems difficult to argue that the public interest test of *Time v. Hill* would still apply in a false light situation involving a private individual. Although it is possible to distinguish false light cases from libel actions—i.e., the facts in the privacy actions may not necessarily be defamatory—the interests protected by the two actions seem almost identical. In *Cantrell v. Forest City Publishing Co.*, 484 F.2d 150 (6th Cir. 1973), *rev'd* and *remanded*, 419 U.S. 245, 250, the Supreme Court again noted that the impact of *Gertz* on false light cases remained an open question:

> This case presents no occasion to consider whether a State may Constitutionally apply a more relaxed standard of liability for a publisher or broadcaster of false statements injurious to a private individual under a false-light theory of invasion of privacy, or whether the Constitutional standard announced in *Time v. Hill* applies to all false-light cases.

[79] 418 U.S. 323, 348 (1974).
[80] 420 U.S. 469, 498 (1975).
[81] *Restatement* (Second) *of Torts*, Tentative Draft No. 21, pp. 86–87.
[82] Defendant Memorandum of Points and Authorities, *Oliver Sipple v. The Chronicle Publishing Company et al.*, Superior Court of San Francisco, California, p. 3.
[83] 189 A.2d 773 (1963).
[84] 297 P. 91, 93 (1931).
[85] It is possible that *Cox Broadcasting* can be interpreted as requiring that all facts which have appeared on a public record—no matter how long ago—automatically receive First Amendment protection.
[86] 297 P. 91, 93 (1931).
[87] Franklin, "A Constitutional Problem in Privacy Protection: Legal Inhibitions on Reporting of Fact," 16 Stan. L. Rev. 107 (1963).
[88] Comment, "The Right of Privacy: Normative-Descriptive Confusion in the Defense of Newsworthiness," 30 U. Chi. L. Rev. 722, 725 (1963).
[89] Kalven, "The Reasonable Man and The First Amendment: Hill, Butts, and Walker," 1967 Sup. Ct. Rev. 267.
[90] *Id*. at 284.
[91] Kalven, "Privacy in Tort Law: Were Warren and Brandeis Wrong?" 31 Law and Contempt. Prob. 326, 336 (1966).
[92] Bloustein, "First Amendment and Privacy," 28 Rut. L. Rev. 41, 57 (1974).
[93] 385 U.S. at 388.
[94] 484 F.2d 150 (6th Cir. 1973), *rev'd* and *remanded*, 419 U.S. 245.
[95] 484 F.2d at 156–7.
[96] See *Miami Herald Publishing Co. v. Tornillo*, 418 U.S. 241 (1974).
[97] The Supreme Court did not pass on the issue of "editor's discretion" standard since it found that the problem was not involved. 419 U.S. at 250.
[98] 527 F.2d at 1130.
[99] Petition for a writ of certiorari to the United States Court of Appeals for the Ninth Circuit, *Time v. Virgil*, see *Virgil v. Time*, 527 F.2d 1122 (9th Cir. 1975), p. 16.
[100] 383 U.S. 75 (1966).
[101] *Id*. at 88, n. 15.
[102] 401 U.S. 265 (1970).
[103] *Id*. at 277.
[104] 401 U.S. 279, 291 (1971).
[105] 376 U.S. 254 (1964).
[106] 388 U.S. 130 (1967).
[107] 379 U.S. 64 (1964).
[108] 527 F.2d at 1130.
[109] 365 F.2d 965 (D.C. Cir. 1966).
[110] *Id*. at 968.

SELECTED BIBLIOGRAPHY

Emerson, *The System of Freedom of Expression*, (New York: Random House, 1970).

Miller, *Assault on Privacy*, (Ann Arbor, Mich.: University of Michigan Press, 1971).

Periodicals

Beytagh, "Privacy and a Free Press: A Contemporary Conflict in Values," 20 N.Y.L.F. 453 (1975).

Bloustein, "First Amendment and Privacy," 28 Rut. L. Rev. 41 (1974).

———, "Privacy as an Aspect of Human Dignity: An Answer to Dean Prosser," 39 N.Y.U.L. Rev. 962 (1964).

———, "Privacy, Tort Law and the Constitution: Is Warren and Brandeis' Tort Petty and Unconstitutional as Well?" 46 Tex. L. Rev. 611 (1966).

Brennan, "The Supreme Court and the Meiklejohn Interpretation of the First Amendment," 79 Harv. L. Rev. 1 (1965).

Franklin, "A Constitutional Problem in Privacy Protection: Legal Inhibitions on Reporting of Fact," 16 Stan. L. Rev. 107 (1963).

Kalven, "Privacy in Tort Law: Were Warren and Brandeis Wrong?" 31 Law and Contemp Prob. 326 (1966).

———, "The Reasonable Man and the First Amendment: Hill, Butts, and Walker, 1967 Sup. Ct. Rev. 267.

Meiklejohn, "The First Amendment as an Absolute," 1961 Sup. Ct. Rev. 245.

Nimmer, "The Right to Speak from *Times* to *Time*: First Amendment Theory Applied to Libel and Misapplied to Privacy," 56 Calif. L. Rev. 935 (1968).

Pember, "Privacy and the Press Since *Time Inc.* v. *Hill*, 50 Wash. L. Rev. 57 (1974).

———, "Privacy and the Press: The Defense of Newsworthiness," *Journalism Quarterly* (Spring 1968), 14.

Prosser, "Privacy," 48 Calif. L. Rev. 383 (1960).

Warren and Brandeis, "The Right of Privacy," 4 Harv. L. Rev. 193 (1890).

Note, "First Amendment and Public Disclosure," 124 U. Pa. 1385 (1976).

Comment, "The First Amendment Privilege and Public Disclosure of Private Facts," 25 Cath. L. Rev. 271 (1976).

Note, "Privacy in the First Amendment," 82 Yale L.J. 140 (1973).

Comment, "The Right of Privacy and Normative-Descriptive Confusion in the Defense of Newsworthiness," 30 U. Chi. L. Rev. 722 (1963).

Comment, *Virgil* v. *Time*," 29 Vand. L. Rev. 870 (1976).

Section 3

Cases

KILIAN v. DOUBLEDAY & CO., INC.
79 A2d 657, 367 Pa. 117 (1951)

Horace Stern, Justice.

In this action for libel the jury rendered a verdict in favor of defendant. Plaintiff appeals from the refusal of the court below to grant him a new trial.

This is the way in which the allegedly libelous article came to be written: At the American University in Washington a course in English was conducted by Don M. Wolfe, the students being disabled veterans of World War II. The course consisted, in part, of the writing by the students of essays or stories about their personal experiences in the war; their compositions would be submitted to Dr. Wolfe, who suggested corrections and revisions. Dr. Wolfe conceived the idea of having these stories published in book form, and, after an original publication by another concern, he entered into a contract with defendant, Doubleday & Company, for that purpose. Each student in the class, 53 in all, contributed at least one article. The book was published under the title "The Purple Testament", and it was advertised in the jacket as consisting of "the native eloquence of *absolute honesty*," and as constituting "the fragments of their (the authors') *own intimate experiences*". Some 9000 copies were sold and distributed throughout the United States. Among the articles was one by Joseph M. O'Connell which gave rise to the present suit.

O'Connell was a soldier who had been seriously injured during the course of the Normandy invasion and was hospitalized from August to October, 1944, at a station hospital about 12 miles from Lichfield, England, where there was a large replacement depot. In the original draft of the article which he wrote he narrated incidents said to have occurred at the Lichfield camp and which, he testified at the trial, were described to him by individuals who had allegedly witnessed them. Dr. Wolfe, to whom he submitted the draft several times, stated that he "thought it was interesting, and that it was the first time he had heard about it", but twice returned it with the suggestion that O'Connell should use "more descriptive detail", that he should "make it more vivid", that it "did not have in it the sights, sounds and bits of conversation necessary to make the story readable". The result was that where as O'Connell had originally written the article in the third person he now wrote it, in order to "make it more vivid", in the first person, purporting that the incidents he narrated occurred under his own personal observation and in his own experience.

The story as it finally appeared in "The Purple Testament", may be condensed as follows: I (O'Connell) and my buddy, while being transferred in an ambulance from one hospital to another in England, reached a big army camp near Lichfield. The camp was dreary and ugly; it reminded me of the rotten filthy German prison camps I had seen in France. As we lay in the ambulance we heard a loud voice outside shouting: "Just let me catch one of you sons o' bitches loaf on this detail and you'll get twenty lashes when you get back tonight." A group of four men came to carry us into the hospital; they were all dressed in blue pants and shirts with a large letter "P" sewed on their clothes. The same loud voice I had heard a few minutes before said: "you're not supposed to talk to these—prisoners." A big heavy-set sergeant stepped closer to me and said, "All they are is a bunch of cowards. They are all too yellow to go back when they finish with this prison." The sergeant ordered them to carry us to the hospital; as they were placing me there in my bed I noticed that one of them had all the fingers of his right hand missing and three fingers of his left. Could such things be allowed in our army? If so, it was being covered up by the brass, and the brass were making suckers of the American people. A ward attendant limping around outside the room came in and said: "I was blown out of a tank; all the muscle of my right leg was blown away. . . . I came through this way on my way (back) to combat. One day the old man (Colonel _____) ordered us out on a ten-mile hike. After about two miles I fell flat on my face. They ordered me on, but I couldn't go. So the next day they took me before the old dictator. He ordered me before a quick court martial. I got six months of hard labor. The doctor said I was unfit for hard labor, so they assigned me to this hospital. I'm still a prisoner. The other night a guard caught me stealing a piece of bread from the kitchen, and I got fifty lashes for it." He showed us the welts on his back; he also rolled his pants leg up so we could see his leg. He said that if the prisoners were caught smoking they were whipped or clubbed. In the morning the old colonel himself came along to inspect the hospital. He wasn't a big guy, but he was stockily built. Behind his glasses his eyes were mean. He looked like a man who enjoys seeing another man suffer. He was surrounded by a lot of other officers. None of them looked good to me. After one scowling glance at Red (my buddy) and me, he left. As we were being carried down the hall of the ward the big sergeant was clubbing a G.I. in the corner, while some officers looked on. I only hoped that some day I would meet up with that big sergeant and the rest of the people that ran that prison. The death chair would be too good for them. But as always, Colonel _____ and the rest of the responsible officers will be protected by the big brass. Mark my work Colonel _____ and his bullies will get off light. That is Lichfield justice.

It is not questioned that by "Colonel _____", the "old dictator", and "the old colonel", was meant Colonel Kilian, the present plaintiff who was the commanding officer of the Lichfield camp. At the end of the article as published there was appended a footnote which Dr. Wolfe himself had added and which stated: "On August 29, 1946, the Associated Press reported that Colonel James A. Kilian was convicted 'of permitting cruel and unusual punishment of American soldiers.' He was reprimanded by the military court and fined $500. — Editor." This insertion was obviously intended to give the impression that what was said or implied in the article in regard to Colonel Kilian was corroborated by his conviction, and further that, as the author of the article had predicted, he "got off light".

The fact in regard to plaintiff's trial before a military court in 1946 is this: He was charged with *authorizing, aiding* and *abetting* the imposition of cruel, unusual and unauthorized punishments upon prisoners in confinement at the depot of which he was the Commanding Officer. The punishments referred to were itemized in the charge. A second specification was that he *knowingly permitted* the imposition of such punishments. As to the first specification—authorizing, aiding and abetting—he was aquitted; as to the second specification—knowingly permitting—he was aquitted of *knowingly* permitting and found guilty merely of *permitting;* in other words, he was convicted of neglect, but not of actual wrongdoing or of acquiescing in what occurred. Moreover, many of the alleged punishments specified in the charge as having been "permitted" were deleted by the court because they were not supported by the evidence.

It will be noted that O'Connell's article purported to describe in factual style a series of specific happenings which he professed to have seen or experienced at Lichfield, thereby giving them the verisimilitude naturally to be expected from the author's statement that he himself witnessed such occurrences as distinguished from assertions made on the basis of hearing only. It will further be noted

602 Defamation and Advertising

that O'Connell alleges that he saw Colonel Kilian face to face, and describes him as having "mean eyes" and looking like a sadist. There is also the possible implication in the article, as a jury might find, that the plaintiff's reprehensible conduct consisted, not merely of neglect properly to supervise the administration of the camp, but, if not of actual participation in the cruelty practiced on the prisoners, at least of knowledge that it was being inflicted and conscious indifference to its perpetration: otherwise the author would scarcely have said of "the people who ran that prison" (who, as the context shows, were meant by him to include plaintiff) that "the death chair would be too good for them"

As affirmative defense to the action defendant pleaded justification on the ground that the publication was *"a true and accurate account of events which were observed by the author of the article in question".* How is that defense supported by the testimony presented at the trial? As far as O'Connell being an eye-witness of any of the alleged happenings at the camp is concerned, he admitted on the witness stand that he never was at Lichfield; therefore, his article, in that respect, was wholly false. Defendant produces as witness three soldiers who *were* at Lichfield, who testified to punishments inflicted on them or observed by them as imposed on others, but none of the incidents they described tended to prove that a single one of the events narrated in the O'Connell article actually occurred; therefore such testimony was not properly admissible to prove the truth of the publication. While in order to support a defense of truth, it is necessary merely to prove that it was *substantially* true, and while, therefore, if the testimony of those witnesses had shown a variance merely in the details of the events described in the article it would nevertheless have been admissible as giving support to the plea of truth, it furnished no such support by proving that other and wholly different incidents occurred although these also may have been equally blameworthy. If, for instance, one were to assert that A had embezzled $50 from the X Bank he would not support the truth of such allegation by testimony that A embezzled $100 from the Y Bank,—especially if he were also falsely to state that he actually saw A committing this other embezzlement. "Specific charges cannot be justified by showing the plaintiff's general bad character; and if the accusation is one of particular misconduct, such as stealing a watch from A, it is not enough to show a different offense, even though it be a more serious one, such as stealing a clock from A, or six watches from B". Prosser on Torts, p. 855, Section 95. "In Skinner v. Powers, 1 Send. 451, it is said by Chief Justice Savage, that a charge of misconduct *of any specific kind* is not justified by proving plaintiff guilty of misconduct of a similar character. The misconduct relied upon in justification must be proved as broad as the charge; and the proof of the truth of one out of many charges does not constitute a justification." *Buford* v. *Wible*, 32 Pa. 95, 96, 97. To the same effect see Rest. Torts, Section 582, comment e. None of defendant's testimony showed any instances at the camp, as alleged in O'Connell's article, of lashing, of cursing prisoners, of having a soldier whose fingers were misssing act as a stretcher bearer, of ordering a badly wounded veteran on a ten-mile hike. It is to be added that defendant's witnesses who testified to what they observed or experienced at Lichfield all admitted that they never saw plaintiff present at any time when any of the alleged occurrences happened; the author of the article himself admitted that when he wrote his story he had never seen plaintiff and did not even know his name. It is obvious that there was not a shred of testimony presented at the trial to prove either that the author of the article saw any of the events he narrated, or that those events or even substantially similar ones occurred, or that plaintiff

---

*Defendant also pleaded as an affirmative defense that the publication was justified on the ground that it was privileged and based upon reasonable or probable cause.

was aware of any such happenings, or that he sanctioned them, or that he was a "dictator", or that in his very appearance he looked like a man who would enjoy seeing another man suffer. The court, therefore, was in error in submitting to the jury, as it did, the question whether the publication was substantially true.

Counsel for plaintiff submitted points for charge requesting the court to declare that there was no evidence to sustain defendant's plea of justification on the ground that the publication was a true and accurate account of the observations of the author; that there was a material difference between statements as to what an author himself observed and what he was told by someone else; that there was no evidence to support the truth of the specific incidents narrated in the published article. Those requests, for the reasons hereinbefore discussed, should have been granted.

Judgment reversed and a new trial awarded.

NEW YORK TIMES COMPANY v. SULLIVAN
376 U.S. 254 (1964)

Mr. Justice Brennan delivered the opinion of the Court.

We are required in this case to determine for the first time the extent to which the Constitutional protections for speech and press limit a State's power to award damages in a libel action brought by a public official against critics of his official conduct.

Respondent L.B. Sullivan is one of the three elected Commissioners of the City of Montgomery, Alabama. He testified that he was "Commissioner of Public Affairs and the duties are supervision of the Police Department, Fire Department, Department of Cemetery, and Department of Scales." He brought this civil libel action against the four individual petitioners, who are Negroes and Alabama clergymen, and against petitioner of New York Times Company, a New York corporation which publishes the *New York Times,* a daily newspaper. A jury in the Circuit Court of Montgomery County awarded him damages of $500,000, the full amount claimed, against all the petitioners, and the Supreme Court of Alabama affirmed.

Respondent's complaint alleged that he had been libeled by statements in a full-page advertisement that was carried in the *New York Times* on March 29, 1960. Entitled "Heed Their Rising Voices," the advertisement began by stating that "As the whole world knows by now, thousands of Southern Negro students are engaged in widespread nonviolent demonstrations in positive affirmation of the right to live in human dignity as guaranteed by the U.S. Constitution and the Bill of Rights." It went on to charge that "in their efforts to uphold these guarantees, they are being met by an unprecedented wave of terror by those who would deny and negate that document which the whole world looks upon as setting the pattern for modern freedom . . . ." Succeeding paragraphs purported to illustrate the "wave of terror" by describing certain alleged events. The text concluded with an appeal for funds for three purposes: support of the student movement, "the struggle for the right-to-vote," and the legal defense of Dr. Martin Luther King, Jr., leader of the movement, against a perjury indictment then pending in Montgomery.

The text appeared over the names of 64 persons, many widely known for their activities in public affairs, religion, trade unions, and the performing arts. Below these names, and under a line reading "We in the south who are struggling daily for dignity and freedom warmly endorse this appeal," appeared the names of the four individual petitioners and of 16 other persons, all but two of whom were identified as clergymen in various Southern cities. The advertisement was signed at the bottom of the page by the "Committee to Defend Martin Luther King and the Struggle for Freedom in the South," and the officers of the Committee were listed.

Of the ten paragraphs of text in the advertisement, the third and a portion of the sixth were the basis of respondent's claim of libel. They read as follows:

Third paragraph:

> In Montgomery, Alabama, after students sang "My Country, 'Tis of Thee" on the State Capitol steps, their leaders were expelled from school, and truckloads of police armed with shotguns and teargas ringed the Alabama State College Campus. When the entire student body protested to state authorities by refusing to re-register, their dining hall was padlocked in an attempt to starve them into submission.

Sixth paragraph:

> Again and again the Southern violators have answered Dr. King's peaceful protests with intimidation and violence. They have bombed his home almost killing his wife and child. They have assaulted his person. They have arrested him seven times—for "speeding, loitering, and similar offenses. And now they have charged him with "perjury"—a *felony* under which they could imprison him for *ten years* . . . .

Although neither of these statements mentions respondent by name, he contended that the word "police" in the third paragraph referred to him as the Montgomery Commissioner who supervised the Police Department, so that he was being accused of "ringing" the campus with police. He further claimed that the paragraph would be read as imputing to the police, and hence to him, the padlocking of the dining hall in order to starve the students into submission. As to the sixth paragraph, he contended that since arrests are ordinarily made by the police, the statement "They have arrested (Dr. King) seven times" would be read as referring to him; he further contended that the "They" who did the arresting would be equated with the "They" who committed the other described acts and with the "Southern violators." Thus, he argued, the paragraph would be read as accusing the Montgomery police, and hence him, of answering Dr. King's protests with "intimidation and violence," bombing his home, assaulting his person, and charging him with perjury. Respondent and six other Montgomery residents testified that they read some of all of the statements as referring to him in his capacity as Commissioner.

It is uncontroverted that some of the statements contained in the two paragraphs were not accurate descriptions of events which occurred in Montgomery. Although Negro students staged a demonstration on the State Capitol steps, they sang the National Anthem and not "My Country, 'Tis of Thee." Although nine students were expelled by the State Board of Education, this was not for leading the demonstration at the Capitol, but for demanding service at a lunch counter in the Montgomery County Courthouse on another day. Not the entire student body, but most of it, had protested the expulsion, not by refusing to register, but by boycotting classes on a single day; virtually all the students did register for the ensuing semester. The campus dining hall was not padlocked on any occasion, and the only students who may have been barred from eating there were the few who had neither signed a preregistration application nor requested temporary meal tickets. Although the police were deployed near the campus in large numbers on three occasions, they did not at any time "ring" the campus, and they were not called to the campus in connection with the demonstration on the State Capitol steps, as the third paragraph implied. Dr. King had not been arrested seven times, but only four; and although he claimed to have been assaulted some years earlier in connection with his arrest for loitering outside a courtroom, one of the officers who made the arrest denied that there was such an assault.

On the premise that the charges in the sixth paragraph could be read as referring to him, respondent was allowed to prove that he had not participated in the events described. Although Dr. King's home had in fact been bombed twice when his wife and child were there, both of these occasions antedated respondent's tenure as Commissioner, and the police were not only not implicated in the bombings, but had made every effort to apprehend those who were. Three of Dr. King's four arrests took place before respondent became Commissioner. Although Dr. King had in fact been indicted (he was subsequently acquitted) and two counts of perjury, each of which carried a possible five-year sentence, respondent had nothing to do with procuring the indictment.

Respondent made no effort to prove that he suffered actual pecuniary loss as a result of the alleged libel. One of his witnesses, a former employer, testified that if he had believed the statements, he doubted whether he "would want to be associated with anybody who would be a party to such things that are stated in the ad," and that he would not re-employ respondent if he believed "that he allowed the Police Department to do the things that the paper say he did." But neither this witness nor any of the others testified that he had actually believed the statements in their supposed reference to respondent.

The cost of the advertisement was approximately $4800, and it was published by the *Times* upon an order from a New York advertising agency acting for the signatory Committee. The agency submitted the advertisement with a letter from A. Philip Randolph, Chairman of the Committee, certifying that the persons whose names appeared on the advertisement had given their permission. Mr. Randolph was known to the *Times* Advertising Acceptability Department as a responsible person, and in accepting the letter as sufficient proof of authorization it followed its established practice.

Alabama law denies a public officer recovery of punitive damages in a libel action brought on account of a publication concerning his official conduct unless he first makes a written demand for a public retraction and the defendant fails or refuses to comply. Respondent served such a demand upon each of the petitioners. None of the individual petitioners responded to the demand, primarily because each took the position that he had not authorized the use of his name on the advertisement and therefore had not published the statements that respondent alleged had libeled him. The *Times* did not publish a retraction in response to the demand, but wrote respondent a letter stating among other things, that "we . . . are somewhat puzzled as to how you think the statements in any way reflect on you," and "you might, if you desire, let us know in what respect you claim that the statements in the advertisement reflect on you." Respondent filed this suit a few days later without answering the letter.

The trial judge submitted the case to the jury under instructions that the statements in the advertisement were "libelous *per se*" and were not privileged, so that petitioners might be held liable if the jury found that they had published the advertisement and that the statements were made "of and concerning" respondent. The jury was instructed that, because the statements were libelous *per se,* "the law . . . implies legal injury from the bare fact of publication itself," "falsity and malice are presumed," "general damages need not be alleged or proved but are presumed," and "punitive damages may be awarded by the jury even though the amount of actual damages is neither found nor shown." An award of punitive damages—as distinguished from "general" damages, which are compensatory in nature—apparently requires proof of actual malice under Alabama law, and the judge charged that "mere negligence or carelessness is not evidence of actual malice or malice in fact, and does not justify an award of exemplary or punitive damages." He refused to charge, however, that the jury must be "convinced" of malice, in the sense of "actual intent" to harm or "gross negligence and recklessness," to make such an award, and he also refused to require that a verdict for respondent differentiate between compensatory and punitive damages. The judge rejected petitioners' contention that his rulings abridged the freedoms of speech and of the press that are guaranteed by the First and Fourteenth Amendments.

In affirming the judgment, the Supreme Court of Alabama sustained the trial judge's rulings and instructions in all respects.

We reverse the judgment. We hold that the rule of law applied by the Alabama courts is Constitutionally deficient for failure to provide the safeguards for freedom of speech and of the press that are required by the First and Fourteenth Amendments in a libel action brought by a public official against critics of his official conduct. We further hold that under the proper safeguards the evidence presented in this case is Constitutionally insufficient to support the judgment for respondent.

I

The . . . contention is that the Constitutional guarantee of freedom of speech and of the press are inapplicable here, at least so far as the *Times* is concerned, because the allegedly libelous statements were published as part of a paid, "commercial" advertisement.

The publication here was not a "commercial" advertisement (because it) . . . communicated information, expressed opinion, recited grievances, protested claimed abuses, and sought financial support on behalf of a movement whose existence and objectives are matters of the highest public interest and concern. That the *Times* was paid for publishing the advertisement is as immaterial in this connection as is the fact that newspapers and books are sold. Any other conclusion would discourage newspapers from carrying "editorial advertisements" of this type, and so might shut off an important outlet for the promulgation of information and ideas by persons who do not themselves have access to publishing facilities—who wish to exercise their freedom of speech even though they are not members of the press. The effect would be to shackle the First Amendment in its attempt to secure "the widest possible dissemination of information from diverse and antagonistic sources." (*Associated Press* v. *United States*.) To avoid placing such a handicap upon the freedoms of expression, we hold that if the allegedly libelous statements would otherwise be Constitutionally protected from the present judgment, they do not forfeit that protection because they were published in the form of a paid advertisement.

II

Once "libel *per se*" has been established, the defendant has no defense as to stated facts unless he can persuade the jury that they were true in all their particulars. His privilege of "fair comment" for expressions of opinion depends on the truth of the facts upon which the comment is based.

The question before us is whether this rule of liability, as applied to an action brought by a public official against critics of his official conduct, abridges the freedom of speech and of the press that is guaranteed by the First and Fourteenth Amendments.

Like insurrection, contempt, advocacy of unlawful acts, breach of the peace, obscenity, solicitation of legal business, and the various other formulae for the repression of expression that have been challenged in this Court, libel can claim no talismanic immunity from Constitutional limitations. It must be measured by standards that satisfy the First Amendment.

The general proposition that freedom of expression upon public questions is secured by the First Amendment has long been settled by our decisions. The Constitutional safeguard, we have said, "was fashioned to assure unfettered interchange of ideas for the bringing about of political and social changes desired by the people." (*Roth* v. *United States*.)

Thus we consider this case against the background of a profound national commitment to the principle that debate on public issues should be uninhibited, robust, and wide-open, and that it may well include vehement, caustic, and sometimes unpleasantly sharp attacks on government and public officials. The present advertisement, as an expression of grievance and protest on one of the major public issues of our time, would seem clearly to qualify for the Constitutional protection. The question is whether it forfeits that protection by the falsity of some of its factual statements and by its alleged defamation of respondent.

Erroneous statement is inevitable in free debate, and . . . it must be protected if the freedoms of expression are to have the "breathing space" that they "need . . . to survive" (*N.A.A.C.P.* v. *Button*).

A rule compelling the critic of official conduct to guarantee the truth of all his factual assertions—and to do so on pain of libel judgments virtually unlimited in amount—leads to a comparable "self-censorship." Allowance of the defense of truth, with the burden of proving it on the defendant, does not mean that only false speech will be deterred. Even courts accepting this defense as an adequate safeguard have recognized the difficulties of adducing legal proofs that the alleged libel was true in all its factual particulars. Under such a rule, would-be critics of official conduct may be deterred from voicing their criticism, even though it is believed to be true and even though it is in fact true, because of doubt whether it can be proved in court or fear of the expense of having to do so. They tend to make only statements which "steer far wider of the unlawful zone." (*Speiser* v. *Randall*.) The rule thus dampens the vigor and limits the variety of public debate. It is inconsistent with the First and Fourteenth Amendments.

The Constitutional guarantees require, we think, a federal rule that prohibits a public official from recovering damages for a defamatory falsehood relating to his official conduct unless he proves that the statement was made with "actual malice"—that is, with knowledge that it was false or with reckless disregard of whether it was false or not.

III

We hold today that the Constitution delimits a State's power to award damages for libel in actions brought by public officials against critics of their official conduct. Since this is such an action, the rule requiring proof of actual malice is applicable. While Alabama law apparently requires proof of actual malice for an award of punitive damages, where general damages are concerned, malice is "presumed." Such a presumption is inconsistent with the federal rule.

The *Times'* failure to retract upon respondent's demand, although it later retracted upon the demand of Governor Patterson, is likewise not adequate evidence of malice for Constitutional purposes. Whether or not a failure to retract may ever constitute such evidence, there are two reasons why it does not here. *First,* the letter written by the *Times* reflected a reasonable doubt on its part as to whether the advertisement could reasonably be taken to refer to respondent at all. *Second,* it was not a final refusal, since it asked for an explanation on this point—a request that respondent chose to ignore.

Finally, there is evidence that the *Times* published the advertisement without checking its accuracy against the news stories in the *Times'* own files. The mere presence of the stories in the files does not, of course, establish that the *Times* "knew" the advertisement was false, since the state of mind required for actual malice would have to be brought home to the persons in the *Times'* organization having responsibility for the publication of the advertisement. With respect to the failure of those persons to make the check, the record shows that they relied upon their knowledge of the good reputation of many of those whose names were listed as sponsors of the advertisement, and upon the letter from A. Philip Randolph, known to them as a responsible individual, certifying that the use of the names was authorized. There was testimony that the persons handling the advertisement saw nothing in it that would render it unacceptable under the *Times'* policy of rejecting advertisements containing "attacks of a personal character;" their failure to reject it on this ground was not unreasonable. We think the evidence against the *Times* supports at most a finding of negligence in failing to discover the misstatements, and is Constitutionally insufficient to show the recklessness that is required for a finding of actual malice.

We also think the evidence was Constitutionally defective in another respect: it was incapable of supporting the jury's finding that the allegedly libelous statements were made "of and concerning" respondent. Respondent relies on the words of the advertisement and the testimony of six witnesses to establish a connection between it and himself.

The judgment of the Supreme Court of Alabama is reversed and the case is remanded to the court for further proceedings not inconsistent with this opinion.

Mr. Justice Black, with whom Mr. Justice Douglas joins, concurring.

I concur in reversing this half-million-dollar judgment against the New York Times Company and the four individual defendants. In reversing, the Court holds that "the Constitution delimits a State's power to award damages for libel in actions brought by public officials against critics of their official conduct." I base my vote to reverse on the belief that the First and Fourteenth Amendments not merely "delimit" a State's power to award damages to "public officials against critics of their official conduct," but completely prohibit a State from exercising such a power. The Court goes on to hold that a State can subject such critics to damages if "actual malice" can be proved against them. "Malice," even as defined by the Court, is an elusive, abstract concept, hard to prove and hard to disprove. The requirement that malice be proved provides at best an evanescent protection for the right critically to discuss public affairs, and certainly does not measure up to the sturdy safeguard embodied in the First Amendment. Unlike the Court, therefore, I vote to reverse exclusively on the ground that the *Times* and the individual defendants had an absolute, unconditional Constitutional right to publish in the *Times* advertisement their criticism of the Montgomery agencies and officials.

We would, I think, more faithfully interpret the First Amendment by holding that at the very least it leaves the people and the press free to criticize officials and discuss public affairs with impunity. This nation, I suspect, can live in peace without libel suits based on public discussions of public affairs and public officials. But I doubt that a country can live in freedom where its people can be made to suffer physically or financially for criticizing their government, its actions, or its officials.

Mr. Justice Goldberg, with whom Mr. Justice Douglas joins, concurring in the result.

The Court today announces a Constitutional standard which prohibits "a public official from recovering damages for a defamatory falsehood relating to his official conduct unless he proves that the statement was made with 'actual malice'—that is, with knowledge that it was false or with reckless disregard of whether it was false or not." The Court thus rules that the Constitution gives citizens and newspapers a "conditional privilege" immunizing nonmalicious misstatements of fact regarding the official conduct of a government officer. The impressive array of history and precedent marshalled by the Court, however, confirms my belief that the Constitution affords greater protection than that provided by the Court's standard to citizen and press in exercising the right of public criticism.

In my view, the First and Fourteenth Amendments to the Constitution afford to the citizen and to the press an absolute, unconditional privilege to criticize official conduct despite the harm which may flow from excesses and abuses. The theory of our Constitution is that every citizen may speak his mind and every newspaper express its view on matters of public concern and may not be barred from speaking or publishing because those in control of government think that what is said or written is unwise, unfair, false, or malicious. In a democratic society, one who assumes to act for the citizens in an executive, legislative, or judicial capacity must expect that his official acts will be commented upon and criticized. Such criticism cannot, in my opinion, be muzzled or deterred by the courts at the instance of public officials under the label of libel.

This is not to say that the Constitution protects defamatory statements directed against the private conduct of a public official or private citizen. Freedom of press and of speech insures that government will respond to the will of the people and that changes may be obtained by peaceful means. Purely private defamation has little to do with the political ends of a self-governing society. The imposition of liability for private defamation does not abridge the freedom of public speech. This, of course, cannot be said "where public officials are concerned or where public matters are involved. (O)ne main function of the First Amendment is to ensure ample opportunity for the people to determine and resolve public issues. Where public matters are involved, the doubts should be resolved in favor of freedom of expression rather than against it." (Douglas, *The Right of the People* (1958), p. 41.)

The conclusion that the Constitution affords the citizen and the press an absolute privilege for criticism of official conduct does not leave the public official without defenses against unsubstantiated opinions or deliberate misstatements. "Under our system of government, counter argument and education are the weapons available to expose these matters, not abridgement . . . of free speech . . . ." The public official certainly has equal if not greater access than most private citizens to media of communication. In any event, despite the possibility that some excesses and abuses may go unremedied, we must recognize that "the people of this nation have ordained in the light of history, that, in spite of the probability of excesses and abuses, (certain) liberties are, in the long view, essential to enlightened opinion and right conduct on the part of the citizens of a democracy."

For these reasons, I strongly believe that the Constitution accords citizens and press an unconditional freedom to criticize official conduct. It necessarily follows that in a case such as this, where all agree that the allegedly defamatory statements related to official conduct, the judgment for libel cannot Constitutionally be sustained.

GERTZ v. ROBERT WELCH, INC.
418 U.S. 323 (1974)

Mr. Justice Powell delivered the opinion of the Court.

This Court has struggled for nearly a decade to define the proper accommodation between the law of defamation and the freedoms of speech and press protected by the First Amendment. With this decision we return to that effort. We granted certiorari to reconsider the extent of a publisher's Constitutional privilege against liability for defamation of a private citizen.

In 1968, a Chicago policeman named Nuccio shot and killed a youth named Nelson. The state authorities prosecuted Nuccio for the homicide and ultimately obtained a conviction for murder in the second degree. The Nelson family retained petitioner Elmer Gertz, a reputable attorney, to represent them in civil litigation against Nuccio.

Respondent publishes *American Opinion,* a monthly outlet for the views of the John Birch Society. Early in the 1960s the magazine began to warn of a nationwide conspiracy to discredit local law enforcement agencies and create in their stead a national police force capable of supporting a communist dictatorship. As part of the continuing effort to alert the public to this assumed danger, the managing editor of *American Opinion* commissioned an article on the murder trial of officer Nuccio.

The article stated that petitioner had been an official of the "Marxist League for Industrial Democracy, originally known as the Intercollegiate Socialist Society, which has advocated the violent seizure of our government." It labelled Gertz a "Leninist" and a "Communist-fronter." It also stated that Gertz had been an officer of the National Lawyers Guild, described as a communist organization that "probably did more than any other outfit to plan the Communist attack on the Chicago police during the 1968 Democratic convention."

These statements contained serious inaccuracies. The implication that petitioner had a criminal record was false. Petitioner had been a member and officer of the National Lawyers Guild some 15 years earlier, but there was no evidence that he or that organization had taken any part in planning the 1968 demonstrations in Chicago. There was also no basis for the charge that petitioner was a "Leninist" or a "Communist-fronter." And he had never been a member of the "Marxist League for Industrial Democracy" or the "Intercollegiate Socialist Society."

The managing editor of *American Opinion* made no effort to verify or substantiate the charges against petitioner. Instead, he appended an editorial introduction stating that the author had "concluded extensive research into the Richard Nuccio case." And he included in the article a photograph of petitioner and wrote the caption that appeared under it: "Elmer Gertz of the Red Guild harasses Nuccio." Respondent placed the issue of *American Opinion* containing the article on sale at newsstands throughout the country and distributed reprinted reprints of the article on the streets of Chicago.

The principal issue in this case is whether a newspaper or broadcaster that publishes defamatory falsehoods about an individual who is neither a public official nor a public figure may claim a Constitutional privilege against liability for the injury inflicted by those statements.

The first remedy of any victim of defamation is self-help—using available opportunities to contradict the lie or correct the error and thereby to minimize its adverse impact on reputation. Public officials and public figures usually enjoy significantly greater access to the channels of effective communication and hence have a more realistic opportunity to counteract false statements than private individuals normally enjoy. Private individuals are therefore more vulnerable to injury, and the state interest in protecting them is correspondingly greater.

More important than the likelihood that private individuals will lack effective opportunities for rebuttal, there is a compelling normative consideration underlying the distinction between public and private defamation plaintiffs. An individual who decides to seek governmental office must accept certain necessary consequences of that involvement in public affairs. He runs the risk of closer public scrutiny than might otherwise be the case. And society's interest in the officers of government is not strictly limited to the formal discharge of official duties.

Those classed as public figures stand in a similar position. Hypothetically, it may be possible for someone to become a public figure through no purposeful action of his own, but the instances of truly involuntary public figures must be exceedingly rare. For the most part, those who attain this status have assumed roles of especial prominence in the affairs of society. Some occupy positions of such persuasive power and influence that they are deemed public figures for all purposes. More commonly, those classed as public figures have thrust themselves to the forefront of particular public controversies in order to influence the resolution of the issues involved. In either event, they invite attention and comment.

Even if the foregoing generalities do not obtain in every instance, the communications media are entitled to act on the assumption that public officials and public figures have voluntarily exposed themselves to increased risk to injury from defamatory falsehoods concerning them. No such assumption is justified with respect to a private individual. He has not accepted public office nor assumed an "influential role in ordering society." He has relinquished no part of his interest in the protection of his own good name, and consequently he has a more compelling call on the courts for redress of injury inflicted by defamatory falsehood. Thus, private individuals are not only more vulnerable to injury than public officials and public figures; they are also more deserving of recovery.

The common law of defamation is an oddity of tort law, for it allows recovery of purportedly compensatory damages without evidence of actual loss. Under the traditional rules pertaining to actions for libel, the existence of injury is presumed from the fact of publication.

It is necessary to restrict defamation plaintiffs who do not prove knowledge of falsity or reckless disregard for the truth to compensation for actual injury. We need not define "actual injury," as trial courts have wide experience in framing appropriate jury instructions in tort action. Suffice it to say that actual injury is not limited to out-of-pocket loss. Indeed, the more customary types of actual harm inflicted by defamatory falsehood include impairment of reputation and standing in the community, personal humiliation, and mental anguish and suffering.

We also find no justification for allowing awards of punitive damages against publishers and broadcasters held liable under state-defined standards of liability for defamation. In most jurisdictions jury discretion over the amounts awarded is limited only by the general rule that they not be excessive. Consequently, juries assess punitive damages in wholly unpredictable amounts bearing no necessary relation to the actual harm caused. And they remain free to use their discretion selectively to punish expressions of unpopular views. Like the doctrine of presumed damages, jury discretion to award punitive damages unnecessarily exacerbates the danger of media self-censorship, but, unlike the former rule, punitive damages are wholly irrelevant to the state interest that justifies a negligence standard for private defamation actions. They are not compensation for injury. Instead, they are private fines levied by civil juries to punish reprehensible conduct and to deter its future occurrence. In short, the private defamation plaintiff who establishes liability under a less demanding standard than that stated by *New York Times* may recover only such damages as are sufficient to compensate him for actual injury.

Notwithstanding our refusal to extend the *New York Times* privilege to defamation of private individuals, respondent contends that we should affirm the judgment below on the ground that petitioner is either a public official or a public figure. There is little basis for the former assertion. Several years prior to the present incident, petitioner had served briefly on housing committees appointed by the mayor of Chicago, but at the time of publication he had never held any remunerative governmental position. Respondent admits this, but argues that petitioner's appearance at the coroner's inquest rendered him a "de facto public official." Our cases recognize no such concept. Respondent's suggestion would sweep all lawyers under the *New York Times* rule as officers of the court and distort the plain meaning of the "public official" category beyond all recognition. We decline to follow it.

Respondent's characterization of petitioner as a public figure raises a different question. That designation may rest on either of two alternative bases. In some instances, an individual may achieve such pervasive fame or notoriety that he becomes a public figure for all purposes and in all contexts. More commonly, an individual voluntarily injects himself or is drawn into a particular public controversy and thereby becomes a public figure for a limited range of issues. In either case, such persons assume special prominence in the resolution of public questions.

Petitioner has long been active in community and professional affairs. He has served an an officer of local civic groups and of various professional organizations, and he has published several books and articles on legal subjects. Although petitioner was consequently well known in some circles, he had achieved no general fame or notoriety in the community. None of the prospective jurors called at the trial had ever heard of petitioner prior to this litigation, and respondent offered no proof that this response was atypical of the local population. We would not lightly assume that a citizen's participation in community and professional affairs rendered him a public figure for all purposes. Absent clear evidence of general fame or notoriety in the community, and pervasive involvement in the affairs of society, an individual should not be deemed a public personality for all aspects of his life. It is preferable to reduce the public figure question to a more meaningful context by looking to the nature and extent of an individual's participation in the particular controversy giving rise to the defamation.

In this context, it is plain that petitioner was not a public figure. He played a minimal role at the coroner's inquest, and his participation related solely to his representation of a private client. He took no part in the criminal prosecution of Officer Nuccio. Moreover, he never discussed either the criminal or civil litigation with the press and was never quoted as having done so. He plainly did not thrust himself into the vortex of this public issue, nor did he engage the public's attention in an attempt to influence its outcome. We are persuaded that the trial court did not err in refusing to characterize petitioner as a public figure for the purpose of this litigation.

We therefore conclude that the *New York Times* standard is inapplicable to this case and that the trial court erred in entering judgment for respondent. Because the jury was allowed to impose liability without fault and was permitted to presume damages without proof of injury, a new trial is necessary. We reverse and remand for further proceedings in accord with this opinion.

Mr. Justice Blackmun, concurring.

The Court today refuses to apply *New York Times* to the private individual, as contrasted with the public official and the public figure. It thus withdraws to the factual limits of the pre-*Rosenbloom* cases. It thereby fixes the outer boundary of the *New York Times* doctrine and says that beyond that boundary, a State is free to define for itself the appropriate standard of a media's liability so long as it does not impose liability without fault. As my joinder in *Rosenbloom*'s plurality opinion would intimate, I sense some illogic in this.

The Court, however, seeks today to strike a balance between competing values where necessarily uncertain assumptions about human behavior color the result. Although the Court's opinion in the present case departs from the rationale of the *Rosenbloom* plurality, in that the Court now conditions a libel action by a private person upon a showing of negligence, as contrasted with a showing of willful or reckless disregard, I am willing to join, and do join, the Court's opinion and its judgment for two reasons:

1. By removing the spectres of presumed and punitive damages in the absence of *New York Times* malice, the Court eliminates significant and powerful motives for self-censorship that otherwise are present in the traditional libel action. By so doing, the Court leaves what should prove to be sufficient and adequate breathing space for a vigorous press. What the Court has done, I believe, will have little, if any, practical effect on the functioning of responsible journalism.

2. The Court was sadly fractionated in *Rosenbloom*. A result of that kind inevitably leads to uncertainty. I feel that it is of profound importance for the Court to come to rest in the defamation area and to have a clearly defined majority position that eliminates the unsureness engendered by *Rosenbloom's* diversity. If my vote were not needed to create a majority, I would adhere to my prior view. A definitive ruling, however is paramount.

Mr. Justice Brennan, dissenting.

The teaching to be distilled from our prior cases is that, while public interest in events may at times be influenced by the notoriety of the individuals involved, "(t)he public's primary interest is in the event(,) . . . the conduct of the participant and the content, effect, and significance of the conduct . . . ." (*Rosenbloom*.) Matters of public or general interest do not "suddenly become less so merely because a private individual is involved, or because in some sense the individual did not 'voluntarily' choose to become involved."

The Court's holding . . . simply den(ies) free expression its "breathing space." Today's decision will exacerbate the rule of self-censorship of legitimate utterances as publishers "steer far wider of the unlawful zone."

The Court does not discount altogether the danger that jurors will punish for the expression of unpopular opinions. This probability accounts for the Court's limitation that "the States may not permit recovery of presumed or punitive damages, at least when liability is not based on a showing of knowledge of falsity or reckless disregard for the truth." But plainly, a jury's latitude to impose liability for want of due care poses a far greater threat of suppressing unpopular views than does a possible recovery of presumed or punitive damages. Moreover, the Court's broad-ranging examples of "actual injury," including impairment of reputation and standing in the community, as well as personal humiliating, and mental anguish and suffering, inevitably allow a jury bent on punishing expression of unpopular views a formidable weapon for doing so. Finally, even a limitation of recovery to "actual injury"—however much it reduces the size or frequency of recoveries—will not provide the necessary elbow room for First Amendment expression.

Mr. Justice White, dissenting.

(T)he Court, in a few printed pages, has federalized major aspects of libel law by declaring unconstitutional in important respects the prevailing defamation law in all or most of the 50 states. That result is accomplished by requiring the plaintiff in each and every defamation action to prove not only the defendant's culpability beyond his act of publishing defamatory material, but also actual damage to reputation resulting from the publication. Moreover, punitive damages may not be recovered by showing malice in the traditional sense of ill will; knowing falsehood or reckless disregard of the truth will now be required.

I assume these sweeping changes will be popular with the press, but this is not the road to salvation for a court of law. As I see it, there are wholly insufficient grounds for scuttling the libel laws of the States in such wholesale fashion, to say nothing of deprecating the reputation interest of ordinary citizens and rendering them powerless to protect themselves. I do not suggest that the decision is illegitimate or beyond the bounds of judicial review, but it is an ill-considered exercise of the power entrusted to this Court, particularly when the Court has not had the benefit of briefs and argument addressed to most of the major issues which the Court now decides. I respectfully dissent.

Lest there be any mistake about it, the changes wrought by the Court's decision cut very deeply.

The impact of today's decision on the traditional law of libel is immediately obvious and indisputable. No longer will the plaintiff be able to rest his case with proof of a libel defamatory on its face or proof of a slander historically actionable *per se*. In addition, he must prove some further degree of culpable conduct on the part of the publisher, such as intentional or reckless falsehood or negligence. And if he succeeds in this respect, he faces still another obstacle: recovery for loss of reputation will be conditioned upon "competent" proof of actual injury to his standing in the community. This will be true regardless of the nature of the defamation and even though it is one of those particularly reprehensible statements that have traditionally made slanderous words actionable without proof of fault by the publisher or of the damaging impact of his publication. The Court rejects the judgment of experience that some publications are so inherently capable of injury, and actual injury so difficult to prove, that the risk of falsehood should be borne by the publisher, not the victim. Plainly, with the additional burden on the plaintiff of proving negligence or other fault, it will be exceedingly difficult, perhaps impossible, for him to vindicate his reputation interest by securing a judgment for nominal damages, the practical effect of such a judgment being a judicial declaration that the publication was indeed false. Under the new rule, the plaintiff can lose, not because the statement is true, but because it was not negligently made.

So too, the requirement of proving special injury to reputation before general damages may be awarded will clearly eliminate the prevailing rule, worked out over a very long period of time, that, in the case of defamations not actionable *per se,* the recovery of general damages for injury to reputation may also be had if some form of material or pecuniary loss is proved. Finally, an inflexible federal standard is imposed for the award of punitive damages. No longer will it be enough to prove ill will and an attempt to injure.

These are radical changes in the law and severe invasions of the prerogatives of the States. They should at least be shown to be required by the First Amendment or necessitated by our present circumstances. Neither has been demonstrated.

GREENBELT COOPERATIVE PUBLISHING ASSN. v. *BRESLER*
398 U.S. 6 (1970)

Mr. Justice Stewart delivered the opinion of the court.

The petitioners are the publishers of a small weekly newspaper, the Greenbelt News Review, in the city of Greenbelt, Maryland. The respondent Bresler is a prominent local real estate developer and builder in Greenbelt, and was, during the period in question, a member of the Maryland House of Delegates from a neighboring district. In the autumn of 1965 Bresler was engaged in negotiations with the Greenbelt City Council to obtain certain zoning variances that would allow the construction of high-density housing on land owned by him. At the same time the city was attempting to acquire another tract of land owned by Bresler for the construction of a new high school. Extensive litigation concerning compensation for the school site seemed imminent, unless there should be an agreement on its price between Bresler and the city authorities, and the concurrent negotiations obviously provided both parties considerable bargaining leverage.

These joint negotiations evoked substantial local controversy, and several tumultuous city council meetings were held at which many members of the community freely expressed their views. The meetings were reported at length in the news columns of the Greenbelt News Review. Two news articles in consecutive weekly editions of the paper stated that at the public meetings some people had characterized Bresler's negotiating position as "blackmail." The word appeared several times, both with and without quotation marks, and was used once as a subheading within a news story.

Bresler reacted to these news articles by filing the present lawsuit for libel, seeking both compensatory and punitive damages. The primary thrust of his complaint was that the articles, individually and along with other items published in the petitioners' newspaper, imputed to him the crime of blackmail. The case went to trial, and the jury awarded Bresler $5,000 in compensatory damages and $12,500 in punitive damages. The Maryland Court of Appeals affirmed the judgment. We granted certiorari to consider the constitutional issues presented. 396 U.S. 874.

In *New York Times Co.* v. *Sullivan,* we held that the Constitution permits a "public official" to recover money damages for libel only if he can show that the defamatory publication was not only false but was uttered with " 'actual malice'—that is, with knowledge that it was false or with reckless disregard of whether it was false or not." In *Curtis Publishing Co.* v. *Butts,* we dealt with the constitutional restrictions upon a libel suit brought by a "public figure."

In the present case Bresler's counsel conceded in his opening statement to the jury that Bresler was a public figure in the community. This concession was clearly correct. Bresler was deeply involved in the future development of the city of Greenbelt. He had entered into agreements with the city for zoning variances in the past, and was again seeking such favors to permit the construction of housing units of a type not contemplated in the original city plan. At the same time the city was trying to obtain a tract of land owned by Bresler for the purpose of building a school. Negotiations of significant public concern were in progress, both with school officials and the city council. Bresler's status thus clearly fell within even the most restrictive definition of a "public figure."

Whether as a state legislator representing another county, or for some other reason, Bresler was a "public official" within the meaning of the *New York Times* rule is a question we need not determine. For the instructions to the jury in this case permitted a finding of liability under an impermissible constitutional standard, whichever status Bresler might be considered to occupy. In his charge to the members of the jury, the trial judge repeatedly instructed them that Bresler could recover if the petitioners' publications had been made with malice or with a reckless disregard of whether they were true or false. This instruction was given in one form or another half a dozen times during the course of the judges' charge. The judge then defined "malice" to include "spite, hostility or deliberate intention to harm." Moreover, he instructed the jury that "malice" could be found from the "language" of the publication itself. Thus the jury was permitted to find liability merely on the basis of a combination of falsehood and general hostility.

This was error of constitutional magnitude, as our decisions have made clear. "This definition of malice is constitutionally insufficient where discussion of public affairs is concerned; 'we held in *New York Times* that a public official might be allowed the civil remedy only if he establishes that the utterance was false and that it was made with knowledge of its falsity or in reckless disregard of whether it was false or true.' " "Even where the utterance is false, the great principles of the Constitution which secure freedom of expression in this area preclude attaching adverse consequences to any except the knowing or reckless falsehood. Debate on public issues will not be uninhibited if the speaker must run the risk that it will be proved in court that he spoke out to hatred . . . ." And the constitutional prohibition in this respect is no different whether the plaintiff be considered a "public official" or a "public figure."

This, however, does not end the inquiry. As we noted in *New York Times,* "this Court's duty is not limited to the elaboration of constitutional principles; we must also in proper cases review the evidence to make certain that those principles have been constitutionally applied . . . . We must 'make an independent examination of the whole record,' . . . so as to assure ourselves that the judgment does not constitute a forbidden intrusion on the field of free expression."

This case involves newspaper reports of public meetings of the citizens of a community concerned with matters of local governmental interest and importance. The very subject matter of the news reports, therefore, is one of particular First Amendment concern. "The maintenance of the opportunity for free political discussion to the end that government may be responsive to the will of the people and that changes may be obtained by lawful means . . . is a fundamental principle of our constitutional system." "Freedom of discussion, if it would fulfill its historic function in this nation, must embrace all issues about which information is needed or appropriate to enable the members of society to cope with the exigencies of their period." Because the threat or actual imposition of pecuniary liability for alleged defamation may impair the unfettered exercise of these First Amendment freedoms, the Constitution imposes stringent limitations upon the permissible scope of such liability.

It is not disputed that the articles published in the petitioners' newspaper were accurate and truthful reports of what had been said at the public hearings before the city council. In this sense, therefore, it cannot even be claimed that the petitioners were guilty of any "departure from the standards of investigation and reporting ordinarily adhered to by responsible publisher," much less the knowing use of falsehood or a reckless disregard of whether the statements made were true or false.

The contention is, rather, that the speakers at the meeting, in using the word "blackmail," and the petitioners in reporting the use of that word in the newspaper articles, were charging Bresler with the crime of blackmail, and that since the petitioners knew that Bresler had committed no such crime, they could be held liable for the knowing use of falsehood. It was upon this theory that the case was submitted to the jury, and upon this theory that the judgment was affirmed by the Maryland Court of Appeals. For the reasons that follow, we hold that the imposition of liability on such a basis was constitutionally impermissible—that as a matter of constitutional law, the word "blackmail" in these circumstances was not slander when spoken, and not libel when reported in the Greenbelt News Review.

There can be no question that the public debates at the sessions of the city council regarding Bresler's negotiations with the city were a subject of substantial concern to all who lived in the community. The debates themselves were heated, as debates about controversial issues usually are. During the course of the arguments Bresler's opponents characterized the position he had taken in his negotiations with the city officials as "blackmail." The Greenbelt News Review was performing its wholly legitimate function as a community newspaper when it published full reports of these public debates in its news columns. If the reports had been truncated or distorted in such a way as to extract the word "blackmail" from the context in which it was used at the public meetings, this would be a different case. But the reports were accurate and full. Their headlines, "School Site Stirs Up Council—Rezoning Deal Offer Debated" and "Council Rejects By 4–1 High School Site Deal," made it clear to all readers that the paper was reporting the public debates on the pending land negotiations. Bresler's proposal was accurately and fully described in each article, along with the accurate statement that some people at the meetings had referred to the proposal as blackmail, and others had indicated they thought Bresler's position not unreasonable.

It is simply impossible to believe that a reader who reached the word "blackmail" in either article would not have understood exactly what was meant: it was Bresler's public and wholly legal negotiating proposals that were being criticized. No reader could have thought that either the speakers at the meetings or the newspaper articles reporting their words were charging Bresler with the commission of a criminal offense. On the contrary, even the most careless reader must have perceived that the word was no more than rhetorical hyperbole, a vigorous epithet used by those who considered Bresler's negotiating position extremely unreasonable. Indeed, the record is completely devoid of evidence that anyone in the city of Greenbelt or anywhere else thought Bresler had been charged with a crime.

To permit the infliction of financial liability upon the petitioners for publishing these two news articles would subvert the most fundamental meaning of a free press, protected by the First and Fourteenth Amendments. Accordingly, we reverse the judgment and remand the case to the Court of Appeals of Maryland for further proceedings not inconsistent with this opinion.

It is so ordered.

TIME, INC. v. FIRESTONE
424 U.S. 448 (1976)

Mr. Justice Rehnquist delivered the opinion of the Court.

Time's editorial staff, headquartered in New York, was alerted to the fact that a judgment had been rendered in the Firestone divorce proceeding by a wire service report and an account in a New York newspaper. The staff subsequently received further information regarding the Florida decision from *Time*'s Miami bureau chief and from a "stringer" working on a special assignment basis in the Palm Beach area. On the basis of these four sources, *Time*'s staff composed the following item, which appeared in the magazine's "Milestones" section the following week:

> DIVORCED. By Russell A. Firestone Jr., heir to the tire fortune: Mary Alice Sullivan Firestone, 32, his third wife; a onetime Palm Beach school teacher; on grounds of extreme cruelty and adultery; after six years of marriage, one son; in West Palm Beach, Fla. The 17-month intermittent trial produced enough testimony of extramarital adventures on both sides, said the judge, "to make Dr. Freud's hair curl."

Within a few weeks of the publication of this article respondent demanded in writing a retraction from petitioner, alleging that a portion of the article was "false, malicious, and defamatory." Petitioner declined to issue the requested retraction.

Respondent then filed this libel action against petitioner in the Florida Circuit Court. Based on a jury verdict for respondent, that court entered judgment against petitioner for $100,000, and after review in both the Florida District Court of Appeal and the Supreme Court of Florida the judgment was ultimately affirmed.

(Mrs. Firestone) did not assume any role of especial prominence in the affairs of society, other than perhaps Palm Beach society, and she did not thrust herself to the forefront of any particular public controversy in order to influence the resolution of the issues involved in it.

Petitioner contends that because the Firestone divorce was characterized by the Florida Supreme Court as a *cause célèbre*, it must have been a public controversy and respondent must be considered a public figure. But in so doing, petitioner seeks to equate "public controversy" with all controversies of interest to the public.

Dissolution of a marriage through judicial proceedings is not the sort of "public controversy" referred to in *Gertz,* even though the marital difficulties of extremely wealthy individuals may be of interest to some portion of the reading public. Nor did respondent freely choose to publicize issues as to the propriety of her married life. She was compelled to go to court by the State in order to obtain legal release from the bonds of matrimony. We have said that in such an instance "(r)esort to the judicial process . . . is no more voluntary in a realistic sense than that of the defendant called upon to defend his interests in court." (*Boddie* v. *Connecticut.*) Her actions, both in instituting the litigation and in its conduct, were quite different from those of General Walker in *Curtis Publishing Co.* She assumed no "special prominence in the resolution of public questions." (*Gertz.*) We hold respondent was not a "public figure" for the purpose of determining the Constitutional protection afforded petitioner's report of the factual and legal basis for her divorce.

For similar reasons, we likewise reject petitioner's claim for automatic extension of the *New York Times* privilege to all reports of judicial proceedings. It is argued that information concerning proceedings in our nation's courts may have such importance to all citizens as to justify extending special First Amendment protection to the press when reporting on such events. We have recently accepted a significantly more confined version of this argument by holding that the Constitution precludes States from imposing civil liability based upon the publication of truthful information contained in official court records open to public inspection. (*Cox Broadcasting Corp.* v. *Cohn.*)

Petitioner has urged throughout this litigation that it could not be held liable for publication of the "Milestones" item because its report of respondent's divorce was factually correct.

For petitioner's report to have been accurate, the divorce granted Russell Firestone must have been based on a finding by the divorce court that his wife had committed extreme cruelty towards him *and* that she had been guilty of adultery. This is indisputably what petitioner reported in its "Milestones" item, but it is equally indisputable that these were not the facts. Russell Firestone alleged in his counterclaim that respondent had been guilty of adultery, but the divorce court never made any such finding. Its judgment provided that Russell Firestone's "counterclaim for divorce be and the same is hereby granted," but did not specify that the basis for the judgment was either of the two grounds alleged in the counterclaim. The Supreme Court of Florida on appeal concluded that the ground actually relied upon by the divorce court was "lack of domestication of the parties," a ground not theretofore recognized by Florida law. The Supreme Court nonetheless affirmed the judgment dissolving the bonds of matrimony because the record contained sufficient evidence to establish the ground of extreme cruelty.

Petitioner may well argue that the meaning of the trial court's decree was unclear, but this does not license it to choose from among several conceivable interpretations the one most damaging to respondent. Having chosen to follow this tack, petitioner must be able to establish not merely that the item reported was a conceivable or plausible interpretation of the decree, but that the item was factually correct.

The trial court charged, consistently with *Gertz,* that the jury should award respondent compensatory damages in "an amount of money that will fairly and adequately compensate her for such damages," and further cautioned that "it is only damages which are a direct and natural result of the alleged libel which may be recovered." There was competent evidence introduced to permit the jury to assess the amount of injury. Several witnesses testified to the extent of respondent's anxiety and concern over *Time* inaccurately reporting that she had been found guilty of adultery, and she herself took the stand to elaborate on her fears that her young son would be adversely affected by this falsehood when he grew older. The jury decided these injuries should be compensated by an award of $100,000. We have no warrant for re-examining this determination.

Gertz established, however, that not only must there be evidence to support an award of compensatory damages, there must also be evidence of some fault on the part of a defendant charged with publishing defamatory material. No question of fault was submitted to the jury in this case, because under Florida law the only findings required for determination of liability were whether the article was defamatory, whether it was true, and whether the defamation, if any, caused respondent harm.

The failure to submit the question of fault to the jury does not, of itself establish noncompliance with the Constitutional requirements established in *Gertz,* however. Nothing in the Constitution requires that assessment of fault in a civil case tried in a state court be made by a jury, nor is there any prohibition against such a finding being made in the first instance by an appellate, rather than a trial, court. The First and Fourteenth Amendments do not impose upon the States any limitations as to how, within their own judicial systems, factfinding tasks shall be allocated. If we were satisfied that one of the Florida courts which considered this case had supportably ascertained petitioner was at fault, we would be required to affirm the judgment below.

But the only alternative source of such a finding, given that the issue was not submitted to the jury, is the opinion of the Supreme Court of Florida. That opinion appears to proceed generally on the assumption that a showing of fault was not required, but then in the penultimate paragraph is recited:

Futhermore, this erroneous reporting is clear and convincing evidence of the negligence in certain segments of the news media in gathering the news. (*Gertz* v. *Welch, Inc., supra.*) Pursuant to Florida law in effect at the time of the divorce judgment (Section 61.08, Florida Statutes), a wife found guilty of adultery could not be awarded alimony. Since petitioner had been awarded alimony, she had not been found guilty of adultery nor had the divorce been granted on the ground of adultery. A careful examination of the final decree prior to publication would have clearly demonstrated that the divorce had been granted on the grounds of extreme cruelty, and thus the wife would have been saved the humiliation of being accused of adultery in a nationwide magazine. This is a flagrant example of "journalistic negligence." (304 So.2d, at 178.)

It may be argued that this is sufficient indication the court found petitioner at fault within the meaning of *Gertz.* Nothing in that decison or in the First or Fourteenth Amendments requires that in a libel action an appellate court treat in detail by written opinion all contentions of the parties, and if the jury or trial judge had found fault in fact, we would be quite willing to read the quoted passage as affirming that conclusion. But without some finding of fault by the judge or jury in the Circuit Court, we would have to attribute to the Supreme Court of Florida, from the quoted language, not merely an intention to affirm the finding of the lower court, but an intention to find such a fact in the first instance.

Even where a question of fact may have Constitutional significance, we normally accord findings of state courts deference in reviewing constitutional claims here. But that deference is predicated on our belief that at some point in the state proceedings some factfinder has made a conscious determination of the existence or nonexistence of the critical fact. Here the record before us affords no basis for such a conclusion.

It may well be that petitioner's account inits "Milestones" section was the product of some fault of its part, and that the libel judgment against it was therefore, entirely consistent with *Gertz*. But in the absence of a finding in some element of the state court system that there was fault, we are not inclined to canvass the record to make such a determination in the first instance. Accordingly, the judgment of the Supreme Court of Florida is vacated and the case remanded for further proceedings not inconsistent with this opinion.

Mr. Justice Brennan, dissenting.

At stake in the present case is the ability of the press to report to the citizenry the events transpiring in the nation's judicial systems. There is simply no meaningful or Constitutionally adequate way to report such events without reference to those persons and transactions that form the subject matter in controversy.

Also no less true than in other areas of government, error in reporting and debate concerning the judicial process is inevitable. Indeed, in view of the complexities of that process and its unfamiliarity to the laymen who report it, the probability of inadvertent error may be substantially greater.

Mr. Justice Marshall dissenting.

Mrs. Firestone brought suit for separate maintenance, with reason to know of the likely public interest in the proceedings. As the Supreme Court of Florida noted, Mr. and Mrs. Firestone's "marital difficulties were . . . well-known," and the lawsuit became "a veritable *cause célèbre* in social circles across the country." The 17-month trial and related events attracted national news coverage, and elicited no fewer than 43 articles in the *Miami Herald* and 45 articles in the *Palm Beach Post* and *Palm Beach Times*. Far from shunning the publicity, Mrs. Firestone held several press conferences in the course of the proceedings.

These facts are sufficient to warrant the conclusion that Mary Alice Firestone was a "public figure" for purposes of reports on the judicial proceedings she initiated.

We assume that it was by choice that Mrs. Firestone became an active member of the "sporting set"—a social group with "especial prominence in the affairs of society," whose lives receive constant media attention. Certainly there is nothing in the record to indicate otherwise, and Mrs. Firestone's subscription to a press clipping service suggests that she was not altogether uninterested in the publicity she received. Having placed herself in a position in which her activities were of interest to a significant segment of the public, Mrs. Firestone chose to initiate a lawsuit for separate maintenance, and most significantly, held several press conferences in the course of the lawsuit. If these actions for some reason fail to establish as a certainty that Mrs. Firestone "voluntarily exposed (herself) to increased risk of injury from defamatory falsehood," surely they are sufficient to entitle the press to act on the assumption that she did.

PAUL v. DAVIS
424 U.S. 693 (1976)

Mr. Justice Rehnquist delivered the opinion of the Court.

(Davis's) due process claim is grounded upon his assertion that the flier, and in particular the phrase "Active Shoplifters" appearing at the head of the page upon which his name and photograph appear, impermissibly deprived him of some "liberty" protected by the Fourteenth Amendment. His complaint asserted that the "active shoplifter" designation would inhibit him from entering business establishments for fear of being suspected of shoplifting and possibly apprehended, and would seriously impair his future employment opportunities. Accepting that such consequences may flow from the flier in question, respondent's complaint would appear to state a classical claim for defamation actionable in the courts of virtually every State. Imputing criminal behavior to an individual is generally considered defamatory *per se,* and actionable without proof of special damages.

Respondent brought his action, however, not in the state courts of Kentucky, but in a United States District Court for that State. He asserted not a claim for defamation under the laws of Kentucky, but a claim that he had been deprived of rights secured to him by the Fourteenth Amendment of the United States Constitution. Concededly, if the same allegations had been made about respondent by a private individual, he would have nothing more than a claim for defamation under state law. But, he contends, since petitioners are respectively an official of city and of county government, his action is thereby transmuted into one for deprivation by the State of rights secured under the Fourteenth Amendment.

The words "liberty" and "property" as used in the Fourteenth Amendment do not in terms single out reputation as a candidate for special protection over and above other interests that may be protected by state law. While we have in a number of our prior cases pointed out the frequently drastic effect of the "stigma" which may result from defamation by the government in a variety of contexts, this line of cases does not establish the proposition that reputation alone, apart from some more tangible interests such as employment, is either "liberty" or "property" by itself sufficient to invoke the procedural protection of the Due Process Clause. The Court of Appeals, in reaching a contrary conclusion relied primarily upon *Wisconsin v. Constantineau.* We think the correct import of that decision, however, must be derived from an examination of the precedents upon which it relied, as well as consideration of the other decisions by this Court, before and after *Constantineau,* which bear upon the relationship between governmental defamation and the guarantees of the Constitution. While not uniform in their treatment of the subject, we think that the weight of our decisions establishes no Constitutional doctrine converting every defamation by a public official into a deprivation of liberty within the meaning of the Due Process Clauses of the Fifth or Fourteenth Amendments.

(In *Constantineau*) the Court held that a Wisconsin statute authorizing the practice of "posting" was unconstitutional because it failed to provide procedural safeguards of notice and an opportunity to be heard, prior to an individual's being "posted."

There is undoubtedly language in *Constantineau,* which is sufficiently ambiguous to justify the reliance upon it by the Court of Appeals:

> While a person's good name, reputation, honor, or integrity is at stake *because of what the government is doing to him,* notice and an opportunity to be heard are essential.

We think that the underscored language . . . referred to the fact that the governmental action taken in that case deprived the individual of a right previously held under state law—the right to purchase or obtain liquor in common with the rest of the citizenry. "Posting," therefore, significantly altered his status as a matter of state law, and it was that alteration of legal status which, combined with the injury resulting from the defamation, justified the invocation of procedural safeguards. The "stigma" resulting from the defamatory character of the posting was doubtless an important factor in evaluating the extent of harm worked by the act, but we do not think that such defamation, standing alone, deprived Constantineau of any "liberty" protected by the procedural guarantees of the Fourteenth Amendment.

While there is no "right of privacy" found in any specific guarantee of the Constitution, the Court has recognized that "zones of privacy" may be created by more specific Constitutional guarantees and thereby impose limits upon government power. Respondent's case, however, comes within none of these areas. He does not seek to suppress evidence seized in the course of an unreasonable search. And our other "right of privacy" cases, while defying categorical description, deal generally with substantive aspects of the Fourteenth Amendment. In *Roe,* the Court pointed out that the personal rights found in the guarantee of personal privacy must be limited to those which are "fundamental." The activities detailed as being within this definition were ones very different from that for which respondent claims constitutional protection—matters relating to marriage, procreation, contraception, family relationships, and child rearing and education. In these areas it has been held that there are limitations on the States' power to substantively regulate conduct.

Respondent's claim is far afield from this line of decisions. He claims Constitutional protection against the disclosure of the fact of his arrest on a shoplifting charge. His claim is based not upon any challenge to the State's ability to restrict his freedom of action in a sphere contended to be "private," but instead on a claim that the State may not publicize a record of an official act such as an arrest. None of our substantive privacy decisions hold this or anything like this, and we decline to enlarge them in this manner.

None of respondent's theories of recovery were based upon rights secured to him by the Fourteenth Amendment. Petitioners therefore were not liable to him under Section 1893. The judgment of the Court of Appeals holding otherwise is

Reversed.

Mr. Justice Brennan, with whom Mr. Justice White and Mr. Justice Marshall concur, dissenting.

I dissent. The Court today holds that police officials, acting in their official capacities as law enforcers, may on their own initiative and without trial Constitutionally condemn innocent individuals as criminals and thereby brand them with one of the most stigmatizing and debilitating labels in our society. If there are no Constitutional restraints on such oppressive behavior, the safeguards Constitutionally accorded an accused in a criminal trial are rendered a sham, and no individual can feel secure that he will not be arbitrarily singled out for similar *ex parte* punishment by those primarily charged with fair enforcement of the law. The Court accomplishes this result by excluding a person's interest in his good name and reputation from all Constitutional protection, regardless of the character of or necessity for the government's actions. The result, which is demonstrably inconsistent with our prior case law and unduly restrictive in its construction of our precious Bill of Rights, is one in which I cannot concur.

If the Court were creating a novel doctrine that state law is in any way relevant, it would be incumbent upon the Court to inquire whether respondent has an adequate remedy under Kentucky law or whether petitioners would be immunized by state doctrines of official or sovereign immunity. The Court, however, undertakes no such inquiry.

The Court by mere fiat and with no analysis wholly excludes personal interest in reputation from the ambit of "life, liberty, or property" under the Fifth and Fourteenth Amendments, thus rendering due process concerns *never* applicable to the official stigmatization, however arbitrary, of an individual. The logical and disturbing corollary of this holding is that no due process infirmities would inhere in a statute constituting a commission to conduct *ex parte* trials of individuals, so long as the only official judgment pronounced was limited to the public condemnation and branding of a person as a Communist, a traitor, an "active murderer," a homosexual, or any other mark that "merely" carries social opprobrium. The potential of today's decision is frightening for a free people. That decision surely finds no support in our relevant Constitutional jurisprudence.

Our precedents clearly mandate that a person's interest in his good name and reputation is cognizable as a "liberty" interest within the meaning of the Due Process Clause, and the Court has simply failed to distinguish those precedents in any rational manner in holding that no invasion of a "liberty" interest was effected in the official stigmatizing of respondent as a criminal without any "process" whatsoever.

I had always thought that one of this Court's most important roles is to provide a formidable bulwark against governmental violation of the Constitutional safeguards, securing in our free society the legitimate expectations of every person to innate human dignity and sense of worth. It is a regrettable abdication of that role and a saddening denigration of our majestic Bill of Rights when the Court tolerates arbitrary and capricious official conduct branding an individual as a criminal without compliance with Constitutional procedures designed to ensure the fair and impartial ascertainment of criminal culpability. Today's decision must surely be a shortlived aberration.

SHARRATT v. HOUSING INNOVATIONS, INC.
365 Mass. 141, 310 N.E.2d 343 (1974)

Hennessey, Justice.

(1) The plaintiffs appeal from an order sustaining the demurrer to both counts of their amended declaration. We first summarize the facts as stated in the amended declaration which, for the purposes of this appeal, we must assume to be true.

The plaintiff John Sharratt is a registered architect and principal stockholder of the plaintiff John Sharratt Associates, Inc. In 1972, the corporate plaintiff entered into a contract with a development corporation to design, as the architect, a project known as "Madison Park Houses." Samuel Glaser and Partners were named as associated architects. Though the defendants knew that the plaintiffs had been awarded the contract as architect and had claimed credit for the award, they published a promotional brochure for the corporate defendant containing the following words: "The project, to be called Madison Park Houses, is in the Campus High School Urban Renewal Area. It will be immediately adjacent to the newly planned 2,500 pupil urban high school that is now under construction. Architects for the Madison Park project are Samuel Glaser and Partners. General contractor for the 12 story building is George B.H. Macomber Company." From this statement it could be inferred that the individual plaintiff was not the architect, nor had the corporate plaintiff contracted to provide these architectural services, despite their representations to the contrary to those with whom they had business dealings.

COUNT 1

1. "It is now well settled that the character of a publication as being libellous or otherwise is not to be judged by what we ourselves would understand it to mean, but that commonly the question is one of fact, and that the court can rule as a matter of law that the publication is not libellous and can withdraw the case from the jury only when it is apparent 'that the publication is not reasonably capable of any defamatory meaning, and cannot reasonably be understood in any defamatory sense.' (Citations omitted.)" (*King* v. *Northeastern Publishing Co.*)

(T)he issue here is whether the determination is to be made by a consideration of the words alone or in the context of the extrinsic facts pleaded.

"The essential question is whether the statement was capable of a derogatory meaning on its face or is to be given such a meaning in consequence of any facts shown in the evidence.

(2, 3) To be actionable as libel, words need not hold a plaintiff up to ridicule or damage his reputation in the community at large, or among all reasonable men. It is enough that they do so among "a considerable and respectable class" of people. Here the plaintiffs have alleged damage to their professional reputation among the real estate development and architectural community in which they work. It would be anomalous at best if words clearly understood in a defamatory sense among that community should fail to be actionable merely because they would appear innocent to the general public.

(4) 2. The defendants' assertion that special damages must be pleaded to survive demurrer is based on the fact that the defamatory meaning of the printed words is apparent only in the context of extrinsic facts, if at all. That extrinsic facts are also needed to determine if the words apply to the plaintiff is irrelevant. "Whether the article was published concerning the plaintiff is generally a question of fact." The facts pleaded "tended to show that such language in the then state of information of the public mind . . . (could) be understood as referring to the plaintiff." "It easily could be learned by those of the public who wished to discover it, aided by the facts and circumstances attending the publication."

Authoritative opinion and case law are both divided on the question of whether or not special damages must be pleaded in a case of *libel per quod*. The disputed issue "concerns cases of libel in which the defamatory meaning, or innuendo, is not apparent on the face of the publication, but must be made out by proof of extrinsic facts; and the question is whether, in such a case, the libel is actionable without proof of special damages, where the same words would not be so actionable if they were slander." (Prosser, "More Libel Per Quod," 79 Harv. L. Rev. 1629, 1630–1631 (1966).) Professor Prosser's view is that *libel per quod* should require the pleading of special damages, and he believes the majority of jurisdictions that have dealt with the issue agree. His views on both policy and law are disputed in Eldredge, "The Spurious Rule of Libel Per Quod," 79 Harv. L. Rev. 733 (1966). Mr. Eldredge argues that there is no justification in law, policy, or history, for distinguishing between different categories of libel regarding a requirement for pleading special damages.

There is certainly language in opinions of this court which supports the view that all libel is actionable *per se*. In *Muchnick* v. *Post Publishing Co.* (1955), we stated at p. 308, 125 N.E.2d at p. 140 concerning an allegation of loss of business that "while not essential to stating a cause of action for libel, the allegation is proper to enable him (the plaintiff) to lay a foundation for proof of an item of damage. Otherwise, he would be limited to these damages naturally and necessarily to be expected from the publication." In the same case, we also stated that we "adopt the rule in the *Restatement:* 'One who is liable either for a libel or for a slander actionable *per se* is also liable for any special harm of which the defamatory publication is the legal cause.' " (*Restatement: Torts,* Section 622. *Restatement: Torts,* Section 569, comment c; compare Section 575, comment b." *Ibid.*) See *King* v. *Northeastern Publishing Co.,* and *Lynch* v. *Lyons,* which imply that the distinction between "meaning on face" and "meaning in context" is irrelevant to the issue of pleading special damages.

(5) Consistent with the implications of these cases, we now hold that all libel is actionable *per se.**

COUNT 2

(6) The cause of action intended to be stated by count 2 is not entirely clear. It may perhaps best be described as a count for intentional falsehood. To the extent that it seeks to recover for a defamatory falsehood, it is repetitive of count 1. The allegation of an intent by the defendants to harm the plaintiffs adds nothing. Punitive damages are not recoverable in a libel action in this Commonwealth (*Ellis* v. *Brockton Publishing Co.*) even in the presence of actual malice toward the plaintiff.

3. The order sustaining the demurrer is reversed. A new order is to be entered overruling the demurrer as to count 1 and sustaining the demurrer as to count 2.

So ordered.

FLAKE v. *GREENSBORO NEWS CO.*
212 N.C. 780, 195 S.E. 55 (1938)

Action by Nancy Flake, by her next friend, Mrs. W.F. Flake, against the Greensboro News Company and others for damages allegedly sustained as the result of a publication of the plaintiff's photograph or likeness in connection with an advertisement which appeared in a newspaper. From an adverse judgment, the defendants appeal.

---

*In view of this holding, it is unnecessary for us to seek further support for our conclusion. However, we do note, additionally, that authorities appear to be unanimously of the opinion that no special damages need be pleaded, whether words are libellous on their face or proved libellous only through extrinsic evidence, if the same words would be actionable *per se* (i.e., without pleading special damages) had they been spoken. (Harper & James, Torts, Section 5.9, pp. 372–373 (1956).) Eldredge, "The Spurious Rule of Libel Per Quod," 79 Harv.L.Rev. 733 (1966). Prosser, "More Libel per Quod," 79 Harv.L.Rev. 1629, 1632–1634 (1966).

"It is settled that words spoken orally are not actionable *per se,* unless they charge the plaintiff with a crime, or state that he is suffering from certain diseases, or prejudice him in his office, profession, or business, or may probably tend to do so." (*Lynch* v. *Lyons,* 303 Mass. 116, 118–119, 20 N.E.2d 953, 955 (1939).) Several cases have interpreted the exception pertaining to professional reputation. *Chaddock* v. *Briggs,* 13 Mass. 248, 252 (1816). *Morasse* v. *Brochu,* 151 Mass. 567, 575, 25 N.E. 74 (1890). See *Craig* v. *Proctor,* 229 Mass. 339, 341, 118 N.E. 647 (1918). Where "spoken words are actionable *per se* . . . (a) *fortiori* the written words to the same effect are actionable . . . under the somewhat broader rule applicable to libel." *Lynch* v. *Lyons,* 303 Mass. 116, 122, 20 N.E.2d 953, 956 (1939); *Friedman* v. *Connors,* 292 Mass. 371, 375, 198 N.E. 513 (1935).

If a jury were to find the words in question in the present case defamatory at all, it would have to be because they impugn the plaintiffs' professional integrity and honesty. Accordingly, for this additional reason, they would be held to be actionable without allegation or proof of special damages.

Folies de Paree was a vaudeville or stage show and advertised its performance through a system of "tie up" advertising. Under this system, some merchant and the local theatre join in the advertisement and it advertises both the product or the merchandise of the merchant and the theatre performance. Pursuant to this plan, the agent of the "Folies de Paree" solicited the defendant L. Melts, who conducted a bakery in Greensboro under the name of "Melts Bakery" and the defendant North Carolina Theatres, Inc., to join in such an advertisement and as a result a two-column advertisement was published in the *Greensboro Daily News* issue of March 11, 1936. In the right portion of the advertisement there was a cut from the plaintiff's photograph showing her standing and wearing a bathing suit. To the left was the following wording, so arranged as to make four distinct statements, as follows:

Keep that Sylph-Like Figure by eating more of Melts' Rye and Whole Wheat Bread, says Mlle. Sally Payne, exotic red haired Venus.

'Folies de Paree' sparkling Parisian Revue, Stage Production, National Theatre two days only, March 11 and 12.

'Melts' Rye and Whole Wheat Bread will give you the necessary energy, pep and vitality without adding extra weight, says Miss Payne. Melts Bakery, 314 N. Elm St., 1829 Spring Garden St.

'Ask for Melts' Bread—Melts in Your Mouth.'

In publishing this advertisement, the photograph or mat made therefrom was used without the consent of the plaintiff and was used by mistake—the defendants intending to use a cut of Sally Payne, the leading lady of Folies de Paree.

The record does not disclose just how the mistake occurred or how the Greensboro News Company came in possession of the plaintiff's photograph, whether the news company had the photograph in its files in connection with the plaintiff's campaign for publicity, or it was furnished by Folies de Paree. In this connection, the plaintiff testified that mats were made from these photographs (referring to the photographs taken in the studios of Columbia Broadcasting Company and including two photographs of her while she was dressed in bathing suit) and that "they were sent to very many places and very many people. There were used to give me publicity and were sent out with my entire consent and approval. I was not compelled by anyone to pose for this photograph, but I did try to cooperate. I posed for this photograph of my own free will and accord."

The mistake having been called to the attention of the defendant Greensboro News Company, it immediately published a full explanation of the mistake and an apology.

Barnhill, Justice.

Libels may be divided into three classes: 1) Publications which are obviously defamatory and which are termed libels per se; 2) publications which are susceptible of two reasonable interpretations, one of which is defamatory and the other is not; and 3) publications which are not obviously defamatory, but which become so when considered in connection with innuendo, colloquium, and explanatory circumstances. This type of libel is termed libel per quod.

When an unauthorized publication is libelous per se, malice and damage are presumed from the fact of publication and no proof is required as to any resulting injury. The law presumes that general damages actually, proximately, and necessarily result from an unauthorized publication which is libelous per se and they are not required to be proved by evidence since they arise by inference of law, and are allowed whenever the immediate tendency of the publication is to impair plaintiff's reputation although no actual pecuniary loss has in fact resulted.

In an action upon a publication coming within the second class, that is, a publication which is susceptible of two interpretations, one of which is defamatory, it is for the jury to determine under the circumstances whether the publication is defamatory and was so understood by those who saw it.

In publications which are libelous per quod, the innuendo and special damages must be alleged and proved.

As the complaint is insufficient to bring the publication under consideration within either the second or the third class—that is, it is not alleged that said publication is susceptible of two meanings, one defamatory, and that the defamatory meaning was intended and was so understood by the public; and there is no allegation or proof of special damages—we must determine whether the publication is defamatory per se. If it is not, the defendants were entitled to judgment of nonsuit as to plaintiff's cause of action upon the publication as a libel.

A libel per se is a malicious publication expressed in writing, printing, pictures, caricatures, signs, or other device, which upon its face and without aid of extrinsic proof is injurious and defamatory, tending either to blacken the memory of one dead or the reputation of one who is alive and expose him to public hatred, contempt, or ridicule.

It may be stated as a general proposition that defamatory matter written or printed, or in the form of caricatures or other signs may be libelous and actionable per se, that is, actionable without any allegations of special damage, if they tend to expose plaintiff to public hatred, contempt, ridicule, aversion, or disgrace and to induce an evil opinion of him in the minds of right thinking persons and to deprive him of their friendly intercourse and society.

In order to be libelous per se, it is not essential that the words should involve an imputation of crime, or otherwise impute the violation of some law, or moral turpitude, or immoral conduct. But defamatory words to be libelous per se must be susceptible of but one meaning and of such nature that the court can presume as a matter of law that they tend to disgrace and degrade the party or hold him up to public hatred, contempt, or ridicule, or cause him to be shunned and avoided. The imputation must be one tending to affect a party in a society whose standard of opinion the court can recognize.

The general rule is that publications are to be taken in the sense which is most obvious and natural and according to the ideas that they are calculated to convey to those who see them. The principle of common sense requires that courts shall understand them as other people would. The question always is, How would ordinary men naturally understand the publication? The fact that supersensitive persons with morbid imaginations may be able, by reading between the lines of an article, to discover some defamatory meaning therein is not sufficient to make it libelous.

In determining whether the article is libelous per se, the article alone must be construed, stripped of all insinuations, innuendo, colloquium, and explanatory circumstances. The article must be defamatory on its face "within the four corners thereof."

"In determining whether language is libelous per se, it must be viewed stripped of any pleaded innuendo. The meaning of the phrase 'per se' is 'taken alone, in itself, by itself.' Words which are libelous per se do not need an innuendo, and, conversely, words which need an innuendo are not libelous per se. 'An innuendo cannot extend the sense of the expressions in the alleged libel beyond their own meaning.' "

The decisions in this jurisdiction, as well as others, clearly establish that a publication is libelous per se, or actionable per se, if, when considered alone without innuendo: 1) it charges that a person has committed an infamous crime; 2) it charges a person with having an infectious disease; 3) it tends to subject one to ridicule, contempt, or disgrace; or 4) it tends to impeach one in his trade or profession.

As the publication is not libelous per se, there is no presumption of resulting damages. The law seeks to compensate for damage to the person, the reputation, or the property of an individual. It cannot and does not undertake to compensate for mere hurt or embarrassment alone.

Plaintiff does not allege or complain that there is any libel through the distortion of her photograph. In fact, she says it is a very good likeness, easily recognizable by her friends and acquaintances. What then does the publication say of and concerning the plaintiff when interpreted in its obvious and natural sense? 1) It represents her as saying that she has a sylph-like figure, which is, or may be, retained by eating more of Melts' rye and whole wheat bread. 2) It represents that she is Sally Payne, an exotic red-haired Venus; Venus being the goddess of beauty. 3) That she is a member of Folies de Paree, a sparkling Parisian Revue stage production, which is to appear at the National Theatre two days only, March 11 and 12. And, 4) that she indorses and recommends Melts' rye and whole wheat bread, and that it will give the necessary energy, pep, and vitality without adding extra weight.

It cannot be said that either one of these representations tends to disgrace and degrade the plaintiff, or to hold her up to public hatred, contempt, or ridicule, or cause her to be shunned or avoided.

Apparently the plaintiff recognized that this publication was not subject to the interpretation that it was libelous per se. The complaint alleges to some extent the innuendo upon which she relies to make it so and she went to considerable length in offering evidence in an effort to establish that the publication when considered in connection with other facts and circumstances could reasonably be construed as a libelous article. That was the theory of the trial below.

As the plaintiff does not allege or attempt to prove any special damages and does not allege or attempt to prove that a libelous construction was placed upon the publication by those who saw it, and it not being libelous per se, it is unnecessary for us to further discuss libel per quod or to determine whether the publication under consideration is sufficient to constitute such a libel.

The defendants were entitled to a judgment of nonsuit on the cause of action for alleged libel.

Plaintiff's second cause of action is based upon the right of privacy, so termed. It is clear that the first issue when considered in connection with the charge of the court was submitted upon the theory of this cause of action.

The question of the existence of this right is a relatively new field in legal jurisprudence. In respect to it the courts are plowing new ground and before the field is fully developed, unquestionably perplexing and harassing stumps and runners will be encountered.

In determining to what extent a newspaper may publish the features of an individual under any given circumstances necessarily involves a consideration of the Constitutional right of free speech and of free press. People do not live in seclusion. When a person goes upon the street or highway or into any other public place, he exhibits his features to public inspection. Is a newspaper violating any right of the individual, or doing more than exercising the right of free press, when it publishes a correct image of such features? Must a distinction be drawn between those in private life and those in public office or public life, and if so, when does a person cease to be a private citizen and become a public character? If a newspaper may publish the features of an individual in connection with an article that is laudatory, does it not also possess the right to publish the same in connection with an article that is critical in its nature so long as it speaks the truth? If the people are entitled to know what their Governor, or their President, or other public servant, is doing and saying, is it reasonable to hold that they are not entitled as a matter of course to ascertain and know through the newspapers his physical features and appearance? These and many other questions which may hereafter arise in connection with this type of litigation are not now before us for decision.

So far as we have been able to ascertain, no court has yet held that it constitutes a tort for a newspaper to publish an image of an individual when such publication is not libelous, except when such publication involves the breach of a trust, the violation of a contract, or when the photograph is used in connection with some commercial enterprise, and we are presently called upon to decide only the right of an individual to prohibit the unauthorized use of an image of her features and figure in connection with and as a part of an advertisement.

The subject is likewise dealt with at length in *Pavesich* v. *New England Life Insurance Co*. All former decisions are likewise fully discussed in this opinion, in which the court holds that the unauthorized publication of plaintiff's photograph in connection with an advertising enterprise gives rise to a cause of action. In the opinion, Cobb, J., quoting at length and with approval from the dissenting opinion of Gray, J., in *Roberson* v. *Rochester Folding-Box Co.,* said in part:

> Instantaneous photography is a modern invention, and affords the means of securing a portraiture of an indivdual's face and form in invitum (of) their owner. While, so far as it merely does that, although a species of aggression, I conceded it to be an irremediable and irrepressible feature of the social evolution. But if it is to be permitted that the portraiture may be put to commercial or other uses for gain, by the publication of prints therefrom, then an act of invasion of the individual's privacy results, possibly more formidable and more painful in its consequences than an actual bodily assault might be. Security of person is as necessary as the security of property, and for that complete personal security which will result in the peaceful and wholesome enjoyment of one's privileges as a member of society there should be afforded protection, not only against the scandalous portraiture and display of one's features and person, but against the display and use thereof for another's commercial purposes or gain. The proposition is to me an inconceivable one that these defendants may unauthorizedly use the likeness of this young woman upon their advertisement as a method of attracting widespread public attention to their wares, and that she must submit to the mortifying notoriety, without right to invoke the exercise of the preventive power of a court of equity.
>
> I think that the plaintiff has the same property in the right to be protected against the use of her face for defendants' commercial purposes as she would have if they were publishing her literary compositions. The right would be conceded if she had sat for her photograph, but, if her face or her portraiture has a value, the value is hers exclusively until the use be granted away to the public. Any other principle of decision, in my opinion, is as repugnant to equity as it is shocking to reason.
>
> It would be, in my opinion, an extraordinary view, which, while conceding the right of a person to be protected against the unauthorized circulation of an unpublished lecture, letter, drawing, or other ideal property, yet would deny the same protection to a person whose portrait was unauthorizedly obtained and made use of for commercial purposes. Whether, as incidental to that equitable relief, she should be able to recover only nominal damages, is not material, for the issuance of the injunction does not, in such a case, depend upon the amount of the damages, in dollars and cents.

We are of the opinion that the reasoning in the *Pavesich* case is sound and establishes the correctness of the conclusion that the unauthorized use of one's photograph in connection with an advertisement or other commercial enterprise gives rise to a cause of action which would entitle the plaintiff, without the allegation and proof of special damages, to a judgment for nominal damages, and to injunctive relief, if and when the wrong is persisted in by the offending parties.

One of the accepted and popular methods of advertising in the present day is to procure and publish the endorsement of the article being advertised by some well-known person whose name supposedly will lend force to the advertisement. If it be conceded that the name of a person is a valuable asset in connection with an advertising enterprise, then it must likewise be conceded that his face or features are likewise of value. Neither can be used for such a purpose without the consent of the owner without giving rise to a cause of action.

We conclude therefore, that there was error in the judgment below and that the motion of the defendants for a judgment of nonsuit should have been sustained as to the plaintiff's cause of action sounding in libel, and that there should be a new trial on the cause of action alleging the unauthorized use of plaintiff's features and person in connection with said advertisement. Upon the present record, from which it appears that said photograph was used by mistake and without malice, and that the defendants immediately desisted from the use thereof upon the discovery of the mistake and made due apology therefore, the plaintiff would be entitled to a judgment for nominal damages only. As the defendants have not and did not persist in the wrong complained of, the right to injunctive relief is not here involved.

New trial.

Chapter VIII

Privacy and Advertising

Section 1

The Role of Advertising and the Right of Privacy

*Daniel M. Rohrer with Martin P. LoMonaco**

INTRODUCTION

Privacy and defamation are separate torts which share some common defenses. "Invasions of privacy and defamation are separate and distinct torts even though they share some of the same elements and often arise out of the same acts. The first is a cause of action based upon injury to plaintiff's emotions and his mental suffering; the second is a remedy for injury to plaintiff reputation. Invasion of privacy torts which require publication and defamation torts share a common defense of privileged communications which grant immunity to otherwise actionable publication" (*Froelich* v. *Adair*, 213 Kan. 357, 516 P.2d 993 (1973)).

Advertising comprises a broad field, as does the area of privacy. The penumbra in which we find these involves use of the plaintiff's name or likeness. This area interrelates more between advertising and privacy, than defamation. Hence, we will concentrate on the former.

Here, the term "advertising purposes" will be conceptualized to include: 1) the use of a person's name or picture for all types of promotional endeavors, such as a photograph as part of an advertisement, a heading on the cover of a magazine, a name or picture as part of a program; or 2) the enhancement of reputation and commercial value for the purpose of increasing trade at the expense of the plaintiff who may be a competitor.

Exceptions will also be considered, as where a person's name or likeness was used in the context of an article published as a matter of public interest; where a partnership or corporation attempts action for invasion of privacy; where the plaintiff has consented to the use of his name or likeness; and where the use of a public figure in a publication is not viewed to be for promotional endeavors.

LIMITS ON USE OF NAME OR LIKENESS FOR ADVERTISING OR TRADE PURPOSES

Introduction

Long ago, the law gave a remedy only for physical interference with life and property, and for trespass. Prior to 1890, every adjucated case involving a right of privacy, in this country and in England, was not based upon the existence of such right, but was founded upon a supposed right of property, or a breach of trust or confidence. Hence, a claim to a right of privacy, independent of a

---

*Our thanks to John McGivney of Boston College Law School for editing this section.

property or contractual right, had until then never been recognized in any decision (*Pavesich* v. *New England Life Ins. Co.*, 122 Ga. 190, 50 SE 68, 69 (1905)).

Centuries' absence of precedent for an asserted right might reasonably cause the courts to proceed with caution, as recognizing that right might invade the province of the law making power. Absence alone, however, is not conclusive of the question as to the existence of the right (*ibid.*).

Shortly before the turn of the 20th Century, Samual Warren and Louis Brandeis wrote that the right to life has come to mean the right to enjoy life, ". . . to be let alone . . . and the term 'property' has grown to comprise every form of possession—intangible, as well as tangible" (4 *Harv. LR* 193 (1890)). Warren and Brandeis cited a limited number of instances in which injunctions had been issued to enjoin certain invasions of privacy (*ibid.* at 208), and they set forth new criteria which should be established to further restrict infractions upon individual privacy (*ibid.* at 214–219).

Little more than a decade after the Warren-Brandeis article was published, the court of appeals heard its first test case on invasion of privacy, *Roberson* v. *Rochester Folding-Box Company*. Here the defendant made use of the picture of an attractive woman to advertise flour without her consent. In a close decision with a strong dissent, the court flatly denied the existence of any right to protection against such conduct, because of the lack of precedent; the purely mental character of the injury; the "vast amount of litigation" which might be expected to follow; the difficulty of drawing a distinction between public and private characters; and the fear of undue restriction of liberty of speech and freedom of the press (171 NY 538, 64 NE 442 (1902)). The court concluded that any such change in the law must rest in the hands of the legislature.

A wave of public disapproval, leading one of the concurring judges to take the unprecedented step of publishing a law review article in defense of the *Roberson* decision. In this article, Judge O'Brien argued that "we may assume that the press is not always a safe guide for either the bar or the public upon legal question or with respect to the real scope and effect of judicial decisions." (2 Col. LR 437 (1902).)

O'Brien's attempted defense of the decision was insufficient. Thus, enactment of a 1903 statute, now New York Civil Rights Law, Sections 50–51, prohibited the use of name, portrait, or picture of any living person without his prior written consent for "advertising purposes" or for "purposes of trade." Similar statutes have been adopted in Virginia, Oklahoma, and Utah.

In order to find an actionable invasion of privacy under these statutes, the courts must first determine that the publication which the plaintiff finds objectionable falls within the meaning of the statute. The courts have tended to be liberal in their interpretation of what constitutes "advertising purposes" or "purposes of trade," as in the following cases where the publication was found to be for such purposes.

In *Pavesich* v. *New England Life Insurance Co.*, a case which arose in Georgia only two years after the passage of the New York privacy law, the defendant's insurance advertising made use of the plaintiff's name and picture, as well as a spurious testimonial from him (122 Ga 190, 50 SE 68 (1905)).

The allegations of the petition were that in an issue of the *Atlanta Constitution* newspaper, there appeared a likeness of the plaintiff, easily recognized by friends and acquaintances, placed by the side of an ill-dressed and sickly looking person. Above the likeness of the plaintiff were the words: "Do it now. The man who did." Above the likeness of the other person were the words: "Do it while you can. The man who didn't." Below the two pictures were the words: "These two pictures tell their own story." Under the plaintiff's picture the following appeared: "In my healthy and productive period of life I bought insurance in the New England Mutual Life Insurance Co., of Boston, Mass., and today my family is protected and I am drawing an annual dividend on my paid-up policies." Under the other person's picture was a statement to the effect that he had not taken insurance, and now he realized his mistake. The picture was made from the negative without the plaintiff's consent, and the publication is peculiarly offensive to him. The statement attributed to the plaintiff in the publication is false and malicious. He never made any such statement, and has not, and never has had, a policy of life insurance with the defendant company, (*supra*).

The petition contained two counts—one for libel, and the other for a violation of the plaintiff's right of privacy. With the example of the New York statute before it, the Georgia court in turn rejected the *Roberson* case, accepted the views of Warren and Brandeis, and recognized the existence of a distinct right of privacy. Although there was no case precedent for this decision, and no Georgia law barring such invasions of privacy, in the words of the court, "the common law will judge according to the law of nature and the public good," (*supra*).

Thus the first form of invasion of privacy to be recognized by the courts consists of the appropriation, for the defendant's benefit or advantages, of the plaintiff's likeness. Consequently, in New York, as well as in many other states, there are a great many decisions in which the plaintiff has recovered when his name or picture, or other likeness, has been used without his consent to advertise the defendant's product, or to accompany an article sold, to add luster to the name of a corporation, or for other business purposes (Prosser, *Torts* (1971), 805).

It is the plaintiff's name as a symbol of his identity that is involved here, and not as a mere name. When the defendant makes use of the name to pirate the plaintiff's identity for some advantage of his own does he become liable (*ibid.*).

Pavesich was not only the first case to establish a right of privacy in advertising and promotional endeavors, but also it was the first to set limits on such protection. These perimeters include public figures and newsworthy items, consent, malice, disclosure, and other elements required for standing.

Public Figures as Newsworthy Items

A number of cases have held that a person who seeks public acclaim or has been thrust into the public limelight has waived his right of privacy to such a degree that even the unauthorized use of his name or likeness for advertising purposes does not constitute an actionable claim upon which relief may be granted. In *Pavesich,* on the other hand, the court held that an artist is not necessarily a "public character," whose position or status might be sufficient to waive his right to privacy, so that his picture might be used for advertising purposes (*supra*). Before identifying a number of cases in which public personages have not been protected because they were viewed as newsworthy, several instances will be cited in which such rights have not been waived.

Right of Privacy Protected

In *Spahn* v. *Messner* the court of appeals upheld a lower court decision that a publication of a fictionalized biography of a well known baseball pitcher, in which the author invented dialogue, incidents, and thoughts, could not be justified on the grounds that these literary techniques were customary for children's books. The court's decision was based on knowing falsity and reckless disregard for the truth on the part of the plaintiff, a criterion which will be explicated later under the heading entitled "Impact of Malice." "To hold that this research effort entitles the defendants to publish the kind of knowing fictionalization presented here, would amount to granting a literary license which is not only unnecessary to the protection of free speech but destructive of an individual's right—albeit a limited one in the case of a public figure—to be free of the commercial exploitation of his name and personality" (21 NY 2d 124, 233 NE 2d 840, 843 (1967)).

Palmer v. *Schonhorn Enterprises, Inc.* involves an action by well-known professional golfers seeking an injunction and damages with respect to use of their names by the defendant corporation in conjunction with a part of a game. The court held that the defendant corporation, which used the names of Arnold Palmer, Gary Player, Doug Sanders, and Jack Nicklaus in connection with a golf game, should not be permitted to commercialize upon such names merely because they had been so highly publicized. The mere fact that the plaintiffs' names were not advertised on the lids of the boxes, so that the purchaser would not know who the "23 famous golfers" were until he purchased and saw the contents of the box, would not mean that the golfers' rights of privacy were not invaded (96 NJ Super. 72, 232 A2d 458 (1967)).

In the following cases, the court concluded that while there may be some instances whereby public figures will not be protected from the commercial exploitation of their likeliness, at least in these cases the defendant is liable for appropriating name or likeness because proper consent had not been obtained: *Harris* v. *H.W. Gossard Co.*, 194 App. Div. 688, 185 NYS 861 (1921); *Sidney* v. *A.S. Beck Shoe Corp.*, 153 Misc. 166, 274 NYS 559 (1934); *Sinclair* v. *Postal Tel. & Cable Co.*, 72 NYS 2d 841 (1935); *Kerby* v. *Hal Roach Studios*, 53 Cal. App. 2d 207, 127 P. 2d 577 (1942); *Jansen* v. *Hilo Packing Co.*, 202 Misc. 900, 118 NYS 2d 162, affd. 282 App. Div. 935, 125 NYS 2d 648 (1952); *Birmingham Broadcasting Co.* v. *Bell*, 259 Ala. 656, So. 2d 314 (1953); *Gieseking* v. *Urania Records, Inc.*, 17 Misc. 2d 1034, 155 NYS 2d 171 (1956); *Wilk* v. *Andrea Radio Corp.*, 200 NYS 2d 522, mod. 13 App. Div. 2d 745. 216 NYS 2d 662 (1960); *Sharman* v. *C. Schmidt & Sons, Inc.*, 216 F. Supp. 401 (DC Pa. 1963); *Reilly* v. *Rapperswill Corp.*, 50 AD 2d 342, 377 NYS 2d 488 (1975).

Right of Privacy Waived

The court heard, in *Clover* v. *Fox Publishing Co.*, the claim of a woman, under legal age, who for several years had been a professional entertainer in the specialty of "high diving." On one occasion a picture was taken of her wearing a costume appropriate to her public performances. A copy of this photograph came into the possession of the defendant who, without the written consent of the plaintiff, or her guardian or parents, published a reproduction of it immediately in its publication known as the *National Police Gazette*. Directly below the picture appeared the words, "May Collier, A Great Trick Diver." On the same page appeared four other pictures of women vaudeville performers, attired in stage costumes. At the bottom of the page were the words: "Five of the Kind on This Page. Most of Them Adorn the Burlesque Stage, All of Them are Favorites with the Bald Headed Boys." Despite her claim that this publication of her picture was a violation of Sections 50 and 51 of the Civil Rights Law, the court decided otherwise. It rejected the proposition that the publication of her picture was a mere advertising sheet sold as a matter of trade. The court concluded that the statute fails to prohibit, under penalty of exemplary damages, a publication in a daily, weekly, or periodical paper or magazine of the portrait of an individual (162 App. Div. 297, 146 NYS 999 (1914)).

Dallesandro v. *Henry Holt and Company, Inc.* involves an action against the publishers of a book for violation of the Civil Rights Law of New York in displaying a picture on the cover showing the subject in conversation with the plaintiff. The court entered an order dismissing complaint and judgment because the picture illustrated an article on a matter of public interest. It therefore was not considered to have been for the purpose of trade or advertising within the prohibition of the statute. Unless it has no real relationship to the article, or unless the article is an advertisement in disguise, it would not be so. The court concluded that it makes no difference whether the article appears in a newspaper, magazine, television, motion picture, or in a book (4 AD 2 470, 166 NYS 2d (1957)).

In *Jenkins* v. *Dell Publishing Co., Inc.* the court held that the widow and children of a man who had been kicked to death by a gang of adolescents could not recover for invasion of their privacy by accurate factual accounting of the homocide in a detective magazine, illustrated with a photograph of the widow and children. It was published about three months after the homocide, when the matter was still newsworthy.

The court argued that: "For the present purposes, news need be defined as comprehending no more than relatively current events such as in common experience are likely to be of public interest. In the verbal and graphic publication of news, it is clear that information and entertainment are not mutually exclusive categories. A large part of the matter which appears in newspapers and news magazines today is not published or read for the value or importance of the information it conveys. Some readers are attracted by shocking news. Others are titillated by sex in the news. Still others are entertained by news which has an incongruous or ironic aspect . . ." (251 F.2d 447 (1958)).

Later in 1958 another complaint purports to allege two causes of action: 1) that defendants printed and published in *Confidential* a sordid article incorporating the plaintiff's name and photographs, without his consent, for the purpose of trade and for the primary purpose of amusing and astonishing the public, and not for the legitimate purpose of disseminating the news or actual events; and 2) that the same charges apply to the plaintiff's wife. The court concluded that although a newspaper or magazine is published for profit, the use of a name or picture in such publications does not *ipso facto* fall within "purpose of trade" under the statute giving right of action for damages to person whose name, portrait, or picture is used for the purpose of trade without written consent being first obtained. "Nor does the statute give a cause of action to those who through their own activities have become public figures" (*Goelet* v. *Confidential, Inc.*, 5 AD 2d 226, 171 NYS 2d 223 (1958)).

Mahaffey v. *Official Detective Stories, Inc.* involves action by the parents of a boy, who was killed by a knife-wielding assailant, against the publisher and distributor of the magazine which contained an article relating events surrounding his death. The lower court held that the mother and father could not recover on the theory of deprivation of property right because the article was published for reader interest and not to promote or publicize a particular product or service. On appeal the case was dismissed (210 F. Supp. 251 (1962)).

A well-known actress brought an action against the publisher of a magazine and its advertising agency for damages for an alleged invasion of her right to privacy in violation of the New York Civil Rights Statute. The Appellate Division held that where a photograph of the actress was properly published by the publisher in its magazine, and subsequently the publisher had the photograph republished in other magazines to advertise the publisher's magazine, the republication of the photograph was not a violation of her right to privacy in violation of the law (15 AD 2d 343, 223 NYS 2d 737 (1962)). The actress appealed, contending that it was undisputed that the publisher and its advertising agency had used her name and picture for advertising purposes without having first obtained her consent. She asserted that she was entitled to judgment as a matter of law, and that the fact that she was a public figure was no bar to her recovery. The court of appeals upheld the lower decision (*Booth* v. *Curtis Publishing Co.*, 11 NY 2d 907, 182 NE 2d 736, 15 AD 2d 343, 223 NYS 2d 737 (1962)).

In an action for invasion of the right of privacy, the court held that a plaintiff, who as a high school student had made important advances in radio communications and received considerable publicity in connection with this accomplishment, was not entitled to be compensated or to share in the profits of a textbook, intended for beginners and persons interested in radio generally, merely because his photograph was used as a frontispiece, followed by a brief summary of his achievements (*Klein v. McGraw-Hill, Inc.*, 263 F. Supp. 919 (1966)).

From the cases described above, it is possible to extrapolate the conclusion that even the name or likeness of a public figure may be exploited at least to some extent for commercial purposes unless the nature of the exploitation becomes extreme. However, the clearest statement of the law relating to public figures appeared in a 1953 case involving an action for inducing breach of contract, *Haelan Laboratories v. Topps Chewing Gum* (202 F. 2d 866 (CA2 1953)).

Molony v. Boy Comics Publishers, Inc. involves an action to recover damages for alleged violation of plaintiff's right to privacy under the Civil Rights Law based on the portrayal of Donald Plummer Molony in the defendant's comic magazine as a hero in a disaster in which plaintiff was a major figure. The court concluded there was no ground for damages under the Civil Rights Law, though there were minor errors in the portrayal (188 Misc. 450, 65 NYS 2d 173, 98 NYS 2d 119 (1950)).

In 1952 professional baseball players brought action to enjoin use of their photographs by Model Airplane Company by contract with Hit Parade, Inc. from whom Theatre Concession, Inc. purchased them. The court held that when the pictures were merely placed in boxes of popcorn without any advertising outside the package that the pictures would be found, an injunction would not be granted, without irreparable damage, *Jansen v. Hilo Packing Co., Inc.* (116 NYS 2d 251 (1952)).

The following cases further denied relief at least in part on the principle that the plaintiff had achieved a degree of public recognition and therefore was not entitled to recovery despite the fact that his name or likeness may have been used by another for promotional purposes: *Harris v. H.W. Gossard Co.*, 194 App. Div. 688, 185 NYS 861 (1921); *Sidney v. A.S. Beck Shoe Corp.*, 153 Misc. 166, 274 NYS 559 (1934); *Hanna Mfg. Co. v. Hillerich & B. Co.*, 78 F.2d 763 (CA5 Ga.), cert. den. 296 U.S. 645 (1935); *Martin v. FIY Theatre Co.*, 10 Ohio Ops 338, 26 Ohio L. ABA 67 (1938); *Paramount Pictures Inc. v. Leader Press, Inc.*, 24 F. Supp. 1004 (DC Okla., 1938); *O'Brien v. Pabst Sales Co.*, 124 F.2d 167 (CA5 Tex.), cert. den. 315 U.S. 823 (1931); *Continental Optical Co. v. Reed*, 119 Ind. App. 643, 86 NE 2d 306, reh. den. 119 Ind. App. 653, 88 NE 2d 55 (1949); *Pallas v. Crowley-Milner & Co.*, 334 Mich. 282, 54 NW 2d 595 (1952); *Cabaniss v. Hipsley*, 114 Ga. App. 367, 151 SE 2d 496 (1966); *Man v. Warner Bros. Inc.*, 317 F. Supp. 50 (DCNY, 1970); *Meeropol v. Nizer*, 381 F. Supp. 29 (DCNY, 1974).

Many of the cases discussed above have been ruled not only on the basis of the public personage and newsworthiness of the item involved, but on other factors as well. Regardless of whether a public figure or newsworthy feature is contained in the publicity, however, the plaintiff's consent is an important factor in determining whether an otherwise right of action may be precluded. The scope, time, and limits upon this condition will now be considered and delineated in the following three sections.

Right of Privacy Precluded by Consent

Obviously, there is no invasion of privacy if consent is given to the use of one's name or likeness. Such consent may be either oral or written. For example, typical of common law, Section 103–4–8,

Utah Code Annotated, 1943, provides among other things that "anyone who uses for advertising purposes or for purposes of trade the name, portrait, or picture of a person, if such person is living, without first having obtained the written consent of such person, or, if such person is dead, without the written consent of his heirs of personal representatives, shall be guilty of a misdemeanor." And Section 103–4–9 provides in part that "any living person, or the heirs or personal representatives of any deceased person, whose name, portrait, or picture is used within the state for advertising purposes or for purposes of trade, without written consent first being obtained, may maintain an action against such person for using his name, portrait, or picture to prevent and restrain the use thereof; and may in the same action recover damages for any injuries sustained by reason of such use, and if the defendant shall have knowingly used such a person's name, portrait, or picture in such manner as is declared to be unlawful, the jury or court, if tried without a jury, may in its discretion award exemplary damages" *(Donahue v. Warner Bros. Pictures, Inc.*, 194 F.2d 6 (1952)).

Earlier in New York, where a privacy statute also existed, the court decided that unless an individual's consent to the publication of his picture in a booklet sold by a corporation to its patrons attending a bicycle race was in writing, there would exist an incomplete defense to invasion of privacy for advertising purposes or for purposes of trade. In this case, the publication was held to be for purposes of advertising *(Miller v. Madison Square Garden Corporation*, 176 Misc. 714, 28 NYS 2d 811 (1941)).

Later in 1961, action for damages for violation of a plaintiff's right of privacy by reason of publication of his name and cartoons in violation of the agreement between an animated cartoon producer and distributor produced the decision that the publication was not for the purpose of advertising or enhancing trade. When the distributor advanced funds to be recouped from profits from distributing efforts, he conferred absolute title to the cartoon on distributor, entitling it to recall the cartoon to a television company without producer's consent *(Fleischer v. WPIX, Inc.*, 21 Misc. 2d 110, 197 NYS 2d 356, affd. 10 AD 2d 688, 199 NYS 2d 423, 213 NYS 2d 632 (1961)).

In 1969, Ayn Rand sued the Hearst Corporation to recover for its use of her name without her consent *(Rand v. Hearst Corporation*, 31 AD 2d 406, 298 NYS 2d 405 (1969)). Ayn Rand brought action against the publisher to recover under the Civil Rights Law of New York because of the reference to a book written by her claiming that she "enjoys" the "same kind of mystique analysis as" the author of the paperback book and that "their underlying drive is the same." The quotation was an excerpt from a review of the paperback book in a newspaper. The state supreme court dismissed the publisher's affirmative defenses; the appellate division reversed the order and dismissed the complaint, holding that the publisher did not violate the Civil Rights Law. On appeal, the case was reversed again, upholding the original decision and granting Ayn Rand's claim for the unauthorized use of her name without her consent (26 NY 2d 806, 257 Ne 2d 895 (1970)).

Other cases relating to these conclusions are as follows: *O'Brien v. Pabst Sales Co.*, 124 F.2d 167 (CA5, Tex, 1941), cert. den. 315 U.S. 823; *Tanner-Brice Co. v. Sims*, 174 Ga. 13, 161 SE 819 (1931); *Marek v. Zanol Products Co.*, 298 Mass. 1, 9 NE 2d 393 (1937); *Harlow v. Buno Co.*, 36 Pa. D & C 101 (1939); *Johnson v. Boeing Airplane Co.*, 175 Kan. 275, 262 P.2d 808 (1953); *Porter v. American Tobacco Co.*, 140 App. Div. 871, 125 NYS 710 (1910); *Sidney v. A.S. Beck Shoe Corp.*, 153 Misc. 166, 274 NYS 559 (1934); *Hammond v. Crowell Pub. Co.*, 253 App. Div. 205, 1 NYS 2d 728 (1938); *Buscelle v. Conde Nast Publications, Inc.*, 173 Misc. 674, 19 NYS 2d 129 (1940); *Metzger v. Dell Publishing Co.*, 207 Misc. 182, 136 NYS 2d 888 (1955); *Durgom v. Columbia Broadcasting System, Inc.*, 29 Misc. 2d 394, 214 NYS 2d 752 (1961); *Lomax v. New Broadcasting Co.*, 18 App. Div. 2d 229, 238 NYS 2d 781 (1963).

Limits of Consent

While in some cases it may be clear that the plaintiff had consented to a particular use of his name or likeness, in other cases dispute may arise as to whether his name or likeness was used in a manner to which he had not agreed. If the plaintiff's consent has been exceeded, there may be a cause of action for invasion of privacy.

Beyond Limits of Consent

Almind v. *Sea Beach Railway Co.* represents a case in which the use of the plaintiff's picture for alleged "advertising purposes of trade," appears to be in violation of the Civil Rights Law. The evidence shows the presence of the plaintiff, her six year old child, and her sister-in-law at a place where a picture was about to be taken and later used to teach passengers a self-protecting way to enter and leave a car. On appeal, the court decided that evidence of her understanding and consent is insufficient, under the statute, to authorize the defendant. If it were, any person making a picture of one willing to sit for it could use it for advertising, by proving that the photographer disclosed the purpose and that she either consented or did not demur. The court further decided that the picture was taken for advertising, but not for trade purposes (157 App. Div. 230, 141 NYS 842 (1913)).

Feeney v. *Young* involved an action brought under the Civil Rights Law of New York for damages in the exhibition of the plaintiff's picture without her written consent. The plaintiff, in giving birth to a child, was compelled to undergo a "Caesarean section" operation. The defendant was her physician. She consented orally with the defendant that a moving picture might be taken of the operation, to be exhibited for medical societies and in the interest of medical science. The picture was then exhibited publicly in two of the leading moving picture houses in New York as part of a picture which was named "Birth." The exhibition was made clearly for the purposes of trade. The court decided that the picture, as presented on the screen, constitutes an offense under the statute (191 App. Div. 501, 181 NYS 481 (1920)).

Another case involving the program, "$64,000 Challenge," produced a similar court ruling. Again the action was brought by the contestant against the broadcasters on the basis of an alleged rigging of the contest. The court ruled that the complaint was insufficient to allege libel, for lack of allegation of special damage, but that the plaintiff should be permitted to replead (*Holt* v. *Columbia Broadcasting Systems, Inc.*, 22 AD 2d 791, 253 NYS 2d 1020 (1964)).

In these cases, the court found the defendant's action and behavior consistent with the plaintiff's claim that consent had been exceeded. An early example of this category involved a complaint alleging that the defendant was a photographer employed to take pictures of guests in the plaintiff's home, and was paid an agreed upon price for such employment. The plaintiff further contended that two photographs were taken of herself without her consent, and with the consent of her husband, with the understanding that they would be their personal property and their exclusive right to dispose of as they so desired. In violation of the plaintiff's rights, and without her consent, the defendant sold a proof or negative to a newspaper, which it published in connection with a false, scandalous, and defamatory article at the expense of the plaintiff, according to the plaintiff. The court ruled for the plaintiff on counts of both defamation and invasion of privacy, requiring the defendant to pay $10 within 10 days (*Holmes* v. *Underwood & Underwood, Inc.*, 225 App Div 360, 233 NYS 153 (1929)).

Additional cases in which the court found the scope of consent to have been exceeded are as follows: *Sinclair* v. *Postal Tel. & Cable Co.*, 72 NYS 2d 841 (1935); *Young* v. *Greneker Studios*, 175 Misc 1027, 26 NYS 2d 357 (1941); *Russell* v. *Marboro Books*, 18 Misc 2d 166, 183 NYS 2d 8 (1959);

Canessa v. *J.I. Kislak, Inc.*, 97 NJ Super 327, 235 A 2d 62 (1967); *Manger* v. *Kree Institute of Electrolysis, Inc.*, 233 F.2d 5 (1956); *Smith* v. *WGN, Inc.*, 47 Ill App 2d 183, 197 NE 2d 482 (1964).

Within Limits of Consent

The courts have not always been in agreement with the plaintiff's contention that consent has been exceeded, however. In fact, at least as many cases have been ruled to the contrary.

For example, after a plaintiff orally consented to use of her picture for any legitimate purpose except for trade or advertising, defendant published her picture in *McCall's* Magazine. A jury returned the verdict that the picture was not used for purposes of trade or advertising (*Donohue* v. *McCall Corporation*, 51 NYS 2d 727 (1944)).

In *Callsa* v. *Whisper, Inc.* the complaint alleges that defendant Harrison owned and published a group of magazines one of which is called *Whisper*. It is asserted that the defendants conspired to induce the plaintiff, then eighteen years old, and who was employed by one of them, to participate in a picture on the assurance that the picture was to be made "solely for the purpose of posing one Gene Haver and that the photograph or others or reproductions thereof of the infant plaintiff would not be used or published in any of their magazines or publications or elsewhere." These representations, it is alleged, were knowingly false and were made for the purpose of using the plaintiff's photograph in the publication of the defendants without her consent and against her will and for "profit and commercial" advantage to the defendants from which they derived. The complaint then indicates that the picture, and its printed caption, were given wide circulation and were intended to and do portray to readers that the infant plaintiff was in a night club with a male companion and that she smoked and drank intoxicating beverages, which was untrue and was known by these defendants to be untrue.

The court decided that in determining whether or not this action may be maintained, it is immaterial whether the use by defendants' of plaintiff's picture holds her up to ridicule or contempt, inasmuch as the action is not one brought for libel (101 NYS 532 (1950)).

In 1953 another plaintiff enrolled in a Model and Charm School of the defendant, at whose request the plaintiff posed for two photographs and submitted a supply of them to be kept on file. Upon completion of the modeling course the plaintiff registered as a professional model with the modeling agency also operated by the defendant. An agreement was signed between the plaintiff and the defendant, which the plaintiff admits, but also raises questions as to its validity and construction. By the terms of the agreement, the defendant was to endeavor to obtain modeling jobs for the plaintiff for one year. In return for this, the plaintiff was to cooperate with the defendant by keeping her supplied with late photographs, and making herself available for publicity stunts and programs. The plaintiff's picture then appeared in the *Chicago Defender* with the statement that she was a contestant in the "Miss Jet Credit" contest.

The court was asked to decide whether there was such a waiver of the right of privacy by the plaintiff's consent as to deny her recovery against the defendants. The court decided that since she had entered into the agreement described above, she was not entitled to recovery on the theory of invasion of privacy by publication of a news item that she had entered a beauty contest to be run in connection with the grand opening of a store and the publication of the accompanying photograph furnished by the agency (*Dabbs* v. *Abbott Publishing Co.*, 44 Ill App 2d 438, 193 NE 2d 876 (1963)).

In a case involving the issues of public personages, sufficiency of a plaintiff's identification, mistaken use of picture, malice, as well as consent, a plaintiff brought an action against the publisher of *Gay Atlanta* magazine and Atlanta's Playboy Club seeking to recover damages for violation of her right of privacy. In count 1 she alleged that for the past six years she had been an "exotic dancer," and in 1960 had had her photograph taken to be used for the purpose of advertising herself and her act at various night clubs and show places throughout the U.S. She contended that the defendants had obtained a copy of the photograph in some unknown manner and, without her knowledge or consent, had published it in an advertisement carried in *Gay Atlanta* for several weeks inviting the public to Atlanta's Playboy Club. Under her photograph in the advertisement she was billed as "Dawn Darling—Provocative and Exciting Exotic Dancer," and with the assertion "She's Terrific." In the picture she was clothed only in two tassels and a scanty G-string.

Plaintiff claimed that she had never appeared at Atlanta's Playboy club nor used the stage name "Dawn Darling." Rather there was another woman dancing at the club under that name. The magazine was distributed weekly in the City of Atlanta and attributed to have a wide circulation among people who are looking for a place of entertainment and who consult it for the purpose of selecting various types of amusement. Proof before a jury trial tended to support these allegations.

Count 2 added the contention that the photograph was used deliberately and maliciously with an intent to mislead the public and thereby damage her reputation.

The court concluded that there are at least three necessary elements for recovery under the theory of public disclosure of embarrassing private facts about the plaintiff: a) the disclosure of private facts must be a public disclosure; b) the facts disclosed to the public must be private, secluded, or secret facts and not public ones; c) the matter made public must be offensive and objectionable to a reasonable man of ordinary sensibilities under the circumstances" (*Cabaniss* v. *Hipsley*, 114 Ga App 367 151 SE 2d 496, 501 (1966)).

The court concluded that: "Plaintiff was what is commonly referred to as a strip-tease, and, by the very nature of her occupation, the facts disclosed were neither private nor embarrassing to her. We prefer not to use the term 'waiver' in our decision here. Without precise analysis this concept may receive indiscriminate application (*supra*, 502).

Before arriving at its judgment, the court emphasized the overlap found in the four distinct kinds of invasion of privacy: 1) intrusion upon the plaintiff's seclusion or solitude, or into his private affairs; 2) public disclosure of embarrassing private facts about the plaintiff; 3) publicity which places the plaintiff in a false light in the public eye; 4) appropriation, for the defendant's advantage, of the plaintiff's name or likeness. We consider this analysis well-founded and take it as a starting point for our deliberations here" (*supra*, 500).

The court conluded that on the basis of none of the four conditions did the defendant invade the privacy of the plaintiff who had not intended to keep her photograph secret or private, and who had sought and consented to the type of publicity which she received through the appearance of the photograph. The court also held, however, that if, on another trial, the jury should find that there was an unauthorized appropriation of the dancer's photograph and that private club's acts and conduct in using such photograph were of a character to import a premeditated or conscious and deliberate continuation of the appropriation, an award of punitive damages in favor of the exotic dancer would be authorized.

A year later, in *Martin* v. *Senators, Inc.*, the court ruled that when a woman authorized the taking of her picture and its use on a bulletin board of a club, membership in which was open to the public, she waived her right of privacy with respect to such photographs. The court further concluded that the club's subsequent use of the photograph in a newspaper advertisement was not unreasonable interference with the woman's right of privacy (418 SW 2d 660 (1967)). Other cases which join consent, advertising, and privacy with intrusion, public figures, false light, and appropriation as they relate to the use of plaintiff's name or likeness are as follows: *O'Brien* v. *Pabst Sales Co.*, 124 F.2d 167, cert den 315 U.S. 823 (1941); *Pallas* v. *Crowley-Milner & Co.*, 334 Mich 282, 54 NW 2d 595 (1952); *Johnson* v. *Boeing Airplane Co.*, 175 Kan. 275, 262 P.2d 808 (1953); *Sherwood* v. *McGowan*, 3 Misc 2d 234, 152 NYS 2d 658 (1956); *Sharman* v. *C. Schmidt & Sons, Inc.*, 216 F. Supp 401 (1963); *Wrangell* v. *C.F. Hathaway Co.*, 22 App Div 2d 649, 253 NYS 2d 41 (1964).

The cases listed above make substantial advances in depicting legal limits of consent in advertising and privacy, as do the preceding descriptions of cases which were held to be either not for purposes of advertising, notwithstanding a plaintiff's claim to the contrary, or if for purposes of advertising, at least not in excess of reasonable limits of consent on the part of the plaintiff for a variety of reasons.

Duration of Consent

The question as to how long consent for the publication of one's name or likeness for advertising purposes remains effective has frequently arisen as a critical issue in privacy cases. Courts have come to a variety of conclusions with regard to the liability of an employer who continues to use the name or likeness of an employee for advertising purposes or for purposes of trade after the termination of the employment relationship. Courts have further questioned the continued validity of consent when a long period of time has elapsed since the agreement was made, or when the plaintiff has formerly revoked his consent to the use of his name or picture for purposes of advertising or trade.

Termination of Employment

Since the State of Texas does not recognize a right of privacy, in awarding damages for the unauthorized continued use by the employers of a branch manager's name on a form letter mailed with advertising matter after the termination of his employment and the right to use the name of an employee, the court ruled that no useful purpose would be served by remanding the case to the court below for another trial (*U.S. Life Ins. Co.* v. *Hamilton*, 238 SW 2d 289, 293 (1951)).

In an earlier case, it had been determined that during the period of time between the termination of employment and termination of employment contract, employers were permitted to send customers monthly statements and delivery tickets bearing the name of a salesman who had already been terminated (*Scharaga* v. *Sinram Brothers*, 275 App Div 967, 90 NYS 2d 705 (1949)).

In an action against an insurance company on a state agency contract for continuing to receive benefits after termination of the contract and for unauthorized use of the plaintiff's facsimile signature on its policies, the court concluded that the plaintiff was owed only his commissions in the amount of $33.37. The court further ruled that the plaintiff could not recover compensation for the use of his facsimile signature stamp for a period after termination of the agency contract even if such use was unauthorized (*Schmieding American Farmers Mut. Ins. Co.*, 138 F Supp. 167 (1955)).

Mrs. Frances P. Tullos brought an action for damages suffered by her due to the publication of her likeness in a certain advertisement that appeared in the *Atlanta Journal*. The advertisement included a picture of "Lustre-Color Home Hair Coloring," various matter describing it, an order form, and a reproduction of her photograph, above the following language: "Miss Elgie Sprague, Lustre-Color authority from New York, will be in Rich's Drug Department, street floor, Tuesday, July 28, through Saturday, August 1, to advise you on your correct Lustre-Color shade." The court held that evidence on the issue of alleged unauthorized use of the plaintiff's portrait for commercial purposes, was sufficient to support a jury verdict for the plaintiff (*Colgate-Palmolive Company* v. *Tullos*, 219 F.2d 617 (CA5, 1955)).

Another complaint shows that for years the plaintiff had been employed under the defendant, posing as "The Man in the Hathaway Shirt;" and the use of the plaintiff's posed photograph in connection with the sale of Hathaway shirts was contemplated by the parties. The plaintiff consented to the defendant filing with the U.S. Patent Office a trademark using his photograph with a black patch over one eye. After the plaintiff left the defendant's employ, the defendant extended its use of the plaintiff's photograph to advertising women's blouses, which prompted the complaint. Plaintiff contends that his contract with the defendant did not authorize the use of his photograph with respect to the sale of women's blouses; and the defendant contends that its right is not so limited.

The court concluded that the plaintiff's grievance is not the breach of his right to privacy, which he does not particularly seek, but the alleged unauthorized use of his photograph in a special way without extra compensation. By his contract of employment and his consent to defendant's use of his photograph in its trademark, plaintiff relinquished his right to privacy. In essence, plaintiff's action is for breach of contract, that is, the use of his photograph in excess of the right and privilege which he granted to defendant. Section 51 of the New York Civil Rights Law does not afford relief for mere breach of contract. The court pointed out from *Sherwood* v. *McGowan* (3 Misc 2d 234, 235, 152 NYS 2d 658, 659) that "resort to the statute under these circumstances perverts its purpose." (*Wrangell* v. *C.F. Hathaway Co.*, 22 AD 2d 649, 253 NYS 2d 41 (1964)).

Lapse of Time or Revocation

In perhaps the first case to consider consent in connection with the right of privacy, the court found it difficult to deny that Mary Garden had agreed to the use of her name and picture. Indeed, for more than 20 years this plaintiff unquestionably permitted defendant to identify her name, her beauty, and her popularity to designate the product as "Parfum—Mary Garden." No other inference could be drawn from the writing signed by her stating that: "I am pleased to give you herewith permission to use my name and portrait in connection with the perfume which you have originated, known as the Perfume—Mary Garden" (*Garden* v. *Parfumerie Riquad*, 151 Misc 692, 271 NYS 187 (1933)).

Nor could belief be extended to the claim that the importance of the document was unknown to her and that she never intended to allow the defendant's predecessor this privilege. Not only did she maintain silence for more than 20 years while he made use of her name and portrait, but entranced, perchance, by the seductiveness of the aroma of the perfume, she indulged herself in poetic flight by writing to the defendant: "How could I object to anything so charming? And thanks a million times for the bottles already received" (*ibid.*).

In *Garden* v. *Parfumerie Riquad, Inc.*, the court concluded that of all the objections raised by the plaintiff, only one was worthy of judicial consideration, sufficient for the maintenance of this action, and entitling the plaintiff to the relief sought: "The one that permission to use name and portrait is revocable stands out with force. It is the well-settled law of this state that a gratuitous license—and that is the best that can be said of the permission granted by the plaintiff—to use name and portrait, is revocable at any time, even though action has been taken upon it. The court cannot lend itself to defendant's claim that, having trademarked the article and invested considerable money to popularize it, no revocation is possible. It may well be that by revocation serious impairment of business results. But that is a danger and risk assumed in accepting a consent unlimited as to time and against which, in the beginning, guard could easily be had. Regardless of plaintiff's reason for her refusal to continue permission to use her name, and even admitting that her reason is ulterior and mercenary, it cannot be denied that her name and her portrait are her own and during life solely at her disposal. She therefore cannot be gainsaid in her refusal, and defendant must be restrained. However, whatever wares have been manufactured by the defendant or are in the process of manufacture may be purveyed by the defendant, but no perfume or other toilet accessory may be produced as Mary Garden perfume or perfumed with Parfum—Mary Garden" (151 Misc 692, 271 NYS 187 (1933)).

All of the cases discussed thus far have involved the issues of consent and/or public figures as they relate to the use of name or likeness in advertising and the right of privacy. Still another condition, which can alter a court's decision with regard to either consent or public figures, is that of malice.

Impact of Malice

Fewer cases of malice have arisen than have other elements of invasion of privacy, and in many cases a lack of malice is completely immaterial to the liability anyway. Nevertheless, in some cases the question of malice, like the question of written consent, may affect the amount of damages that may be recovered. Likewise, malice may be overcome with consent, just as a lack of consent may be overcome by being a public figure.

Probably the most conspicious case which may be useful in defining the malice concept, as it relates to the use of name or likeness in advertising, is that of *Time* v. *Hill*, where the U.S. Supreme Court reversed a lower decision, finding malice to be nonexistent as its basis for ruling that no invasion of privacy had occurred. On the contention that *Life* magazine had falsely reported that a new play portrayed an experience suffered by the Hill family, the court rejected the negligence standard where public figures are involved, holding that the publisher must know that newsworthy reports are false or that he acted in reckless disregard of the truth.

On the malice question the Supreme Court concluded that: "Even negligence would be a most elusive standard, especially when the content of the speech itself affords no warning of prospective harm to another through falsity. A negligence test would place on the press the intolerable burden of guessing how a jury might assess the reasonableness of steps taken by it to verify the accuracy of every reference to a name, picture, or portrait . . ." (385 U.S. 374 (1967)).

Alleging that the *Life* article gave the knowingly false impression that the play depicted the Hill incident, Hill sued for damages under New York statute providing a cause of action to a person whose name or picture is used by another without consent for purposes of trade or advertising. The trial court instructed the jury that liability under the statute depended upon a finding that the *Life* article was published, not to disseminate news, but as a dictionalized version of the Hill incident and for the purpose of advertising the play or increasing the magazine's circulation.

On this issue, the U.S. Supreme Court concluded that: "The requirement that the jury . . . find that the article was published 'for trade purposes,' as defined in the charge, cannot save the charge from Constitutional infirmity. 'That books, newspapers, and magazines are published and sold for profit does not prevent them from being a form of expression whose liberty is safeguarded by the First Amendment.' *Josepf Burstyn, Inc. v. Wilson.*" (*Time v. Hill*, 385 U.S. 374 (1967)).

Although the conviction was not obtained in this case, in dicta *Cabaniss v. Hipsley (supra)* further illustrates the role of malice in the allegedly unauthorized use of name and likeness. Here no evidence was offered of an intentional misuse of the photograph on the part of the defendant. He simply published the photograph given to him by the agent of the other defendant, assuming that it was a photograph of "Dawn Darling." Notification of the mistake was not made to him while the advertisement was running; nor does the evidence disclose any circumstances from which it might be inferred that he had, or was in a position to have, actual knowledge of the mistake.

Without any evidence upon which to predicate liability for punitive damages against defendant Cabaniss, such damages were sought on the basis that not only was the plaintiff's photograph used without her consent, but that it was used deliberately and maliciously with an intention on the part of the defendants to mislead the public and thereby damage petitioner's reputation.

The court concluded that it does not think that there was any duty on the part of defendant Cabaniss to discover and prevent the mistake—"should have known"—so that a failure to do so would authorize an award of punitive damages: "Punitive damages can be awarded upon the same basis as in other torts, where a wrongful motive or state of mind appears, but not in cases where the defendant has acted innocently, as for example in the belief that the plaintiff has given his consent" (*supra*).

Thus it appears that a conviction might have been obtained for lack of consent only if actual malice had been demonstrated in the evidence and if punitive damages had been sought therefrom.

In a later case, a divorced husband brought action against his divorced wife for a decree enjoining her from using his surname for advertising or trade purposes, in contravention of their agreement, and for incidental damages, both compensatory and general. After agreeing not to use plaintiff's name by virtue of their divorce, defendant placed an advertisement in a newspaper setting forth change of business name, a listing in the telephone directory using plaintiff's name. Defendant furthermore used plaintiff's name on the lawn in front of the defendant's place after previously agreeing not to use plaintiff's name in the event of divorce. Since these uses of plaintiff's name for advertising purposes were only isolated instances and not continued for any length of time, the court concluded that in the absence of any showing of malice, one whose name has been wrongfully used cannot recover exemplary damages (*Fullerton v. Kennedy*, 19 Misc 2d 502, 187 NYS 2d 213 (1959)).

The following year, in *Emanuel v. Freelance Photographers Guild, Inc.*, the court concluded that the record satisfactorily establishes that defendants sold plaintiff's photograph in good faith and in the honest belief that it was the photograph of another woman, from whom they had obtained for a consideration a release to sell it, and in the absence of proof that defendants knowingly used plaintiff's portrait or picture, exemplary damages may not be awarded (28 Misc 2d 503, 219 NYS 2d 626 (1960)).

Other cases involving the accidental use of plaintiff's name or likeness for advertising purposes, in which the malice contention was defeated, are as follows: *Peck v. Tribune Co.*, 154 F 330 (CA, 1907)., 214 U.S. 185 (1907); *Flake v. Greensboro News Co.*, 212 NC 780, 195 SE 55 (1938); *MacIver v. George Braziller, Inc.*, 32 Misc 2d 477, 224 NYS 2d 364 (1961); *Man v. Warner Bros., Inc.*, 317 F. Supp. 50 (DCNY, 1970).

Extent of Disclosure of Plaintiff's Name or Likeness

In order for there to be an invasion of privacy for the use of name or likeness for advertising or trade purposes, it must be clear that the defendant's publication or otherwise reproduced and disseminated facsimile clearly identifies or refers to the plaintiff.

Sufficiency of Identification

Loftus v. Greenwich Lithographing Co. involved an action predicated on the provisions of Sections 50 and 51 of the New York Civil Rights Law to enjoin the respondents from using the portrait or picture of the plaintiff for advertising purposes, or for the purposes of trade, without having her written consent, and to recover damages sustained by the plaintiff from such use of her portrait or picture. On appeal, the court reversed a lower judgment and upheld the plaintiffs claim (192 App. Div. 251, 182 NYS 428 (1920)).

In this case, an actress appeared in the Midnight Frolics in a rose garden scene in a special costume called the rose costume. She had her photograph taken in this costume by one who testified that he was taking photographs of several of the artists in that play, representing different parts, and that he made artistic reproductions of Miss Loftus in a red costume representing a rose. There is evidence that this costume was never worn by any person other than the plaintiff, that she so appeared in public, that she became known widely in that character, that she would be readily recognized from the photograph, and particularly from the costume and pose, even though there were, as here, a slight change in the outline of the features and in the poise of her head, incident to enlarging the portrait or picture and adapting it to a particular character by the respondents in the preparation of a poster of a photoplay known as "Shame" (*ibid.*).

This photograph was reproduced in an issue of *Harper's Bazaar,* the *Metropolitan Magazine,* and *Town and Country* without the plaintiff's consent. Furthermore, the plaintiff had no connection with the photoplay "Shame," and she did not pose in the photoplay "Shame." Posters for advertising the photoplay "Shame" were displayed in various parts of the city of New York and vicinity. The word "Shame" in the poster was printed in very large letters. The poster represented a man standing between the advertisement at the extreme left and the advertisement a little to the right of the center, and looking and pointing his right hand in scorn at a woman represented as standing at the extreme right of the poster, with her head slightly bowing (*ibid.*).

Young v. *Greneker Studios* represents a case in which the court determined that a mannequin in the form, features, and likeness of a human model is a "portrait" or "picture" within the New York Civil Rights Law authorizing action for an injunction and damages by any person whose name, portrait, or picture is used for trade purposes if such person has not granted consent (175 Misc. 1027, 26 NYS 2d 357 (1941)).

In *Kerby* v. *Hal Roach Studios, Inc.* the court further decided that the circulating of a letter bearing the plaintiff's name as the apparent signer of a handwritten signature in a feminine hand, of a nature which casts doubt on plaintiff's moral character, when the letter was circulated for purposes of advertising a moving picture, is actionable as constituting an invasion of the plaintiff's right of privacy. Nevertheless, in this case, the court further concluded that, based upon the facts stated above, since the defendants had no intent to refer in the letter to the plaintiff and did not know of her existence, there was no malice and therefore no defense to action for invasion of the plaintiff's right of privacy (53 Cal. App. 2d 207, 127 P.2d 557 1942)).

Adrian v. *Unterman* provided the dicta that a surname alone is within the provision of the New York law authorizing one whose name has been used for advertising purposes without his consent to maintain an action to enjoin such use. Nevertheless, in this case the plaintiff had transferred the right to use his trade name or facsimile of his signature long before the institution of the court action (281 App. Div. 81, 118 NYS 2d 121, affd. 306 NY 771, 118 NE 2d 477 1952)).

By reason of an action for damages for violation of the plaintiff's right of privacy resulting from the publication of his picture without his consent, the case of *Buzinski* v. *Doall Company* suggests that a mechanical science magazine possessed the right to publish the picture of a combination trailer car known as a land yacht, as a matter of public interest, and that the plaintiff, whose appearance therein was reasonably related to the subject of the picture could not maintain an action for invasion of privacy, even though he did not consent to its publication (175 NE 2d 577 (1961)).

In an action which was brought for the alleged invasion of the plaintiff's right of privacy and for libel, the court held that the manufacture and sale of a fabric which reproduced a piece of newspaper with an article reporting the loss of a tennis match by the plaintiff did not constitute an invasion of the plaintiff's right of privacy in violation of the Civil Rights Law of New York or a libel, in the absence of special damage (*Moglen* v. *Varsity Pajamas Inc.*, 13 AD 2d 114, 213 NYS 2d 999 (1961)).

In a case whereby a professional entertainer filed an action to recover damages for invasion of privacy, defamation, and unfair competition, the court concluded that if the legislature had intended that whenever an anonymous speaker extolled a commercial product a cause of action might arise if anyone could substantiate the claim that the voice was mistaken as his. In this case the complaint was not defective in failing to demonstrate competitive interest or purpose served or real confusion of product which would lead to the loss of opportunity in the entertainment field. Merely identifying an individual defendant as an officer of co-defendant corporation is insufficient to prove personal liability of the officer for tortious acts allegedly committed by the corporation, its officers, etc., but the corporate officer is liable for torts in which he personally participated, regardless of whether he was acting within the scope of his authority (*Lahr* v. *Adell Chemical Co.*, 300 F.2d 256 (CAL, 1962)).

The case of *LaForge* v. *Fairchild Publications, Inc.* involved a proceeding on the claim of invasion of privacy by defendants' pictorial story and its publication. From an order denying the defendants' motion to dismiss, an appeal produced the judgment that a publication, without the plaintiff's consent, of a picture of the plaintiff and others garbed in sport jackets of particular material is not for advertising purposes or for the purpose of trade within New York Civil Rights Law and does not invade the plaintiff's privacy, where no one was identified and illustrations related to article of legitimate public interest to more than 20,000 subscribers to a publication largely emphasizing matters of interest to those in men's and boys' wear and textile industries (23 AD 2d 636, 257 NYS 2d 127 (1965)).

The case of *Brauer* v. *The Globe Newspaper Company* rendered the conclusion that publicity which casts the plaintiff in a false light in the public eye through a publication in the defendant's newspaper of a photograph of the plaintiff could not be maintained where the photograph as published did not indicate to the public that it was one of the plaintiff, despite the fact that a small group of neighbors, friends, and relatives to the plaintiff, familiar with him and with the circumstances in which the photograph had been taken, recognized him as the person depicted therein (351 Mass 53, 217 NE 2d 736 (1966)).

Yet in *Flake* v. *Greensboro News Co.* the court determined that the publication of the plaintiff's photograph or likeness in connection with an advertisement was sufficient for her to recover for invasion of privacy despite the fact that the picture bore as a caption the name of a person other than the plaintiff (212 NC 780, 195 SE 55 (1938)).

In *Cabaniss* v. *Hipsley,* however, the court ruled that a publication wrongly identifying the name of another, "Dawn Darling," with the plaintiff's picture served as an insufficient basis to authorize a verdict for general damages to the plaintiff's reputation, since there was no evidence suggesting that the stage name "Dawn Darling" was in a category materially different from that which would include the stage names which plaintiff had used (*infra*).

Incidental Use of Name

As was implied in the previous section, in order to constitute an invasion of privacy under the New York Civil Rights Law, the use of a name must amount to a meaningful commercial purpose rather than a mere incidental taking (*Moglen* v. *Varsity Pajamas, Inc., supra*). There have been several cases in which the reference to the plaintiff has been held too incidental to amount to an invasion of privacy.

In a case of a motion picture entitled "The Inside of the White Slave Traffic," which showed a factory building upon which there was a sign bearing the name and business of the plaintiff, the court held in *Merle* v. *Sociological Research Film Corp.* that the use of the plaintiff's name is not for the purpose of obtaining trade or advertisement, but merely appears in the picture because it was placed upon the building which is a part of the picture. It is therefore a mere incidental part of a photograph which cannot be presumed to add to the value of the photograph for trade or advertising, and even a use that may in a particular instance cause acute annoyance cannot give rise to an action under the statute unless it fairly falls within the terms of the statute (166 App. Div. 376, 152 NYS 829 (1915)).

The case of *Humiston* v. *Universal Film Mfg. Co.* involved the presentation of the plaintiff's name and picture as news in a motion picture film depicting current events, and the publication of the plaintiff's name and picture on certain posters used to announce the subjects of current interest exhibited by the film. The court concluded that if the presentation of this film be not a crime, the use of the plaintiff's name or picture in the approach to the theatre and upon the screen is incidental to the exhibition of the film itself (189 App. Div. 467, 178 NYS 752 (1919)).

In *Stillman* v. *Paramount Pictures Corporation* the plaintiff, in the conduct of a gymnasium for the training of prize fighters in the City of New York, had acquired an excellent world-wide reputation and established valuable good will. The defendants produced and distributed, for public exhibition, a fictional dramatic motion picture entitled "The Country Girl" in which one of the principal characters utters words, carried on the sound track as part of the fictional story, to the effect that he could go to "Stillman's Gym and get a punch-drunk fighter." This action is based on the plaintiff's claim that the defendants used his name, without his consent, for purposes of trade in violation of Civil Rights Law, Sections 50 and 51, and that the reference to the plaintiff was libelous. The court concluded that these sections do not prohibit the incidental, momentary, and isolated use of such words as "Stillman's Gym," even if such place is operated by a living person of the name "Stillman" (2 App. Div. 2d 18, 153 NYS 2d 190, affd. 5 NY 2d 994, 184 NYS 2d 856, 157 NE 2d 728 (1956)).

On the other hand, in *Schneiderman* v. *New York Post Corporation,* the court held that the defendant club's publication at least twice in defendant newspaper of an advertisement story mentioning the plaintiffs as having been recently married following their prior meeting at the club, without written consent of the plaintiffs, did violate the Civil Rights Law and defendants were therefore liable for damages. The court concluded that although a single publication of the alleged news item possibly may take on the posture of "an incidental publishing," its reprint, however, exemplifies an effort towards soliciting and inducing readers to patronize the named country club (31 Misc. 2d 697, 220 NYS 2d 1008 (1961)).

Remaining Limits on Whom May Bring Action Against Whom

Many of the conditions upon which action for the unauthorized use of the plaintiff's identity for advertising or trade purposes will withstand judicial scrutiny have been delineated above. Additional statutory and common law stipulations will be set forth in the following pages. In each case it should be kept in mind, however, that the right of privacy is a personal right and cannot, generally, be asserted by anyone other than the individual whose privacy has been invaded (*Schuman* v. *Loew's Inc.*, 135 NYS 2d 361 (1954)).

1. *Decedent*. This section suggests that while a person, firm, or corporation that uses for advertising or trade purposes the name, portrait, or picture of any living person without having first obtained written consent of such person, may be guilty of an invasion of privacy, such right to privacy does not exist on behalf of any relative or personal representative of any deceased person (*Runyon* v. *United States*, 281 F.2d 590 (CA3, 1960)).

A privacy claim is a peculiarly personal one (*Shibley* v. *Time*, 40 Ohio Misc 51, 59 (1974)). It cannot be asserted by a family member, it cannot be assigned, and it does not survive death (*Young* v. *That Was the Week That Was*, 312 F.Supp. 1337 (ND Ohio, 1969), affd. 423 F.2d 265 (CA6, Ohio 1970)).

A Utah statute, however, forbids the use for advertising purposes or purposes of trade of the name, portrait, or picture of a deceased person without the written consent of his heirs or personal representatives. In *Donahue* v. *Warner Bros. Pictures, Inc.* the court held that a picture within the meaning of the statute included any representation of the person, including such representation by an actor portraying the deceased (194 F.2d 6 (CA10, Utah 1952)).

2. *Corporate Name or Partnership Name*. In the case of *Jaggard* v. *P.H. Macy & Co.* Ginette Jaggard, who was a well-known dress designer, originally filed a certificate to do business under the assumed name of "Ginette deParis," and thereafter engaged in business under that name. In 1935, she caused to be formed a corporation known as Ginette deParis, Inc., and granted to it the sole and exclusive right to use the name she had adopted in connection with the sale of dresses. The violation alleged is the use of the name "Ginette deParis" in connection with the sale of patterns of a dress designed by the plaintiff. It is clear that no cause of action has been established. Neither a partnership name nor a corporate name are within the protection of the New York Civil Rights Law. According to the court it follows logically that a name assumed for business purposes only, the exclusive uses of which has been granted to a corporation, is in the same category. "In no aspect do the facts establish the charge of unfair competition" (176 Misc. 88, 26 NYS 2d 829, affd. 265 App. Div. 15, 37 NYS 2d 570 (1941)).

In *Shubert* v. *Columbia Pictures Corporation* the complaint alleges that the owner of the Winter Garden Theatre, which has become known to the general public as one of the greatest show places in the nation, which possesses a widespread reputation in connection with its presentation of theatrical plays, musical comedies, and other types of entertainment, and which enjoys valuable good will in connection with such entertainment, also owns some kind of property right to the appearance of these qualities. When the defendant produced the motion picture "The Jolson Story," which purports to show the Winter Garden Theatre, both interior and exterior, the famous runway known as "the bridge of thighs," consisting of an extension and elongation of the stage throughout the orchestra, and a large number of plays produced by the individual plaintiffs and their affiliated companies in which Al Jolson appeared and played a prominent role, the plaintiffs brought forth this cause of action.

Here the court announced that in order for the plaintiffs to make out a case of unfair competition, the proof must show the existence of a property right, plaintiffs' ownership of that property, and a misappropriation of that property right by the defendant, or at least a deception of the public occasioning damages to the plaintiffs. It held that notwithstanding the plaintiffs' assertion that they own the good will in and to the Winter Garden Theatre, and that this good will had been appropriated by the defendant, that the plaintiffs do not possess any property right in the name "Winter Garden" (189 Misc. 734, 72 NYS 2d 851, affd. without op. 274 App. Div. 751, 80 NYS 2d 724 (1947)).

3. *Public Domain. Seidelman* v. *State* involved a claim against the State of New York resting upon a violation of the Civil Rights Law and an allegation that the State published and circulated the claimant's picture for trade and advertising purposes without consent. The State moved for an order dismissing the complaint for failure to state a cause of action and for lack of jurisdiction. The court held that the action was maintainable under the statute waiving the State's immunity from suit. This statute waives immunity as to "liability and action," but only where an individual or corporation would be required to answer to an action for the same thing (202 Misc. 817, 110 NYS 2d 380 (1952)).

In the appeal of *Jaccard* v. *P.H. Macy, & Co.*, the court went on to suggest that:

In addition to the reasons upon which the trial court based its decision in awarding judgment to the defendant, we find that such judgment was warranted for the further reason that the dress involved herein had been placed in the public domain without the protection of copyright. Accordingly, in the absence of unfair competition, defendant had the right to copy the dress, or to sell patterns thereof, and in doing so could truthfully state that the dress was designed by the individual . . . Under the circumstances the use of the individual plaintiff's name as the designer of the dress, in connection with the magazine article advertising a pattern thereof, would not afford her any right to damages under Sections 50 and 51 . . . even if her true name, rather than an assumed business name, had been used" (*supra.*, 571).

4. *No Allegation for Advertising or Trade.* In the case of *Pittera* v. *Parade Publications, Inc.* the court examined the pleading and the offending article, annexed to the complaint, and concluded that the cause of action fails to allege that the unauthorized use of the photo and article were used for trade or advertising purposes and is insufficient. The court went on to state that: "The language of the article and the facts set forth in the pleading persuade us that the deficiency could not properly be supplied on a new pleading to meet the requirements of the applicable sections of the Civil Rights Law" (15 AD 2d 882, 225 NYS 2d 478, 479 (1962)).

5. *Abuse of Process.* In *Cardy* v. *Maxwell* the plaintiff alleges that the unauthorized use of his name was for the purpose of extorting money from him to induce defendants to withdraw his wife's deceit action. "This is clearly not a use for advertising purposes," said the court, and it is "not a use for 'the purpose of trade' within the meaning of the statute. Sections 50 and 51 of the Civil Rights Law were, as their language clearly indicates, designed to prevent *commercial* exploitation of a person's name, portrait, or picture" (9 Misc. 2d 329, 169 NYS 2d 547, 550 (1957)). The court concluded that the defendants' use of the plaintiff's name for the purpose of avoiding trial on merits was sufficient to state a cause for action for abuse of process (*ibid.*).

Conclusion

In the above pages a variety of conditions have suggested that when the unauthorized use of identity may have occurred for purposes of advertising or trade under both statute and common law, another variety of reasons sometimes determines the outcome of the case. More often than not, however, a combination of reasons serves to determine the ruling of the court. Whether a case is determined to be for advertising or trade purposes seems to depend at least in part upon how private the defendant is, how malicious the defendant is, how much is given in return for the plaintiff's consent, and so forth. Many of these conditions overlap, and the question remains: how the defendant may know in advance exactly where to draw the line. This dilemma is somewhat mitigated, however, by a rather liberal latitude granted to the defendant by the courts. Such a judicial atmosphere is illustrated above and below.

In *Shubert* v. *Columbia Pictures Corporation* the complaint alleges, for example, that the defendant has caused to be published a circular containing a synopsis describing the story of the motion picture. Here the name "Shubert," the theatre owners' name, is mentioned in two instances—once in connection with the identification of one Baron who is stated to have become manager for the Shuberts, and again in connection with the identification of the individuals who first opened the Winter Garden Theatre (*supra*., 853). Despite the further taking of the theatre's identity mentioned above, the court found that whether or not plaintiffs specifically granted their leasees the right to use the name Winter Garden is immaterial. For the good will of a public building, such as a theatre or hotel, runs with the building, and that good will passes with the lease of the building to the lessee and cannot be severed therefrom even by its first adopter and user (*supra*., 855). The court concluded that despite a 45 year period of shows presented at the Winter Garden prior to its conversion into a movie theatre, and despite the fact that a motion picture showing Jolson performing at the Winter Garden in the shows in which he appeared there has destroyed the possibility of producing a motion picture concerning the history of that theatre and the personalitities who appeared in the shows which were produced there, the court denies the prospect that a picture based upon the plays which took place in the Winter Garden, whether bearing the title "Winter Garden" or some other title, whether using the talent of ex-Winter Garden stars, or whether using the name of the owners of the theatre in its advertisements, could be produced as a box-office or entertainment success (*supra*., 856). The court held that even the combination of the above comprised an insufficient cause of action. Under the Civil Rights Law it could not be for purposes of advertising or trade.

A somewhat similar case occurred in *People* v. *Robert R. McBride & Co*. in which the author's unfolding of the historical narrative of strike breaking includes the name of Stern inside, as well as his picture on the front cover, along with eight others. The court ruled that neither the picture nor the name was used for purposes of advertising the book (159 Misc. 5, 288 NYS 501, 504 (1936)). Consequently, the plaintiff failed to state a claim for which relief could be granted.

One of the most well known and classic cases held not to be for purposes of advertising or trade is that of *Sidis* v. *F-R Pub. Corporation*. While often viewed as a public figure/newsworthy case, it is a consent case as well. Here the court decided that the unauthorized publication of the intimate details of private life are not entitled to an absolute immunity from the prying of the press, and that a limited scrutiny may be had of the private life of any person who has achieved, or has had thrust upon him, the questionable and indefinable status of a "public figure" (113 F. Rep. 2d 806 (CA2, 1940)).

Usage of Name or Likeness as Invasion of Privacy

This section will include the indorsement of products or services, the usage of name on product, the usage of name as part of corporate name, the usage of name or likeness to increase circulation of publication, the usage of pictures for display purposes, in newspapers or other printed publications, and on television or in motion pictures; the usage of name or likeness in cable television, the mistaken usage of picture, and the usage of name or likeness in a false light to misrepresent authorship or statements, or to alter the picture of a plaintiff.

Indorsement of Products or Services

The unauthorized use of someone's identity in an effort to convey the impression that this person indorsed defendant's products or services has been held by the court to comprise an invasion of privacy. For example, the use of the name of the plaintiff, as a noted educator and writer, without his consent by the booksellers in advertising an edition of their standard works as being their selection constitutes a violation of the New York Civil Rights Privacy Law. (*Eliot* v. *Jones*, 66 Misc. 95, 120 NYS 989 (1910).)

In *Schneiderman* v. *New York Post Corporation*, the court considered an action for injunctive relief and damages for the unauthorized use of the plaintiff's names in violation of the Civil Rights Law. It held that the defendant club's publication at least twice in defendant newspaper of advertisement story mentioning plaintiffs as having been recently married following their prior meeting at the club, without written consent of the plaintiffs, violated the statute, and defendants were liable in damages (*supra*).

In another action under the Civil Rights Law, the court held that where plaintiff did not consent in writing to the use of her name and picture for advertising purposes in a camera manual which advertised a camera, publication of the plaintiff's picture in the manual is not within the scope of the statute (*Selsman* v. *Universal Photo Books, Inc.*, 18 AD 2d 151, 238 NYS 2d 686 (1963)).

The court held in *Brociner* v. *Radio Wire Televisions, Inc.* that where the plaintiff was in a contractual relationship with the defendant and designed certain devices for it, truthful statement of the plaintiff's association with product in defendant's advertising would not support a cause of action for breach of the New York Civil Rights Law (15 Misc 2d 843, 183 NYS 2d 743 (1959)).

Thompson v. *G.P. Putnam's Sons* involved an action for alleged violation of the right to privacy statutes and for libel brought against the publisher and others by a literary critic on complaint that the Introduction and Note appearing in a book and allegedly intended to increase the sales of the book used language implying that the plaintiff regarded the book as having literary merit, whereas contrary opinion was the case. The court held that the claims under the right of privacy statute were sufficient as against a dismissal motion but that the claim for libel was insufficient.

On the latter issue, the court felt that: "The mere fact that the plaintiff's personal opinion may be that the work is without literary merit is of no consequence. The reading public may disagree with plaintiff's personal view, in which event his reputation would not be adversely affected by the false attribution to him of a favorable opinion as to the literary merit of the book" (40 Misc. 2d 608, 243 NYS 2d 652, 655 (1963)).

In an action for libel and for invasion of the right to privacy and publicity based on use of plaintiff's picture in an advertising campaign put on by the defendant, the court held that an action for libel on the theory that advertising in which a plaintiff's picture was used to promote the sale of beer subjected plaintiff to conspicious ridicule and scorn could not be maintained where the plaintiff voluntarily permitted his picture to be taken for a consideration and executed at the time releases giving unrestricted permission to the use of his picture, distorted in character or form. Hence the judgment is for the defendant (*Sharman* v. *C. Schmidt & Sons, Inc.*, 216 F. Supp. 401 (ED, Pa. 1963)).

Other cases involving the indorsement of products or services include the following: *Peck* v. *Tribune Co.*, 154 F. 330 (CA7, Ill), revd. on other grounds 214 U.S. 185 (1907); *Foster-Milburn Co.* v. *Chinn*, 134 Ky. 424, 120 SW 364, app. 137 Ky. 834, 127 SW 476 (1909); *Flake* v. *Greensboro News Co.*, supra; *Pallas* v. *Crowley, Milner & Co.*, 322 Mich 411, 33 NW 2d 911 (1948); *Jansen* v. *Hilo Packing Co.*, 116 NYS 2d 251 (1952); *Fairfield* v. *American Photocopy Equipment Co.*, 138 Cal. App.

2d 82, 291 P.2d 194 (1955); *Roberts v. Conde Nast Publications, Inc.*, 286 App. Div. 729, 146 NYS 2d 493 (1955); *Manger v. Kree Institute of Electrolysis, Inc.*, 233 F.2d 5 (CA2, NY 1956).

Thus it appears that one critical perquisite exists for the usage of another's name or likeness for the indorsement of products or services: consent. Without such consent, usually in writing, an action will lie for which relief may be granted provided a substantial relationship exists between the name or likeness employed and the advertisement itself (*Namath v. Sports Illustrated*, 48 AD 2d 487, 371 NYS 2d 10 (1975)).

Usage of Name on Product

Closely related to the use of one's identity for the indorsement of a product is the use of one's name to identify or promote a product. Thus it is in *Jaccard v. R.H. Macy & Co.*, where a designer of exclusive clothes for women, who designed a wedding gown with certain distinctive features using her own name to identify the product. In so doing, without obtaining a copyright on the product, the plaintiff lost the exclusive right to the use of her own name on similar products of defendant (*supra*).

A very different outcome occurs, however, in the case of *Orsini v. Eastern Wine Corporation*. Here the plaintiff sued for damages under Section 51 of the Civil Rights Law, and for an injunction restraining the defendant from using on its label the surname, Orsini, in conjunction with the plaintiff's coat of arms. Alleging that he is the oldest living member of the Orsini family, the plaintiff asserted the right to use the coat of arms. It was claimed that the defendant, without the plaintiff's consent, affixed the name Orsini to labels of certain of its wine products as well as the Orsini coat of arms for commercial and advertising purposes. The court ruled that the complaint here alleging identification by coat of arms and surname satisfies the requirements of the statute with repect to identification (190 Misc. 235, 73 NYS 2d 426 (1947), affd. 273 App. Div. 947, 78 NYS 2d 224, app. den. 273 App. Div. 996, 79 NYS 2d 870 (1948)). On appeal, the court concluded that the name Orsini, together with the family crest and the princely crown, identifies the plaintiff in the public mind as the individual whose name is being used without his consent for trade purposes.

Additional cases involved with the usage of name on products include the following: *Edison v. Edison Polyform & Mfg. Co.*, 73 NY Eq 136, 67 A 392 (1907); *Eliot v. Jones*, 66 Misc. 95, 120 NYS 989, affd. without op 140 App. Div. 911, 125 NYS 1119 (1910); *Prest v. Stein*, 22Q Wis. 354, 265 NW 85 (1936).

Usage of Name as Part of Corporate Name

In a number of cases, the court has confronted concern over the use of the plaintiff's name as part of a corporate designation as it comprises an invasion of privacy. In the case of *Tanner-Brice Co. v. Sims*, the court held that a corporation in the State of New York can by use acquire a right to use a trade name other than its corporate name in connection with its business; that a corporation, in adopting a trade name, can embrace the surname of another person, when this is done with the consent of that person. When the corporation uses such surname and on the faith of the license makes expenditures of money, such license becomes an agreement on a valuable consideration and is irrevocable. The right of a corporation to use the surname of another person with his consent is not prohibited by statute, nor does it violate his right of privacy (174 Ga. 13, 161 SE 819 (1931)).

The case of *Bernham v. Bernham-Stein Furs, Inc.* involved an action to enjoin defendants from using plaintiff's name in corporate defendant's title, and for an accounting. The court held that where the plaintiff and individual defendant entered into an agreement whereby the right to use the name of defendant corporation, which combined the names of plaintiff and individual defendant, would cease if parties disassociated themselves, the subsequent dissociation agreement, by which plaintiff and defendant released each party from any claim against the other, did not excuse breach of agreement not to use the name of corporation, and continued use violated the New York Civil Rights Law (123 NYS 2d 872 (1953)).

Likewise, when a person who has been in business for himself sells stock in such business to others, he loses any privacy right in the continued use of his name in connection with said business. Here by his own voluntary act he gave the corporation his name and the right to use it (*White* v. *William G. White, Inc.*, 160 App. Div. 709, 145 NYS 743 (1914)).

Usage of Name or Likeness to Increase Circulation of Publication

While over the years many common law decisions have sought to protect the privacy of plaintiffs against the unauthorized use of their identity for advertising or trade purposes, the New York Civil Rights Law specifically denies the right to publish a person's picture or to use his name in an article for the purpose of increasing the circulation of the offending publication. A number of decisions illustrate and qualify his intent.

The case of *Middleton* v. *News Syndicate Co., Inc.* involved an action for the unauthorized use of the name and picture of the plaintiff in violation of the Civil Rights Law and for libel. The plaintiff was at the time of the publication an unemployed model. She alleged that her name and picture appeared in the *Daily News* in a column known as *"The Inquiring Photographer."* She further alleged that she was described therein as a cigarette girl employed by the Commodore Hotel. The court concluded that the column which embodied the article containing the plaintiff's name and portrait was not intended or used for advertising purposes or for purposes of trade. Furthermore, the court held that the publication did not injure the plaintiff's reputation (162 Misc. 516, 296 NYS 120 (1937)).

In *Semler* v. *Ultem Publications, Inc.*, the court observed evidence that a professional model was an infant and that consent of her parents or guardian was not obtained for use of her photograph in a negligee which appeared in a magazine of defendant. The court authorized recovery for such unauthorized use regardless of whether the model herself had consented (170 Misc. 551, 9 NYS 2d 319 (1938)).

The case of *Thompson* v. *Close-Up, Inc.* represents an order denying defendant's motion for judgment on the pleadings. The court held that where the amended complaint alleged that plaintiff had no connection with dope selling, which was the subject of the defendant's magazine article, and was not a public figure in such field, it stated a cause of action under the statute protecting the right of privacy if published as part of an advertisement for advertising purposes. In this case the publication of the plaintiff's photograph in connection with the article was unauthorized (227 App. Div. 848, 98 NYS 2d 300, affg. 197 Misc. 921, 99 NYS 2d 864 (1950)).

Shortly thereafter the Levertons sued the Curtis Publishing Company for wrongful invasion of the plaintiff's right of privacy by publication of a photograph of Sue Leverton as she lay in the street immediately after being struck by an automobile. Two decisions rendered the conclusion that the defendant's publication of the photograph had constituted an actionable invasion of the plaintiff's right of privacy (*Leverton* v. *Curtis Publishing Co.*, 97 F.Supp. 181, 192 F.2d 974 (CA3, 1951)).

It has been determined by the court that even a fictionalization of a story based upon an actual trial, because it is not presented for the purpose of providing genuine information, constitutes a sufficient basis to allege a cause of action for invasion of privacy (*Hazlitt* v. *Fawcett Publications, Inc.*, 116 F.Supp. 538 (DC Conn. 1953)).

Yet printing or broadcasting the true facts of a trial, no matter how unpleasant the information may seem to the object, does not constitute an invasion of privacy even if it involves the name or identity of a rape victim (*Cox Broadcasting Corp.* v. *Cohn,* 420 U.S. 469 (1975)). As is pointed out by Lindmark and Fishman in Section Two of this chapter, the use of the name of a rape victim and her picture "would have sold more newspapers."

The principle established in the *Cox Broadcasting* decision was reaffirmed in the similar case of *Oklahoma Publishing Co.* v. *District Court of Oklahoma County.* Here the Supreme Court struck down a decision by Oklahoma courts barring three Oklahoma City newspapers from publishing the name and picture of an 11-year-old boy charged in a shooting death. The high court said that an Oklahoma judge abridged freedom of the press by issuing his gag order. The court said the information barred from publication was obtained in a public hearing and could not be suppressed. The judge issued a pretrial order prohibiting further display, ruling that the boy's right to rehabilitation outweighed any freedom of the press considerations or the public's right to know (429 U.S. 967 (1977)).

Immunity from invasion of privacy is not limited to information obtained as part of the court record, however. In a larger sense, if the name or likeness is used in connection with any newsworthy item, even without consent, it is likely that there will be no invasion of privacy for purposes of advertising or trade despite the fact that the unauthorized appropriation may very probably increase the circulation of the publication. This can be seen readily in the case of *Florida Publishing Company* v. *Fletcher.* Here an action was brought against a newspaper publisher for damages for alleged trespass, invasion of privacy, and for wrongful intentional infliction of emotional distress arising out of the publication of a photograph of the silhouette of the plaintiff's deceased daughter on the floor of the bedroom after a fire at the home of the plaintiff. The plaintiff first learned of the facts surrounding the daughter's death by reading the story and viewing the photographs published in the newspaper. The high court held that the plaintiff could not recover under the theory of trespass, in that there was an implied consent by custom and usage authorizing the photographer's entry into the home under circumstances in which the fire marshall and police officer invited the news media to accompany the marshall and officer in their investigation of a fire. On remand the court held that: "Due to such widespread and longstanding custom, reason and logic support the application of implied consent to enter the premises in the case before us. It, therefore, was not a trespass, and I would affirm the trial court" (340 So. 2d 914, 919 (Fla. 1977)). The trial court had dismissed the count alleging invasion of privacy and granted summary final judgment in favor of the publisher on the counts alleging trespass and emotional distress (see 319 So. 2d 100). Hence the court concluded that the facts of the case failed to constitute intrusion for purposes of invasion of privacy in violation of the plaintiff's Constitutional right.

Other Uses of Name

In a few cases where defendants made an unauthorized use of the plaintiff's name for advertising purposes, recovery for invasion of privacy has been allowed.

Recovery Allowed

Neyland v. *Home Pattern Co., Inc.* involved a magazine publisher who used a painter's name without his written consent to induce trade in patterns for a reproduction of one of his paintings by means of embroidering the painter's artistic production in a magazine offering for sale patterns based upon such reproductions. The court found the publisher liable under Section 51 of the Civil Rights Law as amended (e. 501, 65 F.2d 363, cert. den. 290 U.S. 661 (CA2, NY 1933)).

In *Coleman* v. *Ted's Auto Sales, Inc.*, the court held sufficient under the Civil Rights Law a complaint stating that the defendants falsely used the plaintiff's name, reputation, and widespread legal talent in the automotive business for the purpose of conveying to those with whom they did business and from whom they sought credit, through published credit reports, the notion that the plaintiff was financially connected with their firm and was responsible for its business policies for the purpose of inducing others, on the strength of the plaintiff's reputation, to impart credit to them (34 Misc. 2d 100, 33 Misc. 2d 739, 227 NYS 2d 693 (1962)).

The case of *Hamilton* v. *Lumberman's Mutual Casualty Company* involved a suit to recover for physical pain and suffering, embarrassment, and invasion of the right to privacy as a result of a newspaper advertisement placed by the insurance company in the name of the plaintiff for witnesses to an accident suffered by the plaintiff. The Supreme Court of Louisiana refused to hear the appeal of the insurance company for lack of jurisdiction, transferring it to the Court of Appeals (226 La. 644, 76 2d 916 (1954)). This court held that the evidence showed that the insured had suffered great mental anguish as a result of the invasion of privacy, but found the sum awarded excessive (82 So. 2d 61 (1955)).

Other instances in which recovery has been permitted for advertising or purposes of trade include the following: *Thompson* v. *Tilford*, 152 App. Div. 928, 137 NYS 523 (1912); *Kerby* v. *Hal Roach Studios*, 53 Cal. App. 2d 207, 127 P.2d 577 (1942); *Adrian* v. *Unterman*, 281 App. Div. 81, 118 NYS 2d 121, affd. 306 NY 771, 118 NE 2d 477 (1952); *Gieseking* v. *Urania Records, Inc.*, 17 Misc. 2d 1034, 155 NYS 2d 171 (1956); *Flores* v. *Mosler Safe Co.*, 7 NY 2d 276, 196 NYS 2d 975, 164 NE 2d 853 (1959); *Lahr* v. *Adell Chemical Co.*, 300 F.2d 256 (CA1, Ma 1962); *Palmer* v. *Schonhorn Enterprises, Inc.*, 96 NJ Super. 72, 232 A.2d 458 (1967); *Canessa* v. *J.I. Kislak, Inc.*, 97 NJ Super. 327, 235 A.2d 62 (1967).

Recovery Denied

Under varying circumstances, recovery failed to ensue despite the use of the plaintiff's name for advertising or trade purposes. In one case it was necessary for the wife to use her former husband's name in an advertisement after their divorce in order to publicize the fact that her business was being changed to another name (*Fullerton* v. *Kennedy*, 19 Misc. 2d 502, 187 NYS 2d 213 (1959)).

Another broad area in which recovery is not allowed for the appropriation of one's name even for advertising purposes occurs when the common law right of action is lost as a result of the plaintiff's voluntary use for publication of uncopyrighted material. Once the plaintiff has disseminated such material in connection with his own name and of his own accord, he has no claim against its further dissemination for any reason or purpose (*Rosenthal* v. *Kotler*, 26 Misc. 2d 947, 208 NYS 2d 167 (1960)).

Still another area in which recovery has been denied in a wide range of cases for the unauthorized use of one's name in advertising involves the sale and/or reuse of names from lists, such as subscription lists or lists of employees, without the consent of the individuals involved. On one such case, the court held that claims of privacy violations and deprivations of liberty and property under the Constitution concerning a statute authorizing the sale of copies of motor vehicle registration records by the Commissioner of Motor Vehicles, which allegedly led to considerable annoyance and inconvenience from merchandise solicitation through the mails, by telephone, and in person, were plainly unsubstantial. The complaint was dismissed (269 F.Supp. 880 (SDNY, 1967), 386 F.2d 449 (CA2, NY 1967)). In *Lamont* v. *Commissioner of Motor Vehicles*, the court reasoned that the individuals whose names were reused for advertising purposes had no complaint simply because they were required to register their motor vehicles for the same reason that the court rejects the claim that the outraged listeners may invoke the right of privacy or other Constitutionally protected interests to shut out radio broadcasts regardless of how noxious they may appear (*ibid.*, 882–883).

That same year the court went a step further in a proceeding on a complaint by the National Labor Relations Board which sought an order compelling our employer to produce personnel and payroll records or eligibility lists containing the names and addresses of all employees eligible to vote in a forthcoming union representation election. The court determined that one of the factors that tend to impede a free and reasoned choice in elections is the lack of information with respect to one of the choices available. The court further concluded that the Constitutional right to free association and privacy is not invaded by the removal of this impediment to free choice created by lack of communication. The list simply sets forth the names and addresses of those employed by the defendant. "(I)t tells nothing about their beliefs and associations . . . (T)hose who do not welcome visits to their homes are free to turn the visitors away and will have the protection of the law in doing so" (*National Labor Relations Board* v. *British Auto Parts, Inc.*, 266 F.Supp. 368, 373 (CDCA, 1967)).

In another action for an injunction restraining the defendant from disclosing or selling licensing and registration information, the court rendered its judgment for the defendant, further reinforcing the precedents mentioned above (*Chapin* v. *Tynan*, 158 Conn. 625, 264 A.2d 566 (1969)).

In a more recent case, the plaintiff and members of the class which he represents subscribed to publications or credit card privileges of the defendant who, without permission, sold, rented, or otherwise permitted the names of the plaintiff and the members of the class he represents to be entered into commercial use or distribution to persons not in privity with the publisher whose publication was subscribed for or the credit card company with which the member of the class had a contract. In an action brought to enjoin the publishers and credit card company from selling the subscription lists to direct mail advertisers, the court held that the practice complained of did not constitute an invasion of privacy and that the plaintiff could not adequately represent the interests of the class as a whole. (*Shibley* v. *Time, Inc.*, 40 Ohio Misc. 51 (1974), 45 Ohio App. 2d 69, 341 NE 2d 337 (1975).)

OTHER USES OF PICTURE

For Display Purposes

In general, the use of the plaintiff's picture in advertising displays constitutes an invasion of privacy. Seven years after the passage of the New York statute, the U.S. Supreme Court heard an action for the use of a photographed portrait for advertising purposes without first obtaining written consent. The higher Court upheld two lower court decisons which issued an injunction against the defendant and awarded damages to the plaintiff (*Sperry and Hutchinson Company* v. *Rhodes*, 220 U.S. 502 (1910)).

Shortly thereafter, a case in which consent was exceeded, *Almind* v. *Sea Beach Ry. Co.*, involved a violation of the New York Privacy Act because a street railway company, which took a picture of passengers entering and leaving a car, subsequently used it to teach passengers the proper way to enter and alight with safety. The court held that although one passenger had granted his oral consent, it could not replace the written consent required by the statute (*supra*).

The case of *Lane* v. *F.W. Woolworth Co.* suggests that the use of an actress' picture in a locket sold commercially for the purpose of making lockets more attractive comprised use for advertising purposes or for the purposes of trade within the Civil Rights Law which provides that any person whose portrait is used for advertising purposes or purposes of trade, without his written consent, may recover damages for injuries resulting from such unauthorized use, regardless of the fact that in this case it was printed on the back of the pictures thus allowing the buyer to replace the picture with a photograph more suited to his preference (171 Misc. 66, 11 NYS 2d 199 (1939)).

In a case whereby defendants published a handbill containing the plaintiff's photograph and name as part of a union membership drive, for the purpose of financial gain, and as an advertisement, the court held that a cause of action had been sufficiently stated (*Rubino* v. *Slaughter,* 136 NYS 2d 873 (1954)).

Other cases comprising an invasion of privacy for the display or other use of the plaintiff's picture for advertising purposes include the following: *Kunz* v. *Bosselman,* 131 App. Div. 288, 115 NYS 650 (1921); *Munden* v. *Harris,* 153 Mo. App. 652 (1911); *Harris* v. *H.W. Gossard Co.,* 194 App. Div. 688, 185 NYS 861 (1921); *Bennett* v. *Gusdorf,* 101 Mont. 39, 53 P.2d 91 (1935); *McCreery* v. *Miller's,* 99 Colo 499, 64 P.2d 803 (1936); *Fisher* v. *Murray M. Rosenburg, Inc.,* 175 Misc. 370, 23 NYS 2d 677 (1940); *Young* v. *Greneker Studios,* 175 Misc. 1027, 26 NYS 2d 357 (1941); *Eliot* v. *Jones,* 66 Misc. 95, 120 NYS 989 (1910); *Olan Mills, Inc.* v. *Dodd,* 234 Ark. 495, 353 SW 2d 22 (1962); *Canessa* v. *J.I. Kislak, Inc.,* 97 NJ Super. 327, 235 A.2d 62 (1967); *Fisher* v. *Murray M. Rosenberg, Inc.,* 175 Misc. 370, 23 NYS 2d 677 (1940).

In 1902, the display of a plaintiff's picture was held above any cause of action for the invasion of privacy in *Roberson* v. *Rochester Folding-Box Co. (supra).* While the passage of the Civil Rights Law shortly thereafter attempted to establish the Constitutional right of privacy, many expectations to both statutory and common law have occurred since that time. A few such cases are listed as follows: *Martin* v. *FIY Theatre Co.,* 10 Ohio Ops 338, 26 Ohio L Abs 67 (1938); *Harlow* v. *Buno Co.,* 36 Pa. D & C 101 (1939); *O'Brien* v. *Pabst Sales Co.,* 124 F.2d 167, cert. den. 315 U.S. 823 (CA5, Tex. 1941); *Toscani* v. *Hersey,* 271 App. Div. 445, 65 NYS 2d 814 (1946).

In Newspapers or Other Printed Publications

In a number of cases, the use of the plaintiff's picture in a newspaper or other publication for advertising or trade purposes has been held to comprise an invasion of privacy. For example, while the photographic reproduction of a plaintiff in a newspaper cartoon with statements indicating that the plaintiff had come from the country and "made good" was held by the court to be not libelous in the absence of special damage, the court did find libel in the selling for reproduction in other newspapers a cartoon published without the consent of the plaintiff based upon the New York Privacy Law (*McNulty* v. *Press Pub Co.,* 136 Misc 833, 241 NYS 29 (1930)).

In the case of *Griffin* v. *Medical Soc. of State of New York,* the plaintiff alleged that he was treated by two physicians who took certain photographs which were used under the title "The Saddle Nose" for purposes of advertising and trade when published as "before and after" treatment in a widely distributed journal. The court denied the defendant's motion to dismiss the complaint on the basis of insufficient evidence (7 Misc. 2d 549, 11 NYS 2d 109 (1939)).

One of the few cases in which the court found for the plaintiff on both counts of libel and invasion of privacy is that of *Pittera* v. *Parade Publications, Inc.* Here the court concluded that a complaint for libel charging the defendant's publication of an erroneous statement that the plaintiff had been married to a well-known executive and had terminated their relationship by divorcing him and marrying another stated as a cause of action where details of the entire article exposed the plaintiff to contempt.

Furthermore the court determined that the complaint for violation of the Civil Rights Law by unauthorized use of the plaintiff's photograph was sufficient as presenting a jury question concerning whether the photograph in connection with the entire article was used for purposes of trade (29 Misc. 2d 90, 216 NYS 2d 162 (1961)). It should be noted, however, that this decision was ultimately reversed, which properly places the final disposition of this issue in the section that immediately follows (30 Misc. 2d 706, 219 NYS 2d 998, 15 AD 2d 882, 225 NYS 2d 487 (1962)).

Several additional cases suggest instances in which the use of the plaintiff's picture in a newspaper or similar publication for advertising purposes has been held unacceptable. They are: *Almind* v. *Sea Beach R. Co.,* 157 App. Div. 230, 141 NYS 842 (1913); *Riddle* v. *MacFadden,* 116 App. Div. 353, 101 NYS 606 (1906), 201 NY 215, 94 NE 644 (1911); *Fitzsimmons* v. *Olinger Mortuary Asso.,* 91 Colo. 544, 17 P.2d 535 (1932); *Fisher* v. *Murray M. Rosenberg, Inc.,* 175 Misc. 370, 23 NYS 2d 677 (1940); *Korn* v. *Rennison,* 21 Conn. Supp. 400, 156 A.2d 476 (1959); *Metzger* v. *Dell Pub. Co.,* 207 Misc. 182, 136 NYS 2d 888 (1955); *Gautier* v. *Pro-Football, Inc.,* 304 NY 354, 107 NY 2d 485 (1952); *Rosemont Enterprises, Inc.* v. *Random House, Inc.,* 58 Misc. 2d 1, 294 NYS 2d 122 (1968); *Pagan* v. *New York Herald Tribune,* 32 AD 2d 341, 301 NYS 2d 120, affd. 26 NY 2d 941, 310 NYS 2d 327, 258 NE 2d 727 (1969).

A substantial number of cases have also suggested the converse: that the use of the plaintiff's picture for purposes of advertising or trade in a newspaper or other publication fails to constitute an invasion of privacy. The first such decision was rendered in 1902 when the court heard the case of *Roberson* v. *Rochester Folding-Box Co. (supra).*

Largely resulting from this decision, the New York Civil Rights Law on privacy was quickly passed. In one of the early interpretations of this statute, the court concluded that the use of any person's picture or portrait without his written consent for advertising purposes, or for purposes of trade, so as to warrant an injunction against such use, must be used for the dissemination of information, or for commerce or traffic. (*Jeffries* v. *New York Evening Journal Pub. Co.,* 67 Misc. 570, 124 NYS 780 (1910).)

Likewise an actress has no right of action under this section of the law for the publication of her portrait in a weekly magazine where it is shown that such picture is not used for advertising purposes merely because the magazine contains a number of advertisements. (*Colyer* v. *Richard K. Fox Pub. Co., supra.*)

In the case of *Murray* v. *New York Magazine Company,* the plaintiff brought an action pursuant to Section 51 of the Civil Rights Law to recover damages for an alleged invasion of privacy arising out of the defendant's unauthorized use of the plaintiff's photograph on the cover of an issue of *New York* magazine, which is published and distributed by the defendant. The court felt that a picture illustrating a matter of public interest is not considered to be used for advertising purposes or trade purposes within the prohibitionn of the Civil Rights Law unless it has no real relationship to the article, or unless the article is an advertisement in disguise.

Here, the court held that where a plaintiff was singled out and photographed because his presence in Irish garb constituted visual participation in St. Patrick's Day festivities, publication of his photograph on the magazine cover was in connection with the presentation of matter of legitimate public interest to readers, and bore a reasonable relationship to the presentation. Therefore, it was not a sufficient infringement to be considered actionable as having been used for the purpose of advertising or trade within the prohibition of the Civil Rights Law (27 NY 2d 406, 267 NE 2d 256 (1971)).

Similarly, it had been determined earlier that the use of one's name or picture in a newspaper, magazine, or newsreel, in connection with items of news, or one that is newsworthy, is not a use for advertising or trade within the Civil Rights Law but that an individual cannot be singled out and unduly featured merely because he is on the scene. (*Gautier v. Pro-Football, Inc.,* 304 NY 354, 107 NE 2d 485 (1952).)

Finally, the court held that the defendant's publication and exhibition of a story and photograph which accurately portrayed events underlying the death of the plaintiff's children who suffocated when they trapped themselves in a refrigerator located in the family home were not actionable on the theory of invasion of privacy under the Civil Rights Law because the subject matters was within the area of legitimate public interest. (*Costlow v. Cusimano,* 34 AD 2d 196, 311 NYS 2d 92 (1970).)

A picture illustrating an article on matters of public interest is not considered to be used for advertising or trade purposes as prohibited by the Civil Rights Law unless it has no real relationship to the article to which it refers or unless the article is an advertisement in disguise. (*LaForge v. Fairchild Publications, Inc.,* 23 AD 2d 636, 257 NYS 2d 127 (1965).)

Other cases which further set forth a theory for determining when the use of a plaintiff's picture for advertising purposes in a newspaper or other publication falls short of comprising an invasion of privacy are as follows: *Stern v. Robert R. McGride & Co.,* 159 Misc. 5, 288 NYS 501 (1936); *Pallas v. Crowley-Milner & Co.,* 334 Mich. 282, 54 NW 2d 595 (1952); *Oma v. Hillman Periodicals, Inc.,* 281 App. Div. 340, 118 NYS 2d 720 (1953); *Johnson v. Boeing Airplane Co.,* 175 Kan. 275, 262 P.2d 808 (1953); *Albert v. New York Telephone Co.,* 28 Misc. 2d 296, 204 NYS 2d 36, affd. 11 App. Div. 656, 203 NYS 1019 (1960); *Siequel v. Esquire, Inc.,* 4 App. Div. 2d 477, 167 NYS 2d 246 (1957); *Dabbs v. Robert S. Abbott Publishing Co.,* 44 Ill. App. 2d 438, 193 NE 2d 876 (1963); *Martin v. Senators, Inc.,* 418 SW 2d 660 (1967); *Wendell v. Conduit Mach. Co.,* 74 Misc. 201, 133 NYS 758 (1911); *Toxcani v. Hersey,* 271 App. Div. 445, 65 NYS 2d 814 (1946); *Dallesandro v. Henry Holt & Co.,* 4 AD 2d 470, 166 NYS 2d 805, appeal conditionally dismissed 7 NY 2d 735, 193 NYS 2d 635, 162 NE 2d 726 (1957); *Klein v. McGraw-Hill, Inc.,* 263 F. Supp. 919 (DCDC, 1966); *Murray v. New York Magazine Co.,* 27 NY 2d 406, 318 NYS 2d 474, 267 NE 2d 256 (1971); *Negri v. Schering Corp.,* 333 F.Supp. 101 (DCNY, 1971); *Grant v. Esquire, Inc.,* 367 F. Supp. 876 (DCNY, 1973); *McGraw v. Watkins,* 49 AD 2d 958, 373 NYS 2d 663 (1975); *Wallace v. Weiss,* 82 Misc. 2d 1053, 372 NYS 2d 416 (1975).

On Television or in Motion Picture

The use of one's picture for advertising or trade purposes, without consent, either on television or in the theatre, may be sufficient to warrant an actionable claim for invasion of privacy.

In the case of *Binns v. The Vitagraph Company of America,* a plaintiff, as a wireless telegrapher, had performed acts of great heroism by remaining at his post during a collision between steamships at sea, in which many lives were imperiled. He had refused to allow himself to be publicly exploited as a hero. Nevertheless, the defendant employed an actor to impersonate the plaintiff in scenes representing the disaster, and exhibited photographs so obtained as moving pictures, showing the person representing the plaintiff in ludicrous attitudes, etc. In this case, the jury decided that a verdict of $12,000.00 is not excessive. (147 App. Div. 783, 132 NYS 237 (1911).) On appeal the judgment was affirmed with costs (210 NY 51, 103 NE 1108 (1913)).

William L. Prosser believes the classic case for recovery for this aspect of privacy invasion has been *Melvin v. Reid.* Here Gabrielle Darley, a prostitute, had been tried for murder and acquitted in a famous case. She subsequently married, left the state and "thereafter at all times lived an exemplary, virtuous, honorable, and righteous life." The defendant produced and released a movie entitled "The Red Kimono," based upon the plaintiff's experiences, using her true maiden name and advertisng the film to be a true account (112 Cal. App. 285, 297 (1931)). Subsequent litigation raises several questions concerning the contemporary application of this case. Would this holding be justified in light of *Cox Broadcasting* v. *Cohn* case (*supra*)? Would this holding be justified if the marriage record was a public record? Would this holding have been different if the defendant had publicized the married name of the plaintiff rather than her true maiden name? Would it make any difference if the defendant had identified the plaintiff further by disclosing where she now lived?

In the case of *Blumenthal* v. *Picture Classics, Inc.*, the plaintiff sued under the Civil Rights Law for an injunction to restrain the defendants from unlawfully exhibiting her picture for trade purposes. Without her consent, the defendants had sold and distributed motion pictures of her, depicting her in the act of selling bread and rolls to passersby. These pictures were shown on the screen of various local theatres. The court found the plaintiff entitled to the relief allowed, and the order was affirmed with costs (235 App. Div. 570, 257 NYS 800 (1932), 261 NY 504, 185 NE 713 (1933)).

The case of *Freed* v. *Loew's Incorporated* involved an action in which the plaintiff posed as a sailor being depicted by an artist on world war service recruiting posters, and the artist made such improvements in the physique or features as were deemed desirable on the poster. More than 20 years later the defendant produced a motion picture entitled "Thunder Afloat," having the cooperation of the Navy Department. The pictured story showed fictitious scenes of operations by the U.S. Navy in World War I, especially in respect to the menace of U-boat submarine warfare. The poster appears as part of the dressing for a Navy recruiting office and is carried upon nine feet of film which are shown for six seconds of the 94-minute run. The sailor figure depicted resembles the plaintiff. His friends readily recognized him. Citing *Binns* v. *Vitagraph Co.* (*supra*), the court held that the result cannot be regarded as a portrait or picture of the plaintiff within the meaning of the Civil Rights Law (175 Misc. 616, 24 NYS 2d 679 (1940)).

In the case of *Gautier* v. *Pro-Football, Inc.*, it was determined that a person travelling upon public highways may expect to be televised, but only as an incidental part of a general scene, and a person attending public events may be expected to be televised in the status in which he attends. As a mere spectator he may be taken as part of the general audience, but he may not be picked out of the crowd alone, thrust upon the screen and unduly featured for public view. However, where one is a public personage, an actual participant in a public event, or where some newsworthy incident affecting him is taking place, the right of privacy is not absolute (*supra*).

In 1954, a case arose out of a showing in Salt Lake City Utah, of the movie "Look for the Silver Lining" which was a musical show based on the life story of Marilyn Miller and her rise to fame in vaudeville and musical comedy during the first two decades of this century. Secondarily, the motion picture portrayed the life of Jack Donahue, also a famous singer, dancer, and comedian of that era who in fact did co-star with Marilyn Miller in two famous broadway productions.

Plaintiffs, the widow and daughters of Jack Donahue, sued the defendants for damages and an injunction on the basis of a Utah statute. On appeal, the court held in accord with the trial decision declaring judgment that the semi-fictional portrayal of Jack Donahue was not for purposes of trade within the meaning of the prohibition contained in the state law (*Donahue* v. *Warner Bros. Pictures Distributing Corp.*, 2 Utah 2d 256, 272 P.2d 177 (1954)).

In the case of *Bernstein* v. *National Broadcasting Company*, the court held that where prosecution for murder had been given considerable publicity by newspapers and magazines from the time of trial until the accused's conditional release from imprisonment eight years later, did not invade his privacy. It was also decided that a radio program, which told his story 16 years later, or a television program which did so 20 years later, basing the broadcast upon the plaintiff's past life (yet in no way identifying him by use of his name or by advertisements of the program) did not effectively invade (129 F. Supp. 817 (DCDC, 1955), affd. 232 F.2d 369 (1956)).

It was later decided that the use of a person's name in a picture which is part of a sponsored television program does not *ipso facto* comprise use for advertising purposes as prohibited by the Civil Rights Law unless the name is exploited in commercial announcements or in direct connection with the product itself (*Fleischer* v. *WPIX, Inc.*, 30 Misc. 2d 17, 213 NYS 2d 632 (1961)).

The case of *Youssoupoff* v. *Columbia Broadcasting Systems, Inc.* brought forth the holding that there may be no recovery under the Civil Rights Law for the use of a person's name or photograph in connection with an article of current news or immediate public interest, and that this rule is applicable to television broadcasts (41 Misc. 2d 42, 244 NYS 2d 701, affs 19 AD 2d 865, 244 NYS 2d 1 (1963)).

Nevertheless, the unauthorized use of the name and photograph of a plaintiff, the television personality of "What's the Story, Jerry?" fame, would not be permitted or condoned under the Civil Rights Law. The court determined that such use was, in effect, a theft of valuable property right that the plaintiff had labored mightily to create. (*Rosenberg* v. *Lee's Carpet & Furniture Warehouse Outlet, Inc.*).

In the summer of 1977, the Supreme Court ruled that the First Amendment does not protect a television station from being sued for damages by a "human cannonball" if it broadcasts his entire performance as a news item without his consent. The scope of the decision may prove narrow, however, because it involved a "performance" lasting only 15 seconds. Nevertheless, a broadcaster who films or tapes a performer's entire act and then airs it without permission, even on a news program, may be subjecting the station to a damage suit. Such a broadcast poses a threat to the value of the performance, and the Constitution is not necessarily a protection for the broadcaster involved. In this case, the action involved a film clip of Hugo Zacchini, the self-styled "human cannonball," hurtling 200 feet through the air into a net at an Ohio fairgrounds (*Zacchini* v. *Scripps-Howard Broadcasting Company*, 433 U.S. 562 (1977)).

Other cases involving the use of the plaintiff's picture for advertising or trade purposes, without authorization, on television or in the motion pictures, include the following: *Kunz* v. *Allen,* 102 Kan. 883, 172 P. 532 (1918); *Sherwood* v. *McGowan*, 3 Misc. 2d 234, 152 NYS 2d 658 (1956); *Durgom* v. *Columbia Broadcasting System, Inc.*, 29 Misc. 2d 394, 214 NYS 2d 752 (1961); *Smith* v. *WGN, Inc.*, 47 Ill. App. 2d 183, 197 NE 2d 482 (1964); *Reilly* v. *Rapperswill Corp.*, 50 Ad 2d 342, 377 NYS 2d 488 (1975).

Program Privacy

Program privacy is a relatively new issue because of the inexpensive availability of videotape recording equipment. The burgeoning technology of cable television presents new legal problems which have not yet been defined fully. Hypothetically, a cable operator could videotape a program broadcast by a station which his system is receiving, and then he may show the program over the station, providing the service to his viewers which may attract additional subscribers. Clearly this is a performance for profit.

Recent state laws are now being tested on this question, as are federal regulations. For example, two cases have limited the distance that signals may be carried within the CATV market area. (*Tele-*

prompter Cable Communications v. *FCC*, 565 F.2d 736 (CADC 1977); *Treasure Valley CATV Committee* v. *United States*, 562 F.2d 1182 (CA9 1977).) The effective role in public policy making should be to project potential legal problems and avert their consequences. In this sense, perhaps it should be incumbent upon the judgment of state legislatures to pass laws prohibiting CATV from transmitting any network or station programming without the permission of the broadcasting corporation involved. If the courts will uphold such laws, the integrity of program privacy should be protected. (See *National Association of Broadcaster* v. *Home Box Office, Inc.*, 567 F.2d 9, cert. den., 434 U.S. 829 (1977).)

Another potential illegal practice could be the insertion of local commercials on a popular television program in substitution for the broadcast station or network commercials. What this means is that a local advertiser can receive the benefits of advertising on a network program without paying network rates and indeed reaching his local target audience. The cable system operator could collect a fee for the sale of this time. Again, this is clearly a performance for profit. There is no existing regulation specifically prohibiting these practices, but legal precedents from copyright cases will hold as well as the precedent set forth in the landmark tape piracy case of *Goldstein et al.* v. *California* (412 U.S. 546 (1973)).

Cable television systems developed as a direct result of consumer demand for clearer television reception and more viewing options than were made available under the frequency-allocation system. The first cable television system began service to Mahanoy City, Pennsylvania, in 1948. Federal regulation of cable television services began for the most part in the early 1960s. The statutory basis for regulation by the FCC is section 303(g) of the Communications Act of 1934, which formulates the structure for the Commission "to promote the wider and more effective use of radio." The Commission has the authority under this act to adopt rules and regulations as "reasonably ancillary" to its regulation of television broadcasting. In 1972, the Supreme Court affirmed regulations requiring cable television systems to originate certain kinds of programming as reasonably ancillary to the Commission's general obligation to promote diversity. (*United States* v. *Midwest Video Corp.*, 406 U.S. 649, 622–63 (1972).)

Mistaken Usage of Picture

Where a defendant uses a plaintiff's picture in its advertisement by mistake, there may be sufficient grounds for an invasion of privacy. Such was the case in *Flake* v. *Greensboro News Co.*, which involved the unauthorized publication of a photograph of a radio entertainer in connection with a bread advertisement and an advertisement for a stage show. In light of the publisher's public apology to the entertainer, which included desisting from the use of the photograph, and in the absence of malice and proof of special damages, the plaintiff was entitled to recover nominal damages only for violation of her right of privacy (*supra*).

In the case of *Emanuel* v. *Freelance Photographers Guild, Inc.*, the court continued its liberal interpretation of events in holding that the plaintiff was not entitled to damages where the defendants had sold the plaintiff's photograph in good faith and in honest belief that it was a photograph of another woman, from whom they had obtained for a consideration a release to sell it (28 Misc. 2d 503, 219 NYS 2d 626 (1960)).

The reluctance of the court to hold against the defendant for the mistaken use of another's picture was probably most conspicuous in one of the earliest cases considered. When a defendant published in its newspaper an advertisement for "Duffy's Pure Malt Whiskey," stating that the use of this product was indorsed by one while printing the picture of another, recovery was denied on the ground that the defendant, as printer and distributor of the advertising material, did not mistakenly publish the picture with the demonstrative malice that would be necessary to obtain the conviction desired by the plaintiff (*Peck* v. *Tribune Co.*, 154 F. 330, revd on other grounds 214 U.S. 185 (CA7, 1907)).

It is possible, however, for a plaintiff to win an action for the unauthorized publication of her likeness in a newspaper advertisement. Such was the case when an advertisement included a picture of "Lustre-Color Home Hair Coloring," various matter describing it, a form for ordering it, and a reproduction of a photograph of the plaintiff above the following language: "Miss Elgie Sprague, Luster-Color authority from New York, will be in Rich's Drug Department, street floor . . . to advise you on your correct Lustre-Color shade." The court held that such an advertisement could not be published once the employee used in such advertisement had been terminated by her employer (*Colgate-Palmolive Company* v. *Tullos*, 219 F.2d 617 (CA5, 1955)). The court found that when the plaintiff's continued employment had been discouraged by the defendant, it was too late to remove the relevant advertisement from the publication. Nevertheless, the defendant's "negligent haste in changing the advertisement, which warranted an inference of malice toward the (plaintiff) or wanton disregard of her rights," constituted sufficient unauthorized use of the plaintiff's portrait for commercial purposes to warrant a jury verdict for the plaintiff (*ibid.*).

USAGE OF NAME OR LIKENESS IN FALSE LIGHT

Misrepresenting Authorship or Statements

Closely related to the sections on "Indorsement of Products or Services" and "Usage of Name or Likeness to Increase Circulation of Publication" is the ultimate abuse of these objectives. It represents the unjustifiably extreme attempt to pursue these goals not only without the consent of the plaintiff, but without proper representation of the plaintiff's authorship of an article or statements attributed to him.

For the case of *Thompson* v. *G.P. Putnam's Sons,* described in the section on the "Indorsement of Products or Services," suggests this issue is virtually a closed question. In this case, it was alleged that Putnam published and circulated, and is continuing to publish and circulate, a book entitled "Memoirs of a Woman of Pleasure," containing an "Introduction" and "Note" which are intended to increase the sales of the book by making it appear to be a work of recognized literary merit. It contained language implying that the plaintiff, as literary critic, regarded the book as having such literary merit, whereas his true opinion was that it was tedious and bewildering. The court held this use of plaintiff's name and statement to be sufficient evidence for the rejection of the motion to dismiss the plaintiff's complaint (*supra*).

The court further concluded that altering a plaintiff's research paper so as to suggest that he recommended a substance on which the defendants owned a patent rather than the substance with regard to which the plaintiff physician had conducted research did not render the article libelous per se when published under the plaintiff's name, but it did comprise a sufficient cause of action for violation of the Civil Rights Law as a conspiracy to invade the plaintiff's right of privacy (*Ravich* v. *Kling,* 17 Misc. 2d 683, 187 NYS 2d 272 (1959)).

The case of *Sperry Rand Corporation* v. *Hill* involved an action by a physician against an electric shaver manufacturer for libel and invasion of privacy on the basis of its distribution of reprints of a magazine article allegedly stating falsely that the plaintiff was one of its authors and containing remarks favorable to the defendant. On appeal, the court vacated the judgment and set aside the general verdict which held that no invasion of privacy existed, that the libel question was an issue for the jury, and that no punitive damages should be imposed. The appeal's court asked for another trial to determine the compensatory damages for libel (356 F.2d 181 (CA5, 1966)).

In an out-of-court agreement, on August 4, 1978 a firm dropped its attempt to have a court ban a Scots couple from using the names of characters in the television series, "Upstairs, Downstairs," to market their food products.

The previous week, Sagitta Productions, Ltd., 32 Savile Row, London, was refused interim interdict to stop alleged infringements of copyright it claimed in the format and names of characters in the series.

The company had attempted to sue Mr. Leslie and Mrs. Mary Wallace, of 22 Berryhill Drive, Giffnock, trading as Loyal Scots Foods, and in a second action made similar assertions against Hudson's Pantry Ltd., of the same address.

In each case Sagitta Productions sought a declarator that it owns the copyright and claimed 50,000 pounds. It had sought to prohibit Mr. and Mrs. Wallace from marketing, distributing, or selling food products incorporating the format and names of characters in the series, including "Mrs. Bridges," "Hudson's Pantry," and the title of the program.

Mr. Alan Johnston, for Sagitta Productions, told Lord Scott, of the Court of Session, that certain undertakings agreed between the parties made the motions for interim interdict unnecessary in both cases, and he dropped them. (*Glasgow Herald,* August 5, 1978).

Other cases related to the question of misrepresentation are as follows: *D'Altomonte* v. *New York Herald Co.,* 208 NY 596, 102 NE 1101, modg 154 App Div 453, 139 NYS 200 (1913); *Kerby* v. *Hal Roach studios,* 53 Cal App 2d 207, 127 P.2d 577 (1942); *Manger* v. *Kree Institute of Electrolysis, Inc.,* 233 F.2d 5 (CA2, 1956); *Brociner* v. *Radio Wire Television, Inc.,* 15 Misc 2d 843, NYS 2d 743 (1959)).

Alteration of Picture

Most invasions of privacy involving the usage of name or likeness for advertising or trade purposes occur without the consent of the plaintiff. When the plaintiff authorizes the use of his picture for such purposes, making a substantial change or alteration in the published version of the picture may exceed the consent and therefore be actionable under the Civil Rights Law or its common law equivalent. In *Freed* v. *Loew's Incorporated,* however, it was found that minor distortions may be allowable so long as the portrayal essentially represents the image it was intended to depict (*supra*).

Consistent with this philosophy, the court found in an action by a motion picture actress against a motion picture company alleging libel and violation of her right of privacy that the case should be dismissed. *Dahl* v. *Columbia Pictures Corporation* involved sketches which are used in connection with advertising a photoplay and giving the impression that the character which the actress portrayed was wild and sexually promiscuous. The court decided that the portrayal did not produce an evil opinion of the actress in the minds of right thinking people regardless of whether they felt the role she played was in poor taste, and that the sketches were not actionable by the actress as libel inasmuch as they were based on actual scenes and brought out the main theme, even if exaggerated, of the photoplay and were within permissible limits of motion picture advertising to be unlawful by the last section, the jury, in its discretion, may award exemplary damages.

While the court felt that alterations of the plaintiff's appearance could be made provided that they are insubstantial, the court further held that such alterations could be made where the photograph as published did not indicate to the public that it was one of the plaintiff, even though a small group of neighbors, friends, and relatives of the plaintiff, familiar with him and with the circumstances in which the photograph had been taken, recognized him as the person depicted therein (*Brauer v. Globe Newspaper Co.*, 351 Mass. 53, 217 NE 2d 736 (1966)).

It is also true that if a model signs a release for the unrestricted use of a picture, any oral agreements regarding the use of that picture become irrelevant despite the fact that they may conflict with the objectionable, altered use of the picture along with suggestive captions. Witnesses to the oral agreement were held by the court to be equally irrelevant in the case of *Russell v. Marboro Books* (18 Misc. 2d 166, 183 NYS 2d 8 (1959)).

Other cases involving alteration of the plaintiff's picture include the following: *Loftus v. Greenwich Lithographing Co.*, 192 App. Div. 251, 182 NYS 428 (1920); *Sinclair v. Postal Tel. & Cable Co.*, 72 NYS 2d 841 (1935).

Conclusion

As has been implied throughout this section, the New York Civil Rights Law serves as the model statute on the invasion of privacy. Because it was the first, and because of the amount of advertising business in New York, it has been subject to more test cases than any other statute of its kind. Naturally, more applications of this subject have been made there than in any other state.

Section 50 of this Act sets forth its objective cogently: "A person, firm, or corporation that uses for advertising purposes, or for trade purposes, the name, portrait, or picture of any living person without having first obtained the written consent of such person, or if a minor of his or her parent or guardian, is guilty of a misdemeanor." Here the right of privacy is established. The various ramifications of this right have been delineated above.

Section 51 of this Act further develops the measures which allow action for injunction and for damages when it has been determined that this right has been invaded. In this section it is stipulated that: "Any person whose name, portrait, or picture is used within this state for advertising purposes or for purposes of trade without the written consent first obtained as above provided may maintain an equitable action in the Supreme Court of this state against the person, firm, or corporation so using his name, portrait, or picture, to prevent and restrain the use thereof; and may also sue and recover damages for any injuries sustained by reason of such use, and if the defendant shall have knowingly used such person's name, portrait, or picture in such manner as is forbidden or declared to be unlawful by the last section, the jury in its discretion, may award exemplary damages."

In Section 52 of the New York Civil Rights Law, a prohibition versus media broadcast of filming of procedures relating to the testimony of subpoenaed witnesses exists. Specifically, to prevent the unnecessary and unfair defamation of primary or secondary individuals, subpoenaed testimony given before courts, commissions, committees, or other such constituted tribunals shall not be so broadcast or filmed. Exceptions to this rule essentially concern testimony given before public service commissions, such as those regarding the operation of public utilities; legislatures, where testimony concerns the effective operation of government; and temporary state commissions, insofar as they are partly comprised of legislators, as they relate to similar governmental operations and the public interest.

Section 52 prohibits the televising, broadcasting, or taking motion pictures of certain proceedings: "No person, firm, association, or corporation shall televise, broadcast, take motion pictures, or arrange for the televising, broadcasting, or taking of motion pictures within this statute of proceedings, in which the testimony of witnesses by subpoena or other compulsory process is or may be taken, conducted by a court, commission, committee, administrative agency, or other tribunal in this state; except that the prohibition contained in this section shall not apply to public hearings conducted by the public service commission with regard to rates charged by utilities, or to proceedings by either house of the state legislature or committee or joint committee of the legislature or by a temporary state commission which includes members of the legislature, so long as any testimony of witnesses which is taken without resort to subpoena or other compulsorary process." The Act specifies the conditions as requiring the president or speaker of the assembly, committee, or commission, and the witness testifying to offer their consent in keeping with the philosophy that it is in the public interest to permit the television, broadcasting, or taking of motion pictures of such events. (Standards, 12 Misc. 2d 574, 166 NYS 2d 708 (1957), affd. 7 App. Div. 2d 969, 183 NYS 2d 992 (1959).)

In all such cases, where the Civil Rights Law allows broadcast or film rights; the agreement of the tribunal or assembly leader and that of the witness is to be obtained by the media representatives. Essentially, the objective of the law, and specifically this particular section, is to balance the public's presumed right to know and the privacy and reputation of the witnesses.

Further similarities exist among false light, and appropriation and defamation. In the case of *Hinish* v. *Meier & Frank Co.*, the plaintiff's name without his consent was signed to a telegram to the governor urging defeat of certain legislation (116 Ore. 482, 113 P2d 438 (1941)). "The use of plaintiff's name or picture in advertising without his consent may also often present this form of grievance as well as appropriation. The analogy here, is of course, to defamation, and the overlap might have been thought substantial enough to make an approach via privacy superfluous. It appears, however, that courts are finding it more congenial to assimilate defamation cases to privacy." (Kalven, 31 *Law and Contemporary Problems* 326 (1966).) It would seem somewhat difficult, however, to merge two torts universally when truth is a defense in one and not in the other.

The latter thesis was reinforced in the case of *Cantrell* v. *Forest City Publishing Co.* which applied the *New York Times* v. *Sullivan* standard: "With knowledge that a defamatory statement was false or with reckless disregard of whether it was false or not," (*supra*). In the *Cantrell* case the court explained that: "As so defined, 'actual malice' is a term of art, created to provide a convenient shorthand for the standard of liability that must be established before a State may constitutionally permit public officials to recover for libel in actions brought against publishers .... In a false-light case, common law malice—frequently expressed in terms of either personal ill will toward the plaintiff or reckless disregard or wanton disregard of the plaintiff's rights—would focus on the defendant's attitude toward the plaintiff's privacy, not towards the truth or falsity of the material published" (419 U.S. 245 (1974)).

With the exception of truth, however, privileges are common to both invasion of privacy and defamation of character. The judicial proceeding similarity was related to privacy and defamation in the case of *Cox Broadcasting Corp.* v. *Cohn:* "The developing law surrounding the tort of invasion of privacy recognizes a privilege in the press to report the events of judicial proceedings. The Warren and Brandeis article . . . noted that the proposed new right would be limited in the same manner as actions for libel and slander where such a publication was a privileged communication: 'The right to privacy is not invaded by any publication made in a court of justice . . . and (at least in many jurisdictions) reports of any such proceedings would in some measure be accorded a like privilege' " (*supra*). Such a privilege against invasion of privacy was clearly accorded in the *Cox Broadcasting* and *Ok-*

lahoma Publishing Co. v. District Court of Oklahoma County cases (supra), as it was employed successfully as a defense against liability for defamation of character in the case of *Irwin* v. *Ashurst* (158 Or. 61, 74 P.2d 1127 (1938)).

In the case of *Rosenblatt* v. *Baer,* Justice Douglas took the position that it not matter whether the individuals involved were public or private, but rather" . . . whether a public *issue* not a public official, is involved." (383 U.S. 75 (1966).) Courts struggled with variations of this theme for the following eight years before the high Court ruled on the issue in the case of *Gertz* v. *Robert Welch, Inc.,* and rejected it *(supra).*

Other cases have established that false light and defamation are not generically different, as can be seen in *Zbyszko* v. *New York American, Inc.,* 228 App. Div. 227, 239 NYS 411 (1930), and *John-Frederics, Inc.* v. *Abraham & Strauss, Inc.,* 39 NYS 2d 979 (1942), 53 NYS 2d 658 (1942), 53 NYS 2d 658 (1945). Other cases have involved conviction for both libel and privacy, such as that of *Martin* v. *Johnson Publishing Co.,* 157 NYS 2d 509 (1956). Still others involving successful causes of action for both libel and privacy include *Holmes* v. *Underwood & Underwood (supra).* The examples above are instances in which the name or likeness of the plaintiff has been used for purposes of advertising or trade.

In the section describing the use of name or likeness for purposes of advertising or trade as invasion of privacy and defamation, when both causes of action were raised, cases which involved conviction for invasion of privacy include: *Flake* v. *Greensboro News Co., (supra), Holt* v. *Columbia Broadcasting System, Inc. (supra), Thompson* v. *G.P. Putnam's Sons, (supra), McNulty* v. *Press Pub. Co. (supra), Ravich* v. *Kling (supra), Pavesich* v. *New England Life Ins. (supra), Binns* v. *Vitagraph Co. (supra).*

In other cases, action was brought for invasion of privacy only, which failed, when stronger causes of action for libel may have existed but were not raised. Such cases include: *Rand* v. *Hearst (supra), Callas* v. *Whisper, Inc. (supra), Kerby* v. *Hal Roach Studios, Inc. (supra),* and *Cabaniss* v. *Hipsley (supra).*

Section 2

The First Amendment and the Abridgment of Individual Privacy

*Joyce Lindmark and Donald Fishman**

Both the print and electronic media encounter similar problems in balancing the public's First Amendment right to know with the individual's right of privacy. The key factor in this equation is the notion of "newsworthiness." Yet, no existing media codes define the criterion of newsworthiness, presumably the most essential component of newsgathering. Rather, they describe vague standards of truth, objectivity, and fair play.[1] Consequently, the practicing journalist has been guided only by judicial efforts to define the concept of newsworthiness in cases involving alleged invasions of privacy, and this has involved him in a "seamless web" of problems. Nowhere are the confusing standards enunciated by jurists more evident than in the relationship between the "involuntary public figure" and the media. Overall, the relationship between the mass media and the ordinary citizen is sufficiently defective to warrant the experimental adoption of ethical guidelines which would clarify and modify the relationship.

The involuntary public figure is a private citizen who has been thrust into the public eye by virtue of his alleged "newsworthiness," his unexpected involvement in a situation which supposedly "interests the public."[2] As a result, the individual's privacy—his right to be left alone[3]—is violated in one of two ways: the individual may sustain public disclosure of embarrassing private facts about himself, which he does not want known; or he may be the recipient of publicity that places him in a "false light" in the public eye.[4]

Public disclosure of private facts was the issue in *Jones v. Herald Post Co.* Mrs. Lillian Jones' husband was stabbed to death in her presence on a Louisville street. She pursued the attackers, grappled with them, and when help arrived, screamed, "I would have killed them." The *Louisville Herald Post* published a picture of her at the scene, along with the quotation. Mrs. Jones later sued the paper but was denied relief by the district court which maintained that

> there are times . . . when one, whether willing or not, becomes an actor in an occurrence of public or general interest. When this takes place, he emerges from his seclusion, and it is not an invasion of his right of privacy to publish his photograph with an account of such occurrence.[5]

The most famous—or infamous—case of a plaintiff claiming he was pictured in a false light was *Time Inc. v. Hill.*[6] The James Hill family sued the publishers of *Life*, alleging that *Life* falsely reported that a new play portrayed an experience suffered by Hill and his family. In 1952, three escaped convicts had held the Hill family hostage in their suburban home for 19 hours. The family was released unharmed and reported at that time that the convicts had treated them courteously and had not molested them. By contrast, the play depicted a family that suffered violence in various forms at the hands of the convicts. *Life's* defense was that the article was a subject of "general interest and of value

---

*Joyce Lindmark is chairman of the English Department of Dedham High School (Mass.) and a member of the Freedom of Speech Commission of the Speech Communication Association. Donald Fishman teaches courses in law and communication at Boston College where he is Associate Professor in the Department of Speech Communication.

and concern to the public" and that it was "published in good faith without any malice whatsoever."[7] After an incredibly labored analysis, the United States Supreme Court brought a verdict against Hill; not on the "involuntary figure" issue, but because the jury instructions in the lower court did not clearly define the basis for a verdict of liability.

One reason for the public portrayal of private facts about an individual is the courts' acceptance of journalistic judgments of newsworthiness. In brief, courts generally accept that private information about involuntary public figures becomes newsworthy by virtue of its publication and, hence, it is not a cause for action. A case in point is Bremmer v. *Journal Tribune Publishing Co.,*[8] where parents lost a suit for invasion of privacy when a picture of their eight-year-old son's mutilated, decomposed body was shown on the front page of a Sioux City, Iowa paper. The state court's reasoning:

> From a news standpoint, the public is interested in the appearance of the body of such a local victim. Such appearance may be pictured by words or by photographs or both.

In other "public disclosure" cases, the defense of newsworthiness is expanded to include appearance of the information in a public record, along with public interest in the material. *Hubbard* v. *Journal Publishing Co.* illustrates this journalistic defense. Delores Hubbard brought suit against the publisher of the *Albuquerque Journal* for publishing a story that identified her as the subject of a sexual assault by her sixteen-year-old brother. Being Richard Hubbard's only sister, she alleged that the article, which was printed without her consent, had caused her to suffer "extreme humiliation and distress, to be regarded as unchaste," and to adversely affect her prospects of marriage.[9] The state court ruled against her on three grounds: first, since her name was entered in the public record, the newspaper was privileged to publish the story; second, even though she was an unwilling participant who didn't seek publicity, she was in the unfortunate situation of being drawn into the public eye to have "her misfortunes broadcast to the world;" and finally, the story itself was judged to be "accurate, newsworthy, and exercised in a reasonable manner and for a proper purpose."[10]

A case decided by the United States Supreme Court on March 3, 1975 consolidates and reinforces journalistic defenses on revealing private information about involuntary public figures. In *Cox Broadcasting Corp.* v. *Martin Cohn,* a deceased rape victim's father brought suit for damages against a television station which had obtained his daughter's name from an indictment and published it on a news broadcast. Relying upon a Georgia statute which made it a misdemeanor to broadcast a rape victim's name, he claimed his right to privacy had been invaded. The Court found that the state statute was an illegitimate limitation of the First Amendment's freedom of the press, since the victim's name appeared in public records.[11] The Court reasoned that

> . . . even the prevailing law of invasion of privacy generally recognizes that the interests in privacy fade when the information involved already appears on the public record . . . the freedom of the press to publish that information appears to us to be of critical importance to our type of government in which the citizenry is the final judge of the proper conduct of public business.[12]

Interestingly, the Court chose to back off from the plaintiff's claim of the right to be free from unwanted publicity about his private affairs, which, although wholly true, would be offensive to a person of ordinary sensibilities.[13] The Court found that other case precedents counsel caution by the Court in dealing with the claims of privacy against those of the free press, since "both sides are plainly rooted in the traditions and significant concerns of our society."[14]

In reality, it seems that the United States Supreme Court is caught between a rock and a hard place in attempting to evaluate newsworthiness as an element in public disclosure cases. It is understandable that the court hesitates to rule in favor of individual privacy when to do so erodes a broader societal right to an unfettered press. But on the other hand, to broaden newsworthiness to mean matters of public interest, " . . . a classification that bases the right to First Amendment protection on some estimate of how much general interest there is in the communication, is surely in conflict with the whole idea of the First Amendment."[15] If we are to have a set of standards less permissive than those promulgated by the courts, there is an urgent need for journalists themselves to enter the evaluative process with unambiguous, extralegal standards.

The courts have also made life complicated for the involuntary public figure who is cast in a "false light" in a publication. The problem has developed as the courts have applied the same Constitutional tests as those used in libel cases to cases alleging an invasion of privacy based on false information. *Time* v. *Hill* was especially instrumental in promoting this equation. Within the fact situation previously described, the Court developed three arguments. First, there could be redress for false reports on matters of public interest only with actual malice in the *New York Times* v. *Sullivan* sense; that is, that the defendant published the Hill's story with knowledge of its false elements or in reckless disregard of the truth.[16] Next, the evidence in the *Time* v. *Hill* case could be construed to show one of two things: innocent or merely negligent misstatements by *Life;* or a finding that *Life* portrayed the play as a re-enactment of the Hills' experience, with reckless disregard for its truth or with actual knowledge that it was false. Finally, the court concludes that the instructions to the jury in the lower court did not make clear that actual malice was required for a finding against *Life*.

To determine what this case means to the involuntary public figure cast in a false light is difficult at best. As Thomas Emerson had said, the case provides only "hints" and "implications" of the probable view of the Court.[17] The most obvious conclusion which surfaces is that the Court assiduously avoided reaching a conclusion on the substance of the case. Actual malice seems fairly evident in the fact situation. Hill's charge was that *Life* falsely reported that the play "The Desperate Hours" depicted an incident that the Hill family experienced. He was correct. The reporter Prideaux had contact with the playwright Hayes, but neglected to question him about the play's connection to any real life episode, although he had heard rumors to that effect. In Prideaux' story file were news clippings about the Hill incident which revealed its nonviolent character, and an article by Hayes in which he said the play was based on a variety of incidents. Yet, Prideaux allowed a copy editor to insert the Hill name into the text and to call the play a re-enactment of the Hill's experience. He did this while admitting under questioning that he knew the play was "between a little bit and moderately fictionalized."[18] Certainly, Prideaux behaved "recklessly," in the face of known falsehoods; however, because of the Court's willingness to decide the case on a procedural matter, First Amendment protection was extended to the reporter's article. It seems only fair to conclude that the Supreme Court was reluctant to restrict press activity, even in the face of overwhelming evidence of falsehoods surrounding a private individual.

The Court's reaction in this case clearly demonstrates the need for extralegal, journalistic standards to protect the involuntary public figure in publications where he is cast in a false light. Recently, major United States Supreme Court decisions have evolved standards to protect reputation, but not to protect privacy.[19] Perhaps this is just as well: as Thomas Emerson cautions "It is anomalous to have the issue in privacy cases turn upon falsity at all. The injury is not to reputation, but to feelings. The true could be just as damaging as the false."[20] Others, notably Dean William Prosser and the late

Professor Harry Kalven, support the contention that if a statement is not offensive enough to be defamatory, it is not sufficiently offensive to be an invasion of privacy.[21] Melville Nimmer, Professor of Law at UCLA, in supporting Emerson's position, would respond to these critics by saying

> (their) underlying premise is wrong. An untrue statement may in the same way as a public disclosure of embarrassing private facts constitute an invasion of privacy without in any manner constituting an injury to the subject's reputation . . . the resulting humiliation would have nothing to do with truth or falsity. The unwarranted disclosure of intimate "facts" is no less offensive and hence no less deserving of protection merely because such "facts" are not true.[22]

A number of harms are inflicted on the individual whose right to privacy rests in limbo between journalistic indifference and judicial vacillation. Even with some fast footwork, it is often difficult for an individual to avoid becoming a victim of an assault on his privacy. The reluctant public figure, William Faulkner, speculates on the reason:

> We have no laws against bad taste, perhaps because in a democracy the majority of the people who make the laws don't recognize bad taste when they see it, or perhaps because in our democracy bad taste has been converted into a marketable and therefore taxable and therefore lobbyable commodity by the merchandising federations which at the same simultaneous time create the market (not the appetite: that did not need creating: only pandering to) and the product to serve it.[23]

Ironically, the act of attempting to redress a violation of privacy can injure the involuntary public figure even further. Bringing a court case can be financially and emotionally draining, as well as aggravating the loss of privacy. If a person's reputation is injured by false statements, it can be rehabilitated by additional speech. But the mere fact of publication erodes privacy, and no amount of speech will restore it.

The mental anguish caused by an invasion of privacy is not quantifiable; hence, it is not regarded as "real" by those who have a narrow zone of privacy, or those whose privacy has remained inviolate. Nevertheless, the distress can take several forms. For some, propulsion into the public arena may mean a reawakening of a past agony or the portrayal of a current embarrassment. For others, it represents an exasperating loss of autonomy, a feeling that self-disclosure is no longer within their control. For everyone, the invasion of anyone's privacy is "a blow to human dignity, (because) a private life is transformed into a public spectacle."[24]

Generally, it seems that the right to privacy of the involuntary public figure is ineffectively protected by judicial action or by the individual's own efforts. Yet, many private citizens who unwillingly come to public attention have endured significant harms. It is the potential source of harms—the journalist—who must provide the preventives to future transgressions, hopefully in the form of specific statements of journalistic ethics. The core of the ethical code should be the definition and methods of approaching newsworthy and nonnewsworthy subjects. The following definitions and standards may prove helpful.

    1. Information is newsworthy if it facilitates the "unfettered interchange of ideas for the bringing about of political and social changes desired by the people,"[25] if it has "governing importance."[26]

An individual is newsworthy if he is directly involved in such newsworthy issues. The publisher or journalist need only ask:

> (Is) publication of the name or likeness logically relevant to keeping the public informed for its governing purposes? The issue is one of logic rather than of fact or value. And it is one which is rooted in the First Amendment itself. Is the First Amendment purpose being served by this publication of name or likeness? Can use of the name or likeness in this instance serve any possible basis for any possible governing purpose?[27]

    2. Information is nonnewsworthy when it is intended to satisfy public curiosity and appetite for gossip about private lives. Such information may be sad, terrifying, entertaining, amusing, exciting, but not essential to the purposes of self-government. The press should have an unabridgeable right to comment on persons who voluntarily become involved in nonnewsworthy issues.

    3. If an individual becomes an involuntary public figure through involvement in a non-newsworthy issue, the journalist must observe three standards in reporting about him:

    a. The involuntary public figure must not be identified by name or likeness in any discussion of intimate or private matters involving him. In such circumstances, the public's interest in news reporting is sufficiently served by an account of the event itself without identification of persons innocently involved.[28]

    b. The involuntary public figure must not be identified by name where "the ordinary status he expects to occupy is changed without his volition to a status embarrassing to an ordinary person of reasonable sensitivity. Then he should not be deemed to have forfeited his right to be protected from an indecent and vulgar intrusion of his right of privacy merely because his misfortune overtakes him in a public place."[29]

    c. Generally speaking, if an involuntary public figure is involved in a nonnewsworthy incident, he should choose whether his name is to be used.

Judicial and nonjudicial attempts to expand protection of the involuntary public figure's privacy face recurring challenges. Some journalists equate the price of the protection with an inhibited press which would ignore potentially newsworthy items. But inhibition is not a necessary correlate of journalistic discretion. Edward Bloustein reports a *New York Times* story which carried the headline, "Five Teenagers Hunted in Rape of Visiting Nurse." The name of the victim was withheld but her age was given, along with every detail of the rape except those which would have identified her. This story told the public all they needed to know about the victim of the rape to satisfy their governing obligations under the First Amendment.[30] Most likely, the name of the victim and her picture would have sold more newspapers. But the story without her name fulfilled whatever newsworthiness the incident might have had (e.g., shocking the public into some kind of social action). At the same time, an individual's privacy was preserved.

Other critics question the efficacy of measures to protect the privacy of the involuntary public figure. If the reader knows the individual in the story, so the argument goes, he is probably familiar with that individual's predicament; hence, there exists no real invasion of privacy. Conversely, if the reader is unacquainted with the individual, he cannot be said to invade that stranger's privacy. Such analysis, however, ignores the central focus of the concept of a right to privacy: that the individual *choose* what he wants to reveal to the outside world.[31]

Reporters may question the effectiveness of privacy-protecting measures in another way. They explain that sensitive information is frequently taken from public records, which are readily accessible to everyone. This position ignores the fact that the "average" person does not comb public records any more than the "average" person regularly runs red lights. Therefore, the journalist who reports all types of information found in such records may be thrusting upon the public information it has no need to know, and, perhaps, no interest in knowing, since it did not seek out the information. And if involuntary public figures may be found anywhere it is in situations which must be reported in public records. Those involved in such situations are in a double bind. In attempting to secure certain rights, they must become involved in proceedings which must be recorded. Simultaneously, those individuals automatically surrender their right to privacy, since any reporter may indiscriminately publish any intimate information the individuals were forced to include in the public record to secure another right. It is at best debatable whether such publication furthers the interests of justice or, for that matter, journalistic freedom.

In a society where many people "let it all hang out" all of the time, it becomes difficult to believe that anyone not trying to avoid the FBI would value his privacy. Yet, the hundreds of privacy actions in state and federal courts testify otherwise. However, it has become apparent that legal intervention, at least in regard to published invasions of privacy, does not produce any consistent or lasting protection. Therefore, journalists must debate, adopt, and adhere to ethical standards which demonstrate that they value the people whose personalities and experiences they make "newsworthy."

NOTES

[1] Sigma Delta Chi, "Code of Ethics," 1973, in Lee Brown, *The Reluctant Reformation* (New York: David McKay Co., Inc., 1974), pp. 120–122.
[2] Herold L. Nelson and Dwight Teeter, Jr., *Law of Mass Communications* (Mineola, New York: The Foundation Press, Inc., 1969), p. 176.
[3] Thomas M. Cooley, *A Treatise on the Law of Torts*, 2d ed. (Chicago: Callaghan & Co., 1888), p. 29.
[4] William Prosser, "Privacy," 48 *California Law Review* 383 (1960), pp. 383–386. Prosser identifies two other forms of the right of privacy. One, the appropriation of another's name or likeness for personal advantage, pertains to advertising, and does not bear directly on a reporter's judgment of the newsworthiness of a subject. The other subdivision, intrusion upon a person's seclusion or solitude, has been taken to mean mechanical or physical intrusion.
[5] *Jones v. Herald Post Co.*, 18 S.W. 2d 977 (1929).
[6] *Time, Inc. v. Hill*, 385 U.S. 374 (1967).
[7] *Ibid.*, p. 379.
[8] *Bremmer v. Journal Tribune Publishing Co.*, 247 Iowa 817 (1956), p. 827.
[9] *Hubbard v. Journal Publishing Co.*, 69 N.M. 473 (1962), p. 474.
[10] *Ibid.*
[11] *Cox Broadcasting Corp. v. Martin Cohn*, 420 U.S. 469, 95 S.Ct. 1029 (1975).
[12] *Ibid.*, p. 1046.
[13] *Ibid.*, p. 1043.
[14] *Ibid.*, p. 1044.
[15] Thomas I. Emerson, *The System of Freedom of Expression* (New York: Vintage Books, 1970), pp. 553–554.
[16] *New York Times v. Sullivan*, 376 U.S. 254 (1964), pp. 279–280.
[17] Emerson, p. 552.
[18] *Times, Inc., v. Hill*, p. 393.
[19] See, for instance, *Rosenbloom v. Metromedia*, 403 U.S. 29 (1971) and *Gertz v. Robert Welch*, Inc., 94 S.Ct. 2997 (1974).
[20] Emerson, p. 555.
[21] See William Prosser, "Privacy," p. 400; see also Harry Kalven, "Privacy in Tort Law—Were Warren and Brandeis Wrong?" 31 *Law and Contemporary Problems* 326 (1966), p. 340.
[22] Melville Nimmer, "The Right to Speak from Times to Time: First Amendment Theory Applied to Libel and Misapplied to Privacy," reprinted in Melville B. Nimmer, *Copyright* (St. Paul, Minn.: West Publishing Co., 1971), 745.

[23] William Faulkner, "On Privacy," *Harper's,* July, 1955, p. 36.
[24] Edward J. Bloustein, "Privacy, Tort Law, and the Constitution: Is Warren and Brandeis' Tort Petty and Unconstitutional As Well? *Texas Law Review,* 46, (April, 1968), p. 619.
[25] *Roth v. U.S., 354 U.S. 476* (1957), p. 484.
[26] Alexander Meikeljohn, "The First Amendment Is an Absolute," *Supreme Court Review* 1961 (1961), p. 257.
[27] Edward J. Bloustein, "The First Amendment and Privacy: the Supreme Court Justice and the Philosopher," *Rutgers Law Review,* 28 (1974–75), p. 61.
[28] Nimmer, p. 747.
[29] *Daily Times Democrat v. Graham,* 162 So.2d 474 (1962), p. 478.
[30] Bloustein, "First Amendment and Privacy," pp. 58–9.
[31] Emerson, p. 545.

Section 3

Cases

HAELAN LABORATORIES, INC. v. TOPPS CHEWING GUM, INC.
202 F.2d 866 (CA2 1953)

Frank, Circuit Judge.

After a trial without a jury, the trial judge dismissed the complaint on the merits. The plaintiff maintains that defendant invades plaintiff's exclusive right to use the photographs of leading baseball players. Probably because the trial judge ruled against plaintiff's legal contentions, some of the facts were not too clearly found.

1. So far as we can now tell, there were instances of the following kind:

a) The plaintiff, engaged in selling chewing gum, made a contract with a ball player providing that plaintiff, for a stated term, should have the exclusive right to use the ball player's photograph in connection with the sales of plaintiff's gum; the ball player agreed not to grant any other gum manufacturer a similar right during such term; the contract gave plaintiff an option to extend the term for a designated period.

b) Defendant, a rival chewing gum manufacturer, knowing of plaintiff's contract, deliberately induced the ball player to authorize defendant, by a contract with defendant, to use the player's photograph in connection with the sales of defendant's gum either during the original or extended term of plaintiff's contract, the defendant did so use the photograph.

Defendant argues that, even if such facts are proved, they show no actionable wrong, for this reason: the contract with plaintiff was no more than a release by the ball player to plaintiff of the liability which, absent the release, plaintiff would have incurred in using the ball player's photograph, because such a use, without his consent, would be an invasion of his right of privacy under Section 50 and Section 51 of the New York Civil Rights Law; this statutory right of privacy is personal, not assignable; therefore, plaintiff's contract vested in plaintiff no "property" right or other legal interest which defendant's conduct invaded.

Both parties agree, and so do we, that, on the facts here, New York "law" governs. And we shall assume, for the moment that, under the New York decisions, defendant correctly asserts that any such contract between plaintiff and a ball player, in so far as it merely authorized plaintiff to use the player's photograph, created nothing but a release of liability. On that basis, were there no more to the contract, plaintiff would have no actionable claim against defendant. But defendant's argument neglects the fact that, in the contract, the ball player also promised not to give similar releases to others. If defendant, knowing of the contract, deliberately induced the ball player to break that promise, defendant behaved tortiously.

Some of defendant's contracts were obtained by it through its agent, Players Enterprise, Inc.; others were obtained by Russell Publishing Co., acting independently, and were then assigned by Russell to defendant. Since Players acted as defendant's agent, defendant is liable for any breach of plaintiff's contracts thus induced by Players. However, as Russell did not act as defendant's agent when Russell, having knowledge of plaintiff's contract with a player, but subsequently contracting with that player, induced a breach of plaintiff's contract, defendant is not liable for any breach so induced; nor did there arise such a liability against defendant for such an induced breach when defendant became the assignee of one of those Russell contracts.

2. The foregoing covers the situations where defendant, by itself or through its agent, induced breaches. But in those instances where Russell induced the breach, we have a different problem; and that problem also confronts us in instances—alleged in one paragraph of the complaint and to which the trial judge in his opinion also (although not altogether clearly) refers—where defendant, "with knowledge of plaintiff's exclusive rights," used a photograph of a ball player without his consent during the term of his contract with plaintiff.

With regard to such situations, we must consider defendant's contention that none of plaintiff's contracts created more than a release of liability, because a man has no legal interest in the publication of his picture other than right of privacy, i.e., a personal and nonassignable right not to have his feelings hurt by such a publication.

A majority of this court rejects this contention. We think that, in addition to and independent of that right of privacy (which in New York derives from statute), a man has a right in the publicity value of his photograph, i.e., the right to grant the exclusive privilege of publishing this picture, and that such a grant may validly be made "in gross," i.e., without an accompanying transfer of a business or of anything else. Whether it be labelled a "property" right is immaterial; for here, as often elsewhere, the tag "property" simply symoblizes the fact that courts enforce a claim which has pecuniary worth.

This right might be called a "right of publicity." For it is common knowledge that many prominent persons (especially actors and ball players), far from having their feelings bruised through public exposure of their likenesses, would feel sorely deprived if they no longer received money for authorizing advertisements popularizing their countenances displayed in newspapers, magazines, busses, trains, and subways. This right of publicity would usually yield them no money unless it could be made the subject of an exclusive grant which barred any other advertiser from using their pictures.

We think the New York decisions recognize such a right.

We think *Perkas Co., Inc.* v. *Leslie*, decided in 1915 by Justice Greenbaum sitting in the Supreme Court Term, is not controlling since, apart from a doubt as to whether an opinion of that court must be taken by us as an authoritative exposition of New York law, the opinion shows that the judge had his attention directed by plaintiff exclusively to Sections 50 and 51 of the New York statute, and, accordingly, held that the right of privacy was "purely personal and not assignable" because "rights for outraged feelings are not more assignable than would be a claim arising from a libelous utterance."

We said above that defendant was not liable for a breach of any of plaintiff's contracts induced by Russell, and did not become thus liable (for an induced breach) when there was assigned to defendant a contract between Russell and a ball player, although Russell, in making that contract, knowingly induced a breach of a contract with plaintiff. But plaintiff, in its capacity as exclusive grantee of a player's "right of publicity," has a valid claim against defendant if defendant used that player's photograph during the term of plaintiff's grant and with knowledge of it. It is no defense to such a claim that defendant is the assignee of a subsequent contract between that player and Russell, purporting to make a grant to Russell or its assignees. For the prior grant to plaintiff renders that subsequent grant invalid during the period of the grant (including an exercised option) to plaintiff, but not thereafter.

3. We must remand to the trial court for a determination (on the basis of the present record and of further evidence introduced by either party) of these facts: 1) the date and contents of each of plaintiff's contracts, and whether plaintiff exercised its option to renew; 2) defendant's or Players' conduct with respect to each such contract.

Of course, if defendant made a contract with a ball player which was not executed—or which did not authorize defendant to use the player's photograph—until the expiration of the original or extended term of plaintiff's contract with that player, or which did not induce a breach of the agreement to renew, then defendant did no legal wrong to plaintiff. The same is true of instances where neither defendant nor Players induced a breach of plaintiff's contract, and defendant did not use the player's photograph until after the expiration of such original or extended or option term.

If, upon further exploration of the facts, the trial court, in the light of our opinion, concludes that defendant is liable, it will, of course, ascertain damages and decide what equitable relief is justified.

Reversed and remanded.

TOLLEFSON v. PRICE
45 Or. 398, 430 P.2d 990 (1967)

Fort, Justice pro tem.

Plaintiffs filed a complaint in two counts, each charging an invasion of privacy arising out of the publication of a notice by the defendants respecting money alleged to be due from Mrs. Tollefson. A demurrer to the complaint based on the absence of facts sufficient to state a cause of action was sustained. When the plaintiffs declined to plead further, judgment was rendered against them. They appeal.

Plaintiff husband claims to have suffered embarrassment and humiliation because of the publications respecting his wife. For the purpose of the demurrer, if either plaintiff states a cause of action it must be overruled.

The defendant published in the "Farmers Feed and Seed Store" a document stating in part:

FOR SALE!

The following Judgments, Claims, Notes, and Accounts are offered . . . for sale to the highest bidder. The right is reserved to reject in full, or in part, any offer:

NAMES ADDRESSES AMOUNT

(Names of 28 persons including "Mrs. Roger Tollefson")

The above listed Judgments, Claims, Notes, and Accounts are guaranteed by the owner to be just, correct and undisputed.

It then alleges this notice was published "unlawfully and maliciously . . . without right or legal authority," "that the claim or account against plaintiff . . . is disputed," and that "the defendants . . . well knew that said claim or account was and is disputed by plaintiffs."

After alleging "humiliation, exposure to public contempt and ridicule," it further alleges that the "acts of the defendants . . . in placing and publishing said notice or sign . . . were willful and intentional and committed for the purpose of harrassing (sic), vexing, and annoying the plaintiffs mentally, and that said acts . . . were so reckless, wanton, irresponsible, willful, and malicious that defendants . . . should be punished by assessment against them . . . of exemplary damages . . . ."

A second cause of action is then alleged because of the publication of the above document as an advertisement in the local paper. The complaint also alleges that one of the defendants, Elmer R. Price, is the sole owner of the newspaper and with his wife is the owner of the aforementioned feed and seed store.

The defendants' demurrer admits the allegations and every reasonable intendment to be drawn therefrom.

In *Hinish* v. *Meier & Frank Co.,* this court stated:

> . . . (I)t is well settled that where the wrongful act constitutes an infringement of a legal right, mental suffering may be recovered for, if it is the direct, proximate, and natural result of the wrongful act. Violation of the right of privacy is a wrong of that character.

Dean Wade, in his carefully considered article "Defamation and the Right of Privacy," (15 *Vand. L. Rev.* 1093), points out that the tort of invasion of the right of privacy is, like assault and defamation, in reality "a part of the larger tort of intentional infliction of mental suffering." He states further:

> Privacy is now fully established as a legally protected right in the United States. Of the four recognized types of invasion of the right of privacy, the ones which are most closely analogous to the right of reputation, as protected by the law of defamation, are "public disclosure of embarrassing private facts about the plaintiff" and "publicity which places the plaintiff in a false light in the public eye." These two differ only in that the first involves a true statement and the other a false statement. The hurt to the plaintiff's feelings, the damage to his sensibilities, is essentially the same in both cases.

Prosser, in *Torts,* states as a part of his discussion concerning the public disclosure of private facts as constituting an invasion of the right of privacy:

> . . . It is an invasion of his rights to publish in a newspaper that the plaintiff does not pay his debts, or to post a notice to that effect in a window on the public street, or to cry it aloud in the highway.

He points out that "The facts disclosed to the public must be private facts, and not public ones," and that "the matter made public must be one which would be offensive and objectionable to a reasonable man of ordinary sensibilities."

He states that the elements necessary to establish an invasion of the right of privacy of the kind here involved are first that the disclosure of the private facts must be a public disclosure—that is, that there must be publicity, and, second, the disclosure must be in the form of publicity of a highly objectionable kind. To constitute such a disclosure it must be public in the sense of communication either to the public generally or to a large number of persons as distinguished from one individual or a few.

Whether or not the conduct of the defendants in publishing the notices alleged in the complaint was consistent with what a reasonable man would have done under the same or similar circumstances, is a question of fact to be determined from the evidence in the light of the interest of the plaintiffs to be protected from an invasion of privacy on the one hand, and the legitimate interest of the creditor in seeking the collection of a debt on the other.

Dean Wade states: "There is no reason to believe that the very technical rules of pleading in defamation will be imported into the law of privacy."

Here, the published notice states the owner guarantees the amount to be undisputed. The complaint, reasonably construed, states this to be false and that defendants with that knowledge published the notice for the express purpose of "humiliating, harrassing (sic), vexing, and annoying the plaintiffs" without their consent. We think this complaint meets the requisite tests. It includes allegations sufficient to raise the questions of malice, willfulness, reasonableness of the conduct, and good faith. It also raises the issue of falsity with respect to the matter of the disputed nature of the claim. Finally, it sufficiently alleges under the above authorities that the plaintiffs did not authorize or consent thereto.

We hold that the pleadings, reasonably construed, state a cause of action. It follows that the judgment must be reversed.

Reversed and remanded.

Denecke, Justice (specially concurring.)

I am of the opinion that there should be no cause of action against one who publicizes a debt in the hope that publicity or the fear of publicity will secure collection. If the debt, is not owed, the traditional remedy of defamation is available to the defamed.

I concur in the decision, however, because the plaintiffs alleged that the defendants publicized the debt for the purpose of "harrassing, (sic) vexing, and annoying the plaintiffs." Under this allegation the plaintiffs could prove a purpose other than or in addition to securing collection of the debt.

Perry, C.J., and McAllister, J., join in this concurring opinion.

TIME, INC. v. *HILL*
385 U.S. 374 (1967)

Mr. Justice Brennan delivered the opinion of the Court.

The question in this case is whether appellant, publisher of *Life Magazine,* was denied Constitutional protections for speech and press by the application by the New York courts of Sections 50–51 of the New York Civil Rights Law to award appellee damages on allegations that *Life* falsely reported that a new play portrayed an experience suffered by appellee and his family.

The article appeared in *Life* in February 1955. It was entitled "True Crime Inspires Tense Play," with the subtitle, "The ordeal of a family trapped by convicts gives Broadway a new thriller, 'The Desperate Hours.'" The text of the article reads as follows:

> Three years ago, Americans all over the country read about the desperate ordeal of the James Hill family, who were held prisoners in their home outside Philadelphia by three escaped convicts. Later they read about it in Joseph Hayes' novel, *The Desperate Hours,* inspired by the

family's experience. Now they can see the story re-enacted in Hayes' Broadway play based on the book, and next year will see it in his movie, which has been filmed but is being held up until the play has a chance to pay off.

The play, directed by Robert Montgomery and expertly acted, is a heart-stopping account of how a family rose to heroism in a crisis. *Life* photographed the play during its Philadelphia tryout, transported some of the actors to the actual house where the Hills were besieged. On the next page scenes from the play are re-enacted on the site of the crime.

The pictures on the ensuing two pages included an enactment of the son being "roughed up" by one of the convicts, entitled "brutish convict," a picture of the daughter biting the hand of a convict to make him drop a gun, entitled "daring daughter," and one of the father throwing his gun through the door after a "brave try" to save his family is foiled.

The James Hill referred to in the article is the appellee. He and his wife and five children involuntarily became a front-page news story after being held hostage by three escaped convicts in their suburban, Whitemarsh, Pennsylvania, home for 19 hours on September 11–12, 1952. The family was released unharmed. In an interview with newsmen after the convicts departed, appellee stressed that the convicts had treated the family courteously, had not molested them, and had not been at all violent. The convicts were thereafter apprehended in a widely publicized encounter with the police which resulted in the killing of two of the convicts. Shortly thereafter, the family moved to Connecticut. The appellee discouraged all efforts to keep them in the public spotlight through magazine articles or appearances on television.

In the spring of 1953, James Hayes' novel, *The Desperate Hours,* was published. The story depicted the experience of a family of four held hostage by three escaped convicts in the family's suburban home. But unlike Hill's experience, the family of the story suffer violence at the hands of the convicts; the father and son are beaten and the daughter subjected to verbal sexual insult.

The book was made into a play, also entitled "The Desperate Hours," and it is *Life's* article about the play which is the subject of appellee's action. The complaint sought damages under Sections 50 and 51 on allegations that the *Life* article was intended to, and did, give the impression that the play mirrored the Hill family's experience, which, to the knowledge of defendant, ". . . was false and untrue." Appellant's defense was that the subject of the article was "a subject of legitimate news interest, a subject of general interest and of value and concern to the public" at the time of publication, and that it was "published in good faith without any malice whatsoever . . . ." A motion to dismiss the complaint for substantially these reasons was made at the close of the case and was denied by the trial judge on the ground that the proofs presented a jury question as to the truth of the article.

The jury awarded appellee $50,000 compensatory and $25,000 punitive damages. On appeal, the Appellate Divison of the Supreme Court ordered a new trial as to damages, but sustained the jury verdict of liability. The court said as to liability:

> Although the play was fictionalized, *Life*'s article portrayed it as a re-enactment of the Hill's experience. It is an inescapable conclusion that this was done to advertise and attract further attention to the play, and to increase present and future magazine circulations as well. It is evidence that the article cannot be characterized as a mere dissemination of news, nor even an effort to supply legitimate newsworthy information in which the public had, or might have a proper interest.

At the trial on damages, a jury was waived and the court awarded $30,000 compensatory damages without punitive damages.

We hold that the Constitutional protections for speech and press preclude the application of the New York statute to redress false reports of matters of public interest in the absence of proof that the defendant published the report with knowledge of its falsity or in reckless disregard of the truth.

The guarantees for speech and press are not the preserve of political expression or comment upon public affairs, essential as those are to healthy government. One need only pick up any newspaper or magazine to comprehend the vast range of published matter which exposes persons to public view, both private citizens and public officials. Exposure of the self to others in varying degrees is a concomitant of life in a civilized community. The risk of this exposure is an essential incident of life in a society which places a primary value on freedom of speech and of press. "Freedom of discussion, if it would fulfill its historic function in this nation, must embrace all issues about which information is needed or appropriate to enable the members of society to cope with the exigencies of their period." (*Thornhill* v. *Alabama*.) "No suggestion can be found in the Constitution that the freedom there guaranteed for speech and the press bears an inverse ratio to the timeliness and importance of the ideas seeking expression." (*Bridges* v. *California*.) We have no doubt that the subject of the *Life* article, the opening of a new play linked to an actual incident, is a matter of public interest. "The line between the informing and entertaining is too elusive for the protection of . . . (freedom of the press)." (*Winters* v. *New York*.) Erroneous statement is no less inevitable in such case than in the case of comment upon public affairs, and in both, if innocent or merely negligent, ". . . it must be protected if the freedoms of expression are to have the 'breathing space' that they 'need to survive.'. . ." (*New York Times Co.* v. *Sullivan*.)

As James Madison said, "Some degree of abuse is inseparable from the proper use of everything and in no instance is this more true than of the press." We create grave risk of serious impairment of the indispensable service of a free press in a free society if we saddle the press with the impossible burden of verifying to a certainty the facts associated in news articles with a person's name, picture, or portrait, particularly as related to nondefamatory matter. Even negligence would be a most elusive standard, especially when the content of the speech itself affords no warning of prospective harm to another through falsity. A negligence test would place on the press the intolerable burden of guessing how a jury might assess the reasonableness of steps taken by it to verify the accuracy of every reference to a name, picture, or portrait.

We find applicable here the standard of knowing or reckless falsehood not through blind application of *New York Times Co.* v. *Sullivan*, relating solely to libel actions by public officials, but only upon consideration of the factors which arise in the particular context of the application of the New York statute in cases involving private individuals. This is neither a libel action by a private individual nor a statutory action by a public official. Therefore, although the First Amendment principles pronounced in *New York Times* guide our conclusion, we reach that conclusion only by applying these principles in this discrete context.

The requirement that the jury . . . find that the article was published "for trade purposes," as defined in the charge, cannot save the charge from Constitutional infirmity. "That books, newspapers, and magazines are published and sold for profit does not prevent them from being a form of expression whose liberty is safeguarded by the First Amendment." (*Joseph Burstyn, Inc.* v. *Wilson*.)

The appellant argues that the statute should be declared unconstitutional on its face if construed by the New York courts to impose liability without proof of knowing or reckless falsity. Such a declaration would not be warranted even if it were entirely clear that this had previously been the view of the New York courts. The New York Court of Appeals, as the *Spahn* opinion demonstrated, has been assiduous in construing the statute to avoid invasion of the constitutional protections of speech and press. We, therefore, confidently expect that the New York courts will apply the statute consistently with the constitutional command. Any possible difference with us as to the thrust of the constitutional command is narrowly limited in this case to the failure of the trial judge to instruct the jury that a verdict of liability could be predicated only on a finding of knowing or reckless falsity in the publication of the *Life* article.

The judgment of the Court of Appeals is set aside and the case is remanded for further proceedings not inconsistent with this opinion.

Mr. Justice Black, with whom Mr. Justice Douglas joins, concurring.

I concur in reversal of the judgment in this case based on the grounds and reasons stated in the Court's opinion. I do this, however, in order for the Court to be able at this time to agree on an opinion in this important case based on the prevailing Constitutional doctrine expressed in *New York Times* v. *Sullivan*. The Court's opinion decides the case in accordance with this doctrine, to which the majority adhere. In agreeing to the Court's opinion, I do not recede from any of the views I have previously expressed about the much wider press and speech freedoms I think the First and Fourteenth Amendments were designed to grant to the people of the nation.

I think it not inappropriate to add that it would be difficult, if not impossible, for the Court ever to sustain a judgment against *Times* in this case without using the recently popularized weighing and balancing formula. Some of us have pointed out from time to time that the First Amendment freedoms could not possibly live with the adoption of that Constitution-ignoring-and-destroying-technique, when there are, as here, palpable penalties imposed on speech or press specifically because of the views that are spoken or printed. The prohibitions of the Constitution were written to prohibit certain specific things, and one of the specific things prohibited is a law which abridges freedom of the press. That freedom was written into the Constitution and that Constitution is or should be binding on judges as well as other officers. The "weighing" doctrine plainly encourages and actually invites judges to choose for themselves between conflicting values, even where, as in the First Amendment, the Founders made a choice of values, one of which is a free press.

Mr. Justice Douglas, concurring.

As intimated in my separate opinion in *Rosenblatt* v. *Baer* and in the opinion of my Brother Black in the same case, state action to abridge freedom of the press is barred by the First and Fourteenth Amendments where the discussion concerns matters in the public domain. The episode around which this book was written had been news of the day for some time. The most that can be said is that the novel, the play, and the magazine article revived that interest. A fictionalized treatment of the event is, in my view, as much in the public domain as would be a watercolor of the assassination of a public official. It seems to me irrelevant to talk of any right of privacy in this context. Here a private person is catapulted into the news by events over which he had no control. He and his activities are then in the public domain as fully as the matters at issue in *New York Times Co.* v. *Sullivan*. Such privacy as a person normally has ceases when his life has ceased to be private.

A trial is a chancy thing, no matter what safeguards are provided. To let a jury on this record return a verdict or not as it chooses is to let First Amendment rights ride on capricious or whimsical circumstances, for emotions and prejudices often do carry the day. The exception for "knowing and reckless falsity" is therefore, in my view, an abridgment of speech that is barred by the First and Fourteenth Amendments.

Mr. Justice Fortas, with whom the Chief Justice and Mr. Justice Clark join, dissenting.

The Court's holding here is exceedingly narrow. It declines to hold that the New York "Right of Privacy" statute is unconstitutional. I agree. The Court concludes, however, that the instructions to the jury in this case were fatally defective because they failed to advise the jury that a verdict for the plaintiff could be predicated only on a finding of knowing or reckless falsity in the publication of the *Life* article. Presumably, the plaintiff is entitled to a new trial. If he can stand the emotional and financial burden, there is reason to hope that he will recover damages for the reckless and irresponsible assault upon himself and his family which this article represents. But he has litigated this case for 11 years. He should not be subjected to the burden of a new trial without significant cause.

I fully agree with the views of my Brethren who have stressed the need for a generous construction of the First Amendment. I, too, believe that freedom of the press, of speech, assembly, and religion, and the freedom to petition are of the essence of our liberty and fundamental to our values. But I do not believe that whatever is in words, however much of an aggression it may be upon individual rights, is beyond the reach of law, no matter how heedless of others' rights—how remote from public purpose, how reckless, irresponsible, and untrue it may be. I do not believe that the First Amendment precludes effective protection of the right of privacy—or, for that matter, an effective law of libel. In 1890, Warren and Brandeis published their famous article "The Right to Privacy," in which they eloquently argued that the "excesses" of the press in "overstepping in every direction the obvious bounds of propriety and decency" made it essential that the law recognize a right to privacy, distinct from traditional remedies for defamation, to protect private individuals against the unjustifiable infliction of mental pain and distress. A distinct right of privacy is now recognized, either as a "common law" right or by statute, in at least 35 states. Its exact scope varies in the respective jurisdictions. It is, simply stated, the right to be left alone; to live one's life as one chooses, free from assault, intrusion, or invasion except as they can be justified by the clear needs of community living under a government of law.

The Court today does not repeat the ringing words of so many of its members on so many occasions in exaltation of the right of privacy. Instead, it reverses a decision under the New York "Right of Privacy" statute because of the "failure of the trial judge to instruct the jury that a verdict of liability could be predicated only on a finding of knowing or reckless falsity in the publication of the *Life* article." In my opinion, the jury instructions, although they were not a textbook model, satisfied this standard.

The Courts may not and must not permit either public or private action that censors or inhibits the press. But part of this responsibility is to preserve values and procedures which assure the ordinary citizen that the press is not above the reach of the law—that its special prerogatives, granted because of its special and vital functions, are reasonably equated with its needs in the performance of these functions. For this Court totally to immunize the press—whether forthrightly or by the subtle indirection—in areas far beyond the needs of news, comment on public persons and events, discussion of public issues and the like would be no service to freedom of the press, but an invitation to public hostility to that freedom. This Court cannot and should not refuse to permit under state law the private citizen who is aggrieved by the type of assault which we have here and which is not within the specially protected core of the First Amendment to recover compensatory damages for recklessly inflicted invasion of his rights.

Accordingly, I would affirm.

CABANISS v. HIPSLEY
114 Ga. App. 367, 151 SE 2d 496 (1966)

Eberhardt, Judge.

As Justice Cobb suggested in *Pavesich* v. *New England Life Insurance Co.*, the recognition of the right of privacy, bringing to our law a new concept, made it inevitable that there be developments in its later consideration. Though it has not been pointed out in the subsequent cases before the Supreme Court, and only incidentally by this court in *Ford Motor Co.* v. *Williams*, Dean Prosser has analyzed the many privacy cases in an article entitled "Privacy," published in 48 Calif., L.Rev. 383 in 1960, and in reviewing the cases, he suggests that the invasion of privacy is in reality a complex of four loosely related torts; that there are four distinct kinds of invasion of four different interests of plaintiff; that there are four disparate torts under a common name. These four torts may be described briefly as: 1) intrusion upon the plaintiff's seclusion or solitude, or into his private affairs; 2) public disclosure of embarrassing private facts about the plaintiff; 3) publicity which places the plaintiff in a false light in the public eye; 4) appropriation, for the defendant's advantage, of the plaintiff's name or likeness. We consider this analysis well-founded and take it as a starting point for our deliberations here.*

AS TO BOTH DEFENDANTS

1. Intrusion upon the plaintiff's seclusion or solitude, or into his private affairs

1) This aspect of the right of privacy as a theory of recovery can be disposed of summarily, for the petition was not drawn nor was there evidence to sustain a verdict on it. For cases involving this aspect of the invasion of the right of privacy, see *Newcomb Hotel Co.* v. *Corbett*, where there was an intrusion into plaintiff's hotel room by the house detective who mistakenly believed that unauthorized people were present; *Byfield* v. *Candler*, where there was an unauthorized entry into plaintiff's stateroom; *Young* v. *Western & A.R. Co.*, where there was an unauthorized and unlawful entry into plaintiff's house; *McDaniel* v. *Atlanta Coca-Cola Bottling Co.*, where eavesdropping equipment was placed in plaintiff's hospital room for the purpose of listening to her conversations with her husband and others; *Marcelli* v. *Teasley*, where the owner of the property came upon the premises occupied by plaintiff and threatened eviction in a loud and profane manner in the presence of others; *Walker* v. *Whittle*, where there was a mistaken identity in the making of an arrest without a warrant; and *Ford Motor Co.* v. *Williams* reversed on other grounds, where defendant, wrongfully suspecting plaintiff of having stolen certain goods, went to his house, broke in and removed the goods. See also *Pinkerton National Detective Agency, Inc.* v. *Stevens*, containing elements of "false light" as well as "intru-

---

*There are, of course, other views. See, e.g., Bloustein, "Privacy as an Aspect of Human Dignity: An Answer to Dean Prosser," 39 N.Y.U.L. Rev. 962 (1964), in which it is urged that the cases involving privacy are of one piece, a sort of continuum or a synechiology, and involve a single tort—the affront of human dignity; Green, "The Right of Privacy," 27 Ill.L.Rev. 237 (1932). Dean Green points out that the doctrinal term "right of privacy" threatens to become a catch-all for cases which defy a rule-of-thumb analysis and affords the judicial process a haven for almost any case which raises a novel problem affecting interests of personality or interests in relation with other persons. He states that the tort cases which courts most frequently bring under the "privacy" rubric involve an interest of personality which has been subjected to the harm of appropriation. Interests of personality are broken down into seven phases: 1) physical integrity; 2) feelings or emotions; 3) capacity for activity or service; 4) name; 5) likeness; 6) history; and 7) privacy—privacy being only one of several phases of personality subject to appropriation.

sion," where plaintiff charged defendant with harassingly spying on her in such a manner that neighbors got the impression that plaintiff was engaging in wrongful activity.

Some of these cases overlap and fill in the gaps left by trespass, nuisance, and intentional infliction of mental distress, and whatever remedies there may be for the invasion of constitutional rights.

2. Public disclosure of embarrassing private facts about the plaintiff

1) There are at least three necessary elements for recovery under this theory: a) the disclosure of private facts must be a public disclosure; b) the facts disclosed to the public must be private, secluded or secret facts and not public ones; c) the matter made public must be offensive and objectionable to a reasonable man of ordinary sensibilities under the circumstances.

> The interest protected is that of reputation, with the same overtones of mental distress that are present in libel and slander. It is in reality an extension of defamation, into the field of publications that do not fall within the narrow limits of the old torts, with the elimination of the defense of truth. (Prosser, *supra*. at 398.)

For cases which seem to fall in this category see *Bazemore v. Savannah Hospital*, involving the unauthorized publication of the photograph of a deceased child born with a deformity; *Gouldman-Taber Pontiac, Inc.* v. *Zerbst*, and *Haggard* v. *Shaw*, where plaintiff's creditor had written to plaintiff's employer seeking assitance in the collection of an account; *Davis* v. *General Finance & Thrift Corp.*, where defendant sent a telegram to plaintiff dunning him for an unpaid account; and *Waters* v. *Fleetwood*, also containing elements of appropriation, where a newspaper was charged with unauthorizedly making, publishing, and selling photographs of plaintiff's murdered daughter.

2) In the case sub judice there was no evidence to support elements b) or c) (embarrasing private facts), and consequently the verdict cannot be sustained under this theory.

Plaintiff testified that, as part of her act, she had her photograph taken to send out for advance billing and that the photographs were intended and used for publicity purposes and to sell her act to club owners. Before the occurrence complained of took place, she had played the Club Peachtree and the Gypsy Room in Atlanta. Prior to coming to Altanta for her appearance, she gave her photographs to her agent who in turn supplied them to the club at which she was appearing. Her photograph was customarily put in the window and on advertising boards of the club at which she was playing; it was sent through her New York agent to her Atlanta agent to be used at the Club Peachtree where she was to appear. She knew that Club Peachtree had a copy of her photograph at the time she appeared there and that it was displayed in the glass showcase of the club.

Plaintiff testified that in many circumstances an exotic leaves her photograph behind when leaving town. She usually attempted to pick hers up if it was in the window or showcase, but she did not attempt to do so at the Club Peachtree because it was not in the window or showcase when she left. She did not ask for it, and it was left behind.

After her appearance at Club Peachtree plaintiff gave copies of the photograph involved to her Atlanta agent. Subsequent to the Club Peachtree appearance she played the Gypsy Room, which had her photographs and the right to use them. During the Gypsy Room appearance, and prior to the occurrence complained of, her photograph appeared in the magazine *Gay Atlanta*. She testified that her same photograph had appeared in magazines like *Gay Atlanta* hundreds of times all over the country when she was appearing at various clubs.

It thus appears from plaintiff's testimony that the photograph was not one which she wished to keep private, secluded, or secret, nor was it one which was embarrassing, offensive, or objectionable to her. She testified that this photograph and others similar to it had been put in circulation by her to obtain employment and to publicize herself and the clubs at which she was appearing. We do not think that plaintiff can complain about the disclosure of matters which she has herself disclosed and consciously promoted.

In addition, plaintiff testified on cross examination: "Q. It is a very attractive picture? A. It is a very lovely picture. Q. And shows a charming young lady? A. And I paid a lot of money for it. Q. Fine features and figure? A. I think I look very nice."

Plaintiff was what is commonly referred to as a strip-tease, and, by the very nature of her occupation, the facts disclosed were neither private nor embarrassing to her.

We prefer not to use the term "waiver" in our decision here. Without precise analysis this concept may receive indiscriminate application.

Three reasons are generally given for the loss of the right of privacy by public figures and celebrities: a) they have sought publicity and consented to it and so cannot complain of it; b) their personalities and their affairs already have become public and can no longer be regarded as their own private business; and c) the press has a privilege, guaranteed by the Constitution, to inform the public about those who have become legitimate matters of public interest.

We rest our decision in this division of the opinion on reason a), and we adopt the test as laid down in the crystallization of the right of privacy: "to whatever degree and in whatever connection a man's life has ceased to be private . . . to that extent the protection is to be withdrawn." (Warren and Brandeis, "The Right to Privacy," 4 Harv.L.Rev. 193, 215 (1890).) Or, stated in *Pavesich* in terms of "waiver:" "waiver carries with it the right to an invasion of privacy only to such an extent as may be legitimately necessary and proper in dealing with the matter which has brought about the waiver. It may be waived for one purpose and still asserted for another . . . ." See *Tanner-Brice Co.* v. *Sims* for an application of the "waiver" doctrine, and *O'Brien* v. *Pabst Sales Co.* discussed in division 4 of this opinion.

3. **Publicity which places the plaintiff in false light in the public eye**

Unlike disclosure, this aspect of the invasion of the right of privacy does not require the invasion of something secret, secluded, or private; it does require falsity or fiction.

> The false light cases obviously differ from those of intrusion, or disclosure or private facts. The interest protected is clearly that of reputation, with the same overtones of mental distress as in defamation. There is a resemblance to disclosure; but the two differ in that one involved truth and the other lies, one private or secret facts and the other invention. (Prosser, *supra* at 400.)

For cases involving this aspect of the right of privacy, see *McKown* v. *Great A. & P. Tea Co.*, overruled in *Ford Motor Co.* v. *Williams,* itself reversed on other grounds where defendant went to plaintiff's place of employment charging her with having stolen a pen; *Pinkerton National Detective Agency* v. *Stevens,* also containing elements of "intrusion," where plaintiff charged defendant with harassingly spying on her so that neighbors got the impression she was engaging in wrongful activity; *Meeks* v. *Douglas,* where a search warrant was wrongfully and in bad faith taken against plaintiff to procure evidence of arson; and *Brown* v. *Colonial Stores, Inc.,* where defendant inquired of plaintiff in presence of others as to whether she had signed a check returned by the bank for insufficient funds. In

Goodyear Tire & Rubber Co. v. *Vandergriff,* defendant, by fraudulently impersonating plaintiff, represented him as betraying a confidence by giving secret and confidential prices to a competitor, thus subjecting plaintiff to embarrassment and causing him to be held in contempt and ridicule. The facts of this case might have authorized recovery on the basis of appropriation had it been so presented. See division 4 of this opinion.

"One form in which (the 'false light' invasion) occasionally appears . . . is that of publicity falsely attributing to the plaintiff some opinion or utterance. A good illustration of this might be the fictitious testimonial used in advertising . . . ." (Prosser, *supra* at 398.) *Pavesich,* chiefly relied upon by plaintiff, seems clearly to fall within this category. There a likeness of plaintiff appeared in an advertisement of the defendant insurance company with a testimonial in which plaintiff was made to say, in effect, that he had secured insurance with the defendant company, on account of which his family was protected, and that he was receiving an income from an annual dividend on paid-up policies. Beside the likeness of plaintiff there was a likeness of an ill-dressed, sickly-looking person above which appeared the words, "Do it while you can. The man who didn't." It was alleged that plaintiff did not have, and had never had, a policy of insurance with the defendant company, and that this fact was known to his friends and acquaintances. Hence, in the light of extrinsic facts in which plaintiff became a self-confessed liar, the court in *Pavesich,* in addition to recognizing the right of privacy, held that a cause of action was stated for libel.

We note that in the ficticious testimonial cases, such as *Pavesich,* recovery would also be proper under the theory of "Appropriation," discussed in division 4. Hence, the court in *Pavesich* could have allowed recovery on this theory had it been presented as a basis of liability, but the only damages sought were general damages for bringing plaintiff in contempt and ridicule before the world, and especially before his friends and acquaintances.

We do not think *Pavesich* or similar cases reach the case sub judice. The only falsity or fiction revealed by this evidence is that plaintiff was falsely pictured as appearing at the Atlanta Playboy Club under the stage name of "Dawn Darling." This evidence does not authorize a verdict for general damages for injury to plaintiff's reputation or to her sensibilities. There is no evidence to indicate that the stage name "Dawn Darling" is in a category materially different from that which would include the stage names "Melanie Lark" and "Charming Charmaine De Aire," which plaintiff used, nor is there evidence to indicate that the Atlanta Playboy Club was in any material respect different from the types of clubs plaintiff customarily played, such as Club Peachtree or the Gypsy Room. She was not presented in a false light; she was revealed as an exotic strip-tease, which she was.

3) The evidence does not support the verdict on the theory of publicity which places the plaintiff in a false light in the public eye.

4. Appropriation, for the defendant's advantage, of the plaintiff's name or likeness.

Unlike intrusion, disclosure, or false light, appropriation does not require the invasion of something secret, secluded, or private pertaining to plaintiff, nor does it involve falsity. It consists of the appropriation, for the defendant's benefit, use, or advantage, of the plaintiff's name or likeness.

For cases involving "appropriation" situations see *Pavesich, Tanner-Brice Co.* v. *Sims, Waters* v. *Fleetwood,* and *Goodyear Tire & Rubber Co.* v. *Vandergriff.*

> The interest protected (in the "appropriation" cases) is not so much a mental as a proprietary one, in the exclusive use of the plaintiff's name and likenesses as an aspect of his identity. (Prosser, *supra* at 406.)

Hence, the main distinction between this aspect of privacy and the other three is the distinction between causes of action involving injury to feelings, sensibilities, or reputation and those involving an appropriation of rights in the nature of property rights for commercial exploitation. This distinction was clearly indicated in *Haelan Laboratories, Inc. v. Topps Chewing Gum, Inc.*, where the right of a person or his assignee to protect the publicity value of his photograph was expressly recognized and designated the "right of publicity."

In the *Haelen* case, the plaintiff contracted with prominent baseball players for the exclusive right to use their photographs in connection with the sale of its products. Thereafter defendant was assigned a contract with the same players for the same purpose. In the litigation which followed, plaintiff maintained that defendant invaded plaintiff's exclusive right to use the photographs; defendant, however, contended that none of plaintiff's contracts created more than a release of liability, because a man has a legal interest in the publication of his picture other than his right of privacy, i.e., a personal and nonassignable right not to have his feelings hurt by such a publication.

The court, however, rejected defendant's contention in this manner: "We think that, in addition to and independent of that right of privacy (which in New York derives from statute), a man has a right to the publicity value of his photograph, i.e., the right to grant the exclusive privilege of publishing his picture, and that such a grant may validly be made 'in gross,' i.e., without an accompanying transfer of a business or of anything else. Whether it be labelled a 'property' right is immaterial; for here, as often elsewhere, the tag 'property' simply symbolizes the fact that courts enforce a claim which has pecuniary worth."

> This right might be called a "right of publicity." For it is common knowledge that many prominent persons (especially actors and ball players), far from having their feelings bruised through public exposure of their likenesses, would feel sorely deprived if they no longer received money for authorizing advertisements, popularizing their countenances, displayed in newspapers, magazines, busses, trains, and subways. Prosser states that "(a)lthough this decision has not yet been followed, it would seem clearly to be justified."

4–6) Recognizing, as we do, the fundamental distinction between causes of action involving injury to feelings, sensibilities, or reputation and those involving an appropriation of rights in the nature of property rights for commercial exploitation, it must necessarily follow that there is a fundamental distinction between the two classes of cases in the measure of damages to be applied. In the former class (which we take to include the intrusion, disclosure, and false light aspects of the privacy tort), general damages are recoverable without proof of special damages. In the latter class, the measure of damages is the value of the use of the appropriated publicity.

In the case sub judice it is clear from the record that plaintiff's photograph was appropriated (mistakenly or otherwise) for commercial exploitation without her consent. The difficulty here, however, is that the damages sought and recovered are not the kind of damages which can be awarded under this aspect of the privacy tort.

A similar problem was encountered in *O'Brien* v. *Pabst Sales Co*. In that case plaintiff, a well-publicized football player, posed for football publicity pictures taken by the publicity department of his university and authorized that department to distribute his picture and biographical data to newspapers, magazines, sports journals, and the public generally. Defendant purchased a copy of his picture from the university and published it on a calendar advertising Pabst Blue Ribbon Beer. Plaintiff complained mainly of the fact that the publication impliedly declared that he was endorsing or recommending the use of Pabst beer, whereas he was opposed to the use of alcohol among young people and was greatly embarrassed and humiliated when he realized that his face and name were associated with publicity for the sale of beer.

The court agreed with the trial court that plaintiff was not a "private person," the publicity he received being that which he had been constantly seeking and receiving (in other words, there was no public disclosure of embarrassing private facts, as we have ruled in division 2, *supra*), and that reasonably construed, nothing in the calendar impliedly represented that plaintiff was a user of, or was recommending the use of, Pabst beer (thus holding that there could be no recovery under the false light theory, an even stronger holding under the facts of that case than what we have ruled in division 3, *supra*).

In a dissenting opinion, Judge Holmes, undeterred by procedural points, argued that under the facts pleaded plaintiff was entitled to recover the reasonable value of the use of the picture in trade and commerce for advertising purposes to the extent that such use was appropriated by the defendant. Judge Hutcheson was careful to point out in the majority opinion, however, which affirmed a directed verdict for defendant, the problem similar to the one with which we are faced:

> Nothing in the majority opinion purports to deal with or express an opinion on the matter dealt with in the dissenting opinion, the right of a person to recover on quantum meruit, for the use of his name for advertising purposes. That was not the case pleaded and attempted to be brought. The case was not for the value of plaintiff's name in advertising a product but for damages by way of injury to him in using his name in advertising beer.

Even though, as we have indicated, the evidence here might have supported a verdict under the "appropriation" theory, and indeed plaintiff's testimony reveals that "appropriation" is her real complaint, the damages sought and recovered were not authorized under this theory, because there was no proof of the advertising value of the use of her photograph in the manner and for the time it was appropriated. Recovery was sought and damages were awarded for the injury to feelings, sensibilities, and reputation apparently under the theories of "disclosure" or "false light;" but the evidence does not support the verdict under these theories. Accordingly the judgment must be reversed.

AS TO DEFENDANT CABANISS

5) Under the appropriation theory, it is not enough alone that there be appropriation of plaintiff's name or likeness; there must be an appropriation for the defendant's benefit, use, or advantage upon which to predicate liability against that defendant. (Prosser, *supra* at 405.) Recovery under this theory is measured by the unjust enrichment of the defendant and not by the injury to plaintiff's feelings or reputation (and we assume, but do not decide, to plaintiff's own commercial interests).

7) We have indicated in division 4 that the evidence might have supported a verdict under the appropriation theory had the case been tried and proof made under it. The evidence would not have supported such a verdict, however, against defendant Cabaniss. His participation was merely passive, and his magazine *Gay Atlanta* was merely the conduit through which the advertising and publicity matter of customers was transmitted by the Playboy Club to the public. The appropriation of plaintiff's photograph did not inure to his benefit, use, or advantage, but to that of his advertiser. A

different question might be presented had the evidence shown that Cabaniss used the advertisement of the Atlanta Playboy Club, with its photograph of plaintiff, to publicize or advertise *his magazine* (and had the case been properly tried under such a theory). The evidence did not show, however, that any advantage accrued to Cabaniss by any means. It was uncontradicted that he had received the advertising including plaintiff's photograph without any knowledge of the appropriation. His advertising charges to the customer were on the basis of space used and the number of times the advertisement was run. There was no evidence that he charged or received any more for this advertisement than would have been the case if plaintiff's picture had not appeared in it, or if the photograph of the artist who was in fact appearing at the club had been used. For this reason the evidence did not support the verdict against Cabaniss under any theory.

FLORIDA PUBLISHING COMPANY v. *FLETCHER*
340 So. 2d 914 (1977)

Roberts, Justice.

This cause is before us on petition for writ of certiorari to review the decision of the District Court of Appeal, First District, in *Fletcher* v. *Florida Publishing Co.*, which directly conflicts with *Jacova* v. *Southern Radio and Television Co.,* thereby vesting jurisdiction in this Court.

The facts supported by the record are succinctly stated in the summary final judgment of the trial judge who determined that there was no real dispute as to the material facts. Respondent, Mrs. Fletcher, left Jacksonville for New York on September 15, 1972, to visit a friend. She left in Jacksonville her three young daughters, including seventeen-year-old Cindy. A "baby sitter" was to spend the nights with the children, but there was no one with them in the home during the daytime except a young man who had a room in the house and whom Mrs. Fletcher described as Cindy's "boy friend." On the afternoon of September 15, 1972, while Cindy was alone in the house, a fire of undetermined origin did large damage to the home, and Cindy died.

The fire and police departments were called by a neighbor who discovered the fire, but too late to save the child. A large group of firemen, news media representatives, and onlookers gathered at the scene and on Mrs. Fletcher's property.

When the Fire Marshal and Police Sergeant Short entered the house to make their official investigation, they invited the news media to accompany them, as they desposed was their standard practice. The media representatives entered through the open door; there was no objection to their entry; they entered quietly and peaceably; they did no damage to the property; and their entry was for the purpose of their news coverage of this fire and death.

The Fire Marshal desired a clear picture of the "silhouette" left on the floor after the removal of Cindy's body. He and Sergeant Short in their depositions explained that the picture was important for their respective investigations to show that the body was already on the floor *before* the heat of the fire did any damage in the room. The Fire Marshal took one polaroid picture of the silhouette, but it was not too clear, he had no further film, and he requested photographer Cranford to take the "silhouette" picture which was made a part of the official investigation file of both the Fire and Police.

This picture was not only a part of the investigation but News Photographer Cranford turned it and his other pictures over to the defendant newspaper. It and several other pictures appeared in the news story of The Florida Times-Union on September 16, 1972.

Respondent first learned of the facts surrounding the death of her daughter by reading the newspaper story and viewing the published photographs.

Respondent filed an amended complaint against petitioner alleging 1) trespass and invasion of privacy, 2) invasion of privacy, 3) wrongful intentional infliction of emotional distress—seeking punitive damages.

The trial court dismissed Count II and granted final summary judgment for petitioner as to Counts I and III. Relative to the granting of summary judgment for Petitioner as to Count I, the trial judge cogently explicated:

As to Count I, the question raised by the motion for summary judgment is one of law as there is no genuine issue of material fact. The question raised is whether the trespass alleged in Count I of the complaint was consented to by the doctrine of common custom and usage.

The law is well settled in Florida and elsewhere that there is no unlawful trespass when peaceable entry is made, without objection, under common custom and usage.

On appeal, the District Court of Appeal reversed as to the granting of summary judgment on Count I, stating:

We do not here hold that a trespass or 'intrusion' did in fact occur sub judice: We simply find that such is alleged in Count I of the amended complaint and that the proofs before the learned trial judge are insufficient to resolve the point by summary judgment.

Although recognizing that consent is an absolute defense to an action for trespass and that the defense of custom and usage is but another way of expressing consent by implication—that is consent may be implied from custom, usage or conduct—the District Court commented that the emergency of the fire was over and that there was no contention that petitioner's employees entered the premises to render assistance, explained that respondent did not either impliedly or expressly invite petitioner's employees into her home, and concluded that the proofs before the court were not sufficient to show that there was no genuine issue of material fact as to whether implied consent by custom and usage authorized entry into the premises without invitation by appellant.

As to the other points on appeal, the District Court of Appeal, First District, determined that although punitive damages are recoverable in a proper case for trespass resulting in invasion of privacy, the trial judge did not err in granting summary judgment for petitioner on issue of punitive damages, held that the trial court correctly dismissed Count II with prejudice, and correctly granted summary judgment for petitioner as to Count III.

The District Court erred in reversing summary judgment for petitioners as to Count I. The trial court properly determined from the record before it that there was no genuine issue of material fact insofar as the entry into respondent's home by petitioner's employees became lawful and non-actionable pursuant to the doctrine of common custom, usage, and practice and since it had been shown that it was common usage, custom and practice for news media to enter private premises and homes *under the circumstances present here*.

Judge McCord in his dissenting opinion could not agree with the majority that the news photographer who entered the burned out home was a trespasser or that the photograph published by petitioner and the news story resulting from the entry were an actionable invasion of privacy. We agree with and approve the following well-reasoned explication by Judge McCord in his dissenting opinion:

> The only photographs taken and published were of fire damage—none were of deceased or injured persons. There, is no contention that the particular photograph complained of (the silhouette picture) and the news story were in any way false or inaccurate. There could, therefore, be no recovery under the 'false-light' doctrine of invasion of privacy. Thus, there could be no recovery from the publication if the same photograph had come from a source other than from the news photographer's entry upon the premises. Any recovery in this case and, therefore, the only question is whether or not there was a trespass by the news photographer. The majority opinion discusses the implied consent doctrine under which a person, who does not have express consent from the owner or possessor of premises, may legally enter under circumstances which infer or imply consent (common usage, custom and practice). It is my view that the entry in this case was by implied consent.
>
> It is not questioned that this tragic fire and death were being investigated by the fire department and the sheriff's office and that arson was suspected. The fire was a disaster of great public interest and it is clear that the photographer and other members of the news media entered the burned home at the invitation of the investigating officers. (Numerous members of the general public also went through the burned house.) Many affidavits of news editors throughout Florida and the nation and affidavits of Florida law enforcement officials were filed in support of appellee's motion for summary judgment. These affidavits were to the general effect that it has been a longstanding custom and practice throughout the country for representatives of the news media to enter upon private property where disaster of great public interest has occurred—entering in a peaceful manner, without causing any physical damage, and at the invitation of the officers who are investigating the calamity. The affidavits of law enforcement officers indicate that the presence of the news media at such investigations is often helpful to the investigations in developing leads, etc.
>
> The affidavits as to custom and practice do not delineate between various kinds of property where a tragedy occurs. They apply to any such place. If an entry is or is not a trespass, its character would not change depending upon whether or not the place of the tragedy is a burned out home (as here), an office or other building or place. An analysis of the cases on implied consent by custom and usage, indicates that they do not rest upon the previous nonobjection to entry by the particular owner of the property in question but rest upon custom and practice generally. Implied consent would, of course, vanish if one were informed not to enter at that time by the owner or possessor or by their direction. But here there was not only no objection to the entry, but there was an invitation to enter by the officers investigating the fire. The question of implied consent to news media personnel to enter premises in a circumstance such as this appears to be one of first impression not only in this jurisdiction but elsewhere. This, in itself, tends to indicate that the practice has been accepted by the general public since it is a widespread practice of longstanding. Due to such widespread and long-standing custom, reason and logic support the application of implied consent to enter the premises in the case before us. It, therefore, was not a trespass, and I would affirm the trial court.

Accordingly, that portion of the decision of the District Court of Appeal, First District, reversing summary judgment for petitioner as to Count I is quashed, and the cause is remanded for further proceedings consistent herewith.

JEPPSON v. *UNITED TELEVISION*
3 Med. L. Rptr. 2513 (1978)

Utah Supreme Court

Wilkins, Justice:
Plaintiffs appeal from an order of the District Court, Salt Lake County, granting defendant's motion to dismiss plaintiffs' complaint for failure to state a claim for which relief could be granted. All statutory references are to Utah Code Annotated, 1953.

Plaintiffs allege in their complaint that an agent and employee of defendant, as a part of the television program "Dialing for Dollars," telephoned plaintiffs at their residence on March 11, 1977, and had the following conversation with Plaintiff Jean W. Jeppson:

He: This is "Dialing for Dollars," do you have your T.V. set on?
She: No, I don't.
He: Oh, that is unfortunate, because you could have won $50.00.
She: Well now I'll tell you, I'd rather have peace in my home than all that garbage on television, even for $50.00.

Without the knowledge of Mrs. Jeppson, defendant's agent had announced the Jeppson name and telephone number on the air, and televised the conversation without advising Mrs. Jeppson, and without obtaining her consent. Immediately after this conversation, and continuing all of the remainder of the afternoon, plaintiffs allege they received calls from people all over the state of Utah, who referred to this conversation, and used rude, abusive, obscene and threatening language, all of which caused plaintiffs to be embarrassed, and humiliated, and to fear for their safety and well being.

Plaintiffs pray for relief on three separate theories: 1) invasion of common law right of privacy, 2) abuse of plaintiffs' personal identity in violation of the provisions of Section 76–9–405, and 3) intentional and malicious infliction of emotional and mental harm.

If the allegations contained in plaintiffs' complaint state a claim upon which relief may be granted on any one of these theories the Order of the District Court dismissing the complaint must be reversed.

Section 76–9–405 and 76–9–406, respectively, provide:

1. A person is guilty of abuse of personal identity if, for the purpose of advertising any articles of merchandise for purposes of trade or for any other advertising purposes, he uses the name, picture, or portrait of any individual or uses the name or picture of any public institution of this state, the official title of any public officer of this state, or of any person who is living, without first having obtained the written consent of the person, or if the person be a minor, the written

consent of his parent or guardian, or if the person is dead, without the written consent of his heirs or personal representatives.

Any person or the heirs of any deceased person, who has been injured by a violation of this part may bring an action against the person who committed the violation. If in the action the court finds the defendant is violating or has violated any of the provisions of this part, it shall enjoin the defendant from a continuance thereof. It shall not be necessary that actual damages to the plaintiffs be alleged or proved, but if damages are alleged and proved, the plaintiff in the action shall be entitled to recover from the defendant the actual damages, if any, sustained in addition to injunctive relief. A finding that the defendant is in violation of this part shall entitle the plaintiff to reasonable attorneys' fees. Exemplary damages may be awarded where the violation is found to be malicious.

In the case of *Donahue* v. *Warner Bros. Pictures Distributing Corp.*, this Court construed the predecessor statute to section 76-9-405 in considering whether the showing in the State of Utah of a motion picture based partially on the life of Jack Donahue gave rise to a claim for relief in favor of his heirs on the theory that said motion picture was shown "for purposes of trade".* In that case, this Court rejected the contention that the statute proscribed the publication of a name or picture in all cases when a profit motive is present, and held that the statute proscribes only such use "for advertising or exploitation of the name or picture or for the promotion of the sale of some collateral commodity . . . ."

The statute was changed in 1973 and now clearly contains the limitation adopted by this Court in *Donahue*.

Plaintiffs allege in their complaint that defendant's program, "Dialing for Dollars" is presented solely for the purposes of advertising its television station, and increasing the viewers of its programs. They maintain that defendant's publication of their name and number without their knowledge and consent for the purposes of such advertising is within the proscription of the statute. We agree.

The District Court, in ruling on defendant's motion to dismiss, evidently found that plaintiffs had waived their rights of privacy, and had invited people to call their residence by having their name and number published in the telephone book. The violation of the statute, however, consists of the publication of the name on the air without plaintiffs' prior written consent. Plaintiffs' complaint states a claim for which relief may be granted under the statute.

As this point is dispositive we do not discuss the remainder of plaintiffs' contentions.

Reversed and remanded for further proceedings not inconsistent with this opinion. Costs to plaintiffs. Concurring: Maughan, J., and Hall, J.

NEFF v. TIME, INC.
406 F.Supp. 858 (1976)

Marsh, District Judge.

This diversity action was removed from the Court of Common Pleas of Allegheny County, Pennsylvania, where a complaint had been filed by John W. Neff, the plaintiff, against Time, Inc., the

---

*Section 76-4-8, repealed in 1973, provided in contrast to the present language: "Any person who uses for advertising purposes or for purposes of trade, or upon any postal card, the name, portrait or picture of any person . . . ."

defendant. The complaint was verified by Neff and alleged that the defendant is the owner of a magazine known as *Sports Illustrated* sold weekly throughout Pennsylvania; that Neff is a private citizen employed in education; that in its issue of August 5, 1974, the defendant's magazine used Neff's picture without his prior knowledge and consent to illustrate an article entitled "A Strange Kind of Love;" that the photograph shows Neff with the front zipper of his trousers completely opened implying that he is a "crazy, drunken slob," and combined with the title of the article, "a sexual deviate." Neff alleges that the unauthorized publication and circulation of his picture to illustrate the article invaded his right of privacy and subjected him to public ridicule and contempt, injured his personal esteem and the esteem of his profession, reflected on his character, diminished his high standing reputation among his family, friends, neighbors and business associates, destroying his peace of mind and caused him severe mental and emotional distress to his damage in excess of $5,000, amended to aver in excess of $10,000.

The defendant filed a motion for summary judgment and attached eight affidavits in which the defendant admitted that an authorized employee took Neff's photograph and five others selected it for publication. No counter-affidavits were filed by Neff. There is only one disputed issue of fact: Neff alleges that defendant has used his picture without his prior knowledge and consent; the defendant asserts that his picture was taken for and published in *Sports Illustrated* with his full knowledge and consent.

The undenied facts contained in affidavits filed by defendant establish beyond peradventure that the picture was taken with Neff's knowledge and with his encouragement; that he knew he was being photographed by a photographer for *Sports Illustrated* and thereby implied consent to its publication. Since Neff did not respond by counter-affidavits, in our opinion the motion should be granted.

The affidavits establish that the photograph was taken about 1:00 o'clock P.M. November 25, 1973, while Neff was present on a dugout with a group of fans prior to a professional football game at Cleveland between the Cleveland Browns and the Pittsburgh Steelers. The photographer was on the field intending to take pictures of the Steeler players as they entered the field from the dugout. Neff and the others were jumping up and down in full view of the fans in the stadium; they were waving Steeler banners and drinking beer; they all seemed to be slightly inebriated. One of the group asked the photographer for whom he was working and was told *Sports Illustrated*, whereupon the group began to act as if a television camera had been put on them; as the pictures were taken they began to react even more, screaming and howling and imploring the photographer to take more pictures. The more pictures taken of the group, the more they hammed it up. All were aware that the photographer was covering the game for *Sports Illustrated*. There were no objections; they wanted to be photographed. Thirty pictures were taken of the group on the dugout from different angles.

During the period from July through December, 1973, this photographer took 7,200 pictures pursuant to his assignment to cover the Steelers. As part of his duty he edited the pictures and submitted one hundred to the magazine for selection by a committee of five employees. After several screenings of the thirty pictures of the group on the dugout, the committee selected Neff's picture with his fly open. Although Neff's fly was not open to the point of being revealing, the selection was deliberate and surely in utmost bad taste; subjectively as to Neff the published picture could have been embarrassing, humiliating and offensive to his sensibilities. Without doubt the magazine deliberately exhibited Neff in an embarrassing manner.

It appears that the pictures were taken to illustrate a book being written by one Blount about the Steeler fans, and three excerpts from the book were published in the magazine. Only three pictures, including Neff's, accompanied the article of August 5, 1974. The title to this article "A Strange Kind of Love" could convey to some readers a derogatory connotation. Neff is not mentioned by name in the article; the Steeler-Cleveland game of November, 1973, is not mentioned in the article; Neff's photograph was not selected on the basis of its relationship to that game. The caption appearing adjacent to the photograph reads:

In the fading autumn Sundays at Three Rivers, the fans joined the players in mean pro dreams.

Three Rivers is the name of the stadium in Pittsburgh. Neff's photograph was selected because "it represented the typical Steeler fan: a rowdy, strong rooter, much behind his team, having a good time at the game," and "it fitted in perfectly with the text of the story."

It seems to us that art directors and editors should hesitate to deliberately publish a picture which most likely would be offensive and cause embarrassment to the subject when many other pictures of the same variety are available. Notwithstanding, "(t)he courts are not concerned with establishing canons of good taste for the press or the public."

The right of privacy is firmly established in Pennsylvania despite the fact that its perimeter is not yet clearly defined and its contours remain amorphous.

From *Vogel* it seems that Pennsylvania follows the rules promulgated by the *Restatement* (Second) *of Torts* Sections 652 B through E (Tent. Draft No. 13, 1967); that invasion of privacy is actionable under any one of four distinct but coordinate, torts. These are concisely paraphrased in *Goldman v. Time, Inc.* (1971) as follows:

1. Intrusion upon the plaintiff's seclusion or solitude, or into his private affairs.
2. Public disclosure of embarrassing private facts about the plaintiff.
3. Publicity which places the plaintiff in a false light in the public eye.
4. Appropriation, for the defendant's advantage, of the plaintiff's name or likeness.

Plaintiff's claim is based on "appropriation of name or likeness" and "publicity given to private life," i.e., 4 and 2, *supra*.

As to 4, *supra*, Section 652 C of the *Restatement* (Second) *of Torts* (Tent. Draft No. 21, 1975) states:

One who appropriates to his own use or benefit the name or likeness of another is subject to liability to the other for unreasonable invasion of his privacy.

It is settled that this section is not applicable when a person's picture is used in a non-commercial article dealing with an accident, or the picture of a bystander at a political convention, or parade, *Murray v. N.Y. Magazine Co.* (1971), or generally in the reporting of news. We think actions of excited fans at a football game are news as is a story about the fans of a professional football team. As stated in *Gautier v. Pro-Football, Inc.* (1953): "Once an item has achieved the status of newsworthiness, it retains that status even when no longer current." The fact that *Sports Illustrated* is a magazine published for profit does not constitute a "commercial appropriation of Neff's likeness." The fact that Neff was photographed in a public place for a newsworthy article, entitles the defendant to the protection of the First Amendment. The tort described in 4, *supra*, and Section 652 C *Restatement* (Second) *of Torts* is not applicable to the facts in this case.

As to 2, *supra*, Section 652 D of the *Restatement* (Second) *of Torts* (Tent. Draft No. 13, 1967) states:

One who gives publicity to matters concerning the private life of another, of a kind highly offensive to a reasonable man, is subject to liability to the other for invasion of his privacy."

In the 1975 draft of the *Restatement* (Second) *of Torts* Section 652 D states:

One who gives publicity to a matter concerning the private life of another is subject to liability to to other for unreasonable invasion of his privacy, if the matter publicized is of a kind which:
   a) would be highly offensive to a reasonable person, and
   b) is not of legitimate concern to the public.

The article about Pittsburgh Steeler fans was of legitimate public interest; the football game in Cleveland was of legitimate public interest; Neff's picture was taken in a public place with his knowledge and with his encouragement; he was catapulted into the news by his own actions; nothing was falsified; a photograph taken at a public event which everyone present could see, with his knowledge and implied consent of the subject, is not a matter concerning a private fact. A factually accurate public disclosure is not tortious when connected with a newsworthy event even though offensive to ordinary sensibilities. The Constitutional privilege protects all truthful publications relevant to matters of public interest . . . . The tort described in 2, *supra*, and Section 652 D of the *Restatement* (Second) *of Torts*, *supra*, is not applicable to the facts in this case.

Of course, we are concerned that Neff's picture was deliberately selected by an editorial committee from a number of similar pictures and segregated and published alone. If his picture had appeared as part of the general crowd scene of fans at a game, even though embarrassing, there would be no problem. Although we have some misgivings, it is our opinion that the publication of Neff's photograph taken with this active encouragement and participation, and with knowledge that the photographer was connected with a publication, even though taken without his express consent, is protected by the Constitution.

An appropriate order will be entered.

NOTE I

In the case of *Factors, Etc.* v. *Pro Arts, Inc.* (579 F.2d 215 (CA2 1978)), a professional entertainer's right to publicity, which he exercised during his lifetime by assigning to plaintiff company's client exclusive authority to print, publish, and distribute his name and likeness, was found to constitute a separate, intangible property right that survives the entertainer's death and that can be transferred by the company.

Ingraham, Circuit Judge.

Plaintiffs-Appellees, Factors Etc., Inc. (Factors) and Boxcar Enterprises, Inc. (Boxcar), sued Defendants-Appellants, Pro Arts, Inc. (Pro Arts) and Stop and Shop Companies, Inc. (Stop and Shop), for injunctive relief and damages based upon defendants' alleged misappropriation and unauthorized use of the name and likeness of Elvis Presley (Presley). The trial court granted the plaintiffs' preliminary injunction upon its findings that the exclusive right to market Presley memorabilia survived the death of Presley, and the Presley poster printed by defendants allegedly in derogation of this right was not privileged as the publication of a newsworthy event.

Because the facts are not in dispute, we need not describe them in detail. During Presley's career as an entertainer, Colonel Tom Parker (Parker) served as his close friend, mentor and personal manager. This professional relationship between the two parties began on March 26, 1956, with the execution of the first contract between them. Parker immediately began the task of creating the "Elvis persona." In so doing, both he and Presley capitalized upon the marketing of merchandise bearing the Elvis name and likeness. Parker directed this effort until Presley's death, a task reflected by the numerous extensions of the contract between the two parties.

Boxcar Enterprises, a Tennessee corporation controlled by Presley and Parker, was the vehicle through which the commercial Elvis Presley rights were marketed. Boxcar sublicensed other companies to do the actual manufacturing and distributing of each specific item, receiving royalties from the sales.

On August 16, 1977, Elvis Presley died suddenly and unexpectedly. His father, Vernon Presley, was appointed executor of his estate. On August 18, 1977, two days after Presley's death, Boxcar granted Factors the exclusive license to exploit commercially the name and likeness of Elvis Presley. Factors paid Boxcar $100,000 on execution of the agreement against a guarantee of $150,000. Vernon Presley, as executor of the estate, signed the agreement licensing Factors, at the same time warranting that Boxcar was the sole and exclusive owner of the commercial Elvis Presley rights. The agreement was also approved by Parker.

Immediately following Presley's death, Pro Arts decided that it too wanted a share in the market for Elvis Presley memorabilia. It purchased the copyright in the photograph of Presley from a staff photographer of the Atlanta (Georgia) Journal. On August 19, 1977, three days after his death, Pro Arts published a poster using the photograph and filed an application for registration of copyright. The poster is entitled "In Memory" and below the photograph of Presley the poster bears the dates "1935–1977."

On the same day that the poster was published, Pro Arts began to market it. One of its first customers was co-defendant Stop and Shop Companies, which thereafter sold the poster through its Bradlees Stores Division in the Southern District of New York. On August 24, 1977, five days after its poster was placed on the market, Pro Arts notified Boxcar Enterprises that it was offering "a memorial 'Elvis' poster to meet the public demand." When Factors was informed of the letter, it replied to Pro Arts claiming the exclusive right to manufacture, sell and distribute all merchandise utilizing the name and likeness of Elvis Presley. Factors also warned Pro Arts that if it did not discontinue sale of the poster, it would be subject to a lawsuit for injunctive relief, damages and an accounting.

Instead of ceasing distribution of the poster, Pro Arts filed suit in the United States District Court for the Northern District of Ohio seeking a declaratory judgment of non-infringement of the rights claimed by Factors. When Factors discovered that it had been sued in Ohio, it responded by instituting this action against Pro Arts and Stop and Shop in United States District Court for the Southern District of New York. This later action was filed on September 26, 1977, just five days after Pro Arts' action.

Upon the filing of the complaint in this action, the district judge entered an "order to show cause" requiring Pro Arts to show cause why an injunction should not issue against it. Pro Arts responded with a motion to dismiss, stay or transfer the suit to the Northern District of Ohio. On October 13, 1977, the New York court filed an opinion and order of preliminary injunction against Pro Arts. The injunction restrained Pro Arts during the pendency of the action from manufacturing, selling or distributing (1) any more copies of the poster labeled "In Memory . . . 1935–1977," (2) any other posters, reproductions or copies containing any likeness of Elvis Presley, and (3) utilizing for commercial profit in any manner or form the name or likeness of Elvis Presley. The order also denied Pro Arts' motion to dismiss, stay or transfer.

We now proceed to the determination of the principal issue in this case—whether or not the preliminary injunction was improvidently granted. In order to be granted a preliminary injunction must make "a clear showing of either (1) probable success on the merits *and* possible irreparable injury, *or* (2) sufficiently serious questions going to the merits to make them a fair ground for litigation *and* a balance of hardships tipping decidedly toward the party requesting the preliminary relief." The trial court employed the first prong of the test, finding that Factors had demonstrated probable success on the merits and possible irreparable injury. Because Pro Arts does not challenge the trial court's finding of possible irreparable harm, we need only address the first of the two requirements, that of probable success on the merits.

In concluding that Factors would likely prevail on the merits at trial, the court found that Elvis Presley exercised his right of publicity during his lifetime by giving Parker the exclusive authority to exploit his image through Boxcar Enterprises. This exclusive authority survived Presley's death, after which it was validly assigned to Factors. For this reason Pro Arts was enjoined from manufacturing, distributing, selling or otherwise profiting from merchandise bearing the name or likeness of the late Elvis Presley.

Pro Arts' final argument is that even if Factors possesses the exclusive right to distribute Presley memorabilia, this right does not prevent Pro Arts from publishing what it terms a "memorial poster" commemorating a newsworthy event. In support of this argument, Pro Arts cites a case arising out of the bogus presidential candidacy of the television comedian Pat Paulsen. Paulsen sued defendant for publishing and distributing a poster of Paulsen with the legend "For President." The court refused to enjoin sale of the poster because Paulsen's choice of the political arena for satire made him "newsworthy" in the First Amendment sense. We cannot accept Pro Arts contention that the legend "In Memory . . ." placed its poster in the same category as one picturing a presidential candidate, albeit a mock candidate. We hold, therefore, that Pro Arts' poster of Presley was not privileged as celebrating a newsworthy event.

In conclusion we hold that the district court did not abuse its discretion in granting the injunction since Factors has demonstrated a strong likelihood of success on the merits at trial. Factors possesses the exclusive right to print and distribute Elvis Presley memorabilia, a right which was validly transferred to it from Boxcar following Presley's death. Pro Arts infringed this right by printing and distributing the Elvis Presley poster, a poster whose publication was not privileged as a newsworthy event.

We affirm the action of the district court and remand for further proceedings.

NOTE II

To the extent that the West Virginia Code 49-7-3 (1941) makes it a crime for a newspaper to publish the name of a child in any juvenile proceeding under chapter 49 of the Code, it was found to offend the First Amendment by creating prior restraint on freedom of the press. (*State Ex. Rel. Daily Mail Pub. Co.* v. *Smith,* 248 S.E.2d 269 (1978).) The question presented to the United States Supreme Court was: Does West Virginia code 49-7-3 create prior restraint on freedom of press that violates the First Amendment? (September 21, 1978 petition for certiorari was filed. The Supreme Court granted the request on November 13, 1978. *Smith* v. *Daily Mail Publishing Co.,* 99 S. Ct. 448 (1979).)

In this case the West Virginia court held that to the extent that a statute made it a criminal offense for a newspaper to publish the name of a child in any proceeding under child welfare statutes without prior approval of the trial court, it was unconstitutional as repugnant to the First Amendment because it created impermissible prior restraint on freedom of the press.

In the words of Justice Neely:

These two cases, which have been consolidated for decision, both present a conceptionally indisguisable permutation of a classic First Amendment, freedom-of-the-press issue concerning prior restraint on publication which the United States Supreme Court has addressed numerous times in the last ten years.

Although the Supreme Court has never taken an absolutist position that there can be no abridgment of the freedom of the press under any circumstances, it would appear that outside of the area of pornography there is no governmental interest sufficiently compelling to justify a prior restraint in times of peace. We suspect, although we cannot prove, that the Supreme Court would authorize a prior restraint with regard to publication of military intelligence in a time of serious national peril and concerning a dangerous and indispensable operation such as the Allies' invasion of Normandy in 1944. A relatively concise statement of the two well recognized exceptions to absolute freedom from prior restraint was stated in *Near* v. *Minnesota* and cited with approval by Justice Brennan in his concurring opinion in *Nebraska Press Assn., supra,* as follows: (1) to prevent the disclosure of information that would inevitably, directly, and immediately cause irreparable damage to the Nation in time of war; and (2) to suppress expression which is simply not deemed "speech" within the meaning of the First Amendment, such as obscenity or incitements to violence or revolution by force. In addition to those two exceptions discussed by Justice Brennan, it appears that with regard to acts which are verbal in nature, as for example a parade, a third exception is the regulation of the time, place and manner of expression, without unduly limiting the opportunity for expression. (248 S.E.2d 269 (1978).)

This leads to the question of First Amendment overbreadth which, along with other important issues such as the means of regulating any standard for the First Amendment, may best be addressed in another work at another time.